Acclaim for Benny Morris's

RIGHTEOUS VICTIMS

"A masterly account: detailed but always readable, authoritative but strenuously objective. . . . If you want to understand the Arab-Israeli conflict, rather than sound off about it, the book is essential."
—*Contemporary Review*

"Crisply written, balanced and comprehensive, this is an indispensable work of history." —*Publishers Weekly* (starred review)

"Remarkably objective. . . . Compelling."
—*Financial Times* (London)

"Morris does a wonderful job. . . . [He] describes Jewish-Arab relations evenhandedly and in great detail. . . . Men like him, who can see things from more than one perspective, are sorely needed to prepare the ground for what will hopefully be a peaceful and relatively just settlement of Jewish-Arab problems." —*Austin Chronicle*

"Superb. . . . [Morris's] narrative skill and meticulous attention to historical detail as he shifts from one battleground to another make for absorbing reading." —*National & Financial Post* (Toronto)

"This comprehensive and balanced work is mandatory reading for anyone interested in the long and bitter history of this conflict."
—*Booklist*

BENNY MORRIS

ΠIGHTEOUS VICTIMS

Benny Morris is Professor of History at Ben-Gurion University, Beersheba, Israel, and is the author of a number of books on Middle Eastern history, including *The Birth of the Palestinian Refugee Problem, 1947–1949*.

RIGHTEOUS VICTIMS

A HISTORY OF THE
ZIONIST-ARAB CONFLICT,
1881–2001

BENNY MORRIS

VINTAGE BOOKS
A Division of Random House, Inc.
New York

The Library of Congress has cataloged the Knopf edition as follows:
Morris, Benny.
Righteous victims: a history of the Zionist-Arab conflict, 1881–2001 / by Benny Morris.
p. cm.
Includes bibliographical references and index.
ISBN 0-679-42120-3
1. Arab-Israeli conflict. 2. Jewish-Arab relations—History—1917–1948. 3. Arab-Israeli
conflict—1993—Peace. I. Title
DS119.7.M657 1999
956—dc21 98-42774

Vintage ISBN: 0-679-74475-4

Author photograph © Elena Seibert
Book design by Iris Weinstein

www.vintagebooks.com

Printed in the United States of America
10 9 8 7 6 5 4

For Jeff and Evelyn Abel,
Dubbie and Dvorka Harel,
Mike and Jana Robinson,
Yaron and Nadine Tsur,
With thanks

I and the public know
What all schoolchildren learn,
Those to whom evil is done
Do evil in return.

—W. H. AUDEN, "September 1, 1939"

CONTENTS

ACKNOWLEDGMENTS

I owe a very large debt to Ben-Gurion University, and principally Prof. Jimmy Weinblatt, the dean of Humanities and Social Sciences, as well as to Prof. Nahum Finger, the rector, for a succession of grants that made possible the shortening and shaping of the text of this work to its present size.

I would like to thank Prof. Naomi Chazan and Prof. Moshe Ma'oz, the successive directors of the Truman Institute of the Hebrew University, Jerusalem, for grants, a room, and facilities in the course of the 1990s that helped me carry out the research and write this book. I would also like to thank Prof. Gabriel Sheffer and Prof. Amnon Sela, the successive directors of the Davis Institute of the Hebrew University, and Merle Thorpe's Foundation for Middle East Peace for grants that enabled me to carry out much of the research for chapter 11, which deals with Yishuv-Lebanese relations and the Lebanon War of 1982–85. I also spent an enlightening two weeks in the archives of the French Foreign Ministry, assisted by a grant from the cultural attaché of the French Embassy, Tel Aviv—for which I thank him.

I owe a debt to Prof. David Ruderman and the board of directors of the Center for Judaic Studies, University of Pennsylvania, Philadelphia, for hosting me for a month in early 1997, in which I managed to put final touches to this work.

I also owe a great debt to the Rockefeller Foundation, which hosted me for a month at its estate in Bellagio, Italy, making possible some additions to the manuscript in incomparably wonderful surroundings.

I also owe an incalculable debt to my friend Jeff Abel, who throughout the years of composition was always helpful and available to solve the succession of computer-linked problems that always proved beyond my ken. Evelyn and David also lent an occasional hand.

I am deeply indebted to Pieter Louppen and the Department of Geography and Environmental Development, Ben-Gurion University of the Negev, Beer-sheba, Israel, for producing the book's fine maps.

As usual, I am also indebted to the staffs of various archives and libraries in which I did much of my research—the Israel State Archives and the Central Zionist Archives in Jerusalem; the Israel Defense Forces (IDF) Archive in Giv'atayim, Israel; the National Library in Jerusalem; the Public Record Office in London; and the National Archives in Washington, D.C. I owe a paramount debt to Ronnie Hope, who gently abridged and edited this work— and much of its readability and smoothness is due to his highly competent efforts. Deborah Harris and Beth Elon, my agents, made this book possible and held my hand through the various ups and downs that accompanied its maturation; Susan Ralston was my editor at Knopf—and I thank them all from the bottom of my heart.

I would also like to extend heartfelt thanks to my former teacher and current "blood brother," Prof. Benjamin Z. Kedar, of the Hebrew University, who read through the hardcover edition of *Righteous Victims* and suggested a string of corrections and improvements, which I have introduced into the present edition.

Lastly, thanks to my family—Leah and Erel, Yagi, and Orian—who suffered with dignity the various slings and arrows that accompanied the long labor of research and composition. And I cannot end my expressions of gratitude without a special word of thanks to my friends Dubbie and Dvorka for so many things.

The conflict between Arabs and Zionists is more than a hundred years old. Almost from the start the subject has been treated with emphatic partisanship by commentators and historians from both sides, as well as by foreign observers.

Thousands of books have been written on various aspects and periods of the conflict; this one attempts to relate the entire story in an integrated fashion, covering Israel, the Palestinians, and the Arab states from the 1880s to the present. I hope it will contribute to a good general understanding of what happened, and why.

The book focuses on what, to my mind, are the central components of the conflict in the political and military spheres. I have not given much attention to other aspects, such as the economic and cultural ones. I realize that these have, at certain times, played significant roles, but in a general study of this sort, one must concentrate on the core events, processes, and issues.

I have devoted relatively little space to the internal politics of the societies that inhabit the Middle East, except where these have had a direct bearing on the development of the conflict. My approach has been based on a rejection of the dictum that "there is no foreign policy, only internal politics." It will be for the reader to determine whether I have struck the right balances.

The book is based largely on secondary works and is a synthesis of existing research on the various subjects and periods covered. A history of this subject based mainly on primary sources is, I suspect, beyond the abilities of a single scholar. There are simply too many archives, files, and documents. Nonetheless, parts of the present book—the coverage of the 1948 war and the decade after it, and of certain episodes that occurred during the 1930s and the 1982–85 Lebanon War—are based in large measure on primary sources. Otherwise I have relied on what I regard as the principal scholarly works on given subjects and periods in producing this narrative.

Academic history is necessarily based on a wide range of contemporary documentary material. This book deals, of course, with the early periods from which much of the material is available—but then goes on to cover the 1970s, 1980s, and 1990s, for which it is still largely unavailable. In covering these three decades I have had to make do with secondary works, interviews, newspapers, and memoirs. A full academic history of these latter decades will have to await the opening of the appropriate archival materials.

There is a built-in imbalance in scholarly treatments of the conflict; this study is no exception. The Zionist side tends to be illuminated more thoroughly and with greater precision than the Arab side, and this applies to both political and military aspects. In part this stems from the fact that Zionist and Israeli archives, civil and military, local and national, are relatively well organized and have been open to researchers for many years. By and large, the documents contained in them were written by Zionists, in a Zionist context and from the Zionist perspective. This has almost inevitably affected the historiography based on these documents.

There has been no such access on the Arab side. There are no comparable Palestinian archives, and whatever exists in the archives of the Arab states has been and remains closed to researchers, save for the occasional and usually inconsequential document. Hence "the Arab side," more often than not, has also had to be illuminated on the basis of Zionist-Israeli and Western documentation.

Second, historiography, in the modern sense, has been far more developed on the Jewish-Zionist side than among the Arabs. Indeed, only in recent years have Arab historians—usually living in the West—begun to publish serious historical work connected with the conflict. Unfortunately most Arab historians still labor under the yoke of severe political-ideological restrictions that are characteristic of nondemocratic societies. The same types of censorship and self-censorship have affected the writings of Arab memoirists. Though Jewish officials, generals, and politicians have often also been self-serving and subjective in their published recollections, and past generations of Zionist-Israeli historians have been less than objective, they have been substantially more accurate and informative than their Arab counterparts.

Lastly, there has been a marked quantitative gap between the two sides. The Arabs have simply produced far less historiography and related published materials (autobiographies, collections of documents, and the like) than the Jews.

I have tried to compensate by using relevant Arab materials to the extent that they were accessible, and by ferreting out the "Arab side" or "perspective" as manifested in documentation in Zionist-Israeli and Western archives (for example, by using intelligence documents reporting on thinking and activities from the Arab side) and writings. In doing so, I have attempted to approach the subject as objectively as possible, to bring reason and fairness to my reconstructions of the past. The reader will judge whether I have succeeded.

RIGHTEOUS VICTIS

... its fields and fettered its energies. . . . Nazareth
is forlorn; . . . Jericho . . . accursed . . . Jerusalem . . . a pauper village. . . .
Palestine is desolate and unlovely.

So wrote Mark Twain in 1867.[1] He may have been indulging in hyperbole, but then neither was Palestine, in the mid-nineteenth century, the "land of milk and honey" promised in the Bible.

As it is today, the Holy Land—Eretz Yisrael or the Land of Israel for the Jews, Falastin or Palestine for the Arabs—was defined during the years of British rule (1918–48) as the area bounded in the north by a range of hills just south of the Litani River in Lebanon; in the east by the Jordan River, the Dead Sea, and the Arava Valley (Wadi Araba); in the west by the Mediterranean Sea and the Sinai Peninsula; and in the south by the Gulf of Eilat (or Gulf of Aqaba). In all, it consists of about 26,320 square kilometers (10,162 square miles), an area roughly the size of New Jersey.

Of this landmass, about 50–60 percent, the Negev and the Araba, is a wilderness sprinkled with a handful of oases but largely uninhabitable and uncultivable, as is the area called the Judean Desert, between the hilly spine of Judea—running from Ramallah through Jerusalem to Hebron—and the Jordan River and Dead Sea.

alestine is a dry land, with only one small river—the Jordan—which in is not inside Palestine but rather demarcates the borders between Palestine Syria and, farther south, Palestine and Jordan. Otherwise there are only small streams with perennial water. Most streams run only in winter and dry beds for the rest of the year. Natural springs and wells dot the northern f of the country; in the south they are relatively rare. The naturally habit-le north has rainfall between October and April each year; the remaining onths are dry, with summer temperatures reaching 30–35 degrees Celsius. he Negev has virtually no rain, and temperatures at its southern end reach 0–45 degrees Celsius in summer.

The population has tended to concentrate, in both ancient and modern imes, in the hilly central areas of Judea, Samaria, and Galilee, and in the fer-tile coastal plain and the west-east valley that branches out from it between Haifa and the Jordan River, known as the Jezreel Valley or the Plain of Esdraelon. A further fertile area is the northern Jordan Valley running, from south to north, from Beit Sh'an (Beisan) to the Sea of Galilee and its sur-rounding lowland, to Lake Huleh and then to the Jordan's sources, in the foothills of Mount Hermon.

In ancient times, it is estimated, Palestine contained between 750,000 and 6 million inhabitants, with most scholars giving the figure 2.5 million for about 50 A.D.[2] During the second millennium B.C. it was inhabited by a collec-tion of pagan tribes or peoples—Canaanites, Jebusites, and others—who jostled for control of this or that area. Toward the end of the millennium the Hebrews, or Jews, invaded and settled the land, and for most of the next mil-lennium constituted the majority of the population and governed the bulk of the country. The core of the Jewish state (at one point there were two Jewish kingdoms) was the hill country of Judea, Samaria, and Galilee. Through most of the period there was a minority population of Philistines, and later, Hellenistic and Romanized pagans concentrated in the coastal plain, in such towns as Caesarea, Jaffa, Ashkelon, and Gaza. The chapter of Jewish sovereignty ended when the Romans invaded and then put down two revolts, in A.D. 66–73 and 132–35, and exiled much of the Jewish popula-tion. After successive invasions and counterinvasions by Persians, Arabs, Turks, Crusaders, Mongols, Mamelukes, and (again) Turks, the country—at the beginning of the nineteenth century, under imperial Ottoman rule—had a population of about 275,000 to 300,000 people, of whom 90 percent were Muslim Arabs, 7,000 to 10,000 Jews, and 20,000 to 30,000 Christian Arabs. By 1881, on the eve of the start of the Zionist Jewish influx, Palestine's popu-lation was 457,000—about 400,000 of them Muslims, 13,000–20,000 Jews, and 42,000 Christians (mostly Greek Orthodox).[3] In addition, there were sev-eral thousand more Jews who were permanent residents of Palestine but not Ottoman citizens.

The small pre-Zionist Jewish population of Palestine—usually referred to collectively as the Old Yishuv (literally, the "old settlement")—was largely poor. Many if not most lived on charity from their coreligionists abroad. Both Ashkenazim (Jews of European origin) and Sephardim (Jews of Spanish, North African, and Middle Eastern extraction) were almost exclusively Orthodox and were concentrated, in separate areas, in Judaism's four "holy" towns: Jerusalem, Hebron, Safad, and Tiberias. Most were Ottoman subjects, extremely submissive toward the Turkish authorities and deferential toward the large Muslim communities among which they lived. Many spent their days learning Talmud and Torah; a few were merchants and shopkeepers; more were petty craftsmen. All in all, they were a numerically insignificant minority.

The overwhelming majority of the population was Arab, about 70 percent rural. These were dispersed in seven to eight hundred hamlets and villages ranging in size from fewer than one hundred to nearly one thousand inhabitants. Most of the villages were in the hill country, their location dictated by access to springs or wells and defensive requirements like hilltops or cliffs. Many had been established by invading Bedouin who turned sedentary. The coastal plain and the Jezreel and Jordan valleys were relatively empty, both because of the dangers posed by marauding Bedouin bands and because their swamps presented health hazards and were difficult to cultivate.

Many of the villages fought a continual if low-key battle against the Bedouin, who periodically sortied into the settled areas of Palestine from the desert east of the Jordan, from the Negev, and from the Sinai. There were also protracted land and water disputes between villages and sometimes between clans within villages. These feuds, and rivalries between leading urban families and between various towns, such as Jerusalem and Hebron, were to serve as continuous elements of division and weakness in Palestinian Arab society.

Agriculture was primitive, with little irrigation. During the first half of the nineteenth century, land was usually owned by the villagers privately or collectively. The second half of the century saw the growing impoverishment of the villagers, in large part owing to more efficient Ottoman taxation, and a great deal of rural land was bought up by urban notable families (in Arabic, a'yan), who had accumulated their new wealth as Ottoman agents, especially in tax collection, and through commerce with the West. By the early twentieth century, villagers in dozens of localities no longer owned their land but continued to cultivate it as tenant farmers.

Almost all the large landowners (effendis) were urban notables, some of them living outside Palestine, many in Beirut, Damascus, and Paris. During the last quarter of the nineteenth century, Zionist land purchases from effendis contributed to the roster of dispossessed villagers. The second half of the century witnessed the rapid growth of citrus cultivation, mainly in the humid coastal plain, the produce destined for highly profitable export to Europe. Land became a more attractive investment, and the concomitant price rises led to further sales by impoverished *fellahin*.

By 1881 a third of Palestine's population was urban—up from only 22 percent in 1800. Most of the Jews and Christians lived in the towns, making their relative weight there decidedly greater than in the country as a whole. By 1880 Jerusalem's population numbered 30,000, of whom about half were Jews; Gaza's population was 19,000, Jaffa's 10,000, and Haifa's 6,000. The notables in the towns were nurtured by the Ottoman Empire, which gave them various local positions and tax-collecting functions, and by the British authorities after 1917–18. The elite families—the Khalidis, Husseinis, and Nashashibis in Jerusalem; the Ja'bris and Tamimis of Hebron; the Nabulsis, Masris, and Shak'as of Nablus, and others—supplied municipal officials, judges, police officers, religious officials, and civil servants. Inevitably, given their wealth, power, and influence with the imperial authorities, the *a'yan* emerged as the Palestinian Arabs' local and eventually "national" leadership. A vast gulf—based on disparities in educational level and social, economic, and political position—separated the *a'yan* from the largely illiterate masses.

The second half of the nineteenth century saw a gradual modernization of the country, accompanying the growing urbanization. While most villages and towns were connected by footpaths rather than paved roads, and people and goods still moved on foot or by horse, camel, or mule rather than in wheeled vehicles, a carriage-road, the first in Palestine, was constructed in 1869 between Jaffa and Jerusalem. The first railroad was laid down in 1892 (also between these two towns), and a second railroad, connecting Haifa and Deraa, running through the Jezreel Valley, was constructed in 1903–05.

The century also witnessed a steady increase in literacy. It is estimated that around 1800 only 3 percent of the non-Jewish inhabitants of Palestine were literate (mostly elder sons of the *a'yan*). As the century progressed, an education "system" emerged, mostly owing to the penetration of European missionaries rather than to Ottoman or local Arab initiative.

During the first half of the nineteenth century, lighting was provided by candles and the burning of olive oil. In the 1860s, naphtha was introduced, and generator-produced electricity reached Palestine during the first decade of the twentieth century. Through the nineteenth century the population was plagued by diseases such as malaria, trachoma, dysentery, cholera, and typhoid fever. Water supplies were inadequate and frequently impure. But the first pharmacy opened its doors in 1842; and the first European hospital, in Jerusalem, in 1843. By the end of the century, there were fifteen hospitals in the town, making it the center of European medicine in Palestine and beyond.

THE TURKISH ADMINISTRATION

The Ottoman Empire, which ruled Palestine from 1517 to 1917–18, was aware of the land's importance as the cradle of Judaism and Christianity but never made it a separate, distinct administrative district. In the 1870s Palestine was part of the province (*vilayet*) of Syria, which was ruled by a governor (*wali*) stationed in Damascus. The province was subdivided into districts (*sanjaks*), three of them in Palestine: Acre, including Haifa, the area of today's Hadera, the Jezreel and Jordan Valleys, the Sea of Galilee, Safad, and Tiberias; Nablus, including Beisan, Jenin, and Qalqilya; and Jerusalem, which included Jericho, Jaffa, Gaza, Beersheba, Hebron, and Bethlehem. The *sanjaks* in turn were divided into subdistricts, administered by local governors called *kaymakams*.

In 1887 the *sanjak* of Jerusalem became an independent *mutasarriflik* (sub-governorate) answerable directly to Constantinople rather than to Damascus. The following year, the rest of Palestine—the *sanjaks* of Nablus and Acre—were separated from the *vilayet* of Sam (Syria) and became the responsibility of a newly created *vilayet* of Beirut. The new entity, which consisted of the area of much of present-day Lebanon, thus also controlled the northern half of Palestine.

During a decade of Egyptian rule in Palestine (1831–40), the authorities had managed to impose more or less centralized government. The powerful Egyptian army, led by Ibrahim 'Ali, brushed aside most of the local magnates who had managed to carve out de facto fiefdoms in different areas of the country. They also staved off the Bedouin incursions from the eastern and southern deserts that had done so much to keep Palestine insecure and poor.

On their return, the Turks instituted a wide range of reforms (*tanzimat*)—economic, administrative, legal, military, and political—but with mixed results. The new, more efficient and centralized taxation resulted in massive impoverishment of the rural population, which in turn led to the steady depopulation of villages and an influx into the towns. Efforts to conscript villagers into the Turkish army, a return of brigandage on the roads, and renewed Bedouin incursions—all had the same effect. The village rulers, or sheikhs, who before the Egyptian conquest had had considerable authority, lost much of it as their role as tax collectors for the central government passed into the hands of Ottoman officials and urban notables.

At the same time economic conditions as well as law and order in the towns vastly improved. Trade with the West picked up. The urban notables became wealthier and acquired more land. Turkish reforms of local government, both in Palestine and Syria, including the appointment of town councils, also resulted in increasing the power of the a'yan and religious leaders (the ulema) at the expense of Ottoman governors and subgovernors. These reforms proved to be milestones on the road to the emergence of centrifugal Arab "nationalisms." In other ways, too, the tanzimat—which aimed at centralization and unity—contributed to disunity in the Arab provinces of the empire. The impoverishment of the countryside and the growing prosperity of the towns drove a wedge between townspeople and the fellahin, or peasantry.[4] And the Sublime Porte's firmans (decrees) of 1839 and, more decisively, of 1856—equalizing the status of Muslim and non-Muslim subjects—resulted in short order in the dramatic alienation of Muslims from Christians. The former resented the implied loss of superiority and recurrently assaulted and massacred Christian communities—in Aleppo in 1850, in Nablus in 1856, and in Damascus and Lebanon in 1860. Among the long-term consequences of these bitter internecine conflicts were the emergence of a Christian-dominated Lebanon in the 1920s–40s and the deep fissure between Christian and Muslim Palestinian Arabs as they confronted the Zionist influx after World War I.

ISLAM AND THE JEWS

Islam generally, and the Ottoman Empire in particular, treated the Jews in its midst as second-class citizens. During the Islamic High Middle Ages, c. A.D. 850–1250, Judaism and the Jews had flourished, and would later designate the period a "golden era" of Jewish history. Jews figured prominently in politics, finance, and the arts and sciences in a number of Islamic kingdoms and empires; one or two served as chamberlains and ministers to kings and princes. Moses Maimonides, a physician to a sultan, emerged as one of the major philosophers of the Middle Ages. But thereafter the condition of the Jews in the Islamic world deteriorated, along with the general stagnation of that world; throughout they suffered discrimination, humiliation, and a sense of insecurity. Occasionally they were subjected to persecution and violence.

One distinguished Israeli historian, David Vital, has written pithily of "the unrectifiably inferior role allotted the Jews in the Muslim cosmology."[5] Islam—much like Christianity and Judaism—has traditionally divided the world into "us" and "them," the true believers (Dar al Islam, the "house of Islam") and the infidels (Dar al Harb, the "house of war," those who should or could be put to the sword). The principle of equality—between believer and nonbeliever as between man and woman—is alien to Islam, and the Islamic world, normally in conflict with Dar al Harb in one region or another, has traditionally exhibited a deep xenophobia.

From the beginning, Islam suffered from the natural jealousy of a successor or "child" toward the monotheistic parent religions from which it sprang, Judaism and Christianity. In great measure Muslim attitudes down the centuries were determined by the relations between Muhammad, Islam's prophet and founder, and the Jews of Arabia during the religion's birth in the seventh century, and the way these relations—and Muhammad's teachings—were described and codified in Islam's sacred book, the Koran, and in subsequent traditional texts (hadiths).

Three Jewish tribes in and around the oasis town of Medina, to which Muhammad migrated from Mecca in the year 622, resisted the Prophet and his teachings and were subdued by force. Two of the tribes, the Banu Qaynuka and the Banu al-Nadir, were expelled, losing their lands and much of their other property. Two years later the Nadir were slaughtered by the Muslims at Khaybar, an oasis east of Medina, where they had resettled. The third tribe, the Qurayza, was dealt with more abruptly: Its six to nine hundred menfolk (all but two or three who agreed to convert to Islam) were publicly decapitated, the women and children enslaved and given by Muhammad to his followers.[6] A fourth tribe, which inhabited Khaybar, surrendered and was allowed to stay after agreeing to pay an annual tribute. Jewish and Christian tribes in Yemen and in Nejd and Bahrain, to the east, were similarly subdued.

Inspired by such tales of friction, the Koran is full of anti-Jewish asides and references, such as: "Wretchedness and baseness were stamped upon [the Children of Israel] and they were visited with wrath from Allah. . . . [They] slew the Prophets wrongfully."[7] Muhammad's relations with the Jews, and subsequent Koranic attitudes, were eventually embodied in the treaty of submission to Muslim rule, or writ of protection, known as the dhimma, or Pact of 'Umar,[8] extended by Muhammad's successor, the second caliph, 'Umar 'ibn al-Khaṭṭāb (634–44). The dhimma governed Muslim behavior toward both Jews and Christians, the other "People of the Book," in Muslim parlance. The dhimmi, the subject Jewish or Christian (and later Zoroastrian Persian) communities, were forced to pay a poll tax, the jizya, plus the kharaj, a special tax imposed by the Muslim conquerors on nonbelievers whose lands they had confiscated. By dint of this tax, the dhimmi were allowed to continue to live on and cultivate these lands under Muslim protection, though an apparently later insertion allowed Muslim rulers to tear up the agreement at will and expel the "protected" communities. On this basis 'Umar expelled all the remaining Jews of the Hejaz, the area of western Arabia around Mecca.

The dhimmi were forbidden to strike a Muslim, carry arms, ride horses, build new houses of worship or repair old ones, and they had to wear distinctive clothing. "Contemptuous tolerance," in the phrase of historian Elie Kedourie, came to be the attitude adopted by Muslim states toward their Jewish communities. This stance was generally mixed with a measure of hostility, especially in times of political crisis. Tolerance was then superseded by intolerance, which occasionally erupted into violence. Throughout, Muslims treated the *dhimmi,* and perhaps especially the Jews, as impure.

Nevertheless, in general the Jews under Islam seem to have fared better than the Christians—if only because the former, usually poor, often abject, always powerless, were a threat to no one. The latter, in most places more numerous, and with religious, cultural, commercial, and, sometimes, political links to neighboring Christian states and empires, were a real and powerful threat. Always there lurked the possibility that a Christian fifth column would make common cause with the external enemy.

This situation, which led, for example, to the complete extinction of Christianity in the Maghreb—Muslim North Africa—in the Middle Ages, changed somewhat in the nineteenth century, with the increasing weakness of the Muslim world and the growing assertiveness of the European states. Progressively, Christian minorities in Dar al Islam came under the protection of the European powers and were often shielded from Muslim hostility by the Ottoman authorities, who either feared retaliation or needed European financial and political aid. The Jews, lacking these connections, increasingly fell prey to grassroots hostility. The father of modern Hebrew, Eliezer Ben-Yehuda, put it this way: "The Muslim Arabs hate [the Jews] perhaps less than they hate all other non-Muslims, but they despise them as they do not despise any other creature . . . in the world."[9] Arabs in Palestine in the nineteenth and early twentieth centuries often referred to Jews as *awlad al-maut* (children of death). The *dhimmi*-Muslim relationship, necessarily one of inequality, was also one of injustice. But the extent of the inequality and injustice actually perpetrated was fluid, depending on the circumstances prevailing in each Muslim state or empire at different times.

Some of the restrictions to which the *dhimmi* were subjected no doubt originated in real considerations of security. But they came to be codified in Islamic law, and were later invoked and implemented without reference to changing realities. Jews were forbidden to bear arms; were permitted to ride asses only, not camels or horses, and only sidesaddle rather than astride; and were obliged to wear distinctive garb. Other restrictions had nothing to do with security and everything to do with religious and economic discrimination, and Jewish poverty in most of the Ottoman lands in the nineteenth and early twentieth centuries appears to have been, in some measure at least, the result of discriminatory practices.

Mass violence against Jews, akin to the pogroms in Western Europe in the late Middle Ages and in Eastern Europe during the nineteenth and twentieth centuries, was rare in the Muslim world. But it did occur, often when a Jew who had risen to a senior government position fell from grace, died, or excited the hostility of envious Muslims.[10] In 1066 nearly three thousand Jews were massacred in Granada, Spain. In Fez, Morocco, some six thousand Jews were murdered in 1033,[11] and massacres took place again in 1276 and 1465.[12] There were massacres in Tetuán in Morocco in 1790; in Mashhad and Barfurush in Persia in 1839 and 1867, respectively; and in Baghdad in 1828. The Jewish quarter of Fez was almost destroyed in 1912 by a Muslim mob; and pro-Nazi mobs slaughtered dozens of Jews in Baghdad in 1941. Repeatedly, in various parts of the Islamic world, Jewish communities—contrary to the provisions of the *dhimma*—were given the choice of conversion or death.[13] Usually, though not always, the incidents of mass violence occurred in the vulnerable extremities of the Muslim empire rather than at its more self-confident core. But the underlying attitude, that Jews were infidels and opponents of Islam, and necessarily inferior in the eyes of God, prevailed throughout Muslim lands down the ages.

Maimonides, writing in the twelfth century, lamented: "God has cast us into the midst of this people, the nation of Ishmael, who persecute us severely, and who devise ways to harm us and to debase us. . . . None has matched [them] in debasing and humiliating us. . . ."[14] But generally the Jews' lot was not a matter of violence; rather, it was one of petty mortification and harassment, coupled with a general sense of insecurity.

At least initially, Jews may have been concentrated in the late Middle Ages in urban *mellahs* (ghettos) for their own protection, but this segregation was certainly also a sign of their isolation and marginality. Certainly the *mellahs* established in the sixteenth and seventeenth centuries were founded with the intent of ostracism rather than protection.[15] In the fifteenth and sixteenth centuries the Jews of Ottoman Islam prospered in comparison with their coreligionists in Western Europe. But during the following centuries the condition of the Jews grew increasingly debased and precarious as the empire grew progressively weaker and, as a result, less tolerant, prey to the European powers baying at its heels. A Western traveler spoke of the Jews as "the . . . most degraded of the Turkish non-believer communities . . . their pusillanimity is so excessive, that they will flee before the uplifted hand of a child . . . a sterling proof of the effects of oppression."[16]

One measure and symbol of Jewish degradation was the common phenomenon—amounting in certain places, such as Yemen and Morocco, to a local custom—of stone-throwing at Jews by Muslim children.[17] A nineteenth-century Western traveler wrote: "I have seen a little fellow of six years old, with a troop of fat toddlers of only three and four, teaching [them] to throw stones at a Jew, and one little urchin would, with the greatest coolness, waddle up to the man and literally spit upon his Jewish gabardine. To all this the Jew is obliged to submit; it would be more than his life was worth to offer to strike a Mahommedan."[18]

There was a spate of blood-libel incidents against the Jews during the last decades of the empire. The most famous occurred in Damascus in 1840: A

Capuchin monk from Sardinia disappeared, along with his Muslim servant. The Christian community in the city, egged on by the French consul, Count Ratti-Menton, accused the Jews of killing the monk and using his blood for ritual purposes. The governor, Sharif Pasha, rounded up seven Jewish elders and had them tortured; two died and one converted to Islam to save himself. Sixty-three children were imprisoned, and several homes were destroyed as the authorities searched for the missing bodies. Six months passed before British government pressure persuaded the authorities, meaning the nominally Ottoman governor of Egypt, Muhammad 'Alī Pasha, who was semi-independent of Constantinople, to release the remaining prisoners. Soon afterward Constantinople regained full control of Syria and Palestine (though not of Egypt), and the Sublime Porte issued an edict reaffirming its protection of the Jews and denouncing the blood libel.[19] But such accusations continued to plague the empire for decades.

There was certainly an increase in Christian anti-Semitism—originating with European diplomats, traders, and clerics—in the empire during the second half of the nineteenth century. As it spread among the Christian Arabs, it also irradiated some of the Muslims among whom they lived. It was not just a matter of ideology; as the Jews, like their Christian *dhimmi* compatriots, were gradually emancipated, they became, or were feared as, competitors with the Christian merchants and professionals. European-style anti-Semitism penetrated the Levant. Anti-Semitic literature, which flourished in France against the backdrop of the Dreyfus affair, soon appeared in Syria, Lebanon, and Egypt in Arabic translations. An Arabic edition of *The Protocols of the Elders of Zion*, for example, was published in Cairo in 1927.

However, despite continuing discrimination and occasional acts of violence, both by state bureaucracies and by Muslim mobs and individuals, the nineteenth century witnessed a gradual change for the better in the Jews' status. Both the empire and the Muslim states on its peripheries were subject to emancipatory and egalitarian winds blowing in from Europe.

The penetration of Western influence into Ottoman lands also took a more direct route. British, Prussian, and French consuls were posted in Jerusalem in 1839, 1842, and 1843, respectively.[20] Increasingly the powers took the empire's Christians and subsequently many of its Jews under their wing. Many Jews held European passports. In a series of bilateral treaties with the Sublime Porte, known as the "Capitulations," the European powers established extraterritorial rights within the Empire, especially in Palestine. For example, visiting or resident European nationals who committed crimes could not be detained or tried by the Ottoman authorities without the express permission of their country's consul, which was almost never forthcoming.

A formal change in the status of the *dhimmi* followed shortly. In February 1856 the Sublime Porte promulgated the reformist firman (edict), the Khatt-i

Humayun,[21] which declared all Ottoman subjects equal, regardless of religion, and repealed all restrictions. Almost two decades earlier, in 1839, another firman (the Khatt-i Sherif) had echoed the egalitarianism of the French Declaration of the Rights of Man—but had gone almost completely unimplemented in the various provinces, largely because of local Muslim opposition. Similar opposition, especially among Christians regarding the emancipation of the Jews, was to greet the 1856 firman, but this time the position of the *dhimmi* began to improve substantially, at least in terms of the law and government permits.

In practice, however, the *dhimmi* remained second-class citizens of the empire until its collapse in World War I. As part of the reaction to growing European influence, the Ottoman authorities—in an effort at "Islamization"— transferred tens of thousands of Muslims from the empire's northern and Balkan peripheries (Bukhara, the Caucasus, Albania, and Bosnia) to its Levantine core, including Lebanon, Syria, and Palestine. This increased the Muslim proportion of the population and, perhaps, intensified Islamic consciousness as well.[22] The history and tradition of Muslim attitudes and behavior toward the Jews was to affect profoundly the unfolding of Turkish-Zionist and Arab-Zionist relations in Palestine. The view of the Jews as objects, unassertive and subservient, was to underlie to some degree both the initial weak, irresolute Ottoman and Arab responses to the gradual Zionist influx into Palestine—Why bother, the Jews could achieve nothing anyway!—and the eventual aggressive reactions, including vandalism and murder—the Jews were accursed of God and meant only harm; their lives and property were therefore forfeit. And the traditional view of the Jews as inconsequential weaklings was for decades thereafter to stoke the fires of resentment and humiliation. In the course of the twentieth century the Arabs of the Levant were repeatedly to be humbled by the Jews, and none more so than the Palestinians, ultimately transformed into a weak minority in their own land. Such slights the Muslim world found difficult to countenance; such a situation could not be allowed to endure.

Muslim attitudes to some degree affected the Zionist colonists in Palestine. They drove the colonists, at least during the early decades of Zionism, toward occasional overassertiveness and even aggressiveness in an effort to wipe out the traces of their traditional, and for them humiliating, image. Later, Muslim contempt, as perennially manifested in the Arab states toward their Jewish minorities, redounded against the Arabs when these minorities emigrated to Palestine, and then in much larger numbers to Israel, bringing with them a fiercely inimical attitude toward Arabs in general.

THE RISE OF ZIONISM

Zionism—the drive for the return of the Jews to, and sovereignty in, Eretz Yisrael—was rooted in age-old millenarian impulses and values of Jewish religious tradition and in the flourishing nationalist ideologies of nineteenth-century Europe. Its emergence as a mass political movement was triggered by the outbursts of anti-Semitism to which these ideologies had given rise. The mid- and late-nineteenth century saw the rapid secularization of the millenarian-Zionist goal amid an increasingly secularized Jewish population.

The return to Zion was conceived as a social and political act that would remedy the Jews' abnormal existence as an oppressed minority in the Diaspora. But ever since the Jews' exile from the land at the start of the first millennium A.D., the idea or vision of a return had been closely bound up with the cosmic, messianic theme of collective redemption and salvation. The religious energy generated by this idea over the centuries was transmuted during the decades of Zionist fulfillment into that potent political force which swept all before it and ultimately forged a state in circumstances and in an environment where crude logic dictated that no Jewish state could ever arise. There is no understanding Zionist behavior in Palestine or the development of the Arab-Zionist conflict without comprehending the messianic roots and European background and propellants of Zionism's emergence.

With Zionism, ideology in great measure preceded reality. Its precursors spoke out almost a generation before the start of the Eastern European pogroms that in fact set the movement in motion. But they were not speaking in a void or from their imagination. The reality of Jewish life, when most of the world's Jews lived in the European part of the Russian Empire known as the "Pale of Settlement," running from Memel in the north to Crimea on the Black Sea, was one of continuous discrimination and insecurity and occasional oppression and violence. The historian Elie Kedourie once spoke of the "deep insult of diaspora life." Basic freedoms—of movement, place of residence, language, occupation, and worship—were severely curtailed or regulated by the state. The restrictions, including prohibition of landownership, assured the impoverishment and socioeconomic immobility of most Jews in the Pale. During the mid-nineteenth century, Jews were subjected to a brutal system of twenty-five-year military conscription, which occasionally entailed the virtual kidnapping of their children at the age of twelve, or even sometimes at eight or nine, and their attempted conversion to Christianity by the authorities in special preparatory military schools. Indeed, an official Russian government commission in 1888 defined the Jews' condition as one of "repression and disenfranchisement, discrimination and persecution."[23] The impulse to Zionism arose out of and was a product of this reality.

The three prophetic harbingers of political Zionism, Rabbi Yehuda Alkalai (1798–1878), Rabbi Zvi Hirsch Kalischer (1795–1874), and Moses Hess (1812–1875), preceded by a full generation the actual emergence of the mass movement, and their visionary works had little immediate impact on their milieu. It took the successive shocks of the Russian pogroms of 1881–84 and the Dreyfus affair in France in the 1890s to set the stage for the blossoming of Zionism.

Alkalai, Kalischer, and Hess were all influenced by the plight of the Jews and by contemporary nationalist movements. Both rabbis, Alkalai in Serbia and Kalischer in Poland (then Prussia), saw a return to the Land of Israel as a stage in the redemption of the Jews. Hess was a thoroughly westernized German socialist ideologue who had collaborated with Karl Marx before dramatically returning to the Jewish fold in the 1850s and publishing his major Zionist work, *Rome and Jerusalem: The Last Nationality Question,* in 1862. He sensed the emergence of modern anti-Semitism, which would prevent the Jews from assimilating in Christian society, and he also understood that the Middle East was about to be swept by a wave of national liberation movements in conflict with the Ottoman Empire. He felt that the state the Jews would establish in the heart of the Middle East would serve Western imperial interests and at the same time help bring Western civilization to the backward East.

Alkalai, Kalischer, and Hess were dead by the time the Zionist movement was launched. On March 13, 1881, a band of young Russian revolutionaries assassinated Czar Alexander II, unleashing a wave of political unrest. Anti-Semites spread the rumor that the assassins were Jews (in fact, only one was). A wave of pogroms swept the empire, particularly the Ukraine, where mobs pillaged and destroyed Jewish neighborhoods, beating, raping, and killing the inhabitants. Moshe Leib Lilienblum (1843–1910), who was to emerge as a major Zionist ideologue, spent May 1881 cowering with his family in a cellar in Odessa. His diary entries afford a glimpse of the terror that gripped the millions of Jews in the Pale of Settlement:

May 5: The situation is terrible and frightening! We are virtually under siege. The courtyards are barred up, and we keep peering through the grillwork to see if the mob is coming to swoop down on us. . . . We all sleep in our clothes and without bedding . . . so that if we are attacked we will immediately be able to take the small children . . . and flee. But will they let us flee? . . . Will they have mercy on the youngsters? . . . How long, O God of Israel?

May 7: The rioters approached the house I am staying in. The women shrieked and wailed, hugging the children to their breasts, and didn't

know where to turn. The men stood by dumbfounded. We all imagined
that in a few moments it would be all over with us.[24]

But Lilienblum was fortunate: In Odessa, soldiers intervened, frightening
off the rioters.

The pogroms were followed by a series of laws and edicts institutionalizing
discrimination against Jews, including the numerus clausus, restricting their
entry into secondary schools and universities, hampering them from practic-
ing law, and clamping down on their freedom of movement and residence. In
1891–92, about twenty thousand Jews were expelled from Moscow. The
cumulative effect of the destruction of property and the discriminatory edicts
was the rapid pauperization of the empire's Jewish communities, which had
not been prosperous to begin with.[25]

Most people, including the community leaders in each town (there was no
central national Jewish communal organization), at least initially assured
themselves that all would be well. The pogroms were a passing aberration;
full emancipation was on its way. But many of the better-educated, who had
previously watched with hope the slow penetration of Russia by Western ideas
and had anticipated a gradual liberalization of the czarist realm, began to
despair. Things were only going to get worse. Some Jews had identified with
the revolutionary movement and had believed that the overthrow of the hated
ancien régime would lead to real emancipation. The events of 1881–82 were a
stunning slap in the face to both the liberals and the revolutionaries.

The solution had to lie elsewhere. Jews who had toyed with the possibility
of assimilation, who believed that the march of Westernism and modernity
would bring them to the bright uplands of full and equal integration, at last
acknowledged that history was not necessarily moving in that direction; that
the blood pulse of modern nationalism also led or could lead back to the dark
forests of tribalism and reaction, and to resurgent anti-Semitism.

In the wake of the pogroms, Leo Pinsker (1821–1891), a respected Russian-
Jewish doctor, was moved to dash off his classic, *Auto-Emancipation: A Warning to His Kinsfolk by a Russian Jew* (published anonymously, in German, in
September 1882). Pinsker had been something of an assimilationist, who
regarded the spread of the Russian language among the Jews as a means to
"Russification" and to Jewry's gradual integration into the body social. Then
came the pogroms. A badly shaken Pinsker called, in effect, for a giant exodus. In the Diaspora the Jews were and would forever be unwanted, often
reviled strangers. They must evacuate Europe and move to a "Promised
Land"; that way alone lay both personal salvation and national resurrection.
Pinsker was moved above all by an acute sense of dishonor and shame. The
pogroms had highlighted the Jews' impotence and humiliation: "When we are
ill-used, robbed, plundered and dishonoured we dare not defend ourselves,
and, worse still, we take it almost as a matter of course. . . . Though you prove

patriots a thousand times . . . some fine morning you find yourselves crossing the border and you are reminded by the mob that you are, after all, nothing but vagrants and parasites, outside the protection of the law."[26]

The Jews, "everywhere [guests], and nowhere at home," would, in the Diaspora, always be subject to that "incurable . . . psychic aberration," anti-Semitism. This, Pinsker argued, was not some illogical holdover from medieval Christendom. It had always existed and always would, primarily because the Jews' condition was unnatural and abnormal: Lacking territory, they lacked substance, "like a [people] without a shadow," ghosts, which others perpetually found irritating and threatening. In the modern world this gut abhorrence was compounded by the Jews' emergence from the ghetto as natural economic and professional competitors to the Christians.

The Jew could not save himself individually, only collectively. No one else, neither God nor gentile, would save him; salvation could be achieved only through exodus and concentration in a homeland, in a collective effort of will, through "autoemancipation," the re-creation of the Jewish nation, living on its own soil, in a country of its own. That country must gradually be purchased and settled; eventually the Jews would achieve nationhood and gentile recognition. Only there could Jews at last achieve equality with and independence of the gentiles.

Pinsker did not point to Palestine as the necessary haven. Indeed, he seemed to suggest that the Land of Israel was not really suitable for settlement. Rather, he looked vaguely to some stretch of North America that could be turned into a Jewish homeland.

HIBBAT ZION AND THE BILUIM

The pogroms had a dramatic, vital impact on East European Jewry, even before Pinsker explained their deep historical meaning and offered his solution. Many, at first in a slow trickle, then in a veritable flood tide, reacted with their feet. Unorganized, undirected, the Jews of the Pale of Settlement began to emigrate. It was a sporadic, instinctive response to oppression and violence and the threat of more to come. There was no organized communal response and no way to organize one. But all, or at least most, seemed to understand what history was telling them: Jewish life in Russia was no longer tenable.

Russian Jewry began to make tracks primarily toward the United States; by 1914 approximately 2.5 million were to reach the shores of America. Tens of thousands headed for South America and the British dominions, primarily Canada, South Africa, and Australia. Hundreds of thousands more settled in the cities and towns of central and Western Europe. An infinitely smaller number, more or less simultaneously and initially without coordination, responded to events by setting up in the cities and towns of the Pale and Poland clandestine societies of Hovevei Zion (Lovers of Zion), with the aim of emigrating to Palestine or supporting such emigration. Only a very small minority of Eastern Europe's Jews turned to Zionism, and only a fraction of these actually headed for the Holy Land; this was to remain the situation for decades thereafter.

The dozens of Hovevei Zion groups loosely confederated into what in 1887 was defined as the Hibbat Zion (Love of Zion) movement. *Auto-Emancipation* had provided them with their ideological charter. Indeed, Pinsker himself was rapidly propelled into the leadership. The movement was far from consensual. Almost all the local leaders opposed the impulse to emigrate immediately to Palestine, and few wealthy Jews were prepared to finance what was regarded as a wild venture. Hibbat Zion's fund-raising for settlement in Zion proved almost insignificant. Only from ten to thirty thousand Jews ever participated in the societies, and they managed to raise, altogether, about fifty thousand rubles (about five thousand pounds sterling) a year—a sum thought sufficient to cover the settlement in Palestine of perhaps fifteen families. But rather than fully equipping a dozen or so families with all that they would need, the societies preferred to send out "first aid" in small sums to the various settlements established in Palestine during the 1880s and 1890s—here helping the settlers to purchase a cow, there to fix a roof, elsewhere to buy a small tract of land. Between 1883 and 1899, the Hibbat Zion societies, of which there were several hundred around the Pale, Poland, and Western Europe, managed to raise only some eighty-seven thousand pounds sterling (compare this, say, to the contributions to various Zionist enterprises and charities in Palestine by the French magnate Baron Edmond James de Rothschild [1845–1934] during the same period, amounting to 1.6 million pounds sterling).[27]

One of the societies, set up by students in St. Petersburg, stated that "every son of Israel who admits that there is no salvation for Israel unless they establish a government of their own in the Land of Israel can be considered a member." A group that originated in Kharkov, called the Bilu, which was to leave an enormous stamp on the Zionist enterprise during the following half century, declared in its founding manifesto: "[The Jews have been] sleeping and dreaming the false dream of assimilation. . . . Now, thank God, thou art awakened. . . . The pogroms have awakened thee. . . . We want . . . a home in our country . . . it is ours as registered in the archives of history. . . ." The manifesto vaguely suggested that the Jewish settlers might "help our brother Ishmael [i.e., the Arabs] in his time of need." It also stated that the Biluim aimed to establish in Palestine "a state within a larger [Ottoman] state." A later charter of the association, from 1884, spoke of the need for all male members of Bilu to learn the use of firearms ("very necessary for those inhabiting countries of the East").[28] Fourteen Biluim set out on June 30, 1882, bent at once on "self-redemption" and on national renaissance, through settlement and physical labor in the Land of Israel. Although only fifty or sixty Biluim were to reach Palestine by the end of 1884, they were showing the way. Indeed, they succeeded in establishing at the heart of Zionism what one historian called the "mystique of the pioneer."[29] In July 1882 the first Biluim began working in Palestine as agricultural laborers. In 1884 they set up their own settlement, Gedera, next to the Arab village of Qatra (often, new Zionist settlements retained an approximation of the Arabic name of their sites, much as many Arab place names were derivatives of original Biblical Hebrew names).

Groups of Hovevei Zion began arriving in Palestine in spring 1882. That year the movement established several agricultural settlements, including Rishon Le-Zion, Rosh Pina, and Zikhron Ya'akov, and reestablished Petach Tikva, which had been founded by Jews from Jerusalem in 1878 but then abandoned. A second bout of settlement activity took place around 1890. By 1891 the dozen or so "New Yishuv" settlements had a combined population of less than 2,500.[30] Hovevei Zion's activities came to be known as "practical" Zionism—that is, realization of the dream by day-to-day, dunam-by-dunam[31] settlement of Palestine.

The pioneering enterprise required a great deal of courage and fortitude, and resulted in not a little despair. One of the *olim* ("those who ascend," or immigrants to Palestine) in 1885 aptly described the settlers' travails:

> Nothing frightened them, nothing stopped them, neither the barrenness of the country, nor the wildness of the Arabs . . . nor ignorance of the local language and customs. . . . Nobody knows of all the hardships, sickness, and wretchedness they underwent. No observer from afar can feel what it is like to be without a drop of water for days, to lie for months in cramped tents visited by all sorts of reptiles, or understand what our wives, children, and mothers go through when the Arabs attack us. . . . No one looking at a completed building realizes the sacrifice put into it.[32]

All in all, the movement succeeded in dispatching to Zion in the so-called First Aliyah ("ascension," or wave of immigration to Palestine), between 1881 and 1903, twenty to thirty thousand people, many of whom eventually returned to Russia or headed for the West. They set up nearly two dozen settlements. And, helped by major Western Jewish philanthropists, the movement managed to purchase, by 1890, about 100,000 dunams of Palestine land, and about 200,000 by 1900.[33]

Most of the settlements were fairly quickly overtaken by financial difficulties. But Rothschild, an ardent Zionist, was persuaded to provide assistance, and he carried the new settlements (except Gedera) and others set up later in the 1880s and 1890s until they became more or less self-supporting or found alternative funding.

Having launched the Jewish settlement of Palestine, however, Hovevei Zion failed to arouse, mobilize, and launch world Jewry, or even the mass of Eastern European Jewry, toward the shores of the Holy Land. By the mid-1890s the various societies of Hibbat Zion were in decline. Most eventually joined the Zionist Organization, established by Theodor Herzl toward the end of the decade.

POLITICAL (OR DIPLOMATIC) ZIONISM

In the early 1890s Zionism was an ideology waiting for a leader. Planting the odd settlement in godforsaken corners of Palestine was all very well, but would this trigger mass Jewish immigration or bring about the establishment of a nation-state? Would this solve the "Jewish problem" in Europe?

Theodor Herzl (1860–1904) in effect invented Zionism as a true political movement and as an international force.[34] In many respects Herzl was an unlikely candidate for the role thrust upon him by history. Before assuming the mantle of leadership, he knew next to nothing about the travails and life of Eastern European Jewry. Born to a prosperous, emancipated Budapest family, he was fluent in German and French but lacked Hebrew, Yiddish, and Russian; he was a secular, cosmopolitan intellectual, a doctor of law, and a minor playwright. He earned his living as the Paris correspondent of the Austrian daily *Neue Freie Presse*. Yet, within a few years, this quintessentially Western man was to lead a mass movement composed mainly of religious or observant Eastern European Jews.

What catalyzed Herzl's conversion to Zionism was the Dreyfus affair. In 1894–95 Alfred Dreyfus, a French Jewish officer, was wrongfully convicted of treason and confined to Devil's Island. The trial triggered a wave of anti-Semitism in the cradle and bastion of Western European liberal democracy. Herzl became obsessed with the need to solve the Jewish problem, and, at one point, even toyed with the idea that he was the Messiah, contrasting himself in his diary with Shabbetai Tzvi, a false messiah of the seventeenth century.[35] He set out his analysis of the situation in a prophetic, programmatic thirty-thousand-word pamphlet, *Der Judenstaat* (translatable as The Jews' State or The Jewish State), subtitled "An Attempt at a Modern Solution of the Jewish Question," which appeared in 1896. If France—the home of emancipation, progress, and universalist socialism—could be swept up in an anti-Semitic maelstrom, with Parisian crowds chanting "*À mort les Juifs!*," where could

Jews be safe—except in their own land? Assimilation would not solve the problem because the gentile world would not allow it, as *l'affaire Dreyfus* so clearly proved. The case was a watershed for many Central and Western European Jews, much as the pogroms of 1881–82 had been for Eastern Europeans.

Herzl regarded Zionism's triumph as inevitable, not only because life in Europe was ever more untenable for the Jews, but also because it was in Europe's interest to be rid of the Jews and relieved of anti-Semitism: The European political establishments would eventually be persuaded to promote Zionism. Herzl recognized that anti-Semitism could be harnessed to his own—Zionist—purposes.

Herzl envisioned that settlement in Palestine, and the establishment of a state, would give rise to a "new Jew"—"a wondrous breed of Jews. . . . The Maccabees will rise again."[36] A central aspiration of Zionist ideology was the attainment of honor and respect in place of the shame and contempt that were the hallmarks of Jewish life in the Diaspora, especially in the Czarist empire. Respect was to be attained by the refashioning of the Jew into something akin to a gentile—aggressive, assertive, straight-backed. "Muscular Judaism," in the phrase coined by Max Nordau (1849–1923), later Herzl's deputy at the head of the Zionist movement, was seen as both a means and a goal. Jews, with traditionally well-developed "mental muscles" but physically short and weak, were now also to develop their bodies. Jewish communities across Central and Eastern Europe began to invest resources in physical culture. In 1900 in Berlin a group of Jews set up a sports association called Bar-Kochba, after the Judean leader of the second revolt against Rome in A.D. 132–35.[37] The theme of the assertive "new" Jew was to reverberate through Zionist literature around the turn of the century, and would affect the behavior of the colonists who reached the Promised Land.

In public, Herzl made no explicit reference to the fate of the indigenous Arab population of Palestine, but he was aware of its existence and the problem it represented. In 1899 he wrote to the Arab notable Yusuf Zia al-Khalidi of Jerusalem that Zionism did not pose a threat of displacement for the Arab inhabitants of Palestine; rather, the arrival of the industrious, talented, well-funded Jews would materially benefit them.[38] He adopted a similar line in his utopian novel *Altneuland* (Old-New Land) published in 1902 and set in the Palestine of 1923. The Jews had brought only progress and prosperity to the country's natives, and this was the basis of comity and cooperation. Arabs could become equal citizens in the Jewish commonwealth. In 1903 Herzl reportedly opposed the purchase of the lands of Fula in the Jezreel Valley from the Sursuq family of Beirut, arguing that "poor Arab [tenant] farmers should not be driven off their land."[39]

But in private Herzl sang a different tune—one of displacement and transfer of Arabs, albeit with full financial compensation. In 1895 he wrote in his diary: "We must expropriate gently. . . . We shall try to spirit the penniless population across the border by procuring employment for it in the transit countries, while denying it any employment in our country. . . . Both the process of expropriation and the removal of the poor must be carried out discreetly and circumspectly."[40]

In his 1901 draft charter for a "Jewish-Ottoman Land Corporation," Herzl proposed that the state have the authority to move native populations from one place to another. But he never openly spoke of the need to transfer Palestine's Arabs to pave the way for Zionism; and, as a good liberal, he envisioned the propertied Arabs staying and supporting the Jewish state, living under a regime of exemplary tolerance.[41]

To turn vision into reality required money. Even before fashioning an organization to realize his vision, Herzl began vigorously to seek funds. In mid-1895 he tried to rope in a major Jewish banker, Baron Maurice de Hirsch, to back a Jewish state; subsequently he turned to the Rothschilds. He was unsuccessful with both, as he was with most of the leaders of Western Europe's Jewish communities—though one of the Rothschilds was at the time busy funding a number of settlements in Palestine. Baron Edmond may have feared for the position of French Jewry if a noisy Jewish nationalist movement got under way, but his rebuff to Herzl was delivered in other, strictly "Palestinian" terms: "A mass migration of Jews would arouse the enmity of the Bedouin, the mistrust of the Turkish authorities, the jealousy of the Christian colonies and pilgrims, and would undoubtedly lead to the suppression of the established settlements."[42]

The leaders of British and French Jewry feared that Herzl's loud public advocacy of Jewish nationalist aspirations would undermine their communities' standing and might reinforce Ottoman antagonism toward the ongoing small-scale Zionist enterprise in Palestine. Eastern Europe's Hovevei Zion circles and leaders also, at least initially, reacted to Herzl with extreme wariness: Such a volume of Zionist noise might prove counterproductive. Moreover, Herzl was an outsider, and aloof, and seemed to be dismissing all that Hovevei Zion had accomplished in Palestine. He rejected their piecemeal approach to Zionist realization and, in effect, was supplanting their leadership of the movement.

Eventually, however, the Zionist societies were persuaded that there was no credible alternative, no program better than Herzl's, and no leader better than the journalist from Budapest. Reluctantly they decided to play ball. Unlike the leaders of Western Jewry, prominent Eastern European Jews agreed to attend the First Zionist Congress, the forum chosen by Herzl for launching the movement to realize his goals, after his failure to mobilize the Western magnates.

The Zionist Organization, which was to serve as the movement's core and motor, was founded, under Herzl's orchestration, at the congress convened in Basel on August 29, 1897. It was attended by 200 to 250 delegates from twenty-four countries, with representatives of the Hovevei Zion societies pre-

dominating. There were speeches, debates, and arguments, anger and exultation, before the formula of a "home" (or "homestead"—*Heimstätte*) for the
Jewish people in Palestine was adopted as the goal of Zionism. The final
phrasing was arrived at only after bitter quarrels. But in the end, under Herzl's
guidance, the delegates decided to avoid the term "Jewish state" so as not to
antagonize the Turks, the Russians, and other gentiles.

Immediately after the conclusion of the Congress, on September 3, 1897,
Herzl wrote in his diary: "Were I to sum up the Basel Congress in a word . . . it
would be this: At Basel I founded the Jewish State. . . . Perhaps in five years,
and certainly in 50, everyone will know it."[43] In fact, fifty-one years were to
pass until the fulfillment of his dream.

Many of the ideas upon which Herzl based his "political Zionism" and the
Zionist Organization were to be found in the writings of the largely ignored
forerunners—Kalischer, Alkalai, and Hess—rather than in the praxis of Hovevei Zion. Like these predecessors, Herzl wanted to establish a giant philan-
thropic "Jewish national fund" for the purchase of land (which would then be
state-owned) and the underwriting of large-scale settlement; and, like them,
he proposed to achieve both settlement and statehood through an alliance with
one or more of the Great Powers—Turkey or Germany—or a "charter" by
which one of the powers would grant or lease Palestine to the Jews. Herzl
believed that, given world political realities, only thus could a Jewish commonwealth be established. In his view such a state was in the Great Powers'
interest, as it would form "an outpost of civilization against barbarism";
enable them to be rid of the Jews within their borders; and, at the same time,
offer a useful way of exploiting Jewish power (or potential power), wealth,
and skills.

Herzl's assumptions were echoed by some of Europe's leaders. Kaiser Wilhelm II wrote in 1898 that perhaps "the tribe of Shem would be directed [once
embarked on the Zionist road] to worthier goals than the exploitation of Christians." True, the Jews had "killed our Savior." But, given "the tremendous
power represented by international Jewish capital in all its dangerousness," it
would be well were the Jews to look upon Germany as their pro-Zionist protector.[44]

Without Great Power support the Jews would not succeed, through sporadic immigration, in pushing out the Ottoman rulers or establishing a state.
Indeed, such unauthorized activity, which angered the Ottomans, might well
prove counterproductive. "What is achieved by transporting a few thousand
Jews to another country? Either they come to grief at once, or, if they prosper,
their prosperity gives rise to anti-Semitism. . . . [It] is bound to end badly,"
Herzl once wrote[45]—though he eventually came grudgingly to support the settlement in Palestine of those Zionists under whose feet the Russian soil was
burning and who could not wait for an international charter.

With a ragtag power base and a minuscule treasury, Herzl set about knocking on the doors of presidents and kings to obtain the coveted "charter." The initial and chief object of his diplomacy was the power that physically controlled Palestine. The Ottomans had to be persuaded that a Jewish commonwealth would be to their benefit. The advent of "the financially strong and diligent people of Israel" would bring "undreamt-of prosperity" to the Empire, and the "millions [channeled] into Turkish money-bags" would cure the Sick Man of Europe—this was how Kaiser Wilhelm II put it in a letter to a relative.[46]

Alternatively, if the Turks could not be induced to grant the Jews a charter, perhaps one or more of the Western Powers—Germany or Britain—could be persuaded to back them and either to force a Jewish state upon the reluctant Ottomans or themselves to engineer its establishment. This was to be Herzl's political-diplomatic strategy during the following decade, in the course of which he met, among other potentates, the king of Italy, Pope Pius X, Kaiser Wilhelm himself (twice, in 1898), and the sultan of Turkey, Abdülhamid II (1901). But all the shuttling to and fro, all the meetings and attempted meetings with the world's high and mighty, were to no avail.

The Turks would not budge; in Constantinople—which Herzl came to call that "den of Ali Baba and the 40 thieves"[47] — he encountered only hostility, frustration, delay, and lies. At least initially there had been some encouragement from the Kaiser. But Wilhelm, keen on an alliance with the Turks, saw no reason to go out of his way to offend the Sublime Porte. The pope, various Frenchmen, and the Italians all similarly proved of no use.

Herzl switched his attention to Britain: "England the mighty, England the free, the England that looks out over all the seas, will understand . . . our endeavours." And, indeed, it was England that, at last, in August 1903 offered something concrete—a patch of East Africa (the "Uganda offer")—while denying a coveted stretch of the Sinai Peninsula around Al-'Arīsh, vigorously sought by the Zionists, attracted by its proximity to Palestine.[48] The proposal sparked a major controversy within the movement, ultimately splitting it into two factions: a "territorialist" minority, who favored (against the backdrop of renewed pogroms in Russia) accepting any territory anywhere for the establishment of a Jewish commonwealth and haven, and the "Zionists of Zion," who would accept nothing but Palestine. Crucially, the Russians themselves, led by the young Chaim Weizmann, rejected "Uganda." Herzl, who wavered and then sided with the "Zionists of Zion," died in mid-controversy, on July 3, 1904, and was buried in Vienna. (His remains were symbolically reinterred in Jerusalem in August 1949, a year after the establishment of the State of Israel.) In July 1905 the Seventh Zionist Congress formally rejected "Uganda," and many of the territorialists left the movement. Palestine, and only Palestine, was now the goal. In short order Britain's African offer was withdrawn, never to resurface.

The Zionist movement, which grew rapidly in the years after Basel, received a major boost in 1903–6 from a second wave of Russian pogroms far more vicious than those of the 1880s. The new assaults were a by-product of the grievances and turmoil surrounding the Revolution of 1905, as the Czarist regime tried to thwart the revolutionaries by diverting popular attention and anger from the monarchy to the Jews. A particularly severe jolt was administered by the first pogrom, in Kishinev, on Passover (April 19–20) 1903, when the mobs slaughtered forty-nine people, injured and mutilated hundreds more, and destroyed approximately fifteen hundred Jewish homes and shops.[49] The assaults intensified in 1905, against the backdrop of the Russo-Japanese War and accusations that the Jews were fomenting revolution. The most severe outbreaks—in part organized by government officials and the secret police— occurred in November following the Czar's promise of civil liberties and the establishment of a parliament (duma). There were hundreds of pogroms, in Ukraine, Poland, and Lithuania, leaving altogether about eight hundred Jewish dead; in the worst, in Odessa, about three hundred people died and thousands were wounded. (A third wave of pogroms, during 1917–21, concurrent with the Russian Revolution and the civil wars and mostly carried out by White Russian forces, claimed perhaps as many as sixty thousand lives.)

The pogroms of 1903–06 were a major precipitant of the Second Aliyah, the next wave of Jewish emigration to Palestine. The first pogrom was a turning point: Before, it seemed, Jews accepted slaughter as their fate; after Kishinev they rebelled. No longer would they accept death, beatings, rape, and pillage without resistance. Among a growing militant minority, the rage that had built up over decades, indeed centuries, exploded. Impotence would be replaced by action. Jews would no longer rely on king, baron, or policeman for protection; these had persuasively demonstrated their indifference or malevolence, and could not be trusted. Jews had to protect themselves and their own; at the very least they had to defend or assert their honor and go down fighting.

The single most effective spokesman for Jewish outrage, the man who persuaded the intelligentsia of the need for action, was the poet Hayyim Nahman Bialik. In his epic poem, *In the City of Slaughter,* he described Kishinev after the pogrom, God's indifference, and the Jews going off like sheep to the slaughter. Sarcastically, the poet referred to the victims as "descendants of the Maccabees."

The new wave of immigration to Palestine, even more than the one before it, was an expression of revolt against the helplessness and humiliation of Diaspora life. Some of those who came in the Second Aliyah were veterans of the self-defense groups that had formed inside Russia in the wake of Kishinev. Self-defense was to be a major pillar of their ideology in Palestine. Many of the new *olim* instantly translated their Russian experiences into Palestinian coinage: Arab was equated with gentile, Arab marauding with pogrom, local antagonism and territorial feuding with anti-Semitism. They discerned in their new surroundings, behind every bush, under every tree, the shadow of the

Russian persecutor they had left behind; collectively they were haunted by their awful past. Eventually the Arabs—and they themselves—would pay the price.

THE RISE OF ARAB AND PALESTINIAN-ARAB NATIONALISM

THE HARBINGERS

Zionism emerged about a quarter of a century earlier than Arab nationalism, a head start in political consciousness and organization that proved vital to the Jews' success and to the Palestinian Arabs' failure during the following decades of conflict. There were, during the nineteenth century, centers of disaffection with Ottoman rule in Arab provinces. But the Arabs shared an abiding millennium-old loyalty to the encompassing Islamic polity, buttressed by a vague awareness that the European powers were ready to pounce should the empire falter.

Nevertheless, by the late 1870s a handful of Arabs were urging at least a measure of separation from the empire. Earlier, groups had formed in Damascus and Beirut whose purpose, paradoxically influenced by European currents of thought and American missionaries, was the promotion of Arab culture. The Society of Arts and Sciences was founded in 1847, and the Syrian Scientific Society in 1857. The dominant figures were the Lebanese Christian writers and educators Nasīf Yazijī (1800–71) and Butrus al-Bustāni (1819–83). Separatist impulses and disillusionment with the empire were particularly strong among Lebanese Christians, and grew as a consequence of the Muslim-Druze massacre of Maronites in Mount Lebanon and Damascus in 1860.

Bustāni preached a Syrian consciousness and patriotism that transcended religious-ethnic origins. He regarded the area of present-day Lebanon and Syria as one country (*bilad suriyya*) and wrote that "Syria is our fatherland (*watan*) and the population of Syria, whatever their creed, community, racial origin or groups are the sons of our fatherland."[50] Separatist impulses also existed in Syria proper. In 1858 the British consul in Aleppo, J. H. Skene, reported that the "Mussulman population of Northern Syria harbors hopes of a separation from the Ottoman Empire and the formation of a new Arabian State under the sovereignty of the Shereefs of Mecca."[51]

The years 1876–78 saw a severe crisis in the empire. There were three sultans within eighteen months, the last of whom, Abdülhamid II (1842–1918),

who ruled until 1909, promulgated a new constitution at the end of 1876. The
first parliament was convened in March 1877. The delegates included dozens
of Arabs, for whom this was the first taste of national-level politics. The following month Russia declared war on Constantinople. Thousands of Arab
conscripts from Syria, Lebanon, and Palestine died in the war, which ended in
Ottoman defeat in March 1878, a month after Abdülhamid dissolved parliament and suspended the new constitution. The casualties stoked Arab hostility
toward Constantinople. In 1878 Muslim, Maronite, and Druze leaders from
Syria and Lebanon met with the exiled Algerian rebel leader ʻAbd al-Qadir al-
Jaza'iri, who lived in Damascus, and considered proclaiming an independent
Arab republic with him at its head.[52] But al-Jaza'iri opposed complete independence, and the Ottoman authorities got wind of the movement, exiled
some leaders, and imposed restrictions on others.[53]

A number of insubstantial secret or camouflaged nationalist societies
emerged during 1878–81. Posters appeared sporadically on walls in Damascus, Beirut, Sidon, and Tripoli denouncing Ottoman tyranny and the abolition
of the constitution, and calling for an Arab revolt and Syrian-Lebanese unity
and autonomy.[54] But the poster campaign quickly died down, to be succeeded
by a generation of silence, though covert reverberations of discontent continued. In 1883 a Western traveler, Denis de Rivoyre, reported: "Everywhere
[there is] hatred of the Turks. An Arab movement, newly-risen, is looming in
the distance; and a race hitherto downtrodden will presently claim its due
place in the destinies of Islam."[55]

But the cause of Arab nationalism—never more than the plaything of a thin
layer of intellectuals—abated into quiescence with the passing of the crisis
that had attended the start of Abdülhamid's reign and his heavy-handed stifling of parliament, the press, and all opposition. The later years of his reign
also saw a return to Islamic orthodoxy, with greater subsidies for religious
institutions, which helped blunt the edge of disaffection among Arab notables.[56]

Arab nationalism revived in the first decade of the 1900s. Its main spokesmen, ʻAbd al-Rahman al-Kawakibi (1854–1902), Rashid Rida (1865–1935),
and Najib Azouri (1873?–1916), were apparently unaware of the stirrings of
1877–81 and never mentioned them in their writings. Kawakibi, an Aleppo-
born intellectual, is today seen as the main herald of modern, secular pan-
Arabism. His two books, *Umm al Qura* (The mother of villages, meaning
Mecca; c. 1903) and *Taba'i al Istibdad* (The nature of tyranny; c. 1901),
assailed Ottoman despotism and called for pan-Islamic unity and revival. He
lamented the weakness of the Islamic world and enumerated eighty-six causes
for its inferiority, including fatalism, religious rifts, intolerance, the ban on
freedom of speech, injustice and inequality, uncritical acceptance of the written word, hostility toward the sciences, inefficient use of time, and neglect of

women's education.[57] Though he spoke of Arabia as the heartland of an Arabism uncorrupted by Ottoman values, his message was not really nationalist in the nineteenth-century European sense.[58]

Rida, born near Tripoli, Lebanon, lived most of his life in Egypt, where in 1898 he founded and edited *al-Manar*, a daily newspaper that promoted pan-Islamism and Islamic revival, and, later, Arab nationalism. In 1907 he was among the founders of the Society of the Ottoman Council, which sought to reform the empire, unite its nationalities, and convert the despotism of Abdül-hamid into a constitutional government.[59] But in the face of the Young Turks' "Turkification" policies Rida was gradually converted to pure Arab nationalism, and he founded the secret Society of the Arab Association, whose purpose was to unify the Arab provinces and to counter the Young Turks' Committee of Union and Progress (CUP), which he defined as an "enemy of the Arabs and of Islam." He was prominent in the pre–World War I autonomy-seeking Arab Decentralization Party and in 1915, from Cairo, helped the British establish links with the Hashemites in the Hejaz.[60] In 1920 he served as president of the First Syrian-Arab Congress in Damascus.

Azouri, a Maronite Christian, served as assistant governor of the Jerusalem District between 1898 and 1904, when he fell out with his superiors and fled to Cairo. After publishing articles attacking Ottoman corruption, he was sentenced to death in absentia by a Constantinople court. Moving to Paris, he founded the Ligue de la Patrie Arabe, which in December 1904 and January 1905 published two manifestos denouncing Ottoman oppression and calling for an independent Arab state stretching from the Euphrates to the Suez Canal.[61] Later in 1905 Azouri published *Le Réveil de la Nation Arabe dans l'Asie Turque* (The Awakening of the Arab Nation in Turkish Asia). The first public advocate of a secular Arab nationalism, he wrote:

> A great pacific change is on the eve of occurring in Turkey. The Arabs, whom the Turks tyrannized, have become conscious of their national, historical, and racial homogeneity, and wish to detach themselves from the worm-eaten Ottoman trunk in order to form themselves into an independent State. This new Arab Empire will extend to its natural frontiers, from the valleys of the Tigris and Euphrates to the Isthmus of Suez, from the Mediterranean to the Sea of Oman.[62]

He hoped that France (and perhaps Britain) would assist an Arab rebellion and the establishment of a national state, and probably at times received clandestine French government funding. In 1908 the French chargé d'affaires in Cairo (to which Azouri had by then returned) reported that Azouri had "offered his services to the various diplomatic delegations and most adroitly attempted to exploit his relations with each of them to carry out intrigues." Repeatedly during 1912–14 he asked the Italians and the French to provide him with 100,000 rifles with two hundred bullets apiece and funds to launch a revolt.[63] Nothing came of this.

THE YOUNG TURKS' REVOLUTION AND THE RISE OF ARAB NATIONALISM

The Arab national movement emerged onto the stage of history—although it was not to attain center stage until the Twenties and Thirties—in the wake of the July 1908 revolution of the Young Turks' Movement, which reintroduced the 1876 constitution, freedom of the press, and the Ottoman parliament. In the Arab world, according to a British resident of Syria, there was "universal rejoicing. Muslims were seen embracing Christians and Jews, and inviting one another to receptions and feasts. The pent-up feelings of the populace everywhere burst forth in loud hurrahs in the public streets. Syria has never seen such rejoicing. The Golden Age seemed to be dawning."[64] There were festive rallies and mass meetings in Beirut, Damascus, Haifa, and Jerusalem, though in Palestine the a'yan—linked by tradition and financial benefit to the Hamidian regime—were far from enthusiastic.[65]

Some nationalists feared that the revolution, with its promise of liberalization, might erode the incentive and impetus for Arab liberation and independence.[66] But the Golden Age failed to dawn. Certainly, the 260-man parliament duly reconvened in Constantinople in December, with sixty Arab and 140 Turkish delegates, though the Arabs believed that they were more numerous, by a ratio of 3:2, in the empire than the Turks.[67] (Estimates of the Turkish-Arab ratio in the population vary radically, from 7.5:10.5 million to 12.5:5.3.) Altogether the parliament had 214 Muslims, forty-two Christians, and four Jews. Arab hopes for equality and autonomy were soon dashed. The Young Turks appeared as keen as Abdülhamid to maintain the empire's integrity and to ensure Turkish dominance. A process of Turkification was set in motion: Many Arab officials were replaced by Turks; and Turkish, promoted as the only language of government and the courts, was made compulsory in all schools.[68] An anti-Arab atmosphere suffused the regime. Indeed, leading CUP members in private correspondence wrote derogatorily of the Arabs, one calling them "the dogs of the Turkish nation."[69] The revolution in Constantinople provoked a counterwave of Arab nationalist feeling and paved the way for its organized political expression by allowing a relatively free press and the establishment of political groups. The governor of Jerusalem, 'Ali Akram Bey, warned that local notables would exploit the new freedom for anti-Ottoman purposes: "The promulgation of the constitution and its implementation slowly began to awaken feelings of independence among the Arabs. Though this idea remains for the time being secret and covert, to judge by all that is happening here, [in] the press and other manifestations, one can feel that the tendencies of the populace in all of [Greater] Syria are heading that way."[70]

Among the more important Arab nationalist or autonomy-inclined parties to emerge after the revolution were the Ottoman Party for Administrative Decentralization, founded in Cairo at the end of 1912 and known as the Decentralization Party; and the secret Society of the Young Arab Nation, founded in Paris on November 14, 1909, known as al-Fatat.[71] The former—founded by Syrian, Lebanese, and Palestinian émigrés, both Muslim and Christian, against the backdrop of Ottoman defeat in the Balkan Wars and the loss of Libya to Italy—established secret branches in Damascus, Beirut, Nablus, and Jaffa, and sought the subdivision of the empire into autonomous entities along national-ethnic lines. In part it was motivated by the empire's increasing weakness and a fear that its Arab provinces might be taken over by European powers. The political platform declared: "The best sort of regime is constitutional and the best sort of constitutional regime is decentralized." At the start of World War I the party halfheartedly tried to foment anti-Ottoman rebellions in Lebanon and the Persian Gulf, without success.[72]

The creation of al-Fatat was triggered by a street incident in Istanbul four days after the promulgation of the Young Turks' constitution. Two Arab students, Ahmad Qadri of Damascus and 'Awni 'Abd al-Hadi of Nablus, heard a Turkish officer denouncing "Arab traitors" who had supported the *ancien régime*. Why wasn't he also denouncing the many Turks who had supported Abdülhamid? the two Arabs asked. An argument ensued and the students concluded that the Arabs needed a secret society like that of the Young Turks to obtain equal rights within the empire. What emerged was al Fatat.[73] Two of its founding members, 'Abd al-Hadi and Rafiq al-Tamimi (also of Nablus), were to play prominent parts in the Palestinian Arab national movement. All were of Greater Syrian origin, and all were Muslims. The society initially aimed at preserving the "natural rights" of the Arab nation rather than Arab independence, Arab-Turkish equality within the empire rather than secession. But by 1913 leading members were defining its platform as "the liberation of the Arab nation."[74]

In June 1913 the reformist societies organized the First Arab Congress in Paris. The idea was to publicize Arab grievances in the West and apply indirect pressure on the Turks to agree to reform. Twenty-three delegates—eleven Muslims, eleven Christians, and one Jew—and about 150 observers met in the auditorium of the French Geographical Society and called not for separation but for "political rights" for the Arabs; "decentralized administration" in the Arab provinces; "foreign [non-Ottoman] advisers" for an autonomous

Lebanon; and Arabic to be used—alongside Turkish—in the Ottoman parliament and as an official language in the Arab provinces.

The congress caught the Turks at a particularly difficult moment: The empire had lost Libya to Italy (1912), had just lost the First Balkan War to the Greek-Bulgarian-Serbian-Montenegrin coalition (Treaty of London, May 30, 1913), and was fighting off a renewed challenge in the Balkans (the Second Balkan War would begin on June 29). The grand vizier, Mahmud Shawkat, had been assassinated a week before the congress began. To no avail, Constantinople had attempted to pressure France to cancel the congress. It then mounted an unsuccessful campaign of propaganda and intimidation against the prospective delegates.[75] Constantinople decided to stymie the Arab challenge through appeasement. Senior Ottoman officials traveled to Paris in July and hammered out a compromise with the delegates: "recognition" of Arab rights and the need for reforms; service by Arab soldiers near home; Arabic to be the language of instruction in schools in the Arab districts; and more Arab senior officials in the Constantinople bureaucracies. But these provisions were never put into effect.[76] "A piece of chicanery" was how the first historian of the Arab awakening described the Turkish promises.[77]

The empire lost almost all its remaining European domains in 1912–13. World War I was to deprive it of its Arab lands and, indeed, whittle away its realm until only the bare Turkish rump remained. Moved by hostility toward Russia, and a belief that Germany would win the war—or, alternatively, that if the Allies won, they would in any case carve up the empire among themselves—the Young Turks in November 1914 plunged into the fray on the Central Powers' side. Most of the empire's Arab subjects remained loyal. Al-Fatat, which a year before had been preaching something close to Arab secession, closed ranks with fellow Muslims. It still aimed for the "liberation and independence" of the Arab provinces, but its Supreme Committee in Damascus ruled: ". . . in the event of European designs appearing to materialize, the society shall be bound to work on the side of Turkey in order to resist foreign penetration of whatever kind or form."[78]

A small number of Arabs, mostly Christian, secretly strove for an Allied victory. In Beirut, Maronite notables approached the British and French consuls general to assist a local uprising with troops and funds. But the British and French—their armies heavily committed in Flanders, and unable to help—cautioned against rash action.[79] Nonetheless, the British set about elsewhere fomenting and assisting revolt in the Ottoman rear; the Hejaz, in Arabia, not Lebanon, was to be the focus of British interest. Clandestine contacts between the British and the Hashemite emir of Mecca, Sharif Hussein, and his son, the emir Abdullah, had begun even before the declaration of war. The Sharifians, for their part, established covert contacts with nationalists in Damascus and Beirut. During the following two years the negotiations inched forward, with the Arabs demanding, and the British accepting, the principle of Arab independence in at least part of the crumbling empire. On June 10, 1916, the revolt broke out in Mecca, backed by British and French arms, subsidies, and advisers (of whom the most prominent was to be T. E. Lawrence, "Lawrence of Arabia"). The revolt was seen by the British as mortally subverting Ottoman efforts to turn the war in the East into an anti-Christian *jihad* (Islamic holy war) and as a complement to an Allied military thrust from Egypt up the Mediterranean coast toward Turkey.

From the beginning of the war, the Turks had feared a revolt and fifth-column activities by Arab nationalists in Damascus and Beirut. At first they tried to conquer Egypt; failing in this, they tried to ward off British counter-thrusts toward Palestine and Syria. In 1915–16 Jamal Pasha, commander of the Ottoman Fourth Army and military governor of the Greater Syria region, instituted a reign of terror in which dozens of Arab nationalists were publicly hanged in Damascus and Beirut and hundreds were arrested. Thousands more Palestinian Arabs (as well as Jews) were deported inland, away from the centers of subversion and from likely axes of Allied invasion (and all this even before any concrete anti-Ottoman subversion had taken place). Additional thousands died of disease and starvation, in part as a result of the Ottoman military requisitioning of crops. These events naturally served to intensify Arab nationalist and separatist aspirations. The Turks gradually came to be seen as a vicious (and increasingly weakened) enemy.

The two strands of Arab discontent, the active one backed by Britain in Arabia and the dormant one in Syria and Lebanon, in a sense came together in September–October 1918, as the Arabian rebels, acting as the right flank of Gen. Edmund Allenby's advancing army in Palestine, swept northward through Transjordan and occupied Damascus. There they and their nationalist "hosts" established a Syrian Arab state, with Emir Faisal, Sharif Hussein's son, as ruler, with a cohort of Syrian, Lebanese, Palestinian, and Iraqi advisers.

Jerusalem had fallen to Allenby in December 1917; Beirut, on October 8, 1918—a week after the Arabs entered Damascus. The Ottoman Empire was no more. In the lands south of Turkey there emerged over the years, under French and British tutelage, the states of the Arabian Peninsula, Syria, Lebanon, Transjordan (from 1948 Jordan), and Iraq. And there emerged the problem of Palestine, where, under the umbrella of the British Mandate, two national movements, Arab and Jewish, vied for dominance and, eventually, statehood.

Faisal's brief rule in Damascus was accompanied by hectic political activity, which marked the effective emergence of modern Arab nationalism. In 1919 Faisal's supporters set up the Arab Independence Party, al-Istiqlal, aiming at pan-Arab unity and independence. A succession of large nationalist assemblies, known as the Syrian-Arab Congresses, were convened in Damascus that year and in 1920. They upheld Faisal's territorial claims and advocated his self-proclamation as king of Greater Syria, encompassing Syria, Lebanon, Jordan, and Palestine. Meanwhile, to preempt or stave off Damascene hegemony, Iraqi "nationalists" invited Faisal's brother, Abdullah, to become king of Iraq. In Lebanon a coterie of Christians advocated Lebanese nationhood. And political realities in Transjordan and Palestine quickly subverted the dream of Arab political union. The idea of one large, unitary state or federation evaporated, like a puddle of water in the desert, though during the following decades the motif of Arab unity or pan-Arabism was periodically to bedevil and entrance Arab politics, but to no lasting result.

Complementing and to a great degree overshadowing the centrifugal pull of these national movements, France and Britain were largely to determine the geopolitical character and future of the Middle East over the following two or three decades. Their secret Sykes-Picot Agreement of 1916 had carved up the Arab lands of the soon-to-be-dissected empire in line with traditional, prewar spheres of influence and economic, political, military, and cultural interests. Iraq and, ultimately, Palestine were left to the British. Transjordan, severed from the Palestine Mandate, was declared a separate entity, ruled by Abdullah under British tutelage. In 1920 Faisal was removed by the French from Damascus and reinstalled in Baghdad as a British-protected sovereign. France assumed the mandate over Syria and Lebanon, which were almost from the first administratively separated. National movements and identities soon congealed in each of the mandated territories, each pressing for statehood in its own area, despite the common bonds of language, culture, and history.

It is difficult to categorize the Arab societies and political groupings that emerged before World War I according to Western definitions. Were they nationalist? Of the twenty-odd groups described and analyzed by Israeli historian Eliezer Tauber, only five included the word "Arab" in their names.[80] Most did not aspire to secession, independence, or statehood. They wanted equal rights—cultural, economic, social, and occasionally political—and, perhaps, autonomy. Even the First Arab Congress of 1913 did not aim for secession or statehood. But if nationalism did not figure in these early organizations, some form of "local patriotism"—focusing on Lebanon, Syria, or Iraq—did. Apart from Lebanon, revolt and complete secession were preached only after the outbreak of World War I, when the giant conflagration unleashed apocalyptic expectations. It was only at the start of 1915, when al-Fatat combined with the al-Ahd group formed in 1913 by Arab officers in the Ottoman army, that they called (in the "Damascus Protocol") for Arab independence. Tauber broadly categorizes the clubs, societies, and movements of this period under the headings "Arabism," "Lebanonism," "Syrianism," and "Iraqism," but does not designate any of them "nationalist." The emergence of full-fledged nationalism, he argues, had to wait until World War I and its aftermath. And it was members of these prewar societies, especially al-Ahd and al-Fatat, who emerged after the war as the leaders of the separate, particularist nationalisms of Lebanon, Syria, and Iraq.[81]

It was at this time, too, that a distinct Palestinian local patriotism or proto-nationalism began to emerge. This tendency or orientation—it hardly qualified as a movement—gradually groped its way forward, largely in reaction to the burgeoning Zionist presence. But in part it was also the product of other political, economic, religious, and social developments and realities, dating from the mid-nineteenth century. During the centuries of Ottoman rule, Palestine had not been a single or separate administrative unit. But in the 1880s, as we have seen, the Levantine provinces were reorganized, with most of southern Palestine—including Jerusalem, Jaffa, Lydda, Gaza, Beersheba, Hebron, Bethlehem, and Jericho—transformed into a separate governorate, answerable directly to Constantinople, not to the provincial governors in Syria or Beirut. Thus, the core of the Holy Land had become a distinct administrative and, in some respects, "political" entity. In 1910 the Ottomans established a court of appeals in Jerusalem, which served both the governorate of Jerusalem and the *sanjak* of Nablus (roughly, Samaria) to the north. In the military sphere, too, there was close cooperation, if not unity of command, between the two administrative units.

Perhaps even more important to the development of a distinct "Palestinian" identity were common religious structures, observances, and festivities, both Christian and Muslim. For the Christians, Palestine was a single conceptual entity, the Holy Land. Hence the Greek Orthodox patriarchate of Jerusalem, the Latin patriarchate of Jerusalem, and the Anglican bishopric of Jerusalem were responsible for the whole of Palestine (and Transjordan). Among the Muslims the Nabi Musa festivities, dating from the twelfth-century days of Saladin and celebrating the birth of Moses, each year brought together, at the site near Jericho traditionally accepted as his grave, thousands of pilgrims from the various parts of Palestine.[82] The growing sense of a distinct community was expressed and reinforced by the appearance in Jaffa in 1911 of a daily newspaper named *Filastin*. And in the decade before World War I the term "Palestine"—not used in any political or administrative sense for centuries by the Ottoman Empire—came into common usage among educated Palestinian Arabs. The following two decades would witness the emergence of a full-fledged, separate Palestinian-Arab national movement.[83]

The first quasi-political Palestinian nationalist organizations can be traced to the last months of World War I. In November 1918, veteran Jaffa notables established a local "Muslim-Christian Association" (MCA). Similar MCAs, later all loosely connected, were established—often with clandestine help from British officers—in the following months in other towns. The MCAs, while not defining themselves as political organizations, articulated local political thinking and aspirations, generally espousing self-rule and opposing Zionism, and expressed themselves in posters and petitions to the British administration. Christians were disproportionately represented, perhaps because they were better educated and more advanced politically, perhaps because they felt a greater need to collaborate with others.[84] (In 1931 literacy among Muslims was about 14 percent, compared with 58 percent among Christians.[85])

An important step on the road to a full-fledged Palestinian political identity was the founding at the end of the war, by younger members of the a'yan, of two societies: al-Muntada al-Adabi (the literary club) and al-Nadi al-Arabi (the Arab club). Al-Muntada was led by Jamil al-Husseini, Fakhri al-Nashashibi, Mahmud 'Aziz al-Khalidi, and Hasan Sidqi al-Dajani. Dominated by the Nashashibi family, it promoted Arabic language and culture and Muslim values, and was infused with pan-Arab sentiment, advocating an independent, united Syria-Palestine. Al-Nadi, founded at the end of the war in Damascus as an offshoot of al-Fatat, had similar goals. It was dominated by the Husseini clan (primarily Hajj Muhammad Amin al-Husseini) and by young Nabulsis, including Dr. Hafiz Kan'an. Al-Nadi issued a newspaper, founded in Jerusalem in September 1919, entitled, significantly, *Suriyya al-Janubiyya* (Southern Syria), edited by Muhammad Hassan al-Budayri and 'Arif al-'Arif. Its anti-Zionism was reflected in a play staged in January 1920 by its Nablus branch. In *The Ruin of Palestine,* a Zionist maiden seduces two Arabs and steals their money and land. The play ends with the suicide of the two men, shouting: "The country is ruined, the Jews have robbed us of our land and honor."[86] Al-Muntada and al-Nadi apparently had secret auxiliaries—called Jam'iyyat al-Ikha' wal 'Afaf (association of brotherhood and purity) and al-Fida'iyya (the self-sacrificers), which planned acts of violence against Jews and those who sold them land—but these do not seem ever to have been active.[87]

A handful of Palestinian nationalists had always shied away from pan-Syrian sentiments, preferring a separate national entity. But until 1920 the majority looked to the emergence of an independent Greater Syria, of which Palestine was just the southwestern corner. Indeed, the very idea of Arab sovereignty was linked in their minds to Syria. But events in Palestine and Syria in April–July 1920 abruptly changed this orientation. During this four-month period Palestinian-Arab nationalism can be said to have emerged as a distinct movement, albeit, at this time, the province of a very restricted elite.

The events that resulted in this change began when Arab disturbances around Palestine gave vent to anti-Zionist impulses and to a desire to cast off British rule and unite with Faisal's Syria. In early March, a band of Damascus-affiliated Arabs attacked the Jewish settlement of Tel Hai at the northern tip of Palestine. A second attack, on April 24, by several thousand Bedouin from Syria and the Beisan Valley against a British encampment at Samakh, on the southern shore of the Sea of Galilee, was actively organized in Damascus and seems to have been intended as the trigger to a wider revolt. The defeat of that attack, like the general crushing of the disturbances by the British, reaffirmed Palestine's complete physical and political separation from Syria. The collapse of Faisal's regime in July and the return home of the "national" contingents that helped prop up the Hashemites in Damascus—mainly Palestinians and Iraqis—confirmed the unreality of the "Syrian" option for Palestine's Arabs and persuaded the a'yan that they must go their own way toward independence. Little help could be expected from Faisal, now in exile, and from Syria's Arabs, now under French occupation.

This radical shift can be traced in the successive postwar Palestinian congresses. The first, which met in Jerusalem in January 1919, had voted for unity with Syria. "We see Palestine as part of Arab Syria," it resolved, "[and it should not] be separated from the independent Syrian Arab government."[88] A so-called Second Congress never actually took place. The third, meeting in Haifa in December 1920, called upon the British to establish a "native government" and representative assembly. It made no mention of "Southern Syria" and dropped the demand for unity of Palestine and Syria.[89] The Fourth Congress, meeting in Jerusalem in May 1921, spoke of "the Arab people of Palestine" with no mention of southern Syria[90]— though subsequent congresses generally paid lip service to the idea of Arab unity.[91]

By the end of 1920 "the regional division between Syria and Palestine was complete. The idea of a unified Arab nation gave way to new political divisions along Palestinian and Syrian as well as Iraqi lines."[92] Alongside Syrians, Iraqis, and Egyptians, a Palestinian people was emerging. By 1923 Ze'ev Jabotinsky, who two years later founded the right-wing Revisionist branch of Zionism, was to write:

They look upon Palestine with the same instinctive love and true fervor that any Aztec looked upon Mexico or any Sioux looked upon his prairie. Palestine will remain for the Palestinians not a borderland, but their birthplace, the center and basis of their own national existence.[93]

THE BEGINNING OF THE CONFLICT: JEWS AND ARABS IN PALESTINE, 1881–1914

Who can challenge the rights of the Jews in Palestine? Good Lord, historically it is really your country," wrote Jerusalem Muslim dignitary Yusuf Diya al-Khalidi to Zadok Kahn, chief rabbi of France, on March 1, 1899. In theory the Zionist idea was "completely natural, fine and just." But in practice reality had to be considered—the recognized sanctity of the Holy Land to hundreds of millions of Christians and Muslims. The Jews could only acquire Palestine by war. "It is necessary, therefore, for the peace of the Jews in [the Ottoman Empire] that the Zionist Movement . . . stop. . . . Good Lord, the world is vast enough, there are still uninhabited countries where one could settle millions of poor Jews who may perhaps become happy there and one day constitute a nation. . . . In the name of God, let Palestine be left in peace."

This letter was passed to Herzl, who responded on March 19. He ignored Khalidi's prognosis that Zionism would spark Arab opposition and asserted that the Jews, far from displacing the Arab population, would bring to Palestine only material benefit.[1]

Khalidi had before his eyes the creeping dispossession that began when the first Jewish colonists, with their backers abroad, bought tract after tract of land. In some areas the land was uninhabited and untilled; in others purchase led to the immediate eviction of Arab tenant farmers, many of whose families had themselves once been the proprietors. The fear of territorial displacement and dispossession was to be the chief motor of Arab antagonism to Zionism down to 1948 (and indeed after 1967 as well).

By the outbreak of World War I in 1914, there were probably about sixty thousand Jews in the country,[2] though traditional Zionist historiography puts the figures as high as fifty thousand in 1897[3] and eighty-five thousand in 1914.[4]

Zionist land purchases and settlement in 1880–1914 focused on the coastal plain between just south of Jaffa and Haifa and on the Jezreel and Jordan Valleys. These areas, often swampy, were largely uninhabited and uncultivated. During the second half of the nineteenth century and the early years of the twentieth, they began also to attract Arab families unable to make a living in the crowded hilly spine of the country (Galilee, Samaria, Judea). It was into this still largely uninhabited reserve—these plains and valleys—that the Zionists were pushing, dispossessing some of the Arabs living there or preempting others from moving in. This was to be a demographic-geographic contest the Arabs were destined to lose.

Where they could, the Zionists also picked up land in settled areas of the country, such as the Galilee Panhandle and the Lower Galilee, around Sejera. But hill villagers, who tended to own their lands, were usually averse to selling; the *effendis,* with large holdings in the lowlands, were happy to sell for a good price. Neither the sellers nor the buyers were greatly concerned about the fate of the tenant farmers.

Between 1878 and 1908 Jews purchased about four hundred thousand dunams out of a total land mass of 27 million dunams.[5] The most prominent families—including Nashashibis, Husseinis, and al-'Alamis of Jerusalem, Dajanis of Jaffa, 'Abd al-Hadis of Nablus and Jenin, and Shawas of Gaza—sold land to the Jews. The major incentive was swiftly rising prices, caused largely by Zionist demand. Land prices in Palestine increased between 1910 and 1944 by as much as 5,000 percent.

Land purchase was the underpinning of Zionism. As Menachem Ussishkin (1863–1941) put it in 1904, "Without ownership of the land, Eretz Yisrael will never become Jewish." Purchasing was referred to in Zionist parlance as "redemption" or, indicatively, as "conquest" of the land. Land is acquired in the modern world by three methods, wrote Ussishkin, a Hovevei Zion leader: "By force—that is, by conquest in war, or in other words, by robbing land from its owner; ... by expropriation via governmental authority; or by purchase." The Zionist movement, Ussishkin made clear, was limited to the third choice, "until at some point we become rulers."[6]

The Zionists established ten settlements in Palestine during the 1880s, six in the south (Rishon Le-Zion, Ness Ziona, Ekron, Gedera, Be'er Tuviya, and the reestablished Petach Tikva) and four in the north (Zikhron Ya'akov, Rosh Pina, Yesod HaMa'ala, and Bat Shlomo); in the 1890s, another seven were added in the north (Hadera, Shfeya, 'Ein Zeitim, Sejera, Metulla, Mishmar HaYarden, and Mahanayim) and three in the south (Rehovot, Motza, and Hartuv). By 1908 there were around six thousand Jews in Jaffa and two thousand in Haifa, both previously almost completely Arab cities,[7] and about ten thousand in the twenty-six agricultural settlements.

These Jews were not colonists in the usual sense of sons or agents of an imperial mother country, projecting its power beyond the seas and exploiting Third World natural resources. But the settlements of the First Aliyah were still colonial, with white Europeans living amid and employing a mass of relatively impoverished natives. Things changed somewhat with the Second Aliyah. Many of these newcomers possessed a mixture of socialist and nationalist values, and they eventually succeeded in setting up a separate Jewish economy, based wholly on Jewish labor. But the Second Aliyah's collective settlements, the kibbutzim (the first kibbutz, Degania, was established in 1909), existed alongside the burgeoning First Aliyah moshavot, which were based on private property and exploitation of cheap native labor. The settlers, especially in the moshavot, and the natives quickly developed "normal" colonial relations based on stereotyped images and behavior patterns; exploitation; and mutual dependence, contempt, racism, hatred, and fear.

THE OTTOMAN EMPIRE AND THE ZIONIST MOVEMENT

The Zionists took root in a land ruled by an empire that was antagonistic to their enterprise and that shared religious beliefs and values with the mass of natives rather than with the colonists. Islam posited the inalienability of land conquered by Muslims. Such tracts became automatically part of the divinely sanctioned Dar al Islam. The Sublime Porte's claim to the caliphate, or succession to Muhammad, included the role of protector of Islam's holy places. The sultan was often to declare that he "could never part with Jerusalem."[8] Moreover, there was something unnatural, not to say downright blasphemous, in the notion of the Jews—a *dhimmi,* inferior race—harboring, and attempting to further, political ambitions, and what's more, on Muslim land.

Ottoman officials saw Jewish colonists as strange and alien, people whose manner and actions bespoke subversion. That most of them were Russian did nothing to endear them to the Turks, who for decades had viewed the czarist empire as their archenemy. The Jews were viewed as actual or potential agents of hostile penetration and expansion, at once backed by and enhancing the hated Capitulations, which gave the European powers extraterritorial rights in the empire and subverted Ottoman authority. The Sublime Porte feared, not without foundation, that the European powers were bent on destroying and carving up the empire, and the Zionist movement was seen as but one of their instruments.[9]

From the first a cat-and-mouse game developed, with officials blocking immigration and frustrating settlement construction, and the Jews lying to, bribing, and evading them and abusing Ottoman law and restrictions. Centuries of oppression and discrimination in the Diaspora had bred in the Jews these techniques, so necessary for survival in a hostile environment, and these were among the most important items of baggage the immigrants brought with them to Palestine.[10]

The Ottoman authorities kept close tabs on Zionist activities both within the empire and in Europe, especially Russia. On April 28, 1882, even before the first Biluim set sail for Palestine from Odessa, the Turkish consul general there posted an announcement declaring that no one would be permitted to settle in Palestine.[11] The same day that the first group of fourteen Biluim embarked at Constantinople for Jaffa, June 29, 1882, the governor of Jerusalem was ordered to bar Russian, Rumanian, and Bulgarian Jews from landing in Jaffa and Haifa. On July 1 the governor was ordered to bar Jewish settlement. The following year he was instructed to stop the sale of state lands to Jews, even if they were Ottoman citizens.[12]

A stream of prohibitions—against Jewish tourism, settlement, land purchases, and construction in Palestine—issued forth from Constantinople during the following three decades. Often the restrictions were overlapping or contradictory; sometimes they were downright impracticable, given the inefficiency of Ottoman bureaucracies and their lack of coordination. But the thrust was clear. As Abdülhamid II said in June 1891, after being informed of renewed Zionist pressure on the gates of Palestine: "Why should we accept those whom the cultured Europeans turned back and expelled from their own countries?"

Periodically egging on the central government were Ottoman officials in Palestine—many of whom were Arabs—and the local population. A dialectic soon developed, in which Arab protests prompted Constantinople to clamp down on the Jews, and the resulting restrictions reinforced Arab antagonism and belligerence. Occasionally officials went out of their way to incite Palestinians against the Zionists, as was the case with the *kaymakam* of Nazareth, during a land dispute at Fula in 1910–11 or the *kaymakam* of Tiberias, who in 1910 reportedly told local Arab leaders: "The Jews are traitors, and every act of violence committed against them is a patriotic act."[13]

Between the spring of 1909 and 1911, six Jews were murdered by Arabs in the Tiberias area—but no one was convicted. (By comparison, when Arabs murdered a Christian German settler in Haifa in 1910, within months one was sentenced to death and several others were sent to prison.) The Arabs understood the signals. When Arab bands pillaged two Jewish settlements after a guard at Merhavia killed an Arab during an attack, the authorities looked on impassively, although the guard and ten other Jews who had nothing to do with the Arab's death were arrested. Seven of them spent eleven months in jail without trial.[14]

But the settlers were not easily frustrated. Neither the Ottoman rulers nor the Arabs had the run of the land. The restrictive regulations were opposed, sometimes energetically, by the diplomats of the Great Powers in Constantinople and in Palestine. Some were moved by the Jews' plight, but more importantly they viewed the restrictions on Jews as undermining their countries' rights as embodied in the Capitulations. For instance, at one point the regulations denied Russian Jewish citizens entry into Palestine—despite the explicit provision in the Capitulations giving Russian citizens freedom of movement throughout the Ottoman Empire (save in Arabia). Great Power intercession occasionally led to a reversal of the Sublime Porte's writs, such as those forbidding the sale of land in Palestine to non-Ottoman citizens. Most often, consular protection was simply extended to specific immigrants, preventing their expulsion.

While welcoming, indeed often prompting, intercession by the Great Powers, the Zionists also tried to win the sympathy of the Ottoman rulers. In June 1896 Herzl visited Constantinople and made vague offers of enormous financial assistance in exchange for a Jewish homeland in Palestine. Abdülhamid II would not see him and was not tempted. He responded through an intermediary: "My people have won this empire by fighting for it with their blood and have fertilized it with their blood. We will again cover it with our blood before we allow it to be wrested away from us. . . . Let the Jews save their billions."[15]

In May 1901 Herzl managed to obtain an audience with the sultan, but nothing positive for the Zionists emerged. Indeed, a new set of restrictions on Jewish settlement and land purchases was instituted in 1900–1, though these were somewhat more liberal than many of the previous rules. The new restrictions allowed Ottoman Jewish citizens and foreigners long resident in the empire to purchase state lands, and allowed Jews to enter the empire as pilgrims.

Over the three decades Constantinople's measures certainly curtailed Jewish land purchases and construction. They also deterred many would-be immigrants, but a steady trickle got through, thanks to Ottoman inefficiency, Great Power pressures, and, above all, bribery (baksheesh). Almost every Ottoman official had a price; almost anything could be had for a bribe—residence permits, building permits, land title deeds. Even Herzl's audience with the sultan in 1901 was obtained by means of a 50,000-franc bribe.[16] A British official wrote in 1900: "Foreign Jews are not supposed to be allowed to settle [in Palestine], but Jewish settlers from Europe often arrive in Haifa where there seem to be exceptional facilities for their admission by pecuniary arrangement with the local officials."[17]

Most of the settlers who came in the First and Second Aliyot lived, at least for a time, as illegal residents. They entered as tourists or pilgrims and overstayed their permits, or they entered illegally. Eventually illegal residence was converted into de facto or, often, legal residence; it was usually only a matter of money. Permits for pilgrims and tourists were limited to one or three months, yet not one Jew who stayed longer was expelled from the country in the three decades before World War I.[18] The Yishuv more than doubled between 1882 and 1914, despite a measure of emigration.

THE NEW SETTLERS' ATTITUDE TOWARD THE ARABS

By 1910 Zionist officials had come to realize that not the Turks but the local Arabs were the problem. The Zionist Organization's second president, David Wolffsohn (1855–1914), remarked in September 1908: "One has to pay special attention to the important Arabs who are, after all, the masters of the country." The Zionists had to take care not to arouse their anger.[19]

Many First Aliyah immigrants believed that they were coming to a desolate, empty land and were surprised to find so many Arabs about. After all, they were returning to their Promised Land; no one had spoken of anyone else being there. A character in a work by Yosef Chaim Brenner, the Second Aliyah's leading novelist, says: "Before going to Palestine, the country, for some reason, appeared in my imagination as one city inhabited by non-religious Jews surrounded by many fields, all empty, empty, empty, waiting for more people to come and cultivate them."[20]

"A land without people for a people without a land" was the Zionist slogan—originating, curiously, not with Herzl or one of the forebears, but in Lord Shaftesbury's memoirs, in 1854, and recycled by the Zionist writer Israel Zangwill in an article in 1901.[21] Ahad Ha'Am, the leading Eastern European Jewish essayist, opened many Jewish eyes when he wrote, in 1891, after a three-month visit to Palestine: "We abroad are used to believing that Eretz Yisrael is now almost totally desolate, a desert that is not sowed. . . . But in truth this is not the case. Throughout the country it is difficult to find fields that are not sowed. Only sand dunes and stony mountains . . . are not cultivated."[22]

Moshe Smilansky, one of the founders of Rehovot, wrote years later: "From the inception of the Zionist idea, Zionist propaganda described the country for which we were headed as a desolate and largely neglected land, waiting eagerly for its redeemers."[23]

But the more politically minded immigrants, like the Biluim, were aware of the Arab presence—and possible threat. In a draft of the society's regulations apparently written in the summer of 1883, a year after the arrival of the first Biluim in the country, there is an injunction to "find people who know the language of the country" to help iron out relations with the natives so that they do not greet the immigrants with "rage." Arabic would be taught in the Biluim school, and the children would learn the Arabs' ways "in order that they learn how to live, not fight with them." At the same time the document proscribed the use of Arab laborers on Biluim lands.[24]

Not all the settlers who noticed the Arabs thought in terms of animosity. Some saw them as innocuous, colorful, and generous if primitive desert dwellers, who would not oppose the burgeoning Zionist presence. As Ahad Ha'Am put it: "Abroad, we used to believe that the Arabs are a wild desert people, akin to a mule, who do not see or understand what is happening around them."[25] Many Zionists abroad, even after the start of the *aliyot,* assumed that Arabs and Jews would live in peace and friendship in the Jewish state. An 1884 Hovevei Zion platform argued: "It is untrue that . . . the inhabitants of the country are hostile; rather, it is not possible that they will be more evil or uncultured than the [anti-Semitic] Russian peasants. . . . [Reports of] attacks by Bedouin robbers [on Jews] are merely tall tales."[26] The native population, argued most of the Zionist ideologues down to World War I, were aware that benefits would attend the arrival of Jewish immigrants, capital, and skills.

Nevertheless, the Arabs were generally seen by the *olim* as primitive, dishonest, fatalistic, lazy, savage—much as European colonists viewed the natives elsewhere in Asia or Africa. The Arabs, *olim* reported, frequently cursed and made obscene gestures, practices they feared would be transmitted to their own children by any Arab household staff. The colonists noted the lack of economic development and of hygiene and the rampancy of diseases, especially of the eyes, and the Arabs' low standard of living. All engendered contempt. The settler saw the laborer as "almost always a submissive servant, who may be exploited . . . and accepts lovingly the expressions of his master's power and dominion," to quote Yishuv educator Yosef Vitkin.[27] The settlers "looked down" upon "these barbarians," in the words of Chaim Hissin, one of the Biluim. Three years later, in 1886, Hissin was to write that the Arabs "lacked any patriotic feeling. . . . This is a people in the process of degeneration."[28] Gedera-born Avshalom Feinberg (1889–1917), a child of the Biluim who was to spy for the British during World War I, said of the Arabs: "There is no more cowardly, hypocritical and false race than this race."[29] Nor was the Zionist activist and farmers' leader Moshe Smilansky, who by 1914 was moderate and pragmatic about Jewish-Arab relations, any more complimentary:

We must not forget that we are dealing here with a semi-savage people, which has extremely primitive concepts. And this is his nature: If he senses in you power—he will submit and will hide his hatred for you. And if he senses weakness—he will dominate you. . . . Moreover . . . owing to the many tourists and urban Christians, there developed among the Arabs base values which are not common among other primitive people. . . . to lie, to cheat, to harbor grave [unfounded] suspicions and to tell tales ... and a hidden hatred for the Jews. These Semites—they are anti-Semites.[30]

Some settlers praised and respected the Arabs' presumed martial qualities, their apparent kinship with nature, their hospitality, and even their wildness or untamedness. For some, such as Smilansky, the Arabs were a reminder of what their ancestors, the Jews of biblical Judea, had probably been like.[31] The focus of this ambivalence was the Bedouin (and, sometimes, the Druze). Unlike the somewhat Europeanized urban Arab or the illiterate, debased *fellah* farming the *effendi*'s lands, the Bedouin were often seen as the "real Arabs"— brave, horse-mounted free spirits. But admiration was mixed with fear of the Bedouin's martial prowess. Curiously, this romantic view of the desert Arabs, which closely resembled the British Arabophile's, was most emphatic among the *olim* of the Second Aliyah—or precisely among those who, as we shall see, were to sharpen and deepen Jewish-Arab antagonisms. It became something of a fashion among young Second Aliyah settlers to copy the Bedouin by donning a *keffiyah* (headdress) and robe, riding horses, and shooting.

The sense of the Arabs' savagery and strength was experienced almost immediately by many new immigrants: They were carried ashore at Jaffa by Arab porters. The new Jew, come to Palestine to reassert or rediscover his lost manhood, was embarrassingly shunted from coaster to land by a hefty, illiterate native. But the city Arab was in general perceived somewhat differently. Eliezer Ben-Yehuda was to write that his first encounter with "our cousin Ishmael" was "not a happy one. A depressing feeling of horror ... filled my soul." Reuven Faicovich—a Hovev Zion from Rumania who settled in Palestine in 1882 (father of the 1948 IDF general Yigal Allon)—was impressed by the Jaffa Arabs' hostility. He quickly fashioned truncheons for himself and his brother. The novelist Brenner recalled that soon after landing at Haifa, he was rushed by a group of Arab youths shouting "*Yehud, Yehud*" (Jew, Jew). His initial instinct was to hit them, but his companions warned him that the city was mostly Arab and he should beware. So again "one had to foresuffer the torments of the gentiles."[32] By 1913 Brenner was writing of the hatred that existed between Jews and Arabs—and "so it must be and will continue to be." The Jews must "be ready for the consequences of the hatred ... [and] above all, let us comprehend the true situation, without sentimentality and without idealism."[33]

But not all *olim* came away from first encounters with such negative feelings. David Ben-Gurion met his first Arabs on the way to Jaffa in 1906. "They made a very good impression," Ben-Gurion wrote to his father. "They are nearly all good-hearted, and are easily befriended. One might say that they are like big children." But delight was soon to be mixed with apprehension and anxiety. As the ship carrying Ben-Gurion docked off Jaffa, "the harbor was suddenly filled with skiffs, and Arabs clambered up the sides of our ship. The shouting and shoving were awful." Porters carried the young Ben-Gurion to a skiff and then from the skiff to dry ground. He literally arrived in the Promised Land on the back of an Arab.[34]

Ben-Gurion found Jaffa "not pretty. . . . As in any oriental city, the streets are narrow and winding. An awful dust hangs over the marketplace, for there are no pavement stones." Arabs sat around smoking nargiles. In later years Ben-Gurion was to write: "I saw an uglier exile in Jaffa than in Plonsk," his native town in Poland. He left Jaffa for a colony in the hinterland after a mere seven hours.[35]

THE ARABS' ATTITUDE TOWARD THE *OLIM*

The Jews of the Old Yishuv had been treated by Palestinian Arabs with contempt. The new *olim* sought not only to re-create in Palestine an ancient polity but to refashion the Jews themselves. No longer abject victims, middlemen, peddlers, protected moneylenders, rootless, soft-skinned intellectuals, the Jews were to change into hardy, no-nonsense farmers, who would take abuse from no one. In their encounter with the new *olim,* the Palestinian Arabs often came face to face with, and were surprised and sometimes intimidated by, the "new Jews."

The Arabs, like their Turkish rulers, disliked foreigners. Aliens embodied the threat of Great Power penetration, a foreign culture, and a hostile religion. They were envious of the rights enjoyed by Europeans by virtue of the Capitulations, and both Muslims and Christians, nurtured on the Koran and the New Testament, respectively, were predisposed against Jews. The Christians, a drop in the Muslim ocean, emphasized their anti-Zionism as a way of highlighting their common Arabism.

Few Arabs can have come into direct, protracted contact with Jewish colonists in the 1880s and 1890s; there were very few of them, and they lived in limited areas of Palestine. At first, new settlers may have evoked curiosity and amusement: In Rishon Le-Zion, for example, colonists unsuccessfully tried to harness carts to camels.[36] But gradually there emerged among the Arabs grounds for concern. The immigrants usually had no Arabic (almost no Second Aliyah immigrants learned to read or write the language, though a few mastered passable spoken Arabic[37]), and they knew and cared nothing about Arab customs and mores. "The cause of many of the recent [Arab-Jewish] incidents is apparently a lack of knowledge of how to behave towards our neighbours," wrote Chaim Cohen, of Petach Tikva, in 1911.[38] Many Russian immigrants, especially of the Second Aliyah, were socialists, anarchists, atheists, freethinkers. Back home they had denied or denounced both Jewish tradition and czarist government as well as God. They were no more subdued before Ottoman writ and Arab custom. They brought with them an air and swagger of rebelliousness. They were revolutionaries, come to create a new heaven and a new earth, and their worldview was thoroughly at odds with that of the Arabs. According to a 1914 Arabic pamphlet, the Second Aliyah was "composed of German revolutionaries, Russian nihilists, and vagabonds from other nations."[39]

A Jaffa notable elaborated: "[Hovevei Zion] . . . are doing everything that occurs to [them] as if [they] did not know at all that there is a government in [Palestine], or that there are certain laws." Colonists built houses and planted vineyards without permission.[40] Often they flouted customs in ways injurious to Arabs, as when they forcibly denied local shepherds the use of traditionally common pasturelands. The settlers dressed differently, worshipped (if at all) differently, and acted differently. Their values were alien and antithetical to Arab norms. In short, everything about them was different and in some ways provocative.

In the 1880s there were already Arabs who understood that the threat from Zionists was not merely a local matter or a by-product of cultural estrangement. "The natives are hostile towards us, saying that we have come to drive them out of the country," recorded one Zionist settler.[41] After his visit in 1891, Ahad Ha'Am wrote on the boat back to Odessa that the Arab understood the goals of the Zionist settlers and "had a sharp mind, full of cunning."

RELATIONS BETWEEN *OLIM* AND ARABS AND THE CAUSES OF ARAB-JEWISH ANTAGONISM

The new colonists were in daily contact with the surrounding Arab milieu, for they relied on neighboring villages for food and manure, for seasonal laborers and guards, and for the transporting and marketing of their produce. Colonists in Hadera, Mishmar HaYarden, and Metulla received some agricultural training from Arab neighbors or workers. Some settlements depended on nearby villages for their water, such as Gedera from Qatra in the mid-1880s. Arab women brought water to Metulla in jugs carried on their heads. Contiguous Jewish and Arab fields meant almost daily contact with the *fellahin,* some of whom for a time rented fields belonging to settlements.

The settlers sought to base their relations with their neighbors on mutual respect—something to which the situation was not conducive: On the one hand, the settlers had bought Arab lands and lorded it over, or displaced, the inhabitants; on the other, they depended on Arabs for supplies and labor, and were frequently subject to theft and pillage by them. Jewish efforts to appease Arabs were often interpreted as signs of weakness.

Violence was sometimes triggered by accident or misadventure. In December 1882 a guard at Rosh Pina in the Galilee accidentally shot dead an Arab worker from Safad. In response about two hundred Arabs descended upon the settlement, throwing stones and vandalizing property. Unusually, the inhabitants of a neighboring village, Ja'una, came to Rosh Pina's defense; Ja'una and Rosh Pina shared springs and had a joint interest in denying water to outsiders. The guard was imprisoned for eight months, tried and found innocent, but forced to leave the country for fear of a vendetta; Rosh Pina paid the dead man's family the equivalent of 300 pounds sterling, a relatively large sum.[42]

In the early years of settlement, tension often stemmed from mutual ignorance of one another's customs and languages. Some Zionist leaders called on the settlers to learn local customs and adopt Arab ways. The charter of the Biluim had stressed the need to know Arabic and some moshavot included it in their school curricula. In those places where the settlers abided by Arab agricultural custom, as at Mishmar HaYarden, in the Jordan Valley, they enjoyed good relations with their neighbors. Elsewhere, however, there was often friction, though usually the Arabs reluctantly adapted to the new situation, as at Rehovot, where the settlers refused to allow their neighbors to graze flocks on their harvested fields. When shepherds from nearby Zarnuqa wanted to bring their flocks onto Rehovot lands, they formally asked the managing committee for permission. But marauding Bedouin ignored the new rule and continued to trespass.[43]

Though still a small minority, the settlers quickly began to behave like lords and masters, some apparently resorting to the whip at the slightest provocation. This was a major source of Arab animosity. Some Jewish observers saw it as the "new Jews" compensating for centuries of being at the receiving end of gentile violence. To the Arabs the insult and bewilderment were all the more severe in that the Jews had traditionally been seen as inferior, in terms of legal status and power, and as subservient, dependent, and weak. Explaining an incident in Jaffa in March 1908, the British consul in Jerusalem, Edward Blech, said that some immigrants were "turbulent and aggressive, saturated with socialistic ideas." Zalman David Levontin said the Jews occasionally walked around town provocatively armed.[44]

Ahad Ha'Am in 1891 warned that the new settlers must behave "cautiously . . . [and] act with love and respect" toward Arabs. But the settlers, he wrote, finding themselves in a land "with limitless freedom," as the Turkish authorities were extremely lax, began to exhibit "a tendency to despotism as happens always when a slave turns into a master."[45] Two years later he wrote: "The attitude of the colonists to their tenants and their families is exactly the same as towards their animals." The settlers appear to have commonly referred to their laborers as "mules," an analogy drawn from the Talmudic comparison between asses and Canaanite slaves.[46]

Attitudes translated into deeds. Ahad Ha'Am wrote, with perhaps a measure of exaggeration, that the Zionist colonists "behave towards the Arabs with hostility and cruelty, trespass without justification, beat them shamefully without sufficient cause and then boast about it."[47] Rehovot—exceptionally among the colonies—repeatedly issued rulings forbidding the beating of Arabs. In 1898 a settler was fined 39 grush (there were 100 grush to the Turkish pound [TL], which was worth just under £1), about seven days' pay for a laborer, for beating an Arab who, on the instruction of another settler, drove a cart through his vineyard. The following year a settler was fined TL 4 for "cruelly beating" an Arab. Three-quarters of the fine went to the victim; the settler was also ordered to pay hospital costs.[48] Arabs came so to respect the Rehovot judicial committee that they brought before it complaints against Jewish settlers and at least one dispute among themselves.[49]

But in most moshavot Arabs were treated like the indigenous peoples in other places colonized by Europeans. When Smilansky informed Ahad Ha'Am of this behavior, the latter wrote: "[If] now [we behave] thus, how will we behave towards the others if we really reach the position, at some point, of rulers of Eretz Yisrael?"[50] And besides occasional brutality, some settlers also indulged in a Diaspora practice that had often engendered anti-Semitism in the past—usury. Smilansky charged that some settlers were lending money to Arabs at "30 and 40 per cent interest." At Rehovot the committee explicitly forbade the practice.[51]

ARAB HOSTILITY TOWARD THE NEW JEWS

There was of course another, equally important, side to the coin. The settlers lived in perpetual fear of attack by their employees inside the moshavot or by Arabs from outside.[52] Like white colonists everywhere, they felt perpetually threatened by the surrounding mass, and they were a minority exploiting and occasionally displacing a native population. Moreover, the Arabs often enjoyed the sympathy, if not the backing, of the Ottoman officials and police. They had the right to bear arms and knew how to use them better than did most Jews. The settlers, who regarded Arabs as hot-tempered, naturally violent, and lawbreaking, often feared to fire them lest they be provoked to violence. And dependent as the Jews were on Arab labor, they could not afford to alienate the workers.

But the major cause of tension and violence throughout the period 1882–1914 was not accidents, misunderstandings, or the attitudes and behaviors of either side, but objective historical conditions and the conflicting interests and goals of the two populations. The Arabs sought instinctively to retain the Arab and Muslim character of the region and to maintain their position as its rightful inhabitants; the Zionists sought radically to change the status quo, buy as much land as possible, settle on it, and eventually turn an Arab-populated country into a Jewish homeland.

For decades the Zionists tried to camouflage their real aspirations, for fear of angering the authorities and the Arabs. They were, however, certain of their aims and of the means needed to achieve them. Internal correspondence among the *olim* from the very beginning of the Zionist enterprise leaves little room for doubt. Vladimir (Ze'ev) Dubnow, one of the Biluim, wrote to his brother, the historian Simon Dubnow, in October 1882: "The ultimate goal . . . is, in time, to take over the Land of Israel and to restore to the Jews the political independence they have been deprived of for these two thousand years. . . . The Jews will yet arise and, arms in hand (if need be), declare that they are the masters of their ancient homeland." (Dubnow himself shortly afterward returned to Russia.)[53]

Ben-Yehuda, who settled in Jerusalem in September 1881, wrote in July 1882 to Peretz Smolenskin in Vienna: "The thing we must do now is to become as strong as we can, to conquer the country, covertly, bit by bit. . . . We can only do this covertly, quietly. . . . We will not set up committees so that the Arabs will know what we are after, we shall act like silent spies, we shall buy, buy, buy."[54]

In October 1882 Ben-Yehuda and Yehiel Michal Pines, who had arrived in Palestine in 1878, wrote to Rashi Pin, in Vilna:

We have made it a rule not to say too much, except to those . . . we trust. . . . The goal is to revive our nation on its land . . . *if only we succeed in increasing our numbers here until we are the majority* [Emphasis in original]. . . . There are now only five hundred [thousand] Arabs, who are not very strong, and from whom we shall easily take away the country if only we do it through stratagems [and] without drawing upon us their hostility before we become the strong and populous ones.[55]

The Arabs, both urban and rural, gradually came to feel anxiety and fear. Acute Jewish observers began to sense the changing mood. Ahad Ha'Am, after his visit in 1891, wrote prophetically: "If a time comes when our people in Palestine develop so that, in small or great measure, they push out the native inhabitants, these will not give up their place easily."

Initially opposition to the arrival of the "new Jews" took relatively primitive and benign forms: theft and vandalism against outlying settlements, with
the colonists tending to attribute the incidents to local, specific causes and
grievances and usually failing to discern a "national" or even regional pattern.
But within a decade Arab resentment also found an organized, "national" or
proto-national expression.

LOCAL INCIDENTS

The Arab peasants' fear of being dispossessed was initially personal, tied to
livelihood and, indeed, survival. In time it took on a "local patriotic" dimension—the Jews were "taking over the district." Gradually, as the twentieth
century advanced, feelings of nationalism, and national displacement,
replaced local patriotism.

To begin with, violence was often sparked by the imprecise demarcation of
land. One settler ascribed all the clashes between Petach Tikva and its neighbors to this.[56] Often in contracts the boundaries were roughly described ("a
straight line from the tall tree to the big rock . . ."). Sometimes Arabs tried to
uproot saplings and level ditches, the usual boundary signs. For years they
interfered with efforts to dig a ditch around Rehovot's lands. The Arabs usually knew where boundaries ran, but they were reluctant to concede the loss of
lands they had lived on or tilled for generations. That the colonists, often
shorthanded, rented out some of their newly bought lands or allowed the tenants to remain, for a fee, did nothing to diminish the Arabs' anger when, years
later, they had to move. Some colonists rented plots of land to villagers or former tenants out of an inability to evict them. The longer they were allowed to
stay on, the more difficult they were to evict.[57] Where tenants were not kept
on, there was continual trespassing and encroachment, and even after getting
compensation, tenants often tried to reassert their claims and salvage their
livelihood.

Another major cause of antagonism was the labor controversy. The hard
core of Second Aliyah socialists, who were to become the Yishuv's leaders in
the 1920s and 1930s, believed that the settler economy must not depend on or
exploit Arab labor. Jewish labor was bound up with the Zionist socialist ethos,
which sought to transform the Diaspora middleman, trader, intellectual into a
man of the earth, a productive worker. Moreover, working the land was seen as
giving the cultivator rights over it. The "new Jews" rebelled against the colonialist ethos and praxis of the moshavot, and a curious ideological reversal
took place. Socialists in two political parties, HaPoel HaTza'ir (founded in
1905) and Poalei Zion (founded in 1906), favored the exclusion of Arabs from
the Jewish economy. Poalei Zion, which amalgamated Marxist internationalism with Jewish nationalism, theoretically looked to a common struggle by
the working classes of all nations against capitalists. But in Palestine, partly

because of labor-market competition and the desire to assure every Jew a job, the party faithful, led by Ben-Gurion, advocated complete separation of Arab and Jewish societies and economies.[58] On the other hand, landowners of the moshavot supported the employment of Arab laborers, as they were both cheaper and more experienced than Jews. Poalei Zion ideologue (and later Israel's second president) Yitzhak Ben-Zvi wrote in 1914: "It should have been the case that the Jewish bourgeoisie would be chauvinistic and would demand only Jewish labor. We, the socialists . . . tending toward internationalism . . . should have demanded that workers be employed without regard to national and religious differences. In reality, we see exactly the opposite."[59]

The contradiction was not missed by the socialists' political opponents, the spokesmen of the moshavot: "How can Jews, who demand emancipation in Russia, rob the rights of, and act selfishly toward, other workers upon coming to Eretz Yisrael?" asked Meir Dizengoff (later mayor of Tel Aviv), in 1909.[60] Aaron Aaronsohn of Zikhron Ya'akov condemned the "conquest of labor" (*kibush ha'avoda*) policy as "fanaticism," and as "lack of humanity and of Jewishness."[61] Though it inflamed Arab antagonism to Zionism, the socialists saw the fight over jobs as a struggle for survival, the social struggle meshing with the national one.[62] But, in reality, rather than "meshing," the nationalist ethos had simply overpowered and driven out the socialist ethos.

There were other reasons for the "conquest of labor." The socialists of the Second Aliyah used the term to denote three things: overcoming the Jews' traditional remove from agricultural labor and helping them transform into the "new Jews"; struggling against employers for better conditions; and replacing Arabs with Jews in manual jobs. Continued employment of Arabs would lead to "Arab values" being passed on to Zionist youth and nourish the colonists' tendency to exploit and abuse their workers. Moreover, Arabs living in or on the periphery of colonies were suspected of pilfering and of passing information to hostile villagers and officials. Farsighted Zionists, such as Ussishkin, predicted that if there were no separation between Arab and Jewish economies and societies, the impoverished, exploited Arab would one day "wake up . . . and understand that [the colonists'] prosperity was achieved by dint of his sweat, and he would make demands." Indeed, such grumbling was voiced early on by laborers in the colony of Zikhron Ya'akov.[63]

The Biluim charter of 1883 had declared that the newly acquired lands would be cultivated "without the help of . . . native Arab inhabitants." Ussishkin demanded "Hebrew labor" and the replacement of Arab workers by Jews as early as 1890, more than a decade before the Second Aliyah. But the first *olim,* relatively few in number, needed help. They knew little about agriculture and based their farms on orchards, groves, and vineyards, which required large numbers of field hands, especially at harvest time. When the neighboring villagers were insufficient, Arabs, families in tow, were brought in from far afield, and resided in shanties inside the settlement. They made do with low wages because their standard of living was low and because they relied for their basic subsistence on plots of land they owned or tenanted elsewhere; for many, employment in the colonies meant extra income.

The Arabs were hardy and usually docile. Jewish workers were more expensive, inexperienced, weaker, and often insubordinate. So, despite what some leaders and charters said, during the first decades of settlement most laborers in the moshavot were Arabs. Reality forced Jewish colonial society to reject "Hebrew labor" in all but a few sites and so, to some degree, did the posture of the official Zionist leadership. Dr. Arthur Ruppin (1876–1943), who headed the Palestine Office of the Zionist Organization, wrote: "Though we must, of course, think first of giving work and bread to our own poorer brethren, we must avoid anything that may resemble exclusion of Arabs."[64] Pushing the drive for "Hebrew labor" to extremes would, he felt, raise wages to unacceptable levels and alienate the Arabs, who would "respond with aggression."[65] A pragmatist, Ruppin believed that the settlers must live in peace, "and if possible in friendship," with their neighbors.[66]

There are no firsthand accounts of Arab reactions to the Yishuv's internal controversy. But documentation from this period does contain clear echoes of Arab reaction more generally to Zionist exclusiveness, of which Hebrew labor was but one manifestation. Syrian notable Hakki Bey al-Azm, of the Decentralization Party, said: "We see Jews excluding themselves completely from Arabs in language, school, commerce, customs, their entire economic life. . . . [Hence] the [Arab] population considers them a foreign race."[67]

The controversy over "Hebrew labor" in agriculture did not often result in violence. But relatively severe and persistent violence did occur in a related domain—the guarding of the colonies. Ottoman rule was marked by a serious lack of law and order. Roving Bedouin bands frequently vandalized and stole from Arab as well as Jewish settlements; Arab villagers attacked both their neighbors and passing travelers. Almost from the start, moshavot employed Arabs as guards. The settlers could not guard at night and work during the day, and they lacked experience in the use of firearms. Moreover, if a Muslim guard injured or killed a thief, the colonists would be free of the threat of a blood feud. Some guards developed a vested interest in protecting the colonists; occasionally friendly relations developed. But all too often guards stole from their employers or allowed villagers, for a fee, to trespass with herds or steal; some helped hostile locals to attack Jewish settlements, though, by and large, Arabs desisted from attacking settlements guarded by their fellows.

In September 1907 a group of Poalei Zion activists, led by Israel Shohat (who had helped organize Jewish self-defense in the Pale of Settlement), Israel Gil'adi, and Alexander Zeid founded Bar-Giora, a secret society dedicated to "Hebrew labor" and Jewish guardianship of the settlements. It was named after Shimon Bar-Giora, a hero of the first Jewish Revolt against Rome in the first century A.D. Responding to increased Arab militancy after the Young Turks' revolt of July 1908, its members formed HaShomer (the guard), a semi-clandestine armed organization whose sole purpose was to guard the settlements. The motto of Bar-Giora and HaShomer was: "In blood and fire Judea fell; in blood and fire shall Judea rise," from a poem praising the rebels against Rome.

Within four years HaShomer had contracts to guard Mescha (Kfar Tavor), Hadera, Rishon Le-Zion, and Rehovot. Initially just protecting the settlement perimeters, HaShomer's men soon undertook to guard Jewish farmers in out-lying fields, inevitably coming up against Arab trespassers. Thus HaShomer placed itself in the forefront of the Zionist struggle. Armed might was now backing up purchase and cultivation; settler was becoming soldier. By 1910 the Palestine Office in Jaffa had hired HaShomer to occupy and cultivate recently bought lands before permanent settlers took over; these HaShomer teams were called "conquest groups."[68]

HaShomer's members, who never numbered more than one hundred (the organization also employed some three hundred Jewish hired hands), learned the language and ways of the Arabs, the better to carry out their duties. They often dressed like Arabs, and Bedouin martial prowess and skills were ideal-ized. While asserting Jewish honor, they claimed that they tried to avoid pro-voking or killing Arabs. But the leaders of the moshavot often found their behavior aggressive and provocative. At Rehovot in 1913, HaShomer guards joined Second Aliyah workers in demanding the dismissal of Arab workers and their replacement by Jews. This followed clashes in which two guards and an Arab were killed. HaShomer threatened to quit the moshava if the Arab workers were not dismissed. Unhappy with HaShomer's belligerence, Rehovot decided against renewing their contract. Shmuel Tolkovsky, a promi-nent settler, said the guards' behavior "endangered our moshava's prestige" and complained: ". . . We Jews who ourselves suffered from persecution and ill-treatment for thousands of years, . . . from us a minimally humane approach could have been expected, not to beat unarmed and innocent people with a whip, out of mere caprice."

Tolkovsky agreed with HaShomer's views about the need to maintain Arab respect and fear of the settlers, but believed this did not necessitate "brutal-ity . . . [and] inhumanity." He feared that Rehovot would one day have to pay for HaShomer's "unnecessary provocations."[69] HaShomer was dismissed from Rehovot after Arab village headmen complained that the guards "stole things and were continuously provocative towards the inhabitants of the vil-lages, and [accused them] of committing murders."[70] In Hadera, HaShomer quit when the settlers tried to reintroduce Arab guards.

But Hebrew labor and the guard problem were secondary. Jewish-Arab animosity and violence focused on the land—disputes over ownership and demarcation, quarrels over usage and trespassing, and anger over displacement or dispossession.

Petach Tikva, the first Zionist colony, was established by Jews from Jerusalem in 1878, abandoned, and resettled by First Aliyah *olim* in 1882. The original 14,200-dunam-site had been bought from two Jaffa Christian Arabs, who purchased it from the Ottoman authorities after villagers of Yahudiya and Um Labes, its original owners, had failed to pay their taxes. After the Zionists settled there, villagers continued to cultivate fields rented to them by the settlers. They also laid claim to an area of 2,600 dunams, saying that this had never belonged to the Jaffa *effendis,* and plowed up a road, claiming it ran through their fields. In early 1886 the settlers demanded that the tenants vacate the disputed land. On March 28 a settler using the plowed-over road was attacked and robbed of his horse by Yahudiya Arabs and the settlers confiscated nine mules found grazing in their fields. It is unclear which incident occurred first and which was retaliation. The settlers refused to return the mules, a decision that some Zionist officials, such as Elazar Rokah, viewed as a foolish provocation. The following day, when most of the settlement's menfolk were away, fifty or sixty villagers attacked Petach Tikva, vandalizing houses and fields and carrying off much of the livestock. Four settlers were injured and a fifth, an elderly woman with a heart condition, died four days later. Under pressure from foreign consuls, the authorities eventually arrested thirty-one Arabs, though they were later released without trial after an agreement was reached between the communities.[71]

The raid on Petach Tikva took place a bare four years after the massive Russian pogroms of 1881–82. But observers such as Yehoshua Oussovitzky quickly dismissed comparisons, arguing that the incident had not been triggered by "religious hatred or nationalist jealousy," it was merely a quarrel between neighboring villages.[72] Similar raids, also sparked by disputes over land, occurred at Rehovot in 1892 and 1893.[73] Throughout, the settlers faced a severe dilemma: to adopt a conciliatory posture, which might be interpreted as weakness and invite further depredations, or to display firmness, which might provoke further belligerence. The latter course, it was understood, could result in fatalities and might suck the settlers into a blood-feud cycle.

In 1887 relations between Gedera, which was plagued in its early years by severe economic difficulties, and the neighboring Arabs of Qatra deteriorated. Gedera had been established on land previously owned or tenanted by Qatra *fellahin*; the sale deprived them of much of their livelihood. In early April villagers illegally cultivating Gedera land attacked a settler. In response a group of settlers, armed with whips, descended on the disputed fields with the aim of provoking a fight that would draw in the Ottoman authorities. The outnumbered settlers were soon driven back, but the authorities, as expected, intervened and arrested nine Arabs.

Animosity between Gedera and Qatra peaked the following year when villagers stole a horse. Settlers gave chase, retrieved the horse, and captured one of the thieves. That night, October 17, 1888, the villagers stormed Gedera to free the prisoner. Shots were fired in the air and stones were thrown, both sides taking care not to kill anyone, and the Arabs were driven off. The following day reinforcements arrived in Gedera from two neighboring colonies, Ekron and Rishon Le-Zion. Only the arrival of Turkish soldiers prevented a major clash. The authorities arrested four Qatra Arabs and took away the Arab held by the Jews. The quarrel died down, and the two communities made peace. Qatra thereafter apparently resigned itself to the settlers' presence.[74]

This pattern was repeated in most of the moshavot during the early decades. Once the initial disputes over land were settled, and the Arabs resigned themselves to their loss, hostility abated. Indeed, as predicted by some Zionist ideologues, the moshavot became sources of prosperity for their neighbors: Villagers worked as field hands and guards, earning relatively good pay, and settlers bought Arab produce and manure. The moshavot attracted Arabs, who settled nearby. Some villagers were happy when they heard that Jewish colonists were moving in.[75] For example, after a colony was founded in the area, it was reported that the Arab village of Sarafand, near Ramle, "once a complete ruin . . . has become a big, expansive village, because many families who had deserted the village have settled in it [again], since now there is work for all of them."[76]

Though hostility generally gave way to reasonably good day-to-day relations between each settlement and its Arab neighbors, there can be no doubt that many of the villagers continued to nurture a deep, lasting resentment toward the newcomers.

In 1895 Baron Rothschild's chief officer in the Galilee bought 12,800 dunams from a Lebanese Christian from Sidon. The land, around Metulla, was inhabited and cultivated by more than six hundred Druze tenant farmers. They were paid a paltry compensation and, in the spring of 1896, driven off the land. The moshava of Metulla was established in June. But for years the dislocated families harassed the new settlers, murdering one man in his sleep, stealing farm animals and crops, and firing guns at night. Only in 1904 was the matter settled, when the settlers paid the Druze an additional 60,000 francs (3,000 Turkish pounds) in compensation.[77]

On March 13, 1908, as antagonism grew over the influx of Jews into Jaffa, the center of the New Yishuv, a group of Arabs attacked a Jewish woman and beat her husband, who came to her defense. A group of Second Aliyah youngsters, armed with truncheons and knives, made ready to retaliate. It is unclear who actually started the ensuing skirmish. On Purim eve, March 16, a group of Jews, most of them Russian subjects, chased several Arabs into a shop, destroyed the place, and left one with fourteen stab wounds. The Jews then fled to two hotels. After obtaining permission from the Russian vice consul, the police, accompanied by Arabs brandishing pistols and knives, raided the Spector Hotel (owned by a Russian national). The raiders injured thirteen Jews, some of them severely, and five Jews were arrested. The *kaymakam* of Jaffa was later dismissed, after strenuous Zionist lobbying in Constantinople.

Some Jewish observers and European diplomats believed the Jews were themselves at least partly to blame: The *olim* regularly walked about Jaffa, a mainly Arab town, armed and were "turbulent and aggressive."[78] Ben-Gurion, then a young pioneer in Sejera in the Galilee, offered two explanations for the incident: The fracas had taken place "because the city Arabs . . . hate us." But Arabs were prone to such violent behavior, "more commonly among . . . themselves, between one tribe and another, or one village and another"; it was not really a matter of "Arabs and Jews."[79]

The head of the Palestine Office, Arthur Ruppin, was to adopt a similarly benign view. It was not, as some newspapers declared, a pogrom. Rather it was "an accidental brawl" of the sort that may occur anywhere religiously or culturally different groups in a heterogeneous population come into contact. "Instead of being surprised that disturbances had occurred in Jaffa, one should rather be surprised that the relations between Jews and Arabs here in Palestine are so peaceful notwithstanding all differences."[80] But Ruppin was to change his tune later.

THE EMERGENCE OF THE "NATIONAL" PROBLEM

In the 1890s clear signs appeared of a "nationalist" undertone linking and, in a sense, unifying the various local antagonisms. The first recorded, organized "national" protest against the Jewish influx took place in 1891. Newspapers had reported that a large number of Russian Jews were about to embark for Palestine. On June 24 a group of Jerusalem Arab notables sent a telegram to the grand vizier in Constantinople asking that the government halt Russian Jewish immigration and bar Jews from purchasing land. "The Jews are taking all the lands out of the hands of the Muslims, taking all the commerce into their hands and bringing arms into the country," they complained.[81] In 1899 Taher al-Husseini, the mufti (Muslim religious leader) of Jerusalem, proposed that Jews who had settled in the country after 1891 be either harassed into leaving or expelled.[82]

Arab reactions to the Zionist enterprise picked up, in frequency and animosity, after the turn of the century, with the gradual awakening of an often anti-Ottoman Arab nationalism. The prophet of the Arab response to Zionism was Najib Azouri, the runaway Ottoman civil servant. In his 1905 book *Le Réveil de la Nation Arabe* he called for Arab separation from the Ottoman Empire. The book had clear anti-Semitic as well as anti-Zionist overtones, perhaps influenced by the author's experiences as a student in Paris during the Dreyfus affair. He wrote: "Two important phenomena, of the same nature but opposed, are emerging at this moment in Asiatic Turkey. They are the awakening of the Arab nation and the latent effort of the Jews to reconstitute on a very large scale the ancient kingdom of Israel. These movements are destined to fight each other continually until one of them wins."

The Zionists, Azouri maintained, wanted to establish a state stretching from Mount Hermon to the Arabian Desert and the Suez Canal.[83] Though published in France, the book reverberated in Palestine. Within a few years Ben-Gurion referred to it and to "Azouri's pupils" as "sowing the seed of hatred for the Jews in all levels of Arab society."[84]

There are few other primary written sources relating to the origin of Arab nationalist antagonism to the Zionist enterprise. But its emergence can be traced through Zionist writings and speeches, particularly in the first decade of the twentieth century. In Basel in July, 1905, Max Nordau referred to the "movement" as having "taken hold of a large part of the Arab people."[85] Another speaker, Meir Isser Pines, referred explicitly to "the Arab national movement."[86] At a separate meeting in Basel, a Palestinian Jew, Yitzhak Epstein (1862–1943), delivered a lecture on the "Arab question," charging the Zionist establishment with ignoring it. He had been deeply troubled by the eviction of the Druze tenant farmers at Metulla in 1896. For the time being, he said, there was no "Arab movement in the national or political sense in Palestine," but, he implied, one might develop in the not-so-distant future: "Among the difficult questions connected to the idea of the renaissance of our people on its soil there is one which is equal to all others: the question of our relations with the Arabs. . . . We have forgotten one small matter: There is in our beloved land an entire nation, which has occupied it for hundreds of years and has never thought to leave it."[87]

Epstein took the Zionists severely to task for purchasing land from *effendis* and then pushing out the poor tenants, and he asserted, provocatively, that Palestine in fact belonged to both peoples: "We are making a great psychological error with regard to a great, assertive and jealous people. While we feel a deep love for the land of our forefathers, we forget that the nation who lives in it today has a sensitive heart and a loving soul. The Arab, like every man, is tied to his native land with strong bonds."[88]

Epstein believed that the Zionists required the consent of the Arabs, and that the enterprise could benefit both peoples. He proposed that the Arabs be given access to Jewish hospitals, schools, and libraries. Epstein's lecture, published two years later under the title *The Hidden Question,* was probably the first serious Zionist analysis of the situation and sparked the first major public

Zionist debate on the Arab question. As if responding to Epstein, Ussishkin wrote: "The Arabs live in unequaled peace and friendship with the Jews, [and] acknowledge unreservedly the [Jews'] historic right to Palestine." But another Zionist leader, Hillel Zeitlin, asserted that the enterprise was without hope, given that Palestine was already thoroughly populated and that the Zionists lacked the power to remove the Arabs. Zeitlin proposed that the Jews accept a less problematic venue for their national renaissance.[89]

A direct response to Epstein came from Moshe Smilansky, writing in *Hapoel Hatzair* in spring 1908: "Either the Land of Israel belongs in the national sense to those Arabs who settled there in recent times, and then we have no place there and we must say explicitly: The land of our fathers is lost to us. [Or] if the Land of Israel belongs to us, to the Jewish people, then our national interests come before all else. . . . It is not possible for one country to serve as the homeland of two peoples."

Smilansky said it was disingenuous to believe that the Arabs were interested in Jewish immigration with an eye to improving their own lot. The Zionists should indeed get to know the Arabs, not in order to help them develop but to know better how to fend them off. However, Smilansky warned against behaving toward the Arabs as the European colonists behaved toward native populations elsewhere.[90]

Other, minor Zionist figures went further than Epstein in their calls for Jewish-Arab cooperation. Dr. Nissim Malul, a Safad-born intellectual who worked in the Palestine Office in Jaffa from 1911, felt that the Zionists should learn Arabic and "merge with the Arabs" on the basis of a joint "Semitic nationalism."[91] Ber Borochov, the Marxist Zionist ideologue, tried to give such thinking an historical underpinning: The Arabs of Israel were the descendants of the Canaanite and Judean rural populations who became Muslims with the Muslim conquest, and they were "close to us in blood and spirit."[92]

But the rise of Arab nationalism and the increase in hostility toward the Zionist enterprise also reinforced "exclusivist" tendencies among the settlers. Unlike Malul and Epstein, the "separatists" believed in the impossibility of cooperation and integration, and felt that a conflict was inevitable. Until the Jews had sufficient power to take over Palestine, they must develop politically, socially, and economically in complete separation from their environment.

Some Zionists, like Joseph Klausner, a historian, regarded the Arabs and their culture as inferior, as savage. For Klausner the goal was clear: "Our whole hope is that in the fullness of time we will be the masters of the country."[93] Writers like Moshe Smilansky and his brother, Ze'ev, warned that mixing with the Arabs would lead to infection with the base morals of the *fellahin*. In 1908 Moshe Smilansky wrote that Zionism must strive for a Jewish majority and those who opposed this goal were committing a "national sin." Ze'ev Smilansky denied the Arabs national rights in Palestine, arguing that they were not a nation but a collection of rival tribes or clans.[94]

In 1914 Moshe Smilansky was to become a moderate, calling on Zionists to find a modus vivendi with the Palestinians, to learn Arabic and Arab customs; to refrain from buying land containing Arab villages or sacred sites or from which tenant farmer communities had been removed; and to give Arabs Jewish medical and even educational services.[95]

THE RIPENING OF THE ARAB-ZIONIST CONFLICT AFTER THE YOUNG TURKS' REVOLUTION

The emergence of a militant, activist ethos in the Yishuv preceded the Young Turks' revolution in Constantinople, but nonetheless 1908 was a watershed year. Before 1908 Arab resistance to the Zionist project was mostly local and specific; after it nationalist, or at least protonationalist, resistance appeared. In the preceding twenty-seven years, thirteen Jews had been killed by Arabs— only four in what can be termed nationalist circumstances, the rest in the course of robberies and other crimes.[96] But in the five years 1909–13, twelve Jewish settlement guards were killed by Arabs. Settlers began to speak more and more of Arab "hatred" and "nationalism" lurking behind the increasing depredations, rather than mere "banditry." It is no surprise that 1909 witnessed the first organized effort by the settlements to acquire firearms—five to twenty rifles per moshava, according to its size, suggested Ruppin. Wolffsohn approved an appropriation of five thousand francs for the purchase of weapons.[97]

During the 1880s and 1890s Zionist commentators referred not to the "Arabs" but to the "natives," the "inhabitants," or, sectorally, to *"fellahin,"* "city folk," "Bedouin," "Christians," and so on.[98] From some point around 1908, the use of "Arabs" came to predominate.

Two historic developments that bore heavily on the unfolding conflict occurred at this time. One was the founding by the Zionist Organization, in December 1907, of the Palestine Office, located in Jaffa and, within months, headed by Dr. Ruppin (assisted by Dr. Jacob Thon [1880–1950]). The move marked a partial abandonment of Herzl's all-or-nothing, charter-oriented approach; while continuing to seek Great Power support for their enterprise, Zionists now also looked to put down and develop roots in the country. For the first time the settlement drive had a central guiding hand. The disparate initiatives and activities of immigrant societies, far-flung colonies, and Jewish philanthropists were henceforth to be at least partially coordinated by "the Office," which channeled most of its energies into land purchasing and organizing settlement.

The second development was more dramatic: The revolution that ended the Ottoman Empire broke out on July 24, 1908. The Young Turks reinstated the constitution that Sultan Abdülhamid II had suspended in 1878. Censorship was lifted, and many of the old regime's officials were dismissed. The empire's peoples hoped that a new dawn of enlightenment and liberalization, if not actual freedom, was at hand. But the revolution was dominated by Turks, organized around the CUP; they sought to maintain the empire, albeit with somewhat streamlined and modernized trappings.

Zionist hopes for change were quickly dashed. The CUP saw in Zionism both another secessionist threat and a possible catalyst to Arab secessionism. Nevertheless, the revolution caused a temporary loosening of the reins of autocracy and ignited nationalist spirits in the Levant. In Palestine this resulted in a considerable increase in Arab attacks on Jewish settlements. The trouble focused on Sejera, a Second Aliyah training farm west of Tiberias. The purchase of the eighteen thousand dunams of land in the area in 1899 had triggered demarcation disputes; in 1904 a settler was murdered. In 1907 settlers took over guard duty from Arab employees, causing resentment. In March 1909 Arabs from the village of Shajara, perhaps incited by CUP supporters in Tiberias, began to harass the settlers. In one incident a villager was killed by a Jew; in April a Jewish photographer on his way to Sejera was attacked and robbed by four *fellahin*. He wounded one of his assailants, who died a few days later. During the following week the men of Shajara and Kafr Kanna, both mainly Christian, harassed Sejera, stealing cattle and destroying crops, seriously wounding two settlers and killing a watchman. When the settlers, including Ben-Gurion—armed with a Browning pistol—gave chase, they were ambushed and one of them was shot. Ottoman police eventually pacified the area.[99]

But incidents continued. Walking from Sejera to the nearby colony of Yavniel, Ben-Gurion was attacked by a dagger-wielding robber, who lightly wounded him and made off with his satchel. Years later he was to write that the incident had revealed to him, for the first time, "the severity and dangers of the 'Arab problem.' " In a lecture and a newspaper article in October 1910, he linked his experience to the Young Turks' revolution, which had ignited hope among Zionists but had also opened the floodgates to other nationalisms. "A pitched struggle and intense rivalry" would develop between the empire's various nationalities as they sought to increase their political influence and consolidate their economic development. Ben-Gurion cited Azouri's *Réveil*, which had pitted "the Jewish peril in Palestine" against the "creation of a great Arab empire." Clearly, "our Arab neighbors hate us," Ben-Gurion wrote. It was not merely a matter of one group's ignorance of or insensitivity to the other's customs. The hatred "originates with the Arab workers in Jewish settlements. Like any worker, the Arab worker detests his taskmaster and exploiter. But because this class conflict overlaps a national difference between farmers and workers, this hatred takes a national form. Indeed, the national overwhelms the class aspect of the conflict in the minds of the Arab masses, and inflames an intense hatred toward the Jews."[100]

Ben-Gurion was not alone in sensing the upsurge of anti-Zionist activism. On February 6, 1911, representatives of the moshavot met in Jaffa to discuss "the resurgence of the anti-Jewish movement."[101] But leading Zionist officials continued to describe attacks on settlers either as examples of the Arab, and particularly Bedouin, penchant for violence and pillage directed against all property owners, or as the result of incitement by "unrepresentative" elements: hostile journalists, officials, or Christian Arabs who did not share the Muslims' uncritical, even benevolent, attitude toward the Zionists.[102] The reason for adopting this line of argument was probably psychological. There was a persistent refusal among many Zionists to concede the depth and breadth of Arab antagonism.

But by 1913 leaders such as Ruppin were forced to acknowledge that there was indeed a problem—not merely a matter of Christians or effendis or bandits, but of the majority of Palestine's inhabitants.[103] Initially, said Ruppin, the Zionists had simply been unaware of the Arab presence and hostility. But this hostility was now a fact. And the Arabs, not the Turks, would remain the Zionists' neighbors. The settlers, therefore, must try to reach a modus vivendi with them. Sensitivity must be shown in land purchases, and the leadership must establish friendly contacts with the Arab political elite to persuade them that Zionism would bring them benefit, not harm.[104]

Some Jewish intellectuals, such as Ahad Ha'Am, genuinely tried to promote Zionist-Arab amity. The majority, like Ruppin, more pragmatically sought an accommodation that would last long enough to enable their enterprise to take root irreversibly. And soon enough most of the Zionist leadership—at least in Palestine if not in Europe—came to understand that the two embryonic national movements were in competition and sooner or later would collide. They were engaged in a race against time: "If the national consciousness of the Arabs grows stronger, we shall come up against resistance that it will perhaps be no longer possible to overcome with the help of money. If, in fact, the Arabs reach the stage where they feel it a national disgrace and betrayal to sell their land to the Jews, the situation will become a truly difficult one for us," the Palestine Office reported in February 1913.[105] The Arabs, wrote a Zionist official, "are and will remain our natural opponents. . . . The Jew for them is a competitor who threatens their predominance in Palestine."[106] On the most basic level, Jewish colonization meant expropriation and displacement. As Ruppin later wrote (though his words apply with almost equal relevance to the pre-1914 period): "Land is the most necessary thing for establishing roots in Palestine. Since there are hardly any more arable unsettled lands . . . we are bound in each case . . . to remove the peasants who cultivated the land."[107]

It was all very well to speak of benefits the Jews would bring to Palestine, or of the common ancestry of the two Semitic peoples, or to suggest that the land could be made to yield enough crops to nourish all. The question was whether the Arabs—peasants and urban elite—were buying any of it.

A major controversy was sparked in 1910–11 by Zionist efforts to buy a large tract of land in the Jezreel Valley, around the village of Fula, from the Beiruti Sursuq family. Notables from Haifa protested to Constantinople that "about 100,000 Jewish immigrants" had recently arrived in the country (a gross exaggeration) and that the Zionists were "taking over our farms and our fields." A Nazareth group complained that immigration was "a cause of great political and economic injury. . . . The Zionists nourish the intention of expropriating our properties. For us these intentions are a question of life and death."[108]

The protest against the Fula land sale was spearheaded by the Damascene Shukri al-Asali, who served as the *kaymakam* of Nazareth. He published a series of articles, signing them "Salah a Din al-Ayubi"—Saladin, the twelfth-century Kurdish-born Muslim general who defeated the Crusaders and reconquered Jerusalem for Islam. Fula was the site of a Crusader castle conquered by Saladin in 1187. This appears to have been the first linking in Palestinian polemics of Zionism and the Crusades. From then on, Arab historians and journalists continually compared the two, often prophesying that Zionism would share the Crusaders' fate.

In March 1911, 150 Palestinian notables cabled the Turkish parliament protesting against land sales to Jews.[109] The governor of Jerusalem, Azmi Bey, responded: "We are not xenophobes; we welcome all strangers. We are not anti-Semites; we value the economic superiority of the Jews. But no nation, no government could open its arms to groups . . . aiming to take Palestine from us."

The authorities duly began to prevent purchases of land by noncitizens. But efforts to block sales in the Jezreel Valley were only partially successful.[110] The settlement of Merhavia was established at Fula in January 1911. The farmers who lived there received compensation and left a few weeks before, but then began to harass the settlers. In May an Arab was killed during clashes between HaShomer guards and the former tenants. Intervention by the pro-Arab authorities led to the pillage of Merhavia's fields and houses. Three settlers were held in prison for about a year before bribery secured their release. But the Arabs of the Jezreel Valley gradually resigned themselves to the Jewish presence after HaShomer's show of force.

The historian Neville Mandel has identified the second half of 1911 as a "turning point," when violence that had become endemic in the north spread to the center and south. Three Jews were murdered in 1912 and another two in the summer of 1913. In April 1914 the British consul in Jerusalem reported: "The assaults upon Jews in the outlying districts are increasingly frequent."[111]

Opposition to Zionism, energized by the Young Turks' revolution, was not confined to the countryside. Arab deputies to parliament had been elected in Palestine's towns. These swiftly broadcast the anti-Zionist message in the Ottoman capital. In June 1909 the deputy from Jaffa, Hafiz Bey al-Sa'id, asked in parliament whether Zionism was compatible with the existence of the Empire and called for a ban on Jewish immigration.[112] In November, two other deputies, Ruhi Bey al-Khalidi and Sa'id Bey al-Husseini, of Jerusalem, were interviewed in Eliezer Ben-Yehuda's newspaper, *HaZvi*. Husseini, while paying lip service to the Jews' "many and very important virtues," asserted that there was "no room" for new immigrants, and the arrival of tens of thousands could only harm the country and the Jews themselves. Khalidi noted that the newcomers, "especially the Ashkenazi Jews," made no effort "to draw closer" to the Arabs. Moreover, the Jews, who were rich, threatened "to dispossess the Arabs."[113]

Later that month Husseini argued in parliament that Palestine simply could not sustain a substantial influx (the issue of the country's "absorptive capacity" was to figure large during the following three decades). Khalidi sounded the patriotic alarm: The Jews "will be able to buy many tracts of land, and displace the Arab farmers from their land and their fathers' heritage." His critique marked a change of emphasis. Past Arab protests had tended to focus on Jewish immigration; Khalidi's, on Zionist colonization. New colonies had recently been established: Ben Shemen School, 1906; Hulda, 1907; Be'er Ya'akov, 1907; 'Ein Gannim and Kinneret, 1908; Degania, 1909; and Tel Aviv had been founded earlier that year, just north of Jaffa.[114] Husseini warned that the Zionists were bent on establishing a Jewish state extending from Palestine to "Syria and Iraq."[115] Husseini was not mapping prospective Zionist geography out of thin air. Spokesmen for the movement had declared or implied that Zionism's aim was a Jewish state stretching eastward as far as the Euphrates (referred to in the Bible as the eastern boundary of the Promised Land). Nordau, for example, said the Zionists were coming to the Land of Israel "to expand Europe's moral borders to the Euphrates."[116]

Lobbying by Palestinian deputies continued. In April 1911 the interior minister, Khalil Bey, declared: "To follow the course of Zionism is . . . to go counter to Ottomanism." And the Palestinian political elite sounded the alarm in newspapers that sprang up after the Young Turks' abolition of censorship. *Al Asma'i*, founded by a Jaffa businessman, Hanna 'Abdallah al-'Isa, accused the Zionists of unfair competition with Arab traders and craftsmen, as, due to their foreign citizenship, they were exempt from certain taxes; and their European culture and skills gave them other advantages.[117] The Haifa-based *al-Karmil* was founded late in 1908. In March 1909 a Tiberias-born Protestant of Greek Orthodox origin, Najib al-Khuri Nassar, took it over and ran it until 1914, when the Turks suspended its publication. Nassar had previously worked as a land purchasing agent for the Jewish Colonization Association

and had helped the Jews buy the land on which the moshava of Yavniel was
founded in 1901. He demonstrated that there is no more avid a nationalist than
a repentant collaborator. But, while fervently attacking fellow Christians who
sold land to Jews, he was leery of criticizing Muslims in this respect, perhaps
wishing to avoid stoking Muslim hostility toward Christians.[118]

Nassar supported the CUP. His anti-Zionism was based on Zionism's threat
to the empire's integrity, as well as on the harm it portended for the Arabs.
Jewish efforts to silence *al-Karmil*, through complaints to the Ottoman
authorities, were largely ineffectual. In 1911 Nassar published *al-Sihyuniyya*
(Zionism), the first Arab book on the subject, asserting that the movement's
ambition was to take over Palestine and perhaps to dominate the whole
empire, a goal, according to him, not outside their reach, given the Jews' vast
wealth. Moreover, Zionism enjoyed the support of the Great Powers—
because they themselves wished to be rid of their Jews.[119]

The strongly anti-Zionist paper *Filastin*, founded in Jaffa in 1911 by two
Greek Orthodox brothers, 'Isa Da'ud al-'Isa and Yusuf al-'Isa, was driven by
local patriotism rather than Ottoman sympathies. A letter published in *Filastin*
in May prophetically described Zionism as "an omen of our future exile from
our homeland and of [our] departure from our homes and property." In 1913
'Arif al-'Arif published an article in the paper berating the Ottomans for their
leniency toward land sales, which was enabling "the Zionists [to] gain mastery over our country, village by village, town by town; tomorrow the whole of
Jerusalem will be sold and then Palestine in its entirety."[120] Newspapers in
Beirut and Damascus joined the chorus. Some writers, like Shukri al-Asali,
argued that the ancien régime of Abdülhamid had successfully blunted the
Zionist onslaught but that the flood gates had opened under the more liberal
Young Turks. Asali predicted in 1911: "If the government does not set a limit
to this torrential stream, no time will pass before you see that Palestine has
become a property of the Zionist Organization and its associates."[121]

Activists made several efforts to set up political associations directed
against the Zionist enterprise. At the end of 1910 Nassar, the editor of *al-
Karmil*, established one in Haifa specifically to combat the sale of land to
Jews. A similar group, the Patriotic Ottoman Party, sprang up in Jaffa the following year.[122] In March 1911 fifty Palestinian notables complained to parliament about Jews buying land and using Ottoman citizens as a front. By 1914
the opposition had consolidated. Some Arabs were aware of the "gap"
between the level of political consciousness of their people and that of the
Jews. Their own awakening had been relatively slow to get started. Hakki Bey
al-Azm, a Syrian member of the Decentralization Party, wrote: "The Arabs
have as yet taken no steps on the road to national renaissance . . . they therefore see their very existence threatened by the Jews. . . . The youth of Palestine is already inspired with the idea of assembling in order to take up the
struggle against the Zionist movement."[123]

Different voices were also heard. The empire's gradual breakup, speeded by the Balkan Wars of 1912–13, gave a new impetus to Arab nationalism. Many Arabs saw a need for allies in their struggle to shake off the Turkish yoke and for external assistance in developing the region. Some, with an eye to tapping reputed Jewish economic power and influence, proposed that the two subject peoples make common cause against the Ottomans, or, as Da'ud Barakat, editor of the Cairo daily *al-Ahram*, wrote in early 1913: "It is absolutely imperative that an entente be established between the Zionists and the Arabs, because this war of words can only do evil. The Zionists are necessary for the country; the capital which they will bring, their knowledge and intelligence, and the industriousness which characterizes them, will contribute without doubt to the regeneration of the country."[124]

Barakat was not alone. In spring 1913, leaders of both the Decentralization Party and the Beirut Reform Committee, which sought autonomy for the *vilayet* of Beirut, sent out feelers indicating a desire to reach an accommodation with the Zionists. Similar proposals were made by delegates at the First Arab Congress, held in Paris in June. The chairman, 'Abd al-Hamid al-Zahrawi, a Syrian, spoke privately with a Zionist representative about the need for an agreement allowing even further Jewish immigration to Palestine if the Jews would become Ottoman citizens and did not displace Arabs. The sincerity of these secret proposals remains unclear; possibly they were a tactical maneuver to influence Arab-Ottoman negotiations and obtain autonomy for the Arabs.[125] In any event, nothing came of them.

But not only Arabs were interested in Jewish favors. Late 1913 and early 1914 saw a hesitant shift in Ottoman attitudes. The empire was desperately in need of financial and political support. The Turks began to sound out the Zionists on the possibility of an alliance to unfreeze state lands for sale to Jews, and to ease immigration restrictions. The Arabs took fright, and anti-Zionist activities crested. In July 1913 a clash in the fields of Rehovot left one Jew and one Arab dead. Local mukhtars complained to the governor that the immigrants "kill, pillage, and violate Muslim women and girls." A leading Palestinian, Sheikh Sulayman al-Taji, in November published a poem in *Filastin* declaring:

> Jews, sons of clinking gold, stop your deceit;
> We shall not be cheated into bartering away our country!
> . . . The Jews, the weakest of all peoples and the least of them,
> Are haggling with us for our land;
> How can we slumber on?

An anonymous pamphlet declared: "We are a nation going to its death before the Zionist stream in this land of Palestine."[126] Even more strongly worded was an anonymous petition entitled "General Summons to the Palestinians," published and distributed in June 1914: "Countrymen! We summon you in the name of the country which is in mourning . . . in the name of Arabia, in the name of Syria, in the name of our country, Palestine, whose lot is evil." Calling on the people to cling to Palestine "with their teeth," it continued: "Have pity on your land and do not sell it as merchandise. . . . At least let your children inherit the country which your fathers gave you as an inheritance. . . . Men! Do you . . . want to be slaves and servants to people who are notorious in the world and in history? Do you want to be slaves to the Zionists who have come . . . to expel you from your country, saying that this country is theirs?" The combined local Arab pressures persuaded Constantinople to backpedal and reassert the restrictions on Jews.[127]

The spring of 1914 saw a renewal of secret Zionist-Arab contacts, against the backdrop of Arab disillusion with Ottoman promises of self-government. Zionist leaders professed a keen interest in cooperation. Nahum Sokolow, in an interview with the Cairo daily *al-Muqattam* on April 10, 1914, said the Arabs should view the Jews as fellow Semites "returning home" and that the Zionists, with their skills and capital, could help lift up the local population. The two peoples could prosper together.[128] During these last, pre-war years of Ottoman rule the Zionist Movement invested efforts, and a certain amount of money (by way of bribes), to persuade Arab editors and journalists to publish pro-Zionist articles.

Two Arab-Zionist colloquiums were planned for the summer outside Beirut, but World War I broke out, and neither meeting took place. It is doubtful that anything much could have emerged if they had, as no leading Palestinian had agreed to attend.

THREE

WORLD WAR 1,
THE BALFOUR DECLARATION,
AND THE BRITISH MANDATE

PRELUDES

August 1914 found the world at war, with Britain, France, and Russia pitted against the Central Powers (Germany and the Austro-Hungarian Empire). In November the Ottoman Empire joined the Central Powers. Arab nationalists saw the conflict as an opportunity to detach their provinces from Constantinople and reestablish a vast, independent polity. The Arab Decentralization Party predicted on August 20, 1914: "If the [Ottoman] Empire should enter this war . . . it will never come out of it whole. This war will most likely bring it to its end."[1] By November, Zionists and their supporters were beginning to view the clash of the powers in the same light: "What is to prevent the Jews having Palestine and restoring a real Judaea?" asked H. G. Wells.[2]

The Ottoman Empire had been in retreat since the eighteenth century. Much of the Balkans and North Africa, including Egypt, got out from under the Turkish thumb in the nineteenth century. The Arabian Peninsula, comprising present-day Saudi Arabia, Yemen, Oman, and the United Arab Emirates, enjoyed relative autonomy. Until the 1880s Britain, the main European player in the region, had supported the status quo. Britain was not interested in acquiring more territory, but it was committed to preventing the other imperial powers—France, Russia, Germany, and Austria-Hungary—from expanding at the expense of the Ottomans. But gradually British influence and protection were replaced by those of Germany, which by 1914 was controlling, training, advising, and arming significant parts of the large but only semicompetent Ottoman army.

With the start of World War I, Britain feared for its possessions, especially the Suez Canal, and for the security of its communications with India and the dominions. Whitehall assumed that sooner or later the Ottoman armies would march on the Canal and on Egypt, and a change of policy gradually took place. Turkey, "infected with the virus of German militarism," could not be allowed, after the war, to resume its "control of a country [Palestine] which is the military gate to Egypt and the Suez Canal . . . the nerve-centre of the British Empire," explained Lord George Curzon, the Foreign Secretary.[3] Other Britons were driven by fear of Germany and Russia. Lord Horatio Kitchener, who became war minister in August 1914, argued that Russian policy over the centuries had been constant and clear: to supplant Britain in southern Asia.

Kitchener felt that the postwar settlement must include a "northern tier," stretching from Turkey through present-day Iraq to Persia, to block Russian expansion. Moreover, to give that tier depth, the Arab provinces to the south must be taken over by Britain, and Islam itself mobilized against Constantinople and then against Russia. Britain's old Middle East hands, in touch with émigrés and opinion in Cairo, were in no doubt that the Arabs would cooperate: They had long sought to throw off Ottoman rule and would be pleased to obtain British assistance.[4] Thus was conceived the idea of an Arab revolt in the Ottoman rear, to complement the main frontal assault against the empire. Russia and France, however, coveted parts of the empire. Britain would have to take what it desired, while thwarting its allies' territorial ambitions. The decision-making meetings in Whitehall in 1915–16 concerning the fate of the empire resembled gatherings "of a gang of buccaneers," in the words of Prime Minister Herbert Asquith.[5]

A key figure in the evolution of Britain's thinking from support for the continued integrity of the Ottoman Empire to advocacy of its complete destruction was Sir Mark Sykes, a Tory MP and Kitchener's personal representative in the decision-making forums. Sykes supported Arab independence from the Turks and, eventually, some form of semiautonomous statehood under British tutelage; he dismissed the idea of Arab nationalism as "absurd."[6] These views were in no way mitigated by his belief that urban Arabs were "cowardly," "insolent yet despicable," "vicious as far as their feeble bodies will admit," and that Bedouin Arabs were "rapacious, greedy . . . animals." Sykes also had an obsessive fear of Jews, though he was wont to concede that "even Jews have their good points." But during the war he was converted to Zionism.[7] Aaron Aaronsohn met Sykes in London in October and November 1916, and may have influenced him. In 1916 Sykes had spoken of an Anglo-French condominium in Palestine. But from January–February 1917, he thought in terms of an exclusively British trusteeship, with Zionism flourishing under its aegis.[8]

Britain's alignment with the Arabs and the launching of the Arab Revolt evolved over two years. Initially, in the autumn of 1914, Kitchener, in secret correspondence with Hussein ibn 'Alī, the restive but cautious sharif and emir of Mecca, later king of the Hejaz, agreed that the Arabs should sit tight and do nothing against the Ottomans or to hinder the British war effort. In payment Kitchener dangled before this prince of Mecca the bait of the caliphate—dominion over the whole of Islam. But in the summer of 1915 Hussein demanded British support for an independent kingdom uniting all of the Ottoman Arab provinces. In exchange he promised to rally the Arabs of both Arabia and Greater Syria within months and lead them in a revolt. He appears to have been propelled into pro-Allied action by intelligence that Constantinople planned to depose him.

During the second half of 1915, British Middle East hands were gradually converted to the idea of an Arab revolt. But initially, the high commissioner in Egypt, Sir Henry McMahon, vacillated as to the price. He could not reject Hussein's far-reaching territorial claims, lest he torpedo the prospective revolt. On the other hand, he could not accept them: Britain's own growing territorial interests were at stake, as well as French claims on Syria-Lebanon and other areas. On October 24, 1915, having consulted with London, McMahon took the bull by the horns and replied: "The districts of Mersin and Alexandretta, and portions of Syria lying to the West of the districts or vilayets of Damascus, Homs, Hama and Aleppo, cannot be said to be purely Arab, and must on that account be excepted from the proposed delimitation." McMahon added that the Arabs must recognize "Great Britain's established position and interests" in the vilayets of Baghdad and of Basra, and a "special [British] administrative arrangement" would have to be established there.

Britain was saying that the Syrian coast, including Lebanon, was to be excluded from the Arab area and kept for French or Franco-British dominion. So too was Iraq. Present-day Syria and Jordan, on the other hand, which constituted the Ottoman vilayet of Syria, were to be included, along with the Arabian Peninsula, in the "independent" Arab area.[9]

There remained Palestine, which had nowhere been explicitly mentioned—as, indeed, India Office official Arthur Hirtzel pointed out: "Jerusalem ranks third among the Moslem holy places, and the Arabs will lay great stress on it. But are we going to hand our own holy places to them without conditions?"[10] For decades thereafter the protagonists were to argue about what McMahon had really meant. The British, including McMahon, and the Zionists maintained that he had implicitly included Palestine in the areas "west" of Damascus excluded from prospective Arab rule, though a minority among British officials (Dr. Arnold Toynbee of the Foreign Office Political Intelligence Department for one) held that McMahon had in fact earmarked Palestine as part of the Arab state.[11]

The Arabs argued that, as Palestine was not to the west but to the southwest of Damascus, and as it had not been explicitly excluded, it was to be part of the Arab state. On balance it appears that they were right. McMahon had specifically set aside for "non-Arab" rule Lebanon and the northwestern Syrian coastal regions. Motivated by concern for French sensibilities, he had omitted explicit reference to Palestine, and nowhere in his letters had he concerned himself with Zionism or Jewish claims. But he may well have misunderstood the Foreign Office's brief, for London by this time was clearly seeking to exclude Palestine from the independent Arab sphere.[12]

McMahon's reply to Hussein promised recognition of "the independence of the Arabs" after the war but asserted that their government would need to be advised and assisted by the British—in other words, some form of autonomy under British protection.[13] By "independence" the British meant independence from Turkey; certainly they had not intended to promise or grant the Arabs full-fledged independent statehood. Reginald Wingate, the governor-general of Sudan and a key British Middle East official, put it this way in 1915: "I conceive it to be not impossible that in the dim future a federation of semi-independent Arab States might exist under European guidance and support, linked together by racial and linguistic grounds, owing spiritual allegiance to a single Arab Primate and looking to Great Britain as its patron and protector."[14]

McMahon's promises were contingent on the Arabs rising against the Turks, a revolt in which most British officials placed little faith. Hussein was seen as a slippery customer and Arabs in general as untrustworthy. The feeling in Whitehall was that Britain had traded relatively empty promises for relatively empty assurances from Hussein, whose Arabian cohorts were insignificant and whose following in Syria and Mesopotamia was negligible. The British had "been very careful indeed to commit ourselves to nothing whatsoever," observed Brig. Gen. Gilbert F. Clayton, chief of intelligence in Cairo.[15]

Meanwhile the British had to take account of the views and desires of their allies. (And later, in the course of 1917, American sensibilities, especially the Wilsonian principle of self-determination, had to be considered.) Following McMahon's vague commitments to Hussein, Britain invited France to talks, which began in late November 1915. France was represented by François Georges-Picot, first secretary of their embassy in London, and Britain mainly by Sykes. Picot wanted the area he called "Syria" as a French protectorate, if not as a domain of direct French rule. No French government, he declared, would surrender its claims to Syria, which he defined as roughly comprehending present-day Syria, Lebanon, Israel/Palestine, Jordan, northern Iraq, and part of Anatolia. Britain sought to hold on to Palestine, present-day Jordan, and the bulk of Mesopotamia as areas of direct rule or protection.

In the end what became known as the Sykes-Picot Agreement, concluded on January 3, 1916, gave both sides more or less what they insisted on: France, a promise of direct rule over a greater Lebanon and the northwestern Syrian coastline, and Britain, direct rule over the provinces of Basra and Baghdad in Mesopotamia. The area in between was earmarked for a "confederation of Arab states" but in effect was to be divided in two, with France enjoying protector (or sphere-of-influence) status over the northern half, including the Aleppo-Damascus line and the area to its east as far as Mosul, and Britain enjoying that status over the southern area, including the Negev Desert, Transjordan, and most of Iraq, including Kirkuk and the desert west of the Euphrates. Palestine, from Acre down to Gaza and eastward to the Jordan River, was earmarked for joint Anglo-French rule, with Britain accorded a small enclave of direct rule in the Haifa-Acre coastal area and the right to a railway link from the enclave inland to Transjordan.[16] The Sykes-Picot agreement, as Britain's director of military intelligence, Gen. Sir George Macdonogh, remarked, was like "the hunters who divided up the skin of the bear before they had killed it."[17] But the kill was only a year off.

Britain's Middle East policy abruptly moved into high gear with David Lloyd George's assumption of the premiership on December 7, 1916. Asquith had never regarded the East as a major battleground; the war would be decided on the Western Front, he felt, with the Ottoman provinces at best a sideshow. Lloyd George, taking stock of the protracted stalemate in the trenches of Flanders, realized nothing could be gained there but new piles of corpses. But in the East was the "soft underbelly" of the Central Powers; there Germany's might could be undermined and fatally dissipated. First the Ottoman Empire had to be demolished; then the Austro-Hungarian Empire could be assaulted from the rear. The fall of the two subsidiary empires would portend the demise of the German Hohenzollerns.

Lloyd George was animated by a hatred of the Ottoman Empire mirroring that of the liberal governments of the nineteenth century, which was aroused by the Turkish massacres of Christians in the Balkans. To him the Allied goal was "the liberation of the peoples who now live beneath the murderous tyranny of the Turks, and the expulsion from Europe of the Ottoman Empire, which has proven itself radically alien to Western civilization." But he was also a British imperialist. The Ottoman Empire had to be demolished and the route to India, along with its jugular vein, the Suez Canal, had to be secured.[18] Last, Lloyd George saw Zionism as meshing with his imperial vision, though it also, no doubt, appealed to the "poetic and imaginative qualities of his mind."[19] The Jews in Zion had been a staple of his Welsh chapel upbringing. And, in the circumstances of 1916–18, support of Zionism could always be trotted out as support for Wilsonian self-determination. As Lord Robert Cecil, parliamentary undersecretary of state for foreign affairs, asserted, Britain was not embarked on "a war of conquest" but was striving for "the liberation of peoples oppressed by alien tyranny."[20] Yet, without doubt, Lloyd George believed that a British-protected Jewish colony or commonwealth in Palestine would further the Crown's interests by helping to secure the Suez Canal's eastern approaches. Zionism, in Lloyd George's Whitehall, served as a tool with which both to cloak and to further imperial ambitions.

The outbreak of war, and particularly the Ottoman adhesion to the Central Powers, had unleashed Zionist energies. Among the first to speak out was Sir Herbert Samuel, a Jew who was postmaster general in Asquith's cabinet. From November 1914 onward he pressed his colleagues to make a Jewish state in Palestine a war aim: Such a state would be "the centre of a new culture . . . a fountain of enlightenment," and a strategic asset for the British Empire.[21] In January 1915 he sent Asquith a memorandum proposing large-scale Jewish settlement in Palestine, which, he urged, should become a British protectorate. Two months later he submitted a formal proposal to the cabinet. It was immediately supported by Lloyd George, at that moment primarily interested in keeping the French out of Palestine. Samuel eschewed an immediate drive toward Jewish statehood: A state in which "90,000 or 100,000 Jewish inhabitants" would rule over "400,000 or 500,000 Mohammedans of Arab race . . . might vanish in a series of squalid conflicts with the Arab population." He favored gradual but steady immigration; eventually a Jewish majority would form and, then, a state would naturally follow. Samuel thought in terms of at least "a century."[22] But Kitchener torpedoed the proposal, arguing that Palestine was of little strategic value.[23]

During 1915–16, however, a crucial change in personnel resulted in an unprecedentedly pro-Zionist constellation in Whitehall. Kitchener drowned in the North Sea after a German torpedo attack; Lloyd George replaced Asquith as prime minister and Arthur James Balfour, another philo-Zionist, became foreign secretary. Balfour subsequently explained that he and Lloyd George had been influenced "by the desire to give the Jews their rightful place in the world; a great nation without a home is not right."[24] As for Winston Churchill, First Lord of the Admiralty, in 1908 he had gone on record: "The establishment of a strong, free Jewish state astride the bridge between Europe and Africa, flanking the land roads to the East, would not only be an immense advantage to the British Empire but a notable step toward a harmonious disposition of the world among its peoples."[25]

Moreover, the start of 1916 found three vigorous, opinionated, and powerful assistant secretaries in the all-important war cabinet. One historian wrote that they represented "the moving force behind Lloyd George's Eastern policy . . . and could either collectively or individually shape its course."[26] All three—Sir Mark Sykes; William Ormsby-Gore, MP; and Leopold S. Amery, MP—rapidly became converts to Zionism. Amery had since 1915 pressed for the establishment of a Jewish unit to fight with the Allies against the Turks; Ormsby-Gore, while in Cairo, had run the Palestine Jewish spy ring that supplied the British army with vital information about Ottoman dispositions.

In the Foreign Office, too, pro-Zionists assumed high office or were converted to the cause during the last two years of the war, including Lord Robert Cecil and Sir Ronald Graham, who was to play a major role in formulating the Balfour Declaration. Last, a number of senior pro-Zionist figures from the dominions had been thrust into positions of influence in Whitehall during the war, notably the South African general Jan Smuts. Like other Boers, he had been brought up on the Old Testament, and always believed that "Israel will return to its land."[27] Curiously these ministers and officials saw no incompatibility between furthering both Zionist and Arab aspirations. The Jews, they reasoned, would receive only a small slice of the former Ottoman domains, Palestine; the Arabs would not mind, as they would be receiving the vast reaches of Arabia and Greater Syria (including parts of Mesopotamia). But in Washington, ever more aware of the ascendant Zionist spin on British Middle East policy, not everyone was so sanguine. Witnessing the ravaging by European empire builders of the Wilsonian right to self-determination, Col. Edward Mandell House, the president's aide, wrote: "It is all bad and I told Balfour so. They are making [the Middle East] a breeding place for future war."[28]

THE BALFOUR DECLARATION

The sorry state of the Allies in 1917, with their armies bogged down on the Western Front, was a major factor propelling Britain to issue what was to prove the crucial international warrant for Zionism, the Balfour Declaration. Fears that Russia was about to make a separate peace and a desire to prod the United States into a fuller commitment to the Allied cause persuaded Britain to do what France had done—with far less fanfare—five months earlier. The declaration was partly intended to counter French claims to Palestine—for by endorsing Zionism, Britain was legitimizing its own presence there as the protector of Jewish self-determination.

British officials were perturbed by the belief that world Jewry reviled Russia for its anti-Semitism and opposed Russian victory and expansion. Moreover, they suspected that American Jews, many of them of German and Austro-Hungarian origin, favored the Central Powers. Throughout they held an exaggerated view of Jewish power, influence, and single-mindedness—and support for Zionism. Britain's ambassador to Constantinople, Sir Gerard Lowther, referred to the ruling party there, the CUP, as "the Jew Committee of Union and Progress." The Jews, he wrote, "adept at manipulating occult forces," controlled the Ottoman Empire.[29] Some Britons blamed the war itself on "a syndicate of Jews, financiers, and low-born intriguers."[30]

Britain and France came to believe that rallying American Jews to their cause would help bring the United States into the war and keep Russia involved. Lord Robert Crewe, acting foreign secretary, cabled the British ambassadors in France and Russia, in March 1916: "It is clear that the Zionist idea has in it the most far reaching political possibilities. . . . We might hope to use it in such a way as to bring over to our side the Jewish forces in America, the East and elsewhere which are now largely, if not preponderantly hostile to us."[31]

Lord Balfour put it more concretely at the cabinet deliberation of October 31, 1917, at which the declaration was at last approved: "The vast majority of Jews in Russia and America, as indeed all over the world, now appear to be favorable to Zionism. If we could make a declaration favorable to such an ideal, we should be able to carry on extremely useful propaganda both in Russia and America."[32]

Speed was vital. The Zionist Organization, which had branches in both the Allied and Central Powers, was neutral, and it was feared that Germany might preempt the Allies with a pro-Zionist declaration of its own. A visit to Paris by the Russian Zionist Nahum Sokolow helped convince the Quai d'Orsay that the time had come for a pro-Zionist statement. In exchange Sokolow agreed to rally Jewish support for continued Russian participation in the war. On June 4, 1917, the director general of the French Foreign Ministry, Jules Cambon, issued the declaration that was to serve as a precedent and basis for the more significant Balfour Declaration:

> You [Sokolow] . . . consider that, circumstances permitting, and the independence of the Holy Places being safeguarded . . . it would be a deed of justice and of reparation to assist, by the protection of the Allied Powers, in the renaissance of the Jewish nationality in that land from which the people of Israel were exiled so many centuries ago.
>
> The French Government, which entered this present war to defend a people wrongfully attacked [that is, the Belgians], and which continues to struggle to assure the victory of right over might, cannot but feel sympathy for your cause, the triumph of which is bound up with that of the Allies.[33]

Ironically, the French declaration paved the way for Britain's, which helped secure the exclusion of France from the Promised Land.

Immediately, Cecil and Graham recommended that Balfour issue a similar statement. Washington—suspecting that Britain was bent on a "British Palestine" rather than on furthering the ends of Zionism—advised delay.[34] Lord Curzon, no friend of Zionism, also weighed in against, arguing at the cabinet meeting of October 4, 1917, that Palestine was mostly "barren and desolate . . . a less propitious seat for the future Jewish race could not be imagined." Zionism was "sentimental idealism, which would never be realized." Moreover, how could the Jews hope to displace the far more numerous and stronger Arabs?[35] But Balfour, persuaded by Graham of the imminence of a German declaration that might "throw the Zionists into the arms of the Germans," forced the issue. On October 31 the cabinet authorized him to issue a diluted pro-Zionist statement: "It's a boy," Sykes informed the leading, Russian-born British Zionist activist Chaim Weizmann—the two had done much of the preparatory work in a series of meetings. President Wilson, shown a draft at Balfour's request, privately approved it.[36]

The Balfour Declaration took the form of a letter, dated November 2, 1917, from the foreign secretary to Lord Lionel Walter Rothschild, who headed Britain's Zionist Federation. It read:

> I have much pleasure in conveying to you, on behalf of His Majesty's Government, the following declaration of sympathy with Jewish Zionist aspirations which has been submitted to, and approved by, the Cabinet: "His Majesty's Government view with favor the establishment in Palestine of a national home for the Jewish people and will use their best endeavours to facilitate the achievement of this object, it being clearly understood that nothing shall be done which may prejudice the civil and religious rights of existing non-Jewish communities in Palestine or the rights and political status enjoyed by Jews in any other country."

The declaration was immediately understood by the Zionists to be the most important international statement of support they had ever received. The key term, "national home," was clearly a euphemism for "commonwealth" or "state." All the declaration's architects believed that a state would emerge once the Jews had attained a majority in Palestine. In internal correspondence Zionist officials spoke at the time of their hope for "a Jewish state in Palestine."[37] Representatives of the Yishuv, at their first formal post-Balfour gathering in December 1918, the so-called Eretz-Yisrael Conference, resolved by a vote of 55 to 1 that the Zionist movement intended to establish not a "national home" but a "*medina ivrit*" (a Jewish state).

Everyone was careful not to define the borders of the future state, but in 1918 David Ben-Gurion and Yitzhak Ben-Zvi published (in Yiddish in the United States) a book called *The Land of Israel, Past and Present* in which they described "our country" as stretching from the Litani River in southern Lebanon, the Hermon Mountain foothills and Wadi A'waj (just south of Damascus) in the north, to the Gulf of Aqaba (Eilat) in the south. In the west it would reach as far as Al-'Arīsh in Sinai, and in the east it would stretch to a rough line between Aqaba and Amman.[38]

Balfour himself told a Jewish luncheon gathering on February 7, 1918: "My personal hope is that the Jews will make good in Palestine and eventually found a Jewish State. It is up to them now; we have given them their great opportunity."[39] On November 17, 1919, he argued: "Zionism, be it right or wrong, good or bad, is rooted in age-old traditions, in present needs, in future hopes, of far profounder import than the desires and prejudices of the 700,000 Arabs who now inhabit that ancient land."[40] This was to be the Palestinian Arabs' tragedy: They were seen as insignificant "natives" and usurpers, whereas the incoming Jews were viewed both as Europeans and as the rightful owners of Palestine.

The British did not consult Arab leaders before issuing the declaration or seriously anticipate adverse reaction from them. A leading Arab historian writes that in the Arab Levant the declaration gave rise to "bewilderment and dismay."[41] But there is little evidence for this. More than two months passed before Lt. Col. David Hogarth of the Arab Bureau in Cairo was dispatched to Jedda, where he assured Hussein that "Jewish settlement in Palestine would only be allowed in so far as would be consistent with the political and economic freedom of the Arab population." Hussein replied that the Arabs would not concede sovereignty over Palestine to Jew or Briton. On the other hand, in the daily *al-Qibla,* his official mouthpiece in Mecca, Hussein enjoined the Arabs of Palestine to welcome the expected influx. The Jews, with their known "energies" and "labors," "would improve and develop the country to the benefit of its Arab inhabitants."[42]

In Palestine reactions were muted. It was only a full year later, in November 1918, that about one hundred Arab dignitaries and representatives of political-cultural associations addressed a petition to the British denouncing the declaration. A uniquely empathetic document in Palestinian Arab terms, it stated that they had "always sympathized profoundly with the persecuted Jews and their misfortunes in other countries . . . [but] there is a wide difference between this sympathy and the acceptance of such a nation . . . ruling over us and disposing of our affairs."[43]

THE BRITISH CONQUEST OF PALESTINE

In early June 1916, after almost a year of clandestine Anglo-Arabian contacts, Hussein at last rose in revolt. But it never developed into the grand national movement that he had promised; no large Arab contingents of the Ottoman army defected to join his forces; no grand rebellion engulfed the Levant. The action was limited to a few thousand Hejazi tribesmen who were aided by British gunboats along the Red Sea coast, advisers, and large amounts of gold bullion (in all, London spent 11 million pounds sterling—in today's terms approximately 500 million dollars—subsidizing the revolt). In its first year Hussein managed to capture only Mecca, Medina, and Taif, the last with the aid of British-commanded Muslim troops from the Egyptian army. Only insignificant guerrilla operations followed. Elsewhere in the Arab world Hussein's call to revolt went completely unheeded.

In 1917 Lloyd George placed the Middle East at the top of Britain's strategic agenda. With the Allies bogged down in France, the new prime minister hoped that victory could be achieved by the back door. The capture of Baghdad by an Anglo-Indian army in March 1917 was part of this strategy. So was the British invasion of Palestine, which got off to a poor start when the (British) Egyptian Expeditionary Force, commanded by General Archibald Murray, was repelled at Gaza on March 26, 1917, and again on April 29. In June, a new British commander was appointed—General Edmund Allenby— and instructed by Lloyd George to take Jerusalem before Christmas.

In the autumn, with the Sharifian rebels—now advised by Lawrence and pumped up with new gold—having gradually inched northward along the Saudi Red Sea coast, Allenby launched his offensive. He took an indirect approach, swinging eastward toward Beersheba, on October 31 breaking through the Turkish defense line, which stretched from the Gaza coast to Bir Asluj (a strategy that may have been suggested by the spy Aaronsohn, who had noted the weakness of the Ottoman defenses around Beersheba[44]). Then he headed directly for Jerusalem, which he conquered without a fight and entered on December 11.

Because of a lack of troops, Allenby resumed his offensive only on September 18, 1918, and again he outwitted the Germans and Turks. His left wing took Nazareth, his center routed the Turkish army in the Jezreel Valley, in what came to be known as the "Battle of Megiddo" (the scriptural site of Armageddon), and his right—which included two of the three battalions of the Jewish Legion (British army units composed of Zionist volunteers from Palestine, Britain, and the United States)—crossed the Jordan River near Jericho, taking As Salt in Transjordan, braving logistical problems and appalling climatic conditions. The temperature soared to 120 degrees Fahrenheit; and "the dust on the hills was worse than the smoke in the valley," Jabotinsky—the founder and one of the soldiers of the legion—was to recall.[45] Amman fell on September 25, as did Samakh (Tzemah), the crossroads town at the southern tip of the Sea of Galilee.

To the east of Allenby's forces, Hussein's Arab army, led by his son Faisal and Lawrence, advanced along the Hejaz railway and took Deraa, the last main junction on the road to Damascus, on September 27. Al-Quneitra was taken that day by Allenby's troops, but Allenby decided that it should be Faisal's troops who would first enter and take Damascus—so that the Syrians could not object to a "Christian" occupation. In any event the Turks fled on September 30, and it was local Arabs who hoisted their nationalist flag; a symbolic gesture of self-liberation.[46] And the following day, contrary to plan, Allenby's Australian cavalry brigade rode into and through Damascus on its way to Homs. Lawrence and a vanguard of Hussein's troops followed, and the main body of Arab troops, led by Faisal himself, made their triumphal entry on October 3. Two days later Faisal's forces occupied Beirut and there too raised the Arab flag. French troops arrived on October 6 and took control of the city. The Turks understood that the game was up. On October 30 they signed an armistice agreement that was in effect a surrender, bringing the war in the Middle East to an official close.

According to the Sykes-Picot agreement, France was to have control over Syria-Lebanon, including Damascus. But British attitudes toward imperial expansion had radically changed in the interim. Moreover, the British, not the French, had conquered the Ottoman Middle East. Russia, in the throes of revolutionary upheaval and civil war, was out of the picture altogether. In the Middle East the British no longer needed France as an ally, and London now sought to rescind the agreement. Lloyd George called it "a fatuous arrangement judged from any and every point of view . . . inapplicable . . . and . . . undesirable."[47] Maurice Hankey, the secretary of the war cabinet, recorded Lloyd George as saying that "he wanted . . . to go back on the Sykes-Picot agreement so as to get Palestine for us and to bring Mosul into the British zone, and even to keep the French out of Syria."[48]

Whitehall had decided unilaterally to hold on to Palestine and, what is more, to install their own man, Faisal, in Damascus. A series of maneuvers, parrying both French machinations and local Arab efforts, ended in the establishment of a Hashemite administration, bolstered by local and imported Palestinian officials, in the Syrian capital. Almost two years were to pass before the French managed to make good their claim to Syria. In summer 1920 they invaded the country, crushed the Hashemite forces, and ousted Faisal, who ultimately ended up in Baghdad. Syria became a French Mandatory territory with a Paris-appointed high commissioner.

As for Palestine, France had never really been in the running; it was Britain's to dispose of. So long as the Ottomans had not been crushed and Arab statehood in the Levant in general remained in question, the Hashemite chieftains preferred to leave the question of Palestine on the back burner. But Britain's support of Zionism clearly ran "the risk of alienating the Arabs," in Clayton's phrase.[49] Most British officials believed that the Arabs could be persuaded to live with Zionism. As Lawrence put it: "There would be no difficulty in reconciling Zionists and Arabs in Palestine and Syria, provided that the administration of Palestine remained in British hands."[50] If the Arabs in Syria and elsewhere in the Middle East were assured of independence they would accept Zionist dominance in that small corner of the region called Palestine.

The Zionists were not so sanguine. Though they had perennially tried to make little of it, they had already witnessed two decades of small-scale Arab opposition. The general rise of Arab nationalism in the wake of Turkey's defeat boded ill. In December 1918, Jabotinsky put matters starkly (albeit still in the interrogative):

> This matter is not . . . an issue between the Jewish people and the Arab inhabitants of Palestine, but between the Jewish people and the Arab people. The latter, numbering 35 million, has [territory equal to] half of Europe, while the Jewish people, numbering ten million and wandering the earth, hasn't got a stone. . . . Will the Arab people stand opposed? Will it resist? [Will it insist] that . . . they . . . shall have it [all] for ever and ever, while he who has nothing shall forever have nothing?[51]

In early 1918, with only half of Palestine in British hands, London took steps designed to begin implementing the Balfour Declaration. A nine-man "Zionist Commission," headed by Weizmann and chaperoned by Ormsby-Gore, was dispatched to Palestine to chart the way. Soon after his arrival Weizmann set out—via the Suez Canal and Aqaba, by boat and then on camelback—to meet Faisal, whose army was encamped in Wadi Waheida, near Ma'an, in southern Transjordan. Weizmann had hardly bothered to meet with Palestinian Arab notables; as a group he held them to be "dishonest, uneducated, greedy, and unpatriotic."[52] The Hashemites were something else.

Weizmann and Faisal came face to face on June 4. The British had urged Faisal to come to terms with Zionism. Needing them to fend off potential French claims on Syria, he momentarily acquiesced in a bilateral understanding with Weizmann that was to be translated half a year later into a formal agreement. Later still, once the British had proved a hollow reed and the French had ejected him from Damascus, Faisal allowed his anti-Zionism free rein. Thus, observed historian Bernard Wasserstein, "The Zionist-Sharifian *entente* was . . . a *cul-de-sac* rather than a lost opportunity in the history of Palestine."[53] But for a time at least, perhaps persuaded by Faisal's rhetorical and theatrical powers and his own wishful thinking, Weizmann, who donned a *keffiyah* and posed with Faisal for photographs, came to feel that he had tamed or, at a minimum, charmed the "Arab beast" (as, in the past, he had countless British officials). "He is the first real Arab nationalist I have met," Weizmann wrote of Faisal to his wife, Vera: "He is a leader! He is quite intelligent and a very honest man, handsome as a picture! He is not interested in Palestine, but on the other hand he wants Damascus and the whole of northern Syria. He talks with great animosity against the French. . . . He expects a great deal from collaboration with the Jews. . . . He is contemptuous of the Palestinian Arabs whom he doesn't even regard as Arabs."

For years thereafter the Zionists were to emphasize that a Jewish commonwealth in Palestine would necessarily "have a strong and invigorating effect on the Arab nation outside."[54] Indeed, Weizmann specifically told Faisal that a

"Jewish Palestine" would facilitate the development of an Arab kingdom that would receive Jewish support. Meanwhile the Jews hoped to develop Palestine "under British guidance." One observer, Colonel P. C. Joyce, attached to the Arab rebels at Ma'an, thought that "Faisal really welcomed Jewish cooperation."[55]

Weizmann appeared to have done well with Faisal, but their agreement was to prove as ephemeral and insignificant as a dune in a desert storm. The entente was to have only a few months of dubious life. The two men met for a second time on December 11 at the Carlton Hotel in London, after the Hashemite prince had been installed in Damascus and a month before the opening of the Peace Conference in Paris. A temporary alliance of the two nationalisms striving for postwar Western support was seen as mutually beneficial. Colonel Lawrence served as interpreter. Faisal reassured his guest that "he and his followers would be able to explain to the Arabs that the advent of the Jews into Palestine was for the good of the country, and that the legitimate interests of the Arab peasants would in no way be interfered with." According to Weizmann, Faisal felt that there was land enough for both Jews and Arabs.

Weizmann expected Faisal and the Peace Conference to "recognize the national and historical rights of Jews to Palestine;" that land would be made available for Jewish colonization, so that "four or five million Jews" could settle "without encroaching on the ownership rights of Arab peasantry;" and that Palestinian Jewry would assist Faisal in his own national endeavor. Faisal assured Weizmann that "he would do everything to support Jewish demands, and would declare at the Peace Conference that Zionism and the Arab movement were fellow movements . . . [and in] harmony."[56]

On January 3, 1919, Weizmann and Faisal signed a formal agreement. Referring to the "racial kinship and ancient bonds" between Jews and Arabs, and to the emergent "Arab State" and Palestine as two distinct entities, the agreement asserted:

In the establishment of the Constitution and Administration of Palestine all such measures shall be adopted as will afford the fullest guarantees for carrying into effect the British Government's Declaration of the 2nd of November, 1917 [i.e., the Balfour Declaration]. Moreover, all necessary measures shall be taken to encourage and stimulate immigration of Jews into Palestine on a large scale, and as quickly as possible to settle Jewish immigrants upon the land. . . . In taking such measures, the Arab peasant and tenant farmers shall be protected in their rights, and shall be assisted in forwarding their economic development.[57]

(It is worth noting that while Zionist advocates, both before and after the Weizmann-Faisal agreement, continuously harped upon the favorable economic effect of Jewish colonization on the Palestinian Arabs, not much had changed for the latter between 1882 and 1920. According to Leonard Stein, legal adviser to the Zionist Organization, writing in August 1921, "Little Jewish capital [had] entered the country and . . . there [had] been no conspicuous quickening of economic life. Zionist activity [had] not put enough money into the pockets of the Arabs to make any appreciable impression on their minds."[58])

Faisal added an ambiguously worded proviso meaning that he was bound to carry out the agreement only if an Arab state was indeed established.[59] Without doubt Faisal signed the agreement, with Hussein's blessing, in the hope of mobilizing Zionist support for his own agenda. But at the same time the agreement would appear to show that he was not overly concerned about the fate of Palestine, and that he was not opposed to Jewish colonization and statehood.

But meanwhile the fate of the Levant was to be determined by the Great Powers rather than the Jews or the Arabs. In December 1918, a month before the opening of the Peace Conference, Lloyd George and Georges Clemenceau (who had become premier of France in November 1917) agreed on the inclusion of Mosul and Palestine in the British-Mandated territories.[60] At the conference Faisal—with Lawrence at his side—pleaded on February 6, 1919, for Arab independence, specifically excluding Palestine from the territory he demanded.[61] Weizmann and Sokolow pleaded the Zionist case on February 27. (Between these two sessions Sir Mark Sykes died. Harold Nicolson, then a junior British diplomat attending the conference, recorded: "It was due to his endless push and perseverance, to his enthusiasm and faith, that Arab nationalism and Zionism became two of the most successful of our war causes. To secure recognition of these his beliefs he had to fight ignorance at the F.O. [Foreign Office], suspicion at the I.O. [India Office], parsimony at the Treasury, obstruction at the W.O. [War Office], and idiocy at the Admiralty." Sokolow wrote that Sykes "fell as a hero at our side."[62])

Sokolow called on the conference to recognize "the historic title of the Jewish people to Palestine and the right of the Jews to reconstitute in Palestine their National Home"—echoing and amplifying the Balfour Declaration. He asked that the territory be placed under British Mandate, under League of Nations supervision. The Home was to gradually evolve into "an autonomous Commonwealth," without prejudicing the rights of the existing non-Jewish population of the country. A Jewish government would be established once the Jews formed a majority, which would transpire through steady, large-scale immigration.[63]

Sometime between February 6 and March 1, Faisal began to express public doubts about his previous utterances on Palestine. Perhaps Palestinian Arabs had gotten to him; perhaps his father, Hussein, had expressed dissatisfaction about the agreement with Weizmann. On March 1 the Paris daily *Le Matin* carried an interview with Faisal in which he was quoted as saying that Jews were welcome as refugees in Palestine under a Muslim or Christian government, but if they claimed "sovereign rights in the country, I foresee and fear very serious dangers and conflicts between them and other races." Alarmed, the Zionist leaders dispatched the American jurist Felix Frankfurter to talk to him. Frankfurter was reassured, and the gist of Faisal's position was then written up (by Lawrence) in the form of a letter from Faisal to Frankfurter. It appeared in the *New York Times* on March 5, 1919: "We Arabs, especially the educated among us, look with the deepest sympathy on the Zionist movement. We regard [the Zionist proposals submitted in Paris] as moderate and proper. We will do our best . . . to help them through; we will wish the Jews a most hearty welcome home."[64]

But infidelity was to characterize Faisal's attitude toward Zionism. In May 1920 the new "king" of Damascus appealed to Britain to give Palestine to its Arab inhabitants.[65] In January 1921, after his ouster from Damascus by the French, he told Foreign Office officials that Palestine had in fact been included in the Arab state area in the McMahon-Hussein correspondence: "The Arabs had always regarded both Palestine and the hinterland of Syria as being covered by the pledges," he said.[66]

At the Peace Conference in Balfour's enduring phrase, "These three all-powerful, all-ignorant men [Lloyd George, Clemenceau, and Wilson] [were] sitting there and carving up continents with only a child to lead them" (that is, Maurice Hankey, then forty-one). When it came to Palestine, Lloyd George, using the biblical phrase "from Dan to Beersheba," insisted that Britain have it. He probably had no idea where Dan was. It was only months later that Allenby told him that the remains of biblical Dan had been located (near Metulla, in the Galilee Panhandle)—and that it was somewhat to the south of where Lloyd George wanted the Palestine-Lebanon-Syria frontier to run.[67]

Nevertheless, in the Treaties of Paris, as the peace settlement of 1919 was to be known, the British got more or less what they had wanted. Lloyd George told another participant: "Wilson has gone back home with a bundle of assignats [that is, worthless French revolutionary paper currency]. I have returned with a pocket full of sovereigns in the shape of the German Colonies, Mesopotamia, etc. Everyone to his taste." But not only Britain had emerged from the war with gains, according to Lloyd George. The Arabs, he felt, had also done extremely well, considering which side most of them had been on: "No race has done better out of the fidelity with which the Allies redeemed their promises. . . . Owing to the tremendous sacrifices of the Allied Nations . . . the Arabs have already won independence in Iraq, Arabia, Syria, and Trans-Jordania, although most of the Arab races fought throughout the war for the Turkish oppressors. . . . The Palestinian Arabs [in particular] fought for Turkish rule."[68]

PALESTINE DURING WORLD WAR I

Palestine in World War I was a land occupied by a ravaging power and criss-crossed by warring armies. Ottoman troops, poorly supplied and relatively undisciplined, confiscated pack animals and wagons on a massive scale; much of the country's natural vegetation—never profuse—was cut down for fuel and fortifications; cattle and entire harvests were seized; and stores and flour mills were plundered.[69] Food stocks were also severely depleted by locusts in 1915 and 1916.[70] The war substantially reduced the population. According to various estimates, in 1914 Palestine had 657,000 Muslim inhabitants (including 7,000 Druze), 81,000 Christians, and 60,000 Jews; in 1918 there were 618,000 Muslims, 70,000 Christians, and some 59,000 Jews.[71] This drop was due to both privations and expulsions. "For the majority of the Arabs of the Ottoman Empire, World War I was a time of cruel hardship and unrelieved distress. For the Arabs of Palestine the war was doubly disastrous," wrote historian Samir M. Seikaly.[72]

A few weeks after the conquest of Jerusalem, in January 1918, the new British governor, Ronald Storrs, found a "scarcity of food amounting almost to a famine." A "crowd of veiled Arab women, some of whom tore their garments apart to reveal the bones almost piercing their skin," gathered outside his office window, screaming. At a hospital Storrs saw children with "limbs swollen" from malnutrition.[73] Poorer levels of sanitation, hygiene, and medicine made the Arabs far more vulnerable than the Jews to disease. Outbreaks of typhus, cholera, and smallpox killed thousands of Arabs in 1915–16.[74] Hundreds of Arabs died in battle or from disease while serving in the Ottoman armies, which drafted thousands of Palestinians,[75] leaving some towns and villages with only the elderly, women, and children, and causing serious economic damage.[76] The Jews fared better: Many were foreign nationals or ultra-Orthodox Yeshiva students, exempt from the Ottoman call-up; others managed to buy their way out. But dozens were mobilized by the army or conscripted into special work battalions.[77]

The authorities, aware of the anti-Ottoman pull of both Arab nationalism and Zionism, employed harsh measures to crush rebelliousness. Torture was widespread, with needle pricks, caning of the soles of the feet, and hot boiled eggs in the armpits being among the more common methods.[78] Jamal Pasha, the military governor of Syria-Palestine, "caused very many [Arab] Palestinians to suffer the indignity of arbitrary arrest, savage torture, and summary exile for political crimes never committed."[79] Dozens of Arabs were hanged as subversives in Damascus and Beirut[80] in 1915–16, among them at least two

Palestinians—'Ali 'Umar al-Nashashibi, of Jerusalem, and Muhammad al-Santi (or Shanti), of Jaffa. A number of Arabs were executed in Palestine, including the mufti of Gaza, Ahmad 'Arif al-Husseini, and his son Mustafa,[81] and Salim Ahmad 'Abd al-Hadi, of Nablus. In 1916 alone 120 Arabs were deported from Greater Syria to Anatolia, most of them after the start of the Sharifian revolt.[82] Complaints from neutrals resulted in a rebuke of Jamal Pasha by Constantinople and a general easing of the Ottoman hand in Palestine.[83] When he left the Levant at the end of 1917, the governor was remembered as "Jamal the bloodthirsty, Jamal the fiend, Jamal the tyrant, Jamal the starver of the Land."[84]

The repression was restricted to a thin stratum of the politically active upper classes and did not propel the general population into the arms of the Allies. Neither did the news of the Arab Revolt in the spring of 1916.[85] The upper classes remained by and large pro-Ottoman, for reasons of personal safety and survival, economic and social interests, Islamic confraternity, anti-European xenophobia, or inertia. Many Arabs, especially after the Balfour Declaration, realized that an Allied victory would advance the cause of Zionism.[86] Nonetheless, as Ottoman depredations began to rankle, and as prospects of an Allied victory increased, a small minority of Palestinian Arabs came out in favor of the Arab Revolt and the Allies, primarily as a means of achieving independence.

Most of the Yishuv evinced sympathy for the Turks, castigating those who would publicly express sympathy for the Allies; Anti-Turkish utterances or action, it was rightly argued, would provoke the regime and imperil the Jews. For Zionism the war posed an insoluble dilemma. Most of its cadres and potential immigrants lived in the Russian Empire; thousands of Jews served in the Czar's armies. But Jews everywhere hated Russia. Moreover, Palestine, with its vulnerable, budding colonies and small Jewish population, was still in Ottoman hands. Lastly, the powerful Jewish communities in Germany (the traditional organizational center of Zionism) and Austria-Hungary were patriotic as, indeed, were those of Britain and France. Many thousands of German and Austro-Hungarian Jews, as well as British, French, American, and Italian Jews, served in their countries' armies. Quite wisely, then, at the start of the war the Zionist Organization proclaimed neutrality—while individual leaders generally expressed support for their own countries.

The Turks regarded the largely Russian Zionist colonies and Jaffa–Tel Aviv, the New Yishuv's "capital," with suspicion and hostility based on the belief that these Jews hoped for an Allied victory. The outbreak of the war placed the Yishuv in an extraordinarily difficult position. Most of it, Old and New alike, had depended on monetary contributions from European Jews; for additional manpower, it looked to Russia. At a stroke the links with Western Europe and Russia were severed, and the flow of funds and immigrants ended. Foreign postal services, which had offices in Palestine and which were much more reliable than their Ottoman counterpart, were shut down, and all mail was subjected to strict censorship. The economically crucial citrus exports, by both Jewish and Arab grove owners, were halted. Banks closed, and people hoarded food and other basics. Shops and firms emptied and shut their doors; unemployment and prices soared.

From the Jewish communities urgent appeals went out to the United States. As a neutral power the United States had access to Constantinople and Palestine down to April 1917. The American ambassador to the Sublime Porte, the non-Zionist Jew Henry Morgenthau, quickly organized the dispatch of $50,000 in gold coin, raised among American Jews and conveyed to Jaffa by the battleship *North Carolina* in October 1914. In all, the Yishuv received about $1.25 million in aid from the United States during the war.[87] The money was channeled through the Zionist leadership—thus consolidating its position at the helm of the community. Money and food also reached the Yishuv from the Jews of Germany.[88]

In September 1914, exploiting the outbreak of the war, Constantinople abolished the Capitulations; foreign consuls lost their extraterritorial powers, and those of the Allied nations were soon expelled. Tens of thousands of Jews lost their special rights and became, in effect, enemy aliens. The Arabs, who had long resented the "foreign" Jews' special rights, were jubilant.[89] But though there was renewed anti-Zionist agitation, there was no violence.

Turkey entered the war in November and imposed military rule throughout the Ottoman Levant. Jamal Pasha ordered the settlements to hand over their weapons and mounted search and confiscation operations. (Arab villages and Bedouin tribes were allowed to keep their weapons.) The colonies were forbidden to mount Jewish armed guards; some hid their weapons for the duration. Periodically Jamal cracked down on specific manifestations of Zionism, such as flying the blue-and-white flag, and otherwise harassed the settlements (though, being a Francophile, he occasionally went out of his way to help colonies with a French connection, such as Rishon Le-Zion).[90] His anti-Zionist policy was apparently in part motivated by a desire to balance his anti-Arab-nationalist activities.

On December 17, Constantinople ordered the deportation of all enemy nationals from Palestine—about half the Jewish community.[91] Jaffa's governor, Baha ad-Din—described by one Jewish observer as "a Bedouin . . . swift as a deer, despite his crooked legs, sly as a cat, brutal as a tiger and . . . uncultured and [religiously] zealous"[92]—immediately ordered a roundup. The dragnet—hasty, disorganized, and brutal—scooped men up without their wives and children, and dragged them off to an Italian steamer docked in the harbor. Some were robbed and beaten along the way. Hundreds of other Russian-born Jews, fearing similar treatment or worse, rushed to the harbor of their own volition and got on board. Altogether about seven hundred people were dispatched that day to Alexandria. The Yishuv raised an outcry, and

Morgenthau and the German ambassador in Constantinople intervened. The deportations were immediately halted, and Baha ad-Din was removed from office (though he resurfaced as a special adviser on Jamal's staff).[93]

Foreign nationals were now given the choice of becoming Ottoman citizens or leaving. Though naturalization initially involved a large expense—about TL2 per head, abolished in May 1915—and rendered the applicants eligible for conscription, there was a rush to the "Ottomanization" offices, spurred by the memory of the brutal Jaffa roundup. Jewish leaders, including New Yishuv socialists Ben-Gurion and Ben-Zvi, came out in support of both the Turkish war effort and Ottomanization, arguing that this alone could assure the Yishuv's survival. Jews in Jaffa organized patriotic processions and published pro-Ottoman broadsheets.[94] A handful of Zionist activists, including Moshe Shertok (later Sharett), later second prime minister of the State of Israel, and Dov Hoz, later a Haganah leader, joined the Ottoman army. Only a few Jews managed to obtain citizenship papers. Ottoman officials were lethargic at the best of times, and anti-Zionism may have rendered some deliberately obstructive.

For Jews who decided to leave, the United States sent the warship *Tennessee* to shuttle the emigrants from Jaffa to Egypt. Most went to Alexandria, where by the end of 1915 there were nearly 12,300 Palestinian Jewish exiles.[95] According to Zionist historians,[96] war deaths, voluntary departures, and expulsions during 1914–18 reduced the population of the Yishuv from a pre-war 85,000 to approximately 50,000–57,000.[97] The leading demographer of Ottoman and Mandatory Palestine, Justin McCarthy, argues that the British and some Zionists exaggerated Ottoman oppression and expulsions, lumping together exiles from Palestine with Jews and others who reached Alexandria from Anatolia, Syria-Lebanon, and North Africa. He concludes that only 3,000 to 4,000 Jews were deported or emigrated to Egypt, and the majority of these returned in the wake of the British conquest.[98]

But Zionist activities were certainly curtailed and activists were persecuted. In February 1915 a number of Zionist leaders, including Manya and Yisrael Shohat, Yehoshua Hankin, Ben-Gurion, and Ben-Zvi, were in jail; a handful of others had been exiled.[99] Land sales to Jews were forbidden; Jewish courts and other community institutions were shut down. There were mass arrests and interrogations of activists and leaders. Manya Shohat and Hankin, the main Zionist land purchaser, were both eventually exiled to Anatolia, and Ben-Gurion and Ben-Zvi were deported to Alexandria. Arthur Ruppin was deported to Constantinople, as was David Yellin, a leading Zionist educator.

In 1917 the nine thousand Jewish inhabitants of Jaffa and Tel Aviv, along with Jaffa's Arabs, were evacuated. Unlike the Arabs, the Jews were not allowed to camp near the town; about half of them lived out the time in Petach Tikva and Kfar Sava, which were relatively close by, and many settled temporarily in Galilee moshavot. Many of their homes were plundered: "Hundreds of Bedouin women, Arabs on mules, camels etc. came like flocks of birds and were seen to take valuables: furniture, etc." Two Jews were reported hanged as a warning to those who might try to resist the pillaging.[100] About three hundred Jews were also evicted from Jerusalem.[101] Most of the exiled Jews of Jaffa and Tel Aviv returned to their homes only many months later, after the British conquest.

In the words of one historian, Palestine's Jews "suffered less than any other minority from persecution, harm in battle and executions" during the war, in large measure because of United States and German diplomatic intervention.[102] But at least one group of Jews was involved in active subversion, and was harshly dealt with. In the spring of 1915, Aaron Aaronsohn and Avshalom Feinberg organized a spy ring based on Aaronsohn's family and friends in Zikhron Ya'akov. They named it Nili (an acronym of *Netzah Yisrael Lo Yeshaker*—Hebrew for "the Lord of Israel is not false"). Aaronsohn feared that the Turks' anti-Jewish measures augured far more severe oppression.[103] During 1915–17 the spy ring provided British intelligence with information about the Turkish Fourth Army's order of battle, camps, armaments, and logistics. Nili's activities soon became known to the Zionist leadership, which opposed them, fearing that the Ottomans would collectively punish the whole Yishuv, perhaps to the extent of completely uprooting it. But the Nili men were undeterred.

Feinberg established the first contact with British intelligence in Cairo in September 1915. Aaronsohn, who in 1915–16 supervised the struggle against the locust plagues and who was friendly with Jamal, was well placed to gather information. At the end of 1916 he left Palestine and during 1917 was attached to British HQ, in effect running Nili from Cairo. The ring eventually numbered forty or fifty members.[104] Feinberg was killed by Bedouin near Al-Rafah in January 1917, while trying to reach British lines. On September 4, a carrier pigeon, on its way to Egypt with a coded message, was caught by the Turks in Caesarea. Later that month they captured ring member Na'aman Belkind while he was making his way to British lines in the south. Under interrogation he implicated others. On October 1, Zikhron Ya'akov was surrounded by Turkish troops. Most of the ring was apprehended. Aaronsohn's sister, Sarah Aaronsohn, committed suicide under torture; Belkind and another member, Joseph Lishansky, were hanged in Damascus on December 16.

The Yishuv directly benefited from Nili's operations in two ways: During the first half of 1917 it brought in British funds and distributed them among the needy settlements; and it helped disseminate in the West information (and rumors and misinformation) about Ottoman persecution, raising the outcry that curtailed further similar Turkish actions.[105] But once the ring began to unravel, Zionist leaders were quick to denounce its activities and in one or two cases helped persuade settlements to deny haven to Nili fugitives. Subsequently Nili and the Yishuv leadership made their peace; Aaronsohn himself died on May 15, 1919, in a plane crash in the English Channel.

THE POSTWAR SETTLEMENT AND THE FIRST PALESTINIAN TROUBLES, 1918–21

Almost before the ink had dried on the Treaties of Paris, they began to come unstuck: In the Middle East, the often unnatural territorial divisions and the direct or indirect imperial rule were questioned or defied. Syria, nominally ruled by Faisal, the Hashemite prince who had led the armies of the revolt, attracted a host of Arab nationalists, mostly Palestinian and Iraqi. On June 6, 1919, Faisal convened the "Syrian Arab Congress," which a month later called for "full and absolute political independence" for Greater Syria. It also rejected "Zionist claims for the establishment of a Jewish commonwealth . . . in . . . Palestine" and implictly annulled Faisal's agreement with Weizmann.[106]

Britain and France rejected the congress's resolutions and, in April 1920, at the San Remo Conference, the Allied powers formally granted France and Britain mandates respectively over Syria-Lebanon and Palestine and Iraq. The Arabs immediately condemned these decisions as a betrayal of promises of independence, and Faisal's followers embarked on guerrilla raids against the French in Lebanon. Ignoring Faisal's last-minute unconditional surrender, the French took Damascus on July 26. Faisal was exiled and later was declared king of Iraq, where he ruled under British tutelage until his death in 1933.

France was unhappy with Britain's control of Palestine, which in 1920 included Transjordan, from which pro-Faisal raiders continuously harassed the French in Syria. Paris had never really resigned itself to the scrapping of the Sykes-Picot Agreement, which had given France a half share in the governance of Palestine. But the British managed to exclude France altogether. In April 1918 Allenby established the Occupied Enemy Territory Administration (OETA), headed by Major-General Sir Arthur Money, with Brigadier G. F. Clayton as chief political officer. Though set up more or less on the wings of the Balfour Declaration, OETA from the first dissociated itself from London's declared policy of "Zionizing" Palestine. Many of its senior officers lacked any sympathy for Zionism and understood that British support for it would probably bring them into conflict with the Arabs, making their task of administering a problematic, war-impoverished country that much more difficult. Indeed, some argued that promoting Zionism would result in "an Arab rising" which "would make short shrift of the Hebrews."[107] Aware of the Russian origins of most of the Zionist pioneers, many of the officers also tended to associate or even equate Zionism with Bolshevism.[108]

Anti-Semitism, in varying doses, also touched most of OETA's senior officers. Money, for one, said the Jews of Jerusalem were "bringing up the rising generation in their schools to be dirty, idle wasters. . . . Their men turn out more idle wasters and their women more prostitutes than the rest of the population put together." And he regarded the Jews "as a class inferior morally and intellectually to the bulk of the Muslim and Christian inhabitants of the country."[109] Most British officials also felt a strong antipathy for Palestinian Arabs, however. T. E. Lawrence thought the Palestinian peasants "stupid . . . materialistic and bankrupt."[110] Clayton wrote: "The so-called Arabs of Palestine are not to be compared with the real Arab of the desert or even of other civilized districts in Syria and Mesopotamia." But the officials felt duty bound to protect the Arabs' interests against Zionist encroachment, to resist "a policy of oppression of the local inhabitants in favor of the Jewish minority"[111] and not to antagonize the vast sea of Muslims beyond Palestine's borders. The problem was that Britain's wartime commitment to Zionism ran counter to its vaguer general commitment to Arab independence (the McMahon letters). In April 1919 Money wrote to Lord Curzon: "The Palestinians in fact desire Palestine for themselves: and have no intention of allowing their country to be thrown open to hordes of Jews from Eastern and Central Europe." To implement the Balfour Declaration would involve Britain in the use of force "in opposition to the will of the majority of the population."[112]

OETA severely curbed Jewish immigration, so that only four to five thousand Jews reached Palestine's shores during its two-year rule.[113] It wasn't only a matter of British interference: Zionist leaders failed to raise the funds needed to facilitate large-scale immigration and settlement. The combination of British animosity and their own financial problems, plus increased Arab opposition, caused despondency among Zionists. "Everywhere was a sense of frustration, hope deferred, promise cheated," reported Storrs.[114] By mid-1919 the euphoria that had followed the Balfour Declaration had given way to a measure of hopelessness.[115]

In early April 1918 the Zionist Commission—headed by Weizmann and set up by Whitehall—arrived in Palestine, "to carry out, subject to General Allenby's authority, any steps required to give effect to the Government's declaration in favor of the establishment in Palestine of a national home for the Jewish people." Within a few months it amalgamated with the existing Palestine Office of the Zionist Organization, and represented Zionist interests in Palestine until 1921, when the Zionist Congress at Karlsbad constituted the Palestine Zionist Executive (PZE), which the British recognized as the "Jewish Agency" provided for in article 4 of the Mandate.

Within months of the Balfour Declaration, the Palestine Arab elite began to express its opposition by establishing Muslim-Christian associations and nationalist clubs in Jerusalem, Jaffa, and Ramle. But the continuing war in the northern half of the country—which was to end only in September 1918—necessarily resulted in the curtailment of political activity in the British rear. The end of the war opened the gates to the renewal of Arab anti-Zionist activism, fueled by the changed behavior and status of the Jewish community. The numbers were still small—66,000, according to a report by Clayton from December 1918.[116] But from a persecuted, maligned minority the Jews had become the future masters of the country, part of the machinery of the British administration. After the November 2, 1918, Balfour Day parade in Jewish Jerusalem, more than one hundred Muslim and Christian notables, headed by Musa Kazim al-Husseini, Jerusalem's mayor, handed Storrs a petition that stated: "We have noticed yesterday a large crowd of Jews carrying banners and over-running the streets shouting words which hurt the feelings and wound the soul. They pretend with open voice that Palestine, which is the Holy Land of our fathers and the graveyard of our ancestors, which has been inhabited by the Arabs for long ages, who loved it and died in defending it, is now a national home for them."[117]

A similar petition was submitted by the Jaffa Muslim-Christian Association. Extremist secret societies, pledged to violence, also began to form. In February 1919 an organization called "the Black Hand" was established in Jaffa. Its proclaimed aim was to "kill the snail" of Zionism "while it was [still] young."[118] New Muslim-Christian associations sprang up elsewhere in the country. Soon federated in a national framework, in January 1919 they held the "First Palestine National Congress," which supported the incorporation of Palestine into Syria, which the participants expected would shortly emerge as a fully independent Arab state. Thereafter the associations bombarded the authorities with anti-Zionist petitions and complaints, and the administration briefly banned immigration, stopped land transfers, and even banned the public performance of *HaTikvah,* the Jewish national anthem.[119]

Zionist leaders argued that Arab hostility was "artificial," fomented by self-interested minority groups such as Christians or *effendis,* and not a true reflection of majority feeling,[120] and that British behavior tended to aggravate Arab antagonism toward Zionism. "The official approach is to apologize to the Arabs for a slip of the tongue by Mr. Balfour," wrote Jabotinsky in November 1918.[121] But British officials correctly divined that the outbursts and petitions accurately conveyed "the fundamental antipathy towards Zionism felt by most politically conscious Arabs."[122]

Anti-Zionist activism stopped short of violence, though there had been Arab-Jewish scuffles in Jerusalem after the Balfour Day procession. In early April 1919 anti-Zionism surfaced noisily during the annual Nabi Musa celebrations. Violence was averted largely because of stringent British military precautions. Arab animosity was even more emphatically manifest during the visit of the King-Crane Commission, in June. An agent of the peace conference in Paris, the commission was dispatched to the Middle East to ascertain the wishes of the indigenous populations with respect to their future governance. It consisted of two Americans—Henry King, president of Oberlin College, and Charles Crane, a businessman and Democratic Party contributor. 'Aref Pasha Dajani, a Jerusalem notable, told them that Zionism's triumph would mean Arab enslavement: "It is impossible for us to make an understanding with them [the Jews] or even to live with them. . . . Their history and all their past proves that it is impossible to live with them. In all the countries where they are at present they are not wanted . . . because they always arrive to suck the blood of everybody. . . . If the League of Nations will not listen to the appeal of the Arabs this country will become a river of blood."

Representatives of the Jaffa Muslim-Christian Association put it in the stark terms of a zero-sum game: "We will push the Zionists into the sea—or they will send us back into the desert."[123] Some of the Zionists who appeared before the commission, such as Chaim Margaliut Kalvaryski, tried to downplay the depth and extent of Arab antagonism. But in closed Zionist leadership meetings at this time, there were occasional outpourings of unusual candor. "Everybody sees a difficulty in the question of relations between Arabs and Jews," Ben-Gurion told the members of the Va'ad Zmani (the Temporary Committee, the Yishuv's main governing body) in June 1919: "But not everybody sees that there is no solution to this question. No solution! There is a gulf, and nothing can bridge it. . . . I do not know what Arab will agree that Palestine should belong to the Jews. . . . We, as a nation, want this country to be *ours;* the Arabs, as a nation, want this country to be *theirs*."[124]

Shertok, Ben-Gurion's chief aide in the years prior to statehood and Israel's first foreign minister, five years earlier had written in a similar vein:

> We have forgotten that we have not come to an empty land to inherit it, but we have come to conquer a country from a people inhabiting it, that governs it by virtue of its language and savage culture. . . . Recently, there has been appearing in our newspapers the clarification about "the mutual misunderstanding" between us and the Arabs, about "common interests" [and] about "the possibility of unity and peace between the two fraternal peoples." . . . [But] we must not allow ourselves to be deluded by such illusive hopes . . . for if we cease to look upon our land, the Land of Israel, as ours alone and we allow a partner into our estate—all content and meaning will be lost to our enterprise.[125]

In their report the commissioners spoke of the depth of Palestinian Arab antagonism toward Zionism and disparagingly of the Jewish national movement. King and Crane duly recommended the incorporation of Palestine into Syria in a unified mandated territory. Nothing came of the recommendations.

Arab words were soon to give way to actions. At the end of 1919 animosity toward Zionist settlement focused on the land north of Lake Hula, known today as the Galilee Panhandle. This area, as well as parts of southern Lebanon, was abandoned by British occupation forces and became in effect a no-man's-land between the British and French zones of occupation. A cluster of four Jewish settlements was located at the panhandle's northern end, and the Yishuv pressed for British dominion there. The French were unable to assert sovereignty, and rebellious Bedouin tribesmen, loosely allied with Faisal's increasingly anti-French regime in Damascus, pushed for control. It was a low-key rebellion in which old-fashioned banditry and a bid for a regional fiefdom mixed with protonationalist motives. The Bedouin received arms from Faisal and perhaps enjoyed some clandestine British support as well. They waylaid travelers and attacked the area's allegedly pro-French Christian villages. On December 12, 1919, they mounted a major assault on the village of Abil al-Qamh, killing and looting. That day the marauders also fired on the nearby Jewish settlement of Tel Hai and killed a man.

The rebels announced that they meant no harm to the Jews, only to the French, and repeatedly tried to persuade the four settlements to join their revolt. The settlers opted for neutrality; they did not want to make an enemy of France, though, quite naturally, they preferred to be included in British-controlled Palestine, earmarked for the Jewish National Home. French mobile columns occasionally encamped at two of the settlements, Metulla and Kfar Gil'adi, angering the rebels. Moreover, the logic of the situation—"those who are not with us are against us"—and a natural resentment against the alien Zionist colonies soon persuaded the Arabs to treat the four settlements as enemies.

The settlers felt increasingly isolated. In January 1920 the inhabitants of Metulla decided on evacuation until the political future and security of the area were assured. So did the people at Hamara, to the southeast. But the socialist settlers in nearby Tel Hai and Kfar Gil'adi, reinforced by a handful of volunteers (including Yosef Trumpeldor, a one-armed hero of the Russo-Japanese war of 1905 and of the Gallipoli campaign), stayed put. They—and their backers in the Zionist heartland—were bent on showing that the panhandle was part of the National Home. Besides, as Zionist socialist leader Berl Katznelson wrote, "retreat would be decisive proof of our weakness. . . . The only proof of our right to our land lies in a stiff-necked and desperate stand with no looking back." Ben-Gurion spoke in a similar vein: "If we flee from robbers, then we will have to leave not just Upper Galilee but the whole Land of Israel." "The Arabs respect only force," added Ussishkin. On February 29 he wrote to Weizmann: "If we stood up and fought for every inch of land in Upper Galilee we would show the English and French governments that Upper Galilee is ours, and ours it will have to stay." Ironically, it was the militant Jabotinsky who advocated abandoning the two outposts, arguing that their position was untenable.[126]

The Zionists considered sending a relief column but were deterred by the difficulties involved and by the lack of clarity about the political fate of the panhandle. Bands of volunteers infiltrated through the Arab areas and reached the surrounded settlements. A Zionist emissary to Damascus, Kalvaryski, obtained promises at the beginning of January 1920 from Faisal's men—principally Mahmud al-Fa'ur, a tribal chieftain in the panhandle—that the settlements would be left alone. The remaining settlers resumed work in the fields; but early in February a Tel Hai man was killed by marauders.

On March 1 the Arabs struck. Defending Tel Hai, Kfar Gil'adi, and the reoccupied Metulla were thirty to thirty-five individuals at each site, armed only with rifles, pistols, and grenades, and with insufficient ammunition. The surrounding Arab forces, which included inhabitants of the neighboring village of al-Khalisa as well as Bedouin bands, numbered several hundred. A party of Arabs gained entry into the Tel Hai compound court by saying that they wanted to check whether the Jews were quartering French troops. A fierce firefight erupted, apparently triggered by an unintentional shot by one of the Jewish guards. The "visiting" Arabs were driven out and rejoined those outside, who promptly mounted a number of assaults on the settlement's walls, in which dozens of them died and more were wounded. Altogether six of the defenders were killed or mortally wounded, including Trumpeldor and two women; several others sustained lighter injuries. Trumpeldor died while being carried from Tel Hai to Kfar Gil'adi and is reputed to have said before expiring: "It is good to die for our country"—a statement that became, along with the whole Tel Hai episode, a cornerstone of Zionist mythology.

The assailants failed to take Tel Hai, but the defenders, their ammunition and numbers depleted, understood that the stronghold could not be held. A relief column reached the site during the night and escorted them back to Kfar Gil'adi after putting the settlement to the torch. On March 3, the remaining eighty or ninety defenders of Metulla and Kfar Gil'adi, noting that the surrounding Arab villagers and Bedouin were massing for a final attack, abandoned the two settlements and withdrew. The battle for Tel Hai, which ended in retreat, went down in Zionist history as an epic of courage and fortitude.

The settlers of Kfar Gil'adi, Tel Hai, and Metulla returned to the area only in October 1920, after the French had occupied Damascus and crushed the rebellious Arab bands. In December, France and Britain agreed at San Remo that the panhandle would revert to British rule, and the French withdrew. The three settlements became part of British Mandatory Palestine and the Jewish National Home-to-be.[127]

If in the Galilee Panhandle it appeared that the anti-Zionist hostilities were a sideshow in the wider Arab-French-British struggle, to the south Arab violence took on a clearly anti-Zionist direction, albeit prompted and aggravated by the winds of xenophobic nationalism sweeping through Syria. The Jewish defeat in the panhandle helped fan these winds; in Arab Jerusalem, for example, there was a rumor that sixteen hundred Jews had died in the skirmishes in the North.[128] During February and March there were frequent depredations by Arab villagers and Bedouin bands along the Syrian-Palestinian border south of Lake Hula. Armed marauders regularly crossed the border from the Golan into the Jordan Valley, Jewish field hands were ambushed, farm animals killed or stolen, settlements—Rosh Pina and Yesod Hama'ala—fired upon. A serious attack took place on April 27 against Ayelet HaShahar. About a hundred Arabs, of the neighboring 'Arab al-Heib and 'Arab al-Kirad tribes and from the Golan, surrounded the settlement, which had some thirty arms-bearing adults, and opened fire. The Arabs withdrew three hours later, leaving one dead behind; none of the settlers was hit. Almost two months later, on June 10, marauders murdered a farmer from Yesod Hama'ala, despite the presence in the moshava of a British army platoon.[129]

But the focus of Arab violence against the Jews in 1920 was to be Jerusalem. On February 27, under Zionist pressure, chief OETA administrator Major-General Louis Bols stated in an interview in the Arabic-language daily *Marat al-Sharq* that Britain intended to implement the Balfour Declaration. The announcement coincided with the convening in Damascus of the Second Syrian Arab Congress, where Palestinian delegates called for a renewal of the struggle against Jewish immigration. At home the announcement prompted coordinated demonstrations, shop closures, petitions, and placards reading "Down with Zionism" and "Death to the Jews." A second wave of protests in most of Palestine's towns, in which a number of Jews were assaulted, took place on March 8. The demonstrators were enthused by news of the evacuation of the panhandle and chanted: "Palestine is our land and the Jews are our dogs"and "Kill the Jews" (*Itbah al-Yahud*).[130]

The resolution by the Syrian Congress on March 7, declaring Faisal king of Syria and Palestine, and Arab hopes that Palestine would indeed be incorporated into his kingdom, fueled the demonstrations and helped trigger the climactic outbursts the following month. Though it ran counter to Whitehall policy, Faisal's coronation as king of Palestine as well as Syria had been promoted by OETA officials such as Col. Bertie Harry Waters-Taylor, chief of staff, who on January 20 had encouraged Faisal to insist on an "undivided" Syria, in which Britain would recognize him as "overlord." And on March 8, immediately after Faisal's coronation, chief administrator Bols cabled Whitehall urging it to recognize Faisal. Bols was supported by Allenby, but London demurred: "How would recognition of Faisal as King be reconciled with Zionist claims?" responded Curzon.[131]

The views of these officers were known to the Palestinian Arab leadership (and to Faisal's circle in Damascus); former Ottoman officer and Jerusalem notable Hajj Muhammad Amin al-Husseini, returning from Damascus to Palestine on April 1, told his colleagues that the British administration supported Faisal's kingship over both Syria and Palestine.[132] Such thinking, which could only fire Palestinian Arab anti-Zionism, was complemented by rumors of an impending Arab rising in Palestine. What was about to happen appears to have been clear to everyone but the British. On March 12 Jabotinsky wrote from Jerusalem to Weizmann: "The pogrom is liable to break out here any day."[133]

In the first days of April, Arabs from the surrounding countryside poured into Jerusalem's Old City for the week-long Nabi Musa and Esther celebrations, which fell at the same time as Passover. On the morning of April 4 a procession of nearly six hundred pilgrims from Hebron, a town known for its Muslim orthodoxy, entered the city. There were cheers for "King" Faisal and Arab independence; Jerusalem mayor Musa Kazim al-Husseini swore the gathered crowd to spill their blood for Palestine. 'Arif al-'Arif, the editor of *Suriyya al-Janubiyya*, declared: "If we don't use force against the Zionists and against the Jews, we will never be rid of them." And the crowd chanted *"Nashrab dam al-Yahud"*—we will drink the blood of the Jews.[134]

The rally had a joint Muslim-Christian tone and composition. One placard read: "Shall we give back the country to a people who crucified our Lord Jesus?" As the demonstration drew to a close, the head of the Hebronite pilgrims shouted, *"Itbah al-Yahud"*—and violence erupted. The crowd went on a rampage, moving toward West Jerusalem; Jews on Jaffa Street were stoned and Jewish shops looted. Khalil al-Sakakini, a Christian Arab educator and diarist, described what he saw:

> [A] riot broke out, the people began to run about and stones were thrown at the Jews. The shops were closed and there were screams. . . . I saw a Zionist [that is, Jewish British] soldier covered in dust and blood. . . . Afterwards, I saw one Hebronite approach a Jewish shoeshine boy, who hid behind a sack in one of the [Old City] wall's corners next to Jaffa Gate, and take his box and beat him [the shoeshine boy] over the head. He screamed and began to run, his head bleeding and the Hebronite left him and returned to the procession. . . . The riot reached its zenith. All shouted, "Muhammad's religion was born with the sword" . . . I immediately walked to the municipal garden . . . my soul is nauseated and depressed by the madness of humankind.[135]

Most of the violence took place west of the Old City walls, along Jaffa Road. Arab policemen joined the mob, which, according to Sakakini, tried to stab a British policeman. A British military pilot, on the scene by chance, tried to stop the violence and was clubbed to death. The riotous procession then abruptly turned back from Jaffa Street into the Old City, and the excited pilgrims turned on Jewish shops and pedestrians, brandishing clubs, knives, and stones. The Arab police contingent responsible for the Old City either looked on passively or joined in the mayhem.

Jerusalem's newly formed Jewish self-defense organization, the Haganah, had sent groups, some of them armed, to areas outside the walls but had failed to station a contingent inside the Old City's Jewish Quarter. After the eruption two groups, armed with sticks and metal rods, were dispatched toward the Old City but barred from entering by British troops. The British belatedly sent contingents of Indian troops to protect the Jewish Quarter and disperse the rioters. Inexplicably, that night Governor Storrs ordered the Indian troops to leave the Old City. The following morning (April 5) the rioting resumed. Again British troops at the gates prevented Jewish relief from entering, though a few armed men in medical garb managed to infiltrate in ambulances. The British declared martial law, and troops reentered the Old City and disarmed both sides. The violence continued, but on a low level, the following day as well. The Haganah managed to remove from the Old City approximately three hundred Jews who lived in isolated houses outside the Jewish quarter. Only on April 7 was order fully restored.

Palestinian political associations and branches of the Damascus-based nationalist groups, such as al-Nadi al-Arabi, appear to have had a hand in organizing the episode.[136] The three days of rioting resembled nothing more than a pogrom; nothing like it had been seen in Palestine during the centuries of Ottoman rule. The Arab mobs, sensing the atmosphere in Government House, had shouted, "*Al-Dawla ma'ana*" (the Government is with us). In a number of cases Arabs protected their Jewish neighbors, but six Jews were killed, a number raped, more than two hundred injured, and much property, including several synagogues, was destroyed.[137] Several Arabs were also killed and dozens injured by British troops and police and by Jewish defenders.[138] The British investigation of the outbreak, embodied in the Palin Report, found that "all the evidence goes to show that these attacks were of a cowardly and treacherous description, mostly against old men, women, and children— frequently in the back."[139]

But in a memorandum presented to Bols by Muslim and Christian notables on April 6, the blame for the outbreak was laid squarely on the Jews. "Jewish youngsters," organized by "the Zionist Organization," had "cursed and blasphemed" the Muslim religious leaders, "and the matter ended with the slaughter of Muslims and Christians, including women and children," said the notables. Two of the Arabs' main demands were the disbanding of the Jewish Legion, some of whose members had helped stave off the rioters, and of the Haganah, and the expulsion of the Zionist Commission.[140]

No Jews were killed in Jewish West Jerusalem, which was patrolled by the Haganah. Jabotinsky played a leading role in organizing this new group. In the summer and autumn of 1919, a number of activists, headed by two veterans of HaShomer, Rachel Yana'it and Zvi Nadav, had come together and begun training and acquiring arms. During the winter of 1919–20, they were joined by demobilized soldiers of the American battalion of the Jewish Legion, who brought with them their guns and some ammunition. In September, Jabotinsky was discharged from the Legion for political agitation and joined the self-defense activists, bringing with him members of the Maccabee sports association. In March 1920 the group had crystallized against the backdrop of growing Arab agitation. In Jerusalem a "City Defense Council" was set up, headed by Jabotinsky. Its activities, including training (mostly without weapons), were completely open. Jabotinsky believed and hoped that the British would sanction them. By early April the Haganah (Defense), as it was now called, fielded some two hundred "troops," with about fifty rifles and a handful of pistols and grenades.[141]

On April 7, in an act of appeasement toward the Arabs, the British arrested Jabotinsky and sentenced him to fifteen years' hard labor. More than a dozen other Haganah members were each given three years' hard labor. On the other hand, most of the Arab rioters arrested were given light sentences. Jewish commentators compared the British behavior toward the rioters and the defenders with that of the Russians during the pogroms.

OETA's appeasement of the Arabs was not to end with this. As soon as the rioting started, the military administration halted Jewish immigration and mounted raids on Jewish offices (including Weizmann's) and homes to search for arms. The secretary of the Zionist Commission was arrested, as were dozens of Haganah members. Tight censorship was imposed on all news coming out of Palestine. Only on April 13 was the "Jewish version" of events published in England and the United States.

Months later the report of the Palin commission of inquiry upheld the Jewish complaints of Arab responsibility and (implicitly) the charge of British-Arab collusion. OETA's decision to withdraw the British contingents from Jerusalem on April 5 was roundly condemned as a bad mistake. But the report was never published. One of the more persuasive witnesses before the commission had been Colonel Richard Meinertzhagen, Clayton's replacement (since September 1919) as OETA's chief political officer. He told the board that British officialdom during the riots had taken the side of the Arabs. He also reported to the Foreign Office directly, on April 14, 1920, that Allenby was not carrying out official British policy. Indeed, he accused Bols and his fellow officers of causing the riots. Later Meinertzhagen jotted down in his diary: "I find myself alone out here, among gentiles, in upholding Zionism. . . . And that is the irony of the whole situation, for I am also imbued with anti-Semitic feelings."[142] Meinertzhagen was fired soon after sending his dispatch to the Foreign Office.[143]

On April 26, 1920, the San Remo Conference endorsed the Balfour Declaration and the British Mandate, and on April 28 Bols made an official statement, reiterating, in effect, that the declaration was British policy. In June the (Jewish) Liberal Party politician Herbert Samuel was appointed head of the new civil administration in Palestine, the office he was to hold until 1925, with the title of "high commissioner."

Samuel had strong Zionist convictions. His preparatory visit to Palestine, in January–February 1920, left him profoundly impressed with the settlers' achievements. But it also brought home to him the depth of Arab opposition. In Nablus notables warned him of "a terrible revolution" if immigration persisted. Samuel felt that "the Zionists have not recognized the force . . . of the Arab nationalist movement." As high commissioner, he realized, he could attend and, indeed, advance the rebirth of the Jewish commonwealth, while protecting and advancing Arab interests as well. He chose Brig. Gen. Wyndham Deedes, an ardent Christian Zionist who had been Allenby's chief intelligence officer, as his deputy. "From now," Deedes wrote to Weizmann in May 1920, "the whole of such abilities and strength as God has given me will be devoted unreservedly to the realization of your ideal."[144] Not all of Samuel's appointees were pro-Zionist, however. General Clayton, chief secretary between 1923 and 1925, wrote: "We are pushing an alien and detested element into the very core of Islam."[145]

Samuel took up his position on July 1 and quickly embarked on a policy whose essence was "to create the conditions, political, legal and . . . economic necessary for the Zionists themselves to carry on their work," facilitating rather than encouraging their immigration and settlement.[146] He opted for "cautious colonization" rather than direct progress toward statehood and refrained from subsidizing Zionism. (In the long run this may have helped make "the Yishuv self-reliant and self-sustaining,"[147] much as British failures to protect Jews contributed to the growth of the Haganah.) Samuel immediately released Jewish activists jailed during the April riots, reopened the land registers,[148] and opened Palestine's gates—for the first time—to relatively free Jewish immigration. He granted about one thousand entry visas a month, though not many were used, owing mainly to shortages of jobs and housing in Palestine and the Zionist Organization's lack of funds.

At the same time Samuel tried to calm Arab fears of Zionist intentions and actively promoted the welfare of Palestine's Arab community, "in the same way as a British administration would regard it as a duty to promote the welfare of the local population in any part of the Empire. The measures to foster the well-being of the Arabs should be precisely those which we would adopt in Palestine if there were no Zionist question and if there had been no Balfour Declaration."[149]

On July 8 a general amnesty was declared and all the Arabs convicted following the April riots were released. Hajj Amin al-Husseini and 'Arif al-'Arif, who had played leading roles in the rioting and then fled, were allowed to return. Indeed, both were soon on the British payroll, 'Arif al-'Arif as a senior civil servant and Husseini as the leading Muslim cleric in the country. Samuel would grant a measure of de facto recognition to the Palestine Arab Executive (PAE), set up by the Third Palestinian Congress in Haifa in December 1920 and headed by Musa Kazim al-Husseini, and he declared that the Balfour

Declaration consisted of two equal parts, the promotion of the Jewish National Home and the safeguarding and improvement of the condition of life of Palestine's Arabs.[150] The Zionist leadership took pessimistic note of this even-handed start to Samuel's administration and began to exhibit signs of loss of confidence, even suspicion. The strengthening, in December, of the Haganah and its consolidation under the wing of the newly founded trade union organization, the Histadrut, was one expression of this mindset.[151]

Early April 1920 had witnessed the crest of popular Arab belief in the idea of Palestine as part of an independent Greater Syria. By the end of April, the Palestinian leadership began to accept the country's separate destiny (Zionist officials as early as January had begun to speak of the existence of a distinct "Arab Nationalist Movement of Palestine").[152] By July, the ideological turn-around among the Arabs was more or less complete. The failure of a rumored anti-British revolt to materialize; the flight of Amin al-Husseini; the endorsement of the British Mandate at San Remo; the installation, in July, of a civilian administration, in part in consequence of the rioting; and the ouster that month of Faisal's government in Damascus by the French all contributed to this outcome.[153] In August, Kazim, who had been deposed from the mayoralty of Jerusalem by the British for his part in the April riots, told his fellow nationalists: "Now, after the recent events in Damascus, we must introduce a basic change in our plans here. [The idea of Palestine as] southern Syria no longer exists. We must defend Palestine."[154]

Samuel enjoyed a warm reception and a relatively successful, untroubled first few months in office—"The country is so quiet you could hear a pin drop," he wrote to Weizmann. But Palestine's troubles were only beginning. In December the Third Palestinian Congress denounced the Balfour Declaration as contrary to "the laws of God and man."[155] In March 1921, during Colonial Secretary Winston Churchill's visit to Palestine, he met with an Arab delegation headed by Kazim which attacked Zionism, the declaration, and Samuel himself: "The Jews have been amongst the most active advocates of destruction in many lands. . . . It is well known that the disintegration of Russia was wholly or in great part brought about by the Jews, and a large proportion of the defeat of Germany and Austria must also be put at their door."

Churchill, a lifelong Zionist, dismissed these arguments and assured the Arabs that the Jews would not dispossess them: "It is manifestly right that the scattered Jews should have a national center and a national home and be reunited and where else but in Palestine with which for 3,000 years they have been intimately and profoundly associated? We think it will be good for the world, good for the Jews, good for the British Empire, but also good for the Arabs who dwell in Palestine. . . . They shall share in the benefits and progress of Zionism."[156]

He told the delegation, "You ask me to repudiate the Balfour Declaration and to stop immigration. This is not in my power, and it is not my wish."[157]

Churchill also met a Zionist delegation and cautioned them to take account of "the great alarm" felt by the Arabs. Emir Abdullah of Transjordan asked Churchill whether Britain intended to set up a Jewish kingdom and throw out the Arabs. Britain, Abdullah had said, "appeared to think men could be cut down and transplanted in the same way as trees." Churchill assured him that Britain did not intend mass immigration and that "a very slow process" was anticipated. "There really is nothing for the Arabs to be frightened about," he told the House of Commons in June.[158] And two months later he told another Palestinian delegation, headed by Kazim al-Husseini: The Jews would not "take any man's lands. They cannot dispossess any man of his rights or his property. . . . There is room for all."[159]

Churchill had arrived in Palestine fresh from his meeting with Britain's main Middle East experts, a gathering that came to be known as the Cairo Conference. It decided on a "Hashemite solution" for Mesopotamia (Iraq), offering the country to Faisal, whose brother, Abdullah, was awarded Transjordan as an emirate. This, it was hoped, would at least in part propitiate the Arabs, who claimed that Britain had promised them Palestine within the sphere of prospective Arab sovereignty. In terms of territory, Transjordan represented a full four-fifths of the original Mandatory Palestine; perhaps the Arabs would now waive their claim to the remaining fifth.[160]

The Zionist leadership, though unhappy with the severing of Transjordan from the territory mandated for the National Home, was powerless to change Churchill's decision. In any case, they reasoned—and were to continue reasoning until the end of the 1930s—the arrangement was only temporary: Transjordan might yet be opened up for Jewish settlement and conquest. (The right-wing periphery of the movement, the Revisionists, continued to dream of conquering Transjordan down to the 1950s and 1960s and some, even later; their slogan continued to be "two banks to the Jordan: one is ours and the other too.")

In April–May 1921 Samuel engineered a major conciliatory gesture to the Arabs: the "election" of Hajj Amin al-Husseini (1895/6–1974) as the "Grand Mufti" of Jerusalem, effectively the spiritual leader of the Muslim community in Palestine. Hajj Amin had studied at Cairo's al-Azhar Islamic University before becoming a junior officer in the Ottoman army. He deserted in 1917 and joined the Sharifian army. One source described him as "very pro-British"; another, as a British "informer" or spy in the Sharifian camp.[161] In 1919 he worked for Faisal's regime in Damascus, returning to Palestine early in 1920. He was briefly president of the Jerusalem branch of the nationalist society al-Nadi al-Arabi. In July 1920 he had been sentenced (along with 'Arif al-'Arif) in absentia to ten years in prison for his part in inciting the riots of the previous April. His past was now set aside, however, and even though in the vote (by a committee of Muslim notables selected by the government) for the post of Grand Mufti, Husseini came in fourth, Samuel ignored the results and appointed him on May 8, 1921.[162]

The previous week—giving vent to the Third Palestinian Congress's anti-Zionist resolutions—the Arabs had unleashed a wave of violence far worse than that of spring 1920. It was "not . . . premeditated . . . but [was] . . . the sudden outcome of many months of brooding and fear."[163] Again, the cry of "pogrom" went up. Ben-Gurion charged that at least part of the British administration had encouraged and even assisted the rioters.[164] Without doubt, the military had continued to favor the Arabs. General Sir Walter Congreve (1862–1927), commander of British forces in the Middle East, said in October 1921: "In the case of Palestine [the sympathies of the Army] are rather obviously with the Arabs, . . . the victim[s] of the unjust policy forced upon them by the British Government." Congreve criticized Samuel for trying "to enforce a policy hateful to the majority—a majority which . . . has right on its side."[165]

This time Jaffa (and, to a lesser extent, the Hadera-Tulkarm area) rather than Jerusalem was the focus of the outbreak. Jaffa was then a mixed town of some 26,000 Arabs and 16,000 Jews; neighboring Tel Aviv, to the north, had 3,600 Jewish inhabitants.[166] The violence was triggered by a clash at the southern edge of Tel Aviv between Jewish communist and socialist May Day demonstrators. Police pushed the communists into the sand dunes between Tel Aviv and Jaffa. Arabs in Jaffa's northern Manshiya quarter took up sticks and rushed to the scene, where they were blocked by the police. They then turned back into Manshiya and attacked Jewish pedestrians and shops. Later, Arab spokesmen were to argue that the rioting had resulted from a fear of "Bolshevik penetration" of Jaffa.

The worst violence that day was a mob attack, in which Arab policemen participated, against an immigrants' hostel in Jaffa's Ajami quarter, where thirteen Jews were killed and twenty-six wounded—shot, stabbed, and bludgeoned.[167] The attack occurred more or less simultaneously with the outbreak in Manshiya, which led the Zionist leaders to conclude that the violence had been premeditated. British army contingents arrived on the scene only in the late afternoon. Arab looting and violence continued through the night and the next day in the more remote parts of the city. Not until May 3 did the government impose martial law.

On May 2, in the Jaffa suburb of Abu Kabir, rioters murdered six Jews in an orange grove. One of the victims was Yosef Chaim Brenner. During the following days the attacks spread, encouraged by the government's weak response and the poor showing of the Jewish self-defense groups. East of Tel Aviv, in Petach Tikva, a well-organized assault by villagers and Bedouin tribesmen came at dawn on May 5, simultaneously from the north and the south. The defenders, with an assortment of rifles and insufficient ammunition, managed to hold off the two to three thousand attackers—most of whom were without firearms—for a number of hours until a British relief column arrived and opened up with machine guns on the northern Arab thrust. A lone RAF aircraft bombed the Arabs advancing from the south, and several armored cars joined in. The Arabs fled; British intervention had turned the tide. Four of Petach Tikva's defenders and twenty-eight Arabs died that day.

The following day, May 6, hundreds of Arabs from Tulkarm and the surrounding villages attacked the moshava of Hadera. The British district governor ordered rifles distributed to the settlers and called in army reinforcements. The attackers, advancing from the southeast, managed to set alight a few houses before British intervention—by two aircraft, which dropped bombs and strafed the attackers, and an armored car—routed the mob. No Jews were hurt. Another attack, by several thousand inhabitants of Ramle shouting, "*Itbah al-Yahud*," was launched that day against Rehovot. It, too, was repulsed without any Jewish casualties—this time without British help.

The British imposed heavy fines on a number of Arab villages. Most of the attackers were never identified or brought to trial. Many of those who were, including the assailants of the hostel in Jaffa, were freed by the courts. Only three Arabs received heavy sentences—a tribal chieftain who had fired on British troops, a policeman who had attempted to rape a Jewish woman, and a man who had murdered an elderly Jew in a Jaffa alley. A number of Jews were briefly arrested, including Avraham Shapira, the leader of the Petach Tikva defense, but none were charged.

The attacks, which continued on May 7, were in fact in some measure preplanned, especially the one on Petach Tikva. At the helm were militant younger Palestinian leaders as well as Arab policemen. The traditional leadership of the Muslim-Christian associations and the Palestine Arab Executive had largely opposed the outburst.[168] Indeed, the Fourth Palestinian Congress, meeting in Jerusalem at the end of May, resolved to press its national aims using only legal means.[169] Altogether, 47 Jews and 48 Arabs were killed and 146 Jews and 73 Arabs wounded in the violence.[170] Clashes in November during the celebration of the fourth anniversary of the Balfour Declaration left 5 Jews and 3 Arabs dead.[171]

The massive violence of 1921 left an ineradicable impression on the Zionists, driving home the precariousness of their enterprise. In 1922 Itamar Ben-Avi, a leading journalist, wrote: "The Islamic wave and stormy seas will eventually break loose, and if we don't set a dyke in their way by an agreement . . . they will flood us with their wrath. . . . Tel Aviv in all her splendor, our coast and all its beauty, will be wiped out."[172]

The May disturbances frightened Samuel into conciliating the Arabs. During the week of disturbances a number of ships carrying immigrants who had fled pogroms in Russia were turned away. And on May 14 the high commissioner formally suspended immigration. On June 3, he announced that immigration would resume but would be limited, in effect, by the country's economic absorptive capacity and by "the interests of the present population"—clearly a concession to the rioters. "The British Government," added Samuel, "would never impose upon them a policy that people had reason to think was contrary to their religious, their political, and their economic interests."[173] Husseini's appointment as Grand Mufti was another sop to the Arab crowds. Thereafter, until the 1936–39 rebellion, the Mandatory government invested in and supported Husseini as a means of "preventing people getting too excited and too violent," in Samuel's words[174]—though Husseini was often to oppose the government and, indeed, to instigate, if not actually organize, anti-Zionist and antigovernment violence.

Moreover, in the wake of the May riots the administration went out of its way to promote Arab political frameworks parallel to Zionist institutions. The Supreme Muslim Council, established in January 1922, was given control over all Muslim religious trusts and funds (*awkaf*) and courts (*shari'a*). The government arranged Husseini's election as president of the council, making him the unchallengeable leader of Palestine's Muslims. Husseini commanded vast and unsupervised powers of patronage—the appointment of qadis (religious judges), muftis, and *awkaf* and *shari'a* officials. In 1924 the council employed 1,193 people and had a state-financed budget of some 60,000 pounds sterling, not subject to government audit.[175] The concessions to the Arabs and the limitation of immigration badly undermined Samuel's relations with the Zionists, and there was talk of organizing illegal immigration (though this only came to pass a decade or so later).

On June 30, 1922, after Lloyd George (who had criticized Samuel as "very weak"[176]) was replaced as prime minister by Andrew Bonar-Law, Whitehall issued a "White Paper" redefining British policy in Palestine, couched in far more even-handed language than the Balfour Declaration. Although Britain continued to support Zionism and the creation of the Jewish National Home, the paper assured the Muslim world that His Majesty's Government had not

> at any time contemplated, as appears to be feared, the disappearance or the subordination of the Arab population, language or culture in Palestine. . . . The [Balfour] Declaration . . . does not contemplate that Palestine as a whole should be converted into a Jewish National Home, but that such a Home should be founded in Palestine. . . . [Moreover] the Zionist Commission in Palestine [which had changed into the Palestine Zionist Executive (PZE)] . . . does not possess . . . any share in the general administration of the country.

The document formally detached Transjordan from Mandatory Palestine and spoke not of the eventual creation of a Jewish state but of "a center in which the Jewish people . . . may take . . . an interest and a pride."[177] Following the publication of the White Paper, the League of Nations Council, meeting in London on July 24, 1922, endorsed the British Mandate in Palestine, and on September 28, 1923, it was ratified under the Treaty of Lausanne.

Zionist spokesmen argued, as after previous rounds of violence, that the May rioting had been the work of a few agitators, not a true reflection of majority Arab opinion. The reason: If the violence was widely supported, there was no hope for Zionism. It had to be explained as the work of a small group of criminals, with the Jews—whose "interests were identical" with those of the Arabs—striving for "peace with the Arab nation."[178] This, of course, ran contrary to the truth, and contrary to the findings of the British commission of inquiry, headed by the chief justice of Palestine, Thomas Haycraft, which eventually probed the disturbances. The violence, it concluded, was rooted in political and economic reasons arising from Jewish immigration and Zionist aims and was not caused by envious *effendis,* as the Jews claimed: "The feeling against the Jews was . . . [too] genuine, . . . widespread and . . . intense to be accounted for in this superficial manner."[179]

Zionist officials, though they maintained the fiction in public, were well aware of the truth. As Kalvaryski put it in May 1921: "It is pointless to consider this a question only of effendis. . . . This may be fine as a tactic, but, between ourselves, we should realize that we have to reckon with an Arab national movement. We ourselves—our own [movement]—are speeding the development of the Arab national movement."[180]

But contrary to Kalvaryski's approach—to bring the Arabs around by bribes, especially to newspaper editors and labor leaders—most of his colleagues felt that Arab antagonism could not be bribed or wished away. "The signature of the professional petition-monger or the temporary benevolence of a venal editor [can] have no appreciable effect on the situation," explained Leonard Stein, the secretary of the PZE.[181]

In a sense bribes to *effendis* and editors were merely a microcosm. The Zionist enterprise itself—so its leaders continuously presented it to Arab and gentile politicians—was one giant bribe. Their constant refrain was that if the Arabs allowed Zionism to flourish and prosper, it would materially benefit the native population. But whether this proposition was true or not, the Arabs were unwilling to acquiesce in Zionism's ends even if, in the process, they themselves prospered. Or, to quote historian Bernard Wasserstein:

However great the inflow of Jewish capital, however green the refructified desert, however bright the lamps of westernizing civilization, Zionism . . . could not but arouse the deepest antagonism among most sections of the indigenous Arab population. . . . In fact it was not the effendis, nor as some Zionists believed, anti-Semitic British officials, who were the chief recruiting sergeants for the Arab nationalist movement in Palestine: that was Zionism itself.[182]

While the Yishuv beefed up its defensive capabilities, it also responded to the events of 1920–21 by trying to build bridges to the Arabs. During the twenties and thirties, Zionist officials sporadically attempted to establish such links or at least to define a basis for agreement. In 1919 Kalvaryski tried to organize a joint Jewish-Arab delegation to appear before the King-Crane Commission, and established short-lived Jewish-Arab clubs in Safad and Haifa. But most Zionist leaders resisted his efforts. Ideologically, they preferred the exclusivist, separatist philosophy that had from the start guided their enterprise; tactically, they argued that the Arabs would interpret conciliatory gestures as weakness. They maintained that relations with the Arabs would improve once the Yishuv became so strong that the Arabs recognized that they could not overcome it. Until that time, it was a waste of valuable energy and resources to make fruitless attempts at conciliation.[183]

Following the troubles of 1920–21, a number of top-level meetings took place between the leaders of the two communities. In November 1921, in London, Weizmann, at British insistence, met with an Arab delegation led by Kazim al-Husseini. The Arabs demanded the abandonment of the Balfour Declaration and an end to Jewish immigration, and the encounter ended in fierce disagreement. One British observer described Weizmann's tone as "unfortunate": that of "a conqueror handing to beaten foes the terms of peace."[184]

Intermittent contacts continued. At the end of 1922 Kalvaryski met with Kazim al-Husseini in Lausanne, and a secret arrangement was concluded for Kazim to receive payments from the Zionist Central Office and to preach "moderation" to his fellow Arabs. Money duly changed hands, but there was no consistent change in Kazim al-Husseini's tone.[185] Toward the end of 1924 Kalvaryski met with Jamal Husseini, Hajj Amin's and Kazim's cousin, and discussed a possible compromise regarding the mooted Palestinian legislative council, but nothing came of it after the Yishuv leadership rejected the idea out of hand.[186]

At the grassroots level Kalvaryski stepped up his conciliatory work, with more executive backing than before. Small sums of money were diverted to his projects, which included a mixed Jewish-Arab school at Rosh Pina, mixed clubs, and bribes to editors and writers to plant pro-Zionist articles in the Arab press. In late 1921 he promoted a Muslim National Association (MNA), with branches in the mixed towns, hoping they would serve as a counterweight to the anti-Zionist Muslim-Christian associations. He invested a great deal of his own money in the venture, incurring large debts that he afterwards persuaded the Zionist Executive to cover. The problem was that few Arabs joined, and those who did appear to have been persuaded by the Jewish largesse rather than ideological suasion. Once the subsidies fell away, so did the Arab membership.[187] By mid-1925, Kalvaryski noted pessimistically: "[We] are growing more distant. . . . We have no contact; two separate worlds, each living its own life and fighting the other."[188]

The consistent failure of dialogue and rapprochement had a variety of causes. One problem was that the Zionist officials involved usually regarded their own activities with ambivalence, seeing links with Arabs both as attempts at conciliation and as the cultivation of sources of information. The efforts at conciliation therefore appeared insincere. Kalvaryski embodied this ambivalence: The main advocate of dialogue and accommodation, he was also a key Yishuv intelligence officer. Between 1922 and 1927 he headed, successively, the Arab Secretariat of the National Council of the Yishuv and the Arab Bureau of the Palestine Zionist Executive.[189] (In later years the work of the Jewish Agency Political Department's Arab Division was to be characterized by a similar ambivalence. Its officials—Ya'akov Shimoni, Reuven Zaslani [Shiloah], Ezra Danin, and Eliahu Elath—all worked at building local and national bridges between Jew and Arab; and, at the same time, all used or tried to use their Arab contacts as sources of information. Zaslani, indeed, was to be the founding head of the State of Israel's foreign intelligence service, the Mossad.)

A more important obstacle to peacemaking was the reluctance of the Zionist establishment to back it. Most leaders felt that there were more important things to do with their time and resources, such as organizing immigration, establishing settlements, and buying land. But without doubt the main obstacle was the reluctance of the Arab leadership to join in sincere and open, or even covert, dialogue. None of the peace contacts during the 1920s appears to have been initiated by Arabs. All or nearly all Arabs sought not coexistence but the Yishuv's disappearance. Those who did maintain contacts usually did so for bribes. And the few who were willing to reach an agreement, as a result of a certain empathy with the Jews or, as was more common, out of a feeling that Zionism, backed by Whitehall, was unbeatable, were intimidated into silence by the hard-liners.

1921–1929

Between the summer of 1921 and the summer of 1929 Britain tried to turn Palestine into a unified, working political entity. The Jewish and Arab communities grew in size, strength, and separateness, but these were also years of political tranquillity. Chaim Weizmann wrote: "[O]n the surface at least," relations were "not altogether unsatisfactory."[190] Given the absence of "troubles," the Yishuv could simply ignore the Arabs and the threat they posed. The period was marked by prosperity and development, due to improved infrastructure, efficient administration, cooption into the British imperial economy, and the de facto intercommunal truce. As they developed, Jews and Arabs bred their own social, economic, and political structures, with British officialdom becoming increasingly irrelevant to the internal dynamics of each community—a process that helped lead eventually to the withdrawal of the British and to the partition of the country between Jews and Arabs.

The Yishuv grew in numbers and in economic, social, and political mass far more rapidly than the Arabs. In 1918 there were about 60,000 Jews and close to 700,000 Arabs (611,000 Muslims, 70,000 Christians, and 7,000 Druze).[191] By the end of 1922 there were, according to the first British census, about 84,000 Jews and 760,000 Arabs. The disproportionate Jewish increase was due to immigration: 1,800 in 1919, and more than 8,000 per year in 1920–22, for a three-year total of 27,000.[192] Immigration was to peak in the mid-1920s—around 8,000 in 1923, 14,000 in 1924, 34,000 in 1925, 14,000 in 1926—and then fall off—because of a sharp economic downturn—to 2,000 in 1928 and 5,000 in 1929.[193] There was also a small number of Arab immigrants, estimated by McCarthy at approximately 900 per year after 1931,[194] with probably a smaller annual average during the preceding decade. By 1931—the year of the second (and far more efficient) British census—there were 175,000 Jews and about 880,000 Arabs (775,000 Muslims and 93,000 Christians) in Palestine.[195] The Jews had constituted less than one-tenth of Palestine's population in 1919; by 1931 they represented one-fifth, and their relative demographic weight was to grow even more dramatically during the following decade.

In their immediate post-1918 euphoria Zionist leaders hoped for and anticipated a much larger influx, of perhaps 70,000–80,000 immigrants annually,[196] but most emigrants from Eastern Europe headed for the United States. Nonetheless, between the Balfour Declaration and mid-1926, some 100,000 Jews entered Palestine.[197] The limiting factor on immigration was not so much Mandatory restrictions as Zionist organizational and economic shortcomings and individual preferences. (In November 1920, indeed, Samuel chided Weizmann that the Zionists were bringing too few Jews to Palestine.[198]) Though Jewish landholdings nearly doubled during the first decade of British rule, from 650,000 dunams in 1920 to 1,163,000 in 1929,[199] land purchases too were in large measure constrained less by the government than by lack of funds and initiative.[200] In the late 1920s a severe economic crisis in Palestine led to mass unemployment, a sharp reduction in immigration, and an exodus. Indeed, Jewish emigrants exceeded immigrants by about 2,000 in 1927, the only year this happened during the Mandate.[201] Nonetheless, the National Home developed substantially. Some 40 million pounds sterling came in from Jews abroad during the years 1917–29, and the number of agricultural settlements doubled, to 110. The Hebrew University, the first in the country, opened in Jerusalem in 1925.[202]

In the Zionist movement, the socialist-Zionist parties continued to dominate the center of the political stage, but on the right and on the left new shoots emerged. The most important was the right-wing Revisionist Movement (which eventually evolved into the post-1948 Herut Party, which, in turn, sired the Likud bloc), led and ideologically guided by Ze'ev Jabotinsky. A brilliant orator, Jabotinsky had promoted the establishment of Jewish fighting units within the British Army during World War I and was one of the founders of the Haganah. In 1925 he established the Revisionist Party (so named because it sought to "revise" the terms of the Mandate, particularly to provide for the reinclusion of Transjordan in Mandatory Palestine). He also set up the party's youth movement, Betar, which was characterized by militaristic, some might say fascist, appurtenances (dark brown uniforms), activities (parade ground drill and firearm exercises), slogans and ideology ("in fire and blood Judea will be reborn"), and structure (a rigid hierarchy). Jabotinsky admired Mussolini, and the movement repeatedly sought affiliation with and assistance from Rome. His Zionism was single-minded, exclusivist, rigid. He once declared: "There is no justice, no law, and no God in heaven, only a single law which decides and supersedes all—[Jewish] settlement [of the land]."[203]

Jabotinsky apparently had no emotional animosity toward the Arabs; rather, he regarded them with "polite equanimity."[204] He understood, as he put it in 1926, that "the tragedy lies in the fact that there is a collision here between two truths. . . . But our justice is greater," he concluded.[205] What was unfolding was a clash between two nationalisms. "The Arab," he said, "is culturally backward, but his instinctive patriotism is just as pure and noble as our own; it cannot be bought, it can only be curbed by . . . *force majeure.*"[206] Unlike his compatriots on the left, Jabotinsky had no problem in recognizing that Zionism had a legitimate rival in the Palestinian-Arab nationalist movement. Hence the Jews would have to settle and spread throughout Palestine, and eventually dominate the country, by force. A collision was inevitable. It was partly because of this unpopular message—most people in the Yishuv preferred to pretend that there was no problem or that there was but it would somehow go away—that the Revisionists remained a small, unpopular minority at least until the mid-1930s.[207]

On the left a significant but ultimately marginal development was the establishment in 1925 of Brit Shalom (peace alliance) by a group of intellectuals who sought to replace the traditional Zionist aim of Jewish dominance and statehood with a binational solution: a unitary Jewish-Arab state. They supported continued Jewish immigration but hoped to achieve it peacefully, in agreement with the Arab majority. They placed morality at the heart of their political vision, arguing, in the words of Arthur Ruppin: "Will Zionism deteriorate into pointless chauvinism? Is there no way to earmark in Palestine an area to an increasingly larger number of Jews, without dispossessing the Arabs?"[208] Most of the Yishuv repudiated Brit Shalom as naive and unrealistic. Arab spokesmen, at least in public, lumped all Jews together as seeking their dispossession, and failed to differentiate between socialists, Revisionists, and Brit Shalom.[209]

Following the disturbances of May 1921, Samuel tried to bridge the Arab-Jewish divide by setting up some form of protolegislature to bring together the three corners of the Palestinian triangle. The Mandate had been issued to Britain to prepare the native peoples for self-government, and steps in that direction clearly required that the two communities learn to work and rule together. But the Arabs rejected out of hand a legislature that did not reflect their numerical preponderance (the Jews always insisted on communal parity) and that did not give them real power (the British insisted that the Mandatory government retain veto powers and ultimate authority). The Arabs, guided by the Palestine Arab Executive, by and large boycotted the elections for the legislature, which were held in February 1923. Jewish bribes and British blandishments failed to stimulate Arab participation.

So the problem of Arab representation remained. Early in 1921 Samuel accorded a measure of recognition to the PAE, chaired by Musa Kazim al-Husseini. It was to remain the representative body of the community down to the mid-1930s—but it was outside the government structure and it had no officially sanctioned powers or institutional base.[210] Besides establishing the Supreme Muslim Council (SMC), Samuel in October 1923 tried to set up an Arab Agency as a counterweight to the representative Zionist bodies. But the Arabs rejected the opportunity, partly because the members were to be nominated by Samuel himself.[211] This was not the first or last time that the Palestinians were to shoot themselves in the foot. "Palestine is largely inhabited by unreasonable people," concluded Ormsby-Gore, then Britain's undersecretary of state for the colonies.[212]

The Zionists since 1918 had had the quasi-official Zionist Commission, transformed into the Palestine Zionist Executive (PZE), and then renamed the Jewish Agency Executive (JAE), as a type of internal consultative-executive body. Representing the Yishuv, a second body, Assefat HaNivharim (the representative assembly), with its own executive, the Va'ad Leumi (National Council), served as a type of legislature. By the end of the 1920s, the Jewish Agency, whose establishment had been authorized by a British cabinet ruling in 1920, had turned into the veritable government of the Yishuv. The agency had political, economic, immigrant absorption, settlement, and other departments. Its ruling council, the JAE, was to function as both the Zionist Organization's and the Yishuv's cabinet down to April 1948. The Yishuv had its own school and taxation systems, a carryover from Ottoman days. Other major "national" institutions included the Jewish National Fund (JNF), responsible for land purchase, reclamation, and afforestation; Keren HaYesod, a fund-raising organization; the Histadrut workers' association, which ran the trade unions, a health service, a sports organization, and various industrial and agricultural enterprises; and Irgun HaHaganah (the defense organization usually called simply the Haganah), the labor-affiliated militia or underground.

The quiet of the mid-1920s was broken for a brief moment by Samuel's resignation and the appointment, in 1925, of Field Marshal Lord Plumer, formerly governor of Malta, as his successor. A non-Zionist, Plumer "adhered rigidly to the status quo,"[213] and was remembered for his correctness. But he kicked off his term of office with something of a faux pas. At a Jewish sports meeting in Tel Aviv, Plumer, flanked by his daughter, stood up for "God Save the King," and continued standing when the band went on to play *HaTikvah*, the Zionist (and subsequently Israel's national) anthem. An Arab delegation came to complain. But when he asked: "By the way, have you got a national anthem?" the delegation fell silent. "In that case," Plumer concluded, "I think you had better get one as soon as possible."[214]

Plumer's only important initiative was the appointment of a committee, headed by Palestine Attorney General Norman Bentwich, to improve legislation to protect tenant farmers from eviction. The problem had accompanied, and troubled, the march of Zionism since the 1880s. During the Mandate, the British authorities repeatedly outlawed evictions and tried to curtail land sales that might lead to them. Between 1928 and 1936, the Mandatory authorities issued a flurry of regulations for this purpose, each time trying to close another loophole.[215] Though Arab nationalists made telling and continuous use of the issue for propaganda purposes, it remains unclear how widespread the evictions really were. Still, the repeated efforts at regulation attest to the tenacity of the problem. Zionist purchasers and Arab sellers usually managed to get around the restrictions by such stratagems as compensating and removing the tenants prior to the conclusion of the transaction, enabling the Zionists to claim that they had taken over tenantless lands. One British investigation reportedly found that only 664 Arab tenant farmers were, in fact, evicted because of Jewish acquisitions between 1919 and 1931—in the course of purchases of some 500,000 dunams[216]—and from 1931 to 1939 only 899 Arab families (about 5,000 people all told) were uprooted.[217] It is probably true that a far greater number of Palestinian tenant farmers had been rendered landless by indebtedness or failure to register possession or claims. But it is also true that the British definition of Arab evictees due to Jewish land purchases was severely restrictive, and produced totals that fell far short of the reality.

Many nationalist Palestinian families sold land to Jews, and an element of guilt probably underlay at least some Arab leaders' vituperation against Zionism. Arab politicians and media attacked such sellers, declaring that "by selling land, they sell the blood and remains of their fathers," and charged them with being "dazzled by Zionist gold."[218] Of twenty-nine members of the PAE between 1920 and June 1928, at least one-quarter sold land to Jews or facili-

tated and benefited financially from such purchases, including the PAE's president from 1920 until 1934, Musa Kazim al-Husseini, and Raghib al-
Nashashibi, the mayor of Jerusalem from 1920 to 1934. Zionist land
purchases were limited not by available supply and Arab readiness to sell so
much as by shortage of funds. According to historian Kenneth Stein, "the
quantity of Arab land offered for sale was far in excess of the Jewish ability to
purchase."[219] His conclusion was that "Arab land sales meant the absence of
true commitment to Palestinian nationalism. . . . Individual priorities were
equal to or more important than an emerging national movement. . . . Economic survival was [the] paramount motivation."[220]

THE TROUBLES OF 1929

The Zionist leadership may not have been particularly happy with the rate
of the Yishuv's growth. But from the other side of the fence, the changes in
Palestine—demographic, political, economic, and geographic—looked threatening indeed. By 1929 the Arabs understood that the disproportionate growth
of the Yishuv, nurtured and sustained by Mandatory government measures,[221]
promised to turn them into a minority in their own land. Nonviolent political
protest was proving ineffective, but the alternative would necessarily alienate
British sympathy and involve them in conflict with the Mandatory authorities.
By the end of the 1920s the Arabs realized that what they were witnessing was
separate, exclusivist economic development. According to economic historian
Barbara Smith, "the institutional and ideological basis for separatism had
crystallized. . . . The economic partition of Palestine predated geopolitical
partition and was well under way."[222]

The disparate internal political development of each community also boded
ill for the Arabs. They failed to produce unified leadership or representative institutions, and the 1920s saw a "two-clan system" emerge, with the
dominant Husseinis challenged by their traditional rivals, the Nashashibis.
The Husseinis, who controlled the Palestine Arab Executive and the Supreme
Muslim Council, established an immediate edge, turning the Nashashibis and
their allied notable clans into the "Opposition" (mu'aridun). Generally the
opposition espoused a willingness to cooperate with the government and
occasionally let it be understood that they would compromise with the Jews.
For years they received secret subventions from the Jewish Agency. The Husseinis opposed the government but paradoxically received British support.[223]
This struggle between the two coalitions of clans, and opposition ascendancy

in 1927–28, in part prompted Amin al-Husseini's campaign against the Jews and the violence in August 1929. By exploiting religious passions, he hoped to sway the Muslim masses to back his camp.[224]

On September 23–24, 1928, the eve of Yom Kippur—the Day of Atonement, the holiest day in the Jewish calendar—the SMC complained that Jews had set up a screen to separate men and women at the Wailing Wall (or Western Wall) in Jerusalem's Old City. Judaism's most sacred site, it was the only remaining section then known of the wall that surrounded the Temple Mount, where the First and Second Temples had stood during the first millennium B.C. (since 1967 other sections of the wall have been unearthed). The screen violated the status quo principle that had governed the site since Ottoman days. Failing to persuade the Jews to take it down, the police forcibly removed it. The SMC with great fanfare accused the Jews of "unlimited greedy ambitions" against Islam's holy sites (as well as coveting all the Arab lands lying between the Nile and the Euphrates).

The Temple Mount, called by Arabs al-Haram al-Sharif (the noble compound or sanctuary), is the third-holiest site in Islam. On it the first caliphs built two sacred structures, the Dome of the Rock (covering the rock, according to both Jewish and Arab tradition, on which Abraham—regarded as the common father of the two peoples—prepared to sacrifice his son Isaac) and the al-Aksa Mosque. The Western Wall is called al-Buraq by Muslims, after the Prophet Muhammad's horse, which they believe he tethered there before he ascended to heaven. The contention that the Jews were bent on taking over the compound, destroying the Islamic structures, and rebuilding the Temple had long been a theme in Arab propaganda. For example, the Palestinian delegation to Mecca during the *hajj*, or pilgrimage, of 1922 had declared:

The Islamic Palestine Nation that has been guarding al-Aksa Mosque and Holy Rock ever since 1,300 years declares to the Muslim world that the Holy Places are in great danger on account of the horrible Zionist aggressions. . . . The Zionist Committee, which is endeavoring to establish Jewish rule in Palestine and to rob al Aksa from the Muslims on the plea that it [was] built on the ruins of Solomon's Temple, aims at making Palestine a base of Jewish influence over the [Arabian] peninsula, and the whole East.[225]

In 1928 the Muslims sought British confirmation of their traditional rights at the Wall; after all, they owned the Wall and the adjacent passage where the Jews worshipped.[226] The campaign launched by Hajj Amin in October included an international Muslim congress in Jerusalem and new construction next to and on top of the Wall, in the *haram*. Bricks occasionally fell on the Jewish worshippers below; mules were driven through their praying area, often dropping excrement; and the Temple Mount *muazzins* (criers) turned up the volume on their calls to prayer.[227] The government failed to intervene, and the Zionists turned the affair into a point of national honor, much as for Muslims the conflict over the Wall came to symbolize the struggle against Zionism. Right-wing Zionists began to demand Jewish control of the Wall; and some even publicly advocated rebuilding the Temple, confirming Muslim fears.[228] The crisis simmered until summer 1929, when Sir John Chancellor, an anti-Zionist who had succeeded Plumer as high commissioner in July 1928, went on leave to England, as did many police officers.[229]

On August 14, 1929, some 6,000 Jews marched in Tel Aviv, chanting, "The Wall is ours"; that evening, three thousand gathered at the Wall for prayer. The following day, hundreds of Jews—some of them extremist members of Betar, carrying batons—demonstrated on the site. Rumors, apparently part of an orchestrated campaign, that the Jews intended to march on the *haram* or to attack Arabs swept the populace. Leaflets, which seem to have been printed before August 14, were distributed by Husseini activists in nearby Arab towns and villages, enjoining them to attack Jews and to come to Jerusalem to "save" the holy sites. One flyer, signed by "the Committee of the Holy Warriors in Palestine," stated that the Jews had violated the honor of Islam, and declared: "Hearts are in tumult because of these barbaric deeds, and the people began to break out in shouts of 'war, Jihad . . . rebellion.' . . . O Arab nation, the eyes of your brothers in Palestine are upon you . . . and they awaken your religious feelings and national zealotry to rise up against the enemy who violated the honor of Islam and raped the women and murdered widows and babies."[230]

On Friday, August 16, a mass of SMC-organized demonstrators marched out of the *haram* after an inflammatory sermon, to the Western Wall, where they proceeded to burn prayer books, as well as supplicatory notes left in the Wall's crevices.[231] Responding to Jewish protests, the acting high commissioner, Chief Secretary Harry Luke, declared that "no prayer books had been burnt but only pages of prayer books."[232] The following day, a brawl in Jerusalem's Bukharan Quarter left one Jew dead. The funeral, on August 20, occasioned a mass demonstration, punctuated by cries for vengeance. On the evening of August 22, Arab villagers, many of them armed with sticks and knives, began to pour into the *haram*.[233] British officials organized last-minute Jewish-Arab talks, but it was too late. Following the Muslim morning prayers, just after noon on Friday, August 23, several thousand rioters emerged from the *haram*, attacked Jewish pedestrians, and set shops alight. The riots spread through the city and then to the rest of the country, Arab policemen often joining the mobs.

The British were powerless to halt the escalation. They had only 292 policemen in Palestine[234] and fewer than one hundred soldiers, with six armored cars and five or six serviceable aircraft.[235] Fifty soldiers arrived by air from Egypt on the evening of August 24; another six hundred arrived by train the following day. Several additional battalions were dispatched from Britain by sea.[236] The day following the outbreak, at the government's request, Muslim leaders, including Hajj Amin, Musa Kazim al-Husseini, and Raghib Nashashibi, called on the Arabs to "avoid bloodshed" and to arm themselves with "mercy, wisdom and patience." The statement assured them that the leadership was "making every possible effort to realize your . . . national aspirations by peaceful methods."[237] The Jews suspected that Hajj Amin was clandestinely inciting the rioters while appearing to be working for calm.

The most trying days were August 23 and 24. A number of Jews were killed at the Jaffa Gate while British policemen made only half-hearted rescue efforts (none opened fire). Rioters ran up Jaffa Street, assaulting pedestrians and destroying shops. In Mea She'arim, to the east, Haganah men fired on the mob, which promptly turned tail and ran. Some Christian Arabs sheltered Jewish neighbors. During this rampage, gunmen opened fire on outlying neighborhoods with a simultaneity that, to Jewish minds at least, indicated central organization and preplanning.[238] They shot people and looted houses for several days, during which British police patrols briefly showed up, traded shots with the snipers, and moved on. By the 24th, seventeen Jews had been killed in and around Jerusalem.[239]

Outside the area horrible massacres took place in the two most devout Muslim towns, Hebron and Safad, which had small, Orthodox (and unarmed) Jewish communities. On August 20, Haganah officers had proposed that a squad of militiamen be sent to defend the six hundred Jews in Hebron or that they evacuate. The community rejected both ideas, saying that they trusted the town's *a'yan* to protect them.[240] On Friday, August 23, rioters broke into the yeshiva in Hebron and murdered the lone student they found there. The following day a mob attacked Jewish homes, slaughtering the inhabitants, who tried to fight them off with sticks and knives. British Police Chief Raymond Cafferata and a Jewish policeman fired on the mob, killing eight. But Arab policemen fired only into the air. Hundreds of Jews were saved by Arab neighbors (and, at a later stage, after Cafferata had reimposed his authority, by Arab policemen). Altogether about sixty Jews were killed. Cafferata later testified:

> On hearing screams in a room I went up a sort of tunnel passage and saw an Arab in the act of cutting off a child's head with a sword. He had already hit him and was having another cut, but on seeing me he tried to aim the stroke at me, but missed; he was practically on the muzzle of my rifle. I shot him low in the groin. Behind him was a Jewish woman smothered in blood with a man I recognized as a[n Arab] police constable named Issa Sherif from Jaffa in mufti. He was standing over the woman with a dagger in his hand. He saw me and bolted into a room close by and tried to shut me out—shouting in Arabic, "Your Honor, I am a policeman." . . . I got into the room and shot him.[241]

British reinforcements arrived just after noon. The Jewish dead were buried in mass graves dug by Arab prisoners, who burst into song during the ceremony. Two days later the surviving Jews left Hebron in a British-escorted convoy of trucks and buses, as the Arab townspeople looked on in silence.[242]

On the afternoon of August 29 the riots spread to Safad, which Jews regarded as one of the four "holy cities," alongside Jerusalem, Hebron, and Tiberias. It had about ten thousand Arab and three thousand Jewish inhabitants. A mob charged into the Jewish quarter, killing people and setting fire to the houses. The attack lasted only twenty minutes, during which the British police commander killed two of the rioters. Eighteen Jews died and about eighty were injured. Another two died and several more were accidentally injured by British police fire two days later. The looting and burning lasted for more than two days before British reinforcements reimposed order. Another three Jews were murdered in the nearby settlement of Ein Zeitim.[243]

In Tel Aviv–Jaffa the Arabs struck on August 25. Here the *a'yan,* aware of Jewish power and organization, warned against trouble; one notable was beaten by Arab zealots after he called for calm. A couple of thousand youngsters attacked Tel Aviv's southern neighborhoods. British policemen fired at the mob, killing six and wounding dozens before the rioters fled. Haganah units deployed along Tel Aviv's southern border exchanged fire with Arab snipers. In one incident four Haganah men were killed and five wounded. In retaliation a Haganah unit raided an Arab house, killing four people.[244]

Similar clashes erupted on the evening of August 25 in Haifa, peaking the following day. Haganah squads blocked most encroachments, and a number of their men were arrested for carrying weapons. Arabs from the village of Tira to the south, on their way to join the rioters, were strafed by a British aircraft and fled. On August 27, rioters attacked a Jewish neighborhood. Four hundred British sailors took up positions along the seams between the two communities and put an end to the attacks, though much Jewish property was burned.[245]

Rural settlements were also attacked. Motza, west of Jerusalem, was raided by Arabs who killed most of the Makleff family, whose house was on the edge of the settlement (though one son, Mordechai, survived to become, twenty-three years later, the third chief of the general staff of the IDF), and looted other houses after the inhabitants fled. Four other small Judean Hills settlements—Emeq Arazim, next to Motza, Migdal-Eder, Kfar Uriah, and Har-Tuv—were also abandoned, Har-Tuv after a fight; the inhabitants of the other three were protected by friendly Arab neighbors, but their homes were burned to the ground.[246]

To the west, Kibbutz Khulda put up a spirited defense against an onslaught of several thousand Arabs, but the members were eventually evacuated by a British army convoy, and their homes were torched. More than forty Arabs were killed. Be'er Tuvia was also abandoned. Gedera was saved by the timely arrival on August 27 of British troops as hundreds of villagers assembled for the kill.[247] Settlements in the Jezreel, Jordan, and Beisan Valleys came under similar attacks. Arab police officers protected Jews in Acre, Lydda, and Gaza, prevailing on hotheads not to attack neighboring settlements.[248]

Altogether, in the week of disturbances, 133 Jews and 116 Arabs were killed and 339 Jews and at least 232 Arabs were wounded.[249] The Yishuv emerged profoundly shocked: Their shield, the British government, for a long moment had lost control; the Arabs had bared their true feelings and their teeth. "You cannot build a lasting house, designed as a shelter for a whole people, on a volcano," wrote Moshe Beilinson. The Arabs were described in Zionist publications as "bandits," "oriental savages," and "murderers," their leaders as a "gang";[250] and there was a widespread feeling that they were bent on destroying the Yishuv. Ben-Gurion and his colleagues perceived that this might undermine their whole enterprise, if the Jews (and the Mandatory government) were to lose heart. So, fairly quickly, expressions of vulnerability and assertions of the implacability of Arab antagonism and British impotence and indifference were repressed. Again guarded optimism, and a feeling that the mobs represented but a small proportion of the Arabs, took hold—for without faith in the future, how could the Yishuv develop?[251]

If the aim of the rioters' leaders had been to shake Britain's commitment to the Balfour Declaration, they succeeded, at least in the short term. Sir John Chancellor on September 1 condemned "the atrocious acts committed by bodies of ruthless and bloodthirsty evildoers [and the] . . . murders perpetrated upon defenseless members of the Jewish population . . . accompanied, as at Hebron, by acts of unspeakable savagery."[252] But within hours, he urged Whitehall to reduce, if not completely renege on, its commitment to Zionism. The Balfour Declaration, he wrote, had been "a colossal blunder."[253]

The government appointed a commission of inquiry, headed by Sir Walter Shaw, former Chief Justice of the Straits Settlements, to investigate the outbreak. In its report of March 1930, while blaming the violence wholly on the Arabs, the Shaw Commission concluded that the attacks had been "unpremeditated" and that their "fundamental cause" was "the Arab feeling of animosity and hostility towards the Jews consequent upon the disappointment of their political and national aspirations and fear for their economic future."[254]

The Zionists charged that Hajj Amin—who emerged the uncontested leader of Palestine's Arabs—had fomented the violence. But the commission concluded that "the Mufti of Jerusalem must stand acquitted of the charges of complicity in or incitement to the disturbances"—though it criticized him for not restraining his followers. In his testimony before the commission, the mufti charged the Jews with attacking the Arabs and referred, by way of evidence, to *The Protocols of the Elders of Zion*.[255] The secretary of the PAE, Alfred Rock, called the report "70 per cent favorable to the Arabs."[256] The commission recommended that "excessive" Jewish immigration be halted;

that eviction of Arab peasants be stopped; and that the government look into the issues of land sales to Jews, immigration, and the Western Wall. The panel said the evictions were giving rise to "a landless and discontented class" of evictees.[257]

But the British response to the violence did not end with the Shaw Commission. Some 860 persons, 700 of them Arabs, were put on trial. Fifty-five Arabs were convicted of murder and 25 condemned to death. But massive Arab pressure persuaded the courts and Chancellor to reduce the sentences; only three people were eventually executed for savage murders in Hebron and Safad. The hangings took place on June 17, 1930, the PAE hailing those executed as "forerunners of freedom and independence who met their Lord peacefully without fear and grief . . . victims of the foreign greedy Imperialism."[258] Two Jews were found guilty of murder and condemned to death, but their sentences were commuted to terms of imprisonment.[259]

Whitehall sent Sir John Hope-Simpson, a retired colonial official, to look into immigration, Jewish settlement, and land sales. He wrote in the letter that accompanied his final report: "All British officials tend to become pro-Arab, or, perhaps, more accurately anti-Jew. . . . Personally, I can quite well understand this trait. The helplessness of the fellah appeals to the British official. The offensive assertion of the Jewish immigrant is, on the other hand, repellent."[260] His report, published in October 1930, (mistakenly) stated that there was no room for further settlers so long as Arab agriculture was not developed, and opposed further immigration destined for agricultural settlements.

On October 21, 1930, the British government issued the Passfield White Paper, seriously reducing its commitment to the Balfour Declaration. Colonial Secretary Sydney Webb, the new Lord Passfield, was an anti-Zionist. In 1929 he had commented that in Palestine "there is no room to swing a cat"[261] — meaning there was no room for more immigrants. The white paper stressed that immigration should be limited to "economic absorptive capacity" and promised the Arabs a legislative council in which their numerical preponderance would be accurately reflected. It raised a storm in the Yishuv, and Weizmann denounced it as "inconsistent with the terms of the Mandate."[262]

But the riots ultimately failed to hurt the Zionist enterprise. "We had built too solidly and too well," wrote Weizmann.[263] Britain's partial volte-face was to prove extremely short-lived. By early 1931 well-applied Zionist pressure in the press and lobbying by Weizmann in London bore fruit. Restriction of Jewish immigration and acquisition of land was of questionable legality, given the terms of the Mandate; the Zionist Organization threatened to take it up in the International Court at The Hague. Weizmann himself threatened to resign— the threat being that more militant (and less Anglophile) Zionists would then lead the movement.

On February 14 Prime Minister Ramsay MacDonald wrote to Weizmann reaffirming traditional British policy and, implicitly, reversing the Passfield recommendations on immigration and land purchases. The message was referred to by the Arabs as the "black letter." Weizmann was later to write that "it was under MacDonald's letter to me that the change came about in the Government's attitude, and in the attitude of the Palestine Administration which enabled us to make the magnificent gains of the ensuing years."[264]

Britain's ineffectiveness in protecting the Yishuv in 1929 concentrated Jewish minds wonderfully and led to a major reorganization of the Haganah, a new stage in its evolution into a full-fledged army. In the early 1920s it had sprung out of the minuscule defense organizations that had emerged during the preceding fifteen years. Underlying it was the philosophy encapsulated in May 1921 in a dictum by labor leader Yosef Sprinzak: "We shall not be able to go through our history with an English escort."[265] Jabotinsky said Zionism would have to develop behind an "iron wall"—a protective military shield.[266]

HaShomer, set up in 1907–09 and disbanded in 1920, supplied an early model for the Haganah. During World War I, a group of Palestinian Jews, led by Yosef Trumpeldor and composed mostly of exiles living in Egypt, had decided to assist the Allied war effort by forming a separate fighting unit. The British preferred to set up a 650-strong service unit, designated the Zion Mule Corps. It fought as a transport unit in the Gallipoli Campaign (suffering eight dead and fifty-five wounded) before being demobilized in 1916. Subsequently, Jabotinsky was instrumental in establishing three "Jewish Battalions" (*HaGdudim Ha'Ivriim,* or the Jewish Legion)—the Thirty-eighth, Thirty-ninth, and Fortieth Battalions of the King's Fusiliers, recruited from Russian Jews living in England, exiled Palestinian Jews (including David Ben-Gurion and Yitzhak Ben-Zvi), American Jews, and Jews in southern Palestine—during Allenby's campaign. The Thirty-eighth and Thirty-ninth Battalions participated in Allenby's offensive across the Jordan River in September 1918. Members of the Legion took part in the defense of the Yishuv against rioters in April 1920, after which, under Arab pressure, the units were disbanded.

It became clear to the Yishuv that a defense organization independent of British whim was needed. During January–March 1920 activists, particularly in Jerusalem and Tel Aviv, organized local defense committees, acquired some light weapons, and recruited and trained volunteers. The fall of Tel Hai acted as a major spur. The Jerusalem committee, headed by Jabotinsky and Pinchas Rutenberg, mobilized about two hundred fighters, and dominated the others. In April, during the Passover riots, the Jerusalem Haganah staved off Arab attacks, but many of its members were disarmed and arrested. In May HaShomer formally disbanded and in June, at its convention in Kibbutz Kinneret, Achdut HaAvodah, the leading socialist Zionist party (established in 1919, amalgamating the activist Poalei Zion Party and the Federation of Agricultural Workers) set up the Haganah. A new National Defense Committee was formed to oversee it, composed of three HaShomer veterans and two former members of the Jewish Legion.

The growth of the Haganah was accompanied by painful teething problems. The new Samuel government seemed to assure the Yishuv of security and protection. Was a clandestine militia even needed? Friction developed between HaShomer and Jewish Legion veterans: What was preferable, a popular militia or a tight-knit group of professional conspirators? Each local defense group had its own interests, and resisted subordination to a "national" framework. Internal disputes obstructed growth. In December 1920 the Haganah passed under the jurisdiction of the Histadrut, the trade union federation, which had a wider constituency, but when the May 1921 riots put it to a difficult test, it was found sorely wanting—deficient in organization, weaponry, and training—and barely made itself felt. In Tel Aviv–Jaffa, it was thirty British troops, ex-Jewish Legion, who turned the tide. In Hadera and Petach Tikva it was British army intervention that stopped the rioters. Only in Rehovot were the Haganah members—mostly ex-Jewish Legion—effectively deployed.

A rift opened in late 1921–22 between Haganah commanders and the Yishuv's political leadership, which supported the legalization of the Haganah and its subordination to the British authorities. The impasse led to the organization being deprived of funds by the Zionist Organization. In 1923 friction between HaShomer and Jewish Legion veterans exploded, and the HaShomer stalwarts left. These factors, coupled with the tranquillity of the years 1922–29, impeded development. Although it was overseen by the Histadrut's Executive Committee and directed by a two-man "center," the Haganah was extremely decentralized, local chapters being responsible for their own weapons stores, units, and contingency planning. The core was the three urban chapters, Jerusalem, Tel Aviv, and Haifa; Tel Aviv had 350 members in 1926. The three city commanders served as a sort of general staff and were appointed by the center. In 1924 the organization had 27 machine guns, 750 rifles, 1,050 pistols, and 750 hand grenades, mostly dispersed among the settlements.[267]

The disturbances of August 1929 caught the Yishuv by surprise, despite the considerable forewarning that the Western Wall incidents, which began in September 1928, should have provided. The almost ludicrous inadequacy of the British security deployment left most of the Yishuv's defense up to the Haganah. In 1929 it proved generally successful in the towns, but far less so elsewhere; a number of settlements were abandoned and razed. The small units in the settlements generally acted without coordination or help from outside. But after the start of the disturbances, the Haganah center mobilized about three hundred urban members for a month, dispersing them among the Galilee settlements.[268]

In Jerusalem small Haganah squads using pistols and grenades turned back the mobs. Local cells were also effective in defending northern and western neighborhoods. But in the south, Ramat-Rachel and Mekor-Hayim, at British urging, were briefly abandoned after Haganah squads ran out of ammunition. In Tel Aviv, defenses were efficient, though never really put to the test. In Haifa, the Haganah was successful, with one attack on an Arab bus proving particularly effective.

The upshot of August 1929 was that Zionists were persuaded of the need for a powerful militia. During the following two years, sole control of the Haganah was taken away from the Histadrut and placed in the hands of the Zionist Organization and the Yishuv's civilian authorities. A new executive committee was named and placed in charge.

The riots had another important outcome: In 1930–31 a band of Haganah officers set up their own group, called "Irgun Bet." They wanted the Haganah to abandon its defensive strategy and take an aggressive, retaliatory line. Within months the group veered rightward and in April 1937 renamed itself the Irgun Z'vai Leumi (national military organization; IZL or Irgun), effectively affiliating itself with the Revisionist movement and becoming its military wing.[269]

FOUR

CHE ARABS REBEL

PRELUDES, 1930–35

Following the 1929 riots—which Amin al-Husseini and others were subsequently to call a "revolt"[1]—Palestine enjoyed several years of surface calm. But the conflict became increasingly institutionalized and more radical, due to inter-Arab rivalry and Husseini's dominance of the political scene and the growth in the size and power of the Jewish community. The Arabs felt ever more threatened,[2] and the Yishuv increasingly understood that force alone would decide the issue. The upshot was the rebellion of 1936–39, which saw the Arabs attempt to shake off the British, or at least to bludgeon them into curbing the Yishuv. While ephemerally succeeding in the second objective, the rebellion was to prove counterproductive. Its suppression mortally weakened the Palestinian Arabs in advance of their ultimate confrontation with the Yishuv in 1948.

The 1929 disturbances severely shook the administration and finally persuaded High Commissioner Chancellor that Britain was backing the wrong horse. He revived the proposal to grant the inhabitants of Palestine self-government based on an appointed legislature. In March 1930 a delegation, headed by PAE chairman Musa Kazim al-Husseini and including Raghib Nashashibi and Hajj Amin al-Husseini, left for London to discuss this option. Swayed by its moderate majority (Musa Kazim, trying to fend off the challenge from his cousin Hajj Amin, aligned himself with the opposition), the delegation refrained from demanding full independence and called for majority self-rule under Britain's aegis. Whitehall insisted on retaining its Mandatory powers and implementing, at least partially, its commitments toward Zionism; the delegation returned to Palestine empty handed.[3]

In October 1930 Arab hopes had been raised by the Passfield white paper and the Hope-Simpson Report, but the MacDonald letter of February 1931 effectively blunted the message of both. On February 18 the PAE issued a "Declaration to the Noble Arab Nation," stating: "We must give up the idea of relying on the British Government to safeguard our national and economic existence, because this Government is weak in the face of the forces of World Jewry. . . . Let us seek help from ourselves and the Arab and Islamic World. . . . Mr. MacDonald's new document has destroyed the last vestige of respect every Arab had cherished towards the British Government."[4]

From the summer of 1931 radicalism, pressing upward from the street, took hold of the Palestinian elite,[5] stoked by a dramatic increase in Jewish immigration due to new anti-Semitic measures in Eastern and Central Europe and a drastic reduction of the American intake of immigrants. In 1929–31 Jewish immigration to Palestine stood at 4,000–5,000 people annually; in 1932 there were 9,500; in 1933, 30,000; in 1934, 42,000; and in 1935, 62,000. (Thereafter there was an overall decline: 30,000 in 1936, 10,000 in 1937, 15,000 in 1938; and 31,000 in 1939.)[6] Arab fears were aggravated by the new phenomenon of illegal immigrants, whose numbers were wrongly rumored to be even greater than those of the legal arrivals.[7]

The economic repercussions for the Arabs were severe. Employment had to be found for more and more Jews, leading the secretary of the Arab Labor Federation of Jaffa to declare, in 1937: "The Histadrut's fundamental aim is 'the conquest of labor.' . . . No matter how many Arabs are unemployed, they have no right to take any job which a possible immigrant might occupy. No Arab has the right to work in Jewish undertakings. If Arabs can be displaced in other work, too . . . that is good."[8]

The changes that Palestinian Arab society underwent during the 1930s—urbanization, small-scale industrialization, and unemployment—also bred radicalization, with the traditional, conservative elite threatened and even ousted from leadership by younger men, often from lower social circles.[9]

The Jewish Agency, following its 1929 expansion to embrace non-Zionist Diaspora groups as well, had far more funds at its disposal for immigration.[10] By 1939, there were 1,070,000 Arabs (950,000 of them Muslims) and 460,000 Jews in Palestine. The Arabs declined from more than 82 percent of the population in 1931 to less than 70 percent in 1939.[11] Arab fears of an eventual Jewish majority sharpened. As Ben-Gurion began to state openly: "There is a fundamental conflict. We and they want the same thing. We both want Palestine." And, he explained, for once looking at things from the Arab perspective: "Were I an Arab . . . I would rise up against immigration liable sometime in the future to hand the country . . . over to Jewish rule. What Arab cannot do his math and understand that immigration at the rate of 60,000 a year means a Jewish state in all Palestine?"[12]

The interwar years also saw a major increase in Jewish land ownership. During the 1920s the Yishuv acquired some 533,000 dunams; in the 1930s, another 300,000 dunams.[13] In the 1920s most purchases were of large, relatively empty, mostly uncultivated tracts from absentee *effendi*s; in the 1930s more small, cultivated tracts, owned by their inhabitants, changed hands.[14] During the 1930s the issue of land purchases and tenant evictions was defined by the Arabs as "a matter of life and death," on a par with Jewish immigration. The demand caused a boom in prices, tempting other owners to sell. The average price per dunam leaped from PL 5.3 in 1929 to PL 23.3 in 1935. (The Palestine pound was equal to the pound sterling.)[15] One estimate has it that prices were fifty times greater in 1944 than in 1910.[16] The German consul in Jerusalem, Dr. Heinrich Wolff, observed pithily that Arab nationalists "in daylight were crying out against Jewish immigration and in the darkness of the night were selling lands to the Jews."[17]

The damage these sales caused to Palestinian society was material, psychological, and political. One British report went into the alleged means used by Jews and their Arab agents: "[The Arab cultivators] . . . in the Samakh-Beisan area . . . know that certain simple persons like Yusuf al-Irsan of the [Bani] Saqr receive monthly [Jewish] subsidies and are entertained with wine and women at Tiberias and Haifa, Irsan himself now suffering from venereal disease contracted from such hospitality. . . . Jewish agents and Arab dupes . . . corrupt and intimidate the peasants, with a view to their selling their lands."[18]

Historian Yehoshua Porath writes: "One cannot overestimate the devastating effects of these sales on the Palestinian-Arab National movement. . . . They spread an atmosphere of suspicion, mistrust, and mischief. . . . This situation seriously enfeebled the national movement."[19] The transactions resulted in the eviction of thousands of families from the rural hinterland to the fringes of the big towns and propelled them into a lower socioeconomic status, of tenancy or seasonal agricultural employment, in other sites.[20] The evictees joined the thousands who during the period 1880–1920 moved from the rural areas to the towns or to other villages, as a result of debts, a multiplicity of heirs, famine, or other causes unconnected to Jewish land purchases. But what stuck in the Palestinian collective consciousness were the land losses stemming from Zionist purchases. Many evictees were propelled into nationalist activism by their dispossession.[21] Historians have concluded that only "several thousand" families were displaced following land sales to Jews between the 1880s and the late 1930s.[22] But the Arabs came to feel they faced a galloping process. The effect became more pronounced during the late 1920s and early 1930s, as a result of increased Arab political awareness and literacy and the dramatic growth of the Yishuv.

The Arab radicalization often took on a religious aspect: Increasingly the points of friction with the Zionists were, or became identified with, religious symbols and values. Husseini, dominating Palestinian politics from his perch on the Supreme Muslim Council, was well aware of the political uses of religion. At the end of 1931 he and and Shawkat Ali, a prominent Indian Muslim, organized a World Islamic Conference in Jerusalem, with 130 delegates representing most of the Islamic world. It reaffirmed the sanctity to Islam of the Western Wall, condemned Zionism and land sales to Jews, and elected an executive committee headed by Hajj Amin. The event effectively demonstrated pan-Muslim support for the Palestinians, reinforcing hostility toward Zionism among British officials. Secretaries of state for India, with its large Muslim minority, from this point on adopted an almost automatic anti-Zionist posture.[23]

The years 1930–35 were marked by vocal Opposition-Husseini rivalry. In 1934 the Opposition won the municipal elections in Jaffa and Gaza; the race in Jerusalem was won by the Husseini candidate, Dr. Hussein Fakhri al-Khalidi (paradoxically, with Jewish support, because of his congenial personality and because the Opposition candidate and incumbent mayor, Raghib Nashashibi, had been party to the anti-Zionist Palestinian delegation to London in 1930). Furthermore, since 1930 the mayor's municipal council had been without Jewish representation.[24]

The Opposition—until then a loose coalition of clans and interests—established, in late 1934, the National Defense Party. Its official long-term aims were similar to Husseini's, but it professed willingness to "cooperate" with the government (something the Husseinis resisted). Unofficially its leaders were far more moderate: They met with Zionists, rejected radicals' calls for boycotting the Yishuv, and agreed to a solution that would take account of at least some short-term Zionist goals (continued, if limited, immigration, and so on). They presented an anti-Zionist facade but in private explained that this was necessitated by their struggle with the Husseinis for the support of the population. And they periodically accepted money from the Jewish Agency to fund this or that political campaign or article. A second party identified with the Opposition, the Reform Party, was established by the Khalidi and Budeiri families of Jerusalem in May–June 1935.[25]

In response to Opposition moves, the Husseinis in March 1935 formed the Palestinian Arab Party, whose platform called for resistance to the establishment of a Jewish National Home. It set up its own youth corps, al-Futuwwa (the name of an association of Arab knights during the Middle Ages), which resembled Germany's Hitler Youth and was officially designated the "Nazi Scouts."[26] At the founding meeting on February 11, 1936, Jamal al-Husseini, a principal aide of Hajj Amin, declared that Hitler had started out with only six followers and now had sixty million.[27] The first seventy al-Futuwwa recruits took the following oath: "Life—my right; independence—my aspiration; Arabism—my principle; Palestine—my country, and there is no room in it for any but Arabs. In this I believe and Allah is my witness."[28]

The Husseini-Nazi connection was to crop up repeatedly in the Palestinian struggle against Zionism through the 1930s and early 1940s. Indeed, as early as March 31, 1933, two months after Hitler's assumption of power, Amin al-Husseini told the German consul in Jerusalem that "the Muslims inside and outside Palestine welcome the new regime of Germany and hope for the extension of the fascist anti-democratic, governmental system to other countries." In the name of the Arabs, Husseini expressed a desire to join in the Nazis' anti-Jewish boycott.[29]

The emergence of a better-educated, more politically conscious Arab elite also contributed to the radicalization of the community. The replacement of the Ottomans by the British Mandate changed the political climate from despotism to benign colonialism and soon led to a vast improvement in the school system. The Arab press gained tens of thousands of young readers, all potential activists. While persuading successive high commissioners of his "moderation" (thus earning their political and financial backing), Amin al-Husseini covertly stepped up nationalist agitation (partly through his newspaper, al-Jami'ah al-'Arabiyyah). He understood that the movement was not yet strong enough to openly challenge British rule in armed revolt. But the younger cadres, occasionally organizing themselves in new associations (like the Arab Young Men's Association and the Patriotic Arab Association of Nablus), pressed the leadership for ever more radical steps.[30]

The major political expression of this trend had been the establishment in August 1932 of the Istiqlal (Independence) Party, which espoused pan-Arabism, independence (with Palestine as part of a Greater Syria), and the abrogation of the Balfour Declaration.[31] The Istiqlal was the preeminent expression of the politics of the young rebels, at least for a year, after which its influence plummeted. The first National Congress of Arab Youth, in Jaffa in January 1932, had adopted an "Istiqlalist" platform. Party members patrolled the beaches to prevent illegal immigration, and forced shopkeepers to comply with political strikes.[32]

In 1930–31 the two Husseinis, Amin and Musa Kazim, established a "National Fund," modeled on the Jewish National Fund, to raise money for nationalist activities; but most Palestinians declined to contribute.[33] Its failure stemmed partly from the animosity of landowners associated with the Opposition and possibly from the nature and mentality of Palestinian Arabs: They looked first to the family, the clan, and the village as domains of responsibility. A "national" fund to forestall Jewish purchases in a remote corner of the country proved beyond their ken.

The continuing land sales had nevertheless become the focus of the PAE's struggle by 1933. About five hundred urban notables and village sheikhs met in Jaffa on March 20 and denounced the British for allowing Zionist immigration and their fellow Arabs for selling land. The sellers were threatened with boycott, and some speakers accused Arab leaders (particularly the Nashashibis) of themselves engaging in such sales. On October 13, the PAE organized a one-day general strike and a demonstration in Jerusalem, which was violently dispersed by British security forces at the Old City's New Gate, with no serious injuries. But a second demonstration, in Jaffa on October 27, organized by the Istiqlal without the blessing of the PAE, ended with twenty-six demonstrators and one policeman killed. The outraged PAE responded with a weeklong strike and further demonstrations, but immigration steadily increased.[34] Musa Kazim's death on March 26, 1934, further weakened the PAE and the moderates. The coalition factions could not agree on a successor, and the executive lost the little power it had. The Arabs were left rudderless and split between the Husseinis and the Opposition.

Arab radicalism in the early 1930s was also expressed in clandestine violence. A number of *jihaddiyyah,* or secret fighting societies, emerged. In the Jerusalem area, the Jihad al-Muqaddas (the holy war society) was led by 'Abd al-Qadir al-Husseini (1907–1948), Musa Kazim's son. Organized in five-man cells, it began to collect money and arms in 1934. About 100 rifles and pistols were bought and hundreds of recruits were trained. In 1935, Amin al-Husseini assumed personal control of the society.[35] It is unclear when it began to operate against the British.

The most important clandestine group emerged shortly before the 1929 riots in the Haifa–Lower Galilee area, around the commanding figure of a Syrian-born, Egyptian-educated preacher and cleric, Sheikh 'Izz al-Din al-Qassam (1882–1935). In 1920 he had fled Syria to Palestine after being sentenced to death in absentia by the French for guerrilla activities. He settled in Haifa and preached fundamentalist Islam, calling for *jihad* against both the British and the Yishuv and gathering a host of followers.[36] The British regarded him as "a fanatical religious sheikh of the most dangerous type."[37] He was among the founders of the Haifa branch of the Young Men's Muslim Association and was its president in 1934. At the same time he clandestinely organized a terrorist network called the Black Hand. In a sermon at Haifa's Istiqlal Mosque he declared: "You are a people of rabbits, who are afraid of death and scaffolds and engage in prattle. You must know that nothing will save us but our arms."[38]

Most of al-Qassam's men were poor, uneducated peasants; some had lost land or jobs to Jews. During 1931–32 they launched occasional raids against Jewish settlements and field workers. On April 5, 1931, during the Nabi Musa festivities, they killed three members of Kibbutz Yagur coming home from the fields and wounded four more. The following year, two settlers, one from Balfouriya and the other from Kfar Hassidim, were murdered. On December 23, 1932, a squad penetrated Moshav Nahalal at the western edge of the Jezreel Valley, and threw a bomb into a house, killing a father and son. The murderers were caught and confessed, and at last al-Qassam's organization came to light, though he himself was not named. Subsequently he lay low and refrained from terrorism for almost three years.

In early November 1935 al-Qassam decided to renew his activities, spurred possibly by the "cement barrel incident": On October 16 a shipment of cement barrels that arrived in Jaffa port bound for a Jewish importer was found to contain eight hundred rifles and 400,000 rounds of ammunition.[39] Failing to enlist Hajj Amin's support for either terrorism or all-out rebellion, al-Qassam moved to the Jenin area to recruit and begin operations. On November 6 his group killed a Jewish police sergeant in the Gilboa area, triggering a massive manhunt. On the 21st, they were surrounded by British troops near Ya'bad; al-Qassam and three others were killed. David Ben-Gurion referred to the skirmish as "their Tel Hai."[40] Al-Qassam's funeral in Balad ash Sheikh, a village southeast of Haifa (where his tomb still stands), was a major nationalist demonstration. His deeds and death captured the imagination of a generation of Palestinians and helped spark the Arab revolt that erupted six months later. (At the end of the 1980s, during the uprising called the Intifada, the Muslim fundamentalist Hamas movement named its military-terrorist wing "the Battalions of 'Izz al-Din al-Qassam.") The connection between al-Qassam and his group and the Husseinis is unclear. He almost certainly belonged to the Istiqlal Party and may subsequently have joined Husseini's Palestine Arab Party.[41]

The riots of 1929 radicalized the Jews as well. The Revisionists found support for their belief that Zionism would win through only with military force. The binationalists saw in the violence "proof" that conciliation had to be achieved quickly, before the Arab majority overwhelmed the Yishuv. The socialist mainstream—now represented by Mapai (Mifleget Poalei Eretz Yisrael—the Land of Israel Workers Party), established in 1930 with the amalgamation of Achdut HaAvodah and HaPoel HaZair—was obliged at last to admit that there existed a Palestinian-Arab nationalist movement, and that the Yishuv was not merely confronting a group of bloodthirsty fanatics or incited hooligans.[42] The natural consequence was the growing appreciation, expounded by Chaim Arlosoroff, the director of the Jewish Agency's Political Department from 1931 until 1933, that Zionism would have to use force to achieve its aims.[43] After Arlosoroff was murdered by unknown assailants in Tel Aviv in 1933, Ben-Gurion met repeatedly with Musa al-Alami, a PAE member, and argued that Zionism would develop the country to the benefit of both peoples. Al-Alami replied that he would rather have the country remain desolate for a hundred years than see Zionism succeed.[44] These contacts came to naught, and the stage was set for the outbreak of the Arab revolt.

Among the factors precipitating the explosion were Britain's failure to stop Mussolini's conquest of Abyssinia in 1935–36 and to halt Hitler's remilitarization of the Rhineland in 1936—its military weakness and political irresolution invited challenge. Another was the economic crisis in Palestine. At first the tide of immigration, which also brought in capital, had brought about a major economic upswing. The years 1932–35 saw unprecedented prosperity, for both Jews and Arabs. But when the League of Nations imposed sanctions on Italy, there was a rush on the banks, firms closed, and unemployment spread. The Yishuv tried to limit the damage, and "Hebrew labor" became the order of the day. Arabs were turned out of jobs or could not find any. Resentment grew, exacerbated by active anti-British propaganda directed at the Arab world from Italian-occupied Libya.[45] The crisis was deepened by a drought during 1931–34; in 1932 agricultural production in the Northern District fell to 35 to 70 percent of the annual average, and in the Jerusalem and Southern Districts it stood at 45 percent.[46] The years before the outbreak saw a steady pauperization of the interior hill villages and towns, coupled with a shift of population to the fringes of Haifa and Jaffa, where shantytowns sprouted.[47]

In the meantime, the success of anti-imperialist activities in neighboring states encouraged the Palestinians to take to the streets. Rioting in Cairo in November 1935 gained the Egyptians a treaty with the British, and in Syria in early 1936 a general strike that lasted fifty days persuaded the French to sign a treaty with the Syrians.[48]

After the "cement barrel incident," rumors spread that the weapons were meant for a "massacre" or at least a "war" against the Arabs. A one-day general strike was called; another took place the following month. On November 25, the five Arab political parties submitted a joint protest to the high commissioner demanding a cessation of Jewish immigration, a stop to land transfers, and the establishment of a democratic (that is, Arab-majority) government. Britain's efforts to set up a Legislative Council, in which the British would retain the final say were rejected by the Arabs and the Zionists and were finally shelved when MPs from both sides of the House of Commons roundly condemned them as contrary to the spirit of the Mandate. Inconsequential followup negotiations were interrupted in April 1936 by the beginning of the general strike that marked the first stage of the revolt.

THE REVOLT, 1936–39

THE FIRST STAGE

On the evening of April 15, 1936, a gang of armed Arabs set up a roadblock on a winding road in the hill country east of Tulkarm. From Arab drivers they extorted "contributions" for arms and ammunition. They then shot three Jewish drivers. One died on the spot, another died five days later, and the third survived.[49] They were later seen as the first victims of the Arab rebellion. In an act of revenge two days later, members of Irgun Bet drove up to a shack near Petach Tikva and shot dead its two Arab occupants.

The Tel Aviv funeral of one Jewish victim on April 17 turned into an angry demonstration against the Arabs and the British. The official history of the

Haganah blames this on "hot-tempered and disorganized Oriental [Sephardic] Jews."[50] An Arab passerby and a policeman who came to his defense were badly beaten. The following day several Arab shoeshine boys and peddlers were assaulted. Troops were rushed to Tel Aviv, but it was too late. On April 19 mobs of unemployed peasants and migrant workers from Syria, fired by rumors that an Arab woman and three Syrian laborers had been murdered in Tel Aviv, rampaged through Jaffa, killing nine Jews and injuring almost sixty. Reportedly they were incited by a number of young a'yan leaders, including Fakhri Nashashibi, Opposition leader Raghib Nashashibi's nephew and main aide. Some Arabs saved Jewish pedestrians, and a British police officer killed two rioters. Thousands of Jewish residents of Jaffa fled to Tel Aviv.[51] For the next two days Jews and Arabs in neighborhoods on the Jaffa–Tel Aviv boundary attacked one another, looting and setting fire to shops and homes. Eight more Jews and six Arabs were killed, the latter by police.

The disturbances spread rapidly. Almost from the first, the Arabs referred to them as a revolt (*thawra*) or "the Great Arab Rebellion." Jerusalem educator and diarist Khalil al-Sakakini called it a "life-and-death struggle" and a "revolt" in his diary on April 21.[52] The Jews and the British, wishing to make light of it, respectively called the violence "the events" and "the disturbances." The Arab definition is more accurate. It was to be the biggest and most protracted uprising against the British in any country in the Middle East, and the most significant in Palestinian history until the anti-Israeli Intifada fifty years later. At least in its initial stages, it was a popular movement. Ben-Gurion wrote: The Arabs were "fighting against dispossession. . . . The Arab is fighting a war that cannot be ignored. He goes out on strike, he is killed, he makes great sacrifices."[53] But the rebellion also laid bare the deep rifts in Palestinian society, which ultimately rendered it weak and ineffective: between the a'yan families, between villagers and townspeople, between poor and rich, between Muslims and Christians, and between residents of different districts.[54]

It was the young nationalists, the *shabab*, who took the lead—one of many parallels with the Intifada. The elders were hesitant and Grand Mufti Amin al-Husseini seems, down to the end of June, to have tried to restrain the community from a frontal collision with the Mandatory government.[55] The traditional leaders were sucked in by the unfolding events,[56] but an organizational structure began to emerge in the first days. On April 19 a National Committee was formed in Nablus; similar bodies sprang up during the next few days in other towns, consisting of local representatives of major political factions. Shop closures and strikes broke out in a number of places. It was as if the hay lay ready, just waiting for the spark.

It is unclear what degree of prior organization had gone into the establishment of the National Committees or the launching of the strikes—but they both appear to have occurred almost immediately and almost simultaneously in a number of locations. In some areas the call to strike met resistance. In

Jaffa stevedores and shopkeepers opposed it but were intimidated by national-ist activists.[57] In the mixed cities, militants tried to halt all commerce between the Arab and Jewish sectors. On the night of April 19–20 national-level repre-sentatives of the main factions met in Nablus and decided, with local Istiqlal leader Akram Zu'aytir the driving spirit, on a four-day general strike.

On April 25, representatives of the various factions met in Jerusalem and set up a wall-to-wall eight-man body called the Arab Higher Committee (AHC), which became the successor to the PAE[58] and led the Palestinian struggle during 1936–39 and 1946–48.[59] Amin al-Husseini, elected AHC chairman, emerged as the revolt's leader. At the end of April the AHC declared that the strike would end only when the government put a stop to Zionist immigration and land transfers, and allowed a popularly elected legislature; if the demands were not accepted by May 15, the Palestine Arab community would embark on active resistance, including armed violence.[60] The strike proved only of limited effectiveness—such vital services as Haifa port and the railways continued to function, the peasantry continued sowing and harvest-ing, and Arabs remained at their government posts.[61] Nevertheless it had tremendous political resonance: It was the most significant demonstration of Palestinian-Arab nationalist feeling ever, lasting half a year, until mid-Octo-ber.

Ironically, though causing a shortage of vegetables and delays in construc-tion, the strike significantly aided the Jewish economy by helping to realize the aim of "Hebrew labor" as the jobs of strikers were quickly filled by Jews. It propelled the Jewish sector in the direction of autarchy: The closure of Jaffa port, for example, in short order led to the establishment of a "Jewish" port in Tel Aviv. As Ben-Gurion put it: "The first and principal lesson of these distur-bances . . . is that we must free ourselves from all economic dependence on the Arabs. . . . We must not find ourselves in a situation where our enemies are in a position to starve us, to block our access to the sea, to deny us gravel and stones for construction."[62]

The government readied reinforcements for dispatch from Egypt and deployed roadblocks, curfews, and patrols. But it also tried appeasement, announcing on May 18 a limit to Jewish immigration of 4,500 during the fol-lowing half year. But the AHC, which wanted a complete end to immigration, responded by extending the strike and shifting to urban terrorism and to armed rebellion in the countryside. Bombs were set off near British positions and offices and, to a lesser extent, near Jewish targets. During May forty-one bombs exploded in Jaffa alone; thirty-five more in Haifa. On May 16, an Arab fired on a Jewish crowd leaving a movie theater, killing three and wounding two. Shots were fired at British police stations. In Jaffa, with its narrow alleys, the rebels achieved temporary control, especially at night. The British responded by systematically blowing up parts of the town's Old City.[63] Alto-gether some 220 homes were destroyed.[64] Nablus, too, was brought under control,[65] but the Jewish population of Hebron, which had returned in the early 1930s, had to be evacuated.[66]

The AHC and the local National Committees began to incite the countryside to rebellion. How this mobilization was carried out is indicated in a Haganah intelligence report about a rally in Masmiya al-Kabira on June 1, attended by representatives of fourteen neighboring villages. One speaker declared:

> The inhabitants of Beit Dajan have already rebelled against the government and the Jews and have sacrificed themselves for the homeland. . . . And why should I see the youngsters of this district sleeping as if they are afraid of death and imprisonment? And if you continue doing nothing Palestine will turn into a national home for the Jews. . . . You . . . [must] fight your enemies, the enemies of religion, who wish to destroy your mosques, and who wish to expel you from your land.[67]

The government indirectly facilitated this "incitement" by exiling urban rebels to the countryside, where they duly stirred up the villagers. Moreover, on May 11 members of the AHC themselves began touring the countryside—despite a government demand that they stay in the cities—and preaching rebellion.[68] The government responded by arresting and exiling prominent young Palestinian nationalists, including Akram Zu'aytir and Fakhri Nashashibi.[69]

Since 1930 the British had maintained a fixed military force of two battalions of infantry and an RAF armored car squadron in Palestine. Though the number of policemen increased, the force had not kept up with the general increase in population.[70] It was to be overwhelmed in the first weeks of the revolt.

Initially, there was sporadic sniping against Jewish traffic and settlements but, apart from those in Jaffa, no serious attacks. Jews began to travel in convoys and to put armored sheeting on their vehicles. Most common was the destruction of orchards and groves, a time-honored Arab practice in village feuds. In the course of the rebellion the Arabs uprooted an estimated 200,000 "Jewish" trees.[71] There were also lethal assaults, and on August 17 two Jewish nurses working in Jaffa's government hospital were murdered.[72]

The immediate British response to the unrest was restrained. The government hoped it would blow over, without resort to measures that would permanently scar Anglo-Arab relations. Only on September 7 did Whitehall announce martial law and its intention to restore law and order by drastic means.[73] During the first six months of the revolt, when about two hundred Arabs, eighty Jews, and twenty-eight Britons were killed and thirteen hundred people were wounded,[74] no death sentences were imposed by the courts.[75]

Twenty thousand troops from Britain and Egypt were shipped in, about

2,700 supernumerary Jewish policemen were recruited and armed, and outlying Jewish settlements were given weapons. The British succeeded—using
nightly curfews, patrols, searches, and ambushes—in pushing the terrorists
out of the towns. In Jaffa's Old City, the British blew up dozens of houses to
flush out the rebels. Many militants moved to and began operating in rural
areas. Bands of rebels in the hill country began to ambush traffic and to attack
army camps and settlements. 'Abd al-Qadir al-Husseini left Jerusalem and,
moving from village to village, recruited peasants to his Jihad al-Muqqadas
group. Jamal al-Husseini instructed a Tulkarm leader to "organize bands for
killing, burning houses and uprooting trees. If this opportunity is lost, the
Arabs will have no chance of success."[76]

By mid-May 1936 "the rural sector became the center of gravity of the
revolt."[77] By June armed bands were roaming the hill country of Judea,
Samaria, and Galilee, as well as the Jezreel Valley–Mount Gilboa area. "The
most lawless [area was] Samaria . . . with its center at Nablus," according to
one British dispatch.[78] Prominent among the organizers and leaders were 'Izz
al-Din al-Qassam's veterans.[79]

The rebels were not uniformly or immediately successful in their rural
recruitment drives. There was reluctance among the peasantry to take on the
British, who, despite the weakness they had exhibited in regard to Abyssinia
and the Rhineland, were known to be potentially very strong. Moreover, the
previous decade and a half of British rule had been a boon: Taxes had
decreased; the government afforded some protection against dispossession
and provided occasional loans; and the improvement in security, health, and
other public services was palpable and considerable.

But the succession of dry years in the early 1930s, which had particularly
affected the hill villages, precipitated major movement from the countryside
to the towns. This ate away at the traditional, stabilizing, clan-centered social
fabric; family patriarchs and sheikhs were no longer able to impose their will
on hotheaded youngsters.[80] These socioeconomic developments help explain
the emergence of the rural bands, though this was by no means the main cause
of the peasants' adhesion to the rebellion, according to its leading historian.[81]

The ripening of crops in spring and summer 1936 delayed the peasants'
drift toward rebellion. It was only after the harvest, in late May–June, that they
rose. Moreover, during the first weeks of the revolt they had no representation
in the AHC or the local National Committees.[82] The lead was taken by the
urban activists, with the politically backward peasants following; the villagers
had traditionally looked to the urban a'yan for guidance and leadership.

By the end of summer 1936 much of the countryside was in arms. Ultimately the fellahin were driven by the same political fuel as the urban
rebels—hatred for the foreign ruler, hatred for the infidel, hatred for and fear
of the Zionists. Traditional clan rivalry also played a part: One clan's patrio-

tism could not be outdone by another's.[83] By August the rebel bands were regularly mounting hit-and-run operations, cutting telephone lines and attacking traffic and railway bridges, Jewish settlements, and police outposts. At first, the fighters would go out on a specific mission and then return to their farming. But full-time guerrilla units gradually emerged, with fifty to one hundred men in each. Arab officials and policemen fed them intelligence. During July and August the units began to coordinate their activities.

From the start the AHC denied any connection with the rural "rebellion" or the urban terrorism. But it is clear that it and its subordinate National Committees had a hand in setting up the rural bands and in financing and supplying them as well as in organizing at least some of the urban terrorism. Amin al-Husseini's aides later maintained that he secretly led the revolt during its first two months. But his SMC pointedly refrained from publicly supporting the revolt or giving it a religious imprimatur. And the mufti at this time said that he "opposed violence, since violence would not serve any useful purpose."[84] As usual, it appears, he was "playing a double game," in the words of a British observer.[85] In August, however, the SMC came out explicitly in favor of the revolt. The Husseinis' newspaper, al-Liwa, encouraged the rebels to fight "until God has pronounced his sentence." Arms were stockpiled in the Haram ash Sharif, and Husseini began to raise money and issue instructions.[86]

Largely as a result of feuding between the Husseinis and Nashashibis, the AHC never managed to impose operational control over most of the bands.[87] Money raised for strike relief was often diverted by Amin al-Husseini to the armed bands. Wealthy Palestinians often bypassed the AHC and funded their local bands directly (as in the Nablus area). Often the units used threats and force to exact contributions. Large amounts of weapons and ammunition reached them from Syria and Transjordan, often smuggled in by Bedouin, outside AHC control.

The bands—and the AHC at this time—probably also got funds from Italy, which, at loggerheads with Britain over Abyssinia, wished to disrupt the British rear. In June 1936 British Foreign Secretary Anthony Eden wrote that the "disturbances . . . have been fomented to some extent by Italian money and intrigue." In September 1940, the Italian foreign minister, Count Galeazzo Ciano, spoke of "millions" dispensed to the mufti.[88] Haganah intelligence picked up indications that Germany, too, was transferring funds and arms to the rebels.[89] German and Italian propaganda campaigns supported the rebellion and lambasted the Mandate. In turn, in the words of one Arab commentator, "Feeling the whip of Jewish pressure and influence, the Arabs sympathize[d] with the Nazis and Fascists in their agony and trials at the hands of Jewish intrigues and international financial pressure."[90]

Near the end of summer, a group of two hundred volunteers–from Iraq, Syria, and Transjordan—entered northern Samaria. They were led by Fawzi al-Qawuqji, a former Ottoman officer who had figured prominently in the guerrilla war waged by Faisal's regime in Damascus against the French, and had served as Ibn Saud's military adviser. Backed in some measure by Syria and Iraq, he soon was granted recognition by several large-band leaders as the "commander-in-chief of the revolt in Palestine" (or "Southern Syria," as he sometimes designated it).[91] Qawuqji had good connections with the Nashashibis, and this soon alienated the Husseinis. He seems to have gone out of his way to rebuff the AHC, and the Husseinis no doubt resented his usurpation of the guerrilla leadership.[92]

The AHC mounted major propaganda and fund-raising campaigns in Egypt, Syria, and Iraq, and Whitehall began to fear that the situation would have a direct effect on Anglo-Arab relations in general and on specific imperial interests (such as control of the Suez Canal). Fraternal strikes and demonstrations in Transjordan, Lebanon, Iraq, and Syria, expressing solidarity with the revolt, were followed by efforts by Emir Abdullah of Transjordan and Iraqi Foreign Minister Nuri Sa'id to mediate between the AHC, Britain, and the Yishuv. Abdullah's aim was to "get a foothold in Palestine"; Sa'id's, to advance the cause of a Hashemite federation, encompassing Iraq, Transjordan, and Palestine. The Nashashibis backed Abdullah's *démarche*.[93]

The Husseinis were angered by the Nashashibi-Abdullah connection, and the AHC was reluctant to make concessions to Britain, despite the face-saving measures proposed by the Arab mediators. The Husseinis reinforced their firm stand by assassinating Opposition figures who tended toward compromise. In July 1937, an attempt on the life of Fakhri Nashashibi, apparently by Husseini followers, would result in the Nashashibis' withdrawal from the AHC.[94]

By mid-September 1936 economic and military realities compelled a halt to the rebellion. The Jaffa daily *Filastin* on September 16 called for an end to the five-month-old strike: Jaffa was the center of the Arab citrus industry, and the crop was about to ripen.[95] The Arabs had been hard hit by the strike and wished to return to work and wages. Moreover, at the beginning of September, in reaction to the arrival of Qawuqji's volunteers and because of the growing loss of control in the countryside, the British government had switched from restraint to all-out counterinsurgency warfare, pushing into the hill country to crush the revolt. Houses were blown up as both punishment and deterrence. A full division was shipped to Palestine. This new, vigorous military posture, portending defeat for the rural bands, added to the pressure.

The AHC embarked on an elaborate negotiation with Whitehall, designed to elicit from the kings of Arabia, Yemen, and Iraq, and the emir of Transjordan, an "appeal" to the Palestinians to halt the strike. On October 10 the appeal, whose purpose was to enable the AHC to agree to end the strike without loss of face (and perhaps with some British concessions), was at last published. The potentates urged their "sons, the Arabs of Palestine," to end the bloodshed and to put their trust in "the good intentions of our friend Great Britain, who has declared that she will do justice." The next day the AHC responded by publicly calling on "the noble Arab nation in Palestine to resort to quietness and to put an end to the strike and the disorders."[96]

In secret, the AHC issued a proclamation to the leaders of the militia bands declaring:

> Honored Brethren! Heroes! . . . Our poor tongues cannot express the strength of our love and admiration and the exaltation concealed in our hearts for your self-sacrifice and your devoted war for religion, father-land and all things Arab. Rest assured that your struggle is engraved in letters of flame in the chronicles of the nation. And now . . . we . . . urge you to stop activity until needed. Save the bullets and take care of them. We stand now in a period of hope and expectation. If the Royal Commission comes and judges equitably and gives us all our rights, well and good. If not, the field of battle lies before us. . . . We request . . . self-control and armistice until a new notice.[97]

The British had not agreed to a cessation of Jewish immigration. But they had held out the prospect that a royal commission (promised back in May) would begin investigating Arab grievances as soon as the violence ended. The army was dissatisfied, feeling that it had been on the verge of crushing the rebels. The bands were given a week to disperse and return to their villages, which they promptly did—all but Qawuqji. His force was eventually surrounded, but the British allowed it to cross the Jordan and proceed to Iraq.[98]

In early November the Peel Commission, charged with examining the causes of the "disturbances," set sail for Palestine. Thus ended the first stage of the rebellion. British officials were later—when the revolt resumed with renewed vigor—to bemoan the "weakness" shown at this time and the failure to nip the violence in the bud.[99]

THE JEWISH RESPONSE

The outbreak of the revolt shocked the Yishuv, which had grown accustomed to relative quiet. The Zionist leaders' public attitude was summed up by Chaim Weizmann: "On one side, the forces of destruction, the forces of the desert, have risen, and on the other stand firm the forces of civilization and building. It is the old war of the desert against civilization, but we will not be stopped."[100] Rhetoric aside, however, the Jews realized that they were sitting on a volcano, that the Yishuv's growth could not but spark native resistance. "There is no choice" (*ein breira*) surfaced like a fatalistic battle cry; the Yishuv would have to live by the sword.[101]

Some Jews professed surprise. They had come to Palestine in peace; why were the Arabs reacting in this way? As Mapai's 1936 May Day flyer put it (more than a week after the start of the revolt): "Only narrow reactionary chauvinism cannot see the benefit that our enterprise has already brought, and which it will still bring, to the Arabs of the country." Once more the outbreak was blamed on a minority of "inciters." Again Mapainiks were busy trying to distinguish between "good" and "bad" Arabs;[102] again, the Jews made a conscious effort to minimize the importance of what was afoot; again, anti-Zionist outbreaks were designated "pogroms," a term that belittled the phenomenon, demonized the Arabs, and, in a peculiar way, comforted the Jews—it obviated the need to admit that what they faced was a rival national movement, rather than Arabic-speaking Cossacks and street ruffians. Commentators who ventured to use the term "revolt" always took care to place it in quotation marks, signifying deprecation or doubt. And when they did acknowledge the existence of an Arab nationalist movement, they tried to delegitimize it by branding it immoral and terroristic,[103] or by comparing it to fascism and Nazism. Said Yitzhak Tabenkin, an ideologue of the kibbutz movement: "The swastika, waved aloft in Hitler's Germany, and the green flag, the Arab 'national' flag, now upraised by the reactionary leadership of the Arabs of Palestine—they are the same flag, the flag of national hatred."[104]

Some Zionists, while making certain arguments for public and foreign consumption, believed otherwise. Ben-Gurion and Sharett never disputed the realities of the revolt, and of the Arab nationalist movement having understandable and perhaps even legitimate fears and grievances. "The Arab fear of our power is intensifying," Ben-Gurion said on May 19, 1936: "[Arabs] see . . . exactly the opposite of what we see. It doesn't matter whether or not their view is correct. . . . They see immigration on a giant scale . . . they see the Jews fortifying themselves economically. . . . They see the best lands passing into our hands. They see England identify with Zionism."[105]

The Arabs, he said, felt that they were "fighting dispossession. . . . The fear is not of losing land, but of losing the homeland of the Arab people, which others want to turn into the homeland of the Jewish people."[106] The British and the Yishuv were faced with a "rebellion" and a "bloody war." "There is a fundamental conflict. We and they want the same thing: We both want Palestine. . . . By our very presence and progress here, [we] have nurtured the [Arab] movement."[107] Sharett, Arlosoroff's successor as director of the Jewish Agency's Political Department, spoke in a similar vein: "Fear is the main factor in all [Palestinian] Arab politics. . . . There is no Arab who is not harmed by the Jews' entry into the country."[108]

Yishuv leaders understood that their best interests lay in staying on the sidelines and allowing the British to crush the Arabs. Indulging in operations of their own would push the British toward an even-handed "plague on both your houses" approach. A policy of *havlaga* (restraint) was adopted early on by the mainstream Zionist leaders, and for many months was tacitly adhered to by the Revisionists as well.[109] It had been Ben-Gurion's line from the start:

> Those who today murdered our people in an ambush not only plotted to murder some Jews, but intended to provoke us. . . . The Arabs stand to gain from such a development. They want the country to be in a state of perpetual pogrom. . . . Any further bloodshed [by the Jews] will only bring political advantage to the Arabs and harm us. . . . Our strength is in defense . . . and this strength will give us a political victory if England and the world know that we are defending ourselves rather than attacking.[110]

But within months *havlaga* changed from pure defense to aggressive patrolling and ambushing outside the settlements, though still with the aim of hitting the "guilty" rather than innocent bystanders.[111] Initially, the Arabs restricted themselves to arson in the towns and sniping, crop-burning, and tree destruction in the countryside. Then came attacks on Jewish traffic and farmers in the fields. A convoy system was instituted, with British policemen or troops in armored cars accompanying the vehicles; farmers went out only in armed groups. In the towns the Arabs began throwing bombs and grenades at Jewish homes and cars.

The Haganah devoted its energies mainly to guard duty on the periphery of Jewish neighborhoods in the mixed cities and along the boundary line between Tel Aviv and Jaffa. It and the Revisionist-affiliated Irgun Bet failed to reach formal agreement, so regional commanders hammered out working arrangements. In practice Irgun Bet for months abided by the policy of *havlaga* while the Revisionist press berated the Haganah for cleaving to it. Only in mid-August, after the murder of the two nurses in Jaffa, four Jews in the Mount Carmel forests, and a child in Tel Aviv, did the Haganah briefly deviate from its policy of passive defense. A number of squads crossed through no-man's-land and threw bombs into and sniped at Arab houses on Jaffa's northern perimeter, killing several people; a platoon attacked a Bedouin encampment at Jamasin, just northeast of Tel Aviv; and Haifa contingents attacked pedestrians at Tira, just south of the city, killing a woman and wounding two men. On August 17 Irgun Bet ambushed the Jaffa train, killing an Armenian passenger and wounding five Arabs. Next they murdered two Arabs near Petach Tikva. In the wake of these attacks, the Haganah command, after a stormy debate, reaffirmed the policy of restraint, and no further retaliatory strikes were undertaken during 1936.[112] But in the countryside the Haganah attempted to intercept attackers before they could reach the houses and fields. In the Jerusalem Corridor and elsewhere, Yitzhak Sadeh, a Red Army veteran, set up patrols (*nodedot*) to secure the countryside between settlements.[113]

THE PEEL COMMISSION

In the year between the end of the general strike in October 1936 and the start of the second stage of the revolt in September 1937, the two communities organized for the renewal of hostilities while awaiting the findings of the royal Peel Commission, appointed "to ascertain the . . . causes of the disturbances . . . to ascertain whether . . . either the Arabs or the Jews have any legitimate grievances . . . and to make recommendations for their removal."[114]

The commission, chaired by Lord William Robert Peel, former secretary of state for India, arrived in Palestine on November 11, 1936. The AHC resolved to boycott it unless Britain agreed to suspend immigration. The British duly cut the quota from 4,500 to 1,800, but the AHC stood firm. As so often in the past, however, the Arabs were in fact sawing off the branch they were sitting on. Sir George Rendel, head of the Foreign Office Eastern Department, summed it up: "The Jews have played their cards extraordinarily well," but the Arabs "have been so misguided in the conduct of their case that I sometimes wonder whether Jewish agents are not at work inside the Arab camp."[115] In December, Arab pressure from outside Palestine and Nashashibi opposition inside forced the AHC to agree to submit evidence to the commission, and in January 1937 Hajj Amin al-Husseini himself testified.

The commissioners, sitting in Jerusalem and then London, were lobbied tirelessly by both sides, with the Jews, as usual, proving the more effective persuaders.[116] Weizmann and Ben-Gurion pressed for a solution based on partition. Said Weizmann: "The Jews would be fools not to accept it, even if [the land they were allocated] were the size of a table cloth."[117] Both saw partition as a stepping stone to further expansion and the eventual takeover of the whole of Palestine. "No Zionist can forgo the smallest portion of the Land of Israel," Ben-Gurion was quoted as saying.[118] He wrote to his son Amos: "[A] Jewish state in part [of Palestine] is not an end, but a beginning. . . . Our possession is important not only for itself . . . through this we increase our power, and every increase in power facilitates getting hold of the country in its entirety. Establishing a [small] state . . . will serve as a very potent lever in our historical efforts to redeem the whole country."[119]

The Arabs stridently opposed the Jews' getting any part of the country they viewed as rightfully theirs, and as sacred Muslim soil. And they feared precisely what Ben-Gurion envisioned—that a small Jewish state would be a springboard for future expansion. Said 'Awni 'Abd al-Hadi: "We will fight. We will struggle against the partition of the country and against Jewish immigration. There is no compromise."[120]

The commission's 404-page report, published on July 7, 1937, was based on the premise that the conflict was "irrepressible" and insoluble within the framework of one state, and that the Mandate was unworkable. The main recommendation was to partition the territory. The Jews were to receive less than one-fifth of it: most of Galilee, the Jezreel Valley, and the coastal plain as far south as present-day Ashdod (roughly five thousand square kilometers). The Arab area, comprising the Negev, the southern coastal plain, the Gaza Strip, and the present-day West Bank, was to be united with Transjordan, creating one large, independent Arab state. A small enclave, including Jerusalem, Bethlehem, and a corridor through Ramle and Lydda to the sea at Jaffa, was to remain in British hands (as was a strip along the northwestern shore of the Gulf of Aqaba and possibly also Nazareth and the Sea of Galilee and its shorelines). Britain was also temporarily to hold on to the mixed towns of Haifa, Tiberias, Acre, and Safad.[121]

Peel made a second recommendation as a corollary to partition: an "exchange of population" between the prospective states—the transfer of some 225,000 Arabs and 1,250 Jews. Without this, the Jewish state would have had almost as many Arabs as Jews. The commission thought that the "exchange" should be carried out by agreement, with just compensation to those moved. But if the Arabs objected, the transfer should be implemented by the British, "in the last resort" by compulsion.[122]

Ben-Gurion argued in a letter to his son that the Jews' acceptance of partition—that is, acceptance of only 20 percent or so of their Promised Land—justified the transfer: "[W]e never wanted to dispossess the Arabs. But since England is giving part of the country promised to us—for an Arab state, it is only fair that the Arabs in our state be transferred to the Arab area."[123] The contradiction between this argument and his expectation that the establishment of a Jewish state in a fraction of Palestine was merely a stepping-stone to the eventual conquest of the entire country apparently did not trouble him.

The transfer idea did not originate with the Peel Commission. It goes back to the fathers of modern Zionism and, while rarely given a public airing before 1937, was one of the main currents in Zionist ideology from the movement's inception. It was always clear to the Zionists that a Jewish state would be impossible without a Jewish majority; this could theoretically be achieved through massive immigration, but even then the Arabs would still be a large, threatening minority.

For many Zionists, beginning with Herzl, the only realistic solution lay in transfer. From 1880 to 1920, some entertained the prospect of Jews and Arabs coexisting in peace. But increasingly after 1920, and more emphatically after 1929, for the vast majority a denouement of conflict appeared inescapable. Following the outbreak of 1936, no mainstream leader was able to conceive of future coexistence and peace without a clear physical separation between the two peoples—achievable only by way of transfer and expulsion. Publicly they all continued to speak of coexistence and to attribute the violence to a small minority of zealots and agitators. But this was merely a public pose, designed to calm the worried inhabitants and the troubled British: To speak out loud of inevitable bloodshed and expulsion could only have undermined both internal self-confidence and external support for their cause.

Moreover, transfer was seen as a highly moral solution. The Zionist leaders felt that the Jews' need for a country with empty spaces able to absorb future immigrants morally outweighed the rights of the indigenous Arabs—who were no different than their brothers across the Jordan or Litani and could relocate there with relative ease if the transfer was well compensated and well organized. The Arab states—principally Transjordan, Syria, and Iraq—had vast uninhabited areas and required additional inhabitants for their own development. In any event, separation was preferable to an intermingling, which could only end in a bloodbath.

Transfer would best be accomplished "voluntarily." But Palestine's Arabs did not wish to evacuate the land of their ancestors, and they made this very clear. Moreover, neither the Ottoman Turks nor the British were of a mind to clear out the local population to make room for the Jews. The matter raised ethical questions that troubled the Yishuv from within and inspired opposition to Zionism from without. Yet transfer, however problematic or cruel, offered a way out of the demographic dilemma, and it was sporadically given an airing. Israel Zangwill had declared in April 1905: "[We] must be prepared either to drive out by the sword the tribes in possession as our forefathers did or to grapple with the problem of a large alien population." And fourteen years later he wrote: "We cannot allow the Arabs to block so valuable a piece of historic reconstruction. . . . And therefore we must gently persuade them to 'trek.' After all, they have all Arabia with its million square miles. . . . There is no particular reason for the Arabs to cling to these few kilometers. 'To fold their tents and silently steal away' is their proverbial habit: Let them exemplify it now."[124]

In May 1911 Arthur Ruppin proposed to the Zionist Executive "a limited population transfer" of Palestinian peasants to Syria. Leon Motzkin, one of the founders of the Zionist Organization, declared in a speech in July 1912: "The fact is that around Palestine there are extensive areas. It will be easy for the Arabs to settle there with the money that they will receive from the Jews."[125] The subject of transfer also came up in the Yishuv leadership conference of December 1918. Yitzhak Avigdor Wilkansky, an agronomist and adviser at the Palestine Office in Jaffa, felt that, for practical reasons, it was

impossible to evict the *fellahin,* even if we wanted to. Nevertheless, if it were possible, I would commit an injustice towards the Arabs. There are those among us who are opposed to this from the point of view of supreme righteousness and morality. . . . [But] when you enter into the midst of the Arab nation and do not allow it to unite, here too you are taking its life. . . '. Why don't our moralists dwell on this point? We must be either complete vegetarians or meat eaters: not one-half, one-third or one-quarter vegetarians.[126]

The Arabs soon took note of such utterances. At the meeting in Paris between Faisal and representatives of the Yishuv on April 15, 1919, the emir referred to Zangwill's advocacy of "the removal of the Arab population of Palestine by massive camel-trek." The Jews assured him that Zangwill was "completely outside the [Zionist] camp." Faisal appears to have been placated.[127]

But transfer continued to grip the Zionist imagination. In March 1930 Weizmann told Dr. Drummond Shiels, the British parliamentary undersecretary for the colonies, that the idea of transfer was "a courageous and statesmanlike attempt to grapple with a problem that had been tackled hitherto halfheartedly. . . . Some [of Palestine's Arabs] might flow off into the neighbouring countries, and this quasi-exchange of population could be fostered and encouraged." Weizmann proposed to set up a "development company" to acquire land in Transjordan on which Palestine's Arabs could be resettled.[128] Menachem Ussishkin, one of the founding fathers of Zionism and chairman of the Jewish National Fund, on April 28, 1930, told journalists forthrightly: "[O]ther inhabitants . . . must be transferred to some other place. We must take over the land. We have a greater and nobler ideal than preserving several hundred thousands of Arab fellahin."[129] In March 1936 Moshe Beilinson, a Mapai stalwart, proposed that Britain be approached for "extensive aid for a large development plan, which would enable the evacuation of large Arab tracts of land for our colonization, through an agreement with the *fellahin*."[130]

With the publication of Peel's recommendation, the idea seemed to acquire both "legitimacy" and a measure of "practicability." It remained highly sensitive, but at last was thoroughly discussed in the major Zionist power centers, the Twentieth Zionist Congress and the Jewish Agency Executive. But already in October–early November 1936, even before the arrival in Palestine of the Peel Commission and in preparation for it, the executive debated the issue of landless and land-owning Arab peasants, and reached a near-consensus favoring their transfer to Transjordan. Ben-Gurion observed:

> Why can't we acquire land there for Arabs, who wish to settle in Transjordan? If it was permissible to move an Arab from the Galilee to Judea, why is it impossible to move an Arab from the Hebron area to Transjordan, which is much closer? . . . There are vast expanses of land there and we [in Palestine] are over-crowded. . . . We now want to create concentrated areas of Jewish settlement [in Palestine], and by transferring the land-selling Arab to Transjordan, we can solve the problem of this concentration.
>
> [Query by Mizrahi Party leader and Jewish Agency Executive

member] *Rabbi Yehuda Leib Fishman [Maimon]:* Why not transfer [Arabs] also to Iraq?

Ben-Gurion: Iraq is not [part of] the [Palestine] Mandate [as is officially Transjordan]. If King Ghazi [ibn Faisal of Iraq] will agree to this [and] will not object to this, neither will [I]. . . . Even the high commissioner agrees to a transfer to Transjordan if we equip the peasants with land and money. . . . If the Peel Commission and the London Government accept [this], we'll remove the land problem from the agenda.[131]

It is reasonable to assume that the Zionist leaders played a role in persuading the Peel Commission to adopt the transfer solution, and its eventual support of transfer was greeted by them with joy. But this attitude was not expressed in public, for all understood that rejoicing would arouse vigorous Arab and perhaps British opposition. On July 12, 1937, Ben-Gurion confided to his diary: "The compulsory transfer of the Arabs from the valleys of the proposed Jewish state could give us something which we never had, even when we stood on our own during the days of the First and Second Temples. . . . We are being given an opportunity which we never dared to dream of in our wildest imaginings. This is more than a state, government and sovereignty—this is national consolidation in a free homeland."[132]

Ben-Gurion understood that compulsion would probably be required. And if the British did not exercise force, the Jews would have to do the job. In his mind he merged the possibilities of expansionism and transfer. He refused to resign himself to the minute state that Peel had outlined; the Negev and Transjordan would also have to become Jewish,

because we will not be able to countenance large uninhabited areas which could absorb tens of thousands of Jews remaining empty. . . . And if we have to use force we shall use it without hesitation—but only if we have no choice. We do not want and do not need to expel Arabs and take their places. Our whole desire is based on the assumption—which has been corroborated in the course of all our activity in the country—that there is enough room for us and the Arabs in the country and that if we have to use force—not in order to dispossess the Arabs from the Negev or Transjordan but in order to assure ourselves of the right, which is our due, to settle there—then we have the force.[133]

Ben-Gurion in this passage seems to be saying one thing and its opposite—but the thrust of his thinking in favor of both conquest and transfer seems clear. The attendant contortions merely point to the existence of the severe moral dilemmas occasioned by these issues.

Partition and transfer were debated at length during the Twentieth Zionist

Congress, which met in Zurich in August 1937. A large minority insisted on the indivisibility of the Land of Israel and opposed the Peel recommendations. But the bulk of the delegates accepted the principles of partition and transfer. Many shared an urgent sense that a haven must be created to which the Jews of Europe could emigrate, untrammeled by quotas or restrictions. The final vote was 299 to 160 in qualified favor of the Peel package. The transfer provision is what, at least in part, made partition acceptable. Ben-Gurion told the assembly on August 7:

> We must look carefully at the question of whether transfer is possible, necessary, moral and useful. We do not want to dispossess, [but] transfer of populations occurred before now, in the [Jezreel] Valley, in the Sharon [that is, the coastal plain] and in other places. You are no doubt aware of the JNF's activity in this respect. Now a transfer of a completely different scope will have to be carried out. In many parts of the country new settlement will not be possible without transferring the Arab *fellahin* . . . it is important that this plan comes from the Commission and not from us. . . .
>
> Transfer . . . is what will make possible a comprehensive settlement program. Thankfully, the Arab people have vast, empty areas. Jewish power, which grows steadily, will also increase our possibilities to carry out the transfer on a large scale. You must remember, that this system embodies an important humane and Zionist idea, to transfer parts of a people to their country and to settle empty lands. We believe that this action will also bring us closer to an agreement with the Arabs.[134]

Ben-Gurion suspected that the British would not implement the transfer; but he clearly believed that, in that event, the Jews could carry it out. The plenary sessions of the congress were held behind closed doors, and the whole passage of Ben-Gurion's speech quoted above was completely omitted from the official transcripts. So was the passage in Weizmann's speech in which he proposed setting up a large fund (reverting to his idea of 1930) to buy land in Transjordan on which the Palestinian transferees could be resettled. Weizmann envisioned a piecemeal transfer of population, proceeding at ten thousand a year.[135]

In the ensuing months Whitehall progressively distanced itself from the Peel recommendations, but the JAE discussed the transfer idea repeatedly in June 1938. In one statement Ben-Gurion, chairman of the JAE, proposed policy guidelines, including: "The Jewish State will discuss with the neighboring Arab states the matter of voluntarily transferring Arab tenant-farmers, laborers, and *fellahin* from the Jewish state to the neighboring states."[136]

Various leaders spoke strongly in favor of transfer. Ussishkin said, "We cannot start the Jewish state with . . . half the population being Arab . . . Such a state cannot survive even half an hour." There was nothing immoral about transferring sixty thousand Arab families: "It is most moral. . . . I am ready to come and defend . . . it before the Almighty." Ruppin said: "I do not believe in the transfer of individuals. I believe in the transfer of entire villages." Berl Katznelson, coleader with Ben-Gurion of Mapai, said the transfer would have to be by agreement with Britain and the Arab states: "But the principle should be that there must be a large agreed transfer." Ben-Gurion summed up: "With compulsory transfer we [would] have a vast area [for settlement]. . . . I support compulsory transfer. I don't see anything immoral in it."[137]

While the executive was deliberating, a Transfer Committee of experts was looking into the practical aspects. It was chaired by Jacob Thon, a veteran land purchaser and expert in the eviction of Arab tenant farmers, then head of the Palestine Land Development Company. The committee ended its investigation in June 1938 without producing a final report. Its members were divided on the major issues—how many and what categories of Arabs should be transferred, and to where.[138] But by the summer of 1938 the discussions had become somewhat sterile, as Whitehall had repudiated Peel's recommendations, and the possibility that Britain might actually carry out a transfer had disappeared.

THE SECOND STAGE

In July 1937, the AHC rejected the Peel Report and flatly repudiated the idea of partition.[139] The Arabs of Galilee were especially vehement, regarding the prospect of life under Jewish rule or transfer as equally abhorrent. The British district commissioner reported: "That the Arab population of Galilee should ever be reconciled to the scheme is clearly too much to hope. . . . Christians, Muslims, *fellahin,* and landowners are probably more united in their rejection of the proposal than they have ever been before. Their common feeling . . . is that they have been betrayed and that they will be forced to leave their lands and perish in some unknown desert."[140] The Nashashibi Opposition, while initially supporting partition, under fierce popular pressure about-faced and condemned the report in strong language. The Palestinians asserted that the scheme gave the Jews the best land and seven-eighths of the Arab citrus groves. They also argued that once the Jewish state was flooded with immigrants, it would seek to expand at the Arab state's expense.[141]

In September the rebellion was resumed, with new vigor. Notables who opposed resuming the strike and violence were brushed aside; some, such as Khalil Taha, a Haifa citrus grower, who felt that a renewal would hurt the Arabs economically, were assassinated.[142] The infrastructure of the rebellion was still intact, the British having failed to defeat or disarm the rural bands during the first stage; additional arms and ammunition had been smuggled in during the lull.

It is not clear whether a formal decision to renew the rebellion was ever made by the AHC or any central leadership forum. But all that was needed was a spark—and it came on September 26, when Lewis Andrews, acting district commissioner of the Galilee, was assassinated in Nazareth by Arab gunmen.[143] The AHC once again went through the motions of moderation, formally condemning the murder,[144] while the mufti, from his sanctuary in the Haram ash Sharif, issued a public call for restraint and nonviolence.[145] But on October 1 the government declared the AHC and the regional National Committees illegal. Warrants were issued for the arrest of all AHC members, and Amin al-Husseini was dismissed from the presidency of the SMC. Nearly two hundred prominent Palestinians were rounded up, and a handful were deported to the Seychelles. On the night of October 12, dressed in Bedouin (or, in another version, women's) clothes, al-Husseini clambered down the walls of the Temple Mount compound, reached the coast, and fled by boat to Lebanon.[146] It is possible that just before his escape he convened a group of guerrilla leaders and instructed them to launch a wave of terror[147]—a wave that began on October 14.

Thereafter the revolt proceeded without a central command. Regional commanders and band chieftains forged local alliances and did much as they pleased. The rebellion's second and major stage was emphatically rural; most of the attacks occurred in the countryside and along the roads between towns, with occasional forays into the towns. The overwhelming majority of the rebel commanders were villagers or Bedouin.[148] The number of active participants in the rebellion grew from an estimated 1,000–3,000 in 1936 and early 1937 to between 2,500 and 7,500 in 1938, with an additional 6,000–15,000 part-timers.[149] During 1938 there were "hundreds" of bands, most of them part-time and small (eight–fifteen members).[150] However, many villagers, especially in the coastal and southern areas, were unenthusiastic about the renewed rebellion and refused to join it, mainly out of economic considerations.[151] By late 1938 rebel leaders were even admitting to Jewish officials that "most Palestinian Arabs do not want disturbances."[152]

Overall in 1937, the rebels launched 438 attacks—109 of them against the British police and military, 143 against Jewish settlements, and 109 against "Arab houses." Altogether, 97 persons were killed and 149 wounded.[153] The fighting intensified during 1938, dragged on until April–May 1939, and fizzled out completely in September. The rebellion had peaked during the summer and autumn of 1938, with much of the countryside and many of the towns temporarily falling under rebel sway. The prolongation uncovered and exacerbated the weaknesses of the rebels' organization and mindset. The bands "were [increasingly] torn by political, family and regional dissensions, [and] personal jealousies." The situation deteriorated as the months passed and British military pressure increased. British intelligence (and, to a small extent, the Haganah) exploited the deep cleavages in Palestinian society by sowing false information, setting rebel against rebel, rebel against villager, and villager against townsman.[154] Cases of *fellahin* informing the authorities about rebel movements became so common that one daily newspaper, *al-Jama'a al-Islamiya*, denounced them as "men in appearance but animals in feeling, sinning women who sell their bodies, harmful reptiles and poisonous snakes."[155]

In the cities the Nashashibis, who had severed their links with the AHC and the Husseinis in July 1937, kept aloof from the revolt, triggering a wave of Husseini terrorism against themselves and a power struggle—a low-key civil war within a revolt—in which the Husseinis tried to gain absolute dominance in the Palestinian Arab community. In response the Nashashibis and their allies drifted toward alignment with the British. More anonymous tipsters informing against rebel bands sparked more anti-Nashashibi terrorism. "Streams of blood are now dividing the two factions," Elias Sasson, a senior Jewish Agency Political Department official, wrote in April 1939.[156] Opposition supporters were beaten and intimidated; political moderates, those who sold land to Jews, informers, and Nashashibi supporters—all fell prey to Husseini gunmen. Some suspects were placed in pits with snakes and scorpions; others were flogged. The slain were often left for days in the street, families and clerics fearing to attend to burial.[157]

The AHC members who had evaded the British dragnet and settled abroad, such as Amin and Jamal al-Husseini, tried to regain control over the revolt but met with only limited success. Acting through the Damascus-based Central Committee of the National Jihad in Palestine they repeatedly appointed "commanders-in-chief" of the rebellion. Local leaders, however, ignored the committee's authority and orders. Toward the end of the rebellion, when rebel extortion and brutality against villagers and townspeople became common, the committee also tried to impose a measure of discipline in and between the bands, which often fought among themselves. But repeated orders to cease levying "taxes" or executing suspected miscreants were ignored,[158] and internal differences between rebel commanders frustrated every effort to organize a central command structure.[159] In mid-1938 the committee organized a council of major rebel leaders, called "the office of the Arab Rebellion in Palestine," to supervise all rebel activities. Again, differences and antagonisms between the members themselves and between the office and recalcitrant commanders left the rebellion without an effective central command.[160]

Despite its disorganization, lack of discipline, and internal feuding, the rebellion bit hard into British rule in Palestine. At times, especially in 1938, it may have seemed in Whitehall that Britain was about to lose its grip on the country. Early that year High Commissioner J. Arthur Wauchope, who had been identified since October 1936 with a soft line toward the rebels, was dismissed, and Sir Harold MacMichael, an Arabic scholar and former governor of Tanganyika, was appointed in his place, taking up his duties on March 3, 1938. But the military was given its head only in October, following the conclusion of the Munich Pact, which afforded Britain a respite from the threat of European war and left Whitehall free to send more troops and act more vigorously against the revolt.

Meanwhile Britain's problems in Palestine were aggravated by the advent of Jewish terrorism. Until mid-1937 the Jews had almost completely adhered to the policy of restraint. But the upsurge of Arab terrorism in October 1937 triggered a wave of Irgun bombings against Arab crowds and buses,[161] introducing a new dimension into the conflict. Before, Arabs (and, less frequently, and usually in retaliation, Jews[162]) had sniped at cars and pedestrians and occasionally lobbed a grenade, often killing or injuring a few bystanders or passengers. Now, for the first time, massive bombs were placed in crowded Arab centers, and dozens of people were indiscriminately murdered and maimed—for the first time more or less matching the numbers of Jews murdered in the Arab pogroms and rioting of 1929 and 1936. This "innovation" soon found Arab imitators and became something of a "tradition"; during the coming decades Palestine's (and, later, Israel's) marketplaces, bus stations, movie theaters, and other public buildings became routine targets, lending a particularly brutal flavor to the conflict.

The Irgun bombs of 1937–38 sowed terror in the Arab population and substantially increased its casualties. Until 1937 almost all of these had been caused by British security forces (including British-directed Jewish supernumeraries) and were mostly among the actual rebels, but from now on, a substantial proportion would be caused by Jews and suffered by random victims. The bombs do not appear in any way to have curtailed Arab terrorism, but they do appear to have helped persuade moderate Arabs of the need to resist Zionism and to support the rebellion.

The first Irgun attack occurred on November 11, 1937, killing two Arabs at a bus depot near Jaffa Street in Jerusalem, and wounding five. Three days later, on November 14, a number of Arabs were killed in simultaneous attacks around the country—a day that the Irgun thereafter commemorated as the "Day of the Breaking of the Havlaga (restraint)."[163] On July 6, 1938, an Irgun operative dressed as an Arab placed two large milk cans filled with TNT and shrapnel in the Arab market in downtown Haifa. The subsequent explosions killed twenty-one and wounded fifty-two.[164] On July 15 another bomb killed ten Arabs and wounded more than thirty in David Street in Jerusalem's Old City. A second bomb in the Haifa market—this time disguised as a large can of sour cucumbers—on July 25, 1938, killed at least thirty-nine Arabs and injured at least seventy.[165] On August 26, a bomb in Jaffa's vegetable market killed twenty-four Arabs and wounded thirty-nine.[166] The bombings were condemned by the Jewish Agency and the Yishuv's middle-of-the-road and left-wing political parties and press, which at first refused to believe that the terrorists were Jews.[167]

But the main Jewish response to the renewal of the revolt was a change in strategy and the establishment of new units by the Haganah, developments that were to have a major effect on the conflict down to 1948. "Pure defense" had come to be seen as relatively ineffective in safeguarding settlements and workers in the fields. The Haganah command ordered the creation of "field companies," whose main characteristic was mobility and whose chief function was to speedily aid attacked settlements and to patrol areas and roads between settlements. Yitzhak Sadeh was the driving force behind these units, which were doctrinally an outgrowth of his *nodedot*. The companies were swiftly trained and began functioning in spring 1938, under the command of Haganah district commanders rather than individual settlements, and usually in squad-sized patrols and ambushes.[168]

In early 1939, on Ben-Gurion's orders, Sadeh set up three highly secret squads known as the Pu"m (*pe'ulot meyuhadot,* "special operations"), for retaliatory strikes against Arab terrorists and villages and the elimination of informers. These units were used repeatedly during the last months of the Arab revolt and (also against British targets) during the months that followed. Ben-Gurion controlled the Pu"m directly, bypassing the Haganah general staff.[169]

A major influence on the Haganah's switch to an "aggressive defense" doctrine was Capt. Charles Orde Wingate, a young Scottish intelligence officer with the British Fifth Division. Zionist officials referred to him—both in code and with affection—as "the Friend" (*haYedid*). A mystical Christian philo-Zionist who hoped one day to stand at the head of an apocalyptic Jewish army, he persuaded his superiors to agree to the establishment of a force of Jewish troops and British NCOs, with himself in command, to guard the oil pipeline that ran from Iraq through the Jezreel Valley to Haifa and to prevent Arab attacks and punish saboteurs. About sixty British soldiers and one hundred Jews, many of them supernumerary policemen and Haganah members, participated. The patrols, called the Special Night Squads (SNS), began operating in the Galilee and Jezreel Valley from three kibbutz bases in June 1938. Wingate once told his troops: "The Arabs think that the night is theirs [as] the British troops and police shut themselves up in their camps during the night, but we, the Jews [*sic*], will show them that we can destroy their plans. We will not rest until a fear of the night, as of the day, assails them."[170]

During the first month of their activity the SNS ambushed and killed about sixty Arabs, occasionally launching retaliatory strikes against villages from which rebel bands had operated. Wingate, who was wounded in one such raid, was constantly on the move, training, planning, and leading operations. Sharett described Wingate, toward the end of this period, thus: "I found him completely weakened, his cheekbones stuck out and his eyes were testimony to many sleepless nights, but the internal flame in this extraordinary man burnt with extreme intensity."[171] The SNS were disbanded the following summer.

(Wingate later attained the rank of major general, and died in an air crash on March 24, 1944, in Burma, where he had led the native Burmese Chindit guerrillas against the Japanese.)

There were both Britons and Jews who feared that SNS operations would further antagonize the Arabs and disrupt neighborly relations, and it is possible that Wingate's tactics did have a marginal effect in deepening Arab antagonism. But his operations had a more important influence in shaping Haganah doctrine. In mid-1939, for example, a Haganah squad abducted and executed five villagers from Balad ash Sheikh, southeast of Haifa, after the murder of a Jewish locomotive driver. In a second attack a week later, on June 20, Pu"m, avenging the murder of a member of Kibbutz Afikim, raided a house in the nearby village of Lubiya, killing three people and wounding three others.[172] Such retaliatory behavior was to characterize the Haganah right through the first months of the 1948 war and the IDF in subsequent decades.

The rebellion triggered another major change, in intelligence. The Haganah's main regional headquarters (Tel Aviv and Haifa) had each maintained a minuscule local "intelligence service" (in Haifa, it consisted in the mid-1930s of one man), leaving intelligence-gathering to the Jewish Agency's Political Department and especially its Arab Division. Now the focus had to switch from political to military intelligence. Perpetrators of attacks had to be identified and chains of command traced. Advance warning of raids and intelligence about the flow of volunteers and arms from across the borders were also needed.

As the Peel Commission deliberated, the Arab Division set about laying down a network of Jewish controllers and Arab agents around the country. Merchants, farmers, postmen, delivery men, plumbers, waiters, shepherds, policemen, and cattle buyers—people with natural contacts in the villages and towns—were hired, and they recruited Arab agents, usually by brandishing fistfuls of Palestine pounds, but occasionally by exploiting clan rivalries or personal weaknesses. The key organizers were Ezra Danin and Reuven Zaslani. After the rebellion, in 1940–41, the Haganah and the division reorganized the existing networks into a national organization, called the Information Service (Sherut Yediot, or Shai). The Shai's Arab Department gathered intelligence on Palestine's Arabs while the Internal Department kept tabs on the dissident organizations, primarily the Irgun, Lehi (Stern gang), and the Communists, and the Political Department operated against the British and was responsible for political intelligence.[173]

Following Husseini's flight in October 1937, the centers of gravity of the second stage of the revolt shifted to lower and western Galilee and northern Samaria—areas that were adjacent to centers of Jewish population or were in locales in which Izz ad Din al-Qassam had been active.[174] A number of rebel bands were wiped out, but by August 1938 the Arabs controlled most of the hill country and some towns. Bands were active inside Jerusalem and Jaffa and periodically raided other towns. By September, according to a British report, "the situation was such that civil administration and control of the country was, to all practical purposes, non-existent."[175]

Some rebel bands focused their attacks on Jews rather than on the British. On October 2, raiders attacked the Kiryat Shmuel neighborhood in Tiberias, killing nineteen Jews (eleven of them children), torching the local synagogue, and murdering the curate.[176] A few weeks later, on October 27, Arabs murdered Tiberias's Jewish mayor, Zaki Alhadif.[177]

On October 15, rebel bands penetrated Jerusalem and completely occupied the Old City, hoisting their flag over the walls. By October 20, the army had retaken the area, having used local Arabs as human shields.

Earlier that month, as stated, Whitehall had decided to suppress the revolt with a firm hand. An additional brigade was sent out, bringing the total combat troop strength in Palestine to seventeen battalions, and a succession of repressive, sometimes savage, measures were introduced. Villages identified with the rebels were fined and punished; houses where rebels had hidden were destroyed;[178] orange groves and vineyards were uprooted.[179] Altogether, more than one hundred Arabs were hanged during 1937–39.[180] (One Jewish youngster was also hanged, for firing at an Arab bus, though he hit no one.[181]) Others, some of them related to rebel leaders, were occasionally tied to a flatbed in front of a locomotive in order to prevent sabotage. The Arab population was forced to carry ID cards and subjected to strict travel regulations, and orange exports were curtailed.

Other strategic measures were taken. Roads were laid through parts of the Samarian and Judean hill country to allow mechanized units easy access to remote villages, and a patrol road was built along the Palestine-Lebanon border. Initially, the army forced the *fellahin* to work on the roads without payment.[182] A barbed-wire fence—"Tegart's wall"—was constructed along the borders with Syria and Lebanon to prevent incursions and arms smuggling by rebel bands.

The relentless British pressure—though regularly criticized by the Jews as insufficient—gradually paid off. In the towns the military reoccupied rebel-held neighborhoods. The rural population gradually turned against the rebellion, its disaffection exacerbated by natural causes. A partial drought at the start of the winter of 1937–38 was aggravated by heavy rains toward its end, causing major damage to agriculture. Wheat production, which in 1936 amounted to 76,000 tons and in 1937 to 127,000 tons, fell in 1938 to 50,000 tons. There was also a considerable decline in vegetable production.[183]

During the second half of 1938, the British were substantially aided by Haganah intelligence, which supplied information about the rebel bands and their accomplices. The year saw 986 attacks on British police and military targets and 651 attacks on Jewish targets, with some 720 attacks on telegraph and telephone lines. Seventy-seven Britons and 255 Jews died. An estimated 1,000 rebels were killed that year by British and Jewish forces, and about 2,500 were interned.

THE END OF THE REVOLT

By the start of 1939, some rebel bands had been destroyed; some had lost their commanders or had fled across the Jordan, where Transjordan's army, the Arab Legion, killed or rounded them up. The rebellion had deteriorated into a free-for-all among the rebels themselves. More Arabs were being killed by fellow Palestinians than by the British or the Jews. In the countryside the bands clashed with one another over territory or loot, while villagers and townspeople increasingly resisted their efforts to extort "contributions" and other economic impositions. British counterpressure and rebel counter-counterpressures steadily increased, as did the gradual impoverishment of the rural communities. Psychological warfare also took its toll. Aircraft dropped thousands of leaflets over the villages, telling the *fellahin* that they were the chief sufferers from the rebellion and threatening an increase in taxes. Often the British behaved with great brutality.

Many villagers refused to give the rebels contributions and denied them haven. Some began on the sly to violate the boycott and sell produce to the Jews. The mukhtar of 'Amma was murdered because he refused to give the local rebel band PL50. Other people were beaten for refusing to join up, and some moved to town to avoid intimidation.[184] In Allar, west of Jerusalem, the villagers shot a visiting rebel commander. In January 1938 a Samarian leader, Abdallah al-Khader, complained: "When the fighters reached the village [of Bala'a], they were greeted by the inhabitants with all sorts of harsh and bad words. . . . The inhabitants . . . wanted . . . to steal their weapons . . . and afterwards decided that it was better to drive them out. [The villagers] said that if [al-Khader] came again to their village they would bring the army and order [*sic*] it to destroy all the rebels."[185]

Much of the villagers' anger was due to the repeated humiliations they suffered. In November 1938, according to a Haganah report, the main rebel leader in the Jerusalem area, 'Abd al-Qadir al-Husseini, humbled the elders of Walaja, 'Ein Karim, and Khirbet al-Lauz: "He ordered the *fellahin* to beat them in public. He slapped them . . . [and] ordered Isma' il al Khatib, a lawyer and notable of 'Ein Karim, to pass among the inhabitants while carrying his shoes between his teeth."[186]

By 1939 the intimidation had become unbearable. Ahmad Mahmoud

Hasan ("Abu Bakr"), a rebel commander from the Nablus area, described the situation in May in a letter to the Central Committee in Damascus:

> [W]e found that the spirit of the Revolt was waning. The behavior of the fighters towards the villagers is extremely tyrannical and horrifying: brutal robbery, execution without prior investigation. Conflicts without any reason, disorder, and complete inaction; and the villagers called upon God for help against such behavior. . . . I found the villagers despondent. . . . In the towns there is deep distrust. . . . The spies are everywhere and the loyalists [to the rebellion] crawl into corners.[187]

A few months earlier, in January 1939, a letter from rebel commander 'Abd al-Halim al-Jaulani was published in *The Times* (London) stating: "Complaints are received from the villages in the Jerusalem area regarding robbery, extortion, torture and murder committed by several people wearing the uniform of the Jihad. . . . How did the innocent sin so that their money is stolen, their cattle robbed, their women raped and their jewellery extorted? Our rebellion has become a rebellion against the villages and not against the government or the Jews."[188]

In Jaffa rural bands repeatedly entered the town to raise large "contributions"—so large and with such methods, in fact, that the Central Committee interceded. On December 26, 1938, the committee wrote to Mamduh al-Sukhun, its representative in Nablus, expressing "astonishment" at the PL60,000 "tax" being levied in Jaffa.[189] And it is clear from the repeated admonitions and warnings by the committee that the acts of extortion continued. No doubt, behind at least some of the friction, there was also an element of the traditional mutual rural-urban class antagonism, which was now exacerbated.[190]

Some bands, and also criminals, used the "cover" provided by the rebellion to extort and rob for personal gain. The committee wrote to one of the main commanders, probably 'Abd al-Rahim al-Hajj Muhammad ("Abu Kamal"), praising him for publishing a leaflet warning against using "the name of the rebellion for purposes of robbery and rapine, especially in Jaffa."[191]

The Central Committee and its representatives in Palestine also attempted, periodically, to gain control over the rebel bands and to instill a measure of discipline. Occasionally, the "High Court of Justice of the Rebellion in Palestine" tried, convicted, and sentenced people for deviant behavior. But many of its sentences, especially capital ones, were never executed. For example, Faris al-Azuni, a rebel leader in the western foothills of Samaria, was tried and sentenced to death by firing squad "for disobeying orders issued by the high command; threats to inhabitants, which turned them into enemies of the rebellion, and as a result the number of spies in the country multiplied; the murder of many innocent people . . . ; [and] the use of the weapons of the nation for private purposes." But the sentence was never carried out. After the rebellion, al-Azuni was caught in Syria, extradited to Palestine, and tried, convicted, and hanged by the Mandatory authorities.[192]

But the most important factors in the demise of the rebellion were the enlarged British military presence and its vigorous operations which resulted in the physical destruction of rebel bands, the asphyxiation of their supply routes, and the alienation of the rural population. Another factor was the violent split within the Arab camp, with the Opposition increasingly responding to Husseini terrorism and depredations by counterterrorism and collaboration with the British (and the Yishuv). As early as the winter of 1938, H. H. Wilson, an Englishman who taught at Bir Zeit College, near Ramallah, wrote that "the rebellion seemed now to be turning into a struggle between the two Arab political parties: The Mufti's faction . . . and the Nashashibis, who hoped to get the power away from them by making up to the British."[193] By the revolt's end, in spring 1939, the feuding was so intense that Raghib Nashashibi commented: "We may expect now that for fifty years the Arabs will kill one another to avenge what happened during the disturbances" (and, indeed, his nephew Fakhri Nashashibi was murdered in Baghdad in 1941, and another Opposition leader, Fakhri 'Abd al-Hadi, in Arabe in the Galilee, in 1943).[194]

It was to avoid this internecine killing and extortion that much of Palestine's elite fled the country for the duration.[195] Perhaps as many as thirty thousand Arabs left during 1936–39 (though most returned during World War II). In Beirut during the rebellion, the cafés were full of "Opposition Arabs fleeing from terrorists and of terrorists fleeing from the police."[196]

The exodus consisted largely of the urban elite. Villagers, who could not move out of harm's way so easily, coped by resisting and eventually fighting the rebels. A number of villages and village clusters, apparently without connection to the Nashashibi-Husseini antagonism, set up their own militia units. Such "peace bands," as they came to be known, sprang into existence in the Nablus area, on Mount Carmel (a stronghold of the Druze, who by and large, after 1937, opposed the rebellion[197]), and around Nazareth.[198]

There was also covert resistance, cases in which victims of terrorism or their relatives informed the British about rebel concentrations or operations, for personal or familial revenge.[199] For example, Farhan al-Sa'di, one of Qassam's old followers and a rebel leader, was captured and hanged in November 1937 after being betrayed by the Irshayid family, one of whom had been an informer and had been killed by the rebels. The Irshayids also supplied the information that led to the death of 'Abd al-Rahim al-Hajj Muhammad, the nominal commander-in-chief of the revolt, on March 26, 1939, at Sanur in Samaria. A similar act of betrayal led to the devastation of 'Abd al-Qadir al-Husseini's band near Hebron, in November 1938; al-Husseini himself was badly wounded.[200]

From December 1937 onward, principal Opposition figures approached the

Jewish Agency for money and other assistance with which to combat the Husseinis.[201] The Nashashibis seem to have received clandestine agency funding from early 1938, specifically to launch anti-rebel operations. In March, for example, Raghib Nashashibi asked for a PL5,000 "mortgage," half of which was to be spent "in suppressing terrorism and bringing peace to the country."[202] In July 1938 the Nashashibis began working with villagers in the Jerusalem-Ramallah area. Fakhri Nashashibi's recruitment of the "peace" bands was most successful in the Hebron hills; in one rally, in Yata, in December 1938 about three thousand villagers showed up (with the British military commander of the Jerusalem District, Gen. Richard Nugent O'Connor, also attending).[203]

Some of the peace bands were established through British and Zionist initiative, and were in part funded by the Mandatory authorities. Occasionally they coordinated operations with the British military. Officially Whitehall and Jerusalem were chary of encouraging them, perhaps fearing that open help to such groups might jeopardize the possibility of reaching a settlement with the rebels. But on the ground the British military and some senior officials, such as Alec Kirkbride, the district governor of the Galilee, were supportive.[204]

The fighting between the bands was not just a matter of rural self-defense in face of rebel extortion or an extension of the traditional Nashashibi-Husseini political struggle. Traditional regional family feuds also came into play. Bir Zeit, wrote Wilson, "was little better than a hornets' nest of long-standing family feuds, stirred up afresh in the hope of getting some advantage through the help of this or that party of rebels."[205] The revolt also seemed to bring to the fore, in certain areas, traditional Muslim-Christian antagonisms. Very few Christians participated in the revolt (only 4 of 282 identified rebel "officers" were Christians[206]), and most seem to have opposed it, in their hearts if not actively. The rebels knew this and retaliated, by extorting disproportionately large "contributions" from Christian villages and townspeople, and occasionally by punishing Christians (for example, by raping their daughters[207]). According to a Jewish intelligence report, Christian men in Jaffa were forced to wear traditional Arab headdress, and women a veil. Christian merchants were forced to close their shops on Friday as well as on Sunday.

By May 1939 the revolt was effectively over. Physically decimated, starved of supplies, without popular support, and its leaders dead, in exile, or incarcerated, the rebellion petered out. The authorities, no longer in need of the "peace" bands," dissolved them and confiscated their arms.

THE POLITICAL AFTERMATH

In November 1938 the British announced a basic reconsideration of their Palestine policy. Retreat from partition had been a year in the making. The resumption of the revolt in autumn 1937 had been a major factor; another was the fact that since the mid-1930s, the Empire had been under growing threat from Japan, Italy, and Germany. The possibility loomed that these separate threats might coalesce and bring on a new world war.

The Middle East, astride the route to India and the Far East, rich in oil resources and home to British military bases, was a crucial strategic area and had to be kept calm. The Palestine problem clearly undermined this need for quiet, and had the potential to alienate tens of millions of Arabs and hundreds of millions of Muslims. The Arabs counted for much more, strategically and economically, than the Yishuv and its Jewish supporters abroad. Moreover, the Jews ultimately had no alternative but to support Britain in any conflict with the Third Reich and its allies. The Arabs, on the other hand, with long-burning anti-imperialist resentments and no great admiration for Western democracy, could well plump for Hitler and Mussolini. They had to be bought off. The Middle East subcommittee of the Committee of Imperial Defense noted in its report of January 1939: "We feel it is necessary to point out at the outset . . . the strong feeling which exists in all Arab States in connection with British policy in Palestine. . . . We assume that, immediately on the outbreak of war, the necessary measures would be taken . . . in order to bring about a complete appeasement of Arab opinion in Palestine and in neighbouring countries."[208]

The Foreign Office had always believed partition was unworkable and would, in Foreign Secretary Eden's words, "bring Britain into a collision with the Arab countries and jeopardize British interests"; nothing would antagonize the Arab world more than partition of Palestine and the creation of a Jewish state.

On December 8, 1937, Prime Minister Neville Chamberlain's cabinet had in effect decided against Peel and partition. In March 1938 a "technical committee," headed by Sir John Woodhead, was appointed with the stated purpose of "ascertaining facts and . . . considering in detail the practical possibilities of a scheme of partition." But the terms of reference were in fact a sop to the Zionists—the true purpose was to bury partition. In December 1937, Chamberlain had already gone out of his way to declare that the Government had not accepted the Peel Commission's transfer recommendation.[209] By then Colonial Secretary Ormsby-Gore, once a supporter of Zionism, had lost his sympathy for it. In May 1938 he was to retire from office a broken man and was later to write: "The Arabs are treacherous and untrustworthy, the Jews greedy and, when freed from persecution, aggressive . . . the Arabs cannot be trusted to govern the Jews any more than the Jews can be trusted to govern the Arabs."[210]

The Woodhead Commission arrived in Palestine on April 27, 1938, and left on August 3 after hearing Zionist representatives and British officials. The Arabs completely boycotted it. But the expected tenor of its recommendations was clear to anyone with eyes to see and ears to hear (even though some of the Zionist leaders continued to hope against the evidence that the game was not fixed). Rather ingenuously, Commissioner Thomas Reid at one point told a Jewish Agency Executive member that "Zionism was not a wise movement for the Jews to foster. It was the same nationalism that we objected to in Hitler. The solution of the Jewish problem was that adopted by the Bolsheviks—assimilation."[211]

Reid's opinions were in complete unison with those of the Foreign Office mandarins: The Jews "have waited two thousand years for their 'home' . . . they can afford to wait a bit until we are better able to help them get their last pound of flesh."[212]

The commission published its report on November 9, simultaneously with a government White Paper rejecting partition.[213] The commission formally proposed a new partition scheme: The Galilee; a central area including Jerusalem, Bethlehem, and Jaffa; and the Negev were to remain under British rule, and the remainder divided between a minuscule Jewish state (stretching along the Mediterranean coast from Tel Aviv to Zikhron Ya'akov) and an Arab state (about six times as large, comprising the bulk of the Samarian and Judean hill country as well as the Gaza Strip). The report argued that the Peel scheme was unworkable as a "Jewish" state with a large Arab minority would present insoluble problems, a forcible transfer of Arabs was out of the question, and a "voluntary transfer" was "impossible to assume."[214] The report—as its authors understood—would remain a dead letter, as its proposed Jewish ministate was not only unacceptable to the Zionists but a far cry even from serving as a basis for negotiation. The accompanying White Paper was, in effect, a flat dismissal of the commission's proposal. Woodhead's examination, declared the government, had "shown that the political, administrative and financial difficulties involved in the proposal to create independent Arab and Jewish States inside Palestine are so great that this solution of the problem is impracticable."

Still, Whitehall faced an ongoing revolt in Palestine, and an open admission of defeat might tempt native populations elsewhere to rebel, and induce the dictators to up the ante in Europe or the Far East. A balance had to be struck for Britain to retain credibility. The government decided to crush the rebellion swiftly, and to appease the Arabs with political concessions so that the causes of the rebellion would disappear. Representatives of both sides and of the neighboring Arab states were invited to a conference in London where the modalities of coexistence could be hammered out. The mufti's participation was specifically ruled out: "His record over many years," as the British put it, "makes him wholly unacceptable."[215] They made it clear that should the parties fail to reach agreement, the Crown would be free to formulate a new policy on its own.[216] The British hoped that the presence of delegates from the Arab states might "moderate" Palestinian demands. They vaguely envisioned a future that would assure a permanent Jewish minority; an increase in communal self-rule, giving rise to autonomous cantons; and a Palestine that would be absorbed in a larger, Arab federal structure. In short, there would be neither a Jewish nor a Palestinian Arab state.

The Zionist leaders objected to the invitation to the Arab states and to the fact that they would not be talking directly with the Palestinians. The Arabs sensed victory even though several Palestinian leaders had been barred; violence seemed to be paying political dividends.[217] The London (St. James's) Conference convened on February 7, 1939, in the shadow of the waning but still bloody rebellion. (In 1939 rebel attacks claimed 37 British, 94 Jewish, and 414 Arab lives.) Egypt, Saudi Arabia, Yemen, Iraq, and Transjordan were invited (but not Syria and Lebanon, which were French mandates). Among the Palestinians there were fierce quarrels about who should go. The Husseinis vetoed Fakhri Nashashibi. The British released several AHC detainees, and eventually a delegation comprising representatives of both the AHC and its supporters and the Opposition was formed, with Jamal Husseini as president.

The conference, which, as the Arabs refused to negotiate directly, consisted in effect of separate Anglo-Arab and Anglo-Jewish colloquiums, was doomed to failure. The starting positions were too far apart and both Arabs and Jews thoroughly distrusted the British. The Arabs demanded a cessation of Jewish immigration and land purchases, and an independent state. The neighboring states agreed to support whatever solution the Palestinians accepted. The Jews, led by Ben-Gurion, were adamant that immigration continue, and opposed independence so long as the Arabs were in a majority.[218]

Britain initially insisted on its continued presence, and agreed to limit Jewish immigration to 80,000 to 100,000 during the next ten years. Within weeks, however, Britain agreed to limit immigration to 75,000 in the following five years, and to the principle of an independent Palestinian state, without defining a timetable. The Arabs rejected the proposals and the conference broke up on March 17. Days before, Germany had annexed the Czech part of Czechoslovakia, and Italy conquered Albania the following month. The Middle East was dragged into the unfolding global struggle, as Hitler used the suppression of the revolt to score propaganda points. Palestine, he declared at the end of April, "is having its liberty restricted by the most brutal resort to force, is being robbed of its independence, and is suffering the cruellest maltreatment for the benefit of Jewish interlopers."[219]

Britain's need to appease the Arabs seemed to grow day by day. "We are now compelled to consider the Palestine problem mainly from the point of view of its effect on the international situation. . . . If we must offend one side, let us offend the Jews rather than the Arabs," was Whitehall's bottom line, as enunciated by Chamberlain on April 20, 1939.[220] In a new statement of policy, the White Paper of May 17, 1939,[221] Britain proposed a ceiling of 75,000 on Jewish immigration during the next five years, after which all immigration would require Arab agreement. The White Paper put severe limitations on Jewish land purchasing, completely forbidding it in most districts, and proposed an independent Palestinian state with majority rule within ten years, Arab-Jewish relations permitting.

At this point the Palestinians made a major blunder ("they never missed an opportunity to miss an opportunity," as Abba Eban was later to point out). Having failed in the revolt and nonetheless having been offered major political concessions, the AHC turned around and rejected them, under pressure from the rebels, whose slogan remained, "The English to the sea and the Jews to the graves."[222] The AHC was dissatisfied mainly because the White Paper failed to call an immediate halt to Jewish immigration, and because independence had been deferred and made contingent on Arab-Jewish amity. The Nashashibi Opposition supported the paper ("a good augury," they called it) but Husseini won the AHC's support by a vote of 6 to 4. The Arab states, excepting Transjordan, closed ranks behind the AHC,[223] despite the fact that most Palestinians appeared to favor the paper. "The average Arab one spoke to was triumphant, regarding the White Paper as a concession won by Arab arms," wrote Wilson.[224] The White Paper was the main accomplishment of the rebellion. Husseini subsequently took great pains to justify his decision to reject it. His generally sympathetic Arab biographer, Philip Mattar, later wrote that the mufti's decision "clearly indicated that he was putting personal considerations and his idealism above practical politics."[225]

Though Whitehall's retreat from the Balfour Declaration and the spirit of the Mandate had been years in gestation, the White Paper was a grave shock to the Jews. Britain had turned its back on the idea of a National Home and had surrendered to Arab violence and intimidation at a time when European Jewry was being persecuted and battered. "The need of the Jewish People for a Home was never more acute," declared the Jewish Agency, "and its denial at this time is particularly harsh." The White Paper was denounced as "illegal," as it contradicted the terms of the Mandate, which could only be changed with the agreement of the Council of the League of Nations. The Yishuv declared that it would never acquiesce in the new British policy.[226] The Zionist Organization, and especially its powerful American chapter, vowed to fight it. In Britain, although the Conservatives had a comfortable majority in Parliament, the government was put on the defensive: Two cabinet ministers (Leslie Hore-Belisha and Walter Elliot) and 110 Conservative MPs abstained, and all of

Labour's MPs voted against. Also voting against were twenty Conservative dissidents including Churchill, who called the White Paper another Munich and "a surrender to Arab violence." Capping it all, the Permanent Mandates Commission of the Council of the League of Nations rejected the White Paper as inconsistent with the terms of the Mandate.[227]

While it alienated the Yishuv, the White Paper failed during the subsequent war years to cramp its development. Britain perhaps could no longer be relied upon to realize the dream of a Jewish state, and it would most likely back the Arabs in a showdown. But the White Paper had little effect. Palestine's Arabs remained a mortally stricken community. The Yishuv continued to develop apace: Immigration, affected more by events on the Continent than by British restrictions, continued; the economy burgeoned and the Haganah grew and gained priceless experience. The White Paper did not completely stop Jewish land purchases. A number of settlements were established in the course of the war, most of them in areas prohibited by the British.

If the Jews were left after 1939 with the bitter taste of the White Paper, the Arabs had to contend with the legacy of the failed revolt. Most of their political leadership was imprisoned, exiled, or driven out of politics and public service in disgust. Many, perhaps even most, Palestinian Arabs had breathed a secret sigh of relief when the revolt ended; now they could get back to their normal lives and recoup some of their economic losses.[228] But much of the upper and embryonic middle class was lastingly alienated from politics and many at least temporarily fled the country. Blood feuds between families that had supported the revolt and those who had opposed it were to disrupt society for years.[229] The rift between Husseini and Nashashibi supporters ran so deep that cooperation was impossible. As a result, during 1939–46, political life was paralyzed. The Palestinians were left dependent on the Arab states, whose leadership largely took the place of their own during 1939–48, with grave consequences during the events leading up to the war of 1948. They became "wards" of the Arab states—and were to remain so until 1976, when "Palestine" was accorded Arab League membership.[230]

Estimates put Arab dead in the revolt at between 3,000 and 6,000. One Israeli historian says that 4,500 were killed by other Arabs.[231] By the revolt's end, another 6,000 were in detention.[232] Among the dead, incarcerated, and exiled were many potential leaders, which was vitally to impair Palestinian power in 1948, as was the loss of arms in the course of the rebellion. Hundreds of Arab houses—perhaps as many as 2,000[233]—were destroyed either in the course of warfare or in British punitive actions. The financial cost was enormous. Apart from the losses caused by the general strike of 1936, there were swaths of devastated fields and crops, with many roadside groves and orchards uprooted.[234] The economic boycott of the Yishuv, which was instituted in late

1936 and continued through the revolt (though it was not universally honored), also cost the Arab community dearly, through loss of sales of goods and services, and heightened unemployment.[235]

The Jews' physical losses were relatively insignificant—several hundred people were killed and some property was destroyed or damaged, but no settlement was destroyed; indeed, about three dozen new ones were established during the revolt. More than 50,000 immigrants arrived, and development of the economy and infrastructure accelerated—the port in Tel Aviv, metal works to turn out armored sheeting for vehicles, primitive munitions plants to produce mines and grenades (17,500 of the latter were produced during the revolt). By 1940 the Haganah's arms factories were producing two- and three-inch mortars and mortar bombs. The Yishuv's transportation capabilities expanded to compensate for Arab trucks and buses which were no longer available. Unemployment was offset by the hiring of supernumerary policemen, the Histadrut's public works program, and infrastructure development.[236]

WORLD WAR II AND THE FIRST ARAB-ISRAELI WAR, 1939–49

WORLD WAR II

As the pogroms in Russia in the 1880s had launched modern Zionism, so the largest pogrom of all, the Holocaust, was to propel the movement, almost instantly, into statehood; and much as World War I had issued in the first international support for a Jewish "National Home," so the aftermath of World War II was to result in that decisive international warrant, the United Nations Partition Resolution of November 29, 1947, which was to underpin the emergence of the State of Israel.

The Zionist leadership greeted the outbreak of war with unequivocal declarations of allegiance to Britain. On September 3, the day Britain declared war on Germany, the Jewish Agency Executive announced:

> At this fateful moment, the Jewish community has a threefold concern: the protection of the Jewish homeland, the welfare of the Jewish people, [and] the victory of the British Empire. . . . The war which has now been forced upon Great Britain by Nazi Germany is our war, and all the assistance that we shall be able and permitted to give to the British Army and to the British people we shall render wholeheartedly.[1]

Even the Revisionists, who had embarked on an anti-British campaign of terrorism following the issuance of the White Paper, now offered a truce—and were soon to offer active military assistance. Only the minuscule Lohamei Herut Israel (Lehi, LHI, or the Stern gang), formed at this time by breakaways from the Revisionist Irgun, continued to adhere to a rigidly anti-British line.

The Zionists hoped that loyalty and wartime services would be repaid with the abrogation of the White Paper and support for Jewish statehood. But for the Arabs the war posed difficult choices. By tradition, they lacked any innate sympathy or affinity with democratic and Western values, but current realities also had to be considered: Britain physically controlled the Middle East and had large troop concentrations in Egypt, Palestine, and Iraq; adopting a forthright anti-Allied position could prove self-destructive. On the other hand, common sense dictated support for the future victor, and at least down to mid-1942 it appeared likely that Germany would win and perhaps overrun the Middle East. Hence calculations of expediency cut both ways.

But there were other, more closely felt factors. The British were seen by the Arabs as the protectors of Zionism, and the bitter memory of the crushing defeat of the Palestinian uprising of 1936–39 was still fresh. Support for the Axis seemed only natural, especially as Italian and German propaganda promised the Arabs independence after Britain's defeat. And many Egyptians, Iraqis, Syrians, and Lebanese had the same desire to get out from under the Western imperial boot. True, German racist beliefs and behavior may have put off some Arabs. But Germany was a long way away, while the hated British and French were all too present. The cataclysm of world war appeared to be a good opportunity to achieve complete independence.

Khalil Sakakini was not unrepresentative when he noted in his diary, in mid-1941, that the Arabs of Palestine "had rejoiced when the British bastion at Tobruk fell to the Germans." Indeed: "Not only the Palestinians rejoiced . . . but the whole Arab world, in Egypt and Palestine and Iraq and Syria and Lebanon, and not because they love the Germans, but because they dislike the English . . . because . . . of their policy in Palestine."[2]

The outbreak of war put the triangular struggle for Palestine on temporary hold. Of the major elements of the White Paper, only cessation of Jewish land purchases was fairly effectively implemented. Limiting immigration—to fifteen thousand per year for five years, starting in May 1939—proved more complicated. Since 1934 illegal immigrants had been smuggled into the country, mainly by sea. As the noose tightened around the neck of European Jewry, the Zionist leadership became increasingly desperate. It was not so much fear that the Jews faced annihilation as that the pool of potential *olim*—which could supply the critical mass needed to push on to statehood—was about to dry up, and that the whole Zionist enterprise might thus founder.

Ben-Gurion remarked in December 1938 (a month after the Nazis' pogrom against Germany's Jews, known as *Kristallnacht,* but two years before the start of the Holocaust): "If I knew it was possible to save all the [Jewish] children of Germany by their transfer to England and only half of them by transferring them to Eretz-Yisrael, I would choose the latter—because we are faced not only with the accounting of these children but also with the historical accounting of the Jewish People."[3] Ben-Gurion viewed the Holocaust primarily through the prism of its effect on the Yishuv. "The catastrophe of European Jewry is not, in a direct manner, my business," he said in December 1942.[4]

And, "The destruction of European Jewry is the death-knell of Zionism." In the words of Yitzhak Gruenbaum, a member of the Jewish Agency Executive, "Zionism is above everything."[5]

In mid-1941, after the Germans had started massacring Jews on a large scale but before it was known or, at least, *believed* in Palestine, Ben-Gurion spoke of the need to move three million Jews there over the next ten years. The Colonial Office spoke of a similar number of anticipated postwar refugees— but it opposed their resettlement in Palestine.[6]

The last months of peace and the first months of the war saw a surge of rickety, Haganah-commanded, refugee-laden ships set sail from Balkan ports for Palestine, though such men as Chaim Weizmann, president of the World Zionist Organization, opposed the operation, believing that illegal immigration would do the cause more harm (by provoking the British) than good. In any event, due to the Zionists' meager means, the sealing off of large parts of Europe, and British interference, the campaign never amounted to much, though combating it caused Britain political embarrassment. During the period 1934–38 about forty thousand Jews had entered Palestine illegally, and another nine thousand by September 1939. But less than sixteen thousand made it during the following six years, when the need for sanctuary was at its most acute.[7]

The British viewed illegal immigration as a challenge to the White Paper and to their rule in Palestine, and consequently, as a threat to their position in the Middle East. Given the conflict that already strained resources to the utmost, it is little wonder that Whitehall resorted to severe, sometimes brutal, measures to stop the campaign. At first, they attempted to deport captured individuals back to their countries of origin. This quickly proved impossible (in 1939 only forty-three Jews were so deported; in 1940, seventy-two[8]). For a time, in 1939–40, they resolved to suspend legal immigration until the illegal traffic was stopped. Subsequently they deducted the known illegal entry totals from the annual legal quota of fifteen thousand. Pressure was applied to Balkan states, particularly Rumania and Turkey, to stop the ships from sailing.

In the end, however, Whitehall adopted a policy of capturing and deporting the immigrants en masse to special island camps, in Mauritius and eventually Cyprus. In November 1940 the Haganah tried to subvert the policy by blowing up the *Patria,* a tramp steamer docked in Haifa and crowded with more than 1,700 illegal immigrants from Rumania who were about to be shipped to Mauritius. Miscalculating the explosive charge, the sappers killed 252 of the refugees.

The following month the LHI bombed the immigration office in Haifa to protest Britain's policy. But thousands of Jewish refugees were to spend the war years and beyond in camps in Cyprus, reaching Palestine only after the establishment of the State of Israel. Given the circumstances of global war and strict censorship, the British proved able to weather the occasional tragedy or embarrassment. Thus, when the *Struma,* a ramshackle steamer out of Constantsa, Rumania, with 769 Jewish emigrants aboard, was torpedoed and sunk, probably by a Soviet submarine, in the Black Sea on February 25, 1942, with only one survivor, there were few political waves, though the incident was directly traceable to a British veto on the transshipment of these refugees to Palestine, and British pressure on Ankara. The only change it wrought in Whitehall was the formal cessation of the policy of returning refugees to Europe when caught.[9]

From the Zionist viewpoint, the illegal-immigration campaign was both a disaster and a boon. By September 30, 1941, the midpoint in the White Paper's five-year period, nearly 35,000 Jews had arrived in Palestine, legally and illegally—less than half the 75,000 stipulated. By March 31, 1944, the number was still 20,000 short of the limit.[10]

Very few people were saved from Hitler's death camps or added to the Yishuv's population register; but British policy was highlighted as inhumane, and the need for a sanctuary for the world's oppressed Jews was made clear to the community of nations, especially the United States. The Royal Navy and the security forces in Palestine had managed to keep Jewish immigration down and the Arabs quiescent, but the persistent, cumulative embarrassment that the policy engendered was among the factors that led to Britain's eventual withdrawal from Palestine after the war. Ben-Gurion is said to have greeted the outbreak of war by saying: "We shall fight the White Paper as if there is no war, and we shall fight the war as if there is no White Paper." But in fact the Yishuv confined its struggle against the British to the sphere of illegal immigration. In all else the Yishuv (save for the LHI) laid down its grievances and weapons and joined the war against the Nazis. "Above our regret and bitterness [toward Britain] are higher interests. . . . What the democracies are fighting for is the minimum . . . necessary for Jewish life. Their anxiety is our anxiety, their war our war," explained Weizmann.[11]

The implementation of the White Paper's call for constitutional change that would lead to eventual Arab self-government and dominance in Palestine was shelved for several reasons: internal Arab disarray, Zionist opposition, Whitehall's resentment of the pro-Axis actions of many Arabs, the more pressing tasks at hand, and the fact that the pro-Zionist Churchill was at the helm of government. In general, Britain was loath to do anything that might antagonize American Jewry and hence Washington. Whitehall never got around to appointing Arab heads of Mandatory government departments, the necessary first step on the road to self-government, and repeatedly postponed the establishment of an Executive Council (the mooted Arab-dominated advisory body to the high commissioner).

The Allied defeats in 1939–40 and the Axis gains in North Africa in 1940–41 had a dual effect. They tended to reinforce Britain's desire to appease the Arabs—anything to keep Palestine and the Middle East quiet. But they also tended to persuade the Arabs to support the Axis, creating antipathy among

British officials toward them and their political aspirations. In May–June 1940 the exiled ex-mufti, Amin al-Husseini, reportedly sent agents to Palestine to look into the possibility of inciting a new revolt[12] — but Palestine, which served as a rear base for the British Eighth Army, was awash with Allied troops, and the inhabitants were enjoying an unprecedented bout of prosperity.[13]

Elsewhere in the Middle East, circumstances were more propitious. In Baghdad in April 1941 the Iraqi military, led by deposed Prime Minister Rashid 'Ali al-Kilani, rose in Axis-supported revolt. Britain's fortunes were at a low ebb: General Erwin Rommel's Afrika Korps, encamped in Libya, was potentially poised to invade the Nile Valley. Eclipsing the pro-British Hashemite regime, Rashid 'Ali returned to the premiership and offered Germany air bases and other facilities. But the Reich, husbanding its resources for the coming onslaught on Russia, sent only a squadron of fighter aircraft.

The rebels were assisted by hundreds of Palestinian exiles, including al-Husseini, who appears to have enjoyed subsidies from both the Iraqi government and Berlin. Once Baghdad had fallen to the rebels, he issued a *fatwa* (religious ruling), calling by radio on all Muslims to join in a *jihad* against Britain. But apart from some riots in Syria, he had little success in spreading the conflagration to the rest of the Levant.[14] The British reacted with dispatch; oil and vital supply lines were at stake. On April 18 they landed troops at Basra and marched on Baghdad. At the same time a mixed force of Arab Legionnaires and British troops took the land route from Transjordan. By May 29 it was all over, save for extensive looting and a pogrom by locals on June 1–2 against Baghdad's Jews, in which 120 persons were killed.

Husseini fled to Berlin, where a Foreign Ministry spokesman greeted him as "a great champion of Arab liberation and the most distinguished antagonist of England and Jewry."[15] He had thrown in his lot with the Reich (even though Hitler had once called the Arabs "half-apes"[16]). Amply financed, he was installed as one of the directors in Berlin of a new Arab Office, whose function was to broadcast propaganda and mobilize Arab and Muslim support for the Axis. He also traveled to Yugoslavia and Albania to recruit Muslim prisoners of war for an "Arab Legion" to fight alongside the Axis armies in the East. Occasionally he briefed Arabs about to be parachuted into the Levant as saboteurs.[17] He was later to explain why the Germans had turned on the Jews:

> In return for the [Balfour] Declaration . . . the Jews filled a central role in acts of sabotage and destructive propaganda inside Germany [in World War I]. . . . They acted in every way to bring about its destruction. This was the main reason for Hitler's war against the Jews and for his strong hatred of them. They brought catastrophe upon Germany [in World War I], even though it was winning militarily. Germany's revenge on the Jews was fierce: and it destroyed millions of them during World War II.[18]

On November 28, 1941, al-Husseini met Hitler and promised to organize a new, pan-Arab revolt (similar to the one Hussein, the sharif of Mecca, had organized against the Turks in World War I); and like the British in World War I, Hitler promised the Arabs postwar independence (as well as the abolition of the Jewish National Home). Hitler apparently liked what he heard and saw, including Husseini's blue eyes; he said Husseini must have had "more than one Aryan among his ancestors and one who may be descended from the best Roman stock."[19]

During 1943–44 Husseini wrote to Eastern European leaders asking that they bar the emigration to Palestine of hundreds of Jewish children and adults. In a letter to the Hungarian foreign minister, he suggested that the children be sent to Poland, under German supervision.[20] Whether Husseini was fully aware of the Holocaust, approved of it, or directly aided the Nazis in its implementation, he had without doubt "cooperated with the most barbaric regime in modern times," even in the understated words of his generally sympathetic Arab biographer.[21]

Husseini's activities would weigh against the Palestinians during the following years. Churchill, who replaced Chamberlain as prime minister on May 10, 1940, had never had any great liking for the Arabs, and repeatedly lambasted the "treacherous" Iraqi revolt and the Palestinian support it had enjoyed. Britain, he came to feel, owed the Arabs nothing in a postwar settlement. He found the White Paper's appeasement of them humiliating and politically self-defeating. In April 1943 he said: "I cannot agree that the White Paper is 'the firmly established policy' of the present Government. I have always regarded it as a gross breach of faith committed by the Chamberlain Government in respect of obligations to which I personally was a party."[22]

The anti-Arab feeling in Whitehall was reinforced by the Zionists' readiness to help the war effort. In 1940–41, with the Italians and Rommel at the gates of Egypt, thousands of Palestinian Jews rushed to the colors. Their eagerness to join up was curtailed only by British reluctance to have them. (Eventually from 25,000 to 28,000 of them were to serve in the British Army during the war, with thousands more enlisting as special auxiliary policemen.) Jewish scouts from Palestine assisted the Allied advance into Vichy-controlled Syria and Lebanon in 1941 (it was there that Moshe Dayan lost an eye) and an IZL team, including its commander, David Raziel, assisted in the British push on Baghdad that spring (Raziel was killed by a strafing German aircraft during the campaign). British officials, however, remained acutely mindful of the need to keep the Arab areas of the Middle East—with their vital waterways and land routes—trouble-free, and the area's oil available and flowing.

In this context, during the first years of the war plans were put forward for an Arab "federation" to include Palestine, which might be divided into Arab and Jewish cantons, or ministates, as part of the postwar settlement. But the idea did not attract significant Arab support,[23] and British officials noted the incompatibility of promoting Middle Eastern federation while supporting Jewish national aspirations.

The Palestinian Arab leadership, most of it still in exile, remained silent if not downright contrary about proposals for both constitutional change within the Mandate and a regional Arab "federation." Even more significant was the opposition of the high commissioner himself. Sir Harold MacMichael wrote to the Foreign Office: "I regard it as a fallacy to suppose that to give a few Heads of Departments to Palestinians is likely to turn the politicians of Egypt, Syria and Iraq into likely allies or do more than convince them that we are on the run. The only thing that will achieve the end desired is success in the field of war."[24]

Indeed, MacMichael argued that, despite declining Allied fortunes, Palestine remained quiet; concessions would only whet pan-Arab appetites and cause renewed turmoil.[25] By October 1942 British victories had substantially eroded the urgency for appeasement.

From the start of the war, the Zionists had pressed the British to organize and train a Jewish "army," a demand that enjoyed Churchill's support, at least on paper. In October 1939 he had proposed recruiting several thousand Palestinian Jews to keep law and order in the country and free the British garrison to fight in Europe.[26] Both sides understood that the Jews' offer was partly motivated by the need for a corps of trained troops to protect the Yishuv against the Arabs after the war. And it was understood that, as Colonial Secretary Lord George Lloyd put it bluntly in 1940: "The conversion of Palestine into a Jewish State as a reward for Jewish military assistance is the objective."[27] The Arabs, of course, opposed the creation of a Jewish army, and the British government therefore viewed the idea gingerly. MacMichael even argued that such a force after the war might be used against the Mandatory government itself.[28]

In 1940 the Zionists won an initial, small victory: The British agreed to the raising in Palestine of two battalions—one Jewish, one Arab—to be deployed on guard duty around vital installations. But it was not until September 1944 that Churchill at last pushed down Whitehall's throat the decision to set up a Jewish Brigade, with its own distinct blue-and-white flag. The formation saw action in Italy during the dying months of the war.[29]

THE BILTMORE PROGRAM

In October 1941 Churchill wrote in a secret Cabinet minute: "I may say at once that if Britain and the United States emerge victorious from the war, the creation of a great Jewish state in Palestine inhabited [*sic*] by millions of Jews will be one of the leading features of the Peace Conference discussions."[30]

And two years later Churchill was said to have declared that he intended to see to it that there would be a Jewish state.[31] For the Zionists the quest for statehood had quickened in the tragic circumstances of the Holocaust into a desperate resolve. In July 1942, the Polish government-in-exile in London reported that 700,000 of that country's Jews had already been murdered; in December, Eden told the House of Commons of "hundreds of thousands" of victims.[32]

On September 8, 1939, Ben-Gurion had told the commanders of the Haganah: "The First World War . . . had given us the Balfour Declaration. This time we must bring about a Jewish State."[33] The goal of statehood was thereafter to dominate his thinking. He was soon joined by Weizmann, still the formal head of the Zionist movement. In January 1942 Weizmann, in an article in *Foreign Affairs,* explicitly demanded the establishment of a Jewish state in all of the area west of the River Jordan.[34]

In May 1942 an Extraordinary Zionist Conference in New York, attended by American and European leaders as well as three members of the Palestine Jewish Agency Executive, voted to support what became known as the Biltmore Program, for the hotel in which they met. The program was drafted by Meyer Weisgal, Weizmann's aide, but its essence was later always to be identified with Ben-Gurion. It called for "Palestine to be established as a Jewish Commonwealth integrated in the structure of the new democratic world . . ."; the possibility that the state would be established only in part of Palestine was implicit. The Jewish Agency was to have control of immigration and the development of the country.[35] Ben-Gurion hoped immediately to bring in two million Jews, a number Weizmann dismissed as unfeasible.[36]

In the months before the conference both Weizmann and Ben-Gurion had expressed support for the transfer of the Arabs—preferably in a voluntary move, but by compulsion if necessary. On January 30, 1941, Weizmann met the Soviet ambassador to London, Ivan Maisky. The Zionist report on the meeting read, in part: "Dr. Weizmann said that if half a million Arabs could be transferred, two million Jews could be put in their place. That, of course, would be a first instalment; what might happen afterwards was a matter for history. . . . Weizmann said that . . . they would be transferring the Arabs only into Iraq or Transjordan . . . conditions in Transjordan were not very different from those of the Palestine hill country."[37]

In October 1941 Ben-Gurion set out his thinking on transfer in a memorandum entitled "Outlines of Zionist Policy." He paid the necessary lip service to the traditional Zionist position on the benefits Jews could bring to Palestine without displacing any Arabs, and how neighboring Arab states could easily absorb all of the country's Arabs in the event of transfer. But, he wrote:

"Complete transfer without compulsion—and ruthless compulsion at that—is hardly imaginable." Some—Circassians, Druze, Bedouin, Shi'ites, tenant farmers, and landless laborers—could be persuaded to leave. But "the majority of the Arabs could hardly be expected to leave voluntarily within the short period of time which can materially affect our problem." He concluded that the Jews should not "discourage other people, British or American, who favour transfer from advocating this course, but we should in no way make it part of our programme." As to those Arabs remaining in the prospective Jewish State, they must be treated as equals, even though "our country may . . . suffer from the presence of a considerable illiterate and backward population, and so may our relations with the neighboring Arab countries."[38]

With the support of the American Zionists, Ben-Gurion pushed the Biltmore Program through the Inner Zionist General Council in Jerusalem in August 1942, thus making it the official policy of the Yishuv. A state was now—at last, publicly—what Zionism was all about. Sharett may have dubbed the program "somewhat utopian,"[39] but it was to remain the accepted agenda and, by fits and starts, was to guide the movement to the promised shores of statehood in 1947–48.

As the Peel Commission report had in 1937, the Biltmore Program triggered bitter controversies within the Zionist movement. The group called Faction B (Si'ah Bet), soon to become HaTnu'ah LeAhdut Ha'Avoda (the movement for labor unity), split with Ben-Gurion's mainstream Mapai after refusing to agree to the compromise implicit in Biltmore: that the state would encompass only part of Palestine. Others, such as Weizmann himself, preferred to soft-pedal the demand for statehood. Ben-Gurion resigned in October 1943 as chairman of the Jewish Agency Executive, with the aim of forcing Weizmann back on track, or out of office (he was president of the World Zionist Organization) altogether.[40] In March 1944 Ben-Gurion "reluctantly" agreed to return to office, and in August 1944, in two sets of internal elections (for the Elected Assembly and the Histadrut Executive), finally won the contest. His supporters garnered from 58 to 66 percent of the votes.[41]

But Weizmann's eclipse was not really caused by Biltmore. From its inception and until the mid-1930s, Europe had constituted Zionism's chief base, and Weizmann was the quintessential European. The destruction of European Jewry turned him into a leader without a constituency. The major power centers were now in Palestine and, to a lesser extent, the United States. It was thus natural for that consummate politician Ben-Gurion, head of the Jewish Agency Executive since 1935 and of mainstream Palestinian Zionism, to gain pride of place in the movement as a whole.

Underlying all the disputes between the two men were Weizmann's continued faith in the power of diplomacy and, specifically, in British goodwill—especially after Churchill took the helm—and Ben-Gurion's distrust of those same factors. Ben-Gurion, who matured as a politician on the hard soil of

Palestine, preferred action to faith, facts to talk.[42] The clash between the two men finally ended with Ben-Gurion's complete victory in 1946. Ultimately it was Whitehall's rejection of Jewish statehood that undermined Weizmann. At the Zionist Congress of January 1946 he was removed by Ben-Gurion and his supporters from the presidency of the World Zionist Organization. And, not satisfied with victory, the vindictive Ben-Gurion was to hound him during the years that remained before his death in 1952. To be sure, the ailing elder statesman was installed in 1949 in the (politically neutered) presidency of the State of Israel; but he was firmly kept away from any exercise of influence and was even prevented from signing the new state's Declaration of Independence.[43]

The British victory in North Africa in October 1942 and the Russian victories in Stalingrad and the Caucasus that winter dispelled the German threat to the Middle East, but Britain continued to appease its Arab clients, in order not to rock the boat before the war was won and, in the long term, to exclude American and/or Soviet influence from the region.[44] The war had underlined the region's crucial importance: Oil reserves and production facilities were to become a major issue in the consideration of the postwar future. Moreover, its potential as a vast market for Western goods was beginning to emerge.

But there was a surge of sympathy for the Jews, precipitated by the information gradually leaking out of Europe since mid-1941, and culminating in a formal announcement by the Allies in December 1942, that Hitler was engaged in mass murder of the Jews. The news of the Holocaust seemed to render irrefutable the need for a Palestinian sanctuary. Moreover, American Zionists were gradually pushing a reluctant Democratic administration toward support of Jewish statehood, something Whitehall could not ignore. When the war ended, the problem of the "displaced persons" (DPs) only aggravated the situation. Hundreds of thousands of Jewish survivors refused to remain anywhere near the killing fields, the Western European countries and the United States were unwilling to take them in, and the Zionists wanted them in Palestine.

During 1943–45 Washington continued to view Palestine as London's headache, while in Whitehall, the cumulative thrust of past policy, and a bevy of pro-Arab bureaucrats, prevented the formal abrogation of the White Paper. But in mid-1943 Churchill managed to put together a special cabinet committee, packed with pro-Zionists, to prepare for the postwar settlement. It resurrected the Peel Commission's principle of partition, which the full cabinet endorsed in January 1944, leaving the exact geographical details undefined.[45]

The proposal was that partition "be implemented as soon as the necessary arrangements could be made." But implementation was stymied by a rearguard action in Whitehall. The Chiefs of Staff Committee argued that "the Arab States will object," and the Foreign Office maintained that "the solution to the Palestine question . . . should [not] be determined solely on the basis of world sympathy with the sufferings of the Jews, as contrasted with the alleged failure of the Arabs to assist the war effort."[46] The new scheme, the Foreign Office felt, was a breach of good faith: "When we wanted to keep [the Arabs] quiet, in 1939, we produced the White Paper, but when, after the war, our international difficulties were eased, we decided to betray Arab interests."[47]

Then, on November 6, 1944, Lord Moyne, the British minister resident in the Middle East, was shot dead by LHI terrorists in Cairo.[48] Moyne had been a close friend of Churchill, who took the murder as a personal affront and told the House of Commons: "If our dreams for Zionism are to end in the smoke of assassins' pistols and our labours for its future to produce only a new set of gangsters worthy of Nazi Germany, many like myself will have to reconsider the position we have maintained so consistently in the past."[49]

And he personally prodded the Egyptian government to execute the assassins, who were duly hanged the following March,[50] and withdrew his support of the partition scheme. On July 27, 1945, Churchill and the Conservatives were swept from office, and the Labour Party took over, led by Clement Attlee. The Zionists were now in a completely different ballgame. Though the Labour platform supported Jewish statehood and even transfer, decision-making remained in the hands of the new foreign secretary, Ernest Bevin—a man without a soft spot for Zionism and given to anti-Semitic asides, who thought that Britain's vital interests required support for the Arabs—the cabinet, and the military chiefs.

But during the two-and-a-half years between the end of the war and the start of Arab-Jewish hostilities at the end of 1947, developments in the United States, Palestine, and continental Europe proved more important than the mindset of Whitehall. In Washington the battle for support was decisively won by the Zionists, because of the impact of the Holocaust, effective propaganda, and the electoral and financial clout of the five million American Jews. Until 1944 the administration of President Franklin D. Roosevelt had managed to desist from anything but insignificant expressions of sympathy for Zionism. True, the plight of European Jewry weighed heavily; but American global interests, primarily oil, clearly militated in the other direction. In May 1943 Roosevelt had assured King Ibn Saud that both Arabs and Jews would be heard before a decision was made on the postwar settlement in Palestine.

In March 1944 a shift of attitude began. The White House, under pressure from Arabist officials, persuaded Congress to withdraw a joint resolution calling on Britain to rescind the White Paper and supporting a Jewish state. But, at the same time, Roosevelt assured the Jews that "full justice will be done [after the war] to those who seek a Jewish national home, for which our Government and the American People have always had the deepest sympathy and today more than ever in view of the tragic plight of hundreds of thousands of homeless Jewish refugees."[51]

At Yalta, in February 1945, Roosevelt described himself to Stalin as "a Zionist" (as did the Soviet dictator, though he added that Jews were "middlemen, profiteers, and parasites").[52] The following month Roosevelt assured Ibn Saud that he would support "no action . . . that would prove hostile to the Arab people,"[53] but the growingly Zionist orientation of American public opinion and officialdom proved inexorable. After Roosevelt's death in April, his marginally more pro-Zionist successor Harry S. Truman came out, at the Potsdam summit in August, in support of resettling Jewish DPs in Palestine,[54] and asked Churchill to lift the restrictions on immigration (in response to which the new Arab League's secretary general, 'Abd al-Rahman 'Azzam, declared that this could touch off a new war between Christianity and Islam[55]).

For Palestine's Arabs the war passed without significant change. Their financial assets grew substantially as a result of Allied spending and investment,[56] but militarily and politically, things remained much the same. Few—perhaps five to six thousand men—joined the Allied armed forces or otherwise gained military experience; there was no increment in local military force or organization. And the political (and military) leadership that had been shattered and scattered in 1938–39 remained in exile, neutralized or *hors de combat*.

By mid-1943 it had become clear that the Allies would win the war. To gain anything Palestine's Arabs would require leadership and organization. The former heads of the Istiqlal Party launched an effort to reunite the nationalists, and in November, the fifteenth conference of the Palestinian Arab chambers of commerce met in Jerusalem and set in motion a process to elect new national representation.[57] Owing to the Husseinis' opposition, matters were delayed. But they too began to reorganize. Their major figures were in exile—Hajj Amin in Berlin, serving the Nazis, and Jamal al-Husseini interned in Southern Rhodesia. But in April 1944 the remaining local leadership formally relaunched the Palestine Arab Party; by September the Husseinis were once again the most active and powerful faction,[58] and they led nationwide protests on November 2, Balfour Declaration Day.

This "repoliticization" of the Palestinian community coincided with a British-supported drive for Arab unity. From September 25 to October 7, delegates from seven countries met in Alexandria to found the Arab League, and on March 22, 1945, its pact was formally signed in Cairo.[59] The Palestinians sent Jericho notable Musa al-Alami to the gathering in Alexandria. At first he was designated an "observer," but by the end of the conference he was recognized as a "delegate," the Palestinian community thus enjoying, at least theoretically, an equal footing with the Arab states.

One section of the conference's "Alexandria Protocol" stated: "The rights of the Arabs [of Palestine] cannot be touched without prejudice to peace and stability in the Arab world." The Arab states declared that they were "second to none in regretting the woes which have been inflicted on the Jews of Europe. . . . But the question of these Jews should not be confused with Zionism, for there can be no greater injustice and aggression than solving the problem of the Jews of Europe by . . . inflicting injustice on the Palestine Arabs."[60]

In early 1945 Egypt, Syria, Lebanon, and Saudi Arabia declared war on the Axis, thus assuring themselves membership in the nascent United Nations and a voice in the peace settlement.

The Arab League states collectively put their weight behind the basic demands of Palestine's Arabs but arrogated to themselves the right to select who would represent the Palestinians in their councils, so long as their country was not independent. This, coupled with the deadlock within Palestine, meant that "the initiative in Palestine Arab politics . . . passed to the heads of the Arab states" and "major political decisions on the organization of Arab resistance to Zionism were thereafter taken not at Jerusalem but at Cairo."[61]

And, indeed, it was at the initiative of the Arab League that in November 1945 the Arab Higher Committee was reestablished as the supreme executive body of the Palestine community. A twelve-member committee was appointed, with five Husseini representatives, two independents, and five other members representing the other (now resurrected) pre-1939 parties.[62] But the return of Jamal al-Husseini precipitated quarreling and the disbanding of the committee in March 1946. The opposition set up its own Arab Higher Front (AHF) and Jamal reconstituted the AHC with Husseini family members and affiliates. In June the Arab League foreign ministers imposed upon the Palestinians a new leadership body, the Arab Higher Executive (AHE), with Amin al-Husseini as (absentee) chairman and Jamal al-Husseini as vice-chairman. The Husseinis were now firmly back in the saddle, this time with the imprimatur of the Arab League. Hajj Amin returned to the Middle East and began directing Palestinian affairs from Cairo.[63] In January 1947 he expanded the AHE—now again called the AHC—to nine members, all of them Husseinis or Husseini supporters.[64] The Palestinian Arabs appeared once more to have a somewhat unified, if not particularly representative, leadership.

THE YISHUV RISES

Developments in the Zionist camp proved far more significant. The approaching end of the war obviated the need to maintain solidarity with Britain. Moreover, a home had to be found for the survivors of the Holocaust, but the cabinet in London, the Royal Navy in the Mediterranean, and the security forces in Palestine stood between the DPs and the shores of the Promised Land. On September 27, 1945, the Zionist leadership proclaimed that the blockade was "tantamount to a death sentence upon . . . those liberated Jews . . . still languishing in the internment camps of Germany."[65]

A revolt that had been postponed for six years was now about to break out.

In May 1943 General Harold Alexander, commander of Britain's forces in the Middle East, had warned of the "probability" of revolt after the war: "[The] Jews mean business and are armed and trained."[66] In mid-1942 MI6, Britain's foreign intelligence agency, had estimated, fairly accurately, that the Haganah had thirty thousand members, with arms for 50 to 70 percent of them. The IZL could field another one thousand trained men, with several thousand more supporters and auxiliaries.[67] Jewish estimates put Haganah strength in 1944 at 36,000, with about 14,000 light weapons, including some two- and three-inch mortars and machine guns.[68]

The Yishuv had not wasted the war years. Tens of thousands of its men had joined the Allied (principally, the British) armies and acquired a measure of military training; arms had been stolen or illegally purchased by the Haganah from the vast British stockpiles in Palestine and Egypt. Most significantly, in May–June 1941 the Haganah—with British assistance—had established the Palmah (an abbreviation of *plugot mahatz*, "shock companies"), a fully mobilized strike force, headed by Yitzhak Sadeh, the veteran Red Army soldier and Haganah commando leader. The Jews regarded the Palmah as an instantly available crack force to fend off Arab attacks and a commando unit to be used against the Nazis; the British saw it as the core of a guerrilla army to fight the Germans should Rommel succeed in conquering Palestine. By 1945 the Palmah comprised some two thousand men and women, its platoons dispersed among several dozen kibbutzim and two or three towns. For two weeks each month they worked in the fields to cover their upkeep. The rest of the month was devoted to military training.

The Haganah and Palmah were to join the simmering anti-British struggle, but only after the war ended. The first note had been struck years before by the LHI—led initially by Avraham ("Yair") Stern—which believed that Britain was Zionism's main obstacle and an accomplice in the Nazi crimes against the Jews and, paradoxically, even tried to establish an anti-British alliance with Germany.[69] However, due to its meager resources and manpower, almost consensual Yishuv opposition to anti-British terrorism, and successive, effective British clampdowns, sometimes assisted by tip-offs from the Haganah and the IZL, the LHI's stance was never really translated into action during 1941–43.

On February 1, 1944, several days after Menachem Begin took over command of the IZL, it announced the resumption of the struggle against Britain. The Irgun felt that the war against the Nazis had been decided; London was now the problem. It immediately began blowing up or attacking government immigration and income tax offices and police buildings.[70] The LHI also launched a number of spectacular attacks; on August 8 they even tried to assassinate the high commissioner, MacMichael.[71]

The two groups were roundly condemned by the mainstream leadership and the press. The IZL members were labeled "misguided terrorists," "young fanatics crazed by the sufferings of their people into believing that destruction will bring healing."[72] Efforts by the Jewish Agency Executive and the Haganah to dissuade them failed. Following the attempt on MacMichael and the assassination of Lord Moyne, the LHI agreed to suspend its war on Britain until the larger war ended. But the IZL defied the JAE and the National Committee and continued its attacks. The Haganah declared an "open season" (referred to in Zionist historiography as the "*Saison*," meaning hunting season) against the IZL, and Haganah intelligence and Palmah teams tracked down IZL members, confiscated their weapons, interrogated and beat them, and occasionally handed them over to the British police.

The *Saison* lasted from November 1944 to March 1945.[73] But the changed international situation and growing activist rumblings within the Haganah itself eventually issued in a radical change of tack. The imminent end of the war in Europe signalled the reopening of the struggle for statehood. A memorandum from Weizmann to Churchill in May 1945 served as a prelude to the Haganah campaign: Whitehall should take steps at last to turn Palestine into a Jewish State and concede responsibility for the regulation of immigration to the Jewish Agency. In June a Jewish Agency memorandum pleaded that Britain allow 100,000 immigrants into Palestine immediately.[74] In Ben-Gurion's phrase, the DPs could not be allowed to languish "among the graveyards of the millions of their slaughtered brethren"; their salvation lay in speedy re-settlement in Palestine.[75]

But Churchill and his cabinet were voted out of office. The new foreign secretary, Ernest Bevin, proposed that immigration to Palestine be allowed, even after the expiration of the White Paper's 75,000 quota, at a rate of fifteen hundred per month. Weizmann rejected the proposal out of hand, and Truman implicitly agreed with him. The president had been persuaded by Earl G. Harrison, his representative on the Intergovernmental Committee on Refugees, that Palestine was the best haven for Europe's remaining Jews and that that was what they wanted. Harrison specifically wrote of the need to grant "100,000" additional entry certificates. Truman forwarded the report to Prime Minister Attlee with his personal recommendation that "as many as possible of the non-repatriable Jews who wish it" be resettled in Palestine. Attlee and Bevin managed to dissuade Truman for a time from a public endorsement of the proposal, but the news of his support for it was eventually published, in mid-October.[76]

In the face of British intransigence, the Yishuv resumed the struggle. The IZL's operations had fallen off considerably at the end of 1944 as a result of the British clampdown and the *Saison,* but in May 1945 the group bombed British targets, including police stations, telephone poles, and the IPC (Iraq Petroleum Company) pipeline that ran through the Jezreel Valley to Haifa.[77] In July the LHI came out of hibernation, and, following an agreement with the IZL, a joint team of sappers blew up a bridge near Yavneh.[78] Next, they turned their attention to Labor-affiliated Jewish targets, robbing banks and Histadrut affiliates of money and stocks of explosives.[79]

The Haganah took a few more months to join in, having decided to await the results of the British general elections and, then, Labour's assumption of power. Bevin almost immediately hinted that he intended to push a pro-Arab line, and in early October, the Haganah, IZL, and LHI negotiated an operational pact and formally launched the Hebrew Rebellion Movement (*Tnu'at Hameri Ha'ivri*).[80] The Palmah went into action even before the signing ceremony. On the night of October 9 they raided the British detention camp at Atlit and freed 208 illegal immigrants.[81] In November, Palmah sapper squads sabotaged railway tracks at 153 points around Palestine;[82] a British patrol vessel was sunk; and, in response to the capture of a ship carrying illegal immigrants by the Royal Navy, two British coast guard stations were blown up.[83]

The British responded with raids on several coastal-plain settlements they suspected of harboring Haganah soldiers or illegal immigrants. The troops panicked and opened fire, killing nine civilians and wounding sixty-three. Anti-British emotions peaked.[84] Periodically during the following months the Haganah, IZL, and LHI attacked British targets. The most spectacular action was by Palmah squads on the night of June 17, 1946, when eleven bridges, connecting Palestine to Transjordan, Syria, Lebanon, and the Sinai, were blown up simultaneously.[85]

Meanwhile the illegal immigration campaign was resumed. All but one of the dozens of boats involved were organized and commanded by the Haganah's illegal-immigration branch, the Mossad Le'Aliyah Bet.[86] Many boats were intercepted by the Royal Navy and their passengers interned; but others got through. Between August 1945 and May 14, 1948, about 70,700 illegal immigrants were landed on Palestine's shores.[87]

But the British found themselves under simultaneous pressure from the Arab side. On November 2, 1945, Balfour Declaration Day, there were anti-Zionist demonstrations in Syria, Egypt, Lebanon, and Iraq. In Alexandria, crowds attacked Jewish shops, homes, and synagogues; in British-governed Libya, the mobs slaughtered about one hundred Jews.[88] The dilemma was stark: To turn down Truman's proposal might jeopardize the cornerstone of British foreign policy, the Anglo-American alliance. But to allow 100,000 Jews into Palestine would enrage the Arabs and invite rebellion there and elsewhere in the Middle East.

Whitehall chose the path of least resistance—yet another committee of inquiry into the fate of the Jewish DPs, this one to work jointly with the Americans. The appointment of the committee on November 13 put a temporary halt to Haganah activities. It seemed that Bevin had succeeded in drawing the United States into the Palestine problem. Washington would now share in formulating a solution and might even end up partaking in the expense.

THE ANGLO-AMERICAN COMMITTEE
OF INQUIRY

The committee was directed to determine how many of the remaining European Jews could be reintegrated in their native lands, and how many preferred to migrate to other countries. Both Jews and Arabs were to be consulted about the numbers that could be absorbed in Palestine.

Twelve men—naturally dubbed the "twelve apostles"—were named, six Britons and six Americans.[89] In launching the committee Bevin publicly set out his Palestine policy: Britain would give up the Mandate, and Palestine would be converted into an international "trusteeship"; after a time an independent "Palestinian, not Jewish, state" would be established. He expected the committee to more or less endorse this solution. He warned the Jews not to push their way to "the head of the queue," lest they provoke an anti-Semitic reaction. Meanwhile, there would be a ceiling of fifteen hundred immigration permits per month. The Jewish Agency denounced Bevin's "prejudging" of the committee's findings and formally endorsed illegal immigration.[90]

During February and March 1946 the committee studied the situation of the DPs, toured the Middle East, heard testimony from Arab and Zionist representatives and British officials, and received and read reports from agencies and movements in Palestine and from outside observers. The Palestinian Arab propaganda agency, the Arab Office, headed by Musa al-Alami, submitted a three-volume survey entitled *The Problem of Palestine*. It cautioned the committee against regarding "Jewish colonisation in Palestine and Arab resistance to it in terms of white colonization of North America and Australia and the resistance of the indigenous peoples." Nor would the prosperity Zionism would allegedly bring to Palestine persuade the Arabs to shelve their opposition to a movement that was bent on dispossessing them.[91] The Jewish Agency submitted a thousand-page volume, *The Jewish Case Before the AAC of Inquiry on Palestine*, which contrasted Palestinian Arab backwardness with Zionism's role as a bearer of enlightenment and progress, backed up with reams of statistics and graphs.

Of particular effect was the month the committee spent touring DP centers, especially in Poland. Haganah and Jewish Agency representatives coached the DPs and made sure the AAC met only Jews propounding the Zionist solution.[92] The committee found that the Jews in Poland lived in an "atmosphere of terror," with "pogroms . . . an everyday occurrence."[93] (Indeed, Poles had murdered over a thousand Jews since the end of the war.) The testimony of American and British officials on the spot confirmed this, and most of the committee members became convinced of the need for immigration of the DPs to Palestine.

Before reaching Palestine, the committee subdivided and visited several Arab capitals. At Riyadh, King Abdul Aziz ibn Saud told his visitors: "The

Jews are our enemies everywhere. Wherever they are found, they intrigue and work against us. . . . With the power of the sword, we drove the Romans out of Palestine. How, after all this sacrifice, would a merchant [that is, a Jew] come and take Palestine out of our hands for money?"

He then presented each member with a golden dagger and an Arabian robe and headdress, and showed them his harem. He offered to find the AAC chairman, Judge Sir John Singleton, a wife.[94]

At the hearings in Palestine in March, the Jewish leaders presented the Zionist case forcefully, citing facts and figures. Ben-Gurion banned all but mainstream spokesmen from appearing (though, defying the leadership, Hebrew University president Yehuda Leib Magnes testified on behalf of a binational solution). The Arabs, according to an American observer, preferred to impress the committee with "a sumptuous luncheon at Katy Antonius's or a ceremonial visit to a large estate rather than with any systematic marshaling of facts and figures to make a convincing presentation."[95]

But perhaps more important than all the testimony were the committee's travels around the country. The diverse realities of the cities and countryside left an abiding impression. One American committee member, Frank Aydelotte, later wrote: "I left Washington pretty strongly anti-Zionist. . . . But when you see at first hand what these Jews have done in Palestine . . . the greatest creative effort in the modern world. The Arabs are not equal to anything like it and would destroy all that the Jews have done. . . . This we must not let them do."

Frank Buxton, another American member, wrote: "How my Vermont father . . . would have been amazed at the greater deeds of the Palestinian Jews. . . . I came away from those farms less cocky and more humble and not quite so certain that American pioneers left no successors."[96] Buxton later compared the Haganah to the American Revolutionary army, "a rabble in arms in the fine sense."[97]

British committee member R. H. S. Crossman later recalled, by contrast, visiting "the stenchiest Arab village" he had ever seen.[98] The main findings of the report, which was released on May 1, were that the great majority of DPs wished to settle in Palestine and that 100,000 visas should be issued and immigration expedited "as rapidly as conditions will permit." The committee rejected partition as unworkable; independence, when given, should be within a single, binational framework. But independence should be postponed for now, and the Mandate continued as a United Nations Trusteeship. If Bevin had hoped that the committee would produce an agreed Anglo-American policy, he was sorely disappointed. Truman again endorsed the passage of 100,000 DPs to Palestine and approved the scrapping of the White Paper's land sale provisions, which the committee had deemed discriminatory. Attlee ruled out mass immigration until the Jewish military undergrounds were disbanded and the Yishuv disarmed.[99]

The Jewish Agency greeted the report with limited approval, endorsing the immigration recommendation. The Arabs rejected it completely. There were riots and demonstrations in Baghdad and Palestine, and in Beirut the United States Information Center was set on fire. The report was officially condemned by the Arab League Council, but it resisted calls for severe measures against Britain and the United States should the recommendations be implemented.[100]

Publication of the report did nothing to stop Jewish attacks on British targets, culminating in the Palmah's "Night of the Bridges" (June 17). On June 29, in response, the British launched "Operation Agatha," aimed at seriously reducing Jewish military capabilities.[101] Haganah intelligence had obtained advance warning, and most commanders escaped the dragnet. The operation, in which hundreds were arrested, including four members of the JAE, only marginally affected the Haganah's strength and did nothing to improve Britain's image in the United States. But on the political plane, it paralyzed the Yishuv decision-makers and persuaded the JAE (meeting in Paris in August 1946) to abandon the path of military confrontation with the British.[102]

However, the operation also provoked a desire for revenge, as the IZL, rather ironically, took up the cudgels for its sometime enemy, the Haganah, on July 22. Without coordinating with the Haganah, sappers placed a number of bomb-laden milk containers in the basement of the King David Hotel in Jerusalem, which served as a British military and administrative headquarters. The resulting explosion, which demolished an entire wing of the building and killed ninety-one people—Britons, Arabs, and Jews—was the biggest terrorist action in the organization's history. The IZL subsequently claimed it had given the occupants ample warning, but they had failed to evacuate the building; the British maintained that no such warning had been issued. In response, the commander of the British forces in Palestine, Lt. Gen. Sir Evelyn Barker, issued a nonfraternization order in which he accused all of Palestine's Jews of complicity in the outrage. Personnel were barred from frequenting any Jewish home or business or having "any social intercourse with any Jew," in order to punish "the Jews in a way the race dislikes as much as any, by striking at their pockets." Barker was subsequently rebuked by Attlee but was not removed from his command.[103]

The Haganah, always opposed to terrorism (which it distinguished from legitimate anti-imperialist guerrilla warfare), condemned the attack, disbanded the Hebrew Resistance Movement, and called a halt to its anti-British military actions. Once again, each of the three Jewish underground organizations went its own way.

The upshot of the Anglo-American talks in the summer of 1946, and of the violence in Palestine, was Britain's floating of the Morrison-Grady, or Provincial Autonomy, Plan, London's last effort to find a compromise solution. It left defense, foreign affairs, and most economic matters in British—or "International Trusteeship"—hands, while, subdivided into four "provinces" or cantons,

Jews and Arabs were offered a measure of local autonomy over municipal affairs, agriculture, education, and so on. Provision was made for the immediate transfer of 100,000 DPs and eventual independence for Palestine as a unitary (or binational) state.

In September, British officials and representatives of the Arab states met in London to discuss the plan. There was no Palestinian Arab or Jewish representation; British insistence on determining the composition of the two delegations resulted in a double boycott. Like all its predecessors, the Morrison-Grady Plan was rejected, both by the Zionists (who insisted on "Jewish statehood") and the Arabs ("immediate Arab independence") as well as by the United States. Indeed, on October 4, 1946, consummating a steady process that had begun in 1945, President Truman formally enunciated U.S. support of partition and Jewish statehood and called for an immediate start to "substantial" immigration.[104] This statement, in large measure prompted by the heated contest for Jewish votes in New York in the upcoming midterm elections, was a bitter blow to Attlee. "I am astonished that you did not wait to acquaint yourself with the reasons" for the British plan, he cabled Truman. Within weeks his cabinet was to decide to abandon the Mandate: Britain understood that its position in Palestine was untenable without an Anglo-American understanding—and clearly no such accord was in the cards.

On January 27, 1947, the London Conference was reconvened. This time the AHC was represented—but the Jewish Agency continued its boycott and the United States refused even to send an observer. The British formally negotiated with Palestinian and other Arab representatives while informally meeting Zionist officials behind the scenes. But there was no basis for an agreement. The agency refused to consider anything less than partition; the Palestinians, anything less than majority-rule independence for all of Palestine.

UNSCOP

On February 14, 1947, the British cabinet decided, in effect, to wash its hands of Palestine and dump the problem in the lap of the United Nations. "We are unable to accept the scheme put forward either by the Arabs or by the Jews, or to impose ourselves a solution of our own," Bevin told the Commons on February 18.[105] The Arabs were not averse to the matter going before the UN, where they anticipated a favorable outcome; the Zionists were wary of a "UN solution." These attitudes may well have affected Bevin's decision.

Some historians have suggested that by threatening the sides with the unknown and the unpredictable, Britain may have been aiming to force them to accept its latest proposals, or to accede in a prolongation of the Mandate. Others believe Britain was simply too weak and poor to soldier on. IZL and LHI adherents claim it was their constant attacks that persuaded the British to cast off the burden. The Haganah operations of 1945–46 have also been seen as portending a clash with the main Zionist militia that Whitehall was unwilling to contemplate, while the struggle against illegal immigration was a headache of major proportions. Most historians agree that given the Cold War context, in which the need for Anglo-American amity was seen as paramount, and Britain's insolvency, Whitehall could ill afford to alienate Washington over a highly emotional issue that, when all was said and done, was not a vital British interest.

The political developments of 1947 were played out against a background of Jewish violence and reprisals spiraling almost out of control. Efforts to block and punish illegal immigration took on new, bloody dimensions, though by and large the British displayed restraint and humanity in face of terrorism.[106] With evacuation only months away, Britain appeared no longer capable of properly governing Palestine and to have lost the will to continue. And, without doubt, the decision to withdraw heightened the terrorists' expectations. The British had close to 100,000 troops in Palestine, five times as many as had been used to crush the Arab Revolt of 1936–39 (a tribute, perhaps, to the greater efficiency and deadliness of the Jewish militants), but there were strict limits to what they could allow themselves to do in the way of effective counterterrorism.

On March 1, 1947, IZL gunmen killed more than twenty British servicemen, twelve of them in a grenade attack on their Officers Club in Tel Aviv, and injured thirty. On March 31 the LHI sabotaged the Haifa oil refinery; the fire took three weeks to put out. And on May 4 the IZL penetrated the British prison in Acre and set free two dozen of its incarcerated members (and, unintentionally, some two hundred Arab prisoners), but nine of the attackers were killed and eight captured. The latter were tried, and on July 8 death sentences were confirmed against three of them.

On July 12, the IZL abducted two British sergeants, Clifford Martin (apparently a Jew) and Mervyn Paice, and hanged them after their three comrades were executed on July 29. The Britons' bodies were booby-trapped and a British captain was injured when they were cut down.[107] "The bestialities practised by the Nazis themselves could go no further," commented *The Times* of London.[108] But bestiality was by no means a monopoly of the Jewish terrorists. On the evening of July 30 British troops and police went on a retaliatory rampage in Tel Aviv, destroying shops and beating up Jews. In one area, berserk security men sprayed pedestrians and shops with gunfire, killing five and injuring ten.

In Parliament, meeting in special session on August 12, there was an all-party consensus to quit Palestine, quickly; "no British interest" was safeguarded by staying on, said Churchill. The judgment of historians familiar with the British state archives is that "the IZL's draconian methods, morally reprehensible as they were, were decisive in transforming the evacuation option of February 1947 into a determined resolve to give up the burdens of the Mandate."[109]

The British had by now dumped the problem in the lap of the UN. Responding, in April–May 1947 the General Assembly met in special session in New York and established yet another committee to examine the problem. Over Arab objections the UN Special Committee on Palestine (UNSCOP) was empowered to probe the DP problem, and also to determine guidelines for a settlement. The Netherlands, Sweden, Czechoslovakia, Yugoslavia, Canada, Australia, India, Iran, Peru, Guatemala, and Uruguay were asked to send representatives. The Arab states were not dismayed, expecting an easy victory at the UN.

With a Swedish judge, Emil Sandstrom, as its chairman, UNSCOP spent five weeks in Palestine that summer, hearing Jewish and British officials. Ben-Gurion at first spoke of a Jewish state in all of Palestine, then agreed to partition; Weizmann spoke of partition from the start. The Jews enjoyed a clandestine advantage: They had bugged the committee's rooms and knew what every committee member and witness was saying.[110]

The committee toured the country and again, the face-to-face encounter with the two sides in the settlements and villages was to prove persuasive. The committee members were warmly welcomed by their Jewish hosts, and the Jewish Agency made sure they met with settlers who spoke their languages (Swedish, Spanish, Serbo-Croat, and so on). The Arabs, on the other hand, everywhere greeted them with sourness, suspicion, or aggressiveness. The committee was impressed by the cleanliness and development in the Jewish areas and, conversely, by the dirt and backwardness of the Arab villages and towns. The Jewish community appeared to be "European, modern, dynamic . . . a state in the making."[111]

Though officially the AHC boycotted UNSCOP, the Arab position did not go completely unrepresented. Acting "independently," Musa al-Alami and Cecil Hourani, secretary of the Arab Office in Washington, submitted a memorandum setting out the Arab viewpoint.[112] UNSCOP also heard representatives of the Arab states who rejected partition and advocated a unitary, democratic state from which the illegal immigrants would be expelled, and where the remaining Jews would have no political rights.[113]

A factor that dramatically influenced UNSCOP was the *Exodus* affair.[114] Since August 1946 the British had been sending captured illegal immigrants to detention camps in Cyprus. But with about twelve thousand prisoners in the island's camps, there was no more room. In spring 1947, under the hammer blows of IZL terror and the Haganah illegal immigration campaign, the

British decided to tighten the screws. MI6 unleashed a campaign of sabotage against the Haganah's ships in European harbors: The *Vrisi* was sunk in Genoa on July 11; the *Pan Crescent* was damaged and grounded near Venice on the night of August 30–31.[115] Whitehall also decided to send captured illegal immigrants back to Europe.

On July 12, the *Exodus 1947* set sail from southern France, with 4,500 DPs aboard. On July 18 it was intercepted and boarded by Royal Marines some 30 kilometers off the coast of Palestine, opposite Gaza. A nightlong hand-to-hand battle followed, which the Haganah decided to exploit to show how poor and weak and helpless the Jews were, and how cruel the British. Three Jews died and twenty-eight were seriously wounded, but the desperate plight of the DPs had been highlighted and their fate linked to Palestine. As if to drive home the grim message, the British then proceeded to tow the boat into Haifa harbor, disembark the dead and wounded, and then transfer the bulk of the DPs to three seaworthy ships—under the watchful eye of UNSCOP chairman Sandstrom—and ship them back to France. Increasing Britain's embarrassment, the French refused to cooperate; the French Communist Party daily *L'Humanité* described the vessels as "a floating Auschwitz." The great majority of the passengers refused to leave the ships, and the British, maneuvered into a corner of their own making, sailed on to Hamburg, where the army on September 8 forcibly disembarked the passengers. Jews, this time shepherded by British troops, had been returned to the land of their persecution. The ordeal of the *Exodus* seemed to symbolize contemporary Jewish history and British insensitivity. Nothing could have done more to promote the Zionist cause at this crucial juncture.[116] The almost simultaneous British execution of the three IZL operatives and the IZL hanging of the two sergeants apparently had a much smaller impact on the UNSCOP members—though perhaps the *Exodus* affair had indirectly cast light on the wellsprings of the IZL's behavior.[117]

The committee moved to Europe in late July to interview DPs and officials dealing with the problem. The DPs—as with the AAC before—unanimously asserted that they wanted to immigrate to Palestine.[118] UNSCOP's report, submitted to the General Assembly on September 1, was unanimous about the need to terminate the Mandate. A majority of eight proposed partitioning Palestine into Jewish and Arab states, with an international trusteeship for Jerusalem and Bethlehem. The two states would be bound in economic union, and Britain would continue to administer the country for two years, during which 150,000 Jews would be allowed in. The minority report—written by the Yugoslav, Iranian, and Indian representatives—proposed that Palestine be given independence as a "federal state," meaning a unitary entity under Arab domination.

The immediate British cabinet reaction was initially a secret decision, on September 20, to evacuate Palestine completely.[119] Either the UN would set up the machinery for an orderly transfer of power or else the Arabs and the Jews would settle the problem on their own, by force of arms. In either case, it was no longer Britain's responsibility.

THE GENERAL ASSEMBLY PARTITION RESOLUTION, NOVEMBER 29, 1947

The Zionists mounted a powerful campaign in the United States to pressure President Truman into endorsing the UNSCOP majority report. As he had supported partition back in October 1946, and, moreover, the Soviets had recently adopted a propartition stance,[120] he could hardly do otherwise, despite a last-ditch struggle by the State Department. Two weeks after Britain announced its intention to evacuate,[121] both the United States (October 11) and the Soviet Union (October 13) publicly reiterated their support for partition. On November 13 Britain announced that it would withdraw all its troops from Palestine by August 1, 1948.

Before the General Assembly vote on November 29, 1947, the State Department made frantic efforts to award the Negev—which the UNSCOP majority had earmarked for the Jews—to the Arabs. Only Weizmann's personal intervention with Truman saved the bulk of the desert for the Jews.[122] In exchange the Jewish Agency reluctantly agreed to concede Beersheba and a strip of territory along the Sinai-Negev border—awarded to the Jews in the majority report—to the Arabs. Jaffa was made an Arab enclave in the Jewish state, while the Jews were given a little more land in the Galilee.[123] With these changes the prospective Jewish state was to have 55 percent of Palestine and a population of approximately 500,000 Jews with an Arab minority of close to 400,000. (Another 100,000 Jews lived in Jerusalem.)

The UN Charter required that the resolution pass by a two-thirds majority. Despite the majority in UNSCOP and despite U.S. and Soviet support, the Zionists were initially far from optimistic. On November 26 three wavering nations—Haiti, Greece, and the Philippines—indicated that they would vote against the resolution. The desperate Zionists turned to the United States, realizing that without direct American pressure on its client states the vote might be lost. Zionist lobbying was crude and effective—as was the arm-twisting the Americans, in turn, applied to a dozen smaller nations. Truman's original instruction of November 24—"[not] to use threats or improper pressure of any kind on other Delegations to vote for the majority report"[124]—was cast aside. Greece was threatened with a foreign aid cutoff, Liberia with a rubber embargo.

UN Partition Plan, November 1947

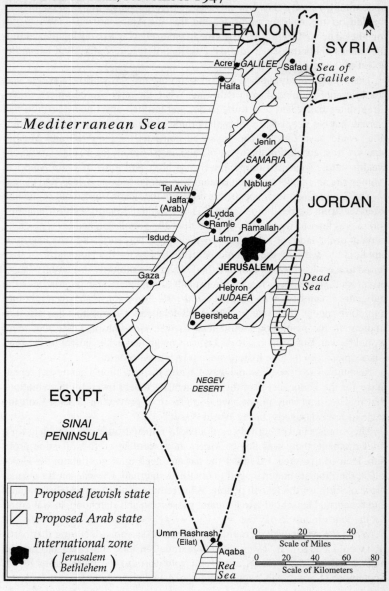

LEBANON

SYRIA

N

Acre • *GALILEE* • Safad *Sea of Galilee*

Haifa

Mediterranean Sea

Jenin •

SAMARIA

Nablus •

Tel Aviv • JORDAN

Jaffa • (Arab)

Lydda • Ramallah
Ramle • Ramallah •
Latrun

Isdud •

JERUSALEM

Gaza • Hebron • *Dead Sea*
JUDAEA

Beersheba •

NEGEV DESERT

EGYPT

SINAI PENINSULA

Proposed Jewish state

Proposed Arab state

International zone
(*Jerusalem Bethlehem*)

Umm Rashrash (Eilat) •

Aqaba •

Red Sea

0   20   40
Scale of Miles

0 20 40 60 80
Scale of Kilometers

On November 28, in the hours before the crucial vote, the Arabs succeeded in obtaining a short delay. But only a serious compromise proposal could have warded off the vote for partition, and this the Arabs proved unable to put together. The AHC representatives made themselves scarce during the behind-the-scenes deliberations, as did the Pakistani delegate, Zufferallah Khan, the ablest of the Muslim spokesmen.

The voting was broadcast live on radio around the world. Nowhere was attention more riveted than in Palestine. When the tally was complete, thirty-three states had voted yes, thirteen no, and ten had abstained. Partition had passed, but not very comfortably (had three of the ayes voted nay, the resolution would have failed). The nays had consisted of the Arab and Muslim states, Cuba, and India; the ayes, of the United States, the British Commonwealth states, Western Europe, the Soviet bloc, and most of Latin America. Among the abstainers had been Britain, Argentina, Mexico, Chile, and China.

The Zionists and their supporters rejoiced; the Arabs walked out of the hall after declaring the resolution invalid. They could not fathom, a Palestinian historian was later to write, why 37 percent of the population had been given 55 percent of the land (of which they owned only 7 percent). And "the Palestinians failed to see why they should be made to pay for the Holocaust . . . they failed to see why it was *not* fair for the Jews to be a minority in a unitary Palestinian state, while it *was* fair for almost half of the Palestinian population—the indigenous majority on its own ancestral soil—to be converted overnight into a minority under alien rule."[125] The Arab delegates asserted that any effort to implement the resolution would lead to war. Ben-Gurion knew that there would be war. But still, he said, "I know of no greater achievement by the Jewish people . . . in its long history since it became a people."[126]

Resolution 181 was, in some way, "Western civilization's gesture of repentance for the Holocaust . . . , the repayment of a debt owed by those nations that realized that they might have done more to prevent or at least limit the scale of Jewish tragedy during World War II."[127]

The Zionists had effectively exploited the unusual situation, in which, for a brief moment, there was Soviet-American agreement on the Palestine problem. Helped to a great extent by the nations' feeling of guilt about the Holocaust, the Zionists had managed to obtain an international warrant for a small piece of earth for the Jewish people. What remained was for the Jews to translate the formal leasehold into concrete possession and statehood, in war—and for the Palestinians to pay the price.

When the Arabs walked out of the General Assembly declaring that partition would lead to war, it was not an idle threat. In June 1946 the Arab League had secretly pledged funds, arms, and volunteers to the Palestinians.[128] On September 16, 1947, the league decided to establish an Arab Liberation Army (ALA), composed of Palestinians and volunteers from the Arab states. In November the Syrian army began registering volunteers and set up a training camp. Fawzi al-Qawuqji, who had sat out the war years in Germany, broadcasting the Nazi message to the Arab world, was named commander.[129] Amin al-Husseini bitterly opposed the appointment. Since the Arab Revolt he had seen Qawuqji as a rival, and their animosity was to undermine the Palestinian war effort in 1948. The forces aligned with Husseini would operate without coordination with, and often at cross-purposes to, the ALA.[130]

Even before the vote in the UN, the Arab League had set up a Military Committee, to be headed by Gen. Ismail Safwat, former chief of staff of the Iraqi army, to assist the Palestinians. To pressure Britain and the UN it decided to deploy troops along Palestine's frontiers. Damascus sent several battalions to the border, giving the British a scare and jolting the Yishuv into vigilance. Indeed, on October 20, 1947, a small Syrian force crossed the frontier at Tel al-Qadi, perhaps by mistake, perhaps with the intention of testing the British, who immediately drove them back.[131]

In a bleak report to the League, General Safwat said that the Zionists possessed "political, military and administrative institutions and organizations, characterized by a very high degree of efficiency." They could field twenty thousand troops, and had forty thousand reserves, good lines of communication and well-defended settlements. The Palestinians had none of these things. The Arab states must mobilize and come to their aid, or, he implied, the Zionists would win.[132] But the other League members were not yet ready to be sucked into the conflict. Consistently it was the Iraqis who were the most militant, "breathing brimstone for home consumption."[133] Being farthest from the prospective battlefield, they apparently felt free to exhibit less caution than the front-line states. A few days after the passage of the partition resolution and the start of hostilities in Palestine, Iraq proposed that the regular Arab armies intervene to "save" Palestine even before the Jews proclaimed a state and the British departed. This was rejected, but the League decided on indirect, minimal intervention, by sending ten thousand rifles[134] and three thousand "volunteers."[135]

Husseini, forever showing up uninvited at Arab League meetings, forever saw his proposals rejected.[136] He had been deeply unhappy with Safwat's proposal for intervention, understanding that it would provide an opportunity for land grabs by Jordan, Syria, and Egypt.[137] The meetings were marked by disunity, mutual suspicion, and bitter enmities. Most of the Arab rulers had developed a strong antagonism toward Husseini, whom they regarded as an inveterate plotter, and this undermined any hope of realistic decision-making in their councils. Moderates—such as Abdullah of Jordan—allowed themselves to be pushed into extremist pronouncements, lest they be charged with showing insufficient zeal. All paid lip service to Arab unity and the Palestinian cause, and all opposed partition—but all were really at a loss about what to do to prevent it. Most knew their armies were weak and in no state to take on a serious enemy, certainly not while the British were still in Palestine.[138] Still, the Arab leaders felt that they had to do something. Some felt opposition politicians nipping at their heels; most, especially some of the monarchs, suffered from unpopularity and questionable legitimacy. Non-intervention in Palestine might well doom their regimes. The public bluster, the leaders' fear of their own populations, whom they had whipped up to a frenzy with militant rhetoric, and the pressure of their fellows all combined to egg them on. They had embarked on a course almost inevitably leading to war.

Ben-Gurion understood that the decisive battle for statehood would be waged not against the British or in the diplomatic arena but against the Arabs. Between 1936 and 1945 the Haganah grew by leaps and bounds, steadily improving its command structures and soldiering abilities, adding fresh units, particularly the Palmah, and enlarging its armory and arms-producing capabilities. In 1945 its agents in the United States had managed to buy war-surplus arms-making machine tools and smuggle them into Palestine. By the end of 1947 Haganah arms factories were producing two- and three-inch mortars, Sten submachine guns, and grenades and bullets in large numbers. The buildup extended also to the air. In the 1930s the Haganah had bought planes and, under civilian camouflage, had begun training pilots. In November 1947 the Air Service was formed, and some light civil aircraft were armed.

In May 1946 the Haganah General Staff put together its Plan C, a response to organized attacks and guidelines for retaliation. Plan B, devised in 1945, had outlined the defense of the Yishuv in the event of a renewed Arab rebellion, with the Haganah serving as an auxiliary to the British forces. In October and December 1946, in two addenda to Plan C, instructions were issued to regional commanders regarding retaliation against British forces should they come to the aid of the Arabs. Formerly an organization that saw itself as an appendage of the British Army, cooperating with the Mandate government, the Haganah now took on sole responsibility for the defense of the Yishuv, against the British if necessary.[139]

In December the Zionist leadership made Ben-Gurion responsible for defense in addition to his function as Jewish Agency chairman—effectively, the prime minister of the state within a state. From the spring of 1947 he devoted most of his time and energy to preparing the Yishuv for war, leaving the conduct of the political-diplomatic battle to Moshe Sharett, Abba Hillel Silver in the United States, and others. He spent long hours with Haganah and Palmah officers and veterans of the Jewish Brigade, studying the Yishuv's strategic problems and defense needs.

During this period the Haganah-Palmah brass battled for dominance against the regular (mainly British) army veterans, who had returned to the Haganah after 1945 or were waiting for commissions. It was a matter of both military philosophies and personnel: What outlook and which group of commanders would fashion the emergent Jewish army? Each group sought to win

Ben-Gurion over: the hit-and-run, informal, small-unit approach versus the big-unit, strict-regimen, regular army way.

Unlike most of his colleagues, Ben-Gurion believed:

> Until recently there was only the problem of how to defend [the Yishuv] against the Palestinian Arabs. . . . But now we face a completely new situation. The Land of Israel is surrounded by independent Arab states . . . that have the right to purchase and produce arms, to set up armies and train them. . . . Attack by the Palestinian Arabs does not endanger the Yishuv, but there is a danger, that the neighboring Arab states will send their armies to attack and destroy the Yishuv.[140]

The preparations set in train by the Haganah in 1947 were for conventional war against a coalition of Arab states rather than for limited guerrilla warfare against the Palestinians. Ben-Gurion tended to belittle the Haganah and apparently doubted its ability to convert itself efficiently and quickly into a competent regular army. He surrounded himself with military advisers drawn largely from the pool of regular army veterans, as a counterweight to the existing Haganah leadership.[141] Nonetheless, apart from appointment to command posts of a few regular army veterans and the adoption of certain regular army norms in the fields of logistics, staff work, and intelligence, it was the Haganah that eventually expanded and in mid-1948 became the Israel Defense Forces (IDF).

This conversion was left until very late in the day, largely because Palestine remained under British control and the Haganah was by nature an illegal, underground organization. Only in November 1947 did Ben-Gurion and the Haganah command shift to an active mode and begin to reorganize for war. Even though Ben-Gurion believed as late as April 1948 that the British intended to manipulate events so that they could stay on in Palestine, the reorganization of the Haganah was based on the assumption that they were, indeed, leaving and that the Palestinians and the Arab states were the enemies the Haganah would have to face.

THE WAR BEGINS

Though everyone in the Yishuv expected conflict at some point in the future, and violence indeed erupted on November 30, within hours of the General Assembly vote, no one was certain that this was the start of a "war." It appeared to be just another spontaneous outbreak, akin to those of 1920–21 and 1929, one that would pass. Indeed, the general opinion in the Haganah Intelligence Service (Shai) before November 29 was that the Arab states were disunited, and that the Arabs of Palestine were unprepared for war and would not react belligerently to a pro-partition vote.[142] But David Shaltiel, the Shai's commander, was more guarded: "None of us knows what may happen tomorrow, or, indeed, today," he wrote on the night of November 29.[143]

That night passed in the Yishuv's towns and settlements in noisy public rejoicing. Almost everyone had sat glued to the live radio broadcast of the vote, and a giant, collective cry went up when the two-thirds majority was achieved. The young poured into the streets and danced and celebrated around bonfires through the night. In the courtyard of the National Institutions Buildings in Jerusalem, Golda Myerson (Meir), acting director of the Jewish Agency's Political Department (Sharett was in New York), addressed the crowd below: "For two thousand years we have waited for our deliverance. Now that it is here it is so great and wonderful that it surpasses human words. Jews, *mazel tov*, good luck!"[144]

But some, like Yosef Nahmani, a veteran of HaShomer, a Tiberias city councillor and head of the JNF office there, were more sober. He had been carried aloft through the streets of his lakeside town by the celebrants, but "in my heart," he told his diary, "there was joy mixed with sadness: joy that the nations had at last acknowledged that we are a nation with a state, and sadness that we lost half the country, Judea and Samaria, and, in addition, that we [would] have [in our state] 400,000 Arabs."[145] And Ben-Gurion was later to recall: "I could not dance, I could not sing that night. I looked at them so happy dancing, and I could only think that they were all going to war."[146]

Not far from each celebrating Jewish throng was an Arab village or neighborhood where the mood was grim. What the Palestinians had most feared had now come to pass. The initial reactions were spontaneous and explosive, and apparently unorganized. On the morning of November 30 a band of Arabs ambushed a bus near Kfar Syrkin, killing five Jews and wounding several others. Twenty-five minutes later they let loose at a second bus, killing two more people. It is unclear whether the ambushes were triggered by the passage of the UN resolution or by a desire to avenge an earlier LHI raid, which had left five Arabs dead. Another Jew was murdered on November 30 by Arabs on the border between Jaffa and Tel Aviv. These were the first casualties of the first Arab-Israeli war.[147]

Guided by Husseini from Cairo, the AHC on December 1 declared a three-day general strike of the Palestinian Arab community, to begin the following day. On December 2 a large mob, armed with sticks and knives, burst out of Jerusalem's Old City gates and attacked Jewish pedestrians and shops. The mob reached City Hall. A number of people were injured, one seriously, and buildings were set alight. Haganah intelligence identified AHC officials leading the mob.[148] Haganah units fired above and into the crowds; British police and troops generally looked on, inactive. Some policemen joined in the vandalism and looting, though others helped evacuate the Jewish wounded—a range of behavior that was to characterize the Mandate's security forces during the following six months.[149] The mob eventually turned back and dispersed. But the war had begun.

THE CIVIL WAR: NOVEMBER 1947– MAY 14, 1948

The first Arab-Israeli war was to have two distinct stages: a civil war, starting at the end of November 1947 and ending in mid-May 1948, largely characterized by a guerrilla struggle between the Yishuv and the Palestinian Arab community; and a conventional war, from May 15, 1948 until early 1949, between the newly founded State of Israel and the armies of Syria, Jordan, Egypt, Lebanon, and Iraq, and small expeditionary forces from a number of other Arab countries, including Yemen and Saudi Arabia.

During the civil war most of the fighting occurred in the areas earmarked for Jewish statehood, where the Jews enjoyed a demographic edge: Jerusalem, Jaffa–Tel Aviv, Tiberias, eastern Galilee, the Jezreel Valley, and the coastal plain. In western Palestine and parts of the Galilee the communities were thoroughly intermingled. In the main cities and in some of the towns—Haifa, Jaffa–Tel Aviv, Jerusalem, Safad, Tiberias—the populations were mixed, overlooking and often sitting astride routes to one another's neighborhoods. In both urban and rural areas the mix of Jewish and Arab settlements along the roads enabled each side to interdict the other's traffic at will.

The British still nominally ruled the country, and their units were deployed in the various regions. Both sides had to take account of this factor, and each suspected the British of favoring the other. Without doubt, until late March 1948, the British presence severely inhibited the Haganah, which had to operate under the assumption that large-scale attacks by its forces would be blocked or rolled back. At the same time, the British presence prevented the Arab states' armies from interfering. For months British troops protected Jewish convoys and, occasionally, settlements.

THE RELATIVE STRENGTH OF THE TWO SIDES

At the start of the war Whitehall believed the Arabs would prevail. "In the long run the Jews would not be able to cope . . . and would be thrown out of Palestine unless they came to terms with [the Arabs]," was the considered judgment of the Imperial Chiefs of Staff.[150] And indeed, the battle seemed, at least on paper, extremely unequal. The Palestinian Arabs enjoyed a roughly 2-to-1 population advantage—1.2 or 1.3 million to 650,000 Jews. Moreover, they benefited from a vast hinterland of sympathetic Arab states, which were able to supply them with volunteers, supplies, and safe havens. The Jewish "hinterland"—the Diaspora—lay many hundreds of miles away; aid consignments had to penetrate the Royal Navy blockade or the RAF-patrolled skies.

But the Yishuv enjoyed basic advantages over the Palestinian Arabs in all other indices of strength—"national" organization for war, trained manpower, weaponry, weapons production, morale and motivation, and, above all, command and control. Moreover, the Yishuv enjoyed a demographic advantage in army-age males,[151] resulting in part from the deliberate policy during the previous years of bringing in as many young male immigrants as possible. The disparities between the military strengths of the two sides were rooted in the nature of the two societies as well as in historical circumstances. Facing off in 1947–48 were a highly motivated, literate, organized, semi-industrial society and a backward, largely illiterate, disorganized, agricultural one. For the average Arab villager, political independence and nationhood were vague abstractions; his loyalties were to his family, clan, and village and, occasionally, to his region. Moreover, decades of feuding had left Palestinian society deeply divided. Underlying all, politically, was the pervasive antagonism between Husseinis and Nashashibis.

The 1936–39 rebellion had, moreover, left the community decapitated, politically and militarily: Some leaders had been killed or wounded, some were in exile. Many others had retired. There was a general weariness of armed struggle. The war years had provided an extended breathing space, but the society as a whole had failed to get over the devastation inflicted by the internal divisions and the crushing of the rebellion, and to develop self-governing institutions. Its sole autonomous executive body was the SMC, which dealt with religious affairs. The AHC was largely unrepresentative and controlled no administrative structures. The Palestinian leadership during the 1930s and 1940s may have talked often and loudly about "independence," but it never made any of the necessary nuts-and-bolts preparations for self-government. After centuries of Ottoman rule, the Arab elite had no tradition of public service; it was essentially corrupt and venal. Under the Mandate, the leading "nationalist" families had sold land to the Zionists and taken Jewish Agency bribes and "loans." Few Arabs had acquired either governmental or military experience during the Mandate years. During the period 1936–47 the Palestinians had developed a reliance on the Arab states to pull their chestnuts out of the fire.

The contrast with Zionist society was stark. No national collective was more self-reliant or motivated, the Holocaust having convincingly demonstrated that there was no relying for survival on anyone else, and that massacre would as likely as not follow upon military defeat. By the late 1940s the Yishuv was probably one of the most politically conscious, committed, and well-organized communities in the world. Over the decades of benign British rule, the infrastructure of a state-within-a-state had been fashioned. In addition to the Haganah, the Yishuv had a protogovernment—the Jewish Agency—with a cabinet (the Executive), a foreign ministry (the Political Department), a treasury (the Finance Department), and most other departments and agencies of government, including a well-functioning, autonomous school system, a taxation system, settlement and land reclamation agencies, and even a powerful labor union organization (the Histadrut). Unlike the Arabs, the Yishuv had a highly talented, sophisticated public-service-oriented elite, experienced in diplomacy, economic development, and military affairs.

The Yishuv also enjoyed the well-organized backing of the World Zionist Organization, with powerful branches in the United States and Britain that could, at crucial junctures, tap the resources of the Jewish communities. In an emergency fund-raising tour of the States in January–March 1948, Golda Meir collected $50 million for the Haganah—twice the sum Ben-Gurion had asked for. In a second whirlwind tour in May–June, she raised another $50 million. These funds paid for crucial arms shipments from Czechoslovakia.[152]

Theoretically the Palestinian Arabs had the whole Arab world to fall back on, but that world, less organized and less generous than Jewry, gave them little in their hour of need, in money and arms; the thin stream of Arab volunteers, perhaps five thousand all told, even fell short of the number, and certainly of the quality, of the foreign volunteers—both Jewish and non-Jewish—who came to fight for the Yishuv.

On the eve of the war, the Haganah had altogether 35,000 members. Of these, the Palmah, in November 1947, fielded 2,100 troops and had another 1,000 reservists, who were instantly called up. The IZL had from two to three thousand members, the LHI three to five hundred. Throughout the "civil war," the three organizations did not clash with one another or operate at cross-purposes. Indeed, during the latter stages the IZL occasionally coordinated its actions with the Haganah. In short, the Yishuv enjoyed the advantage of a unified national defense force, something the Palestinian Arabs completely lacked. Moreover, the Haganah's effective general staff and organizational structure ensured that forces could be supplied and deployed in a manner that assured overwhelming superiority on any given battlefield.

At the end of November 1947 the Haganah had some 16,000 light weapons—rifles, submachine guns, and pistols, about 1,000 machine guns, and 750 light mortars—and the Jewish Settlement Police, under British supervision but in fact loyal to the Haganah, legally held another 6,800 rifles and 48 machine guns. Most of the three hundred-odd Jewish settlements entered the war with well-prepared trenchworks, bunkers, and bomb shelters, with

barbed-wire perimeter fences and minefields. They were, in fact, small fortified encampments. But the Haganah had weak points too. It had no artillery or
tanks and only a small number of ramshackle, homemade armored vehicles. It
had a small fleet of civilian aircraft but no combat aircraft. And it had only a
very limited supply of ammunition.

The Palestinian Arabs' efforts in the 1930s and mid-1940s to set up
"national" military structures produced meager fruit in the form of two small,
poorly organized, armed and trained militias—the Najada, headed by
Nazareth lawyer Muhammad Nimr al-Hawari, and the Husseini-dominated
Futuwa, headed by ex–police officer Kamal Arikat. Under Husseini pressure
and intimidation they ultimately amalgamated into the Arab Youth Organization (AYO), and Hawari fled to Jordan. But the AYO never got off the
ground, and the Palestinians entered the fray without a "national" military
organization.[153]

During the early weeks of the war, in December 1947–January 1948, a
number of large Arab bands sprang up. The two largest were led by 'Abd al-
Qadir al-Husseini, who operated in the hills around Ramallah and Jerusalem,
and Hassan Salame, in the Lydda area. Each band had a hard core of about
three to five hundred fighters, who moved about the countryside quartering in
successive villages. Some villages refused to host them, for fear of Jewish retribution. They were lightly armed, their heaviest weapons running to two- and
three-inch mortars and medium machine guns. The Haganah's opinion of the
bands' abilities was low, as was Qawuqji's, who reportedly described them as
"unreliable, excitable and difficult to control and in organized warfare virtually unemployable."[154]

The largest and best-organized Arab formation in Palestine until the invasion of May 1948 was Qawuqji's ALA, consisting mainly of the volunteers
mustered by the Arab League in Syria. At its height, it comprised five to six
thousand troops and could call on hundreds of local volunteers in each locality. It was equipped with a diverse collection of light weapons, a number of
medium-sized mortars and some 75 mm and 105 mm guns, with a very small
stock of shells. After leaving Palestine in May 1948, the ALA reorganized in
Syria and returned with a slightly improved armory.[155] In October 1948, it
consisted on paper of eight battalions, but in reality it mustered no more than
three to four standard battalions. Each ALA battalion operated on its own.
They entered Palestine piecemeal from Syria and Jordan in January 1948, and
concentrated in Samaria and the Galilee. They were repeatedly defeated in
encounters with the Haganah, and were finally crushed and ejected from
Palestine by the IDF at the end of October.

In the main, Palestinian military strength was based on the separate forces
in the 800 or so villages and towns, only about 450 of which were involved in
the war. (The others, almost all of which lay in the territory which became the

West Bank, barely contributed to the war effort.) Each had its own "militia" of ten to one hundred men, armed with pistols or rifles and a small stock of ammunition. There was no "national" framework; at best they would coordinate on a regional basis, usually in offensive actions. The militiamen of a number of neighboring villages, for example, hearing of an approaching Jewish convoy, would mount an ambush together. The firefight over, they would disperse until the next such *fazza* (summons) took place a month or two later. Occasionally a *fazza* lasting from two to four days was mounted against a Jewish settlement or cluster of settlements, as in May 1948 at the Etzion Bloc. In defense each village was almost always on its own, and Jewish units were able to pick them off one at a time. Territorial or clan disputes often underlay this noncooperation.[156]

A number of villages and clans preferred to assist the Jews—with information and sometimes even with arms—because of a deep-seated hatred for their Arab neighbors or because they thought that the Jews would win and they preferred to be on the winning side. Most of the Druze villages in the Galilee threw in their lot with the Jews during 1948; some were to participate in Haganah or IDF attacks against their neighbors, and a Druze unit was eventually established in the IDF.[157]

All the Palestinian forces suffered from acute supply problems, especially the villages. Most received no outside supplies of any kind for the duration of the war: The ALA and the large bands had none to spare, and when the Arab countries or the Military Committee sent in arms and ammunition, they ended up in the hands of the larger units or, occasionally, the urban militias of Jaffa, Haifa, or Jerusalem. Once a village militia ran out of ammunition or guns, it ceased operations.

The ALA, the larger bands, and the urban militias relied on neighboring Arab countries for supplies. But these states were poor, corrupt, and badly organized, and the Arab League Military Committee in Damascus, which nominally supervised the war effort in Palestine, and the AHC leaders in exile proved unable to raise the necessary funds or to organize the dispatch of the war matériel on time. Yishuv intelligence reports are crammed with intercepts of messages from Palestinian towns and villages, and from the bands, desperately calling upon this or that Arab state, the Military Committee, or the AHC to rush in supplies. The response was almost invariably: "Soon, God willing."

According to one report,[158] by March 23 the Arab states had contributed to the Military Committee 9,800 rifles and almost 4 million rounds of ammunition. But the bulk went to the ALA; only a small part was distributed among the urban militias, and the villages got almost nothing. Moreover, much of the weaponry was of different types, and many of the rifles were unserviceable (particularly unusable were the Saudi contributions). Only the ALA seems to have enjoyed an effective logistical infrastructure, with fairly standardized weaponry and ammunition. Complicating matters, supply convoys were illegal and had to get around British patrols and checkpoints. They were also sometimes interdicted by the Haganah.

Still more critical than the problem of supplies was that of command and control. There were simply too many diverse units in the field (in Jaffa alone there were three or four separate militias) and too many bodies pulling the strings from outside. The Military Committee proved incapable of coordinating the disparate, often competing bodies, and itself had to fend off challenges from the AHC, while individual Arab states and the AHC manipulated the various militias to their own, separate advantage. Meeting in Damascus on February 5, 1948, the members of the Military Committee and Amin al-Husseini, 'Abd al-Qadir al-Husseini, and Hassan Salame decided more or less to formalize the existing situation. Palestine was divided into four zones, with the Galilee and Samaria under Qawuqji (ALA), the Jerusalem district under 'Abd al-Qadir, the Lydda area under Salame, and activities in the South to be overseen by an Egyptian commander. Safwat was named commander, and Taha al-Hashimi "inspector general," of all Arab forces in Palestine. Hajj Amin al-Husseini was given no area of responsibility.[159]

In practice, the attempt to impose central authority over and operational coordination between the various commands proved a dead letter. Moreover, the militia forces in the large towns by and large failed to accept the authority of the commanders or to coordinate activities with them. The death of 'Abd al-Qadir in early April left the crucial Jerusalem hills bereft of central command for the remaining six weeks of the battle. The absence of coordination was probably the single most important factor in the eventual Palestinian defeat and the relative ease with which this was accomplished by the Haganah.

THE FIRST PERIOD OF THE "CIVIL WAR"

The first, "civil war" stage of the conflict can be roughly divided in two. From December 1947 to March 1948, the Arabs held the initiative and the Haganah remained on the strategic defensive. Then, in early April, the Haganah went over to the offensive, by mid-May crushing Palestinian resistance. During the first period, the Arabs appeared to have the edge, especially in the battle for the main roads, the lifelines to western (Jewish) Jerusalem and a number of isolated settlement concentrations. It was not a concerted campaign; separate bands launched occasional attacks against Jewish vehicles, urban neighborhoods, and settlements. The Haganah, busy organizing its forces and wary of the British, adopted a defensive posture, though it did launch occasional, usually retaliatory, raids on Arab villages and urban sites.

As early as mid-December, pure defense had already given way to an "active" or "aggressive" defense; restraint (*havlaga*), as practiced through most of 1936–39, was not to be the Haganah's way this time. Moreover, its reprisal raids tended to be disproportionate to the original Arab offense. This strategy tended to spread the conflagration to areas that had so far been untroubled by the hostilities. From the first, the IZL and LHI, and to a lesser degree the Haganah, used terror attacks against civilian and militia centers. The Arabs responded by planting large bombs in Jewish civilian centers, especially in Jerusalem.

Almost from the outset the Arabs perceived that the Jewish towns and settlements, even the remote ones, presented formidable challenges, given their own meager resources and disorganization. But the roads were quickly understood to be softer targets. In March 1948 the bands' efforts to interdict Jewish traffic, by then running in convoys, succeeded to a remarkable degree: Isolated Jewish settlements and western Jerusalem, with its 100,000 Jewish inhabitants, faced siege and possible strangulation. It was this, as well as a growing assessment that the British were interested principally in their own safe withdrawal and would not interfere in the hostilities, that prompted the Haganah's switch to the offensive at the start of April, setting the stage for the second half of the "civil war."

Much of the fighting in the first months took place in and on the edges of the mixed cities—Jerusalem, Tel Aviv–Jaffa, and Haifa—in most cases initiated by the Arabs. But the IZL and LHI, using terrorism against civilians, had a major hand in turning what were sporadic Arab riots and armed attacks into a bitter, full-scale war. The first organized, armed attack on a Jewish urban neighborhood occurred on December 8, against the Hatikvah quarter of Tel Aviv. On December 4, Arabs had opened fire at the quarter and attempted to take a few houses; Haganah defenders fired back, killing several Arabs; and British troops intervened, killing two Haganah men and wounding others. On December 7, the Haganah retaliated by blowing up a house on the outskirts of the neighboring village of Salame.

The following day hundreds of Arab irregulars, led by Hassan Salame, launched a frontal assault in an attempt to conquer Hatikvah. A few of the quarter's peripheral houses fell as British troops looked on without interfering. The Arabs began looting and torching houses. Haganah reinforcements arrived, infiltrating between the British patrols, as did a squad of Jewish policemen. The attackers were pushed back to Salame. About 60 Arabs and 2 Jews were killed, and after the battle, a British officer returned a baby the Arabs had found and abducted. The British suspected that the attack had been carried out on direct orders from Husseini.[160]

With the British still heavily deployed in Jerusalem, the Mandate's capital, full-scale attacks on the Jewish neighborhoods ran the risk of forceful intervention and counterattack. Nonetheless on February 10, 1948, 150 Arabs from the Old City attacked the Yemin Moshe quarter to the west, across the Vale of Hinnom. The Haganah, aided by British troops, beat them off.[161] (That week, also in Jerusalem, the British displayed a contrary face when a squad of their troops disarmed four Haganah men and handed them over to an Arab crowd, which promptly lynched them. The troops responsible were later said to have acted in revenge for the murder of several of their comrades by LHI or IZL men back in November.[162])

Attacks on Jewish rural settlements also began in early December 1947, generally resulting in the Arabs being beaten off, sometimes with British assistance. The largest raid took place on January 9, 1948, when more than 300 Arabs, mostly Syrian Bedouin, stormed the frontier kibbutz of Kfar Szold, probably in response to a Palmah raid of December 18 on nearby Khisas (see below). The local British battalion commander sent eight armored cars to help the defenders, and the Arabs were driven off. One Haganah man was killed and four wounded; 24 Arabs died and 67 were wounded.[163]

In Tel Aviv, Jaffa, Haifa, and Jerusalem, in December and early January 1948, hundreds of Arab civilians were killed or wounded by IZL terror. In Jerusalem alone, 37 Arabs were killed and 80 wounded in two bombings on December 13 and 29.[164] Another such operation set in motion one of the bloodiest, most vicious cycles of terror and retaliation of the period: On December 30, an IZL squad threw a number of bombs into a crowd at a bus stop outside the Haifa Oil Refinery, killing six people and wounding dozens more. In a spontaneous response, the Arab workers in the refinery turned on their Jewish coworkers with hammers, chisels, stones, and clubs, massacring 39 of them and wounding another 50 before British forces intervened.[165]

The Haganah General Staff felt that the massacre could not go unanswered, whatever its causes. On the night of December 31 the suburban villages of Balad ash Sheikh and Hawassa, southeast of Haifa, where many of the Arab refinery workers lived, were raided by Palmah and Haganah units. The order at Balad ash Sheikh was to "kill a maximal number of adult males, destroy furniture, etc." but to avoid killing women and children. The raiders moved from house to house, pulling men out and executing them. Sometimes they simply threw grenades into houses and sprayed the interior with automatic fire. The villagers suffered more than 60 dead, some of them women and children. In Hawassa 16 men were killed and 10 wounded.[166]

The LHI also contributed to the carnage. On January 4, 1948, it detonated a truck loaded with explosives outside the Jaffa city hall, which housed the local Arab National Committee offices, demolishing the building and killing 26 persons and wounding many more. The operation badly damaged the morale of Jaffa's inhabitants and defenders.[167]

The Haganah also contributed to the terrorist campaign, though its intended targets were what were believed to be Arab terrorist concentrations rather than civilians. On the night of January 5, a Haganah unit blew up part of the Semiramis Hotel in Jerusalem, where it suspected an Arab irregulars headquarters was located, killing 26 civilians.[168] On February 28 some 30 Arabs died and 70 were wounded by a car bomb placed by a Palmah unit in the Abu

Sham garage in downtown Arab Haifa, where it suspected similar bombs were being assembled for use against Jews.[169]

Haganah retaliatory strikes contributed to the intensification and spread of the conflict. The organization entered the war with a mindset attuned to retaliation: Arab attacks should be countered with even more forceful Jewish responses, targeted, where possible, against the perpetrators themselves, and, if not, against a relevant collective target—the attackers' village, traffic on a nearby road, and the like. There were several such reprisals around the country on December 11, following Arab roadside ambushes in which 5 Jews were killed.[170]

A major raid took place on December 18 against the village of Khisas, in Upper Galilee. A Jewish guard had shot dead an Arab from Khisas; the British arrested him, and the villagers began to snipe at Jews in nearby fields. Then Arabs ambushed and killed a cart driver near Kibbutz Ma'ayan Baruch. That night the Palmah raided Khisas and a large nearby house (the "Palace") belonging to the main Arab landowner in the area, the Emir Fa'ur. In Khisas the Palmahniks blew up a house and killed three men, a woman, and four children; at the "Palace" they killed 4 men. Several Yishuv politicians and Arab experts later condemned the raid, saying that it had spread the conflagration to a hitherto quiet area.[171]

Attacks on Jewish vehicles were one of the components of the first stage of the war. Early in December, Jewish traffic began to move in Haganah-protected convoys, sometimes accompanied by British armored cars. The Haganah began to equip trucks and pickup trucks with armor-plating. But the ambushes grew in number and organization. On December 11, a convoy making its way from Jerusalem to the isolated Etzion Bloc of Jewish settlements south of Bethlehem was ambushed by a *fazza* of Arab villagers; 10 Jews died. On December 14 a second convoy was shot up near Ben Shemen. Most of the 14 Jewish dead were killed by Arab Legionnaires seconded to the British army in Palestine.[172] The Jews struck back with a series of ambushes of their own. On December 12, for example, a Palmah unit attacked an Arab bus, apparently filled with irregulars, near Safad, killing 6 and wounding 30. On December 16 the Alexandroni Brigade set up ambushes along roads near Beit Naballah in the central coastal area, and a number of Arabs were killed or wounded.[173]

Within weeks of the start of hostilities, foreign volunteers began arriving from Syria and Lebanon. A number of Iraqis and Syrians had accompanied both 'Abd al-Qadir al-Husseini and Hassan Salame, exiles since 1939, when they returned to Palestine at the start of December 1947, and set up armed bands. About six hundred volunteers who crossed into Palestine from Syria and Lebanon in late December were dispersed among the local militias in Jaffa, Haifa, Gaza, Safad, Acre, and Jerusalem.[174]

In the first half of January 1948, the advance units of the ALA—having completed a superficial training course in Qatana—crossed into Palestine. The

Second Yarmukh Battalion, of more than three hundred troops, mostly Syrians, crossed from Lebanon; and the First Yarmukh Battalion, with about six hundred men, from Jordan. The British did nothing about the crossings, save for exacting a worthless promise from the commander of one of the units that he would not engage the Jews until after the British themselves had departed. A third battalion, the Hittin, composed mostly of Iraqi volunteers, arrived in Palestine, also via Jordan, at the end of January, and joined the First Battalion near Nablus.[175]

On January 20 the Second Yarmukh attacked Kibbutz Yehiam, in western Galilee, taking its Haganah defenders by surprise, but it failed to overcome the settlement and withdrew after five hours.[176] The First Yarmukh went into action only on February 16, assailing Kibbutz Tirat-Zvi, in the Beit Shean (Beisan) Valley.[177] During the night of February 15 Haganah wiretappers had picked up coded messages telephoned from Jenin to Nablus and the Arab town of Beisan: "The sheikh is on his way. All is ready," and "Tonight a hot rain will fall near Beisan."[178] The kibbutz was reinforced, and on that same night a Palmah force attacked and blew up the Sheikh Hussein Bridge over the Jordan, to cut the ALA units off from their bases in Syria. When the assault on the kibbutz began, the Haganah was ready: Its counterfire, new barbed-wire fences, and pouring rain and mud proved too much for the attackers. The Arabs broke and retreated. A British armored column arrived on the scene and asked the commander, Muhammad Safa, to leave. Safa requested that they let loose with their mortars and machine guns so that he could later explain that he had withdrawn under British fire. They complied and the First Battalion withdrew, leaving behind their dead. The demoralizing news of the defeat swiftly spread through Arab Palestine.[179]

The failure of the irregulars to penetrate Jewish urban neighborhoods, and the retaliatory attacks on Arab neighborhoods, persuaded Husseini and his followers to switch their focus from the towns to the countryside. Moreover, delegations of Arab notables from Haifa, Jerusalem, and Jaffa had traveled to Egypt and pleaded with Husseini to let the towns alone. (Indeed, in December 1947, partly to enable both sides to export their citrus crop, Jewish Tel Aviv and Arab Jaffa representatives signed a nonaggression agreement.) The shift produced mixed results, with relatively successful attacks on traffic but failures in assaults on the fortified settlements. The irregulars, and to some degree the ALA as well, during January–March 1948 focused mainly on the roads, the area of maximum Jewish vulnerability. There the Arabs usually enjoyed the advantages of initiative, surprise, numbers, and firepower. And the results of successful ambushes could be far-reaching if not decisive. If supplies failed to get through, especially to Jewish Jerusalem, the Yishuv's morale and war effort might collapse. The gradual withdrawal of British troops from successive regions—they had already gone from Tel Aviv in December 1947— meant that in more and more areas it was possible to attack the roads without fear of interference. On December 31 the Shai had reported: "The Arabs intend, in the coming days, to paralyze all Jewish traffic on the roads." In early February 1948 the Shai learned that 'Abd al-Qadir intended to halt all Jewish traffic on the Tel Aviv–Jerusalem highway.[180]

As a complement to the battle for the roads, the Husseini-affiliated irregulars also turned to urban terrorism, despite the growing difficulty in penetrating Jewish neighborhoods, which had more and more patrols on the streets, and more and more British and Jewish barbed-wire cordons and checkposts separating the Arab and Jewish districts. The Arabs had noted the devastating effects of a few well-placed Jewish bombs in Jerusalem, Jaffa, and Haifa. The period January–March saw a succession of major urban terrorist attacks, probably mounted with Husseini's personal blessing.

The Arabs may well have learned the value of terrorist bombings from the Jews, as Arab Legion officer Abdullah Tal was later to write.[181] But the Husseinis' chief bomb maker, Fawzi al-Kutub, had learned his craft in an SS course in Nazi Germany.[182] On the night of February 1 two British deserters and an Arab used a British Army truck packed with explosives by Kutub to blast the offices of the *Palestine Post* in downtown Jerusalem. (British vehicles were still able to move freely through Jerusalem's various neighborhoods.) One Jew died and more than twenty were injured.[183]

The next bombing had far graver results. Haganah intelligence had ample forewarning—that it would be carried out by British deserters using a convoy of official army trucks being readied in the village of Immwas, near Latrun— but took no heed. Kutub used three stolen trucks and an armored car, with at least six British deserters and policemen. On the morning of February 22 the convoy drove to Ben-Yehuda Street, in the heart of Jewish Jerusalem. The Britons primed the bombs, shot a suspicious guard, got into the armored car, and drove off. The trucks then blew up, completely leveling four buildings and killing fifty-eight people and seriously wounding thirty-two. There was shock and anger in Jewish Jerusalem. Vengeful IZL and LHI members roamed the streets and killed sixteen British troops and policemen. On February 29 a bomb planted by the LHI near Rehovot derailed a British troop train traveling from Cairo to Haifa, killing twenty-seven soldiers.[184]

The third Arab bombing of the series was the most audacious. On March 11 a Husseini agent drove an American consulate car, rigged with a bomb, into the courtyard of the Yishuv's National Institutions compound, which included the headquarters of the Jewish Agency, the Jerusalem Haganah, and the JNF. When it went off, twelve people were killed and ten seriously wounded. The blow to Jewish morale was enormous.[185]

But ultimately the bombing campaigns were a sideshow; the roads were far more important. During January and February, Arab ambushes took a heavy toll. Supplying isolated outposts, such as Kibbutz Manara or Kibbutz Yehiam, in the Galilee, or the Etzion Bloc in the Judean Hills and the 100,000 Jews in

Jerusalem, became a major problem, and Palmah units were deployed to guard convoys. But while Jewish defensive tactics and means improved, so did the Arabs' organization and weaponry. It was essentially an unequal struggle between small Haganah units in lightly armed, cramped, hot, highly inflammable, makeshift armored cars and masses of Arabs enfilading the road from behind rocks on surrounding hills. Narrow roads made maneuver all but impossible. Communication between vehicles was often lost, and communications between the convoy and Haganah headquarters were impaired by poor equipment. There was usually nowhere to retreat to: Jewish settlements were often far away, with only unfriendly Arab villages in all directions.

Quite often British troops protected the convoys and intervened in firefights.[186] But this gradually ceased in March as more and more units were withdrawn to the Haifa enclave, from which they boarded ships to Britain. Their willingness to protect the Jews was dampened by the LHI's and IZL's terror attacks against them.[187] In any event, assuring the safety of the withdrawing forces had become Whitehall's chief concern—though, to be sure, a second major interest was maintaining good relations with the Arabs, so that Britain's position in the Middle East after the withdrawal would still be robust.

Jewish pressure on Arab traffic was maintained throughout. In some areas, such as Haifa, topography and demography combined to give the Jews the upper hand. But ultimately the Yishuv proved more vulnerable, because while most Arabs lived in autarchic or semiautarchic villages, most Jews were concentrated in towns that required continuous supply.

In late March, the Haganah endured a series of major disasters on the roads that portended final defeat in the war—or, alternatively, showed the need for a basic switch in strategy that would give the Yishuv the initiative and allow it to divert its energies away from protecting the convoys to defeating the Arab militias in their home bases. In the course of two weeks the Haganah lost most of its armored vehicles and hundreds of its best troops.

First came three serious setbacks in the Jerusalem area, in which the Haganah lost twenty-six men killed and eighteen vehicles.[188] Then, on March 27, a large convoy—some three dozen supply trucks, five buses full of troops, and seven armored cars—made its way from Jerusalem to the Etzion Bloc. The Arabs decided to attack the convoy on its way back. Kamal 'Arikat, 'Abd al-Qadir's deputy, mobilized thousands of armed villagers and townsmen from Hebron, Bethlehem, and Jerusalem; it was to be the biggest convoy ambush of the war. The British warned the Haganah that they would not intervene and advised that the convoy postpone its return. But the men and vehicles were needed back in Jerusalem, and the convoy set out.

A Haganah spotter plane warned that there were more than a dozen roadblocks and Arabs were massed along the route, but the commanders believed that they had superior firepower. A British colonel in an armored car drove southward through the roadblocks, met the convoy, and again warned them what to expect. The convoy plowed on. Just south of Bethlehem, the Arabs opened fire. An obstacle-busting vehicle, with a steel V-front, cleared six of the barriers before coming to a halt at the seventh. Heavy fire poured down on the stalled convoy from the hillsides. A relief column of four armored cars sent from Kibbutz Ramat Rachel, south of Jerusalem, was unable to reach the convoy and turned back after it, too, encountered an ambush and took casualties. The British rejected Haganah requests to intervene.

Most of the Haganah troops, 186 men and women all told, left the buses, which had become death traps, and took refuge in an empty stone house by the road. A few of the armored cars, like a wagon train, took up positions around the house. Six others, including the convoy commander's, managed to turn around and retreat. For the next thirty hours, the troopers were besieged by several thousand Arabs. Spotter planes, mounting Bren guns, periodically strafed the ambushers and dropped primitive bombs and supplies as the Haganah in Jerusalem tried unsuccessfully to put together a large relief force or, alternatively, prod the British into action.[189]

On the morning of March 28 a relief column of British armored cars at last set out from Jerusalem. Arab roadblocks repeatedly delayed it. The British halted a couple of kilometers from the besieged house, and a protracted three-way negotiation began. Eventually, the Haganah agreed to demands that its aircraft cease attacking and that the besieged troops give up their weapons before the British extricated them. The Haganah troops left under British escort and the British then handed over their arms to the Arabs.

Haganah losses were fifteen dead and seventy-three wounded, as well as a number of vehicles. Arab losses, according to the Shai, were approximately sixty dead and two hundred wounded. The engagement left a bitter residue in the Haganah. The commander in the besieged house, Arye Tepper (Amit), later wrote to Ben-Gurion and other Haganah chiefs implicitly blaming them for the fiasco and proposing that the isolated Jewish outposts around Jerusalem, including the Etzion Bloc, be evacuated; the price of holding on was too high.[190]

The losses were even greater when, also on March 27, a second Haganah convoy was attacked on the road to the isolated, besieged settlement of Yehiam, in western Galilee. Seven vehicles were ambushed by militiamen from the surrounding villages and units of the Second Yarmukh. The Shai had warned the convoy commander that the Arabs were massing—but, in light of Yehiam's plight, he decided to go ahead. The bulk of the convoy was destroyed. About three dozen men managed, under cover of darkness, to escape from the burning vehicles and make their way through the Arab lines. Only the following morning did British and Haganah men arrive at the scene and collect the bodies, many of them mutilated. The Haganah had suffered forty-seven dead and seven wounded. Arab losses were three to six dead and a handful of wounded.[191]

By the end of March, the food situation in Jewish Jerusalem was growing desperate: "There is panic in the city regarding supplies. . . . There may be food riots," wrote the head of the Shai in Jerusalem, Yitzhak Levy, to his commander, Isser Be'eri. The Haganah command believed that the city was on the verge of collapse.[192] On March 31, a large supply convoy was ambushed near Kibbutz Khulda. The area had been fairly quiet for weeks; a mutual Jewish-Arab agreement not to attack each other's transport had been reached. But the night before, Haganah troops had blown up a house and killed some fifteen Arabs in a nearby village, in reprisal for the killing of a Jewish watchman. And on the morning of March 31, Haganah troops fired on an Arab bus near Khulda, killing the driver and several passengers—in contravention of an order from Palmah headquarters.

The Arabs of the area and assorted irregulars gathered for a *fazza* with the convoy as their target. The dozens of trucks and armored cars, guarded by two companies of Palmahniks, came to a stop near Khulda after some trucks overturned. Arabs in the surrounding hills sniped at the vehicles, and were joined by a number of armored cars. A full-scale battle developed, and most of the convoy retreated back to Khulda. The Palmahniks extricated themselves and, with nightfall, reached Khulda. But twenty-two Haganah men died in the attack and sixteen were wounded. The crew of a Palmah armored car, abandoned by the convoy commanders, had blown themselves up rather than fall into Arab hands—Jews taken prisoner during convoy battles were generally put to death and often mutilated by their captors. Arab losses were eight dead. It was the first time a convoy had failed to make it to Jerusalem.[193]

THE SECOND STAGE OF THE CIVIL WAR

The loss of the convoys prompted a decisive switch in Haganah strategy. If the Arab bands could not be defeated on the roads, the Haganah would have to destroy them in their bases by attacking and conquering Arab villages and districts. Only thus could the pressure on embattled Jewish neighborhoods and settlements be permanently relieved. Moreover, with British evacuation drawing near, the emergent Jewish state's interior lines of communication and border areas had to be secured to facilitate defense against the expected invasion by the regular Arab armies. The Arabs' dispersed military capabilities inside the country, in the rear areas, had to be extinguished so that the Haganah's strength could be deployed along the borders.

The switch to the offensive in early April also had a political trigger: By mid-March the international community was beginning to entertain second thoughts about the partition resolution of November 1947. On March 19 the United States delegation to the United Nations introduced a motion to defer partition and establish an international trusteeship regime in Palestine. Truman was badly embarrassed. Only the day before, he had solemnly assured

Weizmann that the United States still backed partition. On March 25, egged on by Zionist lobbyists, the president reiterated his support for partition, but Washington's commitment had been revealed as shaky. A Haganah victory was clearly necessary to persuade a doubting world that the Jews would defeat the Palestinians and effectively establish a Jewish state.[194]

The gradual withdrawal of the British was now to help the Yishuv. By early April, the Haganah felt relatively certain that they would not interfere with its planned offensives. And, given the state of the Yishuv after the terrible losses along the roads, it had no choice: Either it went on the offensive or it would lose Jewish Jerusalem and, perhaps, the war.

One last reason for the change of strategy was that it had now become physically possible. Until early April, the Haganah had been in the throes of reorganization from an underground militia into a regular army, and incapable of mounting large offensive operations; its brigades lacked trained manpower and weaponry and had not yet solidified as effective large units. The Palmah, engaged daily in eastern Galilee, the Jerusalem Corridor, and the Negev, had provided the shield behind which the bulk of the Haganah had reorganized. By the end of March, many of the formations were more or less ready.

Finally, at the beginning of April, the first major injection of arms reached the Haganah, from Czechoslovakia—some 4,700 rifles, 240 machine guns, and 5 million rounds of ammunition.[195] This relatively massive shipment allowed the Haganah, at last, to concentrate a large number of weapons with sufficient ammunition in a single area for offensive operations, without dangerously stripping the localities. As Ben-Gurion observed at the time, "[F]ollowing the absorption of part of the Czech assistance, the situation changed radically in our favor."[196] The Haganah was transformed overnight from a "militia" into an "amateur army"; in a few months it was to become a "professional" army.[197]

Palestinian Arab strengths were well suited to the nature of the early months of the war, when fighting was dispersed, disorganized, small-scale, and highly localized. The moment the Haganah switched to the offensive and launched large-scale, highly organized, and sustained operations, the enemy's weaknesses came to the fore—and its military formations fell apart. But the Yishuv's leaders had no clear grasp of the essential weakness of Palestinian society; indeed, they felt they faced a far more formidable foe—and they were for the most part surprised, even shocked, by the swiftness of its collapse.

The change in strategy was decided on incrementally in the course of the first week of April: Each decision appeared to be a response to a particular, local problem. But by the end of the week it was clear that a dramatic conceptual change had taken place and that the Yishuv was now fighting a war of conquest as well as survival. This was prefigured in the Haganah's Plan D, drawn up by Haganah operations chief Yigael Yadin and his staff and submitted to the general staff on March 10. The plan was to have been set in motion in May, as the last British troops were withdrawing. Its aim was to take over strategic areas vacated by the British, gain control of the main towns and the internal lines of communication, and secure the emergent state's border areas in preparation for the expected invasion by the Arab armies. Implementation in effect meant crushing the Palestinian Arabs' military power and subduing their urban neighborhoods and rural settlements in the areas earmarked for Jewish statehood. The various areas held by the Haganah were to be soldered together by conquest of those lying in between into a single geographic-political-military continuum. Blocs of settlements outside the statehood areas—such as the Etzion Bloc and Nahariya—were also to be secured and linked up. Brigade and battalion commanders were given permission to raze or empty and mine hostile or potentially hostile Arab villages.

In effect, the implementation of Plan D was now brought forward. On the night of March 31, Ben-Gurion met in Tel Aviv with the Haganah command and made the crucial strategic decisions. The main immediate problem was Jewish Jerusalem, which he had decided must be held at all costs: The loss of the city, whose symbolic importance was incalculable and which contained one-sixth of the Yishuv's population, would, he felt, be a death blow to the Zionist cause. It was decided to mobilize a brigade-sized force of fifteen hundred troops and break through to Jerusalem with one or more massive convoys, neutralizing the main Arab militia bases (villages) along the way.[198]

Operation Nahshon, as it was called, started on the night of April 2, when a Palmah company captured the hilltop village of al-Kastal, five kilometers east of Jerusalem, dominating the highway into the city; in a second key action, on the night of April 4, a Giv'ati Brigade company blew up the headquarters near Ramle of Hassan Salame, commander of the band of Arab irregulars in the area. Though Salame himself was uninjured, at least seventeen of his men were killed, and the blow to morale was tremendous.[199] Meanwhile, Operation Nahshon unfolded smoothly. The relief convoy from Khulda—twenty-five supply-laden trucks, five armored buses, and eighteen armored cars—reached Jerusalem almost without incident.

The battle for al-Kastal turned out to be crucial, though the Haganah didn't realize it at the time. The Palmah unit which had captured the village was withdrawn and replaced by a second-line unit of the Etzioni (Jerusalem) Brigade. 'Abd al-Qadir al-Husseini realized the site's importance: Who controls al-Kastal controls the western entrance to Jerusalem. He organized a bid to retake it, but it failed. At dawn on April 8, 'Abd al-Qadir, in the belief apparently that the village was again in Arab hands, walked up the hill and was shot dead by a Jewish sentry. The death of the most prominent Palestinian military figure and the commander of the militias in the Judean Hills–Jerusalem area proved to be a turning point in the "civil war."

Word that Husseini was missing spread rapidly, and thousands of armed Arabs poured into the area. They wanted Husseini back—alive or dead. At about noon on April 8, they stormed the hill and eventually retook it. They found Husseini's body and took it to Jerusalem, where, on the Temple Mount, he was buried in a mass funeral, next to his father, Musa Kazim, the late mayor. Most of the fighters who had retaken al-Kastal accompanied the body to Jerusalem or left their positions to attend the funeral, and in the early hours of April 9 a Palmah force found the village completely deserted and captured it once again. The original operational order of April 2 had not instructed the troops to raze the village, but the order of April 8 specifically mandated destruction, an indication of the radical change in the Haganah's strategic thinking.[200]

But in the long run, the most important event during Operation Nahshon was probably the conquest by the IZL and LHI, assisted by the Haganah, of the village of Deir Yassin, which lay roughly between Jerusalem and al-Kastal, and the slaughter of many of its inhabitants. During the first months of the war, the village enjoyed relatively good relations with the nearby Jewish neighborhoods of western Jerusalem. In March, the villagers had dissuaded Husseini's men from attacking Giv'at Shaul and, later, refused to host ALA or irregular units. It is possible that—as often asserted by Israeli historians—a group of irregulars did bivouac in the village and fight in the subsequent battle, but the evidence for this is far from definitive.[201]

The Haganah command in Jerusalem, which had a good working relationship with the local IZL, tried to persuade its commanders to join the battle at al-Kastal. The IZL men declined, saying they had no transport and were, in any case, interested in mounting a separate, independent operation. Deir Yassin was targeted. In the planning meetings between IZL and LHI officers, they agreed to expel the inhabitants. The LHI men proposed that villagers who did not run away should be killed in order to terrify the country's Arabs. Most of the IZL and LHI officers present said they favored killing adult male prisoners, but the IZL command rejected these suggestions.[202] According to one IZL officer, the troops were ordered not to kill women and children or prisoners.[203]

The attack, on the morning of April 9, was carried out with the prior approval of, and in cooperation with, the Jerusalem command of the Haganah. Some 130 IZL and LHI fighters took part. During the battle, Haganah machine-gunners stationed nearby supplied covering fire, and two Palmah squads in armored cars joined in the actual battle. Palmah squads also helped evacuate the wounded, and the Haganah helped the combatants with ammunition.

The advance through the village proved far more difficult than anticipated. By its end the IZL and LHI had suffered five dead and more than thirty wounded—or more than one-quarter of the attacking force. The units, pinned down by sniper fire, advanced slowly, throwing grenades through windows and dynamiting house after house. Much of the population, including most of the able-bodied males, fled.[204] Soon after the start of the battle an IZL armored truck with a loudspeaker began calling on the villagers to lay down their arms and flee. But the truck got stuck in a ditch some 30 meters from the village and apparently went unheard.

Deir Yassin is remembered not as a military operation, but rather for the atrocities committed by the IZL and LHI troops during and immediately after the drawn-out battle: Whole families were riddled with bullets and grenade fragments and buried when houses were blown up on top of them;[205] men, women, and children were mowed down as they emerged from houses;[206] individuals were taken aside and shot.[207] At the end of the battle, groups of old men, women, and children were trucked through West Jerusalem's streets in a kind of "victory parade" and then dumped in (Arab) East Jerusalem.

According to Jerusalem Shai commander Levy (reporting on April 12), "the conquest of the village was carried out with great cruelty. Whole families—women, old people, children—were killed, and there were piles of dead [in various places]. Some of the prisoners moved to places of incarceration, including women and children, were murdered viciously by their captors." In a report the following day, he added: "LHI members tell of the barbaric behavior [*hitnahagut barbarit*] of the IZL toward the prisoners and the dead. They also relate that the IZL men raped a number of Arab girls and murdered them afterward (we don't know if this is true)." The Shai operative who visited the site hours after the event, Mordechai Gichon, reported on April 10: "Their [i.e., the IZL?] commander says that the order was: to capture the adult males and to send the women and children to Motza. In the afternoon [of April 9], the order was changed and became to kill all the prisoners. . . . The adult males were taken to town in trucks and paraded in the city streets, then taken back to the site and killed with rifle and machine-gun fire. Before they were put on the trucks, the IZL and LHI men searched the women, men, and children [and] took from them all the jewelry and stole their money. The behavior toward them was especially barbaric [and included] kicks, shoves with rifle butts, spitting and cursing (people from [the Western Jerusalem neighborhood of] Giv'at Shaul took part in the torture)."[208]

The Jewish Agency and the Haganah leadership immediately condemned the massacre. Deir Yassin became the one Jewish atrocity that it was permissible to write about—and to condemn. The Haganah made great efforts to hide its part in the operation, and during the following decades, Menachem Begin's Herut Party and its successor, the Likud, were continually berated for Deir Yassin in internal Israeli political squabbling. And over the years, the incident came to be used in Arab propaganda to blacken the name of the Yishuv as a whole.

During the next three days a variety of outsiders—Israeli doctors, Haganah officers, a Red Cross representative named Jacques de Reynier—visited the village to investigate. All saw bullet-riddled, sometimes charred bodies of men, women, and children. In 1948 participants, observers, and journalists wrote that as many as 254 villagers were killed that day. Everyone had an interest in publicizing a high Arab casualty figure: the Haganah, to tarnish the IZL and LHI; the Arabs and British, to blacken the Jews; the IZL and LHI, to provoke terror and frighten Arabs into fleeing the country. Recent Arab and Jewish investigations, and supporting interviews, however, suggest that these numbers were an exaggeration and that the real number of Arab dead was 100–110.[209]

Deir Yassin had a profound political and demographic effect. Despite a formal Jewish Agency Executive letter of apology and explanation to King Abdullah,[210] the incident seemed to push Jordan into the arms of those pressing for direct intervention by the Arab states, and to undermine the secret Yishuv-Abdullah agreement (see below). It may also have contributed to the decision of leaders of other nations—principally Egypt—to join the fray. Certainly the news enraged Arab fighting men, and "Deir Yassin!" became a rallying cry for combatants bent on revenge.

At the same time, however, the news of what had happened—extensively covered and exaggerated in the Arab media for weeks—had a profoundly demoralizing effect on the Palestinian Arabs and was a major factor in their massive flight during the following weeks and months. The IDF Intelligence Service called Deir Yassin "a decisive accelerating factor" in the general Arab exodus.[211]

The affair had an immediate and brutal aftermath. On April 13, Arab militiamen from Jerusalem and surrounding villages attacked a ten-vehicle convoy of mostly unarmed lecturers, nurses, and doctors on their way to the Hadassah Hospital–Hebrew University campus on Mount Scopus. (The convoy was also carrying two IZL fighters who had been wounded at Deir Yassin.) Four vehicles, including two packed buses, were trapped. For hours the British refrained from intervening and warned the Haganah not to do so. Three Palmah armored cars arrived on the scene but were overwhelmed by the ambushers. The shooting continued for more than six hours, the Arabs eventually dousing the armored buses with gasoline and setting them alight. When the British finally intervened, more than seventy Jews had died. Deir Yassin and the death of 'Abd al-Qadir had been avenged.[212]

Operation Nahshon had been only partially successful: Three large convoys had pushed through to Jerusalem and a number of Arab localities had been taken and either permanently occupied or leveled. But other villages remained and continued intermittently to block passage along the Tel Aviv–Jerusalem road. The Haganah launched a series of operations designed to either lift or ease the siege, but without achieving a strategic result. The road to Jerusalem remained closed.

While the Haganah was trying to break the back of the Arab forces in the Jerusalem Corridor, two battles took place in the north. Both were initiated by the Arabs but ended in Haganah victories and the wholesale flight of the local communities.

The battle for Kibbutz Mishmar Ha'Emek between Qawuqji's ALA and the settlement's defenders, eventually reinforced by Haganah companies, lasted from April 4 to 15. The kibbutz sat on the main road from Jenin to Haifa and was surrounded by Arab villages, whose militiamen helped Qawuqji's troops. ALA artillery reduced many buildings to rubble, but the settlers held out, repulsing an infantry assault. On April 8 the Haganah forces went over to the offensive and in six days took and leveled all ten surrounding villages. The inhabitants either fled or were expelled. The Haganah's measures were approved, in principle, by Ben-Gurion on April 8 or 9.[213] By April 15 the area around Mishmar Ha'Emek had been cleared of Arabs, and the ALA had withdrawn to the hill country to the east.

In the battle around Kibbutz Ramat Yohanan, Haganah troops, after repelling attacks on April 12 by the ALA's Druze unit, counterattacked and on April 16 captured the villages of Khirbet Kasayir and Hosha. The inhabitants fled. Nine Druze attempts to retake the two villages—they advanced "with large knives sparkling between their teeth in the sunlight"[214]—were beaten off, and the Haganah then razed the two villages to the ground. The Druze retreated and proceeded to abandon the ALA and make peace with the Haganah, marking the start of the Israeli-Druze alliance that continued through the 1990s.[215]

Later that month Jewish forces conquered key Arab urban areas, in effect delivering a death blow to Palestinian Arab military power and political aspirations. In a two-week period, Tiberias and Haifa and the districts of Manshiya in Jaffa and Qatamon in Jerusalem, fell in quick succession.

The Arab neighborhoods of Tiberias dominated the road linking the Jewish settlements in the Upper Galilee and the Jordan and Jezreel Valleys. In March 1948, in large measure as a result of Haganah provocations,[216] relations between the town's communities rapidly deteriorated, and the general staff decided to resolve the problem of Tiberias once and for all. On April 12 Haganah units raided the hilltop village of Khirbet Nasir ad Din, which overlooked Tiberias's Jewish districts. Atrocities were apparently committed, and the villagers fled to Arab Tiberias, sowing panic.[217] On the night of April 16 the Haganah attacked the Arab part of town with mortars, and took several houses in close-quarters combat. The British declined to intervene and Arab pleas for help from outside went unheeded. Within twenty-four hours resistance collapsed, and after the Haganah rejected a truce, the notables decided on evacuation. The British imposed a curfew, and the Arab population was trucked out to Jordan and Nazareth. The Jews looted the abandoned quarters.[218]

Haifa was the next to fall. In late 1947 Haifa had about seventy thousand Jews and an equal number of Arabs, making it, along with Jaffa, the largest

Arab concentration in Palestine. The Jews and Arabs had lived there in relative harmony for decades. But relations deteriorated during the first months of the war, with the two sides exchanging shots along the border between the two communities and planting bombs in each other's neighborhoods. The Haganah's onslaught, in line with Plan D, came on April 21; Arab disorganization and isolation, and a general feeling of weakness and of Jewish superiority, aggressiveness, and self-confidence, determined the outcome in just twenty-four hours.

On the night of April 20–21 the British units deployed along the seam between the Arab and Jewish neighborhoods were abruptly pulled out, and Jewish and Arab militiamen fought for control of the dominant positions. The Arabs had 500–1,000 militiamen; the Haganah's Carmeli Brigade had roughly the same number of troops but far superior command and control and better arms. Arab resistance gradually evaporated, and civilian morale broke, most of the population fleeing. Repeated pleas by Arab leaders for reinforcements from outside the city went unanswered; at one point British troops turned back a column that tried to reach the city from the village of Tira, to the south. A number of prominent Arab military leaders left Haifa just before or during the battle, ostensibly to seek aid. Throughout, the Haganah had the advantages of the initiative and topography (they dominated the high ground). Nonetheless the Carmeli's commanders were surprised by the speed of the Arab collapse.

Arab efforts on April 22 to obtain a truce were turned down by the Haganah, which demanded what amounted to unconditional surrender. The Arab leaders, preferring not to surrender, announced that they and their community intended to evacuate the town, despite a plea by the Jewish mayor that they stay. During the following week, all but three or four thousand of the Arabs left, and the town came completely under Jewish control (save for a small enclave that was to remain British until the departure of the last British troops from Palestine at the beginning of July).[219]

To the south, the IZL—after assembling its forces in the greater Tel Aviv area, some six companies in all—on April 25 launched an offensive, without coordination with the Haganah, with the aim of taking the northern, Manshiya, neighborhood of Jaffa, undermining morale in the town and precipitating a mass exodus of its inhabitants. IZL gunners let loose for seventy-two hours on downtown Jaffa with a hail of three-inch mortar bombs. The panic and flight unleashed by this incessant barrage served as background to the IZL's ground thrust toward the sea, through the southern part of Manshiya. The troops, poorly trained, led, and armed, found the house-to-house slog hard going. However, after losing some forty dead and at least twice that number wounded, the attackers at last reached the sea on April 27. As they advanced the inhabitants fled southward, toward the center of Jaffa, reinforcing the panic already created by the mortar barrage.

Palestinian and outside Arab spokesmen had blamed Whitehall for the fall of Arab Haifa and the subsequent exodus, which undermined Britain's standing in the Middle East. Now, with the IZL assault on Jaffa, Bevin and the military chiefs in London instructed the army to take a hard line. On April 28 High Commissioner Gen. Sir Alan Cunningham ordered the IZL to quit Manshiya; and British troops, accompanied by a mortar barrage and swooping Spitfires overhead, moved into Jaffa as Royal Navy vessels hove into view. The IZL withdrew after blowing up the district police fort.

But the show of force did not stem the Arab flight. A Haganah offensive on April 27–28, in which a string of Arab villages east of Jaffa fell to the Jewish forces, boosted the exodus. The behavior of Jaffa's Arab militiamen also contributed: They looted the empty houses and occasionally robbed and abused the remaining inhabitants. The townspeople knew that, whatever the motive behind Britain's aid, in two weeks the troops would be gone, and unable to help them. Hence Bevin's dramatic intervention did little or nothing to stem the flow of refugees. By the time the remaining city notables surrendered to the Haganah, on May 13, only four or five thousand of the eighty thousand inhabitants remained. On May 18, after visiting the conquered town, Ben-Gurion wrote in his diary: "I couldn't understand. Why did the inhabitants . . . leave?"[220]

The conquest of Tiberias and Haifa was quickly followed by two major Haganah offensives in the countryside, also in line with Plan D: the occupation of the Arab villages of eastern Galilee and the Arab quarters of Safad (Operation Yiftah), and the conquest of western Galilee (Operation Ben-Ami).

Operation Yiftah, which began on April 15, moved into high gear on May 1, when Palmah units took the villages of Biriya and 'Ein az Zeitun, just north of Safad. During the following two days, sappers demolished the villages as Safad's Arabs looked on. On May 4, the Palmah First Battalion pushed southeastward from Rosh Pina and cleared the whole area as far as the northern shore of the Sea of Galilee of its Bedouin inhabitants, who fled eastward, to Syria. This suboperation, code-named Operation Broom, had "a tremendous psychological impact" on the Arabs of Safad and the Hula Valley, said Palmah commander Yigal Allon, who directed Operation Yiftah.[221]

Safad, with ten to twelve thousand Arab inhabitants and fifteen hundred Jews, was the political and commercial hub of eastern Galilee. The British had evacuated it on April 16. The Arab neighborhoods were defended by several hundred ALA fighters and several hundred local militiamen; the Haganah had about two to three hundred troops plus a thirty-five-man Palmah platoon. But the Arab population was already demoralized when battle was joined on May 6. When the Palmah's Third Battalion attempted to storm the Arab strongpoints, it was beaten back; nonetheless the Arabs sought a truce. Allon rejected the terms, and the Arab states failed to send help. Starting on May 2, inhabitants began to trickle out of the town.[222] The Palmah attacked again on the evening of May 10, beginning with a strong mortar barrage. The Arab irregulars collapsed and fled, and by the early hours of May 12, the town had been secured, almost all the Arab inhabitants fleeing eastward across the Jordan.

The fall of Safad and the flight of its inhabitants shocked the Arab villagers of the Hula Valley, to the north. Allon launched a psychological warfare campaign ("If you don't flee immediately, you will all be slaughtered, your daughters will be raped," and the like), and almost all the villagers fled to Lebanon and Syria.[223]

Complementing Operation Yiftah, the Golani Brigade cleared the Arab villages of the Jordan and Beit Shean Valleys as well as the town of Beisan, which fell on May 13, with most of the inhabitants fleeing, or being driven across the river, to Transjordan. A day or two short of the pan-Arab invasion, all of eastern Galilee was in Jewish hands.

The battle for western Galilee was launched by the Carmeli Brigade on May 13. It was a last-second effort to secure and physically incorporate in the Jewish state an area that had been designated Palestinian Arab territory in the partition resolution. The scattered Jewish settlements in the area—Hanita, Eilon, Matzuba, Yehiam, all kibbutzim, and the town of Nahariya—had been cut off from reinforcement and supplies for weeks and looked bleakly towards a future under Arab rule. They mounted an effective lobbying campaign among the Haganah brass and the Jewish Agency Executive. The result was Operation Ben-Ami. Ostensibly the aim was to push through supplies and reinforcements to the isolated outposts; in effect, the result was conquest, incorporation, and the clearing of the area of Arabs.

Initially a cluster of villages was overrun. Then, on May 18–19, Acre fell to Carmeli Brigade units, and much of its population fled, though five to six thousand inhabitants remained.[224] On May 21–22 the troops pushed eastward from the coast and took a string of Arab villages in the overlooking hills. Western Galilee, from the Mediterranean to a line about ten to thirteen kilometers to the east, was thus secured for the Jewish state.[225]

The final weeks of the Mandate had seen the conquest of many of Palestine's Arab population centers and the destruction of their military power, which for all practical purposes was not exercised again for the rest of the war. Moreover, the Jews had secured crucial border areas and territorial continuity between them and the Jewish population centers; likely Arab invasion routes had been fully or partially blocked.

But in the last days of the Mandate, too, a number of offensives were carried out by external Arab forces. In the south Egypt-backed Muslim Brotherhood irregulars attacked Negev outposts; Kibbutz Kfar Darom's forty-five defenders beat off attacks by hundreds of "brothers," most of them Egyptians.[226]

In the center of the country Arab Legion units, supported by hundreds of villagers, managed to overcome and conquer the isolated Etzion Bloc (four Jewish settlements north of Hebron). Under intermittent siege since January, it was defended by about four hundred men and one hundred women (the children had been evacuated). The Haganah command refused to evacuate the settlers as a matter of principle ("[N]o Jewish outpost must be abandoned"). In addition, the bloc harassed Arab traffic along the Hebron-Jerusalem road and diverted Arab attention and resources, easing the pressure on Jewish Jerusalem. Local militiamen and Arab Legionnaires—which, though seconded to the Mandate, during the waning period of British rule acted as an independent, Arab army—were bent on destroying the bloc. On May 4, following an ambush by bloc fighters against Arab traffic, a Legion armored column backed by hundreds of local villagers attacked, and about forty of the defenders were killed or wounded.[227]

On May 12 the assault was renewed; Legion Sixth Battalion units and thousands of armed villagers gathered for the kill. The defenders had no adequate answer to the Legion's artillery and armored cars. The next day the legionnaires broke into the main settlement, Kfar Etzion. Villagers shouting "Deir Yassin, Deir Yassin" poured through the breach. The remaining defenders laid down their weapons and walked, hands in the air, into the center of the compound. There, according to one of the few survivors, the villagers (and perhaps some legionnaires as well) proceeded to mow them down.[228]

In all, about 120 defenders, 21 of them women, died that day. Of the 4 survivors, 3 were saved by Arabs. The remaining three kibbutzim held on until the morning of May 14, but their position was hopeless. The Haganah general staff gave them permission to surrender, and all the defenders and settlers, except four more who were murdered by their captors, were trucked off to a Legion prison camp near Mafraq, Jordan. About 350 of the bloc's defenders ended up in captivity.[229]

Despite the fall of the Etzion Bloc, the result of the five-and-a-half months of fighting was a convincing Jewish victory. Palestinian Arab society and military strength had been dealt crushing blows. Important areas assigned in the UN resolution to Palestinian or international control—including Jaffa and parts of western Jerusalem—fell under Zionist sway as hundreds of thousands of Palestinians were driven from or fled their homes. The Haganah consolidated its hold on a continuous strip of territory along the coastal plain, the Jezreel Valley, and the Jordan Valley, which it proved able to hold against combined Arab attack from without and from which it was able, eventually, to expand, at the expense of additional territory earmarked for Palestinian sovereignty. The victory gave the Haganah the experience and self-confidence necessary to later defeat the invading Arab armies and earned the new State of Israel sufficient credit to enable the international community to accord it diplomatic recognition.

The Second Half of the War:
Israel Versus the Arab States,
May 15, 1948–Spring 1949

RELATIVE STRENGTHS

On the afternoon of May 14 the leaders of the Yishuv gathered in the Tel Aviv Museum and heard Ben-Gurion read the Declaration of Independence, announcing the establishment of the State of Israel. At the end of the thirty-two-minute gathering, Ben-Gurion announced simply: "The State of Israel has arisen! This meeting is over." In his diary he noted: "In the country there is celebration and profound joy—and once again I am a mourner among the celebrants, as on 29 November [1947]."[230] The Yishuv faced invasion by the Arab states and full-scale conventional war. Two days before, Haganah commanders had told him the chances of victory were "50–50."[231]

The civil war had ended with the Haganah in control of two connected north–south strips of Palestine: One consisted of the Galilee Panhandle and the Jordan and Beit Shean Valleys; the other ran along the Mediterranean coastline, from the Lebanese border through western Galilee, Haifa, and Tel Aviv–Jaffa, and ended in the southern coastal plain around Rehovot. The strips were linked by the Jewish-held Jezreel Valley. In addition a narrow corridor ran to western Jerusalem; and in the south the northern Negev settlement bloc was connected to the coastal area by a thin strip of land around Negba.

The Arabs held the central Galilee, including Nazareth; the southern coastal plain; an expanded West Bank (Judea and Samaria), stretching westward to Lydda and Ramle and southward as far as Beersheba; and the bulk of the Negev. They also held a small enclave just south of Haifa, which included four villages.

The Jewish areas were defended by nine Haganah brigades. Three more were to be organized during the following weeks. On May 15, the Haganah had a total of thirty to thirty-five thousand men; the IZL and LHI, another three thousand together.[232] About six thousand of the Haganah men were in the three Palmah brigades. By June, the IDF had 42,000 men and women under arms.[233] Large shipments of light arms had poured into the country during May, and by June, according to Ben-Gurion, the IDF "had a surfeit" of light weapons.[234] The Yishuv's own weapons plants had already produced seven thousand Sten guns; by October, sixteen thousand. By the end of May, they were producing all the IDF's needs in submachine guns and their ammunition; in light and medium mortars; in antitank rockets; and in grenades, mines, and bombs.[235]

Arab Invasion of Palestine, May 1948

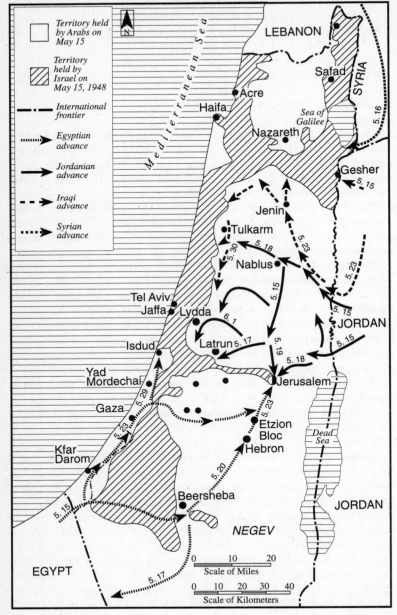

The Haganah's main problem during the first two weeks of the Arab invasion was in the field of heavy weapons. It had managed to steal or buy from the departing British units three tanks, twelve armored cars (four of them mounting cannon), three half-tracks and three coastal patrol vessels.[236] By the end of May ten additional tanks and a dozen or so half-tracks purchased abroad had arrived. In addition, by May 15 there were four or five small field artillery pieces (forty-five by the end of the month), twenty-four antiaircraft or antitank cannon, seventy-five PIAT (projectors, infantry, antitank) launchers and about one hundred armored trucks and personnel carriers, the great majority of them converted trucks fitted with armor plating. The Haganah also had about seven hundred two-inch mortars and one hundred three-inch mortars, plus a few crude, locally made heavy ("Davidka") mortars—all of which compensated, to some degree, for the initial lack of artillery.

The Haganah had twenty-eight light reconnaissance and transport airplanes but no combat aircraft (though some light aircraft were fitted with machine guns and used as makeshift bombers). By May 29, Israel had received, assembled, and sent into action four Czech-made Messerschmitt Avia 199 fighters.[237]

Each side tended to exaggerate the other's strength; the Yishuv's strategy cannot be understood without taking into account its very real fears of defeat and possible annihilation, which began to dissipate only after the Arab armies proved smaller and less efficient than anticipated. In mid-1947 Ben-Gurion believed that Transjordan's Arab Legion consisted of no less than "15–18,000" troops, with "400 tanks,"[238] though in fact it had no tanks at all and, at the time, only about six thousand soldiers. All the Arab armies were much smaller than the Haganah believed and, in any event, deployed only part of their strength in Palestine.[239] Only the Transjordanian regime felt secure enough to commit most of its army.

The Arab forces in Palestine consisted (until the end of May) of not more than 28,000 troops—some 5,500 Egyptians, 6,000–9,000 Arab Legionnaires, 6,000 from Syria, 4,500 from Iraq, a handful of Lebanese, and the remainder Palestinian irregulars and foreign volunteers.[240] On paper, according to Haganah estimates, the combined Arab armies had some 75 combat aircraft, 40 tanks, 500 armored vehicles, 140 field guns, and 220 antiaircraft and antitank guns. In practice they had far less, much of the equipment (especially the aircraft) being unserviceable, and some of the remainder never reaching Palestine.

After the invasion both sides substantially increased their forces, the Jews handily winning the manpower race. By mid-July the IDF was fielding nearly 65,000 troops; by early spring 1949, 115,000. The Arab armies probably had about 40,000 troops in Palestine and Sinai by mid-July, and 55,000 in October, [241] the number perhaps rising slightly by the spring of 1949.[242]

There was, however, a relative decline in Arab strength during the course of the war, which by September–October 1948, resulted in clear if not over-whelming Jewish superiority. This was a result of Israel's "victory" in the struggle against the international arms embargo imposed by the UN Security Council on all the Middle East combatants from May 29, 1948, until August 11, 1949. Even before this, on December 14, 1947, the United States had unilater-ally declared an embargo. And beginning in February 1948, Britain—the sole supplier of weapons and ammunition to the Iraqi, Egyptian, and Transjordan-ian armies—began to curtail such shipments to the entire Middle East.[243] The embargo was applied with great rigor by the United States and Britain as well as by France, the traditional arms supplier of Syria and Lebanon. In retrospect it clearly hurt the Arab cause badly but only minimally harmed the Yishuv.

The Arab states had no alternative sources; from July onward their armies suffered from severe shortages in weapons, ammunition, and spare parts. The Egyptian Air Force in October 1948 nominally had thirty-six fighters and six-teen bombers; in practice it was able to fly less than a dozen of the fighters and only three or four of the bombers, and those with ill-trained crews and inade-quate munitions.[244] The Haganah had laid down an extensive secret arms-procurement network in Europe and the Americas. Some $129 million, in cash and pledges, was raised from Jews abroad; $78.3 million was spent between October 1947 and March 1949, on arms purchases.[245] Early in the war deals were concluded with Czechoslovakia, which was hungry for dollars, and with private dealers in Western Europe and the United States, and relatively large arms shipments began to arrive from March 30, 1948, the bulk after the decla-ration of statehood on May 14. Neither the Czechs nor the private dealers paid any attention to the UN arms embargo. But the Arab states lacked the cash and the contacts to buy from them.

Thousands of trained Jewish and gentile volunteers flocked from abroad to join the Jewish forces. More than three hundred Americans and Canadians—mostly with World War II experience—served in the IAF in 1948, 198 of them as air crew.[246] The IAF had far more trained personnel than were needed; the Arabs far too few. Thus, in October 1948, flying only a dozen or so fighters, the IAF gained immediate air superiority against the Egyptians. The surfeit of per-sonnel and the availability of spare parts and munitions made all the difference.

PLANNING—OR NOT PLANNING— THE ARAB INVASION OF PALESTINE

On the eve of the pan-Arab invasion, 'Abd al-Rahman Azzam Pasha, the Arab League's secretary general, who for months had sounded dubious about the prospective invasion, fearing Jewish power and Arab disunity and incompetence, changed his tune, declaring: "This will be a war of extermination and a momentous massacre, which will be spoken of like the Mongolian massacres and the Crusades." Ahmed Shukeiry, one of Hajj Amin al-Husseini's aides, described the aim of the invasion as "the elimination of the Jewish state."[247] But such utterances hid deep doubts, fissures, and disagreements in the Arab camp. There was no political agreement about the goals of the war; there was no unity of military command, agreed military aims, or operational procedures and timetables; and there was no political-military coordination.

General Ismail Safwat, in charge of the external Arab involvement in Palestine since autumn 1947, was initially designated supreme commander of the invasion armies but was replaced at the last minute by a more politically acceptable candidate, Gen. Nur al-Din Mahmud, also an Iraqi. Safwat, in his Damascus headquarters, had spent weeks trying to hammer out a joint strategy and a detailed invasion plan for May 15: "A swarm of Syrian and Iraqi officers buzzed around the building seemingly more familiar with the science of political intrigue than with that of warfare. The distribution of funds, of commands, of rank, of operational zones, of arms and materials, all were objects of bargaining as intensive as any displayed in the city's souks."[248]

With the exception of the Arab Legion, none of the Arab armies had really prepared for war. All had assumed either that the day would never come or that, if it came, it would be a walkover or that the UN would intervene before the going got tough; no preparations would be needed. Indeed, none—again excepting the Legion—had ever fought in a war. In the last days before the invasion, military and political leaders oscillated between overoptimistic contempt for the Jews and a fatalistic pessimism. "Tel Aviv in a fortnight," "a parade without any risks whatsoever," was how the Egyptian army presented the coming adventure to its political superiors—even though, only weeks before, they had spoken clearly and firmly against intervention in Palestine, arguing lack of training, arms, ammunition, and so on. "We shall never even contemplate entering an official war. We are not mad . . . ," the Egyptian defense minister, General Muhammad Haidar, had told one journalist. General Ali Ahmed al-Mawawi, commander-designate of the Egyptian invasion force, told Haidar that his troops were not "trained for war."[249]

'Azzam Pasha, meeting in Amman with a British representative a week before the invasion, stated: "It does not matter how many [Jews] there are. We will sweep them into the sea."[250] But Prince Talal, son of Abdullah, openly predicted Arab defeat.[251] And at the last moment several leaders, including the Saudi king and 'Azzam Pasha himself, appealed to the British to prolong their stay in Palestine.[252] Of course the pessimists were right. The Arabs had done no proper planning or intelligence work, logistics were in a shambles, armaments and ammunition were in piteously short supply. Officers and soldiers alike were unprepared for what faced them—a tenacious enemy, well dug in, superior to them in organization and numbers, and soon to be better equipped.

But by the start of May the Arab leaders had no other option but war. "The politicians, the demagogues, the Press and the mob were in charge—not the soldiers. Warnings went unheeded. Doubters were denounced as traitors," recalled the Arab Legion's British commander, Gen. John Bagot Glubb.[253] The leaders found themselves enmeshed in a snare of pro-war rhetoric of their own making. By May 15 not to go to war appeared more difficult and dangerous than actually taking the plunge, whatever the eventual outcome.

It is unclear whether the armies had agreed on a plan of war when they invaded Palestine, even of a most general, strategic kind.[254] Certainly there was nothing that could be considered a "detailed" plan. Nevertheless, a plan of sorts had apparently been produced by Capt. Wasfi Tal, a young Arab Legionnaire who served as Safwat's head of operations. It foresaw an eleven-day campaign, with the Lebanese army pushing down along the coast from Ras al-Naqurah to Acre; the Syrian army, in two columns, thrusting southward from Bint Jbail in southern Lebanon and westward, from the Sea of Galilee area, toward Afula; units of the Iraqi army crossing the Jordan at Beisan and thrusting northwestward toward Afula; and Arab Legion units, after crossing the Jordan, driving for Afula from Jenin. The pincer around Afula would then turn into a massive combined drive on Haifa. At the same time other Legion units would drive westward through Judea and Samaria, soon to become known as the West Bank, toward Lydda and Ramle and perhaps the Mediterranean shore. The Egyptians would drive straight up the coast through Majdal toward Jaffa–Tel Aviv. Tal's "plan" appeared to call for far greater forces than were actually allocated by the Arab states.

The League Political Committee approved the plan on May 12.[255] Just before the meeting, 'Azzam Pasha traveled to Amman, to try to persuade Abdullah and Glubb to become the supreme commanders of the invasion forces. Glubb declined, apparently regarding 'Azzam (and perhaps the plan itself) as "naive and impractical."[256] A day or two later, the plan was revised downward by the League Military Committee. The northern objective now became to cut off Jewish-held eastern Galilee (the area from Beisan to Metulla) from Haifa. Afula, rather than Haifa, now became the main objective of the planned offensive.[257]

But Abdullah was not primarily interested in the north or Haifa. He wanted eastern Palestine. On May 13, unilaterally changing the plan, he instructed Glubb (and perhaps his Iraqi allies, whose expeditionary force was in his kingdom), that the West Bank was the real objective: The Legion would fan out in and occupy the hilly Samarian-Judean area, including Jericho, Ramallah, Nablus, and Hebron, and areas around Jerusalem.[258] Abdullah and Glubb were chary about attacking Jerusalem itself, for both political and military reasons. The Iraqis intended to make a minor thrust in the Beisan area, toward

Kibbutz Gesher, and were later instructed to take over northern Samaria (the Jenin-Tulkarm-Nablus triangle) from the Legion.

This confronted the Egyptians with a major political dilemma. Their rivals, the Hashemites, clearly intended to grab as much as they could of Arab Palestine. The Egyptians responded by changing their planned unitary offensive, up the coast to Tel Aviv, to a two-pronged attack: one toward the Arab coastal towns of Majdal and Isdud (and perhaps, later, Tel Aviv); the other eastward, toward Beersheba, and then northeastward, toward Hebron and Jerusalem. Egypt intended to acquire a chunk of the West Bank (and perhaps of Jerusalem).[259] Thus the Arab war plan changed in conception and essence from a united effort to conquer parts of the nascent Jewish state and perhaps destroy it, into a multilateral land grab focusing on the Arab areas of the country. The evolving Arab "plans" failed to assign any task whatsoever to the Palestinians or to consider their political aspirations. Moreover, the ALA was ordered by the Jordanians to leave the West Bank and move to Galilee—that is, out of the area they themselves intended to occupy.[260]

The key to understanding what was happening, and Arab disunity, lay in Amman. For two years Abdullah had been locked in intermittent, secret negotiations with the Jewish Agency with the aim of annexing eastern Palestine. He favored partition, but between himself and the Jews. His preference was a federative solution in which the Jews would have an enclave with autonomous rights within a Hashemite kingdom. But the Jews insisted on full independence, and by the end of 1947 he had resigned himself to their statehood.

At a secret meeting with Golda Meir on November 17, 1947, Abdullah expressed this resignation and asked how the Jews would view his takeover of the Arab part of Palestine. Meir responded favorably and reported later that Abdullah had said he wanted compromise, not war, and that "he would not allow his forces to clash with us nor cooperate with other forces against us." His idea was to take over the Arab areas in order to enforce law and order and forestall the mufti. Meir in effect agreed to the proposed Jordanian takeover of the West Bank. A mutual nonbelligerency deal had been struck.[261] On the night of May 10, 1948—disguised as an Arab in flowing black robes—Meir arrived in Amman for her second meeting with Abdullah. The king revived his proposal, of Jewish autonomy within a Hashemite Arab state. He said the situation had changed; there had been Deir Yassin, and he was now only one of a coalition of five war-bound rulers, no longer a free agent. "He is going to this business [of war] not out of joy or confidence, but as a person who is in a trap and can't get out," Meir later explained to her colleagues. Abdullah had pointedly declined to recommit himself to the November 1947 understanding. But at the same time, he seemed to imply that a Jewish state would arise and that he would make peace with it after the war.[262]

After the meeting, Yishuv officials were left unsure whether or not the Legion would attack Jewish territory—but in fact it didn't. Abdullah was far from confident of Arab victory and preferred a Jewish state as his neighbor to one run by the ex-mufti. "The Jews are too strong—it is a mistake to make war," he told Glubb, just before the invasion,[263] ". . . —though without doubt many of his soldiers believed that they were embarked on a crusade to destroy the Yishuv and liberate all of Palestine."[264]

A key feature of the Arabs' plans was the complete marginalization of the Palestinians. Their remaining militia formations were either ignored or destined to serve as auxiliaries to the regular armies. This aptly reflected the political reality: The military defeats of April–May had rendered them insignificant. The Arab League through the first half of 1948 had consistently rejected Husseini's appeals to establish a government-in-exile. But the May 15 invasion, with Jordan's occupation of much of eastern Palestine, was to change the situation. Under strong pressure from Egypt, which feared complete Hashemite control over the Palestinians, the League Political Committee in mid-September authorized the establishment of a Palestinian "government." On September 22, the Arab Higher Committee proclaimed the establishment, in Egyptian-ruled Gaza, of the "All-Palestine Government," and on September 30 a constituent assembly, the "Palestine National Council," with about eighty delegates, was convened. Escaping his Egyptian "protectors," Husseini managed to reach Gaza on September 27 and was named president of the council.

But it was all farce. On September 30, King Abdullah convened in Amman the rival "First Palestinian Congress," which promptly denounced the Gaza "government." The Egyptians, for their part, soon bundled Hajj Amin back to Cairo. The Gaza "government" and "Council" did not long outlast his departure. Though it was rapidly recognized by most of the Arab governments, the skeleton administration hastily put together in Gaza managed to carve out no real fiefdom; under tight Egyptian military administration, it had no real powers or funds. Moreover, most of the little land that was nominally under its control (that is, the area of Palestine held by the Egyptian army) was overrun in mid-October by the IDF. At the same time, the Arab Legion disarmed the few Palestinian militiamen in the West Bank who might have owed it allegiance. The "All-Palestine Government" maintained a paper existence as a subsection within the Arab League until 1959, when it was finally disbanded by Col. Gamal Abdel Nasser.[265]

On the eve of the 1948 invasion, both sides enjoyed major strategic advantages and disadvantages. The Arabs held the initiative and could count on a measure of strategic and tactical surprise: They would be striking first, when and where they chose, and could expect to enjoy at least temporary local superiority, in manpower and weaponry. Moreover, the Arabs held much of the high ground—in Galilee, Samaria, and Judea; Jewish control was largely limited to the coastal plain and the Jezreel and Jordan Valleys. The Arabs also had an overwhelming preponderance in heavy weapons—artillery, armor, and aircraft.

The Haganah enjoyed superiority in both quality and quantity of manpower, unity of command, and relatively short lines of communication that facilitated resupply and the rapid shift of forces. By and large the Haganah had better trained, more capable commanders—though the Arab Legion's mostly British senior officers were probably as good, if not better. Initially on the defensive, the Haganah for the most part enjoyed the home-court advantage: greater familiarity with the terrain and the morale-boosting stimulus of fighting for one's own home and fields (in many cases literally) and in defense of one's loved ones. Moreover, as during the first "civil" half of the war, the Jews felt that they faced slaughter should they be defeated. With the memory of the Holocaust still fresh in their minds, the Haganah troopers were imbued with unlimited motivation. The soldiers and officers in the Arab armies were less motivated. While eager to defeat the Jews—infidels and usurpers—and to right the wrong done to the Palestinians, their countries, homes, and families were not in the balance. The Arab soldiers were and remained invaders, fighting a great way from home for a remote, largely abstract cause.

The Haganah enjoyed an unquantifiable though very real advantage owing to its victory in the "civil war." It had crushed Palestinian military power and, as a result, enjoyed a self-confidence based on proven capabilities. The Arab armies—bar the Legion, whose officers and some troops had seen combat in World War II—had no such victory under their belts and had no tangible basis for confidence in their own abilities.

THE JORDANIAN FRONT

The force the Yishuv feared most was the Arab Legion: The Jews had come to respect it during the months it had served with the British army in Palestine. It had assisted the British campaigns in Iraq and Syria in 1941. A professional, efficient, small army, its total strength in May 1948 was about eight thousand.[266] It was highly mechanized, with effective auxiliary and service units, and was led by fifty to seventy-five experienced British officers and noncommissioned officers, including the chief of staff, General Glubb.[267] The Legion—soon to be renamed the "Royal Jordanian Army"—had no air force and no tanks, but it had some 120 armored cars, about 70 of them armed with two-pounder guns, and a highly professional artillery arm.

From October 1947 to May 1948 the Legion underwent substantial reorganization, manpower expansion, and reinforcement in matériel, in preparation for the British withdrawal from Palestine. By mid-May it consisted of three brigades, each with two battalions (called regiments). During the war Glubb mounted a massive recruitment and training campaign, and by May 1949 his army consisted of fourteen thousand soldiers.[268]

The Legion was very short of ammunition, especially for its artillery, and suffered severely from the embargo imposed soon after the start of hostilities.[269] It embarked on the invasion with artillery shells for ten days' combat and light weapons ammunition for thirty days.[270] The officers, not expecting an embargo, expended their shells and bullets with little restraint. On May 30, the Fourth Battalion, fighting in Latrun, ran completely out of ammunition.[271]

When the Legion crossed into Palestine before dawn on May 15, "the troops themselves were in jubilation. . . . Many of the vehicles had been decorated with green branches or bunches of pink oleander flowers, which grew beside the road. The procession seemed more like a carnival than an army going to war," its commander was later to recall.[272] But some of the soldiers, at least, embarked on the expedition with a touch of bitterness. Capt. Mahmud al-Ghussan, a staff officer in the Fourth Battalion, later recalled that the inhabitants of Amman had virtually ignored the troops as they passed through the city on their way "to save [Palestine] from the Zionists and the West."[273]

The Legion's First Brigade headed northwest for Nablus; the Third Brigade headed due west, occupying Ramallah, Latrun, Lydda, and Ramle. The aim was to take control of and protect the key Arab areas. There was no resistance. In most places the Legionnaires were showered with rice by cheering Palestinian crowds. The original plan had been to bypass Jerusalem, both not to embarrass Britain, which secretly supported Amman's takeover of the West Bank, and to avoid costly battles in built-up areas. But the desperate pleas of the Arab inhabitants and defenders to save them from the Haganah—which on May 13–18, in two efficiently executed operations, took over all the former British compounds and camps—compelled Abdullah, on May 17, to order the Legion to Jerusalem.[274] Glubb understood that the city, beyond its political and religious significance, was also the strategic key to the West Bank: If the Jews conquered East Jerusalem and headed down the road to Jericho, they could sever the Legion from its bases in Transjordan, with catastrophic results.[275]

On May 18—with "the King . . . haggard with anxiety lest the Jews enter the Old City and the Temple area, with the Great Mosques. His father, the late King Husayn . . . was buried in the precincts"[276]— Glubb sent an infantry company into the Old City to succor its defenders; a second company joined them the following day.

And that morning, May 19, a Legion armored force drove down the main road from Ramallah toward the Sheikh Jarrah neighborhood, which had been partly occupied by IZL and Palmah troops on May 14. The Legion retook the area and launched probes westward—designed to widen and safeguard their axis of advance—which the Haganah feared were offensive assaults and which Zionist historians later mistakenly described as attempts to conquer West Jerusalem. In these encounters the outgunned Israelis put the Legionnaires to flight after hitting the lead armored cars with PIAT shells and machine guns. But the bulk of the column entered the Old City.

Meanwhile, at the southern edge of Jerusalem, several platoons of the

Legion stationed in Hebron (they had never pulled out of Palestine, remaining along with several other units seconded to the British army before May 15) joined a band of irregulars to attack Kibbutz Ramat Rachel. Muslim Brotherhood units of the Egyptian expeditionary force arrived on May 22–23 and pitched in. The seesaw battle, in which the settlement changed hands three times, ended in the evening of May 25, when the Haganah finally dislodged the Legionnaires.[277]

But the main battles took place in the center of the city. On May 21–22 the Jordanians threw in the Legion's Third Battalion with the aim of taking the vast Hospice of Notre Dame de France, which dominated the Old City's northern walls and the Damascus Gate. The five-hundred-room building, completed in 1888, had been occupied by the Haganah on the night of May 17–18. For three days—May 22–24—the defenders and the Legionnaires battled from room to room with grenades and submachine guns, before the Legionnaires at last withdrew. Their six-pounder guns and mortars had been of little use against Nôtre Dame's stout stone walls: "The Holy Catholic Church seemed to have built for eternity," wrote Glubb.[278] But the Third Battalion had linked up with the units already in the Old City, and the Legionnaires, supported by irregulars, went on to attack the Jewish Quarter. The Jews had suffered some setbacks, too. During May 14–16 the communities of 'Atarot and Neveh Ya'akov, just north of Jerusalem, were attacked repeatedly by irregulars and Legion units and then were abandoned. And on May 17–20 the militarily untenable settlements of Kalia and Beit Ha'Aravah, at the northern end of the Dead Sea, just south of Jericho, were also abandoned.

But the most significant Jewish defeat was to occur in the Old City itself. The Jewish Quarter's fifteen hundred almost uniformly ultra-Orthodox inhabitants had been under intermittent attack since March but had been protected by the British until the latter evacuated the Old City on May 13, when the defense was assumed by the Haganah. On May 15 hundreds of Arab irregulars attacked. During May 16–18 the Haganah made several attempts to reinforce and resupply the quarter and establish a permanent corridor to West Jerusalem through Zion Gate, but they proved unable to keep the passage open after the Legion entered the Old City. For 10 days the Legionnaires, commanded by Abdullah Tal, battled the defenders, house by house, gradually compressing the Jewish area. Then, on May 28, "two old rabbis, their backs bent with age, came forward down a narrow lane carrying white flags." The quarter had fallen. Almost all the inhabitants and seriously wounded combatants were allowed to cross into Jewish Jerusalem; nearly three hundred able-bodied defenders were taken prisoner.[279]

In the partition plan Jerusalem had been designated an international zone and therefore lay outside the tacit nonaggression agreement concluded between Golda Meir and Abdullah. It was up for grabs, and force would determine the outcome. The Legion and the Haganah fought fiercely over parts of the seam between the eastern and western sectors. But when the dust settled, it emerged that each side had more or less held on to its own part of the city.

The battle for Latrun, though vitally connected to the battle of Jerusalem, was another matter. The small hillock, topped by a large police fort, and five surrounding Arab villages sat astride the junction of the Tel Aviv–Jerusalem and Ramallah-Majdal highways. The occupation of the area by the Legion on May 17 meant that the road from Tel Aviv to Jerusalem would remain closed. Ben-Gurion feared that without supplies and reinforcements Jewish West Jerusalem would fall. Latrun, earmarked in the partition plan for Arab sovereignty, had to be taken—even though this meant attacking the Legion and violating the tacit nonaggression agreement with Abdullah. Three times during the following three weeks the Israelis attacked—and three times they were repulsed, with heavy losses. The assaults were poorly organized, and the professionalism of the Legion's artillery and mortar men proved decisive.

The first two battles at Latrun, on May 25 and 30, were to go down in Israeli military mythology as prime examples of ill-planned attack and of waste of manpower and matériel. Indeed, the numbers of those killed in the battles—seventy-four and forty-four respectively—were traditionally to be vastly exaggerated.[280] Moreover, it was commonly charged, and believed, that many or most of those killed had been new immigrants sent into battle without even minimal training. In fact most of those killed were either sabras or long-settled immigrants.[281]

The Palmah made another unsuccessful attempt against Latrun, on June 8–9. The following day, June 10, the Legion mounted a surprise counterattack, in which it captured the settlement of Gezer and thirty of its defenders. But that evening, after the Legionnaires withdrew, Palmah units counterattacked and retook the ravaged kibbutz from the irregulars who had been left to defend the site.[282]

The UN-sponsored First Truce came into effect on June 11, aborting any thought of another IDF effort against Latrun. The road to Jerusalem remained closed. But almost accidentally, an alternative emerged. A Palmah squad, on foot, discovered that dirt tracks linking three abandoned Arab villages in the area could be negotiated by vehicles. Jeeps were sent in to try out the route and, a few days later, engineers with earth-moving equipment prepared the new "Burma Road" (named after the British supply route from Burma to China in World War II). The Latrun salient was bypassed, and convoys of jeeps, mules, camels, and—by June 11—trucks, traveling at night and without lights, began plying their way up the hills from Khulda to Jerusalem.[283] A steady trickle of supplies began reaching the city—the siege had been lifted.

By the start of the First Truce, both sides were generally satisfied. Abdullah had taken control of much of the Arab-designated area of eastern Palestine, stretching from Jericho to Lydda-Ramle and Tulkarm in the west and from Jenin in the north to Bethlehem-Hebron in the south. He had also managed to save East Jerusalem for the Arabs, take the Jewish Quarter of the Old City, and administer some severe setbacks and shocks to the Yishuv. The IDF, for its part, had managed to deny the Legion even a toehold in West Jerusalem and, despite defeats in Latrun, had found a way to resupply the city. It had held its own against a professional, British-led army. Both sides had managed to avoid a war to the finish.

But the Legion had suffered serious losses (some companies in Jerusalem taking as many as 20 percent casualties), and its stocks of ammunition were extremely low. For the rest of the war the Legion's commanders, and its patrons in London, lived in constant fear that the IDF would encircle and destroy the force, the main prop of the Hashemite monarchy as well as the only serious obstacle to Israeli conquest of the whole of the West Bank.[284] The IDF—many times larger than the Legion and steadily resupplied from Czechoslovakia—more than made up for its losses. Within weeks it was far stronger than it had been on the eve of the engagements with the Legion.

THE EGYPTIAN INVASION AND ITS CONTAINMENT

The Egyptian invasion, a poorly organized affair,[285] unfolded along two axes, a brigade group advancing along each. The invasion force was composed of somewhat more than six thousand troops; by October, its size had increased to fourteen thousand.[286] At the end of April, Gen. Ahmed 'Ali al-Mawawi was appointed to command the expeditionary force; Col. Muhammad Naguib was his deputy. The force which crossed into Israel on May 15 and 16 and pushed northward into the area later known as the Gaza Strip, up the coast road, consisted of three infantry battalions: a support battalion of three-inch mortars and machine guns; an artillery battalion with twenty-four twenty-five-pounders; and a battalion of twenty-four armored cars, and support units. Throughout his push Mawawi sacrificed speed to caution. Fearing that the settlements on his route would attempt to cut off his forward units, he devoted major energies to subduing them.

The second brigade, commanded by Col. Ahmad 'Abd al-'Aziz, included several battalions of irregulars, mostly Muslim Brotherhood volunteers, supported by a number of Egyptian army units. It advanced eastward to Beersheba, and then northward through the Hebron hills and Bethlehem, on May 22–23 joining in the attack on Ramat Rachel.[287]

On paper the expeditionary force was backed by an air force consisting of five squadrons, two of them of Spitfires, and two of makeshift bombers (mostly DC-3s). But the Egyptian Air Force (EAF) had few good pilots or ground crews and suffered from a severe shortage of spare parts. After the first three weeks of combat, in which it lost nineteen aircraft, the force was almost completely grounded.[288]

The Haganah held the northern Negev approaches and the settlement enclave in the northern Negev with two brigades, consisting of four to five thousand troops, and several dozen armored cars and two- and three-inch mortars but, in the first days of the invasion, no field artillery or proper armor.

The invasion was heralded at dawn on May 15 by a flight of some fourteen bombers and fighter-bombers, attacking targets in Tel Aviv, including the Sdeh Dov Airfield and the Reading Power Station. One aircraft was downed by Israeli flak. Ground forces then proceeded to attack the settlements of Nirim, on the western edge of the enclave, and Kfar Darom, which sat astride the Rafa–Gaza road inside the Gaza Strip. The two kibbutzim and several neighboring settlements were the Yishuv's first line of defense and were to prove exceptionally hard nuts to crack for successive waves of Egyptian troops, who were severely bled and stalled at each outpost. When Yitzhak Sadeh, Ben-Gurion's military adviser, proposed abandoning some of the isolated southern settlements (which, ultimately, were militarily untenable) Ben-Gurion responded: "There is no hurry. Gaining time is a big thing."[289] He was proved right. The Egyptian thrust lost its momentum, and the Haganah gained time in which to reposition its forces and to deploy the heavy arms—fighter aircraft, armor, and guns—that it had been unable to bring into the country before the end of the Mandate.

At Nirim, the Egyptian Sixth Battalion (whose operations officer was Major Gamal Abdel Nasser)—five hundred to six hundred infantrymen supported by six armored cars mounting two- and six-pounders, twenty armored Bren gun carriers, a battery of twenty-five-pounder artillery, and a battery of three-inch mortars—faced forty-five well-entrenched defenders armed only with light weapons (their heaviest armament was a two-inch mortar). The settlement perimeter was mined and well fenced. After a short, sharp battle the attackers were beaten off. The Egyptians shelled the settlement for another nine hours and then withdrew to Rafa (where they held a "victory rally," with Cairo Radio announcing that they had conquered the settlement). A Palmah commander, Chaim Bar-Lev, commented afterward that for him the outcome of the war had been settled by the "Battle of Nirim": If forty-five lightly armed Jews could best an expanded, well-supported Egyptian battalion, then the Yishuv would defeat the invading Arab armies.[290] The Egyptian First Battalion's attack on Kfar Darom on May 15 had a similar result.

The Egyptians spent the next days reorganizing, and on the 19th resumed their advance northward, immediately encountering fire from Kibbutz Yad Mordechai. The Egyptians could not afford to bypass this settlement, which dominated the coastal road. On the night of May 18 a small Israeli armored column had quietly managed to reach the kibbutz and evacuate its children. Left behind were 110 adults and two squads of Palmahniks, with light weapons, a medium machine gun, and a PIAT. Just after dawn on May 19, the Egyptians launched their assault. Fighter-bombers attacked from the air; batteries of 25-pounders and mortars laid down a heavy barrage. But the ground assault that followed was driven back, taking dozens of casualties. Again Cairo Radio announced that an Israeli settlement had fallen.[291]

The next morning, May 20, the Egyptians resumed the assault, this time supported by a tank and armored cars. In desperate hand-to-hand fighting along the perimeter fence, with much of the kibbutz on fire behind them, the defenders beat back seven attacks. That night the Palmah sent in a platoon of reinforcements (including six British deserters who had thrown in their lot with the Jews) with another PIAT. The Egyptians attacked again on May 23, this time with two infantry battalions supported by artillery and armor. By nightfall, Yad Mordechai had suffered, all told, twenty-three dead and forty wounded. After the wounded were evacuated, the remaining defenders decided that the situation was hopeless and left; two of them—carrying a wounded man on a stretcher—were caught and murdered by Egyptian troops.

Yad Mordechai fell on May 24, after the Egyptians shelled the now-empty settlement for hours. They had taken some four hundred casualties in all and, more importantly, had lost five precious days, in which the Giv'ati Brigade, responsible for the area between the Gaza Strip and Tel Aviv, was able to make adequate preparations to halt the advancing column.[292]

The Egyptians made similar energetic efforts to take Kibbutz Negba, which sat astride the road from Majdal to Beit Jibrin and Hebron, and Kibbutz Nitzanim, which overlooked the road north. At Negba they failed, but in Nitzanim, on June 7, they succeeded. The victory came too late, however. By then all thought of further advance northward had long vanished from the minds of the senior commanders. The stubborn resistance of the kibbutzim had demonstrated that the expeditionary force lacked the wherewithal even to push beyond Isdud, let alone on to Tel Aviv. Perhaps, too, Mawawi was instructed to call a halt, as his column had reached the border of the coastal strip assigned to Arab control by the United Nations. At the end of May he decided to dig in just north of Isdud, about twenty miles short of Tel Aviv—at least until he was given substantial reinforcements.[293] The Egyptian battalions were thus dispersed and stretched along long lines of communication, absorbed in defense, and incapable of further offensive action.[294]

The Israeli command, however, did not know this and feared that the Egyptians intended to continue their push to Tel Aviv. On June 2–3 the IDF launched Mivtza Pleshet (Operation Philistia). Four days before, on May 29, the IDF had mounted its first official air attack, by a foursome of Messerschmitt 109s against the column at Isdud. Though it caused little damage and one aircraft was shot down, the attack caused alarm among the Egyptians, who understood that they had lost dominance of the skies.

The operation, designed to stop an Egyptian advance that had come to a halt days before, ended in a shambles. In the Battle of Isdud—mistakenly portrayed in traditional Israeli military historiography as the crucial action in which the Egyptian advance on Tel Aviv was frustrated—around two thousand IDF soldiers, mainly of the Giv'ati Brigade, faced about 2,500 Egyptians of the First, Second, and Ninth battalions. But the Israelis dispersed their effort in such a way as to be at extreme numerical disadvantage in most points of engagement.

IDF losses amounted to fifty dead and missing and fifty wounded; Egyptian losses are unknown. But the counterattack had caused alarm, amounting almost to panic, in the Egyptian command, which feared that its forces north of Majdal might be cut off. One Egyptian military diarist recorded at the time: "The commander of the Isdud front [Naguib] reports that his forces were bombarded from the air, by artillery and by mortars and that the Jews launched an assault which was barely beaten off. The headquarters was badly damaged and the telephone lines were cut."[295]

For Israel, Operation Philistia had positive consequences. An Arab chronicler, Kamal Isma'il ash Sharif, concluded: "[T]he Jewish attack . . . was a turning point . . . from this point on the Egyptian command was forced to change its plans: Instead of continuing to chase after the Zionist gangs, the command decided to limit itself to severing the Negev from the rest of the country."[296]

All thought of pushing on to Tel Aviv had been definitively abandoned. There was no change in the front lines before the start of the First Truce on June 11.

THE INVASIONS IN THE NORTH

THE IRAQIS

In the spring of 1948 the Iraqi army consisted of two underequipped infantry "divisions" and a poorly equipped armored "brigade," which had about 120 armored cars. There were two artillery battalions, one equipped with modern twenty-five-pounders and the other with obsolescent 3.7-inch and 4.5-inch howitzers. There were also two batteries of 6-inch howitzers in extremely poor condition. Most of the artillery ammunition was old and undependable; some of the shells that reached Palestine during the war dated from 1916–17. The Iraqi Air Force boasted sixty-two aircraft, of which only three were modern fighters, Furies, and all the rest were old and poorly maintained.[297]

In May, Iraq dispatched three brigade groups, numbering around five thousand men, to Palestine. During the first truce, in June and July, two more brigades joined them, and by September, the Iraqi expeditionary force totaled eighteen thousand men,[298] making it the largest Arab army in Palestine.[299] This force was meant to constitute the Arab Legion's "junior partner" and right flank. But it had an agenda of its own. Apart from helping to crush the Jewish state, the Iraqis appeared interested in reaching Haifa, on the way conquering and securing the area on either side of the length of the IPC pipeline that conveyed oil from Mosul through Lower Galilee to the refinery in Haifa.[300]

On the morning of May 15, units of the Second Brigade Group forded the Jordan where the pipeline crossed it, and the following day attacked Kibbutz Gesher and the nearby police fort, which was held by the Haganah. They were twice repulsed after suffering heavy losses, but besieged the settlement for the next five days. Their situation, stranded on the west bank of the Jordan, was unproductive and, in the long run, strategically precarious. Glubb ordered them to move to Nablus, to replace a Legion battalion needed in Jerusalem. On May 22 the Iraqis withdrew back across the Jordan, having failed to take Gesher or establish a secure bridgehead across the river. Reinforced by another brigade and additional armor, they redeployed in the Arab-held Samaria "triangle" of Nablus-Tulkarm-Jenin on May 22–23[301] and mounted a small local attack on the Jewish settlement of Geulim, but were eventually repulsed. On May 30 an Iraqi column was strafed with telling effect by Israel's remaining two Messerschmitt fighters, with one brigade commander reportedly killed.[302] It is likely that this IAF attack helped disabuse the remaining Iraqi commanders of all further thought of offensive action.

Fearing an Iraqi thrust—the logical move—across the narrow waist of the coastal plain, the Haganah command decided to preempt by striking at the northern sector of the Iraqi perimeter, at Jenin. A secondary Haganah aim was to remove the potential threat posed by the Iraqis to the Jezreel Valley settlements. On June 1 Gen. Moshe Carmel, commander of the northern front, launched his two-brigade offensive. Carmeli and Golani brigade troops easily overran four Arab villages along the route of advance, and on the morning of June 3 moved on Jenin itself in three columns. One column occupied three hills overlooking the town from the west, but the others failed to take some of their objectives. The troops suffered severely from the intense heat and were unable to dig in on the rocky hills. Jenin's defenders, consisting of several companies of Iraqi troops and local irregulars, put up a stubborn resistance until a fresh battalion, with a battery of artillery, arrived from Nablus. A confused seesaw battle ensued. Iraqi air attacks and the arrival of the ground reinforcements broke the back of one Israeli battalion, after a chance shell hit its command post, killing and injuring several officers, and a rumor spread that a retreat had been ordered. The companies in the hilltops to the west, taking severe losses, broke and fled, sowing panic in other units as well.

Meanwhile, throwing in his reserves, Carmel managed to push fresh troops into Jenin, by nightfall occupying the center of the abandoned town but remaining seriously exposed. Carmel warned the IDF general staff that if an assault was not mounted on Tulkarm to relieve the pressure on Jenin, he could not hold. Headquarters responded that no such attack could be launched, and Carmel ordered a retreat to a line north of the town. All told the IDF lost thirty-four dead and about one hundred wounded; the Iraqis and irregulars, perhaps two hundred dead and a similar number of wounded. The IDF had narrowly missed delivering a mortal blow to the Iraqis;[303] indeed, superior Israeli forces had been routed by a small number of Iraqis and irregulars. But as often happens in war, defeat can sometimes produce positive strategic dividends. The attack on Jenin definitively persuaded the Iraqis—much as had happened with the Egyptians after Isdud—not to venture out of the Arab-populated "triangle" and attack Haifa or push westward toward the coast.

THE SYRIANS

On paper the Syrian army mustered about fifteen thousand soldiers.[304] But due to lack of weapons, ammunition, and trained manpower, it was in fact much smaller. By May 14, only one brigade was more or less ready—and it was that brigade that initially constituted the Syrian expeditionary force. Its two infantry battalions were equipped mainly with obsolescent French rifles; it also had a company of light Renault-35 and -39 tanks (mounting 37 mm cannon), and a battalion of 75 mm and 105 mm artillery. The Syrian Air Force consisted of some twenty Harvard trainers, converted for use as fighters or bombers, and a number of light aircraft. Many of the planes were unfit for action, as were many of the pilots.[305]

Early on May 16, after wasting the previous day moving from southern Lebanon to the Golan Heights, the Syrians crossed the border at al-Hama, near the southern end of the Sea of Galilee. A few minutes later their artillery began shelling Kibbutz Ein Gev, on the eastern shore of the lake. Facing them was a battalion of the Golani Brigade and local Haganah territorials, dispersed in the area's kibbutzim. A company of the Palmah, and territorial platoons from settlements farther afield, joined the battle during the following days. The Jordan Valley settlements had evacuated their women and children, and the Jews of Tiberias began building barricades and fortifications south of the town.

On May 18 the Syrians took the former British camp and police fort at Samakh and then repeatedly attacked the abandoned, now Israeli-occupied Arab village. The defenders retreated in disorder, leaving wounded and dying among the rubble. At the same time, the defenders of nearby Kibbutzim Sha'ar HaGolan and Masada abandoned their settlements (without permission of Haganah headquarters). Lt. Col. Moshe Dayan, the Haganah commander in the battle, that night threw in a Palmah company in a counterattack, but it was driven back with losses.

During the following two days the Syrians assaulted the twin kibbutzim to the west, Degania Aleph (Dayan's birthplace) and Degania Bet. The Haganah, pressed by the kibbutzim for reinforcements, was able to offer only a battery of 65 mm cannon for twenty-four hours. The defenders of the two Deganias were ordered to fight where they stood and, with their homes literally a few yards behind them, they held the Syrian tanks and armored cars off with PIATs and Molotov cocktails. On May 20, the 65 mm guns opened up from the heights of Alumot. For the Syrians it was the last straw: The fight at the Deganias had been bloody and frustrating, and they had been told the Jews had no cannon. They beat a hasty retreat, abandoning Samakh, Masada, and Sha'ar HaGolan.

Two weeks later the Syrians launched a new attack into the Galilee, just south of Lake Hula, around the settlement of Mishmar HaYarden, which dominated the Bnot Ya'akov Bridge across the Jordan. This time, the aim was not to cut through the Galilee and defeat the Jewish state, but just to conquer one or more small chunks of territory to reach the start of the expected UN truce with some achievement in hand. After a first effort, on June 5, ended in failure, the Syrians tried again on June 10. Mishmar HaYarden, defended only by several dozen of its members, fell after a fierce fight. The Syrians had gained a toehold west of the Jordan, giving them the military potential to renew operations in the Galilee and a political bargaining card in future negotiations about territory and borders.

THE LEBANESE FRONT

The Galilee Panhandle, bordered on the west and north by Lebanon and on the east by Syria, was defended by the Palmah's Yiftah Brigade. Facing them was a Lebanese army whose total strength was four battalions. Two of these, supported by armored cars and two batteries of 75 mm artillery, were deployed in southern Lebanon for the planned invasion,[306] but they apparently never crossed the border.

On May 15 a Palmah unit in the abandoned Arab village of al-Malikiya on the heights west of the Hula Valley was driven out by a column of Arabs from Lebanon, who also occupied the village of Qadas. But they had suffered serious losses at al-Malikiya and had lost their will to advance farther.

It appears that the attack was mounted by irregulars—Lebanese, Palestinian, and Syrian—who were backed, logistically and with mortars, by regular troops. The original Arab plan had called for at least a token—one battalion—Lebanese contribution to the invasion. But according to Haganah intelligence, the American and French representatives in Beirut had warned the Lebanese to stay out;[307] moreover, the most powerful community in the country, the Maronite Christians, staunchly opposed participation, regarding the Jews as possible allies in the struggle against the surrounding Muslim world.

It appears that, at the last minute, the Lebanese chief of staff, Gen. Fuad

Shihab, and Col. Adel Shihab, the commander of the unit designated to cross the border, resisted the politicians' blandishments and refused to march. But in order to demonstrate "participation" or at least pan-Arab solidarity, they either organized or simply allowed a group of several hundred irregulars—from the border villages and from among Qawuqji's men—to cross into al-Malikiya. It is probable that Lebanese army artillery provided the covering fire.

Subsequently Beirut Radio repeatedly announced that "the Lebanese army" had invaded Palestine. The broadcasts were no doubt intended to fend off criticism of Lebanon's failure to participate in the invasion. Haganah Intelligence Service agents later explained, variously, that "the Lebanese army . . . did not join the invasion as its main forces were concentrated between Tyre and Ras al-Naqura [to the west]"[308] and that General Shihab had "refused to invade [Palestine] and argued that his army is only a defensive army and [incapable] of offense, but opened fire against [Kibbutz] Hanita with a mortar barrage in order to show that the Lebanese too were taking part in the war."[309] But there are also several Haganah Intelligence Service reports from the same period implying that Lebanese army units did participate in the battle at al-Malikiya.[310]

In any event Yiftah retook al-Malikiya on the night of May 28,[311] but on June 6 the Arabs—again, probably irregulars supported by Lebanese army logistics and artillery—reconquered it. Israel was to retake it, this time definitively, only at the end of October.

THE AIR AND NAVAL WAR UNTIL JUNE 11, 1948

Air and naval operations during the civil war and the first, Arab-invasion stage of the conventional war were peripheral and had almost no impact on the fighting, mainly owing to the absence on both sides of serious air and naval capabilities. However, the Haganah had in its ranks about half a dozen trained (British and American) pilots, soon joined by dozens of experienced North American and West European fliers, who were to constitute the backbone of the new Israel Air Force, which grew by leaps and bounds. Initially there were light civilian aircraft converted to military use. The first fighter arrived (in parts) on May 20 —a Messerschmitt M-109 from Czechoslovakia. By May 29 a foursome had been assembled. By June 11, eleven Messerschmitts were operational; by August 12, twenty-five.[312] Several IAF aircraft bombed Amman on the night of June 1, and an IAF Dakota dropped two tons of bombs on Damascus on the night of June 10. Little damage was done, but the Arabs were caught by surprise, and their morale may have been affected.[313]

The Egyptian Air Force, using bombers and Spitfires, repeatedly attacked Israeli airfields, ground forces, rural settlements, and towns. There were relatively few casualties, and the attacks gradually fell off as Israeli air power grew and interception became more effective. In Tel Aviv, which was hit several times by Egyptian air raids, more than forty-two civilians were killed, most of them on May 18, when the city's central bus station was bombed.

At sea the only significant operation occurred on June 4, when a three-boat Egyptian squadron (a corvette, a landing craft, and an armed troop carrier) tried to reach Tel Aviv to shell the city or launch an amphibious raid. An effort by the Israeli navy's only armed ship, a small frigate, to intercept failed, as the larger Egyptian guns kept the vessel at bay. Three IAF light aircraft intervened when the squadron reached the coast off Jaffa, strafing and bombing the Egyptians. One boat was hit, and the Egyptians retreated, heading back to Port Said. One Israeli aircraft was shot down.

TRUCE

The UN Security Council on May 20 appointed Count Folke Bernadotte, a Swede who had helped rescue Jews during World War II, as special mediator for Palestine, empowered to seek a quick end to the fighting and a comprehensive, lasting settlement of the conflict. He got nowhere on the latter. As to a cease-fire, first one side and then the other balked, each interested in making as many gains as possible on the ground. But the weeks of the Arab invasion were intense and exhausting for both sides, and eventually Bernadotte's efforts were crowned with success. The "First Truce," as it came to be known, went into effect on June 11, and the fronts fell silent, each army digging in in place. The truce held for almost a month, until July 8, when battle was renewed.

The result of the four weeks of battle were a clear Israeli victory. Israeli intelligence estimated, on June 27, that during the invasion period (May 15–June 11), Syria lost three hundred dead and four hundred wounded, Iraq two hundred dead and five hundred wounded, the Jordanians three hundred dead and four hundred wounded, and the Egyptians six hundred dead and eight hundred wounded. The report made no mention of any Lebanese casualties—acknowledging, in effect, that the Lebanese had not taken part.[314]

The Israelis had suffered a large number of casualties, but they had withstood the four-pronged assault. The invaders had made very few territorial gains, had failed to destroy any large IDF units, and had been effectively halted in their tracks. The Israelis had held on to most of the areas earmarked by the UN for their state (bar much of the unpopulated Negev), and in some areas, after the initial battles of containment, the IDF had swung over to the counteroffensive and had managed to roll back the Arabs and capture territory. And even in the major, brigade-size counterattacks—against the Iraqis in Jenin, the Arab Legion at Latrun, and the Egyptian army around Isdud—in which the Israelis had been repulsed, they had inflicted sufficient casualties and shock to persuade the Arab commanders to shelve any thought of further advance. The initiative had thus passed from Arab into Israeli hands and was to remain so for the duration of the war. But, like the Arabs, the Israelis were thankful for the long breather. "It came to us as dew from heaven," an Israeli commander was quoted as saying of the first truce.[315]

During the period of the invasion and the truce, the Haganah quickly made the transformation from a semilegal underground/militia into a full-fledged army—the IDF was formally established on the basis of the Haganah on May 31—and by the start of the truce the Haganah was far stronger in terms of command and control, manpower, and weaponry than it had been on May 15. With the arrival from abroad of immigrants, volunteers, and returning Palestinian Jews, and more efficient mobilization procedures at home, the manpower pool almost doubled between May 15 and July 9, the number under arms rising from around thirty-five thousand to sixty-five thousand. Several thousand of the recruits—perhaps as many as four thousand—were veterans of the Allied armies (British, American, Canadian, Czech) of World War II who came to help the Israelis win the war. They included specialists, such as sailors, doctors, and logistics and communications experts; most of the IAF's pilots during the war were such volunteers, many of them non-Jews.

At the same time, exploiting holes in the UN-supervised arms embargo, the IDF managed to bring into the country great quantities of armaments including artillery, armored vehicles, and military aircraft.[316] In the course of June, most of the existing brigades were substantially beefed up, the companies and battalions filling out to more or less regulation size, and two new brigades were added to the roster. The army that confronted the Arab states on July 8 was radically different from, and far stronger than, the one they had met on May 15.

THE DISMANTLING OF THE DISSIDENT ORGANIZATIONS

On June 1, Ben-Gurion's aide, Israel Galili, and IZL commander Menachem Begin signed an agreement disbanding the IZL and transferring its troops to the IDF, where they were to constitute a number of separate battalions in the Alexandroni and Giv'ati brigades. However, the IZL (and LHI) units in Jerusalem continued to maintain a separate, independent existence—Jerusalem officially not being part of the State of Israel.

But on June 19–20 there occurred what Ben-Gurion and his ministers regarded—or said they regarded—as a rebellion. An IZL ship, the *Altalena,* carrying about nine hundred immigrants and members of the organization, as well as arms, arrived off Israel's shores from France. The IZL demanded that the weapons be distributed to "its" battalions in the IDF and the independent IZL troops in Jerusalem; the government refused. Ben-Gurion maintained that the country could have only one army, the IDF. IZL troops took control of a beach area near Kfar Vitkin, north of Netanya, and began to offload the vessel. Government troops surrounded the area and a number of firefights ensued. On June 21 the IZL troops surrendered, but the *Altalena* sailed south to Tel Aviv where, on Ben-Gurion's orders, IDF artillery opened fire on it. At the same time Palmah troops took over the IZL's headquarters in downtown Tel Aviv and arrested and disarmed the dissidents. The *Altalena,* hit and on fire, soon sank; most of the arms were lost. Eighteen men died in the clashes, most of them IZL members.

The IZL troops were subsequently dispersed among the IDF's different units, and there were no longer "IZL battalions." The IZL and LHI units in Jerusalem remained separate from the IDF until mid-September, when they were disbanded in the wake of the LHI's assassination of Count Bernadotte.

THE "TEN DAYS" (JULY 8–18, 1948)

At the end of June, Bernadotte proposed that Palestine, including Transjordan, be redivided into two states, the one Jewish and consisting of most of the areas allotted to the Jews in 1947 (without the Negev but including western Galilee), and the other consisting of the Arab parts of Palestine and Transjordan. The states should be joined in a federal union. Jewish immigration, after two years, should be governed by UN decision, and the Arab refugees should be allowed to return to their homes "without restriction." Lydda Airport and the city of Haifa should become international "free ports," while Jerusalem was to be included in the Arab-ruled area, with the Jews of the city retaining "municipal autonomy."[317] Both the Arabs and the Jews rejected the plan—the Arabs arguing that it was merely a reiteration of partition, which they had always opposed, and the Jews, that the nature of the political settlement and the borders would be determined by the results of the fighting.[318] However, Israel agreed to the extension of the truce by a further thirty days. But the Arabs, misjudging the balance of military power, rejected an extension, and fighting resumed on July 8. The hostilities up to July 18 were to be known in Israeli historiography as "the Ten Days."[319]

THE SOUTH

During the truce the IDF had planned a major offensive against the Egyptians, who held a thin wedge of territory on either side of the Majdal–Faluja–Beit Jibrin road, separating the Giv'ati Brigade to the north (the Negba-Yavneh area) from the two dozen or so northern Negev kibbutzim, held by the Negev

Brigade. The aim of the offensive, code-named Operation An-Far (anti-Farouq), was to link up the two brigades and thus cut off the Egyptians' forward bases along the coast from their right wing, strung out from Faluja to the Hebron hills and the southern outskirts of Jerusalem.

But the Egyptians, having used the truce to beef up their forces to a level of four brigades, including small Saudi Arabian and Sudanese contingents, pre-empted the IDF, striking at dawn on July 8, a day before the truce was officially to end. In his memoirs, Nasser noted a "laxity" about the Egyptian preparations, and a "lack of conviction."[320] But the main thrusts, starting out from Majdal, were partially successful. Their goal was to widen the wedge and assure that the Giv'ati and the Negev Brigades remained apart, increasing the pressure on and the isolation of the settlements south of the road.

When the IDF counterattacked that night, July 8–9, with An-Far, Negev Brigade units failed in a bid to take the large Iraq Suweidan police fort, southeast of Negba.[321] On July 12, the Egyptians launched their most determined counterattack, using the Fourth Brigade, commanded by Muhammad Naguib. The main force struck at Negba, the hinge of the Israeli line. The kibbutz was defended by about one hundred members and Giv'ati soldiers. Beginning at dawn, repeated infantry assaults, backed by armor and artillery, failed to breach the perimeter fences, and by sunset the Egyptians retired, leaving dozens of dead in the field. They had poured nearly four thousand artillery and mortar shells onto the kibbutz, but the fortifications had held. Negba lost five of its defenders and sixteen were wounded; Egyptian losses were two to three hundred dead and wounded. The battle was the turning point of the "Ten Days" in the south.[322]

Until the beginning of the second truce on July 18, the initiative now lay with the IDF; in Operation Death to the Invaders (Mivtza Mavet LaPolshim), the Giv'ati Brigade expanded its areas of control and weakened the Egyptians.[323] At 7 p.m. on July 18, the second truce, ordered by the UN Security Council, went into effect. The "Ten Days" in the south had been indecisive, though the IDF had retained a slight edge, capturing some territory along the peripheries of its former holdings but failing to establish a corridor to the northern Negev settlements or to cut the link between the two Egyptian prongs. On the other hand, the Egyptians had failed to take any territory (except Kibbutz Kfar Darom, whose situation, as an isolated outpost along the Egyptians' route of march, had become untenable; its defenders slipped out during the night of July 8 and evaded capture).

THE NORTH

In the northern and central theaters, the IDF had the initiative. The main offensive in the north was Mivtza Dekel (Operation Palm Tree), designed to expand the Jewish-held coastal strip of western Galilee into the mountains to the east and to capture Nazareth and the surrounding area, in which much of the ALA was concentrated. Two undersize brigades were deployed against a considerably weaker force of two battalions, probably mustering about one thousand troops in all, backed by a small number of irregulars in the towns and villages. The Arabs were further weakened by the desertion of the Druze, who threw in their lot with the stronger side and made secret agreements with the IDF, assuring the bloodless capture of several Druze villages.[324]

A string of Arab villages was taken after preliminary barrages on July 9–10. These achievements persuaded the Israelis to mount a deeper push into ALA territory[325] and to capture Qawuqji's headquarters in Nazareth. IDF units surrounded the town on three sides, and it fell on July 16 almost without a fight, after a column of ALA armored cars encountered north of the town was destroyed. Qawuqji and his staff, and most of the town's ALA garrison, managed to slip out during the evening.[326]

The IDF advance was facilitated by Qawuqji's ill-timed diversion of most of the ALA's firepower against Ilaniya (Sejera, where HaShomer had been founded during the Second Aliyah), west of the Sea of Galilee, which constituted a Jewish-held promontory deep in ALA territory. As in the attacks on Yehiam, Tirat Zvi, and Mishmar Ha'Emek in January and April, Qawuqji appears to have been driven by a desire to conquer at least one settlement. But again, his wish was denied. Repeated assaults during July 11–16 failed to break the staunch defense.[327] After the fall of Nazareth the IDF conquered a swath of villages around the town.

To the north the IDF launched a brigade-size effort (Mivtza Brosh—Operation Cypress) on July 9 to destroy the Syrian bridgehead around Mishmar HaYarden. The Syrians were holding the enclave, about six miles from north to south and three miles wide, with more than three thousand troops. The Israelis managed to reduce the enclave by half but failed to eradicate it. The well-dug-in Syrians persisted doggedly and both sides suffered attrition in ten days of seesaw battle. The area was to remain in Arab hands until the Syrian withdrawal under the armistice agreement of July 1949. The IDF lost ninety-five dead and about two hundred wounded; the Syrians, according to IDF estimates, about two hundred dead and four hundred wounded.[328]

CENTRAL FRONT

The IDF's major effort during the "Ten Days" was Mivtza Dani (Operation Dani), geared to clearing Arab-held sections of the Tel Aviv–Jerusalem road and the ridge of hills to the north, stretching from Latrun to Ramallah—which again meant taking on the Arab Legion. Despite the "Burma Road," Jewish Jerusalem was still felt to be in jeopardy. Moreover, the Legion's occupation since mid-May of the towns of Lydda and Ramle, some ten miles southeast of Tel Aviv, was regarded as a threat to the city. The IDF did not realize how thinly stretched the Legion was (on June 26 it estimated that there were "1,400–1,500" Legionnaires in the Lydda-Ramle area—when in fact there were only about 150[329]) and feared that, at some point, Gen. Glubb might push toward Tel Aviv.

With Gen. Yigal Allon in command, the IDF was to enjoy a massive superiority in numbers and firepower, concentrating its largest force ever: two Palmah brigades, Harel and Yiftah (together consisting of five battalions), the Eighth (Armored) Brigade, and several battalions of Kiryati and Alexandroni infantrymen, backed by some thirty artillery pieces.[330] The initial stage, a two-brigade pincer movement to surround the Lydda-Ramle area and the rural hinterland to its east, began during the night of July 9 and continued without respite until July 13. The IDF forces faced disparate, uncoordinated irregular contingents, beefed up by several hundred poorly armed Bedouin tribesmen from Transjordan; two Legion companies; and the (overstrength) First Battalion, the Legion's strategic reserve, which was sent in to counterattack on July 10.[331]

The Israelis encountered only light resistance in the early morning hours of July 10, when they took a string of villages and Lydda international airport. Things turned difficult in the afternoon, when the Legion's First Battalion arrived and engaged the Eighth Brigade. However, despite initial success, the battalion made no effort to push toward Lydda and Ramle: Glubb refused to commit any troops to saving the two towns, which he regarded as untenable. (Indeed, the Legion company in Lydda withdrew on the night of July 11.)

On the morning of July 11, Yiftah troops pushed toward Lydda itself, but failed to penetrate the town's defenses. Allon threw in the Eighty-ninth Battalion, commanded by Lieutenant Colonel Dayan. Its armored cars and machine-gun-mounting jeeps burst into Lydda, shooting up everything in their path before withdrawing. The raid and the knowledge that the Legion would not defend them apparently sent the irregulars into shock; the will to fight deserted them. That evening the town fell to the IDF after minor skirmishing. The following morning Ramle's notables surrendered their town without a fight.

But the battle for Lydda was not quite over. At around noon on July 12, three Legion armored cars entered the town on a reconnaissance mission, only to find it occupied by Israeli troops. Some of the locals joined in the ensuing firefight, sniping at the Israelis. The jittery troops responded harshly, massacring young men detained in the mosque compound, and shooting indiscriminately into houses; "at least 250" of the townspeople died, according to Palmah records. Immediately after this, with Ben-Gurion's authorization, the troops expelled the inhabitants of Lydda and Ramle and drove them toward the Legion lines to the east. By the evening of July 13, the two towns had been completely emptied (though several hundred Arabs were to infiltrate back in the following months, and both today have substantial Arab minorities).

But the advances of July 9–13 seem to have spent Operation Dani's offensive potential. An effort on the night of July 15 to take the hilly ridge east of

Latrun failed, as did a last-minute frontal attack on the Latrun police fort an hour or two before the start of the second truce.

Meanwhile, in a series of parallel, minor attacks the Harel Brigade expanded Israel's holdings in the Jerusalem Corridor south of the Tel Aviv–Jerusalem highway, taking a series of Arab villages during July 13–18. At the eastern end of the corridor, on the western peripheries of Jerusalem, units of the IZL and the Etzioni (Jerusalem) Brigade took the villages of Beit Safafa, 'Ein Karim, and al-Maliha. The result was that a new, less vulnerable axis to Jerusalem became available, running parallel to and south of the so-called Burma Road.

By the end of Operation Dani the IDF had made substantial territorial gains but it had failed in its major strategic objective, to take Latrun. Nonetheless, the fort and its satellite villages, while heavily defended and fortified, were now precariously held, constituting a thin wedge of land jutting out into Israeli territory.[332]

The most striking air operation during the "Ten Days" was the bombing of Cairo by a lone IAF B-17. Three B-17s purchased by the Haganah in the United States had been flown to Czechoslovakia to be outfitted and armed. On July 15 they set out for Israel, ordered to bomb Egyptian targets on the way. One headed for Cairo, where it failed to hit its target, King Farouq's palace, but caused some damage nearby.[333] The two others bombed Rafa before landing in Israel.[334] During the following days the B-17s bombed Al-'Arīsh and Syrian positions around Mishmar HaYarden and al-Maza Airport outside Damascus. On July 17 two IAF Dakotas bombed Damascus. The Arab air forces' only effective missions were flown by the Syrians against IDF troops around Mishmar HaYarden.

THE SECOND TRUCE,
JULY 19–OCTOBER 15, 1948

Again, the three months' respite from the fighting during the second truce was used far more effectively by the IDF than by its Arab counterparts. By October 1948 the IDF had eighty-eight thousand troops to the combined Arab presence in and around Palestine of sixty-seven thousand troops.[335]

By October 15 the Israelis, with twelve brigades, deployed about 300 armored cars and half-tracks, 15 tanks, close to 150 artillery pieces, 57 heavy mortars, 109 antiaircraft and antitank guns, more than a dozen fighter aircraft (the first of 50 Spitfires purchased from the Czechs began to arrive at the end of September), and 16 bombers. It also had around 50 light and transport aircraft and 5 combat naval craft, with 10 coastal patrol vessels. The combined Arab armies, on paper, probably had something like twice this amount of weaponry but much of it, especially the aircraft, was unserviceable. They also lacked spare parts and ammunition. The combined Arab artillery may have had parity with, or even a slight edge over, the IDF in the number of guns; but the IDF had an overwhelming advantage in ammunition.[336] Moreover, in effect the armies of Syria, Jordan, and Iraq were not engaged in the hostilities after July 18: The IDF engaged, and focused its might, only on the Egyptian army and the ALA. Relatively insubstantial forces were left to fend off possible moves by the others. Hence the IDF enjoyed overwhelming superiority in manpower and in most categories of weaponry during the battles that followed the second truce.

Toward the end of September it appeard that the IDF might turn its attention, at the end of the truce, on Jordan rather than Egypt. At Latrun the Jordanians constantly halted the flow of water from the Ras al-Ayin springs to West Jerusalem; and on September 22 Legionnaires ambushed an unarmed Israeli supply convoy, with a UN escort, on its way to Jerusalem. (One of the conditions of the truce had been that Israeli traffic could travel more or less freely past Latrun along the old Jerusalem–Tel Aviv road.) Four people (an American, a Dutchwoman, and two Israeli officers) were killed. Two days later, on September 24, Legionnaires, supported by local irregulars, attacked an IDF position north of Latrun. Twenty-three Israelis were killed, though the IDF managed to recapture the site.

On September 26 Ben-Gurion proposed to the cabinet that the IDF immediately attack and conquer the whole Judea-Hebron region (including Latrun, Ramallah, East Jerusalem, Bethlehem, Hebron, and Jericho). But the ministers voted down the proposal by a margin of 7 to 6 (in another report 7 to 5), implying that when the war resumed, it should be directed against the Egyptians rather than Jordan.[337] Underlying the cabinet's decision were the following calculations: Attacking in Jerusalem and the West Bank (*a*) might involve Israel in war with Britain (which was bound to Jordan and Iraq by treaties of defense); (*b*) would result in a renewal of the war with Jordan (and Iraq), which Israel preferred to avoid—indeed, the Israeli decision-makers were still hoping that peace might be achieved with Abdullah; (*c*) might burden Israel, if the area was conquered, with more than half a million additional Arabs (that is, the regular population of the West Bank plus several hundred thousand refugees); and (*d*) might alienate Christendom, which would resent any damage that occurred to Christian sites in Jerusalem and Bethlehem and Jewish domination of these sites.

The reasons for tackling Egypt were: It had the most powerful Arab army and potentially threatened the center of the Jewish population in the Tel Aviv area; the precarious situation of the besieged Negev Brigade and the two dozen Jewish settlements in the northern Negev; and the Egyptian threat to Israel's possession of the Negev, the main potential site for the absorption of millions of Jewish immigrants (or so it was then believed).

Ben-Gurion was later repeatedly to blame this cabinet vote for (and thus clear himself of) the "loss" of East Jerusalem, a cause for "lamentation for generations."[338]

On October 6 the cabinet voted to order the IDF to break the siege of the Negev settlements. The Egyptians had persistently violated the truce terms by preventing Israel from resupplying the northern Negev pocket. Bernadotte's proposal that the whole of the Negev be given to the Arabs in a peace settlement was an additional spur to action.

Bernadotte's proposal, which, except for its new call to internationalize Jerusalem, greatly resembled his plan of late June, was published two days after he was assassinated, on September 17, by LHI terrorists. The proposal was seen by the international community as the martyred diplomat's "testament," giving it powerful moral sanction. The Israeli government, which flatly rejected the plan, felt impelled to block it by cutting open a corridor to the northern Negev and by crushing the Egyptian army.

OPERATION YOAV (TEN PLAGUES), OCTOBER–NOVEMBER 1948

On the eve of Operation Yoav, the Egyptian force in Palestine consisted of the equivalent of four brigades, with some fifteen thousand men deployed mostly from Al-'Arīsh in Sinai along the coast to Isdud, and more thinly in the curving strip of territory stretching northeast from 'Auja al-Khafir on the Negev-Sinai frontier, through Beersheba, to the Hebron hills and Bethlehem.[339] The main Egyptian formations along the coast were supported by armor and artillery, but they were severely lacking in ammunition, and some of their shells and mortar bombs were of World War I vintage.[340]

The IDF struck on October 15. A supply convoy was launched toward Egyptian lines east of Negba; the Egyptian troops duly opened fire, and the IDF, having concentrated four brigades under the command of Yigal Allon, unleashed its offensive. The main effort was a direct thrust by Giv'ati, starting on the night of October 16 and ending on October 20, from Julis-Negba southward through the main Egyptian positions. A corridor was at last punched through the Egyptian wedge to the northern Negev settlements, severing the Egyptian forces in the east from those in the coastal plain. Israeli forces pushed southward and took Beersheba on the night of October 20–21. The defending Egyptian battalion and the local irregulars put up only a token fight.[341]

In a secondary effort, other units mopped up the Arab villages in the area and cut a second north–south corridor to the northern Negev enclave, at the same time sealing off a further section of the Egyptian-held Majdal–Bethlehem road. In the middle, around the police fort of Iraq Suweidan and the villages of Faluja and Iraq al-Manshiya, a four-thousand-strong Egyptian brigade was surrounded in an area to be known as the "Faluja Pocket."[342]

The Egyptian expeditionary force's situation became precarious. Starting on the night of October 15, units of the Negev and Yiftah Brigades—the latter had been infiltrated into the Negev enclave during the Second Truce—seriously threatened the main south–north road linking Rafa with Isdud. The Egyptians feared that the bulk of their units were about to be cut off. On October 19 the divisional headquarters retreated from Majdal to Gaza, with most of the units to the north following suit during the next days. By November 4, IDF units had entered the abandoned Kibbutz Nitzanim, Isdud (today Ashdod), Majdal (Ashkelon), and Yad Mordechai. The Egyptians were left in control only of the area along the coast known thereafter as the Gaza Strip.

The police fort at Iraq Suweidan, dubbed "the Monster on the Hill" by Israeli troops, which had defied seven IDF attempts at conquest, fell at last—without Israeli casualties—on November 9, the battle having been decided by an unprecedentedly massive preliminary IDF barrage followed by an armored advance. The "Faluja Pocket" was to remain encircled until the implementation of the armistice agreement in late February 1949.[343] The Egyptian forces in the Bethlehem-Hebron area also began retreating, and on October 22 Glubb put together a hastily assembled mechanized force and sent it dashing southward, skirting around East Jerusalem and on to Bethlehem and Hebron, to take over from the Egyptians.[344] Throughout the operation, the Jordanians had watched from the sidelines as the IDF had mauled the Egyptians.

During Operation Yoav the IAF had mastery of the air. Though the contending forces each had only fifteen or so serviceable fighter aircraft and bombers, the IAF had an overwhelming advantage in air and ground crews, which enabled it to fly some 240 missions; the Egyptians flew only 30–50 missions. The Egyptians also suffered from a severe shortage in munitions and parts.[345]

As an appendage to Operation Yoav, on November 23–25 the Negev Brigade, unopposed, pushed from Beersheba to Sodom on the Dead Sea (Operation Lot) and to Ein Husub and Bir Maliha in the Arava. Sodom had been held throughout the war by Jewish troops but from May 20 had been completely isolated and supplied only by air. The linkup extended Israeli territory through the northern Negev to the southern Dead Sea.[346]

Throughout the operation, Israeli navy flotillas patrolled off the Majdal-

Gaza coastline, repeatedly shelling the Egyptians from the sea. On October 22, the naval commando unit, using four newly acquired speedboats loaded with explosives, attacked the Egyptian flagship, the *Emir Farouq,* and an accompanying minesweeper, off Gaza. The *Emir Farouq* was sunk and the minesweeper damaged.

In the north, Qawuqji's ALA provided the IDF with just cause to mount a major assault on the north-central Galilee, which was still in Arab hands. On October 22, taking the Carmeli Brigade by surprise, Qawuqji's troops captured a series of positions in the Galilee Panhandle north and south of Kibbutz Manara. On the night of October 28 the IDF attacked the ALA enclave, held by Qawuqji's three thousand irregulars supported by two companies of regular Syrian infantry, from both west and east. The four-brigade attack was called Operation Hiram, after the Lebanese king of Tyre who had been King Solomon's ally three millennia before. On October 30 al-Malikiya, which had been the sole ALA-Lebanese gain during the war, was conquered. The Carmeli Brigade on October 31 crossed the international border in several columns, took some fifteen Lebanese villages bordering on the panhandle, and reached the Litani River. Operation Hiram resulted in the IDF occupying all of northern Palestine up to the international frontier, as well as a small slice of southern Lebanon, and in the crushing of the ALA, which ceased to be a military force. The Syrian and Lebanese armies failed to interfere significantly in the fighting, leaving Qawuqji for all practical purposes to fight alone. During Hiram, IDF troops carried out at least nine massacres of Palestinian civilians and prisoners of war (at Eilaboun, Saliha, Safsaf, Jish, Hule, Majd al-Kurum, Bi'na, Deir al-Assad, and Arab al-Mawassa).[347]

OPERATION HOREV

Yoav and Hiram were followed by a lull in the fighting, and the fronts remained largely quiet during the second half of November and most of December. But the Egyptians still held substantial chunks of Palestine: the Gaza Strip, the "Faluja Pocket," and a large part of the western Negev, much of which was earmarked by the UN Partition Resolution for the Jewish state. Moreover, with a renewal of hostilities possible at any time, the IDF had to remain at full strength: A full seventh of the total Jewish population—more than half of the healthy adult males—remained under arms, away from their families and work.

On December 19 the cabinet decided to renew the war in the south with the aim of driving the Egyptians out and, if possible, destroying their army. They could then be expected to agree to an armistice—and the other Arab states would be likely to follow suit.[348] The IDF plan was simple. A major diversionary attack would be launched against the Gaza Strip, threatening the main Rafa–Gaza road, while the bulk of the Israeli army, starting out from Beersheba, would drive in a deep enveloping sweep southwestward through the Egyptian positions in the Negev, veer westward into Sinai, and then push north to Al-'Arīsh and the Mediterranean coast. If successful, the sweep would result in the destruction of the Egyptian brigade in the south and the encirclement of most of the Egyptian Expeditionary Force strung out along the coast between Al-'Arīsh and Gaza.

The IDF deployed four brigades for the main thrust, Operation Horev ("Horev" being another name for Mount Sinai), commanded by Allon. On the night of December 22 the diversionary attack was staged, persuading the Egyptians, who repulsed it, that the IDF intended a frontal assault on the core of their army in the Gaza Strip.[349] But the main Israeli thrust, southward, by the Eighth and Negev Brigades, both completely mechanized and in large part armored, unfolded like a classic desert operation. The force faced two Egyptian brigades dug in in a chain of hilltop fortifications. It was tank and half-track against trenchwork, artillery, and antitank gun—movement versus immobility. Given the paucity of Egyptian artillery, the result was a foregone conclusion: The defenses were overwhelmed.[350]

Regrouping and exploiting its success, the Israeli force on December 28 pushed across the border into Sinai. Once pierced, the Egyptian defense lines tended to crumble: Poor command and control, an inadequate officer corps, lack of air support and ammunition, and a lack of motivation were among the most telling factors. Israeli units were soon close to Al-'Arīsh, ready to close the ring at the Mediterranean.

But the thrust into Sinai was to encounter opponents far more powerful than the Egyptian army: An international frontier had been violated, and the vital interests of a Great Power were under vague threat. Britain had a defense treaty with Egypt dating from 1936. If not stopped, the Israelis might even reach and jeopardize the Suez Canal.

Britain gave the United States notice of possible impending action, and President Truman expressed his "deep" concern at the development, which, he said, tended to "prove" the State Department's view of "Israel's aggressiveness" and "complete disregard of the United Nations."[351] On December 31 James McDonald, the U.S. special representative (soon to be ambassador) to Israel, handed Foreign Minister Sharett an official protest and caution from Truman. The British also threatened to lift the arms embargo and resupply the Arab armies. McDonald insisted on also conveying the message directly to Ben-Gurion, who was vacationing in Tiberias.

Ben-Gurion reassured McDonald that the IDF had only crossed the border as a "maneuver" and had already been ordered to return to Israel (a lie). The prime minister added: "I am surprised by the harsh tone. Is there any need for a friendly power to approach a small and weak nation in such a tone?"[352] To blunt American anger Ben-Gurion and Sharett asked Weizmann to intercede personally with Truman. In a letter to the president, Weizmann averred that the Israeli forces had "accidentally crossed the Egyptian frontier" (another lie) and "had no intention of destroying the Kingdom of Egypt."[353]

On December 29, a day or so before the Anglo-American démarche in Tel Aviv, Yadin had ordered Allon to halt the armored thrust toward Al-'Arīsh, implying that it did not have formal IDF general staff sanction. Allon flew to Tel Aviv to try to persuade Ben-Gurion to give the advance the go-ahead. Ben-Gurion approved a compromise: Allon would withdraw from the interior of Sinai but mount a new thrust northward, just west (on the Egyptian side) of the international boundary, toward Rafa, with the aim of closing the ring at the international border rather than at Al-'Arīsh. The Israeli units were accordingly redeployed[354] and the new offensive northward was launched on the night of January 3, 1949. After a series of attacks (some on the Egyptian side of the border) and counterattacks, the Harel Brigade's Fourth Battalion on the night of January 6 advanced unnoticed through the dunes and cut the vital Al-'Arīsh–Rafa coast road at Sheikh Zuweid. The bulk of the Egyptian Expeditionary Force in Palestine, dug in the length of the Gaza Strip, was now cut off and encircled.[355]

But the Western powers again protested that the IDF was operating across the international frontier. On January 5, the Egyptian government, fearing its army was about to be annihilated, and under pressure from London, announced its readiness to enter into armistice negotiations if Israel halted its attack. On January 6 Israel's representative in Washington, Eliahu Elath, cabled Sharett: "Public and official Washington opinion dangerously tense, almost hostile. . . . Threats regarding further [U.S. financial] support [for Israel]."[356]

Tel Aviv caved in. The following day it agreed to an immediate ceasefire and armistice talks and the IDF withdrew from the area around Rafa west of the international frontier—though not before IDF commandos laid a large mine that on the night of January 7 blew up a train from Rafa bound for Egypt carrying hundreds of wounded troops.[357] But the vise around the Egyptian brigades in the Strip had been removed.

Israel's agreement to end the fighting and withdraw from the Rafa area was clinched by a series of encounters on January 7 over eastern Sinai between Israeli and British aircraft, the latter sent up from Canal-side bases to reconnoiter the battlefields. The Israeli Spitfires shot down five of the British planes (four Spitfires and one Tempest), all or most of which were unarmed. But the British patrols had ascertained that IDF units were still in Egypt (contradicting

Ben-Gurion's explicit assurances).[358] Britain strongly protested the downing of the aircraft and threatened unspecified "actions"—and landed a small tank force in Aqaba, an oblique warning to Tel Aviv to rein in the IDF.[359]

Operation Horev had two epilogues. In Mivtza Uvda (Operation Fact), the last military act of the first Arab-Israeli war, from March 7 to 10, 1949, the IDF occupied the central and southern Negev down to Um Rashrash (later Eilat) on the northern shore of the Gulf of Aqaba. At midnight on March 10 "our flag was raised above the waters of the Red Sea. . . . This is perhaps the greatest event in the past months, if not in the whole war of independence and conquest. And not one drop of blood was spilt!" Ben-Gurion, with some hyperbole, noted in his diary.[360] The following day, March 11, Israeli and Jordanian representatives signed a tentative ceasefire agreement.[361] And on March 7–9, a company of Alexandroni Brigade troops advanced from Beersheba, via Kurnub and Ein Hatzeva, to Sodom and then by boat northward to Ein Gedi, occupying the area's springs as well as Masada, the hilltop site of the Jews' last stand against Rome during the great revolt that ended in A.D. 73. Thus the central and southern Negev, down to the Gulf of Eilat (Aqaba) coastline, and much of the western shore of the Dead Sea—areas designated by the UN for the Jewish state (which is why Jordan and Britain did not resist either IDF advance)—were occupied by Israel, and without battle.

The first Arab-Israeli war ended in a clear Israeli victory and a humiliating Arab defeat. The Yishuv suffered some six thousand dead and about twice that number wounded; Palestinian losses, in civilians and armed irregulars, may have been similar and perhaps even higher. In the 1950s, al-Husseini claimed that "about" twelve thousand Palestinians had died during the war.[362] Egyptian losses, according to an official announcement made in June 1950, amounted to some 1,400 dead and 3,731 "permanently invalided."[363] The Jordanian, Iraqi, and Syrian armies each suffered several hundred dead, and the Lebanese several dozen.

Of the Arab armies only the Arab Legion had performed well and had more or less held its own against the Israelis. Jordan had gained—and was eventually to annex—the core of Arab-populated Palestine, the West Bank. But this was to prove an ambivalent blessing. At a stroke Jordan's demography vitally changed from a largely loyal Bedouin majority to a suspicious if not downright hostile Palestinian one, which was perennially to attempt to subvert the Hashemite hold on the territory and which, after 1967, managed to cast off altogether allegiance to Amman. Egypt, likewise, emerged from the war with a small chunk of Palestine, the Gaza Strip. But it, too, would prove a dubious asset. For the next twenty years Cairo was to rule over and periodically suppress the Strip's impoverished, disaffected Palestinian population.

The Jews, despite the heavy losses, had managed to establish and protect their state while enlarging its borders, and had both crushed the Palestinians and administered a stinging defeat to the Arab states. The outcome had sent shock waves through the Arab world that were to be felt for decades, subverting regimes and traumatizing societies. A Jewish state stuck at the core of the Arab and Muslim worlds was now a fait accompli. Thereafter the Arabs would tangle with it at their peril.

Economically the war had done a limited amount of harm to Israel, in terms of houses and fields destroyed, production impeded, and the like. But this was largely offset by the massive financial contributions sent in by world Jewry and by the grants and loans that soon began to arrive from various Western countries. A giant demographic and agrarian revolution took place that, within five years, led to the doubling of the number of Jewish settlements in the country, with all that this implied in terms of agricultural productivity and demographic expansion and dispersion. The war had also been a boon to Israel's fledgling industrial sector.

The Arab states had notched up only losses. Their already weak economies were further weakened by an increase in foreign debt. And all, to one degree or another, after 1948 were forced to cope with the burden of the Palestinian refugees on their soil. However, this by and large did not harm them economically, as the 1950 advent of the UN Relief and Works Agency for Palestine Refugees in the Near East (UNRWA)—which cared for the refugees' education, medical services, and, more generally, economic well-being—and a steady flow of Western relief capital more than compensated for any losses they may initially have incurred. The major economic harm was to the Palestinians, who lost much of their property to the victors.

The Armistice Agreements

Operation Uvda took place midway between the signing of the Israel-Egypt and Israel-Jordan armistice agreements. Indeed, it was facilitated by the conclusion of the first pact, which obviated the possibility of Egyptian intervention in the march to Um Rashrash; and it was, in part, timed by the Israelis to precede the conclusion of the armistice with Jordan. Ben-Gurion wanted to establish the facts of Israeli occupancy of, and Jordanian withdrawal from, the central-southern Negev before a ceasefire was signed and before the armistice negotiations moved into high gear. (Jordan had deployed a reconnaissance company in the southern Negev since November 1948.)

The Israeli-Egyptian talks opened on the Greek island of Rhodes on January 13, 1949, and lasted four weeks. In the chair was the UN acting mediator for Palestine, Bernadotte's successor, Dr. Ralph Bunche, from the United

States. The compromise eventually hammered out and signed on February 24, largely through Bunche's good offices, provided for the continued Egyptian military occupation of the Gaza Strip, with the IDF withdrawing from positions it still held there. The 'Auja area became a demilitarized zone, with a somewhat larger "limited forces" zone in the area of Sinai immediately across the border. The Egyptian forces were to withdraw from the "Faluja Pocket," with all their equipment.

The Israeli-Lebanese talks, held near Rosh HaNiqra (Ras al-Naqurah), began on March 1, the Lebanese having stalled until after the Egyptians had signed. Henri Vigier, one of Bunche's assistants, mediated. The armistice agreement, signed on March 23, provided for Israeli withdrawal from the Lebanese villages occupied by the IDF at the end of Operation Hiram, and recognition of the old Lebanon-Palestine international frontier as the boundary between the two states. In a separate understanding with the UN, the Lebanese agreed that the Syrian troops stationed in southern Lebanon would leave.

The Jordanian front presented the gravest problems when Israeli and Hashemite negotiators informally began discussing an armistice on December 26, 1948. The long, unnatural serpentine lines; the large concentrations of population, including refugees, close to the borders; and the presence of Iraqi troops in Samaria and vestigial Egyptian forces around Bethlehem all posed serious difficulties. Jordan sought an armistice based on the 1947 partition plan, while Israel wanted a settlement based on the military-territorial status quo. Jordan's demands included part of the southern Negev, Lydda and Ramle (or at least the repatriation of the refugees from those towns), special enclave status for Arab Jaffa, and small exchanges of territory in and around Jerusalem. Israel, for its part, demanded that its "waist" in the coastal plain be widened and the Arabs withdraw from the Latrun salient.

The formal Israel-Jordan armistice talks began, with Bunche mediating, in Rhodes on March 4, 1949; there were also parallel direct, secret negotiations between King Abdullah and his advisers and Israeli representatives. Over both sets of talks hovered the threat of Israeli military action to alter the existing lines unilaterally. Indeed, on March 7–10, as described, Israel occupied the central-southern Negev down to the Gulf of Aqaba, frustrating Jordan's desire to be recognized as sovereign over the southern Negev. In mid-March, Israel openly threatened to conquer areas in the northwestern and western foothills of Samaria if Jordan did not agree to cede them. At one point the threats included a twenty-four-hour ultimatum, to which Abdullah acquiesced on March 23. He feared that if the IDF reopened hostilities, it would go on to take the whole of the West Bank rather than merely a strip of territory on its periphery. Abdullah's last-minute efforts to mobilize British and American support failed. Neither power was willing to guarantee the existing lines as international frontiers, or Jordanian control of the West Bank.[364]

In the agreement finally signed on April 3, Jordan agreed to cede to Israel a continuous strip of territory, about three to five miles wide, running from just southwest of Qalqilya northward to Wadi 'Ara and from there eastward to a point just north of Jenin. Israel agreed to cede to Jordan a far smaller patch of territory—though it enabled Abdullah to claim that he had merely "exchanged" territory—southeast of Dhahiriya (southeast of Hebron). Included in the Jordanian-ceded strip (known thereafter in Israeli historiography as "the little triangle") were about fifteen villages, adding about twenty thousand Arabs to Israel's minority population. Jordan agreed that Iraq's troops in Samaria would be withdrawn (no Iraqi-Israeli negotiations took place, and no separate armistice was ever signed).

The Israeli-Syrian negotiations began on April 5, on the edge of the Syrian-held enclave at Mishmar HaYarden. Vigier mediated, but on matters of substance (and often also in matters of minute detail) was guided from New York by Bunche. Israel demanded that the Syrians withdraw to the old international Syria-Palestine frontier—that is, withdraw from the Mishmar HaYarden enclave, from the Tel al-Qasir strip east of the Sea of Galilee, and from a small strip of land between Kibbutz Dan and the village of Banias, at the northern edge of the Galilee Panhandle. The Syrians—this time echoing the Israeli stance in the talks with Egypt and Jordan—claimed that the boundaries should reflect the status quo post bellum.

The talks dragged on for more than a month, until Bunche proposed that Syria withdraw from the areas west of the old international line in exchange for their demilitarization, with neither Syria nor Israel obtaining formal sovereignty over them. Haggling over the exact constitution of the demilitarized zones (DMZs) followed, and the two countries signed the armistice agreement on July 20. Syria agreed to withdraw its forces back to the old international frontier. A small area between Kibbutz Dan and Banias, a larger area around Mishmar HaYarden, and the whole strip of territory east of the Sea of Galilee, from Nuqeib through 'Ein Gev to Al Hama, were designated DMZs. No Israeli or Syrian troops were allowed in; Israeli bureaucrats and police administered the Jewish-inhabited areas and Syrians, the Arab-inhabited areas. In practice, as the Arab inhabitants had by then been largely bought or pushed out of the southern area, the region—save for Nuqeib and El Hama—became de facto sovereign Israeli territory, as did almost all the central DMZ. The Syrians took control of most of the much smaller northern DMZ. Both sides agreed to limited-forces zones the length of the border.[365]

The signing of the armistice agreements marked the formal end of the first Arab-Israeli war. The state of war had been replaced by a de jure state of non-belligerency. Subsequently the international community and, to a somewhat lesser degree, the former combatants themselves, were to recognize the armistice lines as de facto international frontiers. The agreements also provided for the establishment of four separate UN-chaired mixed armistice commissions (MACs) to supervise their implementation.

The armistice agreements were not peace treaties and did not provide for many of the features that normally govern the relations between neighboring states at peace with each other, such as diplomatic and trade ties. During the following years Arab leaders made abundantly clear their uniform view that the armistice accords were merely elaborate cease-fire agreements, implicitly temporary and qualitatively different from and well short of full peace treaties.

In Israel a more complex perception of the armistice agreements took hold, with some leaders, including Ben-Gurion, viewing them as de facto peace agreements, which effectively freed them from the need to pursue full peace accords, while others took the "Arab view" that they were overblown cease-fire agreements that would have to be superseded by peace treaties—or else they might result in renewed fighting when one or both sides felt it to be in their interest. The armistice accords in large measure governed Israeli-Arab relations—both through what they lacked and through what they stipulated—during the following years, though they were eventually more honored in the breach than in the observance.

The Birth of the Palestinian Refugee Problem

Besides the emergence of the State of Israel, the other major result of the 1948 war was the destruction of Palestinian society and the birth of the refugee problem. About 700,000 Arabs—the figure was later to be a major point of dispute, the Israelis officially speaking of some 520,000, the Palestinian themselves of 900,000–1,000,000—fled or were ejected from the areas that became the Jewish state and resettled in the territories that became known as the West Bank and the Gaza Strip, as well as Transjordan, Syria, and Lebanon, with additional small communities in Egypt, Iraq, and the states of the Arabian Peninsula. The war's end found less than half of the Palestinians in their original homes—fewer than 150,000 in Israel, some 400,000 in the West Bank, and 60,000 in the Gaza Strip.

Why 700,000 people became refugees was subsequently hotly disputed between Israel and its supporters and the Arabs and theirs. Israeli spokesmen—including "official" historians and writers of textbooks—maintained that the Arabs had fled "voluntarily," or because the Palestinian and Arab states' leaders had urged or ordered them to leave, to clear the ground for the invasion of May 15 and enable their spokesmen to claim that they had been systematically expelled. Arab spokesmen countered that Israel had systematically and with premeditation expelled the refugees. Documentation that surfaced in massive quantities during the 1980s in Israeli and Western archives has demonstrated that neither "official" version is accurate or sufficient.

The creation of the problem was almost inevitable, given the geographical intermixing of the population, the history of Arab-Jewish hostility since 1917, the rejection by both sides of a binational solution, and the depth of Arab animosity toward the Jews and fears of coming under Jewish rule.

The structural weaknesses that characterized Palestinian society on the eve of the war made it especially susceptible to collapse and flight. It was poorly organized, with little social or political cohesion. There were deep divisions between rural and urban populations, between Muslims and Christians, and between various elite clans, and there was a complete absence of representative leaders and effective national institutions.

As a result of economic and social processes that had begun in the mid-nineteenth century, large parts of the rural population had been rendered landless by the 1940s. In consequence there was a constant, growing shift of population from the countryside to urban shantytowns and slums; to some degree this led to both physical and psychological divorce from the land. Moreover, 70 or 80 percent of the people were illiterate. In some measure this resulted in and was mirrored by a low level of political consciousness and activism. The "nationalism" of the urban elite was shared little, if at all, by the urban poor and the peasantry. And finally, the Arab economy in Palestine had failed to make the shift from a primitive, agricultural economy to a preindustrial one—as the Yishuv had done. Equally relevant, in the towns very few Arab workers were unionized; none, except the small number in British government service, enjoyed the benefit of unemployment insurance. Effectively ejected from Jewish enterprises and farms when Arab factories and offices closed down, they lost their means of livelihood. For some, exile may have become an attractive option, at least until Palestine calmed down.

Another crucial precondition was the penchant among Yishuv leaders to regard transfer as a legitimate solution to the "Arab problem." Recently declassified Zionist documents demonstrate that a virtual consensus emerged among the Zionist leadership, in the wake of the publication in July 1937 of the Peel Commission recommendations, in favor of the transfer of at least several hundred thousand Palestinian Arabs—if not all of them—out of the areas of the Jewish state-to-be. The tone was set by Ben-Gurion himself in June 1938: "I support compulsory transfer. I do not see in it anything immoral."[366]

Ben-Gurion's views did not change—though he was aware of the need, for tactical reasons, to be discreet. In 1944, at a meeting of the Jewish Agency Executive discussing how the Zionist movement should deal with a British Labour Party decision to recommend the transfer of Palestinian Arabs, he said:

When I heard these things . . . I had to ponder the matter long and hard. . . . [but] I reached the conclusion that this matter [had best] remain [in the Labour Party Program]. . . . Were I asked what should be our program, it would not occur to me to tell them transfer . . . because speaking about the matter might harm [us] . . . in world opinion, because it might give the impression that there is no room in the Land of Israel without ousting the Arabs [and] . . . it would alert and antagonize the Arabs. . . .

Ben-Gurion added, "The transfer of Arabs is easier than the the transfer of any other [people]. There are Arab states around. . . . And it is clear that if the [Palestinian] Arabs are transferred this would improve their situation and not the opposite."

None of the members of the Executive opposed or questioned these views; most spoke in favor. Moshe Sharett, director of the Jewish Agency's Political Department, declared: "Transfer could be the crowning achievement, the final stage in the development of [our] policy, but certainly not the point of departure. By [speaking publicly and prematurely] we would be mobilizing vast forces against the matter and cause it to fail, in advance." And he added: "[W]hen the Jewish state is established—it is very possible that the result will be transfer of Arabs."[367] On February 7, 1948, three months into the war, Ben-Gurion told Mapai's Central Committee that in Jerusalem's western neighborhoods, from which the Arabs had fled or been expelled, he had seen

no strangers [Arabs]. Not since Jerusalem's destruction in the days of the Romans has it been so Jewish. . . . I do not assume this will change. . . . And what happened in Jerusalem . . . could well happen in great parts of the country . . . if we hold on, it is very possible that in the coming six or eight or ten months of the war there will take place great changes. . . . Certainly there will be great changes in the composition of the population of the country.[368]

These "great changes" took place in four stages. The first was between December 1947 and March 1948, when the Yishuv was on the defensive and upper- and middle-class Arabs—perhaps as many as seventy-five thousand—fled, mainly from the mixed cities, or sent their dependents to the West Bank, Lebanon, Egypt, Syria, or Transjordan. In this context there can be no exaggerating the detrimental effect on Arab morale of the IZL and LHI bombing campaigns in the big towns.

These families had the wherewithal to settle comfortably in Cairo, Nablus, Amman, or Beirut, and in any case most viewed their exile as temporary. As in the exodus of 1936–39, they expected to return once the hostilities had ended.

Many notable families also resented or feared the domination of the Husseinis, and indeed may have feared a Husseini-ruled Palestine as much as they did life under Jewish rule. It was at this time that many of the political leaders and/or their families left the country—including most members of the AHC and of the Haifa National Committee. Jewish-Arab hostilities were only one aspect of a more general breakdown of law and order in Palestine after the UN Partition Resolution. There was also a gradual collapse of public services and a withdrawal of British authority, and an influx into both urban and rural districts of Arab irregulars, who extorted money from prosperous families and occasionally abused people in the streets.

Arabs also abandoned a number of villages in areas earmarked for Jewish statehood and with a Jewish majority, such as the coastal plain. In villages on the edge of Jewish urban centers, a combination of fear of the Jews and actual intimidation, principally by the IZL and LHI, prompted flight. In at least one case there was also outright expulsion by the Haganah—on February 20 at Caesarea, midway between Tel Aviv and Haifa.

The flight of the upper and middle classes entailed the closure of schools, clinics and hospitals, businesses and offices, and in turn engendered unemployment and impoverishment. This was the background to the second stage, the mass flight from urban neighborhoods and rural areas overrun by the Jewish forces during spring 1948. The earlier flight of the elite sapped popular morale and gave the masses an example to emulate.

The principal cause of the mass flight of April–June was Jewish military attack, or fears of such attack. Almost every instance—the exodus from Haifa on April 21–May 1; from Jaffa, during late April–early May; from Tiberias on April 17-18; from Safad on May 10—was the direct and immediate result of an attack on and conquest of Arab neighborhoods and towns. In no case did a population abandon its homes before an attack; in almost all cases it did so on the very day of the attack and in the days immediately following. And flight proved to be contagious. The fall of, and flight from, the big cities—principally Haifa and Jaffa—radiated pessimism and despair to surrounding villages. In the countryside flight by one clan led to that of neighboring clans, and flight from one village to flight from neighboring villages.

Haganah documents described "a psychosis of flight" gripping the Palestinian population during this period. The echo of the slaughter on April 9 of the villagers of Deir Yassin, augmented by Arab atrocity propaganda regarding what had happened there, both reinforced and symbolized this. Fear that the same fate might befall them propelled villagers to flight, and this "atrocity factor" was reinforced periodically during the months of fighting by other Jewish massacres, especially in October. Residents of a small number of villages—more than a dozen—were expelled before the start of the first truce (June 11) by Jewish troops; and some were intimidated by propaganda disseminated by Haganah agents. In most areas there was no need for direct expulsion. Villagers and townspeople usually abandoned hearth and home at the first whiff of grapeshot.

In some areas Arab commanders ordered the villagers to evacuate to clear the ground for military purposes or to prevent surrender. More than half a dozen villages—just north of Jerusalem and in the Lower Galilee—were abandoned during these months as a result of such orders. Elsewhere, in East Jerusalem and in many villages around the country, the commanders ordered women, old people, and children to be sent away to be out of harm's way.[369] Indeed, psychological preparation for the removal of dependents from the battlefield had begun in 1946–47, when the AHC and the Arab League had periodically endorsed such a move when contemplating the future war in Palestine. Altogether about two to three hundred thousand Arabs fled their homes during this second stage of the exodus.

During the first stage, there was no Zionist policy to expel the Arabs or intimidate them into flight, though many Jews, including Ben-Gurion, were happy to see the backs of as many Arabs as possible. And, without doubt, Jewish—both Haganah and IZL—retaliatory policies and the IZL/LHI terror bombings were precipitants. And there was no Arab policy, aside from sporadic AHC efforts, to stem the tide of upper- and middle-class departures.

During the second stage, while there was no blanket policy of expulsion, the Haganah's Plan D clearly resulted in mass flight. Commanders were authorized to clear the populace out of villages and certain urban districts, and to raze the villages if they felt a military need. Many commanders identified with the aim of ending up with a Jewish state with as small an Arab minority as possible. Some generals, such as Allon, clearly acted as if driven by such a goal.

On the Arab side there was general confusion at this time about everything concerning the exodus. The governments appear simply not to have understood what was happening and, initially, did not try to stop it. Indeed, Arab Higher Committee agents instructed the population of Haifa, after the flight from the town had begun, to continue to leave. But the exodus, as far as the evidence goes, was not initiated—as Jewish spokesmen later claimed—by an order from the AHC. It is quite possible that both Arab states and Palestinian leaders were happy to see it happen in order to have good cause to intervene once the British departed. By early May, however, some Arab states and the AHC began to take action. Transjordan, the AHC, and the ALA repeatedly cautioned the inhabitants to stay put and tried to pressure those who had already fled the country to return, to no avail. Meanwhile the Haganah, certainly from mid-May on, adopted a policy of preventing refugees from returning to their homes, using live fire when necessary.

The pan-Arab invasion of May 15 clearly hardened Israel's resolve regarding the Palestinian civilian population, for good military and political reasons.

On June 16, the cabinet, without a formal vote, resolved to bar the return of refugees. The IDF general staff ordered its units to stop would-be returnees with live fire. At the same time the army, the settlements, and the JNF Lands Department took a number of initiatives designed to obviate a return. Abandoned villages were razed or mined or, later, filled with new Jewish immigrants, as were abandoned urban neighborhoods; fields were set alight, and landowners still in place were urged to sell out and leave; and new settlements were established on Arab sites and began to cultivate the abandoned fields.

In the third and fourth stages of the exodus, in July and October–November 1948, about three hundred thousand more Arabs became refugees, including the sixty thousand inhabitants of Lydda and Ramle who were expelled by IDF troops. However, many of Nazareth's Arabs were allowed to stay, apparently to avert the prospect of negative reactions by Western Christian states.

Israel's readiness to expel the Arabs was to some degree counterbalanced by a newfound Arab desire to stay put. By October, villagers in the Galilee had heard of the poverty and homelessness of those who had already fled, and understood that their return was far from imminent. So, during the second half of the war, there was far less "spontaneous" flight. Most of the exodus at this time was due to clear, direct causes, including brutal expulsions and deliberate harassment.

Ben-Gurion clearly wanted as few Arabs as possible to remain in the Jewish state. But there was still no systematic expulsion policy; it was never, as far as we know, discussed or decided upon at Cabinet or IDF general staff meetings. Yet Israeli troops, both in the "Ten Days" in July and during Operations Yoav and Hiram in October–November 1948, were far more inclined to expel Palestinians than they had been during the first half of the war. In Operation Yoav, Allon took care to leave almost no Arab communities along his lines of advance. In Operation Hiram, in the north, where Moshe Carmel commanded the Israeli forces, there was confusion and ambivalence. Despite Carmel's October 31 guideline "to assist the Arabs to depart,"[370] some units expelled villagers, others left them in place. And while in general the attitude towards Muslim villages was more severe, there were expulsions and massacres of Christians and many Muslim villagers, such as in Majd al-Kurum, were allowed to stay. During November, when the IDF cleared a strip from five to fifteen kilometers deep along the border with Lebanon, for security reasons, both Christians and Muslims were transferred.

But while military attacks or expulsions were the major precipitant to flight, the exodus was, overall, the result of a cumulative process and a set of causes. A Haifa merchant did not leave only because of months of sniping and bombing, or only because business was getting bad, or because he saw his neighbors flee, or because of extortion by Arab irregulars, or because of the collapse of law and order and the gradual withdrawal of the British, or because of a Haganah attack, or because he feared to live under Jewish rule. He left because of an accumulation of these factors. In the countryside, too, many factors often combined: isolation among a cluster of Jewish settlements, a feeling of being cut off from Arab centers, a lack of direction by national leaders and a feeling of abandonment by the Arab world, fear of Jewish assault, reports and rumors about massacres by the Jews, and actual attacks and massacres.

From April 1948 onward, the Yishuv was pressed to allow refugees to return. Arab leaders and spokesmen for various groups (inhabitants of Jaffa, Maronites from the Galilee, and so on) demanded repatriation, as did international figures, including Count Bernadotte, and the United States and Britain.

Western pressures brought about two Israeli offers to allow a measure of repatriation as part of an overall peace settlement. In July 1949 Israel said it would take back "100,000" (65,000, once those who had already returned or were in the pipeline were deducted), if the Arab states agreed to resettle the rest in their own lands and conclude a peace settlement. Alternatively, Israel might be willing to incorporate the Gaza Strip into its territory and absorb the Strip's population of 60,000 native inhabitants and 200,000 refugees. In this way, Israel would have done more than its fair share toward resolving the problem—which, its officials tirelessly argued, was not of their own making. (Or, as Ben-Gurion was fond of telling Western interlocutors, "Israel did not expel a single Arab."[371])

The offer was seen by the Arabs as far too little, and most of the Arab states insisted that Israel take back all the refugees. Egypt was unwilling to hand over the Gaza Strip—its sole territorial gain of the war—even though this would have relieved Cairo of the burden of a large, impoverished, and subversive population. During the following years the refugees themselves rejected efforts to resettle them in the Arab states. They wanted to "go home," and the Arab states—save Jordan, which gave them citizenship—did little to absorb them, seeing in them and their misery a useful tool against Israel. Israel refused to allow them back, both because it needed the abandoned lands and houses for new immigrants and because it feared the refugees' potential for destabilization—so the problem remained to plague the Middle East, and indeed the world.[372]

SIX

1949–1956

THE MISSED PEACE
AND THE SINAI WAR

T he end of the war found Israel firmly established, the Arab states humiliatingly defeated and their regimes in disrepute, and Palestinian society shattered.

The new state had borders that were more or less internationally accepted, to which the Arab world had at least temporarily resigned itself. In great measure, and especially around the West Bank and the Gaza Strip, they followed no natural topographical contours. Often they abruptly severed Arabs from their lands and kin. A few villages were even cut in two, one part in Israel, the other in the West Bank.

Israel faced a strategist's nightmare—it was surrounded by hostile states, its cities were within enemy artillery range, and it had a narrow, ten-mile-wide waist between the West Bank border and the Mediterranean. Theoretically the eight-thousand-square-mile country could be cut in half in less than an hour by a determined armored thrust. Israel's population regarded the country as highly vulnerable. The Arab minority, 150,000 out of a total population of 850,000–900,000, was justly regarded by the Jews as, at best, an unknown quantity, and at worst a potential fifth column. The Arab countries waged unremitting economic, diplomatic, and propaganda warfare against the new nation. The Egyptians barred Israeli shipping from the Suez Canal and, eventually, also blockaded Eilat. Occasionally Arab states initiated violence along the borders, though by and large they avoided it, if only out of fear of Israeli retaliation.

The government's attention was focused on economic consolidation and absorbing as many immigrants in as short a time as possible. Ben-Gurion believed that a certain demographic mass was necessary for the country's survival, and a massive influx during the three years after the war doubled the

Jewish population. The original 650,000 Jews, with the aid of contributions from American Jewry, housed, fed, and provided employment and schools for another 700,000 people. Most had arrived destitute, many traumatized. Of those coming from the Muslim world, many were illiterate and lacked skills useful in a semi-European, twentieth-century state. The newcomers were settled in the abandoned Arab urban neighborhoods or sent to establish settlements along the borders and in the emptied areas of the interior. In the course of 1949–50, most of the abandoned Arab fields, groves, and orchards were parceled out to and cultivated by kibbutzim or immigrant settlements.

In the summer of 1948, refugees—propelled by poverty, homesickness, or the desire for revenge—began to infiltrate in large numbers into Israel. Many West Bank farmers, from about eighty villages that had fields on the Israeli side of the new border, also regularly crossed over to work "their lands," even though these were now increasingly cultivated by Jewish settlers. Another kind of border problem arose from the creation of the DMZs on the Israeli side of the borders with Egypt and Syria, where no country was officially sovereign. The 1950s saw frequent clashes over control of the zones.

It was mainly the plight of the Palestinian refugees that fueled Arab animosity toward Israel. Their massive presence served as testimony to the Arab world's humiliation, as proof of the injustice that had befallen the Palestinian people, and as a spur to anti-Israel action. Of the 700,000 or so refugees, about half were in Jordan, most of them in the West Bank. Another 200,000 were in the Gaza Strip; about 100,000 in Lebanon; and more than 60,000 in Syria. About half of all the refugees settled in existing towns and villages; the other half, in camps.

The refugees represented an element of social and political destabilization: They became a focus for political disaffection and, in some cases, the bearers of revolutionary threats to the existing regimes. Palestinians such as George Habash and Wadi'a Haddad, both of them Marxists, were among the founders of the radical Kawmyun al-Arab movement in Beirut in 1949–50, which saw salvation in pan-Arab unity. The refugees helped to destabilize the Lebanese polity, a process that culminated in the civil war that began in 1975.

The threat to the status quo was most persistent and pronounced in Jordan, the country with the largest number of refugees; after the takeover and annexation of the West Bank, Palestinians—refugee and non-refugee—constituted 70 percent of the country's population. Jordan treated its Palestinians better than any other Arab country, granting all of them citizenship while most of those in the camps of Gaza, Syria, and Lebanon, and their descendants, remained stateless. But Palestinian Jordanians came to constitute a disaffected majority. They were by and large barred from the Arab Legion's combat formations, as they were from most senior positions in the civil bureaucracy. Their animosity toward the Hashemites found expression on July 20, 1951, in the assassination of Abdullah by Husseini supporters, at Jerusalem's al-Aqsa Mosque.

The war and its consequences also shook the other Arab countries. In Egypt, after a period of unrest, a coterie of young army officers—most of them veterans of the defeat in Palestine—on July 22, 1952, launched a coup d'état, ousting King Farouq and his court and establishing a republican revolutionary regime. In Syria the army overthrew Prime Minister Khalid al-Azm and took control in March 1949. That coup was to prove only the start of a protracted period of military rule and instability, marked by two decades of almost annual coups and countercoups.[1]

Arab leaders and media spoke obliquely or explicitly of the need for or possibility of a redeeming "second round," of "wiping out the traces of Zionist aggression" or "righting Palestinian wrongs." Before 1955 the Arabs did nothing to occasion or prepare for it, but many Israelis feared that such an attack was in fact being planned, and believed that Israel should strike first, before the Arabs were ready and while they were off guard. Such key figures as David Ben-Gurion, the new state's prime minister and defense minister, and Moshe Dayan, a key IDF general from 1949 through 1957, felt that the 1948 war should have ended with Israel occupying the whole country, from the Jordan to the Mediterranean, and that a great opportunity had been lost to redeem the "Land of Israel" up to its natural frontiers. There were powerful forces, including the socialist Ahdut Ha'Avodah and Herut (Revisionist) parties, who had not given up the dream of Jews controlling "the Complete Land of Israel"; and there were many in the defense establishment who believed that this was essential for the country's security.[2] A number of politicians and generals, including Dayan, repeatedly voiced the hope that an opportunity would arise in which Israel could complete its historic mission and round out its borders (as well as expel its own, inconvenient Arab minority). Indeed, they toyed repeatedly with the idea of provoking a "second round" and in 1955–56 they at last managed to do so.

But not everything in the Middle East between 1949 and 1956 militated toward a war. Both sides had suffered greatly in 1948 and were loath to embark on a new bout. Moreover, in the Arab world, the massive shock inflicted by the defeat, in some cases compounded by the overthrow of the old order, initiated a period of flux that appeared to hold out hopes for peace; the postwar situation had not yet calcified in a mold of permanent belligerence and inflexibility.

In Arab eyes, Israel appeared to be a power in its own right, and one that enjoyed the backing and sympathy of the superpowers and of world Jewry (usually perceived in the Arab world as a unified entity of far greater potency than it actually possessed). Perhaps, some surmised, Israel could not be uprooted; perhaps an accommodation should be reached with the Jews. And perhaps—so it seemed to some, like the king in Amman—the new situation was preferable to the alternatives: a Husseini-dominated or an Egyptian-governed Palestine.

During the spring and summer of 1949, under the auspices of the UN's Palestine Conciliation Commission (PCC), representatives of the Arab states and Israel convened in Lausanne, Switzerland, and held indirect talks through the three PCC mediators. But the gaps proved too wide. The Israeli public, "drunk with victory"—in Ben-Gurion's phrase in the cabinet meeting of December 19, 1948[3] —was unwilling to give up any of its hard-won territory or to allow back the refugees, the two consistent Arab demands. The offer to take back sixty-five to one hundred thousand refugees was, as expected in Tel Aviv, flatly refused, and the conference dissolved in September, a total failure.[4]

The Israelis—and the PCC—had noticed a tendency among Arab delegates in multilateral gatherings to slide toward the most uncompromising position presented by any of their number. In Tel Aviv, at least, it was felt that secret, bilateral negotiations might offer a more realistic chance of compromise.

ISRAEL AND JORDAN, 1948–1951

Among the Arab leaders, King Abdullah had been exceptional in almost consistently adopting a conciliatory position. During the 1920s and 1930s, in fact, he was the happy recipient of clandestine largesse from the Jewish Agency.[5] During 1946–48 he had agreed, albeit somewhat ambiguously, to limit Arab Legion operations in Palestine to its Arab-populated areas and to avoid Jordanian-Israeli hostilities. With Jordan emerging as the only Arab state to have made substantial territorial gains and to have avoided military defeat, Abdullah and the Jews resumed their secret dialogue, this time with a peace treaty as the avowed purpose.

Israel's leaders, Prime Minister Ben-Gurion and Foreign Minister Sharett, acknowledged that Abdullah sincerely sought peace. But they themselves were not quite so eager, because peace carried a price. As Sharett noted in his report on a meeting on May 5, 1949, with Abdullah: "Transjordan said—we are ready for peace immediately. We said—of course, we too want peace, but we cannot run, we have to walk."[6]

Initially Abdullah demanded the return of Jaffa, Lydda, and Ramle (all designated in the 1947 Partition Resolution for Palestinian Arab sovereignty) to Arab control. Israel refused, and itself demanded the Legion-held Latrun salient and areas around Jerusalem. By the end of 1949 Abdullah had whittled down his major demands to a two-kilometer-wide strip of land from the Hebron hills to the Mediterranean at Gaza or Ashkelon. Israel proposed allowing Jordan access to the sea—but without a sovereign corridor. Months passed and eventually, Israel agreed to a fifty- or one-hundred-meter-wide corridor. But it was too late; Abdullah had lost his room for maneuver and was unable to overcome the opposition of his cabinet ministers to a peace treaty involving only minor Israeli concessions.

In February 1950 Jordan proposed, in lieu of a full peace treaty, a five-year nonbelligerency agreement, and a draft was eventually initialed by representatives of the two countries. But Abdullah seems to have gotten cold feet and suspended negotiations; there was too much internal opposition in Amman, and it is likely that he felt he could not sell such a pact to his people—by now mostly Palestinians—and to his fellow Arab leaders. And Israel, for its part, also began to reconsider the worth and viability of an agreement with Jordan. Perhaps it was better first to make peace with Egypt; perhaps Israel should strive to destroy Jordan and share out its territory with its Arab neighbors rather than shore up Abdullah's "unnatural" kingdom with a peace treaty.[7] By July 1951 Abdullah was dead—and with him any hope of a speedy peace with Jordan.[8] Israel's postwar inflexibility was in part due to its success in negotiating the armistice agreements. The threat of renewed war had been pushed back, well over the horizon. So why strain to make a peace involving major territorial concessions? Ben-Gurion told a visiting American journalist in July 1949: "I am not in a hurry, and I can wait ten years. We are under no pressure whatsoever."[9]

Israel had other, more urgent worries and interests: the absorption and settlement of the masses of new immigrants, the creation and consolidation of the infrastructure of statehood, the reconstruction and expansion of the economy.[10] The land that Abdullah and other Arabs were demanding was precisely that needed for the immigrants. In April 1949, even before Israel had signed armistice agreements with all its neighbors, Ben-Gurion stated: "The main thing is the absorption of the immigrants . . . for many years, until . . . a regime takes hold in the [Arab] world that does not threaten our existence. . . . The state's fate is dependent upon 'Aliyah . . . 'Aliyah must determine our policy in negotiations." Not peace but substantially increasing Israel's population was Ben-Gurion's priority. Clearly he looked to peacemaking mainly as a facilitator of demographic growth which in turn would enhance the country's security and power.[11]

If Israel was unwilling to pay a price for peace, "minimal or maximal," in the words of one Israeli negotiator at Lausanne, Elias Sasson,[12] the Arab leaders proved incapable of withstanding the combined pressure of their hard-line colleagues, domestic political elites, and public opinion. Certainly they felt that they could not take the plunge without a substantial quid pro quo—and none was forthcoming. "I could justify a peace by pointing to concessions made by the Jews. But without any concessions from them, I am defeated before I even start," said Abdullah three weeks before his death.[13]

THE ZA'IM PEACE OVERTURE, SPRING 1949

On March 30, 1949, Col. Husni Za'im, chief of staff of the Syrian army, took power in Damascus in a bloodless coup d'état. On August 14 he himself was overthrown—and executed—in another military coup. During his brief regime Za'im proposed a "separate" peace settlement with Israel, but got nowhere.

In mid-April, shortly after the start of the Israeli-Syrian armistice talks, Za'im asked for a meeting with Ben-Gurion to negotiate a peace settlement. "They want to immediately sign a peace and not an armistice and to immediately exchange ambassadors," Yigael Yadin told a meeting of senior Israeli officials on April 19.[14] Za'im sought—as he told an American diplomat— "give and take provided he [was] not . . . asked to give all while [the] other side takes all." Za'im offered to absorb 250,000–500,000 Palestinian refugees in Syria, with the West paying for their resettlement and related development projects. In return, Israel was asked to agree that the new frontier would run down the middle of the Jordan River and the Sea of Galilee rather than follow the old Palestine-Syria border, which ran along the east bank of the Jordan River and slightly to the east of the sea—leaving both wholly inside Palestine/Israel. Syria would withdraw from the Mishmar HaYarden salient, west of the river, and would receive the eastern shore of the Sea of Galilee (the 'Ein Gev–HaOn strip) and half its water and half the waters of the River Jordan.

Ben-Gurion refused to meet Za'im (as he had, previously, refused to meet King Abdullah) and rejected any concession of territory or water. Syria, he argued, must first recognize the existing frontier, withdraw from the salient, and sign an armistice agreement; afterwards Israel and Syria could discuss peace. In an angry cable to Washington, the U.S. ambassador in Damascus concluded:

> Unless Israel can be brought to understand that it cannot have all of its cake (partition boundaries) and gravy as well (area captured in violation of truce, Jerusalem and resettlement of Arab refugees elsewhere) it may find that it has won Pal[estine] war but lost peace. It should be evident that Israel's continued insistence upon her pound of flesh and more is driving Arab states slowly (and perhaps surely) to gird their loins (politically and economically if not yet militarily) for long range struggle.[15]

Ben-Gurion's response sealed the fate of the Za'im initiative.[16] The armistice agreement, which met most of Israel's territorial demands, including Syrian withdrawal from the salient, was signed on July 20. An Israeli effort to revive contacts came to nought, and two weeks later Za'im was dead.

Israel's leaders may have suspected that Za'im's proposals were merely a ploy to win territory and water resources. He had an unwholesome reputation, both at home and abroad. In exile in Paris before the war, he had repeated contacts with Zionist and American officials—and was apparently regarded as an intelligence asset by both. On assuming the Syrian presidency he took on the rank of marshal, complete with a $3,000 baton, and had been overheard telling his wife: "One day you shall be queen."[17] Ben-Gurion expressed "strong dislike and suspicion of Za'im," and even characterized him as "a little Mussolini."[18] But he acknowledged that Za'im "for some reason . . . wants good relations with us."[19] Yet he was, or pretended to be, perturbed precisely by those traits of Za'im's—pragmatism and lack of strong ideological convictions—that had enabled the Syrian to make his overture to Israel.

Of course, it was not Za'im's sincerity or seriousness that was of paramount concern. Israel's leaders simply refused to contemplate a concession of territory or water to achieve peace. As in their dealings with Abdullah, they were remarkably single-minded and rigid, convinced that the Arabs would eventually agree to make peace without Israel having to make such concessions. Meanwhile, the armistice agreements would suffice.

Throughout, Ben-Gurion took the crucial decisions alone. His ministers, apart from Sharett, knew nothing about Za'im's offer. And the Israeli public was left enwrapped in an even thicker veil of ignorance.[20]

ISRAEL AND EGYPT, 1948–1952

During this period there also occurred secret, intermittent Egyptian-Israeli contacts in which possible peace terms were discussed. Initially, King Farouq's representatives signaled that Egypt would be willing to reach a settlement if Israel relinquished part or all of the Negev (with an eye to reestablishing the territorial continuity of the Arab world). But the Israeli negotiators refused to budge. As Ben-Gurion put it in a cable to Sharett a few years later: "Israel will not discuss a peace involving the concession of any piece of territory. The neighboring states do not deserve an inch of Israel's land. . . . We are ready for peace in exchange for peace."[21]

Egypt first sent out peace feelers in September–October 1948, during the Second Truce. On September 21 Kamal Riad, a Farouq court official, met in Paris with Elias Sasson of the Israeli Foreign Ministry and sounded him out on Israel's readiness to sign a separate peace. Sasson hammered out a fourteen-point draft treaty and submitted it to Riad, who transmitted it to Cairo. The Egyptians hinted that they wanted the Negev in exchange for peace. But Ben-Gurion parried the overture with questions about details—meanwhile pushing through the cabinet the decision, on October 6, to renew the offensive (Operation Yoav) against the Egyptian army. Perhaps he viewed the peace feelers as insincere and designed merely to deflect the expected IDF offensive. In any event, he kept the matter to himself and failed to bring it before the cabinet.[22]

At the beginning of November, with Operation Yoav nearing completion, Cairo renewed its initiative, asserting its interest in armistice talks and in retaining the Gaza Strip and parts or all of the Negev. This time, the matter was brought before the cabinet, but Ben-Gurion—and, apparently, the majority of the ministers—objected to the Egyptians' retaining any part of Palestine, and the negotiations were suspended. In December 1948–January 1949 the IDF launched Operation Horev, driving the Egyptian army out of Palestine, except for the Gaza Strip.[23]

After Israel and Egypt signed the general armistice agreement, on February 24, officials of both nations met periodically, in secret, often in Paris. The Egyptians consistently demanded the Negev in return for peace.[24] During the following two years, down to the July 1952 revolution, their negotiators, while moderate in tone, shied away from discussing peace terms, arguing that Egypt's delicate position in the Arab world precluded any dramatic moves vis-à-vis Israel.[25] Underlying this lack of movement was also Egypt's appreciation that Israel was not going to budge from its standard "no territorial concessions" position, clearly laid out in the contacts of 1949–50.

Things changed, or appeared to change, dramatically with the overthrow of the Farouq regime and the assumption of power by the junta of the Free Officers Movement. The Revolutionary Command Council (RCC), led by Gen. Mohammed Naguib, was soon dominated by Col. Gamal 'Abdel Nasser, who eventually emerged as Egypt's prime minister and then president.

Would the Free Officers, who preached modernity, progress, and socialism, proceed where their predecessors had feared to tread? A certain stream of Israeli thinking had it that there was no possibility of peacemaking between the Arab world's reactionary regimes and Israel. Only a forward-looking, progressive regime—one enjoying popular support and caring more for its people's welfare than foreign adventures—would be capable of making peace.

In August 1952 Ben-Gurion, speaking in the Knesset, welcomed Farouq's deposition and formally extended the new regime an offer of peace, arguing that there were no natural conflicts of interest between Israel and Egypt. Simultaneously, secret contacts were initiated with Egyptian diplomats in Paris. An internal Israel Foreign Ministry memorandum said: "We do not regard Naguib's regime as hostile. . . . Farouq's overthrow has removed from the arena one of the main bearers of the drive for revenge against Israel. . . . One should not assume that the new regime . . . is headed for a renewal of the aggression against Israel by a second round."[26]

During its first two years in power the RCC showed little interest in Israel. In their public utterances, the junta's leaders continued to toe the rejectionist Arab line, though there was an appreciable reduction of incidents along the Gaza Strip border. Israeli peace feelers were politely ignored. In early 1953 Egypt secretly informed Israel that it preferred to maintain the "no war, no peace" status quo; the Egyptian emissary, 'Abd al-Rahman Sadiq, said the RCC was split on the issue, and while Nasser and Gen. 'Abd al-Hakim 'Amr favored progress toward a settlement, they were curbed by those, like Anwar Sadat and Salah Salem, who opposed any peacemaking initiatives. Hence no movement was possible, despite Egypt's desire for Israeli help in facilitating Britain's withdrawal from the Canal area and obtaining American economic assistance. Israel, for its part, set major preconditions that had to be met before peace was officially negotiated: Egyptian guarantees of free passage for

Israeli ships and Israel-bound goods through the Canal, the lifting of the economic boycott, and stricter adherence to the armistice agreement.

In 1953–54 Prime Ministers Sharett (Ben-Gurion had retired temporarily)
and Nasser exchanged secret messages—Nasser's arrived unsigned—expressing a desire for "a peaceful solution." But no progress toward a solution, or
indeed, formal, open talks, was achieved. Nasser's attitude was ambivalent.
Like most Arabs, he had felt personally humiliated by 1948 (he himself had
been trapped by the IDF in the "Faluja Pocket") and resented the establishment of a divisive Jewish state in the heart of the Arab world. Palestine, he
wrote in 1953, was "a home illegally stolen from its owners," and Israel was a
"fruit of imperialism."[27] But he respected Israel's strength and understood that
it was in the Middle East to stay, at least in the short term. In January 1955 he
published his views in *Foreign Affairs*: "Israel's policy is aggressive and
expansionist. . . . However, we do not want to start any conflict. War has no
place in the constructive policy which we have designed to improve the lot of
our people. We have much to do in Egypt. . . . A war would cause us to
lose . . . much of what we seek to achieve."[28]

During the second half of 1954 and early 1955, Nasser's attitude toward
Israel visibly hardened—much as Ben-Gurion's attitude toward Egypt and
Nasser grew progressively more hostile. During 1955 the direct, if highly
clandestine, Israeli-Egyptian feelers and talks were replaced by third-party
mediation, with a succession of Western officials, businessmen, and clergy-
men acting as go-betweens. Tension between the two countries, in part resulting from cross-border forays and clashes, in part from Israeli provocations
such as the Bat-Galim affair and the Esek HaBish sabotage affair (see below),
now precluded direct and, indeed, meaningful contacts.[29]

The most comprehensive, protracted, and intensive third-party mediation
effort was to be Project Alpha, the Anglo-American initiative of 1955. The
goal was an Israeli-Egyptian peace settlement (or something short of it) in
which Israel would cede all or parts of the southern Negev and agree to absorb
some of the refugees and to compensate the rest. The two powers promised to
guarantee the settlement and offered Nasser, as added bait, economic and military aid.

Nasser responded by demanding the whole of the Negev, and Israel by
rejecting any cession of territory or substantial refugee repatriation. The two
major powers then suggested a compromise based on Israel's yielding up two
"kissing" triangles in the southern Negev in a way that would connect Egypt
to Jordan without disconnecting Israel from its access to Eilat and the Gulf of
Aqaba (a tunnel or bridge was envisaged). Both sides rejected the idea
(though the Egyptians at one point, albeit informally, agreed to drop the
refugee repatriation demand), and Alpha fizzled out and died. Neither of the
Western powers had fully comprehended the depth of Israeli opposition to any

ceding of territory.[30] By the end of 1955 Israel and Egypt were set on a more or less inevitable collision course. The 1956 Sinai/Suez war was the outcome.

Israeli and Western documentation indicates that windows of opportunity for peacemaking between Israel and several of its neighbors certainly existed during late 1948–July 1952. However, the opportunities were not exploited, certainly not to the full, because Israel was unwilling to make concessions for peace, and the Arab leaders felt too weak and threatened by their own people and their neighbors to embark on, or even contemplate, peace unless it included substantial Israeli concessions.

Abdullah, it is clear from the documents, was sincerely interested in a settlement, and Israel's leaders appreciated this. Syria's Za'im offered a more problematic prospect—but he, too, it would seem, was ready to reach an agreement, if not with quite as much enthusiasm as Abdullah. The Egyptians present a more ambivalent picture: King Farouq, after 1948, was at best lukewarm, while some members of his court and other senior Egyptian officials occasionally met in secret with Israelis and discussed mutual interests and this or that possibility of peacemaking and coexistence. But all in all, neither the Farouq nor the RCC regime appears to have been "ripe" for peace.

It is unclear whether, had Israel been more forthcoming, the Arab leaders would have followed through—or whether they would have flinched at the last moment; or how long such treaties, if signed, would have lasted. What is certain is that several proposals were tabled and considered, and that they were ultimately rejected or finessed, leaving the state of war between Israel and each of its neighbors intact. The leaders on both sides failed to rise to these occasions and adequately to pursue the opportunities offered.

The Arab regimes—all of them autocracies or dictatorships—subsequently hid from their constituencies the facts about what had transpired. No Arab archive opened its papers to the scrutiny of historians. In Israel, a democracy, the situation was somewhat different. For decades Ben-Gurion, and successive administrations after his, lied to the Israeli public about the post-1948 peace overtures and about Arab interest in a deal. The Arab leaders (with the possible exception of Abdullah) were presented, one and all, as a recalcitrant collection of warmongers, hell-bent on Israel's destruction. The recent opening of the Israeli archives offers a far more complex picture.

A somewhat ironic (in retrospect) postscript to the issue of the "missed" peace was afforded by Ben-Gurion in a Knesset address in August 1952:

> All my life down to today—as a Zionist and a Jew—I regarded peace and understanding with the Arabs as a basic and primary value. . . . I would regard it as a grievous sin not only against our generation but also against future generations were we not to do everything possible to reach mutual understanding with our Arab neighbors and were the coming generations able to blame the Israeli government with missing any

opportunity whatsoever for peace. . . . I would not want to be the person that our grandchildren or great-grandchildren would charge with having missed, at some point, a possible chance for Israeli-Arab peace.[31]

THE INFILTRATION PROBLEM

But the essential reality of Israeli-Arab relations during 1949–56 was not these failed efforts at peacemaking but unremitting, if generally low-key, conflict. Leaders and news media on both sides regularly voiced propaganda and traded threats, and the Arab world closed ranks in waging massive political warfare against Israel, regarding it as a pariah state and attempting to persuade the rest of the world to follow suit. The Arabs refused to recognize Israel's existence or right to exist—leaders and writers avoided using the word "Israel"; maps left its area blank or called it Palestine. They closed their frontiers to all traffic to or from Israel, barring even non-Israelis who had Israeli visas in their passports; voted en bloc against Israel in all international institutions; and refused any association with Israelis in cultural and sports activities. A comprehensive Arab economic boycott was imposed, including the closure by Egypt of the Suez Canal and the Straits of Tiran to Israeli shipping and to specific goods (such as oil) bound for Israel, carried on third-country vessels, and a ban on deals with companies doing business with Israel.[32]

The most grinding and visible expressions of animosity were border clashes. Most of the tension along the frontiers resulted from Arab infiltration. The daily trespassing and shooting incidents, the occasional murder of Israelis, and the retaliations generated fresh hostility which gradually built up to a crescendo in the second Arab-Israeli war of 1956.

There was little infiltration of any kind on the Israel-Lebanon border and almost none at all on the Syrian border. Along the Negev-Sinai line, where there were few settlements, Bedouin would cross in both directions to meet seasonal grazing needs and there were intertribal raids, mainly to steal sheep and cattle. But along the West Bank and Gaza borders, massive infiltration began in the summer of 1948, during the First Truce. Roughly ten to fifteen thousand incidents occurred annually during 1949–54, the number falling off to six to seven thousand annually in 1955–56. During 1948–49, most of the infiltrators crossed the borders to harvest crops left behind, to plant new crops in their abandoned lands, or to retrieve goods. Many others came to resettle in their old villages or elsewhere inside Israel, or to visit relatives, or simply to get a glimpse of their abandoned homes and fields.

During the following years the vast majority came to steal crops, irrigation pipes, farm animals, or other property belonging to settlers, or to graze their flocks. Some engaged in smuggling goods or mail—certain items, such as Bedouin clothing, were often unavailable in Israel, and there were no postal services between Israel and the Arab states. Others moved through Israeli territory in order to reach other Arab countries, most frequently from the Gaza Strip to the West Bank.

Most of the infiltrators were unarmed individuals, though it appears that the proportion who came armed and in groups steadily increased after 1950, largely in reaction to the IDF's violent measures. Many of the Israeli victims of infiltration were incidental casualties of raids whose aim was theft or smuggling. Of the approximately thirty nonmilitary Israelis killed by infiltrators in 1952, seventeen were civilian guards and two were policemen.[33]

Only a very small proportion, certainly far less than 10 percent, of the infiltrators came with the express purpose of attacking people or sabotaging Israeli targets. Some of these sought revenge. Others were supporters of the exiled ex-mufti, Hajj Amin al-Husseini, who resorted to terrorism for political reasons, such as to spark conflict between Israel and Jordan. During 1954–56, however, the Egyptian military intelligence office in Gaza sent infiltrators called *fedayeen* ("self-sacrificers") to retaliate for Israeli attacks in the Strip. Jordanian officers appear to have begun recruiting their own *fedayeen* in 1956. Moreover, throughout 1949–56, Arab armies sent scouts into Israel on intelligence-gathering missions; occasionally they attacked Israelis.

Until 1955 the Arab states officially opposed infiltration and generally attempted to curb it. But the frontiers were long and unnatural, and the Arab authorities operated with insufficient vigor and means. Often infiltrators and local civil and military authorities collaborated. Many of the latter turned a blind eye in return for bribes, especially the men of the Jordanian National Guard, a frontier militia created in 1950. Moreover, Arab officials and policemen felt there was nothing intrinsically wrong with repossessing crops or stealing from and otherwise harming Israelis. They saw Israel as an immoral robber state that had driven the Palestinians out and stolen their homes. Curbing infiltration and punishing infiltrators was unpopular, in both Jordan and Gaza.

Israeli officials understood the Arab dilemma. As Dayan observed in 1955:

> It is not easy for an Arab government and its forces to fight infiltration. Most of the Arabs do not see theft from the foreigner as a sin at all, and as to Israel—in the wake of the War of Independence there has been added a will for revenge and feelings of enmity. . . . The Arab policeman has no facile answer when, coming to arrest an Arab from Qalqilya who is returning with a cow from Israel, he is asked: "What do you care if I steal a cow from Kibbutz Ramat-HaKovesh?"[34]

Even so, both the Jordanian Legion and the Egyptian military made efforts to curtail infiltration. Glubb repeatedly imposed restrictions on border villages and farmers, and Jordanian magistrates frequently punished infiltrators—though usually too lightly for Israeli tastes. During the period December 1950–February 1952, according to Jordanian statistics, 2,575 infiltrators were tried and convicted, receiving fines or short jail terms.[35] During 1950–53 Israel and Jordan signed and implemented "Local Commanders Agreements," providing for local military cooperation in curbing infiltration. Along the Israeli-Egyptian border, the two countries in 1949–50 ran joint military patrols, with the same aim.

Major IDF retaliatory raids during this period were often followed by Arab action against infiltration. After the IDF raid on the West Bank border village of Qibya in October 1953, the Legion deployed along the border in an effort to halt infiltration, as well as to deter IDF incursions. But enlarged Legion and IDF presence along the border almost inevitably resulted in firefights. Egypt invested too little in its efforts to have any significant effect. "Egyptian [anti-infiltration] policy is not being implemented," IDF Intelligence complained in 1952.[36] Local officials and military or paramilitary border units were mostly Palestinians. In July 1954 the head of Egyptian military intelligence in the Gaza Strip wrote: "The main objective of the military presence along the armistice line is to prevent infiltration, but the Palestinian troops encourage the movement of infiltrators and carry out attacks along the line."[37]

Israel routinely accused Jordan and Egypt of doing nothing to stop infiltration, and of encouraging or directing it. Spokesmen including Ben-Gurion publicly charged the Arab states with deliberately using infiltration as a "guerrilla war" against Israel. In the words of an internal Israeli report: "It disturbs the peace; engenders an atmosphere of war; [and] harms the economy, both directly and by necessitating extensive security measures."[38]

During 1948–56 about two hundred Israeli civilians and scores of soldiers were killed by infiltrators. In addition, dozens of Israeli soldiers were killed in the course of IDF retaliatory strikes triggered by incursions. Infiltrators stole or damaged each year, on average, several hundred thousand Israel pounds' worth of property, for which the government reimbursed the settlers. One cooperative settlement, Beit Arif, east of Tel Aviv, summarized its losses due to infiltration during June–November 1950 thus: "We lost the autumn agricultural season . . . [had] poor corn [and] potato crops . . . [lost] three cows worth IL600, one horse worth IL100, two goats worth IL50 . . . laundry worth IL10, various [irrigation] pipes worth IL1,610." In 1952 infiltrators stole or damaged property worth IL517,000, according to Israel Police records.[39] (The state budget stood at IL300 million in fiscal 1952/3—about $200 million.)

Infiltration also resulted in major indirect economic damage, much of it stemming from the need to pay for large numbers of civilian guards. In the mid-1950s, the Treasury and the Jewish Agency each spent close to IL1.5 million a year on guards. Further large sums were expended on perimeter fences, lighting, and other measures. Still other indirect costs were incurred because the settlers put in many hours of guard duty, reducing their agricultural productivity. Fear of infiltrators caused settlers to leave remote fields fallow and to sell off livestock, which might be stolen.

For a time, during 1950–53, infiltration threatened to subvert the whole border-settlement venture. In certain areas, the population lived in perpetual fear. In Moshav Mishmar Ayalon, west of Jerusalem, it was reported in December 1951: "In the evenings the women are afraid to remain in their homes and they gather together with their children in a number of houses in the center of the settlement." (Many of the menfolk worked outside the settlement during the week, returning home only on the weekends.) And a year and a half later, Mishmar Ayalon's inhabitants still left their houses at night "to join 4–5 [other] families in one room, so that there's a feeling of security."[40]

The most serious result of this demoralization was the abandonment of border settlements. Some half dozen moshavim, populated by new immigrants mainly from Muslim countries, were completely deserted during this period, and more than a dozen others suffered major population depletion. In large measure this was due to depredations by infiltrators. The departure of some families inevitably increased the guard-duty burden of the males who remained, further undermining the settlers' staying power.

For a time, there was something close to panic in the Jewish Agency Settlement Department. "The new immigrants, because of their wanderings, anomie and lethargy, are like leaves in the wind, who will tremble before any storm. . . . We fear day and night for them," wrote the department's director, Levi Eshkol (Shkolnik), in the early 1950s, and warned of impending "catastrophe."[41] The agency, assisted by the police, took stringent measures to halt this flight. Would-be leavers were occasionally harassed and penalties were imposed on those arriving in the center of the country from the frontier areas. The IDF added patrols and more paid guards. In the end most of the settlers hung on, if only because they really had no viable options: Housing and jobs were extremely difficult to find in the country's urban centers.

THE ISRAELI RESPONSES

During the second half of 1948, 1949, and the early 1950s, immigrants were settled in abandoned Arab villages and neighborhoods, and new settlements were established on the lands of abandoned villages, which were leveled, to deter refugees from returning and to deny infiltrators hiding places and way-stations.

But the chief response to infiltration was military. The IDF policy, adopted during the First Truce (June 11–July 8, 1948), was to shoot at any Arab who crossed the lines. Most of those shot were refugees trying to get back to their lands and homes, shepherds and harvesters. This policy was carried over by the

IDF—on the government's orders—into the postarmistice years. It was both a matter of consolidating the lines marked out as the borders and preventing the return of refugees and depredations by infiltrators. No one wanted to lose any of the small, hard-won country marked out in the armistice accords—and if Arab cultivators were allowed to move into border areas, these would quickly revert de facto to Arab sovereignty—and no one wanted an increase of Israel's Arab minority. From mid-1949, IDF orders to the front-line units were at night to fire at anything that moved, no questions asked, and during daylight hours to fire at every adult male. But the troops were allowed to open fire at will from several hundred yards away, at which distance it was often impossible to distinguish the gender or age of the target. They were also often instructed during daylight to issue a halt order, and to open fire only if the "target" disobeyed. In practice, however, many infiltrators preferred to make a run for it; they may have assumed that the soldiers had little chance of hitting them, or they may have heard that the IDF treated captives with incarceration, beatings, deportation across a distant border, and, occasionally, torture and murder.

The thrust of IDF policy is apparent, for example, in orders issued by the Fifth (Giv'ati) Brigade to one of its battalions on the line in 1953: "The battle against infiltration in the border areas at all times of day and at night will be carried out mainly by opening fire, without giving warning, on any individual or group that cannot be identified from afar by our troops as Israeli citizens and who are, at the moment they are spotted, [infiltrating] into Israeli territory."[42] Ultimately the troops' behavior depended on the discretion of local commanders: Some fired over the heads of infiltrators to drive them off.

Arab governments—particularly Jordan—repeatedly complained about the free-fire policy, claiming that it caused death and injury to innocuous trespassers; moreover, Israeli troops quite often fired on farmers in no-man's-land or even on the Jordanian side of the line. According to the British Legation in Amman, Israeli troops, between February and July 1950, killed twenty-six Arabs near the line inside Israel, eleven in no-man's-land, and twenty-three on the Jordanian side.[43]

A large number of infiltrators were killed by mines and booby-traps. Hundreds of mines were laid each night along suspected infiltrator routes and anticipated targets, such as irrigation piping and water pumps, were booby-trapped. The office diary for the first half of 1950 of the secretary of Kibbutz Erez, on the Gaza border, gives an indication of the success of these measures: "8 January: Five Arabs killed by shrapnel mine laid by Aharonik [a kibbutz member]. . . . 8 April: Successful ambush: Two Arabs killed. . . . 10 April: An Arab and donkey killed by mine. . . . 11 April: An Arab killed by a mine. . . . 13 April: An Arab killed by a mine. . . . 12 June: Two Arabs killed by a mine . . . 14 June: An Arab killed by a mine."[44] Mines were sometimes laid for infiltrators coming to retrieve the bodies of others killed the night before. In Kibbutz Yad Mordechai, also on the Gaza border, the settlers in May 1953 booby-trapped a water pump they knew Arab infiltrators were coming to take, killing a dozen or more of them.[45] Israel's defensive measures resulted in the death of between 2,700 and 5,000 infiltrators, mostly unarmed, during 1949–56, the vast majority during the first four or five years.[46]

Another anti-infiltration measure was expulsion. In February–March 1949, during the Israel-Jordan armistice negotiations, Israeli troops expelled to the West Bank, as infiltrators, a large number of refugees living along the front lines, especially in the "wild" Beit Jibrin (Beit Govrin) area. During June–October 1950, the IDF transferred to the Gaza Strip the approximately 2,500 Arab inhabitants of Ashkelon, many of whom were believed to have fled the country during the war and infiltrated back.

From the end of 1948 the IDF and police regularly searched the country's remaining Arab villages, mostly in the Galilee and the "Little Triangle," ferreting out suspected infiltrators and their families. These were promptly thrown across the border, usually into the West Bank, though occasionally into Lebanon or across the Arava border. Charles Freeman, an American Quaker working in refugee relief, visited Kafr Yasif, in the Galilee, in early March 1949 and found that 239 people who had been in the village the previous month were no longer there: "In each case whole families were removed. . . . Some of the refugees were allowed to take whatever they could of household equipment and clothing, but others were given only a few minutes' notice." They had been taken by trucks to the West Bank border and herded across.[47]

In May 1950 a kibbutz member witnessed one of these truck convoys on its way to the border:

We were waiting for a lift beside one of the big army camps [in the South]. . . . Suddenly two large trucks arrived, packed with blindfolded Arabs (men, women and children). Several of the soldiers guarding them got down to drink and eat a little, while the rest stayed on guard. To our question "Who are these Arabs?" they responded: "These are infiltrators, on their way to being returned over the borders." The way the Arabs were crowded together was inhuman. Then one of the soldiers called his friend the "expert" to make some order. Those of us standing nearby had witnessed no misbehavior on the part of the Arabs, who sat frightened, almost one on top of the other. But the soldiers were quick to teach us what they meant by "order." The "expert" jumped [onto the truck] and began to . . . hit [the Arabs] across their blindfolded eyes, and when he had finished, he stamped on all of them and then, in the end, laughed uproariously and with satisfaction at his heroism. We were shocked by this despicable act.[48]

Perhaps the most brutal of the mass expulsions occurred at the end of May 1950, when more than one hundred suspected infiltrators were pushed across the Jordanian frontier in the Arava. Most eventually reached safety, but about thirty died of dehydration and exhaustion, triggering rebukes of Israel in the international press and of the government and IDF inside Mapai and Mapam. Responding to criticism by Foreign Minister Sharett, the head of IDF Southern Command, General Dayan, expatiated on the whole anti-infiltration policy:

> Using the moral yardstick mentioned by [Sharett], I must ask: Are [we justified] in opening fire on the Arabs who cross [the border] to reap the crops they planted in our territory; they, their women, and their children? Will this stand up to moral scrutiny . . .? We shoot at those from among the 200,000 hungry Arabs who cross the line [to graze their flocks]—will this stand up to moral review? Arabs cross to collect the grain that they left in the abandoned villages and we set mines for them and they go back without an arm or a leg. . . . [It may be that this] cannot pass review, but I know no other method of guarding the borders. If the Arab shepherds and harvesters are allowed to cross the borders, then tomorrow the State of Israel will have no borders.[49]

Among those expelled to Jordan or the Sinai Peninsula during 1949 and the early 1950s were a number of Bedouin tribes and subtribes, believed to have infiltrated into the Negev since 1948, or to be troublesome. Israel probably expelled more than 10,000 suspected infiltrators during the period 1949–56. In 1952 alone, the number was 3,181.[50]

The atmosphere that equated "infiltrator" with "terrorist" and the various brutal measures permitted led to a succession of atrocities during 1949–53. Many of them went unrecorded: Victims cannot talk and the perpetrators do not usually want to. But occasionally there was physical evidence; less often there were survivors or witnesses of the murder or rape of infiltrators. More commonly captives were beaten and then shoved back across the border or sent inland to detention centers. Often infiltrators who were seriously injured by a mine or in an ambush were finished off by their captors.[51]

In addition to these defensive measures, Israel, starting at the end of 1948, adopted a policy of retaliatory strikes. The policy had three main aims: revenge ("[T]he [public's] rage must be defused," said Sharett in 1955[52]), punishment, and deterrence. As Dayan enunciated the policy:

> The only method that proved effective, not justified or moral but effective, when Arabs plant mines on our side [is retaliation]. If we try to search for that [particular] Arab [who planted mines], it has no value. But if we harass the nearby village . . . then the population there comes out against the [infiltrators] . . . and the Egyptian Government and the Transjordanian Government are [driven] to prevent such incidents,

because their prestige is [assailed], as the Jews have opened fire, and they are unready to begin a war. . . . The method of collective punishment so far has proved effective.[53]

During the years 1950–56 it emerged that retaliatory strikes were actually not particularly effective; they rarely stopped terroristic infiltration for long. But Dayan and others argued—unassailably—that the situation would have grown far worse had there been none. The Arab leaders, it was argued, had to be motivated to curb the infiltrators, and the retaliatory raids, by humiliating the targeted countries, provided such motivation. Moreover, the strikes sent a message of strategic deterrence to the Arab states. They demonstrated, for all to see, that the IDF was far more powerful and efficient than any of the Arab armies, thus pushing back the day—and possibility—of a "second round." Paradoxically, during the years 1955–56 (and perhaps as early as 1954), retaliatory strikes were also launched by the IDF in order to draw the Arab states into a premature war.

The strikes also served to bolster Israeli morale and to harden and prepare the IDF, physically and morally, for the coming war. And there was a negative political consideration as well: In the absence of retaliatory responses, it was feared in government circles, the public might abandon Mapai and throw its support to the more militant-sounding Herut Party or the "activist" Ahdut Ha'Avodah Party.[54]

Occasionally during 1949 and the early 1950s, the IDF used mortars and aircraft to bombard and strafe villages or encampments from which infiltrators had set out. But the most frequent method of retaliation was a cross-border raid by a small unit of infantrymen. Usually operating at night, they would snipe at field hands and lay mines, or attack a Bedouin encampment, a village, Arab traffic, or a military post, and then return to Israeli territory. From the end of 1953 the strikes became bigger affairs, usually involving whole battalions and even brigades, with the target usually an Arab military installation. The crucial policy shift from mainly civilian objectives to mainly military targets was a consequence of the IDF raid on the West Bank village of Qibya, in which about sixty civilians were massacred, and the resultant political-diplomatic fallout.

One of the first relatively large-scale strikes was against the village of Sharafat, just south of Jerusalem, on the night of February 6, 1951. Two houses, one of them the village mukhtar's (headman's), were blown up to avenge a murder and rape at Manahat (al-Maliha), southwest of Jerusalem. About a dozen Arabs—mostly women and children—were killed. Most were apparently related to the Mansi gang, which had carried out the attack in Manahat. The raid raised a political storm in Jordan and at least temporarily persuaded King Abdullah and his ministers that taking a conciliatory line with

Israel would avail them nothing, and rendered the chances of peace more remote.[55]

The years 1951–53 were marked by a steadily increasing cycle of infiltration and counterraids along the Israeli-Jordanian border. There were also occasional terrorist attacks and Israeli counterstrikes across the Israel-Gaza frontier.

The rape and murder of a young Jerusalem woman triggered a raid on the night of January 6, 1952, on the village of Beit Jala, near Bethlehem. The target was several houses belonging to the Mansi clan, which had been displaced in 1948 from the Jerusalem Corridor village of Walaja. Israeli intelligence believed that they were responsible for the murder as well as several previous outrages. The attacking platoon blew up two houses and raided a third, killing six persons, including two women and two girls, and injuring three more. They left behind a leaflet stating that this was revenge for an "unpardonable crime." Israel officially denied any involvement in or knowledge of the raid. The Jordanian authorities temporarily clamped down on infiltration in the area.[56]

The severity and frequency of retaliatory raids went up a notch in 1953. In a series of singularly inefficient IDF operations in January, a handful of Arabs were killed and wounded—but the raiders suffered casualties and failed to complete their missions. There were also diplomatic and military repercussions. Jordan invoked its defense treaty with Britain—but Whitehall responded by issuing vague reassurances coupled with a refusal to activate the treaty. Washington made representations to Jerusalem. The Arab Legion deployed two of its battalions along the frontier, previously manned only by National Guard militia units based in each village.

The inept raids and their diplomatic consequences triggered some soul-searching in the IDF (focusing on the incompetence) and in the Foreign Ministry (focusing on the principle of retaliation). Observers discerned a rift in the government between "activists" in the Defense Ministry and IDF, and "moderates" in the Foreign Ministry, who considered retaliation ineffectual, possibly counterproductive, and morally dubious.

February, March, and April 1953 witnessed spasmodic infiltrator attacks, which included abductions and murders. Incidents in and around Jerusalem brought about a massive, unprecedented IDF response. At dawn on April 22 a company of snipers let loose a fusillade of shots into Arab Jerusalem, killing six and wounding fourteen, and during the following months reprisals against West Bank villages caused the death or injury of more than a dozen Arabs, including women and children. These attacks were marked by incompetence and lack of resolution. Major Ariel ("Arik") Sharon, the Israeli officer who came to embody the retaliatory policy, wrote: "Army units proved unable to locate their targets at night and wandered around aimlessly in the dark. If they did manage to find their objectives, they would exchange a few shots with Arab guards, then withdraw. At best, they managed to occupy a few outlying buildings and blow them up before leaving."[57]

To solve the problem, in August 1953 the general staff established a special commando unit, named Unit 101, commanded by Sharon, which operated until January 1954. It was characterized by exacting training, which included regular forays into the West Bank and the Gaza Strip, and efficient and brutal performance.

On the night of October 12, 1953, a grenade was lobbed into a house in the settlement of Yehud, east of Tel Aviv, killing a woman and two children. To retaliate, the IDF sent Unit 101 and a paratroop company into the border village of Qibya on the night of October 14. About sixty of the inhabitants were killed, as were a handful of Legionnaires ambushed as they tried to come to the village's aid. There were no IDF casualties.

Foreign Minister Sharett noted in his diary on October 15: "A reprisal of this magnitude . . . has never been carried out before. I paced back and forth in my room perplexed and completely depressed, feeling helpless."[58] Sharett had rather halfheartedly tried to halt the operation. But had he known in advance that there would be "so much killing," he subsequently wrote, "I would have screamed to high heaven."[59]

Sharon and the IDF subsequently claimed the villagers had hidden in cellars and attics and the troops had been unaware of this when they blew up the buildings. But in truth the troops had moved from house to house, firing through windows and doorways, and Jordanian pathologists reported that most of the dead had been killed by bullets and shrapnel rather than by falling masonry or explosions. In any event, the operational orders, from CO Central Command to the units involved, dated October 13, had explicitly ordered "destruction and maximum killing." Hence no one criticized Sharon or his troops—though there were questions about how the original general staff order, which had called for "blowing up a number of houses . . . and hitting the inhabitants," had changed, while proceeding down the chain of command, into an order for "maximum killing."[60]

The Qibya operation triggered a wave of strident international condemnation. Whitehall issued a veiled threat to activate its treaty with Jordan; Washington suspended economic aid to Israel (officially linking the suspension to a dispute in the Israel-Syria DMZs). Even American Jewry, normally quick to defend Israel, right or wrong, distanced itself from the raid. In Jordan there was an uproar, specifically directed against Britain—seen as Israel's "ally"— and the Arab Legion, which had failed to protect Qibya.

The Israeli public was left ignorant of the facts by the heavily censored press and the government-controlled radio. The government reacted to the foreign criticism by instructing its diplomats to stress the murderous attacks that had provoked the raid and by demanding high-level talks with the Jordanians to iron out border problems. If the Jordanians refused—as they eventually did—they could be blamed for the troubles. On October 19, Ben-Gurion went on the air with a wholly fictitious account of what had happened. In line with past disclaimers of IDF responsibility for or knowledge of reprisals, he announced that after the attack on the family in Yehud, the patience of Israel's frontier settlers had been exhausted and they had taken the law into their own hands, attacking Qibya: "None deplores it more than the Government of Israel, if . . . innocent blood was spilled. . . . The Government of Israel rejects with all vigor the absurd and fantastic allegation that 600 men of the IDF took part in the action. . . . We have carried out a searching investigation and it is clear beyond doubt that not a single army unit was absent from its base on the night of the attack on Qibya."[61] But everyone understood that the military was responsible and that the operation had been authorized by the government. The UN Security Council duly condemned Israel in the "strongest" terms, on November 24.

Following the operation more Arab Legion battalions were deployed along the Israel-Jordan line to block infiltration (and to deter further IDF assaults). There was a sharp decline in infiltration in the immediate area of Qibya and, briefly, an overall reduction in incursions all along that frontier. But the Legion presence inevitably increased the frequency of confrontations with Israeli troops—during 1954, there were 145 such clashes, where there had been only 47 in 1953.

After Qibya the IDF switched from civilian to military targets. Arab civilian casualties declined markedly, reducing Western condemnation of "indiscriminate" Israeli reprisals. But the sorties increased in size and firepower: Many more troops and guns were needed to conquer a well-fortified military camp or police fort than to overrun a village. IDF casualties increased dramatically. At Qibya no Israelis died; in conquering the police fort at Qalqilya, in October 1956, the IDF was to lose eighteen dead and more than fifty wounded. Moreover, the strategy involved a more powerful challenge to the Arab states: Now it was their armies—the mainstays of the Nasserist and Hashemite regimes—that were being hit.

Toward the end of 1953 Ben-Gurion went on leave; in December he announced his resignation and went to live in Kibbutz Sde Boker, in the Negev. On January 26, 1954, Sharett was sworn in as prime minister (retaining his post as foreign minister). The defense portfolio went to Pinchas Lavon, who was to serve in that capacity until February 1955, when Ben-Gurion returned to the cabinet.

A deep political rift had gradually opened between the activists led by Ben-Gurion, backed by the army and the intelligence services, and the moderates, led by Sharett, who was supported only in the Foreign Ministry. The hard-liners enjoyed the support of the bulk of the public, though occasionally Sharett mustered a cabinet majority to thwart this or that plan or action.

In 1957 Sharett defined the two approaches:

> The activists believe that the Arabs understand only the language
> of force. . . . The State of Israel must, from time to time, prove clearly
> that it is strong, and able and willing to use force, in a devastating and
> highly effective way. If it does not prove this, it will be swallowed up,
> and perhaps wiped off the face of the earth. As to peace—this approach
> states—it is in any case doubtful; in any case, very remote. If peace
> comes, it will come only if [the Arabs] are convinced that this country
> cannot be beaten. . . . If [retaliatory] operations . . . rekindle the fires of
> hatred, that is no cause for fear for the fires will be fuelled in any
> event. . . .
> The other approach [is that] not even for one moment must the
> matter of peace vanish from our calculations. This is not only a political
> calculation; in the long run, this is a decisive security consideration [as
> well] . . . We must restrain our responses [to Arab attacks]. And there is
> always the question: is it really proven that retaliatory actions solve the
> security problem?

The "activist" position, according to Sharett, lacked empathy with or
understanding of the Arab side, and was wholly Judeo- or Israel-centric.[62]

Though western diplomats in Tel Aviv sensed the Ben-Gurion–Sharett
split, and periodically reported on it to their capitals, the Israeli public
remained largely unaware of its existence down to the Sinai-Suez war of 1956.
The rift rarely made it into the pages of newspapers or into the public pronouncements of Israel's leaders. But it weighed continuously on the minds of
those leaders and poisoned their relations. In August 1953 Ben-Gurion wrote
in his diary: "Contrary to Moshe [Sharett]'s opinion . . . reprisals are imperative. There is no relying for our security on UN observers and foreign states. If
we do not put an end to these murders [by infiltrators] now, the situation will
get worse."[63]

Activists such as Dayan (OC Southern Command in 1949–52, head of the
general staff branch in 1953, and chief of general staff [CGS] from December
1953 until January 1958) periodically toyed with the idea of expanding
Israel's borders, at least eastward to the Jordan, to give the country strategic
depth and more logical, natural, and defensible frontiers. Occasionally during
1954–56 Ben-Gurion, Dayan, and Lavon also proposed conquering the Golan
Heights, southern Lebanon, the Gaza Strip, or parts of Sinai.

The activist line dominated Israeli policy in the period 1949–56. During the
Sharett interregnum there was something of a shift in emphasis if not in basic
substance. Sharett himself acknowledged that to some degree activism
reduced terrorist infiltration, for a time in a given area. And, more important,
he found that the weight of past tradition, the power of the military establish-

ment, the opinions of his own Mapai Party colleagues, and pressure from a revenge-bent public narrowed his room for maneuver.

In March–April 1954 Sharett managed to persuade the cabinet to resort to diplomatic measures rather than military retaliation after the worst Arab terrorist atrocity in the interwar years: On March 16 infiltrators ambushed a bus traveling from Eilat to Tel Aviv at Scorpions Pass in the Negev, murdering eleven passengers. (Israel claimed that the raiders came from Jordan, but the point remained in dispute. This was a factor that stayed Israel's hand; subsequently it emerged that the raiders were probably Sinai Bedouin.[64]) Israel took the matter to the UN, without responding in the usual military manner.

But other terrorist attacks did not go unanswered. As prime minister Sharett felt bound to take into account, or even put to the fore, the thrust of public and military opinion and hit back after the murder of civilians and soldiers. He was able to stop particular retaliatory actions or reduce their scope. But paradoxically, while he was prime minister, the reprisals increased in magnitude and in the number of casualties inflicted on the Arabs. This was due to the shift from civilian to military targets, and to the growing incidence of terrorism—some state-directed—from the Gaza Strip.

During 1949–53 there had been massive infiltration across the Gaza Strip border, but terrorist attacks were relatively rare. When they occurred they were usually followed by IDF raids. (Israeli casualty statistics show that 7 or 8 Israelis were killed by infiltrators on the Gaza border annually from 1951 to 1954, with a dramatic rise to 48 in 1955. On the Jordan border, 11 Israelis were killed by infiltrators in 1949, 18 in 1950, 44 in 1951, 46 in 1952, 57 in 1953, 34 in 1954, and 11 in 1955.[65]) The situation began to deteriorate in 1954. The two-year-old Egyptian revolutionary regime had by the middle of that year consolidated its hold on power. Gamal 'Abdel Nasser, who had emerged as the leader of the new regime, was bent on achieving dominance of both the Arab and Muslim worlds, as well as the wider nonaligned Bloc.

Nasser's claim was bolstered by the success of Egypt's main foreign policy objective—ousting Britain from his country and the Middle East. During the years 1952–54 he had mounted a staggered political and guerrilla campaign against the British troop presence. On October 19, 1954, the Egyptian and British governments signed an agreement providing for Britain to withdraw completely from its large military bases in the Suez Canal Zone by June 1956.

Israel's strategists quite naturally feared that if the British evacuated the bases, leaving Egypt free to attack Israel, its next objective would be "the Palestine question." Acting on these concerns Israel launched two initiatives designed to stymie the withdrawal. The first was a sabotage campaign in Cairo and Alexandria against Western, and particularly British, targets, designed to cause bad blood between Egypt and Britain and the United States; the second was the dispatch of an Israeli merchant vessel into the Canal, where, it was assumed, the Egyptians—in flagrant breach of international law and accepted norms of maritime behavior—would intercept and impound it, highlighting the danger inherent in a British withdrawal.

At the beginning of July 1954, Unit 131, a psychological warfare department of IDF Intelligence, launched a long-dormant Egyptian-Jewish network on a bombing campaign in the streets of Cairo and Alexandria, targeting American and British cultural centers and other sensitive Western sites. Unfortunately for the Israelis, one of the saboteurs was caught on July 23, as a bomb he was carrying in his pocket began to emit smoke. Under torture he revealed names and addresses, and within forty-eight hours the whole network was in Egyptian hands. Israel dissociated itself from the affair, but nobody believed it. One of the captured saboteurs was tortured to death, and an Israeli agent, picked up along with the network, committed suicide. In January 1955 most of the network were given stiff prison sentences, two were acquitted, and two were sentenced to death—and almost immediately executed, contrary to assurances which Western intermediaries felt they had been given by Nasser that no capital sentences would be carried out.

What became known in Israel as the "Esek Bish" (the bad affair) or the "Lavon affair" had immediate, powerful repercussions within the defense establishment. It vitally undermined the position of both Defense Minister Lavon and the director of military intelligence, Col. Binyamin Givli—each of whom accused the other of initiating the provocative scheme and both of whom were suspected of covering up their responsibility. By February 1955 the two had been ousted, and Ben-Gurion was summoned back from retirement to replace Lavon at the Defense Ministry.

The Israelis were infuriated by the torture of their agents and by the death of four of them; they had, after all, caused no Egyptian fatalities. And the Egyptians were outraged by the operation, which had threatened to embroil them in conflict with the Western powers.

With somewhat less justification, the Egyptians reacted similarly in the *Bat Galim* affair. That ship, sailing from Mombasa, Kenya, reached the Canal in September 1954 and was promptly impounded, and its crew beaten and tortured. Again the Egyptians saw the action as a deliberate provocation designed to harm their relations with the British. The Israelis were angered by the treatment meted out to seamen who, after all, were simply trying to use an international waterway that the Egyptians were illegally blockading.

In the Gaza Strip too the Egyptians were to feel the growing Israeli militancy, in part inspired by the newly installed, aggressive CGS, Moshe Dayan. The Israelis, for their part, noted a greater Egyptian readiness to take chances and challenge them. In April 1954, for the first time, the Egyptian military authorities sent squads of "official" infiltrators across the border—in reaction to an Israeli military sortie a few days before. In July and again in September, more commandos went into Israel for the purpose of revenge and terrorism. A handful of Israelis died or were injured in each of these incursions, which involved ambushes and minelaying along IDF patrol roads. The operations were directed by the commander of Egyptian military intelligence in the Strip, Maj. Mustafa Hafiz, and it is likely that they were authorized from Cairo as responses to Israeli raids and the provocations of the sabotage ring and the *Bat Galim* affair.

By February 1955 the situation was ripe for a massive explosion. In Cairo there was deep suspicion (monitored by IDF Intelligence Branch[66]) of Israel's aggressive intentions; and in Jerusalem there were both real and feigned suspicions and antipathy toward the Egyptian dictator. The Cairo death sentences, aggravated by what was seen as Nasser's duplicity, and Ben-Gurion's return to the Defense Ministry, signifying a weakening of Sharett's moderate approach, were the two important precipitants of what was about to happen. But the immediate trigger, as usual, was provided by the Arab side: In the last week of February a team of Egyptian intelligence scouts penetrated deep into Israel, reconnoitered a number of sensitive defense facilities, and on February 25 gratuitously shot and killed an Israeli cyclist on a road near Rehovot.

The response came on the night of February 28. In Operation Black Arrow, two IDF paratroop companies raided an Egyptian army camp near Gaza and a nearby train station and subsequently ambushed an Egyptian relief column. About forty Egyptians died. The IDF suffered eight dead and thirteen wounded. The shock and sense of humiliation in Cairo were acute. Egyptian arms had not sustained such a blow since the 1948 war.

For months thereafter Nasser was to tell almost every Western and UN official he met that the Gaza raid had caused him radically to rethink his position vis-à-vis Israel, which, he maintained, was interested not in peace but in expansion. In part this was propaganda, designed to justify his subsequent moves, but it also reflected genuine shock. Senior British Foreign Office official Anthony Nutting understood at the time that the Gaza raid was not something a military dictatorship such as Nasser's could take lying down.[67] In future, Nasser declared, it would be "an eye for an eye."

In the third week of March, Nasser unleashed a campaign of continuous, low-level, daily harassment of Israeli border patrols and observation posts with small-arms fire, cross-border ambushes, and minelaying. An Egyptian squad attacked an Israeli wedding celebration at Moshav Patish, killing one person and wounding twenty-two others. Meanwhile Hafiz's small intelligence scout unit was expanded—by early 1956 reaching battalion size—and trained for protracted, deep-penetration terrorist attacks. Similarly *fedayeen* squads were recruited and armed by Egyptian agents in Jordan and Lebanon and prepared for cross-border raiding.

After Patish, Ben-Gurion had proposed that Israel conquer the Strip, but Sharett managed to mobilize a cabinet majority against the idea. And when Israel responded to the border harassment by storming, capturing, and briefly occupying the offending Egyptian front-line positions on May 18 and August

22, the Egyptians countered with a large-scale *fedayeen* terror campaign against southern Israel. Four squads crossed the border on the night of August 25; more pressed into Israel during the following nights. The raids went on for a week. The raiders laid mines, ambushed civilian and military vehicles, and attacked settlements, killing more than a dozen Israelis. The attacks ended only after an IDF paratroop battalion on the night of August 31 took and destroyed the Khan Yunis police fort in the Gaza Strip.[68]

On September 12 Egypt tightened its blockade of the Straits of Tiran and closed the air space over the Gulf of Aqaba to Israeli aircraft, forcing Israel to halt civilian flights to South Africa. During the following weeks Egyptian-directed *fedayeen* attacked Israeli settlements and traffic across the Lebanese and Jordanian borders. And on September 27 Nasser announced that Egypt had concluded a major arms deal with Czechoslovakia (in effect, with the Soviet Union), which promised radically to alter the balance of military power. Egypt explained that it had been forced by the Israeli raids to reinforce its army and make it capable of deterring IDF attack. It had turned to the Soviet bloc because the West had refused to supply the quantity of arms it had requested on acceptable terms.

The arms were scheduled to arrive in the course of the following twelve months, and Israeli analysts believed that the Egyptian army could absorb them by autumn 1956. Israel had to acquire a similar quantity of arms, or to attack and destroy the Egyptian army while it was relatively weak. In fact Israel did both, setting in motion arms acquisition drives and planning—and, in late October 1955, trying to provoke—a preemptive war with Egypt. The United States was asked to offset the Soviet shipments to Egypt with arms sales and a security guarantee to Israel. The Americans, trying to avoid antagonizing the Arabs and to draw Nasser back into the Western fold, stalled. Washington's policy was one protracted and dishonest evasion. "The question that confronted the American administration was not whether to supply Israel with arms but how to hide from her the decision not to supply them," is how one historian later put it.[69] Only at the end of March 1956 did Secretary of State John Foster Dulles tell Abba Eban, Israel's ambassador in Washington, that there would be no American arms.

Israel's leaders had long been dubious about Washington's intentions. Ben-Gurion and Defense Ministry Director General Shimon Peres for months had focused their efforts on France. And in November 1955, when Ben-Gurion resumed the premiership, Israel and France signed their first big arms deal, with 100 French AMX-13 light tanks and up-gunned Sherman M-3s as the major items. Larger sales followed, encompassing dozens of Mystère IV fighters and hundreds of tanks. Behind the agreements was a swiftly growing recognition of a mutuality of interests. Nasser, the chief political backer and military supplier of the FLN rebels fighting against French rule in Algeria, had become a common enemy. With his nationalization of the British- and French-owned Canal in July 1956, the die was cast. France actively sought an alliance with Israel and provided it with the tools to attain absolute military superiority over Egypt. As it turned out, the IDF, supported by the French air force, secured the left flank of the Franco-English invasion force as it descended upon the Canal in November 1956.

But the invasion of Egypt—the Sinai-Suez war—was still a year off. In late September 1955 the future, from Jerusalem's perspective, looked bleak. Preemption seemed a safer course than waiting for Western succor.

In seeking to provoke a war with Egypt, Israel had ready-made pretexts in the DMZs along the border in the western Negev, as well as those on the border with Syria along the Jordan River and the Sea of Galilee. The three countries were barred from introducing soldiers into the zones—though Israel continually, and Syria occasionally, violated these provisions. Since 1949 all three countries had been jockeying for position within them.

Before 1953 the struggle between Israel and Egypt over the DMZ around 'Auja (Nitzana in Hebrew) had been low-key, though incursions into the area—and through it into Israel proper—by Bedouin tribes (no doubt in part at least encouraged by Egypt) had triggered repeated IDF counterincursions designed to push the marauders back into Sinai. But in September 1953 Israel established a permanent military camp, in the form of a Nahal[70] outpost, inside the DMZ. The troops mounted patrols and ambushes against the Bedouin. Israel argued—falsely—that the outpost, named Giv'at Rachel, was not a military base. (Eventually, renamed Ketzi'ot, it became a civilian settlement.) With tension rising, the Egyptians in late 1954 set up three checkpoints along the western edge of the DMZ (to curtail "smuggling," they said). And in December of that year they set up another checkpoint just inside the zone. In July 1955 Israel unilaterally began to mark the international frontier on the western edge of the DMZ; the following month the Egyptians destroyed twenty-one of the border markers, apparently in response to the IDF assault on August 22 on a position on the Gaza border. Events in the DMZ became entangled with developments along the Gaza Strip line.

On September 20 IDF units took over the UN-controlled camp of the Egyptian-Israel Mixed Armistice Commission at 'Auja, wounding two Egyptian guards. They dug trenches and laid minefields, and said they would leave the DMZ only after the Egyptians pulled out their checkpoints. Israel maintained that two of these were inside the zone. Under a UN-mediated agreement, Egypt removed the checkpoints, and most of the Israeli troops withdrew. But on October 26 the Egyptians raided an Israeli "police" (in reality, IDF) outpost in the DMZ, killing one soldier, wounding four, and taking two prisoner. The raid followed Israel's abduction on October 23 of five Syrian soldiers near the Jordan River; four days earlier, Egypt and Syria had signed a mutual defense pact, and Nasser apparently felt obliged to show solidarity.

Here was the opportunity the Israelis had been waiting for. On October 23, at Dayan's prodding, Ben-Gurion had agreed to a policy of retaliating massively after small border incidents, forcing an Egyptian counterstrike, which would provide Israel with the pretext to go to war and destroy the Egyptian army before it absorbed its new Soviet weaponry and became too strong.

On the night of October 27, a paratroop unit commanded by Sharon (now a lieutenant colonel) assaulted the Egyptian police fort at Kuntilla, some three kilometers inside Sinai, about midway between 'Auja and Eilat. They killed twelve Egyptians and captured twenty-nine (to exchange for the two captured Israeli "policemen"); two Israelis died. Ben-Gurion's instructions were that if the Egyptians retaliated, the IDF, raising the stakes, would attack bases in the Gaza Strip; if they launched air raids, the IAF would attack Canal-side air bases.[71] But the Egyptian response proved too feeble to justify escalation. On October 28, Egyptian commandos assaulted an IDF outpost on the Gaza border but retreated under fire, without causing Israeli casualties.

Jerusalem felt that something further was needed. On the night of November 2, a brigade-sized force attacked a string of Egyptian positions inside the DMZ and on the Egyptian side of the border at al-Sabha and Wadi Siram. The Egyptians lost eighty-one killed and fifty-five captured; the IDF five dead. Dayan wanted the troops to stay in the captured positions for twenty-four hours in the hope that the Egyptians would counterattack, thus provoking the desired escalation. But Ben-Gurion got cold feet and turned down the request. The IDF withdrew and, as expected, on November 3 the Egyptian army launched a massive "counterattack" against the now empty positions and retook them.

Dayan turned his gaze northward. Perhaps the desired war could be triggered by an action along the Syrian border that would activate the October 19 Egyptian-Syrian mutual defense accord. But the Israeli-Syrian DMZs had been essentially quiet since a series of clashes in the central DMZ, just north of the Sea of Galilee, in 1951. Since then the Syrians had occasionally fired at soldiers and farmers along the border and at fishermen in the Sea of Galilee, and had sent its own fishermen into the northeastern corner of the lake—even though the whole of the lake was sovereign Israeli territory.

On December 10, 1955, Israel sent a police patrol boat close to the northeastern shore hoping to provoke Syrian fire. The Syrians obliged, and on the night of December 11 an IDF brigade launched Operation Olive Leaves. The raiders overran a string of Syrian positions along the shores of the lake, from the Jordan estuary to Nuqeib, just north of Kibbutz Ein Gev, killing fifty-four Syrians (six of them civilians) and taking thirty prisoners. Six Israelis died.

Despite this devastating blow, neither Syria nor Egypt moved. Only bluster issued from Cairo. Both countries were keenly aware of the IDF's superiority. Dayan and Ben-Gurion were again denied their war, though Operation Olive Leaves appeared to have a major fringe benefit: In the Sinai war less than a year later, Syria watched from the sidelines; it had no stomach to fight the IDF.

But the major site of border troubles since spring 1955, the Gaza Strip, continued to fester: During December 1955–February 1956 the Egyptians appear to have clamped down on civilian infiltration, but their troops fired across the line at Israeli patrols almost every day, and during March and early April there were repeated mining attacks and ambushes along the IDF's patrol roads. On April 4, a patrol was caught in a cross fire, and three soldiers died.

The following day Dayan was ready. It remains unclear which side fired the first shot, but by midday much of the line was ablaze with small-arms fire. By early afternoon the two sides were trading mortar and artillery rounds. Some of the Egyptian fire was directed at border kibbutzim, and in response Israeli mortars opened up on downtown Gaza. Within an hour fifty-eight Egyptian and Palestinian civilians, thirty-three of them women and thirteen children, lay dead, with about one hundred wounded; four Egyptian soldiers also died. Sharett was later to call the attack "a crime."[72]

Nasser clearly could not let this deed pass without answer. An "eye for an eye" was what he was after—but not war, so he told the American ambassador to Cairo, Henry Byroade.[73] On the night of April 6 some two hundred *fedayeen* were sent across the border in small squads. The IDF was put on a war alert, and for a day or two the Middle East was on the brink of war. On April 11, *fedayeen* penetrated Moshav Shafrir and attacked the local yeshiva/synagogue, murdering five pupils and teachers and wounding twenty.[74] By the time the operation ended on April 12, nine Israeli civilians and two soldiers lay dead and about fifty civilians and soldiers had been wounded. The *fedayeen* themselves lost sixteen dead, two missing, and five captured. The Egyptians, as Cairo Radio put it somewhat hyperbolically on April 10, had succeeded in putting "an end to the tranquillity the Israelis enjoyed. . . . The whole of the Negev is in a state of tension, readiness and panic."[75]

On April 13 Ben-Gurion proposed a strike against a *fedayeen* base in Gaza, which in the circumstances would probably have provoked wide-ranging hostilities. But the cabinet made its approval of the plan contingent upon a renewal of *fedayeen* attacks. Sharett, though depressed, had again won the day. With UN Secretary-General Dag Hammarskjöld in the area and mediating, the Egyptians ceased their raiding, and the April crisis ended in a renewed truce.

The month was to end on a sad note for the Israeli border settlers. On April 29, a well-prepared Egyptian ambush cut down the security officer of Kibbutz Nahal-'Oz, Ro'i Rothberg. Dayan delivered a eulogy that is one of the most candid and revealing statements by an Israeli about the crux of Israeli-Palestinian relations:

> Yesterday at dawn Ro'i was murdered. The quiet of the spring morning blinded him, and he did not see those who sought his life hiding behind the furrow. Let us not today cast blame on the murderers. What can we

say against their terrible hatred of us? For eight years now, they have sat in the refugee camps of Gaza, and have watched how, before their very eyes, we have turned their lands and villages, where they and their forefathers previously dwelled, into our home. It is not among the Arabs of Gaza, but in our own midst that we must seek Ro'i's blood. How did we shut our eyes and refuse to look squarely at our fate and see, in all its brutality, the fate of our generation? Can we forget that this group of youngsters, sitting in Nahal-'Oz, carries the heavy gates of Gaza on their shoulders?

Beyond the border surges a sea of hatred and revenge; revenge that looks toward the day when the calm will blunt our alertness, the day when we shall listen to the envoys of malign hypocrisy [a reference to Hammarskjöld, whom Israeli officialdom regarded as anti-Israel] who call upon us to lay down our arms. . . . We are a generation of settlement, and without the steel helmet and the gun's muzzle we will not be able to plant a tree or build a house. Let us not fear to look squarely at the hatred that consumes and fills the lives of . . . Arabs who live around us. . . . That is the fate of our generation. This is our choice—to be ready and armed, tough and harsh—or to let the sword fall from our hands and our lives be cut short.[76]

The epilogue to the April *fedayeen* campaign was the assassination, by IDF Intelligence on July 11 in Gaza, of the commander of the *fedayeen* operations, Lt. Col. Mustafa Hafiz, head of Egyptian military intelligence in the Gaza Strip, and of his representative in Amman, Lt. Col. Mahmud Mustafa, on July 14. Both were dispatched by cleverly crafted and delivered parcel bombs (the second was hidden inside a volume of memoirs by Gerd von Rundstedt, the World War II German tank general).

April had passed without war, and a cease-fire of sorts was reinstituted along the Israeli-Egyptian border. But the simmering crisis was steadily moving toward a climax, despite efforts at pacification by the UN and the United States. Washington had sent Robert Anderson, a former deputy secretary of defense and friend of President Dwight D. Eisenhower, on a secret shuttle between Jerusalem and Cairo during January–March.[77] Arms from the Czech deal were steadily pouring into Egypt. Israel had effected major arms deals with France, and the two nations' intelligence services had begun cooperating in the clandestine battle against the common Arab (Algerian/Egyptian) enemy.[78]

The French arms were to offset the Soviet weaponry reaching Nasser—theoretically, once equilibrium was reached the need for a preemptive war would have disappeared. In reality Israel's leaders had set a course for war, prodded by the persistent pinpricks of the infiltrators, by militant public opinion, by an officer corps bent on hostilities, by the vision of the potential "second round" threat from Egypt and the rest of the Arab world, and by France. During the summer of 1956,. only two questions remained: When? and What target? There were two real possibilities. Egypt, which in 1948 had fielded one of the largest of the Arab armies, remained, especially after the "Czech deal," the most serious military threat to Israel's existence. But it was Jordanian territory, namely the West Bank down to the Jordan River, that Israeli leaders had long coveted, for a heady mixture of strategic and historical reasons.

During the autumn of 1956 it seemed to many in the West that Israel had chosen the "Jordanian option": conquest of the West Bank. Jordan had recently veered sharply toward the radical, Nasserist camp. In March, King Hussein abruptly dismissed his long-serving British commander in chief, General Glubb, and almost all the British officers of the Arab Legion, at a stroke Arabizing his armed forces (as Nasser and Jordanian radicals had long demanded). Moreover, the Arab Legion set about recruiting its own *fedayeen* units and hosting those that had crossed from Gaza to the West Bank after carrying out missions in Israel.

In September and October the IDF launched four massive attacks against Jordanian police and military installations,[79] one of them in response to a massacre of Israeli archaeologists and officials (four killed, sixteen wounded) at Ramat Rachel, south of Jerusalem. Israel deliberately gave the impression that Jordan was being readied for the coup de grâce, in order to divert American (and perhaps Soviet) suspicions, but it had already been decided that Egypt was the true target (though some, including Dayan, still hoped that Jordan would be sucked into the conflict, enabling Israel to conquer the West Bank). In a series of clandestine conferences during June–October 1956, Israeli and French leaders had hammered out an agreement on a joint attack aimed at toppling Nasser and destroying the Egyptian armed forces. Egyptian subversion of pro-Western regimes in the Middle East, principally Jordan and Iraq, coupled with the "Czech deal," had strengthened Western suspicions that Nasser was steadily moving toward alignment with the Communist bloc. French and British antipathy toward Egypt had been strengthened in the last week of July when Nasser had unilaterally nationalized the Suez Canal, divesting France and Britain of their seventy-year-old control of the vital waterway.

At the secret Sèvres Conference, in a villa outside Paris, on October 22–24, Ben-Gurion and French premier Guy Mollet, joined by British Foreign Secretary Selwyn Lloyd, agreed on a tripartite assault on Egypt. France and Britain would conquer, and resume control of, the Suez Canal and reestablish the Western military bases from which Britain had withdrawn four months earlier. Israel would destroy the Egyptian army in Sinai and the Gaza Strip *fedayeen* bases, and ultimately annex all Sinai, or at least its eastern third, east of a line running from Al-'Arīsh southward to Sharm ash-Sheikh. Perhaps, once and for all, Egypt's ability to launch terror attacks against Israel would be ended.

At Sèvres, the three allies—after the British reluctantly agreed to Israel's participation—hammered out an operational plan. Ben-Gurion at first presented a grandiose scheme for the complete reordering of the Middle East: Jordan would be "dissolved," with Iraq annexing the East Bank, and Israel, in effect, acquiring the West Bank; Lebanon would divest itself of some of its heavily Muslim eastern and southern provinces and reconstitute itself as an overwhelmingly Christian republic, aligned with Israel, while Israel would annex southern Lebanon up to the Litani River and retain at least a strip of eastern Sinai down to and including Sharm ash-Sheikh.[80] The French gently brought Ben-Gurion down to earth and suggested that they focus on Egypt, promising ships to guard Israel's coastline and aircraft to guard its skies to alleviate his fear of aerial bombardment. (He had been in London during the Blitz, and knew what air power could do to a crowded city.)

The British proposed a staggered attack, with Israel striking first and "threatening" the Canal Zone with a paratroop drop. At the same time, columns of armor would race westward through Sinai to link up with the paras, destroying the Egyptian army along the way. Only subsequently would the British and French intervene in order to "separate" the combatants and safeguard the Canal. The two powers would issue an ultimatum to both sides to stay clear of, or remove their forces from, the Canal area. The Egyptians could be expected not to comply, and Britain and France would then invade the Canal Zone, intervening not as aggressors but as (somewhat forceful) peacemakers and protectors of an international waterway.

The Israelis initially objected, rejecting a scenario in which they were cast as the robbers and the European powers as the cops. Moreover, the plan would leave Israel alone against Egypt for a full thirty-six hours, during which time its cities would be vulnerable.[81] But the French, with their promise of protection, and Ben-Gurion's advisers, Dayan and Shimon Peres, persuaded him of Britain's sincerity and of the workability of the plan.

In the package, agreed and signed by the three parties at Sèvres on October 24, Israel promised not to attack Jordan, and Britain agreed not to come to Jordan's assistance if it attacked Israel. (During Sèvres, much to London's chagrin, Jordan announced the "union" of its army with Egypt's and Syria's, under the chairmanship of the Egyptian chief of general staff, Gen. 'Abd al-Hakim 'Amr.[82])

Britain and France went full steam ahead and concentrated their forces within striking distance of Egypt's shores and airfields. Large quantities of armaments were rushed to Israel (two hundred vital six-wheel-drive trucks reached Haifa on October 27, about forty-eight hours before H-hour) and French units began deploying in Israel's airfields and off its shores. Israel instituted a full-scale mobilization of its reserves, letting everyone know that it was worried by the possible movement of Iraqi troops into Jordan, and that matters might well come to war with Jordan and Iraq.

On the morning of October 28 Ben-Gurion presented his cabinet with the fait accompli—an alliance with France and Britain and a detailed war plan. He said that, if it were at all possible, Israel would remain in occupation of Sinai "until the end of time," and that it had Anglo-French agreement to the permanent occupation of Tiran and Sanafir, the two islands at the entrance of the Gulf of Aqaba. The cabinet, without its chief dissident (Sharett had been fired by Ben-Gurion in June), approved the plan.[83]

The forces that faced each other across the Negev-Sinai border were unevenly matched—even without taking account of the superior quality of IDF manpower and organization and the French backup air and naval units. On paper the Egyptians, with five "divisions," fielded the stronger force. In reality the Israeli forces were vastly superior, both in manpower and equipment. During the summer Egyptian intelligence had concluded that the threat of large-scale Israeli attack had diminished, while the threat of British or Anglo-French attack on the Canal and the Nile Valley had increased. One of three divisions, and several armored units, were withdrawn from the peninsula.[84] The Gaza Strip was left in the charge of a Palestinian infantry division.[85]

The Israeli half of the war went almost like clockwork and is regarded as a classic of armored desert warfare, largely owing to the element of surprise: The Egyptian high command did not anticipate the Israeli thrust into Sinai (or, in fact, the Anglo-French assault on the Canal Zone that followed). Israel's rumblings against Jordan and Anglo-French agreement to open talks with the Egyptians on October 29 in Geneva clearly misled their leadership—on October 25 a military delegation, led by Chief of Staff 'Amr, left for a visit to Jordan and Syria.[86]

And the war in fact began with a little-known IDF operation connected with that visit. On the night of October 28 IDF intelligence pinpointed the flight path of a lone Ilyushin-14 military transport flying from Syria to Egypt over the Mediterranean. A Meteor jet fighter, sent up to intercept, shot the transport out of the sky. The Israelis had hoped to kill 'Amr. In any event, eighteen Egyptian general staff officers died, while 'Amr himself returned to Egypt on a later flight. But it was still a serious blow for the Egyptian army. "That's the first half of the war over. Let's drink to the second half," Dayan reportedly said at the welcome given the returning fighter pilot after the mission.[87] One other operation preceded the actual start of the offensive: During the afternoon of October 29 a foursome of IAF Mustangs flew across Sinai and, using their propellers, cut telephone lines in a number of key junctions, causing a breakdown in Egyptian communications.

The Israeli war plan was simple, in large measure dictated by topographical realities and by political requirements. Its first move made no military sense and served no strategic purpose. On October 29 about four hundred paratroops were dropped and dug in, without incident, at the eastern entrance to the Mitla Pass, deep in Sinai, within striking distance of the Canal, in order to provide the British and French with the pretext to issue their ultimatum. The rest of the

Paratroop Brigade, commanded by Sharon, plus a company of light tanks and artillery, crossed the border on half-track armored personnel carriers and trucks and sped across Sinai, linking up with the Mitla force the next night.

The main IDF offensives were unleashed in staggered fashion in the center and north, along the two main east-west axes that cross Sinai; here the battle for the peninsula was to be won or lost. Along the central axis, which linked Nitzana ('Auja) and Ismailia, an IDF division that crossed the border on the night of October 29 met fierce Egyptian resistance and suffered heavy losses. But on November 1 the remaining Egyptian forces in the Umm Katef-Abu Awgeila area, which had held their ground impressively, were ordered to retreat to the Canal.[88] The directive was probably part of the general Egyptian high command order to its troops in Sinai to withdraw in order to meet the by now expected Anglo-French assault (whose aerial component had begun the previous day). The IDF occupied the defensive complex the following morning, November 2, uncontested, though there was a hitch: In a fierce fight between two IDF tank units, each side mistaking the other for Egyptians, about a dozen vehicles were knocked out.

To the north on the night of October 31 an IDF division crossed the border just south of Rafa at the southern end of the Gaza Strip, and ran into intense artillery fire and minefields. The Egyptians apparently fought tenaciously,[89] but early on November 1 all Egyptian troops still in the Rafa area were ordered to retreat.

The Egyptians fought, and lost to, each IDF thrust without movement or initiative. Each battalion- or brigade-size position essentially fought alone, without reinforcement or aerial backup and with little artillery support. The troops fought from their trenches and pillboxes until outflanked and over-powered by the superior maneuverability and firepower of the Israelis. One Egyptian commentator was to blame 'Amr for the lack of initiative: Local commanders were regularly instructed to desist from individual initiatives and to take action only after receiving approval from him.[90]

By the morning of October 30 the high command in Cairo had understood what was happening in Sinai and, that day and the next, sent three brigades across the Canal. Their apparent aim was to reinforce the Egyptian garrisons that were still fighting to the east and hurl back the IDF. But the speed of the IDF ground advance and the IAF's complete mastery of the skies over Sinai by November 1 (reinforced by flights of Israel-based French Mystères) stymied these efforts and led to the destruction of the eastward-pressing Egyptian columns by the roving IAF and French foursomes.

One Egyptian armored brigade had been ordered to advance from the Canal and to extricate the Sixth Brigade from Umm Katef. But on the night of October 31, following the repeated Israeli air attacks, its commander ordered the brigade to retreat toward the Canal, ignoring orders to push eastward. The order was repeated on November 1, but the brigade continued inching west-

The Sinai Campaign, 1956

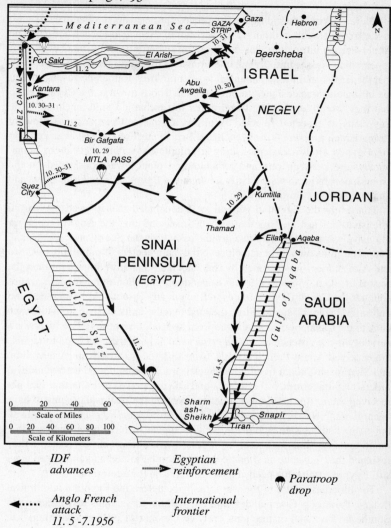

IDF advances

Anglo French attack 11. 5 -7.1956

Egyptian reinforcement

International frontier

Paratroop drop

ward, and on the night of November 2 most of it crossed back to the Canal's west bank.[91]

There is no understanding the Egyptians' confused and ineffective response to the Israeli assault without taking account of the Anglo-French actions. The Anglo-French ultimatum was delivered on the afternoon of October 30.[92] It appears that Nasser initially misinterpreted its meaning. He could not believe that the British and French intended to act militarily. Rather, he suspected that the ultimatum was designed to pin Egyptian troops down in the Canal area so that they would not be sent to reinforce the embattled units in Sinai.[93] The Egyptians, as expected, rejected the ultimatum and on October 31—following strong Israeli pressure—the French and British air forces at last began attacking Egypt's air force, demolishing it completely within forty-eight hours. Somewhere between one and two hundred planes were destroyed on the ground; dozens more were hastily flown out of Egypt, to airfields in Libya and Sudan, to avoid a similar fate.

That night the Egyptian general staff concluded that it faced a tripartite offensive, not just an Israeli attack in Sinai, and that the Anglo-French air offensive was a preliminary to a ground assault on the Suez Canal. The Canal, important in its own right and close to the main centers of population—Cairo and Alexandria—was deemed by the leadership far more important than the wastes of Sinai. Moreover, it was understood that should the Western armies conquer the Canal, Egypt's forces in Sinai in any case would be stranded and unreinforceable. Logic therefore dictated that the units in Sinai be withdrawn back to the Canal, both to save them from destruction by the IDF (which was a certainty in the absence of any air cover) and to have them on hand to repulse the expected Anglo-French assault. 'Amr ordered his troops in eastern Sinai and Sharm ash-Sheikh to withdraw westward. Without doubt, the withdrawal orders also undermined the morale and staying power of units that had not received them. But no blanket order to abandon the peninsula seems to have been given.[94] Nasser reportedly had favored ordering a general withdrawal, but 'Amr had resisted.[95] But the Israelis appear to have been unaware that many units in Sinai had received orders to withdraw. On November 1 they resumed their advance as if battle were still to be joined and as if there were still Egyptian units that needed to be driven from the peninsula.

The bloodiest battle of the war took place before the Egyptian withdrawal orders. Paratroop Commander Sharon, itching for a fight and contrary to Southern Command instructions, early on October 31 pushed a battalion-size combat team into the Mitla Pass. (His superiors had authorized only a nonviolent, reconnaissance sortie.) Unknown to him, an Egyptian infantry battalion, supported by units of 120 mm mortars, antitank guns, and recoilless guns, had dug in on both sides of the pass. When the combat team entered the pass, the Egyptians opened up from both sides, and their aircraft strafed and bombed the column. Sharon sent in reinforcements and in bitter hand-to-hand fighting that lasted through the night, the Israeli paratroops took one Egyptian position after another. By morning the pass was in Israeli hands—but the IDF had suffered 38 dead and 120 wounded. Egyptian losses were over 200 dead.[96]

Elsewhere the IDF columns advanced smoothly, Israeli and French jets clearing the path. On November 2, the Twenty-seventh Brigade took Al-'Arīsh (which had already been evacuated) and drove headlong down the coast road, hard on the heels of the retreating Egyptians. In a feat of mobility the Twenty-seventh managed to cover 120 kilometers in eight hours, coming to a halt the next day within artillery range of the Canal. To the south the Seventh Armored Brigade had proceeded, without encountering any serious resistance, along the central east-west route, halting just short of the Canal opposite Ismailia.

The Gaza Strip—apart from Rafa, which had fallen on November 1–2—was conquered on November 2–3. The defending Eighth Palestinian Division was a ragtag, under-strength formation.[97] The soldiers were largely Palestinian and the officers Egyptian. They offered only sporadic, poorly organized resistance. The fact that by November 2 the Strip had been cut off from the rest of Sinai and that the Egyptian army had been decimated and was in headlong retreat had caused morale to plummet. None of the Eighth Division's senior officers believed that the Strip could hold out for more than a few hours. The Egyptian high command had ordered the division to stand fast in order to pin down as many Israeli troops as possible—even though on November 1 it had already ordered most of its forces in eastern Sinai to withdraw to the Canal. (Perhaps the division's assignment was specifically designed to facilitate the withdrawal to the Canal of the rest of the Egyptian army.) But hundreds of the division's soldiers also made good their escape—by heading, along with many *fedayeen,* across the northern Negev waist to the West Bank.

The Israeli conquest and its aftermath were characterized by a great deal of unwarranted killing, especially of retreating or captured Egyptian soldiers. In all, Israeli troops killed about five hundred Palestinian civilians during and after the conquest of the Strip. About two hundred of these were killed in the course of massacres in Khan Yunis (on November 3) and in Rafa (on November 12). Several dozen suspected *fedayeen* who had fallen into Israeli hands were summarily executed. During and immediately after the conquest, there was a great deal of looting. At least one senior officer, Col. Uri Ben-Ari, commander of the Seventh Brigade, was tried and dismissed from his post as a result (an accomplished armored commander, however, he was to be returned to active service in June 1967 and again in October 1973, retiring as a brigadier general).[98]

The Israeli record was to be blemished during 1956 by one other atrocity. On October 29, border police units massacred forty-nine Israeli Arabs in and near the village of Kafr Kasim in the "Little Triangle." The villagers, returning from work, had broken a curfew of which they had not been informed.

One last conquest remained: Sharm ash-Sheikh and the Straits of Tiran, whose blockade by the Egyptians had been a primary cause of the war. The area was held by roughly two Egyptian battalions. The IDF brigade that had set out down the eastern Sinai coastline had advanced through near-impassable dunes and wadis, reaching the outskirts of Sharm on November 4; by the next morning the Egyptian headquarters, airfield, and harbor had fallen.[99]

Air operations during the battle for Sinai were extremely important and were characterized by Israeli supremacy and large-scale aerial resupply missions for the advancing ground troops. Egyptian aerial efforts to intervene in the ground fighting or to destroy Israeli aircraft were few and largely without result. With the Allies taking care of the Egyptian air bases and protecting Israel's cities and airfields, the IDF used all its air power in a ground support role. Beside protecting the troops, particularly the Paratroop Brigade on the southern east-west axis, the IAF, bolstered from November 1 by two of the three French fighter-bomber squadrons stationed in Israel, throughout the campaign continuously harassed the Egyptian columns in eastern and western Sinai. Retreating Egyptian troops were severely hurt, but most, including much of their heavy weaponry, managed to make it safely back across the Canal.[100]

Only one noteworthy action occurred at sea during the Sinai Campaign. The Egyptian destroyer *Ibrahim al-Awal* early on the morning of October 31 shelled Haifa (causing neither damage nor casualties) and was then chased and captured by the Israeli navy, assisted by the IAF, after being hit and disabled. Subsequently the vessel was renamed the *Haifa* and entered service with the Israeli navy.

The IDF lost about 190 soldiers killed, 20 captured, and 800 injured in the Sinai Campaign. The Egyptian army lost several thousand killed and much of its equipment. Some four thousand Egyptians fell into Israeli hands.

The Anglo-French plan to conquer the Suez Canal suffered from a basic flaw that was vitally to undermine its implementation. The flaw stemmed from the pretense that Britain and France were intervening to separate two warring states, rather than acting as full-fledged belligerents in cahoots with Israel. But they had actually begun planning the war following Nasser's nationalization of the Canal on July 26, 1956, with the aim of taking over the Canal Zone and ousting the Egyptian dictator. Britain's Prime Minister Anthony Eden considered him a reborn Hitler, whose "aggressions" had to be stopped.[101]

In August, French and British units began to assemble at Malta and Cyprus. Altogether, some fifty thousand British and thirty thousand French soldiers, as well as hundreds of aircraft and more than one hundred ships (including seven aircraft carriers) were involved. But precisely because of the agreed scenario, with Operation Musketeer beginning only *after* Egypt rejected the Anglo-French ultimatum, the invasion force could not be poised to strike on October 29. Indeed, its bulk could only begin to move from Malta after the start of

Israel's attack and after Egyptian rejection of the ultimatum. These factors, compounded by inefficiency in movement and coordination and by an over-estimation of Egyptian military strength—necessitating the adoption of great margins of safety—created a six-day hiatus between the start of Anglo-French air operations and the actual ground assault on the northern end of the Canal. This was to prove the political and military undoing of the enterprise.

The air offensive that began on October 31 lasted three days. The invasion itself began on November 5, with paratroop drops at Port Said, at the northern entrance of the Suez Canal, and at Port Fuad, just across the waterway. On November 6 British and French amphibious units landed and swept through Port Said. Resistance was sporadic and light. But it was Soviet and American diplomatic maneuvering and threats, rather than Egyptian resistance, that won the day. The allied thrust southward along the Canal came to a halt, obeying a UN Security Council cease-fire call, at 0200 hours, November 7, about one hundred miles short of the objective, Suez City. The Anglo-French part of the war had ended.

On November 5, both Israel and Egypt had accepted the UN demand for a cease-fire, substantially undercutting the Anglo-French invasion even before it had begun. The following day Soviet prime minister Nikolai Bulganin sent Eden, Mollet, Ben-Gurion, and Eisenhower threatening messages. The letter to Israel was particularly menacing: Israel's attack on Egypt "was sowing a hatred for the State of Israel among the peoples of the East such as cannot but make itself felt with regard to the future of Israel and which puts in jeopardy the very existence of Israel as a state."

The Israelis were both angry and frightened. Ben-Gurion noted in his diary: "Bulganin's dispatch could have been written by Hitler. . . . The pande-monium of Russian tanks running loose in Hungary [where Soviet troops were busy crushing an anti-Communist revolt] are evidence of what these Communist Nazis are capable of. It worries me because Soviet arms are flowing into Syria and we must presume that the arms are accompanied by 'volunteers.' "[102]

But it was American action that persuaded Britain and, in its wake, France to call it quits. The war reportedly had precipitated a run on sterling; Washing-ton, very pointedly, was not coming to its rescue. Britain's "special relation-ship" with the United States appeared to be imperiled. Eden and the French leadership got cold feet. As both Egypt and Israel had accepted the idea of a cease-fire, the pretext for intervention was no longer valid. In both Britain and France growing opposition to the operation cut across party lines.

The situation on the ground on November 7 was highly embarrassing for both London and Paris. The Anglo-French force had failed in its goal of con-quering the length of the Suez Canal and a ten-mile-deep buffer area on either bank, let alone toppling Nasser. All it held was the northern end, with most of the force still on ships offshore; militarily it was precariously positioned, with only a toehold on Egyptian soil, vulnerable to air attack and guerrilla warfare. The Canal itself was closed—Egypt had scuttled ships and bridges every few kilometers, preventing any passage until a massive salvage operation was undertaken.[103]

Ironically, after the British accepted the cease-fire, U.S. Secretary of State John Foster Dulles, from his sickbed (he was dying of cancer), privately berated them for having stopped their operation midway. "Why didn't you go through with it and get Nasser down?" Dulles asked his visitor, Foreign Secretary Lloyd.[104]

Britain and France had accepted the principle of withdrawal from the Canal Zone with alacrity, indeed, even before their troops had landed, but on condition that a UN force be deployed that could effectively secure their interests in the area, thus saving their collective face. A UN Emergency Force was established by the General Assembly on November 7, and the first contingents, from Scandinavia, reached Port Said on November 21. On December 3 Britain announced the impending withdrawal and on the 22nd and 23rd the Anglo-French forces evacuated Egyptian soil under UNEF guard. The following day, Egyptian sappers blew up the statue in Port Said harbor of Ferdinand de Lesseps, the French planner of the Canal. Eden resigned two weeks later.

Both Britain and France suffered irreparable harm in the Middle East as a result of Suez. Their position as coprotectors of Western interests in the region was largely taken over by the United States. For decades the stigma of (incompetent) neo-imperialism was to stick to them. As expected, the Soviet Union made further inroads, pouring money, arms, and advisers into a succession of "progressive" Arab states.

The Israeli withdrawal from Egypt was not as rapid as that of the British and French, whose leaders had only pretended to believe that Nasser's Egypt was a mortal threat to their countries (on the order of Nazi Germany). Israel's motives were more legitimate: Egypt's army had invaded Palestine and threatened Tel Aviv in May 1948 and had been busy intensively rearming (and it was to pose the most serious Arab challenge to the IDF in 1967 and again in 1973). After 1956 Nasser was often to speak of the need to destroy Israel. Israel's leaders believed and continued to believe that the Arab states—primarily Egypt—posed a threat to the existence of their country.

On November 7 Ben-Gurion declared that the 1949 armistice agreement with Egypt was dead and that Israel would permit no UN force to be stationed in its territory or in any part of Sinai and the Gaza Strip that it occupied. He also obliquely referred to Israel's historic right to the island of Tiran, which he identified with Yodfat, where a Jewish kingdom had existed in the sixth century A.D. The message was clear—Israel had no intention of withdrawing from Sinai.

A few hours later, the UN General Assembly passed a resolution calling for the immediate withdrawal of the three invading armies from Egyptian soil. The vote was 65 to 1 (Israel was the lone dissenter; Britain and France abstained). Herbert Hoover Jr., acting U.S. secretary of state, threatened that his government would cut off all public and private aid to Israel; there would be UN sanctions; and Israel would be expelled from the organization.[105] President Eisenhower had just been elected to a second term; he could allow himself to ignore Jewish lobbying. Ben-Gurion noted Abba Eban's terror and remarked that his cables from the United States to Jerusalem "sowed fear and horror. . . . A nightmarish day," he called it.[106]

Israel proved incapable of withstanding the pressure. On November 8 Eban announced acceptance in principle of the UN resolution, provided the withdrawal would be gradual, and subject to specific conditions relating to UNEF's role and deployment. As the weeks stretched out, Ben-Gurion reasoned, the world might grow used to Israel's occupation of the Gaza Strip and Sharm ash-Sheikh. Indeed, on November 11 the Israeli cabinet formally decided that, while withdrawing from the bulk of Sinai, Israel would retain the Straits of Tiran and a coastal strip linking them and Eilat. Moreover, there would be no Egyptian troops in Sinai, and UNEF would remain, as a buffer, in the Canal Zone.[107]

But, bowing to continuing American and international pressure, the IDF began withdrawing from Sinai during the last week of November. Behind it, on Ben-Gurion's instructions, it left scorched earth. All military camps and buildings were destroyed; railway lines were dismantled and carted back to Israel; roads were plowed up and certain areas mined. By January 15, 1957, the IDF was back on the old international frontier, retaining only Sharm ash-Sheikh and the Gaza Strip.

The Israeli cabinet agreed in principle to the eventual evacuation of Sharm ash-Sheikh—on condition that Israel's rights of maritime passage through the straits be firmly guaranteed by the international community. But Israel would not quit the Gaza Strip "even if the U.S. imposes sanctions," Ben-Gurion declared. The Strip—its northern edge a mere thirty miles from Tel Aviv—had been the source of continuous border trouble between 1949 and 1956 and represented a clear strategic threat to Israel. But it contained more than 300,000 Arabs, most of them refugees, a burden Israel was not eager to shoulder.

From the available documentation there can be little doubt that on balance, Ben-Gurion would have preferred to hold on to Sharm, even if it meant no international guarantees for Israel, and to the Gaza Strip, despite the masses crowded into its miserable refugee camps. But Washington remained insistent on complete withdrawal. Ben-Gurion was at a loss to understand this: "Here is a president [Eisenhower] who . . . spends his time playing bridge or golf. In the morning he reads a little sheet of paper . . . about what's going on in the world—and of all things, he picks this issue to get completely involved in."

Ben-Gurion did not grasp that in the wake of the Anglo-French debacle the United States felt responsible for the West's interests—and that it had to vie against Soviet influence. And to win over the Arabs, Washington had to act tougher with Israel.[108]

January and February 1957 witnessed Israel's dogged rearguard efforts to squeeze out of the UN and United States appropriate guarantees and security arrangements before withdrawing. By mid-February Jerusalem caved in, and on March 1 Foreign Minister Golda Meir announced Israel's readiness to withdraw. In exchange the United States had indirectly promised to guarantee Israel's right of passage through the straits and its right to self-defense if the Egyptians closed them. As to Gaza, the U.S. had somewhat vaguely promised to try to install UN administration and to keep Egypt from returning. UNEF would be deployed as a buffer along the border, stationed on Egyptian or formerly Egyptian-controlled territory.

The IDF evacuated Gaza on March 6 and Sharm ash-Sheikh two days later. UNEF tried to impose its control over the Strip, but Egyptian agitators immediately provoked riots and stone-throwing. The UN gave up, and on March 14 Egyptian officials took over. But the UNEF presence, and Nasser's fear of another Israeli offensive, prevented reactivation of the *fedayeen* and of a threatening military deployment in eastern Sinai.

The consequences of the Anglo-French defeat were profound. Through manipulation of the media, Nasser persuaded his people, and many other Arabs, that Egypt had won. The Canal was more Egyptian than before, and his regime was firmly in the saddle, with great popular support throughout the Arab world. Egypt enjoyed massive Soviet military, political, and economic backing. Israel had completely cleared out of Sinai and the Gaza Strip. And the terms of UNEF's deployment gave Cairo the prerogative to send it packing at will. Egypt had attained the position of undisputed leader of the Arab world.

The Anglo-French collusion with the Zionist enemy against Egypt and the ex-imperialists' invasion of Arab soil set in motion a tidal wave of Nasserist radicalism throughout the Arab world. The idea of a unified state, this time under Nasser's leadership, was once again in the air. Within two years, in February 1958, his popularity was translated into a (short-lived) political union between Egypt and Syria—the United Arab Republic (UAR).

More violent fallout was to follow, with the pro-Western regimes in Baghdad, Amman, and Beirut all targeted; Egyptian subversion intermixed with locally bred disaffection. In Iraq on July 14, 1958 the army took power, and King Faisal II and Prime Minister Nuri Said were murdered. However, once in control, the leaders of the revolt, Brig. 'Abd al-Karim Qassem and Col. 'Abd al-Salam 'Aref, resisted the pan-Arab currents, rejected Nasser's blandishments, and maintained Iraqi independence.

In March 1957 Jordan annulled its Treaty of Alliance with Britain after Egypt, Syria, and Saudi Arabia agreed to pay it an annual subsidy of 12.5 million pounds sterling in lieu of the British grant. But none of this forestalled Egyptian and pan-Arab plotting against King Hussein's regime. In April 1957 the king had managed to turn the tables on a military coup supported, if not engineered, by Cairo; and in July 1958, at Hussein's request, British paratroopers flew into Amman as the regime tottered in the aftershocks of the Baghdad coup. Within months the situation stabilized, and the British troops withdrew. During the following years Nasser continued intermittently—and unsuccessfully—to try to subvert the last remaining Hashemite monarchy.[109]

Lebanon, a traditional French client, also suffered severe aftershocks in the wake of Suez. The establishment of the UAR acted as a catalyst—Lebanon had always been influenced by developments in nearby Damascus. Egyptian funding of radicals stirred the pot. The country's left-wing and Muslim leaders demanded integration into what they believed was an emerging pan-Arab federation; the Christian elite resisted. By May 1958 clashes between the two camps spiraled into a low-key civil war. The Christian-dominated government charged that the UAR was behind the outbreak. In July, against the backdrop of the Baghdad coup, Lebanese President Camille Chamoun appealed to Washington, and U.S. Marines landed in Beirut to shore up the regime. They were withdrawn in October, once the crisis had blown over; and Chamoun was replaced, after elections, by Gen. Fuad Shihab, with the establishment of a government in which Nasserists and right-wingers were evenly balanced. Thereafter Lebanon's foreign policy was to be closely aligned with Egypt's.

The 1956 war resulted in a significant reduction of Egyptian-Israeli and Jordanian-Israeli border tensions. Egypt refrained from reactivating the *fedayeen,* and the security forces of Egypt and Jordan made great efforts to curb infiltration. The Arab armies, bearing in mind what had happened in Sinai, took great care not to provoke the Israeli tiger. Moreover, the Egypt-Israel border was patrolled by buffering UN troops.

Paradoxically the political outcome of the war was a clear and substantial radicalization of the conflict. Nasser and other Arab leaders began to speak openly of the need for a "third round," in which Israel would be destroyed. In a letter to Hussein on March 13, 1961, Nasser wrote: "On . . . Israel, we believe that the evil introduced into the heart of the Arab world must be uprooted."[110]

If the destruction of Israel was not Arab *policy* before, after 1956 it most certainly was. While border clashes and terrorist infiltration remained rare during 1957–62, the political will to belligerence had vastly increased in the Arab world as a result of Israel's collusion with the ex-imperialist powers and the onslaught against Egypt. What many Arab leaders had long claimed had now been "proved"—Israel was the imperialists' cat's-paw in the Middle East.

SEVEN

THE SIX-DAY WAR, 1967

THE ROAD TO WAR

On the evening of May 14, 1967, while Israel's leaders were milling about on the terrace outside Prime Minister Levi Eshkol's office overlooking the stadium where an Independence Day tattoo was about to begin, Lt. Gen. Yitzhak Rabin, chief of the IDF general staff, took Eshkol (who had succeeded Ben-Gurion in 1963) aside and reported unusual Egyptian troop movements across the Suez Canal into the Sinai Peninsula.

Within three weeks the equivalent of seven divisions—about 100,000 troops with eight to nine hundred tanks and more than seven hundred pieces of artillery—would be deployed in defensive positions, in depth, along the border with Israel. Previously the Egyptians had had less than one division in Sinai. Since 1956 the Israel border and Sharm ash-Sheikh had been patrolled by the UNEF. The new Egyptian deployment fatally undermined the order that had assured relative tranquility for a decade. It posed a strategic threat to Israel and a major challenge to the country's ability to deter invasion. Moreover, it compelled Israel to mobilize a large number of reserve units, gravely and indefinitely disrupting the economy.

The Egyptian initiative and the subsequent Israeli responses, culminating in the Six-Day War that erupted on June 5, were in large part a product of error and mutual miscalculation. Rabin assumed—probably correctly—that the Egyptian move was deterrent and political, meant to persuade Israel not to attack Syria, and to demonstrate Egypt's fraternity, resolve, and strength to the Arab world. IDF intelligence had concluded only a few weeks before, in its annual "national strategic assessment," that war was highly unlikely in the near future. A large part of the Egyptian army was tied up in a civil war in Yemen, supporting the republicans against the Saudi-backed royalists. So Egypt would probably not seek war with Israel; and without the Egyptians, the other Arab states were not likely to march. (However, Prime Minister Eshkol, who had no military background but was naturally cautious, had told a group of officers in February that war could break out "soon."[1])

With hindsight, however, a drift toward belligerency had been discernible for months, if not years. The Palestinians had been quiescent for more than a decade, but in May 1964 they signaled a return to the arena, establishing the Palestine Liberation Organization (PLO) with the stated aim of righting the wrong done to their people and the dismantling of the "Zionist entity." The principal component of the PLO was to be al-Fatah, founded by a group of exiles in the late 1950s. On January 2, 1965, al-Fatah carried out its first military operation, sabotaging a section of Israel's National Water Carrier (a partly open canal that carried water from the Sea of Galilee to the center and south of the country). Guerrilla groups—mainly Fatah—carried out some 122 raids, most of them abortive, between January 1965 and June 1967.

Most of the incursions were from Jordan and Lebanon, but Fatah, at least after February 1966, was largely armed, trained, and run by the Syrian general staff. The latter preferred the raiders to cross into Israel from other Arab states, reducing the danger of IDF retaliation against their own country.[2] Jordan and to a lesser extent Lebanon tried to halt the raids, without much success, and Israel reverted to retaliation, to nudge King Hussein into acting more effectively.

The biggest reprisal was on November 13, 1966, two days after a mine killed three Israeli paratroopers on the West Bank border, south of Hebron. Unusually, the attack was conducted in daylight and involved a relatively large force of tanks, half-track-borne paratroops, self-propelled artillery pieces, and air cover. The main target was the hill village of As Samu'; in addition, an IDF blocking unit ambushed a Legion relief column.[3] The planners appear to have ignored possible political repercussions. The raid rocked Hussein's kingdom, and the West Bank was swept by violent anti-Hashemite demonstrations. The state-directed Jordanian media lambasted Nasser for breaking promises to come to Jordan's aid and "hiding behind UNEF's skirts."

Another, more important, factor in the heightening tension was a series of Israeli-Syrian clashes stemming from disagreements about the use of Jordan River waters and Israeli cultivation of land along the border. Exacerbating matters, in February 1966 a radical "Socialist" Ba'athist regime took power in Damascus. It often spoke of waging a "war of liberation" in Palestine, giving confrontations in the field a threatening ideological context.

After Israel began pumping water from the Sea of Galilee into its National Water Carrier on June 5, 1964, Syria responded with a plan to divert the Jordan's sources into its own territory. Israel stepped up patrols in areas adjacent to the sources, around Kibbutz Dan. In November, Syrian positions fired on the patrols, drawing artillery and tank counterfire and, eventually, air power, which silenced the guns. In 1965 there were three major incidents in which IDF tanks and artillery destroyed tanks and earth-moving equipment after the Syrians fired at border patrols or farmers. The water-diversion effort was finally halted in July 1966, when Israeli aircraft bombed a concentration of earth-moving equipment and downed a Syrian MiG-21 which tried to interfere.[4]

In August the Syrians opened fire on an Israeli patrol boat that had run aground in the northeastern corner of the Sea of Galilee, and beginning in January 1967, they sporadically attacked patrols and farmers in the DMZ east of the lake. On April 7, the conflict escalated. Both sides used tanks. The IAF bombed and strafed seventeen Syrian positions, and six Syrian MiG-21s were shot down, two of them over Damascus.[5] The Syrians found their inability to stop the flight of Israeli aircraft over their capital particularly humiliating. A few weeks later Syrian intelligence sent an agent using a British passport to set off explosions in Jerusalem during the forthcoming Independence Day celebrations. He was caught before he could do any harm.[6]

Against this backdrop of increasing hostilities, Rabin declared in mid-May: "The type of reaction adopted against Jordan and Lebanon is applicable only against states that do not favor the acts of sabotage mounted from their territory. . . . In Syria the problem is different, because the government activates the saboteurs. Therefore the objective of the action in Syria is different."[7]

Some observers interpreted this to mean that Israel aimed, through military action, to topple the Syrian regime. Eshkol reprimanded Rabin for the statement, which many ministers regarded as gravely improper. But it clearly reflected what was on the government's mind. In an interview published on May 11, Eshkol stated: "In view of the 14 [border] incidents in the past month alone it is possible that we will have to adopt measures no less drastic than those of April 7" (when the six MiGs were downed).[8] And on May 12 United Press International (UPI) reported that a "high Israeli source said Israel would take limited military action designed to topple the Damascus army regime if Syrian terrorists continued sabotage raids inside Israel. It would be a telling blow against the Syrian Government." The source, who had spoken, in another version, of "a military operation of great size and strength," was the director of military intelligence, Gen. Aharon Yariv, at a briefing for the foreign press.[9]

Ultimately it was the sputtering Syrian-Israeli border that triggered the process that led to the Six-Day War. Warnings that Israel was building up its forces along the frontier in preparation for an assault against the Golan Heights emanated periodically from Damascus during the weeks following the April 7 dogfight. Initially they went unheeded and were put down to understandable Syrian nervousness. On May 12, however, a Soviet intelligence officer in Cairo apparently confirmed the vague Syrian reports to senior Egyptian officials. On May 13, the Soviets officially informed Egypt—both in Cairo and to a visiting Egyptian delegation, led by Anwar Sadat, speaker of the National Assembly, in Moscow—that Israel was massing troops and intended to invade Syria. The Soviets spoke of ten to twelve IDF brigades and mentioned May 17 as the date set for the assault.[10]

The same day Syrian defense minister Hafez Assad requested that the Egyptians act to deter an Israeli attack. The chief of staff of the Egyptian army, Muhammad Fawzi, flew to Damascus to consult. Damascus seemed genuinely scared. But, saber-rattling by Israel's leaders notwithstanding, there was in fact no IDF buildup along the border, no unusual reserve call-ups, and no nonroutine deployment of troops or armor. This was confirmed by Fawzi, who later recalled: "I did not find any concrete evidence to support the information received. On the contrary, aerial photographs taken by Syrian reconnaissance on 12 and 13 May showed no change in normal [Israeli] military positions."[11]

Fawzi had apparently reported this from Damascus to Cairo on May 14 (or 15), adding that the Syrian army itself had not gone on alert. Fawzi returned to Cairo on May 15 and reported on his findings in person to War Minister 'Amr.[12]

Why the Kremlin had "confirmed" something that had not happened may become clear when the relevant files are declassified. Some Soviet leaders may truly have believed that Israel intended to strike, and that their warning would act as a deterrent; it is more likely that they wished to increase Arab-Israeli tensions or to elicit Egyptian support for the Syrian regime. Moscow probably did not imagine that its actions would lead to drastic Egyptian moves or to war. Its ambassador, Leonid Chuvakhin, declined Eshkol's invitation to inspect Israel's side of the border. On May 15, the chief of the UN Truce Supervision Organization, the Norwegian general Odd Bull, reported that he "had no reports of any build-up" from observers on the border.

Why the Egyptians reacted the way they did is not clear either. According to Fawzi's memoirs, 'Amr failed to respond on May 15 to his report that the accounts of an Israeli buildup were incorrect: "Consequently, I began to believe that from his perspective the business of troop concentrations was not the principal reason for mobilization or the troop movements which we had been asked to undertake in such a hurry."[13]

The implication, borne out by an Egyptian staff officer, Gen. 'Abd al-Ghani al-Gamasy, was that 'Amr, perhaps with Nasser's agreement, had decided to exploit the situation to annul Israel's gains from the 1956 war: remilitarize Sinai, secure the withdrawal of UNEF, and again close the Gulf of Eilat to Israeli shipping.[14]

So the Egyptian divisions moved into Sinai. The IDF's initial assessment was that Nasser was merely flexing his muscles to deter a strike against Syria; he had been affected, if not actually driven, by the stinging Arab criticism of his inaction after the Samu' raid and the dogfight over Damascus. But on May 16–18 Egypt abruptly turned ostentatious display into deep political-military crisis, by demanding the evacuation of the 3,400 UNEF troops from Sinai and Gaza.

And Secretary-General U Thant unquestioningly accepted Cairo's right to demand the withdrawal: On May 20–21, UNEF withdrew from Sharm ash-Sheikh, and Egyptian troops immediately occupied the site. The UN's compliant response certainly surprised the Israelis. It may also have taken Nasser aback: He may have hoped that the matter would be referred to the Security Council or General Assembly, where it would be turned down—leaving his forces in Sinai, having challenged Israel, but with a UN buffer still firmly in place. With the news of U Thant's agreement to the withdrawal, IDF intelligence began changing its tune. Its assessment on May 17 stated: "If the UN forces withdraw . . . a new situation could arise, which would give the Egyptian [deployment] an offensive . . . character." Yet the overall Israeli estimate on May 18 remained that war was still "a remote possibility."[15]

At this point Nasser appears to have submitted to the momentum of his (or 'Amr's) previous actions. He may have thought that he was on the verge of a major, cost-free political victory. Having already moved six divisions into Sinai and returned at least two brigades from Yemen, on May 21 he declared a general mobilization of the Egyptian army. He appears to have believed—perhaps persuaded by 'Amr—that his army could defeat or at least hold off the IDF; perhaps the war fever of the Cairo crowds, reproduced in a dozen Arab capitals, got the better of his judgment.

Israeli intelligence still believed that Nasser would halt at the brink, and on the morning of May 22 thought it "unlikely" that he would announce the closure of the Straits of Tiran to Israeli shipping.[16] But around noon the same day, Nasser visited the Bir Gafgafa air base in Sinai and declared that Egypt was about to do just that, re-creating the situation that Israel had always regarded as a *casus belli*. 'Amr instructed his units to bar the Gulf of Eilat, from noon on May 23, to all vessels flying the Israeli flag and to all oil tankers bound for Eilat.[17] That night, just after midnight, the formal announcement was made.

In retrospect this can be seen as the decisive act that made war inevitable—though Nasser apparently did not realize it.[18] He was subsequently to imply—as during his speech of May 26 to Arab trade union leaders—that the whole sequence of moves, culminating in the closure of the straits, had been planned to trigger war with Israel, with the ultimate aim of "liberating Palestine." Not the Straits of Tiran but Israel's "existence" was the issue, he said on May 29.[19] Clearly the situation had changed dramatically. At the IDF general staff meeting on the morning of May 23, Yariv declared: "The post-Suez period is over. It is not merely a matter of freedom of navigation. If Israel does not respond to the closure of the Straits, there will be no value to its credibility or to the IDF's deterrent power, because the Arab states will interpret Israel's weakness as an opportunity to assail her security and her very existence." Rabin and the deputy chief of general staff, Gen. Ezer Weizman, agreed.

The IDF had more or less completed mobilizing by the end of May. The army favored war immediately, but Eshkol hesitated. The United States, which strongly condemned the closure of the straits as "illegal" and "potentially disastrous to the cause of peace,"[20] had firmly signaled, since May 15, its opposition to "unilateral" Israeli action. Washington proposed to put together a multinational flotilla—"the Red Sea Regatta," as it was later called—to break the Egyptian blockade. Eshkol preferred to give the superpowers time to resolve the crisis without war.

The week of growing tension had another—at the time secret—effect: Rabin suffered what amounted to a nervous breakdown, which he later described as "nicotine poisoning" or "a state of mental and physical exhaustion,"[21] incapacitating him for forty-eight hours during May 22–24.[22] The collapse may have been triggered by a meeting on May 22 with the retired elder statesman Ben-Gurion, who told Rabin that his "mistaken" mobilization of reserves had made the crisis acute and that he was responsible for "leading the nation into a grave situation," isolated and with war a fearful possibility.[23]

The Egyptian command on May 24–25 briefly considered and planned a preemptive air offensive against Israeli targets—including the Dimona nuclear plant, set up with French help in the late 1950s and early 1960s. Western governments suspected (or knew) that it was designed to produce weapons. 'Amr apparently issued orders, on May 25, for a massive assault on the morning of May 27. The IDF learned of it,[24] and Nasser countermanded the order on May 26, deterred perhaps by American (and possibly Soviet) warnings.[25] On May 25 the Egyptians also apparently considered striking across the southern Negev from Sinai to the Jordanian border to isolate Eilat. But Nasser argued that Israel might respond by conquering the Gaza Strip, where Egypt's forces were vulnerable.[26]

Throughout the crisis Israeli decision-makers were worried by the possibility of an attack on the Dimona plant. In 1965 Nasser's confidant, the journalist Muhammad Hassnin Heikal, had written that Arab experts believed Israel would go nuclear in three years' time and that the Arab world would have to take preemptive action. In 1966 Nasser himself had declared that if Israel developed an atomic bomb, Egypt's response would be a "preemptive war," directed in the first instance against the nuclear production facilities.[27] On May 21, Eshkol had told the cabinet Defense Committee that Egypt wanted to close the straits and "to bomb the reactor in Dimona."[28]

Two primitive devices appear to have been assembled during the "waiting period" of May–early June. Munya Mardor, the director of Rafael, Israel's Weapons Development Authority, published the following oblique passage from his diary for May 28:

> When I reached the site, I found Dr. Jenka . . . supervising the project work teams under his authority. The teams were engaged in assembling and checking the weapons system, whose development and production they succeeded in completing before the war. It was after midnight.

Engineers and technicians, most of them young, were concentrating on their work. They looked serious and reserved, as ones who recognized the great—perhaps fateful—importance of the weapons system that they had succeeded in bringing to an operational level.[29]

Ben-Gurion's aide, Shimon Peres had overseen the nuclear program since its inception in 1953 and can rightly be viewed as the "father of the Israeli A-option." In May 1967 Peres, then a senior Knesset member, had proposed to a small circle of ministers that Israel take a certain dramatic measure as a warning to the Arab states, but the ministers turned it down.[30]

The air space above and around the plant was declared off limits to all aircraft, and indeed, on June 5, the first day of the Six-Day War, the antiaircraft missile battery guarding the plant shot down a damaged IAF fighter that had strayed over Dimona while returning from an attack mission in Jordan. The (apparently) wounded Israeli pilot was killed.[31] Hence the shock in Jerusalem when, on May 26, two Egyptian Air Force MiG-21s overflew the reactor (at 52,000 feet) on a photographic reconnaissance mission, and interceptors and missiles failed to bring them down. The Israelis linked the mission to a possible preemptive strike on the plant. Some of the generals, including Weizman, who suspected that Egypt intended to bomb the reactor that day or the next, wanted to attack Egypt immediately, a proposal rejected by Eshkol.[32]

For more than a week diplomats shuttled fruitlessly back and forth among Jerusalem, New York, Washington, and Cairo. Washington, though still pressing Israel to hold its fire ("Israel will not be alone unless it decides to go alone," said Secretary of State Dean Rusk), had made no headway organizing the "Red Sea Regatta."[33] Ultimately only Holland and Australia signed up; when the war broke out, Britain and Canada had not yet decided.[34]

With mobilization in Israel, the economy slowed down. The generals feared that the Arabs were using the time to improve their defenses, but Eshkol insisted on delay.[35] Morale began to slump. Empty lots were consecrated as makeshift cemeteries; tens of thousands were expected to die. There was a widespread feeling among the civilian population—though not in the army—that a "Second Holocaust" was a definite possibility. Newspapers explicitly likened Nasser to Hitler: *HaAretz*, the leading daily, even ran Nasser's declaration of May 26: "If Israel wants war—well then, Israel will be destroyed!" alongside Hitler's of January 30, 1939: "If the Jews drag the world into war—world Jewry will be destroyed."[36] A low point came on the evening of May 28, when the prime minister broadcast a rather hesitant, faltering speech to the nation; later designated "the stammering speech," it projected fear and irresolution.

The cabinet that morning had deferred taking military action for "two–three weeks," motivated by repeated warnings from Washington, which offered Jerusalem vague reassurances that it would engineer a diplomatic or multinational solution to the crisis. On February 11, 1957, the United States had committed itself to freedom of passage through the Straits of Tiran in an aide-mémoire sent by Secretary of State John Foster Dulles to Israel's ambassador to Washington, Abba Eban. Dulles had also pledged American support for Israeli self-defensive action to force open the straits, should this prove necessary. But in May 1967 the White House and Department of State were in no mood to reiterate this commitment.

Following his broadcast, Eshkol met with the IDF general staff—and was subjected to a frank, and extremely unusual, tongue-lashing by the assembled generals. The cabinet—and the prime minister—were accused of hesitancy and indecision. Similar charges were also hurled more and more openly by opposition parties, chiefly the right-wing Herut, led by Menachem Begin, and the activist Rafi, Ben-Gurion's new political home. The political commotion soon produced a single chorus: that Eshkol was unfit to lead the country into war, and that he should at least give up the Defense Ministry in favor of someone who could generate greater public confidence.

Public opinion, opposition leaders, and much of the IDF command favored Moshe Dayan, a Rafi leader and the victorious chief of general staff in 1956. Eshkol had become a figure of fun. Rafi leaders, said Rabin, "laughed at him and berated his character and publicized his weaknesses and made up stories about him and argued that, in effect, 'the country, in its hour of desperation, had no defense minister.' Eshkol was weary. The burden of the hour and the defamatory campaign combined to undermine his position."[37] On June 1, a very reluctant Eshkol caved in, bringing Dayan in as defense minister and two right-wing opposition figures, one of them Begin, as ministers without portfolio. Some commentators designated what had occurred a "putsch."[38]

Realignments were also taking place in the Arab world. On May 30, King Hussein flew to Cairo and signed a mutual defense pact with President Nasser.[39] An Egyptian general, 'Abd al-Mun'im Riad, was appointed, at least on paper, overall commander of Jordan's army. On June 3 two Egyptian commando battalions were flown to Jordan, and on the following morning an Iraqi mechanized brigade crossed into Jordan and began to move toward the Jordan River. Egypt and Iraq, traditional enemies, also signed a mutual defense pact. The crisis had precipitated what appeared to be that ancient, coveted will-o'-the-wisp, Arab unity. The Arab world was rallying around its new leader, Nasser. Even the long-standing enmity between Hussein and PLO chairman Ahmed Shukeiry seemed to dissipate as the latter visited Amman.

The masses, meanwhile, had been whipped up by politicians and the media into a state of war hysteria and exultation. In Israel, which could not but be influenced by the hourly radio reports of Arab war frenzy and announcements of Israel's impending demise, there was a feeling of a noose tightening around the nation's neck—especially among Holocaust survivors. Damascus Radio told its listeners on May 23: "Arab masses, this is your day. Rush to the battlefield. . . . Let them know that we shall hang the last imperialist soldier with the entrails of the last Zionist." The director of the Voice of the Arabs (Cairo), Ahmed Said, chimed in: "The Zionist barracks in Palestine is about to collapse and be destroyed. . . . Every . . . Arab has been living for the past 19 years on one hope— . . . to see the day Israel is liquidated."[40] The prime minister of Iraq spoke of "a rendezvous with our brothers in Tel Aviv," and Shukeiry declared: "[T]here will be practically no Jewish survivors."[41]

In the first days of June the feeling of asphyxiation intensified, as did the sense that the Arab states might launch an attack within days. There was particular fear of a limited Jordanian or Jordanian-Egyptian offensive against Eilat.[42] The military leadership felt that each day's delay strengthened the Arabs' hand and weakened Israel's. The troops camping in the desert opposite the Egyptian army were chafing at the bit and might become demoralized by the situation.

Tensions peaked on June 2, when, at a joint meeting of the cabinet and the general staff, Israel decided in principle on war, but no date was set. "Every day that passes substantially lessens the chances of Israel attaining air superiority," Yariv told the ministers. "What are we waiting for?" asked the quartermaster-general, Mattityahu Peled (who after demobilization became a prominent political dove).

Eshkol managed to restrain the dogs of war for two more days. But on June 4, the cabinet gave the army the green light to attack when ready. Eshkol had finally been persuaded by the director of the Mossad, Meir Amit, who had spent the previous three days in Washington and returned to Tel Aviv certain that the United States would "bless an operation if we succeed in shattering Nasser." Foreign Minister Abba Eban had independently reached the same conclusion.[43] American intelligence accurately predicted that Israel would defeat any possible Arab coalition within a few days, perhaps a week, and by the start of June Washington had come round to the view that war was inevitable. Israel was given to understand that it could go ahead. The change in President Lyndon Johnson's thinking apparently occurred during the long Memorial Day weekend (May 27–31), which he spent on his Texas ranch with a number of Jewish friends and advisers. Efforts to put together a multinational policy and flotilla had failed. Johnson was apparently shaken by Hussein's decision to align with Egypt. The president now expected the Israelis to strike.[44]

The road to the Six-Day War had been lined by Israeli intelligence failures. On June 13, Dayan was to lambaste the intelligence agencies on three major counts: failing to evaluate correctly the effect on Egypt of the IDF actions against Jordan at Samu' in 1966 and against Syria in April 1967, failing to grasp the significance of the Egyptian push into Sinai, and failing to anticipate Nasser's order to UNEF to withdraw.

THE WAR

THE LINE-UP

The armies were extremely ill-matched. Israelis, throughout their history, have tended to see themselves as the "weaker side," their army smaller and less well armed than their Arab enemies'. The truth, in 1967 as at other times, was different.

To begin with, there was certainly a vast difference in levels of motivation. The Egyptian, Syrian, or Jordanian soldier may have been filled with hatred, or at least animosity, toward the usurping Israeli—but he failed to regard the battle with Israel as a war for very survival. The Israeli believed he was fighting for his life, his family, and his home. Beyond that, there was a mortal fear for the very existence of the national collective. A Herut Party Knesset member, Arye Ben-Eliezer, said after the war: "We were not so few in number as there is a tendency to believe. By our side fought the six million, who whispered in our ear the eleventh commandment: Do not get murdered—the commandment that was omitted at Mount Sinai and was given back to us in the recent battles in Sinai."[45]

Israel's army, numbering about 250,000 troops, was about three-quarters reserve formations and one-quarter conscript. Men between the ages of eighteen and twenty-one usually served two-and-a-half years, and women two years. The men then served in the reserves until approximately the age of fifty, usually doing a month or so of training or operational duty annually. The army, leavened by several thousand professional soldiers, was thoroughly mechanized and, in large part, armored. The air force—the IDF's most powerful component, in both defense and offense—and the navy were composed mainly of conscripts and long-term professionals. In May 1967 the IDF had 192 airworthy jet fighters and fighter-bombers (with another 40 trainers convertible to ground attack missions). There were on average three pilots per aircraft, highly competent ground crews and air controllers, and a finely tuned command system.

The land forces had some four hundred artillery pieces and heavy mortars and eleven hundred tanks. They were divided into twelve–thirteen artillery brigades and six armored brigades, with six or seven additional independent armored battalions; eleven infantry brigades (most of them second-line territorial units); two paratroop brigades; and the equivalent of two or three independent battalions of paratroops and special forces and three mechanized infantry brigades. The infantry was largely transported in 2,500–3,000 World War II–vintage, renovated armored half-tracks.

The Arab armies were mostly professional forces, relatively poorly trained, and not properly mechanized. The Egyptian army suffered from a basic weakness owing to the politicization of its command echelons, which resulted in the appointment of incompetent and inexperienced senior commanders, and structural weaknesses that were to prove fatal in wartime. On May 15 'Amr made a series of top-level appointments, among them Gen. 'Abd al-Muhsen Kamal Murtaji—the longtime head of the Egyptian expeditionary force in Yemen, who was unfamiliar with the plans for the defense of Sinai or the units and commanders involved—to lead the Sinai Front Command, a new headquarters unit. At a stroke 'Amr thus threw the whole command structure in Sinai into confusion.

The effect of the last-minute personnel changes was aggravated by 'Amr's and Nasser's last-minute alterations in the deployments in Sinai. In the days before the war and during the fighting itself, 'Amr repeatedly bypassed various headquarters and issued orders directly to the divisional commanders.[46]

In 1965 (and there was little growth between 1965 and 1967) the Egyptian army had numbered 150,000–180,000 troops.[47] The rapid expansion of the army in the preceding decade (from 80,000 in 1955) had resulted in a shortfall of experienced officers. Men attained ranks and positions for which they had no training or ability. 'Amr himself had risen in a period of two years (1952–54) from major to major general, and effectively commanded the armed forces from 1953 on. He then filled the officer corps with political appointees, resulting in its "deprofessionalization."[48]

The Egyptians had deployed in Sinai and along the Suez Canal almost all their combat units: eighteen infantry brigades, one paratroop brigade, and four or five independent special forces battalions; six armored brigades with seventeen additional independent armored or semi-armored battalions; and two mechanized brigades. They fielded around nine hundred tanks and eight hundred artillery pieces. The air force consisted of 242 fighter aircraft, many poorly maintained, and fewer trained pilots than aircraft. It also lacked radar capable of picking up low-flying aircraft.[49] Last, the intelligence services were incompetent and were focused mainly on rooting out internal dissension rather than on Israel.[50]

The Jordanian Army, with 56,000 troops, consisted of nine infantry brigades, two armored brigades, and a mechanized brigade. Jordan was reinforced by an Iraqi brigade, two Egyptian commando battalions, and one Iraqi-Palestinian battalion. In all, the Jordanians had 264 tanks, plus 30 belonging to the Iraqis, 160 artillery pieces and heavy mortars, and thirty-four Iraqi guns.

The air force consisted of twenty-four Hawker Hunter jet fighters.

The Syrian army fielded 70,000 troops, most of them at the front, in six infantry brigades; two paratroop and special forces battalions; two armored brigades (and an independent armored battalion); one mechanized brigade; and 265 artillery pieces and heavy mortars. The armor consisted of about 300 tanks, and the air force comprised ninety-two fighters and two bombers.

THE PLAN AND ITS EXECUTION

The Six-Day War was in all essentials a clockwork war carried out by the IDF against three relatively passive, ineffective Arab armies; indeed, the Israeli offensives in most areas proceeded more rapidly than the planners had envisioned. Throughout, the initiative lay with the IDF; occasionally the Arabs "responded" to an Israeli move; most often they served as rather bewildered, sluggish punching bags.

The main and initial objective of the Israelis was the destruction of the Egyptian army in Sinai. From the first it was understood that the implementation of their plan would be severely circumscribed by limitations of time imposed by the superpowers. Before June 5 Foreign Minister Eban estimated that the IDF would have no more than twenty-four to seventy-two hours at its disposal.[51] Israel's diplomatic missions, and particularly its delegations in Washington and at the UN, were ordered to stall for as long as possible, to allow the IDF to complete its work. As it turned out, the Security Council called for a cease-fire on the evening of June 7 (Israel time). Egypt and Jordan gave their agreement the following day but Syria accepted only on June 10, the cease-fire taking effect late that afternoon. By then, of course, it was all over.

WAR AIMS

In his message to the troops, broadcast shortly after the start of the battle on the morning of June 5, Dayan declared: "The Egyptian General Mortaji, who commands the Arab forces in Sinai, has broadcast to his troops ... to conquer ... 'the plundered land of Palestine.' Soldiers of the IDF, we have no objectives of conquest. Our goal is to frustrate the attempt of the Arab armies to conquer our country, and to break the ring of isolation and aggression surrounding us."[52]

Later, at a meeting with Eshkol and others in the early hours of June 7, Dayan put Israel's war aims somewhat differently—"to destroy the Egyptian army and to open the Straits to Israeli shipping." Israel's explicit, publicly stated assumption was that Egypt was intent on attacking the Negev. But captured Egyptian documents show that Egypt's army was in fact preparing for a defensive battle, to absorb and repel an initial IDF blow.

Israel's stated war aims were confined to Egypt. The documentation so far available concerning June 2–5, as well as the reality of IDF deployments, show that it was not part of Israel's original intentions to conquer the West Bank or parts of Syria.[53] Thinking about the results and consequences of the war appears to have been generally fuzzy. During the waiting period and the first days, most people were focused on the here-and-now: the battle against the Arab armies, the efforts to stave off a cease-fire imposed by the Great Powers, and the threat of Soviet intervention. Almost no thought was devoted to the aftermath. It was not clear until nearly the end of the conflict what areas would be taken by the IDF. Only late on Day 1 was it clear that East Jerusalem and parts of the West Bank would be conquered (though on the morning of June 5, even before the Jordanians started shooting, a special West Bank Command was set up under Gen. (Res.) Chaim Herzog, whose function was to administer the area in the event of Israeli takeover).[54] Not until the end of Day 3 was it understood that the army would advance as far as the Canal; only at the end of Day 4 was it apparent that the IDF intended to conquer parts of the Golan Heights.

Of Israel's political leadership, only Dayan appears to have contemplated, before the outbreak of the fighting, conquering the West Bank. Over the years he had repeatedly lamented the failure of the IDF to achieve this during the 1948 war. Ever since, and especially between 1949 and 1956, he had openly avowed or strongly hinted at his desire to see the territory annexed by Israel. In the events leading to the 1967 conflict, he seems to have been one of the few to have envisaged the impending clash as an opportunity to do so. It was this wish, perhaps, that underlay his opposition to the proposal by the prime minister's special military adviser, former IDF chief of general staff Yadin, on June 4, that Israel issue a specific, forceful warning to Jordan to stay out of the war (such a warning was in fact issued).[55] Until May 30, when King Hussein flew to Egypt to sign his military pact with Nasser, the Israeli leaders were uncertain whether Jordan would join the battle. Israel would not initiate hostilities against Jordan, and its response to Jordanian actions would be ad hoc and specific. Indeed, the forces that eventually conquered the northern West Bank had been earmarked purely for defense, not offense, and were in many ways unsuitable for the role that eventually devolved upon them.[56]

The same type of thinking dominated considerations regarding the Syrian front—no IDF offensive unless provoked by Syria. But here, clearly, the Israeli ministers and army command were uniformly itching to strike a major blow. After all, Syria had triggered the whole crisis; there would be no logic to ending the war without "solving" the Syrian problem. It was assumed that Syria would join in; the impending war was regarded as a golden opportunity to avenge and put an end to what was seen as Damascus's belligerency and harassment.[57]

Israel's Conquests in the 1967 War

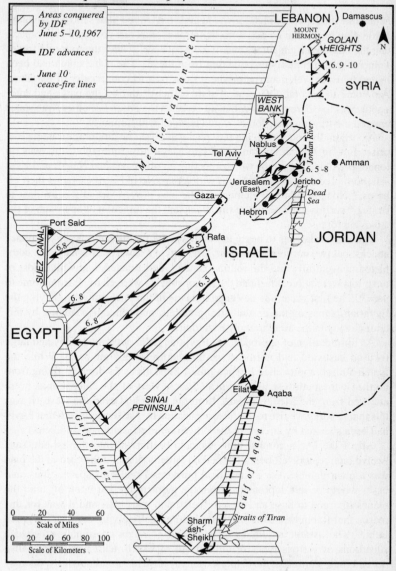

Areas conquered
by IDF
June 5–10, 1967

IDF advances

June 10
cease-fire lines

LEBANON

Damascus

MOUNT
HERMON

GOLAN
HEIGHTS

N

6. 9 -10

SYRIA

Mediterranean Sea

WEST
BANK

Nablus

Jordan River

Tel Aviv

Amman

6. 5 -8

Jerusalem
(East)

Jericho

Gaza

*Dead
Sea*

Hebron

Port Said

JORDAN

Rafa

6. 5

ISRAEL

SUEZ CANAL

6.8

6. 5

6. 8

6. 8

EGYPT

SINAI
PENINSULA

Eilat

Aqaba

Gulf of Suez

Gulf of Aqaba

0   20   40   60
Scale of Miles

0   20 40 60 80 100
Scale of Kilometers

Sharm
ash-
Sheikh

Straits of Tiran

THE AIR ASSAULT

Much like the Japanese plan for war against the United States in 1941, the IDF battle plan hinged on an aerial master stroke—this one designed to incapacitate the opponents' air forces and, in consequence, render their ground forces vulnerable to a continuous pounding from the air. The plan, which had been honed by Ezer Weizman (before he left his post as commander of the Israel Air Force to become OC general staff branch)[58] during the early and mid-1960s, was to destroy the Egyptian air force on the ground. If other Arab states entered the fray, their air forces would be dealt with similarly.

As originally conceived, the IDF plan was based on attaining strategic surprise. But, in the circumstances of late May–early June 1967, this was no longer possible. The Arabs were expecting an offensive, and Nasser and Hussein both predicted it would begin with a massive IAF strike against their air bases.[59] Nonetheless, two elements in the plan proved virtually equivalent to strategic surprise: the timing of the attack and the direction of approach of the attacking forces.

The IAF strike was to begin not at dawn, the traditional time of "surprise" attacks, but two or three hours later, after Egypt's dawn patrols had been completed uneventfully and the routine general alert relaxed, and while most of the pilots were at breakfast and the senior officers were en route from home to base.[60] The first wave was designed to take out the vital runways, leaving the Egyptian planes on the ground sitting targets, and rendering landing by aircraft already in the air extremely hazardous.

As for direction of approach, the Egyptian radar network was by and large focused eastward and northeastward, towards Israel's air bases. While the Israeli aircraft approached Egypt's minor Sinai air bases directly, flying from northeast to southwest, the main air bases, west of the Suez Canal, were attacked from the Mediterranean, from the north and even the west. (It was this that in part gave rise to the false accusation by Nasser on June 6 that Egypt had been attacked by aircraft of the U.S. Sixth Fleet, stationed off Crete.)

All of the IAF's combat units were to be thrown into the assault, save twelve interceptors left behind to defend Israel's skies. At the core of the plan was a giant gamble. For all practical purposes Israel's air space, cities, and bases would be left unprotected from the moment the IAF took off until the planes returned to base and were refueled and rearmed—and it was for this reason that Rabin hesitated for weeks before finally giving the plan the green light.[61] The assault required precision and complex coordination between squadrons of various types of aircraft, all of which, taking off from half a dozen bases, were to hit the dispersed enemy airfields simultaneously. Secrecy was of the essence. It was only on June 4 that the IAF base commanders briefed their deputies and the squadron commanders; and it was only on the morning of D-Day, June 5, hours before takeoff, that the pilots themselves were told of their missions.[62]

The key to success was comprehensive, detailed, and accurate intelligence on orders of battle, bases, aircraft deployment and capabilities, the thickness and composition of Arab airstrip tarmacs, antiaircraft defenses and radar stations, and so on. As the commander of the IAF, Gen. Mordechai ("Motti") Hod, reported at the June 2 cabinet meeting: "The IAF knows precisely . . . the location of every Egyptian aircraft, what it is doing, what it is capable of doing."[63] Or, as King Hussein later observed: "Their pilots knew exactly what to expect. . . . [they] had a complete catalogue of the most minute details of each of the thirty-two Arab air bases, what objectives to strike, where and how. We had nothing like that."[64]

On the morning of June 5, the IAF enjoyed the unexpected "help" of Egypt's antiaircraft command, which had ordered its units not to fire at overflying aircraft—because Defense Minister 'Amr and his air force commander, Gen. Mohammed Sidki, were flying to inspect the Egyptian positions in Sinai.[65]

Hod, who had succeeded Weizman as IAF commander in 1966, said in his prewar order of the day: "Fly, descend upon the enemy . . . disperse him in the desert in all directions so that the people of Israel may live safely on their land." And just before takeoff, one fighter-bomber squadron commander, Maj. Yosef Salant, told his pilots: "With you, in the cockpit, sit the People of Israel, generations of Jews, and each one of them is confident that you will do it right."[66]

And, indeed, the pilots "did it right." Between 7:14 and 7:30 A.M. 183 planes took off. In this first wave were a full 95 percent of the IAF's front-line aircraft. Most headed westward, toward the Mediterranean. Then, after flying eighteen minutes, each formation rolled southward, toward the bases in Sinai and Egypt proper. They flew low to avoid radar detection, hugging the waves and desert, all maintaining complete radio silence. The senior IAF and IDF command—Dayan, Rabin, Weizman, Yadin, and Hod among them—were gathered in the IAF underground command bunker, known as "The Hole" (HaBor).[67]

Approaching their targets, the attacking Israeli jets soared upward to get into position for their bombing runs. The lead foursomes all reached and attacked their targets, eleven bases in all, at precisely 7:45 A.M. They first released their large bombs at one-third and two-thirds the length of the runways, ripping up the tarmacs, rendering them useless. Then they made additional runs, bombing, rocketing, and machine-gunning the MiGs waiting on the runways or in their hangars and antiaircraft batteries and radar sites, before heading for home. The Egyptians were caught almost completely by surprise; antiaircraft fire was meager and ineffective. At Fayid air base, Israeli Mystères

left sixteen MiGs burning on the tarmac—but narrowly missed a large transport plane that had just landed, bringing 'Amr and most of his senior staff back
from their visit to Bir Gafgafa.[68]

By 9:00 A.M. the picture was clear. The IAF had scored a victory of historic
proportions, destroying 197 aircraft (189 caught on the ground, 8 in dogfights)
and demolishing or damaging eight radar stations. The six Egyptian forward
air bases—in Sinai and along the Suez Canal—were rendered completely
inoperative. Hod received the news impassively, uttering not a word: "[H]is
features were rocklike . . . not a muscle moved," Rabin later recalled.[69]

Thanks to efficient ground crews, the IAF turnaround (rearming, refueling,
and minor repairs) was rapid. The second wave, 164 aircraft, took off about an
hour after the return of the first. Fourteen air bases were hit and another 107
aircraft were destroyed. In the two waves of attack, the IAF had demolished
304 of Egypt's 419 planes, itself losing nine aircraft with six more seriously
damaged. Six Israeli air crewmen were killed, two captured, and three
wounded.[70] At about 10 o'clock—just minutes after the second wave had
begun to hit the Egyptian airfields—Weizman telephoned his wife and told
her: "We have won the war."[71] Shortly after 11:00, Hod at last broke his
silence and said to Rabin: "The Egyptian Air Force has ceased to exist."[72]

Beginning at 12:45, a third assault wave struck Syria, Iraq, and Jordan,
whose warplanes had begun to attack Israeli targets about fifty minutes before.
The whole Jordanian air force (twenty-eight aircraft) was destroyed, as was
half the Syrian air force, fifty-three aircraft. The Syrians then hastily moved
the rest to bases beyond Israel's reach. In Iraq the IAF bagged ten aircraft.

The day's air offensives gave Israel almost unhindered superiority over the
battlefields of Sinai, the West Bank, and the Golan Heights and freed the IAF
for continuous support missions against the Arab ground forces. The Israeli
planes were to bomb, napalm, and strafe the Arab positions and armored
columns almost at will; the main problems were to be fatigue, turnaround
times, repairs, maintenance, and friend-or-foe identification of ground forces.
The constant Israeli air attacks were a major factor in the successive demoralization and collapse of the Egyptian, Jordanian, and Syrian armies.

By the war's end Israel had destroyed about 450 enemy aircraft, some 70 of
them in dogfights and the rest on the ground, at a cost of about twenty dead
airmen and about forty aircraft (almost all of them lost to ground fire). One
combat jet in five had been lost.[73]

THE GROUND ASSAULT IN SINAI

On the ground, IDF planning called for a massive offensive against the Egyptian army in Sinai while leaving relatively sparse defensive forces on the Jordanian and Syrian fronts. The aim was to destroy the Egyptian army and then
deal if forced to—and if time and the powers permitted—with the Syrians and

Jordanians. As modified after June 1 by the new defense minister, Dayan, the plan called for a three-pronged east-west offensive across northern Sinai, initially bypassing the Gaza Strip. (At a June 2 consultation in the prime minister's office attended by Eshkol, Dayan, Labor Minister Yigal Allon, and Eban, Allon proposed, as part of the planned ground offensive, to transfer to Egypt the hundreds of thousands of refugees in the Gaza Strip. Dayan rejected the idea: The Egyptians would not agree, and Israel would be forced to carry out an "unparalleled inhumane and barbaric expulsion," he said.[74])

The thrusts would eventually loop southward, effectively trapping the bulk of the Egyptian forces. These were later to be destroyed by the flanking Israeli units.[75] Sharm ash-Sheikh and Gaza would be left for a later stage.[76] Dayan planned to halt the advance well short of the Suez Canal, apparently out of fear of Soviet intervention if the heart of Egypt was threatened.[77]

The assault began at 8:00 A.M. on June 5, just as the first wave of the IAF strike was ending and before anyone knew how well it had fared. Three divisional task forces, comprising the IDF's best conscript units and armor, crossed the border almost simultaneously and rapidly overcame the opposition, achieving their breakthroughs south of Rafa and at Abu Awgeila well ahead of schedule and leaving much of Egypt's armored and mechanized forces stranded in central-eastern Sinai, unable or unprepared to join the battle. The Egyptian commanders had no clear idea of the situation and no orders what to do—advance, counterattack, or retreat—though they had a growing sense that they were about to be outflanked and assailed from the north and west. In short order they came under air attack and understood that no succor would be offered by their air force.[78] On June 6–7 some of these units succeeded in reaching the Canal (without their heavy equipment), outdistancing the IDF columns advancing from the northeast, who were poised to cut off their routes of retreat.

But for most of the Egyptian units the peninsula had become one giant trap. The Israeli tankmen and gunners exploited their breakthroughs relentlessly; they barely slept for three days. Advancing continuously, except when refueling and ammunitioning, they ravaged the retreating foe. Many Egyptian soldiers, discarding their weapons, took to the sands. The IDF units, who did not want to advance encumbered with prisoners, often let them get away, though some mowed down those fleeing or trying to surrender.

'Amr, sensing what was about to happen, and apparently with Nasser's agreement, on the evening of June 6 (a bare thirty-six hours after the start of the war) issued a general order to his troops in the peninsula to retreat to the Mitla and Jidi passes in western Sinai, some twenty miles from the Canal, and, if necessary, subsequently to cross the Canal westward.[79] Fawzi recalled that by that afternoon, 'Amr "was psychologically worn out and seemed on the verge of nervous collapse." 'Amr claimed that Nasser had approved the general withdrawal, but his subordinates were dismayed by the order.[80] The full significance of the Israeli air victory on Day 1 took about twenty-four hours to dawn on the Egyptian command, at which point they apparently panicked. Or perhaps they sincerely believed that they could pull back and regroup their divisions and hold the Israelis at the passes, keeping them away from the vital waterway.

The general retreat order, however, demoralized and disoriented the troops. The Egyptians were fairly competent at static, defensive warfare; given a position or chain of positions to hold, they more or less stuck to their guns and knew what to do. But now the various units in eastern Sinai were called on to retreat in orderly fashion while conducting a rearguard defense, without air cover or proper antiaircraft defenses, against slashing Israeli tank thrusts and continuous IAF assault. Their lack of intelligence was total. Neither the high command in Cairo nor the front and divisional commanders nor the lower echelon commanders had any knowledge about Israeli deployment and intentions—or indeed about where their own units were. The jamming of their radio communications by the Israelis added to the chaos. In effect they conducted what their commanders had hoped would be a fighting retreat while totally blind.[81]

Sensing the problem, on June 7 the high command canceled the general retreat order. Some units were told to stand fast at the passes, others to retreat westward across the Canal. But this only added to the confusion and demoralization.[82] Most were already in headlong flight, and some units, such as the Sixth Division, were specifically ordered to discard their heavy equipment to facilitate retreat. Harried uninterruptedly from the air, dogged on their flanks by Israeli armor, and threatened with interdiction from their rear, many of the commanders panicked. Some abandoned prepared positions and set out for the Canal; others tried to counterattack, but without coordination with other units they were doomed to failure. Israeli control of the skies, besides enabling strafing and rocketing attacks to proceed unhindered, also assured the advancing IDF commanders of good intelligence while denying it to the Egyptians.

Most of the units that tried to retreat to the Canal fared poorly. Israeli tank brigades successively shot up and destroyed them. In almost every case, the speed of Israeli movement and poor communications between the Egyptian units and between the units and their headquarters—and their habit of transmitting to each other inaccurate or misleading information and rumors—left the Egyptians confused, surprised, and outflanked.

The June 7 order to stand fast at the entrances to the Jidi and Mitla Passes and at Bir Gafgafa to the north resulted in a series of abortive rearguard actions the following day that served to delay but not to prevent the inevitable. The Egyptians threw into the Sinai battles two and a half brigades that had spent the first days of the war beside the Canal. But they too were unable to withstand the aerial pounding that accompanied the Israeli tank thrusts. After the IAF knocked out his antiaircraft batteries, said one Egyptian general in his memoirs, his troops tried to fight off the fighter-bombers "with rifles and pistols."[83] Journalists visiting the battlefields after the war were astonished by the sight of the miles-long armored columns, blackened by fire or stuck in the sand, inside and at both ends of the Jidi and Mitla Passes.

By June 7 the IDF had taken the Gaza Strip, and a day later Israeli units were at the Canal. The Egyptian army had been defeated without offering real opposition. Most of its units, indeed, had had no chance to fight. Poorly commanded, moved confusedly back and forth, and battered from all sides and, most important, from above, they had never had a chance.[84]

JORDAN ENTERS THE WAR

Israel had hoped on the morning of June 5 to confine the war to Egypt; its military planning and strategy were geared to this prospect, including the initial commitment of the whole IAF to the southern front. But IDF planning also took into account the possible entry of Jordan and Syria into the war. In that event the IAF was to take out their air forces while, on the ground, the IDF was to remain on the defensive until the Egyptian army had been destroyed. Only subsequently, if circumstances permitted, was the army to shift to the offensive and invade Jordanian and/or Syrian territory as well.

But as things turned out, Israel found itself almost instantaneously engaged against Jordan and, at the same time, so successful against the Egyptians that it was able to switch to the offensive on the Jordanian front by the end of Day 1.

The groundswell of popular passions in the Arab world in a sense made Jordan's entry into the war inevitable; staying out, Hussein reasoned, would probably prove more hazardous than joining in, and could cost him his throne. The king's dramatic flight to Cairo and the hastily concluded defense pact of May 30 in effect set the seal on Jordan's prospective participation in the war.

Israel's leaders understood Hussein's predicament. But there were those among them who were eager to "exploit to the full" any rash actions by him.[85] After all, since 1949 Ben-Gurion had been calling Israel's failure to conquer East Jerusalem and, by extension, the whole of the West Bank "a lamentation for generations"—a phrase that was in continuous use among Herut and Ahdut Ha'Avoda politicians between 1949 and 1967. In an article published shortly before the outbreak of the war, Allon wrote: "In . . . a new war, we must avoid the historic mistake of the War of Independence [1948] . . . and must not cease fighting until we achieve total victory, the territorial fulfilment of the Land of Israel."[86]

Before the outbreak of war the IDF anticipated that Hussein would take the fatal plunge. In the final decision-making meeting, on the evening of June 4, Defense Minister Dayan had "strongly opposed" a proposal by Yadin, Prime

Minister Eshkol's adviser, that Israel warn Jordan to keep out. Eshkol's military aide-de-camp, Gen. Yisrael Lior, was later to reflect that Dayan, even before the first shot had been fired, was "pondering the possibility of opening up a second front, on the Israeli-Jordanian border, aimed at conquering the Old City."[87]

But the Israeli government *did* issue the warning—and Hussein ignored it. The IDF then thrust into the West Bank without a clear plan for conquering the territory[88] and occupied it piecemeal, responding, at least initially, to specific Arab initiatives and threats. One reason for this "defensive" outlook, clearly, was the IDF's relative weakness on the Jordanian front.

On the morning of June 5, the Arab Legion had the equivalent of six or seven infantry brigades, two armored brigades, and two independent tank battalions in the West Bank and East Jerusalem (with 255 tanks all told); another three infantry brigades were left in the East Bank. The Jordanian forces in the West Bank had 144 artillery pieces. They had been joined, two days before, by two Egyptian commando battalions, and on June 5 the Iraqi expeditionary force, consisting of four brigades, one of them armored and one mechanized, began moving into eastern Jordan. (Only one was ultimately engaged by the Israelis: It was bombed and strafed by the IAF as it reached the Jordan River crossings. The Saudis also sent elements of a brigade to Jordan's aid, though these, too, never crossed into the West Bank.)

Facing them that morning was a far smaller Israeli force, consisting of three and a half second-line or territorial infantry brigades, and an armored brigade, with an independent armored battalion: altogether 128 tanks, mostly aged Super-Shermans. The Israeli forces had 177 guns, most of them 120 mm mortars. By the end of Day 1 and the start of Day 2 (June 6), these forces had been joined by three more brigades. More than making up for this imbalance in ground forces, from about noon on June 5, the Israelis had the all-important advantage of complete mastery of the skies.

It was the Arab Legion that initiated the hostilities, on the morning of June 5. The Israeli Foreign Ministry had summoned UN Truce Supervision Organization chief General Bull to the ministry at 8:30 A.M.—less than an hour after the IAF had hit the Egyptian air force but before anyone had exchanged shots along the Israel-Jordan border. He was handed an urgent message for Hussein cautioning the king against entering the war and promising that no harm would befall Jordan if it stayed out. Bull quickly transmitted the message to Amman, but apparently it did not reach Hussein himself until 11:00. The king then rejected it, implying that his aircraft were already on their way to attack Israeli targets.

Jordanian snipers and machine-gunners in Jerusalem fired a few rounds at about 10:15, and sporadic light-weapons fire continued for an hour.[89] Then Legion headquarters issued a directive to open fire when ready, and at 11:45[90] the heavy mortars began pounding targets in West Jerusalem in organized fashion, while their artillery began to shell targets east of Tel Aviv and in the southern Jezreel Valley. Jordan's aggressiveness was apparently prompted by misinformation and deliberate deception. Hussein, it seems, had been persuaded by false Egyptian reports of early victories, Israeli air losses, and Egyptian air raids on Tel Aviv and IAF bases.[91]

The IDF returned fire, but at the same time Israel issued one last appeal to the Jordanians via the United Nations and the American Embassy—to cease fire or bear the consequences. The warnings were ignored.[92] At 13:30 hours Jordanian infantry occupied the strategic compound—in no-man's-land, between Israeli and Jordanian territory—of Government House, the high commissioner's office during British Mandate days and now UN headquarters in the Middle East, in southern Jerusalem. Israeli troops quickly assembled for a counterattack, which was mounted less than two hours later. By evening Government House and several Jordanian positions directly to the south had fallen, effectively cutting the road from East Jerusalem to Bethlehem and Hebron.

Soon after the Jordanians began shelling, Dayan had proposed taking two or three small areas of the West Bank for tactical defensive reasons. But by the evening of June 5 General Lior was aware that these proposals were not just a matter of safeguarding Israeli territory: The cabinet had begun to inch toward a decision fraught with major political significance—to "liberate Jerusalem."[93] Once the fate of the Egyptian army had become clear to the decision-makers, thoughts of offense began to supersede defense in Israeli thinking vis-à-vis the West Bank and East Jerusalem.

Much of a cabinet meeting that evening was devoted to the possibility of conquering the West Bank and East Jerusalem "without any advance preparation, without working papers, without knowing anything about political or military plans." Allon and Begin proposed, in response to the Jordanian shelling, that Israel conquer the Old City. Begin argued that "this is an historic moment of opportunity." Eshkol wavered,[94] and the cabinet remained deadlocked.

Later that night Dayan proposed a new attempt to open talks with Jordan. At the same time, assuming that the attempt would fail, he proposed that the IDF "conquer the Old City and perhaps also the [whole of] the West Bank."[95] Eshkol declined to decide. Dayan went ahead and gave orders to conquer the Jenin area and a path from West Jerusalem to the Israeli enclave on Mount Scopus, both described as precautionary measures. Columns of tanks, half-tracks, and trucks immediately crossed the border in the northern West Bank and advanced on Jenin.

By noon on June 6, the Tenth Armored Brigade had cut the Jerusalem-Ramallah road, and the hills just north of Jerusalem were in Israeli hands, with Mount Scopus only a few hundred yards away. In the meantime a paratroop brigade, the Fifty-fifth, had pushed directly into northeast Jerusalem, aiming to cut a corridor to Mount Scopus. This brigade's battles at Ammunition Hill and Sheikh Jarrah were among the most difficult and bloodiest of the war.

Another brigade was ordered to take the Latrun salient, dominated by the police fort that in 1948 had eluded capture despite three costly assaults, and crossed the border in the early hours. The Jordanians had left it only lightly defended, and it soon fell, with the Israeli force pressing on eastward and linking up in the afternoon with the brigade that had cut the Ramallah road. In the early evening the two brigades pushed into Ramallah without a fight.

During the afternoon of June 6, a ministerial meeting, chaired by Eshkol, decided on conquest of the Old City—without an explicit resolution. The ministers agreed to the encirclement of the city (which had already been half accomplished) and empowered Dayan to send troops in, but only if military circumstances necessitated it. They also empowered the IDF to go ahead and conquer the mountainous, heavily populated spine of the West Bank—meaning Hebron, Bethlehem, Ramallah, and Nablus.[96]

The director of the Mossad, General Amit, was one of the few individuals at this session who seemed to understand the momentousness of the questions that the conquest would raise even if the answers remained extremely unclear: "We must understand what we want in the West Bank. Are we interested in sitting in it? Do we want union? Are we interested in some other proposal?" Eshkol himself had commented the day before: "Even if we conquer the Old City and the West Bank, in the end we will have to leave them."[97] Few of the other attendees, civilian or military, appeared at this point overly perturbed by such problems.

A UN Security Council call for a cease-fire on the Jordanian front persuaded them, prodded by Dayan, that they had to act fast. At dawn on June 7 Dayan ordered the IDF to take the Old City. Paratroops broke through the Lion's Gate and were soon joined by an infantry battalion that pushed through the Dung Gate. Within minutes—encountering only light resistance from snipers—the troops fanned out through the narrow alleys, broke onto the Temple Mount, and took the Western Wall. The city's Jordanian governor, Anwar al-Khatib, quickly signed an instrument of surrender, and just after noon all resistance in the town came to an end.

The only tank battle in the Israeli-Jordanian confrontation developed in the Dotan Valley, south of Jenin, which had fallen to the IDF in the early hours of June 6. After a bitter, bloody battle, the Israelis got the upper hand, and the remnants of the battered Jordanian force retreated, leaving the way open for an advance on Nablus, the largest town in the West Bank. The units that reached the outskirts of the city on the morning of June 7 were greeted by the local inhabitants with enthusiastic cheering—they had been mistaken for Iraqi reinforcements.[98]

On June 7–8, Nablus, Bethlehem, Hebron, and Jericho fell to the IDF, with the Legion putting up resistance only in Nablus. The next morning Israeli sappers blew up the Abdullah and Hussein Bridges over the Jordan. Thus, symbolically and physically, the West Bank was severed from the East.

CONQUERING THE HEIGHTS

From the beginning of the crisis in mid-May, the head of IDF Northern Command, Gen. David ("Dado") Elazar, maintained that the war would inevitably spread to the Syrian front and that it would be necessary to capture the Golan Heights. Dayan wasn't convinced.[99] He argued that assaulting the heights might trigger Soviet intervention and prove prohibitively costly in Israeli lives. But after Egypt and Jordan had been taken care of, he changed his tune. The signal to proceed reached Elazar in the early hours of June 9.

The Golan Heights, stretching from Mount Hermon (9,000 feet) in the north to the Yarmuk River and the border with Jordan in the south, is a plateau 13–20 miles wide at the southwestern edge of Syria, traversed by a chain of volcanic hills (tels) and studded with basalt boulders and outcrops. The northern half of the heights rises gradually from the Jordan River basin, leveling off into a plateau a few miles west of Quneitra. In the south, the rise is steep and abrupt from the narrow plain surrounding the Sea of Galilee. The Syrian army had turned the western edge of the heights into fortified emplacements backed by artillery and antiaircraft batteries. The basalt- and concrete-clad fortifications were strung out in depth, so that they covered and overlooked one another to a depth of three miles from the border. Tanks were dug in at various points overlooking the escarpment.

Despite his declared objections to conquering the heights, it was Dayan who—without consulting his cabinet colleagues—on the morning of June 9 ordered the IDF to storm the slopes. Eshkol was shocked and angry, calling Dayan "contemptible"—both because he had bypassed the prime minister and cabinet and because, by personally issuing the order, he would be reaping all the postwar political rewards. Why Dayan changed his mind so abruptly is not completely clear. At first, he explained that he had received intelligence reports on June 8 that the Syrian defenses and army were crumbling and he felt that the IDF should exploit the situation. Later, he said that intelligence had picked up a message from Nasser saying the IDF would switch its focus to the Golan and advising Syria immediately to agree to a cease-fire: This forced Dayan to move, lest the long-awaited chance to strike a blow against Syria be lost.[100] Whether or why Dayan's assessment of possible Soviet intentions had become more sanguine is also not clear.

On June 5, before the destruction of their air force, Syrian aircraft had carried out small-scale, ineffective attacks against Israeli targets, and on June 6 IDF positions and settlements at the foot of the Golan had been intermittently shelled. But Israel's decision to attack had little to do with these jabs and everything to do with the harassment of the border settlements during the previous five years, and a desire for territorial expansion pressed by these self-same settlements, which coveted the lands on the Golan. These were chronic problems begging for a solution; the Six-Day War afforded the opportunity.

On the evening of June 6, Elazar requested permission to launch "Macbeth North," a plan to conquer the northern Golan Heights.[101] The request was turned down, perhaps partly because Elazar had too few units at his disposal; no one was interested in a failure. But as the battles in the south and central area were decided, the IDF dispatched units northward, taking advantage of Israel's short internal lines of communication.

Opposite the relatively meager Israeli lineup—about five brigades—fielded on the morning of June 9 were seven Syrian infantry brigades, most of them well dug in among the western escarpment's fortifications. But their positions had been pounded continuously during the previous days by artillery, and, more importantly, by fighter-bombers. Efforts to supply and reinforce the front-line positions had been repeatedly interdicted by roving Israeli aircraft. The troops knew that the Egyptian and Jordanian armies had been routed, that they were now alone. They were thoroughly demoralized and, with some exceptions, put up only brief, lackadaisical resistance or retreated posthaste.

The ground assault was preceded by two hours of aerial bombardment. Under heavy artillery fire, the Eighth Armored and Golani Infantry brigades advanced in a slow, grueling climb up the escarpment just south of Mount Hermon, and fought a succession of head-on skirmishes with dug-in Syrian tanks and antitank-gun positions. The Israeli tanks, mostly aged though up-gunned Super-Shermans, had difficulty advancing through the boulder-strewn landscape. The infantry, meanwhile, stormed a series of fortified positions.

The first day ended with elements of four IDF brigades having scaled either halfway up the escarpment or, in the north, all the way, and the Syrian army in disarray or in retreat. At first light on June 10, with the IDF under severe pressure due to the imminent UN cease-fire deadline, the units already on the escarpment, and several newly arrived brigades, dashed across the Golan to a natural defense line as far east as possible.

Most of the positions overrun that morning were deserted: The Syrian general staff had ordered the withdrawal of all its units, and many had begun to retreat even earlier, without orders. Damascus Radio prematurely announced the fall of Quneitra, the Golan's "capital," sowing panic among the retreating soldiers, who feared that they had been cut off by the Israeli columns. Quneitra did fall, but only about four hours later; Syria feared that the IDF would march on Damascus and issued the false announcement to pressure the Security Council to impose a cease-fire as quickly as possible.[102]

The advance halted on the afternoon of June 10, as the cease-fire came into effect, but the conquest of the Golan was completed only on June 12, when troops were helicoptered to the Hermon mountainside Druze village of Maj-dal Shams and to one of the mountain's peaks.

THE WAR AT SEA

The Six-Day War saw intense activity by both the Israeli and Egyptian navies. Both sides proved largely ineffectual, but Israel attained its strategic objective of keeping the far larger enemy fleets away from its own shores and restricting the naval warfare to the Arab coastlines. Israeli torpedo boats occupied Sharm ash-Sheikh's deserted harbor, having sailed past the unmanned Egyptian naval guns at Ras Nasrani.

In the Mediterranean, Israeli naval units engaged and turned back three Egyptian submarines approaching the Israeli coastline. But apart from the sinking of an Egyptian missile boat outside Port Said on June 6 by the destroyer *Yaffo,* Israel's own offensive efforts were also abortive. Naval commandos raided both Port Said and Alexandria harbors but failed to destroy any Egyptian combat vessels; the six frogmen at Alexandria were captured and severely tortured.[103]

On June 8, off Al-'Arīsh, Israeli torpedo boats and aircraft attacked and badly mauled the American spy ship *Liberty,* which they apparently mistook for an Egyptian vessel. Thirty-four American servicemen died and seventy-five were injured.[104]

CASUALTIES

Israel had anticipated heavy losses;[105] in fact they were relatively light. Arab casualties were far heavier. In the battle for Sinai, Israel lost 338 dead and some 1,400 wounded. Between 10,000 and 15,000 Egyptians were killed and some 5,000 taken prisoner.[106]

On the Jordanian front Israel suffered about 300 dead, 183 in the battle for Jerusalem. Around 800 Jordanians were killed and 636 taken prisoner. About 20 Iraqi soldiers were killed in IAF attacks. In the conquest of the Golan Heights, 141 Israelis died. The Syrians, according to Israeli estimates, lost some 500 dead and 2,500 wounded; another 578 were taken prisoner.[107]

In general, the war did not leave much physical destruction in its wake. It was very brief and the fighting in built-up areas was extremely limited. Israel took care to use its air power and artillery sparingly in populated areas. But in several locations Arab houses were deliberately destroyed after the fighting ended. A number of IDF commanders, apparently without cabinet authorization, though most probably with Dayan's approval, tried to repeat the experience of 1948—to drive Palestinians into exile and demolish their homes. Altogether, some 200–300,000 Arabs fled or were driven from the West Bank and the Gaza Strip, most of them going to the East Bank of the Jordan, during the war and in the weeks immediately after. Another eighty to ninety thousand civilians fled or were driven from the Golan Heights.

In the town of Qalqilya, in a number of villages in the southern West Bank border area, and, to a smaller degree, in Tulkarm, IDF troops systematically destroyed Arab homes. In addition, four villages in the Latrun salient—Imwas, Yalu, Beit Nuba, and Deir Aiyub—were leveled and their inhabitants sent into exile, with at least postfactum Cabinet agreement. Dayan later explained that Israel's international airport at Lydda had been shelled from the salient, so Israel could not allow the area to revert to Arab rule. There may also have been an element of revenge for the events of 1948.[108] (The destruction, it was understood, would also facilitate Israel's retention of the salient under any future peace settlement.) An element of revenge for 1948 certainly characterized the leveling of the village of An Nabi Samwil, north of Jerusalem.[109]

In Jerusalem the Israeli authorities swiftly exploited the shock of war and conquest to destroy the so-called Mughrabi Quarter, a cluster of houses inhabited by Muslims next to the Western Wall in the Old City, in an operation that began on June 10 and ended on October 14. The result was a large plaza that afforded a place for assembly in front of Judaism's holiest shrine.[110]

In three villages southwest of Jerusalem and at Qalqilya, houses were destroyed "not in battle, but as punishment . . . and in order to chase away the inhabitants . . . —contrary to government . . . policy," Dayan wrote in his memoirs. In Qalqilya, about a third of the homes were razed and about twelve thousand inhabitants were evicted, though many then camped out in the environs.[111] The evictees in both areas were allowed to stay and later were given cement and tools by the Israeli authorities to rebuild at least some of their dwellings.[112]

But many thousands of other Palestinians now took to the roads. Perhaps as many as seventy thousand, mostly from the Jericho area, fled during the fighting; tens of thousands more left over the following months. Altogether, about one-quarter of the population of the West Bank, about 200–250,000 people, went into exile.[113] Many of them were refugees from 1948 and their descendants who had lived in camps, mostly around Jericho. They simply walked to the Jordan River crossings and made their way on foot to the East Bank. It is unclear how many were intimidated or forced out by the Israeli troops and how many left voluntarily, in panic and fear. There is some evidence of IDF soldiers going around with loudspeakers ordering West Bankers to leave their homes and cross the Jordan.[114] Some left because they had relatives or sources of livelihood on the East Bank and feared being permanently cut off.

Thousands of Arabs were taken by bus from East Jerusalem to the Allenby Bridge, though there is no evidence of coercion. The free Israeli-organized transportation, which began on June 11, 1967, went on for about a month. At the bridge they had to sign a document stating that they were leaving of their own free will.[115] Perhaps as many as seventy thousand people emigrated from the Gaza Strip to Egypt and elsewhere in the Arab world.[116]

On July 2 the Israeli government announced that it would allow the return of those 1967 refugees who desired to do so, but no later than August 10, later extended to September 13. The Jordanian authorities probably pressured many of the refugees, who constituted an enormous burden, to sign up to return. In practice only 14,000 of the 120,000 who applied were actually allowed by Israel back into the West Bank by the beginning of September. After that, only a trickle of "special cases" were allowed back, perhaps 3,000 in all.[117]

THE AFTERMATH

ISRAEL'S NEW TERRITORIES — THE SETTLEMENT MOVEMENT

"We were like dreamers," said Prime Minister Eshkol's aide, General Lior, describing the mood among Israelis when the guns fell silent. A messianic, expansionist wind swept over the country. Religious folk spoke of a "miracle" and of "salvation"; the ancient lands of Israel had been restored to God's people. Secular individuals were also swept up—on June 8 an editorial in the liberal daily *HaAretz* stated: "The glory of past ages no longer is to be seen at a distance but is, from now on, part of the new state, and its illumination will irradiate the constructive enterprise of a Jewish society that is a link in the long chain of the history of the people in its country . . . Jerusalem is all ours. Rejoice and celebrate, O dweller in Zion!"

The war did wonders for the state's international standing, almost overnight converting it from a minuscule backwater into a focus of the world's attention. Israel was now seen by the West, and primarily Washington, as a regional superpower and a desirable ally among a bevy of fickle, weak Arab states. The May crisis and the war also generated a surge of unity and self-confidence among the world's Jews; it even gave rise to a modest wave of immigration to Israel from western Jewish communities.

But the most important consequences were in the Middle East itself. The cease-fire found the IDF deployed on the Suez Canal, on the Jordan River, and on the Golan, along the "line of the tels," roughly sixteen miles east of the old frontier. All of Sinai (61,000 square kilometers), the Gaza Strip (363 square kilometers), the West Bank, including East Jerusalem (5,700), and the Golan Heights (1,200), were in Israeli hands. The IDF had conquered an area three-and-a-half times larger than Israel itself, as well as more than one million Palestinians living in the West Bank and Gaza.

In six days the geopolitical balance of the region had been radically subverted—or, rather, as the war itself had demonstrated, the existing military imbalance had been aggravated. Three sovereign states had been thoroughly humiliated,[118] and now the Israeli government hoped to convert the stunning military victory into political achievement: The conquered territories could be traded for peace. Dayan was quoted as saying that he was "waiting for a telephone call from King Hussein"—presumably to discuss such a tradeoff. The cabinet on June 19 resolved that the former international boundaries between Israel and Egypt and between Israel and Syria would be the basis for permanent borders—Israel would withdraw to them and give up Sinai and the Golan in exchange for peace. This decision was never made public. It was transmitted to the United States government to pass on to Egypt and Syria.[119] Within days both countries had rejected the overture.[120]

The resolution did not mention the Gaza Strip, implying that Israel would keep it, and postponed a decision concerning the West Bank, about which the ministers disagreed. There was a consensus not to return to the prewar borders—which Foreign Minister Abba Eban, nothing if not a dove, was to immortalize as the "Auschwitz" lines.[121] Some ministers, including Begin and those of the National Religious Party (NRP), wanted the West Bank and Gaza annexed as historic parts of the "Land of Israel"; others were willing to trade all or almost all of these territories for peace. Dayan sat on the fence, at times enigmatically hinting at a preference for annexation, at other times suggesting that it would be disastrous.

The majority eventually coalesced around the plan proposed by Yigal Allon at the end of July 1967: to divide the West Bank between Israel and Jordan—a "territorial compromise," as Labor Party platforms were to call it.[122] Israel would retain a six–seven-mile-deep strip along the west bank of the Jordan as a "security belt," while the rest of the territory, save for some narrow border strips (such as the Latrun salient), would revert to Jordan. The so-called "Allon Plan," submitted to the cabinet on July 26,[123] was never formally adopted as government (or even Labor Party) policy; but it was to remain the unwritten platform of Israel's Labor-led governments down to 1977, and of Labor in opposition thereafter.

Within months, partly because of renewed Arab belligerency, Israel's positions hardened. The cabinet secretly decided in October to qualify the June 19 decision. It resolved not to return to the prewar frontiers, to base future boundaries on Israel's "security" needs, and not to withdraw from the Gaza Strip, Sharm ash-Sheikh, or a strip of coast linking Eilat and Sharm.[124]

Nevertheless, the war had opened the way for a possible solution: The Israelis at last had something they could give the Arabs in exchange for peace, and the Arabs gradually would come round. But the war also unleashed currents within Israeli society that militated against yielding occupied territory and against compromise. Expansionism, fueled by fundamentalist messianism and primal nationalistic greed, took hold of a growing minority, both religious and secular, getting its cue, and eventually creeping support, from the government itself.

"There is nothing so dreadful as a great victory, except of course a great defeat," historian Walter Laqueur has written.[125] Jewish settlement in the West Bank began, in effect, in Jerusalem and its environs during the first days after the guns fell silent. On June 14, Allon proposed to the cabinet that Israel immediately begin to reconstruct and settle the Jewish Quarter of the Old City, and to surround Arab East Jerusalem with a ring of new Jewish neighborhoods. The aim was to turn all of Jerusalem into an inalienable part of Israel. "If we don't [start doing] it in a day or two, we never will," he said.

The Jewish Quarter was actually inhabited by Arab families who had moved in after the Jews were expelled in 1948. Allon proposed that the Arabs be evicted; he was backed by Dayan, the cabinet approved, and about three hundred families were removed.[126] The eviction, Lior was to write, "passed without violence and in a pleasant enough atmosphere." What he meant was that the shock of the war and the fear of the Jews were such that the inhabitants were submissive and frightened and readily packed up and left when ordered out.[127]

On June 25–27, East Jerusalem and West Bank areas immediately to its north and south were officially annexed and declared part of Jerusalem's expanded municipal area.[128] Within days the physical unification of the city was completed with the destruction of concrete walls—mostly built between 1949 and 1967 as protection from sniper fire—along the no-man's-land that had divided the city. Ben-Gurion, then a Rafi Knesset member, called for the removal of the Old City's sixteenth-century walls as well, so that the city "would not again be divided"—but his proposal was, fortunately, rejected by the government.[129] (It was, however, indicative of the mind-set of most of the new conquerors, who were almost obsessively interested in archaeological relics that related to the Jewish past—and were relatively indifferent to the antiquities of non-Jews.)

The precedents set in Jerusalem by the government were soon to be followed and borne along by a tide of nationalist fervor throughout the West Bank. An early development was the establishment, in September, of the Land of Israel Movement, whose founding manifesto (published in *HaAretz* on September 22) advocated the retention of the borders reached by the IDF on June 10. The seventy-two prominent signatories included both traditional territorial maximalists from the Right and some Labor Party stalwarts.

But this largely secular group was almost immediately overshadowed by religious nationalists who declared that the "miraculous" conquests were *at'halta dege'ula*, the start of divine redemption, and that the settlement and annexation of the conquered territories were a divine command, in accordance with the teachings of the historic sage of their movement, Rabbi Avraham

Yitzhak Hacohen Kook (Ashkenazic chief rabbi of Palestine during the 1920s), as interpreted by his son, Rabbi Zvi Yehuda Hacohen Kook. Rabbi Zvi's Jerusalem yeshiva, Mercaz HaRav, became the focal point of the new messianic politics and spawned most of its cadres. Until 1967 the NRP had been a rather placid, bourgeois, pragmatic, and obedient partner of the Labor Party. The Six-Day War sent it, with its Bnei Akiva youth movement and yeshivot, identified by their colored knitted skullcap (the ultra-Orthodox wore black skullcaps and hats), into paroxysms of jingoism. On May 14 Zvi Kook had delivered a sermon bewailing the partition of Palestine and declaring the situation intolerable. And on June 7, minutes after the conquest of the Old City, some of his protégés rushed the elderly rabbi in a jeep to the Western Wall, where he solemnly announced: "We hereby inform the people of Israel and the entire world that under heavenly command we have just returned home. . . . We shall never move out."[130]

The NRP's rabbis, with Kook in the lead, hailed the IDF conquests as the first peal of the Deliverance, and the party's youngsters, grafting religion onto history, made ready to usurp from Labor and its kibbutzim and youth movements the position of torchbearers of Zionism. They were the new pioneers, and the occupied lands would be their frontier. The admixture of messianism and nationalism proved heady and powerful. Casting caution and pragmatism to the wind, God's skullcapped legions and their vigorous, bearded rabbis forayed into the hills and dales of Judea and Samaria to choose sites for settlements. They skirted government policies and army roadblocks to map out the new "Greater Israel." At site after site they coerced the government into giving way to their pioneering zeal and acceding to the establishment of a chain of settlements that would define and secure the new territories. In March 1974 these cadres and this spirit were formally consolidated in an extraparliamentary movement, Gush Emunim (Bloc of the Faithful), loosely affiliated with the NRP. Its leaders would set the tone and content of right-wing activism with regard to the territories and push the Labor movement, that historical agent of Zionist expansionism and pioneering, onto the perennial defensive.[131] The goal was massive, irreversible settlement leading, inevitably, to annexation.

Both opponents and promoters of this project immediately understood what was happening: Settlement spelled a will to permanent retention. And, as many Israeli, Arab, and American politicians were to note during the 1980s and 1990s, the settlements were a major obstacle to peace.

Jewish settlement proceeded, both geographically and conceptually, from politically "easy" areas, those that had once been inhabited by Jews, like the Etzion Bloc, or were relatively uninhabited, to the more problematic areas with dense Arab populations. The process unfolded gradually and seemed to advance almost as a matter of course, without any overall plan. Looking back, some ministers were amazed by how it had taken them almost unawares, without a cabinet decision to annex any territory, except Jerusalem, until the Golan Law of 1981 (effectively annexing the heights).

By one year after the Six-Day War there were six Israeli settlements on the Golan. In June 1967 the IDF—again without cabinet authorization—had begun to raze empty villages, and that autumn the Defense Ministry decided systematically to destroy those remaining.[132] In early July the cabinet approved the establishment of "two or three" temporary "work camps" inside the former DMZs of which Syria had gained control in the 1950s but that were not officially Syrian territory.[133] On July 19 the first settlement group moved into a wood next to the abandoned village of 'Aleika; the IDF provided guards and equipment. On August 27, the cabinet approved Israeli cultivation of fields on the heights. Within weeks Dayan, Allon, and Agriculture Minister Haim Gvati—without full cabinet discussion or approval—decided on the establishment of a chain of Nahal outposts, or settlements inhabited by soldiers, which usually became civilian and permanent after a while, with the first one, Nahal Snir, going up in September near Banias.[134]

Decision-making regarding settlement in the West Bank was even more ad hoc. Individual ministers raised specific proposals, and the cabinet or its settlement committee approved or rejected them (often after the fact). In September 1967 Eshkol informed the cabinet that a settlement was being established in the Etzion Bloc, between Bethlehem and Hebron, roughly where Kfar Etzion had stood in 1948 before its destruction by the Arab Legion, intimating that he had given permission. The resettlement of the bloc was propelled by NRP lobbying, and on September 30 the committee approved the establishment of a regional-rural center there.[135]

In January 1968 the cabinet formally approved the establishment of two Nahal outposts in the Jordan Rift (the southern Jordan Valley).[136] During the following years others sprang up in various parts of the Golan, the Gaza Strip, and the rift. They were established both for security reasons—they "covered" the border, dominated strategic crossroads, and so on—and as part of the settlement drive. Almost all were in areas without large Arab concentrations.

But the movement that eventually became Gush Emunim built on these hesitant beginnings and, in a sense, acted in parallel to them, aiming primarily at the Arab-populated hill country of the West Bank and the Gaza Strip. Where they could, the activists merely lobbied and pressed the government to set up settlements. Where they met reluctance or hesitation, they took matters into their own hands, in the belief that the government would not oppose them and that many ministers were "closet" supporters.

Often, at least initially, the settlers encountered an ambivalent government. Some dovish ministers, such as Finance Minister Pinchas Sapir, consistently opposed new settlement ventures; others, such as Herut's Begin, gave enthusiastic support. Allon and Dayan remained equivocal throughout, the latter often evincing a readiness to trade land for peace, even as regards the West

Bank, but at other times radiating an unwillingness to part with any of the biblical Land of Israel. On June 8, hard on the IDF conquest of Bethlehem and Hebron, Dayan told a colleague that "Jerusalem and the Hebron Hills will remain in our hands forever."[137] Many of the ministers proved not unwilling victims of the settlement movement's pressure. Veteran Ahdut Ha'Avodah politicians, such as Allon and Galili, wedded from youth to the concept of "the whole Land of Israel," quietly sympathized with the lawbreaking settlers' aims. Indeed, to a degree they came to accept their self-image as heirs of the early pioneers, who had added dunam after dunam to the Zionist domain. Support for or opposition to new ventures soon became a function of internal political rivalries within the Labor Party, especially between Dayan and Allon.

The movement's first organized effort was prefigured by Allon's proposal in the cabinet on January 14, 1968, "to encourage the establishment of a Jewish neighborhood next to Hebron."[138] In April a group of activists led by Rabbi Moshe Levinger checked into the Nahar al-Khalid Hotel, later renamed the Park Hotel, on the outskirts of Hebron, to hold a traditional Passover seder. They had obtained permission for a one-night stay, promising the head of Central Command, Gen. Uzi Narkiss, to return to Israel the following day. Instead, they hoisted an Israeli flag over the hotel and announced their intention to remain.

Levinger's initiative benefited from two incidental factors that hobbled the military government in those crucial days: Dayan was in the hospital after nearly being buried alive on an archaeological dig; and Col. Shlomo Gazit, coordinator of activities in the territories, was at home mourning the death of his father.[139]

The Hebron incident set two precedents. The settlers and their first patron in the defense establishment, Lt. Col. Yehoshua Varbin (who in 1950 had engineered the transfer to Gaza of Ashkelon's Arab community and until 1966 headed the IDF's Military Government Department), had deliberately deceived Narkiss. This pattern was to recur during the following decade as the movement with impunity hoodwinked and circumvented the authorities. Then, the government did not eject the settlers immediately, a failure that stemmed in large measure from the presence in the coalition of NRP and Herut ministers, and the key Labor-linked ministers, Dayan and Allon. (In the specific case of Hebron, Dayan sat on the fence, and Allon firmly supported the settlers.) Moreover, there was a reluctance to authorize the use of force to dislodge Jews—and the settlers made it clear that only force could curb their activities.

The compromise eventually reached in Hebron—to allow the settlers to move into the town's police fort—was to typify the future give-and-take between the government and the settler movement.[140] Within months this toehold was translated into government agreement to the establishment of a large

Jewish neighborhood on the outskirts of Hebron, the present-day Kiryat Arba, and several years later—after further squatting demonstrations—into Jewish settlement in the very heart of the Arab town, in buildings owned by Jews before the 1929 massacre and then in new buildings.

Almost invariably, the government provided settlers—whether state-organized or illegal—with the wherewithal to carry through with their ventures. This support was often crucial in the early days. Troops protected them from attack by Palestinians; water was trucked or piped in; electricity generators were supplied. But even more telling was the government's land policy. A few scattered tracts purchased by Jews before 1948 were immediately available for settlement. But much of the land in the territories was state owned, and Israel immediately expropriated it all—in the West Bank more than 50 percent of the land surface. Once this happened the indigenous population of the West Bank and Gaza Strip lost most of its potential for natural growth and physical expansion.

In addition the authorities and the settler associations began to purchase land from local landowners and arbitrarily to lay hold of uncultivated tracts, including many bordering on Arab villages and claimed by Arabs. Frequently Arab-owned lands were expropriated on ostensible security grounds but were earmarked for settlement. Efforts by Israeli peace activists to block such expropriations through petitions to the High Court of Justice almost always failed.

Within two to three years a gigantic settlement venture was afoot. One early stratagem was the establishment of Nahal outposts. The soldier-settlers would do sentry duty, mount patrols, and in some sites, farm land. Within a few years many of these ostensible military camps, especially in the West Bank, became full-fledged civilian settlements. Quite separately hundreds, and then thousands, of Jews, driven by ideological motives ("Greater Israel") and economic incentives (free or cheap land, big mortgages at low interest, outright grants), began to move to the territories. By the late 1970s areas where there had been no Jews became, physically and demographically, Jewish. By the end of 1973 Israel had established seventeen settlements in the West Bank (most of them in the Jordan Valley), and by May 1977, when the right-wing nationalist Likud Party (formerly Herut) came to power under Menachem Begin, there were thirty-six. By 1973 seven settlements had been established in the Gaza Strip and in the northwestern corner of the Sinai Peninsula (the Rafa approaches); by 1977, sixteen. In Sinai proper, by 1973, there were three settlements; by 1977, seven. In the Golan, by 1973, there were nineteen settlements; by 1977, twenty-seven. By 1977, about eleven thousand Israelis were living in the territories.

The settlement enterprise was revolutionized following the Likud victory in the 1977 Knesset elections. Vast sums of money went into settling the territories, and by the mid-1990s the number of settlements in the West Bank alone surpassed a hundred, with the Jewish population of the territories, including Jerusalem's satellite neighborhoods, passing the 150,000 mark.

THE PALESTINIANS COME UNDER ISRAELI CONTROL

Israel's conquest of the West Bank and Gaza Strip reawakened the Palestinian issue, largely dormant since 1949. In the main the Palestinians had endured the first two decades of exile quietly, "living and partly living" in the Arab states on handouts from UNRWA and waiting for eventual deliverance at the hands of the Arab armies.

Before June 1967 about half the Palestinians, close to 1.5 million, lived in Jordan, where they received citizenship and were gradually integrated into the sociopolitical fabric. Fewer than half lived in the East Bank, the rest—perhaps 800,000—in the West Bank. Of the total, 600,000 to 700,000 were refugees or children of refugees, of whom 40 percent lived in camps. Another 350,000 to 400,000 Palestinians lived in the Gaza Strip, three-quarters of them refugees. Another 300,000 lived in Lebanon and Syria, mostly in camps.

The Six-Day War made Israel the country with the largest Palestinian population: In round figures, 400,000 lived within its pre-1967 borders (the Israeli Arab minority), and 1.1 million in the now-occupied territories—600,000 in the West Bank (200,000 or more, mostly denizens of refugee camps, had fled during the war and its immediate aftermath to the East Bank), 70,000 in East Jerusalem, and 350,000 in the Gaza Strip. Of the West Bank population, only 60,000 now lived in camps; in the Gaza Strip, some 210,000 had refugee status, 170,000 of them in camps.

The traumatic demolition of the status quo reawakened Palestinian identity and quickened nationalist aspirations in the conquered territories and in the Arab states. The hated enemy, who had driven the Palestinians from their homes in 1948, was now in control of their lives, lands, and property. The impotence and dependence of Palestinian existence was again starkly apparent. "I myself was crying," recalled Khalil al-Wazir (Abu Jihad), one of Yasser Arafat's lieutenants in Fatah, the main resistance group. "Some were talking about giving up the struggle and making new lives outside the Arab world."[141] Those who in May 1967 had enthusiastically hailed Nasser's brinkmanship, expecting victory and a return to the lost lands of 1948, now saw their world shattered.

Before the conquered Palestinians managed to catch their breath, Israel had imposed military government and set up the usual repressive infrastructure of occupation and control. Planning in the IDF general staff for the eventuality of conquest of the West Bank had begun in 1963, when a crisis shook the

Hashemite kingdom and the possibility of war had loomed. A skeleton staff was formed, with General Herzog, former director of military intelligence, designated as governor. In midwar, on the evening of June 7, he and a number of aides moved into the Ambassador Hotel in East Jerusalem and set up shop.

The task of determining the nature of the regime that developed in the occupied territories in the weeks and months ahead was immediately taken up by Defense Minister Dayan, initially without cabinet approval. The cabinet preferred not to get involved and Dayan emerged as the architect and then the arbiter of policy in the territories. Some of his decisions resulted in the faits accomplis that were severely to curtail future governments' options on the ultimate fate of the territories. Because of internal political constraints and external circumstances, successive Labor-led governments proved unable to decide what to do with the territories. In the absence of a strategy Dayan had to rule on each issue without knowing whether the territories would be annexed or given up, or how long the temporary military government was to go on. For daily management, he established an interdepartmental "coordinating committee," chaired by a coordinator of activities in the Administered Territories. The first incumbent was Colonel Gazit, of IDF intelligence.

Dayan set several (in part contradictory) principles to guide IDF behavior. A spirit of pragmatism informed them, reflecting that side of his nature. One principle was noninterference: to allow the inhabitants to run their own lives as freely as possible, and to ensure normalcy, including contacts with the Arab world. Economic and familial dislocation was to be kept to a minimum. From August 1967 Dayan instituted the "Open Bridges" policy, by which the West Bank could continue to trade and maintain other economic ties with the East Bank. After being taken to a ford near the ruins of the Allenby Bridge and watching West Bank trucks, loaded with agricultural produce, making their way through the shallow water to the East Bank, he proposed that Israel or Jordan rebuild the bridge and maintain free, orderly movement in both directions. The decision was taken on the spur of the moment, without any planning or staff work.

West Bank and East Jerusalem schools were to retain Jordan's curriculums, and the Gaza Strip Egypt's. But the Arabic textbooks were scoured, and anti-Israeli and anti-Semitic statements and cartoons were excised.

Jerusalem's holy sites were to be governed by the pre-1967 arrangements, but with free access for all. Immediately on entering the Temple Mount compound (Haram ash-Sharif) on June 7, Dayan had ordered the paratroops to take down a hastily hoisted Israeli flag flying over the Dome of the Rock. Administration of and security in the site were left essentially in the hands of the Wakf, the Muslim religious trust, though the IDF was given control of one gate, to oversee Jewish civilian and tourist traffic into the compound. At the Tomb of the Patriarchs (the Ibrahimiyya Mosque) in Hebron, Dayan worked out a compromise enabling both Muslim and Jewish worship. (Between 1948 and 1967, Jordan had completely prevented Jews from reaching the Temple Mount, Western Wall, and Tomb of the Patriarchs.)

Early in the summer of 1967 Dayan rejected the idea of autonomy—proposed by West Bank notables—for the inhabitants of the territories, fearing it would evolve into Palestinian statehood. He, like the rest of the Labor Party leadership, firmly opposed such statehood, deeming it a mortal threat to Israel's existence.

Side by side with his pragmatic strain—and despite his desire not to add more than a million Arabs to Israel's citizenry—Dayan was also an annexationist. He was a prime mover in the annexation of Arab East Jerusalem and its "unification" on June 27 with West Jerusalem. For deeply felt reasons, both historical and strategic, he believed Israel should retain control of the West Bank. He consistently advocated the integration into Israel of the economies and infrastructures of the territories—a policy that gradually turned them into appendages of Israel. (Critics were later to refer to this policy as "creeping annexation.") The West Bank and Gaza economies were rapidly fused with Israel's in a binding, colonial relationship: Tens of thousands of Palestinians, rising to somewhere between 100,000 and 150,000 (or 40 percent of the workforce of the two territories) by the mid-1980s, provided cheap labor—ironically, many of them, construction workers, actually built the new settlements.

Alongside "creeping annexation" Dayan from the start instituted a policy of creeping transfer. In the course of the war he and the IDF to some extent pushed along the process by which 200,000 to 300,000 of the inhabitants of the Palestinian territories, most of them refugee families from 1948, fled to Transjordan. On June 7, 1967, when informed that the inhabitants of Tulkarm were fleeing eastward, "the minister reacted positively. The roads [eastward] must be left open, he said, and the advance of the 45th Brigade slowed down . . . in this way, he thought, the population of the West Bank would be reduced and Israel freed of severe problems."[142]

In the war's immediate wake and during the years that followed, the defense minister and his military government staff made serious efforts to bring about the emigration of as many of the territories' remaining inhabitants as possible. The government always denied that there was such a policy or that such efforts were being made. But evidence has recently surfaced that points in the opposite direction. In September 1967 Dayan told a meeting of the IDF's senior staff that some 200,000 Arabs had left the Palestinian territories and "we must understand the motives and causes for the continued emigration of the Arabs, from both the Gaza Strip and the West Bank, and not undermine these causes, even if they are lack of security and lack of employment, because after all, we want to create a new map."[143] In November he was quoted as saying: "We want emigration, we want a normal standard of living, we want to encourage emigration according to a selective program."[144] On

July 14, 1968, at a meeting in his office, he said: "The proposed policy [of raising the level of public services in the territories] may clash with our intention to encourage emigration from both the Strip and Judea and Samaria. Anyone who has practical ideas or proposals to encourage emigration—let him speak up. No idea or proposal is to be dismissed out of hand."[145]

Dayan's mode of thinking was shared by his subordinates. A meeting of IDF governors in the West Bank on November 22, 1967, concluded with a decision "to seek ways to increase Arab emigration from the West Bank . . . we must not go out of our way to meet every request they send our way."[146] General Narkiss, on a visit to Bethlehem, is quoted as saying: "We are talking about emigration of the Arabs. Everything must be done—even paying them money—to get them to leave."[147]

Israeli thinking was to some degree governed by the notion that the Arabs of the territories, starved of land and resources (primarily water), and denied the possibility of industrial development, would gradually drift away. Though never clearly enunciated, this was the government's aim—especially after 1977. And, indeed, over the decades a steady trickle of West Bank and Gaza Arabs left their homes to find an easier life abroad. Economists estimate that twenty thousand more Palestinians left the territories each year on average than entered—many of them moving to the rich Gulf States, from which they sent remittances that became a major pillar of the West Bank–Gaza economy.[148]

Various economic measures were adopted to make life difficult for the local population. These measures also had another purpose. Dayan and the military government consistently frustrated industrial development in the territories so that they would not compete with Israel's own industries. Protectionist policy gradually turned the territories into major buyers of, or dumping grounds for, Israeli goods. By the 1980s they had become Israel's second largest export market (after the United States). In agriculture Israeli experts advised the locals on ways to increase their productivity, but the military government also took care to prevent farmers from competing with Israel on home or foreign markets. The territories' utility grids—electricity, telephones, transportation, and water—were all linked up to Israel's. Dayan overcame Labor Party doves, such as Sapir, who argued that such integration would inevitably result in annexation.

In theory Dayan favored allowing Palestinians complete freedom of political expression, drawing the line only at anti-Israel activity. But in practice political freedoms were severely curtailed, all parties and associations being regarded as potential cores of resistance to the occupation.[149] Strict censorship of news publications, journals, and books was imposed, prohibiting all material deemed seditious. Most were anti-Israeli or pro-Palestinian works in Arabic. But occasionally the censors indulged in absurd excesses, for example banning Shakespeare's *Merchant of Venice* as anti-Semitic, and Yigal Allon's works on the creation of the IDF. Hundreds of works available in Israel (and in Arab East Jerusalem) were banned in the territories.

After the conquest of the West Bank many of the notables and middle class hoped for a quick return of Jordanian rule. During the 1950s and 1960s they had established strong links with the monarchy and its bureaucracies; indeed, they were Jordanian citizens. In some measure they had repressed their Palestinian identity and regarded the alternative to Jordanian rule, a small Palestinian state, as "artificial" and "economically hopeless."[150] But the Israelis stifled all efforts toward a return of Jordanian control, threatening and occasionally carrying out arrests and deportations. In the routine fashion of conquerors, they also practiced "divide and rule," setting nationalists and republicans against pro-Hashemites.

In late 1967 several senior officials, including, apparently, Prime Minister Eshkol, contemplated an Israeli-dominated autonomous entity in the West Bank. There was strong opposition to the idea within the bureaucracies, especially in the army, where the fear was that autonomy, however controlled, would evolve into statehood. Threats and acts of violence by Palestinian nationalists against fellow Arabs assured the idea's demise.[151] It was with some such "third alternative" in mind that Israeli governments in the mid-1970s set up and bankrolled the "Village Leagues," associations of West Bank rural families who tacitly accepted Israeli rule, occasionally made pro-Jordanian noises, and struggled against the nationalists. But league members were dismissed as traitors and "collaborators" by most Palestinians, and, by the early 1980s, after several leading figures were attacked by terrorists, the leagues faded away.

The overwhelming majority of West Bank and Gaza Arabs from the first hated the occupation. The first signs of resistance were manifested about a month after the war, in early July 1967, when Israel's annexation of East Jerusalem sparked a number of small demonstrations and graffiti. At the end of the month, twenty Arab notables, led by Anwar al-Khatib, the former Jordanian governor of Jerusalem, sent a petition to the authorities protesting against the annexation. The authorities struck back by temporarily exiling four of the signatories. In August and September, there were larger demonstrations and transport and commercial strikes. Stone-throwing protesters and baton-wielding Israeli troops clashed.

The initial wave of West Bank protests, which were relatively widespread though far from universal, culminated in a call for a general strike on September 19. Though it failed, the Israelis retaliated firmly. On September 25, they dispatched 'Abd al-Hamid a Seih, the chief Muslim religious judge in the West Bank and one of the strike's organizers, into open-ended exile. In Nablus, the only West Bank town that had universally heeded the strike call, the Israelis cracked down with a series of collective punitive measures. These included an indefinite nightlong (5 P.M. to 7 A.M.) curfew, severely hurting those employed outside of town. Also, public transport was shut down; twenty shops that had closed during the strike were arbitrarily sealed shut; the town's telephone system was closed down; a daytime curfew was imposed on a number of neighborhoods with the ostensible aim of facilitating searches (though the real aim, it was later admitted, was "intimidation"[152]); the business licenses of some wholesalers were revoked; and the town's main outlet to Jordan, the Damiyeh (Adam) Bridge, was closed. Within days the resistance collapsed.

There was a clear lesson for the inhabitants of the territories and the Palestinian diaspora in these events: Israel intended to stay in the West Bank, and its rule would not be overthrown or ended through civil disobedience and civil resistance, which were easily crushed. The only real option was armed struggle.

Israelis liked to believe, and tell the world, that they were running an "enlightened" or "benign" occupation, qualitatively different from other military occupations the world had seen. The truth was radically different. Like all occupations, Israel's was founded on brute force, repression and fear, collaboration and treachery, beatings and torture chambers, and daily intimidation, humiliation, and manipulation. True, the relative lack of resistance and civil disobedience over the years enabled the Israelis to maintain a facade of normalcy and implement their rule with a relatively small force, consisting of a handful of IDF battalions, a few dozen police officers (rank-and-file policemen were recruited from among the Palestinians), and a hundred or so General Security Service (GSS) case officers and investigators.

But the "active" occupying units enjoyed the passive backup of much larger forces permanently stationed in the area after June 1967, when many IDF bases were transferred to the West Bank and their troops were on tap for occupation duties (such as the imposition of a curfew or a search operation). Moreover, the proximity to the territories of the many IDF, border police, and GSS bases in Israel proper meant that the occupation forces could draw on a large pool of support units from across the "Green Line," as the border between the territories and Israel proper came to be called.

Military administration, uncurbed by the civil rights considerations that applied in Israel, possessed ample measures to suppress dissidence and protest. These included curfews; house arrest, with resulting loss of wages; judicial proceedings, ending in prison terms or fines—the work of the military courts in the territories, and the Supreme Court which backed them, will surely go down as a dark age in the annals of Israel's judicial system—or expulsions; administrative detentions, or imprisonment without trial, for renewable six-month terms; and commercial and school shutdowns, usually in response to shopkeepers' strikes or disturbances by students. The Israelis could withhold or, alternatively, grant to collaborators, travel permits, commercial or building licenses, family reunion approvals, and marketing and work permits. Such measures were often used selectively and, occasionally, collectively. Sometimes whole towns were denied the right to receive visitors from the Arab states, such as Ramallah in the summer of 1968.[153]

By the end of 1969, Israel had sent into indefinite exile seventy-one West Bankers and Gazans, mostly notables who had had a hand in organizing strikes and demonstrations. A few of the deportees were teachers or parents of schoolchildren who had demonstrated. In one case, that of banker and Jordanian senator Anton 'Atallah, of Jerusalem, the deportation order was issued because, while in Jordan trying to organize the reopening of an Arab bank in the West Bank, he had been compelled by the authorities to swear allegiance to the Hashemite crown.[154]

With the crushing of civil dissent and disobedience in September 1967, opponents of Israeli rule began to turn to armed resistance—grenades were thrown at patrols, bombs planted in the cities. The resistance met with quick and brutal repression. Midnight sweeps and arrests; beatings, sensory deprivation measures, and simple, old-style torture to extract information and confessions; a system of military courts which bore no resemblance to the administration of justice in Western democracies (or, for that matter, in Israel proper); the demolition (or sealing) of suspects' houses; long periods of administrative detention; and deportations—all were systematically employed. Most of the measures had been introduced by the British during their suppression of the Arab rebellion of 1936–39 and were still on the statute books in the form of "emergency regulations."

When demolishing buildings where suspected terrorists lived or had hidden, the authorities rarely waited for anyone to be convicted before acting. For example, on October 21 and 25, 1969, IDF sappers blew up 18 houses in the town of Halhul, after an officer was killed there by Palestinian gunmen.[155] There are no complete figures, but according to the Palestinian civil rights organization al-Haq, 1,265 houses were destroyed or sealed during 1967–81, 72 during 1981–84, and 143 during 1985–87. According to Be'tselem, the Israeli human rights organization, the IDF destroyed 434 houses and sealed 314 between December 1987 and December 1993, when punitive demolition virtually stopped.

Civil and military controls—identity cards, travel and movement permits, IDF and border police body searches and roadblocks—sufficed to keep most of the population in check. Behind these visible forces of occupation stood the apparatus of the GSS. Before 1967 it had been a very small, secret agency of two to three hundred officers. Immediately following the war it doubled and then tripled in size, and a net of case officers and informants, recruited by money, intimidation, or manipulation, was thrown over the territories. The GSS efficiently insinuated itself into all areas of Palestinian life, penetrating every town and village and almost every clan. It effectively exploited clan, village, generational, and religious rivalries and made extensive use of underworld figures and lowlifes, thieves, pimps, drug dealers, addicts, and prostitutes.

The Palestinians turned out to be relatively easy to manipulate, intimidate, or buy off (reinforcing the Israeli security agency's considerable contempt for the occupied population). With very little effort or expenditure, the GSS managed to corrupt large sectors of Palestinian society and to create an atmosphere of animosity, suspicion, and fear. Inevitably, the corrupting effects of the occupation soon affected the conquerors as well as the occupied. Behavior by IDF and security personnel that had been inconceivable before June 1967 became the norm. GSS officers who engaged in torture systematically lied in court about how confessions were extracted; and GSS executives lied, both in court and to their political bosses, to cover up for their subordinates. Bribe-taking by Israeli officials—who gave out the travel, building, and business permits—also became rife.

Intellectuals such as theologian and scientist Yishayahu Leibowitz and writers Amos Oz and Yizhar Smilansky (S. Yizhar), who warned of the corrupting effects of occupation, were belittled. Golda Meir, the ever-self-righteous prime minister, told a Mapai Party meeting: "I am shocked. All of me rebels against Oz, Smilansky and professors and intellectuals who have introduced the moral issue. For me the supreme morality is that the Jewish people has a right to exist. Without that there is no morality in the world."[156]

The war and its aftermath of occupation, repression, and expansionism swiftly reignited the tinder of Palestinian nationalism, propelling thousands of young men, especially from among the dispossessed and hopeless of the refugee camps in East Jordan, Syria, and Lebanon, into the burgeoning resistance organizations. At the same time, much as the growing Zionist enterprise had helped trigger early Palestinian nationalism, so the daily contact and friction with Israel and the Israeli authorities inside the territories now reawakened it.

INTERNATIONAL CONSEQUENCES

Until 1948 the Jewish-Arab conflict had been largely a local affair, between two ethnic or national communities under Ottoman or British rule. After the 1948–49 war it was a struggle primarily between the new Jewish state and the Arab states. The Palestinians, broken and mostly exiled, had been temporarily sidelined. The 1967 war brought more than a million Palestinians under Israeli rule, heightening their national consciousness. Now represented by the PLO and local leaders in the occupied territories, the Palestinians quickly returned to center stage. They became once more the focus of the conflict and of international diplomacy. Soon, in terms of the conflict, they achieved status equal to the Arab states, with the right to veto any solution reached between the latter and Israel. They became the standard bearers of the military struggle against the Jewish state. The Arab armies had been crushed and could offer Israel no serious challenge; perhaps, it was reasoned, a guerrilla movement could do better. Thus emerged the Palestinian resistance movement, which was to harry Israel on its border on the Jordan River and, eventually, on its northern border with Lebanon.

The Palestinians lost a great deal but also gained much from the war. Egypt was clearly the chief loser: its army destroyed; the Suez Canal, a main source of revenue, blocked indefinitely; the Sinai oil fields, another major financial asset, in Israeli hands; tourism abruptly falling off. But, above all, Egypt—and its leader, Nasser—had suffered severe loss of face. As the Arab world's strongest power, and the active precipitator of the crisis, Egypt was the most severely humiliated.

The army's lost equipment was replaced fairly quickly by the Soviet Union, which also afforded Egypt immediate economic relief, sending three hundred thousand tons of wheat in three months to overcome food shortages. In exchange, in line with a secret accord of April 1968, the Soviet fleet received "maintenance facilities" in Egyptian harbors. The Soviets were also allowed to post a squadron of surveillance aircraft in Egyptian air bases to track the United States Sixth Fleet in the eastern Mediterranean.[157] Arab "reactionary" regimes, Saudi Arabia, Kuwait, and Libya, also came to Egypt's assistance, agreeing to dole out $266 million annually.[158]

The military and political weakness of the Arab states and the fragility of their regimes translated into increased Soviet influence. Arms and economic aid were turned into a powerful political lever; American support for Israel was exploited to further Soviet penetration of the Arab countries. Partly to reaffirm its new status as patron of the Arab world, the USSR on June 10, 1967, broke off diplomatic relations with Israel. Moscow's lead was shortly followed by the rest of the Eastern bloc, including Yugoslavia but excepting Rumania.

Nasser's regime had suffered a near-fatal blow in Sinai. No longer could he claim to be the savior of the Arab world; he had palpably dragged it into the abyss. (The defeat also apparently shattered his health. Within days he lost thirty pounds, his diabetes worsened, and he developed circulatory and heart problems.[159]) His and the Arab world's bankruptcy was now clear for all to see. If the years of mutual subversion of Arab regimes and of fraternal warfare in Yemen had been papered over in various ways, usually in a manner not compatible with any definition of integrity, 1967 could not be. The newsreel footage of long, burned-out Egyptian armored columns in the desert and of shattered, blackened MiGs on their tarmacs told it all; nothing could be hidden except, perhaps, from the most gullible.

But the Arab masses were to prove just that, under the efficient manipulation of the state-run media. On the afternoon of June 9, Cairo Radio reported the resignations of Egypt's top military commanders, Field Marshal 'Amr and

War Minister Shamsedin Badran, and followed this up with the announcement of Nasser's own resignation, which had been extracted that morning, when 'Amr, Badran, and senior generals had met with the "Rais" and demanded that he too resign.[160] The streets of Cairo suddenly filled with masses of people calling on Nasser to recant and stay on. His *baraka* (divine charm) had apparently not deserted him. For the masses he was still the savior. As one observer recorded: "It was an extraordinary spectacle, to see all those people hurrying from all sides, shouting, weeping, some wearing pyjamas, some barefoot, women in nightdresses, children, all tormented by a suffering beyond endurance and imploring: 'Nasser, we need you. . . .' Women fell to the ground, men burst into tears."[161]

The wild, hysterical demonstrations, it later emerged, were in some measure orchestrated by Nasser's staff. Be that as it may, the following day he announced that he was not, after all, resigning. In early September 'Amr and Badran were arrested on conspiracy charges, and on September 15 it was announced that 'Amr had committed suicide. The armed forces were purged, and hundreds of senior officers were dismissed.[162]

In Syria the Ba'athist dictatorship had a tight grip, especially on the army and media. But the defeat had been complete and humiliating—some reverberations were unavoidable. In a two-stage coup in October 1969–November 1970, Defense Minister Hafez Assad—who was directly responsible for the defeat—became prime minister. In 1971 he became president, with 99.2 percent of the votes, in a plebiscite. His regime, which still continues in power, emphasized the rebuilding of the armed forces for "the day of reckoning."

Though what had happened in those six days in June was clear (indeed, perhaps, because of this), the Arab world proved unable to come to grips with it. Like the aftermath of 1948, there was an almost automatic inclination to blame others. Intellectuals, religious leaders, and journalists, following the politicians' lead, took to blaming the United States: "Washington had launched Israel to destroy the Arabs" and "American Sixth Fleet warplanes had taken part in the air strikes of 5 June" were the most frequent charges heard. Here was an acceptable explanation for what had happened: Defeat at the hands of puny Israel was unthinkable, but there was no disgrace in defeat by a superpower.

The debacle did not, at least immediately, lead to a reevaluation of basic assumptions or a revolution in government and society. Few Arab analysts agreed, certainly not in public, to look frankly at the mortal weaknesses of their societies and polities and at the incompetent political and military leaderships.[163] Similarly (and commensurately), neither did the fiasco inspire a challenge to standard Arab policies. Rather, there was reiteration and a digging in of heels. At the Arab summit meeting at Khartoum in August–September 1967, the leaders, showing resolution—or obduracy and inflexibility—in defeat, hammered out a defiant, rejectionist platform that was to bedevil all peace moves in the region for a decade. On September 2, the summit resolved that the Arab world would unite in its efforts to "wipe out the consequences of the aggression" and "assure the withdrawal of Israel's aggressive forces from the Arab lands conquered since the aggression of 5 June." The Arab states committed themselves to the principles of "no peace with Israel," "no recognition of Israel," and "no agreement to negotiation with Israel" and upheld "the Palestinian people's right to a state of its own." In part, their stand was a response to Israel's unwillingness or inability to consider withdrawal from the West Bank and Gaza as part of any peace settlement.

What became known as the "three nos" of Khartoum—which in fact were three "nos" and a "yes"—contributed to the crystallization of Israel's counterposition, which was "direct negotiations" with the Arab states and "defensible borders," a euphemism for nonwithdrawal to the 1967 lines. Arab rejectionism was thus, in part at least, responsible for the gradual emergence of Israeli rejectionism and expansionism; the Arab stance prompted the partial Israeli retreat from the cabinet decision of June 19, which had implicitly affirmed the principle of territory for peace, and its replacement by the concept of "defensible borders" and the practice of creeping annexation.

The West's response was UN Security Council Resolution 242, of November 22, 1967, which was to be the cornerstone of all future peace efforts in the Middle East down to the late 1990s. The Soviet Union had sought a clear-cut condemnation of Israel and a demand that it unilaterally withdraw its troops to the June 4 borders. But Western and Israeli opposition resulted in the compromise of 242, which, while "emphasizing the inadmissibility of the acquisition of territory by war," called for a "just and lasting peace" in the Middle East based on a trade-off of land for peace. Israel had to withdraw "from territories occupied" in June 1967 (the Arabs preferred the French version of the document, which spoke of "the territories")[164] but the Arabs had to agree to terminate the state of belligerency and "acknowledge . . . the sovereignty, territorial integrity and political independence of every state in the area and their right to live in peace within secure and recognized boundaries." The resolution affirmed the "freedom of navigation through international waterways in the area." The council also affirmed the need to solve the "refugee" problem (not "the national Palestinian problem"), and empowered the secretary-general to appoint a special representative to assist in efforts to achieve this peaceful settlement.

EIGHT

THE WAR OF ATTRITION

Defeat left Colonel Nasser, his army, and his people with a deep sense of shame and a driving urge for revenge. At the least, Sinai and the Gaza Strip had to be retrieved: "What was taken by force must be restored by force," Nasser declared. And Egypt's military recovery was to take far less time than the Israelis expected. Within months, following a June visit to Egypt by Soviet President Nikolai Podgorny and Chief of Staff Marshal Matvei Vasilievich Zakharov, the Soviets made good all the lost equipment—generally providing more modern weaponry, virtually gratis, in place of what had been destroyed.[1] But replacing the incinerated tankmen and pilots was to take as long as three years.

The months following the war saw relative calm along the Suez Canal, apart from occasional local shooting incidents and commando forays. But there were clashes in the Mediterranean off the Sinai coast, with one Israeli destroyer sunk; and on October 24–25 the IDF shelled the outskirts of Suez, destroying a major petrochemical complex, and Ismailia, causing Egypt serious economic damage and precipitating a massive flight of inhabitants. Within months, as many as 700,000 people had become refugees.[2]

The two armies dug in on either side of the Canal, the Israelis in a series of small, strung-out, poorly fortified positions along a 100-mile line, and the Egyptians in depth along three lines. Soviet advisers, whose numbers rose from a prewar five hundred to fifteen hundred, were to be seen in most headquarters down to the battalion level,[3] and hundreds of pilots were sent to the Soviet Union for training, though apparently only a small fraction returned qualified. Particular emphasis was placed on antiaircraft defenses. In February 1968 an air defense command—equal to and independent of the army, air force, and naval commands—was established.

The UN mediator appointed in the wake of Security Council Resolution 242, Gunnar Jarring of Sweden, tried his hand at finding a diplomatic solution, as did the two superpowers directly. But to no avail. Israel wanted full peace with the Arab world in exchange for withdrawal from parts or all of

Sinai and the Golan Heights; Egypt wanted all the territories, including the Gaza Strip and the West Bank, restored to Arab sovereignty but without giving Israel full peace in exchange, speaking instead vaguely of some form of non-belligerency.

Nasser realized that only a military initiative could exert the kind of pressure on Israel and, indirectly, on the superpowers, that could get Israel to withdraw. He told his cabinet in February 1968: "We will cooperate with Jarring. . . . We will listen to the U.S. . . . We will work with the Devil himself, [but] we know from the start that we must be the ones to liberate our land by the force of arms."[4] Given the growing, direct Soviet involvement, Egyptian-Israeli hostilities threatened to result in East-West confrontation.

Cairo opted for a form of limited warfare, later dubbed a "war of attrition," based on intermittent, staggered artillery bombardment of IDF front-line positions, leavened by occasional cross-Canal commando raids. The Egyptians would enjoy the twin advantages of superior firepower—they had far more artillery pieces than the IDF—and the ability to dictate when and where there would be a flareup. By the autumn of 1968 they felt that they were ready. They had deployed two armies, altogether about one hundred thousand troops, with hundreds of tanks and guns along the Canal, dug in in depth.[5]

The Egyptians correctly assessed that such warfare would put Israel in a severe quandary, unwilling as it was to sustain continuous casualties and large-scale mobilization, and reluctant to embark on a major Canal-crossing operation that might draw Soviet intervention. Nasser's confidant, the journalist Heikal, explained Egypt's strategic thinking: "If the enemy succeeds in inflicting on us 50,000 casualties in this campaign, we can go on fighting nevertheless, because we have manpower reserves. If we succeed in inflicting 10,000 casualties, he will unavoidably find himself compelled to stop fighting, because he has no manpower reserves."[6]

Egypt began the hostilities with two bombardments of Israeli positions in June 1968; Israel responded only with local counterfire. Then, on the morning of September 8, the Egyptians unleashed a sudden, massive artillery barrage in the northern sector of the Canal, between Kantara and Port Said, followed six weeks later, on October 26, by a second massive barrage, this time all along the Canal, killing fifteen Israelis.[7] Visiting the Canal the following day, Defense Minister Dayan was shocked to see that one of the hardest-hit forts "looked as if [it had been] struck by a typhoon." A heavy shell had crashed through the roof of a bunker and killed or wounded all inside.[8]

This latest attack, it was felt, could not go unanswered. It was clear that Egypt had embarked on a new, provocative policy; nonreaction would be seen as weakness. Israel decided to strike at targets in Egypt's vulnerable underbelly, the Nile Valley. On the night of October 30 IDF heli-borne commandos, using special explosives, destroyed a bridge at Kina, in Upper Egypt, and a dam and an electricity transformer and switching station at nearby Naj

Hamadi.[9] As anticipated, the ensuing blackout and transportation difficulties sent Egypt into shock. A de facto 'cease-fire emerged. Cairo suspended the Canal-side shelling and spent the following months building a "People's Militia" and fortifications to guard the hundreds of "soft" civilian targets in the Nile Valley. Defenses around rear headquarters and base camps were considerably reinforced, and the Egyptian radar network was enlarged to cover Upper Egypt and the Gulf of Suez, from which the IAF helicopters had approached Naj Hamadi.

Israel used the respite to turn its superficial Canal-side fortifications into what became known as the "Bar-Lev Line" (named for the chief of staff at the time, Gen. Chaim Bar-Lev). This chain of thirty-five forts on the waterline (one or a cluster of two or three every six miles) was impregnable to any weight of artillery, surrounded by barbed wire and minefields and each holding a platoon of infantry. Along the length of the Canal a sandbank was erected several yards high, which effectively hid all movement on the east bank from Egyptian eyes and housed firing positions for tanks. A few kilometers behind were walled tank laagers and artillery positions. The forts were connected by a paved north–south road. Six miles or so behind the waterline ran a second artery called the Artillery Road, along which tanks and guns could move speedily to reinforce or relieve forts under attack. Some thirteen miles behind the Artillery Road ran a third road, connecting the IDF rear bases of Baluza and Tasa with the Mitla Pass. Here were positioned several battalions of tanks, which could quickly reach the Canal to fight off an Egyptian crossing. The Bar-Lev Line, perhaps initially conceived merely as an early-warning mechanism, was to emerge after 1969 as something more than that, but less than a true defense line. But gradually between 1969 and 1973, without giving the matter thought, Israel's strategists began to relate to the line of forts as a solid, Maginot-like defense line.

The basic design of the forts and the Bar-Lev Line was approved by the IDF general staff in November 1968, and work began at the end of the month. The cabinet allocated an initial fifty million dollars and a thousand workers, with hundreds of earth-moving vehicles. They worked around the clock. The Egyptians did not interfere in any serious way, beyond a few commando sorties for intelligence-gathering and minelaying purposes, and a gradual increase in small-arms fire attacks.[10] By the end of February 1969 the forts were more or less ready.

In late February, Nasser ordered a renewal of the war of attrition. On March 3, Cairo announced that it no longer recognized the previous November's cease-fire. And on the morning of March 8, Egyptian artillery unleashed a massive bombardment along the length of the Canal. Several MiG-21 fighters were sent in, and one was shot down. The Israelis were heavily outgunned, but the following day their mortars killed the Egyptian chief of staff, Gen. 'Abdul Munim Riad, at a bunker just north of Ismailia.[11]

The Egyptians stepped up the war: In March there had been altogether 140 firing incidents; in April, 570.[12] In addition to intensifying the shelling they launched commando attacks on forts and ambushes every night between April 19 and 26.[13] The Israelis lived under continuous shellfire. Some forts were cut off for days on end and casualties often had to wait for many hours and, in one or two cases, for days, for evacuation.[14]

The IDF reverted to raiding deep in Egypt, attacking, on the night of April 28, the same bridge and dam near Naj Hamadi that had been damaged the previous November, and twice blowing up high-tension electricity pylons. On the night of June 21, a force of about forty naval commandos raided a small Egyptian coast guard camp at Ras Adabiya, on the Gulf of Suez, six miles south of Suez City. IDF intelligence mistakenly believed that the camp, manned by about forty Egyptian soldiers, contained a naval radar station.[15]

Egypt kept up the artillery barrages and raids, killing 47 IDF soldiers and wounding 157 in May, June, and July. Superpower diplomatic maneuvering brought no alleviation. Starting on March 18, the United States and the Soviet Union held intensive talks, exchanging proposals designed to end the Israeli-Arab conflict or, at least, the eruption along the Canal. The talks continued intermittently until mid-July, but got nowhere, with Egypt rejecting the American proposals, which called, among other things, for a "contractual agreement" between Israel and Egypt, a cease-fire, Egyptian recognition of Israel's right to exist, and freedom of Israeli navigation in the region's waterways. Washington realized that either the Soviets were not really interested in Middle East peacemaking or they just could not deliver the Arabs, and that it would be better to engineer direct American-Egyptian talks. Israel saw the superpower talks (and the American proposals) as concessions to Egyptian belligerency, presaging an externally imposed settlement—whereas Israel had traditionally sought a settlement achieved voluntarily through direct Israeli-Arab negotiation. (Israel believed that it would get a better deal in direct negotiations.)

But military developments did not portend a quick end to the fighting. Israel seemed able to sustain high casualty levels, though in the general staff there were increasing demands to shift to the offensive, cross the Canal, and end a situation in which the Egyptians enjoyed overwhelming advantages.

A change of strategy amounting to an escalation was definitely in the air. On June 17, 1969, a pair of IAF Mirages, coming in low, flew over Nasser's Cairo home and Cairo-West airport, creating sonic booms audible all around the Egyptian capital. Nasser was embarrassed and angry; he promptly fired the heads of the air force and the air defense command. Later that month, and during the first half of July, Israel initiated a series of dogfights over the Gulf of Suez and over Egyptian territory to a depth of twenty miles, downing nine Egyptian MiG-21s, to no IAF losses.[16] But these signals of the IAF's potential to cause Egypt grave harm went unheeded; the Egyptian artillery along the Canal continued to pound the forts.

The rising graph of IDF losses at last pushed Israel into unleashing its air power. A successful Egyptian commando raid against an IDF tank laager next to a fort at the southern end of the Canal, on the night of July 10, in which six Israeli soldiers were killed, helped tip the scales.[17] The cabinet Defense Committee on July 16 approved a sustained aerial assault on the northern sector of the Canal. Instrumental in the decision was the former commander of the IAF, Gen. Ezer Weizman, now head of the general staff branch. He visited the Canal in early July, received "the shelling of [his] life—a hell of fire," and came away shocked.[18]

Jerusalem had Washington's backing for the offensive. "A man would have to be blind, deaf and dumb not to sense how much the administration favors our military operations," Yitzhak Rabin, ambassador to Washington, reported. U.S. readiness to supply additional weapons "depends on us stepping up the military activity against Egypt, not reducing it," he wrote a few weeks after the start of the Israeli air offensive.[19]

The air offensive had three stages. From July 20 to December the whole Egyptian air defense system—front-line positions; artillery, SAM, and antiaircraft gun batteries; and radar stations—was destroyed; from January 7, 1970, to April 13, Egyptian base camps and headquarters in the Nile Valley and Delta were hit in a series of deep-penetration raids; and from mid-April until the cease-fire of August 8, the IAF tried to halt Soviet-Egyptian efforts to push the air defense system toward the Canal, and continued to hammer the Egyptian front line.

The air offensive was preceded by a daring commando raid on the night of July 19 against Green Island (al-Ahdar), a small artificial island south of Suez City, dominating the southern entrance of the Canal. IDF intelligence believed it was a major antiaircraft position, with radar and gun emplacements, but in fact Green Island was not, when attacked, any sort of hindrance to the IAF. "Many believed the operation was superfluous," wrote an Israel Navy historian.[20] The raid was followed by bitter recriminations and criticism within the IDF. The site could have been taken out by air or artillery; no radar was found, only a dummy antenna, and the guns appear to have been heavy machine guns and obsolete, rusty cannon rather than working antiaircraft artillery.

On the afternoon of July 20 almost the entire combat strength of the IAF, maintaining radio silence, hit the northern Canal sector, with dramatic results. The targets were antiaircraft positions, tank and artillery compounds, and infantry fortifications. Altogether 159 tons of bombs and seventy-two canisters of napalm were dropped. Hundreds of Egyptian soldiers were killed or injured, and within hours, troops all along the sector began to throw down their arms and flee. The Israelis lost a Mirage to ground fire and another to Egyptian interceptors. Five Egyptian aircraft were downed.

On July 24, the IAF went into action again, this time taking out SAM-2 sites and artillery in the central and southern sectors. Most of Egypt's SAM-2 bases were destroyed. The Egyptian air force belatedly sent up dozens of interceptors; seven were shot down. Again, Egyptian troops exhibited demoralization and panic.[21] The air raids substantially reduced Egyptian artillery fire. But there was an increase in mortar and light weapons attacks and there were more hostile "incidents" in August than there had been in June or July (515 compared with 404 and 355).[22] Israel renewed the counteroffensive, meshing commando operations with a stepped-up, systematic air offensive facilitated by the arrival in Israel of the first batch of four Phantom F-4 fighter-bombers,[23] the sturdy, powerful aircraft that were to be the mainstay of the IAF for the rest of the War of Attrition and during the 1973 war.

On the night of September 7, naval commandos blew up two Egyptian P-183 MTBs at Ras Sadat,[24] clearing the way for one of the IDF's most daring, ingenious raids ever. In Operation Raviv, on September 9 six tanks and three armored personnel carriers (all Soviet-built and captured in June 1967 and then converted to IDF use, and all in Egyptian army colors) were ferried in three landing craft across the Gulf of Suez to a point some seventeen miles south of Ras Sadat. They drove for seven hours southward along the Egyptian coastline, destroying vehicles, shore batteries, lookout posts, two army camps, a number of radar stations, and telephone poles before being picked up by the navy just north of Ras Za'afrana and ferried back to Sinai. The raiders cleared fifty miles of coastline of Egyptian troops, killing more than one hundred of them, including a general.[25]

Neither the Egyptian chief of staff nor the director of military intelligence was informed of the raid before it was over. Nasser learned of it from the news media, and suffered a heart attack that day or on September 10. He dismissed the chief of staff, Gen. Ahmad Ismail 'Ali, the OC navy, Adm. Fouad Zikri, and the Gulf of Suez sector commander.[26] He later reportedly said that the Egyptian army had, during the whole episode, reverted to its "1967 ways."

The Egyptians attempted revenge on September 11 and 12, sending dozens of aircraft to attack Israeli positions on the Canal. Seventeen of the jets were shot down; the IAF lost one. The Israelis also pounded Egyptian positions behind the Canal and along the Gulf of Suez,[27] and from then on raided the Egyptian front line and rear almost daily until the end of the war. By winter Israel had two squadrons of Phantoms.[28] Twice as heavy as the Mirage, the Phantom could carry seven tons of bombs to the Mirage's one; it also had better armaments and maneuverability, and greater range and speed. September and October saw a systematic campaign against Egypt's air defense units, particularly its SAM-2 batteries. By the end, the skies west of the Canal were all but free of antiaircraft fire and the IAF was able to devastate the Egyptian ground units at will.

In early December the Egyptians made a last effort to reconstruct their air defense system, pushing new SAM-2 batteries toward the Canal. On December 25 the IAF countered in a massive eight-hour bombing campaign involving hundreds of missions. It was the largest Israeli aerial operation since the Six-Day War. Seven new SAM sites as well as a large number of artillery batteries were taken out. Efforts by Egyptian interceptors to interfere came to naught.[29] Between July 20 and the end of December, the Egyptians lost thirty-eight aircraft.[30]

Commando raids, principally against targets along the Gulf of Suez coastline, also continued. The Israelis became particularly adept at long-range 120 mm mortar raids. A small unit with one or two mortar tubes would be helilifted to a site a few miles from an Egyptian naval base or military camp. The commandos would set up their mortars, range in on the target, and then unleash a bomb barrage, pack up, and fly back to Israel before the stunned Egyptians could identify the source of the attack and respond.

The IDF crowned this series of raids on the night of December 26, when paratroops flew to Ras Gharib on the Gulf of Suez coast, overpowered radar operators and guards, and brought back to Israel—suspended under two large helicopters—a Soviet-made P-12 radar designed to track low-flying aircraft. The raid was kept secret for several days but eventually found its way into the media: One western newspaper ran a cartoon showing IDF helicopters carrying away the Pyramids. Several Egyptian officers were subsequently executed, and others were jailed on Nasser's orders.[31]

But Egypt's devastated gunners and infantry units continued to exact a daily toll on the Bar-Lev Line that Israel could ill afford. And there was a notable increase in the number and success of Egyptian cross-Canal raids in November and December 1969. Egyptian-inspired "incidents" remained level or actually increased—with 448 in September, 642 in October, 495 in November, and 461 in December (as compared with 355 in July and 515 in August). But there was a considerable reduction in Egyptian artillery activity and consequently in IDF casualties.

In November the Egyptians launched a series of daring naval commando operations of their own. One team took up residence in a beachside apartment in Aqaba, the Jordanian port two miles east of Eilat, and began keeping tabs on the Israeli port. On the night of November 15 they swam across the bay and, using magnetic limpet mines, blew holes in two Israeli civilian boats.[32] On the night of February 5, 1970, the commandos sank an armed merchantman, and badly damaged a landing craft in the harbor. The IDF retaliated immediately, bombing and sinking an Egyptian minesweeper at Ghardaka harbor on the Red Sea.

Egypt then launched a spectacular, if little-publicized, strike against an Israeli target far afield—in Abidjan, capital of Ivory Coast in West Africa. On March 7 commandos attached limpet mines to a Canadian oil-drilling rig making its way toward the Israel-controlled Abu Rodeis oilfields off Sinai in the Gulf of Suez. It was only slightly damaged.

On the night of May 14, the Egyptians' Aqaba team, despite stepped-up

Israeli patrolling, managed once again to penetrate Eilat harbor, this time with fatal results. They planted mines near the sunken hull of the merchantman, which later killed an Israeli frogman and injured two more. Israel retaliated the following day, sending jets to bomb and sink an Egyptian destroyer and a missile boat in the southern Egyptian port of Ras Banas.[33]

But the real battle was along the Canal. The destruction of the Egyptian air defense network had changed the military situation dramatically: The IAF could operate at will both along the Canal and in the heartland. The Egyptian army was again on the verge of defeat. Could Moscow allow this? Feelers from the Kremlin resulted in renewed U.S.-Soviet talks, starting on October 17, and in what came to be known as the Rogers Plan—named after Secretary of State William Rogers—which was made public on December 9. Rogers spoke generally of the need for Israel to withdraw to the 1967 borders. Egypt was called on to "agree to a binding and specific commitment to peace," not, it was noted in Jerusalem, to an actual peace treaty. Rogers had also worked out a plan for Israeli withdrawal from all, or almost all, of the West Bank.

The Israeli cabinet publicly rejected the plan in communiques issued on December 10 and 22, calling it "an attempt to appease [the Arabs] at the expense of Israel."[34] A consensus had already formed around the desire to retain Sharm ash-Sheikh and a strip of land in eastern Sinai connecting Sharm to southern Israel. Besides, even the cabinet decision of June 19, 1967, to which the government no longer subscribed (though it was never officially repudiated), had spoken of full withdrawal only in exchange for real peace. Curiously, the Israelis found some encouragement in Washington: The national security adviser, Henry Kissinger—perpetually at odds with the secretary of state—hinted at his displeasure with the Rogers Plan, and seemed to have President Nixon's ear.[35]

But it was Egypt and the USSR who in fact definitively shot down the plan. The Soviets dismissed it as "one-sided" and "pro-Israeli." Nasser rejected a separate deal with Israel (even if he recovered all of Sinai) as well as demilitarization of the peninsula after Israeli withdrawal, freedom of maritime passage for Israeli vessels, and various security arrangements—all stipulated in the Rogers Plan as part of the quid pro quo.[36] Instead the Egyptians, bent on a military solution, sought to restore their fortunes by obtaining a heightened Soviet commitment and new weaponry.

A delegation led by Anwar Sadat, speaker of the National Assembly and soon to be vice president, Defense Minister Fawzi, and Foreign Minister Riad rushed to Moscow on December 9 to plead for more sophisticated weapons to withstand the Israeli air assault. They also asked for long-range bombers. The Soviets stalled, in effect rejecting the plea. They understood that it would require a major commitment of military personnel, as the Egyptians were unable to operate the systems they were requesting: In effect the Soviets were being asked to take over, at least for a time, Egypt's air defenses, and they were not ready to do that.[37]

The Rogers Plan having been turned down, Israel and the United States were now back on the same track. Superpower negotiation and agreement on an imposed settlement had failed: A restoration of the cease-fire through military action seemed the only road open. Israel would now try to make good its strategic advantage, born of the destruction of the Egyptian air defense network.

If blows to front lines and antiaircraft systems were insufficient to silence the Egyptian guns, perhaps a sustained assault on the rear bases, headquarters, and main depots would do the trick. The arrival of the Phantom F-4s made possible massive, deep-penetration bombing. On January 6, 1970, the cabinet Defense Committee decided to allow the IAF to begin bombing major military targets around Cairo and in the Nile Delta. For months the cabinet had been prodded from Washington to take such a decision by Rabin—who held cabinet rank. He believed that Washington expected, indeed wanted, Israel to deliver a major body blow to the Egyptian regime and to see it topple.[38]

IDF Intelligence Branch—the ministers concurring—predicted that the Soviets would bluster but do nothing. They were seen in Jerusalem as something of a "paper tiger";[39] since 1956 they had often threatened but never actually intervened. What Israel—or the United States—would do if the USSR did act was, apparently, never seriously debated. But these international question marks gave the decision makers some pause. The decision to bomb in depth was not open ended. The bombings were to be intermittent, not daily, each new raid requiring the specific approval of the prime minister and defense minister. After each raid the IAF and the cabinet would reassess the situation.

On January 7, the IAF hit three "deep" targets—a SAM-2 training facility and depot and a commando headquarters near Cairo, and camps at Tel al-Kebir. There were similar raids on January 13, 18, 23, and 28. In the last attack the Phantoms struck at a camp at Ma'adi, a suburb of Cairo—which briefly panicked the American diplomatic contingent in the Egyptian capital, many of whom lived or sent their children to school in the neighborhood.[40] The Ma'adi raid resulted in an American démarche to Jerusalem—the first since the deep-penetration raids began—but it had no impact.[41]

The primary aim of the raids was to force Egypt to accept a cease-fire. A secondary aim may well have been to overthrow Nasser. "We shall not go into mourning if Nasser falls . . . I don't know if Nasser's successor would be any better than he is, but I don't think he could be much worse," said Golda Meir, who had replaced Eshkol as prime minister in March 1969. Foreign Minister Abba Eban put things more positively: "[T]he possibility of peace would be improved if the Egyptian people were blessed with a different regime. . . . A new regime would be free . . . to see a way out of the dilemma it is caught in."[42] The Americans also seem to have looked forward to Nasser's demise.[43]

Confronted with the Israeli escalation, which threatened to bring about a complete military collapse, a desperate Nasser secretly flew to Moscow on January 22, 1970—though, in retrospect, the immediate danger to the regime appears to have been negligible.[44] The Soviet leaders were willing to supply Egypt with the new SAM-3s as well as improved SAM-2s. But six months or more of training were required to operate the sophisticated missiles, and squadrons of aircraft would be needed to protect their deployment. Egypt did not have the time or the competent pilots. Soviet personnel, in large numbers, would be needed, at least until the Egyptians were trained, said Nasser. Communist Party secretary Leonid Brezhnev was reluctant. Nasser then played his trump card: He threatened to resign, suggesting that someone pro-American might replace him.

Nasser was the key to the Soviets' position in the region, and they had already invested in him heavily. Brezhnev caved in and agreed to provide a full air defense umbrella—thus agreeing to intervene directly in the war.

The decision was kept secret: Soviet personnel in Egypt were to wear Egyptian uniforms, and the aircraft were marked with Egyptian insignia. The Americans were told on January 31 that if "Israel continues its adventurism," the Kremlin would be forced to see to it that the Arab states would "have the means at their disposal . . . to rebuff . . . the arrogant aggressor."[45] But the Americans ignored the implied warning and made no effort to stop the Israeli bombing.

Neither the Israelis nor the Americans had an inkling of this decision. As late as February 20, General Bar-Lev discounted possible direct Soviet intervention. By the end of the month, the Egyptians were busy ten to twenty miles west of the Canal building SAM emplacements, and the IAF began to bomb them.[46] In March three Soviet MiG-21 squadrons were deployed around Cairo, Aswan, and Alexandria.[47]

In January 1970 there were 2,500–4,000 Soviet personnel in Egypt, mostly military advisers. By March 31, the total was 6,500–8,000, 4,000 of them missile crewmen and 60–80 pilots; by June 30, the number had reached 10,600–12,150, including 8,000 SAM crewmen and 100-150 pilots; and by September 30, 12,650–14,000, including 10,000 SAM crewmen and 150 pilots.[48]

The Israelis continued their deep-penetration bombing, as well as Canalside attacks. In early February, at al-Khanka, eleven miles north of Cairo, a Phantom, put off its bombing run by SAM-2s, mistakenly released its payload over the Abu Zaabel metalworks. About seventy civilians were killed and another fifty injured. The IDF promptly acknowledged its mistake and warned the Egyptians that among the bombs was one with a delayed-action fuse. Instructions on how to defuse it were passed to Egypt through UNTSO.[49] Ambassador Rabin was summoned to the State Department and, for the first time, heard of Washington's "strong disapproval" of the deep-penetration raids.[50] In early March this disapprobation was translated into postponement of the sale of twenty-five more Phantoms and one hundred more Skyhawks to Israel. Washington now felt that the campaign was unwise, having provoked direct Soviet military intervention. The United States was not going to be seen assisting the IAF campaign, even though, as Kissinger was to argue, the non-sale would be interpreted in Moscow as a sign of weakness. But Washington did quietly agree to replace all Israeli aircraft losses.[51]

The following two months of raids concentrated on Egypt's burgeoning antiaircraft network. The Canal-side SAMs and antiaircraft batteries had for the most part been taken out in December 1969; but the batteries in the Nile Valley (especially around Cairo), around the Mediterranean naval bases, and at other strategic sites were still troublesome. Between February 17 and April 3 the IAF attacked SAM bases eight times, eventually shifting to targets away from Cairo. Soviet personnel and SAM-3 missiles were deployed around the city and nearby military bases in March. Israel feared that a head-on collision resulting in large Soviet losses would have repercussions, so the focus of the strikes moved to the delta, which—apart from Alexandria—was still clear of their presence.[52]

Moshe Dayan put in a special appearance on Israeli television on March 20, speaking somberly of the possible "Sovietization" of the conflict. The IAF, he hinted, would stay clear of Cairo and the Nile Valley as well as the delta, into which the Israelis knew the Soviets were about to move, but would continue to attack Canal-side fortifications. On April 9, in a speech at Tel Aviv University, he spelled this out—in effect offering Moscow a deal: "We have no pretensions of making ourselves at home in the skies over Cairo . . . or Alexandria . . . or Aswan. However, we must assure our ability to maintain military control . . . along the Suez Canal for as long as the fighting continues."

The end of the deep-penetration bombing may have been hastened by the events of April 8 at Salahiya, twenty miles west of al-Kantara: Some forty-seven Egyptian schoolchildren were killed and thirty wounded when a military installation—inside which the Egyptians had located an elementary school—was bombed.[53] The last raids were on April 13. Moscow had not even bothered to respond to Dayan's offer of a deal, and Jerusalem made the decision to stay clear of them unilaterally.

All in all, deep-penetration bombing had been a failure. It had not ended Egyptian belligerency along the Canal, and it had led to direct Soviet intervention, vastly complicating Israel's political and military position. And it had not reduced IDF casualties. January–February 1970 saw 829 Egyptian-initiated incidents along the Canal (compared with 956 for November–December 1969) and twenty-three Israeli dead and sixty-four wounded (compared with the November–December 1969 total of twenty-five dead and forty-eight wounded). There were more Egyptian artillery attacks in January–February 1970 than in the previous two months.[54] In March–July the IDF suffered an average of fifteen killed a month.[55]

The strategic picture, from Israel's perspective, had grown darker. Having secured the Nile Valley and delta, the Soviets began to push their missiles toward the Canal. At the end of March and beginning of April, the Egyptians renewed work on the SAM emplacements twenty miles from the Canal that the IAF had bombed in late February. In the second half of April the Soviets began to provide the construction sites with air cover, and on April 18 they directly challenged the IAF over the Canal Zone. A flight of eight Soviet-flown MiG-21s tried to intercept and shoot down a pair of Phantoms. Breaking radio silence, the pilots spoke in Russian, intent on revealing their identity; the warning could not have been clearer.[56] But the IDF signaled that it would not be deterred. Dayan had publicly drawn a red line, which Israel would not allow the Soviets to cross, twenty to twenty-five miles west of the Canal. If the IAF could not operate along the Canal, the Bar-Lev Line would be at the mercy of Egyptian artillery and would collapse. "Israel is not Czechoslovakia" became a recurring phrase in speeches by Israel's leaders. (The Czech army had offered no resistance when the country was overrun by the Soviets in August 1968.[57])

During late spring and early summer, Soviet MiGs stayed clear of the Canal. But the SAM crews, with thousands of Egyptian workers and anti-aircraft batteries, made repeated efforts to push toward the waterway, accompanied by a stepped-up artillery war and commando raids. What was for Israel the worst raid of the War of Attrition took place on May 30 at the northern end of the Bar-Lev Line, where patrols were restricted to a narrow road bounded by the Canal and impassable marshes with no room for maneuver. A well-laid Egyptian ambush, in daylight, hit an armored patrol and relief columns, killing eighteen soldiers, wounding six, and taking three prisoner.[58] The IDF struck back hard, in eleven days of intensive air raids and a commando operation across the Canal in the northern sector that cleared two miles of Egyptian infantry fortifications. At least twenty-one Egyptians were killed. The IDF suffered four dead and more than a dozen wounded, a cost deemed prohibitive, and such frontal assaults were not repeated.[59]

In early May, within the space of a few days, the Soviets, using thousands of workers around the clock, built a large number of SAM emplacements thirteen to twenty-five miles west of the Canal. The IAF responded with relentless bombing. Egyptian reports subsequently spoke of one to two thousand workers killed.[60] The Soviets and Egyptians gave up the attempt.

In early June a new method was tried—"missile ambushes." Small numbers of well-camouflaged SAM launchers with radar vans were sent at night into the "forbidden" zone, to fire at overflying IAF aircraft. The IAF eventually located them and took out some of the launchers.[61] The Egyptians continued to construct regular fortified SAM sites, and the IAF to hit them.

Secretary of State Rogers and his assistant, Joseph Sisco, reinforced Israel's military efforts by warning Moscow against trying to push the SAMs up to the Canal.[62] But the Soviets were not impressed and, together with the

Egyptians, worked out a new plan. On the night of June 29, they simultaneously pushed fourteen SAM batteries into a narrow fifty-mile stretch. Each
battery covered its neighbor, so that any aircraft entering the "SAM box"
would face a barrage of missiles. The following day, Phantoms managed to
destroy two of the batteries—but two aircraft were shot down, the largest
Israeli loss in a single day since the Six-Day War.[63] The "box" was gradually
rolled forward. By July 13 the SAM-2s were only twenty miles from the
Canal, with the SAM-3s six miles behind them.[64]

During the following weeks, in what was to be dubbed the "electronic war,"
the IAF repeatedly attacked the "box," destroying several more SAM batteries
but losing three more Phantoms. On July 13, on President Nixon's instructions, the U.S. Air Force rushed a supply of Electronic Counter-Measure
(ECM) pods to the IAF, hoping to right the military balance. But the new
equipment failed to live up to expectations. Twenty Phantoms backed by
Skyhawk-mounted jamming equipment struck along the length of the Canal
on July 18. The pods worked against the SAM-2s but failed against the SAM-
3s. Four batteries were knocked out and three damaged, but the Israelis lost a
Phantom piloted by a squadron commander, whose death badly dented IAF
morale. Another Phantom had to crash-land.[65] The Soviets were winning the
"electronic war"; the SAM screen would soon reach the Canal.

Pressure on Israel now mounted with an upsurge of belligerency by Syria.
Damascus, apparently prodded by Cairo—and perhaps Moscow—to display
some fraternal Arab feeling while its allies were heavily engaged in the south,
unleashed a massive artillery barrage along the Golan line on June 24. Three
days of combat ensued.[66]

At the Canal the Soviets decided to up the ante and provide the eastward-
inching SAMs with air cover. On July 21 and again on the 25th, Soviet-piloted
MiGs chased IAF fighter-bombers in the west bank back to the Canal (in one
case even flying over into Sinai). The challenge that Dayan had long feared
had materialized. The CO of the IAF, General Hod, bluntly told the cabinet
that the Soviets had to be stopped. The ministers reluctantly agreed. On July
30, the IAF set a large, complex ambush which resulted in five MiGs being
shot down with no Israeli losses. There were victory parties that night at the
IAF bases.[67]

The commander of the Soviet air force, Marshal Pavel Kutakov, rushed to
Cairo to find out what had happened and to plan a reprisal. On August 3 the
Soviets were ready to avenge their dead pilots. An SAM ambush was prepared, and an IAF raiding mission, decoyed by fake SAM sites, was intercepted by a barrage of missiles. One Phantom was downed and another badly
damaged, though its wounded pilot managed to land at Bir Gafgafa.[68]

As seen from Jerusalem, the situation had turned critical. The IAF had been
able to contain the missile advance—but only just, and with heavy losses. By
early August "the handful of Mirage and Phantom crews who [had] carried the

brunt of the endless war had reached their breaking point."[69] The Soviets had managed to push a handful of SAM batteries beyond the Israeli-defined "red line," but they needed to put more into place in order to achieve an interlinked, mutually supportive belt.

If this activity persisted, the IAF would be relentlessly rolled back, unless it was willing to fight the Soviets. To do this it would have to be considerably reinforced, and to face heavy, perhaps unsustainable, losses. It might lose air supremacy over the west bank of the Canal, resulting in the destruction of the Bar-Lev Line by Egyptian artillery—unless Israel escalated the War of Attrition by mobilizing its reserves and launching a major Canal-crossing ground offensive to destroy the Egyptian artillery batteries and the SAM belt protecting them. But such a massive escalation posed grave dangers—overextension (did the IDF really want to occupy parts of the west bank of the Canal?); a major confrontation with Soviet power (could the Soviets allow themselves to lose?); a breach with the United States (was Washington willing to supply Israel with the necessary weapons and, possibly, to be sucked into a war with the Soviets over the Bar-Lev Line?); and the extension of the war to Israel's other borders (would Syria and Jordan sit still if there was a full-scale Israeli-Egyptian war?). From a struggle over the Bar-Lev Line, the War of Attrition had seemingly turned into an existential matter. As Eban told the Knesset in July, "[T]he battle on the canal line is the battle to preserve the very existence of the State of Israel."[70]

Neither the Soviets nor the Israelis wanted full-scale war. The United States now moved to prevent matters from spinning out of control. Following the repeated failures in 1969 of American-Soviet efforts to promote an Israeli-Arab peace process, or even a superpower-imposed settlement, in January 1970 Washington had begun to reopen direct channels with Cairo (which had severed diplomatic relations with the United States in June 1967). Washington in effect had decided to bypass Moscow and deal directly with the Egyptians, who reluctantly agreed to play ball.

Serious negotiations began in April. Sisco arrived in Cairo and met Nasser. He tried to sell the Egyptians on the renewal of talks under the auspices of Ambassador Jarring—with negotiations to begin after Egypt and Israel instituted a cease-fire. The United States promised Egypt that it supported a settlement on the basis of the Rogers Plan, and complex trilateral negotiations followed. On July 22–23 Nasser accepted the U.S. proposal; Israel accepted, reluctantly, on July 31, and on August 6 formally agreed to the terms of the cease-fire. Egypt did so a few hours later, on August 7. The key provisions were that both sides would cease all fire and incursions, on the ground and in the air, and that "both sides will refrain from changing the military status quo within zones extending 50 kilometers to the east and the west of the cease-fire line. Neither side will introduce or construct any new military installations in these zones."

The agreement was to last for three months, by which time the Jarring talks were to be resumed.

That night, with the cease-fire just five minutes away, an IAF patrol spotted "convoys of vehicles [on the Egyptian side] beginning to move in the direction of the canal." Another patrol, the next morning, showed the start of work on the Egyptian side on several new missile sites and the arrival in the standstill zone of new missile batteries. On August 9, with the work continuing at the SAM sites, Israel complained to Washington.

The Israelis were not really surprised. IDF Intelligence had predicted the Egyptian move ten days before. Indeed, during the months of negotiation, Nasser had never taken the emerging agreement seriously. But he played along. For Egypt, it was a no-lose situation: If Israel proceeded to negotiate on the basis of the Rogers Plan, which assured the Arabs of virtually complete Israeli withdrawal from the occupied territories, Egypt would get what it wanted. If Israel demurred, as Nasser suspected it would, Egypt would still have emerged with substantial gains—because, under cover of the cease-fire, it planned to advance the SAM umbrella close to the Canal in preparation for a future cross-Canal offensive.

Nasser had repeatedly signaled this intention. He would advance his missiles, come hell or high water. On June 25, at Benghazi, Nasser told a Libyan audience: "Once Egypt secures . . . parity in the air, then no power on earth can prevent it from crossing the Canal."[71] A month later, at a meeting of his Arab Socialist Union party, he was asked: What if Israel refused to withdraw from the Canal after the three months of cease-fire were up? He replied: "If . . . Israel has refused to withdraw, we will have the right to continue the battle. . . . Will the ceasefire enable us to install a [SAM] network? . . . This we will answer in a closed session."[72] In short, Nasser's intention was to go to war under infinitely improved starting conditions.

On August 10, the United States initiated U-2 spy plane flights over the standstill zones and confirmed the Israeli reports. Rogers for days refused to believe that the Egyptians had so blatantly violated an agreement they had just signed, and that he had brokered. Only on August 19 did the State Department rather hesitantly announce that the Egyptians had committed violations; only in September did the Americans endorse the Israeli accusations in full. Egypt brazenly maintained that it had not violated the agreement.[73]

Dayan pressed for an immediate air strike against the new missile sites. Bar-Lev said that a limited strike would not avail, and, if Israel wanted to renew hostilities, it must go for a full-scale cross-Canal offensive against the Egyptian line. But the cabinet, having just ended a long, indecisive, and agonizing war, was in no mood to renew hostilities; the threat of a major collision with the Soviet Union loomed over the proceedings. Bar-Lev and Dayan were rebuffed.[74]

By September the Americans had identified twenty-four SAM sites either wholly or partly constructed in violation of the standstill clause; Israel claimed there were forty. By October there were about one hundred SAM sites in the zone, with 40–50 operational batteries installed. The Egyptians refused to move the missiles. Israel reacted by refusing to renew the Jarring talks.

Nasser geared up for war at the end of the three-month cease-fire. Months before, he had decided that in the absence of Israeli agreement to withdraw from the territories Egypt would launch a "war of liberation."[75] But Nasser was not to be in at the kill. Three years were to pass before Egypt made its move—and then, with Anwar Sadat, the self-effacing vice president, rather than Nasser, at the helm. On September 28, 1970, Nasser died of a heart attack; Sadat took over.

Egyptian public statements during the War of Attrition were highly inaccurate: The cost of the war was hidden from the people, and Israeli losses were vastly exaggerated. For example, official announcements in the course of 1969–70 spoke, all told, of "190" Israeli aircraft shot down (or, approximately, the full front-line strength of the IAF). The true figure—as reported by the IDF—was fourteen. Egypt conceded that eleven of its aircraft were shot down during the two years; IDF spokesmen told of ninety-eight.[76]

There are no accurate figures for Egyptian casualties in the War of Attrition. A reasonable estimate would probably be about ten thousand—civilians and military—killed.[77] Between the Six-Day War and mid-August 1970, 367 Israelis died on the Egyptian front,[78] 260 of them between March 1969 and August 1970.[79]

Given the small size of Israel's population and its close-knit society, the IDF was in no position to lie about casualties, even had it wanted to. But the government and the army (and the media in their wake) all made a deliberate effort to downplay the effects on morale of the almost daily casualty toll during 1969–70, the awful realities of life in the Bar-Lev Line and, in the later stages of the war, the IAF pilots' difficulties in combating the "missile wall." The end of the war was greeted by the Israeli public with a vast sigh of relief.

The War of Attrition had an important impact on the future of the Middle East. Egypt had set out to push the IDF away from the Canal's eastern shore; the IDF had managed to hold on and had forced the Egyptians into a cease-fire. The Israeli cabinet, the army, and the public believed that Israel had won. This had several consequences: First, they assumed that the Egyptians realized that they had been beaten, that their army was weaker than the IDF, and that therefore they could not—especially so long as their air arm was palpably inferior—go to war. So Israelis felt no real incentive to reach political agreement with the Arabs based on withdrawal from occupied territories: Continued occupation was both possible and desirable for "strategic depth," and concessions were unnecessary.

Second, the war instilled a sense of complacency regarding the Bar-Lev

Line. There was a belief that the forts could hold out and "stop" even a major Egyptian Canal-crossing offensive. The Israelis forgot that the war had ended with the Egyptians using even more artillery and light weapons fire than when it began, and that, but for the continuous IAF bombing campaign, the line would have crumbled.

Third, and most important, the IAF's success in hammering the Egyptians until Cairo acquiesced in a cease-fire left the Israelis with the illusion of an all-powerful air arm. The IAF's difficulties against the SAM network in May–June 1970, and the creeping Israeli aerial withdrawals in July–August, were forgotten. Somehow it came to be assumed that in any future confrontation, the Phantoms would beat the SAM network and protect the Bar-Lev Line. Overlooked too was the fact that, in any future war, the IAF would face a vast and well-organized SAM network already in place and dug in close to the Canal's banks, with the ability to shoot down Israeli aircraft over the east as well as the west bank.

From Egypt's point of view the War of Attrition had been a success. If, in the past, the Egyptians had always suffered defeat and, even, humiliating rout, now their army—albeit with important Soviet input—had held its own. Thousands had died, sensitive targets had been devastated, but on the whole the army had been able, right down to the cease-fire, to pound the Bar-Lev line and inflict casualties on its defenders. The Egyptians acquired a self-confidence that seemed to have been irreparably damaged in the defeats of 1948, 1956, and 1967.

Indeed, during the last stages of the war it seemed that the Soviet-Egyptian air defense command had found a way to solve or at least neutralize the problem posed by the IAF. The war and the massive violation of the cease-fire terms that followed placed Egypt in a supremely advantageous starting position for October 1973. Egypt's General Gamasy thus concluded his account by writing that though the War of Attrition had been "a tremendous burden on both Egypt and Israel, . . . in the final analysis it was beneficial to Egypt and proved harmful to Israel."[80]

THE RISE OF THE PLO AND THE START OF THE ARMED STRUGGLE

The start of Palestinian military operations against Israel had preceded the Six-Day War. The 1950s had seen sporadic raiding across the armistice lines by Palestinians acting independently, or as agents of political organizations such as the Muslim Brotherhood, or of Egyptian military intelligence. Following the

1956 Sinai war, a handful of students and intellectuals began to think in terms of a national resistance organization. A cell of like-minded militants, inspired by the Algerian nationalist FLN and by Nasser's ejection of the British, gathered around Yasser Arafat, head of the Palestinian Students' Union in Cairo.

Arafat, according to PLO tradition a scion of the notable Husseini family, was born in 1929, probably in Cairo. His father was a relatively prosperous Gaza food merchant. He claims to have taken part in the Egyptian army's invasion of the Negev in May 1948, though this seems unlikely. After studying civil engineering at Cairo University he drifted to Kuwait, where in 1959 he and other exiles set up the clandestine Palestine National Liberation Movement, or Fatah, and embarked on five years of fund-raising, propaganda, and armchair warfare.

On the night of January 2, 1965, a Fatah squad crossed the border and planted an explosive charge next to the National Water Carrier in the Galilee. The charge was discovered and defused before it could explode. On its way back the squad was intercepted by a Jordanian patrol. The leader was shot dead and the other members were arrested. Such was the fate of the first raid against Israel by Fatah, or rather by al-Assifa (meaning "the storm"), Fatah's military wing.

The Arab regimes feared that the Palestinians would drag them into a premature war with Israel, and Jordan and Egypt proceeded to clamp down on Fatah cells in their territory. Nevertheless, by the outbreak of the Six-Day War, al-Assifa had carried out about one hundred raids.[81] The start of the armed struggle won Fatah, and Arafat personally, a growing following in the Palestinian dispersion, soon enabling him to take over the PLO.

The PLO came into being as a result of a resolution engineered by Nasser at the first Arab Summit Meeting in Cairo, January 13–16, 1964. Nasser, aided by Syrian prime minister Amin al-Hafez and Iraqi president 'Abd al-Salam 'Aref, sought to forge a subservient Palestinian instrument with which to batter Israel, while at the same time restraining independent initiatives. (The first Fatah or al-Assifa operations were launched partly in reaction to the establishment of the PLO—to show the world that the Palestinians were not going to be ruled or manipulated by fellow Arabs.)

The Acre-born Ahmed Shukeiry, a veteran Palestinian-Arab diplomat, who had served as both Syrian and Saudi ambassador to the UN, was called on to set up the organization. At the end of May, the founding conference convened in Jerusalem's Palace Hall movie house. About four hundred representatives of the Palestinian diaspora and various organizations, including twelve delegates from Fatah, took part. The conference in effect constituted itself into the Palestine National Council (PNC), a parliament-in-exile, and on May 28 issued the Palestinian National Charter, which denied Israel's right to exist and posited the establishment in its place of an Arab state. The charter affirmed the Palestinians' right to "return" to the country and asserted that "armed struggle is the only way to liberate Palestine." The PLO "aims at the elimination of Zionism in Palestine," it stated. The 1947 partition was deemed "illegal" and all of Palestine's political history, from "the Balfour Declaration" to the establishment of Israel, was declared "null and void." The Jews' "claims of historical or religious ties . . . with Palestine" and to a distinct "nationality" were denied. The charter stated that Judaism was only a "religion" and Zionism was deemed "racist and fanatic . . . aggressive, expansionist and colonialist in its aims, and fascist in its methods." In effect the charter called for Israel's destruction and provided for only a minority of the Jews resident in the country to continue to live there.

Fatah's operations—backed by Syria—were a major catalyst in the deterioration of Israeli-Arab relations that led to the Six-Day War. But the "war of popular liberation," as advocated in the charter, only got off the ground in the wake of that disaster. Largely unsuccessful, it unfolded over the following three years, at the same time as Egypt's 'War of Attrition' along the Canal; some observers regarded the Palestinian effort as the "eastern adjunct" of that war. The Palestinians' war had two theaters: the "interior," in which guerrillas and terrorists acted against targets inside the occupied territories and in Israel proper; and the "exterior," in which raiding squads crossed the border from the East Bank of Jordan and Lebanon and attacked IDF patrols and installations along the borders, or civilian targets inside the country.

The "interior" campaign came first. On June 12, 1967, two days after the Six-Day War ended, the heads of Fatah met in Damascus and resolved to renew the guerrilla war, but only inside the occupied territories and Israel rather than across the borders from the Arab states. They decided to open an emergency fund-raising campaign; to establish new bases along the Jordanian and Lebanese borders; to collect arms; and to organize resistance cells in the territories, particularly the West Bank.[82] Fatah announced: "Our organization has decided to continue struggling against the Zionist conqueror. We are planning to operate far from the Arab states so that they will not suffer Israeli reprisals for fedayeen actions. . . . We are united in our resolve to free our stolen homeland from the hands of the Zionists."[83]

Recruits streamed in from the refugee camps of Syria and the East Bank, and from among the Palestinian student communities in Germany, Italy, and Spain. Perhaps as many as 1,000 were sent to Algeria and Syria for military training during July and August. Many were then sent across into the West Bank, where they faded into the landscape. Apparently the Fatah leadership hoped that the resistance activities of these recruits and of indigenous cells would spark a popular uprising. Arms and money were provided by Syria and Iraq. Yasser Arafat crossed into the West Bank in early July and moved through a succession of safe houses in Qabatiya, Nablus, and Ramallah. Periodically he appears to have crossed back into East Jordan to meet the other Fatah leaders before returning to the occupied territory. He finally returned to the East Bank in late September (some sources claim in December), apparently just in time: A squad of GSS men raided his Ramallah hideaway only minutes after his departure; the mattress was still warm.

On August 31 the Fatah Central Committee decided to launch the "popular rebellion." In September there were thirteen acts of sabotage against Israeli targets, almost all of them in Israel proper. (The saboteurs were reluctant to hit targets in the occupied territory lest Israel vent its wrath on the local population.) Most of the attacks were ineffectual, but the GSS, backed by the IDF and police, struck back efficiently and ruthlessly. In massive, nightly raids the Israelis netted hundreds of the infiltrators as well as many of their local accomplices. Caves and orchards were searched and weapons dumps destroyed. Houses where guerrillas had been harbored were demolished; long, economically injurious curfews were imposed.

The Israelis' aim was to separate the local population from the resistance operatives, who in many ways made the task fairly easy. They were often careless and unprofessional, and many broke down under interrogation (which was normally accompanied by some form of physical abuse), quickly dispensing information about their comrades. As General Narkiss told a British journalist: "For every guerrilla captured in action . . . 40 were rounded up through denunciation."[84] Their networks suffered from an absence of compartmentalization.

The Israelis won this round hands down. They had built up their apparatus far more swiftly and efficiently than had their opponents. In October, Fatah launched ten sabotage attacks; in November, eighteen and in December, twenty. But thereafter it was all downhill. By the end of 1967 the Israeli security forces had arrested about one thousand Palestinian operatives and killed about two hundred. In January 1968 the Palestinians launched only six attacks. By then the Fatah leadership had acknowledged defeat: The popular uprising had failed to materialize.

During the months of unequal struggle in the West Bank, other resistance organizations entered the picture. The first to emerge was the Popular Front for the Liberation of Palestine (PFLP), founded and led by George Habash, a Lydda-born physician from a landowning Greek Orthodox family. Exiled from Palestine in 1948, he studied medicine at the American University in Beirut, along with Wadi'a Haddad, who was to become the PFLP's head of operations. In the 1950s Habash and Haddad moved to Amman, where, on December 11, 1967, they established the PFLP. The new movement was forthrightly Marxist but also paradoxically emphasized Palestinian nationalism. It berated "American imperialism" and propounded "revolutionary" armed struggle against Zionism. Asserting ideological differences, it initially boycotted the PLO, joining only in 1970. The PFLP, which never had more than about two thousand members, was to lead the field in international terrorism during 1968–71.

The PFLP spawned a number of breakaway organizations. On February 22, 1969, Naif Hawatmeh, a thirty-four-year-old Greek Orthodox native of As Salt in Jordan, announced the establishment of the Popular Democratic Front for the Liberation of Palestine, later renamed the Democratic Front for the Liberation of Palestine (PDFLP or DFLP). Habash and Haddad, he charged, were insufficiently Marxist. Hawatmeh received Syrian backing and made Damascus his headquarters. He called for the overthrow of most current Arab regimes and their replacement with Eastern bloc–style "people's democracies," and he maintained links with ultra-left-wing Israelis. The DFLP at its height had perhaps one thousand members. A smaller breakaway from the PFLP was the "PFLP–General Command," founded on April 24, 1968, by Ahmed Jibril, an ex-major in the Syrian army, who was born in the village of Yazur, outside Jaffa. His organization saw the gun as the only means of struggle and the liberation of all of Palestine as the only goal. During the 1970s and 1980s it carried out a number of spectacular terrorist atrocities against Israeli and Western targets.

Al-Sa'iqa (meaning "thunder and lightning," also known as "the Vanguards of the Liberation War"), the second-largest organization in the PLO after Fatah, was set up in September 1967 as an instrument of the Syrian government. Between 1970 and 1979 it was headed by Zuhair Muhsein, a Ba'ath party apparatchik. He was assassinated in 1979, apparently by agents of the Iraqi-backed Abu Nidal group, also known as "Fatah—the Revolutionary Council," which had broken away from Fatah in 1973. For the first six years of its existence, the Abu Nidal group, while occasionally attacking Israeli targets, served Iraqi intelligence interests. In 1979 Abu Nidal switched allegiances and residences and began to work for Syria. In the mid-1980s the organization moved to Libya. Its main target was Fatah, which it accused of willingness to compromise with Israel.

At a meeting of the PNC on July 10, 1968, in Cairo, the resistance organizations in effect came to dominate both the council and the PLO. The Palestinian National Charter was amended to give greater weight to the concept of "armed struggle." In February 1969 the takeover was completed: At the next PNC meeting Arafat was named chairman of the fifteen-man PLO Executive Committee (a position he was to hold into the late 1990s). Fatah's takeover of the PLO was backed by all the Arab states.

CROSSING THE RIVER

The destruction of the Fatah networks in the West Bank during the autumn and winter of 1967 persuaded the movement's leadership to switch strategy. Banking on a popular uprising in the occupied territories had proved misguided. From the beginning of 1968 the guerrillas would attack Israel from bases on the Jordanian side of the border. The IDF usually succeeded in interdicting

them, thanks to a blocking system that consisted of ambushes; a string of fortified riverside positions dominating the Jordan fords; a barbed-wire-fence-
and-minefield complex, with electronic sensors; a "smudge trail," checked
each morning for telltale footprints or erasures; and a chain of Nahal outposts
a few kilometers to the rear.

The guerrilla incursions, which grew in number and sophistication, continued down to September 1970. IDF countermeasures, including raids across
the Jordan, also grew apace. Most of the guerrilla squads were intercepted and
destroyed along the river; the few that reached the West Bank's towns were
eventually rounded up. But their guns and mines also took a steady if much
smaller toll of Israeli lives.

Arab Legion infantrymen and gunners along the Jordan often gave withdrawing Fatah squads covering fire. This resulted in frequent IDF-Legion
skirmishing. On February 14–15, 1968, the whole frontier, from the Sea of
Galilee to the northern tip of the Dead Sea, erupted in artillery duels after Jordanian mortarmen hit a string of Israeli settlements in the Beit Shean and Jordan Valleys. IDF artillery and the IAF hit Jordanian bases, artillery batteries,
and the Ghor Canal (which supplied the eastern Jordan Valley villages with
fresh water, drawn from the Yarmuk River). American mediators eventually
arranged a cease-fire, but thousands of Jordanian farmers fled eastward, abandoning homes and fields; more and more guerrillas moved into the valley.
King Hussein, fearful of a clash with Israel, repeatedly declared he would prevent the guerrillas from using Jordan as a base. But he proved unable to make
good on his word.[85]

March 1968 saw the largest Israeli assault ever against the guerrillas in Jordan, provoked by a raid, on March 18, in which an Israeli school bus was
blown up by a mine near the settlement of Be'er Ora in the Arava, killing two
adults and wounding ten children.[86]

The Israeli forces went in on March 21, hastily and with poor intelligence.
The main target was a complex of Fatah bases in the Jordan Valley, in and
around the village of Karameh (the name means "honor" in Arabic), where
Arafat had his forward headquarters. Several hundred civilian inhabitants
lived there, alongside about nine hundred lightly armed guerrillas, mostly
belonging to Fatah. But the Israelis' main antagonist was to be the Arab
Legion, with an infantry division, artillery, and an armored brigade dug in on
the heights overlooking the Jordan. The Jordanians enjoyed a topographical
advantage, and the raiders were hampered by politically motivated orders forbidding them to advance too far eastward into Jordan, as well as by wet
ground. But throughout, the Israelis enjoyed complete air superiority.

The IDF deployed three reduced brigade groups—two of paratroops and
one of armor. The aim was to surround and isolate Karameh and destroy its
PLO bases and personnel. The expectation, soon confounded, was that the
Legion would stay out of the fight. In his memoirs Abu Iyad, Arafat's deputy,

claimed that he and Arafat had been tipped off about the impending raid by Legion officers, who learned of it from the CIA. The PLO leaders decided to stand and fight.[87] The Legion had declared an alert on March 18 and, judging from events three days later, was well prepared for the IDF assault.

Soon after the attack began, Israeli tanks, advancing in three separate columns, ran into trouble, with the lead vehicles sinking in wet ground and the Jordanians knocking them out, one after the other. Almost all the tanks were engaged all day in extricating those stuck in the mud or in fending off the Jordanians, or were themselves hit; none actually performed their task—to block reinforcements from reaching Karameh or guerrillas from escaping. Fierce Jordanian resistance was maintained despite continuous IAF strafing and rocketing attacks against Legion positions. A fourth IDF blocking force—a heliborne elite reconnaissance company—found the area they were set down in, in the hills east of Karameh, crawling with PLO fighters, many of them firing from well-prepared foxholes. "Only by a miracle was a major catastrophe avoided," the IDF historian of the operation later wrote.[88]

While these battles were raging, the paratroops reached Karameh, shortly before 7:00 A.M. Although outnumbered and heavily outgunned, dozens of guerrillas stood their ground and fought them, though many, including Arafat, fled eastward. At 11:00 the paratroops were ordered to withdraw, before they had completed their mission—but first they blew up about 175 of Karameh's houses.[89]

Simultaneously with the Karameh action, the IDF mounted an operation against a number of small guerrilla bases south of the Dead Sea. About twenty Jordanian soldiers and policemen and twenty Fatah men were killed, and twenty-seven prisoners were taken back to Israel for interrogation. The operation went smoothly and the raiders suffered no casualties.

Altogether the IDF lost 33 dead and 161 wounded at Karameh; 27 Israeli tanks were hit, four of them left behind. One fighter-bomber was shot down and a Mirage had to crash-land. The PLO lost 156 dead and 141 captured.[90] The Arab Legion lost 84 dead and 250 wounded.[91]

The guerrillas and the Jordanians had put up far fiercer resistance than anticipated; the IDF had failed to complete its assigned missions and had been forced to withdraw earlier than planned; most of the guerrillas had slipped through the net. Nevertheless it was hardly the great Palestinian (and Jordanian) victory that Arab spokesmen subsequently hailed. For the first time in decades, the propaganda broadcasts maintained, the Arabs had stood up to IDF armor and routed it. Karameh was to serve a generation of Palestinian fighters as a symbol of heroic resistance and proof of the IDF's vulnerability.

The instant legend was to have an immediate result. Thousands of young Palestinians, abandoning high school and university, flocked to Fatah, whose numbers rose within a few months from a couple of thousand to ten to fifteen thousand.[92] The battle also temporarily closed Arab ranks: Even Hussein declared, "I am becoming a guerrilla."[93] Karameh gave renewed impetus to the guerrillas' war against Israel—though immediately after the battle they moved their bases eastward, to be out of reach of the IDF's armor.

The expansion of the guerrilla movements was made possible by large donations from rich Arab states. Kuwait, after Karameh, imposed a 5 percent surtax for this purpose on its hundreds of thousands of Palestinian residents. The injections of capital and prestige enabled the PLO to cast off the restraining fetters of the Arab states and to become more independent. Hussein proved less able to control the guerrilla groups within his borders, while Syria lost control over various groups outside its borders.

Within months the Palestinian bases and refugee camps around Amman and in northern Jordan effectively turned into a state-within-a-state. Fatah's headquarters moved from Damascus to Amman. The guerrillas, AK-47s always slung over their shoulders, began to roam arrogantly around the towns; Hashemite sovereignty was challenged daily. Hussein's troops and police took offense, and there were periodic clashes in the streets of Amman.

During the following two years, while the *fedayeen* persistently tried to penetrate the Israeli defensive line, the IDF itself mounted hundreds of cross-border patrols and ambushes, infantry and armored raids, and air attacks on PLO targets and Jordanian units thought to be assisting the guerrillas. The continual blows threatened to undermine the Hashemite regime, and ultimately they were to prod it into crushing the guerrillas.

In the Gaza Strip, Palestinian terrorism and guerrilla warfare arrived somewhat belatedly. Relative quiet prevailed in 1967 and 1968. In 1969 there was a sudden surge in anti-Israeli operations, some seven hundred incidents, and by 1970, the guerrillas—especially the PFLP—more or less controlled a number of refugee camps.[94] Dozens of local residents, suspected of collaborating with the Israelis or merely working in Israel, were murdered.

A grenade attack on January 2, 1971, in the center of Gaza, in which two Israeli children were killed and their father and mother injured, was the last straw. The grenade had been thrown by a fifteen-year-old boy—according to Israel, paid the equivalent of $10 by PFLP officers.[95] Southern Command was instructed to crush the terrorists in the Strip ruthlessly. From Jerusalem's point of view the right man was on the spot: General Sharon, CO Southern Command, who launched the "cleansing" operation later that month. It was to last a year, and by its end, terrorism in the Strip, for all practical purposes, had been extirpated, with almost all the terrorists killed, captured, or driven across the border to Jordan and Egypt.[96]

At the start of 1971 there were seven to eight hundred guerrillas in the Strip. They hid during the day, coming out mostly at night to attack collaborators and Israelis, receiving orders from PLO, mainly PFLP, executives in Egypt and Jordan. Sharon's campaign was heralded by the dismissal, on January 4, of Gaza's mayor and Dayan's announcement that a string of Israeli settlements would be set up in the Strip. (The first had been established the previous month, December 1970. It was named "Kfar Darom" after the Jewish settlement destroyed by the Egyptian army in 1948.)

The operation was launched in mid-January, after the replacement of most of the rather easygoing IDF reservists who until then had patrolled Gaza's streets by crack conscript infantrymen, who mounted day and night patrols inside the towns and refugee camps and in the surrounding orange groves, without letup. Among the most feared Israeli troops were Druze border policemen who, within a week of their arrival, had shot twelve Arabs (five fatally) who failed to halt when challenged. Locals complained of numerous cases of beating and systematic humiliation at the hands of the Israeli soldiers.[97]

Sharon also made use of a small undercover unit—"Rimon"—whose members, mostly kibbutzniks, worked closely with the GSS and, dressing as Arabs, mingled with the local population. In 1970–71 the unit was expanded and given a key role in hunting down and killing terrorists. According to one journalistic investigation, Rimon executed "dozens" of captives, occasionally shooting suspects in the back who had supposedly "attempted to escape."[98]

The Gaza-Israel border was sealed off with a barbed-wire fence; roads were driven through the crowded refugee camps after rows of houses were demolished, and their inhabitants were moved elsewhere in the Strip. The roads sectionalized the camps and made them controllable by IDF patrols and observation posts.

Using both carrot and stick, the Israeli authorities steadily weaned the local population away from the guerrillas. Infantry squads relentlessly hunted them and shot them down. On November 21, 1971, Ziad al-Husseini ("Abu Nimr"), the PFLP commander in the Strip, committed suicide. The back of the resistance movement had been broken, with some 100 guerrillas killed and 700 captured. For about a decade, the area was to be almost completely free of guerrilla warfare or terrorism.

During 1968–70 there were occasional pinprick guerrilla raids from Syria across the Golan border, and sporadic Israeli retaliatory strikes. The Syrian authorities kept the guerrillas on a tight leash, generally preferring that they strike at Israel across other borders. But occasionally they decided to remind Jerusalem that they still wanted back the Golan Heights. On February 24, 1969, after an upsurge in guerrilla raiding, Israel responded with a major air attack on Fatah and Saiqa training camps deep in Syria.

The main secondary theater of Palestinian guerrilla operations was the Lebanese-Israeli border, which had been largely quiet since 1948. The intense IDF pressure on Fatah bases in Jordan during 1968 forced the guerrilla leaders to seek another sanctuary and front. In October 1968 Fatah and Saiqa established their first small bases in southern Lebanon.[99] In December and January 1969 the *fedayeen* launched their first rocket attacks from Lebanon against the

Israeli town of Kiryat Shmona, in the Galilee Panhandle. Hundreds of Palestinian guerrillas moved in, turning the town of Nabatiya into a regional headquarters and dominating the Arkoub, the area north of Mount Hermon.

The Christian-led Lebanese government and army realized the dangers—the
emergence of a PLO state-within-a-state and the provocation of IDF retaliatory
strikes, as had happened in Jordan. But Beirut was too weak to stop the process,
which was backed by Syria. Early in 1969 the guerrillas also took control of the
refugee camps in Lebanon. Local Muslims supported the guerrilla influx, viewing it as a means of shaking Christian dominance in the country.

October 1969 witnessed the first serious fighting between the Lebanese
army and PLO guerrillas stationed on the fringes of the Arkoub. Syria pointedly dispatched a relatively large force of guerrilla reinforcements along the
"Arafat Trail," linking Syria to the Arkoub. Lebanese troops also clashed with
Palestinians in Tripoli, Beirut, and Sidon. The fighting shook the Lebanese
polity, which in 1958 had endured a Muslim-Christian civil war. Some Muslim groups openly supported the guerrillas, and the threat of open Syrian
intervention hovered in the air. Nasser and the Lebanese leaders decided to
call it quits. In Egyptian-brokered talks the guerrillas and the Lebanese later
that month secretly signed an agreement (subsequently known as "the Cairo
Agreement") which effectively turned the Arkoub into sovereign PLO territory and assured it a safe supply line eastward to Syria. The guerrillas agreed
not to shell Israeli settlements from Lebanese territory, but they were left in
control of most of the refugee camps on the peripheries of Lebanon's cities,
assuring the development of a full-fledged Palestinian state-within-a-state
during the following decade. The PLO also promised to give the Lebanese
advance notice of any operation against Israel (a clause they never fulfilled).

What the Lebanese authorities had always feared soon came to pass. After
repeated PLO cross-border raids and rocket attacks, the IDF began to raid the
Arkoub, using both fighter-bombers and ground troops. But these raids and
the Cairo Agreement brought no relief to the border. On May 12–13, 1970, the
IDF launched its largest operation yet in this theater, aimed at clearing the
guerrillas out of most of the Arkoub, which the Israelis had begun calling
"Fatahland." The raiders briefly took and cleaned out a string of villages.
Lebanese army tanks and artillery, asserting Lebanese sovereignty rather than
feelings of fraternity with the embattled Palestinians, interfered and were
engaged by the Israelis. Three Syrian MiG-17s which tried to interfere were
shot down. Syria was goaded into counterattacking, but its artillery, which
opened up on IDF positions on the Golan, was in short order silenced by the
IAF.

Yet, despite its local successes, the IDF had failed to solve the problem of
Fatahland. The Syrians quickly moved hundreds of fresh guerrillas into the
area, and the raids on Israel were renewed. On May 22 a PFLP squad
ambushed an Israeli school bus near Moshav Avivim, killing twelve passen

gers (eight of them children) and wounding another nineteen. Israel, enraged, responded with massive artillery attacks on southern Lebanon, killing twenty villagers and wounding forty. The message was directed at Beirut: Either get rid of the guerrillas or suffer the consequences. Thousands of villagers fled northward.

After Avivim the IDF instituted regular armored patrols inside southern Lebanon. That summer Israeli engineering units pushed a road through the southern fringes of Fatahland to Jabal Russ (Har Dov, or Bear Mountain), a Hermon-range foothill that dominated the Arkoub. In July the IDF constructed a large fortress on the mountaintop. In effect Israel had annexed a small sliver of Lebanese territory.

But the Lebanese front remained secondary to Jordan, where the guerrilla organizations continued to grow and to harry the Israelis along the river. (And increasingly they began to target Israeli institutions and officials abroad.) But as their power increased, so did friction between them and the Jordanian army, and pressure on the Hashemite monarchy by the *fedayeen,* the Israelis, and neighboring Arab states. Fear grew that the upshot might be the overthrow of the monarchy.

Clashes broke out in May between Jordanian units and Palestinian fighters. On June 9, Hussein's tanks and artillery pounded several of Amman's refugee camps after guerrillas tried to free incarcerated *fedayeen* from a Jordanian prison; in four days of fighting about 400 people died and 750 were wounded. Hussein's motorcade came under guerrilla fire, and an assistant U.S. military attaché in Amman was murdered by Palestinians. On June 11 PFLP gunmen took hostage thirty-three Americans, Britons, and West Germans in two Amman hotels—and demanded the dismissal of the commander in chief, the interior minister, and the brigadier whose tanks had fired on the refugee camps.

Hussein caved in, and calm was temporarily restored. His government signed an agreement with Arafat on July 10, giving the PLO complete control over the refugee camps, while the guerrillas undertook to keep their armed men out of Amman city center. But the guerrillas failed to keep their part of the bargain. The signing on August 7 of the Israeli-Egyptian cease-fire agreement and the announcement of the Rogers peace plan only exacerbated matters, making the guerrillas in Jordan feel threatened. Indeed, Nasser cautioned the PLO to do nothing that might upset the cease-fire. And Hussein, heartened by the accord, publicly endorsed the Rogers initiative and warned that his government and army would not tolerate challenges to their authority. Once again the PLO leaders felt alone in the field against Israel—and perhaps against Hussein as well.

Within hours Hashemite policy and resolve became clear. On August 30, the army began to shell Fatah positions around Amman. On September 1 Hussein's motorcade was again attacked by guerrillas—the second assassination attempt in three months. The skirmishing ended on September 5, when a cease-fire was arranged and the army withdrew to the outskirts of Amman, but the climactic explosion was at hand. The spark was provided by the PFLP hijacking of three Western jetliners (TWA, Swissair, and Pan Am) and the taking of hundreds of British, American, and German hostages on September 6. Two of the planes were landed at a disused RAF base outside Amman—posing a direct, embarrassing challenge to Jordan's monarch. The aircraft, the hostages, and their captors were ringed by Jordanian army units that stood by helplessly.

Arafat and the majority in the PLO opposed the hijackings, understood that the Arab states were being alienated, and moved to eject the PFLP from the organization. To preempt PLO pressures, the PFLP on September 12 blew up the three aircraft and released most of the hostages. But it kept and dispersed among Jordan's refugee camps fifty-four of them, including twenty-four Jews. In response Israel arrested in the occupied territories about five hundred "counterhostages," most of them relatives of PFLP members. The message was clear: "Do not harm the hostages." But the emboldened guerrillas, acting as if the die had been cast, took control of swaths of northern Jordan, including the town of Irbid. On the 15th the local Fatah commander declared the area the "First Arab Soviet." Roadblocks were set up around the town and on the way to Jerash, effectively marking off the area as sovereign Palestinian territory. In the south a Fatah rebellion was put down by army units, backed by local Bedouin.

Hussein abruptly replaced his civilian cabinet with a twelve-man military government. On September 17 the army unleashed a full-scale assault, which came to be known as "Black September," on PLO camps and bases in Amman. It was a major gamble. Much of Jordan's population opposed the king, and almost all the Arab states were to side, with varying degrees of enthusiasm, with the PLO. Slaughtering those perennial victims, the Palestinians, was far from popular among the Arab masses. Two-thirds of all Jordanians and a full one-third of the Arab Legion were Palestinians. But the elite armored brigades were almost exclusively Bedouin, and these spearheaded the assault. It was an unequal battle: The guerrillas lacked both heavy weapons and proper organization.

Hundreds of Palestinian civilians were killed or wounded; there were also reports of looting and rape by the Legionnaires. By September 23, the Legion was in possession of the city center and most of the dominant heights, though much-battered concentrations of guerrillas held out in several camps; but it was only a matter of time before they succumbed to vastly superior firepower. Simultaneously with the fighting in Amman, clashes between troops and guerrillas erupted in the north in Zarka, Irbid, Kerak, and As Salt. Syria, the PLO's main backer in the Arab world, moved on September 18, sending three brigades across the border. On the 22nd, as the Syrian columns advanced toward Amman, Jordanian armor engaged the invaders and Jordanian jets ravaged them. (Syria refrained from committing air power, fearing that this might draw in the IAF on Jordan's side.) The Syrians came to a halt.[100]

But more telling still was the indirect intervention of Israel and the United States.[101] On September 20, Secretary of State Rogers denounced the invasion. President Nixon and National Security Adviser Kissinger contacted Israel and endorsed an IAF strike against the Syrians, if they captured Irbid and the surrounding area. Israeli armor was readied for action on the Golan and in the Beit She'an Valley, opposite Irbid. It was against this favorable international background that Hussein decided to gamble and commit his armor to repel the Syrians; he knew he had a safety net.

Assad caved in. On the afternoon of September 22 the Syrian tanks began to withdraw, and two days later the PLO sued for peace.[102] Hussein and his generals initially wished to complete the destruction of the *fedayeen* in Jordan, but were pressed by their allies to negotiate and sign (on September 27) the fourteen-point Cairo Agreement bringing the civil war to an end. The following day Nasser collapsed and died.

The PLO emerged from the war severely battered. Hussein said the Legion had lost two hundred soldiers, while the PLO spoke of 3,500 civilians and nine hundred guerrillas killed.[103] But the organization retained its presence in Jordan and the right to operate against Israel. The last guerrillas left Amman on November 7, the majority moving northward to the Irbid-Jerash-Ajlun triangle (which remained their stronghold until summer 1971). The following months were marked by recurrent clashes between the guerrillas and the Jordanian army, which more or less systematically harassed them. They lived in makeshift camps in the hills, caves, and woods south of Irbid and still constituted something of a state-within-a-state and a threat to Israel, though their raiding across the Jordan ceased almost completely after September 1970. Palestinian terrorist energies were diverted to targets abroad—Jordanian, Israeli, and Western.

However, Hussein still wanted to end the problem once and for all. After a string of skirmishes, on July 13, 1971, he ordered his troops to wipe out the guerrillas. The campaign around Ajlun lasted six days. Arafat's appeals for renewed Syrian intervention fell on deaf ears; the Iraqis, too, refused all assistance. The guerrillas were isolated and heavily outgunned, and their concentrations were picked off one after another. Arafat "declared war" on Jordan, which countered by pronouncing the Cairo Agreement null and void. By July 19, Jordan reported that 2,300 guerrillas had been captured. Most of the others—perhaps as many as 5,000—escaped to Syria, and during the following months many of them moved on to Lebanon. By November 1971 there were about 4,000 guerrillas in Fatahland.[104]

Southern Lebanon now became—and remained, until the Israeli invasion of 1982—the main PLO concentration and the principal theater of guerrilla operations. In response to an upsurge in January 1972 of guerrilla attacks on Israel—ambushes and long-distance rocketing—the IDF raided a number of Lebanese villages. In the wake of one such raid, an enlarged Lebanese army battalion moved into the area and effectively prevented further attacks on Israel until the summer.

On June 20 a squad of guerrillas crossed the border and rocketed an Israeli bus, wounding two persons. The following day Israel retaliated by bombing the Druze village of Hasbaya, from which the guerrillas had come. But the Israeli bombs apparently killed only Druze villagers—forty-eight in number, according to the official Lebanese tally. Israel conceded that the bombing had been an error. The renewal of serious attacks along the border (and a series of PLO attacks abroad) prompted the IDF to advance deep into central-southern Lebanon, on September 16–17, clearing out guerrillas and engaging a series of Lebanese army units, which had opened fire on the raiders.

THE WAR OF THE SPOOKS, 1968–73

On July 23, 1968, three Palestinians, members of the PFLP, brandishing pistols and grenades, hijacked an El Al jetliner traveling from Rome to Tel Aviv. They forced the pilot to land at Algiers and were then quietly allowed to leave Algeria. The Israeli passengers were released by the Algerian authorities only some five weeks later, after Israel agreed to release fifteen jailed Palestinians.

The hijacking, in effect, was the first shot in a Palestinian terror campaign against Israeli targets abroad. Later it also targeted "pro-Israeli" Western states and, occasionally, moderate Arab states, such as Jordan, as well as Jewish leaders and institutions around the world. The incidence of international terrorism was linked to the nature and level of operations along Israel's borders: Palestinian groups looked abroad for softer targets when cross-border raiding became difficult. It was also a function of ideological postulates and political changes within the different Palestinian military organizations, and of competition between them. Fatah, the main component of the PLO, generally opposed terrorist operations abroad as counterproductive. But after the PLO's expulsion from Jordan, Fatah unleashed a wave of terror initially against Jordanian targets, and subsequently against Israeli and Western objectives. A second wave of anti-Israeli operations abroad followed the 1982 invasion of Lebanon and the infighting in the PLO and the Fatah that ensued.

George Habash's PFLP, on the other hand, generally supported such operations on organizational and ideological grounds but tempered its actual activities in relation to various political and military realities inside the PLO and the

Middle East. As the PFLP was very small, it could hardly expect to make its weight felt in cross-border raiding, even if that had been possible; but spectacular, attention-grabbing attacks abroad were another matter altogether. This factor also underlay the international terrorist campaigns of other minuscule Palestinian groups. Organizations such as Abu Nidal never suffered from ideological inhibitions and periodically unleashed murderous attacks against European, Arab, and moderate Palestinian targets during the following decades. It also, though rarely, attacked Israeli and Jewish targets.

Aerial hijacking was "invented" in the 1960s by Cuban-connected Latin American terrorists. But the Palestinians, though not its authors, perfected the genre. In all, their organizations between 1968 and 1977 hijacked or attempted to hijack twenty-nine aircraft. And they were the first to turn jetliners into targets of light weapons and rocket attacks: On December 26, 1968, PFLP terrorists shot up an El Al liner on the ground in Athens, killing one passenger and wounding a stewardess. They were also the first to bomb jetliners out of the skies with time- or altimeter-detonated bombs: On February 21, 1970, a Swissair jetliner en route from Zurich to Israel was blown up by a bomb placed by the PFLP–General Command (the PFLP breakaway headed by Ahmed Jibril), killing all forty-seven crew and passengers, thirteen of whom were Israelis. A second bomb, planted that day by the group in an Austrian Airlines plane flying from Frankfurt to Vienna, exploded in the luggage compartment but failed to down the aircraft or cause casualties.

Palestinian terrorists were also the first to massacre passengers at airport check-in counters and in preflight waiting rooms, and the first to take over hotels or meeting halls and take large numbers of bystanders or participants hostage for political purposes. And they were the first to poison food—Israeli-exported oranges in Europe, in 1978—for political reasons.[105]

In the course of the international terror campaign, which reached its peak in 1972–73, the Palestinian groups established contacts and, occasionally, close relations with assorted terrorist and guerrilla organizations in Europe, Japan, and the Third World (the West German Red Army Faction, the French Action Directe, the Japanese Red Army, and so on) and occasionally undertook joint operations with them. In one or two cases non-Arab terrorist groups carried out anti-Israeli operations as "subcontractors" for their Palestinian allies; the Palestinians apparently rendered similar (and other) services to these foreign groups. Palestinian organizations during the 1970s trained cadres of European and Third World terrorists in their base camps in Lebanon. Some of the Palestinian groups also developed close relations with the intelligence services of the Eastern European states (principally the Soviet KGB and the East German Stasi), which supplied them with training, arms, safe havens, and false documents. Groups that were active abroad enjoyed the logistical services of friendly embassies, mostly of the radical Arab states.

In response to the attacks on El Al airliners, embassies, and consulates, the

GSS considerably beefed up its protection of all potential targets, turning each embassy and consulate into a virtual fortress and seating teams of air marshals on every El Al flight. Subsequently attacks on such targets fell off sharply. But these measures involved an outlay of many millions of dollars and a great deal of high-grade manpower.

In addition to defensive measures, Israel periodically unleashed its own counter-terrorist operations. The first of these was probably the raid by the General Staff Reconnaissance Unit (Sayeret Matkal) on Beirut International Airport on December 28, 1968, which was a direct response to a PFLP attack two days before in Athens and, more distantly, to the hijacking of the jetliner to Algiers the previous July. Landing in four helicopters, the commandos blew up thirteen empty Arab airliners and, by mistake, a Ghanaian one as well. Israel charged that the PFLP terrorists had been trained in Lebanon and had embarked on their missions from Beirut.

In 1968–69 the PFLP was responsible for almost all the Palestinian attacks abroad, including one (on February 18, 1969) on an El Al plane in Zurich airport; two bomb attacks on Jewish-owned stores in London (July 18); the hijacking of a TWA jetliner between Rome and Lydda to Damascus (August 29); grenade attacks on the El Al office in Brussels and on the Israel embassies in The Hague and Bonn (all on September 8); and a time bomb in the Jewish Community Center in West Berlin (defused September 9). Three PFLP terrorists who had planned to hijack a TWA jetliner were arrested in Athens on December 21.

From June 1970 on, PFLP activities were directed against Jordan and the United States rather than Israel: There were attacks on the Philadelphia and Intercontinental Hotels in Amman, and the abduction of an American diplomat and murder of an American assistant military attaché occurred there. The triple hijacking on September 6 precipitated King Hussein's "Black September" crackdown, which in turn gave birth to the Black September organization, the PFLP's successor in the field of international terrorism. Having been trounced and humbled by the Arab Legion, and denied their main theater of operations against Israel (the Jordanian-Israeli frontier), the Fatah leadership, using Beirut as its base, decided also to embark on such headline-grabbing activities, initially against Jordan and subsequently against Saudi Arabia, Israel, and Israel's western backers.

Salah Khalaf (Abu Iyad), the Fatah leader who secretly headed Black September, described his organization's purpose: "to make the world feel that the [Palestinian] people exists." In January 1973, at the height of its activities, he told a Palestinian student conference: "We shall find the enemy [Israel] in every place . . . hunt the enemy down in every place we can reach him."[106] But Black September operations also had other motives: to undermine relations between Arab and Western governments and to inspire Palestinian youth. There was also a problem of internal PLO or Fatah cohesion, with extremists

constantly demanding greater militancy. The moderates apparently acquiesced in the creation of Black September in order to survive.

The establishment of Black September was secretly resolved upon at a
Fatah congress in Damascus in August–September 1971, as a compromise
between moderates and extremists.[107] It was based on Fatah's existing special
intelligence and security apparatus, Jihad al-Rasad, and on the PLO offices
and representatives in the various European capitals. From very early on there
was cooperation with the PFLP. A number of Black September operations
were clearly planned and carried out jointly by Fatah and PFLP personnel,
such as the October 1972 hijacking of a Lufthansa aircraft. The aircraft was
hijacked by a PFLP team—but with the purpose of freeing Black September–
Fatah operatives from German jails.[108]

The three-year period 1971–73 witnessed—principally as a result of the
activities of Black September—the greatest concentration ever of terrorist
attacks by Palestinians outside "Palestine," with sixty operations in 1973
alone, compared, for example, with only two in 1968.[109] Even before Black
September was "officially" founded at the end of 1971, Fatah, in the summer
of that year, unleashed a series of attacks against Jordanian targets abroad.
Then, because of the negative diplomatic fallout, its leaders were persuaded to
officially quit the international terror arena and to replace it with a hitherto
unknown, deniable organization that would be smaller and more efficient than
the large, cumbersome Fatah. Moreover, as its leaders knew, Fatah had long
before been penetrated by both the Israeli and Jordanian intelligence services.
The creation of a new, smaller organization would enhance security.

The lull ended on November 28 in Cairo, with Black September's dramatic
first operation: A team of terrorists gunned down Jordan's prime minister,
Wasfi Tal—who was regarded as an architect of the Arab Legion onslaught
against the PLO in September 1970 and July 1971—and then proceeded
"symbolically" to drink some of the dead man's blood off the sidewalk. Black
September—probably as a result of inter-Arab political developments—then
suspended operations against Jordan, and in December 1971 began to attack
Israeli targets. A new method was adopted—letter bombs were mailed to
Israelis, Jews, and even to President Nixon, Secretary of State Rogers, and
Secretary of Defense Melvyn Laird. In September 1972 an Israeli diplomat in
London was killed by one of these devices.[110]

On May 8, 1972, a Sabena jetliner, en route from Brussels to Tel Aviv, was
hijacked. At Lydda Airport the hijackers demanded that Israel release hundreds of jailed Palestinian guerrillas and terrorists. Israel, as usual, stuck to its
traditional line of not succumbing to such extortion. The following day, after
"negotiations" designed to buy time, members of the IDF's Sayeret Matkal,
dressed in airport technicians' white overalls, stormed the aircraft and killed
two of the terrorists and captured the other two. One passenger was killed in
the crossfire. Under interrogation, the prisoners revealed that they had been

sent on their mission by 'Ali Hassan Salameh, the Black September chief of operations.[111]

Much more bloody was the PFLP-engineered raid on Lydda Airport three weeks later, on May 30. Using its links with non-Arab groups, the PFLP in April brought over for training from North Korea to Lebanon a group of Japanese Red Army terrorists. A three-man team then made its way to Rome, where it boarded an Air France jetliner bound for Lydda. Their suitcases were packed with Kalashnikov AK-47 assault rifles and grenades. After disembarking, the terrorists picked up their luggage and opened fire in all directions. The Israeli security personnel were taken by surprise and their response was slow and ineffectual. Twenty-seven people were killed and 71 wounded, many of them Catholic Puerto Rican pilgrims to the Holy Land. Two of the Japanese terrorists also lay dead, killed by their own weapons; the third was captured.

Black September and the PFLP became primary targets of Israeli retaliation. On July 8, agents in Beirut placed a bomb in the car of the PFLP's spokesman, writer Ghassan Kanafani, who was blown up, along with his seventeen-year-old niece. On July 11 rockets hit the Beirut rooms of Wadi'a Haddad, the PFLP's head of foreign operations, though he himself was not injured. Kanafani's successor, Bassam Abu Sharif, was badly injured on July 25 in his Beirut office by a parcel bomb.

Black September's attacks had ranged wide and far, but initially Israel restricted its antiterrorist operations to the Arab world. The next major Black September operation—the most spectacular of them all—was to change all that. In the early morning hours of September 5, a squad of gunmen penetrated the athletes' dormitories in the Munich Olympic Village, at the height of the 1972 Olympic Games, and took over the Israeli team's rooms. Two team members who tried to bar the way and warn their colleagues were shot dead, and nine athletes were taken hostage. The operation was clearly designed to exploit the enormous media coverage of the games. In negotiations with the terrorists, the West German authorities agreed to allow the gunmen and their hostages to fly out to Cairo. The hostages, bound hand and foot, were then driven to waiting helicopters and flown to a military airport outside Munich. Israel had rejected the terrorists' demand to release about two hundred imprisoned Palestinians, and the Germans had decided on a rescue operation.

Ten minutes after the helicopters landed, a waiting German Border Police team opened fire. The terrorists shot and threw grenades at their captives before they themselves were hit. All nine Israelis died. Five of the terrorists were killed, three wounded and captured. A German policeman was killed, and one of the German helicopter pilots was wounded in the inept rescue attempt.[112] On November 29 the three captured terrorists were released by the Germans after a Lufthansa jetliner, en route from Frankfurt to Beirut, was hijacked by Black September terrorists over Zagreb.

The Israeli cabinet viewed the Munich assault as a challenge that could not go unanswered. The IDF immediately bombed PLO bases in Lebanon and Syria, most of them inside refugee camps, killing or wounding about two hundred Palestinians. But more significant was a secret decision by Golda Meir and the cabinet Defense Committee authorizing the Mossad to kill Black September and PFLP officers wherever they could be found. The Mossad set up a special hit team that, aided by the agency's stations in Europe, was to locate and eliminate the terrorists.

Using information gathered from "turned" PLO personnel, Palestinians in the occupied territories (some of them sent especially to Europe to gather information), and friendly European intelligence services, the Mossad compiled a target list and went to work. The first to go was Wael 'Aadel Zwaiter, suspected member of Black September and the official PLO representative in Italy, gunned down on October 16. (Abu Iyad later wrote that Zwaiter was not connected to Black September and was "fiercely opposed . . . to all forms of terrorism."[113]) This was followed by letter bomb attacks on the PLO representatives in Algeria and Libya, on the Red Crescent representative in Stockholm, and on Palestinian student activists in Bonn and Copenhagen, all of whom were wounded.

The attacks grew increasingly sophisticated as the potential targets became more cautious. On December 8, 1972, the PLO's representative in Paris, Muhammad Hamshari, was assassinated by a radio-detonated bomb under his desk—the detonation signal was sent over the telephone when he lifted the receiver. Over the next three months, four operatives of the PLO, PFLP, and PFLP-GC were dispatched in Cyprus, Greece, and Paris.

On the night of April 9, 1973, in the heart of Beirut, came the most complex, daring, and telling attack: Operation Springtime of Youth, conducted by the Mossad with the IDF's Sayeret Matkal and naval commandos, combined accurate intelligence and operational efficiency. The targets were Muhammad Yusuf al-Najjar ("Abu Yusuf"), head of Fatah's intelligence arm (which ran Black September); Kamal Adwan, who headed the PLO's "Western Sector," responsible for PLO activities in Israel and the occupied territories; and Kamal Nassir, the PLO's spokesman.

Nine missile boats and a small fleet of Dabbur patrol boats carried the commandos to a point south of Beirut; they came ashore on a deserted beach in rubber dinghies and set off for their targets in cars prepared by a Mossad advance team. One detachment drove in two cars to downtown Beirut, killed a guard, and broke into three flats in two apartment houses. There, with silenced pistols, the commandos—led by Lt. Col. Ehud Barak, the CO of Sayeret Matkal—cut down Adwan, Nassir, and Najjar (as well as Najjar's wife, who had tried to shield him). Najjar's children and Adwan's family were spared. The commandos collected documents before getting out and driving back to the waiting dinghies.

A second detail, commanded by Col. Amnon Lipkin-Shahak, drove to south Beirut's Sabra district, to the seven-story headquarters of Naif Hawatmeh's PDFLP. After a brief skirmish the commandos planted a large explosive charge inside, and detonated it before retreating. Part of the building collapsed. Two raiders were killed and one was wounded; dozens of PDFLP men died. Two secondary forces attacked the Fatah headquarters for Gaza operations and a Fatah workshop in Beirut's southern Uza'i district. A third independent force, of naval commandos, landed in northern Beirut and blew up a small Fatah explosives plant, and a paratroop unit destroyed the PLO's main garage, just south of Sidon.[114]

"Springtime" was followed by one further Mossad success. On June 28, 1973, the Algerian-born suspected director of Black September's operations in Europe, Muhammad Boudia, was killed by a bomb placed in his car in a Paris street.

Then came the fall, in the Norwegian resort town of Lillehammer. The Mossad hit team gathered there after an informant mistakenly placed 'Ali Hassan Salameh in town. On July 21, the Israelis shot dead a Moroccan waiter in the belief that he was Salameh. The planners had also gravely underestimated Norwegian efficiency. Within hours, police had netted six of the operatives, though a number of others slipped away. Five Israelis, including two women, were subsequently tried and jailed.[115]

Following Lillehammer, the Mossad's war against Black September and the PFLP was effectively suspended. Almost simultaneously, Black September stopped its activities and vanished forever. Its executives had been forced to expend far more resources and energy than before on protecting themselves, but the Mossad campaign had failed to crush the shadowy organization. Throughout the "war of the spooks," Black September continued to function, carrying out operations like the takeover of the Israeli Embassy in Bangkok (December 28, 1972); a letter-bomb campaign against Israeli missions abroad (January–February 1973); the planting on March 6 of car bombs at Israeli targets in New York (all were discovered in time and neutralized); the murder on April 27 of an El Al employee in Rome; and the murder on July 1 of the Israeli air attaché in Washington. On September 5 a SAM-7 attack on an El Al jetliner in Rome was thwarted and five Arabs were arrested.

As for those responsible for Munich: On January 22, 1979, the Mossad at last caught up with and killed Salameh in Beirut (along with several bodyguards) using a remote-controlled car bomb. Abu Daoud was shot and seriously wounded on July 27, 1981, in a Warsaw coffee shop. Salah Khalaf (Abu Iyad), who had become Arafat's deputy and ironically a leading PLO moderate, was murdered—allegedly by an Abu Nidal agent—on January 14, 1991, in Tunis, though this may have been an Israeli "false flag" operation.

The PLO closed down Black September in autumn 1973, prompted, above all, by the political calculation that no more good would come of terrorism abroad. The October War pushed the Palestinian problem to the top of the international agenda once again and opened up diplomatic avenues for progress. Continued international terrorism, it was now felt by Arafat and his colleagues, would tend to subvert political opportunities. In March 1974, in an interview with an Austrian newspaper, Arafat spoke out against it; in July 1974 the PLO formally came out against it, while supporting a stepped-up armed struggle in the occupied territories. The PLO even began to punish Arabs who committed acts of terrorism abroad, though it still sought to overthrow the Hashemite monarchy in Jordan, if necessary through the assassination of King Hussein.[116]

A similar trend had become apparent in the PFLP during the summer of 1973, when Habash publicly cautioned against airplane hijacking. His "moderation" caused the breakaway of his more radical head of foreign operations, Wadi'a Haddad, and some of his officers, but Habash continued to oppose hijacking thereafter, though he did support other types of international terrorist activity.[117]

Both the PFLP and Haddad's faction still attacked Israeli targets abroad. The PFLP was responsible for a series of car bomb attacks against Jewish targets in Paris on August 3, 1974; two abortive rocket attacks against El Al aircraft in Paris on January 13 and 19, 1975; and attacks on El Al passengers in Istanbul and Paris in 1978.

Black September imitators plagued Israeli targets abroad well into the 1980s. While they did not enjoy the firepower, logistical infrastructure, and political connections of Fatah, they often proved to be more difficult to penetrate. The Haddad and Abu Nidal groups were among the more deadly splinter groups. On December 21, 1975, a group of Haddad's men, led by the Venezuelan terrorist "Carlos" ("the Jackal"), raided an OPEC ministers' meeting in Vienna and took twenty hostages, whom they flew to Algeria. Five people were killed in the raid. Three of Haddad's men and two German terrorists tried to bring down an El Al jetliner with a SAM-7 in Nairobi airport on January 25, 1976, but they were captured, deported, and tried and jailed in Israel.

Five months later, on June 27, 1976, four Haddad terrorists (two Palestinians and two Germans) hijacked an Air France Airbus with 268 passengers and twelve crew en route from Lydda via Athens to Paris, and diverted it to the airport at Entebbe in Uganda, on the northwestern shore of Lake Victoria. The passengers and crew were herded into a terminal, guarded by a company of Ugandan troops. The local dictator, Idi Amin (probably bribed), was apparently working with the terrorists. During the following days, additional German and Arab terrorists joined the hijackers. Non-Israeli passengers were released; the one hundred or so Israelis remained, along with the French crew, who opted to stay with their passengers. The terrorists demanded the release of fifty-three of their comrades jailed in Israel, Kenya, Switzerland, France, and Germany.

After days of agonizing, the Israeli cabinet on July 1 decided to begin negotiating a prisoner release with the terrorists.[118] But hours after the cabinet vote, Defense Minister Peres persuaded a hesitant Prime Minister Rabin to approve an IDF rescue plan.[119]

On the afternoon of July 3, about half an hour after the bulk of the task force had taken off, the mission got its final go-ahead from the cabinet.[120] Generals and ministers realized they had approved a daring gamble—an airborne operation involving an eight-thousand-kilometer round trip over mostly unfriendly territory, with no possibility of reinforcing or rescuing the force should a disaster occur. Hundreds of Israeli lives were at risk, and any number of things could go wrong. But the decision-makers realized that to submit to terrorism would involve major costs, with further acts of extortion and national humiliation.

The four Hercules transport aircraft, each with three pilots and three navigators, took off from Sharm ash-Sheikh. They were packed to the gills, carrying a 150-man commando force and tons of equipment and fuel. They were followed by two Boeing 707s—an airborne command and communications center and a field hospital. To avoid radar detection, they flew low over the Red Sea and then climbed to 20,000 feet, proceeding along the Sudanese-Ethiopian border in complete radio silence and without lights through thick clouds and violent thunderstorms.

A British transport plane was scheduled to land at Entebbe at 11:00 P.M. (Israel time). The lead Hercules landed, without lights, in its wake, "hiding" behind its radar image and exploiting the runway lights, which had been turned on. The other three followed. The assault force, commanded by Yonatan ("Yoni") Netanyahu (brother of the future prime minister), quickly disembarked. The spearhead unit, faces blackened, dressed in Ugandan camouflage uniforms, headed straight for the terminal in a long black Mercedes (like the vehicle used by Idi Amin) and two Land Rovers, lights blazing. They stormed the building, killing the terrorists and about a dozen Ugandan soldiers. From the initial firefight to the takeover of the main hall, where the hostages were sleeping on the floor, took twenty to thirty seconds. Netanyahu was shot dead outside the building by a Ugandan sniper. The Israelis suppressed the Ugandan fire and quickly shepherded the hostages to a waiting Hercules.

By 12:41 A.M., July 4, all four Hercules were back in the air, on their way to Nairobi for refueling. Three of the hostages had been killed and six wounded in the cross fire inside the terminal. A fourth, an elderly woman who had been removed to a Kampala hospital a day or two before, was subsequently murdered by Amin's men. Netanyahu was the only IDF fatality in the operation; another soldier was badly wounded. Eight German and Arab terrorists died in the shootout, and the Ugandans suffered twenty to forty dead.

On July 4, at 8:00 A.M., the aircraft landed in Israel to a tumultuous welcome. The "Entebbe Raid," as it was to be known, was a brilliant, daring, and successful rescue operation and is still studied in special forces training schools around the world. It was to be more than a year before Haddad mounted another major international operation—the hijacking on October 13, 1977, of a Lufthansa jetliner, en route from Majorca to Frankfurt, to Mogadishu, Somalia. A year later, on August 20, 1978, Haddad's men attacked a bus carrying El Al crew members in London, killing a stewardess and wounding three others. Haddad was also apparently responsible for an attempt to blow up an El Al liner in midair between Switzerland and Israel on April 21, 1980, and for a bomb outside a Paris synagogue in which three bystanders (including an Israeli tourist) were killed on October 4, 1980.

During the mid-1970s the Abu Nidal group swiftly outpaced Haddad and the other Palestinian groups in the field of international terrorism. Its favored targets were "moderate" Arabs. In 1978 it dispatched several PLO representatives interested in reaching a settlement with Israel. In 1981–82 it began to attack Jewish targets such as synagogues in Vienna, Brussels, and Rome and a Jewish restaurant in the Marais district of Paris.[121] The main target in 1982–83 was to be Jordan and its allies in the Arab world. The purpose of these operations was extortion. After a series of murders of diplomats and the blowing up of a Gulf Air jetliner over Abu Dhabi on September 23, 1983, killing 111 passengers and crew, the Emirates apparently agreed to pay Abu Nidal $17 million, in installments. The Kuwaitis also secretly began to pay a monthly stipend.[122]

Abu Nidal's attacks continued in the mid-1980s with a series of outrages. On December 24, 1985, teams of gunmen opened fire almost simultaneously near the El Al ticket counters at airports in Rome and Vienna, killing 18 persons and wounding 110, mostly Western tourists and businessmen. A year later, on September 26, Abu Nidal gunmen murdered twenty-one worshippers in Istanbul's Neve Shalom Synagogue during the Sabbath morning service.

The Israeli occupation of the West Bank and Gaza Strip and the crushing of the Arab armies in June 1967 reenergized the Palestinian people and put the Palestinian problem back on the international agenda. An issue dead for close to twenty years had suddenly come alive; it was kept alive, and the Palestinian people were mobilized and motivated, by dint of the unremitting guerrilla/terrorist activities against Israel. A desperate people both rediscovered its identity and found a means of expressing its political will through violence. Palestinian guerrilla warfare across the Jordan River and over the Lebanese-Israeli frontier may have been of no more than nuisance value, militarily speaking. But it gave Jerusalem and the world no respite and in various ways kept the Arab states, generally unenthusiastic about doing battle with Israel, mobilized in varying degrees behind the Palestinian cause.

Until 1987 Israel proved easily able to control the Palestinian population of the West Bank and Gaza. But it could not staunch either their nationalism or international pressures to alleviate their plight. At the same time, controlling the territories subverted Israel's democratic and legal norms and increasingly fissured society along bitter fault lines. An ever more militant, annexationist, racist right wing came to the fore and increasingly determined government policy and behavior.

Ultimately, the thrust of Israeli policy and the weight of the occupier's boot were to give rise among the conquered population to powerful fundamentalist Muslim currents—in various ways mirroring developments among Israel's Jews—which were subsequently to mount serious challenges to moderate opinions and parties. To some degree, the growth of Palestinian guerrilla and terrorist activity against Israel was a response not just to the occupation, which involved daily humiliation of the population by the occupiers, but also to the annexationist spirit that had laid hold of the Israeli polity. It was understood that Israel was not going to release its grip on the territories unless it was forced to. And if attacking Israelis in the occupied territories or in Israel proper grew more difficult, then Palestinians were just going to have to find more vulnerable targets farther afield.

In retrospect, the various Palestinian campaigns from the late 1960s through the 1980s outside the Middle East had a dual and contradictory effect. They put the "Palestinian problem" on the world agenda while substantially undermining world sympathy for the Palestinian cause; the terrorist outrages were both useful and important to the cause while at the same time putting it into disrepute.

The mainstream bodies—the PLO and Fatah—were aware of this. Sometimes they distanced themselves from the outrages and claimed to have had no part in them—while clandestinely organizing them, such as the Black September operations of 1971–73. At other times they renounced international terrorism in principle and as policy, while periodically mounting individual terrorist acts to achieve specific objectives. Usually such attacks were carried out by nonmainstream PLO groups, and could subsequently be disavowed by the leadership. Without doubt, Arafat recognized the value of the terrorist splinter groups; they could be relied upon both to keep the Palestinian issue alive and to hurt Israel—while he himself could denounce these groups as anti-PLO renegades, or at least dissociate himself from their actions.

NINE

CHE OCTOBER WAR, 1973

I n the October war, also known as the Yom Kippur or Ramadan war, Presidents Anwar Sadat of Egypt and Hafez Assad of Syria sought to regain the territories lost in 1967. Neither aimed to destroy Israel, though during the opening hours of the conflict, its leaders could not be sure of this; both Sadat and Assad knew that this was beyond their powers and that Israel, if mortally threatened, would unleash devastating nuclear strikes.[1] There was, however, a major disparity between their aims, stemming in part from the difference in size between the Sinai Peninsula and the Golan Heights. Syrian defense minister Tlass later wrote: "We sought to liberate the conquered Arab lands, while Egypt sought to cross the Canal and remain on [both] its banks . . . out of a desire to push things forward on the international plane"[2] (that is, to get hold of a strip of territory on the east bank of the Canal[3] so as to jolt Israel and the world community into breaking the political deadlock). The Syrians wished to reconquer all of the heights, something they believed could be achieved in a few days.[4]

For both Sadat and Assad, the war promised major gains, beginning with a restoration of Arab pride. (After the war Arab chroniclers would even speak of "the rebirth" of "Egyptian man."[5]) Merely daring to go to war against the invincible IDF would be seen as profoundly courageous; wiping out the shame of 1967, indeed the shame of Arab history since 1948, would bring both regimes rewards in terms of popularity, legitimacy, and longevity, as well as large contributions from the oil kingdoms.

COUNTDOWN TO WAR

On February 4, 1971, in a speech to the Egyptian parliament, Sadat launched what he called a peace "initiative" designed to obtain Israel's withdrawal from the Canal area and a reopening of the waterway, with a lasting cease-fire. He suggested that the six-month cease-fire brokered by the United States the previous August, which was due to expire the following day, might serve as the first stage of a process leading to a final peace settlement. On December 28, 1970, in an interview with the *New York Times*, Sadat had explicitly spoken of the possibility of "peace" with Israel if it withdrew from every inch of Arab land occupied in 1967 (a radical departure from the position taken in Khartoum, though the reference to "peace" was deleted from the version of the interview published in Arabic in Cairo's *al-Ahram*).[6] In January 1971 an Egyptian general, a "close friend of Sadat," approached the American chargé d'affaires in Cairo and proposed a partial settlement, based on Israel withdrawing twenty-five miles and Egypt reopening the Canal and agreeing to extend the cease-fire. Yitzhak Rabin, then ambassador in Washington, recommended pursuing the overture, but Prime Minister Golda Meir would not consider withdrawing from the Canal without a full peace treaty.[7]

The Sadat initiative in fact originated in a proposal by Defense Minister Moshe Dayan, who had outlined a possible interim separation of forces agreement to Meir on September 4, 1970: the IDF to be redeployed twenty miles east of the Canal, and Egypt to reopen the waterway and rebuild the Canalside cities to demonstrate commitment to nonbelligerency.

The proposal met with a cool reception among his fellow ministers, including Meir. Nonetheless, Dayan broached it again, apparently with her reluctant agreement, at a meeting with National Security Adviser Henry Kissinger in Washington in December. Sadat, in his February 1971 speech, proposed both an interim agreement and negotiation of a peace agreement with the help of Gunnar Jarring.[8] Israel rejected the overture. Years later Gad Ya'acobi, a Labor Party cabinet minister, wrote: "Israel did not take in the full significance of Sadat's speech."[9]

Israel's response was to ask if its shipping would be allowed through the Canal during the interim arrangement, and to declare that it opposed any Egyptian military presence east of the Canal. It also insisted that Egyptian forces on the Canal's west bank would have to be severely reduced. Moreover, Israel opposed complete withdrawal to the pre–June 1967 borders, and said withdrawal would be correlated in depth to the extent of the continued cease-fire.[10] When the full cabinet discussed the Egyptian proposals on February 7,

Meir and others were unenthusiastic.[11] Rabin again recommended serious consideration of the overture. But on February 9, addressing the Knesset, Meir rejected the initiative and the idea of an "interim settlement": Israel wanted a full peace treaty, not partial arrangements; Sadat's address "was not a peace speech."[12] Meir was later to write of herself: "Intransigence was to become my middle name."[13]

Meir reinforced the impression of Israeli inflexibility by declaring, on March 13, that Sinai must be demilitarized, and that Sharm ash-Sheikh, with an access road from Eilat, as well as the Golan Heights and united Jerusalem, must remain under Israeli rule.[14] Dayan said bluntly that he preferred "Sharm ash-Sheikh without peace to peace without Sharm ash-Sheikh."[15] The United States and the United Nations pressed the Israelis to reconsider. In response to a memorandum from Jarring, Egypt expressed explicit readiness for "peace" with Israel for the first time in an official document. It was to be based on complete withdrawal from the occupied territories.[16] The Israeli response to the memorandum insisted that there could be no return to the pre-1967 borders. Assistant Secretary of State Sisco commented: "Israel will be considered responsible for the rejection of the best opportunity to achieve peace since the establishment of the state."[17]

Nonetheless, Dayan still hoped for a settlement. On March 22 he formally presented his proposal to the cabinet, this time suggesting that the IDF withdraw thirteen to twenty miles, to the western entrances of the Sinai passes, in exchange for the reopening of the Canal, the rebuilding of the Canal-side cities, and an "end-of-belligerency agreement"—not full peace. Moreover, the areas evacuated by Israel were to become demilitarized.[18] But the cabinet demurred. While setting aside its routine insistence on nothing less than a comprehensive peace treaty, it ruled that the interim withdrawal should be only five to eight miles in depth, leaving the IDF within immediate striking range of the Canal's east bank. The ministers refused to link the interim agreement to a commitment to withdraw from all of Sinai in exchange for peace, as Egypt was demanding. Indeed, on March 31, the cabinet insisted on retaining the Gaza Strip and Sharm with a land connection, in any final settlement.[19]

Egypt rejected these terms. Sadat saw the interim settlement as a stage on the way to a comprehensive settlement based on complete withdrawal to the June 4, 1967, borders. He also rejected demilitarization of the east bank of the Canal.

U.S. Secretary of State Rogers believed that Sadat sincerely wanted peace—but, in exchange, had to have all of Sinai. This was the gist of Rogers's message to the Israeli leadership in Jerusalem in May 1971. Again the ministers rejected the implied deal, and returned to the idea of an interim arrangement—but without accepting the Egyptian conditions or countenancing even a symbolic crossing of the Canal by Egyptian troops.[20] Months later, Meir and other ministers apparently came around to accepting a token crossing by a small number of "uniformed" Egyptians and a withdrawal of the IDF twenty-five miles eastward, to the Sinai passes. But by then the Egyptians had abandoned the idea of negotiation and had probably decided on war.[21]

In retrospect, it seems that in February–May 1971 Israel "missed an historic opportunity" for peace, in the words of Dayan's aide at the time, Col. Arie Braun.[22] Gad Ya'acobi, then a Dayan protégé, echoed Braun's judgment.[23] But Meir, in her 1975 autobiography, remembered things differently: Apart from "talk about reopening the Suez Canal," the Arabs "continued to refuse to meet us or deal with us in any way . . . in 1971 or 1972."[24]

By May 1971, Sadat was persuaded that war was his only option. Egypt and the Soviet Union, represented by President Podgorny, signed a pact in Cairo, committing the Soviets to help Egypt "erase the consequences of [Israeli] aggression." In early June, Sadat announced that he was willing "to sacrifice a million Egyptian soldiers" to recover the lost lands. On June 22, he called 1971 "the year of decision." In July he declared that Egypt could no longer accept the state of "no war, no peace"; there had to be a resolution one way or another.[25] He publicly compared the Zionists to the medieval Crusaders who, like a wave, would eventually recede and vanish.[26]

Egypt pressed the USSR for large quantities of relatively sophisticated weapons, including Scud medium-range ground-to-ground missiles, which could reach Israel's population centers. Sadat viewed the Scuds as a deterrent, however limited, to Israel's nuclear weaponry. The Soviets stepped up arms deliveries but apparently remained unenthusiastic about war, perhaps fearing a repeat of 1967 or a confrontation with the United States. Moscow's misgivings sparked a measure of disaffection in Egypt. Moreover, some Soviet military advisers exhibited what their hosts regarded as contempt, which was deeply resented by the Egyptian officer corps. Last, the Soviets dragged their feet over delivery of more sophisticated weapons, without which the Egyptians felt they could not go to war.

Sadat's "year of decision," embarrassingly, came and went without war. He blamed Moscow for the mockery to which he was subsequently subjected.[27] At the same time, he began to view the thousands of Soviet officers in Egypt as both a restraining presence (they apparently tended to sow defeatism and opposition to the war policy in the units to which they were attached) and as an impediment to improved relations with the United States, which he now understood was the only power that could influence Israel. Like Nasser, Sadat had never been happy with the image of Egypt as a Soviet client.

Resentment of the Soviet Union came to a head in May 1972, when Sadat was enraged by a joint American-Soviet communiqué, issued during President Nixon's visit to Moscow, which implicitly called for Arab restraint in the Middle East. He feared that a superpower détente would freeze the situation, with Israel indefinitely continuing its occupation of Arab lands.[28]

In July, Sadat, with his penchant for the dramatic, announced the expulsion of thousands of Soviet military advisers. Perhaps this would jar the Kremlin into giving Egypt what it wanted: sophisticated weaponry and a free hand in deciding to go to war. At the same time it would earn Sadat points in Washington. By August the fifteen thousand or so Soviet personnel (air and antiaircraft units as well as almost all the advisers) had left. Israel (and the United States) misinterpreted Sadat's move as signaling abandonment of the idea of confrontation. They reasoned that Egypt, by expelling these personnel, had substantially weakened its air and antiaircraft capabilities: Would Sadat have done this had he been bent on war? This misinterpretation of events, Sadat later wrote, helped Egypt attain strategic surprise in October 1973. Moreover, his gamble paid off. Unwilling to lose their position in the Middle East, the Soviets, after a few weeks in a huff, agreed to supply him with MiG-23s and SU-20s, SAMs, Scuds, antitank missiles, and tanks.

Egypt's war minister, Gen. Ahmed Sadek, was lukewarm about Sadat's plans: without adequate air power, which was years away, he argued, Egypt could not risk war. He made his views clear at a meeting, chaired by Sadat, of the Egyptian Armed Forces Supreme Council in October 1972. Two days later Sadat replaced him with the more militant Gen. Ahmed Ismail 'Ali.[29]

Nasser and Sadat had spent the period 1967–70 preparing the Egyptian army for war. The result, apparent during Sadat's first years in power, was a considerable improvement in the caliber of the senior officers and the streamlining and simplification of the command structure.[30] Egypt had also quietly marshaled its allies. Agreement with Syria to go to war together before the end of the year appears to have been reached in April 1973, during a secret visit to Egypt by Assad.[31] The plans were finalized in August meetings of the military commanders, and later that month Sadat secretly visited Syria, where he and Assad decided that D-Day would be October 6 (the tenth day of Ramadan, as well as Yom Kippur).[32] On September 22 they informed their chiefs of general staff of the chosen date.[33] A main consideration in the choice was moonlight: The moon would shine that night (October 6–7) from sunset to midnight, after which there would be pitch darkness, which would make the identification of the Egyptians' Canal-crossing bridges more difficult. Another consideration was the water level: October 6 promised a minimal difference between high and low tide, facilitating the initial boat crossings and the bridge-building.[34] Last, on Yom Kippur many Israeli soldiers would be home on leave, and only a skeleton force would be on duty in front-line positions and rear headquarters. General Gamasy, the Egyptian head of operations (and later chief of general staff and defense minister) added in his memoirs that Yom Kippur was designated because all of Israel's radio and TV stations would be shut down that day, making a speedy mobilization—usually effected through the broadcast of special code-words over the radio—more difficult.[35] The Arab leaders do not seem to have been aware that on Yom Kippur all traffic in Israel comes to a halt, affording unparalleled conditions for swift mobilization and deployment of the reserves: The roads are unclogged and everyone is at home and can be called quickly.

Sadat and Assad, while not wishing to share their secret, needed and wanted the help of other Arab states. If Jordan was sounded out, it declined to join in as a full-fledged partner. Having been badly scorched (and deceived by Egypt) in 1967, Hussein was unwilling to plunge into a second adventure. Moreover, Jordan's relations with Egypt and Syria were badly strained: Cairo had severed diplomatic ties with Amman in March 1972; Damascus had done so in 1971. But the preparations for war required a smoothing of ruffled feathers, so in September 1973 Egypt and Syria initiated a last-minute restoration of relations with Amman.

Other Arab states were also solicited. Sadat obtained pledges for hundreds of millions of dollars in grants and loans from a number of oil-rich rulers, including those of Saudi Arabia and Qatar.[36] Gen. Saad ad Din al-Shazly, the Egyptian chief of staff, personally toured the Arab capitals to elicit promises of financial support, weaponry, and personnel. But all he told them was that at some point in the near future, Egypt and Syria were going to war against Israel. He did not reveal even the approximate date, thus ruling out the possibility of these states sending contingents to the front before the war. Most of the pledges were for the dispatch of military units after battle had been joined; most of those which were sent arrived too late. Two Algerian brigades and some jets eventually reached the Egyptian front. Morocco already had an infantry brigade in Syria; another arrived in Egypt after the fighting ended. So did a Sudanese infantry brigade.[37] The Libyans sent an armored brigade; it was deployed on the Egyptian front only after the fighting had ended. Libya and Iraq also pledged and sent dozens of aircraft. Kuwait contributed a brigade of infantry, with about forty tanks, and a handful of aircraft to the Syrian war effort; Saudi Arabia sent a battalion of paratroops and a battalion of armored personnel carriers and moved several brigades of infantry and a number of tanks to Jordan, though these did not participate in the fighting. By far the largest and most important contributions to the Syrians were made by Iraq, which sent two armored divisions, with some 500 tanks and 700 armored personnel carriers (APCs), and by Jordan, which sent two armored brigades, with 170 tanks and 100 APCs. The Iraqis and Jordanians were to play a major part in the battle for the Bashan, the area east of the Golan.

Sadat simultaneously made a major effort to improve relations with the West, going out of his way to ingratiate himself with Kissinger and the United States, and in June 1973 restoring diplomatic relations—broken off in 1967—with France, Britain, and West Germany.[38]

Specific planning for the 1973 war apparently began soon after Shazly became chief of staff in May 1971.[39] The chief architect of the eventual plan was Gen. Gamasy, who headed the Operations Department of the Egyptian general staff from January 1972. After analyzing the 1967 defeat, the general staff pinpointed two crucial areas of Egyptian inferiority: the absence of an air force that could challenge, let alone overpower, the IAF, and the absence of an armored corps that could match its Israeli counterpart. The IDF's machines, both in the air and on the ground, were simply superior. So was its manpower: Israeli pilots, maintenance and ground control staffs, tank officers, and men were far better trained and led than their Arab counterparts. In 1973, says Shazly, the IAF was "ten years ahead" of his own air force.[40]

The Egyptians and Syrians hoped at least partially to offset Israel's aerial advantage by mobilizing contingents of combat aircraft from the Arab world and elsewhere. The need became particularly acute after the Soviet contingents were expelled in July 1972. Among the first to send aid was North Korea—twenty MiG-21 pilots, eight air controllers, and various support personnel served from June 1973 with the Egyptian air force, taking part in defensive operations during the war.[41] The Egyptians' "international air brigade" also included three squadrons from Algeria, two from Libya, and one from Iraq (which the Egyptians sent on attack missions into Sinai on October 13). Iraq also supplied Syria with four squadrons of MiGs.[42]

But, as it turned out, none of this aid did much to change the strategic picture. Even the two-front Arab war plan, which necessarily divided the IAF's attention and resources between two simultaneous threats, was insufficient. The two air forces, while together outnumbering the IAF by 2 to 1 in combat aircraft, remained inferior to it. The planners were obliged to look elsewhere for a means of offsetting the IAF (which, in their view, had been the decisive factor in the 1967 war). Their focus, during 1968–73, turned to ground antiaircraft defenses, primarily SAMs. Both Syria and Egypt, with massive Soviet help, constructed large antiaircraft networks.

But reliance on such a network, much of it static, meant that advancing troops would be "covered" only as far as the range of the SAMs; beyond it they would be prey to Israeli aircraft. This underlay Shazly's decision to send his ground forces only as far as the antiaircraft missile umbrella would stretch. Their objective would have to be to capture only a six-mile-deep strip of the Israeli-held side of the Canal.[43] The offensive planned by Syria also took account of this; but Syria's SAM network covered most of the Golan's air space.

Egypt's qualitative inferiority in armor dictated a similar course: The Egyptians could not allow their armored formations to push deep into Sinai, where they would be without antiaircraft cover and outmaneuvered, outgunned, and destroyed by Israeli armor. As in the air, a defensive solution was found. Disproportionate numbers of antitank guns were deployed, and Egyptian infantry divisions were supplied with large numbers of antitank guided missiles (NATO code-named "Saggers") and short-range rocket launchers.

Egypt faced not only the routine, if substantial, amphibious challenge of efficiently ferrying troops and building bridges across a large waterway under fire. In addition, along both sides of the Canal stretched giant banks of earth and sand, on the Israeli side sixty feet high. Vehicles could not scale such steep embankments, nor could heavily laden troops. In his two years as chief of staff Shazly had put together forty new battalions of engineers specifically to tackle this problem.[44] Their task was speedily to cut holes in the bank on the Egyptian side, to allow the troops, boats, bridges, and vehicles to reach the water's edge, and then to punch gaps on the Israeli side so that the assault forces could push into Sinai and establish a viable bridgehead. About 450 giant water cannon were acquired from West Germany and Britain—unnoticed by Israeli intelligence—to gouge out holes in the embankments far more quickly and efficiently than explosives or bulldozers.[45]

Planning for war also meant a major expansion of Egypt's military manpower. The armed forces, which in 1971 had numbered 800,000 troops, many of them deployed in the Nile Valley to protect bridges, electricity lines, dams, factories, by October 1973 had been increased to 1,050,000, plus 150,000 reserves.[46]

The Arab war plan was based on the achievement of limited tactical surprise through the deployment of antiaircraft missiles, antitank missiles, rockets, and water cannon. The IDF anticipated neither the use of some of these items—certainly not in the quantities that were deployed—nor their effectiveness. Equally important to the Arab plan was major strategic surprise. For months the two Arab armies steadily pushed units and equipment to the front, reaching an unprecedented concentration of forces by October 6. Yet Israel held fast to intelligence assessments of a low probability of war.

The Arabs' success in springing this strategic surprise—a feat that has taken its place in military history alongside Hitler's invasion of Russia and the Japanese attack on Pearl Harbor—owed much to the Israeli perception of the Arab forces as inherently incompetent, weak, and incapable of mounting such a deception. Zvi Zamir, then director of the Mossad, explained: "We simply did not believe that they could do it. . . . We scorned them. 'Put all their paratroops with Saggers on a hill—and I'll wipe them out with two tanks,' one major-general told me. Even when we received reliable information about the water cannon . . . there was the same dismissive reaction.[47]

And Defense Minister Dayan and CGS Lieutenant General Elazar both felt—on the basis of a skeleton exercise held in 1972—that 300 tanks in the south and 180 on the Golan would suffice to beat off any offensive.[48] As events of October 6 and 7 were to prove, these forces were simply inadequate, especially when not properly deployed.

Israeli intelligence officers assumed that decades of defeat had persuaded the Arabs that they were bound to lose any war, and therefore they would not embark on one. It did not occur to them that the Arabs might go to war even believing they could not win. Their assessment of Arab intentions focused on alliances—neither Syria nor Egypt would contemplate attacking Israel alone—and on aerial and antiaircraft capabilities—without having achieved parity in the air, including a capability of hitting strategic targets deep inside Israel, the Arabs would not go to war. The Israeli commanders, repressing memories of the SAM-aircraft confrontations of July 1970, did not believe that the Arabs' antiaircraft networks provided an adequate defensive umbrella. In April–May 1973 they held that the IAF could destroy the Syrian air force "in two hours"[49] and that if the Egyptians launched a cross-Canal offensive, IDF armor could wipe them up and the IAF could demolish their air and anti-aircraft forces in "a day or two," with the IDF itself crossing the Canal on day 2 or day 3.[50] These assumptions were later lumped together and designated *hakonseptziya*, meaning "the preconception."[51] As a senior Israeli official later put it, the military set the politicians' minds at rest, and the national mood bred complacency among the military.[52] So, during the three years leading up to the October War, all IDF intelligence assessments consistently stated that war was "improbable" or "highly improbable." Only on October 5–6 did this confidence abruptly give way to a realization that war was about to break out.

Another perception that dulled the Israelis' judgment was their poor opinion of Sadat. He was seen by them (and, indeed, by most Egyptians) as a small-time politician, a waverer, a stopgap measure after Nasser while the "real" candidates maneuvered for primacy. His success in consolidating power failed to impress Israeli intelligence. An image of indecisiveness and buffoonery also affected American opinion. Kissinger reportedly said: "Who is Sadat? We all thought he was a fool, a clown."[53] Sadat helped reinforce that image. He repeatedly declared that 1971 was "the year of decision"; in 1972 his May Day declaration that "I am willing to sacrifice a million people in this battle" was followed in November by his promise that Egypt would go to war within half a year. These instances of promise and nonfulfillment helped to lull the Israeli leadership. Even Cairo Radio's announcement on September 11, 1973, an intelligence gaffe if ever there was one, that Sadat and Hussein were "discussing the preparations for the fateful battle against Israel," turned on no warning lights in Tel Aviv.[54]

And as for Cairo's expulsion of Soviet troops and advisers: Israeli observers saw it as a serious weakening of Egypt's military capability—would a country knowingly weaken itself if it was planning war?

Syria and Egypt also carried out a well-orchestrated political and military plan of deception. Right up to October 1973, Egypt engaged in dialogue with American and UN officials (and, indirectly, Israel) concerning a range of peace proposals.[55] At the end of September, Arab foreign ministers agreed to meet secretly with Israel in the United States in November to discuss negotiating procedures. Egypt and Syria used the media extensively, issuing a succession of reports that implied business as usual. *Al-Ahram* on October 4 reported that Egyptian defense minister 'Ali would be meeting his Rumanian counterpart in Cairo on October 8. Damascus Radio announced, also on October 4, that President Assad would begin a nine-day tour of Syria's eastern provinces on October 10. On the morning of October 6, Sadat sent New Year's greetings to Egypt's Jewish community. The Egyptian media reported that he would fly to New York later in the month to attend the UN General Assembly.[56] During the last days of September and early October, newspapers in both countries reported a deep political rift between the two leaders.

Sadat personally contributed to the campaign of deception. In four speeches in July he spoke of a "25-year strategy," with a focus on internal reform and the need to solve the Israeli-Arab problem. IDF Intelligence Branch took this to mean that he had accepted the status quo along the Canal. On September 28, in a speech on the anniversary of Nasser's death, Sadat all but avoided mention of the struggle against Israel, a stark deviation from his usual aggressive bluster. Israeli analysts failed to identify this as a warning sign.[57]

The last, perhaps crucial brick in the construct of deception—whether intended as such or just by luck—was the "Schönau Incident." On September 28, two Arab terrorists attacked a train carrying Soviet Jews on their way to Israel from Czechoslovakia at the Austrian border. They took some hostages and demanded the closure of the Schönau Castle transit camp outside Vienna. Austria quickly capitulated. Israel was outraged, and on October 1 Golda Meir flew from Strasbourg, where she was attending a Council of Europe meeting, to Vienna, where she tried unsuccessfully to persuade the Austrians to rescind the decision.[58]

The hijacking and Meir's mission to Vienna diverted Israel's attention from Arab war preparations. Indeed, since the late 1960s Israeli intelligence services, especially the Mossad, had been paying increased attention to combatting terrorism and less to watching the Arab states and armies. Moreover, the prime minister was out of position for a crucial three days. Evidence suggests that Schönau was part of the Arab deception plan: The gunmen belonged to as Saiqa, which is unlikely to have launched such a mission without a green light from Damascus.

On the military level, the Egyptians and Syrians invested a great deal in achieving both strategic and tactical surprise. Both started out with a major advantage: Their standing armies, based on a long-term professional core and conscripts, were very large (more than 1,000,000 for Egypt, more than 600,000 for Syria) and their main combat formations, since the late 1960s, had mostly been deployed in depth along the front lines. In Syria, only relatively small changes in deployment and organization were needed to switch from a defensive to an offensive posture.

To deceive Israel the Arab leaders consistently "deceived" their own armies, all the way up to senior field and staff officers; very few soldiers knew that they were going to war until a few minutes before the offensive was launched. The highest-ranking Egyptian to fall into Israeli hands during the war, a colonel, told his interrogators that the first he heard of the war was just after 1:30 P.M., October 6, when he and other senior officers were summoned to their army's commander, a lieutenant general. They found him on his knees, at prayer. When the general concluded his prayers, he informed them that war was about to begin. At that moment they heard the first attack aircraft winging their way overhead on their way to targets in Sinai.[59]

The Egyptian half of the war plan was integrated into and camouflaged by a large military exercise near the Canal, simulating a Canal crossing. The Egyptian army had regularly held such exercises since 1968, each one larger and more realistic than its predecessor, and all code-named Tahrir (Liberation). "Tahrir 41" began on October 1, 1973, and was scheduled, according to Egyptian announcements, to end on October 7. It provided the army with cover for moving large numbers of men and masses of equipment to the Canal. Egypt also had mobilized reserves, in varying numbers, twenty-two times in the first nine months of 1973. The twenty-third mobilization, of 150,000 men in late September, caused no concern in Israel.[60]

Among other measures calculated to keep Israeli intelligence off guard were orders to units to release cadets and reserve soldiers participating in Tahrir 41 on October 7 and 8. Various units and bridging equipment, moved to the Canal weeks before, were ostentatiously moved back to the Nile Valley in early October. (But by October 6 they were back in place, transported eastward during the nights.) Special squads of troops moved about on October 5 and the morning of October 6 on the ramps on the west bank of the Canal without helmets or weapons, eating oranges or sucking on sugarcane.[61] Others swam or fished in the Canal itself.[62]

Parts of the Egyptian and Syrian armies were put on high alert in the days before October 6. But both governments let it be known that, for different reasons, they feared that Israel was about to attack them.[63] Egypt explained its alert as stemming from fear that Israel might exploit Tahrir 41 to launch a blow against the army while it was otherwise occupied. Gen. Eli Zeira, director of Israeli military intelligence, even used this explanation in support of his assessment of "low probability" of war at a meeting of senior IDF officers on October 5, twenty-six hours before the Arab armies struck.[64]

In both May and August there had been unusual Egyptian and Syrian troop concentrations and movements; in both cases Israel had reacted by mobilizing reserves, despite Zeira's assessment that there was no threat of war. Sadat claimed later that on both occasions his army had deliberately "let slip" indications that it was about to launch a war[65] as part of the deception plan. Israel later suspected that the Arabs had in fact intended to strike but were deterred by its degree of preparedness. In October the memory of those costly and unnecessary mobilizations reinforced its reluctance to mobilize the reserves yet again.

During the fortnight before the war, Egyptian and Syrian general staff officers kept to their normal schedules.[66] Knowledge of the impending assault was restricted, until the beginning of October, to the dozen or so political leaders and top military commanders; the Arabs' Soviet patrons were informed only on October 4. In a secret directive of October 5 to Minister of War Ahmad Ismail 'Ali, Sadat outlined Egypt's war aims as ending "the present military inertia," inflicting high casualties and heavy damage on Israel, and "liberating the occupied territory in progressive stages."[67]

SIGNS OF WAR

The Israelis were deceived and taken by surprise, despite the general awareness of Defense Minister Dayan and others that the Arabs sooner or later had to go to war. Dayan understood the depth of the Arabs' humiliation in 1967. The failure of UN- and American-sponsored peace proposals had proved that Israel was not going to give up territory through negotiation; by now the Arabs had come to believe that their honor and land could be restored only through war. Moreover, Dayan understood that they did not actually have to win a war; all they needed was not to lose it too decisively. The logic of events was thus propelling Egypt toward war, Dayan told the cabinet on December 3, 1972.[68] And on May 14, 1973, he told the IDF general staff that he believed that the Arab states had embarked on a course that would lead to war. The Egyptians did not think they could conquer Sinai, but they hoped that a war at the Canal would generate international pressures that would result in Israeli withdrawal.[69]

But the Arabs' repeated failure to launch a war when expected, in May and again in August 1973, seems to have eaten away at Dayan's conviction. Perhaps Zeira was right, and war *was* "highly improbable." By the end of September, Dayan was far from sure that the myriad signs that had been picked up lately were indeed indications of impending war.

In April, when Mossad chief Zamir had joined Dayan in suggesting that war was "probable," Zeira rejected their analysis and promised the IDF a "five-six day" advance warning if and when the Arabs decided to attack—and "a 48-hour warning" in a worst-case ("catastrophic") scenario.[70] As described, during the following months Syria and Egypt were to supply Israeli intelligence with countless indications of danger. Among the evident preparations for war in both the civilian and military spheres, perhaps the most revealing occurred on October 4–5: Soviet naval vessels steamed out of Mersa Matrūh and Alexandria harbors into the Mediterranean, and six giant Soviet aircraft landed in Cairo and began to evacuate the families of the advisers still in Egypt. Photographs taken by the IAF that day showed a massive increase in

Egyptian artillery along the Canal, and the positioning of pontoon boats and bridging equipment in large quantities. Platoons of tanks had taken up positions atop many of the Canal-side ramparts. At dawn on October 6, Egypt armed, fueled, and readied its Scuds for firing.[71]

Another warning Israel ignored came from Jordan. On the evening of September 25, King Hussein, at his request, was flown by IAF helicopter to the Tel Aviv area for a meeting with Meir, whom he had secretly met eight times since her taking office in 1969. On his own initiative he remarked that the Syrian army had deployed in its "pre-jump-off positions" for an offensive war. Meir asked whether Syria would go to war without Egypt. Hussein said that he thought not—implying, perhaps, that Egypt, too, was getting ready. Perhaps the prime minister understood him to mean that only the Syrians had moved onto a war footing and that therefore no war was likely to ensue. In any case she apparently failed to ask him about a possible date of attack or its possible objectives.[72] Hussein may not have been completely sure that Damascus and Cairo were going to war and was probably unaware of the October 6 date. For he and Meir agreed that on October 7 the Jordanian crown prince, Hassan, would secretly meet with Israeli agriculture minister Haim Gvati to discuss joint exploitation of Dead Sea mineral resources.

Meir called Dayan and informed him of Hussein's message. Dayan passed the information on to a senior intelligence officer, who promptly called the prime minister and told her not to worry. But not all in Intelligence Branch were equally sanguine. Hearing of Hussein's warning, the head of the Jordanian and Syrian desks in the Research Department concluded that Egypt and Syria were going to war. But Zeira brushed aside Hussein's warning and called the two officers "panicky" and "alarmist."

Meir was sufficiently reassured to fly off to Strasbourg the following day. General Elazar, too, was unfazed by Hussein's warning. At a senior staff gathering on September 26, the day after the Meir-Hussein meeting, he said he did not think it should be taken seriously.[73]

Well before D-day, Israeli intelligence had most of the facts. But because of preconceptions, errors, and the Arabs' deliberate deception measures, it was unable to separate the telling signals from the background noise. The few who read them correctly went unheeded.[74]

But even Zeira's certainty began to crumble on October 4, and by the early morning hours of October 6 he, too, believed that war would break out that day. Four critical developments had convinced him: the abrupt (and, to IDF intelligence, inexplicable) departure from Cairo and Damascus of the Soviet advisers' families; the analysis of the October 4 aerial reconnaissance photographs; the movement of Soviet naval vessels out of Egyptian waters on October 5; and the arrival of two messages from a top Israeli agent that war was about to break out.

On October 4, the agent informed his Israeli controller in Europe that war was imminent. The controller advised Mossad headquarters, which informed Zamir, who then told Zeira. Zeira later testified that he had not understood from Zamir that the message had said that war was certain. At the time Zamir, sensing Zeira's indifference, had also reported to Dayan. But he too had not been particularly perturbed.

Around midnight on October 5–6 Zamir met with the agent somewhere in Europe and was told that war would break out that day "at around 1800 hours [6:00 P.M.]."[75] Zamir then telephoned Zeira, finally persuading him, Dayan, and Meir that war was indeed imminent.[76]

The arrival of the message only hours before the outbreak of hostilities was, of course, the chief reason for the IDF's state of unpreparedness when the Syrian and Egyptian guns at last opened up, a few minutes before 2:00 P.M. on October 6. But the mistake in the time of the attack proved almost equally harmful, going a long way to explain the weak Israeli response to the initial Arab onslaughts. Units of the armored division in Sinai responsible for blocking the Egyptian offensive began to move out of their rear bases toward the front only during the afternoon hours, too late to meet the Canal crossers before, or as, they reached the east bank. Zeira has since maintained that the crucial misinformation about the timing of the beginning of the offensive was deliberate and clearly indicates that the agent was a "double."[77]

THE MORNING OF OCTOBER 6

Clearly Israel had to mobilize its reserves—the bulk of its army. Only a handful of specialists—air force mechanics and ground controllers and electronic intelligence experts—had been called up already. At a dawn meeting with Dayan, Elazar pressed for complete and open mobilization. This would involve some 200,000 troops and would take from forty-eight to seventy-two hours. Dayan agreed to mobilize only two divisions and their support troops, some fifty thousand men, contending that if the IDF mobilized fully, the Arab states could argue that they had felt threatened and had launched a preemptive strike. Elazar also pressed for an IAF preemptive attack against Syrian SAM sites or airfields during the early afternoon. (He was assuming that the Arabs were scheduled to move at around 6 P.M.) Dayan opposed this idea too.

Both options were submitted for decision to Prime Minister Meir and her senior ministers. Dayan said that American support would be crucial in the coming days, both politically and in terms of supplies, and Israel must not be seen as the aggressor. He knew they were far from persuaded that Egypt and Syria intended to launch a war. If Israel struck first or mobilized fully, there

The Syrian Offensive and Israeli Counteroffensive, October 1973

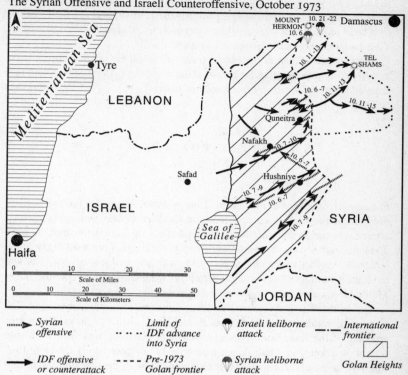

| Syrian offensive | Limit of IDF advance into Syria | Israeli heliborne attack | International frontier |
| IDF offensive or counterattack | Pre-1973 Golan frontier | Syrian heliborne attack | Golan Heights |

would be no way of proving that subsequent Egyptian and Syrian offensives were not merely reactions to aggression; American support for Israel would then be in jeopardy. In any case, like everyone else, Dayan assumed that Israel would win handily once the fighting erupted.

Meir backed Dayan in opposing an air strike and Elazar in favoring mass mobilization, which got under way at about 10:00 A.M. The disagreement had delayed the mobilization by four precious hours.[78]

THE BATTLE FOR THE GOLAN

Facing each other across the "Purple Line"—Israel's name for the 1967 cease-fire line in the Golan—at 2:00 P.M. on October 6 were two very unequal armies. On the Syrian side were the equivalent of three reinforced infantry divisions, 930 tanks, around 930 artillery pieces, and more than thirty SAM batteries. Another two armored divisions, with 460 tanks, were positioned in the rear. A number of commando battalions were deployed to take the IDF's Mount Hermon position and to support the infantry.

Facing these five divisions was the equivalent of one undermanned IDF division, commanded by Brig. Gen. Rafael Eitan, with 177 tanks. The northern half of the line, from Quneitra to Mount Hermon, was held by a thin screen of infantry in a half dozen platoon-size positions along the front line. The IDF command foresaw that the principal Syrian thrust would be in that sector, and 137 tanks were dispersed behind and between the positions. Some of the units were concentrated on or behind volcanic *tels* that offered protection and good vantage points. The southern half of the Golan, from Quneitra down to the Yarmuk River and the Jordanian border, was lightly defended by the remaining 40 tanks and a paratroop battalion, strung out in the half dozen front-line forts, some on hills overlooking the southern sector of the border, a deep wadi with cliffs impassable to armor. The eleven artillery batteries on the heights had forty-four guns, and there was one SAM battery. Overall, the Israelis were outnumbered by more than 5 to 1 in armor and 20 to 1 in guns.

The objective of the Syrian offensive was to sweep through and destroy the IDF forces and reach the Jordan River in eighteen to twenty-four hours.[79] The offensive began a minute or two before 2:00 P.M. As a hundred jets streaked toward IDF headquarters and depots on the Golan, a thousand artillery pieces opened up against infantry emplacements and armor and artillery concentrations. An hour later, Syrian engineers and infantry, followed by tanks, began to push across the border. What followed during the next four days was the biggest tank battle since World War II.

Crucial to the Syrian offensive was the success of a minor commando attack at the northern end of the front, against the IDF's electronic intelligence base atop Mount Hermon. Apart from its symbolic and morale value, the base also monitored all Syrian air and ground traffic and dominated the northern Golan and southern Lebanon. It was manned by about forty intelligence and technical personnel and only fourteen infantrymen. The crack Syrian Eighty-second Special Forces Battalion, which had trained on a model for three years, quickly penetrated the fort. Within hours most of the defenders were dead or captured, though a few escaped. A Syrian flag flew above the fort for the next sixteen days.[80]

Except for this action, the Syrian battle plan had been known to Israeli intelligence for months; an updated version had reached the IDF from Washington (originating from an Arab source) on September 29.[81] But at this moment, with the reserves not yet mobilized, Israel was in no position to exploit the information. The Golan Heights were, at their widest, only seventeen miles deep. Unlike Sinai, where space could be traded for time to complete mobilization, or for advantages in positioning, the Golan offered little room to maneuver. The IDF had to fight where it stood.

In the northern sector two Syrian divisions, reinforced by hundreds of tanks, crashed into the Israeli lines and, bypassing infantry positions, pressed forward a few hundred meters before coming up against a deep antitank ditch and well-placed tanks of the Seventh Brigade, which offered fierce and effective resistance. The Israeli gunners had the advantage of having the sun behind them and in the Syrians' eyes. The major battle, fought day and night until the afternoon of October 9, took place just north of Quneitra, often with only a few dozen yards separating the two sides. The outcome was determined largely by the Israelis' superior gunnery and tenacity, though they were heavily outnumbered and fought under massive artillery fire. Throughout they retained the advantage of the high ground, dominating the plain below, which came to be called "the Vale of Tears." The Seventh Brigade's commander, Col. Avigdor Ben-Gal, made clever use of his units, always retaining small reserves and throwing them into the breach at crucial moments. The efficiency and bravery of the units that repaired, refueled, and munitioned tanks coming off the line proved vital.[82]

Israeli strategic planning had assumed that the IDF would have five or six days or, in the worst case, at least forty-eight hours to deploy its reserve armor and match the Syrians, almost tank for tank. But should the Syrians somehow achieve surprise—as occurred on October 6–7—IAF jets would serve as flying tank killers and hold them at bay until the reserves arrived.[83] But the planners failed to foresee the effectiveness of the Syrian SAMs, which greatly reduced the effectiveness of the IAF's ground support.[84]

During the afternoon and evening of October 6, and on through the night, while the general staff was persuaded that the conscript brigades in the Golan were holding, almost all the IAF's offensive power was directed against the Egyptian Canal-crossing units and bridges. But in the early hours of October 7, anxiety focused on the Golan, where the Syrians had broken through in the southern sector, and the IAF redirected its main energies there. Skyhawks bombed and strafed the Syrian columns, helping the small scattered IDF tank formations to block the advance toward the Sea of Galilee. At Northern Command headquarters, Reserves General Hod, who had commanded the IAF in 1967, personally guided the fighters to their targets.[85] But, while IAF Mirages flying cover shot down a number of Syrian jets that tried to interfere, SAMs took a steady toll of the Skyhawks.

At 11:30 A.M. on October 7, Elazar—in the worst possible circumstances—launched the operation originally conceived as a preemptive strike (which Meir had vetoed). The whole of the IAF should have been unleashed against the Syrian missile screen's thirty-one batteries and half dozen radar sites.[86] Now the IAF was sent to take out the missiles while some of its resources were devoted to providing ground support to embattled units on the Golan and along the Suez Canal. About fifty Phantoms[87] charged into the missile field and encountered masses of shoulder-launched SAM-7s as well as radar-guided antiaircraft guns before coming up against a steady stream of SAM-2s, -3s, and -6s. Few of the aircraft found targets. Only one SAM battery was destroyed and one damaged—at a cost of six Phantoms, their crews killed or captured.[88] The operation had failed.

On the ground in the northern sector, the Syrians' initial efforts to break through were repelled with heavy losses. Their final thrust, a joint effort on the morning of October 9 by some two hundred fresh tanks and Assad's palace guards contingent, almost managed to breach the line, held by some four dozen Israeli Centurions. The Syrians set several tanks alight and captured some of the high ground. Toward the end of the battle, almost all the Israeli tanks were without ammunition, and the men, after three days of battle, were exhausted. Dayan had given orders that morning not to withdraw "even one meter." The Syrians, he said, must "find an army in which everyone fights until the last bullet and let us see whether they can break [us]. [Our troops] . . . are fighting like Maccabees, let us hope that they will not be broken, and that the Golan will remain [ours]."[89]

For long moments the situation was desperate. For days the Israeli tankmen had known that they were all that stood between the Syrians and Israel; most fought as Dayan had expected.

On the morning of October 9, senior Israeli ministers apparently discussed the possible use of nuclear weapons. It is unclear whether, as some reports have it, Dayan and Meir in fact ordered the arming of Israel's missiles with nuclear warheads. Nuclear weapons may also have been loaded onto a squadron of Phantom F-4s at Tel Nof air base in the center of the country. Accurate information about the failure of the IDF counteroffensive in Sinai (see below) had trickled in during the night, shocking the Israelis, who had initially been led to believe that it was succeeding. The renewed, powerful Syrian offensive near Quneitra threatened to overwhelm the defenses. Israel knew that any nuclear deployment would be monitored by the superpowers, indirectly warn the Arabs not to push across the pre-1967 borders, and pressure—or blackmail—the United States into immediately resupplying the IDF with major weapons systems that had been ground up in the war.[90]

At one stage in the battle late that morning, with smoke lying heavy over the "Vale of Tears," Syrian tanks were interspersed among the Israeli ones. Colonel Ben-Gal, the brigade commander, was later to say: "I was already set to order all [my] forces to withdraw. I had already picked up the radiotelephone. But I said to myself: Let's wait a little longer. . . . I was sure we had lost the battle. Had it gone on for another half an hour, an hour, we would have lost. For some reason, the Syrians broke first and decided to retreat."

One reason was the arrival at the last minute of the Seventh Brigade's final reserve of thirteen tanks.[91] Then, just before noon, General Eitan received a report that Syrian tank crews were fleeing eastward. Eitan immediately called Ben-Gal, and the news was then reported down the chain of command. It was a great boost to morale. The Israeli tankmen fought on, and, within minutes, the remaining Syrian tanks turned around and retreated.

Ben-Gal later observed: "You never know the condition of the other side. You always assume that he is in better shape than you. The Syrians, apparently, assumed that they had no chance of success. They did not know the truth, that our situation was desperate."[92]

During the four days of battle north of Quneitra, one hundred Israeli tanks had engaged altogether five to six hundred Syrian tanks. By noon on October 9, the Syrians had lost about two hundred of these and several hundred other armored and light-skinned vehicles.[93] The Seventh Brigade's stand on the Golan has entered the military textbooks as an unparalleled example of defensive armored warfare.

In the southern Golan, where Israeli forces were more thinly spread, the Syrians fared much better. By evening on October 6, three brigades had broken through. During the following hours and for much of the next day, the plateau resembled an expansive ocher sea, in which vast fleets of green Syrian tanks and APCs were engaged by small packs of brown IDF tanks, darting this way and that, now forward, now back, trading shells, occasionally bursting into flames. Everywhere the steel treads and roaring motors threw up plumes of smoke and dust; everywhere earth and rock were blown into the sky by salvos of tank, artillery, rocket, and mortar fire.

During the first night the Syrians pushed four more brigades into the sector. One force penetrated as far as Nafakh, the site of Eitan's divisional headquarters, at the Golan's key strategic crossroads. Another almost reached the escarpment overlooking the Jordan Valley but was halted by three tanks of an

IDF reserve brigade, which was moving piecemeal onto the heights. Farther to the south a Syrian mechanized brigade came to a halt at the abandoned Israeli settlement of Ramat Magshimim. Despite the Syrians' accomplishments their drive had been blocked by a ragtag array of tattered and battered Israeli units. The Syrians' inertia and hesitancy may have been due to logistical problems and to the traditional disinclination of Arab armies to move and fight at night, even when, like this time, they were equipped with night-vision devices.

At first light on October 7 the Syrians, still hoping to reach the river, threw in key units of their second armored echelon, in two thrusts: northwestward against the divisional headquarters at Nafakh, and southwestward, toward the junction of the Yarmuk and Jordan Rivers (and the Jordan-Israel border). One battalion, taking a wrong turn, headed due west, and at 3:00 P.M. achieved the Syrians' westernmost penetration of the war, reaching the escarpment above the Sea of Galilee just west of Gamla, before being engaged and pushed back.[94]

The Israeli settlements on the Golan, planted there between 1967 and 1973, were abandoned on October 6 and 7. Some of the settlers left only as shells began to fall around them. Within twenty-four hours of the start of hostilities, the situation was seen as so desperate that IDF Northern Command ordered the six Jordan River bridges connecting the Golan with the Galilee prepared for demolition. The commander of the unit who supervised the preparations told the Agranat Commission (which later investigated the IDF's performance during this period) that "the feeling was that there was going to be a holocaust."[95] CO Northern Command Gen. Yitzhak Hofi was reported to have been seen, on the first or second day of the war, by one divisional commander, "lying on his camp bed . . . a broken man, lacking all spirit, and muttering: 'All is lost, all is lost.'"[96]

The Syrian armored probes toward Nafakh were initially blocked, but the conscript units in the southern Golan were overwhelmed by firepower and numbers; and Israeli air power was blunted by the SAMs. The battle, at Nafakh as for the Golan as a whole, would in fact be decided between the Israeli reserve formations and the Syrian second-echelon armored divisions. In the end, at Nafakh, the Israelis won by a hair.

The reserve tank brigades had mobilized in record time, often setting out from their bases in the Galilee without adequate equipment or sufficient supplies of shells. Their main objective was to get up the Golan escarpment and onto the plateau before the Syrian armor reached the edge and began to descend to the Jordan Valley and the Sea of Galilee. In the early hours of October 7, four fresh reserve armored brigades (the lead elements of two new divisions assigned to the Golan) reached the escarpment and began to push up and eastward, some of them, as described, engaging the lead Syrian tanks on the edge of the plateau. Much of that day's fighting was highly disorganized. IDF companies, platoons, and even single tanks climbed the slopes and engaged the Syrians wherever they found them.

The most important action of the day took place at and around Nafakh, where a few remaining tanks of one of the conscript brigades put up a last-ditch stand against the Syrian advance. Reserve tanks began to arrive in support, but the brigade commander, his deputy, and his operations officer were all killed outside the perimeter fences. Eitan abandoned Nafakh and moved his command post a mile to the north. Only seven infantrymen, commanded by a first lieutenant and armed with bazookas and other light weapons, remained there and, for an hour or so, were all that stood between the Syrians and the main road to the river.[97] But then tanks arrived, and the Syrians pulled back.

That afternoon witnessed a general turnaround in the battle. The Syrians, meeting tenacious resistance on the ground and fresh Israeli armor as well as air attacks, ran out of steam. More and more Israeli armor—much of it antiquated Sherman tanks but with the standard, modern IDF 105 mm gun—slowly made it up to the plateau. The Syrian offensive, irresistible on paper, was halted. The Israelis' superior determination and gunnery, occasionally assisted by almost suicidal air support, had made the difference.

During October 7–8 the Israelis reorganized their forces into three divisions, and on the morning of October 8 launched a two-division counterattack in the southern Golan. They made rapid progress. By the next day what remained of the Syrian thrust was effectively surrounded in an area that became known as the Hushniye pocket.[98] By the morning of October 10, the back of Syrian resistance had been broken by successive waves of airplanes bombing the armor and infantry positions. The remaining units retreated eastward, across the "Purple Line," leaving hundreds of tanks, armored vehicles, and artillery pieces behind.[99] Hushniye, like the "Vale of Tears," had turned into an armor graveyard. With the exception of Mount Hermon, both armies were now back at their starting positions; but both, and especially the Syrians, had incurred severe losses.[100]

Simultaneously with the start of the assault on Hushniye, Israel began bombing Syria. General Elazar sought to force the Syrians "to scream stop," and sue for peace,[101] freeing the IDF to face only the Egyptians. (And even short of such a success, an attack on Syria's strategic targets could dissuade other Arab states, and especially Jordan, from joining the fray.) The bombing of Syria's military airfields began on October 8; by the fourteenth, most of them were out of commission. On the morning of October 9 Dayan persuaded Meir of the need to destroy Syrian strategic installations. Salvos of FROG missiles had been fired at northern Israel—aiming at the Ramat David air base—during the previous three nights, inflicting about two dozen civilian and military casualties. Dayan had his rationale, if any was needed.[102]

In the late morning of October 9, eight Phantom F-4s, braving poor visibility, clouds, and strong winds, dove into the center of Damascus and accurately bombed the General Staff and Air Force Headquarters buildings, heavily damaging both. Syrian air defenses had been caught completely by surprise. A number of bombs, off target, damaged the nearby Damascus TV building and the Soviet Cultural Center. One Phantom was shot down. Another eight, due to attack the same buildings in a second wave, failed to reach the city because of thick clouds, so they dropped fifty-six tons of bombs on a large Syrian tank concentration near Hushniye, in what proved to be a major contribution to the subsequent conquest of the area by Israeli armor.[103]

The Damascus raid kicked off a protracted air and naval campaign, during which an oil refinery and power plant at Homs, a central Syrian radar station in Lebanon, and a number of major industrial and communications targets were destroyed. The power stations outside Damascus, which supplied three-quarters of Syria's electricity, were demolished on October 10, as were oil storage facilities at Homs, Aleppo, and Damascus airports and the Syrian naval headquarters north of Latakia. The Israeli navy attacked oil storage facilities at Latakia and Tartus, and port installations at Latakia, Tartus, and Banias. Parts of Syria remained blacked out for months after the war; the damage inflicted amounted to hundreds of millions of dollars.

But the Syrian army, though driven from the Golan, was still far from collapse, as the IDF general staff—based on the precedent of 1967—initially believed. An Israeli division, exploiting the success at Hushniye, tried to push across the "Purple Line" into Syria at four points on October 10. But the attack was hastily mounted and with exhausted and undertanked brigades.[104] The drive encountered a complex of minefields as well as fierce artillery and antitank missile fire, and it stalled in no-man's-land, taking serious losses before it was called off.[105]

A more massive and determined effort would be needed, complementing the strategic bombing campaign. A major thrust across the "Purple Line" into the Bashan was decided upon, to knock Syria out of the war. With Damascus (only some thirty-five miles away) under threat by ground forces, the Syrians would have to stand and fight; perhaps they could then be decisively defeated. But the command failed to draw appropriate conclusions from the experience of the day before. As the Syrian army's offensive performance no longer resembled its showing in 1948, so its performance in defense in no way recalled the dismal showing of 1967. No one was about to cut and run.

On the morning of October 11, two IDF divisions, after a day or so of rest and reorganization, went into action. The attack, launched from the Golan's northern sector, was directed straight at the jugular: "The aim is to reach Damascus" or at least "the gates of Damascus," was how Dayan described its purpose that day. Two days later, somewhat more modestly, he and Elazar were to redefine the goal as to "bring Damascus within artillery range"[106] or, in Eitan's blunter phrase, "to shell Damascus."[107] But, more important, the aim of the offensive was to rout and destroy the Syrian army, which had lost much of its heavy equipment in the offensive on the Golan and was presumed to be demoralized and ready for the coup de grâce.

To their surprise the Israelis encountered two solid defense lines, in depth, with massive artillery backup and antitank weaponry, and with able and determined defenders. The Syrians may have lost most of their offensive capability in the mine- and basalt-strewn fields of the Golan, but in defense they still carried considerable punch. A new, important element of motivation and morale now entered the picture: The Syrian troops were defending their homeland and specifically their capital city. Moreover, their SAM network, covering the Golan and Bashan skies, was almost completely intact (though some of its batteries were short of missiles, having fired off large numbers during the previous five days), and still put a considerable brake on the IAF's ability to provide ground support. Seven Israeli aircraft were lost to Syrian ground fire the first morning of the offensive.

In addition, the attacking units were considerably under strength, having lost a great deal of equipment and many men in repelling the opening Syrian offensive. The two divisions together deployed about 180 tanks, or less than half their prewar total. The IAF, too, was licking its wounds and trying to husband its dwindling resources.

Eitan's division, in the north, crossed the "Purple Line" first, at two points south of the Hermon. The Syrian lines were manned by an understrength infantry division. Eitan's tanks and APCs made relatively quick progress, encountering only light resistance. General Dan Lanner's division, to the south, was less fortunate. His brigades advanced on either side of the main Quneitra–Damascus road, which was heavily defended; the Syrians put up stiff and efficient resistance. Altogether, the division that day lost a third of its tanks.[108]

The following day proved even more grueling, as the Syrians marshaled most of their remaining armored and air forces in a last-ditch effort to stop what they believed was a lunge at their capital. The two lead brigades of the Iraqi expeditionary force also arrived on the scene, five days after they crossed into Syria. They proved to be not very effective. As Eitan later put it, from the first their actions were characterized by "confusion. . . . They moved from place to place [without reason]. They lacked maps. The Syrian guides failed to reach them. . . . [Occasionally] the Syrians fired at them [thinking that they were Israelis] . . . and the Iraqis fired back."[109] But their mere appearance, at various places at different times, was to have great psychological impact and a cautionary effect on the Israelis.[110] They relieved the pressure on the retreating Syrians and diverted the advancing IDF from pushing deeper into Syria and inflicting further, major blows on the battered Syrian army. The Iraqis bought the Syrians time to regroup, absorb replacement equipment, and build new defense lines. The Iraqis were later to claim that their intervention had "saved Damascus."[111]

During the night of October 13–14 the Israelis at last took Tel Shams, a dominant hillock on the way to Damascus. Where armored forces had twice failed in daylight (October 12), a force composed mainly of paratroops, mostly on foot, now succeeded. A few days later Israeli artillery sent a strong signal to Assad, firing a few salvos from Tel Shams at the Mazar neighborhood, on the outskirts of Damascus.[112]

The air assault on selected strategic targets in the Syrian rear continued. The IAF found the going relatively easy: Its pilots had learned to cope with the SAM-2s and -3s, and by the second week of the war the Syrians had expended their entire stock of SAM-6s.[113]

By October 14 the Israelis had conquered a twenty-square-mile box of territory in the Bashan and were barely twenty miles from Damascus. But no more great advances were achieved on the ground. Northern Command's units and equipment had been churned up in the continuous fighting; the IDF's focus—and the bulk of its air power—was now switched to the Suez Canal; and the counterattacks mounted by the Syrians and their allies prevented a return to the offensive. A major Syrian-Iraqi-Jordanian effort took place on October 16. (King Hussein had kept Jordan out of the war during the first week—but the Syrian defeats and the IDF offensive apparently forced his hand, and on October 12 he dispatched his crack Fortieth Armored Brigade into southern Syria.) Poor coordination led to only minimal Iraqi participation, and to Iraqi artillery strikes and Syrian tank fire against the retreating Jordanian force, which they mistook for Israelis, as both the IDF and the Arab Legion deployed Centurion tanks.

The largest and final Arab counterattack against the Bashan enclave took place on October 19. There too the Iraqis failed; at crucial moments they tended to display a lack of resolve.[114] In the end, the Iraqis retreated, leaving behind some fifty tanks, most of them badly hit.[115]

The last battle in the north, and one of the costliest, was the recapture on October 21–22 of Mount Hermon. Snow-covered much of the year, Mount Hermon is a nine-thousand-foot-high limestone outcrop at the northern end of the Golan, on which Israel had located its main electronic surveillance station against Syria. Almost without vegetation, it rises gradually in a series of sheer cliffs. It dominates the Golan plateau to the south and the Damascus approaches to the east. The Israeli position was on the western shoulder of the mountain. To the northeast lay a strip of no-man's-land and then two Syrian positions. Still farther to the northeast is the summit. The IDF now decided both to retake its own Hermon position and to take the Syrian positions and the summit.

The Syrians held the mountain with two elite battalions, one of special forces and the other paratroops. The Israeli Golani Brigade, supported by tanks, was assigned the task of reconquering the Israeli position, where most of the Syrian forces were concentrated. A reserve paratroop brigade, transported by helicopters, was to take the Syrian positions. The operation was supported by dozens of IAF missions, both of ground support and interdiction of

Syrian aerial interference. The paratroop brigade had a relatively easy time, as the Syrians had left their positions only lightly defended.[116]

The soldiers of the Golani Brigade began their trek up the mountain as night fell on October 21, two columns on foot, and one, taking the serpentine road up, on half-tracks, accompanied by tanks and engineers. For the foot-sloggers, weighed down with weapons, ammunition, food, and water, it was a supreme test of stamina as well as courage. The hundreds of Syrian defenders, dug in behind rocks and often equipped with night sights and rocket-propelled grenade launchers, put up a dogged resistance, but the Israeli advance was relentless, and by 11:00 A.M. the mountain was in Israeli hands. Most of the defenders managed to scramble down the slopes and eventually reach Syrian territory.[117]

THE SOUTHERN FRONT

As on the Syrian front, the armies facing each other across the Suez Canal on October 6 were ill matched in both size and preparedness. Israel held the whole of the Sinai Peninsula with one armored division, which mustered about three hundred tanks. When the Egyptians launched their offensive, only the forward elements—about eighty tanks and forty guns all told—were in position along the Canal or on the internal north–south road six miles to the rear. Deployed in the sixteen manned Canal-side forts was the equivalent of an infantry battalion, mostly middle-aged reservists of the Jerusalem Brigade. Along the internal road (the Artillery Road) was a chain of eleven secondary fortifications manned by service personnel and the equivalent of two battalions of tanks. Together the double line of forts constituted the "Bar-Lev Line."

Even had it been properly deployed, the IDF division would have been seriously outnumbered, 5 to 1 in tanks and 20 to 1 in guns. But when the Egyptians struck, the remaining armor and artillery were still in their rear bases, or just beginning to move out in the direction of the Canal. The misinformation about the timing of the offensive—6:00 P.M. instead of the actual 2:00 P.M.—had caught the bulk of the Sinai division on the hop, far from their planned war stations. The Agranat Commission later found CO Southern Command Maj. Gen. Shmuel Gonnen (Gorodish) negligent in not having deployed his troops earlier. Gonnen had taken over from Sharon on June 15 and had had less than four months to learn the command's ropes.

During 1968–72, the IDF had debated how best to defend Sinai. After the August 1970 cease-fire, a number of generals, led by Sharon and Israel Tal, argued that the Bar-Lev Line forts, while sufficient to repel commandos and

The Egyptian Offensives and Israeli Counteroffensive, October 1973

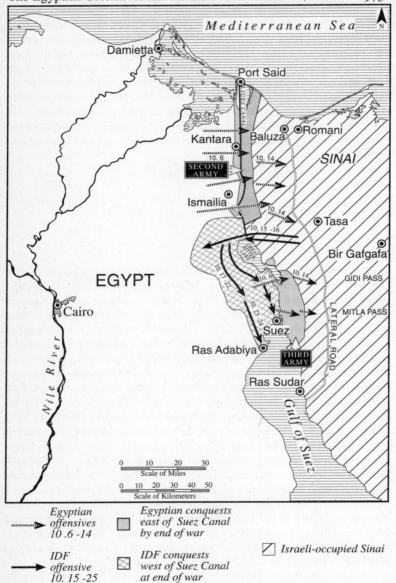

Mediterranean Sea

Damietta

Port Said

Kantara   Baluza   Romani

SINAI

10.6
SECOND ARMY   10.14

Ismailia   10.14

10.15 -16   Tasa

Bir Gafgafa

EGYPT   GREEN ISLAND   10.6   10.14   GIDI PASS

10.17 -22   MITLA PASS

Cairo   10.23 -24   LATERAL ROAD

Suez

Ras Adabiya   THIRD ARMY

Nile River   Ras Sudar

Gulf of Suez

0   10   20   30
Scale of Miles

0   10   20   30   40   50
Scale of Kilometers

- - - ▷ Egyptian offensives 10.6 -14

▬▬▶ IDF offensive 10.15 -25

▨ Egyptian conquests east of Suez Canal by end of war

⊠ IDF conquests west of Suez Canal at end of war

⧄ Israeli-occupied Sinai

protect their defenders against shellfire, would be overwhelmed should Egypt launch an invasion. They sought to replace the static line with a mobile, aggressive defense made up of tank and armored infantry units based at a distance from the Canal but continuously patrolling the waterline.[118] Sharon, appointed to head Southern Command at the start of 1970, set about gradually implementing his ideas. But he was unable to impose his will fully on the general staff. What resulted was a synthesis of the Bar-Lev and the mobile defense concepts. By October 1973, fifteen of the original thirty-one forts had been closed down and the rest reduced to about twenty men each.

Facing the Sinai Division were the Egyptian Second and Third Armies, consisting together of eight to nine divisions. The Second Army was responsible for the northern sector, the Third held the south. The two had some twelve hundred guns and heavy mortars[119] and about fifteen hundred tanks.

The Israeli defense plan had called for the entire Sinai Division to be deployed forward in anticipation of an attack, but Southern Command's expectations of the first days of the war were completely unrealistic—in line with the *Konseptziya* prevailing in IDF headquarters. (Indeed, on October 5 the commander of the division, Gen. Avraham Mendler, discussed the possibility that one of his brigades, alone, would cross the Canal and capture Port Said. The Egyptian army was not taken seriously.[120]) And the plan had not been implemented when the blow fell on October 6. Thus the Sinai Division had very little, initially, with which to stop the Egyptians at the waterline.

The Egyptians had a two-stage plan of attack: First, five infantry divisions would cross the Canal and establish bridgeheads. Then, after an "operational pause" allowing for unsuccessful IDF counterattacks, a second, armored wave would cross and push eastward to the Mitla and Gidi Passes.

The campaign kicked off with an air assault: 150–200 planes flew low over the Canal and the Gulf of Suez and simultaneously struck IDF camps, radar installations, airfields, and intelligence bases deep in Sinai, from Al-'Arīsh to Sharm ash-Sheikh. The attackers inflicted some damage but lost thirty-seven aircraft in dogfights and to ground fire.[121] At the same time, in an attempt to strike at targets in Israel proper, two bombers flew low across the Mediterranean and launched two KELT missiles at Tel Aviv. But one missile fell into the sea and the other was shot down by an IAF interceptor. Egypt's aim may have been to deter Israel from "strategic" bombing by signaling in advance that it, too, had a capacity to hit civilian centers.

On the ground, the massed Egyptian artillery began raining thousands of shells on the Israeli lines. Gamasy says that during the first minute of the Egyptian offensive, 10,500 artillery and mortar rounds fell on the Bar-Lev Line.[122]

During the previous twenty-four hours, on October 5 and during the early hours of October 6, the Egyptians had sent several dozen reconnaissance teams—some dressed as Bedouin—across the Canal to scout out any last-minute Israeli redeployments. The scouts reported back: "The Israelis are asleep." One two-man team, with a radio transmitter, in fact, was captured by a patrol, but the Israelis didn't know what to make of them.[123] That night, October 5–6, a number of commando units had also apparently crossed over and penetrated deep into Sinai, their task being to ambush the expected Israeli tank reinforcements as they approached the waterline. Just after the start of the bombardment, commando units laden with antitank Saggers and rocket propelled grenades (RPGs) crossed the waterway at a number of sites, scaled the ramparts on the east bank, and raced for the empty Israeli ramps in order to deny the IDF tanks their preplanned, commanding firing positions. At about 2:20 P.M., the first main wave of the assault got under way along the length of the Canal, the Egyptians launching around four thousand of their best infantrymen. The crossings were effected in the "dead" areas between the manned Israeli forts, which were able effectively to "cover" with their mortars and machine guns only the areas facing them and a kilometer or so to either side.[124] General Shazly described the infantry crossing thus: "The . . . men . . . poured over the ramparts and slithered in disciplined lines down to the water's edge. The dinghies were readied, 720 of them, and a few minutes after 14:20 hours, as the canisters began to belch clouds of covering smoke, our first assault wave was paddling furiously across the Canal, their strokes falling into the rhythm of their chant 'Allahu Akbar, Allahu Akbar' [Allah is great]."[125]

For months they had practiced the crossing, running up and down sand ramps, paddling furiously in the sand; Israelis who had seen them had been amused.[126] By 4:15, eight infantry waves were across, some 25,000 soldiers in all—ten brigades, concentrated in five divisional bridgeheads. The troops had fanned out south and north, cutting off and attacking the forts; they had occupied the tank ramps and pressed eastward a mile or two.[127]

During the first three hours of the assault Egyptian engineers began to scour sixty passages through the sand barrier on the east bank while others brought bridge sections up to the water's edge on the west bank.[128] By 6:30 P.M., according to Shazly, they had completed the first breach in the east bank rampart; by 8:30, the first bridge was completed and functioning and the first tanks began to trundle across. By 11:00, the Second Army had six functioning heavy bridges.[129] In the southern, Third Army, sector, however, things did not proceed according to schedule. The engineers encountered a serious problem when the banks scoured by the water cannon turned into mushy mud. Two bridges were completed by the morning of October 7.

During the night of October 6–7 the Egyptians managed to push across the Canal about five hundred tanks and another three thousand artillery pieces, trucks, APCs, and so on—mostly in the Second Army's sector. Very little heavy equipment managed to get across in the southern sector. By the late morning of October 7, five infantry divisions had crossed the Canal, each with a brigade of tanks, as well as battalions of SU-100 armor-mounted antitank guns and armored Sagger launchers. In the north the troops, backed by tanks, advanced four to six miles into Sinai.[130]

The Israeli command had long known the outline of the Egyptian war plan. On April 16, 1972, the director of military intelligence, Maj. Gen. Aharon Yariv, had passed detailed copies to the general staff and Southern Command.[131] But the general staff, on October 6–7, was unaware of a planned "operational pause" after the crossing, and feared that the Egyptians, in the wake of the success of their infantry on the east bank of the Canal, intended immediately to bring over the reserve armored and mechanized divisions and push inland.[132]

Hence Southern Command tried with everything at its disposal to halt the crossing at the waterline and, later, at the Artillery Road (the planned limit of the first stage of the Egyptian offensive) in the hope of preventing a breakout toward the passes. But, in fact, the Egyptians at this time had no intention of advancing beyond the Artillery Road. Spreading out as their numbers and equipment increased at the five bridgeheads, they quickly encountered IDF tanks, which they ambushed before the Israelis reached their prepared battle stations.

But the Israeli command's confusion and misreading of events was such that General Elazar, at 6:35 P.M. on October 6, described the situation on the Canal as "reasonable."[133] He and his commanders spoke of crossing the Canal the next day—even though the necessary bridging equipment was to become available only on October 12! As one historian put it, during the first three days the battle in the south was enveloped, for the Israeli command, not by the "fog of war" but by "utter darkness."[134]

The IDF's sporadic armored attacks on the bridgeheads caused few Egyptian casualties. By evening on October 7, "100,000 men, 1,020 tanks, and 13,500 vehicles" crossed the waterway.[135] Nonetheless, at this time the Egyptian commanders in both the Second and Third Army sectors made little effort to expand their bridgeheads toward the Artillery Road.[136]

The IAF accomplished no more than the Israeli tanks. During the late afternoon of October 6 it flew dozens of ground support missions against the bridgeheads. During the night, using flares, it tried to locate and destroy the bridges, but its night-bombing capabilities were minimal, and these efforts succeeded only marginally, if at all, in affecting the Egyptian timetables.[137]

The Israeli failures of October 6–7 confirmed the dictum of Frederick the Great: "[He] who defends everything defends nothing." But by any standards, and the weakness of the Israeli response notwithstanding, the Egyptians had scored a major achievement, of both logistics and combat, and their offensive would enter the textbooks as a classic in the genres of both surprise and assault across a major water obstacle.

On October 7, with the Egyptian bridgeheads firmly in place, the IDF platoons in the isolated forts, some of which had withstood repeated assault, were given permission to retreat. For many this came too late. Two forts surrendered; five others were abandoned, some of their troops making it to Israeli lines on foot or on the back of relieving tanks. Several platoons were wiped out on their way east toward the Artillery Road and safety, ambushed by Egyptian infantrymen.

By morning, 60 percent (153) of the Sinai Division's tanks had been put out of commission, many of them left behind in the Egyptian bridgeheads. Hundreds of men had been killed or were missing in action. The badly mauled division had certainly inflicted casualties[138] and had made some of the Egyptian units pause, but in general it had failed, and dismally. The surviving soldiers, noted Sharon, now a reserve divisional commander, when he arrived at the Tasa base on October 7, were bewildered: "Suddenly something was happening to them that had never happened before. These were soldiers who had been brought up on victories. . . . It was a generation that had never lost. Now they were in a state of shock. . . . How was it that [the Egyptians] were moving forward and we were defeated?"[139]

By now this state of dismay had, to a degree, gripped Southern Command headquarters as well. And panic could also be sensed higher up. Early that morning the general staff decided, for the moment, to disregard the Golan (where the troops were believed to be holding) and throw the bulk of the IAF against the Egyptians. Specifically, the Phantom and Mirage squadrons were to destroy the antiaircraft missile network between the Canal and Cairo, thus clearing the sky over the Canal for ground support missions. The jets took off just before 7:00 A.M. and, penetrating the missile screen, successfully hit a number of radar sites and Egyptian Canal-side and Nile Valley airfields. But having successfully completed this first phase, and while refueling and rearming for the second, main stage—the massed attack on the antiaircraft missile network—the force was abruptly retargeted. In a panicky early morning telephone call, Dayan, bypassing normal channels, directly warned IAF commander Benny Peled that "the Third Temple [the State of Israel] is in danger," that Syrian armor had broken through the Golan defenses and was rolling down the slopes toward the Jordan Valley, and that the IAF had to stop it. "The Sinai is sand. Here [the Golan and Jordan Valley] are homes," Dayan told Peled.

To the astonishment of his senior staff, Peled redirected the IAF toward the Golan. Meanwhile the Egyptian antiaircraft network had been left intact, severely curbing the IAF's ability to provide the embattled tank brigades with air support.[140] That day Dayan, taking note of the failure to crush the Egyptian bridgeheads and of the continuing advance of the Syrian divisions on the Golan, repeated his dire "Third Temple" warnings to all and sundry.[141] He recommended that the IDF retreat to a new defense line in Sinai—in effect, to abandon all the territory west of the passes.[142]

During October 6–8, Egyptian heliborne commandos tried repeatedly to disrupt the movement of Israeli units toward the front and to facilitate a Third

Army breakthrough southward, down the Gulf of Suez coast toward Sharm ash-Sheikh.[143] The commandos caused only a handful of Israeli casualties and failed to delay substantially the arrival of the reserves. But their unexpected presence did force the IDF repeatedly to divert reconnaissance units from front-line duties. Moreover, they managed to instill in the Israeli divisions a measure of trepidation, which, in turn, led to travel restrictions on roads in western Sinai at night. Less quantifiably, the commandos marginally threw the Israeli command off balance.[144]

On the morning of October 8 the IDF launched its first coordinated, full-scale response to the offensive—a concentrated two-division (or what was planned as such) assault on the bridgeheads. The stunning surprise of October 6 and the weakness of the Sinai Division's response had given the Egyptians time to consolidate. But now General Avraham Adan's and Sharon's divisions were poised to counterattack.

The IDF leadership—at this time almost to a man Armored Corps veterans—still believed in the near-miraculous powers of the concentrated armored punch. Debating the events of the past two days, Elazar, Gonnen, and the others concluded that the fault lay not with the doctrine but with its uncoordinated, piecemeal application: Platoons and companies of tanks had, indeed, been mauled by Egyptian armor and artillery, and particularly by infantry; but brigade and divisional assaults would be something else. Elazar and Gonnen believed that a two-division armored thrust would succeed in throwing at least some of the Egyptian infantry back across the Canal—and might well develop into an Israeli crossing to the west bank. Dayan, badly affected by the Egyptian successes, was not optimistic but let the generals have their way.[145]

The two fresh reserve divisions would attack the bridgeheads, starting from a point across from Ismailia, and push southward. Elazar and Gonnen had received reports about the masses of antitank rockets and missiles on which the Egyptians relied, but had not really digested their meaning. Thus the Israeli plan both took them into account and ignored them, a fatal contradiction at its heart. For the orders to Adan and Sharon were both to sweep up the Egyptian bridgeheads and reach the water's edge, and to stay out of range of the Egyptian Saggers (one to two miles). There was no way that both guidelines could be carried out.

The primary objective was to roll up the bridgeheads. If successful, the divisions were then to exploit the momentum, somehow cross the Canal (very little thought and apparently no planning at all were actually invested in the notion), and establish their own bridgeheads on the other side. But a difference in nuance soon became apparent. Elazar both before and during the offensive stressed the aim of smashing the east-bank bridgeheads; Gonnen, of "exploiting the success" and crossing the Canal. He instructed the IAF representative in Southern Command to stop planes bombing the Egyptian bridge just north of the Great Bitter Lake, as he had earmarked it for the IDF's later use.[146]

At the very least the commanders hoped to delay or subvert the consolidation of the enemy bridgeheads. Unaware of the Egyptians' imminent activation of an "operational pause,"[147] the Israelis feared that they intended to push their armored divisions across the Canal and race for the passes. The counteroffensive was thus, to some degree, designed to blunt their eagerness to launch this second-stage offensive.[148]

Adan's division set out without even minimal artillery support; the self-propelled cannon, with their long ammunition trains, were still crossing central Sinai. Moreover, the IAF was apparently not informed in time that Southern Command was about to launch a major counteroffensive and managed to provide only sixty-two ground support missions on that front between 8:00 A.M. and 3:00 P.M.[149] Wherever they approached the bridgeheads, the battalions were badly mauled by the Egyptians, and many tanks were damaged or destroyed.

For hours Adan failed to understand what was happening; it took Gonnen even longer. At 9:15 Adan reported to Gonnen: "Slowly we are succeeding in sweeping up everything."[150] At 9:30 Gonnen ordered Adan "to destroy all the [Egyptian] forces in the area . . . and only then to cross [the Canal] . . . try to put across a small unit that will stay on the [west] bank."[151] At 10:40 Gonnen instructed Adan to capture Egyptian bridges on the Canal and transfer platoons of tanks to their western side. Only at 11:50 did Adan inform Gonnen: "We have taken a lot of casualties, a great many. Vehicles [tanks] are burning from missiles." Yet at 12:45 P.M. Gonnen again informed Adan that he had permission to cross the Canal and establish a bridgehead on the west bank.[152]

The wild optimism (and misinformation) of Adan's and Gonnen's early communications infected the general staff back in Tel Aviv. At 9:32 and again at 9:50 Gonnen reported that small reconnaissance units of Adan's division had already crossed the Canal. At 10:19 he asked Elazar's permission to cross the Canal with armor; permission was radioed back a minute later. Elazar's briefing of the cabinet that morning was similarly tinged with optimistic misinformation; he read out a note he had received to the ministers: "A bridgehead has been established on the west bank of the Suez Canal." Responding to this, Dayan said the IDF must take Port Said as well.[153] At around noon Elazar approved a further request by Gonnen: to allow Sharon's division to cross the Canal that afternoon and capture Suez City.[154]

These euphoric assessments were quickly overtaken by realism and gloom, compounded by the successive failures of the IDF's columns to reach objectives or, even, to come to grips with the enemy. Some of the heaviest fighting took place at Hammutal, a large fortification in the central sector, occupied by the Egyptians. Israeli tankmen spoke highly of the Egyptians' courage in beating off their attacks: "The Arabs fired with all their weapons, from each dugout. They fought with terrible fanaticism. [They] competed with each other in acts of heroism."[155]

The following day, October 9, the Israeli units were ordered to withdraw, and the attack ended with nothing accomplished but the destruction of some eighty Israeli and eighty Egyptian tanks.

At a press conference in Tel Aviv that evening Elazar failed to clarify that the counteroffensive had gone badly wrong. Rather, he said: "We reached [the Canal], we destroyed [enemy units], we pushed back [the enemy]. . . ." But at the same time he grimly conceded that the Egyptians had not been "broken" and were not retreating. He promised, however, that in the end "[W]e shall break their bones."[156] He was visibly enraged.

One of the few Israeli successes of October 8–9 was the retention and relief of "Budapest," the northernmost position of the Bar-Lev Line. It was the only Bar-Lev fortification not to fall.[157] Less fortunate was the reinforced paratroop platoon defending the Mezakh fort at the southern tip of the Canal. Repeated amphibious and infantry assaults during October 6–10 were beaten off, but one by one all the defending tanks were put out of action, as were most of the paratroops. On October 13 the defenders surrendered.[158] The Mezakh was the last Canal-side fort to fall into Egyptian hands.

The IDF's armored attacks against the bridgeheads had been spectacularly unsuccessful, but cumulatively they had sapped the Egyptians' energies and dented their composure. As Egyptian documents later captured by the IDF were to demonstrate, the counterattacks, however incompetent, managed to retard the planned advance. In the northern sector some Egyptian units had penetrated Sinai to the depth of about six miles; but in the south, the Third Army fell well short of that.[159]

The counteroffensive of October 8 had been, in Sharon's phrase, "a tankman's nightmare."[160] Its net outcome was the mauling of Adan's and Sharon's divisions and the expansion of the Egyptian bridgeheads eastward (in one or two areas their troops reached the Artillery Road). It left Israel's military and political leadership in shock and acutely depressed. The failures of the first two days could, perhaps, be chalked up to experience. But this was something else: The initiative was with the IDF, and relatively large forces had been deployed, but the traditional doctrine of concentrated armored punches and breakthroughs had failed. The fact that the implementation had been poor was irrelevant—or, indeed, was an additional cause for concern. Moreover, the Egyptian troops had proved to be of radically different stuff from those encountered in 1948, 1956, and 1967.

Regaining the east bank of the Canal, it was now understood in Tel Aviv, was going to be a difficult, if not impossible, task. Both Prime Minister Meir and the IDF generals were "shocked" by Dayan's appearances at the ministerial and general staff meetings on the night of October 8. The successive blows had clearly jolted him. He spoke of mobilizing high school students (twelfth- and even eleventh-graders) and individuals who had passed the age of reserve duty, and he recommended readying a new defense line deep in Sinai, along or east of the passes, "with or without Umm Hashiba [the IDF headquarters and electronic intelligence base, northeast of the Gidi Pass]."[161]

Dayan and the general staff reached three conclusions: First, given the proven strength of the Arab armies, the IDF was incapable of mounting simultaneous major offensives both in the north and the south. During the offensive in the South on October 8 most of the air force had been engaged in trying to stop the Syrians on the Golan. Second, the IDF would have to wait until it had amassed sufficient strength to mount a new offensive in the South. Third, the army could not successfully—and certainly not at an acceptable cost—attack the Egyptian bridgeheads frontally, pitting tanks and infantrymen against large concentrations of well-dug-in, profusely well-armed, highly motivated troops. The Egyptians would have to be defeated using an indirect approach.

Dayan and Elazar were persuaded that much of the confusion and lack of coordination had stemmed from incompetent command and friction between the generals. Gonnen had functioned poorly. Neither Adan nor Sharon got along with him, and neither hid his view that Gonnen was incompetent. Moreover, Elazar and Adan also had uneasy relationships with Sharon, who tended to regard everyone around him as less capable than he. Dayan and Elazar felt they had to act. On the night of October 9–10, Gonnen, while nominally remaining CO of Southern Command, was in effect replaced by Lieutenant General Bar-Lev, a cabinet minister and Elazar's predecessor as chief of general staff. Bar-Lev was rushed to Sinai and given the title of the "CGS's representative" at the command, with Uri Ben-Ari as his assistant.

Dayan and the general staff were at something of a loss about how to proceed. In the north things were clear: The Syrians had to be pushed out of the Golan and perhaps beyond, with the IDF implicitly threatening Damascus. But with much of the armor committed in the North, the options in the south seemed somewhat opaque. The Egyptians might or might not launch their second-stage armored offensive toward the passes. If they did not, then a battle of attrition, consisting mainly of artillery duels, would ensue, with the IDF less able than the Egyptians to sustain losses in men and matériel (as well as the economic losses stemming from the massive mobilization of the reserves).

IDF planning since the late 1960s had called for a cross-Canal offensive, albeit under more agreeable conditions. This idea, propounded loudly and persistently by Sharon since October 6–7, might provide the required strategic volte-face that could bring the war to a successful conclusion. But it was extremely risky. One or more "soft spots" had to be found in the Second and Third Army defenses, through which the IDF could advance to the Canal's banks. The attackers, while vulnerable and crossing the Canal—for which they would need to span the waterway with a number of armor-sustaining bridges—would have to fend off one or both of the armies. Then the crossing force would have to be able to secure bridgeheads on the west bank and beat off counterattacks. In effect this meant that Israel could undertake the crossing only after the Egyptians had transferred their reserve armored divisions from the west bank to the east and, perhaps, after these had been substantially battered in combat. Otherwise the mass of armor might crush the vulnerable bridgehead before it was firmly established.

If no such second-stage offensive materialized, and quickly, then a cease-fire—even with Egypt still holding its initial territorial gains—might be best. It was certainly better than an open-ended war of attrition. One relevant factor was the state of the IAF. On October 12 General Peled warned Elazar that in two days his command, mainly because of the continued air offensive against Syria, would reach a "red line" in terms of serviceable aircraft and pilots, and would no longer be able to provide effective support for another major ground offensive.[162]

The matter was brought to a meeting of the War Cabinet for decision. But before the ministers could vote, IDF Intelligence Branch informed them that, at last, the Egyptian armored divisions on the west bank were on the move, would cross the Canal, and on October 13 or 14 would launch the long-mooted offensive. Thus, almost at the last moment, the Egyptians had solved Israel's strategic dilemma: The IDF and the ministers would wait for the offensive—and decide on the next step in light of its outcome.[163]

On the nights of October 12 and 13 Egypt's Twenty-first Armored Division, parts of the Fourth Armored Division and of two mechanized divisions, and a large number of mobile SAM-6 batteries, crossed the Canal.[164] At dawn on October 14, they launched the second-stage offensive.

In his memoirs the Egyptian commander, Shazly, maintains that he had always resisted the concept of a deep "second-stage" thrust but was overridden by President Sadat and War Minister Ismail 'Ali, who apparently were motivated, at least in part, by a desire to relieve Israel's pressure on Syria. (On October 11 the IDF columns began pushing toward Damascus.) He believed that Egypt lacked sufficient armor, and that pushing two armored divisions into Sinai would be a strategic mistake, stripping the rear of reserves. Shazly also feared that the force would be beaten back with heavy casualties; the tanks, advancing beyond much of their SAM cover, would be sitting ducks for the well-entrenched Israeli gunners and the IAF.

In the event Shazly proved to be right. But the Egyptians also tripped up in the execution: They dispersed their offensive effort both geographically and chronologically—not one concentrated push but six separate thrusts along the one-hundred-mile front launched in staggered fashion. In a sense it was a replay of the IDF's counterattack of October 8, but this time the Egyptians were caught out in the open.[165]

Just after dawn on October 14, hundreds of Egyptian guns opened up along the Artillery Road while warplanes attacked Israeli targets, including the forward headquarters at Baluza. The previous night a hundred commandos had been helilifted to a point just south of Tasa, in order to cause chaos in the

Israeli rear. But they were located and killed or captured before they could do any damage.

The six prongs of Egyptian armor, deploying altogether about 1,000 tanks and hundreds of APCs and guns, got under way during the morning. "A river of armor flowing over the desert," was one Israeli colonel's description of the sight that unfolded.[166] They were awaited by 750 Israeli tanks.

"The outcome was predictable," Shazly wrote later.[167] His T-55 and T-62 tanks charged forward, with the sun in their crews' eyes, against superior Pattons and Centurions and against superior gunnery. In the southern sector the columns were also subjected to devastating attacks by waves of IAF fighter-bombers. The Egyptians that day lost hundreds of men, and between 200 and 250 tanks; the IDF lost 20 to 25 tanks.[168] In several sectors the IDF drew the Egyptians in by dissembling retreat, the better to destroy their tanks as they pushed forward. Bar-Lev reported at the end of the day that "the Egyptians are again acting in their traditional way, and we are resuming our old ways."[169]

In retrospect both sides would regard the battle as the turning point of the war, when Egypt lost the initiative and the IDF acquired it, smoothing the way for its own cross-Canal offensive. Certainly the battle of October 14 was a severe psychological blow to the Egyptians, who had just become accustomed to victory; the Israelis had once again shown their mettle when it came to fighting a mobile armored battle in open desert. And once again the Egyptians witnessed the devastation the IAF could wreak if their ground forces were caught outside the SAM umbrella.

The long-awaited precondition for an Israeli counterthrust was now reality (the west bank of the Canal was shorn of the large, threatening Egyptian tank formations). Just as the Egyptian cross-Canal assault had suited that army's character and capabilities, the Israeli counteroffensive was to be characteristic of the IDF. The Egyptian crossing had involved masses of men, with substantial artillery and antiaircraft cover, spread over a wide front. Years of planning had gone into it, each officer and soldier meticulously drilled on his own particular actions at each stage. The Israeli crossing was a concentrated (almost pinpoint) attack. It began with something akin to a large commando raid, and gradually unfolded into a full-fledged invasion. It was hastily planned, and a great deal was to hinge on improvisation and local initiative at various echelons of command. The Egyptians had crossed in broad daylight, relying on main strength, with the booming support of more than a thousand guns; the Israelis crossed at night, stealthily and covertly, at first barely discernible, almost inaudible. For days the Egyptian high command could not make out what was happening. Was it a mere raid or a feint? Or was it the overture to the real thing? Were the Israelis *still* on the west bank? Egyptian commanders and politicians were to ask during the following days, unable to fully grasp the significance of the dangerous Israeli gamble.

Sharon had been chafing at the bit since October 7–8 to launch the crossing, which he singlemindedly regarded as the only way to destabilize and defeat the Egyptian army. Given the fact that it was essentially his plan and that it was to be his division that punched the initial hole through the Egyptian lines and onto the west bank, he can justifiably be regarded as the architect of the crossing. The operation was given the final green light at a meeting at Southern Command headquarters just before midnight (October 14–15); the cabinet had already given Dayan and the army carte blanche for the offensive, which all understood would be highly risky, and Israel's last chance to reverse the tide.

To secure the crossing point, near the Matzmed fort just north of the Great Bitter Lake, the Israeli forces had to get past two Egyptian divisions, which were holding the "Missouri" complex of fortifications and the "Chinese Farm" (a large desert agriculture project set up by the Egyptians in the 1960s, so called because IDF troops who came upon the site in 1967, inexpert in Oriental languages, found machinery with Japanese inscriptions). Sharon hoped that a surprise approach (from the west) by an armored brigade would result in the fall of "Missouri." But the Israelis once again underestimated Egyptian strength and resolve. All their efforts were unsuccessful. However, the successive attacks caused the defenders heavy casualties and ultimately wore them down.

The focus of the battle was a junction of two axes code-named "Lexicon" and "Tirtur." The Egyptians fought bravely and stubbornly, expending hundreds of Saggers and thousands of shells. The point Israeli brigade lost some sixty tanks and 120 men; the Egyptians lost even more. Sharon later described the crossroads that morning: "I . . . saw hundreds and hundreds of burned and twisted vehicles. . . . Here and there Israeli and Egyptian tanks had destroyed each other at a distance of a few meters barrel to barrel. . . . Inside those tanks and next to them lay their dead crews. . . . No picture could capture the horror of the scene."[170]

But the IDF losses had not been in vain; indeed, they were crucial to the success of the Canal-crossing plan. While the Egyptians were occupied with Tirtur, the Fifty-fifth Paratroop Brigade, commanded by the legendary Col. Danny Matt, stole past a few kilometers to the south and reached the Canal in half-tracks, carrying rubber dinghies. By 5:00 A.M. on October 16, most of the understrength brigade, about 750 troops, was across and digging in. After three large passages were gouged by the engineers through the Israeli Canal-side sandbank, amphibious craft, which had followed Matt's column, began to ferry armor across the Canal. Within minutes twenty-seven tanks and seven APCs were across. The landing took the Egyptians completely by surprise; there was no opposition on the west bank. The paratroops radioed Sharon "Acapulco," the code-word for success.

But the general staff's timetable had gone seriously awry. The plan had called not for piecemeal ferrying but for a solid bridge (or two bridges) to be established across the Canal by first light. However, because of enormous traffic jams, the blockage at Tirtur, and the heavy Egyptian fire, the bridges had remained stuck east of the Chinese Farm, partially damaged, and unable to reach the waterway. A small Israeli force was on the west bank. But behind it there was no bridge, and the routes to Matzmed and the Canal were effectively blocked. The general staff forbade any further shift of troops across the waterway until the routes were secure and at least one bridge firmly in place.

At sunrise on October 16 perhaps the main ray of light (from the Israeli perspective) was afforded by the fact that the Egyptians appeared to be confused by the battles around Missouri and Tirtur and completely indifferent to what was going on around Matzmed. They failed to understand that IDF forces were already on the west bank and that a major offensive, albeit one in grave trouble, was under way. Only around midday did they receive reports about the presence of Israeli tanks on the west bank.[171] But they appear to have thought in terms of a small amphibious raid, not of a major offensive. The Egyptian general staff communiqué spoke of seven Israeli tanks that had somehow "infiltrated" to the west bank.[172] Sadat, addressing his parliament at noon, announced his intention to reopen the Canal—and failed altogether to mention the Israeli presence on the west bank.[173]

Only with Golda Meir's late-afternoon announcement in the Knesset that IDF units were fighting on the west bank—an intelligence indiscretion if there ever was one—did the Egyptian high command begin to fathom what was happening and hastily draw up plans to block the crossing and order the shelling of the crossing point.[174] According to Soviet sources, the news had created "a situation of near-panic among many Egyptian political and military leaders." Some even considered withdrawing the government to Asyut in Upper Egypt, from there to wage a war of "popular resistance" against the Israeli invaders.[175]

To the Israelis the situation on October 16 still looked bleak, though the small force on the west bank had given some grounds for optimism: That morning a column of about a dozen armored vehicles had sortied out of the bridgehead westward and, traversing a twenty-mile arc, in six hours had destroyed, among other objectives, four SAM bases.[176] But the bridgehead appeared vulnerable and not viable: Either a bridge and a secure east–west corridor to it would be established, quickly, or the task force would have to be pulled out. Withdrawal was seriously discussed but rejected, at Sharon's insistence. With Sharon's division now split on either side of the Canal and badly battered, Adan was charged with securing the corridor and bridging the waterway.

An initial effort by Adan's tanks on October 16 to clear the Tirtur axis failed that night. A second assault was launched, this time by a battalion of paratroops, commanded by Lt. Col. Yitzhak Mordechai and overseen by his deputy brigade commander, Amnon Lipkin-Shahak, against the missile-carrying infantry dug in at the Chinese Farm.[177]

The site consisted of a handful of buildings and more than sixty miles of crisscrossing irrigation canals and ditches. The paratroops stormed into the farm and came under a hail of missiles and shells. Unable to advance, they dug in opposite the Egyptian infantry. The two sides traded fire through the night, the paratroops unable to maneuver or withdraw. The Israelis came off worse, targeted relentlessly by dozens of artillery batteries and missile launchers. The following morning a tank force, commanded by Col. Ehud Barak, broke through and pulled out the remnants of the paratroop battalion.

The operation failed to unblock Tirtur, but it had inflicted severe losses on the Egyptians and disrupted the Second Army's preparations for an offensive southward, against the Israeli crossing. And, under cover of the battle at Tirtur, Adan—taking a serious gamble—had managed to push a tank column, dragging along most of the parts for a bridge, down the more southerly axis, Akavish. The vital rafts reached the Matzmed crossing point at 6:30 A.M. on October 17.[178]

The Egyptian plan for that morning had been to attack Matzmed from north and south, and the bridgehead itself from the west. Shazly subsequently claimed that he had opposed the plan, calling for elements of the Third Army to be moved back across the Canal and then to drive northward along the western shores of the Bitter Lakes, to attack the bridgehead itself from the south. But he had been overruled by Ismail 'Ali and Sadat, who angrily opposed withdrawing troops from the east bank to the west, for whatever purpose.[179]

The Egyptian plans spun out of kilter because Adan, following up the paratroop assault, had that morning launched a multipronged attack on the Chinese Farm–Missouri complex from the east, south, and west, and succeeded in pushing the Egyptians northward. At the same time the bulk of his division was deployed to the south in a classic ambush, trapping an Egyptian armored brigade moving northward along the eastern shore of the Great Bitter Lake. Caught between the lake, Israeli minefields, and well-positioned Israeli tanks in superior numbers, the bulk of the brigade, strung out along six to seven miles, was demolished, including about fifty of its tanks and dozens of armored cars. Shazly put it dramatically: "When night came, there were only a few survivors to pull back to the Third Army bridgehead. It was an utter waste." Adan lost three tanks in the engagement, two of them to mines.[180] The destruction of the brigade had sealed the fate of the Egyptian offensive against the Israeli crossing.

Meanwhile IDF engineers assembled a sectional raft bridge across the Canal, working under an intensive artillery bombardment. Egyptian aircraft, which for days had lain doggo in their Nile Valley bases, also began to interfere. Sharon, a few years later, described the situation that day in the "courtyard," where the bridging operation was being marshaled: "[A] tremendous Egyptian artillery barrage brought a curtain of shells crashing down on us. . . . MiG fighters swarmed over the yard . . . [turning] the compound into an inferno. With incredible courage soldiers were standing outside in this storm of fire directing traffic. . . . [Meanwhile] others worked at . . . assembling and launching the rafts. . . . The chaos was mind-boggling."[181]

But by 4:30 P.M., the bridge was complete, and before dawn on October 18 Adan was across with two brigades of tanks. The next two days saw the widening of the IDF's east–west corridor to the Canal and the breakout from the bridgehead. As before, the Egyptian counteroperations were mounted by inadequate forces acting without coordination. All the while the Egyptians continued to announce that the Israeli presence on the west bank amounted to "seven tanks hiding in the thickets around Deversoir."[182]

By now the high command had come around to Shazly's way of thinking, and saw the necessity of quickly moving armored formations back from the east bank to the west. But the units were too small, moved too slowly, and arrived too late. And efforts by the strategic reserve, which had remained on the west bank throughout, also proved unavailing. The Egyptian units acted without due coordination, arriving separately on the scene and without an accurate picture of the constantly changing Israeli dispositions.[183]

By October 20 the IDF on the east bank had cleared an area three miles north of Tirtur. But the decisive action was to unfold on the west side. The Israeli bridgehead, between October 16 and dawn on the 18th, was a constricted thing, about a mile deep and two to three miles from north to south, bounded on the east by the Canal, on the south by the Great Bitter Lake, and on the west by the Sweet Water Canal (SWC), which channeled water from the Nile Valley eastward to the Ismailia area and then turned south parallel to the Canal and the Great Bitter Lake, as far as Suez City. The land immediately on either side of the SWC was agricultural, heavily vegetated, in parts swampy, and crisscrossed with irrigation ditches. Passable though problematic for either tracked or wheeled vehicles, the area was known to Israeli troops as the "agricultural buffer." To the west lay the desert, duned and bare, as far as the Nile Valley.

With the bulk of Adan's and Sharon's divisions in the bridgehead on October 18, the stage was set for the Israeli thrust that was to overturn the results of Egypt's initial successes in the war. Both sides were racing against time. For the Egyptians the challenge was to set up a new, solid defense line west of the bridgehead before the Israelis could break out and cut off their armies on the east bank; for the Israelis, to get out into the open desert, destroy the rear echelons and SAM bases of the Second and Third Armies, and cut them off before the Egyptians could set up a viable line of containment. But the Israelis faced an additional, political race against the clock—to achieve their strategic objectives (the destruction or at least entrapment of one or both of the Egyptian armies) before the superpowers and the UN Security Council imposed a cease-fire.

At first light on October 18 three brigades lunged out of the bridgehead heading northwest, west, and south. The Egyptians, slow to understand developments and incompetent in improvisation, had not yet managed to set up a viable line. Nonetheless the going was not easy. The Egyptians had rushed units into the area around the bridgehead, most simply reinvesting defensive complexes that before October 6 had served as the Egyptian second and third lines.

As the tanks punched their way out of the bridgehead, the Egyptian air force made a last desperate effort to destroy the Israeli bridge on the Canal. Several dozen MiGs and Sukhois mounted what Adan was to call "suicide" attacks on the bridgehead. These were followed by a number of large, slow MI-8 helicopters, from which the Egyptians rolled out fuel drums (perhaps hoping for a napalm effect). The attackers met with a hail of ground fire; IAF interceptors soon joined the melée. In all, Egypt lost sixteen airplanes and seven helicopters over the bridgehead that day.

The same day the IAF had one last major go at the remaining Egyptian missile complex between Port Said and Ismailia, destroying six of the fifteen sites using bombs and Shrike anti-SAM missiles—but at a cost of six Phantoms. Thereafter the IAF reverted to piecemeal hit-and-run tactics. During the following four days around forty SAM sites were destroyed with no further Phantom losses.[184]

But the main battle was fought on the ground. On October 19 the breakout turned into the start of a massive strategic envelopment. By now the IDF had about 350 tanks on the east bank. The general staff had decided that the main push would be southward by two divisions—Adan's and Gen. Kalman Magen's (Magen had taken over and reconstituted the Sinai Division after its commander, Albert Mendler, was killed by an Egyptian shell)—to cut off and surround the Third Army. A secondary effort, by elements of Sharon's division, would at the same time press northward along the Canal's west bank, toward Ismailia, in order at least partially to cut off the Second Army and destroy its rear bases, artillery, and SAMs.

By dawn on October 19 President Sadat grasped what was happening and acceded to Soviet importuning for a cease-fire. Soviet Premier Alexei Kosygin, in Cairo since October 16, had reportedly shown him Soviet spy satellite photographs highlighting the burgeoning IDF presence on the west bank. Sadat was at last persuaded. He promptly transmitted his agreement to a cease-fire to Assad, who was astonished and angry. The two men had apparently agreed before the war that they would start it together and end it only in agreement. Yet here was Sadat, without consultation, informing Assad of his decision, leaving the Syrian leader in the lurch and, in reality, with no choice but to follow suit. Assad, hard-pressed in any case, could not carry on the war alone.

That night, just before midnight, the Egyptian high command, together with Sadat, held an emergency conference. Shazly's views were clear: The army's efforts during the previous three days to destroy or cut off the Israeli bridgehead had failed; efforts at containment, as things stood, would be use-less; the Third Army would be surrounded and trapped, and subsequently the Second might suffer a similar fate. Drastic action was called for—that is, withdrawal of the four key armored brigades of the Third and Second Armies (Sadat later claimed that Shazly had recommended withdrawing both armies in toto) from the east bank back to the west, to help contain the Israelis. Sadat reportedly had responded: "We will not withdraw a single soldier from the east to the west." Shazly felt that the Egyptian leadership was unwilling to face reality: "The regime was falling victim to its own lies." Sadat in his mem-oirs claimed that Shazly suffered a nervous breakdown and that he fired Shazly that night, replacing him with General Gamasy; Shazly denies this, claiming he was dismissed only on December 13, long after the war. But in effect that night Shazly was shunted aside from the army command in all but name.[185]

Just after dawn on October 19, Adan's and Magen's tanks had started out on their southward sweep. At last leaving the cramped, swampy, overgrown "agricultual buffer," they were now out in the open desert plains, "as if a prize had been given to the armor that had fought so hard . . . and [at last] had achieved the long-coveted freedom of maneuver."[186] Overrunning Egyptian positions and SAM batteries, the two divisions had entered classic tank coun-try and were dispersed over an enormous dusty plain, raising vast clouds as far as the eye could see.[187] By evening they had advanced some twenty-five miles. Sharon's division, meanwhile, pushing northward along the SWC, encoun-tered stiff resistance from hastily deployed Egyptian paratroops and com-mando battalions, and managed to gain only one or two miles.[188] The Egyptians understood that Ismailia and the fate of the Second Army were at stake.

That night, as Henry Kissinger flew to Moscow to discuss a superpower-imposed cease-fire, the Israeli command knew it had, at most, three days left in which to encircle the Third Army. With the Egyptians still shelling the Canal-crossing bridges (the IDF had completed a second bridge on the morn-ing of October 19), the Israeli divisions faced serious problems of re-resupply. Meanwhile, the Third Army—despite Sadat's professed opposition to any Egyptian troops crossing from the east to the west bank—moved more and more units back, to stave off the threatened envelopment.[189]

Adan's and Magen's divisions resumed their southward march with first light on October 20, destroying a succession of SAM sites and ragtag tank and artillery units thrown in to defend them. Many of them were taken completely by surprise and had no idea that the IDF had penetrated the west bank to such an extent. The two divisions continued their main thrust some fifteen to twenty-five miles west of the lakes and the Canal, while devoting secondary efforts to taking sections of the roads which ran beside the lakes and Canal banks. Both Magen's and Adan's columns advanced fourteen miles, reaching the Cairo–Suez railroad. Sharon's division had gained only another two to three miles in its push northward, through the "agricultural buffer," toward Ismailia.

By October 21, Egyptian resistance to the southward thrust had stiffened considerably, bringing Magen to a temporary halt. But the Egyptians sustained casualties and made no real inroads. Adan, too, made little progress that day, though his brigades managed to clear further areas on the east bank of the Great Bitter Lake. Sharon's forces again advanced a mile or two.

The Israelis now had hours, rather than days, to complete their task. Since the evening of October 20, Kissinger had been in emergency session with Soviet Communist Party Secretary Brezhnev and his aides, hammering out acceptable cease-fire terms. The Egyptians and Soviets had gradually abandoned their demand for an Israeli commitment to withdraw, on all fronts, back to the June 1967 lines. Indeed, Egypt's recognition of the dire military position was such that in the early morning hours of October 21 Sadat twice called in the Soviet ambassador to Cairo, Vladimir Vinogradov, and made a "desperate appeal" to the Kremlin to "take all possible measures to arrange an immediate cease-fire." At the first meeting, Sadat's aide, Hafiz Ismail, "acknowledged a serious threat to Cairo." Later that day Kissinger and Brezhnev reached agreement on a joint draft for what was to become Security Council Resolution 338, providing for a cease-fire in place no later than twelve hours after its adoption and calling on the parties to begin negotiations for "a just and durable peace in the Middle East," on the basis of Security Council Resolution 242. The resolution was adopted by the council, by a vote of 14 to 0 (China did not participate), at 00:52 A.M., October 22 (New York time).[190]

With hours in hand, the Israeli offensive continued. Adan still had 175 tanks in good repair.[191] Two of his brigades attacked the large Egyptian pockets along the southwestern shore of the Bitter Lakes. Adan's Third Brigade and Magen's division completed the envelopment of the Third Army by advancing due south and cutting off the main Cairo–Suez road (code-named "Sareg"), the Third Army's last supply line. The Third Army made a last desperate effort to keep Sareg open. The Israelis beat off the early morning attacks, but were surprised by their tenacity, despite a continuous pounding by the IAF.[192]

Adan's progress, southeastward, to reach the Canal's west bank, was slow, hampered by minefields and stubborn resistance. The Egyptians even threw in Libya's Mirage fighter-bombers to hamper him; dozens of IAF interceptors went up to stymie them. Meanwhile, Magen's division continued to push south. At 3:00 P.M., the two divisions were informed that the cease-fire would go into force just after 6:00 P.M. (Israel-Egypt time), leaving Adan barely three hours to reach the Canal. Thousands of Egyptian troops fled in all directions, but the Israelis had no time to take prisoners. By 6:50, Adan's lead units had reached the southern end of the Small Bitter Lake and the Suez Canal at three points. Magen's division had blocked Sareg at two points. Sharon's division had advanced a few more miles, stopping just south of Ismailia.[193]

At around 6:00, the Soviet-manned brigade of Scud medium-range missiles stationed near Cairo fired off a volley that was aimed at, but failed to hit, the Israeli troop concentrations at the Canal crossing point. The firing—the only use of Scuds during the war—was ordered directly by Soviet Defense Minister Andrei Grechko, without authorization from Brezhnev.[194]

The situation after the cease-fire took effect, during the evening of October 22, was "full of complex problems," as Adan later put it.[195] Israeli and Egyptian units were intermixed; thousands of Egyptian troops were on the loose, some armed, others not, inside and behind areas already captured by the IDF; units in both armies were at half cock, having only partially fulfilled missions; and several Egyptian battalions had lost touch with their headquarters and did not know of the cease-fire orders.

Almost immediately after it nominally took effect, the cease-fire was violated by both sides.[196] Southern Command wanted to complete the envelopment of the Third Army by reaching the Gulf of Suez and to clear the whole area occupied in the west bank of Egyptian units. In several places enemy troops had fired on the Israelis during the night: the latter thus felt they had a good excuse themselves to violate the cease-fire. The following morning Adan's troops slowly cleared the area along the western shore of the Small Bitter Lake and the Canal's west bank, where pockets of stranded Egyptians still held out. They captured some 4,500 soldiers, who by then were thoroughly demoralized and offered minimal resistance.

Meanwhile, there were grueling deliberations in the Israeli cabinet and general staff about whether to allow the generals to complete their task of encirclement. Though the main Cairo–Suez axes had been cut, the Egyptians could still supply the army by taking a roundabout route to the Gulf of Suez, and then north along the gulf road to Suez City and across to the east bank on the still-intact Egyptian bridges. But it was clear that strong American pressure, and perhaps even more strident Soviet pressures, would be unleashed. Nonetheless the IDF got the green light. According to Dayan the reasons were Syria's continued rejection of the cease-fire resolution (Damascus only announced its acceptance that evening, October 23, at 6:15 P.M.) and Egyptian violations, which included efforts to advance in all sectors as well as air activity over the west bank.[197]

The orders went out at about noon to Magen's and Adan's divisions. Shazly later charged that the Israeli decision was made without legitimate cause. It is likely that there was an element of truth in both sides' contentions: Egyptian units, not necessarily under central direction, had violated the cease-fire by fire and movement; Israeli units, on the night of October 22, had already violated the standstill provisions. They went on to violate the cease-fire, in coordinated fashion, on October 23.

Adan launched two brigades due south, to race the last thirteen miles to Suez City's outskirts. They encountered a succession of "soft," rear-echelon targets—truck laagers, headquarters units, and artillery batteries—but few tanks or infantry units, and made excellent time. Adan's division reached the vital crossroads on the northwestern outskirts of Suez City at 8:00 P.M. Above, the sky swarmed with dogfights as the Egyptians threw in the remnants of their air force to try to thwart the Israeli advance. IAF interceptors that day bagged fourteen more Egyptian aircraft.

The Third Army's formations in the west bank had completely collapsed. Shazly somewhat ludicrously described the Israeli thrust southward on October 23 thus: "Driving unopposed past administrative bases and rest camps full of wounded men, through checkpoints manned by weary soldiers relaxing in the knowledge of a cease-fire, does not strike me as particularly gallant, but perhaps I am old-fashioned." Magen's brigades, taking a more westerly route, raced south, to Ras 'Adabiya on the Gulf, the southernmost point of the Israeli encirclement. They reached and occupied the site just before midnight on October 23.

But one last battle was in store for Adan's division and the Egyptians. After midnight on October 23, Adan was ordered by Southern Command to take Suez City, "if the city was empty" or, in a variation, "if it was not Stalingrad."[198] IDF intelligence knew that the city—which had been emptied of its civilian population during the 1968–70 War of Attrition—was held by two battalions of mechanized infantry and an antitank (Sagger) company as well as a commando battalion. But the Egyptians were believed to be demoralized and ineffective; their poor showing on October 23, during Adan's race southward, was taken as a foretaste of what was in store in Suez City.

The Israelis couldn't have been more wrong. Sensing that an attack on the city was impending, the Egyptians had organized a lively reception. The Israelis were to suffer the usual fate of troops fighting in an unfamiliar, fortified, built-up area. Moreover, Adan's two-brigade attack on October 24 was hastily conceived and organized. At one stage a battalion of paratroops was stranded, surrounded and under heavy Egyptian fire. By evening dozens of the besieged troops were dead or wounded, before the unit was extricated by an armored relief column. Suez City remained in Egyptian hands—though, like part of the Third Army, it was now completely surrounded by Israeli forces.

Security Council Resolutions 339 and 340 of October 23 and 25, respectively, reiterating the call for an immediate cease-fire, which were implicitly backed by the threat of Soviet military intervention, ended the Yom Kippur War. By October 27–28, UN observers had deployed along the front lines.

All told, in the October war Israel lost about 2,300 dead (half of them tankmen), 5,500 wounded, and 294 prisoners (most of them from the forts of the Bar-Lev Line). Egyptian casualties were some 12,000 dead, 35,000 wounded, and 8,400 prisoners. Syria lost some 3,000 dead, 5,600 wounded, and 411 captured (including 13 Iraqis and 6 Moroccans).

Arab losses in equipment were even more disproportionate, largely because damaged Arab equipment fell into Israeli hands, while most damaged Israeli equipment was retrieved and later repaired. Hundreds of captured (damaged and undamaged) Arab tanks and APCs were repaired and converted for Israeli use after 1973. Egypt lost about 1,000 tanks, Syria 1,150, and Israel 400 (many more were hit but repaired after the war).

Israel lost 102 airplanes—or about thirty percent of its combat aircraft— and 5 helicopters (101 of the total to antiaircraft fire), the Egyptians 235 airplanes and 42 helicopters, and the Syrians 135 airplanes and 13 helicopters. More than two-thirds of Arab aerial losses were in dogfights.

Egyptian losses in SAM missile batteries were severe—forty-three, mostly overrun or battered from the air in the IDF offensive in the west bank. The Syrians lost four SAM batteries and Israel one. Sixteen more Egyptian and Syrian SAM batteries were damaged.

At sea Israel lost no vessels, the Egyptians seven missile boats and four torpedo boats and coastal defense craft, and the Syrians five missile boats, one minesweeper, and one coastal defense vessel. Though relatively small, Israel's navy was the only arm of the IDF that was properly prepared for the war. The Armored Corps was completely unprepared for the massive deployment of Saggers, recoilless antitank guns, and RPGs by the Arab infantry; the IAF had no suitable response to the Egyptian and Syrian interlocking SAM networks; and Israel's infantry, equipped with outdated bazooka rocket launchers, FN semiautomatic rifles, and Uzi submachine guns, was no match in firepower for the Egyptian and Syrian infantry, who were equipped with RPG-7s and AK-47 (Kalashnikov) automatic assault rifles. Only in the course of the war did the United States airlift to Israel large quantities of automatic rifles (M-16s), TOW antitank guided missiles, and LAW antitank rockets.

But at sea Israel entered the war with superior weaponry, with its thirteen Reshef- and Sa'ar-class missile boats mounting Gabriel sea-to-sea missiles and effective electronic jamming and deflection systems. These, operated by highly trained seamen, easily outclassed the Arab navies' thirty-two Soviet Komar and Ossa boats, with their antiquated Styx missile systems.

Israeli naval activity was not restricted to the missile boats. On the night of October 16 a team of naval commandos, using minisubmarines, penetrated Port Said harbor and sank an Ossa missile boat, a rocket-launching ship, an MTB, and a landing craft. Two of the commandos went missing, presumed dead, in the attack.[199] And naval commandos raided the main Egyptian Red Sea base at Ghardaka four times, sinking two missile boats. The Egyptians managed to block the Red Sea's exit to Israeli shipping at Bab al-Mandab and to stop (with mines) the movement of Israeli oil tankers from the Abu Rodeis oilfields to Eilat.

The conclusion of the October war, in a military sense, in no way conformed to the model set in 1967: Neither the Syrian nor the Egyptian armies had been routed. Both, though eventually bested, had emerged with solid, initial accomplishments and had managed to retain organized military structures and a strong defensive capability, even after defeat. On both fronts, the war—unlike 1967—had ended without a decisive result. Hence on both fronts the Arabs were able to apply military pressure (sporadic shelling and raiding) against the IDF troops dug in in their territory in the course of the protracted postwar disengagement-of-forces negotiations.

The Syrian army had been defeated and pushed back into Syria. The IDF had then pushed into the Bashan and conquered a chunk of territory (about five hundred square kilometers, in all), including the Syrian Hermon peaks and Tel Shams, which brought it to within twenty miles of Damascus. But despite severe losses the Syrian army (reinforced by Iraqi and Jordanian expeditionary forces) had not been broken, and still presented a tenacious opponent in defense, barring substantive IDF advances after October 14.

In the south the situation was more complex. Most of the Third Army's combat formations were surrounded and stranded on the east bank of the Canal and its rear echelons had fallen to Israeli assault, with thousands of troops captured. Had the war continued, the army could have been pounded into submission within days. To the north the Second Army still had open supply lines and intact rear echelons, but Ismailia was within range of medium Israeli weaponry. Its armored and mechanized forces had largely been shattered, its SAM defenses were badly battered, and its troops on the east bank were exposed to artillery fire and aerial bombardment. They faced the threat of envelopment, should the war be renewed.

But as things stood on October 25, Egypt had chalked up two big achievements: Its armed forces had broken through a major psychological barrier, wiping out the "shame" of earlier defeats, and they had conquered and held on to two strips of territory, about six miles in depth, in Israeli-occupied Sinai, thus definitively shattering the political-military status quo ante bellum.

THE POLITICS OF WAR AND AFTEREFFECTS

The superpowers had a major impact on the conduct and course of the war—through their policies on military supply and a cease-fire.

In the nineteen days of combat the two sides expended vast amounts of munitions, and lost thousands of tanks, APCs, and artillery pieces and hundreds of aircraft.[200] Within a few days both sides were in urgent need of resupply.

The USSR stuck by its clients; it had little choice if it wished to maintain its position in the Middle East. Beginning on October 10, the Soviets mounted "the biggest airlift in their history," in Shazly's words. In the course of the war and in its immediate aftermath, about fifteen thousand tons of war matériel were flown to Egypt and Syria, and a sealift of sixty-three thousand tons of equipment, mostly tanks and guns, reached the Arab states (mainly Syria) by October 30. Altogether Syria and Egypt received approximately twelve hundred tanks and three hundred MiG-21 aircraft.[201] The airlift prevented the collapse of their armed forces and probably underlay, at least in part, Assad's resolve, up to October 23 and despite a continuous trouncing, to stay in the fight.

The American airlift to Israel, which began on the night of October 13, was even larger. It was in response both to the Soviet effort and to Israel's increasingly shrill requests (which may have included an at least implicit threat to use nuclear weapons if the supply of conventional arms ran out—Secretary of State Kissinger used the phrase "hysteria or blackmail" in his memoirs[202]). The delay between President Nixon's initial order on October 9 to rush supplies to Israel and the actual start of the airlift was, according to Kissinger, the fault principally of the Pentagon;[203] but some Israelis suspected that he had been playing a double game, reassuring them of imminent resupply while delaying it in order to gain leverage.[204]

American planes flew 22,400 tons of supplies to Israel between October 14 and November 15. El Al brought in another 11,000 tons from the United States and from American bases in Europe. During the war Israel also received about forty Phantom F4 fighter-bombers and thirty-six Skyhawks as well as twelve C-130 Hercules transports. By October 30, the United States had also sent 33,000 tons of equipment—mostly tanks—by sea, in ships which started to arrive on November 15. But the Israeli generals were far from satisfied. After a week of battle the hunger for weapons and ammunition was acute, and the initial delays were seen as political manipulations. The equipment that eventually reached Israel fell short of the needs and requests.[205]

At crucial junctures such as the offensive against Syria on October 11 and the Canal crossing of October 15–16, knowledge of the delivery or impending arrival of fresh American supplies—especially aircraft—contributed to the IDF's decisions to go ahead. And Washington was aware of the effect of the airlift. On October 10, for example, Kissinger told Israeli ambassador Simcha Dinitz: "The IDF must attack [Syria] with all its strength, as if it had another 40 aircraft in hand, and not stint on ammunition or aircraft, because the United States will supply everything."[206] On October 13 he advised the Israelis "to continue the offensive" against Syria in the knowledge that the airlift was about to begin.[207]

Superpower influence was wielded in an even more telling way by changing policies toward a cease-fire. During the first days, when Arab fortunes seemed to soar, the Soviets made no effort to promote one. Only on the night of October 12 did they propose a halt to the hostilities, driven by the apparent collapse of the Syrian army. But the frustration of the IDF drive toward Damascus, plus Egypt's demands for more time, persuaded Moscow to think again.

And only on October 18, as the IDF offensive unfolded on the west bank of the Canal, did Moscow's call for a cease-fire turn into an unequivocal demand. On October 19, hours after Premier Kosygin's return from Cairo, Kissinger was "urgently" summoned to Russia.[208] A note of desperation crept into Soviet utterances as the defeat of Egypt (and perhaps of Syria) drew closer. By October 23, the demand had become an ultimatum, backed by the threat of the dispatch of Soviet troops to the battle zone.

Initially the United States, buoyed by Israeli assurances that all was well and that the IDF was about to get the upper hand, made no effort to arrange a cease-fire. On the contrary, Kissinger virtually egged the Israelis on; on October 12 he approved their intention to shell the outskirts of Damascus.[209] But that night Washington persuaded Israel—whose forces were by then inside the Bashan in the north and whose leaders were suspicious about the delays in the start of the American airlift and somewhat pessimistic about the ultimate outcome in the south—not to oppose a cease-fire "in place."[210] Kissinger, apparently, had concluded that the fact that both sides by then could claim military gains had created a type of equilibrium. He may also have begun to fear a violent Soviet reaction to Israel's advance on Damascus.[211]

But Egypt rejected the cease-fire proposal. Then Israel's military successes (and Soviet inaction) persuaded Washington to give Israel time to turn the war around.[212] But Soviet pressure, triggered by Egyptian cries for help, persuaded Washington to join Moscow's demand, as did the threat to the Western economies posed by the Arab states' October 19 declaration of a general oil embargo against the "pro-Israel" United States and Holland.

According to Gamasy the unleashing of the oil weapon against the West was Egypt's doing. On October 10 Sadat sent a deputy to Saudi Arabia and the Gulf States to solicit help for the war effort.[213] On October 16 these states announced a blanket 70 percent increase in oil prices and a progressive, monthly 5 percent reduction in output until Israel withdrew completely from the occupied territories and restored the "legal rights" of the Palestinians. The screws were tightened with the announcement of the embargo against Israel's "friends" and, a few months later, on December 23, with OPEC's decision to double oil prices.[214]

The superpowers hammered out the cease-fire terms in Moscow on October 21.[215] The following afternoon Kissinger arrived in Israel and persuaded the reluctant ministers to comply. But he also told the Israelis "that he would not complain if Israeli forces continued their advance that night. After all, it was customary that after a cease-fire comes into effect, units continue to attack."[216] Kissinger had apparently spoken of "a few hours' slippage."[217] But as described, Israel exploited the ongoing fighting along the Canal (as well as

Syria's continued rejection of a cease-fire) to fight on until the morning of October 25, by then completing the encirclement of the Third Army.

The Syrians, with Damascus under threat, had been keen on a cease-fire from October 9 to 14. But thereafter, seeing the IDF offensive grinding to a halt, they sought to keep the war alive until they could drive the Israelis out of the Bashan. Their resolve was reinforced by the arrival, beginning on October 12, of the contingents from Iraq and Jordan. On October 22, they still opposed a cease-fire, but Egypt's acceptance, coupled with Soviet pressure, eventually turned them around, and on the evening of October 23 Assad too at last agreed.

The Egyptians refused to agree to a cease-fire until October 19, when they at last realized that the IDF Canal-crossing offensive could result in a catastrophe. From then on their enthusiasm to end the war increased daily. So long as Egyptian troops held fast to the east bank of the Canal, and so long as the Third Army remained more or less intact, Arab honor remained satisfied. This—as Kissinger realized—enabled Sadat to agree to a cease-fire. But, if the Israeli offensive in the South was allowed to continue and the Third Army demolished, the Arab accomplishments of October 6–7 would be erased.

With both Israel and Egypt violating the October 22 resolution, and with Syria still rejecting it, the Security Council reconvened on October 23 and passed Resolution 339, reiterating the call for an immediate cease-fire, and "urging" that both sides draw back to the positions they had occupied at 6:52 P.M. on October 22. The resolution also empowered the secretary general to send a United Nations Emergency Force to supervise the cease-fire between Israel and Egypt.

The USSR blamed Israel for the breakdown of the initial cease-fire, and, to be sure, it was Israel that had strategically exploited that breakdown, whereas Egypt, perhaps for lack of means, had not. After October 22 Egypt had called for the dispatch of a joint Soviet-American force to assure the cease-fire, and had demanded Israel's return to that day's lines.[218] But Israel refused.

The United States was in the difficult position of battling both its client, Israel, and its global rival, the Soviet Union. The Americans pressed Israel to withdraw to the October 22 lines and, at the same time, rejected the Egyptian demand for American-Soviet military involvement, viewing this as a barely veiled ploy to inject Soviet troops into the area in order to intimidate Israel and to force open a passage between Cairo and the Third Army.

Late on October 23, with Magen's tanks racing to the Gulf of Suez, the Soviets placed their seven airborne divisions in Eastern Europe on standby and threatened to send them in unilaterally. Washington countered early on October 25 by putting its nuclear forces on alert,[219] simultaneously demanding that Israel cease all fire and movement and withdraw to the October 22 positions. Israel ceased fire but refused to withdraw—but in a conciliatory gesture agreed to allow a "onetime" shipment of one hundred trucks with "humanitarian" supplies to pass through its lines to the Third Army, after the United States threatened to supply it unilaterally with Sixth Fleet aircraft; a breach with Washington was the last thing Jerusalem needed. The Soviets were deterred from unilateral intervention and at last agreed to the positioning of a UN force, without Soviet or American troops, in the area.

The cease-fire that finally went into effect left a complex political and military situation. On the wide political front, the Security Council resolutions pointed the way to an accommodation based on 1967 Resolution 242—the trading of land for peace, and direct negotiations between Israel and each of its Arab enemies. The war—as intended by Sadat—had loosened the political logjam that had existed since 1967. For the Arabs it had paved the road to a settlement. Their honor had been restored, enabling their leaders at last to contemplate direct dialogue and peace with Israel, but not from a position of humiliating inferiority. However, Israel's military prowess had once again been demonstrated and had perhaps definitively persuaded the Arab leaders that their foe could not be defeated, let alone destroyed, in battle: The return of their territories could be achieved only through negotiation.

On the other hand, the war had given Israel a stinging slap in the face. The 1948, 1956, and 1967 wars had conditioned them to stunning victories over the Arabs and to Arab military (and political) incompetence; 1973 proved to be something else altogether. Many Israelis were now persuaded that the territories could not be held indefinitely by force and that continued occupation would necessarily lead to further bouts of painful warfare. At last, and for the first time since June 1967, most people were willing to contemplate giving up large chunks of land for peace.

On the narrower, military front, both sides, severely bled and wearied, felt that there was a pressing need to disengage their armies, especially in the south, where the Egyptians were hard-pressed to negotiate the relief of the Third Army which, in the absence of supplies, would swiftly expire. Moreover, Israel's occupation of sixteen hundred square kilometers of territory on the west bank of the Canal, within sixty miles of Cairo, severely irked the Egyptian leadership—as Israel's presence in the Bashan, only twenty-five miles from Damascus, clearly rankled Assad. At the same time, Israel's strategic situation, with its army split on the two banks of the Canal and with a narrow, linking passage, and with the Egyptians, now resupplied, in the rear of the IDF forces on the west bank, was highly uncomfortable. The leadership was also under pressure at home, both to demobilize the two hundred thousand combat reservists, who were much needed in the economy and by their families, and to bring home some three hundred soldiers being held prisoner by Egypt and Syria.

Kissinger understood that these two levels of dilemma and opportunity—political and military—could be combined to produce a "peace process." Both sides had in past years been reluctant to move—Israel to concede territory and the Arabs to talk peace. But the direct talks necessary to achieve a military separation of forces could be expanded into something more, perhaps fulfledged peace negotiations.

On November 11, 1973, at "Kilometer 101" on the Cairo–Suez road, Egypt and Israel signed a formal cease-fire agreement, stipulating the need for a "disengagement of forces" agreement, and setting in motion an exchange of POWs and the provision of nonmilitary supplies to Suez City and the Third Army. The first exchange took place on November 15; within a week 241 Israelis and 8,300 Egyptians had been repatriated.

But negotiations for disengagement bogged down over Israel's demand for "reciprocity"—that its withdrawal from the west bank of the Canal be matched by Egyptian withdrawal from the east bank. Egypt insisted on retaining its hard-won gains in Sinai. Kissinger stepped into the breach and, in an intensive shuttle between Cairo and Jerusalem, persuaded the two sides to sign what became known as the first Egyptian-Israeli Disengagement of Forces Agreement (or "Sinai I"), on January 18, 1974. The agreement, underpinned by secret Israeli-American and Egyptian-American understandings, provided for complete IDF withdrawal from the west bank and redeployment along a line some ten to fifteen miles from the Canal. A strip of land six miles deep along the east bank was left in Egypt's hands, though its military presence there was severely curtailed.[220] (When informed of the troop-limitation provisions, Gamasy, by now chief of staff of the Egyptian army, "left the meeting room [with Kissinger and Sadat] angry, with tears in my eyes, and I went to the bathroom." Kissinger couldn't understand Gamasy's emotional reaction: "[Kissinger's] face grew pale and he kept muttering '[W]as there anything wrong in what I said?'"[221])

The agreement thus reflected the Egyptian military accomplishment of October 6 rather than Israel's subsequent victories. But there were elements in the accord that conformed with Israel's desire to reach peace or at least some sort of normalization of relations with its Arab neighbors. A two-to-four-mile buffer zone was established between the Egyptian and Israeli lines, to be manned and patrolled by the UNEF, in effect ruling out any possibility of further Egyptian attacks on the IDF, which retained the vast bulk of Sinai. And the agreement defined itself as "a first step toward a final, just, and durable peace" based on Resolution 338.

Egyptian forces on the east bank and Israeli forces in the strip west of the UNEF zone were limited to seven thousand troops each. Egypt agreed to clear and open the Suez Canal and to rebuild and repopulate the abandoned Canalside cities, Suez and Ismailia—measures that would greatly curtail its freedom to renew warfare. Israeli goods, though not vessels, were to be allowed through the Canal. The IDF completed its withdrawal from the west bank to Sinai on March 3, 1974.

An Israeli-Syrian agreement proved trickier. No cease-fire agreement was signed between the two countries, and Syria for months refused to give Israel even a list of POWs, stalling the negotiations and causing a great deal of anger in Israel. And, unlike the Egyptians, the Syrians refused to meet and negotiate directly with the Israelis. Israel was willing to withdraw to the pre-October 1973 "Purple Line" but was averse to ceding part of the Golan, which Syria insisted on. The Syrians proceeded to unleash a miniwar of attrition against the Israeli forces occupying the Bashan enclave, using incessant artillery bombardments and sniping. The two sides also fought a small infantry engagement over control of the Syrian Hermon peaks in mid-April 1974. Assad, always the tough negotiator, correctly calculated that the continuous drip of Israeli casualties would undermine Jerusalem's staying power but that Israel would not respond with full-scale hostilities. The Israeli public was in no mood for renewed war and, besides, the United States would veto such a denouement.

Kissinger repeatedly traveled to Damascus and Jerusalem, with an intense period of nonstop shuttling and negotiations in May. The "Agreement on Disengagement between Israeli and Syrian Forces" was finally signed by the sides in Geneva on May 31, 1974. Israel withdrew from the Bashan, the Syrian Hermon, and a thin strip of territory to the west of the old "Purple Line." This area, with a little no-man's-land and some Syrian territory to the east, was turned into a separation-of-forces zone—one to five miles wide—to be held and patrolled by a new, 1,250-man United Nations Disengagement Observer Force (UNDOF). The strip included the derelict town of Quneitra. Israeli and Syrian forces were barred from the zone, though it was placed under Syrian civilian administration. The establishment of the buffer zone, mirroring the arrangement in Sinai, reflected both sides' successes—Syria's, in getting Israel to withdraw from all of the Bashan and from a thin, token strip of the Golan; Israel's, in forcing on Syria a UN-guarded zone that would effectively prevent it from repeating its recent surprise attack. The agreement also provided for limited forces zones on both sides of the buffer, and the two sides agreed to an exchange of POWs. The agreement was implemented by the end of June.[222]

The disengagement agreements did not solve the major underlying causes of tension. Most Arabs continued to regard Israel as an alien, unwelcome presence in the region; and Israel still occupied the West Bank of the Jordan and the Gaza Strip and lorded it over their Palestinian inhabitants, and continued to occupy the bulk of the Sinai Peninsula and the Golan Heights. Clearly Egypt and Syria could not rest. But the second half of 1974 witnessed no further political movement. Syria periodically hinted that a resumption of hostilities was imminent. The biannual renewal of the mandates of UNDOF and UNEF served as occasions for subversion of the status quo, with both Syria and Egypt threatening nonrenewal. It was clear—as it had been before the October war—that the status quo was untenable and, in the absence of peace or at least progress toward peace, hostilities would eventually erupt. Massive rearmament by both Syria and Israel underlined the threat.

Secretary of State Kissinger had decided that the only way forward was by gradual, staggered, partial, bilateral agreements. Multilateral peace conferences would gain nothing. The separation-of-forces agreements seemed to point the way, as long as the road to a comprehensive settlement was blocked by the thorny Palestinian/PLO issue. It was best to advance by way of successive, separate agreements between Israel and the main confrontation states, Egypt and Syria.

At the end of 1974 and the beginning of 1975, with Kissinger as intermediary, Israeli and Egyptian leaders began to discuss a new, "interim" agreement. Israel sought a firm commitment to "nonbelligerency" and elements of normalization of relations; Egypt sought the return of Sinai, or at least further chunks of the peninsula. Here, clearly, were the makings of a partial "land-for-peace" deal. What remained was to sort out how much land for how much peace.

February–September 1975 saw increasingly intensive three-way negotiations. The talks advanced by fits and starts. Kissinger's good offices, as he shuttled between Cairo and Jerusalem, were crucial; so was American pressure on Israel. In March, after Israel displayed what Washington considered inflexibility, the United States announced suspension of the talks and a "reassessment" of its relations with Israel, during which time negotiations on new arms agreements (and perhaps some deliveries) were suspended. Kissinger, after visiting Masada, where two thousand years earlier hundreds of Jews had committed suicide rather than surrender to Rome, told the new prime minister, Rabin (he replaced Meir in spring 1974): "This is a real tragedy. . . . It's tragic to see people dooming themselves to a course of unbelievable peril."[223]

By the end of August the two sides were on the brink of agreement; on September 1, the pact—sometimes called "Sinai II"—was initialed, and on September 4 it was signed in Geneva.[224]

Israel obtained something less than an explicit declaration of nonbelligerency. The two sides undertook "not to resort to the threat or use of force or military blockade against each other" and agreed that the conflict "shall not be resolved by military force but by peaceful means." They agreed to reach a "final and just peace settlement" on the basis of Resolution 338. While the actual sovereign Egyptian holding in Sinai was not extended, the "separation of forces" (UNEF) buffer zone was expanded eastward, making it ten to twenty-five miles wide, and Israeli forces were to withdraw to the zone's eastern edge, which now ran through the eastern side of the Gidi and Mitla Passes. A new Israeli limited-forces zone was established east of the buffer zone, and both sides were allowed to maintain or establish early warning stations (in the buffer zone) near the Gidi Pass. These were to be reinforced by a number of American-manned early warning stations. Egypt was given control of the Abu Rodeis oilfields, now part of the UN buffer zone. The agreement was to be in force until superseded by a further one.

The pact was supported by a number of separate Israeli-American and Egyptian-American agreements and understandings. Egypt agreed to renew UNEF's mandate annually for at least three years, and reiterated its permission for the passage of Israeli cargoes through the Suez Canal. The United States undertook to meet Israel's defense, energy, and economic needs, including an assurance of "essential" oil supplies, and agreed to supply it with advanced F-16 aircraft. The United States also agreed in principle to mount another military resupply operation if a new "emergency situation" arose, and recognized Israel's right of free passage through international waterways and straits, including, specifically, Bab al-Mandeb and the Straits of Gibraltar, and Israel's right to fly over the Red Sea. The United States also committed itself not to recognize or negotiate with the PLO "as long as the PLO does not recognize Israel's right to exist and does not accept" Resolutions 242 and 338.[225] By November 30 the IDF was redeployed eastward, Israeli goods were passing through the Canal, and Egypt was given the Ras Sudar and Abu Rodeis oilfields.

Sadat's gamble, to achieve a breakthrough in Arab-Israeli relations through the application of shock treatment, had paid off. What Israel had been unwilling to contemplate in 1971—a partial withdrawal from the Canal in exchange for partial nonbelligerency with Egypt—it acceded to after the Yom Kippur war. And the interim accords of 1974–75, in turn, set the two states firmly on the path toward one further and final deal—full peace in exchange for the whole of Sinai. That, too, had apparently been offered, or at least more than intimated, by Sadat back in 1971; that, too, had been rejected by Jerusalem. But the shock of the war, followed by the interim accords and Egypt's palpable, convincing readiness to parley, at last persuaded Israel to move toward the next stage—the peace agreements of 1977–79.

On the other hand, the more limited 1974 Israeli-Syrian disengagement-of-forces agreement—which the Syrians had throughout insisted should have no civilian or normalization-of-relations components—lacked any intimation of anything more comprehensive or dramatic. As Assad had eschewed any desire for peace with Israel before 1973, so he shunned all hints of it or normalized relations afterward.

THE AGRANAT COMMISSION, 1973–75

The Yom Kippur war proved to be not only a catalyst to peacemaking; it also thoroughly shook Israeli society. Its major aftereffect proved to be political, when, four years later, Menachem Begin's right-wing alliance, the Likud, took power in the wake of the 1977 general elections, bringing to an end Labor's three-decade-long dominance of the polity.

But the war had important, immediate internal effects. In the December 1973 Knesset elections, while many of the troops were still doing reserve duty along the front lines, the Labor Alignment lost five of its fifty-six seats. And it was the first war to set off mass public protest. Neither the IDF's occasional incompetence in 1948 nor the unforced, indeed enthusiastic, march to war in 1956 had elicited more than low background rumblings; 1967, for obvious reasons, set off only a few voices in the wilderness, protesting against expansionism and the ugly prospect of Israeli rule over a million hostile Palestinians. But 1973, with its myriad examples of unfounded overconfidence by the government, of intelligence failures, and, in the first days, of military unreadiness and incompetence, was something else.

Trickling back from the fronts, some soldiers and officers raised the banner of protest. Who was responsible for the army's unpreparedness (tanks going to war on the Golan without night sights and sufficient ammunition, troops rushing to the Canal unaware of the quantity and lethality of the Saggers)? Who was to blame for the failure of the initial counteroffensives? Who had mistakenly assured the nation that it faced unprecedented years of security and prosperity, but now was accountable for more than two thousand dead and an unclear military victory followed by what amounted, for many, to political defeat?

The protests were kicked off by Capt. Motti Ashkenazi, the commander of "Budapest," the only Bar-Lev Line fort that had held out. At first alone, Ashkenazi stood in silence, day after day, opposite the Defense Ministry in Tel Aviv. He was soon joined by others, demanding the resignation of the minister, Moshe Dayan. These protests occurred against a background of acrimonious public controversy, in which Ariel Sharon—by now a Likud Knesset member—took the lead. Sharon demanded General Elazar's resignation; Gonnen, for his part, charged Sharon with disobeying his orders during the war. The released reservists only embodied, if somewhat more vociferously, a general public disquiet with what had happened.

The demand for a top-level investigation into the events leading up to the war and its conduct was almost immediate. On November 8, the senior cabinet ministers debated the form and timing of such an inquiry. Golda Meir and Dayan both acknowledged the need, and on November 18 the full cabinet empowered the president of the Supreme Court, Justice Shimon Agranat, to appoint a judicial commission of inquiry. Agranat assembled a formidable panel, with himself as chairman. The other members were former IDF chiefs of general staff Yigael Yadin and Haim Laskov, Supreme Court Justice Moshe Landau, and State Comptroller Itzhak Nebenzahl. The commission's terms of reference, as set out by the cabinet, were to probe the functioning of the intelligence services before the war; the army's preparations; and its performance during the first, "containment" phase of the war.[226]

On April 2, 1974, the commission issued an interim report that contained major operative conclusions; the final report came on January 30, 1975. The interim report rebuked the IDF Intelligence Branch for its "overconfidence" and for its subscription to the incorrect *konseptziya* of Arab unreadiness and unwillingness to go to war. The commission found that the agency had failed to distinguish between the hundreds of "signals" it had picked up indicating imminent war and the background "noises" in which these signals had been incidentally enmeshed or deliberately camouflaged by Egypt and Syria.

The commission recommended a substantial reorganization of the intelligence services and the dismissal not only of Ze'ira and several other senior intelligence officers, but of Chief of General Staff Elazar, who was blamed both for incorrectly assessing the intelligence that had reached him and for failing to prepare the army adequately for war. A further recommendation was that CO Southern Command Gonnen be "suspended" and barred from filling any senior command. In the final report both were also severely faulted for the mismanagement of the IDF's counterattacks along the Canal on October 6–8.

In a surprise decision, the commission declined to go into the issue of "ministerial responsibility." It effectively exonerated Meir and Dayan from blame, though it noted the latter's refusal on the morning of October 6 to agree to a full mobilization of reserves, which cost several hours. But this failed to stem the tide of public pressure, which included major rumblings also from within the Labor Alignment. On April 11, 1974, Meir announced her resignation, which meant the resignation of the whole cabinet. The successor government, which took office in June, was led by Yitzhak Rabin, the former IDF Chief of Staff who was untainted by the failures of the war. Neither Meir nor Dayan was in the new cabinet. The war had thus led, within months, to the ouster from public office of Israel's two preeminent political leaders, of the IDF's commander, and of its senior intelligence officer.

Che Israeli-Egyptian Peace, 1977–79

Launching Peace

The two Israel-Egypt disengagement agreements paved the way, again with the help of American mediation, for the process that culminated in the signing of the peace treaty in 1979.

From the perspective of its chief architect, Anwar Sadat, the October war had broken the political-diplomatic logjam and had regained for Egypt a slice of Sinai. But it had failed to recover the bulk of the peninsula or to shake Israel's hold on the Palestinian-populated territories; nor had the Golan been restored to its Syrian owners.

The peacemaking momentum was halted after Sinai II by the collapse of the Nixon administration as a result of the Watergate affair, and the prospect of elections in both the United States and Israel. The election of Jimmy Carter as president in November 1976 set in train the renewal of the peace process. Carter, innocent of foreign policy experience, set his sights on a comprehensive Middle East settlement based on Security Council Resolution 242. He believed that Israel must withdraw from the territories occupied in 1967, with only minor border changes; and the Palestinians must get "self-determination" and a "homeland." He regarded Israeli military rule over the Palestinians as a gross violation of human rights.

Carter's attitude towards Israel was "ambivalent," observed Zbigniew Brzezinski, his national security adviser: "On the one hand, he felt that Israel was being intransigent; on the other, he had a genuine attachment to the country as 'the Land of the Bible' [and] he explicitly disassociated himself from the more critical anti-Israeli view."[1] As a devout Christian, Carter was emotionally involved with the fate of the Jews.[2] He believed that a major foreign policy success was possible, and he understood that lack of movement could result in renewed hostilities, possible West–East confrontation, and an oil cut-off severely damaging to Western economies. But when he assumed office, he apparently had no idea just how difficult the road ahead was to be.

Among American officials a consensus formed around the idea of a large, multilateral negotiation. A framework, with the superpowers in a brokering role, already existed in the form of the Geneva Conference, which had convened once in December 1973. The front-line Arab states all rejected one-on-one, separate negotiations, each fearing that its neighbor would strike a separate deal with Israel, weakening its own bargaining position. Israel argued that multilateral talks were a recipe for disaster, as the Arab states would push each other into extreme positions.

But Washington believed that separate, bilateral Israeli-Egyptian or Israeli-Jordanian negotiations would get nowhere, because of outside Arab pressures or threats; and that even if a bilateral treaty was signed, it would in short order be undermined by the other Arab states, perhaps encouraged by the Soviet Union. Multilateral talks in Geneva seemed the best option, though the State Department was not keen on giving the Soviets an equal role. But only with all parties present could a comprehensive settlement be hammered out, with the two superpowers acting as mediators and, eventually, guarantors.[3] In the spring of 1977, Carter and Secretary of State Cyrus Vance held a series of meetings in Washington and the Middle East to promote the reconvening of Geneva. From Jerusalem, Geneva was seen as a giant trap to be avoided. The Israelis feared that the Americans and Soviets would gang up on them and try to impose a pro-Arab compromise. But subtlety was required; Israel could not afford bluntly to refuse to attend.

Henry Kissinger, and then Carter in his first months in office, had been dealing with Labor-led Israeli governments under Golda Meir and Yitzhak Rabin. Labor, at least in theory, accepted the notion of territorial compromise and the "land-for-peace" formula. But on May 17, 1977, in an unexpected turnaround, the majority of the Israeli electorate voted the right-wing Likud, led by Menachem Begin, into power.

Until that very sweet moment Begin had lived his life in the political wilderness, an unusual cross between pariah and jester. During the 1940s he had led the Revisionist Movement, which claimed all of Palestine and the East Bank of the Jordan for Jewish sovereignty, and its terrorist-military wing, the IZL. He had been hunted by the British and renounced and denounced by most of the Yishuv. With statehood the Revisionist Movement became the Herut Party, which won 14 of the 120 seats in the first Knesset. Ben-Gurion rarely acknowledged Begin's existence, let alone his words (despite, or perhaps because of, the high level of his oratory); when he did it was usually with contempt. Between 1949 and 1977—except for the interlude in which Begin served in Eshkol's 1967–70 National Emergency Government—Begin and Herut were continuously in opposition, impotent and often risible.

Now Begin was to govern Israel with great authority for six years. Vance saw him as "a combination of Old Testament prophet and courtly European. He can be harsh and acerbic at one moment and warm and gracious the next." Others had less charitable descriptions. But all agreed that he had "a powerful sense of history" and that his outlook had been "deeply influenced by his exposure to anti-Semitism as a youth in Poland . . . and, above all, by the Holocaust."[4]

Begin's coalition government, composed of a bevy of small right-wing, centrist, and religious parties clustered around Herut and its Liberal Party affiliate in the Likud, assumed office on June 21, 1977. Seven years before, Begin had resigned from the Emergency Government precisely because of its acceptance of Resolution 242 and the "land-for-peace" formula. Herut viewed the West Bank and Gaza Strip as inalienable parts of the Jewish patrimony. To Begin these territories were "as Jewish as Tel Aviv," and were never to be given over to Arab rule.

Carter's first meeting with Begin, in Washington on July 19, probably went better than expected by both sides. Begin agreed to Resolution 242 as the basis for the prospective peace talks. He opposed Palestinian self-determination and was dubious about an international or American guarantee of whatever settlement was reached: "In the whole world, there is no guarantee that can guarantee a guarantee," he told Vance.[5] However, he told Carter, who failed to appreciate the full significance of the statement, that he planned to meet with Sadat.[6] Carter demanded a freeze on new settlements in the territories, and Begin made a vague promise to "try to accommodate" the United States on the issue. Bad blood arose when Begin, back in Israel, announced "legalization" of three settlements set up under the previous government. Carter felt that Begin had breached the spirit, though not the letter, of his promise.[7]

Relations between Washington and Jerusalem soured further during Vance's trip to the Middle East in August. Sadat presented him with a draft peace plan and asked him to elicit similar drafts from Israel, Syria, and Jordan, and then to begin bridging between the different positions. Sadat also asked Vance to tell Begin that he was interested in a meeting.[8] In Jerusalem, Vance encountered a truculent Begin, who compared American willingness to deal with the PLO to Chamberlain's readiness to appease Hitler. He made it clear that he had no intention of withdrawing from the West Bank and Gaza, though the Arabs in these territories could be granted "cultural autonomy." The draft peace treaty he eventually presented to the Americans[9] made no mention of territorial concessions. And a September 2 letter to Vance from Begin's foreign minister, Moshe Dayan—he had bolted Labor and joined the new government as a nonparty expert—spoke of Israel's intention to retain the Gaza Strip, Sharm ash-Sheikh, and a strip of eastern Sinai linking the two. Dayan also implied that Israel would retain control of the West Bank, but that part of the Golan Heights was negotiable.[10]

Simultaneously with the American initiative, a separate, secret Israeli-Egyptian dialogue began to unfold. In August, Begin flew to Bucharest and asked Romanian president Nicolae Ceauşescu to inform Sadat he was interested in a meeting. On September 4 Dayan—"transformed beyond all recognition" by makeup artists, with the "mane of a beatnik . . . the moustache of a dandy; and . . . large dark sun-glasses"[11]—secretly flew to Morocco to ask King Hassan to arrange a meeting with the Egyptians. Hassan moved quickly, and on September 16 Dayan returned to Morocco and there secretly met Hassan Tuhami, the Egyptian deputy prime minister.

Tuhami's message was simple: Sadat was "deadly serious in his quest for peace," but peace was only possible in exchange for complete withdrawal from the occupied territories, including East Jerusalem. Sadat believed that successful Israeli-Egyptian negotiations would result in Syria and Jordan joining the peace process. He would not sign a separate peace, and would meet with Begin only if Israel committed itself in advance to withdraw from all occupied Arab land. Dayan countered that the two leaders should meet to discuss the basic issues, and Israel and Egypt could sort out their differences. Begin subsequently informed Cairo that Israel would not undertake to withdraw from all the territories in exchange for a meeting with Sadat.

Subsequently Tuhami claimed that Dayan had undertaken that Israel would withdraw from all of Sinai in exchange for peace with Egypt. Dayan always denied this, arguing that he had only spoken of the need for demilitarization of Sinai in any peace settlement.[12] David Kimche, the ex-Mossad executive who during the 1980s was director general of the Israel Foreign Ministry, subsequently wrote that Dayan had handed Tuhami "a three-line, hand-written message . . . for Sadat's eyes only," declaring Israel's willingness to hand over the whole of Sinai in exchange for peace.[13]

Available evidence indicates that Dayan avoided making a clear commitment, but gave Tuhami good cause to believe that Israel would agree to full withdrawal from Sinai in exchange for peace.[14] Dayan emerged from the talks "reasonably sure" that Egypt would sign a separate peace if it got back the peninsula.[15]

On September 19 Dayan flew to Washington and, contrary to his promise of secrecy to Tuhami, informed his American hosts of the Rabat meeting.[16] Egypt's foreign minister, Ismail Fahmy, followed him to Washington two days later. Carter apparently told him that he could not put effective pressure on Israel because of internal political considerations; this may have contributed to Sadat's decision a few weeks later to bypass the Americans and deal directly with Israel.[17]

Sadat was strongly influenced by the joint U.S.–Soviet communiqué of October 1, 1977, which spoke of the need for "withdrawal of Israeli armed forces from territories occupied in the 1967 conflict; [and] the resolution of the Palestinian question, including insuring the legitimate rights of the Palestinian people."[18] The statement fell short of basic Arab demands. It implicitly accepted the Israeli reading of Resolution 242—withdrawal from "territories" rather than from "the territories." And it made no mention of the PLO or Palestinian statehood. But far worse, from Sadat's perspective, was Carter's retreat[19] from the spirit of the communiqué. Roundly attacked by American Jewish spokesmen and Israeli politicians for caving in to Arab and Soviet pressures, Carter told the UN General Assembly on October 4 that the United States would not try to impose a Middle East peace settlement. And, following meetings later that day between American leaders and Dayan, the United States and Israel issued a joint communiqué of their own, declaring: "Acceptance of the Joint U.S.–U.S.S.R. Statement of October 1, 1977, by the parties is not a prerequisite for the reconvening and conduct of the Geneva Conference."

In the Arab view, Carter had attempted to edge slightly toward the Arab position ("legitimate rights" of the "Palestinian people")—and had been swiftly reined in by Israeli and American Jewish pressure. The United States, it appeared, could not "deliver" Israeli flexibility or concessions.[20] Sadat would have to look not to Washington, not to Geneva, but to Jerusalem to obtain the concessions he sought. Always prone to the theatrical gesture, Sadat was no man for the nit-picking and hairsplitting of international diplomacy. He believed that what stood in the way of Arab-Israeli understanding was a "psychological barrier," a basic mutual distrust that translated into an inability to move forward. A dramatic act was needed to shatter the barrier.[21]

Such, at least, was Sadat's own postfactum explanation of his decision to fly to Jerusalem. Underlying it, without doubt, was a deep and genuine desire for peace, fueled by the succession of wars and the suffering they had caused, and by the belief that Israel's powerful army and its nonconventional weapons precluded a military solution favorable to the Arabs. Israel could not be beaten and destroyed, certainly not without bringing down upon the Arab world— and particularly the Nile Valley, the vulnerable core of the Egyptian state— catastrophic, permanent ruin.

There were also economic reasons for Sadat's decision. Despite substantial Saudi Arabian subsidies, the October war had severely depleted Egypt's coffers, as had postwar rearmament. His country, Sadat felt, was simply too poor to carry the burden of the endless fight against Israel. This message was underlined in January 1977, when thousands of Egyptians rioted in the streets of Cairo and Alexandria to protest an announced cut in food subsidies; clashes with the security forces left scores of people dead (seventy-seven in Cairo alone, according to the official count).[22] Peace with Israel could well result in American aid, something that the state of war had perennially stymied. Gen. Kamal Hassan 'Ali, Egypt's war minister in 1978, later calculated that the United States had provided Egypt with $6.6 billion in aid in the years 1978–82 (and was to continue to grant it $1.5 to $2 billion annually thereafter). By contrast, the oil-rich Arab states had granted their Egyptian "brothers" only $5 billion during the period October 1973–November 1977. To highlight how little this really was, 'Ali pointed out that Egypt's initial artillery and air strikes on October 6, 1973, alone had cost £400 million.[23]

Sadat may also have been motivated by a sense that time was running out. If peace was not achieved soon, a new war would erupt. And for him—aged fifty-seven—personally, it was now or never. He had suffered two heart attacks; how long did he have left to fulfill his historic mission?[24]

The immediate chain of events that led to Sadat's journey to Jerusalem can be said to have begun with Carter's personal, handwritten, hand-delivered appeal of October 21. "I need your help," he wrote, to remove the obstacles barring the road to Geneva.[25] Sadat's response, also handwritten, of October 31, promised Carter a "bold step." He had apparently started toying with the idea of traveling to Jerusalem. He first broached the idea to Foreign Minister Fahmy on October 28 while on a visit to Rumania (after President Ceauşescu told him that Begin was interested in a face-to-face meeting). Fahmy was appalled, viewing such a trip as an admission of defeat and potentially disastrous for Egypt's position in the Arab world. It would mean automatic recognition of Israel and the termination of the state of belligerency, two of the main negotiating cards held by Egypt. Sadat appeared bent on giving these up without obtaining an Israeli quid pro quo.[26] Fahmy tried to dissuade him and proposed, instead, either meeting Begin on neutral territory or calling a giant summit conference in East Jerusalem, to be attended by the UN secretary-general and the leaders of the Arab confrontation states (including PLO chairman Arafat) and of the permanent member states of the Security Council.[27] Sadat agreed and on November 3 wrote to Carter proposing the idea. Brzezinski thought it "rather droll" and "nothing if not imaginative," and was to record in his diary that "Sadat does not seem to differentiate clearly between fact and fiction." American foreign policy executives "worried about Sadat and wondered whether he was not losing his sense of reality."[28] Washington gently advised him to keep his eyes focused on Geneva.[29]

But he had already given up on Geneva. On November 5 he told the Egyptian National Security Council: "I am ready to go to Jerusalem and to give a speech in the Israeli Knesset if this will save the blood of my sons."[30] And four days later, on November 9, he delivered his bombshell in public. Addressing the Egyptian National Assembly, with Arafat specially invited and present in the audience, Sadat departed from his text and declared: "I am prepared to go to the end of the earth, and Israel will be surprised to hear me say to you: I am ready to go to their home, to the Knesset itself and to argue with them there. We have no time to waste." A hush fell upon the hall, broken long seconds later by loud clapping. Even Arafat joined in; like others, he appears to have believed that Sadat had merely used a figure of speech.[31]

But Foreign Minister Fahmy, Defense Minister Gamasy, and others were horrified. Having heard Sadat in the National Security Council only days before, they knew that he was in dead earnest, and that he was proposing a course that flew in the face of accepted Arab wisdom and of their better judgment.

Though the sentence about Jerusalem was deleted the next day—according to Fahmy, on Sadat's instructions—from reports of the speech in Egypt's official newspapers, the foreign press gave it due prominence.[32] Initially neither the Americans nor the Israelis believed that Sadat actually intended to travel to Jerusalem (even though Sadat had informed Carter the day before that he was indeed considering such a step.[33]) The Americans thought they were on the verge of success in reconvening Geneva. They could not fathom Sadat's impetuosity, which, they felt, would leave him "isolated and exposed" in the Arab world—and deprive themselves of the diplomatic initiative.[34]

In Jerusalem, despite the Tuhami-Dayan meeting in September, the disbelief was, if anything, even more extreme. Begin was wont privately to call Sadat "the *Chudak*," Russian for "the flaky one"; the Egyptian's frequent brainstorms should not be given undue credence, it was felt.[35] This view was reinforced by the IDF intelligence assessment, submitted to Defense Minister Ezer Weizman in September, that Egypt, having lost faith in the diplomatic process, had decided on a further round of warfare. There had been "no shift of mood in Egypt's ruling circles . . . no change far-reaching enough to induce them to come to terms with the existence of Israel." The experts suggested that Egypt might renew hostilities as early as October.[36]

But the IDF and Weizman knew nothing of the Tuhami-Dayan meeting or other Israeli-Egyptian diplomatic exchanges. These had been kept under tight wraps by Begin and Dayan. It was not until November 18, the day before Sadat's arrival in Jerusalem, that Begin informed them of all that had gone before. Hence Sadat's announcement caught the Israeli defense and intelligence establishment by complete surprise. Only four years after the bitter shock of October 1973, it could not fail to conjure up the specter of yet another grand Egyptian deception.

The Israelis began intensively to study the new situation. A number of memorandums were produced and submitted to the prime minister. None was particularly encouraging. In a pessimistic personal note to Begin, Gen. Shlomo Gazit, the director of military intelligence, described the Sadat initiative as a "well-laid trap." Between November 12 and 17 he tried repeatedly to arrange a meeting with Begin—but without success.[37]

Begin knew what Gazit wanted—and understood the situation better than his intelligence chief. Tuhami and the Americans had provided him with a clear key to Sadat's radically altered thinking. Begin may not have been certain that Sadat really intended to come to Jerusalem. But he decided to play it straight and forthrightly. "If the President of Egypt decides to come to Jerusalem, he will be greeted with all the respect due a president," he declared. And he added (to Egyptian consternation): "I will also be happy to visit Cairo and look at the pyramids. . . . After all, our forefathers helped build them."[38]

During the following days Sadat reiterated his declaration of intent, and Begin firmed up his prospective welcome. But a discordant note came on November 15, from the Israeli chief of general staff, Gen. Mordechai ("Motta") Gur. "President Sadat must realize that if his intention is a second deception, like in the Yom Kippur War, his intention is clear to us," Gur declared in an interview. "We know that the Egyptian army is in the midst of preparations to start a war against Israel, [scheduled] for 1978, despite Sadat's announcement of readiness to come to Jerusalem."[39] Begin and Weizman were furious. Gur was ordered home—he was on a trip abroad—and on his return received an official reprimand (the first ever given to an officer of his rank by a defense minister).[40]

But the episode had no effect on the unfolding preparations. The Egyptians ignored it, and on November 15 Begin sent a formal invitation, repeating it in a well-publicized Knesset address. The owner of a small flag-producing workshop in Jerusalem, sensing that the visit was on, decided to take a chance—and began manufacturing dozens of Egyptian flags.[41]

Meanwhile, Sadat tried to salvage what he could in the Arab world. Egyptian-Syrian relations had been soured by Sinai II in 1975 and further undermined by the recent negotiations over Geneva. Sadat now sought to avert an irreparable rupture. On November 16, he flew to Damascus to try to persuade Assad at least to acquiesce in his Jerusalem expedition. Assad refused, and warned of dire consequences. The following day Syria declared an official day of mourning. Black flags were draped on the facades of public buildings and on street corners. In Baghdad, giant crowds gathered to denounce Sadat. In Cairo, small spontaneous student demonstrations were roughly broken up by security men. Sadat also had problems within his government. Fahmy and his deputy, Mohammed Riad, resigned.[42]

On November 18 Begin informed his military and intelligence chiefs of the diplomatic background to the Sadat visit. Deputy Prime Minister and Acting Defense Minister (following a car crash, Weizman was in hospital with broken ribs and a broken leg) Yadin, voicing the military's concern, spoke of a possible deception and proposed mobilizing a reserve division. But Begin, now supported by Gur and Gazit, blocked the idea. The visit was on.[43]

SADAT IN JERUSALEM

"I will watch you on TV, as will the whole world," Carter told Sadat on the telephone on the eve of his departure for Jerusalem. Another call came from Hassan of Morocco: "I admire your courage," said the king.[44]

Sadat's plane landed at Ben-Gurion International Airport at 8:00 P.M. Saturday, November 19. Giant searchlights lit up the aircraft. A thousand journalists, including dozens of TV crews, covered the event. When Sadat appeared in the doorway, he was welcomed by spontaneous applause from the tarmac, where Israel's political and military leaders were waiting. "Disbelief prevailed and people were stunned," Sadat was later to record.[45]

Begin led him down the line of dignitaries. To former Prime Minister Golda Meir, Sadat said: "For a long time I have looked forward to meeting you." "But you never came," she replied. "But now I'm here," he responded.[46] To Ariel Sharon, who had led the IDF thrust across the Suez Canal in October 1973 and was now agriculture minister, he said: "If you attempt to cross to the west bank again, I will have you arrested."[47] To General Gur he said: "I wasn't deceiving you." Gur burst out laughing. Invited Palestinian dignitaries had preferred to stay at home, either in fear of extremist reprisals or in protest against Sadat's peace initiative.

At the King David Hotel, Begin and Sadat had an unscheduled tête-à-tête. Sadat insisted that he had come to Jerusalem only to plead the Palestinian case, not to reach a separate Egyptian-Israeli deal. Begin responded that Israel would be willing to give back all of Sinai in exchange for peace. Sadat declared that he would agree not to move his army east of the passes, implying a demilitarization of the bulk of the peninsula after it was restored to Egyptian sovereignty. "Whatever happens, we shall remain friends," Sadat reportedly declared. "There is a real bond between us. We exchanged jokes," Begin said later.[48]

Sadat began the next day, November 20, at dawn prayers in the al-Aqsa Mosque. It was Id al-Adha, or the Holiday of Sacrifice, which closes the month-long Ramadan fast. Despite serious jitters among the Israeli security men—King Abdullah had been assassinated by a gunman on that very spot twenty-six years earlier—some six thousand Palestinians were allowed into the compound. The imam called on Sadat not to give up East Jerusalem and to protect Palestinian rights. From there, Sadat, accompanied by Begin, proceeded to Yad Vashem, the Holocaust memorial in West Jerusalem. He declined to don a skullcap, perhaps fearing that his enemies might exploit a photograph showing him in Jewish headdress. Begin, always the preacher, explained that the Holocaust happened because the Jews had had no country of their own.

The central event of the visit, Sadat's speech in the Knesset, took place that afternoon. He spoke, in Arabic, of the two countries' war casualties and the feelings of personal and collective bereavement, which he knew to be the most telling point in favor of peace among the Israeli public: "We all still bear the consequences of four fierce wars waged within 30 years. . . . A wife who becomes a widow is a human being entitled to a happy family life, whether she be an Arab or an Israeli. . . . For the sake of the lives of all our sons and brothers . . . for the generations to come, for a smile on the face of every child born in our land, for all that I have taken my decision to come to you, despite all the hazards."

He blamed "suspicion" and "lack of confidence" for the months wasted in "fruitless discussions" about reconvening the Geneva Conference. The time had come for "a bold drive towards new horizons." He referred to his previous efforts to achieve peace, in February 1971 and in mid-war in October 1973—but "I was not heard." He then spelled out his terms:

> I have not come here for a separate agreement between Egypt and Israel. . . . I have come . . . to build a durable peace based on justice. . . . Israel has become a fait accompli . . . we really and truly welcome you to live among us in peace and security. . . . [But Israel must] give up once and for all the dreams of conquest and give up the belief that force is the best method for dealing with the Arabs. . . . Expansion does not pay. . . . There are Arab territories that Israel has occupied and still occupies by force. We insist on complete withdrawal from these territories, including Arab Jerusalem. . . . Any talk about peace based on justice . . . would become meaningless while you occupy Arab territories by force of arms. . . . There can be no peace without the Palestinians. . . . It is no use to refrain from recognizing the Palestinian people and their right to statehood.

Sadat outlined the principles for a peace agreement: Withdrawal from "the Arab territories," Palestinian "self-determination," the "right of all states in the area to live in peace within . . . secure boundaries . . . [with] appropriate international guarantees." He then appealed directly to the Israeli people: "Encourage your leadership to struggle for peace."[49]

Though Sadat never mentioned the PLO, and he endorsed "secure boundaries" for all, the speech sounded to Israeli ears uncompromising. Begin reportedly muttered: "This is an ultimatum." Weizman—who was to emerge as the firmest advocate of peace in the Israeli cabinet—later wrote: "The words surprised me by their intransigence. There was a menacing undertone I didn't like." He passed Dayan a note saying: "We have to prepare for war."[50] But the participants—and history—were soon to forget the inflexibility. Jimmy Carter observed: "The meaning of the words themselves was muted by the fact that he was standing there alone, before his ancient enemies, holding out an olive branch."

In his response Begin was uncompromising as to the contours of the envisioned settlement. He recounted the history of Arab aggression aimed at destroying the Jewish state, and he asserted Israel's desire to make peace. But, he said, "We have a different position regarding the final borders between us and our neighbors." Leaving the door open to further dialogue, he said: "I suggest that everything will be open to negotiation." Somewhat contradictorily, he declared that Jerusalem would never again be divided.

The essential difference between the two leaders was evident in these speeches, and was to loom large during the following two years. Weizman later put it pithily: "Both desired peace. But whereas Sadat wanted to take it by storm . . . Begin preferred to creep forward inch by inch. He took the dream of peace and ground it down into the fine, dry powder of details, legal clauses, and quotes from international law."[51] The Egyptians were taken aback by Begin's speech, especially by his intransigence on the Palestinian issue. They had expected some flexibility in response to Sadat's grand overture. But it had failed "to produce the basic shifts in Israeli . . . positions that he was seeking."[52]

The festive dinner that night was overshadowed by the afternoon's speeches. "Everyone seated at the table—Egyptians no less than Israelis—looked as though they had just returned from a funeral," recorded Weizman.[53] The gloom was deepened by references to close relatives of some of those present who had been killed or invalided in past wars. Weizman spoke of his son, badly injured by an Egyptian sniper during the War of Attrition; Tuhami, of Sadat's half-brother, killed in October 1973; Begin, of Dayan's brother and of Deputy Prime Minister Yadin's brother, both killed in 1948.

After dinner Weizman, Yadin, Egyptian acting Foreign Minister Butros Butros Ghali and Mustafa Khalil, the secretary-general of Egypt's ruling Socialist Unity Party, conversed long into the night. Khalil spoke at length of Egypt's poverty and inability to continue to shoulder the burden of the struggle against Israel and added: "We know that we have no chance of winning in war, and we also know that you have the atomic bomb. . . . Egypt has no military solution, and we must seek another solution."[54]

Sadat took an instant liking to Weizman. At a meeting the next morning they exchanged reminiscences, and Sadat said that he would arrange a meeting for Weizman with his Egyptian counterpart, General Gamasy. Sadat then met with a delegation of West Bank and Gaza notables, with whom he got nowhere. Some supported the PLO and a Palestinian state; others, a federated West Bank–Jordanian "state."

The visit ended with a joint press conference. Standing beside an upbeat, jocular Begin, Sadat spoke of a future follow-up meeting; both promised that there would be "no more war" between their two states.

Despite the broad gap between the positions of the two countries, starkly apparent in the Knesset speeches, the visit was a major milestone on the road to peace. Agreement—informal, undetailed, vague, but still agreement—had been reached between Begin and Sadat on the foundation of a separate Israeli-Egyptian peace: Israeli withdrawal from all of Sinai and the effective demilitarization of the peninsula.[55] But the significance of the visit went far deeper. The Israelis, long fed on a diet of unswerving Arab enmity and barbarism, now came face to face with the most important leader in the Arab world, the man who had engineered the costly surprise attack of 1973—and found a smiling, somewhat paternal, soft-spoken, dignified idealist who clearly wanted peace and was willing to put his life on the line to achieve it.[56]

Throughout Israel's history, and especially in 1948–51 and again in the early 1970s, the government had successfully hidden from the public the fact that there were Arab leaders who were willing to make peace and to make concessions to achieve it. But now there was obviously "someone to talk to" out there, someone ready to make a deal.

In Egypt, too, the visit broke a psychological barrier. Traditional demonization of the Zionist enemy gave way to a more rational approach. The Egyptians clearly were won over by the warm welcome accorded their president. Thereafter Cairo's radio stations stopped referring to Israel as the "enemy," instead calling it a "rival." Egyptian journalists visited Israel and met its leaders, officials, and people for the first time—and wrote reports describing the country more or less as it was, not as thirty years of propaganda had fashioned it in their readers' imagination.[57]

Sadat's visit shocked the rest of the Arab world. The rejectionists saw it as a prelude to a sellout—a separate Israeli-Egyptian deal, which would remove the strongest Arab country from the arena. The Palestinians took it worst. The number two man in the PLO, Salah Khalaf (Abu Iyad), wrote that "tears were streaming down the cheeks of some of my comrades" as they watched the visit on television. On November 22 Arafat and Assad issued a joint communiqué condemning the visit and announcing their "readiness to apply all their resources to the elimination of its consequences." Both called on the Egyptian people to "resist this treason to the Arab nation." The next day Sadat ordered the PLO office in Cairo and its Voice of Palestine radio transmitters shut down.[58]

AFTER JERUSALEM

Most American officials were disconcerted by the visit, viewing it as subversive of their attempt to reconvene the Geneva Conference. In the ensuing flurry of Israeli-Egyptian contacts, sometimes Americans participated, more often not. But the impasse that had starkly surfaced in the Knesset speeches continued to characterize relations between the two countries, and the United States was inexorably drawn back into the process.

By December 1977 it dawned on Washington that Israel and Egypt were moving toward a separate peace. While not opposed to such a denouement,

Washington hoped to exploit the momentum generated by the bilateral process to achieve a wider agreement, which might include at least the Palestinians if not Syria, Lebanon, and Jordan as well. A basic fear remained that a separate Israeli-Egyptian peace would unravel if the Palestinian problem were not at least partially resolved.

But the Begin government regarded the continued occupation of and settlement in the West Bank as its historic, divine mission. Begin and his colleagues always spoke of the Israeli "liberation"—rather than "conquest" or "occupation"—of the West Bank and the Gaza Strip. But diplomacy, and continued American goodwill, demanded a measure of Israeli give on the Palestinian issue. Begin's solution—harking back to plans by Jabotinsky and Ben-Gurion—was "autonomy," meaning a very limited measure of self-rule for the Arab inhabitants of the West Bank (which Begin invariably called "Judea and Samaria") and the Gaza District, with Israel retaining military control and overall governmental oversight, as well as specific control over land and water. The plan that began to take shape "did not include . . . the withdrawal of Israel's civilian population or military forces" from the territories.[59]

On December 2-3, 1977, at their second secret meeting, in the royal palace at Marrakech, Morocco, Dayan told Tuhami of the evolving "autonomy" plan. He also said that Israel wanted full normalization of relations between Israel and Egypt, and was ready to give up almost all of Sinai in exchange for peace, but wanted to retain the Rafa Approaches, which included the new Jewish town of Yamit and the surrounding agricultural settlements. Tuhami responded that all the settlements in Sinai would have to go: "The President and the people of Egypt will not agree to a single Israeli settlement or soldier remaining in Sinai." Tuhami was clearly embarrassed by Israel's interest in a separate pact and spoke of the need to reach a comprehensive peace, which would include Palestinian independence.

The negotiations were at an impasse. Dayan concluded that "unless the Americans could . . . throw their weight behind the negotiations, the wheels of peace would remain at a standstill."[60] His impression was reinforced by the Cairo Conference, which took place eleven days later at the Mena House Hotel. It was initiated by Sadat, with the aim of preparing for Geneva. Israel, the United States, and the UN were represented by senior officials rather than ministers. Both sides stuck to their guns, and no progress was achieved. None of the other Arab states participated—Sadat had failed to mobilize any Arab support for his moves. Rejectionist Arab states, led by Syria and Iraq, supported by the PLO, had gathered on December 2 in Tripoli, Libya, and declared an economic and diplomatic boycott of Egypt. Sadat had responded on December 5 by breaking off relations with the countries represented in Tripoli. One ray of light, from Cairo's viewpoint, was that Saudi Arabia and Jordan, for the moment at least, preferred to sit on the fence.[61]

Begin had reached his strategic decision to cede all of Sinai in exchange for peace without consulting the military, Defense Minister Weizman, or the cabinet. Only on December 13 did he submit his plan to the Ministerial Defense Committee. Chief of General Staff Gur dissented. He argued that Palestinian "autonomy" would lead to statehood and that Israel should retain eastern Sinai as a security zone. But the ministers unanimously supported the prime minister.[62]

Begin flew to Washington to get U.S. backing. On December 16, he explained to Carter that Israel would withdraw from Sinai in stages, over a three- to five-year period, with each stage matched by additional normalization measures between the two countries (exchange of ambassadors, commercial ties, and so on). Egypt would receive sovereignty over all of Sinai—but the Israeli settlements in the Rafa Approaches would remain protected by Israeli and UN troops. Israel would not impose its sovereignty over the West Bank and Gaza, and would grant the Palestinians a measure of self-government but would not withdraw militarily.[63]

On December 20 Weizman flew to Egypt for meetings in Ismailia with Sadat, Vice President Hosni Mubarak (like Weizman a former combat pilot), and Defense Minister Gamasy. The talks took place at the presidential villa overlooking the Canal; sitting on the veranda, the participants could clearly see the ruins of one of the forts on the east bank that had fallen to the Egyptian army in October 1973. Weizman later recorded: "I have to admit that I felt my heart wrench as I saw the Bar-Lev Line in ruins. From time to time I would sneak a glimpse at it. . . . [I]t is obvious that this meeting could not take place except after the Egyptians had succeeded in crossing the Canal in 1973, but the price we paid was extremely dear."[64]

Gamasy wrote: "As for me, I felt satisfied whenever I saw Weisman [sic] look at their fortified line destroyed by our forces on October 6; I hoped that this would be a lesson for the Israelis—to turn to a real peace rather than resort to repeated aggressions against Arab countries."[65]

Sadat conceded the need for full normalization of relations after peace was achieved—including an exchange of ambassadors (previously he had resisted the idea). But he reiterated his traditional formula: Peace was possible only if Israel withdrew from every inch of Arab territory, and the Israeli settlements in northeastern Sinai would have to be uprooted.

Gamasy, the reserved, cerebral architect of the 1973 Canal crossing, was more forthcoming when he met with Weizman alone. He acknowledged Israel's security problems and expressed agreement to the continued existence of the settlements, so long as they accepted Egyptian sovereignty ("like the Jews of Cairo"). Gamasy also promised that after the signing of a peace agreement, Egypt would reduce the size of its army and pull most of it back from the Canal zone to the Cairo area. However, he insisted that Israel's air force be reduced and that Egyptian ground troops and aircraft be stationed in Al-'Arīsh. Weizman countered that Sadat had already agreed in principle to the demilitarization of Sinai east of the passes. "My surprise was great and my shock was even greater," recorded Gamasy in his memoirs. Sadat apparently had not consulted him in the matter. "Sadat is not a military man. . . . [He is] a statesman," he argued. But Weizman quite naturally "clung to the promise that Sadat had made." Gamasy also rejected Israel's demand for early warning stations in Sinai to monitor Egyptian military activity.[66]

On the subject of occupied Arab territory Gamasy was as unrelenting as Sadat. There could be no border changes. He also suggested that, as part of the settlement, Israel sign the nuclear nonproliferation agreement.[67]

The Weizman-Sadat-Gamasy meetings provided an accurate foretaste of the Begin-Sadat summit in Ismailia on December 25. It was Begin's first visit to Egypt. The two men, in the words of one American historian, "were unable to agree on anything of substance."[68] Begin presented his "peace plan," providing for withdrawal from Sinai, but with Israeli settlers, troops, and air bases remaining in the Rafa Approaches and along Sinai's eastern shore; and limited "self-rule" for the Palestinians, with Israeli settlers and troops remaining in and controlling the territories, though the question of ultimate sovereignty was left open.[69] Egypt's new foreign minister, Mohamed Ibrahim Kamel, subsequently defined the proposals as "insults to our intelligence."[70] Sadat, for his part, reiterated Egypt's positions: complete Israeli withdrawal from the territories and Palestinian statehood in the West Bank and Gaza. The impasse remained. The only progress was the creation of military and political committees to discuss the prospective settlement. "It was one of the worst conferences I have ever attended . . . a complete failure," concluded Gamasy.[71]

Sadat had expected the Israelis to reciprocate his grand gesture of traveling to Jerusalem. But Begin offered nothing. For weeks after Ismailia, Sadat and the Egyptian press portrayed the Israelis as a group of Shylock-like merchants, bent on swindling the Arabs.[72] The Egyptians became convinced that only the Americans could persuade Israel to be more flexible and that it was imperative that they be brought into the process.[73] On January 4, 1978, on his way from Riyadh to Europe, Carter met Sadat in Aswan and issued a statement, subsequently known as the "Aswan Declaration":

> First, peace must be based on normal relations among the parties. . . . Second, there must be withdrawal by Israel from territories occupied in 1967 and agreement on secure and recognized borders. . . . Third, there must be a resolution of the Palestinian problem in all its aspects. The solution must recognize the legitimate rights of the Palestinian people and enable the Palestinians to participate in the determination of their own future."[74]

The declaration, with its new (for the United States) wording on Palestinian "legitimate rights" and self-determination, helped keep an increasingly disillusioned Sadat in play. But news that day that Israel had started work on four new settlements in Sinai[75] pushed in the contrary direction. And it strengthened Carter's feeling that Begin was not a man of his word.[76]

The meeting in Jerusalem on January 16-18 of the political committee set up at Ismailia, with Secretary of State Cyrus Vance heading the American delegation, only reinforced the Egyptian and American conviction that the talks were getting nowhere. The Israelis continued to insist that the settlements, troops, and air bases must remain in eastern Sinai, and were inflexible over the West Bank and Gaza Strip. On the third day Sadat abruptly ordered his delegation home and told Carter on the telephone that Begin obviously preferred land to peace.[77] Weizman, of whom Carter later wrote that he was capable of "a degree of objectivity . . . rare among any of the Middle East leaders,"[78] presented the same positions in the military committee talks with Gamasy later that month.[79] Following their failure Weizman commented: "It was a meeting between the Middle East [the Egyptian mentality] and Eastern Europe [the Israeli mentality]."[80]

Two days after Egypt withdrew from the political committee talks, Carter, for the first time, in a talk with Brzezinski, raised the possibility of bringing Begin and Sadat face to face at Camp David to thrash the issues out.[81] But it was to take several more months before conditions ripened. Meanwhile, Carter invited Sadat to Washington to hammer out, and subsequently confront Begin with, joint positions he would find it difficult to resist. National Security Council Middle East expert William Quandt called this policy, pushed by Brzezinski and himself, a "secret strategy of collusion" between the United States and Egypt.[82] Motivating the effort was knowledge of Sadat's deepening depression and talk of resignation.[83] A boost from his American friends was definitely in order.

Sadat arrived at Camp David, outside Washington, on February 3. He was ready, he said, to suspend all contacts with Israel. Only the United States could pressure Begin to change his positions—Washington must make its views clear. Carter agreed but had to take care not to appear to be in collusion with Egypt against Begin; this could raise a storm in American domestic politics and frustrate all movement toward peace. But by the end of the talks Carter went public on a number of points that indicated a pro-Sadat shift: He declared that Israel's settlements in the territories were illegal and an obstacle to peace, and that Resolution 242, regarding Israeli withdrawal, applied to *all* fronts, not just to Sinai. Meanwhile, Sadat, in a series of television interviews, displaying charm and openness, "conquered the hearts of the [American] people," in Dayan's phrase.[84]

As the months passed, Sadat seemed increasingly concerned only with a bilateral Egyptian-Israeli accord. Perhaps he had never cared that much about the Palestinians to begin with; without doubt, PLO opposition to his peace efforts had taken its toll; perhaps Begin's rigidity over the West Bank and

Gaza had persuaded him that only a deal on Sinai was possible. It took the Americans several months to digest the deep conceptual change that was taking place in Sadat's thinking, perhaps because he never actually put it in so many words.[85] Between the flight to Jerusalem (November 1977) and the signing of the Camp David Accords (September 1978), there was a succession of Palestinian terrorist attacks against Egyptian, Israeli, and Western targets. The outrage that probably affected Sadat most deeply was the murder in Cyprus on February 18, 1978, of Yusuf al-Siba'i, editor-in-chief of the leading Cairo daily, *al-Ahram*, who had flown with him to Jerusalem. Though the killers apparently belonged to the breakaway Abu Nidal faction, Sadat subsequently publicly called the PLO leaders "pygmies and hired killers" and Egyptian-PLO relations went into a deep freeze, with Palestinians regularly burning Sadat in effigy in demonstrations around the Arab world.

Sadat's public response was mild compared to his private rage. "I have excluded the PLO from my lexicon. By their behavior, they have excluded themselves from the negotiations," he told Weizman in March. There should be no Palestinian state, and the West Bank and Gaza should be ruled by Jordan, Israel, and representatives of the local population, he said.[86]

That month Israel was the target of a major PLO operation against the peace process. On March 11, a dozen Fatah terrorists disembarked from rubber dinghies on a beach south of Haifa, murdered an American woman, and commandeered a bus on the Haifa–Tel Aviv highway. Heading south, they fired on passing cars before slamming into a roadblock just north of Tel Aviv. The hastily gathered collection of policemen and soldiers opened fire, the terrorists responded, and several grenades exploded. Within minutes thirty-seven of the passengers and nine terrorists were dead.

Three days later, the IDF invaded southern Lebanon, destroyed PLO bases, and conquered the area up to the Litani River, severely embarrassing Sadat. Here were the Israelis, with whom he was trying to negotiate peace, killing hundreds of Arabs, including civilians, and invading Arab territory (albeit with serious provocation). Carter, too, was disturbed by the disproportion between the PLO attack and the Israeli response. But Lebanon and the PLO, as it turned out, were marginal. In reality, negotiations were stalled because of differences over specific bilateral, Israeli-Egyptian issues.

Sadat's frustration was understandable. Five months after his Jerusalem visit, not only had there not been a reciprocal gesture on the part of Begin, but Israeli policy had hardened, particularly with regard to the West Bank. Indeed, in March, Weizman threatened to resign from the government in order to block efforts by Dayan and Sharon to begin construction of a new settlement in the territory. Weizman that month also proposed taking the Labor Party into the government, deepening his growing rift with Begin.[87]

During the first months of 1978 Arab rejectionists inside and outside Egypt stepped up their pressure on Sadat to withdraw from the peace process.

Israel's inflexibility also contributed to the decision of Arab "moderates," like King Hussein of Jordan and King Fahd of Saudi Arabia, to stay out of it, exacerbating Egypt's isolation. Begin, too, began in early 1978 to feel the weight of large-scale domestic dissent. From March he was forced to take account of an increasingly questioning, indeed protesting, public and press that feared that through rigidity, pedantry, and myopia, he was letting the historic chance for peace with Egypt slip through his fingers.

The main Israeli peace movement, Peace Now, emerged as the expression of the mood of suspicion and disenchantment that prevailed mainly among middle-class, Ashkenazic Israelis. It was born after the publication of a letter to Begin signed by 348 IDF reserve officers and soldiers, among them more than a dozen lieutenant colonels and majors and a handful of decorated war heroes.

The so-called "Officers' Letter," dated March 7, 1978, declared:

We see it as our duty to call on you to avoid taking steps that might be a cause for lamentation for generations for our people and country. . . . A government that prefers the existence of the State of Israel within the boundaries of Greater Israel to its existence in peace with friendly neighborly relations will awaken in us grave doubts . . . regarding the justice of our cause.[88]

Almost instantly a movement coalesced around the letter and its signatories. Thousands quickly added their names to petitions circulated around the country. On March 30, when the activists held their first demonstration outside Begin's residence in Jerusalem, the demand "Peace Now" appeared on placards for the first time. A few days later it was adopted as the movement's name. On April 1, 40,000 people attended Peace Now's first mass rally, in Tel Aviv, making it Israel's largest political demonstration ever.

By the end of May some 100,000 people had signed the petitions. The movement was particularly strong in the kibbutzim, the universities, and among the intelligentsia; but while Begin and the Likud dismissed the protesters as just another group of leftists and Labor-supporters, it was clear to the ministers that the will to peace was shared by large sections of the public, well beyond the Likud's traditional foes on the left.[89] While not necessarily bowing to it, Begin was forced to take account of the popular groundswell.

Between March and August, American diplomats whittled away at the major areas of disagreement. The key to bridging the antithetical Israeli and Egyptian positions regarding the West Bank and Gaza Strip—no withdrawal versus full withdrawal, including from East Jerusalem—was the concept of a "transitional period." Egypt accepted the American premise that Israel could not implement an immediate withdrawal and that there would have to be an interim period, during which Israel relinquished some powers to the local population but remained effectively in overall control. After the interim period either the Palestinians would be allowed to determine their own future or the parties would sit down and negotiate the ultimate fate of the territories. The Americans began to speak of a five-year transitional period, and both Israel and, with some reluctance, Egypt began to fall into line.

But the Israelis could not be persuaded to declare an intention to withdraw from the West Bank and Gaza or to agree to Palestinian "self-determination" at the end of the five-year period; they would agree only to begin negotiating the question of sovereignty at that point. Moreover, they would not even contemplate withdrawal from eastern Sinai. In mid-July, at a meeting with Weizman, Sadat said that if no progress was made by October, he would resign;[90] he wanted Israel to make a grand gesture such as a unilateral withdrawal from Al-'Arīsh and Saint Catherine (Mount Moses) well in advance of the signing of a peace treaty. At the latter site Sadat wished to build a mosque, synagogue, and church complex.[91] Weizman urged Begin to agree, but the prime minister refused. "One does not give something for nothing," he angrily told reporters.[92] Weizman declared publicly: "I am not sure the Government wants peace."[93] Relations between the two neared the breaking point.

Talks in July that focused on the Palestinian issue produced nothing, but Dayan apparently agreed in principle that the Palestinians uprooted in 1967 be allowed to return to the West Bank and Gaza. Egyptian Foreign Minister Kamel had demanded that Israel allow the return of all the refugees, from 1948 as well as 1967, but Dayan had rejected this.[94] At one point, after Egypt had turned down all of Israel's autonomy proposals, Dayan suggested: "Would it not be correct for Israel now to withdraw its previous proposals [as well], regarding complete withdrawal from Sinai?"[95]

By the end of July a frustrated, unhappy Sadat, feeling that the talks were getting nowhere, told Carter that there was no point in further meetings with the Israelis. If his purpose was to jolt Washington into some dramatic action, he succeeded. On July 30, Carter told his advisers that he had decided to call a tripartite summit at Camp David. "None of us thought we had much chance of success," he was later to write.[96] But with the real decision-makers, Sadat and Begin, on hand and with himself mediating and cajoling, he hoped real bridging would be possible.[97] Carter was ready to make this "last major effort."[98]

By the summer of 1978, Carter sensed that Sadat's advocacy of the Palestinian cause had become more feigned than real, a matter of lip service and fig leaf rather than substance. Sadat's real interest lay in the recovery of Sinai. At the same time Carter at last appreciated that whereas Begin's attempts to keep a grip on the eastern fringes of Sinai with their settlements and air bases were tactical and security oriented, his insistence on retaining the West Bank was deeply ideological, basic, and inexorable: Begin was simply not going to give it up. But he could be induced to give up every inch of Sinai, given adequate security provisions that might offset the loss of territorial depth. The contours of a potential deal were at last emerging.[99]

Both Sadat and Begin quickly accepted Carter's invitations to Camp David, though Begin feared that he might be heading into a trap. He genuinely wanted peace, and the meeting would offer a major opportunity to achieve it, but he also knew he had no choice: If he refused to attend he would be blamed for blocking the peace process. And Peace Now provided a timely, forceful reminder of his domestic problem. On September 2, on the eve of his departure for the United States, the movement organized a mammoth send-off rally of 100,000 people in Tel Aviv. The message was simple: You have the support of the Israeli public to make the concessions necessary to achieve peace. Begin was later to write to novelist and Peace Now supporter Amos Oz that at Camp David he was unable to shake off the memory of the "100,000 rally." And both Weizman and Moshe Arens, Israel's ambassador to Washington, later testified that the rally and the movement behind it had helped persuade the Israeli negotiators to make concessions.[100]

Other considerations also affected Begin's thinking. Knesset members from the middle-of-the-road Dash Party threatened to leave his coalition if he missed the opportunity for peace. Failure might result in early elections and endanger Begin's chances of reelection. Moreover, Israel's relations with its chief ally, the United States, would suffer grave damage if Begin refused to attend the summit or if his government was perceived as the chief cause of its failure. He simply could not afford to say no, not with the president putting all his prestige on the line. Last, Begin wanted to go down in history as the man who had made peace, dispelling that image of "Begin the warmonger" that Ben-Gurion had cultivated since the 1940s. Carter understood: "Begin . . . seemed to look on himself as a man of destiny, cast in a biblical role as one charged with the future of God's chosen people."[101]

In preparing for Camp David, the Israeli leadership was united: No withdrawal of settlers or soldiers from the West Bank and Gaza, and no Palestinian self-determination; and both of the air bases in eastern Sinai must remain in Israeli hands, as must all or most of the settlements. Sadat was equally adamant: No settlements and no Israeli troops or air bases must remain in Sinai. As to the linkage between an agreement on Sinai and the Palestinian issue, Sadat over the months had fluctuated between insistence on complete Israeli withdrawal from the West Bank and Gaza and pragmatism. It was the latter that prevailed at Camp David, to the chagrin of his hard-line aides.[102]

Carter went into Camp David with an open mind and expectations of success.[103] He had planned for a three-day meeting, a week at most.[104] In the end it took almost two weeks to reach agreement. From the first, Begin suspected American-Egyptian collusion. The repeated hugs Sadat got from Carter, which went well beyond the bounds of protocol, when he arrived on

September 5, fed this suspicion in Begin, forever on guard against the smallest slight. But ceremony and formality were deliberately banished by the hosts from the marathon get-together, perhaps to Begin's discomfort. The guests were asked not to wear ties, though Begin wore a suit and tie throughout, and the Egyptians generally wore jackets "of studied elegance."[105] There were no regular or formal working hours. A swimming pool, a movie theater, and a billiards table were available, and Brzezinski and others occasionally played chess.

The Egyptians and Israelis were asked not to discuss the proceedings with journalists and to channel everything through Carter's press secretary. "It was imperative that there be a minimum of posturing," Carter explained.[106] He rejected Brzezinski's suggestion that the guest quarters be bugged to give the Americans an intelligence edge.[107]

Sadat's party included Kamel, Butros Ghali, and Osama al-Baz, under secretary for foreign affairs to the president. (Gamasy was conspicuously absent.) Begin had Dayan, Weizman, and Attorney General Aharon Barak. And Carter brought Vance, Brzezinski, and Assistant Secretary of State Harold Saunders. Sadat decided on everything more or less alone, while Begin relied heavily on the advice of his aides; Carter was thankful, because "in Sadat's case, the leader was much more forthcoming than his chief advisers, and in Begin's case, the advisers were more inclined to work out difficult problems than was their leader."[108] But Begin was prodded toward inflexibility by regular calls from his son, Binyamin Ze'ev Begin, then working on a Ph.D. in geology in Colorado.[109]

Brzezinski rated the Israelis the "least cohesive negotiating team." Begin, Dayan, and Weizman "did little to mask their mutual dislike. . . . [Dayan managed] to convey his contempt for Begin," while Begin regarded Weizman as "not to be taken seriously." Weizman thought Begin was "mindlessly" missing the opportunity for peace and regarded Dayan as "deceitful."[110]

The Americans had greater sympathy for and rapport with Sadat: "We all felt that the Egyptian leader had gone out on a limb . . . and Begin was busily sawing the limb off."[111] Carter and Sadat enjoyed excellent relations; relations between Carter and Begin were very tense to begin with and grew worse as the conference went on. Carter spent the first few days trying to "establish a rapport among the three leaders. He sought [particularly] to break down the mistrust and animosity between Begin and Sadat."[112] (On September 6 Sadat told Carter: "Begin is full of complexes and bitterness; he has completely ignored my great gesture."[113])

The negotiations began on September 5 with a brief Carter-Sadat tête-à-tête. Sadat said he would be flexible on everything including diplomatic and trade relations with Israel, but not over "land and sovereignty."[114] Carter then met Begin, hoping both to allay his fears of American-Egyptian collusion and to restore trust. This proved no easy matter, as already there was a sediment of mutual antagonism and distrust left over from their previous meetings, which had resulted in a number of deceptions or misunderstandings concerning the problem of the settlements.

At that first meeting Carter tried to put Begin "at ease and to assure him there would be no surprises."[115] But the conversation was marked by a series of differences, including those over the settlements and Israeli aid to the Christians in southern Lebanon. Begin said that he sought agreement "on general principles," with more detailed negotiations to follow between the respective ministers of foreign affairs and defense. Carter retorted bluntly: "We must emerge from this meeting with a detailed agreement. . . . After a failure there will be little chance for a successful follow-up. . . . A reconciliation between Israel and Egypt is even more important to me than . . . reelection."[116]

The next day Carter, Begin, and Sadat met. Earlier, Sadat had handed Carter a document entitled "Framework for the Comprehensive Peace Settlement of the Middle East Problem," characterized by hard-line positions. Carter found the document to be "extremely harsh and filled with all the unacceptable Arab rhetoric."[117] But Sadat also handed him a three-page modification of the "Framework" that Carter could, if necessary, introduce during his talks with the Israelis. In other words, Sadat had given Carter a list of Egyptian fallback positions and concessions, such as full diplomatic relations and the indivisibility of Jerusalem, *in advance of* the start of the negotiations with the Israelis. (One result was that Carter tended to disregard all opening Egyptian positions and to believe that Sadat could always be persuaded to make concessions.)[118]

Just before the three men met, Carter asked to see Begin privately and warned him that Sadat's position paper would be "aggressive." Begin was cautioned not to "over-react."[119] At the tripartite meeting, Sadat spent ninety minutes reading out his "Framework." Begin listened patiently. At the end Carter suggested that if Begin would just sign, it would save everybody a lot of time.[120] There were "gales of genuine laughter"[121] and the meeting ended in good cheer. Begin postponed his response until the following day. Carter had expected him to react immediately and angrily; he later interpreted Begin's upbeat mood as stemming precisely from the harshness of the "Framework:" It highlighted the unreasonableness of the Egyptians. And Sadat was cheerful, according to Carter, because the Israelis had not reacted angrily.[122] But just to keep the lid on the Israelis' temper, Carter telephoned Begin and, calling the "Framework" an "extreme" document, explained that it was merely an "opening position."[123] But the Israelis were not to be mollified. Consulting back in Begin's cabin, the delegation was unanimous in flatly rejecting the "Framework."[124]

Begin and Sadat met again the following day, September 7, but not before there had been a near blowup between Carter and Begin at an earlier meeting without the Egyptians. Begin denounced the "Framework" and went on to insist that Israel must retain its settlements in Sinai and its settlements and army in the West Bank and Gaza. Carter insisted that the Israelis must withdraw from the bulk of the West Bank, with appropriate arrangements to safeguard their security. Begin refused to discuss it. Carter accused him of being "evasive" and said that the whole Israeli "autonomy" plan was a "subterfuge" to enable Israel to hold on to the Palestinian territories. Begin threatened to demand that Egypt withdraw the "Framework." In the end, Carter persuaded him simply to declare it "unacceptable" as a basis for negotiation.[125]

Begin told Sadat that his grand gesture had been reciprocated by the warm welcome accorded him in Jerusalem. He then tore apart the "Framework:" "You address us as if we are a routed nation," Begin charged. Sadat misunderstood and thought that Begin had referred to Egypt as a "routed nation." He was enraged. "We are not routed! We are not routed," he said. "All restraint was now gone. Their faces were flushed, and the niceties of diplomatic language and protocol were stripped away. . . . I thought Sadat would explode. He pounded the table, shouting that land was not negotiable," recorded Carter.

Begin rejected Sadat's demand that Israel pay Egypt reparations for war damage and for the oil pumped out of Sinai since 1967. The two men raised their voices. Carter tried to calm them down. Sadat: "We give you peace and you want land. You do not want peace!" Begin rejected Sadat's call for a Palestinian state. Sadat reiterated his demand for the complete removal of Israeli settlements and air bases from Sinai and then condemned Israel's intervention in Lebanon. Begin rejoined (looking at Carter) that Israel had intervened to "save the Christians," and that, "were it not for Israel, no one would have come to their aid." The session broke up in a grim mood.[126]

The three leaders met again that afternoon, the talk focusing immediately on the settlements in eastern Sinai. "Neither I nor my people can accept them," said Sadat. Begin: "We will not agree to the dismantling of the settlements." Carter: If the agreement stands or falls over the settlements, "I am sure you will get an overwhelming majority [in the Knesset in favor] of their dismantling, Mr. Begin." Again the meeting broke up without progress and in bad humor. Begin and Sadat "left [the room] without speaking to each other," and were not to meet again until ten days later, on the final day of Camp David. "The talks had broken down," concluded Carter.[127]

But neither Sadat nor Begin had any thought of quitting Camp David: The political costs of being the first to leave were calculated as inordinately high. During the following days it was left to the United States to pick up the pieces and battle on. "A sense of gloom and foreboding still prevailed," but, under Carter's leadership, the American team began to work "on formulations which might possibly break the deadlock."[128] Carter was indefatigable, putting in twenty-hour days, exhibiting "bulldoglike persistence" as well as a mastery of every problem and argument, however minor.[129]

On September 8 Carter told Begin that the Egyptian proposals were only opening positions; there were also fallback positions. But he refused to divulge them, and Begin declined to suggest what Israel's were. Instead, Begin asked that the United States refrain from putting forward a plan of its own, and especially from pressing Israel on the issue of settlements. Carter dug in his heels: "We are going to present a comprehensive proposal for peace. . . . I can see no other possibility for progress."[130]

The Americans worked on their draft proposal (there were eventually to be twenty-three such drafts) the following day while Weizman twice met with Sadat, on Carter's initiative. Sadat was not particularly flexible but did agree that Israel could have two years in which to withdraw from the Etzion air base, northwest of Eilat. Discussing the draft proposals with his staff, Carter for the first time made it clear that the United States must strive for the attainable, meaning a separate Israeli-Egyptian peace deal. The deal should not be conditionally linked to the fate of the West Bank and Gaza, which could also be determined in ten years.[131]

Presenting the American draft to the Israelis,[132] Carter said he believed Sadat would accept its essentials. Begin argued over almost every word, particularly a passage relating to the inadmissibility of acquiring territory by force. Carter: "Do you reject UN Resolution 242? . . . What you say convinces me that Sadat was right—what you want is land!" Begin declined to commit himself explicitly on 242 but then asked to delete all reference to that resolution from the document. Carter: "If you had openly disavowed UN Resolution 242, I would not have invited you to Camp David." Begin parried with some banality—which Carter, in his memoirs, dismissed as "gobbledygook." "If you don't espouse 242, it is a terrible blow to peace," the president said. "If I were an Arab, I would prefer the present Israeli occupation to this proposal of yours," he added.[133] The president later apparently described Begin as a "psycho."[134]

Carter took Dayan—whom he regarded as "level-headed" and reasonable—aside and called Begin "unreasonable" and "an obstacle to progress." They sat together on the porch of Carter's cabin until 4 A.M.[135] Dayan reassured Carter that Begin really did want an agreement and promised to do what he could; Carter came away considering the Israeli foreign minister "a friend and a proper ally."[136] Vance wrote that Dayan was "brilliant, imaginative and honest" and "very helpful in the darkest moments in helping us thread our way through the thickets."[137] Carter and Vance also established a respectful, trusting relationship with Barak, whom Brzezinski described as "the sleeper in the Israeli delegation—clearheaded and obviously determined to conciliate. . . . In private conversation he has told me that many of the Israeli positions have no merit but are essentially psychological in origin."[138]

On September 11, Sadat told Carter that the Israeli settlements in eastern Sinai would have to go. Jews, he said, would be permitted to live in "Cairo or in Aswan"—but not in Sinai. Carter pointed out that this seemed illogical.

Sadat: "Some things in the Middle East are not logical or reasonable. For Egypt, this is one of them." At Carter's insistence Sadat agreed to stretch the deadline for the IDF's withdrawal from Sinai from two to three years.

The Israelis remained adamant about retaining the settlements in the Rafa Approaches. Their reasoning was made clear to Carter by Barak: Uprooting them would provide an unwanted precedent for the fate of the West Bank and Golan Heights settlements; and if Egypt at some point violated the agreement and moved troops east of the passes, Israel would be justified in sending troops to protect the settlers. If there were no settlements left, it would be difficult for Israel to send the IDF into the peninsula in response to Egyptian troop movements that fell short of actual hostilities.[139]

At this point the Americans, urged on by Dayan,[140] began to draft two documents—one on Egyptian-Israeli relations and the other on the Palestinian issue, which would also set principles for a comprehensive Israeli-Arab peace. On September 12, they continued to push the draft agreement along, this time with the Egyptians, while beginning work on the separate Egyptian-Israeli Sinai accord. The Egyptians were disappointed that the draft failed to determine what would happen to the West Bank and Gaza after the transitional period, leaving open the possibility of permanent Israeli control. Moreover, East Jerusalem, they noted, was not mentioned. Sadat's advisers, al-Baz and Kamel, apparently had persuaded Sadat to harden his position on the Palestinians in deference to outside Arab—particularly Saudi—pressure.[141] Carter penned a "Framework for a Settlement in Sinai," restoring Egyptian sovereignty in all of the peninsula. Sadat read it and said: "It's all right." The basis for the future Israeli-Egyptian peace treaty had been laid.[142]

But it was not going to be clear sailing. In a private conversation Begin told Brzezinski: "My right eye will fall out, my right hand will fall off, before I ever agree to the dismantling of a single Jewish settlement."[143] He was speaking about Sinai as well as the West Bank and Gaza. In a private meeting with Carter, Begin urged that Resolution 242 be left out of the agreement and implied that there could be no territorial compromise regarding the West Bank. He could not go against the will of the Israeli people, he argued. Carter responded that most Israelis were willing to give up the Sinai settlements for peace and were willing to withdraw from "substantial portions" of the West Bank as well. In stating this position, Carter argued, he represented the Israeli people more accurately than Begin. The two men then chewed over and over the same points, and Carter accused Begin of being willing to forgo peace "just to keep a few illegal settlers on Egyptian land"—in a "heated . . . unpleasant" discussion.[144]

The next few days were marked by crisis and a sense among the Americans that the talks had reached an impasse. There was a feeling of "claustrophobia" and that time was "running out."[145] With the help of Barak and al-Baz, Carter and Vance hammered out the basis of an agreement on the Palestinian issue:

the mechanism for a transitional period and future negotiations. The basic problems—withdrawal and sovereignty—were left for the future.

On Sinai neither side would budge. Weizman told his fellow Israelis: "Evacuation of the [Sinai] settlements is necessary, if we want peace." Dayan refused to support him, perhaps wary of an open clash with Begin. And Begin angrily rejected the idea.[146] A crisis was clearly at hand. On September 15, after a meeting with an unrelenting Dayan that broke down over the settlements and air bases, Sadat announced that the Egyptians were leaving.[147] Sadat had always been wary of Dayan, perhaps seeing him as the embodiment of the Israel that had beaten Egypt's armies in Sinai in 1956 and 1967.[148] The meeting had apparently induced in Sadat a mixture of rage and despair. He felt trapped between the Israeli hammer and the American anvil—in Kamel's phrase—with Camp David itself exerting a prisonlike effect on his psyche. (Begin, too, at one point commented: "It is beginning to feel like a concentration camp."[149]) No doubt the constant pressure from within the Egyptian delegation also took its toll. That evening Sadat accused Kamel of regarding him, Sadat, as an "idiot," and peremptorily ordered all of his aides to leave his cabin. Kamel—a longtime personal friend—protested this treatment.[150]

The following day, arguing that Sadat had "capitulated unconditionally" to both Carter and Begin, Kamel announced his intention to resign.[151] He objected, in general terms, to the emergence of a separate Egyptian-Israeli peace, to Sadat's agreement to an exchange of ambassadors with Israel before the completion of the IDF pullout from Sinai, and to Israel's offer of "autonomy" for the Palestinians, which he, like Carter, regarded as nothing more than a gimmick.[152] On the morning of September 16, he made one last effort to dissuade Sadat from signing the agreements. Then, having failed, he resigned, as did two senior Foreign Ministry officials.[153]

The deep misgivings in the Egyptian ranks contributed to Sadat's surprise decision on September 15 to leave Camp David. A white-faced Vance reported this to a "shocked" Carter,[154] who put on a suit and tie and walked over to Sadat's cottage to explain the gravity of what was about to happen: Egypt would be blamed for the failure of the conference; American-Egyptian relations would be ruptured; the Soviet Union would return to the Middle East and Egypt; Sadat's enemies, who had opposed his trip to Jerusalem and the peace process, would rejoice and say they had been right all along. Carter added that failure at Camp David could result in the end of Sadat's presidency and would endanger their friendship. According to a report that he later denied, Carter also dangled before Sadat the bait of massive American aid.[155]

Sadat said he would stay, on condition that whatever concessions he made would be the last. Carter agreed. But Sadat still needed major Israeli concessions in order to sell a deal to his cabinet, army, and people. Carter understood that Begin, too, had to be given something in return for backing off from his previous "nonnegotiable" positions. It was time for conclusive tradeoffs. The rough lines were clear: Egypt would drop its demand that Israel commit itself explicitly and in advance to eventual withdrawal from the Palestinian territories in exchange for Israeli agreement to give up the northern Sinai settlements and air bases along with Sinai itself. Moreover, Egypt could throw into the pot full normalization of relations with Israel. Such a tradeoff, Carter realized, took account of the key Egyptian and Israeli "red lines"—complete Egyptian control of Sinai and open-ended Israeli control of the West Bank and Gaza. All three leaders understood that the alternative to a tradeoff was a continued impasse, a breakdown of the talks, public confrontation between Carter and Begin, damage to American-Egyptian relations, and, possibly, a new Middle East war.[156]

A key element in the tradeoff had fallen into place in talks on September 15 between Weizman, Vance, and Secretary of Defense Harold Brown. The Americans had approved the idea of granting Israel $3 billion in easy-term loans to construct two modern air bases in the Negev in place of those to be evacuated in Sinai. Also, both Weizman and Agriculture Minister Sharon, the latter calling Begin from Jerusalem, argued that if peace with Egypt depended on uprooting the settlements, then the price had to be paid.[157]

The following morning Dayan told Carter that Begin would undertake not to establish any new settlements in the territories. But that evening Begin began a meeting with Carter by shouting words like "ultimatum" and "political suicide" concerning the demand for the complete evacuation of the Sinai settlements. But gradually he backed down, eventually agreeing that the Knesset would decide within two weeks whether or not Israel should give up the settlements for peace. Begin refused to say how he himself would vote but said that the members of his party would be free to vote as they wished. The following day Weizman promised Carter to do his best to shepherd the agreement through the house.[158] "I believed this concession would be enough for Sadat. Breakthrough!" wrote Carter in his memoirs.[159]

Begin's change of position on the Sinai settlements was due to the relentless American pressure; to the dissent within the Israeli leadership, culminating in Weizman's blunt statement that it was either peace or the settlements, and in Sharon's telephone call; and to Begin's own realization that Sadat (and Carter) would not budge on this issue and the historic chance for peace must not be allowed to slip away. Thus, having promised the settlers' representatives hours before leaving for Camp David that he would sooner "pack his bags and return home" than uproot them, and despite his dramatic pledge to Brzezinski three days earlier, Begin capitulated.

To facilitate the signing of the "Framework" agreement concerning the Palestinians, many issues were left deliberately vague. Begin eventually agreed that the full text of UN Resolution 242 could be appended to the agreement, thus signifying—at least in American and Arab eyes—Israel's implicit acceptance of the provisions concerning its eventual withdrawal and the acquisition of territory by force. Begin had flatly refused to include either article in the text of the actual agreement. The issue of East Jerusalem was resolved by agreement on an exchange of letters, in which each country would simply restate its position. Begin reluctantly agreed to a reference to "the legitimate rights of the Palestinian people," a phrase he had hitherto strenuously rejected. According to Carter, Begin also agreed to sign a letter committing Israel to build no new settlements in the territories until the autonomy negotiations ended. Begin subsequently said he had only agreed to a three-month freeze during the expected duration of the negotiations.

The truth appears to be that Carter had requested an indefinite, open-ended suspension; that Begin had said he would think about it and had added that he would agree to three months, which possibly could be extended; and that the duration of the freeze had been linked to the prospective autonomy talks rather than to the bilateral Israeli-Egyptian peace negotiations.[160]

By September 17, the thirteenth day of the talks, "everyone was exhausted."[161] Carter informed Sadat of the breakthrough, and the Americans rewrote the draft "Framework" and peace accord for the last time.[162] But a number of major snags remained. When the Israelis were informed of the content of the prospective American letter on the status of Jerusalem—defined as occupied territory whose future must be determined in negotiations—Begin threatened to pack up and go home. The Americans backed down and agreed to refer to, but not quote from, their previous statements that had called East Jerusalem occupied territory, subject to the Geneva Convention of 1949.[163]

On the other hand, the content of Begin's two draft letters—on the Knesset vote to determine the fate of the Sinai settlements and on the freeze on West Bank–Gaza settlement—jolted Carter. Neither quite matched what he believed had been agreed upon.[164] But time was pressing. Carter objected to the West Bank settlements letter—but instructed his aides to go ahead and complete the polishing of the accords. Begin, a master of brinkmanship, gambled that Carter would proceed with the signing ceremony and that after it, neither Carter nor Sadat would be in a position to do anything about it, even if he referred only to a "three-month" freeze. Meanwhile Carter had to obtain Sadat's agreement to the final wording of the accords themselves—and Sadat "was far from enthusiastic. . . . There was no sense of victory or elation." By 5:30 the texts were finally ready, and Carter gave the green light for the signing ceremony.[165] Begin, whom Quandt later called "the most able negotiator at Camp David,"[166] telephoned Sadat and congratulated him on the agreement, and then came over to the Egyptian president's lodge to shake hands. It was the first time they had met in ten days.[167]

Just after 10:00 that night, September 17, 1978, Carter, Begin, and Sadat gathered in the East Room of the White House and signed the two documents. They had reached substantial agreement on the contours of an Israeli-Egyptian peace and on the mechanism for negotiating a resolution to the problem of the

West Bank and Gaza Strip, which would include some measure of self-rule for the Palestinian inhabitants during a protracted interim period. Though fatigued, they "were a happy and beaming trio."[168] As Carter put it, "[A]ll three of us were flushed with pride and good will toward one another because of our unexpected success."[169]

The agreements signed by Begin and Sadat and witnessed by Carter[170] were not full-fledged, detailed peace treaties. But they were to constitute the basis for the Israel-Egypt peace treaty that was signed half a year later and the Israel-PLO accords signed in Oslo, Cairo, and Washington a decade and a half later, in 1993–95. Their imprint can also be found in the Israel-Jordan peace treaty of 1994.

The first document, called simply the "Framework," was straightforward and simple: Israel would completely evacuate Sinai in exchange for diplomatic recognition by Egypt, peace, and the establishment of normal relations; during the following three months, the two sides would negotiate a bilateral peace treaty, based on "all of the principles of UN Resolution 242." The terms of the treaty were to be implemented within two to three years of the signing. All Israeli forces were to be withdrawn from Sinai. Israeli shipping was to enjoy unimpeded passage through the Suez Canal, the Gulf of Suez, the Straits of Tiran, and the Gulf of Aqaba, and Israeli aircraft were to have "freedom of . . . overflight" over the straits and the Gulf of Aqaba. Most of Sinai was to be effectively demilitarized, with Egypt allowed a force of up to one division to a depth of thirty-three miles from the Suez Canal and the Gulf of Suez. UN forces and Egyptian policemen were to patrol and control the area adjacent to and west of the old Egypt-Palestine frontier, to a depth of thirteen to twenty-five miles. To a depth of two miles east of the frontier, Israeli military forces were to be limited to four infantry battalions. UN forces were to be stationed in the Rafa Approaches and at Sharm ash-Sheikh. The Framework provided for the establishment of early warning stations—though their number and location were not stated.

The Israeli evacuation was to be carried out in two stages, with the first, "interim" withdrawal, to a line running from just east of Al-'Arīsh to Ras Muhammad, just south of Sharm ash-Sheikh, between three and nine months after the signing of the peace treaty. Following this, "normal relations" were to be established between the two countries, with "full recognition, including diplomatic, economic and cultural relations; [and] termination of economic boycotts and barriers." The IDF was then to withdraw from the remainder of Sinai.

The second document, the "Framework for Peace," declared that UN Resolutions 242 and 338 must serve as the basis for a peaceful settlement of the conflict between Israel and its neighbors and that "the sovereignty, territorial integrity and political independence of every state in the area and their right to live in peace within secure and recognized boundaries" must be assured in such a settlement. It suggested that the peace treaties would include provisions for "demilitarized zones, limited armaments areas, early warning stations, the presence of international forces," and "agreed measures for monitoring" military movements, which would enhance security. It also stipulated that these treaties should provide for the establishment of "relationships normal to states at peace with one another . . . [including] full recognition . . . and abolishing economic boycotts." The United States was invited to participate in the talks on the "modalities of the implementation" of all agreements reached, and the UN Security Council was requested to "underwrite" the prospective peace treaties and to guarantee the implementation of their provisions.

Most of the "Framework for Peace" was devoted to negotiations on the Palestinian problem. These were to be undertaken by representatives of Israel, Egypt, Jordan, and "the Palestinian people" and were to take place in three stages: (a) "In order to ensure a peaceful and orderly transfer of authority" in the West Bank and Gaza, there should be "transitional arrangements" for a period of up to five years. The Arab inhabitants should receive "full autonomy," while Israel should withdraw its military government and civil administration, which would be replaced by an elected, Arab "self-governing authority." (b) Egypt, Israel, and Jordan would negotiate the "modalities" for establishing the self-governing authority and its "powers and responsibilities," though the Egyptian and Jordanian delegations "may include Palestinians from the West Bank and Gaza" and other "mutually agreed" Palestinian representatives. Israeli troops would withdraw to "specified security locations" and a "strong local police force," composed of inhabitants of the West Bank and Gaza, would be established. (c) The five-year transitional period was to begin with the establishment of the self-governing authority or "administrative council." (Begin had insisted on the use of the term "administrative council" rather than "legislative council" or "legislature"—as a legislative body could enact laws, giving it de facto sovereignty in its territory.) No later than three years after the start of this transitional period negotiations were to begin (between representatives of Israel, Egypt, and Jordan and those elected in the West Bank and Gaza) "to determine the final status of the West Bank and Gaza" and the relationship between these areas and their neighbors (that is, Egypt, Jordan, and Israel) and to conclude a peace treaty between Israel and Jordan. The "final status" negotiations were to be concluded by the end of the five-year transitional period and were to be based on "all the provisions and principles" of Resolution 242. The negotiations would determine boundaries and security arrangements, and would "recognize the legitimate rights of the Palestinian people and their just requirements. In this way the Palestinians will participate in the determination of their own future." This phrase was included at Carter's and Sadat's insistence, to Begin's discomfort, but fell short of explicit reference to Palestinian "self-determination" and "statehood," as Sadat had initially demanded.

The "Framework for Peace" also made provision for some form of return of "persons displaced from the West Bank and Gaza in 1967," to be regulated by a committee that would include Israeli representatives. How many were to be allowed back was left unclear. Even more vaguely, the agreement stipulated that there was also to be a "resolution of the [1948] refugee problem"— though how exactly, and by whom and in what form, was not stated.

While the Israeli-Egyptian "Framework" was clear in its main points, the "Framework for Peace" left vast areas of uncertainty. What was to be the role of the PLO, the Palestinian people's representative body, both in the negotiations and in the implementation of each of the stages agreed upon? What was to be the extent of withdrawal of the IDF, and where was it to withdraw to? Who would join the large Palestinian police force, and who was to determine its constitution, and who, in effect, would control it? Who would determine the fate of the West Bank and Gaza's land and water, crucial elements that concerned present and future Israeli settlements and the Israeli and Palestinian economies? What was to be the fate of the Israeli settlers and settlements? None of these issues was addressed.

The two agreements were accompanied by a series of letters, from Begin to Carter, Carter to Begin, Secretary of Defense Brown to Defense Minister Weizman, Sadat to Carter, and Carter to Sadat. Begin promised to submit the issue of the evacuation of the Sinai settlements to a Knesset vote within two weeks of his return to Israel. Sadat stated that if Israel decided against the withdrawal of the settlements, the whole "Framework" agreement would be rendered "void and invalid"; and he asserted Arab sovereignty over East Jerusalem though the city, in terms of "essential functions," should remain "undivided." Begin declared that Jerusalem should remain "one city, indivisible, the Capital of the State of Israel." Brown promised United States–Israeli consultations "on the scope and costs of the two new airbases" to be constructed in the Negev to replace those Israel would relinquish in Sinai, and stated that "the President is prepared to seek the necessary Congressional approvals" for financial assistance toward their construction.[171]

For Carter, their chief engineer, the Camp David accords represented a personal triumph. All who attended agreed subsequently that without his authority, mastery of detail, ready grasp of the issues, empathy, persuasive charm, and occasionally firmness, no agreement would have been possible.

In the West, public opinion and governments by and large welcomed the agreements, often enthusiastically. The USSR was strongly critical, saying that "the Israelis had won everything and the Arabs . . . nothing," and urged Carter to abandon the Camp David track (which had excluded them).[172] In the Middle East, the responses were vociferous and mixed. Against a backdrop of loud opposition by the rejectionist states, the moderate kings—Hussein, Hassan, and Khāled—preferred to sit on the fence and imply that the accords, in effect, were a separate Egyptian-Israeli peace, concluded at the expense of the Palestinians.[173]

In Egypt, the response was also mixed. For almost thirty years the country had been at war with Israel. Tens of thousands of people had died or suffered injury; many more had suffered materially, directly and indirectly, from the state of belligerency. Until the 1970s all mention of possible peace with Israel had been taboo, at least in public. But the relative successes in the 1973 war and the negotiations and agreements with Israel in its wake had begun to dent the facade. Moreover, Sadat's winning smile notwithstanding, Egypt was a dictatorship: Up to a point, most of the media and public could be manipulated and "persuaded" to toe the official line. But there was also popular enthusiasm. Upon his arrival home, Sadat was greeted by vast cheering crowds, only in part mobilized by the state and the ruling party apparatus. Many no doubt viewed Camp David as a genuine achievement for Egypt and greeted the dawn of peace with relief. After all, it seemed to spell an end to war, to long stints in the army and recurrent bloodletting, and, possibly, to the grinding poverty that was the pervasive reality of their lives.

The press, too, was by and large favorable; some newspapers were even effusive. Most approved of the accords. No longer would the people have to fight and shed their blood, as they had done for three decades, for the Palestinians; now at last the nation could look to its own welfare, needs, and interests. This was a common refrain.

But there were loci of dissent as well, on left and right. Communist Party and Muslim Brotherhood publications uniformly condemned the agreements as a betrayal. So did hard-line Nasserists, like Heikal, Nasser's old mouthpiece and former editor of *al-Ahram*. In the universities, posters went up. In the mosques, preachers delivered sermons against the accords, and street vendors sold cassette tapes vilifying both the peace and Sadat himself.[174]

Moreover, much of Egyptian officialdom was unhappy with the accords. As described, successive foreign ministers and various aides had resigned in the course of the negotiations; other officials, including the draftsman of the treaty, Osama al-Baz, had boycotted the signing ceremony at the White House. Sadat, it was muttered, had "sold out" the Palestinians. Perhaps he had done this to regain Sinai, but even the restoration of the peninsula to Egypt was marred by the prospective demilitarization of most of it and the stationing of international forces and warning stations on Egyptian soil (but not, reciprocally, on the Israeli side of the border). Sinai was not returning to full Egyptian sovereignty.

Defense Minister Gamasy had not attended Camp David and had not been consulted about the accords. Subsequently he apparently supported the gist of what had been agreed,[175] but he also had misgivings. Whether he expressed them, and if so to whom, is unclear. What is certain is that on October 3 Sadat summoned Gamasy to his villa on the Nile and informed him of his impending dismissal. Some sources have suggested that Sadat's action stemmed not from Gamasy's concerns about Camp David but from his rivalry with Vice President Mubarak.[176] In his memoirs Gamasy bluntly charged that the accord "removed Egypt from the arena of the Arab-Israeli conflict, thereby weakening the Arab position both politically and militarily. It put Israel in a stronger strategic position, gave it freedom of action to swallow up the rest of Palestine in the short term, and to expand at the expense of its Arab neighbors in the future." And while Egypt recovered all of Sinai, it was subjected to serious restrictions on its sovereignty there.[177]

The Palestinians, almost to a man, saw the accords much as they had viewed Sadat's visit to Jerusalem, as heralding a sellout of their interests. "Autonomy" was seen as a cover for continued Israeli occupation of the West Bank and Gaza, spelling the demise of their hopes for statehood. In the territories, the PLO-affiliated National Guidance Committee fulminated against Sadat. The PLO Executive Committee called on the population of the occupied territories to launch a general, one-day protest strike on September 20. Camp David was designated an anti-Palestinian "conspiracy," which would be followed by "just retribution."[178]

The ninth Arab Summit Meeting held in Baghdad in the first week of November 1978—attended also by Jordanian and Saudi representatives—decided on a series of sanctions that would automatically be imposed on Egypt should it go ahead and conclude a bilateral peace treaty, as prefigured in the Camp David accords. Egypt would be expelled from the Arab League, the league's headquarters would be removed from Cairo, and Egyptian bodies maintaining relations with Israel would be boycotted. The summit also set up a $3.5 billion fund to finance continued "resistance" to Israel.[179]

An overwhelming majority of Israelis favored the agreements, though Dayan complained that the delegation, on arriving home, received "a cold reception."[180] In reality it was only a small right-wing minority—mainly from within Begin's Likud and parties to its right—that opposed the accords, though the head of the Labor opposition, Shimon Peres, accused Begin of mishandling the negotiations. Better terms could have been extracted, he argued.

The two-day Knesset debate ended on September 27, when 84 of the 120 members voted to approve the agreements and only 19 voted against (with 17 abstaining). Of the 45 Likud members, 29 voted aye, 7 nay, and 9 abstained; of the Labor Alignment's 31, 24 voted aye, 4 nay, and 3 abstained. By Begin's design the members were forced to vote to accept or reject the accords in toto; they were not allowed to vote separately on the provisions concerning the Sinai settlements (as some had initially demanded). The vote accurately reflected the popular mood. One opinion poll, conducted just before the vote, found that 75 percent were satisfied with the outcome of Camp David, and 78 percent supported the government's concessions.[181]

In the Likud there were deep doubts about the agreements, even among those who had voted aye. Many were unhappy with the autonomy provisions, fearing that they would lead to the establishment of a Palestinian state. (A decade and a half later, after the signing of the PLO-Israeli Oslo Accords, many Palestinians were to bemoan the failure to accept the autonomy offered at Camp David.) Outside the Knesset there was a spate of demonstrations by Gush Emunim members, Greater Land of Israel activists, and Sinai settlers. But they found little support among the general public. Some of the deepest misgivings were on the Left (especially from Labor's Ahdut Ha'Avodah wing). After all, it had been a Labor-led government that had established the Rafa Approaches settlements. This was the first time the Zionist movement had agreed to uproot a bloc of settlements. And there were serious doubts in the IDF as well. The generals viewed the Jordan River, reached in June 1967, as Israel's natural strategic frontier, but the accords seemed to signal possible Israeli withdrawal from all or parts of the West Bank, possibly endangering the Jordan line. Moreover, the evacuation of the Sinai Peninsula involved vast logistical problems and the loss of territorial depth, bases, training areas (especially for aircraft), intelligence and early warning stations, and warning time. Should the agreement collapse and Israel and Egypt revert to a state of belligerency, the front line would again be on Israel's doorstep, less than fifty miles from Tel Aviv and Beersheba.

THE ISRAEL-EGYPT PEACE TREATY, 1979

"Camp David represented a possibility of peace, but did not guarantee its achievement," wrote Quandt.[182] The two short framework accords had to be translated into detailed agreements. Not until March 26, 1979, did Israel and Egypt sign their peace treaty, and this only after a string of crises.

Back in the real world after the cloistered venue of Camp David, Sadat came under strong and immediate pressure from fellow Arab leaders and from internal critics, including the Egyptian left and the fundamentalists. He was accused of having abandoned the other Arab states to face Israel alone, and of having sold out the Palestinians. He was forced to harden his positions: During the post–Camp David months he was to insist—contrary to what had been agreed upon—on clear linkage between implementation of the Israeli-

Egyptian accord and progress on the Palestinian issue. Even though he was wont to call his fellow leaders "dwarfs and pygmies," he felt compelled to justify what he had done and to prove that he had not betrayed the Palestinians.

In Israel, opposition to the Camp David agreements, seen in perspective, never amounted to much. Nevertheless, Begin inclined in public to exaggerate and highlight his domestic difficulties in order to fend off American and Arab demands for further concessions. Begin's real problems lay not in selling Camp David to his electorate but in soothing his own conscience: He had reneged on his promise not to uproot Israeli settlements in Sinai and had thus provided a precedent for the future eradication of those in the West Bank, Gaza, and the Golan Heights; he had abandoned important military positions in eastern Sinai; and he had provided a possible opening via autonomy for the eventual emergence in the West Bank and Gaza of a Palestinian state. He had also committed himself to at least a temporary suspension of settlement in the territories.

Begin spent the next months trying to salvage some of what he had conceded to Sadat and Carter. Above all, he resisted any clear, formal linkage between the Israeli-Egyptian and the Israeli-Palestinian tracks. Israel, as Carter correctly perceived, still wanted "a separate peace with Egypt; they want to keep the West Bank and Gaza permanently."[183]

Both Begin and Sadat were keenly aware of the limited time frame imposed by the looming U.S. presidential elections of November 1980. From some point in 1979 Carter would be otherwise engaged and increasingly unable to apply any pressure on Israel, for fear of alienating the financially and electorally powerful American Jewish community. Thus Begin had a distinct interest in pushing the real decision making in the negotiations as far forward into 1979 as possible.[184]

Another external influence was the revolutionary rumblings in Iran, soon to topple the shah's regime. In both Washington and Cairo it was understood that a fundamentalist victory would further impair Sadat's ability to make a deal with "the Little Satan" under the tutelage of "the Great Satan"—as the Iranian leader Ayatollah Khomeini called Israel and the United States. Sadat had one further fear: that the negotiations would drag out until the U.S. election, when Carter might be succeeded by someone less "even-handed."[185] An Israeli-Egyptian treaty therefore had to be achieved quickly.

The Americans tried unsuccessfully to get Begin to undertake to halt the establishment of new settlements in the territories for the duration of the autonomy talks, in place of his letter of September 18, 1978, which had promised only a three-month suspension. Secretary of State Vance tried, also unsuccessfully, to persuade the kings of Jordan and Saudi Arabia to endorse Camp David and, in the case of Hussein, to actively join the peace process. Most important, the State Department, with help from other branches of the government, drew up a draft for a full-blown Israeli-Egyptian peace treaty.

Despite the agreements, Camp David had done little to bolster mutual confidence. The Egyptians feared that Israel wanted a separate peace or none at all; the Israelis, that the Egyptians only wanted to get Sinai back and then tear up the treaty. From the start Israel sought normalization of relations, including the exchange of ambassadors, as soon as possible after completion of the first stage of the withdrawal from Sinai. Such measures, it was felt, would make it that much more difficult to renege on the treaty. Egypt, for its part, sought to link the exchange of ambassadors to the start of Palestinian autonomy, and an explicit Israeli commitment in the Israeli-Egyptian treaty to a timetable for negotiating and implementing autonomy.

Another vital issue was "priority of obligations": Israel wanted explicit agreement that the treaty would override any Egyptian obligation to come to the aid of another Arab country, should a new war erupt between Israel and that country. Sadat found it extremely difficult to make such a commitment. In effect, he was being asked to put Israel's interests before those of his country's traditional allies, further alienating Egypt from the Arab world.[186]

From October 1978 to March 1979, Sadat, Begin, and Carter were less personally involved in the negotiations. Carter appointed Vance to head the American team. Israel was represented by Dayan and Weizman, assisted by Barak and Foreign Ministry legal adviser Meir Rosenne; Begin gave them very little independence. The Egyptian team consisted of the new foreign minister, Hassan Kamal 'Ali, Butros Ghali, and Osama al-Baz. The delegations convened in Washington, on October 12, 1978. After five fruitless days Carter stepped in and hammered out a draft treaty, agreed upon by both sides on October 22.

Despite some unresolved issues on October 26 Begin pushed this draft through his cabinet "in principle."[187] But, to appease the hard-liners (and, perhaps, his own conscience), he also agreed to an expansion of the existing settlements in the West Bank. (The agreed three-month suspension had covered the establishment of new settlements, not the expansion of existing ones.)[188] Washington believed, probably correctly, that this move by Begin was in part designed to prevent the Palestinians and Jordan from joining the peace process—facilitating continued Israeli retention of the territories.[189]

Carter was furious. He wrote Begin on October 26: "At a time when we are trying to organize the negotiations dealing with the West Bank and Gaza, no step by the Israeli Government could be more damaging. I have to tell you with gravest concern and regret that taking this step at this time will have the most serious consequences for our relationship." Begin and Sadat were awarded the Nobel Peace Prize the following day.[190]

The negotiations were renewed at the end of October. The main problem remained the West Bank and Gaza. Dayan and Weizman had left for Washington under a domestic cloud: Their fellow ministers suspected that, in their eagerness to conclude a treaty, the two ex-generals were ready to sacrifice essential Israeli interests. Moreover, Dayan and Weizman were somewhat suspicious of each other.[191] Israel sought to focus the negotiations on the modalities of the prospective autonomy elections. But the Egyptians countered that unless the powers and responsibilities of the council-to-be were first agreed, the elections would be meaningless. Dayan accurately predicted that discussion of the powers and responsibilities of the autonomous authority would prove interminable and inconclusive. Meanwhile, he told the Americans, Israel intended to perpetuate the military government and to set up a string of new settlements ("18 to 20") in the Jordan Valley, on the eastern edge of the West Bank. Washington felt that Begin was trying to dilute the commitments he had made at Camp David.[192]

Sadat's position became increasingly difficult. On the one hand, Israel was making no concessions on the Palestinian front—and on the other, on November 5 the Arab Summit Meeting in Baghdad roundly condemned the Camp David accords and the impending peace treaty. In public Sadat brushed this off as the "hissing of snakes."[193] But the criticism had an impact. Sadat demanded the start of self-government, at least in Gaza, during the first stage of the IDF withdrawal from Sinai, and agreement on a target date for the West Bank–Gaza elections. Moreover, he demanded special status—including the stationing of Egyptian liaison officers—in the Gaza Strip during the transitional autonomy period. This stance was backed by a Saudi emissary, who arrived in Washington in November and suggested that Riyadh would support Camp David if there was effective "linkage" and if the Palestinians were assured of some concrete gains.

A similar hardening took place on the Israeli side. When Weizman arrived on November 5 to report to the cabinet, even before he opened his mouth Education Minister Zevulun Hammer piped up: "Well, what did you sell out on today?"[194] Begin rejected the idea of a target date for autonomy elections (even though Dayan had earlier implied a readiness to agree to a date); rejected any linkage between the elections and the withdrawal from Sinai; and refused to bring forward the completion of the first-stage withdrawal, as Dayan had proposed. But, unlike Egypt, Israel accepted the American draft treaty in toto, demurring only at the American-Egyptian insistence on a target date for the elections. Israel still sought American commitment on financing the withdrawal (Israeli estimates said it would cost $3.8 billion) and an Egyptian commitment on the supply of oil, to make up for the oil lost to Israel by its withdrawal from the Sinai fields. Israel's fears on this latter score were now compounded by the fundamentalist unrest in Iran, its other main source of fuel. Egypt was reluctant to commit itself to supplying Israel with oil.[195]

Right-wing opposition to Begin increased appreciably. On November 19 he and Weizman were pelted with eggs and tomatoes by Gush Emunim demonstrators;[196] some called Begin a "traitor." He may have been shaken, but he remained undeterred. As he told a meeting of the Central Committee of the Herut Party (the main component of the Likud bloc) that day:

> All the years our rivals lied, claiming that I am a man of war. . . . All the time I argued that the Herut Party is the peace party in Israel, and therefore my first duty is to make this effort, to put an end to the state of war. . . . There is much pain in this. . . . But if there is a serious attempt to reach peace, we should make painful decisions.

Begin won an overwhelming Central Committee endorsement, 306 votes to 51. He now had a clear party mandate to continue negotiating.[197]

By the end of November, Sadat was in a foul mood—and, in messages to Begin and Carter, he reneged on a series of major commitments. He no longer agreed to send his ambassador to Tel Aviv within a month of the completion of the Israeli first-stage withdrawal or to permanent limitations on Egypt's military forces in Sinai; he insisted on the presence of Egyptian liaison officers in the Gaza Strip during the autonomy period; and he rejected outright the "priority of obligations" clause.[198] The Israeli cabinet "firmly but politely" rejected his demands.[199]

To break the deadlock Vance flew to the Middle East. At their meetings on December 10–12 Sadat was conciliatory, agreeing to a number of accompanying letters, American and Egyptian, that would accommodate Egyptian views on various issues. But ambassadors could only be exchanged, he said, after the establishment of West Bank–Gaza autonomy. Begin greeted Vance and the new Egyptian positions, which the United States now endorsed, with anger. He felt that Israel was now facing that old bugbear, "American-Egyptian collusion." As Vance headed home the Israeli cabinet declared: "The Government of Israel rejects the attitude and the interpretation of the United States Government with regard to the Egyptian proposals." The impasse continued. Once again, Begin and Sadat were engaged in a "test of wills . . . [with] the United States in the middle. . . . Each side would wait to see who would flinch first."[200] But Begin had the clear advantage: He was under no deadline— whereas Carter was nearing Election Day and Sadat remained under continuing Arab pressure, with nothing to show the Egyptians or the Palestinians for his iconoclastic trip to Jerusalem and his brave handshake with Begin in the White House.

By the end of 1978 the prospects for peace in the Middle East looked "dim."[201] But the impasse was broken by events in Iran rather than Jerusalem, Cairo, or Washington. The revolution that toppled Shah Reza Pahlavi—he fled his kingdom on January 16, 1979—threatened America's overall position in the region and forced Carter to try to bring the Egyptian-Israeli peace process to a swift, successful conclusion.[202] It persuaded Sadat that if peace was not achieved quickly, the fundamentalist tide might overwhelm the Middle East and torpedo the peace process, and Egypt would lose the chance to retrieve the Sinai Peninsula in the foreseeable future. At the same time, the revolution underlined Egypt's need to be able to show that it was acting in the Palestinian interest and not simply cutting a separate deal with Israel.

But Carter read the cards right. By the start of 1979 he had reached the conclusion that Sadat really "did not give a damn about the West Bank"[203] and could be persuaded to drop his insistence on "linkage" far more easily than Begin could be persuaded to withdraw from that territory. And this dovetailed with Carter's own domestic political reasons not to rekindle the confrontation with Israel. The Americans would ease off on the Palestinian problem.

Following an unsuccessful meeting of Dayan, Vance, and Mustafa Khalil, Egypt's new prime minister, at Camp David on February 20-22, Carter invited Begin for what he saw as a conclusive round of talks, which began on March 2. The prime minister arrived without Dayan and Weizman—a bad sign, from Carter's perspective. At their first meeting, Begin let loose with all his ammunition: Israel was America's only reliable ally in the Middle East and stood in the path of a Soviet takeover of Saudi Arabia; Article 6 ("priority of obligations") must be left intact, otherwise Sadat or a successor would tear up the treaty the moment any of Egypt's Arab allies engaged in conflict with Israel; and Israel was "under no obligation to discuss the West Bank unless Jordan joined the negotiations," and would not agree to a target date for autonomy elections. Last, Egypt must guarantee Israel a substantial supply of Sinai oil.[204] He even added, according to Carter's diary, "that Sadat still wants to destroy Israel." Carter, much taken aback, was "convinced [that] the peace effort was at an end."[205] "Frustrated [by] Begin's insistence on debating every issue at length and angry with his skepticism about Sadat's sincerity," Carter argued that Sadat had "proved he wanted peace." On the other hand, Begin's continuous bickering about the language of the treaty and its addenda were, in Vance's phrase, "inconsequential and an exercise in semantics."[206]

But Carter, so close to the finish line, relented a little—on the wording of Article 6, on oil supplies, and on the "target date"—and Begin "realized that the moment had come to clinch the bilateral deal." Carter promptly sent Brzezinski to Cairo to persuade Sadat that he had better give in. Somewhat to Brzezinski's surprise, Sadat agreed to the revised terms and invited Carter to come to the Middle East to wrap up the treaty. Carter landed in Cairo on March 7, sure of impending success.[207] Meanwhile, Begin informed his ministers of the revised provisions and recommended that the cabinet approve them.[208] Carter spent three days in Egypt, basking in a popularity that eluded him back home, and dispensing explicit and implicit promises of post-treaty largesse. He expected the treaty to be signed in a day or two, himself affixing his signature as witness.

On March 10 Carter flew to Israel—and immediately hit snags. Begin made it clear that there would be no signing during Carter's trip; the cabinet and then the Knesset, he said, would have to debate the issues and decide. This would take at least two weeks. Carter, furious, recorded in his diary: "I asked him if he actually wanted a peace treaty, because my impression was that everything he could do to obstruct it, he did with apparent relish. He came right up and looked into my eyes about a foot away and said . . . that he wanted peace as much as anything in the world."[209]

Begin refused either to change anything in Article 6, to consider instituting autonomy first in Gaza, or to countenance Egyptian "liaison officers" moving into the Strip. It was clear to Carter that Begin was "obsessed with keeping all the occupied territory except the Sinai."[210] Carter, after a "moving" visit to Yad Vashem, produced a string of concessions: The United States would guarantee Israel's oil supplies; Egypt, he was sure, would agree to exchange ambassadors after the first-stage withdrawal from Sinai; and the United States would sign a memorandum of understanding with Israel on what it would do if Egypt violated the treaty. But he wanted the treaty signed that day.

"I can't leave Israel with nothing in hand, you will have to sign," Carter declared at a March 11 meeting of the American delegation with the full Israeli cabinet.[211] Carter had been happy at the prospect of this session, hoping to bypass Begin's objections and reach the ministers directly. The ministers were taken aback: This sounded like a *diktat*. Begin promptly rejoined: "Mr. President, you will forgive us, but surely you know that we will sign only what we want to sign and we will not sign anything that we do not wish to sign!"[212] Trying Carter's patience further, Ariel Sharon declared that "Jordan is Palestine" and said that within twenty years there would be one million Jews in the West Bank, which was an inseparable part of Israel.[213]

For the rest of the day the two delegations "por[ed] over a dictionary and a thesaurus," trying to solve the problem raised by the use of the words "derogate" and "contravene" in Article 6. The matter was eventually resolved.[214] But Israel refused to concede on an Egyptian presence in Gaza and demanded Egypt's explicit commitment to sell Israel oil, as well as a concession on the exchange of ambassadors. Later that day Carter and Begin addressed the Knesset. Begin was continuously heckled by opponents of the treaty—a display he relished as proof of both Israeli democratic norms and the extent of the opposition he was facing.

A last negotiating session was held the following day (March 12), with the Israelis as unconciliatory as ever. There could be no Egyptian presence in Gaza, and Israel must be guaranteed 2.5 million tons of Egyptian oil annually. It was clear that no treaty was to be signed that day or the next. "A bitterly disappointed" Carter prepared to leave for the United States the following morning.[215]

But the dissenters in Begin's cabinet began to protest loudly. Weizman apparently threatened to resign, and Dayan asked to see Vance. On March 13 a compromise was hammered out—an Israeli concession on oil in exchange for an American-Egyptian retreat over Gaza and the early exchange of ambassadors—and Carter flew off to Cairo to inform Sadat of his success. On March 20–21, after a long and noisy debate, the Knesset voted 95 to 18 in favor of the treaty. Earlier the cabinet had approved it, with only two ministers dissenting, one of them Sharon.[216]

Begin and Sadat flew to Washington, and at 2:00 P.M., on March 26, 1979, signed the treaty and its three annexes in a huge tent on the White House lawn, Carter bearing witness. Again there was the much-photographed triple handshake. This time, wrote Brzezinski,

> . . . not only was there joy but a sense of real reconciliation. . . . Weizman had his son with him. . . . Sadat made some reference to the Palestinians. . . . [But] much to our joint surprise Begin's response was peaceful, warm, cordial. . . . I was amazed and gratified. Peace can be contagious. There was electricity in the air, a sense of joy, people mixing, shaking hands, patting [each other] on the back.[217]

THE TREATY

The "Preamble" of the "Treaty of Peace Between the Arab Republic of Egypt and the State of Israel" alluded to "the urgent necessity of the establishment of a just, comprehensive and lasting peace . . . in accordance with resolutions 242 and 338" and spoke of the treaty as "an important step" on the road to this peace. The other Arab states were invited to join the process on the basis of the Camp David "Framework for Peace."

The treaty provided for withdrawal of all Israeli armed forces and civilians from Sinai and full Egyptian sovereignty there. The old Palestine-Egypt frontier was recognized as the permanent boundary "without prejudice to . . . the status of the Gaza Strip." A "normal relationship" was to be established, with "full recognition, diplomatic, economic and cultural relations, termination of economic boycotts and discriminatory barriers to the free movement of people and goods." Israeli ships were to be allowed through the Suez Canal, and navigation and overflight would be allowed all parties, "unimpeded and unsuspendable," through the Straits of Tiran and in the Gulf of Aqaba.

Article 6 stated: "The Parties undertake to fulfill in good faith their obligations under this Treaty, without regard to action or inaction of any other party and independently of any instrument external to this Treaty." If a conflict arose "between the obligations of the Parties under the present Treaty and any of their other obligations, the obligations under this Treaty will be binding and implemented."

The treaty established limited-forces zones and called for the continued stationing of UN personnel in Sinai. Annex I provided for the completion of the Israeli withdrawal within three years of the exchange of instruments of ratification, to be accomplished in two phases. Within nine months Israel was to withdraw to a line east of Al-'Arīsh–Ras Muhammad, and within three years, to the international frontier. Egyptian forces were to be limited in western Sinai ("Zone A") to one mechanized division, with no more than 230 tanks, seven artillery battalions, and seven antiaircraft battalions; in central Sinai ("Zone B") to four border guard battalions; and in eastern Sinai ("Zone C") to civil police forces, with light weapons. In "Zone D," an area about three miles deep running the length of the Israeli side of the international frontier, Israeli forces were to be limited to four infantry battalions. Egypt was not allowed to station combat aircraft anywhere in Sinai, though it was allowed to overfly "Zone A"; Israel was not to have combat aircaft in "Zone D" but was allowed to overfly it. The Egyptians were allowed unarmed helicopters and unarmed transport aircraft in "Zone B" and police helicopters in "Zone C." The UN Force was to be stationed in and patrol "Zone C" and along the international frontier, and UN observers were to patrol "Zone D" to verify compliance with the treaty's provisions.

The two sides agreed in Annex III to establish diplomatic relations and to exchange ambassadors "upon completion of the interim [first-phase] withdrawal." The Egyptian economic boycott was to be lifted and economic relations to be established. In clarificatory letters the two sides committed themselves "to proceed with the implementation" of the provisions in the Camp David accords relating to the West Bank and Gaza (Sadat to Carter and Begin to Carter, March 26, 1979). Autonomy negotiations on the modalities of the election of the self-governing authority and its powers and responsibilities would begin within one month of the exchange of instruments of ratification, with Jordan invited to attend. Palestinians would be included in the Jordanian and Egyptian delegations, and the negotiations were to be concluded "at the earliest possible date," the goal being within one year. The five-year interim "autonomy" period would begin once the self-governing authority had been established.

In a letter to Begin (March 26, 1979), Carter committed himself to ensuring the establishment of an "alternative multinational force" should the Security Council balk at establishing a UN force to patrol eastern Sinai—and, indeed, it was a non-UN force, the Multinational Force and Observers (MFO), mostly Americans, that was eventually deployed there, where it remains to this day. In a letter of the same date, Sadat informed Carter that within one month of the completion of the interim withdrawal, he would "send a resident ambassador to Israel and will receive a resident Israeli ambassador in Egypt."[218] Secretary of

Defense Brown, in letters to his Israeli and Egyptian counterparts, promised Israel $3 billion ($800 million of it in grants, the rest as a loan) to cover the construction of two airfields in the Negev, and Egypt $1.5 billion in aid.[219]

Last, Israel and the United States signed a "Memorandum of Agreement," outlining steps the United States would "consider" should Egypt violate the treaty provisions, including "strengthening [its] presence in the area, the providing of emergency supplies to Israel, and the exercise of maritime rights in order to put an end to the violation." In a separate memorandum, also dated March 26, 1979, the United States guaranteed Israel's oil supplies for fifteen years (though Sadat had promised he would sell Sinai oil to Israel at market prices).[220]

All three sides were satisfied, and the treaty has held sway over Israeli-Egyptian relations ever since. Sadat had won back all of Sinai and had freed Egypt from the economic and military burden entailed by its conflict with Israel; Carter had registered a major, historic foreign policy achievement, one that substantially reduced the danger of future East-West confrontation; and Begin had won peace with Egypt and a far less dangerous Middle East, for it was doubtful whether the remaining Arab states could contemplate war against Israel without Egypt.

Begin was probably the most satisfied. He had successfully warded off all efforts to pin him down on the Palestinian problem; and he had avoided a commitment to withdraw from any part of the West Bank and Gaza. Sadat (and Carter) had gained nothing tangible for the Palestinians and Sadat ended up with a thinly veiled separate peace, something he had always tried to avoid. The Arab states reacted accordingly, by implementing the decisions taken at the Baghdad summit. All save Oman and Sudan severed relations with Cairo; the headquarters of the Arab League were moved to Tunis, and Egypt's membership in the League was suspended; the export to Egypt of oil and its derivatives was suspended; and all grants and loans to Egypt were stopped.[221]

Sadat had gambled that as his country was the natural center of the Arab world, the others would have to patch up their differences with Egypt and eventually invite it back into the League, and even follow it into the peace process. He was right: By 1989 all the Arab states had resumed diplomatic relations with Cairo, and the League headquarters had returned to Egypt—and by the early 1990s the PLO, Syria, and Jordan were engaged in the peace process, while several other League members had established various levels of formal relations with Israel.

IMPLEMENTATION

The IDF withdrew from successive chunks of western and central Sinai on May 25, 1979, and completed the interim (first-stage) withdrawal to the Al-'Arīsh–Ras Muhammad line on January 25, 1980. The second and final stage, back to the international frontier, was completed on April 25, 1982.

The settlers' physical opposition began in May 1979, when Israel had to evacuate the vegetable garden of Neot Sinai, near Al-'Arīsh. The settlers, backed by Gush Emunim supporters from the West Bank—who regarded this uprooting as an ominous precedent—resisted. The government was reluctant to use force, and the settlers were pacified by promises or hints of increased financial compensation.[222]

Meanwhile, normalization of relations proceeded apace. In June and July, Egyptian tourists and businessmen arrived in Israel for the first time. During the summer and autumn, agreements were reached on the reciprocal granting of visas and on the sale of two million tons of Egyptian oil annually to Israel. Israel evacuated the St. Catherine's area of Sinai on November 15, two months ahead of schedule.

Begin and Weizman both visited Egypt in April 1979 and reached a variety of tentative agreements. On April 29, the first Israeli cargo vessel traversed the Suez Canal; a naval flotilla passed through on May 29. On May 25, on schedule, Al-'Arīsh was handed over to Egyptian control. Two days later Sadat and Begin met there and flew on to Beersheba, inaugurating an Israel-Egypt civil air corridor. At the reception in Beersheba, Israeli president Yitzhak Navon declared: "We have now handed over to you El 'Arish." Sadat responded: "I can't agree that anyone will say: 'We handed El 'Arish over to you.' . . . We retrieved it in bitter fighting and with precious blood."[223]

In February 1980, a month after the completion of the interim withdrawal, Israel and Egypt exchanged ambassadors. Israel pressed for further, speedy normalization measures. But, because of internal and outside Arab criticism, Egypt proved reluctant to speed up the process. In effect Cairo tried to correlate further normalization with the progress of the autonomy talks—in other words, to bring about in practice the "linkage" that had eluded it in the treaty itself. Israeli hints that a freeze in normalization might result in nonimplementation of the final withdrawal resulted in a series of agreements relating to an overland route for goods, food purchases from Israel, and the study of joint economic projects.

Begin had never seriously contemplated giving the West Bank and Gaza Arabs any substantial measure of self-rule. Or, as Weizman later wrote: "Alarmed by the peace treaty they had just concluded, Begin and his supporters . . . withdrew into their mental ghetto . . . into his pipe dreams."[224] The autonomy talks began in late May 1979 and ended—in complete failure—in 1982. Sadat first broke off the talks in May 1980 and again after the Knesset, on July 30, passed the Jerusalem Law, imposing Israeli law in East Jerusalem (which Sadat demanded be included in the autonomous area). The three sides met again briefly in October and November 1980 and September 1981, but with no result.

Given the nature of the Israeli government and of Egyptian and Palestinian demands, the autonomy talks were doomed to fail. From the start, Israel had excluded the PLO, and neither the West Bank and Gaza inhabitants nor Jordan had agreed to participate. Moreover, Israel's concept of autonomy did not include giving the Palestinians control over land, water, defense, or foreign policy; the military occupation would continue and the settlement network would remain intact (indeed, Begin planned to beef up the settlements during the negotiations). Thus it was a nonstarter for both the Egyptians and the Americans, not to mention the Palestinians. The Arabs wanted substantial self-rule that would naturally evolve into statehood. They and the Americans quite accurately saw the Begin scheme as mere camouflage for continued Israeli control.

Begin made his intentions clear in May 1979, when he appointed Interior Minister Yosef Burg to head the negotiating team—rather than Dayan, who begged off after being told that he would have no authority. The choice of the interior minister signaled Begin's view that the fate of the West Bank and Gaza was an internal, domestic Israeli matter—not an international issue. In June both Dayan and Weizman withdrew from the Israeli team and within months resigned from the cabinet.[225]

During the summer and autumn of 1979 Israel established a string of new settlements in the West Bank and mapped out plans for more at the southern end of the Gaza Strip. When the Likud came to power in May 1977, there had been thirty-four settlements in the West Bank (excluding Jerusalem's new outlying districts), containing about 4,000 inhabitants. By 1978 there were 7,500 settlers; by 1979, 10,000; by 1980, 12,500; and by 1981, 16,000, living in about seventy settlements. Moreover, during the first Likud years, the emphasis of new settlement had shifted from the eastern and western peripheries of the West Bank to its heavily Arab-populated spine, and from small, rural communities to urban or semiurban centers. Soon after coming to power, the government adopted in principle a plan that envisaged raising the number of settlements to well over one hundred and the number of Jews in the West Bank to one hundred thousand by 1983.[226]

The settlement policy, while accurately reflecting Begin's deeply held views on Jewish rights to the territories, also served to deflect right-wing opposition to the peace treaty with Egypt and withdrawal from Sinai. Given their head in the West Bank and Gaza, Gush Emunim and the Greater Israel Movement could be expected to go easy on Sinai. Repeated antisettlement protest rallies by Peace Now in Tel Aviv proved of little avail.[227]

Two major challenges were to confront the implementers of the Israeli-Egyptian treaty after the completion of the interim withdrawal: the assassination of President Sadat and the Israeli withdrawal from the remainder of Sinai. The first put to the test Egypt's determination to abide by the treaty even after its architect had been murdered; the second tested the Israeli government's resolve to confront and overpower the treaty's right-wing opponents. Both governments passed the tests with good marks.

Begin received considerable indirect help in implementing the treaty from the Israeli public. He was returned to power in the June 1981 general elections, with a renewed mandate to carry out the treaty provisions. His Likud bloc substantially increased in strength, to forty-eight Knesset seats. The opposition Labor Alignment also made substantial gains, winning forty-seven seats—but, as Labor supported the treaty, the election results meant that Begin now enjoyed a much larger popular mandate to carry out the withdrawal. Indeed, Tehiya, the main antiwithdrawal party, won only three seats.

The new Begin coalition, however, based on the Likud and a group of right-wing and religious parties, was more right-wing and hardline than the first Begin government (in which Yadin and his centrist Dash Party and such moderates as Dayan and Weizman had curbed the hawks). The moderates were now out, and the new cabinet sported two hardliners in central positions, Ariel Sharon as defense minister and Yitzhak Shamir—the former head of the LHI terrorist underground, who had opposed the peace treaty—as foreign minister. (Shamir took over when Dayan resigned in October 1979.) Yet, despite the cabinet's hawkish complexion, the antiwithdrawal activists geared for battle. In September 1981 they set up an umbrella organization, the Movement to Stop the Withdrawal (MSW), which began campaigning against implementation of the second and final stage of the pullback.

Sadat and Begin met in Alexandria in August 1981, discussed advancing the normalization process, and agreed to renew the autonomy talks the following month. Then, on October 6, Sadat was murdered during a military parade commemorating the Egyptian-Syrian "victory" in the October 1973 war. The four assassins, members of the Jihad Organization (an offshoot of the Muslim Brotherhood), were motivated by Islamic fundamentalism, opposition to the peace treaty with Israel, and hatred of Sadat, who was seen as a "tyrant."[228] Egyptian leaders feared that the attack was part of a wider plot to take over the country. But apart from a small clash in Asyut, the nation remained calm and the changeover in rulers—Vice President Mubarak was sworn in as president within hours—was effected smoothly.

In Israel, for a few tense days, there were fears that Mubarak, who had been beside Sadat on the grandstand but had emerged unscathed, might revoke the treaty. But on October 10, during the funeral ceremony, the new president promised Begin that the provisions of the treaty would be carried out. This commitment was underlined in November, when Egypt joined Israel in declaring the adherence "of [the] governments to the framework of the Camp David agreement,"[229] and reiterated by Cairo on April 16, 1982, in formal letters to the United States and Israel.[230] Thus, while Israel remained unhappy about the pace of normalization—as Shamir put it in December 1981, "[T]he normalization . . . is not full and on the Egyptian side it is being implemented as if it were forced by the devil"—the treaty survived the assassination.[231]

But as the final evacuation day approached, Israeli-Egyptian relations grew increasingly tense. Underlying the tension was the Israeli fear that once the withdrawal was completed, Egypt might renege on all or parts of the treaty. But there were also concrete bones of contention. The autonomy talks were clearly getting nowhere; Mubarak pointedly refused to visit Jerusalem; and in March 1982 the Taba controversy came to a head.

Over the years, many of the old markers along the old international frontier between Egypt and British mandatory Palestine had been destroyed or moved. Fourteen points along the frontier—meant to become the permanent border between Israel and Egypt—were now in dispute. The most important was Taba, a triangle of land of less than one square mile at the northern end of the Gulf of Aqaba, southwest of Eilat. Egypt charged that Israel had deliberately destroyed the old border markers.[232] Israel's interest in retaining Taba was understandable: Eilat had a relatively limited coastline, and the Taba area contained a fine beach and a luxury hotel that Begin had permitted contractors to build in 1979–80. The Egyptians, who had offered Israel $56 million for the hotel,[233] viewed Israel's refusal to evacuate Taba as a provocation, a last-minute attempt to "steal" a piece of valuable Egyptian real estate.

Egypt maintained that Taba was, and had always been, part of Sinai (Egypt) and pointed out that Israel had implicitly recognized this both in 1949, when the Egypt-Israel General Armistice Agreement had left Taba on the Egyptian side of the line, and in 1957, when, in the wake of the Sinai-Suez War, Israel had withdrawn from all of Sinai, including Taba. Now Israel was arguing that the Egyptian (British)-Ottoman demarcation agreement of 1906 had placed Taba on the Ottoman (Palestine) side of the border, and that Israel had erred in allowing it to remain in Egyptian hands during 1949–67.

The impasse gradually cast its shadow over the entire peace process, and Egypt proposed international arbitration. Israel refused, and threatened to remain in Sinai until the issue was settled to its satisfaction. At Sharon's insistence Israel apparently rejected a hinted Egyptian proposal that the area be split between the two countries (with Israel retaining the northern half of the triangle, including the hotel).[234]

Clearly, however, Taba was not worth the breakdown of the peace process, and at the end of March the two sides agreed to go ahead and complete the Sinai evacuation, with Taba meanwhile remaining "neutral" territory (but under Israeli control), and to submit the matter to arbitration if bilateral efforts to solve the problem failed.[235]

Some minor Egyptian violations of the treaty's demilitarization clauses raised hackles in Jerusalem during March and early April,[236] but with the aid of American mediation these were smoothed over, and on April 20–21 both Mubarak and U.S. president Ronald Reagan reaffirmed their commitment to the Camp David accords. On April 21 the Israeli cabinet voted to complete the withdrawal as scheduled, by April 25.[237]

There remained the problem of Begin's domestic opponents, who since the summer of 1981 had mounted a campaign of harassment and demonstrations. From July 1981 onward Gush Emunim members and West Bank settlers began moving illegally into empty apartments in Yamit, the main Jewish settlement in northeastern Sinai, and into other sites in the Rafa Approaches. The government's main counter was the formulation of a generous compensation package to the settlers evacuating Sinai, which would enable them easily to buy houses and put down roots in Israel proper. Many of the settlers did move back to Israel. But the political squatters stayed put.

On March 3, after persistent wavering, the cabinet ordered the IDF to clear the remaining inhabitants—almost all of them MSW squatters—out of the northern Sinai settlements. The evacuation proceeded smoothly and quickly, without much resistance. But the protestors regrouped, and the real and decisive showdown took place on April 21–25, when twenty thousand IDF troops surrounded and then "liberated" Yamit from the fifteen hundred squatters who had occupied the town. The soldiers used water cannon and foam sprayers; the squatters, stones, bottles, and clubs. The military's overwhelmingly superior numbers won out, without anyone suffering serious injury. (Both sides pointedly avoided bloodshed. Some of the militants had vowed to commit mass suicide—but at the last moment thought better of it.)

With the withdrawal from Sinai, almost all the settlements were razed to the ground. Only the town of Ofira (Sharm ash-Sheikh), at the southern end, was left largely intact; Yamit and all its satellites at the northeastern end of the peninsula were razed by bulldozers. "The town looked as if an atomic bomb hit it," one of the militants later wrote of Yamit.[238] Egypt had offered $50 million for the lot,[239] but Israel had refused.

The decision to destroy the settlements was made by Begin, on Defense Minister Sharon's prompting; there was no prior cabinet discussion or vote.[240] Sharon and Begin had decided to leave behind scorched earth in order to deny the Egyptians readymade forward bases or jumpoff points should Cairo decide to violate the treaty and remilitarize northeastern Sinai. A well-based Egyptian military presence in the Rafa Approaches was seen as a serious strategic threat to Israel. Moreover, Sharon argued that should the buildings and infrastructure be left intact, Egypt could move a large civilian population into the area, and such a presence would cause unnecessary friction. Or MSW supporters and former Sinai settlers might infiltrate back and cause major diplomatic embarrassment. Sharon and Begin may also have been motivated by vengefulness, as well as by a desire to impress on the world in graphic television footage the cost of Israel's sacrifices for peace and on the Israeli public the sheer awfulness of evacuating settlements (a caution, perhaps, for those bent on the evacuation of the West Bank and the Golan Heights).[241]

Like the memory of the "Battle of Yamit," the dispute over Taba was to haunt relations between Israel and Egypt for the better part of a decade. For years, under the orchestration of Foreign Minister and then Prime Minister

Yitzhak Shamir, Israel attempted to avoid arbitration. But finally, when Foreign Minister Peres threatened in 1986–87 to resign and bring down the coalition, Shamir agreed to it.[242] A tribunal consisting of one representative each
from Israel and Egypt and three distinguished international jurists from
France, Sweden, and Switzerland delivered its judgment on September 29,
1988. On the appropriate location of four of the fourteen disputed border pil-
lars or markers it favored Israel; on the other ten—including Taba—it favored
Egypt. Israel had lost.[243] By December the disputed areas had been properly
demarcated, and Taba and its hotel were transferred to Egyptian hands. The
Israeli withdrawal from Sinai had, at last, been completed.

Another loose end had been international supervision. The USSR objected
to the positioning of a new UN peacekeeping force in Sinai. In line with the
promise in Carter's letters to Begin and Sadat of March 26, 1979, the three
countries agreed in September that the United States would conduct routine
supervisory overflights, to assure that the two sides were abiding by the treaty
provisions. In addition parts of Sinai evacuated by Israel would be monitored
by the Sinai Field Mission, the body of American civilians who had manned
electronic surveillance stations that, since 1975, had monitored the second
Israeli-Egyptian disengagement agreement.

But a more comprehensive and permanent arrangement was needed. On
August 3, 1981, American, Israeli, and Egyptian representatives signed a protocol in Washington establishing the MFO, with the three parties sharing
equally in the $100 million-plus annual cost. The force, headed by an Ameri-
can, began operating from bases located north of Sharm ash-Sheikh and
southwest of Rafa (formerly the IAF's Eitam air base). A small force of UN
observers, belonging to UNTSO, was to continue to assist the MFO in monitoring the international border.

The MFO consists of three thousand troops and civilians. About half the
personnel are Americans, and the rest come from ten other countries, with
Colombia, Fiji, Italy, and Australia supplying the largest contingents.[244] The
force can be withdrawn only with the agreement of both Israel and Egypt.

Apart from the Taba hiccup, the withdrawal from Sinai, like the parallel
measures of normalization of relations between Israel and Egypt, proceeded
smoothly and on schedule. Indeed, few observers in 1977–79 would have predicted that the implementation of the treaty would proceed with so few snags,
and few in Israel believed that events like the assassination of Sadat and their
own invasion of Lebanon in 1982 would leave intact both the peace treaty and
relations between the two nations. But so it happened.

However, Israelis were to complain repeatedly that Egypt never really fully
normalized relations. Cairo abided by the letter of the treaty—ambassadors
were exchanged, Sinai remained largely demilitarized, commercial treaties
were signed—but undermined its spirit by preventing the development of
proper economic and cultural ties between the two countries. Egypt purchased

almost no Israeli goods and—barring oil—exported almost nothing to Israel; and while each year Israelis in their thousands visited Egypt, Egyptians by and large were prevented by their government from visiting Israel. Occasionally terrorists attacked Israeli diplomats and tourists in Egypt, and much of the Egyptian media kept up its traditional, anti-Israeli propaganda (in some measure as an oblique way of giving vent to its antigovernment attitudes). Moreover, Egyptian institutions and professional associations continued to boycott Israel.

Israeli protests over the years had little impact. For their part, the Egyptians maintained that Israel had almost completely failed to deliver the goods promised in Camp David regarding the Palestinians—had never taken the autonomy plan and the negotiations seriously, and continued to oppress the Palestinians in the territories. Indeed, the very neutralization of Egypt through the bilateral peace treaty enabled Begin to avoid making any concessions on the Palestinian issue, assuring the demise of the autonomy talks and the continuation of the occupation. Moreover, having safeguarded its southern flank through peace, Israel felt free in 1981 to bomb the Iraqi nuclear reactor outside Baghdad and in 1982 to invade Lebanon. Both assaults gravely embarrassed Cairo, which considered them contrary to the spirit of the peace process if not actually a violation of any of the treaty's provisions.

But, taken all in all, the Israeli-Egyptian peace held, and through the 1980s and early 1990s served as a beacon to the rest of the Arab world, attracting moderates and offering a viable alternative to continued, endless hostilities. And, during the 1990s, for a variety of reasons, that world gradually gravitated toward the Egyptian model, abandoning the rejectionism that had over the decades achieved very little for the Palestinians or anyone else.

ELEVEN

THE LEBANON WAR, 1982–85

With Egypt sidelined by the provisions of its treaty with Israel, the Begin government was able to plan a major assault against the PLO in Lebanon relatively untroubled by the risk of an escalation into general war. It was extremely unlikely that Jordan would get involved, and with both Egypt and Jordan out, Syria would not open a second front on the Golan Heights. But the treaty was a precondition, not a cause, of war. The IDF invasion of Lebanon in June 1982 had deep historical roots.

THE YISHUV/ISRAEL AND LEBANON

The map of the prospective Jewish state presented by the Zionist Organization at the Versailles Peace Conference in 1919 included southern Lebanon up to the Litani River.[1] This area contains two of the three main headwaters of the Jordan—the Hasbani and Wazani Rivers (the third, the Banias, lies in the Golan)—as well as the Litani itself, another large source of water. Moreover, the Zionists wanted their state to border on the Lebanese Christian heartland north of the Litani, which they hoped would emerge as a Maronite-dominated state in its own right.

Southern Lebanon, populated largely by Muslims, might become a wedge between the two states—a fact that worried the heads of the Jewish Agency in 1937–38, after the Peel Commission recommended awarding the Galilee to the Jews.[2] Ben-Gurion wrote at that time of "a political need for a common frontier with Lebanon, a country with a large Christian community that could hold on only precariously in a Muslim ocean. The Lebanese Christians [are] in a similar situation to ours, and it [is] important for both [of us] that we should be neighbors."[3]

Moshe Sharett believed that "it is vitally important for the Jews that the area of their settlement should remain contiguous with the [Christian] Lebanon."[4]

The possibility of a Zionist-Christian alliance captured the Zionists' and, to a lesser extent, the Maronites' imagination for decades. The latter were the largest, most powerful, and geographically closest community the Yishuv could look to for such a relationship. The two communities shared a commonality of interests, periodically underlined by expressions of Muslim hostility toward both. Both were minorities—by 1952, according to a French diplomatic report, citing Lebanese sources, about 60 percent of Lebanon's population was Muslim[5]—and both felt under perpetual demographic and physical threat. (The Maronites had suffered massacres at the hands of Lebanese and Syrian Muslims and Druze in 1860[6] and smaller-scale depredations during the early 1920s.) Both feared that if the protective French or British shield was removed, they would face violence and, at least in the case of Lebanon, Syrian expansionism.[7]

The Maronites, who had escaped from Muslim persecution to Mount Lebanon in the seventh century, saw their land as a haven for victimized Christians from other parts of the Levant, much as the Zionists regarded Palestine as a refuge for persecuted Jews. Both communities encouraged the return of their brethren from abroad to "the homeland." Moreover, both had a commercial bent, and trade between them increased dramatically during the 1930s. (The Christians' economic-mindedness led the Zionist leadership to view them as people who could always be bought. No doubt, Maronites harbored similar attitudes toward the Yishuv.)[8]

Throughout the relationship, however, the Maronites were "torn between taboo and temptation"[9]—the Arab ban on cooperation with the Zionists versus the allure of making common cause against the Muslims. Most saw their welfare as dependent upon amicable relations with the majority. They might, for a time, cooperate with the Yishuv and benefit from its assistance, but long-term interest dictated coexistence with the Muslims, even if this might require lining up with them against the Jews. And many Maronites feared Zionist territorial designs on Lebanon.[10]

The minority who favored alliance with the Yishuv believed that Muslim enmity toward the Maronites was permanent and inexorable; that Syrian ambitions vis-à-vis Lebanon were immutable; and that their community's salvation ultimately lay in military and political strength rather than diplomacy and conciliation. They tended to stress their Francophone cultural affiliations and saw their ethnic roots as lying in ancient Phoenicia rather than in Arabia.

Many Zionist leaders, at least until 1948, felt that their basic interest was to reach accommodation with the Arab states and their Muslim majorities. Some minor benefits and short-term gains might accrue from alliances with Christian or non-Arab minorities, but these were no substitute for reconciliation with the Muslims. As Eliahu Epstein stated in 1937, after serving as the Jewish Agency representative in Beirut: "We need to reach agreement first of all with the Muslims and only afterwards with the Christians. With Christian Lebanon we can link up only after we firm up good neighborly relations with Syria, otherwise we will not so much win over the Maronites as alienate the Muslims, who are the majority in Palestine as in the whole of the Middle East."[11]

Nor, most Zionists felt by the 1940s, could the Maronites be trusted to forge a lasting alliance or stick to it, given their real and justified fear of the Muslims and the cultural, financial, and political bonds that joined them and the Muslim Arabs of Lebanon and Syria. All Arabs were seen by the Zionists as essentially untrustworthy, not to say treacherous, and the Maronites were Arabs.

Nonetheless, the political realities time and again pushed the Maronites toward an understanding with the Yishuv. According to the leading historian of this connection, Laura Eisenberg, as early as 1913 some of their spokesmen expressed support for the Zionists and posited an alliance with them.[12] In the 1930s major Maronite figures, among them the patriarch, Antoine Pierre Arida; the archbishop of Beirut, Ignatius Mubarak; with less enthusiasm, Emile Edde, the president of Lebanon from 1936 to 1941; and the prominent Naccache family supported an alliance.[13] Edde was wont to point to the "superiority" of the "two Occidental cultures" over "that of the Arab neighbors" and to the common "goal" of both communities, to build a "bridge between eastern and western cultures";[14] Arida wrote to Weizmann of the "brave Israelites"[15] and spoke to another Zionist official of "the sea of savage Muslims" among whom, unfortunately, the Christians lived.[16] All of them met (in secret) during the thirties and forties with Zionist officials.

The covert political contacts as well as more overt economic relations— including Jewish patronage of Lebanese resorts—peaked in the mid-1930s. But during the Arab rebellion Lebanon served for the first time as a haven for Palestinian Arab guerrillas and as a staging post for attacks on the British and the Jews in northern Palestine. The mufti himself found sanctuary in Beirut and from there directed the rebellion's second stage.

The Jewish Agency tried to make Lebanon less hospitable to Palestinian leaders. A propaganda battle was fought on the pages of the country's dailies, and the agency's Political Department subsidized a bevy of Lebanese journalists.[17] A prominent Sunni Muslim journalist-turned-politician, Khayr ad Din al-Ahdab, had the distinction of being one of the few Arab prime ministers in Zionist pay.[18]

Zionist-Maronite contacts and relations reached a nadir during World War II, but after the war the Zionist leadership and the committed "pro-Zionists" in the Maronite camp rushed toward a formal alliance. Pierre Gemayel, the expharmacist founder and leader of the Maronite Phalange Party—established on the model of Europe's fascist movements after Gemayel visited the 1936 Olympic Games in Berlin[19]—took an unfriendly tack,[20] as did Lebanese government spokesmen; but Edde, Arida, and Mubarak testified before the 1946 Anglo-American Committee and the 1947 UN Special Committee on Palestine, in favor of Zionism and Jewish statehood.[21] Mubarak, perhaps, was the most outspoken: "If you oppose Zionism in Palestine it means returning the people to the domination of savagery and the country to the state of anarchy and bribery in which it existed under the Ottoman Sultans . . . here is a struggle between civilisation and regression, and the Jews represent civilisation."[22]

On May 30, 1946, Arida and the Jewish Agency concluded a secret treaty. The Maronites recognized the Jews' right to statehood in Palestine, and the Jews affirmed the independent, Christian character of Lebanon. The agency foreswore any territorial designs on Lebanon.[23] But the treaty was historically irrelevant: The "National Pact" (or "Contract") of 1943-44 instituted Christian-Muslim cooperation in Lebanon, acceptance of its "Arab" character, and membership in the Arab League. The Christians were assured of the presidency and the command of the army, while the prime ministership was assigned to the Sunni Muslims.[24] The balance between the various groups was fragile in the extreme, as the civil wars of 1958 and 1975-90 were to demonstrate. The Lebanese polity, while trumpeting and partially embodying such Western tenets as openness, tolerance, and pluralism, was, at the same time, inherently "artificial and archaic, built on shaky demographic and political foundations."[25] Realizing this, Lebanese governments were perennially wary of striking out on new or bold courses that might prove radically destabilizing. The preservation of the status quo, in internal politics as well as in foreign policy, became an overriding goal.

During the 1948 war Israeli officials hoped for a Maronite-led rebellion that would perhaps lead Lebanon toward a peace treaty with Israel.[26] Ben-Gurion wrote: "The weak link in the Arab coalition is Lebanon. The Muslim rule is artificial and easy to undermine. A Christian state must be established, whose southern border will be the Litani. We will sign a treaty with it."[27] No rebellion occurred, but Prime Minister Riad as Sulh in effect kept Lebanon out of the conflict, going through the motions of hostility rather than actually fighting.

After the war the Phalange Party sought Israeli arms and funds to help it in the parliamentary elections of 1951. A covert token of two thousand dollars was passed—though the Israelis were not particularly optimistic about the prospects of a genuine partnership. They focused on the possibility of organizing a coup in which a Christian military leader would reduce Lebanon to its Christian "core," divested of the Muslim-inhabited eastern and southern peripheries, and strike a deal with Israel. Ben-Gurion and Dayan raised the idea whenever periods of inter-Arab turmoil and stress appeared to provide opportunities to meddle.[28]

Ben-Gurion's views verged on the apocalyptic; in 1954 he told Prime Minister Sharett that the establishment of a friendly, Christian Lebanon would "decisively re-arrange the Middle East and a new age would dawn."[29] Sharett responded that any attempt to subvert the government and body-politic of Lebanon would fail and would bring on Israel only "opprobrium,"[30] views which corresponded with those of his Foreign Ministry experts.[31]

Ben-Gurion was not deterred. He again took up the theme in 1955, after returning to the cabinet as defense minister. And this time he was strongly supported by Dayan, who was now chief of the general staff. Their plan depended upon Iraq first conquering Syria. According to Dayan, recorded Sharett, "all that is needed is to find an officer, even of the rank of captain, to win him over or bribe him so that he agrees to declare himself the savior of the Maronite population. Then the IDF will enter Lebanon, conquer the necessary territory and establish a Christian government that will be allied to Israel. The area south of the Litani will be annexed completely to Israel."[32]

Again, Sharett, still prime minister, flatly rejected the idea—and wrote in his diary that "the lack of seriousness exhibited by the [military brass, including Ben-Gurion] . . . in its approach to the affairs of the neighboring countries and especially toward the most complicated problem of Lebanon's internal and external situation was simply horrifying."[33]

Three decades were to elapse before Ben-Gurion's and Dayan's dream was to be resurrected by Menachem Begin and Ariel Sharon when they launched the invasion of Lebanon in 1982. In the interim Israel, which never found a strong, reliable Maronite leader or faction with whom it could do business, was preoccupied with the border situation along the West Bank and Gaza Strip, the PLO, and the threat posed by Nasser's Egypt.

Yet, through the 1950s and 1960s, Israeli officials maintained secret though largely unfruitful contacts with Lebanese leaders, Muslim as well as Christian, the thought of alliance or strategic cooperation always at the back of their minds. In 1958, during the first Lebanese civil war, when American marines were sent to Beirut to protect the government of President Chamoun (a deployment for which Israel vigorously lobbied[34]), they returned to the idea of helping to create a "reduced," Christian-dominated state. One official spoke of the need to "trim" Lebanon of its Muslim-populated northern, eastern, and southern fringes, with the (largely Shi'ite) population of the south (Jabal 'Amal) to be transferred to Syria and replaced by Christians with "the aim" of achieving "territorial continuity between Israel and the Christian community in Lebanon."[35]

ISRAEL AND THE PLO IN LEBANON

During the following decade, there was no change in Israeli-Lebanese relations. Lebanon had wisely kept out of the 1967 war. During 1968–69 the Palestinian guerrilla groups conducted a massive recruitment campaign in Lebanese refugee camps, which turned into PLO-ruled enclaves. Forward bases were set up near the Israeli border, around Nabatiya, and in the hill country to its east. Pinprick raids against Israel were launched, opening a second front in addition to the main theater of operations along the Jordan River. Periodically the IDF retaliated, striking with aircraft, commandos, and armor at Palestinian targets in southern Lebanon.

The September 1970 and July 1971 Jordanian assaults on the PLO resulted in a massive movement of guerrillas to Lebanon, which was too weak to resist. Some Muslims welcomed them. Arafat and the PLO command set up shop in Beirut and the refugee camps. Much of the south and all of the camps became an armed state-within-a-state, where Lebanon's writ ceased to operate. PLO strongholds came to serve as bases of a number of terrorist groups, including Black September, the German Baader-Meinhof Gang, and the Japanese Red Army Faction. Ariel Sharon, with a large measure of accuracy, was later to call Lebanon in the 1970s "a true kingdom of terror" and "the center of world terrorism."[36] Because of its weakness, stemming mainly from the delicate Christian-Muslim internal balance, the government proved unwilling or unable to restrain the guerrillas, even though their raids brought massive Israeli retribution down upon the border villages.

The years 1970–75 witnessed a vast increase in Palestinian guerrilla and terrorist operations from Lebanon against targets in northern Israel and outside the Middle East. In 1974 alone terrorists from Lebanon killed sixty-one Israelis, most of them civilians. Dozens of terrorist squads were intercepted by Israeli ground troops and naval units before they managed to cross the border or reach their objectives, and many PLO fighters died in IDF raids.

By 1975–76 the IDF had managed substantially to seal the northern border and the Mediterranean coastline against PLO incursions. The main means were the electronically monitored barbed-wire fence, flanked by minefields, which stretched from the slopes of Mount Hermon to the Mediterranean; ambushes and patrols, many of them inside Lebanese territory; and land, air, and sea radar and other surveillance systems.

The outbreak of the Lebanese civil war in April 1975 also hampered the terrorists. The war, in which more than 100,000 people were to die,[37] sputtered on, in fits and starts, until 1990. "Long-suppressed hatreds, resentments, fears, and loathing"[38] came to a head in no small measure because of destabilizing Palestinian armed activity, primarily against Israel but also against the Lebanese security forces, although the basic cause of the conflict was the long-simmering Christian-Muslim antagonism. Despite Arafat's initial efforts to stay out, the PLO and his own Fatah organization were sucked in on the Muslim side by the radical Palestinian organizations—much as had occurred in Amman five years earlier.

During the first years of the war, the Palestinians were to suffer a number of major setbacks. In Beirut two refugee camps fell to Christian assault, and many of their inhabitants were massacred. Areas of the south fell to Israeli-assisted Christian forces, and during September–October 1976 large areas fell under direct Syrian domination. Both the Christians and the Muslims sought assistance from Syria—but both feared their neighbor's expansionist ambitions. In the end, the Syrians intervened to prevent an outright PLO-Muslim victory. Syria was motivated primarily by its historic goal of bringing Lebanon under its rule, but also by fear that the civil war would spill over into its own territory. Israel feared that the war could spiral out of control and involve it in war with the Arab world; the United States sought pacification as an end in itself. So, with what amounted to Israeli, American, Phalange, and partial Arab agreement under Syria's belt, on the night of May 31, 1976, it invaded Lebanon.[39]

The Israelis were happy that the Syrians, rather than the IDF, were going in to save the Maronites, and perhaps to savage the PLO. The main Syrian efforts were blocked by hastily deployed Muslim-PLO forces seven kilometers east of Beirut and outside Sidon. A cease-fire was instituted on June 9, but during the following weeks the Syrians intermittently punished the recalcitrant Muslims and Palestinians with artillery and enabled the Christians to gain local victories. But this too failed to bring the Muslims and PLO to heel. Following the failure of PLO-Lebanese-Syrian talks on September 17–19,[40] the Syrians sought a pretext to deliver a decisive stroke. This was supplied by the breakaway Abu Nidal faction (much as it was to supply Israel with the excuse to invade Lebanon six years later): On September 26 its gunmen briefly took over the Semiramis Hotel in Damascus. Syria blamed Arafat's mainstream Fatah group (as Begin was to blame the PLO for the Abu Nidal action six years later) and on September 28 launched its offensive. In coordination with the Phalange, the Syrians occupied much of the PLO-Muslim-held area north of the Damascus–Beirut highway and advanced to the outskirts of Beirut and Sidon meeting little resistance;[41] by October 16, both cities were at the mercy of Syrian guns. But the Syrians stopped short of smashing the PLO.

The Arab states duly legitimized the Syrian thrust by dubbing the occupation force the "Arab Deterrent Force."[42] In November, Syria extended its control to parts of West Beirut, Sidon, and Tripoli. It failed to disarm the warring militias but pressed on with a gradual imposition of the "pax Syriana." America and Israel consented to the move, but the Israelis set a number of limits, or "red lines": Syria tacitly agreed not to introduce aircraft or SAM batteries in Lebanon, or to deploy armor and artillery south of a line thirteen to twenty miles north of the Israeli border.

But in the Middle East, defeats—and victories—tend to be relative and short-lived. The PLO had been battered by the Syrians but emerged from the battles of 1975–76 far stronger. It had consolidated its hold over the south and the refugee camps around Beirut and Tripoli, was better armed than before, and occupied additional, formerly Christian territory. In January 1976 PLO forces had captured the Christian town of Damour, south of Beirut, massacring 150 to 200 of its inhabitants[43] and expelling the rest.

The PLO state-within-a-state had consolidated with its own embryonic regular army (perhaps thirty thousand strong), a taxation system, a police force and judiciary, and schools and health care facilities. Palestinian historian Rashid Khalidi observes that his people viewed this period as "a high point in the re-creation of their national identity" and that the war served as "a primary impetus to the expansion of [the PLO's] presence in Lebanon," in part as a result of military exigencies, in part because the Palestinians were forced to provide services that previously had been provided by the Lebanese state.[44]

During 1977–81 the PLO continued to raid northern Israel. The IDF retaliated with shelling, aerial and naval bombardment, and ground raids of its own. The high point in this duel was reached after the March 1978 bus hijacking near Haifa. The large number of casualties and the blow to Israel's heartland meant that restraint was not an option. Nor was the target of retaliation ever in doubt. Israeli intelligence estimated there were some 4,000 "terrorists" in Lebanon in and around refugee camps, villages, caves, and hilltop positions south of the Litani. On March 15, three IDF brigades, with powerful artillery and air support, invaded the area. The aim of "Operation Litani" was to kill as many guerrillas as possible and to destroy the military infrastructure—camps, munitions dumps, artillery pieces. A secondary aim was to expand, and create continuity between, the existing Christian-held enclaves on the Lebanese side of the border. By March 21, the IDF had taken all of the area south of the Litani (except for Tyre and its environs). The Syrians refrained from interfering, and American and Western European protests were mild and ineffectual.

The IDF had used a great deal of artillery fire to keep down its own casualties. But many PLO fighters were thus given ample warning and were able to escape. Altogether the IDF lost 18 dead and 113 wounded; about 300 Palestinian fighters were killed, several hundred wounded, and several dozen captured.[45] During the week-long operation the IDF fired or dropped twenty-two thousand shells and bombs. Hundreds of Lebanese homes were destroyed and tens of thousands of villagers fled.

The IDF accomplishment may not have been very considerable in military terms. But a continuous Christian-dominated "Security Zone" was established inside Lebanon, to a depth of some six miles from the frontier. Moreover, adding a further layer of security to northern Israel, a new force, the United Nations Interim Force in Lebanon (UNIFIL), was established by Security Council Resolution 425 of March 19 and deployed in the area between the zone and the Litani (save for the Tyre coastal strip, which remained in PLO hands). By July the force was composed of six thousand troops, rising to seven thousand in the late 1980s.[46] Its mandate was to oversee an Israeli withdrawal and to assure the future demilitarization of the evacuated area. In effect the IDF withdrew only back to the Security Zone, and UNIFIL was charged with keeping PLO fighters out of the area to its north. Israel repeatedly complained during the following years that UNIFIL was ineffective, but its presence in camps, fixed positions, and patrols was a major impediment to the PLO's freedom of action. It also curtailed Israel's ability to operate in the area north of the zone.

Nonetheless, Palestinians and Israelis were still able to get at each other. During 1978–81, despite periodic clashes with the Syrians, the Phalange, and Lebanese army forces to the north, PLO guerrillas repeatedly launched artillery and rocket attacks against Israel or crossed through the UNIFIL area and attacked targets in the Security Zone and in Israel. Israeli commandos, aircraft, artillery, and missile boats periodically retaliated against Palestinian targets inside and north of UNIFIL's area.

THE FORGING OF THE ISRAELI-CHRISTIAN ALLIANCE, 1975–82

The outbreak of the civil war was the crucial event in the forging of the Israeli-Christian alliance. That alliance was to take two tracks: a local one, along the border, and a national one, involving IDF aid to the Phalange militia in the Christian heartland around Jounieh–East Beirut.

In the course of 1975–76 several Christian border villages, assisted by Lebanese army defectors, set up local militias to fend off attacks by the Palestinian-Muslim forces. The main Maronite Phalange militia was heavily engaged in the north and was unwilling or unable to help in the south. Within months three clearly defined pockets of Christian militia control had emerged in the south, adjoining the Israeli border. Israel extended them military, financial, and medical aid, and loosely organized their defenses under the direction of Maj. Sa'ad Haddad, formerly of the Lebanese army.[47] During 1976–77 the IDF provided the enclaves with limited military support during their sporadic battles against PLO forces. In September 1977, in a little-known incident, Israel intervened directly with ground troops in the civil war. A paratroop battalion, accompanied by artillery and armored units, crossed the border to help Haddad's troops take and hold the PLO position at Tel a Sharifa.[48]

In 1978, during Operation Litani, Israel assisted Haddad in expanding the enclaves into a continuous strip known as the Security Zone, with 100,000 mainly Christian inhabitants, stretching from Ras al-Naqurah in the west to the Mount Hermon foothills in the east. With Israeli arms, money, training, and technical and artillery backup, Haddad's ragtag units were streamlined into a Christian militia brigade; a number of affiliated local Muslim units were also established. The militia, initially designated the Army of Free Lebanon, was eventually renamed the South Lebanese Army (SLA). At first, Haddad's fifteen hundred or so troops served two weeks out of four in or near their villages. In 1980 the militia was converted into a fully professional standing force, the troops serving in Israeli-built fortified hilltop positions, strung out along the northern edge of the zone, or in patrols between the positions.[49] During the 1980s the SLA was 70 percent Christian, 20 percent Shi'ite, and 10 percent Druze.[50] By the 1990s about half its 2,300 soldiers were Christian, the rest Muslims and Druze.

But Israel's main Christian partner was to be the Maronite Phalange Party, based in East Beirut, the port town of Jounieh, and Bikfaya, the native village of the Gemayel clan on Mount Lebanon to the east.

On the night of March 12, 1976, the Phalange chief of operations, Joseph Abu Khalil, with Pierre Gemayel's blessing, boarded an Israeli missile boat off the coast of Beirut and traveled to Haifa to meet Prime Minister Yitzhak Rabin and Foreign Minister Yigal Allon. It was the height of the civil war, and the Christians were close to defeat. Having gotten nowhere with the French or with any of the Arab regimes, the Phalangists were ready to sup with what Gemayel regarded as the devil: Abu Khalil had come to Israel to plead for weapons and ammunition.[51]

The Israelis were cautious. Within days, an intelligence team was dispatched to Jounieh to look over the Phalange and assess its needs. Additional investigative teams followed, plying the nighttime route between Haifa and Jounieh on fast missile boats. They were briefed by Phalange officers; they poked about, they evaluated. In July 1976 an intelligence executive, Col. Binyamin Ben-Eliezer, was taken to the Phalange command post to view the last days of the battle for the Tel al-Za'atar refugee camp. He and other Israeli officers quickly identified Bashir Gemayel, Pierre's son and the new commander of the Phalange-led militia, as a powerful ally and rising star. Bashir, then twenty-nine, charismatic and persuasive, had matured rapidly during the civil war. He was a doer, not a talker, and he led from the front—to the Israelis' liking. They had never had much time for the run-of-the-mill Lebanese politicians and army commanders, who "played at politics [and] played at war."[52] Bashir put in twenty-hour days, and was "cool and calculating," single-minded, and ruthless in the pursuit of power: "His pragmatism was boundless."[53]

A suspicious Israeli establishment began to inch toward commitment. But months passed before the decision-makers settled on the Gemayels. First, they heard out their Maronite rivals. In August, Camille Chamoun, the former Lebanese president (1952–58) and then a cabinet minister, journeyed to Haifa to meet Rabin.[54] When asked by Chamoun whether Israel was ready to intervene, Rabin responded: "Our guiding principle is that we are prepared to help you help yourselves." During the following months, Rabin met repeatedly with Chamoun, and with Pierre Gemayel and his two sons, Bashir and Amin.

Pierre Gemayel, at least, was honest: "I have been forced to turn to you, but I am filled with shame and dismay." Still, Rabin was persuaded to send aid— obsolescent Sherman tanks, LAW antitank rockets, M-16 rifles, and eventually Soviet-made T-54s and T-55s captured from Egypt and Syria and improved by the Israelis. In June 1982, Israeli officials estimated that during the previous six years the Lebanese Christians had bought $118.5 million worth of arms from Israel.[55]

Initially, the Maronites had also turned to Syria. It was partly in response to their appeals that the Syrians began pushing military units into Lebanon in June 1976. But the longed-for decisive campaign against the PLO and its Muslim allies failed to materialize; Assad preferred to maneuver between the parties rather than crush one of them outright, and during 1977 there was a gradual Syrian-PLO rapprochement. At the same time, the Syrian army of occupation began to rub the Christians the wrong way. Within months the saviors became resented occupiers.[56] During 1977–78 the understanding fell apart, to be replaced by ever-bloodier hostilities between the Christian militiamen and the Syrian army and its Lebanese allies.[57]

The Christians soon realized that scattered harassment was not going to drive the Syrians out, and that they were too weak to manage it in open battle. Bashir Gemayel began to look to Jerusalem for salvation: The Israelis might both destroy the PLO (which Damascus had declined to do) and expel the Syrians into the bargain. He found a ready ally in the Mossad. The IDF Intelligence Branch was always suspicious of the Maronites and their promises; the Mossad—as embodied in David Kimche, then deputy director and head of its foreign relations division—thought otherwise, constantly pushing for an expanded and deeper relationship.[58]

The general election of May 1977 thrust Menachem Begin into the premiership. The Maronite appeal for Israeli aid struck a deep psychological chord in this very history-minded man. For millennia the Christian world had oppressed and killed the Jews. Now a Christian community was appealing to the Jews for succor—after Europe, particularly France, had turned its back. Begin was not one to resist the opportunity of showing the world how his people, in their magnanimity and humanity, would help and protect the Christians of Lebanon from Muslim "genocide" as Europe and the United States had failed to do for the Jews during the Holocaust. He also shared Ben-Gurion's vision of an anti-Muslim alliance of the Middle East's minorities.

During the 1977-79 Maronite-Syrian clashes, the Christians were the main instigators, but the Syrians were not to be driven out by a band of unprofessional militiamen. The weaker, more vulnerable Maronites were usually worsted in battle, the Syrians tending to retaliate massively and brutally, in complete disproportion to the provocation and without any effort to spare civilians. They bombarded Maronite villages and Christian East Beirut in June-July 1978, and again in September-October. Hundreds of civilians died.

Gemayel's strategy was simple: to provoke the Syrians into such brutal retribution that Israel could no longer stand aside. It worked, though perhaps not as speedily as he had hoped. Syria's behavior gradually compelled the Israeli public to take a sympathetic interest in the Christians' plight. During and after each clash Bashir (and Chamoun) would appeal to Jerusalem for salvation. For a while Jerusalem merely advised them to be patient. But in autumn 1978 Begin publicly declared that Israel would prevent the "genocide" of Lebanon's Christians. Israeli reinforcement of its armor on the Golan and IAF flights over Beirut persuaded the Syrians to agree to a cease-fire.[59] But Israel rejected Christian appeals to intervene directly.[60]

Israeli aid went up a notch the following year, when hundreds of Phalange officers and NCOs began to train in Israel, and senior officers attended courses at the IDF Staff and Command College.[61] Additional weaponry reached Jounieh, and Israeli military advisers and intelligence experts, now stationed on a semipermanent basis in the Christian enclave, pressed Gemayel to unite the militias. In the course of 1978-81 he bloodily dismantled the rival units, incorporating their survivors in his militia, which had been renamed the "Lebanese Forces" (LF).[62]

The burgeoning Israeli-Phalange relationship was facilitated, according to Sharon, by the gradual transformation of Bashir Gemayel from "an emotional and hate-filled gang leader [into] a relatively careful and perceptive political leader. As the days passed, his deeds—despite his pronouncements—became more moderate. His political carefulness increased, and his urges toward undisciplined actions were curbed by a realistic perception geared to his expected position as president of all the Lebanese. This remodeling of Bashir Gemayel was characteristic of the whole leadership of the Phalange."

Though this view was not shared by many in IDF Intelligence Branch and the Mossad, by 1981, says Sharon, the relationship with the Phalange had become a "political-strategic alliance," which included "far-reaching political understandings and military coordination in joint operations in the future."[63]

The background to this consolidation was an upsurge of Christian-Syrian fighting. In late 1980 Begin gave Gemayel a long-coveted guarantee: "Should the Christians be attacked by the Syrian Air Force, we will help you with our air force." Begin read this text from the Knesset podium on June 3, 1981, adding that the "security and survival" of Lebanon's Christians was of "vital interest" to Israel.[64]

With this promise in his pocket, Gemayel once again set out to challenge the Syrians, by introducing his militia into the eastern city of Zahle and by cutting a supply road to it from Mount Senin, in the Maronite heartland. Undaunted, Assad ordered an offensive in both areas; hundreds of civilians died in the ensuing artillery exchanges, most of them Christians.[65] Gemayel and Chamoun, at a hastily organized meeting with Begin, warned that if Mount Senin fell, the whole of Maronite Lebanon might fall. But the Syrians had signaled Jerusalem to keep out—by rapidly digging emplacements in the Beka'a Valley for four SAM-6 batteries. Syria would bring in the SAMs and radically change the status quo if Israel intervened.[66]

The Israeli leadership picked up the gauntlet on April 28. The chief of general staff, Lt. Gen. Rafael Eitan, proposed to the cabinet a limited air strike against the Syrians. The director of military intelligence, Maj. Gen. Yehoshua Saguy, demurred, predicting that the Syrians would respond by deploying SAMs in the Beka'a. A number of ministers joined Saguy—but Begin backed Eitan ("We won't let them perpetrate genocide in Lebanon"), and the majority swung behind him. That afternoon Israeli jet fighters streaked over Zahle and shot down two Syrian transport helicopters above Mount Senin.[67]

Within twenty-four hours Assad called Israel's bluff, moving SAM-6s into the Beka'a and deploying medium-range Scud surface-to-surface missile batteries aimed at Israel, near Damascus. The meaning was clear: Syria would now deny Israel freedom of the skies over Zahle and the Beka'a—and was backing this up with the strategic deterrent of the Scuds. Begin vowed to destroy the SAMs and obtained cabinet approval for an air strike.[68] No doubt influencing the ministers' judgment were the impending general elections: The Likud could not afford to back down in face of the Syrian challenge. An anti-SAM strike was set for the afternoon of April 30, but cloud cover forced postponement. Washington hastily announced that it would secure withdrawal of the SAMs through diplomacy, and Begin reluctantly acquiesced.

During the following weeks U.S. Special Ambassador Philip Habib shuttled fruitlessly between Jerusalem, Beirut, and Damascus. Assad wouldn't budge. In June, Syrian commandos took Mount Senin. Gemayel agreed to withdraw from Zahle, and the last Phalange contingent, their situation now completely untenable and with even the townspeople clamoring for their withdrawal, left the town on June 30. Having obtained what they had all along demanded, the Syrians lifted the siege.[69] The round had definitely gone to Assad.

By then the Israelis had put the SAM issue on the back burner. The political urgency of taking out the Syrian missiles had been diluted by two separate military operations: the daring, successful June 7 IAF strike against Iraq's Osirak nuclear reactor, outside Baghdad, which the Israelis charged was designed to facilitate the production of nuclear weapons; and the IAF campaign, beginning on May 28, against PLO concentrations in southern Lebanon. Both were clearly softer targets, both militarily and politically, than the Syrian missile complex, and clearly preferable in a run-up to elections.

The PLO avoided retaliating against the Galilee border settlements, fearing that Israel would launch another ground invasion. Having shown that it was no paper tiger, the Begin government on June 3 halted the bombardment of southern Lebanon, probably in large measure to avoid a major flare-up along the border just before polling day.

Begin narrowly won the June 30 elections and, within days, put together a coalition of right-wing and religious parties. With the relatively dovish ministers now out, the new cabinet gave Begin far more freedom of maneuver than had its predecessor. Moreover, Sharon was slated to become the new defense minister.

On July 10 the IAF renewed its assault on Palestinian targets in southern Lebanon. The PLO was ready[70] and responded with a salvo of rockets against the Galilee Panhandle town of Kiryat Shmonah, in which a number of civilians were injured.[71] On July 12 and 14 the Israelis upped the stakes: They repeatedly bombed PLO bases in Damour, ten miles south of Beirut, and Nabatiya. This time the PLO threw caution to the winds. On July 15 rockets and artillery hit Kiryat Shmonah and the resort town of Nahariya. Three Israelis were killed and twenty-five wounded. The beginnings of panic took hold in the Israeli border settlements; normal life ceased, schools and factories closed, and the inhabitants took to air-raid shelters until further notice. Many families jumped into their cars and fled.

Begin, incensed, ordered the gloves off. On July 16 the IAF destroyed several bridges in southern Lebanon and attacked PLO installations in Damour and the 'Ein al-Hilwe refugee camp in Sidon, killing at least twenty people and wounding many more. The PLO kept up sporadic fire against the border settlements, and on July 17 the IAF launched the crowning raid of the series, attacking PLO buildings in downtown Beirut. Perhaps as many as three hundred people died, and eight hundred were wounded, the great majority of them civilians. PLO spokesman Mahmoud Labadi charged that Israel had unleashed "a war of genocide against the Palestinians."[72] But, though outgunned, the PLO remained defiant, sending more rockets and shells against Kiryat Shmonah and Nahariya.[73] And there was a political gain as well: Following the raid on Beirut, the United States announced a delay in the delivery of new fighter aircraft to Israel.

The Begin government was severely shaken, not least by the knowledge that the IDF was proving incapable of silencing the PLO guns and rocket launchers. The PLO's strategy of widely dispersing artillery and ammunition stockpiles had largely neutralized the far more powerful Israeli aircraft and artillery. Nor, during the two-week duel, were the Israelis able to interdict supplies of shells and rockets, despite the destruction of roads and bridges.[74] During the following five days aircraft and gunners bombarded southern Lebanon, killing dozens more PLO fighters and civilians but failing to silence the batteries. Thousands of border settlers headed south; one report said that during the fortnight of fighting about 40 percent of Kiryat Shmonah's inhabitants left the town.[75]

Both sides needed a cease-fire. Ambassador Habib had begun negotiating with the Israelis and the PLO (the latter through Saudi and Lebanese mediators) soon after the start of the fighting. On July 24 the guns at last fell silent.

The American-mediated agreement forbade all acts of belligerence from Lebanese territory against Israel and the Security Zone, and from Israel and the Security Zone against targets in Lebanon, "from the air, from the sea or on land."[76] Subsequently crucial differences of interpretation surfaced. Israel argued that the cease-fire applied to its other borders as well, and to Israeli targets abroad, as all Palestinian "terrorist" activity ultimately stemmed from PLO headquarters in Lebanon. But Washington tended toward the narrower PLO interpretation: that the agreement applied only to the Israeli-Lebanese theater of operations. Moreover, all agreed, the accord enabled the PLO to reconstitute and, indeed, expand its military—including artillery—infrastructure in southern Lebanon. Here were the foci of future contention.

In Jerusalem the feeling at the end of July was of military and political defeat. The formidable IAF and IDF artillery had failed to break the PLO in southern Lebanon. Moreover, Israel and the United States had been forced, however indirectly, to negotiate with the hated PLO and to reach an agreement, seemingly spelling some form of parity between that organization and Israel. Some felt that the cease-fire implied the beginning of Israeli recognition of the PLO; certainly the PLO state-within-a-state had been at least unofficially recognized.

The fighting and the agreement that followed, coming on top of Syria's refusal to withdraw the SAMs from the Beka'a, carried the seeds of Israel's invasion of Lebanon a year later. The government emerged with a deep sense of frustration and humiliation—and a burning desire to settle accounts with the PLO and the Syrians. In a sense the PLO guns and rockets seemed to hold northern Israel hostage and limited the IDF's freedom of action. From Begin's perspective it was clear that a major new operation would be necessary, to drive the PLO out of southern Lebanon and demolish its threatening military infrastructure and perhaps to destroy the organization itself. The PLO, too, soon came to recognize that a new, full-scale Israeli attack was almost inevitable. In early August, Begin appointed as his defense minister the hardliner Sharon, who for months had been openly preaching war against the PLO and had "strenuously opposed" the accord negotiated by Habib.[77] The move clearly indicated the direction in which events were heading.[78]

Israel spent the months between August 1981 and June 1982 seeking a pretext to invade Lebanon. Diplomacy had failed to dislodge the SAMs and had only aggravated the problem posed by the PLO, whose firepower had steadily increased after Habib's mission. Nor had diplomatic efforts done much to shore up the Christians' flagging fortunes. In all three spheres the solution, for Begin and Sharon, lay in a massive offensive.

The most immediate problem was the PLO's military infrastructure, which posed a standing threat to the security of northern Israeli settlements. The removal of this threat was to be the battle cry to rouse the Israeli cabinet and public, despite the fact that the PLO took great pains not to violate the agreement of July 1981. Indeed, subsequent Israeli propaganda notwithstanding, the border between July 1981 and June 1982 enjoyed a state of calm unprecedented since 1968.[79]

But Sharon and Begin had a broader objective: the destruction of the PLO and its ejection from Lebanon. Once the organization was crushed, they reasoned, Israel would have a far freer hand to determine the fate of the West Bank and Gaza Strip. Indeed, the Palestinians might give up their national political aspirations altogether or look to their fulfillment in Jordan. To further this "Jordan is Palestine" solution, Israel might be willing to help overthrow the Hashemites, Sharon told a group of his associates at the end of June 1982.[80] Palestinian historian Rashid Khalidi later wrote: "'Operation Peace for Galilee' was in a very real sense a war for the future disposition of Palestine."[81]

Another objective was the restoration of Christian dominance in Lebanon, which would then sign a peace treaty with Israel. Sharon also hoped to achieve the removal of Palestinian population concentrations from Israel's borders. It was known in Jerusalem that Bashir Gemayel hoped to remove all of the Palestinians and their subversive refugee camps from the country.[82]

The ejection of the Syrian army from Lebanon was another goal.[83] The IDF's plan to attack the SAM network necessitated an advance on the ground up the Beka'a, through the protective crust of Syrian armor and infantry, to bring the batteries within artillery range. Though Sharon understood that a clash with the Syrians was inevitable, it is not clear whether Begin shared this assessment in the planning stages or came to realize this only after the war started.[84] Eitan apparently genuinely hoped to avoid such a clash.

Damascus knew that Israel would eventually mount a large-scale operation in Lebanon, but apparently felt this would be limited to in-and-out attacks against the PLO, perhaps a repeat of Operation Litani. Assad could live with this. The Syrians were to remain ignorant of Sharon's real aims until June 8–9, 1982. Assad may have reasoned that the Israelis were too smart to plunge headlong into the Lebanese swamp—in which he himself had been floundering since 1976.

During the summer of 1981 the IDF general staff began to improve two basic operational plans. "Little Pines" covered an invasion of southern Lebanon somewhat more ambitious than Operation Litani, designed to destroy the PLO military presence up to the Zaharani or the Awali River. Implicit in Little Pines was avoidance of a clash with the Syrians. "Big Pines" posited a more massive invasion, reaching as far north as Beirut, linking up with the Christian enclave, severing the Beirut-Damascus highway, and possibly also ejecting Syrian units from southern and central Lebanon and the southern Beka'a but, it was hoped, "without tackling the main Syrian deployment in the Beka'a."[85]

From the start Sharon pushed Big Pines. The PLO's headquarters and leadership, many of its weapons and ammunition stores, and many of its units were in and around Beirut. To destroy the PLO militarily and politically meant driving it out of Beirut. Similarly, to get the Syrian army out of southern and central Lebanon necessarily meant coming to grips with it, in the southern Beka'a, around Beirut, and along the Beirut–Damascus highway. Last, to install and assure a Christian-dominated regime meant reaching Beirut. To Sharon these objectives were always clear (even if he sometimes camouflaged them). In October 1981 he told the general staff: "When I speak of destroying the terrorists, it means *a priori* that [the operation] includes Beirut."[86] A few weeks before, he had told a political meeting: "Israel's objective is to see to it that Lebanon becomes an independent state that will live with us in peace . . . as well as to solve the problem of the Syrian presence in that country." But this "cannot happen so long as the terrorists control southern Lebanon and two-thirds of Beirut, and as long as the Syrians control whole sections of Lebanon. In other words, it is impossible to deal with this subject without taking care of the Syrians."[87]

But Sharon was usually cagey, leaving room for various interpretations: "We would much rather not deal with the Syrians . . . and avoid going to war against them," he said. Or: "The aim must be to reach Beirut, that is, Beirut's suburbs, or to wherever you [the general staff] decide." He always left loopholes and openings; ministers, generals, and future historians would never quite be able to pin him down. Over the months, he had recommended fighting the Syrians—and not fighting them; reaching Beirut—and not reaching it.[88]

Sharon and Begin's chief obstacle was not the PLO, the Syrians, or Washington but their own cabinet. Despite its narrowly right-wing character, too many ministers refused to approve Big Pines in the absence of clear provocation—something the PLO and the Syrians declined to provide. Begin was loath to launch an invasion without a cabinet consensus. But Begin, Sharon, and Eitan eventually managed to manipulate the ministers into approving Big

Pines after a hard, deceitful slog. First, in early June 1982, they exploited a Palestinian provocation to ram through ministerial approval of an escalation leading to war. Then, with cabinet approval of Little Pines under his belt, Sharon stretched the endorsement into a de facto "rolling" implementation of Big Pines. At each stage Sharon obtained piecemeal cabinet approval of a military operation either just before or just after its implementation, at a time when the ministers barely understood what was happening. Each time, they were browbeaten into approval by the argument that to withhold permission would result in needless loss of Israeli lives.

When Sharon submitted Big Pines to the ministers for the first time, on December 20, 1981, they were "stunned." When he unrolled his campaign map, with a black arrow reaching the Beirut–Damascus highway, their consternation increased. No, he said, the IDF did not intend to assault Beirut— that would be left to the Phalange, if they wanted to do it. Begin demanded that the ministers approve the plan immediately, in principle. But the cabinet, led by Interior Minister Yosef Burg, would not be jostled peremptorily into war. Begin backed down and adjourned the meeting without a decision.[89] Nevertheless, military and political preparations continued apace. The planners hoped the operation could be timed to promote Bashir Gemayel's prospects in the Lebanese presidential elections scheduled to take place in August.[90]

In the second week of January 1982 Sharon, with a large entourage, made his first secret visit, by helicopter, to the Lebanese Christian enclave. He was met by Gemayel, who hugged him and declared: "I knew you would be the one to come. Even though they didn't tell me, I was sure it would be you."[91] Gemayel took him around East Beirut and other points of interest, including Mount Senin (from which the Syrians had withdrawn). He lunched with Gemayel, Gemayel's father, Pierre, and Camille Chamoun at Bashir's home in Beirut. "Everything . . . was exquisite, elegant. A magnificent dinner was served, table manners were perfect, the most beautiful French was spoken— and all of it against this backdrop of assassination and death."[92] Chamoun asked whether the IDF would really come to Beirut, "or is all this just talk." Sharon: "We'll get there. Don't you worry." Pierre Gemayel wept as he pleaded for Israeli help. But when asked about the possibility of a Lebanese-Israeli peace treaty, he countered (according to Ze'ev Schiff and Ehud Ya'ari, the foremost chroniclers of the war): "We are not like [Maj. Sa'ad] Haddad. We are not traitors! . . . We must remain on good terms with the Arab world. We are part of it." Chamoun, too, was skeptical. But Sharon was not disheartened—and Bashir Gemayel more or less told him not to mind "the old men." Sharon declared that Israel would yet crown Bashir president.[93]

Sharon said later that it was during these meetings that Israel and the Phalange had sealed their "political-strategic alliance" and reached agreement on coordinating "joint military moves," an oblique reference to the planned IDF invasion.[94] Eitan visited the enclave in February and March, and other senior IDF officers went in April.

Repeatedly during the first months of 1982 Sharon and Eitan pounced on this or that incident, usually far from the Lebanese-Israeli border, that might serve as the necessary detonator. On January 28 a squad of Palestinians tried to infiltrate into Israel across the border with Jordan. Sharon and Eitan proposed to retaliate with an air attack on PLO targets in Lebanon. They hoped these would trigger a PLO artillery response against Israel's northern border settlements—providing the *casus belli*. But most of the participants at the decision-making meeting, including Begin himself, voted no.[95] Another attempt, on March 25, was triggered by a grenade attack on an IDF vehicle in the Gaza Strip, in which a soldier was killed.[96] This time Begin supported Sharon, but all the other ministers were opposed.[97]

The PLO commanders studiously reined in their units. But there were unruly non-PLO terrorist groups, such as the Abu Nidal faction; and there were dissident groups within the PLO. On April 3, 1982, a Mossad officer was shot dead in Paris. A group calling itself the "Lebanese Armed Revolutionary Factions" (possibly a cover name for the Abu Nidal group) claimed responsibility, but Israel blamed the PLO and labeled the murder a violation of the terms of the July 1981 cease-fire.[98] For its part, the PLO both denied responsibility and claimed—with Washington discreetly supporting this interpretation—that the agreement pertained only to the Israel-Lebanon border.

On April 21 an IDF officer was killed and another soldier wounded by a land mine inside the Security Zone. It was unclear whether this was the work of PLO men, a provocation by others, or an old mine triggered accidentally. Nonetheless Israel struck back. That afternoon IAF jets hit PLO targets south of Beirut, in Damour and Khalde, killing twenty-three people. Two Syrian MiG-23s that tried to interfere were shot down.[99] Arafat declined to be drawn into the trap; the PLO held its fire. Two weeks later, Israel charged the PLO with responsibility for two minings on the border, a bombing in the Israeli town of Ashkelon, and a bus-bombing in Jerusalem. On May 9 the IAF struck targets in Damour and southern Lebanon, and this time the PLO struck back, unleashing a barrage of rockets and shells. But none of the projectiles hit an Israeli settlement;[100] the gunners had been ordered to miss.

Nonetheless, Begin was eager to respond to the "provocation" and the cabinet was assembled the following day. Sharon and Eitan, this time presenting Little Pines, asked for a green light for a "policing operation," set to start on May 17. The meeting was characterized by a measure of ambiguity. While the maps unfurled by Sharon and Eitan distinctly showed arrows reaching the outskirts of Beirut, Sharon made no mention of reaching the capital, linking up with the Phalange, or attacking the Syrians. Indeed, he spoke of a "24-hour" operation. Communications Minister Mordechai Zippori, an ex-general himself, commented that the action would not remain "limited," as Sharon had postulated, but would snowball into a real war, implying that it would involve the Syrians as well. Begin blandly dismissed Zippori's prognosis.[101] But about half the ministers still shied away from war.[102]

Sharon was later repeatedly to state that on May 10 the ministers had in fact approved Big Pines, including the "link-up with the Phalange and a joint operation to take control of the city of Beirut."[103] It is unclear whether Begin, at this stage, understood that the IDF was going all the way to Beirut or that it intended to take on and drive out the Syrians.[104]

Sharon had made a point of explaining that Israel would not attack the Syrians. For example, in his December 5, 1981, meeting with Habib and William Brown, the American chargé d'affaires in Tel Aviv, Sharon had said: "We can free Israel and Lebanon of the PLO without fighting the Syrians. Assad won't intervene."[105] But the Israeli generals knew better. At the general staff meeting on May 13, 1982, intelligence chief Saguy predicted that, given the IDF plans, which involved outflanking the Syrian division in the Beka'a, a battle with the Syrians would ensue. Moreover, the Phalange, whatever its promises, would not lift a finger to help the IDF. Saguy spoke of the lack of Israeli national consensus in favor of the war and predicted major political problems in its wake: The IDF would find it much more difficult to leave Lebanon than it had to enter it.[106]

During the first half of 1982, the Reagan administration was repeatedly informed by Israeli officials of the resolve to invade Lebanon. Washington tended to sympathize with the Christians; the PLO, the Syrians, and their Lebanese allies were seen as Soviet clients. But, to the Americans, a more compelling consideration was the desire to maintain the status quo; with all its pitfalls, it left them uninvolved. On the other hand, a major crisis could lead to an Israeli-Syrian war or an Israeli-Soviet showdown, and might drag the United States into a confrontation with the USSR.

According to the memoirs of Secretary of State Alexander Haig, he repeatedly and consistently "cautioned" Israel against attacking, at least not "disproportionately" or without adequate provocation. In January, after meeting Begin, he had written to him saying that "only" a "strictly proportional response" to "an internationally recognized provocation" would be acceptable. But Haig recognized the limitations of Washington's influence over Israel. So, while "duty" perhaps obliged him to try to prevent an Israeli assault, his "ability to do so [was] questionable."[107]

The crucial American-Israeli exchange was to take place when Haig and Sharon met in Washington on May 19-20. It appears that Sharon obtained a limited green light for the invasion—or "a dim yellow light," in the words of one American analyst,[108] though in his memoirs Haig again emphasized that he told Sharon that if Israel acted without due provocation, the effect on the United States would be "devastating."[109] Most sources agree that Sharon told

Haig that while "we do not intend to attack Syria . . . it is almost impossible to act without hitting the Syrians." How far did the Israelis intend to go? asked an American official. "As far as we have to," replied Sharon. Haig let Sharon understand that, if Israel was adequately provoked, he would support a swift, sharp operation; he spoke of a "lobotomy." Sharon went home pleased.[110] A few days later, on May 29, Haig met Israel's Ambassador Arens and left him with the clear impression that the United States would support a forty-kilometer (twenty-five-mile)-deep offensive.[111]

But Washington was far more equivocal than Haig's remarks indicate. Haig himself, under pressure from his aides (and perhaps Reagan), on May 20 wrote directly to Begin expressing concern over a possible offensive and called on Israel to exercise "absolute restraint."[112] Begin had been warned: There might or might not be American support for a forty-kilometer anti-PLO venture; but certainly there would be none for anything that went beyond.

On the night of June 3, Israel's ambassador in London, Shlomo Argov, was shot in the head and severely wounded by members of the Abu Nidal group. The attack had probably been ordered by Abu Nidal himself, or by his Iraqi paymasters (who provided the weapons), specifically in order to provoke an Israeli assault on the PLO in Lebanon. If this was the motive, it worked. Although the shooting clearly was not a PLO operation, Begin was not to be deterred; here was the provocation for his long-sought war. "The ambassador represents Israel. An attack on him is tantamount to an attack on the state," he told the ministers.[113] He was not perturbed by the fact that the deed had been carried out by anti-PLO gunmen. "They're all PLO. Abu Nidal, Abu Schmidal. We have to strike at the PLO," he said.[114]

Begin's enthusiasm was fueled by his view of the PLO as a reincarnation of Nazism, and of Yasser Arafat as a latter-day Hitler. He was wont to call Arafat a "two-legged beast" and to compare the Palestinian National Covenant—which called for the dismantling of Israel—to *Mein Kampf*. In the final cabinet session before the invasion of Lebanon, on the evening of June 5, Begin told his ministers: "Believe me, the alternative to this [attacking the PLO in Lebanon] is Treblinka, and we have decided that there will not be another Treblinka." Later he was to write to President Reagan that the destruction of Arafat's headquarters in Beirut had given him the anachronistic feeling that he had sent the IDF into Berlin to destroy Hitler's bunker.[115] Amos Oz was later to write an open letter to Begin: "But Mr. Prime Minister . . . Hitler died 37 years ago. . . . Hitler is not hiding in Nabatiya, Sidon, or Beirut. He died and was burned." Dr. Herzl Rosenblum, the editor of Israel's most popular daily newspaper, *Yediot Aharonot*, responded to Oz's letter:

Arafat, were he stronger, would do to us things that Hitler never even dreamed of. . . . Hitler killed us with a measure of restraint. . . . If Arafat were to reach power, he would not amuse himself with such "small

things." He will cut off our children's heads with a cry and in broad daylight and will rape our women before tearing them to pieces and will
throw us down from all the rooftops and will skin us as do hungry leop-
ards in the jungle . . . without the famous "order" of the Germans. . . .
Hitler is a pussycat compared to what Arafat will bring upon us.[116]

Weeks later a Holocaust survivor, Dr. Shlomo Schmalzman, was to declare
a hunger strike at Yad Vashem to protest Begin's exploitation of the Holocaust
to justify the Lebanon war.[117]

On June 4, Eitan, with Begin's approval, proposed a massive air attack on
sixteen PLO targets, nine of them in the heart of Beirut,[118] saying that the raid
would most likely trigger a PLO bombardment of northern Galilee. The ministers understood that this would precipitate the long-planned IDF ground
assault on southern Lebanon. Wishing to limit civilian casualties, they gave
Eitan permission to attack only five of the proposed targets, including downtown Beirut's disused football stadium, where the PLO housed large quantities of weapons and munitions. Not one minister dissented, though all knew
that their vote was leading to war; none took account of the PLO's statement
that day deploring the attack on Argov.[119]

That afternoon Israeli jets hit Beirut and a number of PLO bases in southern Lebanon.[120] Two hours later, apparently after receiving Arafat's approval,
PLO gunners opened fire on Israel's northern border settlements, from
Nahariya in the west to Kiryat Shmonah in the east. The Israelis continued to
pound southern Lebanon throughout June 5.[121]

When the Israeli cabinet reconvened that night, a vote to invade was a foregone conclusion. The plan Sharon and Eitan presented was Little Pines,
whose defined and only purpose was to push back PLO artillery and rocket
launchers some forty kilometers, so that the Galilee settlements would be out
of their range. No mention was made of "destroying the PLO", reaching Beirut, linking up with the Phalange forces and enclave and establishing a pro-
Israeli Christian government, or fighting and driving out the Syrians.[122] On the
contrary, Sharon said there was no intention of clashing with them. But, by
thrusting northward, the IDF would "outflank" the Syrians in the Beka'a, if
possible forcing them to retreat northward, together with the PLO forces in
their sector.[123]

The only participant who voiced a suspicion of "foul play" was Communications Minister Zippori. He pointedly asked Sharon and Eitan for map references regarding the forty-kilometer limit of the advance and declared that, "in
simple Hebrew, we are going to attack the Syrians. I think this is wrong."
Begin angrily responded: "I said we will not attack the Syrians." Zippori: "It
does not matter what decisions we take. The moves described here will bring
us into contact with the Syrians." Sharon and Eitan spoke of Sidon and Lake
Karoun as the northernmost points of the prospective IDF thrust.

"What about Beirut . . . ?" asked Deputy Prime Minister Simcha Ehrlich.

Sharon: "Beirut is out of the picture. We mustn't enter Beirut. It is a capital city. . . . [But] if the Christians want to liberate their capital, that's their right. . . . We're talking about a range of 40 kilometers." As to the timetable, Sharon at first spoke of "12 hours," and then of "24 hours," to complete the operation.[124] (In his memoirs Eitan was to claim that the cabinet had approved the "Big Plan" [Big Pines]—" which explicitly included . . . conquest of a section of the Beirut–Damascus road.") On the evening of June 6, Eitan informed Bashir Gemayel that the IDF "goal" was to reach the road and "to link up with the Christians." He later flatly denied that the cabinet or the general staff had at any time spoken of a forty-to-forty-five-kilometer limit to the operation.[125]

Interestingly, at that decisive cabinet meeting on June 5, Begin was somewhat vaguer about the exact distance the IDF intended to advance. "One always knows how a war begins, but not how it ends. But I declare here that nothing will roll ahead of its own volition, as happened in Israel's previous wars. The cabinet will meet every day," he promised.[126]

In selling the war—that is, Little Pines—to the cabinet, Sharon had spoken of a "24-hour" campaign. No one seems to have asked how long he expected the IDF to stay in Lebanon *after the fighting*. To his aides, earlier, he had spoken of "six weeks"—long enough to assure Bashir Gemayel's election as president. (Saguy had spoken at the time of "not a day less than three months.")[127]

Despite the outrage over the Argov shooting and despite Sharon's declarations about the limited scope of the operation, there was still some hesitancy. A number of ministers held back. In the vote, three of them—Interior Minister Yosef Burg, Ehrlich, and Energy Minister Yitzhak Berman—abstained. But the other fourteen voted for Sharon's proposal.[128]

Earlier that day, June 5, Eitan—certain of the impending cabinet decision—had flown to the Christian enclave to inform Bashir Gemayel of the coming invasion and to make two requests: that, at the start of the hostilities, Bashir order his militiamen to open fire along the front lines in Beirut (to keep the PLO fighters in the capital occupied), and that he allow an IDF combat team to land in Jounieh, to be in position to attack the PLO from the rear. Gemayel turned down both requests.[129]

OPPOSING FORCES AND AIMS

Thanks to the peace treaty with Egypt, Israel was able to commit its entire standing, conscript army to the campaign in Lebanon. A number of reserve divisions were mobilized and held ready in northern Galilee. Altogether the IDF threw into the fray six to seven divisional task forces and an independent reinforced armored brigade,[130] with more than fifteen hundred tanks, as well as the whole of the air force and navy.

Facing this massive deployment were the PLO's military formations and part of the Syrian army. During 1978–81 Arafat had turned his forces in southern Lebanon from a loose array of guerrilla forces into a semiregular "army." In mid-1981 the PLO had only about 80 artillery pieces and Katyusha rocket launchers in the south; by June 1982, some 250.[131] Three infantry "brigades" were strung out between the sea and the Hermon, and a fourth in and around Beirut. These had about one hundred obsolescent tanks and several dozen antiaircraft guns.[132] The infantry had a few shoulder-held SAM-7s. The antiaircraft weaponry lacked radar and command-and-control systems.[133]

In April 1982 Arafat ordered his troops in the south onto an emergency footing and deployed two of the brigades northward, so that they were positioned within or adjacent to the Syrian First Division's defensive complex in the southern Beka'a.[134] The IDF estimated there were six to seven thousand PLO fighters in southern Lebanon, fifteen hundred of them south of the Litani and fifteen hundred in the foothills of Mount Hermon, known as "Fatahland."[135]

The PLO officers knew they could not defeat or halt an IDF offensive. But they could—and these were their orders—cause a large number of casualties and slow the Israelis down, in the hope that Arab or superpower intervention would force a halt before the invaders achieved their objectives.[136] The greatest shortcomings of the PLO forces in southern Lebanon, aside from inferiority in firepower and numbers, lay in command and control, communications, and logistics. Units fought, or ran away, alone. Israel's complete control of sky and coastline, and IDF interference with PLO communications, rendered Beirut unable to provide logistical support, reinforcement, or overall direction. The PLO enjoyed only rudimentary field intelligence, and through most of the crucial first week of fighting, Beirut remained in the dark about what was happening in the south.[137] The level of the PLO officer corps, trained by various Arab armies and in the Eastern Bloc, was low, and the training of the rank and file was deficient in all that pertained to conventional warfare.

Contributing to the PLO's ineffectiveness was the element of surprise. During the months and weeks before June 6, 1982, the leadership, on the basis of intelligence gleaned from contacts in the Phalange,[138] France, and the Arab states, and from observation of the Israeli buildup in northern Galilee, had understood that an assault was impending. Documents captured by the IDF show clearly that the PLO high command, various regional commanders, and the Syrian army all anticipated a major military strike.[139] On May 9, 1982, the PLO issued "Operational Order No. 1," which predicted: "Following the completion of its withdrawal from Sinai [in April 1982], Israel will attempt to realize its expansionist aims in Lebanon and to weaken the PLO. . . . Israel might try to achieve this by a main thrust along the Marj Ayoun–Nabatiya–Sidon axis . . . accompanied by intensive aerial support . . . a bombing of the revolutionary headquarters in Beirut, and this may trigger a direct conflict with the Syrian ground forces."

The document also predicted a secondary IDF thrust northward, up the Beka'a, toward the Syrian headquarters at Shtoura "in order to force the Syrian forces . . . to withdraw from Lebanon."[140] When the war actually began, however, the PLO was caught totally by surprise. So often since July 1981 had its leaders declared that invasion was imminent that when it happened, they couldn't believe they were seeing the real thing.

Thus, despite orders issued by the PLO's Supreme Military Council on April 28 predicting that the IDF assault would reach "the outskirts of Beirut and include marine and paratroop landings, especially at Damour,"[141] Arafat himself was off the scene in Saudi Arabia, trying to arrange a truce between Iraq and Iran.[142]

Until the Israelis reached the gates of Beirut on June 10 and came up against the Syrian Eighty-fifth Infantry Brigade, the PLO fought alone. The Arab states failed to intervene or even send substantial material assistance. Several planeloads of arms and medical supplies from Saudi Arabia and Algeria reached Damascus—but failed to get to Beirut. A force of several hundred Arab Legionnaires of Palestinian origin actually left Jordan but did not reach Beirut before it was sealed off by IDF siege.[143] Nor did the PLO's Lebanese allies come to its aid: The Sunni, Druze, and Shi'ite militias all watched from the sidelines.[144]

Syria, the most radical of the confrontation states, desperately tried to avoid battle and scrupulously refrained from assisting the PLO. The IDF was perceived as much stronger than the Syrian army and if Syria was to fight Israel, it would be on its own terms. So long as the Israelis left the Syrian units alone and stayed out of the Beka'a, the Syrians would not interfere. (Assad may also have been motivated by his distaste for Arafat, who for almost two decades had energetically parried his efforts to turn the PLO into a Syrian vassal.)[145]

By mid-1982 the Syrian army had almost completed the process, accelerated after 1973, of becoming fully mechanized and armored. It consisted of four armored and two mechanized infantry divisions, two independent armored and two independent mechanized infantry brigades, and two dozen or so "commando"—that is, elite infantry—battalions and a number of reserve armored, artillery, and infantry brigades. The bulk of this force was deployed between the Golan Heights and Damascus and in bases around the capital. (Perhaps the IDF's goal of engaging the Syrians in June 1982 stemmed, at least partly, from a desire to maul their army before it completed its renovation.[146])

The Syrian expeditionary force, whose advance elements had entered Lebanon in June 1976, at this time consisted of some three hundred tanks, about three hundred artillery pieces and heavy mortars, eighty APCs, and around thirty thousand troops. It was widely dispersed, protecting a number of separate strategic locations—Beirut itself, the Beirut–Damascus highway, and the Beka'a, where since April 1981, the Syrians had introduced about fifteen SAM-2, -3, and -6 batteries.[147]

Once Israel's intentions became clear, as IDF units pushed toward vital junctions and Syrian troop concentrations, Assad could choose between humiliating withdrawal or battle against superior forces. He opted to fight, as Saguy and Zippori had predicted he would. Israel suspected that his strategic aim was a "Greater Syria," or the annexation of Lebanon. However, it is possible to put a less imperialistic gloss on his actions: Lebanon was a natural area of Syrian influence, and Assad was bent on putting a stop to its civil wars, which perennially threatened to suck Syria—with its own mosaic of sometimes restless groupings—into the conflict or to propel it into conflict with Iraq or the PLO or Israel. In this reading Assad was reluctantly drawn into the Lebanese quagmire and then found it impossible to withdraw without damaging Syrian interests and credibility.

In 1982 Syria regarded its continued military control of and presence in the Beka'a as imperative. The crucial factor was Israel rather than Lebanese faction fighting or economic interests (though Assad's brother, Rif'at, reportedly was heavily engaged in trafficking drugs grown in the valley—and some of the revenue reached the Syrian Treasury). The Beka'a was seen as the strategic back door to Damascus. In a future conflict, the IDF might well decide to bypass the thick swathe of Syrian defenses between the Golan and Damascus and swing an indirect "left hook" through the Beka'a. Syria's deployment there was largely geared to neutralizing this threat. And it was to keep this back door to Damascus firmly shut that, on June 9, the Syrians rushed their Third Armored Division and fresh SAM batteries into the valley, bringing their forces in Lebanon up to the fifty-to-sixty-thousand mark.

Sharon's aims were to crush the PLO and drive its remnants out of Lebanon; to push the Syrians out; and to install a pro-Israeli government. It was the contradiction between the real and the official aims—and the different military actions required for each—that hamstrung the planning and conduct of the offensive. In early spring 1982 the generals had been told to prepare their troops for Big Pines. But following the cabinet veto of Big Pines in May, orders went out to prepare for Little Pines. Some generals, such as Eitan and Amir Drori, OC Northern Command, knew that the real goal was Beirut and the Beirut–Damascus highway, inevitably leading to a clash with the Syrians. But the operational orders could not be explicit, and the initial troop movements could be directed only at the more limited, formal war aim.

Hence, none of the originally planned Big Pines opening moves—such as a preliminary assault against the Syrian antiaircraft system in the Beka'a and deep-penetration landings around Beirut or along the highway—could be set

Israel's Invasion of Lebanon, June 1982

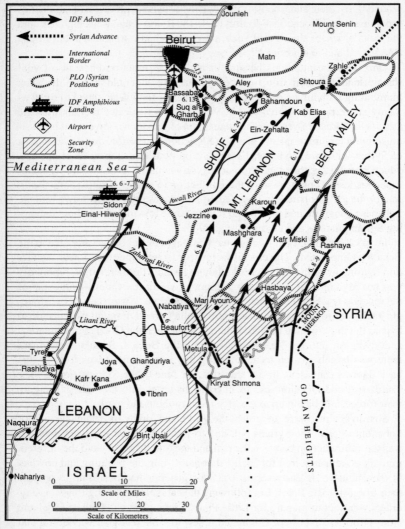

in motion; the long-planned frontal thrust up the southern Beka'a could not begin until *after* Israeli and Syrian forces had clashed elsewhere. Nor could the IDF land heliborne forces in the rear of the Syrian First Division, to cut off its path of retreat and, at the same time, to block the entry into the valley of Syrian units sent to reinforce the First Division.[148]

The IAF began bombing Lebanon on June 4; the ground forces crossed the border at 11:00 A.M. on June 6. The giant armored columns—a divisional column, consisting of a thousand or so vehicles, could stretch back for miles—proceeded along three principal axes, pushing through Haddad's Security Zone and brushing past the UNIFIL checkposts to the north before pouring into Lebanon. The 91st Division,[149] commanded by Gen. Yitzhak Mordechai, pushed directly north along the coast road and along several roads to its east, heading for Tyre and the surrounding refugee camps; the 36th Division, commanded by Gen. Avigdor Kahalani, entered Lebanon from the Galilee Panhandle and headed northwest to link up with Mordechai's south of Sidon; and the 162nd division, commanded by Gen. Menachem Einan, followed Kahalani across the Litani but then headed due north, aiming to reach the Beirut–Damascus highway.

Einan's projected advance was a key element in the Israeli plan to leave the Syrian Eighty-fifth Brigade stranded in Beirut and at the same time threaten to cut off the First Division in the southern Beka'a. But speed was essential and because of the paucity of useable axes and the heavy, competing traffic, Einan got off to a slow start. Damascus ordered its troops not to fire unless fired on and not to redeploy to face the Israelis. No effort was made to reinforce the First Division or, indeed, the forces facing the Israelis on the Golan. Assad clearly sought to avoid battle.[150]

That morning Begin took steps to cover his political flanks. He wrote to President Reagan explaining the aim of the war, which he dubbed "Operation Peace for Galilee" (shades of Orwell's "War Is Peace"): to push the PLO back forty kilometers, so that the settlements of northern Israel would be beyond the range of its guns and rockets.[151] And he briefed the leaders of the main opposition Labor Party. On May 16 Begin and Sharon had told Labor's leaders—Peres, Rabin, and Chaim Bar-Lev—that the planned thrust northward would include the Sidon area, the implication being that it would not reach as far as Beirut.[152] On the morning of June 6 Begin explained that forty kilometers was the limit—and shrugged off Bar-Lev's warning that the Syrians would be sucked in.[153] Labor reluctantly gave its blessing.[154]

Late that night the UN Security Council, as expected, demanded in Resolution 509 that Israel withdraw immediately and unconditionally to the international frontier. The United States voted for the resolution—but only for form's sake. Reagan and Haig, though perhaps troubled by the Israeli operation, were not going to rein Begin in before he achieved his professed forty-kilometer goal. American policy on Lebanon was founded on keeping the Soviets out and their local clients out of power. During the 1975–76 civil war, Washington had vaguely supported the Christians and, more emphatically, opposed the PLO's destabilization of the Lebanese state and a clear Muslim-Palestinian victory—and supported the Syrian intervention to save the Maronites and pacify the country. From 1980 the Reagan administration's primary goal had been to prevent a major Israeli-Syrian conflict, partly because it could lead to an East-West confrontation. The reaction to the invasion was ambivalent: Haig supported giving Israel time and freedom to destroy the PLO and oust the Syrians. But others, eventually including Reagan, feared the outbreak of full-scale Israeli-Arab war and Soviet involvement, and felt that a halt to military operations and speedy Israeli (and, they hoped, Syrian) evacuation were desirable.

Half an hour after crossing the line at Ras al-Naqurah, Mordechai's lead unit, the 211th Armored Brigade, commanded by Col. Eli Geva, encountered a PLO ambush just south of Tyre. The Palestinian fighters showed great courage, taking on armor with RPGs and light weapons, but eventually the Israeli tanks took and crossed the Kasmiya Bridge. That evening, according to Sharon, Begin and the full cabinet "formally approved" the extension of the IDF push beyond the forty-kilometer limit, mainly with the aim of threatening the Syrian rear so that the First Division would pull back northward.[155]

That night, June 6–7, an IDF naval flotilla landed two battalions of paratroops, with several companies of tanks and supporting artillery and mortars, on a beach just north of Sidon and the Awali River.[156] Coming as a complete surprise, the landing encountered only light opposition, despite the prediction weeks before that the IDF would in fact make an amphibious effort in the rear of the PLO forces. As anticipated by the IDF, the landing had a tremendous psychological impact and hastened the collapse of organized PLO resistance south of the Awali.[157] The PLO's Kastel Brigade, responsible for the Tyre-Sidon sector, fell apart; its commanders departed the scene, and many of the troops fled north.[158]

The brigade's failure to attack the Israeli beachhead reflected the lack of intelligence and organization, and the infirmity at the top, in most PLO regular formations. Almost from the first moment, the brigade and its six constituent battalions failed to function as regular military units. Instead, junior officers and NCOs independently took small units—squads and platoons—and either resolutely engaged the Israelis or ran away. By and large, the officers and men of the regular PLO brigades tended to flee. Only one senior officer—Lt. Col. 'Azmi Sghayir, commander of the Fatah battalion in Tyre—stayed at his post and fought till death.

In contrast, the dispersed local garrisons and militiamen offered real resistance, often to the last. Among those who gave battle were a platoon of Palestinians manning the hilltop Beaufort position, overlooking the Litani River and the Hardala Bridge. Here the Golani Brigade's crack reconnaissance company had to fight through the night of June 6–7 to overcome fierce opposition. By daybreak the remains of the medieval Crusader fortress—periodically bombed and shelled by the IDF for a decade—were in Israeli hands, and all the defenders were dead. So were six members of the assaulting company.[159] Beaufort had a panoramic view of the Security Zone and northeastern Israel. Begin was flown there by helicopter that morning (June 7) in his brief and only visit to Lebanon during the war. Sharon misinformed him that no Israelis had died in conquering the position—and an irate Golani lieutenant promptly set the record straight. In a somewhat ludicrous ceremony, Begin turned over control of the fortress to Haddad and his SLA militiamen.[160]

Along the coastal road, concentrations of militiamen in the big towns and refugee camps were putting up a fight in guerrilla fashion. General Saguy had predicted as much on June 4:

> [T]here will be strong Palestinian resistance in these places. You can flee from a [rural] outpost, but it's not so easy to get up and run when you're in a city, and especially not in a refugee camp, where there are families—old people and children. They'll fight in these places; these are the vital centers of their lives. They'll lay mines, fire off RPGs from every nook and cranny. Wherever we advance, when night falls we'll find ourselves cut off from behind.[161]

Having bypassed Tyre and its refugee camps, Geva's brigade had rushed northward. But it took infantry units four days to quell resistance and take the Rashidiya camp; three and a half days to take Burj ash-Shamali; three days at al-Bass. The camps had organized well for defense, each crisscrossed with bunkers, trench networks, and firing positions. And the local militiamen, using Kalashnikov assault rifles, RPGs, and grenades, were determined. The Israelis' advantage in armor and firepower was often offset by the narrow alleyways and by the presence of large numbers of civilians, whom the IDF was reluctant to harm. In order to avoid casualties on both sides, the Israeli commanders proceeded in each camp in what became a standard, step-by-step fashion. First, the residents of successive sections of the camp were warned by loudspeakers of impending attack. Next, each targeted section was heavily shelled; often air strikes were called in. Then infantry moved in, advancing cautiously from house to house. The defenders fought grimly, occasionally using civilians as human shields. By June 9, all the Tyre area camps had fallen. About half the buildings in Rashidiya were destroyed; other camps also suffered substantial damage. Hundreds of Palestinians lay dead; twenty-one Israelis died and ninety-five were wounded.[162]

Geva's tanks—followed by dozens of empty APCs that were destined for Gen. Amos Yaron's undersized amphibious division waiting at the Awali

Estuary—sped northward on June 7. By evening the brigade, with the bulk of Mordechai's division in its wake, was on the outskirts of Sidon. But there it was to stay for almost two days, halted by strong resistance along the main streets and by the militiamen in the 'Ein al-Hilwe refugee camp on the south-eastern edge of town.[163] An effort by paratroops to take central Sidon and clear the south–north route through the city failed.

With the through-road blocked, Geva decided to skirt Sidon. During the night of June 8, his tanks and APCs made a difficult detour through the hills to the east. By dawn they had made it to the Awali and linked up with Yaron's division, whose core was the Thirty-Fifth Paratroop Brigade.[164]

That same morning, another force of paratroops, backed by armor and massive air support and artillery, inched its way along two axes through central Sidon. By evening, a south–north route had been cleared; most of the buildings on either side had been badly damaged and their inhabitants evacuated. Kahalani's division was now able to traverse the city and link up with Geva's and Yaron's troops on the Awali. Mordechai's paratroops were left to take care of 'Ein al-Hilwe camp and the old Kasbah area, to the west of the south–north axis.

The battle for the camp lasted a full week, and was dubbed by Schiff and Ya'ari "suicidal," the Palestinian "Masada." The camp defenders, PLO militiamen and Muslim fundamentalists, fought like "men possessed," though their struggle no longer had a strategic purpose—the IDF had already secured the south–north route and bypassed the camp. On June 10, a mixed force of Golani and armor attacked the camp, while the paratroops, led by armored bulldozers, tackled the old part of Sidon. It took three days to complete the capture of the Kasbah. Advancing from house to house with extreme caution, they suffered no casualties. Golani, at 'Ein al-Hilwe, had a different experience. There the defenders fought over each alley and house; the mosques and the camp hospital proved to be formidable strongholds. Civilians who pleaded for surrender were shot dead by the fundamentalists. The IDF pounded section after section of the camp with air and artillery fire, gradually reducing it to rubble. During pauses in the shelling the Israelis, on the advice of psychologists, sent in delegation after delegation of Lebanese civilians and captured PLO officers to persuade the defenders to give up. All were rebuffed.

Meanwhile, Golani, now joined by paratroops, gnawed at 'Ein al-Hilwe's fringes, gradually closing in on the center of the camp. By Saturday, June 12, the scene was set for the main assault on the command bunker. Artillery and tanks flattened each section as the ground troops inched forward. That evening the paratroops reached the bunker and blew it up with an enormous charge of TNT. Mopping-up operations continued for two more days, with Palestinian squads offering haphazard resistance. A last stand took place in one of the camp mosques, ending only with its demolition by IDF sappers. The last of the defenders was killed on June 14.[165]

Starting on June 7, Yaron's undersized division inched northward out of the Awali beachhead without waiting for Kahalani's and Mordechai's divisions. No one, apparently, had informed Yaron of Begin's "forty-kilometer" limit, and by the following day, June 8, he and Yoram Yair, CO of the Thirty-fifth Paratroop Brigade, were telling their troops that the goal was Beirut.[166] Indeed, according to Yair's memoir of the war, "all those present" at a briefing on the morning of June 9 knew that "the real aims in our sector were to reach the Beirut–Damascus road in order to cut off the Syrian forces in Beirut, and to link up with the Christian forces."[167]

Throughout, the paratroops took care not to harm Lebanese and Palestinian civilians living in the houses along the route, and to fire only when fired upon and only at the sources of fire. Underlining the somewhat bizarre nature of the war, Lebanese families watched the sporadic IDF-PLO firefights from nearby balconies and rooftops. Occasionally the Lebanese offered the Israelis soft drinks and sweets.

At Damour, the division split in two. The bulk of Yaron's troops—two armored brigades and a paratroop battalion—set off at noon on June 9 along the shortest route, straight up the coastal highway to the southern edge of Beirut. At the same time the bulk of Yair's paratroops took the longer, mountainous route northeastward toward the hills dominating the Lebanese capital from the southeast.

FIGHTING THE SYRIANS

On June 8 Begin had told the Knesset: "[W]e are not interested in a war with Syria. . . . I call upon President Assad to order the Syrian army not to harm Israeli soldiers and no harm will befall them in return. . . . Once we reach a line forty kilometers from our border, our job will be done; the fighting will stop."[168] In his memoirs Eitan claimed that he and Sharon agreed that the IDF's objective "was the terrorists, not the Syrians," and that if they "did not stand in our way . . . it was best that the operation end without a clash with the Syrians."[169] It had been repeated Syrian attacks and threatening troop movements that ultimately forced the IDF to "counterattack," he wrote, citing a "Syrian" artillery salvo (which may well have been loosed by PLO guns inside the Syrian-controlled Beka'a) on June 7. By June 8, maintained Eitan, it became clear to the general staff that the Syrians had decided to fight.[170]

The Syrians initially seem to have believed the Israeli declarations of intent. As Defense Minister Tlass later put it: "[T]he [Israeli] act of aggression itself did not come at all as a surprise. But the scope of the aggression did not become apparent to us until the morning of June 9, when the enemy widened the geographical scope of his activities."[171]

U.S. Secretary of State Haig was equally unaware that the Syrian expeditionary force and the SAM complex in the Beka'a were among Sharon's targets, and that an IDF division was heading for the Beirut–Damascus highway, far beyond the forty-kilometer limit. On the first day of the war Haig had relayed Begin's assurances to Damascus. And as late as June 8–9 these assurances were directly conveyed to Assad in Damascus by Ambassador Habib, after he had met with Begin in Jerusalem. But they were accompanied by demands that the Syrian army refrain from firing at the IDF, pull back the PLO forces in the Beka'a to a line forty kilometers north of the border, and pull back those of its troops that over June 7–8 had advanced southward and westward. If Syria complied, Israel would not attack its army. As expected in Jerusalem, Assad rejected these demands.[172]

Begin and Sharon may have hoped that as the IDF crossed the border, Assad would take fright and simply order his forces out of Lebanon, or at least out of the southern and central sectors. But such behavior would have been out of character, as the intelligence chiefs had made clear. Sharon certainly believed, on June 6–7, that the IDF was heading for a major clash with the Syrians, and it is likely that Begin also thought so. It would appear that Begin's public utterances and diplomatic footwork during June 6–8 were part of a deliberate effort to deceive Assad (and the Americans) about Israel's real intentions.[173]

On June 7 Israeli forces had already destroyed a Syrian APC, killing five men, near Sidon. More tellingly the IAF had demolished the Syrian-manned radar stations at Damour, south of Beirut, and at Rayak in the northern Beka'a, with the aim of blinding Syrian air defenses. The Syrians failed to respond, seemingly giving more credence to Begin's public utterances than to the IDF's very concrete signals.[174]

On June 8—just as Begin was telling the Knesset of his desire to avoid battle—Israeli troops clashed, on their own initiative, with a reinforced Syrian brigade around the town of Jezzine, a vital east–west and north–south junction.[175] The brigade was protecting the right flank of the First Division. Israeli aircraft attacked tanks heading for the town from the Beka'a. But some reinforcements reached Jezzine and an armored brigade was ordered to eject them.[176] The Israeli column approached, and the Syrians opened fire;[177] as Sharon had intended, they had risen to the bait. What followed was a concentrated Israeli assault on the town, with the remnants of the Syrian brigade fleeing eastward, to the Beka'a. It was quite beside the point who had fired the first shot, though later Israeli spokesmen were falsely to describe the battle as a "Syrian initiative."[178]

The Syrians responded to the fall of Jezzine by rushing five more SAM batteries into the Beka'a, bringing the total to nineteen, and dispatching several commando battalions to block the route along which Einan's division was advancing. They also launched Gazelle helicopters, armed with HOT missiles, against Einan's tanks,[179] which bypassed Jezzine, taking serpentine, mountainous northward routes. Einan advanced unopposed along an axis roughly midway between the PLO concentrations along the coast (then being overrun by Mordechai's and Kahalani's divisions) and the Syrian forces in the Beka'a. By evening on June 8 his lead units were on the outskirts of the Druze village of Ein Zahalta, perched along a winding, wooded mountain defile four miles short of the Beirut–Damascus highway. The Syrians had been thrashed at Jezzine but had simultaneously prepared a new line of defense farther north with orders to stop Einan's advance at all costs. It was the worst possible terrain for armored advance and combat. The vehicles could not get off the road and presented the Syrian commandos with easy targets. The fighting, involving tanks and missile-carrying infantry and paratroops, was bitter and protracted. The Syrians managed to hold up Einan's advance for sixty hours,[180] and he had failed to gain his objective—the Beirut–Damascus highway—when, at noon on June 11, an American-engineered cease-fire went into effect.[181]

For Israel, the most acute strategic problem left by the October 1973 war had been the Soviet-built SAM systems in Syria and Egypt. The best minds in the IAF and IDF—pilots, electronics and communications experts, and munitions scientists—had labored to solve the problem, and by June 1982 they had put together a package—consisting of special ordnance, electronic countermeasures (ECM) and radar-tracking equipment, communications and radar jamming pods, drones, and a complex, synchronized plan of attack—that was equal to the task. The destruction of the missile system in the Beka'a was to be clean and swift, and the shock to the Syrians and the Soviets immense. Afterward there were Israeli military experts who were to bewail the "waste" (and exposure) of the surprise package in a minor affair when it should have been kept under wraps for use in a full-scale war.

Be that as it may, Begin had sworn back in the spring of 1981 to take out the missile system, and on June 6, 1982, Sharon remarked: "There is no way that we will end this operation while these missiles remain in place."[182] The opportunity, to Sharon's mind, arose immediately after the conquest of Jezzine. Two days after the IDF assault on the Beka'a missile network, he publicly explained his reasoning: "The Syrians cheated the mediator Habib and moved more troops into Lebanon, and so we were forced to act against them. . . . The Syrians exploited [Habib's] stay in Damascus [June 8–9] to [commit] an act of deception by reinforcing the missile network in the Beka'a."[183]

On the morning of June 9, Sharon proposed to the cabinet that the IDF attack and destroy the missile system. He had delayed submitting the proposal because of anticipated opposition and political problems—both internal and with the Americans—that the strike would surely generate. Moreover, during the war's first days senior commanders had objected to the expansion of the campaign to include a clash with the Syrians. Eitan, Drori, and air force commander Maj. Gen. David Ivri had all expressed reservations about attacking the missile system. But by that morning, with Einan stuck at 'Ein Zahalta, and with the Syrian Third Armored Division about to join the First in the Beka'a, the attack—and its corollary, Ben-Gal's multidivisional thrust up the Beka'a—could be delayed no longer.

Sharon failed to inform the cabinet of the IDF's reservations or of the possible repercussions of the move. He argued that the army was hard-pressed and taking casualties. To reduce losses, the air force had to provide effective ground support, and the missile system must be taken out first. Gen. Amos Amir, the deputy commander of the IAF, told the cabinet that aircraft losses were expected to be minimal.[184] Thus confronted, the ministers really had no choice. And the implied corollary to their approval of the antimissile strike was, in effect, a green light for the full-scale advance of two divisions into and up the Beka'a—though this too, apparently, was never clearly spelled out. Indeed, they appear to have been unaware that Sharon had in effect asked for, and that they, in effect, had given, approval for a major ground offensive against the Syrians as well as the anti-SAM strike.[185]

The two-hour attack on June 9 was an historic event in modern warfare—for the first time, a Western air force successfully tackled and annihilated a complex, sophisticated Soviet-built SAM network. Neither Israel nor Syria has ever published a clear description of the attack, and how the IDF destroyed the missiles remains one of the best-kept Israeli military secrets. What is known is that the Israelis employed a staggered mix of long-range shelling and rocketing from the ground, communications and radar jammers, pilotless decoy and radar-tracking aircraft, airborne electronic countermeasures, and strike aircraft delivering a mix of steel, cluster, and smart bombs.[186] It is possible that the assault was aided by a preliminary commando attack on a crucial air defense control center inside Syria. The Beka'a SAM complex straddled the Syrian-Lebanese border and "many" of the missiles hit (with advance cabinet knowledge and approval), according to Ivri's testimony at the Israeli cabinet meeting of September 5, 1982, were on the Syrian side.

By 4:00 P.M. it was all over: Almost all of the nineteen batteries were completely destroyed and others sustained severe damage.[187] In the latter part of the attack, the Syrians threw in about one hundred MiG-21 and MiG-23 aircraft in an effort to save their SAMs. Some two dozen MiGs were shot down by IAF interceptors, the Syrians losing many of their best pilots and navigators. The IAF sustained no losses in the attack on the SAMs and in the subsequent mass dogfight. The Syrian forces in the Beka'a were left without substantive air defenses.[188]

That night the IAF devastated the Syrian Forty-seventh Armored Brigade north of Baalbek, as it made its way southward,[189] and the following day destroyed another six SAM batteries—two that had survived from the original nineteen and four more that the Syrians had pushed into the Beka'a on the night of June 9–10. Two weeks later, the IAF destroyed three more batteries deployed after the original assaults.[190]

The June 9 antimissile strike "changed the timetable of the war."[191] The possibility of a full-scale Israeli-Syrian war, encompassing both Lebanon and the Golan, now loomed, and with it, possible superpower intervention, including an imposed cease-fire. Assad sent Defense Minister Tlass scrambling to Moscow to seek a comprehensive Soviet air umbrella. The Soviets refused but began massing large quantities of military equipment at airfields for immediate dispatch to Syria.[192] On the night of June 9 the Soviets sent their air defense chief, Marshal Pavel Kutakhov, to Syria to find out what had happened in the Beka'a: If Israel could wipe out a SAM network with such ease, perhaps NATO could do the same in Eastern Europe.

In Jerusalem, it was clear that the IDF was fast running out of time. And, on cue, Washington stepped in. On June 9 Assad had rejected Habib's terms and demanded Israel's withdrawal from Lebanon as a condition for Syria's acceptance of a cease-fire. President Reagan had sent personal cease-fire demands to both Assad and Begin. He assured Assad that, should he agree to a cease-fire, Washington would see to it that Israel would withdraw. To Begin, Reagan added open reproof of the prime minister's deceit.[193] "I am extremely concerned" about reports of the IDF advance, he wrote, which had gone "significantly beyond the objectives that you have described to me." There was a danger of a wider Israeli-Syrian war and of possible Soviet involvement, Reagan warned. He called on Begin and Assad to accept a cease-fire effective at 6:00 A.M., on June 10.[194]

Haig's green light had quickly changed to orange and was fast turning red. The Israelis assumed that Haig's enemies in Washington had gained the upper hand. (They were right—by June 25 Haig was forced to resign, to be succeeded as Secretary of State by George Shultz.[195]) Begin convened his cabinet at 4:00 A.M. on June 10. The mood was grim. The war was taking much longer than anyone had projected; Israeli casualties were higher; and the army was now fully engaged against the Syrians. And, with the IDF having wiped out the Syrian air defense system without loss and on the verge of trouncing their army of occupation in the Beka'a, the powers seemed bent on snatching victory from Israel's grasp. The ministers were in no mood to bow to an American *diktat*. For once Sharon spoke for the majority when he called Reagan's message an "ultimatum, which should not be acquiesced in." Instead, the ministers decided to play for time. The cabinet empowered Begin to respond that Israel accepted a cease-fire in principle, but Syria had to agree to a set of (for it unacceptable) conditions, including withdrawal of the Third Division northward and withdrawal of all PLO forces from the forty-kilometer zone north of Metulla. In a telephone conversation with Haig, Begin made it clear that the

IDF would not halt before conquering territory to the depth of forty kilometers up the Beka'a.[196]

Assad, too, declined to accept the American terms promptly and unreservedly. He demanded that the IDF immediately agree to a complete pullback from Lebanon. Needless to say, this was unacceptable to Jerusalem (and to Washington). Thus Begin and Sharon won a few more hours for their armored columns. But clearly, time was very short.

Begin's delaying tactics had been designed primarily to facilitate Ben-Gal's offensive, which had haltingly begun on the afternoon of June 9, just as the antimissile strike ended. On the morning of June 10, it was resumed, this time with great vigor. Ben-Gal's main objective was the Beirut–Damascus highway. But to take this he had to crush, and get past, the Syrian First Division, dug in in the southern Beka'a, and elements of the Third Armored Division that had crossed into Lebanon and begun to push down the valley from the north.

Ben-Gal's force, initially two divisions (the 252nd and 36th) reinforced by a third large task force, enjoyed the benefits of complete air superiority and an overwhelming advantage in firepower and numbers, though the terrain, especially on his mountainous, eastern flank, did not always allow these to be brought to bear. He had less than forty-four hours in which to accomplish his task. Everything was to depend on offensive determination and speed of advance and, obversely, on Syrian resolve in defense. Thus for both armies, it was a race against time. The Israelis had to destroy the First Division and reach the highway before a cease-fire was in place; and the Syrians, to reinforce the First before it was wiped out and to hold fast south of the road. As it turned out, the Syrians won the race.[197] On June 10, Ben-Gal's columns demolished the bulk of the First Division, and in the early morning hours of June 11, his westernmost task force, commanded by Gen. Yossi Peled, reached Kab Elias, a point about three miles short of the vital highway, when he was ordered to halt.

The battle for the lower Beka'a ended with an effective cease-fire in place at noon on June 11. The Israelis had gained ground, wiped out the Syrian air defense system, and virtually destroyed the First Armored Division; but they had been denied their main objective.[198] Generals and officials were subsequently to criticize the government's acceptance of the cease-fire, which had saved the Syrian army from decisive defeat—a fact that was to have important repercussions in the following months and years.

Defense Minister Tlass was later to maintain that it had been the resolute Syrian opposition and the heavy Israeli losses that had prompted the Israelis to seek a cease-fire and to halt their advance up the Beka'a. In fact, the cease-fire was forced on Israel by the Americans, themselves prodded by implicit Soviet threats. Internal opposition to the invasion also contributed to the Israeli decision. But it was primarily the looming cease-fire rather than their own losses or Syrian military effectiveness that halted the advance (though stiff Syrian resistance had, in fact, substantially slowed it down).[199]

As things turned out, however, Ben-Gal's failure to cut the highway was not crucial. The thrust along the western axis by General Yaron's division—just after both Ben-Gal and Einan had come to a stop—solved the problem.

As Yair's paratroops made their way northeastward, up the escarpment overlooking the coast road, Yaron's tanks slowly pressed northward along the coast, eventually coming up against Syrian and PLO forces dug in at the Khalde junction, the southern entrance to the capital, on June 12. By early the next morning the Israelis had complete control of the junction, affording them a dominant position overlooking the runways of Beirut International Airport.[200]

But the strategically more significant advance was that of the paratroops slogging on foot up a series of ridges east of the coast road. The area, mountainous, rocky, and heavily wooded, was stubbornly if sporadically defended by Syrian commandos and Palestinian irregulars. On June 11, Yair was told to halt the fighting at noon, in deference to the UN resolution. But almost immediately afterward, he was ordered to resume the attack, in line with what Sharon told a group of journalists the same day: "We have no cease-fire with the terrorists. We did not decide on a cease-fire and did not sign a cease-fire agreement with them."[201] The paratroops pressed northward, toward the Christian enclave. "The Christian forces are awaiting us. For years they have waited for this moment, when IDF forces would reach them and tilt the scales in their favor in their brutal and desperate war against the Syrian army and the Palestinian terrorists," wrote Yair.[202] At noon on June 13 the paratroops reached Phalange-held territory at Bassaba, cutting the Beirut–Damascus road just east of the capital.[203]

Sharon had repeatedly told the cabinet that his forces had no intention of linking up with the Christians—but the Christians were free to push southward and connect with them.[204] The truth was somewhat different. On June 11 in Jounieh, Sharon and Bashir Gemayel finalized the details of the link-up[205]—and it was the IDF that did the pushing, with the Phalange sitting tight and waiting. Moreover, the Phalange consistently rejected Israeli requests that its forces advance into PLO-held Beirut.[206] But Sharon was subsequently to argue that it was the IDF command that had "avoided activating" the Lebanese Forces during the first stages of the war, and that they had increasingly intervened in the fighting during its later stages—while conceding that they had not evinced "the full usefulness that the IDF had expected."[207]

The week-long IDF campaign had split Lebanon into four quarters. The Syrians occupied the Beka'a in the east and part of the north; the Israelis were in the south up to Beirut and the Damascus road; the Christians controlled East Beirut and the mountainous hinterland to its east and northeast; and Syrian units and the PLO held West Beirut, surrounded on three sides by IDF and Christian forces and on the fourth by the Mediterranean Sea, controlled and patrolled by the Israeli navy. The IAF had complete mastery of the skies. The Syrian Eighty-fifth Brigade and the PLO's leadership and surviving military forces, as well as the crowded refugee camps on the city's southern fringes, were isolated and virtually at Israel's mercy.

The IDF-Phalange linkup had taken place several days later than planned. During June 13–14 the IDF occupied more suburbs southeast of Beirut— including Yarze, the site of the Lebanese Defense Ministry, and Ba'abda, the site of the presidential palace. Units also moved into Christian neighborhoods of East Beirut proper. This deployment in and around the capital was unsanctioned by the Israeli cabinet. The first Prime Minister Begin heard of the armored presence in Ba'abda was when Habib informed him of it.[208] Indeed, on June 13, Sharon told the cabinet that the IDF was not "in Beirut," only in suburbs outside the municipal boundaries—and that this had happened because the "terrorists" had broken the cease-fire.[209] IDF units took Beirut International Airport on June 14–16.

The Phalange avoided fighting the PLO. Bashir always told Israelis that he was willing to engage the Palestinians and/or the Muslim militias—"but in that case you will find me at the head of a small Christian state within a divided Lebanon."[210] Throughout the summer of 1982 he argued that joining the fight against the PLO would jeopardize his chances of becoming president—and only as president, he argued, could he help realize Israel's goals.[211]

The IDF's position around Beirut was uncomfortable. To the east the Syrians still occupied the 'Aley-Bahamdoun Ridge. There were daily skirmishes and artillery duels, with the IDF in inferior topographical positions. From June 19, without cabinet knowledge or sanction, Yaron's and Einan's divisions began to slowly inch northward, occupying one hill and then another; the Syrians bitterly contested each ridge. The first some ministers heard about this unilateral violation of the cease-fire was on the radio. When they complained, Sharon countered that the Syrians and PLO had broken the cease-fire and that the IDF troops could not be left in perilous positions. Indeed, on June 23–24 he unleashed a two-divisional attack on 'Aley and Bahamdoun to finally resolve the situation along the road. Faced with a fait accompli, the cabinet approved the action retroactively on the 24th—though six ministers spoke up against Sharon's machinations.

By June 25 the IDF had control of 'Aley and Bahamdoun and the section of the Beirut–Damascus highway that ran between them. Reserve paratroops who had taken part in the clandestine "creep" forward and had taken several dozen casualties subsequently expressed their bitterness in a confrontation with the deputy commander of the general staff, Gen. Moshe Levy: What had this road to do with "Peace for Galilee"? they asked. Why had Israel Radio reported at the time, quoting army spokesmen, that all was quiet along the front, or that the Syrians and PLO were harassing the Israelis with fire when the truth was quite the opposite?

Following the offensive a new cease-fire was instituted with the Syrians.[212] But the Israelis gradually tightened the noose around the PLO and Syrian defenders of Beirut in what was to be a bloody nine-week siege characterized by almost daily artillery barrages and aerial attacks, punctuated by intermittent ground assaults. The staggered cutoff of food supplies, fuel, electricity, and water to the embattled population and massive use of IDF firepower against civilians traumatized Israeli society, caused rents in the military itself, and raised hackles in the West. The artillery and the air force tried to pinpoint military targets, but inevitably many civilians were hit. Western television showed the Israeli gunners and planes doing their worst, with brown-and-black smoke clouds over the dying city. Approval of Israel plummeted, reaching an all-time low in American opinion polls.

Curiously, Arab governments were relatively indifferent to the agony of Beirut, though the televised images of the bombardment deeply embarrassed leaders who felt unable to intervene. The Egyptians, who had just signed a peace treaty with Israel, were perhaps the most deeply chagrined. But Lebanon's Christians rejoiced, seeing in the punishment meted out to their foes divine justice and revenge for the years in which they had been subjected to similar treatment by the Syrians and, to a lesser degree, by the PLO. Indeed, the Christians in various ways assisted the Israelis, including by cutting off the water to Muslim West Beirut.[213]

At a meeting on June 16 with Eitan, Col. Johnny 'Abdu, the (Christian) director of Lebanon's military intelligence, encouraged the Israelis "to continue with the aerial bombardments . . . as the artillery bombardments are ineffective, as they have grown used to them." ('Abdu added that "it is difficult for the Lebanese army to carry out a massacre in the refugee camps, as there are many Muslims (about 70 percent) in the army.")[214]

The siege and bombardment continued through July. Israel's goal, on reaching the gates of Beirut, had been clearly stated: The PLO and its satellite "terrorist" organizations, and the Syrian forces, must leave the city (and preferably Lebanon). If they did not agree to do this, Begin and Sharon had warned Habib, the IDF would force them, even if it meant conquering West Beirut. Habib spent late June and July trying to fend off the threatened ground assault and to persuade Arafat and the Syrians to leave.

The PLO leaders dug in their heels, heartened by Western European (especially French) opposition to the siege, by American irresolution, by the world media coverage that portrayed them as courageous victims, and by criticism of the Begin government, and especially of Sharon, by the Labor opposition and Peace Now inside Israel.[215] At the same time, as Habib discovered, Arab governments were reluctant to take in the PLO fighters and bureaucracy. They had long accounts with Arafat and no great desire to host such potentially

subversive and unruly elements; perhaps, too, they were interested in perpetu-
ating Israel's embarrassment. These factors added to Arafat's natural resistance; he seemed to be playing for time. Sharon began to press the cabinet to
approve a major offensive, but the ministers agreed only to "incremental military advances" combined with "intermittent shutoffs of electricity and water,
and psychological warfare techniques such as leafleting and mock air
raids."[216]

West Beirut's Lebanese population also began to pressure the PLO to leave,
but its leaders could not do so openly lest they be accused of making common
cause with the Israelis. Indeed several of them, including former Sunni Muslim premiers Rashid Karameh and Salim al-Hoss, Druze leader Walid Jum-
blatt and Shi'ite leader Nabih Berri, came out in support of the PLO's
defiance.[217] But over time the continuous bombardment and the power and
water cutoffs made local leaders bolder and bolder in their advocacy of a PLO
evacuation. (The interdiction of foodstuffs and medical supplies had little
effect, as the various factions had learned their lesson from the early years of
the civil war and had built up large stockpiles. Moreover, Christian militiamen
could be bribed to allow fresh supplies to cross from East to West Beirut.[218])

A major reason for the PLO's reluctance to leave the city was fear for the
fate of the tens of thousands of Palestinian civilians in West Beirut, who
included the families of the fighters and bureaucrats. On July 3 the first scent
of a possible solution reached Jerusalem: U.S. Ambassador to Israel Samuel
Lewis informed Begin that the United States and France were prepared to
send troops to Beirut to "cover" the PLO's departure and to protect the Palestinians left behind.[219] During July and early August, American diplomats in
the Middle East and North Africa tried to persuade their hosts to take in PLO
evacuees from Beirut. Gradually they managed to elicit commitments from
several states, including Syria, to accept a proportion of the Palestinian fighters and bureaucrats if and when they agreed to withdraw.

The drawn-out nature of the negotiations persuaded Sharon, despite
Habib's assurances to the contrary, that the PLO was determined to remain in
Beirut and was just playing for time—rather than actually trying to obtain better conditions for evacuation. On July 11 he told senior officers that the IDF
would have to assault Beirut, or at least those southern districts containing the
refugee camps, and PLO headquarters. The aim would also be to destroy the
refugee camps so that Beirut would once and for all be rid of the "terrorist"
presence. (Sharon often used the word "terrorist" as a synonym for "Palestinian.")[220] Israel was interested in the Palestinians "moving elsewhere. Lebanon
will deal with this and we must [first] create the background," Sharon said. His
views complemented Economics Minister Ya'akov Meridor's position that the
refugees living in southern Lebanon must be rehabilitated north of the Awali,
and Gemayel's that "a large proportion" of them must be expelled. Gemayel
was bent on "liquidating the Palestinian problem in Lebanon, even if unusual

measures . . . had to be taken," in the words of the subsequent Kahan Commission of Inquiry report on the massacres of September 1982.[221]

On July 12 Sharon and Eitan obtained Begin's support for the planned offensive. Begin's main argument was that, because of international and local pressures, Israel could not continue the siege of Beirut long enough to achieve the evacuation of the PLO. Hence a massive assault and conquest were necessary. The implication was that the political and propaganda damage to Israel was and would be greater from a lengthy, inconclusive siege than from a swift and successful operation.[222] But the full cabinet, four days later, in effect rejected the proposal—it passed by only one vote (9 to 8, with two ministers absent), which Begin deemed insufficient for an inevitably bloody and controversial action. Perhaps he himself was not completely persuaded. The prospect of heavy casualties weighed heavily on his mind and those of several ministers; others were not convinced that the offensive could be completed within three days, as Eitan predicted; most were also concerned by the political consequences, both at home and in Washington, of an assault on a heavily populated Arab capital. Two coalition partners, the National Religious Party and Agudat Yisrael, hinted that they would withdraw from the government, precipitating its fall, if the offensive were launched. The opposition Labor Party leaders also made their objections clear.[223] Begin dropped the idea.[224]

But military preparations continued apace. General Drori presented the draft plan at a meeting of brigade commanders. A number raised objections, especially to the two-day period allotted for implementation (the less time, the less caution would be shown and the greater would be the casualties, it was reasoned). Col. Eli Geva, a highly esteemed officer, also voiced objections of principle: What was the point of the proposed assault? Was it worth the lives that would be expended, Israeli and Arab? What would Israel gain? A few days later, Geva's opposition crystallized into the clearest dissent within the army regarding the war's conduct and aims. In an unprecedented step he informed his superiors that he wished to be relieved of command of his brigade if it was ordered to advance into Beirut—and offered to continue to fight with it, in the ranks, as a private. The offer was rejected, and after Eitan, Sharon, and Begin failed to persuade him to back down, he was cashiered. The publication of the affair in the press in late July raised a storm, and the opponents of the war had found an instant symbol and hero.

At the end of July, with negotiations still deadlocked, the IDF stepped up its attacks. The Mossad, using Phalangist contacts, began to send Arab agents with car bombs into Beirut to terrorize the Palestinians into submission and the Lebanese into increasing the pressure on them to depart. Dozens of people were killed. Some of the bombers were caught and confessed.[225] The IAF was also frequently activated, some of its missions specifically designed to target Arafat, Abu Jihad, and Abu Iyad in their bunkers. An American journalist later called it "the world's first manhunt by air."[226] Sharon told the cabinet on July

19: "Arafat appears at the stadium, in the Fakahani neighborhood. . . . This is the area that, ultimately, we will destroy. The commanders and the headquarters—all of these are to be found here."[227] The feeling was that if the PLO leaders were eliminated, the defense of West Beirut would collapse. A number of large apartment houses were destroyed, with hundreds of Palestinians and Lebanese killed or wounded, but the leaders evaded the hunters from the sky, who were assisted by agents with transmitters on the ground.[228] At one point in the indirect negotiations with Habib, Arafat threatened to blow up the PLO's three hundred ammunition dumps around the city, causing a major catastrophe. Begin and Sharon were unimpressed. Begin, with his view of Arafat as a resurrected Hitler and Beirut as Nazi Berlin in 1945, seemed to feel that the city deserved its fate.[229]

In early August, Sharon, with Begin's approval, intensified the campaign. The IAF and navy were given their head, and ground troops were thrown against several of Beirut's southern suburbs. The aim was to show the PLO that the IDF would not be deterred by American or internal Israeli opposition, or by the fear of casualties in a major ground assault, should it be necessary. On August 1 Israeli fighter-bombers flew 127 sorties[230] against the city, bombing and strafing suspected PLO strongholds; and missile boats fired cannon and Gabriel missiles from offshore. Several paratroop companies, with armor, pushed into West Beirut simultaneously from east and south, taking a district, Khai as Salum, whose capture the cabinet had specifically forbidden,[231] and the northern end of the airport's runways, after rolling back PLO and Syrian defenders.[232] Officially Israeli spokesmen maintained that the PLO had broken the cease-fire, and the IDF had had to "improve positions," for the safety of the troops.[233]

On July 2 Arafat had handed Lebanese premier Shafiq Wazzan a memorandum conveying the PLO's readiness to evacuate Beirut.[234] But not until August 1 was Arafat convinced that evacuation was the only option.[235] Contributing to his decision was the Arab states' near-unanimous endorsement of an American-brokered evacuation plan. As announced at the Jedda Arab League conference on July 29, they wanted the PLO out of Beirut. Even PLO officers who had held out until then for a fight to the finish were now persuaded of the need for withdrawal.[236]

The PLO's readiness to leave wasn't apparent to, or fully understood by, the Israeli leadership: "Nibbling" away at Beirut's extremities and massive aerial attacks continued during the following fortnight. On August 4 IDF units breached the lines in southern Beirut and advanced about a mile, taking the Ouzai neighborhood and a Lebanese army camp. Simultaneously, an armored force pushed a few hundred yards into central Beirut and took the city's large museum building and part of the racetrack to its north.[237]

These assaults prompted a strong American protest, including a demand that the IDF withdraw back to the August 1 lines, and though Begin hung tough—"Jews do not kneel except to God," he said—the army was ordered to desist from further major ground pushes.[238] Frustrated on the ground, Sharon stepped up the offensive from the air. On August 9 the IAF renewed its bombings, targeting the PLO's central command bunker, which kept skipping from site to site.[239] The campaign climaxed on August 12, with seventy-two sorties and a massive artillery bombardment (the unofficial Arab death toll that day was three hundred[240]). Sharon later wrote that that evening Arafat, under pressure from Habib, at last agreed to leave Beirut.[241]

But the bombings of August 11–12 appear to have been superfluous. By then the Syrians had agreed to take in as many as four thousand PLO men, and the PLO had agreed to leave Beirut. Habib's evacuation package had been presented to Israel on August 10 and approved by the cabinet, with several minor reservations, the following day. Reagan called Begin twice on August 12, protesting that the air raids were "unfathomable and senseless," demanding an immediate IDF cessation of fire, and threatening to break off Habib's mediation. Earlier that day, unknown to Reagan, Sharon had been roundly attacked in the cabinet for jeopardizing the negotiations and the PLO agreement to pull out. Sharon sought cabinet approval to mount a new, limited ground offensive in central Beirut; the ministers said no, and then proceeded to deny him the right to activate IDF artillery, the navy, and the IAF without prime-ministerial or full cabinet approval. The meeting was marked by sharp exchanges, with Begin reprimanding Sharon: "I ask that you not interrupt me. You cannot force me to listen to you," and the like.[242] Yet Begin, who on June 29 had told the Knesset: "Blessed is the country whose defense minister is Ariel Sharon,"[243] was seemingly to continue to put his trust in Sharon.

Over the long haul, Sharon's brutal measures worked: They persuaded Arafat that the PLO no longer had a choice. On the night of August 12–13, he dropped his last conditions and agreed to Habib's terms. No Arab state, it appeared, would support a PLO "Stalingrad," and the Lebanese were almost up in arms. A Muslim leader had pleaded with Arafat: "We'll all die, we'll all die!"[244] On August 21 the evacuation began, many of the Palestinians sailing out of Beirut harbor in Greek and Italian ships, under American Sixth Fleet escort.

A multinational force, composed of eight hundred Americans, eight hundred Frenchmen, four hundred Italians, and three thousand soldiers of the Lebanese army, had deployed to guard the departure and the evacuated areas of West Beirut.[245] Some PLO troops, the PLA brigades, and the remains of the Syrian Eighty-fifth Brigade rolled out of the city on trucks, bound for the Beka'a and Syria. The PLO evacuees were allowed to retain their light weapons; heavy weapons and vehicles were handed over to the Lebanese army. Drawing a curious historical parallel, Begin explained: "They will leave like the Crusaders. The Crusaders left [the Holy Land] with their swords in their hands, and they will leave with their Kalashnikovs."[246]

During the eleven days of the evacuation, which ended on August 31, 14,398 Palestinians and Syrians, including 664 women and children—the families of the PLO brass—left the city. The Syrians and PLA troops redeployed in the Beka'a and northern Lebanon. The PLO men dispersed to Syria, Algeria, South and North Yemen, Iraq, Jordan, and Sudan, and the leadership reestablished its headquarters in Tunisia. Its duty done, the multinational force sailed out of Beirut on September 11–13.[247]

Two days after the start of the evacuation, on August 23, the Lebanese parliament gathered in the Military College at Ba'abda and, in the words of Syrian Defense Minister Tlass, "under the influence of the Israeli occupation and bayonets,"[248] elected Bashir Gemayel president. His inauguration was set for a month later. Israel had forcefully lobbied for Gemayel's election and, indeed, its troops escorted a number of deputies to the session. One elderly Shi'ite from the Beka'a was flown in by Israeli helicopter; other votes were bought (the going rate was half a million US dollars).[249]

The Israelis were soon disappointed. A few hours after the election, Gemayel told a group of Israeli visitors at his home in Bikfaya: "Personally, I shall always be with you. Politically, however, I shall opt for my father's [neutral or pro-Syrian] line."[250] He set as his initial objective the "reunification" of Beirut under Lebanese sovereign control. This posed somewhat contradictory, if not mutually exclusive, challenges. He would have to make his peace with the traditional Muslim leadership in West Beirut, and disarm and arrest or expel the remaining Palestinian and leftist militiamen. (The idea of such a cleanup meshed, of course, with Sharon's own desires and plans.) As his second and third objectives, the president-elect aimed, once firmly established in Beirut, to extend his control to contiguous areas (the Shouf, southern Lebanon) and to achieve a settlement that would see the withdrawal of both Syrian and Israeli forces from Lebanese soil.[251]

On September 1 an IDF helicopter flew Gemayel to Nahariya, in northern Israel, where he met Begin, who had just been informed of the "Reagan Plan," the new American initiative for Israeli withdrawal from most of the occupied territories in exchange for Arab recognition and peace. By invading Lebanon, Begin had hoped to neutralize Palestinian nationalism and facilitate Israeli annexation, at least de facto, of the West Bank. But the invasion had brought home to the Americans the plight of the Palestinians and the imperative of resolving their problem, with Israeli withdrawal from the West Bank among the necessary preconditions. The Reagan initiative ruled out a final settlement that would involve either Israeli annexation of the territories or full-fledged Palestinian statehood.[252]

The Reagan Plan had left Begin shocked and angry, and he directed some of his anger at the young Gemayel. He opened by speaking of the need for an early Israeli-Lebanese peace treaty and for an official visit by Gemayel to "Jerusalem or . . . Tel Aviv." He chided Gemayel on a number of issues and denied his request to allow a large number of Phalange troops to enter the Shouf and suppress the local Druze militia.

Gemayel countered that "Hasty signing of a treaty is not justified," and added insult to injury by suggesting that the commander of the SLA, Major Sa'ad Haddad—a Begin favorite—would have to stand trial in Beirut. Moreover, Gemayel had avoided making any clear commitments regarding the open alliance coveted by Jerusalem. He was not ready to become an Israeli pawn and was not going to sign a treaty that would immediately delegitimize his presidency in the eyes of more than half the Lebanese population (and Syria). Both men came away from the meeting disappointed and resentful. But Gemayel had also felt ill used on a personal level: "He treated me like a child," he later told his father.[253]

The results of the battle of the Beka'a were a clear political defeat for Israel. The Syrian army as a whole was fighting fit, with its high command confident it had weathered the storm.[254] At the same time the trouncing Syria had taken and the humiliation its air force and air defense system had suffered had left Assad—an air force man himself—with a strong motive for revenge. From now on he was single-mindedly to deny Israel any gains in Lebanon and to assert Syria's complete control over that country. The Syrians suspected that the IDF intended to stay. "Syria has declared a long-term struggle, a war of attrition . . . with the aim of defeating Israel and forcing it to withdraw [from Lebanon]," announced a commentator on Damascus Radio. Israel would not remain in Lebanon, "however high the cost [to Syria]."[255]

In gradual, escalating fashion in the period after the of June 11 cease-fire, the Syrians were to go over to the strategic offensive. But from the start, aware of their army's inferiority, they employed proxies: local Lebanese agents and guerrilla-terrorist groups and militias, primarily the Shi'ite 'Amal and Hizbullah, assorted PLO groups, and the Lebanese Syrian National Party, which advocated the incorporation of Lebanon into a Greater Syria.

During June and July 1982 the Syrians harassed the Israelis in the Beka'a, where the two armies faced each other just south of the highway. PLO and PLA forces sniped at Israeli patrols and occasionally crossed the lines to plant mines and ambushes; only occasionally did Syrian artillery and troops join in. With cabinet approval the IDF retaliated massively on July 22, using tanks, helicopter gunships, and fighters. The Syrians lost seventy tanks and two dozen APCs.[256] Following this the Syrians removed all PLO forces to the rear and set up checkpoints to prevent continued Palestinian operations in the Beka'a. PLO activity on the eastern front decreased considerably.

RETREATING FROM LEBANON,
SEPTEMBER 1982–JUNE 1985

Although the fighting of June–August 1982 was characterized by almost complete IDF dominance and initiative, the following three years were to be marked by Syrian initiative and the gradual success of their stratagems and proxy forces, with the IDF, for the first time in its history, suffering a clear and painful defeat.

The turning point was the assassination in September of Bashir Gemayel, Israel's great hope and the only Lebanese Maronite politician of stature and charisma. Thereafter Israel managed to alienate almost every faction in Lebanon before finally pulling back in mid-1985 to its starting position in the border-hugging Security Zone. It left behind a country dominated as never before by Syria and an efficient and resolute guerrilla movement, spearheaded by the Hizbullah, which was to hound the IDF and SLA through the late 1980s and 1990s. Throughout, the Syrians, wary of a renewed frontal clash with the IDF, made clever and effective use of its assorted local allies.

Following the PLO withdrawal from Beirut at the end of August 1982, senior IDF and Mossad officials met with the LF's commanders and discussed the coming "cleanup" of Muslim West Beirut. The remaining militiamen were to be disarmed and arrested, and weapons stockpiles confiscated. The Israelis and Phalangists agreed that it was best to start with the Palestinian neighborhoods and only afterward to move on to the Lebanese Muslim districts. Joseph Abu Khalil, the Phalange operations chief, said that the cleanup would be carried out immediately after Bashir Gemayel's election as president, by the Lebanese army, assisted by the security apparatus of the LF, led by Elie Khobeika, which would take care of extremist elements. The Mossad's deputy director, Nahum Admoni, said that the Palestinians should not be treated with the "magnanimity of victors."[257]

On the night of September 12–13 Sharon and Gemayel met in the latter's home village of Bikfaya and smoothed out ruffled feathers. Gemayel was due to be sworn in on September 23. The two men agreed on joint short- and long-term plans of action: Sometime toward the end of the month, Israel and the Lebanese Christians were to uproot the remaining "terrorist" presence in West Beirut; later, Bashir and Israel would sign a full bilateral peace agreement.

Regarding stage one, the IDF was to march into West Beirut and take control of major buildings, roads, and junctions while the Phalange would do the dirty work in the refugee camps, carrying out arrests, interrogations, and demolition of buildings.[258] Lebanon had more than 300,000 Palestinian inhabitants, one-third of them in refugee camps. The Phalange regarded them as the "poisoners" of Christian-Muslim relations, who had helped tilt the ethnic balance against the Christians. Gemayel had long harbored the idea of expelling them and saw the Israeli invasion of the south as a heaven-sent opportunity to carry this out. This dovetailed with Begin's thinking. At a meeting with the Knesset Defense and Foreign Affairs Committee on June 10, 1982, he had spoken of the need to "transfer" the Palestinians out of southern Lebanon.[259]

Bashir was more militant. In July he had tried to intimidate the inhabitants of the Mieh Mieh refugee camp outside Sidon into leaving, but local IDF commanders put a stop to it.[260] Now, in September, he spoke explicitly of razing the refugee camps around Beirut and establishing "a large zoo" in their stead and of "dispatching the Palestinians to Syria on air-conditioned buses."[261] At a meeting that summer with the director general of Israel's Foreign Ministry, he said: "If the refugee camps in [southwestern Beirut] are destroyed, this will not cause great sorrow among the local Muslims, who live in the northwestern part of the city, and some of them may even cooperate."[262]

Gemayel and Sharon seem to have been in agreement; Sharon, according to some reports, hoped that, with a little nudging, all or many of Lebanon's Palestinians could be persuaded ultimately to move to Jordan, which he had earmarked as "the Palestinian state."[263] Their agreement of September 12-13 was subsequently to serve as the quasi-legal basis for the IDF's entry into West Beirut three days later—but in completely unforeseen circumstances.

Israeli intelligence assessments of the various Arab reactions to Gemayel's election predicted that Syria would not take military action against the Christians, for fear of IDF intervention; "but attempts by Syria to assassinate Bashir or encourage its supporters [in Lebanon] to act against him should not be discounted."[264]

The Syrians may have been worsted in the Beka'a and expelled from Beirut, but they were far from giving up the fight. At 4:10 P.M. on September 14, a Syrian agent named Habib Tanious Shartouni activated by remote control a large bomb he had planted in his sister's empty apartment in the Ashrafiya quarter in East Beirut. On the floor below, in the local Phalange headquarters, Bashir Gemayel was delivering a lecture to a group of young female activists. Within seconds the building collapsed; dozens of dead and wounded lay strewn among the debris, among them the president-elect. Outgoing president Elias Sarkis wryly commented: "Bashir was hasty in everything he did, even in going to his death."[265]

"The assassination . . . threatened to destroy the foundation of the whole military and political structure that underpinned the war," Sharon was later to write.[266] The Israelis moved quickly. Even before Gemayel's corpse had been identified, Sharon discussed the occupation of West Beirut with Begin and Eitan. He even spoke that evening of sending the Phalangists into the refugee camps.[267]

Sharon and Israeli intelligence believed—perhaps based on erroneous information[268]—or at least conjectured that the PLO, in violation of the Habib-mediated evacuation agreement, had left behind a clandestine terrorist/guerrilla infrastructure, comprising about 2,000–2,500 fighters, and feared that these along with their Lebanese Muslim allies, principally the Sunni Mourabitoun militia, would take control of West Beirut, threatening Israel's long-term goals in Lebanon.[269] In the short term Gemayel's murder raised a giant question mark over the LF's intention—as agreed between him and Sharon on September 12–13—to clean up West Beirut, but it also gave the Israelis an excuse to take over the city and carry out, or oversee, the long-mooted operation.

There was also—at least according to Israeli spokesmen—a humanitarian consideration, which soon came to the fore as the main pretext for what was about to happen: The Christians could be expected to exact massive revenge for the assassination, and the IDF had to prevent this. Such, at least, was Begin's argument in favor of the IDF takeover of West Beirut, in conversations with Eitan on the evening of September 14 and subsequently.[270] However, Sharon's aides were later to stress the contrary: that the Phalange leadership at that moment had appeared "quiet, calm and in control . . . matter-of-fact and moderate" and were not "emotional"—and therefore unlikely to react to the assassination by massacring their enemies.[271]

But this, of course, was nonsense—as a stream of previous intelligence indicated. For example, a June 23 Mossad document had asserted: "In recent days, the Christians detained some five hundred Muslims at their roadblocks and afterward liquidated them." On July 6 Sharon had cautioned Gemayel that murders, rapes, and robberies by his men were having a bad effect on Israeli public opinion. Sharon reported to Mossad executive Nahum Admoni that Khobeika had recently "caused the disappearance" of twelve hundred persons in Beirut.[272] Yet Sharon and Eitan were later to argue that the LF had given no grounds for supposing that it would commit atrocities against Muslims or Palestinians.[273]

With Gemayel dead and the IDF about to enter West Beirut, who was going to clean up the refugee camps, clearly a distasteful and possibly dangerous job? On September 14 the IDF asked the Lebanese Army to do it. Its high command politely refused but agreed not to interfere with the Israeli takeover of West Beirut. Simultaneously Eitan and Drori sounded out the Phalangists at their headquarters. The Phalangists agreed to carry out the task.[274]

What Israel's director of military intelligence, General Saguy, had predicted well before the assassination, at a meeting with Sharon on August 12, was about to happen: "The Phalange will find a way to . . . settle old scores.

One day the murders will start, and they will just go on and on without end."[275] But the exact scenario was unforeseen by Saguy. As it turned out, the Phalange would not have to "find a way" to get at the Palestinians—they would be going in at Israel's invitation and with IDF support.

Early on September 15 the first IDF units crossed the line into West Beirut, some of the troops arriving by airlift from Israel at Beirut airport. Yaron's division moved in from south to north, taking over the southern districts; Mordechai's division entered from the east, driving towards the sea. The advance was almost unopposed, the Syrians and the PLO having departed the previous month. Sharon met with Phalange commanders Fadi Frem, Khobeika, and others to coordinate the impending action in the camps. He spoke of killing the "terrorists": "I don't want a single one of them left."

Khobeika asked: "How do you single them out?"

Sharon: "We'll discuss that in a more restricted session." He then flew off to Bikfaya to pay a condolence call on the Gemayel family. What exactly passed between Sharon and Pierre and Amin Gemayel that afternoon is unknown. Sharon later denied that they had spoken of the need for revenge or of the impending massacre.[276]

By the following morning, the IDF completed the occupation of West Beirut. Sharon met Eitan and told him the Phalangists were preparing to enter the camps. Eitan said: "They're thirsty for revenge. There could be torrents of blood." But neither man seems to have paid attention to what they themselves were saying; Sharon later told the Kahan Commission that not one officer or intelligence official warned him at this time that sending the Phalange into the refugee camps would result in a massacre.[277] That afternoon, September 16, Khobeika arrived at Yaron's headquarters to finalize details. Yaron, echoing Drori, warned against atrocities. In Jerusalem, meanwhile, American special envoy Morris Draper and American ambassador Lewis were meeting with Sharon and Eitan, just back from Lebanon. Eitan said: "Lebanon is at the point of exploding into a frenzy of revenge. No one can stop them. The Phalange . . . are obsessed with the idea of revenge. . . . Some of their commanders visited me and I could see in their eyes that it's going to be a relentless slaughter."[278]

At that very moment or minutes after, at around 6:00 P.M., under loose, distant IDF monitoring, 150 of Khobeika's men entered the Sabra and Shatilla refugee camps, from the west and south, through IDF lines. At the request of the Phalange's liaison officer with Yaron's division, Jesse Soker, an IDF battery of 81 mm mortars began to send illumination rounds into the sky, to light the Phalangists' way. (Later IAF aircraft were to drop larger illumination flares.)

At 6:50 Yaron's aides monitored an exchange between Khobeika and one of his subordinates, who asked what to do with fifty women and children he had rounded up.

Khobeika: "That's the last time you ask me. You know what to do."

Yaron, hearing of this exchange, again cautioned Khobeika not to harm civilians.[279]

The cabinet meeting in Jerusalem convened a few minutes later. Some ministers complained that they had not approved the occupation of West Beirut. Begin explained that there simply hadn't been time to consult or inform the cabinet. Sharon then gave an hourlong survey of events since the assassination, ending with an explanation of the current situation. He failed to mention that the Phalangists had been sent into the Palestinian camps, let alone that they were massacring the inhabitants. It was only later, at about 9:00, that the ministers—including Begin—were informed by Eitan that the Phalangists were at that moment operating in Sabra and Shatilla. Again Eitan vaguely predicted an "outburst of vengeance"—but failed to connect this forecast to what the Phalange was at that moment actually doing. Only one minister, David Levy, seemed to partly take in what was being said, commenting: "When I hear that the Phalangists have already gone into certain neighborhoods—and I know what vengeance means to them, the kind of slaughter; no one is going to believe that we were there to maintain order, and we'll bear the blame." None of the ministers reacted or responded.[280]

Just as Sharon was failing to give his colleagues the full picture of what was happening and Eitan was failing to connect between his intuitive forecasts and unfolding reality, liaison officer Soker was asked by a Phalange commander inside the camps what to do with forty-five captives. "Do God's will," replied Soker. The radio exchange was monitored by Yaron's divisional intelligence officer.[281]

Israeli warnings went unheeded; revenge against their longtime foes after the assassination of their leader was more important to the Phalangists. Perhaps the Lebanese sensed—or thought they sensed—that the Israelis were not really averse to what was happening. After all, the IDF had sent them into the camps and was providing them with illumination; moreover, killing Palestinians had been the aim of the IDF invasion in the first place. At least some of the Phalangist commanders regarded the slaughter as a necessary catalyst to a Palestinian exodus—and this was a goal at least partly shared with key Israeli leaders.

Khobeika's force, having split up into small squads, moved from house to house through Sabra and Shatilla murdering the inhabitants. They encountered almost no resistance; apparently the last exchange of fire took place just after 6:00. Thereafter the massacre went on uninterruptedly for more than thirty hours; the Phalangists slaughtered civilians—individuals and whole families—with consistency and deliberation. An infant was trampled to death by a man wearing spiked shoes; others were killed with grenades hung around their necks; still others were raped and then butchered with knives.[282]

During the night of September 16–17 reports of the killing reached a number of Israeli headquarters, mostly from IDF troops monitoring the action from observation posts or over the radio. But all were treated as specious, and nothing was done. In the camps themselves, many of the thousands of residents appear to have slept through the night without knowing that there were Phalangists inside or that their neighbors were being murdered. They had grown used to hearing light weapons fire, even close by.

The next morning, reports continued to filter to the IDF headquarters. A tank company commander, looking into one of the camps, noticed Phalangists leading away some Palestinians. He then heard shots and saw the Phalangists return without their captives. That afternoon, he saw Phalangists shooting a group of women and children.[283] Ze'ev Schiff, the military correspondent of *HaAretz*, spoke with officers in general staff headquarters in Tel Aviv and, worried, contacted Communications Minister Zippori. In turn Zippori contacted Foreign Minister Shamir—but Shamir did nothing.[284] Yaron, though sensing that something was wrong, allowed a second, fresh force of Phalangists, led by the LF chief of operations, Fuad Abu Nader, into the camps to complete the "cleanup." It was ostensibly to have replaced Khobeika's force, but the latter's men remained in the camps. That afternoon, Eitan, Drori, and other senior officers met with Khobeika, Abu Nader, and other Phalange commanders and heard about the "difficult battle against the terrorists." No one, on either side, spoke of the ongoing slaughter of civilians or of the reports and rumors to this effect. Indeed, Eitan explicitly gave the Phalangists permission to continue the cleanup until the following morning and agreed to supply them with two bulldozers "to knock down illegal structures." The Phalange used the equipment to cover some of the dead with earth and rubble.[285]

That night journalist Ron Ben-Yishai of Israel Television called Sharon at his home and told him that IDF officers in Beirut were reporting a massacre. Sharon did nothing, apparently calmed by Eitan's assurances that the Phalange would be leaving the camps in the morning.[286] The following morning, the 18th, Yaron saw a procession of medical staff of the Gaza Hospital next to Shatilla being escorted by Phalangists out of the camp; they told him of the corpses they had seen along the way. Yaron ordered the Phalange to evacuate the camps. Ben-Yishai later described in a personal letter to Begin what he had observed that morning:

The Phalangists were driving a long line of women, children, and elderly people ahead of them at a run. Some of these people were covered with blood, others were wailing and shouting. . . . [The refugees] shouted to us that they had been separated from their menfolk, whom the Phalangists had marched off elsewhere. While we were arguing with them, a senior IDF officer brought the procession to a halt and ordered [the Phalangists] to leave the area.[287]

Thus ended the massacre (though reports continued to filter out that day and even the following day that some Phalangists were still in the camps killing people[288]). Loading the weapons they had found in the camps onto waiting trucks, most of the militiamen at last drove off. As journalists and IDF officers entered the camps, reports about piles of corpses and of the wide-scale killings began to pour out. But Begin, who had spent much of September 18 at prayer in synagogue—it was Rosh Hashanah, the Jewish New Year—claimed that he first learned of the massacre from a BBC report that afternoon at 5:00. He promptly called Sharon, who ordered an investigation.

At Israel's request, units of the Lebanese Army entered the camps at last on September 19. Meanwhile, official Lebanese and Phalange radio stations began to broadcast that it was Haddad's militia that had perpetrated the massacre and that the Phalange had had nothing to do with it. Eitan demanded that the Phalange admit publicly—at a press conference—to their troops' misdeeds, perhaps explaining that the massacre had not been Phalange policy or intention. They refused. "In the current political situation this is impossible," declared Abu Khalil. He was referring to Amin Gemayel's impending election as president: The Phalange was not about to jeopardize his chances with a public admission of a mass slaughter of Muslims.

Abu Khalil then asked Eitan and Drori to brief the Israeli press so that it, too, would not blame the Phalange, "at least not during the coming days, in order to gain political time." Eitan retorted that Israel had a free press, which would publish whatever it wanted; the fact that the Phalange had committed the massacre could not be hidden. With unmitigated effrontery, Abu Khalil then offered to deny that "the IDF had carried it out."[289] During the following days, the Phalange flatly denied any connection with the massacre. On September 24, at a meeting of the Knesset Foreign Affairs and Defense Committee, Sharon described a meeting with Phalange leaders: "I asked them, why did you do it? They looked into my eyes, like I'm looking at you now, and they didn't bat an eyelid. They said: 'We didn't do it, it wasn't us.' And . . . we are talking here about engineers and lawyers, the whole young upper crust, the intelligentsia."[290]

Curiously, Muslim and PLO leaders joined in this campaign of disinformation. The massacre was now a thing of the past. What was important was national reconciliation and future cooperation with Amin Gemayel and the Phalange, not further hatred and bloodshed. Besides, Amin was the only Lebanese Christian leader who, since the civil war, had maintained good relations with the PLO, the Syrians, and the Lebanese Muslim leaders. Tlass wrote: "Amin was graced by wisdom, flexibility and moderation."[291] For the

Lebanese, the PLO, and Syria, it was convenient to cast the blame on the IDF and its proxy, the Haddad militia.[292]

The Israeli cabinet, too, preferred, in its first public pronouncement after the massacre, not to clearly point a finger at its ally the Phalange, or admit any form of IDF complicity. In its official communiqué the cabinet charged that the murders had been committed by "a Lebanese unit" that had entered the camps "at a point far from the IDF position."[293] Reinforcing this lie, army and Foreign Ministry spokesmen declared during the following days that the Phalangists entered from the east, not through IDF lines, without coordination with, and without the knowledge of, the IDF.[294]

On September 21 Amin Gemayel was elected president by the Lebanese parliament. The Israelis had wanted Sarkis to be reelected, with Lebanon's intelligence chief, Col. Johnny 'Abdu, serving as the power behind the scenes. But following Bashir Gemayel's death and the massacre, Israel's influence on Lebanese politics—despite the continued occupation of all of Beirut—was no longer what it had been.

The numbers of those murdered by the Phalange in the massacre remained in dispute. The Lebanese army's chief prosecutor, Assad Germanos, who probed the affair on orders from President Gemayel, found that a total of 460 persons had been killed, 15 of them women and 20 children. Most—328— were Palestinian males; 109 Lebanese were among the dead, as were a handful of Iranians, Syrians, Algerians, and Pakistanis who had lived in Sabra and Shatilla. Israeli intelligence reached a higher estimate, 700–800 dead.[295]

If Begin and the cabinet had hoped that the storm would simply blow over, they were seriously mistaken. News of the full extent of the atrocities, including TV clips of the batches of victims lying in West Beirut's alleyways, was to dominate the headlines around the world for days—leading the Israeli public and the IDF to a widespread feeling of revulsion, which gradually extended to cover the whole Lebanese adventure. For many Israelis, the massacre came to symbolize the war itself.[296]

At first, Begin and his colleagues resisted public pressure for an independent judicial commission of inquiry. But the groundswell proved irresistible. One general, Amram Mitzna, in effect called for Sharon's resignation; others protested and, in a gathering of the senior IDF command, Yaron blamed himself, and the whole command system, for "callousness"; "We were all insensitive, that's all."[297] Yaron had a point: 1948 and the subsequent decades of battle against the Palestinians, culminating in the war against the PLO in summer 1982, had substantially desensitized Israeli society, and the IDF in particular, to their suffering and death. In some vague, general way, this had paved the way for Sabra and Shatilla.[298]

Key civilian figures spoke up as well. Energy Minister Yitzhak Berman resigned from the cabinet, and President Yitzhak Navon and the president of Israel's Academy of Sciences and Humanities, Prof. Ephraim Urbach, both publicly called for a judicial inquiry. Labor Party leaders decried the Begin-Phalange partnership. The general public added its voice on September 25, when, in Israel's largest political rally ever, the opposition parties and Peace Now assembled hundreds of thousands of demonstrators (the organizers claimed 400,000) in Tel Aviv to call for the establishment of a commission of inquiry and the resignation of the government. In effect, the protest was against the war itself.[299]

Begin caved in. On September 28 the cabinet appointed the president of the Supreme Court, Yitzhak Kahan, with Supreme Court Justice Aharon Barak and Maj. Gen. (Res.) Yona Efrat, to investigate the massacre. The commission interviewed dozens of witnesses, read affidavits from many dozens more, and scrutinized thousands of documents. The inquiry focused on Israel's role and the Israeli-Phalange connection.

On February 8, 1983, the Kahan Commission published its unanimous findings, attributing to the IDF and Israel indirect responsibility for the massacre. Indeed, the commissioners compared Israel's responsibility to that of the Russian or Polish authorities when pogroms were carried out against Jews in the nineteenth century.[300] The commission accepted as proven beyond doubt that the massacre itself had been committed by the Phalange ("the Lebanese Forces"),[301] even though in secret testimony to the commission the heads of the LF, including their new commanding officer, Fadi Frem, argued that the killing had been an indirect consequence of the heavy fighting against terrorists. (The LF apparently suffered two dead and a dozen or more wounded during the two days in the camps.[302]) The commission found that no unit of Haddad's militia had participated in the massacre (as some witnesses alleged), though conceded that individuals from among Haddad's troops could have taken part. (Haddad and a group of his troops had passed through Beirut twice on September 17.) No IDF soldiers had participated.[303]

On the political level, the commission attributed "a certain degree of responsibility" to Begin and rebuked Foreign Minister Shamir for failing to follow up the report on the massacre that he was given on September 17. The main blame was directed at Sharon. He was found to have been "remiss in his duties," and the commission recommended that he resign or be removed from office by the prime minister. Sharon refused to resign, and Begin agonized over the decision to dismiss him, until, under popular pressure, he was finally removed from the Defense Ministry—but remained in the cabinet as a minister without portfolio.

The commission found Chief of General Staff Eitan to have been grossly negligent and remiss in his duties. But as he was about to complete his tour of duty, the commission declared that it would not pass judgment on his suitability for that office. Drori was mildly rebuked, and Yaron was found to have failed to carry out his duties. The commission recommended that Yaron be removed from any position of command for at least three years. (He subsequently was appointed military attaché to Washington and promoted.) The director of military intelligence, Major General Saguy, was found grossly negligent and was removed from command. (He retired from the army and in 1988 was elected to the Knesset on the Likud ticket.) The deputy director and then director of the Mossad, Nahum Admoni, was lightly reprimanded and continued in his position for seven more years.

The report concluded with a very mild rebuke to the IDF in general: "It is regrettable that the reaction by IDF soldiers to such deeds was not always forceful enough to bring a halt to the despicable acts."[304]

Under intense American pressure the IDF withdrew from Beirut on September 26, more or less back to the positions it had occupied before the massacre. On September 27–29 a hastily reconstituted, American-led Multi-National Force (MNF) returned to the city, at Gemayel's invitation and much to Israel's chagrin,[305] with a mandate to help the Lebanese government reassume its authority in and around Beirut. The core of the force was a contingent of American marines; French and Italian units (later joined by a small British group) were charged mainly with protecting the Palestinians. The Americans were soon to be caught in the middle of the various struggles, between Israel and Syria and its proxies and between the Gemayel government and the Palestinian, Druze, and Shi'ite militias.

But Israel remained in control of most of southern Lebanon and at this point upped the ante: The IDF would withdraw from Lebanon only along with "all foreign forces"—meaning the Syrian army—and only after adequate security arrangements had been assured in the areas evacuated. And it wanted these arrangements to be enshrined in a formal peace accord. But the Lebanese were far from eager to sign an agreement. Even before the Israeli invasion Bashir Gemayel had hinted at this reluctance; his brother Amin followed suit. But the United States, always interested in widening the circle of Israeli-Arab peace-making, over November 1982–May 1983 helped Israel and Lebanon negotiate peace, or at least "nonbelligerency." An initial framework agreement, reached secretly in December 1982, was publicized by Sharon with much fanfare but never signed[306]—the Lebanese were outraged by its publication—and the formal talks dragged on, with Syria exerting ever greater pressure on Beirut to avoid a successful conclusion.[307] Syria opposed the negotiations as it opposed any Arab-Israeli agreements. Moreover, perhaps unwisely, the Americans and Israelis had made a point of leaving Damascus entirely out of the picture.

From the start (as Damascus had maintained), the negotiation was unbalanced. It was a dialogue between a powerful state that had invaded and still occupied a third of the territory of the weak country with which it was negotiating. The Lebanese wanted the Israelis out and had no choice but to negotiate.[308] But Israel's position, too, was inherently weak. Syria still occupied about half of Lebanon and various local factions—the remainder of the PLO in the north, Shi'ites, and Sunnis—opposed dealing with Israel, let alone concluding a peace treaty. From the first Gemayel refused to agree to a full peace settlement and rejected various Israeli security demands.

The Lebanese delegation was headed by a professional diplomat, Antoine Fattal, a Christian. The Israeli team was led by David Kimche,[309] who later called the agreement signed on May 17, 1983, "an impressive document" and "an important achievement."[310] In fact it was never more than a scrap of paper. The agreement[311] provided for Israel's withdrawal back to the international frontier and the termination of the state of war between the two countries, formally in existence since 1948. But it predicated these on the withdrawal from Lebanon of Syria's army of occupation, and Assad had no such intention.

The document outlined arrangements to safeguard the security of northern Israel and provided for various measures of "normalization"—falling somewhat short of full peace—in the relations between the two countries. The agreement was swiftly ratified by the Lebanese parliament, but in spring 1984 it was abrogated by Gemayel on orders from Damascus.

Since the siege of Beirut there had been a steady disenchantment with the whole Lebanese adventure among large parts of the Israeli public as well as elements in the army and government. In particular, there was a radical disaffection from the Phalange. The Israeli-Maronite alliance proved "too ambiguous and too slight for the baggage it had to carry."[312] A consensus began to develop around the notion of getting out of Lebanon and cutting losses.

Once the agreement was signed—affording Jerusalem something of a fig leaf behind which to retire—a staggered withdrawal soon followed. This was facilitated by the departure of Eitan, whose term had now ended, and of Sharon, who, following the publication of the Kahan Commission report, was replaced as defense minister by the more pragmatic Moshe Arens.

Syria's campaign against the agreement became intertwined with Druze-Christian hostilities in the Shouf Mountains, southeast of Beirut. Israel wished to alienate neither faction. Yet these were, increasingly, at each other's throats in an area formally under IDF control—and the Druze, from May 1983 on, received weaponry and support from Syria. In part to resolve this dilemma, on September 3–4 the IDF withdrew from Beirut's environs and the Shouf back to a line along the Awali River, after rejecting American requests to delay the move. The Americans feared it would precipitate large-scale fighting and expose their marines around Beirut airport to fire from the Shouf by the Syrian proxy forces. The Israelis had repeatedly tried but failed to persuade the Lebanese army to move into the area in their wake.

As expected, the IDF withdrawal led to an intensification of the interfactional battles, with Syrian and Syrian-proxy artillery pouring shells down on Christian East Beirut and the Druze massacring hundreds of Christians in the Shouf and driving the rest out. The Maronites came to regard their violent ejection from the Shouf as a product of deliberate Israeli betrayal. Now, with the Christians on the run, the Israeli-Phalange alliance shattered and, the Israelis having withdrawn from the main Lebanese pressure points, Syria's proxies—Shi'ite, Druze, and Palestinian—backed by Syrian army artillery and intelligence, proceeded to battle simultaneously against Gemayel and his Lebanese army; the MNF (principally the Americans), Gemayel's chief prop; and the IDF, which still occupied much of the south. This tactic was to pay handsome dividends: Damascus proved able to bring to heel the Gemayel regime and drive out the Americans and Israelis while avoiding punishment at the hands of their powerful armies. (During September–December 1983 the Syrians also cleverly used proxy Palestinian forces to eject Arafat's main-stream PLO forces from their last toehold in Lebanon, in the northern town of Tripoli and its satellite refugee camps.[313])

The Syrians and their Lebanese allies had opposed the presence of the MNF—seen as "Western imperialists" and supporters of the Christians—since late 1982. Their campaign against the Americans began in March 1983, when, in two coordinated attacks, five Marines were injured by a grenade in southern Beirut and six Italian soldiers were injured in a rocket attack near the airport. Then, on April 18, a Shi'ite suicide bomber in a disguised van destroyed the American Embassy in Beirut, killing sixty-three people, of whom seventeen were Americans, including the CIA station chief, Robert Ames. Another one hundred or so were wounded.[314] (A year and a half later, on September 20, 1984, another Shi'ite car-bomber succeeded in destroying the new American Embassy building, killing twenty-five persons, two of them Americans.) The high point in the Syrian-orchestrated campaign came on October 23, 1983, when a Shi'ite suicide bomber drove a truck-bomb into the marine barracks in Beirut and blew it up, killing 241 servicemen. Another truck-bomb that morning destroyed the nearby French military compound, killing 59 soldiers.[315]

The bombers belonged to a group of devout families, led by a handful of Teheran-trained Shi'ite clerics, who drew their spiritual and financial suste-nance from Iran.[316] Immediately after the IDF invasion in summer 1982, these families broke away from the mainstream Shi'ite 'Amal militia—which was seen as insufficiently militant, primarily because it had not opposed the Israelis—and rather loosely organized themselves into Hizbullah, or the "Party of God," founded and led by Hussein Mussawi, a fundamentalist cleric and former 'Amal official. Its immediate aim was to drive all the foreigners—especially the infidel Israelis and the MNF—from Lebanon; eventually it hoped to turn the country into an Islamic republic modeled after Iran. The party's longer-range goals were to launch a jihad against Israel, to restore Jerusalem and Palestine to Islam, and to defeat the Christian West, or at least uproot its influence in the Muslim world.

The Hizbullah drew its recruits and power mainly from the poor Shi'ite fringes of southern Beirut, populated largely by evacuees from Tyre and the villages in the south pummeled for years by IDF artillery and air power and from the eastern, largely Shi'ite, Syrian-occupied Beka'a Valley, where several hundred Iranian Revolutionary Guard volunteers had set up camp in late summer 1982 and established training and supply bases, behind the Syrian front lines. During late 1982–84 the Revolutionary Guards and the Hizbullah militants converted the Beka'a and parts of southern Beirut into a Shi'ite state-within-a-state. It was from these areas that the militants set out to do battle against the MNF and, later, the Israelis. From the first, the Hizbullah had close links with the Iranian Embassy in Beirut and with the Iranian and Syrian intelligence services, and received funds, arms, information, and training from both countries.

The massive loss of life at the marine compound instantly broke Washington's resolve, and the MNF pulled out of Lebanon in February 1984. Following the successive blows to its American patrons and to its own army, Amin Gemayel's government crumbled, the president himself being forced to travel to Damascus and pay homage to his new overlord, Assad, and to assure the Syrians that the previous year's Israeli-Lebanese agreement was "null and void." An official declaration to this effect was published by the Lebanese government on March 5;[317] a Syrian-dominated "Government of National Unity," with Rashid Karameh as prime minister, was established; and in July, the Israeli "liaison office," which had opened in September 1982 at Debayya outside Beirut and combined the functions of an embassy and intelligence station, was closed down.[318]

The primary engine of Israel's gradual withdrawal from Lebanon was the increasingly violent guerrilla campaign against the IDF presence. It began on October 3, 1982, when Palestinian guerrillas killed six Israeli soldiers in an ambush near 'Aley, southeast of Beirut. In a second incident, twenty-one soldiers were injured when their bus was attacked on January 7, 1983. The pace gradually picked up, not a week passing without one or more Israelis injured or dead. At first, the "resisters" were largely PLO men who had stayed on in Lebanon and their left-wing allies, from such organizations as the Lebanese Communist Party and the Syrian National Party. But from spring 1983 on, the brunt of the guerrilla war was borne by the newly militant and freshly armed Shi'ite militias. The Hizbullah was to lead the way, with 'Amal soon following.

In June 1982 the Shi'ites of the south had welcomed the advancing IDF forces, if only because these had, at a stroke, rid them of their Palestinian tormentors. But with the PLO beaten and gone, and with the occupation now stretching out indefinitely, the Shi'ites began to grow restive. The Israelis seemed uninterested in their welfare or interests, or in contacts with them. 'Amal began to stockpile weapons. But 'Amal leader Nabih Berri still counseled and imposed patience; for more than a year, 'Amal lived in uneasy peace with the Israelis. But 'Amal soon found itself in competition for Shi'ite hearts and minds. Hizbullah sought to give the traditionally downtrodden Shi'ites more say, to replace the multiconfessional Lebanese polity with a rigid, monolithic Islamic republic, and to evict the Israelis. From spring 1983 on, the Hizbullah, usually calling itself the Islamic Jihad, dominated the anti-Israeli guerrilla campaign, with the Syrians apparently footing the bill.

Following the IDF withdrawal from the Shouf, the guerrillas stepped up their activities, perhaps animated by the suspicion that the Israelis intended to hold on to the rest of southern Lebanon forever. They (and the Syrians) knew of the promised boundaries sketched out in the Bible, and no doubt had heard of the post–World War I Zionist maps showing a Jewish state stretching to the Litani.[319] Their fears may have been aggravated by the Israeli census conducted in the area in 1983, with a twenty-seven-page questionnaire that covered every aspect of daily life. The census seemed to augur a very long stay—while Israel's leaders, hamstrung by various political and diplomatic calculations, never convincingly announced that the IDF intended to leave.[320]

The resistance spearheaded by the Hizbullah was assisted by the Iranian Revolutionary Guards and by Syrian intelligence, with Palestinians occasionally joining in particular attacks (though the Druze pointedly resisted Syrian pressures and stayed out of the fight, not wishing to turn the Israelis into lasting enemies). In February 1984, with the MNF leaving the country and the Gemayel regime on the verge of collapse, 'Amal at last joined the Hizbullah in the campaign, Berri publicly declaring that 'Amal would "force an Israeli withdrawal from the last foot of southern Lebanon."[321]

The guerrilla war soon donned the usual features. The population was warned off cooperating with the Israelis; collaborators were shot; and Israeli troops were sporadically attacked, from ambush and with mines. The Israeli reactions also followed the timeworn patterns of curfews, searches, mass arrests, torture of suspects, vandalism, looting,[322] and occasional on-the-spot executions—all fueling local anger and support for the guerrillas. Perhaps a harsher policy, with mass executions and expulsions, and the destruction of whole villages, could have halted the Shi'ite campaign. But given Israel's behavioral and democratic norms, this was never an option. At the same time, the alternative—an abrupt, unilateral withdrawal back to the Security Zone without an agreement with, or guarantees by, the Shi'ites—was rejected by Jerusalem as amounting to an admission that the whole project had been folly. For the Likud, this was politically unacceptable.

So, for two years southern Lebanon was engulfed by a bloody cycle of violence in which hundreds of people died and thousands of Lebanese were incarcerated—and Israel's will to hang on was relentlessly undermined. There were two crucial events: the IDF withdrawal from the Shouf and the "Ashura" incident of October 16, 1983, when an IDF convoy accidentally barged into a large Shi'ite religious gathering in Nabatiya (the Ashura festival commemorates the martyrdom of the Shi'ites' prophet, the Imam Hussein, Muhammad's grandson). The trucks were stoned and set alight, and the Israelis opened fire, killing two Shi'ites and wounding seven. Several Israelis were injured. The incident, subsequently exaggerated by local clerics and Hizbullah operatives into a "massacre," crystallized and popularized the Shi'ites' hatred.[323]

The most potent weapon in the Shi'ite armory once again proved to be the suicide bomber. "Death for us is merely a custom; God's generosity is martyrdom," reads a local mosque inscription.[324] The suicide bomber, spiritually chaperoned by a cleric and operationally supplied and directed by a Hizbullah agent, believed that killing Israelis was God's will and that his sacrifice would send him straight to heaven, where he would be enveloped by God's grace and seventy lascivious maidens.

The Israelis, forewarned by the Americans' experience in Beirut, beefed up their guard contingents at the entrances to military bases and installed concrete blocks and other obstacles on approach roads. But the Shi'ites were infinitely determined, courageous, and resourceful. On November 4, 1983, a truck broke through and demolished the IDF General Security Service (Shin Bet) headquarters in Tyre, killing twenty-three Israeli soldiers and five GSS officers—as well as thirty-two Arabs who were being held in the interrogation cells. Another thirty or so Israelis were wounded. From then on, the war took on an ever more bitter and dirty face. The Israelis closed the Awali bridges, effectively cutting off the Shi'ites of the south from their brethren in southern Beirut and the Beka'a. In response the locals increased their aid to the guerrillas.[325]

The Israelis expanded their use of psychological warfare, dropping leaflets warning of the consequences of attacking Israel. "We would take people in and feed them dirt about people we were against: He's an embezzler, he's a homosexual, he's a coward, and so on. . . . We funded broadcasting stations and newspapers and got them to print articles about hospitals and medical services we were running for the people's benefit."[326]

The Israelis deployed units of Haddad's SLA north of the Security Zone (for a time Haddad even set up headquarters in Sidon) to assist them. The Arabic-speaking SLA men helped round up suspects; occasionally they carried out raids and committed atrocities on their own, as on September 20, 1984, at Suhmour, where Druze SLA troops lined up and murdered more than a dozen Shi'ite villagers and wounded two dozen, after a number of their comrades had been killed in an ambush nearby.[327] But the SLA was always too small and stretched too thin to be of great significance. Haddad died of cancer in January 1984 and was replaced by another professional Lebanese Christian soldier, Gen. Antoine Lahad.

Exploiting clan feuds and local criminal elements, the Israelis went about setting up their own local militias in Shi'ite villages and Sunni towns. Few joined; and many of those who—tempted by money or otherwise—did, soon resigned.[328]

But nothing seemed to work. The usual cycle of insurgency and repression spun out of control. Shi'ite gunmen shot at and blew up Israeli convoys. Israeli troops, except on patrol, rarely ventured out of their camps at night. During daytime they moved about in increasingly armored convoys. Defensive measures were matched by an increase in Shi'ite offensive capabilities—more and bigger mines, powerful booby-trapped roadside bombs, and suicide bombers on foot, bicycles, donkeys, cars, and trucks.[329]

The IDF and GSS retaliated after each major incident with mass arrests, wholesale torture, and the occasional assassination of suspected Shi'ite militants. During the first year of the occupation, the primary target of Israeli security operations had been the remnants of the PLO infrastructure and leadership; from autumn 1983 it was the Shi'ites. Initially, the counterinsurgency efforts were largely defensive and in the hands of the IDF. Mass arrests were the main measure (in August 1982, for example, the Israelis were holding some ten thousand mostly Palestinian prisoners in the new, large detention camp established at Ansar, southeast of Sidon) and the Shin Bet's role was limited to interrogation. But over time, the Shin Bet's input became more critical and multifaceted. Injecting more and more agents into the area, the security service attempted to reproduce its coverage of the West Bank and Gaza Strip through local recruitment and a large web of informants and collaborators. Extortion, intimidation, beatings, and torture became the norm, and Shi'ite militants from time to time were liquidated in their homes and villages by locally hired assassins or Shin Bet operatives.

Moving in two-car convoys (usually beat-up Mercedeses, indistinguishable from Lebanese civilian cars) with IDF soldiers (in civilian clothing) riding shotgun, the Shin Bet teams roamed the countryside, arresting and interrogating suspects, delivering threats and warnings, occasionally meting out punishment, often very publicly and very definitively. Some of their operations were reported by Robert Fisk of *The Times* (London), who had excellent sources in the south. In February 1984 a leading Shi'ite cleric was killed in the village of Jibshit, hit in the back by three bullets.[330] On June 14, in the village of Bidias, fifteen Shin Bet men in three vehicles stopped outside a garage owned by Murshid Nakhas, a local 'Amal commander. One of the Israelis called out Nakhas's name while two cars drove around the square to keep away spectators. When Nakhas appeared, he was bundled into one of the cars, dragged off, and shot dead. His body was later found nearby. Israel announced that he had been shot "resisting arrest."[331]

On March 3, 1985, the IDF raided the village of Ma'arake and then withdrew. Under cover of the raid, Shin Bet operatives had concealed a bomb on the roof of the mosque, above the office of the local Hizbullah commander. The following day the bomb was triggered—probably by remote control—as the village militants gathered for a meeting. Among the twelve dead were three prominent Hizbullah commanders; another thirty-four people were injured. An Israeli spokesman announced that the bombing was part of "an internal 'Amal conflict." The Israelis crowned the operation by arresting dozens of participants in the mass funeral on March 5–6.[332]

Rafi Malka, a senior Shin Bet executive, later had this to say about the counterinsurgency activities: "Lebanon gave us Lebanonization, levantinization. . . . In order to stay sane and stay alive, you had to do things that were unacceptable. The Shin Bet was no exception. It was a struggle in a 'Wild West,' and people paid with their lives if they tried to behave according to accepted standards."[333]

The Israelis also took casualties, mostly in roadside ambushes. They would routinely fire wildly as soon as they came under fire, often hitting innocent bystanders, and destroy buildings and groves or orchards near ambush sites, to deter future attacks. But the Shi'ites, with their courage, belief in their cause, and contempt for death, proved better able to endure casualties than Israel, where public opinion had turned thoroughly against the war and its seemingly endless, aimless bloodletting. By mid-1984 the Shi'ites were mounting about one hundred attacks a month. Israeli intelligence, which had successfully penetrated the Palestinians in southern Lebanon, proved largely unsuccessful in gleaning information from the Shi'ites. Detainees were commonly beaten and placed for hours in the sun, handcuffed, with sacks over their heads. Informers were used liberally. The resistance movement regularly hung posters in the streets naming the collaborators; one list had forty-nine names, another twenty-six. Most of those named eventually fled to the Israeli-controlled Security Zone, or were shot.[334]

By the first months of 1985 patrols, in the countryside and in the cities, were usually carried out or accompanied by tanks. Still, the ambushes and roadside explosions, and the reprisals, went on, even though the Israeli government had already announced its intention to withdraw—and had begun to do so, in stages—from southern Lebanon. The Shi'ite suicide bombers were now emulated by Syrian-dispatched agents of the Syrian National Party. The SNP introduced female car-bombers under the assumption that Israeli soldiers, at least initially, would be less suspicious of women drivers. On April 9 a sixteen-year-old girl blew up her car near an Israeli truck convoy outside Jezzine, killing two IDF soldiers (and two Lebanese) and wounding two more.[335]

The IDF withdrawal back to the Security Zone was finally completed in June 1985. It was made possible by the Likud's failure to win a majority in the general elections of July 23, 1984, largely due to the Israeli public's disaffection with the war (as well as with the party's inflationary economics). With a virtual tie between the two main political blocs, neither Labor nor the Likud proved able to establish a viable coalition government without the other. Labor's Shimon Peres and the Likud's Yitzhak Shamir (who had taken over as premier from Begin when the latter resigned in September 1983) entered into a partnership in a so-called National Unity Government. Peres was designated prime minister until 1986, when he was to be replaced by Shamir. In early 1985 the cabinet, successfully steered by Peres—with two Likud ministers joining the Laborites—at last approved a withdrawal plan and in June unilaterally extricated the IDF and GSS from the quagmire. The Israelis withdrew without having received any political or military agreements or assurances from Syria, the Lebanese government, or the various factions.

In May 1985, Syria's President Assad aptly summed up the Israeli experience in Lebanon:

> Israel assumed that the invasion [of Lebanon] would be like a rural excursion in a beautiful mountainous land and that in its wake Lebanon would become an Israeli puppet-state. . . . Begin . . . told the Israelis: Your security will be assured for forty years. But he did not manage to assure their security even for forty days. The people of Lebanon refused to resign themselves to [foreign] oppression, and the Israelis in Lebanon found no rest and tranquillity but were forced, rather, to live in fear and dread, while all their resources during these three years were devoted to finding an escape and better protective measures. . . . They didn't know and do not know when and where they will be fired upon or blown up . . . whether in their camps, patrols or convoys. Because the spirit of sacrifice in the ranks of the Lebanese National Resistance movement knows no bounds.[336]

But the resistance forces—led by Hizbullah and the SNP—wanted the Israelis out of all of Lebanon, including the Security Zone, and swiftly moved to make their point. Again suicide bombers were the favored weapon. On July 9, mere days after the completion of the Israeli withdrawal, two SNP bombers drove into IDF/SLA checkposts at Ras al-Baida and Hasbaya, leaving twelve Lebanese (mostly civilians) dead and six injured, and two Israelis lightly wounded. Afterward, as became their wont, the organizers broadcast a video made before the event, in which the prospective bomber explained: "I hope to kill as many Jews and their agents as possible." Nine such suicide attacks took place during the first three months after the pullback.[337]

The Hizbullah, occasionally assisted by 'Amal and Palestinian guerrillas, was to continue its campaign against the Israelis and SLA in the Security Zone after 1985 and down to the end of the 1990s. The Shi'ite leaders demanded that the IDF withdraw from the last inch of Lebanese soil; the Israelis feared that were they to comply, the Hizbullah would then begin to harry the border settlements in Israel itself.

Between June 1982 and June 1985, Israel suffered some 650 dead and close to 3,000 wounded in Lebanon. Syrian losses were anywhere from 500 to 1,000 dead.[338] The PLO suffered more than 1,000 dead. There were also substantial Palestinian and Lebanese civilian casualties, mostly caused by IDF artillery and air strikes, largely in and around Beirut. No accurate or reliable figures exist. A Lebanese police report from late 1982 speaks of 19,085 persons killed and 30,000 wounded, but this seems a vast exaggeration.[339] Israeli spokesmen usually claimed that Lebanese and Palestinian civilian dead during the war ran into the hundreds rather than the thousands.

"Born of the ambition of one willful, reckless man [Sharon], Israel's 1982 invasion of Lebanon was anchored in delusion, propelled by deceit, and bound to end in calamity," concluded Schiff and Ya'ari.[340]

Israel did achieve a number of undoubted successes: The PLO military infrastructure in southern Lebanon was destroyed, and the organization was driven out of Beirut. Many PLO fighters were killed, and it lost most of its heavy equipment and ammunition stockpiles. Its headquarters was reestablished in faraway Tunisia, and its military units were dispersed in camps around the Middle East and North Africa, no longer posing a threat along or near Israel's borders. The PLO and Arafat emerged from the fray considerably weakened.

But the PLO was not destroyed or mortally wounded, as Sharon and Begin had hoped and planned. Indeed, it could well be argued that the drubbing the organization received drove it, in the end, to moderate its positions, a process that culminated in Arafat's 1988 declaration recognizing Israel and repudiating terrorism. Thus, instead of demolishing the PLO and preparing the ground for Israeli annexation of the West Bank and the Gaza Strip, it can be argued that the invasion of Lebanon had, albeit very violently, groomed the PLO for participation in the diplomacy and peace process that was to characterize the 1990s and was to pave the way for its assumption of authority in parts of the West Bank and Gaza: In sum, Begin and Sharon, by invading Lebanon, can be said to have made a major contribution to the establishment of a Palestinian state.

In the course of the war the IDF had delivered a major blow to Syria's military power, badly mauling its air force and air defense systems. But Israeli commentators and generals were later to argue that (*a*) the thrashing had been insufficient, leaving Assad not greatly weakened—but certainly hugely antagonized and thirsting for revenge; and (*b*) Israel had "wasted" its anti-SAM technology and tactics in a superfluous war, enabling the Syrians (and Soviets) to prepare their air defense systems for the next round, when Israel might be faced with a real fight for survival. Moreover, the Soviets quickly replenished Syria's losses in matériel and, indeed, substantially beefed up its air defense capabilities with batteries of long-range SAM-5s, which theoretically extended Syria's aircraft-killing capabilities into Israel proper. As well, Syrian armored power was enhanced with large shipments of T-72 tanks.

But the debit side of the war, from Israel's perspective, did not end there. Having set out to destroy the Palestinian threat from Lebanon, the Israelis withdrew only to find that they had installed in its place a far more fanatical and efficient foe in the form of the 'Amal and, particularly, the Hizbullah military organizations. The latter was to prove far more deadly and determined than the PLO. After the withdrawal the Hizbullah (and, to a lesser degree, other Lebanese and Lebanon-based groups) continued to hound and pound the IDF in the Security Zone and, on occasion, on the Israeli side of the international frontier. Indeed, by the mid-1990s the guerrilla campaign in the south was dubbed by Israeli generals a "war of attrition." Clearly Begin (and Sharon) had dismally failed to deliver "forty years of peace" along Israel's northern frontier.

In the short term, the war did Israel harm in the propaganda war fought across the newspaper pages and television screens of the West, though it failed to do long-term damage to the country's international standing. However, it left Israeli society bitterly divided and the government and military with a sense of failure. The alliance with the Maronites was shattered and Christian military power in Lebanon was definitively vanquished. The Christians lost about sixty villages (mostly to the Druze in the Shouf) and thousands of casualties, and emerged from the war much weaker than they had entered it. Indeed, in the course of the battles and occupation of 1982–85, Israel succeeded in antagonizing and alienating most of Lebanon's different communities and factions, particularly the Shi'ites.

Syria had effectively prevented Lebanon from becoming the second Arab state to make peace (or at least achieve contractual nonbelligerency) with Israel. Moreover, Syria effectively filled the vacuum created by the IDF withdrawal, gradually gaining far greater power in the country than it had enjoyed before 1982. After a series of ups and downs and a succession of showdowns with different groups (Phalangists, the Lebanese Army, Shi'ites, Palestinians, and so on), the Syrians in 1990 succeeded in imposing complete military and political control over all of northern and central Lebanon, including all of Beirut, with their troops patrolling as far south as Sidon. By the end of the 1990s Lebanese presidents and prime ministers had become no more than puppets dancing to Damascus's tune. Moreover, the Syrians—avenging their defeat at the gates of Sidon in 1976 and completing the IDF's own campaign—succeeded in driving Arafat and the mainstream PLO factions out of

Lebanon altogether, though the aim of dominating the PLO continued to elude Damascus as it did Beirut. In the mid-1990s the PLO went its own way, in defiance of Syria, in its peacemaking with Israel.

It is perhaps worth adding that during the 1990s Syrian hegemony in Lebanon brought with it an almost complete stifling of the internecine fighting that had characterized that country since 1975. Given the Israeli and American experiences of intervention, this was no mean achievement—and one for which many Lebanese probably remain reluctantly, ambivalently thankful.

TWELVE

The Intifada

Causes

O n the evening of November 25, 1987, two hang gliders flown by members of the PFLP–General Command took off from a hilltop just north of Israel's Security Zone in southern Lebanon. One of them made it over the zone into the Galilee Panhandle. He landed outside the headquarters camp of an IDF infantry brigade, ran past a somnolent guard, shot everyone in his path, and tossed grenades. Six soldiers died and seven were injured before he was shot dead.[1] The courageous escapade fired the imagination of the Palestinians, and the airborne raider was adopted as a national hero.[2] Demonstrating youths later taunted Israeli troops with the cry "six to one," and "6:1" soon also adorned the walls in the alleyways of Gaza.[3]

Two weeks later, the Intifada—Arabic for "shaking off," like a dog shaking off a flea[4]—erupted. The uprising began on December 8–9, 1987, fully two decades after Yasser Arafat first called for a revolt against the Israeli occupation in the West Bank and the Gaza Strip. It came as a complete surprise to the PLO, and took a course totally different from that preached by the organization's leaders. It was not an armed rebellion but a massive, persistent campaign of civil resistance, with strikes and commercial shutdowns, accompanied by violent (though unarmed) demonstrations against the occupying forces. The stone and, occasionally, the Molotov cocktail and knife were its symbols and weapons, not guns and bombs.

The Intifada—the Palestinians' "war for independence from Israel"[5]—was a political struggle, though it started as a mass protest against unbearable economic conditions,[6] which in turn were largely a result of political realities. Only after its outbreak were the Palestinians' energies clearly channeled toward nationalist goals by political leaders who gained partial control over the enraged populace. The main energizing force of the Intifada was the frustration of the national aspirations of the 650,000 inhabitants of the Gaza Strip, 900,000 of the West Bank, and 130,000 of East Jerusalem, who wanted to live in a Palestinian state and not as stateless inhabitants under a brutal, foreign military occupation.

Nationalist feeling had been immensely reinforced during the decades of Israeli rule. Not least, this was a result of what the inhabitants saw as a process of "creeping annexation." Three days after the start of the Intifada, Rashad a-Shawa, former mayor of Gaza, explained it thus:

> One can expect such events after 20 years of harsh occupation. People have lost all hope. They are completely frustrated. They don't know what to do. They have adopted a line of religious fundamentalism, which for them is the last resort. They have lost hope that Israel will ever give them rights. They feel that the Arab states are incapable of achieving anything [for them]. They feel that the PLO, which they regard as their representative, failed to achieve anything. . . . What has happened is an expression of the frustration and the pain over the continuing Israeli occupation.

In another interview a-Shawa said that the people of the Gaza Strip "have a sense of injustice and discrimination, that they have nothing more to lose. They work for [Israel] as garbage collectors and dish-washers, and feel like slaves. The wave of demonstrations is . . . a spontaneous expression of the people, which begins with the small pupil in elementary school and ends with the laborer who returns day in day out from Israel, where he sees the good life, and here he is forced to live in sub-human conditions."[7]

In two decades of struggle the PLO had achieved close to nothing. Following its ejection from Lebanon, it appeared feebler than ever. In November 1987 the Palestinians were afforded humiliating confirmation of the PLO's weakness as an Arab summit meeting virtually ignored their problem and focused on the Iraq-Iran war. The assembly in Amman endorsed the reestablishment of diplomatic relations between their states and Egypt, bowing to the fait accompli of the Egyptian-Israeli peace. The meeting clearly signaled that the Palestinians were at the bottom of the Arab agenda.[8]

Israel appeared determined that there would be no negotiation with the PLO and no Palestinian state. Nor, it appeared, would salvation come from outside: Washington was solidly in the Israeli camp, the UN as impotent as ever, and the Kremlin under the sway of a reformer, Mikhail Gorbachev, who was rapidly casting off Cold War baggage, such as the Soviets' traditional pro-Arab posture, and dispatching tens of thousands of Jewish emigrants to Israel, strengthening it and providing a vast pool of potential settlers for the occupied territories. If the Palestinians' situation was to be ameliorated, it would have to be by their own hand, and quickly.

Though harsh and often brutal, Israeli rule in general was never as restrictive or repressive as the Palestinians made out. Over the decades of occupation, the Israelis had allowed the establishment of a web of institutional kernels of self-rule and political resistance. Some had been properly licensed—such as the seven West Bank and Gaza universities (there had been no universities in the territories before 1967) and the Islamic Association, the front organization of the Muslim Brotherhood that was soon to become the Hamas. Israeli indifference, ignorance, or goodwill allowed other institutions to bloom by default, such as the local "popular committees," conscious replications of the National Committees that had emerged in the Palestinian population centers in 1936 and again in 1947–48. The seventies and eighties had seen the blossoming of a range of self-help and potential self-governmental organizations, such as trade unions, professional associations, students' committees, charities, newspapers, research institutes, and women's groups.

Two "national" institutions or networks are worthy of note: Fatah's youth wing, the Shabiba (or, in full, the Youth Committees for Social Activity), and the Islamic Association. Established in 1981, the Shabiba gave the Fatah control over young people who might otherwise have drifted into crime and drugs, or into the Islamicist camp. Its clubs afforded a venue for social mixing, sports, and games, and provided manpower for community services, such as repairing sewage systems and roads, and rebuilding homes demolished by the Israelis. By 1987 tens of thousands of youngsters belonged, throughout the West Bank and Gaza Strip.[9]

The Muslim Brotherhood centered around the Islamic University and the mosques of Gaza, where, following Israel's victory in 1967, with the yoke of Nasserist oppression removed, Islam enjoyed a revival. During the first decade of the occupation, the Brotherhood was ignored by the authorities, who were concerned above all about nationalists of the Fatah and PFLP stamp. The members, keeping to their mosques and clubs, appeared to be innocuous; the GSS ignored their anti-Semitic teachings. The movement expanded quietly, eschewing anti-Israeli resistance. During the 1970s the return to the Strip of graduates of Egypt's increasingly Islamicized universities supplied fresh energy and cadres. At the same time Gazan students enrolled in the universities in Nablus, Hebron, and Bir Zeit and spread the word of Allah to the West Bank.

The growth of the Brotherhood—and Islamic fundamentalism in general—among Palestinians owed much to the organizational skills of Sheikh Ahmad Ismail Hassan Yassin. Born in 1936 near Ashkelon, in 1948 he fled with his family to the Strip. In 1952 he was crippled in a sports accident.[10] He became an elementary school teacher, and from 1968 on directed the Brotherhood's activities in the Gaza Strip and oversaw a massive if gradual program of expansion. During the 1970s and 1980s the movement took over the various Muslim Trust (*waqf*) institutions, including the Gaza Islamic University and most of the Strip's mosques, giving it an institutional and financial power base. Despite his disabilities—which grew progressively worse—Yassin frequently traveled to mosques in the West Bank and Israel, which by then were also in the grip of a steady Islamic revival. (Between 1967 and 1987 the number of Muslim worshippers in the Gaza Strip doubled, the number of mosques rising from 77 to 160. In the West Bank, by the 1980s, 40 new mosques were being built each year.[11])

Yassin stayed clear of explicit political incitement, though his movement's publications often struck a crude anti-Semitic note. (One fundamentalist detainee told his Israeli interrogators that "the resurrection of the dead at the End of Days was conditional upon every last Jew being destroyed."[12]) Yassin directed his efforts to saving Muslims' souls and providing the poor with economic and social benefits and institutions. He combined fervent religious enthusiasm with a cold, precise intellect, both housed in a body that by the 1980s was paralyzed from the neck down. Israeli officials were repeatedly struck by the contrast between his inability to move his own limbs and his power to control, with the twitch of an eyelash, a massive political movement.[13]

By the late 1970s the Brotherhood—operating under the legal cloak of the Islamic Association, a social and religious welfare organization—provided the believers and their families not only with a clandestine political affiliation and religious services, but with kindergartens, elementary and high schools, libraries, day-care centers, clinics, sports clubs, even a blood bank. A network employing hundreds of workers and servicing tens of thousands of families had emerged, and the Brotherhood offered a serious challenge to the PLO for the loyalties of the populace.[14]

In many towns and villages, the fundamentalists imposed new norms of behavior. Movie houses were shut down; shop windows displaying models of women in dresses were vandalized; cafés selling alcoholic beverages were set alight; people who used the left hand in eating (contrary to the tradition of the Prophet) were beaten. Women increasingly took the veil, and young men began sporting beards.[15]

Such institutions and associations, secular and Islamic, and the leadership cadres that emerged during the occupation, particularly in its second decade, were to supply the organizational infrastructure for the Intifada. But the factors that made individual Palestinians take to the streets and endure beatings, imprisonment, and economic privation were predominantly socioeconomic and psychological. One researcher compared the Gaza Strip on the eve of the Intifada to a pressure cooker, containing "overcrowding, poverty, hatred, violence, oppression, poor sanitation, anger, frustration, drugs and crime."[16]

Between 1967 and the early 1980s, annual per capita income in the Gaza Strip rose from $80 to $1,700; in the West Bank, the gross domestic product more than tripled in that period.[17] The number of cars in the territories increased tenfold, the number of telephones sixfold, the number of tractors ninefold.[18] The rise in personal income and expenditure fueled a general growth in the economy, with the West Bank enjoying an average annual GNP increase, between 1968 and 1978, of 12.9 percent; in the Gaza Strip, it was 12.1 percent, while in Israel itself it was 5.5 percent.[19] Roads were vastly improved (though this had more to do with Israeli security considerations and servicing the new Jewish settlements than with care for the welfare of the Arab inhabitants). Most homes were linked up to Israel's electricity grid—in 1967 only 18 percent of Gaza households had electricity; in 1981, 89 percent.[20] Health care, too, got much better, with many of the sick enjoying the services of Israel's hospitals, which led to a dramatic expansion of the population and overcrowding, especially in Gaza.

But none of this sufficed to erase—though it may for a time have tempered—the inhabitants' political frustration and anger or their feelings of discrimination and inequality compared with the Israelis. Moreover, despite the average increases in income and living standards, vast pockets of abject poverty continued to exist and grow.

In the years immediately preceding the Intifada, both territories experienced major economic slumps. During 1981–86 the average annual GNP increase was only 3.2 percent in the West Bank and 1.7 percent in the Gaza Strip. Commensurately, during 1981–85 the per capita GNP declined on average by 1.8 percent per year in the Gaza Strip and by 0.7 percent in the West Bank.[21] The effects were most acutely felt in the refugee camps, populated by the dispossessed of 1948, who were to be the heart and driving force of the Intifada.

In 1987, the Gaza Strip had one of the highest population densities in the world—1,600 persons per square kilometer. Many homes in the camps lacked running water, and sewage ran in the streets. About half the inhabitants lived in "subhuman" conditions.[22] In 1986–87 the increase in births ran at double the pace of new housing construction.[23] A few months before the Intifada broke out, an Israeli study used two images to describe Gaza: "a cancer," which would eat away at the Israeli polity, and "a time bomb," economic, social, and demographic, of almost unimaginable potency. With the population exploding, land and water resources were shrinking: By 1987 the 2,500 Israeli settlers in the Strip—or 0.4 percent of the territory's total population—had control over some 28 percent of its state lands.[24] Similarly, much of the underground water reserves, in both territories, were diverted to the use of Israel itself or Jewish settlers. On average, West Bank settlers used twelve times as much water as did Palestinians.[25] The amount of irrigated Arab land in the West Bank declined by 30 percent between 1967 and 1987.[26]

Government policies subordinated the territories to Israeli economic needs and stultified Palestinian development. The overall policy was described by analysts Ze'ev Schiff and Ehud Ya'ari as one of "sheer despotism, selfishness and greed," with the territories serving as a type of "slave market" for the Israeli economy.[27] To protect Israeli industries the civil administration—the civilian arm of the military government—blocked Arabs from setting up manufacturing plants. Through a system of permits (required to travel, to import funds and materials, to construct buildings) the territories were turned into a vast market, if not a dumping ground, for Israeli goods.[28]

While barring the territories' farmers from producing certain agricultural products (to prevent them from competing with Israeli exports), the authorities encouraged, and even assisted in various ways (loans, expert advice, and so on), in the production of other fruit and vegetables (tomatoes, cucumbers) that could meet Israel's internal needs. Israeli farmers were thus freed to invest in foreign-currency-earners—such as flowers and out-of-season or tropical fruits and vegetables.

With little or no indigenous industrial or agricultural development, a large part of the territories' labor pool was forced to seek work in Israel. In 1987 some 120,000 West Bank and Gaza Arabs, or more than 40 percent of the labor force, were employed in Israel.[29] Most of them had menial jobs and earned very little, even compared with the few Israelis in similar employment, and most were denied all social and fringe benefits.

A number of Israeli economic sectors—construction, agriculture—became dependent on Arab labor, and the employers turned a nice profit for as long as the arrangement lasted. Curiously, through most of the Intifada many of these workers continued to pour into Israel and even to construct the homes of the settlers. Only in the mid-1990s, against the backdrop of Islamic fundamentalist terrorism, did Israel cut back on the use of such laborers, replacing most of them with foreign workers imported from, among other countries, Thailand and Romania, and leaving the former Arab workers stranded in the territories, where they could not find alternative employment.

All the universities and most of the other institutions of higher education in the territories were established in the years of Israeli rule,[30] but the military government prevented the growth of an economy to absorb their graduates. Tens of thousands of high school and university graduates took menial jobs. Others suffered prolonged stints of unemployment or sought work in the Gulf States or in the West. During the 1970s more than ten thousand, and in some years as many as twenty thousand, Palestinians left the territories annually,[31] remitting to their families hundreds of millions of dollars each year. But during the mid-1980s the Iraq-Iran war gradually closed this opening; thousands of Palestinians were forced to return to the territories from the Gulf States. The loss of these petrodollars both contributed to the outbreak of the Intifada and fueled it. Then, during 1988–94, hundreds of thousands of Soviet Jews poured into Israel and took many of the menial jobs previously held by Palestinians; unemployment among the latter soared.[32]

Palestinians interpreted Israel's settlement policy and its discriminatory economic policies as signifying the government's ultimate intent to dispossess and drive them out and to replace them with Jews—a continuation of 1948 by other means. The Likud's assumption of power in 1977 and its reinforced settlement drive during the following seven years—which saw the establishment of about one hundred new settlements, including large urban centers near Jerusalem and east of Tel Aviv—seemed to bring that anticipated displacement giant strides closer.

As described, the July 1984 elections ended in a tie between Labor and the Likud. In the National Unity Government the two parties shared power, and their respective leaders, Shimon Peres and Yitzhak Shamir, rotated as prime minister. (Peres served as premier during 1984–86 and Shamir during 1986–88, with Labor's hard-liner, Yitzhak Rabin, holding the defense portfolio throughout, as he was to do in the next unity government, in 1988–90, as well.) Though few new settlements were established in the territories during this hybrid government's years in office, the settler population was substantially boosted as existing settlements were expanded. In the West Bank alone, the Jewish population, in some 125 settlements, increased from 35,000 in 1984 to 64,000 in 1988 (reaching 130,000 by the mid-1990s).

The settlement effort was accompanied by a continual crackdown, or "iron fist" policy, as it was called, against Palestinian nationalism. Indeed, in some respects (such as the number of demolitions of terrorists' or suspected terrorists' houses), the National Unity Governments' rule in the territories, as overseen by Rabin, was harsher than that of the 1977–84 Likud administration.[33] The government's measures were paralleled by increasing militancy on the part of some of the settlers, who periodically indulged in retaliatory vigilantism—smashing car windows, firing at houses, and so on—while the authorities failed to interfere.

Through the 1980s, the Arabs picked up signals that Israel ultimately intended to evict them—not merely from extremists such as the Moledet Party's Rehav'am Ze'evi, the former IDF general who publicly preached "voluntary transfer" in "air-conditioned buses," but from mainstream politicians as well. In July 1987 Deputy Defense Minister Michael Dekel, who was close to Prime Minister Shamir, publicly called for the transfer of Palestinians to Jordan. Cabinet minister Mordechai Zippori, not at all a hard-liner, in 1982 told Jewish settlers near Nablus: "Don't worry about the demographic density of the Arabs. When I was born in Petach Tikva, we were entirely surrounded by Arab villages. They have all since disappeared."[34] Another minister, Yosef Shapira, of the National Religious Party, proposed offering US$20,000 to any Palestinian willing to emigrate.[35] In early December 1987 Ariel Sharon, then the industry and trade minister, moved into an apartment in the Old City's

Muslim Quarter.[36] In Arab eyes the move portended displacement; it was a "dangerous and infuriating" development, said the mufti of Jerusalem.[37] (For years Sharon had been saying that Jordan should be the Palestinians' "homeland."[38])

There was also the all-pervading element of humiliation, which some observers regard as the key to understanding the outbreak of the Intifada.[39] The protracted state of political subjugation and economic dependence, and the day-to-day realities of military occupation, meant a continuous trampling on the basic rights and dignity of the inhabitants. Israeli propagandists tried to project an image of an "enlightened occupation." But in fact it was always a brutal and mortifying experience for the occupied (as well as a brutalizing experience for the occupiers), involving daily, often rough, identity checks and body searches of laborers and students, accompanied by verbal abuse and, more rarely though not uncommonly, by physical abuse.[40]

Attacks against Israelis were followed by added elements of brutality and collective punishment. Curfews, sometimes lasting for days, were common. Soldiers and GSS operatives, in search of suspects, weapons, or subversive literature, broke into homes in the middle of the night, pulling whole families out of bed, overturning beds, wardrobes, and jars of oil and cereals, leaving crying mothers and babies in their wake. The men were taken to the village or town squares and screened. Some were bundled off blindfolded and manacled for further interrogation at GSS facilities and police stations—their families learning of their whereabouts only days or weeks later. In many cases, close relatives of suspects were themselves detained as a means of acquiring information or applying pressure on fugitives.

Over the decades the security forces detained tens of thousands of inhabitants, holding them for weeks and months on end, often without trial. Interrogation involved physical and psychological abuse and, frequently, varying degrees of torture. These experiences left the population of the territories thirsting for revenge. The troops, policemen, and GSS officers, themselves ground down by the routine and abasement of the occupation, rarely paid attention to the dignity of those they dealt with, and often deliberately humiliated them.[41]

Ironically, the prisons and detention camps provided effective ideological indoctrination, group consolidation, and terrorism training centers for the inmates. Almost all the leaders of the Intifada went through these facilities, most notoriously the "Ansar Camp," originally in the Gaza Strip, and later in the Negev. Of fifty-three such leaders deported during 1988–89, forty-two had served long stints in Israeli prisons.[42]

THE TRIGGERS OF THE INTIFADA

The mid-1980s witnessed a steady decline in Israel's deterrent image, precipitated by the successful Shi'ite guerrilla campaign against the IDF in southern Lebanon.[43] A series of armed clashes in the territories were similarly to boost Palestinian morale and to deflate the IDF's reputation. The discrediting of the GSS during 1985–87 as a result of the public exposure of grave human rights abuses also played a role: It emerged as immoral, brutal, and incompetent. Other important elements in this process were the stabbing of Israeli civilians and security personnel by Palestinians (twenty in 1985, seventeen in 1986, and fifteen in 1987[44]), and the May 1987 escape from Gaza Prison of six Islamic Jihad terrorists. Taken as a whole, the incidents projected a sense of Israeli vulnerability and Palestinian daring and sacrifice.

During the 1970s and early 1980s the Muslim Brotherhood had shied away from violence. Consequently, the military government, advised by the GSS, had tacitly and perhaps also actively assisted in its growth, seeing it as a counterweight to the PLO. But the climate among the fundamentalists began to change in the wake of the success of Khomeini in Iran and the Shi'ites in southern Lebanon. The ayatollahs were exporting their fiery brand of Islam around the Middle East; Sunni fundamentalists assassinated the symbol of Arab reconciliation with Israel, Anwar Sadat. The PLO's demise in Lebanon had left many Palestinians bereft of hope of national salvation. Islam seemed to provide an answer. The Likud's rise to power, the ascendancy of Jewish fundamentalism, and the threat these posed to the Palestinian patrimony and the Islamic holy sites on the Temple Mount—all helped pave the way for many Palestinians to Islamic fundamentalism. Following the July 1983 massacre of students at the Islamic University of Hebron by Jewish terrorists, West Bank fundamentalists distributed a leaflet stating: "[L]ook what the Jews, scions of apes and pigs, are doing to us. . . . The Jews' aim is and always was . . . settlement, oppression . . . massacre . . . wholesale [Arab] emigration. . . . They spit hatred at Islam in preparation for . . . demolishing al-Aqsa Mosque and to build again their false temple."[45]

During this period the Muslim Brotherhood underwent a process of "Palestinization." The universalist Islamic core of its preaching and activities gradually gave way to a narrower, nationalistic focus. More and more fundamentalists began to speak of "Palestine" and Palestinian political goals—a shift that went unnoticed by the authorities. Few Israelis made the connection between Sheikh Yassin and the Khomeinist model: preacher turned political revolutionary and terrorist mastermind.

In 1983–84 Yassin took an early, hesitant, clandestine stab at political militancy. He instructed his followers to set up a secret military/terrorist wing inside the Brotherhood. They began to stockpile arms, mostly stolen from IDF bases. But in June 1984 the GSS got wind of this and discovered a cache of rifles and pistols in Yassin's mosque. (The fundamentalists made a practice of hiding weapons and seditious material in mosques, knowing that, because such raids prompted foreign criticism and, often, mass rioting, the Israelis were extremely reluctant to raid places of worship.) Yassin was arrested, tried, and given a thirteen-year prison term. Released the following year as part of a mass IDF-Palestinian prisoner exchange deal, he reverted to preaching nonviolence. But in secret, in June 1987, the Brotherhood again set up a military wing, acquiring arms and organizing fighting squads. In addition Yassin set up an intelligence wing, which murdered collaborators and "moral deviants."[46]

But the political shift among the fundamentalists had begun years earlier. In 1980–81 a group of Gaza intellectuals led by an Egyptian-trained Gaza doctor, Fathi Shkaki, and 'Abd al-'Aziz 'Odeh, a cleric from Jibalya, broke with the Brotherhood and began to preach violent rebellion against the occupation as well as radical Islamic reform of Arab society, both inside and outside Palestine. Shkaki and his colleagues had a deep, Koran-based hatred and contempt for Jews, which was fed by the abuses of the occupation and by what the fundamentalists saw as the blasphemous, religiously subversive Israeli culture. Moreover, influenced by the GSS practice of using drug pushers and prostitutes as collaborators, they identified Israeli rule with the spread of drugs and moral laxity in general in their own society. They inveighed against "the spread of Jewish corruption [in Palestine]. Israel is a central part of a plan to fragment the Islamic nation, to westernize it, to subjugate it, to enslave it, to paralyze its will and to cast an eternal yoke over its neck." The Muslims were duty-bound to "eliminate the element of corruption, Israel."[47]

Shkaki hoped that the militants' attacks would provoke the Israelis into harsh countermeasures and drive the Palestinians to rebellion. He set up an underground organization of several dozen activists, based largely on recruits from the student body of Gaza's Islamic University and on the congregation of 'Odeh's Sheikh 'Izz a Din al-Qassam Mosque and affiliated Gaza mosques. The members were organized in tightly compartmentalized five- to seven-man cells. Eventually they adopted the name "Islamic Jihad for Palestine" and in 1985 or 1986 began pinprick attacks against the Israelis. Shkaki himself was arrested in 1986 and deported on August 1, 1988.[48] He subsequently directed the organization from an office in Damascus.

Islamic Jihad members often acted in coordination or alliance with Fatah activists, having grown close in Israeli jails. Though at odds regarding their visions of the future of Palestine—Islamic fundamentalist republic versus "secular democratic" state—they shared the goal of overthrowing the occupation. On October 15, 1986, they jointly carried out a spectacular grenade attack on an IDF swearing-in ceremony at the Western Wall, in which one person was killed and close to seventy injured.

The May 1987 breakout of the Islamic Jihad militants from Gaza Prison set in motion a new guerrilla campaign that, through its mixture of successes and self-sacrifice, was within months to help set the territories ablaze. Only one of the six was caught immediately. The remaining five made contact with other Islamic Jihad activists, reconstructed a number of guerrilla cells, and embarked on operations. On August 8, an IDF military police captain was shot dead in the center of Gaza. Subsequently grenades were thrown at the military government headquarters in Gaza, a GSS vehicle was ambushed, and two Arab collaborators were killed.

The militants' luck ran out at the beginning of October—but with a bang that shook the Gaza Strip. On October 1, a squad of Islamic Jihad gunmen in a car tried to break through an IDF roadblock. All three passengers, who included one of the escapees, died in the exchange of gunfire.[49] Five days later GSS agents, backed by border police, ambushed two cars carrying the rest of the fugitives in Gaza's Saja'iya quarter. Four gunmen (including two of the escapees) were killed;[50] two managed to escape to Egypt. Muslim preachers and activists turned the firefight of October 6 into a heroic tale of resistance and martyrdom. A one-day general strike called by the Islamic Jihad on October 10 to commemorate its fallen was obeyed throughout the Strip, accompanied by giant demonstrations and stone-throwing attacks on Gaza's police station, ending only after some two dozen persons were wounded by Israeli gunfire. Unwisely, the authorities helped stoke tempers by demolishing the homes of four of the Islamic Jihad activists.[51] The territories would never be the same again—and, indeed, Islamic Jihad spokesmen later dated the start of the Intifada as October 6.

Through November there were clashes in the Strip. On the 10th, an Arab schoolgirl was shot dead by a Jewish settler near Deir al-Balah after his car was stoned. The following day, in another stoning incident, two more schoolgirls were shot and wounded by settlers,[52] and the Islamic University was shut down. The military authorities announced the impending deportation of Sheikh 'Odeh. The Brotherhood, coming to the Islamic Jihad's help, reacted by issuing leaflets denouncing the deportation and maintaining that "throughout history the Jews have remained crooks, charlatans, and schemers who trample our honor and kill women, children and old people." Days of rioting followed, with the unarmed participants showing unwonted courage, even storming the fence surrounding the IDF outpost inside the Jibalya refugee camp.[53] The level and frequency of the violence were unprecedented. An Israeli salesman was stabbed to death in Gaza; a curfew was imposed and hundreds were detained for interrogation.[54] By early December, to avoid confrontations, official vehicles began to use side roads. Israeli inspectors refrained from visiting schools.[55] Israel's loss of control was palpable.

Jerusalem and the West Bank were also affected. Increased Palestinian militancy, often expressed in stone-throwing incidents, triggered an increase in Jewish vigilantism. Groups of extremist settlers, particularly in and around Hebron, raided Palestinian villages and refugee camps, shot up cars and rooftop solar heaters, and intimidated the inhabitants. Occasionally the vigilantes beat up and shot Arab bystanders.[56]

One expression of this Jewish militancy was the emergence of an organization known as the Faithful of the Temple Mount, whose members believed that the "End of Days" was near and that the al-Aqsa Mosque and the Dome of the Rock should be destroyed and be replaced by a "Third [Jewish] Temple." They regularly tried to get into the Temple Mount compound to stage mass prayers but were barred by the police.[57] In October 1987 they redoubled their efforts. On the 11th, about two thousand Muslims gathered outside al-Aqsa to protest. Troops and police moved in to clear the area and several dozen Arabs (and policemen) were injured. Subsequently a commercial strike and demonstrations swept East Jerusalem and nearby West Bank towns.[58] There was also a brawl between Jewish and Muslim worshippers at the Tomb of the Patriarchs in Hebron.

The Israeli government regularly dissociated itself from, and sometimes explicitly condemned, acts of Jewish vigilantism—but did little to stop them. Arabs began to feel that the IDF could no longer protect them from the settlers, mirroring the settlers' own feelings about the army. The security forces were still fighting terrorism, more or less as efficiently and resolutely as in the past. But there seemed to be a loss of will to confront unarmed, mass opposition, a slackness and irresolution when it came to civil protest and disobedience—a certain tiredness.

Arab high school pupils took to the streets, stone-throwing attacks on Israeli buses multiplied, and the police seemed powerless to stop them. Through much of the year the West Bank universities—hotbeds of nationalism—remained shut, either by order of the Israeli military or because of student-administration disputes whose background was usually political. Thousands of students sat around, waiting for something to do, for something to happen.

But the major augury of Israel's loss of control took place in the Balata refugee camp, on the eastern edge of Nablus. It was the largest and most crowded of the West Bank refugee camps. By spring 1987 the camp's internal affairs were run by the local Shabiba chapter. During the previous months almost every IDF patrol and lookout post in the camp had been challenged by stone-throwing and Molotov cocktail attacks. In the end, the IDF (and the civil government) simply withdrew. Bands of Shabiba members roamed the alleyways, masked and armed with knives and chains, punishing and occasionally expelling suspected informers (and their families) and pimps and drug dealers. On the constructive side the Shabiba organized mosque renovation, sewage upkeep, garbage collection, and sports activities. For several months the Fatah held sway in Balata—and the camp's "liberation" reverberated throughout the territories.

At last, on May 31, the IDF moved in. A curfew was imposed, and units surrounded and drove into the camp in search of wanted terrorists, political activists, and weapons. But the operation soured almost immediately. After several thousand young males were rounded up for questioning, the bulk of the population, led by masses of women and children, rioted, pelting the Israeli troops with stones and bottles. Some of the detainees broke free of their captors and joined in. The troops had either to let loose with live fire—or else withdraw without accomplishing their mission. The commanding officer, Gen. Amram Mitzna, chose the second course.[59] In effect, the Shabiba had won the "Battle of Balata"—and the camp remained under de facto Fatah control. The Israeli coordinator of activities in the territories, Shmuel Goren, later described what had happened in the camp as a "mini-Intifada" that had helped precipitate the wider, real uprising.[60]

All that was needed now was a spark—and that, ironically, was provided by a traffic accident rather than by any blatant act of repression or defiance. On the morning of December 8 an IDF tank transporter traveling just north of the Strip hit a number of vans carrying workers from the Jibalya refugee camp to construction sites in Israel. Four of the Arabs died, and six were wounded.[61] A rumor—that the driver had deliberately hit the van in revenge for the murder of an Israeli two days before—swept through the Strip and West Bank like a brush fire.[62] On December 9, thousands poured out of the alleys of Jibalya and other Gaza camps for the funerals, shouting "*Jihad, Jihad!*"[63] At Jibalya the IDF outpost was surrounded by mourners and pelted with stones. But no IDF reinforcements were deemed necessary or rushed to the scene. The following day Jibalya's inhabitants again took to the streets and set up roadblocks. Israeli APCs were turned back by stone throwers. Troops fired on the crowd, wounding a number of people and killing a seventeen-year-old boy.[64] The Intifada had started.

The rioters of December 1987 and the years that followed wanted to get rid of the Israeli occupation and to better their economic conditions. Most Palestinians certainly regarded independence and the establishment of their own state as a further, major objective.[65] Among many, and certainly among the Islamic fundamentalists, there also lurked the ultimate aim of destroying the State of Israel and ejecting its Jewish population. As Sheikh Ibrahim al-Quqa, a Hamas leader, put it: The Intifada is "a phase, and a prelude to a more serious process of getting rid of the Zionist presence on this land."[66] Many refugees saw the Intifada as an instrument that would help them repossess what they had lost in 1948.

The activists aimed to weaken Israel and its hold on the territories by inflicting both casualties and political damage, to push the Palestinian problem to the top of the international agenda, and to initiate a dynamic that would empower the PLO and force its inclusion in the Middle East peace process. They understood that, to achieve any of these goals, the Intifada must encompass not only the refugee camps and urban centers but also the rural population. They hoped to force the IDF out of as many areas as possible and to institute, for as long as possible, some form of Palestinian "independence" there, as a means to consolidate and spread the rebellion and to draw nearer to their ultimate goal.

Within hours of the first rioting in Jibalya, the Intifada had spread to the Gaza Strip's other refugee camps and soon after to camps in the West Bank. A day or two later it pressed outward, from the camps into Gaza's towns and then to West Bank towns.[67] Spontaneously hundreds and then thousands of people poured into the streets, flinging stones, burning tires, and building barricades.

The sporadic, unsuccessful attempts by small IDF patrols to confront and break up the enormous, raging crowds only aggravated matters, especially as the clashes often ended with soldiers firing into the mob. The funerals of slain demonstrators, who were immediately dubbed "martyrs," themselves turned into violent protests. The rioters showed great courage and a willingness for self-sacrifice that the Israelis had rarely encountered before. Photographs from those early days show youngsters tearing open their shirts and challenging the soldiers to shoot them.

Wrote Schiff and Ya'ari: "The long tradition of capitulation to Israel was supplanted, almost magically, by a mood of defiance. . . . In a matter of days the West Bank and the Gaza Strip had become the scene of an all-out fray between a native population and an occupying power. . . . The system that had enabled the occupation to continue for over two decades simply collapsed in the face of the violence. . . . None of the old rules applied any more."[68]

Twelve consecutive days of rioting turned the refugee camps and urban poor into the dominant force in Palestinian society. Demonstration leaders took to masking their faces with keffiyahs (a symbol of Palestinian resistance at least since the 1930s), both to prevent identification and to reduce the effects of tear gas—red-and-white scarves for leftists (PFLP, DFLP, and so on), green-and-white ones for Muslim fundamentalists, black-and-white for Fatah.[69] No national organizing hand was apparent, though on the local level, in the Gaza Strip, Islamic Jihad and other fundamentalists immediately took a leading role, with the mosques serving as focal points of incitement and leadership.[70] Many of the local agitators were ex-prisoners released in the May 1985 exchange for a handful of Israeli soldiers captured in Lebanon. The Israelis had released 1,150 Palestinians, allowing 650 of them to remain in the territories.[71]

The man who ran the activities of Fatah in the territories from Tunis was Arafat's deputy, Khalil al-Wazir, known as Abu Jihad. Within days of the outbreak in Jibalya, he was somewhat halfheartedly prodding his men in the territories to try to assume the lead. But he and Arafat were slow to grasp that they were witnessing not just another ephemeral state of rioting but the start of a sustained rebellion which would continue for years.[72]

Only in mid-January did they understand and harness the rebellious energies that had been unleashed. By then a web of local and national organizations had taken hold and set certain patterns. Local committees had sprung up in each village, refugee camp, and town, replicating the revolutionary experience of 1936–37. Prominent figures representing the various political factions in each locality came together in the "popular committees," which would then direct the course of protest. "Revolutionary," or "shock," committees served as the executive arm of the Intifada in each area, imposing commercial closedowns, levying funds, harassing and punishing collaborators or lawbreakers, and clashing with Israeli troops.

In the West Bank, above the various local committees, there emerged a loose umbrella organization, the "United National Leadership of the Uprising" (UNLU) (also known as the "Unified National Command"), comprising national-level representatives of the Fatah, PFLP, DFLP, and Communist Party (though the heads of each party, mostly resident in East Jerusalem, remained in the background, directing their men in the UNLU, much as they themselves were controlled by PLO-Tunis). The UNLU was based on a four-party committee that had loosely coordinated Palestinian political activities prior to the Intifada.[73]

Two Ramallah brothers, thirty-three-year-old Muhammad Labadi, an electrician, and twenty-eight-year-old Majid Labadi, a construction worker, were the moving spirits behind the formation and functioning of the UNLU, assisted by Nasser Ju'abah, a Ramallah bookshop owner. The Labadis had long been active in Naif Hawatmeh's DFLP, had established a Print Workers Trade Union, and had done time in Israeli prisons. They decided to bring East Jerusalem into the circle of violence—with the help of "imported" PLO activists from the Gaza Strip. Riots broke out and barricades were erected simultaneously in a number of places around East Jerusalem on December 19. Israeli banks and vehicles were trashed and set alight; vehicles were stoned; eight villages around Jerusalem put up barricades and declared their "independence." One such, Sur Bahir, was to remain effectively "liberated" for six weeks, with no Israeli daring to enter.[74] Only on February 5 did the police "retake" most of the "liberated" villages and neighborhoods. The authorities hesitated because of Jerusalem's international sensitivity and because it was considered part of Israel, annexed in 1967, rather than of the West Bank. No IDF troops were used, and the police were forbidden to use firearms.[75]

The Labadis' major contribution to the Intifada, apart from the establishment of the UNLU, was the production of its first series of handbills, making the UNLU immediately the heart of the rebellion. The first broadside, published on January 10, 1988, called on "the heroes of the stone and firebomb war" to "redouble the revolutionary content" of their protest and "shake the oppressive regime down to its foundations. . . . All roads must be closed to the occupation forces. . . . Its cowardly soldiers must be prevented from entering the refugee camps and large population centers by barricades and burning tires. . . . Palestinian flags are to be flown from minarets, churches, rooftops, and electricity poles everywhere. . . . We must set the ground alight under the feet of the occupiers."

It also called for a three-day general strike (on January 11–13).[76] The Labadis and their leaflets gave the rioting masses a feeling that there were a guiding mind and hand behind the seeming anarchy.[77] They proved a major means of mobilizing the Palestinians to action, both in the various localities and on a national level: "Behind the youngsters and the stones and the roadblocks are the words. They set the style, and delineate what is allowed and what forbidden, and send the people into the streets and instruct them what, when, and how to do things. And the population abides by the written instructions."[78]

The UNLU debated strategy and tactics with PLO-Tunis through faxes and then, by means of leaflets, directed the course of the Intifada. The UNLU also received and distributed PLO funds.[79] Gradually, during the spring and summer of 1988, the PLO became the dominant partner partly because it was the source of the money, partly because successive UNLU committees were smashed by the GSS, and partly because UNLU members feared retribution should they fail to accept the PLO's leadership.[80]

PLO bankrolling involved $120–300 million annually,[81] the main outlays being salaries for leaders and activists and compensation for the families of those killed (the "martyrs"), injured, or arrested. The PLO also often gave large onetime sums to families whose houses had been demolished. The local committees reported to UNLU about the doings in each area, requests for aid, complaints, and so on. Schiff and Ya'ari reproduce one such report, from the Tulkarm area:

> [W]e burned a minibus belonging to the collaborator Khalid al-Masrieh. . . . We torched the offices of *An Nahar* and threw three Molotov cocktails at army cars. . . . The women led two processions in the city to the offices of the Red Crescent and to City Hall. . . . Each day we also set up roadblocks and [we] burned tires in two neighborhoods. . . . As for money, so far I have received 500 dinars in three payments in addition to 500 shekels. Out of this sum we have paid comrade J.S. (who left his place of work) for gasoline to distribute handbills.[82]

The fundamentalists had not been co-opted into the UNLU, though their activists had been in the forefront of the demonstrations in December 1987. Yassin's Muslim Brotherhood switched from educational-social activity to political-military activism. Pressure from the rank and file, and the need to avoid being outdone either by the secular PLO or the Islamic Jihad, combined to generate an abrupt, radical shift that was to result in the emergence of the Hamas. Perhaps, too, Yassin somehow sensed that this time the Palestinians would succeed.

According to movement lore, Hamas was established by Yassin and six of his aides in his Gaza home on December 9–10, 1987.[83] *Hamas*—an Arabic word meaning "enthusiasm" and "courage," also an acronym for *harakat al-mukawma al-islamiya,* the Islamic Resistance Movement—emerged from the Muslim Brotherhood like a butterfly from a cocoon. The Brotherhood was not structured for political and military struggle, but it had the necessary dedicated manpower, organized in cells, and funds as well as several squads already recruited by Shehadeh, head of the military wing. Yassin simply drew on these and established a new, clandestine framework. There were to be six operational districts, each headed by one of his aides, with Sheikh Jamil Hamami of 'Anata village charged with setting up a parallel Hamas structure in the West Bank.

By the spring of 1988 the Hamas was a major component of the rebellion in the Strip and, to a lesser extent, the West Bank.[84] Its cadres and supporters mounted demonstrations or joined those initiated by Fatah, threw stones and firebombs, raised barricades. Almost from the start Yassin approved the use of "hot" weapons against Israeli troops,[85] but lack of equipment and training resulted in continuous delays. Only in March 1988 did the Hamas mount its first "military" operation, with an ambush in Gaza in which an Israeli water engineer was injured.[86]

On December 14, 1987, the six-man steering committee put out a flyer listing the Brotherhood's goals in the rebellion. (Later it was referred to as the first Hamas leaflet, though the first one actually carrying the name "Hamas" appeared in January 1988.[87]) And here, for the first time, the word "Intifada" appeared in print. The goals were: to wage a holy war against the Zionist enemy, to oppose any peace efforts, and to convert the Arab states to the way of Islam and to draw them into the conflict. The flyer spoke of the ideal Muslim youngsters as those more eager to enter paradise by way of martyrdom in the struggle against Israel "than is our enemy to continue living in this world."[88]

Still the government was slow to notice the advent of the new organization. In April 1988, a full five months after the eruption, the civil administration wrote, in a survey called *Islamic Activity in the West Bank,* that the Muslim Brotherhood "does not initiate . . . sabotage, rejects Palestinian nationalism

and . . . the PLO . . . [and] is not involved in subversive acts and does not initiate political subversion."[89] And the authorities were still turning a blind eye to
the passing of funds to the Hamas—while making every effort to block funds
going to PLO activists.[90]

The official attitude changed only later that year, when Hamas activists
were identified with several acts of terrorism. By then, according to the GSS,
the Hamas's military wing, headed by Shehadeh, had around 200 men. During
the summer the GSS pounced on the network and captured about 120 of its
members, temporarily breaking its back.[91] Yassin himself was not arrested,
partly because of his infirm state. The Israelis appeared not to know how
deeply he was involved in the military side of the organization.

Israel's about-face vis-à-vis the Hamas was finalized by the publication, in
mid-August, of the organization's "Covenant," which defined the achievement
of Palestinian national aspirations as a stepping-stone to the country's "Islamization." It also made the destruction of Israel the movement's official goal. As
Palestine was sacred Muslim territory, "until the day of judgment," no Muslim
or Arab had the right to cede any part of it. Participation in the anti-Zionist
jihad was defined as the "personal obligation" of every Muslim. All compromise and negotiation with the Zionists were forbidden: "Only the jihad can
solve the Palestine issue." The Jews were collectively described as an "instrument of evil." The "Covenant" is forthrightly anti-Semitic as well as anti-
Zionist. It specifically cites *The Protocols of the Elders of Zion* as its source
for understanding the Jews' expansionist ambitions, which include control of
all the territory between the Nile and the Euphrates rivers and, then, the whole
world. The Jews are also blamed for the French and Russian Revolutions,
World War I (with the aim of destroying the Islamic Ottoman caliphate), and
World War II. They also "founded the United Nations and the Security Council in order to rule over the world." In a softening of the traditional Brotherhood line, the PLO is described as "a father, brother, relative or friend" of the
Hamas. "Can the Muslim be alienated from his father, brother, relative, or
friend?"[92] A few months later a Muslim Brotherhood pamphlet described the
Jews as "the dirtiest and meanest of all races, [and they] are defiling the most
sanctified and honored spot on earth."[93]

Far less important than Hamas to the Intifada's success was the Islamic
Jihad—mainly because of its small numbers and lack of leaders. At the outset,
both Shkaki and 'Odeh were in Israeli jails (Shkaki was to be deported in
August 1988). It was partly to offset its secondary position that the Jihad, after
the first few days, reverted to supporting armed attacks, and, in summer 1988,
resumed its propaganda in favor of suicide attacks.[94] No doubt the Islamic
Jihad's readoption of armed struggle was among the factors that prompted
Yassin and the Hamas also to break with Fatah on this issue. Needless to say,
this resulted in successive Israeli crackdowns. Eventually, in May 1989, after

an upsurge of Islamic terrorism, the Israelis took off the gloves. Yassin himself was arrested along with 260 activists, including Shehadeh.[95]

From the start the Hamas and Islamic Jihad dominated the rebellion in the Gaza Strip. The West Bank–based, PLO-affiliated UNLU tried in January 1988 to wrest control from the fundamentalists. The Labadis set in motion the establishment of a similar "national" coordinating committee for the Strip. The Gaza committee generally replicated the UNLU's leaflets in the West Bank but never managed to supplant the Hamas.[96]

Throughout, the UNLU's relations with PLO-Tunis were tense. The latter, fearing the loss of its authority in the territories, tried to impose its will on the UNLU and direct every aspect of the struggle; it publicly described the UNLU as its "arm." But its instructions were not always attuned to the realities of the situation on the ground and the UNLU and the local leaders by and large maintained a measure of operational independence, often sidestepping Tunis's orders.[97]

From February 1988 most UNLU broadsides were worked out in fax exchanges with Tunis, each personally approved by Arafat.[98] During 1988 the UNLU issued thirty-one of them; Hamas, thirty-three.[99] They were distributed and plastered on walls in the towns and villages, and from August 1988, read out over PLO radio stations in Baghdad and Damascus. Apart from aiming to raise the Palestinians' morale, they usually carried instructions—to strike on such and such days, or demonstrate in the main streets, or stop paying taxes, or throw stones or Molotov cocktails. UNLU leaflets occasionally laid out PLO policy or addressed themselves to Israel, calling for an end to the demolition of houses, for example, or for expressions of solidarity by pro-peace forces.

Hamas's handbills were more colorful—"the Jews, brothers of apes, the murderers of prophets"[100] —and denounced all efforts to reach a settlement. Palestine must be liberated "down to the last grain of sand." Liberation would be costly, but "this is part of the price of glory and salvation. This is the dowry of the dark-eyed girls in Paradise." The liberation of Palestine would lead to an Islamic renaissance.[101]

From the first, the GSS took great pains to stop distribution of the leaflets, which were seen as the Intifada's glue. It repeatedly arrested UNLU members and printers. In early February 1988, 35,000 copies of "Leaflet No. 6" were discovered in a pickup truck whose driver quickly implicated the whole network. But Muhammad Labadi escaped the dragnet, and the UNLU was reconstituted with new members.[102] On March 19 the GSS again nabbed members of the UNLU, as they met in an apartment in Ramallah, formulating "Leaflet No. 11." But again it reemerged with new members.[103]

But the essence of the Intifada lay not in the printed word but in the daily, bloody confrontations. By the end of the first month twenty-six Palestinians lay dead from Israeli gunfire and some 320 injured; fifty-six Israeli soldiers and thirty civilians had been injured by stones and bottles. More than a hundred Molotov cocktails and three grenades had been thrown at Israeli traffic and troops. There had been some fourteen hundred incidents of stone-throwing, demonstrations, tire-burning, and roadblocking.[104]

The frenzied first month was followed by a brief lull in the rioting. But within weeks it resumed, with added intensity, moving from the alleyways to the main thoroughfares within and between the cities. The shock committees also began to impose a routine of commercial shutdowns and strikes, which the Israeli security forces proved unable to quell. As one merchant explained, the shopkeepers feared the wrath of the *shabab* (the "youngsters") far more than anything the Israelis might do to them.[105]

At first, the activists would close down the shops for days on end. The merchants protested that this would bankrupt them. Eventually a compromise was reached, with shops generally being allowed to open for three hours each morning. In general, the youngsters dictated the behavior of the middle class. From the rebels' perspective, this was the point of the exercise: to demonstrate to Palestinians, Israelis, and the world at large precisely who ruled the streets.

From the start the activists abjured the use of firearms, understanding that fire-power was the Israelis' strong suit. It was better to fight the enemy with what they weren't equipped for, and what was at hand in every alleyway and hill-side village—stones, bricks, and slingshots, using pebbles or metal balls. Many activists also bore clubs, knives, and hatchets. Nails and oil were spread on roads to cause accidents. The closest the activists came to employing firearms was the massive use, for a time, of Molotov cocktails, mainly against traffic, though occasionally also against troops.

Israeli intelligence believed that there were thousands of rifles, shotguns, and pistols in private hands in the territories. But these were rarely used. The UNLU and local Intifada leaders, in a decision endorsed by PLO-Tunis, made a point of barring guns. Naif Hawatmeh explained: "We wanted to prevent a situation in which the occupying authorities would lose self-control and carry out massacres."[106] More important, the aim was to maintain the revolt's "popular" image, with the Palestinians cast as David to Israel's Goliath. The use of guns, it was feared, would serve Israel's public relations purposes. It was better that the troops be seen using rifles against youngsters armed only with stones. The Palestinians understood that the struggle would be largely won or lost on Western television screens.

The daring of the rioters grew in the course of the rebellion—in part as a result of Israel's self-imposed curbs on the use of weapons by its forces, in part because of a feeling that victory was attainable.[107] Towns and villages that during the previous twenty years had enjoyed good relations with the Israeli authorities soon became prominent bastions of rebellion—the townspeople perhaps feeling, or being made to feel, that they had to compensate for the years of tranquillity.[108]

During the first eighteen months of the rebellion, the IDF registered around 41,000 "violent incidents," including the throwing of Molotov cocktails and stones, arson, and grenade and knife attacks. By and large the violence was more muted in Jerusalem than elsewhere.[109] Overall, the main targets were soldiers and traffic, mostly civilian but also military.[110]

The Palestinians also revived a practice popular during the 1936–39 rebellion: setting fire to cultivated fields and forests, both in the territories and in Israel proper. This began in May 1988; Arafat formally gave it his blessing the following month. In 1988 about 36,000 acres of forest and cultivated fields were burned in 3,100 incidents, most of them during May–July. Another 485 fires in the first half of 1989 resulted in the destruction of 11,000 acres. This decrease was the result, in part, of orders from above, after the leaders realized that the fires were doing their cause harm in Western public opinion and among Israeli leftists.[111]

About a year after the start of the rebellion, Intifada activists zeroed in on a new target: collaborators. By the end of June 1989, about ninety Arabs who had given intelligence to the Israelis or had helped sell them land had been killed, many savagely tortured before being dispatched.[112]

Much of the Intifada consisted of nonviolent, passive resistance, including a campaign against the purchase of Israeli goods and efforts to raise vegetables and poultry to reduce dependence on imports from Israel.[113] Since 1984 Dr. Mubarak 'Awad, a Palestinian-American resident in the West Bank, had been preaching noncooperation with the authorities and the establishment of parallel self-governing institutions, that would both detach the population from the civil government apparatus and contribute to the emergence of a Palestinian state. Over American objections, 'Awad was deported back to the United States in May 1988. But by then the idea of establishing Palestinian institutions and services that would compete with Israel's had taken root.[114]

Hanna Siniora, editor of the Fatah-affiliated East Jerusalem daily *al-Fajr*, in January 1988 publicly advocated the nonpayment of taxes as well as a trade boycott and commercial strikes—the closing of all shops in a locality during certain hours, days, or weeks.[115] But in general, while shutdowns and a measure of economic boycott were to characterize the Intifada,[116] the rioting masses and their leaders in effect rejected the nonviolent route. And the Israeli authorities made sure that the 'Awad-Siniora initiative would be almost stillborn, by silencing the two men.[117]

Nonetheless, various elements of civil disobedience were employed: From early January 1988 the UNLU called for occasional strike days or "days of rage"—usually one or two per week—in which commercial activity, travel, and work would come to a halt. Often the population would simply be called upon to stay home or occasionally to demonstrate in the streets on the strike days.[118] Commercial strikes were also called. In general throughout the Intifada the leaders tried to keep shops and gas stations closed for all but three hours a day. This enabled the population to purchase necessary provisions—while still creating the impression of a general shutdown of commercial activity and of Intifada control. In March 1988 merchants were told to stop paying value-added and other taxes, and local tax officials in the civil administration were ordered to resign. Tax collection came to a halt. In July, Rabin announced in the Knesset that tax revenue in the territories had decreased by 40 percent since the start of the Intifada.[119] The Israelis countered with tax sweeps, backed by confiscation orders and troops. In the Gaza Strip new identity cards and car license plates were withheld from people who owed taxes, gradually forcing many to pay up.[120]

In early March 1988 the UNLU called on all West Bank and Gaza policemen to resign, under threat of dire punishment. A policeman who refused was shot dead in Jericho. Immediately, despite Israeli counterpressures, some 500 of the 800 local policemen in the West Bank and Gaza quit. By May 1989 only 20 or so remained in the Gaza Strip (out of 430 in December 1987). Those who formally stayed on by and large refrained from carrying out their duties. Because of a sense of national unity and purpose, crime rates in the territories dropped significantly, despite the absence of police and the impoverishment of the population.[121]

The activists also demanded the resignation of mayors and members of city and local councils appointed by the Israelis during the previous decade. Most struck private deals with the PLO that allowed them to stay on; only the mayor of Nablus actually resigned. Some councillors were driven from their posts because they were suspected of collaboration.

Within months of the start of the rebellion, a range of self-governing institutions sprang up to replace certain civil administration services. "Aid committees" were set up in each locality to assist the needy, and education committees tried to assure the continuation of classes in makeshift premises after schools were shut down. Most educational institutions were closed in December 1987 and the beginning of 1988, the Israelis accurately charging that they were centers of rioting and militancy. The Intifada leaders called on the population either to defy the Israelis and open the schools or to provide alternative venues for classes, such as mosques. But the schools—save for the one hundred or so that were privately run (that is, nonstate and non-UNRWA)—remained shut during the riot-ridden first two years and alternative teaching proved beyond the abilities of most communities. Many, perhaps most, pupils simply lost years of schooling. But some of the postsecondary institutions, including the universities, which were also closed, continued to function partially off-campus.[122]

A leadership effort that was ultimately aborted by individual self-interest was the call, beginning in January 1988, for Palestinians to stop working in

Israel. Most continued to commute to Israel (and even to the settlements in the West Bank), however, except on general strike days and when Israeli curfews or area closures prevented it. Periodically the activists would stone and torch buses taking workers to Israel or threaten the workers. But after several months of tussling, the leadership realized that in order to continue the struggle, the population must enjoy at least a minimal income.

Despite the PLO prohibition there were occasional terrorist incidents, though fewer than in previous years and almost invariably carried out by the Hamas or Islamic Jihad. During the first eighteen months of the rebellion, there were altogether forty-one light-weapons attacks; thirty-nine with grenades; 127 bombs; and 102 incidents involving "cold" weapons such as knives and hatchets.[123]

Beyond the routine, the Intifada years were punctuated by a series of dramatic incidents that provide insights into the nature of the protagonists and the character and complexity of the struggle. Three of the most prominent are worth examination.

On April 6, 1988, a group of fifteen Israeli high school pupils accompanied by three armed adults, all from Eilon Moreh, a major Gush Emunim settlement outside Nablus, went on a hike in the hills several kilometers from their settlement. The excursion—conceived as if Samaria were wholly Jewish and there were no Intifada—was typical of Gush Emunim behavior during this period: The group failed to coordinate the hike with the IDF, as required by law. Near the village of Beita they encountered a group of Arab youngsters, who pelted them with stones. One of the adults opened fire with his M-16 rifle, killing an Arab youth and wounding an adult. Scores of Arabs surrounded the group and, in effect, frog-marched them, under threat, into the center of Beita. There they were stoned again, and the sister of the slain youth threw a large stone at the killer's head. Badly injured, as he collapsed he let off a long burst from his rifle, accidentally killing one of the Jewish girls. Two villagers were also killed, and some of the Israeli youngsters were injured in the melee. A number of Arabs then protected the hikers until IDF troops arrived.

The enraged Israeli Right shouted "pogrom!" Sharon demanded that the village be razed and called for a mass deportation. Subsequently about two dozen villagers were arrested and tried for stone-throwing and the IDF demolished thirteen houses. It later emerged that several of those left homeless had taken no part in the rioting and that one of them had in fact saved hikers from the mob. Eventually the IDF paid him compensation. Six villagers were deported to Jordan.[124]

A more representative incident was the lynching, on February 24, 1988, of an Arab collaborator in the northern West Bank village of Kabatiya. Attacked by a mob, he opened fire with his Israeli-supplied Uzi submachine gun, killing a four-year-old child and injuring thirteen people. The enraged crowd set his house alight and dragged him out. He was beaten, strangled, and strung up on a telephone pole.[125] The Israelis sealed the village off from the outside world for weeks, destroyed two houses, detained about one hundred villagers, and later tried and sentenced a number to long prison terms. But the image that captivated the Palestinian imagination was that of the punished collaborator. During the following weeks dozens of collaborators broke off their links with the authorities and even took part in attacks on Israeli security personnel as evidence of their change of heart. In April eight more collaborators were killed; in September, four more.

By the end of 1989, the GSS's web of informants, indeed, its whole modus operandi in the territories, had unraveled. The population was more afraid of the rebels than of anything the Israelis could throw at them. Collaboration more or less came to an end, and the GSS's sources of information—which had made possible the smooth running of the occupation—dried up.

The third, and by far the most serious, incident was the Temple Mount Massacre. Saddam Hussein's invasion of Kuwait in August 1990 revitalized the then somewhat-flagging Intifada. The Arabs had discovered a new Saladin, a potential savior who defied the West and threatened Israel with apparent impunity. To divert attention from his rape of Kuwait, Saddam portrayed himself as protector of the Palestinians and promised to recover the holy places in Jerusalem for Islam. He spoke of scorching half of Israel with chemical weapons.

In response, preachers in the mosques of the Haram ash-Sharif gave sermons in support of the Iraqi dictator. An Israeli police intelligence report of August 24 predicted: "In light of the recent developments in the Gulf crisis and of various statements regarding the imminence of salvation, extremist elements might awaken and begin actions around the issue of the Temple Mount."[126]

Tension was already running high in Jerusalem. On the night of August 4–5 Arab terrorists had abducted and murdered two Jewish youths, igniting an orgy of stone-throwing by Jewish extremists against Arab traffic and pedestrians. An Arab was killed and several dozen were injured. In reaction the Intifada surged. Jewish buses running through Arab areas were regularly stoned.[127]

The head of the Temple Mount Faithful, Gershon Salomon, announced that he intended to lay a foundation stone for the Third Temple on the Mount, during the Feast of Tabernacles (Sukkoth) in October. On September 26 the Hamas issued a leaflet declaring October 11 a special day of fasting and rebellion, in light of the Jewish "threat." On September 29 police clashed with a procession of young Arabs trying to reach the Western Wall plaza abutting the Mount. Dozens were injured and arrested.[128] Israeli intelligence warned that there would be disturbances on the Temple Mount itself. On Friday, October 5, Muslim notables called on the faithful to gather on the Mount to prevent the stone-laying ceremony and to "defend the mosques." Arabs duly began to assemble on the evening of the 7th. Some piled up stones, others brought along sticks and metal bars. The police informed Muslim officials that no Jews would be allowed onto the Mount on the 8th, but these assurances failed to calm them.

By late morning October 8 about 30,000 Jews had gathered in the Western Wall plaza for a regular Sukkoth service. The rumor had spread among the Arabs that Salomon's Faithful had actually entered the compound. A number of Arab children on the Mount began throwing stones at the forty-four border policemen inside the compound, whose job was to protect the Jewish worshippers below. One of the policemen accidentally dropped or deliberately lobbed a tear-gas grenade, which rolled toward a group of Arab women. The Arab crowd began pushing toward the policemen. The border police commander placed himself between the crowd and his men, but he was trampled on and beaten. He fired some shots into the air and was rescued by his men. The crowd began to hurl stones, concrete blocks, metal bars, pieces of glass, and other objects at the policemen, who opened fire and hurled tear gas to keep the rioters at bay. But stones began falling on the crowd in the plaza, which fled in panic. The police retreated from the Temple Mount, and the way was clear for the Arabs to stone the Jewish worshippers thirty-one meters below. But by then the plaza was almost empty, and only a few people were slightly injured.

Two policemen, both Arabs, were still trapped, and being stoned, at their post on the Mount and were appealing for rescue. When radio contact with them was suddenly lost, the Jerusalem district police chief, fearing that they were in the hands of the mob and seeking to retake the site as a matter of principle, decided to break back onto the Temple Mount. His men pushed in through the Mughrabi Gate. A hail of stones greeted them as they advanced toward al-Aqsa. They responded with fusillades of live rounds and tear gas. Dozens of Arabs were hit, but the stone-throwing continued. The Mount looked like a battlefield, enveloped in smoke and tear gas, the floors of al-Aqsa covered by the blood of the dead and wounded who had been taken into the mosque for safety or treatment. Within an hour it was all over, with the Mount firmly in the hands of the border police and the stone-throwing at an end.

Altogether, eighteen or nineteen Arabs aged fifteen to sixty-three were killed and another hundred wounded; thirty-four Israelis—civilians and policemen—were slightly injured.[129]

The incident sent a jolt of vengeful energy through the fundamentalists in the territories. There was a spree of revenge stabbings, especially in Jerusalem, where three Israelis—a woman soldier, a policeman, and a civilian— were killed in one incident. Almost all the attackers said under interrogation that they were avenging the Temple Mount Massacre.[130] Within two months, in nineteen incidents, eight Israelis were killed and about a dozen wounded.[131] Three more were killed on the first anniversary of the event.[132]

The government set up a commission of inquiry that spent its days interviewing Israeli civilians and policemen, though almost no Arabs. It concluded that the fault for the incident lay wholly with the Arabs and that the Jewish authorities were blameless, though it mildly criticized some of the police commanders' tactical decisions. The Muslim authorities rejected these findings, and the Supreme Muslim Council published a report of its own, saying the massacre had been preplanned by the police, had been unprovoked, and was wholly the Israelis' fault. A third investigation, by a Jewish Jerusalem district court judge, ruled that no policeman involved in the incident should be charged, but that the police had been "too quick on the trigger" and that not all the firing had been justified by "clear and imminent danger."[133]

ISRAEL'S RESPONSE

The cabinet, IDF Intelligence, the GSS—all failed to anticipate the uprising or immediately to understand its nature, once it had erupted. The initial response, echoing the Yishuv's reaction to the "disturbances" of prestate days, was to describe the rioting as "disturbances instigated by a minority."[134] The territories had repeatedly witnessed flurries of rioting; here was just another bout of the same, albeit more intense and widespread; give it a few days and it too would soon fade away. On December 23, 1987, Shmuel Goren reported that the riots were "dying down."[135]

Indicative of this misreading of events was the fact that Defense Minister Rabin, the man responsible for law and order in the territories, felt able on December 10 to fly off to the United States, to shun advice from experts to cut short his visit, and to return to Israel only on December 21—when he told a waiting press conference that the unrest in the territories was a result of Syrian and Iranian incitement.[136] He was not alone in dismissing the disturbances as insignificant. At the IDF general staff meeting of December 14, most participants rejected the opinion of Deputy CGS Barak that the territories were on the verge of a civil rebellion.[137] Voices like that of Middle East expert Prof. Yehoshua Porath—who said that the events were the "first signs of an uprising by the population" and that there was mass participation—went unheeded.[138]

In the past the West Bank and Gaza had seen sporadic, isolated demonstrations involving dozens or hundreds of participants, usually youngsters. During the first months of the Intifada, there were many thousands in the streets—in many places simultaneously—with children, youths, adult men and, even more unusual, women taking part.[139] Nevertheless, it took Israel's military and political establishments about a month to grasp and concede that what they faced was in fact a homegrown political uprising.

How was Israel to respond? Almost everything was tried: shooting to kill, shooting to injure, beatings, mass arrests, torture, trials, administrative detention, and economic sanctions. The Israelis made great efforts to stop the flow of PLO (and, later, Hamas) money into the territories.[140] They closed down print shops and arrested printers, they forced merchants to keep their shops open, and they conducted mass sweeps and arrests. All failed. Ultimately the territories quieted down only after Israel and the Palestinians began political negotiations four years later.

As a democracy bound by respect for the rule of law and subject to internal and external public scrutiny, there were measures that Israel could not undertake. And there were means that at least some of the Israeli public, and Western governments—principally Washington—and public opinion, would not countenance. CGS Dan Shomron said that the Intifada could be suppressed completely if very extreme measures, "such as transfer [that is, mass expulsion], starvation, and genocide, were applied—but none of these methods is acceptable to the State of Israel."[141]

At first, the government debated whether military measures could indeed halt the Intifada. How could a sophisticated modern army fight an essentially unarmed popular revolt? Had the Palestinians found a way to neutralize Israel's vastly superior military strength, something the Arab states had tried and failed to do for forty years? As early as January 13, 1988, Defense Minister Rabin concluded that the solution would have to be "political"—through negotiation leading to a political settlement, rather than through military means.[142]

Within weeks Israel set itself the limited goal of reducing the disturbances to an "acceptable" minimum, to contain rather than extinguish the uprising—and this was in effect to remain the policy during the years that followed. Implicit was the understanding that the rebellion could not be brought to an end by (acceptable) military measures.[143] One initial problem was that the occupation forces were not equipped or trained for riot control. They were armed, as in the past, for warfare against armies or guerrillas—they lacked large quantities of shields, riot helmets, truncheons, tear gas launchers, and the other paraphernalia of riot control. During the first weeks of the Intifada a special airlift was organized to bring in tear gas when local production fell far behind demand.[144] There were similar problems with batons and shields. The IDF and the Finance Ministry expected that the rioting would die down "soon" and shrank from making the necessary large-scale orders. Only once it became clear that the Intifada was there to stay was it decided to equip the troops for the tasks at hand.

In the course of the Intifada the Defense Ministry developed, manufactured, and deployed a number of novel weapons—including a half-track mounting a pebble- or stone-launcher to counter the stone-throwers with their own ammunition. It was not particularly effective. A number of defensive innovations were also introduced, to protect soldiers and settlers using the beleaguered territorial roads. Vehicles were fitted with wire-mesh screens and defensive plastic glass; jeeps were mounted with fixtures to cut wire strung across the roads or to break through stone barricades. Many vehicles were also provided with bulletproof glass and metal plating.

During the first month the IDF refrained from reinforcing the units in the West Bank, after the commanding officer, General Mitzna, said he could cope with the forces at hand. At Southern Command, General Mordechai said he would need substantial reinforcements to restore order in the Gaza Strip, but he got them only in the last week of December.[145] The general staff was loath to send in more troops, as this would be tantamount to admitting that the riots had been successful and that Israel was afraid of losing its grip. So the small units patrolling urban alleyways and villages found themselves confronting masses of demonstrators in what the soldiers time and again felt were life-threatening situations—and they responded with live fire. Resultant killings enraged the populace and still larger and more violent funeral-riots followed.

From the start, regulations governing open-fire procedures were a hot moral and political issue. Before the Intifada there were two sets of circumstances in which troops were allowed to shoot: if their lives were in immediate danger or if a person suspected of "grave crimes" was escaping and ignored a shouted warning and a shot in the air. Fire was then to be directed at the fugitive's legs.[146] The radically changed circumstances of the Intifada inevitably gave rise to new definitions of what was permissible. Field commanders and troops, and those responsible for them—the heads of Southern and Central commands—continuously pressed for greater freedom to open fire. The judge advocate general's office, supported by liberal and left-wing politicians and the media, and some members of the general staff, fought these pressures. Gray areas and situations emerged, in which the traditional rules could no longer apply. For example, the IDF's activation of small undercover units dressed as Arabs inside Palestinian towns and villages raised a host of questions with regard to when and how to open fire; so did the Arab activists' practice of wearing masks. Were they legitimate targets, even if they were only spraying graffiti on walls?[147] In general, the IDF tried to restrict the use of firearms to life-threatening situations—but trigger-happy troops, provocation, or complex situations often resulted in the death of Arabs, even though no Israeli life had, in fact, been threatened.

Early in January 1988 the IDF flooded the territories with thousands of conscript and reserve troops.[148] The massive influx—by mid-1988 the IDF deployed what amounted to two divisions in the West Bank and a third in the Gaza Strip[149]—gradually cowed much of the population and caused a reduction in the numbers involved in each incident. The reinforcements also allowed the resumption of patrols—which had more or less ceased—into more remote West Bank villages. But the very arrival of the patrols often provoked riots, bringing journalists to the area, which in turn sparked further rioting.

Almost from the start the IDF response to the Intifada came under attack. Left-wingers accused the army of brutality; right-wingers, of hesitancy and weakness. There was constant criticism inside the cabinet, especially when General Shomron came to report. A frequent target was the liberal-minded General Mitzna, whom right-wingers charged with being "soft" on the rioting "criminals."[150] The generals all stressed that the IDF could deal with specific incidents, but the Intifada as a whole could only be brought to an end by a negotiated settlement. Likud ministers were incensed by this position, which reflected that of the Labor Defense Minister Rabin.[151]

But despite the persistent attacks, some of them directed at Rabin personally, the cabinet majority beat back all proposals for more drastic military measures, such as sending tanks into the streets. The unity government enjoyed broad public support, and the extremists outside the coalition and the wild men within it were easily rebuffed by the solid, sober majority, as embodied by Rabin and, to a great degree, Prime Minister Shamir himself.

In January 1988 the IDF began imposing curfews—usually a few days long—whenever and wherever trouble broke out. Anyone caught outside his home was to be shot on sight, except for a half-hour time-out each day. But the curfew turned out to be a two-edged weapon, like almost every other measure employed: Rioting was suppressed for a while, but the restrictions were deeply resented and the circle of hatred and confrontation was widened. The army sometimes imposed area closure orders—meaning inhabitants could leave their homes but not the town. Like the curfew, closure prevented Palestinians from reaching their workplaces and earning a living.

Once the reinforcements were in place, the IDF began to suppress the demonstrations. Rabin ordered the intensive use of riot sticks to break up riots. The thinking behind this "beatings policy," as it came to be called, was that it would cause fewer deaths than shooting, which resulted in large, violent funerals and in bad publicity abroad. Broken bones, moreover, would put the demonstrators out of commission for long stretches. But the policy, apparently adopted in haste and in anger, was of dubious legality and was introduced over the objections of the army's legal service. According to the judge advocate general, Brig. Amnon Straschnov, in the course of 1988 it led to "the death of several Arabs and severe physical injury [including permanent disability] to thousands of others."[152]

Throughout the ranks confusion reigned as to how exactly the newly distributed clubs were to be used. Rabin had let slip in a television interview that the intention simply was to "break [the rioters'] bones."[153] Many understood his orders to mean that clubbing was to be used as a form of punishment. Rabin later denied this. After a great deal of public criticism, he made it clear that force, including beating, would be used against those using violence themselves: stone-throwers, road-blockers, and people resisting arrest. The implication was that there was to be no clubbing *after* suspects were arrested.[154] But there is no doubt that the defense minister's early statements "encouraged commanders and soldiers in the field to act as they did . . . and to give his words a loose practical interpretation."[155]

While the beatings policy, at least briefly, proved an effective deterrent to the rioting, it also intensified the Arabs' hatred of Israel. An intelligence officer observed: "The hundreds, perhaps thousands of people left in plaster casts by Israeli soldiers will translate into thousands of others who will wish to avenge them: fathers who have seen their sons battered, and children who watched in terror as their fathers were clubbed."[156] In short, "[T]he troops were brutalizing the Palestinian population because the Intifada had brutalized the IDF."[157] Gaza Strip brigade commanders reported quite openly that their men beat suspects, occasionally to death.[158] In some cases the troops were later brought to trial; in others, charges were never brought or were dropped.

The nature of the Intifada and of the IDF's response gave rise to a stream of excesses. In one famous case, in February 1988, at a village near Nablus, soldiers tried to bury alive four Palestinians, who were saved at the last minute. Though the IDF placed restrictions on media crews, beatings were often captured on film and broadcast worldwide. And while such material was rarely shown on state-run Israeli TV, it eventually reached Israeli households via satellite and cable. Officers and enlisted men, usually reservists, turned to the press and "told their story" after completing stints of duty in the territories. There was major unease among the troops, some of whom refused to beat prisoners.

In late January 1988 the IDF legal adviser in the West Bank, Col. David Yahav, warned Straschnov that "the law was being trampled upon, there is no longer rule of law in Judea and Samaria," and requested permission to resign. Straschnov himself clashed repeatedly with Rabin and General Mordechai, one of the major proponents of the beatings policy.[159]

With battered Intifada activists becoming instant heroes, the IDF began to rethink its policy. At Straschnov's insistence on February 23, 1988, an order was issued to all commanders by CGS Shomron: Soldiers were not to use truncheons after "the demonstration has been broken up and after a person is in our hands and does not display resistance."[160] Follow-up orders issued soon led to a general letup in the beatings policy.[161] But beatings, and other excesses, continued during the following years.

One of the more shameful episodes occurred a mere two days after Shomron's orders were issued: Four soldiers were caught by a CBS television crew beating up two Palestinian youngsters for fifteen minutes on a bare hilltop near Nablus. The footage clearly showed the soldiers punching the kneeling Arabs, pulling their hair, and then hammering them with a large rock (though in the end, curiously, there were no broken limbs). Broadcast round the world, even on Israeli television, the clip raised a public storm, forcing the judge advocate general to investigate. Shomron urged an internal disciplinary proceeding, chiding Straschnov: "When will you lift your eyes from your lawbooks and look around, not only dry laws have to be protected, but also the troops and the whole army?" Three of the culprits were tried in a military court, and two other soldiers linked to the affair faced a disciplinary hearing. Ironically, these two were given ten- and twenty-one-day prison sentences, while the other three were given suspended sentences.[162]

The IDF now reverted to engaging the rioters from a distance, shooting to injure, not to kill. The troops had the right to open fire with regular ammunition if they were in a life-threatening situation, but firing to kill was forbidden, except at people who threw grenades or Molotov cocktails. In practice, though gunfire was more carefully supervised and limited than during the first weeks of the Intifada, a large proportion of the Palestinian dead were not shot in life-threatening situations, and a great many of these were children.

Two new types of ammunition were introduced in order to reduce the number of deaths: rubber and plastic bullets. Rubber bullets—large, hard rubber balls—are designed to stun and injure at ranges under fifteen meters. The plastic bullet, used by the British in Northern Ireland since the 1970s, was introduced in July 1988. Shaped like a regular bullet, its impact is somewhere between that of a regular one and a rubber one at ranges of 70–110 meters. In principle, only specifically trained and authorized troops were allowed to use them, and they were instructed to fire only below knee level.[163] In practice, the bullets were often fired by unauthorized troops, sometimes at lethal ranges under 70 meters, and above the knees. During the period July 1988–June 1989, the IDF recorded eighty-two Palestinians killed by plastic bullets, whereas during the Intifada's first eight months, when only regular ammunition was used, there were 178 Palestinian fatalities.[164] As a rule the IDF refrained from shooting at children, but the problem was that about 60 percent of the stone-throwers, as Rabin said in February 1989, were between six and fourteen years old.[165] Snipers were introduced into IDF antiriot units, in particular against throwers of Molotov cocktails—and the number thrown declined from an average of 130 to about 65 per month by September 1988.[166]

In 1988 the IDF set up and introduced two undercover units into the territories—Shimshon (Samson) in the Gaza Strip and Duvdevan (cherry) in the West Bank. Additional undercover units, belonging to the border police and other arms of the security establishment, eventually joined them. The troops, disguised as Arabs, on foot or in vehicles with territorial plates, operated in small teams, night and day, capturing or, more often, killing riot leaders as well as "wanted" terrorists. The foreign press charged that some of these units operated like death squads, shooting suspects without warning and usually finishing off those who had already been wounded.

The Israeli human rights organization Be'tselem published in 1992 a 108-page report containing detailed descriptions of several dozen incidents involving these undercover units. A fairly typical operation occurred on the afternoon of March 22, 1992: A four-man squad, apparently of border police in civilian dress, burst onto a soccer field in Tulkarm, pulled out pistols, and shot dead a young player who was on the GSS's "wanted" list, without warning and without trying to shoot him in the legs. He was unarmed and had no way of escaping.[167]

The most routine measure was arrest and detention. Before the uprising, military courts annually tried some 1,200 West Bank and Gaza Arabs for rioting. In its first three years, approximately 30,000 were tried on Intifada-related charges.[168] Apart from those detained in the West Bank and Gaza Strip, 2,700 East Jerusalemites were arrested in the course of 1988.[169] In addition, by December 1990 about 14,000 West Bank and Gaza Arabs had been in administrative detention—in prison without trial—usually for periods of six months and more.[170]

As the Intifada waned in the early 1990s, and Israel and the PLO began their peace process, the number of Palestinians in Israeli prisons at any given point gradually declined. In December 1991 there were just over 8,000; in January 1993, 6,800; in February 1995, 5,700; by June 1996, 3,300.[171]

The penalties imposed by the military courts were severe. Stone-throwers who caused no injuries got three to six months in jail and a fine; if anyone was injured or property was damaged the sentence was one to two years. If the miscreants were under twelve, their parents were compelled to pay large fines.[172]

The IDF also resorted to collective punishments, such as sealing off a village from the outside world for weeks and cutting off its electricity.[173] A major measure against instigators, terrorists, and occasionally stone-throwers[174] was the demolition or sealing up of houses, which also rendered the imprisoned offender's family homeless.[175] This measure was based on Defense (Emergency) Regulations 1945, which the Knesset had adopted from the British Mandate. The practice ran counter to most conventions and precepts of international law but was upheld as legal by the Israeli Supreme Court.[176] A comparison made by Arye Shalev of the numbers of houses demolished each month during the Intifada and the number of violent Intifada incidents during the same and subsequent months seems to demonstrate that this policy did not have the deterrent effect hoped for by its initiators—and may actually, by inspiring additional hatred, have contributed to an increase in the number of incidents.[177]

Another Israeli measure—again based on Defense (Emergency) Regulations 1945 and upheld by the Supreme Court, though contrary to international law (specifically Article 49, Fourth Geneva Convention, 1949)—was deportation. There had been deportations, for a specified period or open-ended, on and off throughout the occupation. About 850 persons were deported from the West Bank and Gaza Strip during 1967–74, when Dayan was defense minister;[178] the number declined thereafter. But during the Intifada the expulsions appear to have had little deterrent effect—as with the demolition of houses— and may well have led to more violence. Indeed, the number of violent incidents increased after each batch of deportations (though other factors may have been at play).[179] Between December 1987 and December 1991 Israel expelled altogether sixty-six persons. The largest deportation took place (when Rabin was both prime minister and defense minister) in December 1992, after a particularly provocative Hamas murder: 415 fundamentalists were rounded up and dumped across the border just north of the Security Zone, where they camped out for a year before being allowed to return as a result of an Israeli Supreme Court ruling.[180]

Israel also responded to the Intifada by attacking the PLO outside the territories; the fact that the organization was encouraging not terrorism but essentially nonlethal violence was ignored. On February 14, 1988, three PLO officers were killed when a bomb exploded in a car in the port of Limassol, Cyprus.[181] According to Israel, the three had had a hand in planning terrorist strikes in Israel and the territories; shortly before their deaths they had been deported from Jordan at Israeli and American insistence. The following day a limpet mine disabled the *Soi Phryne*, a small steamer, in Limassol harbor without causing casualties. The PLO had recently bought the ship in order to mount a propaganda extravaganza: It would be packed with several hundred refugees, dubbed "the Ship of Return," and launched toward Haifa, where the passengers would demand to be allowed to disembark in their "homeland."[182]

A more powerful blow was struck by the Mossad and the IDF two months later, in Tunis. On April 16 an army commando team disembarked from a missile boat in the Mediterranean and was ferried to shore by naval commandos in rubber dinghies. There they boarded three waiting cars rented by Mossad agents and drove to the suburban residence of Arafat's deputy, Khalil al-Wazir. They killed several guards, broke in and, in full view of Wazir's wife, "Um Jihad," and the couple's children, gunned down the PLO commander. The operation was controlled directly by Deputy CGS Barak, flying overhead in a converted IAF "eye in the sky" Boeing 707.[183]

Ostensibly the assassination was a belated response to the killing of three Israeli civilians on March 6, when a PLO squad had crossed from Sinai into the Negev and hijacked a bus near the Dimona nuclear plant. Israel charged that Abu Jihad had planned the attack, as he had other terrorist episodes before the Intifada. Prime Minister Shamir and Defense Minister Rabin may have hoped that killing Abu Jihad, who had a reputation as an efficient operations officer, would harm the Intifada. Shimon Peres apparently opposed the assassination.[184] It was strongly criticized by Israeli doves such as Minister without Portfolio Ezer Weizman, who remarked, "liquidating individuals will not advance the peace process." In the end, the assassination proved of marginal importance.[185] Indeed, in the territories it triggered a wave of riots that ended in the death of at least fourteen Palestinians and in a revitalization of the Intifada.[186]

LAST STAGE

The Intifada was called off in September 1993, when the PLO and Israel signed their first peace accord in Oslo. But the end of October 1991, when an international Middle East peace conference was convened in Madrid, might be viewed as a more accurate cutoff date. After that the popular demonstrations and mass violence began to die down, to be replaced by an upsurge of fundamentalist Islamic terrorism, aimed specifically at undermining the unfolding peace process. This continued into the late 1990s and exacted a far higher toll: 39 Israelis had died in Intifada violence between December 1987 and 1991; more than four times that many—165—were killed by Arab terrorists between 1992 and early 1996.

That the Intifada had come to an end, on the psychological plane at least, was evident in the October 1991 spectacle of the return to the territories of the Palestinian delegation to Madrid. Young Palestinians handed out flowers and olive branches to the Israeli troops, as the masses defied an IDF closure order in Jericho and flooded the town to greet the arriving delegates; in Jerusalem and elsewhere in the West Bank, Palestinian flags sprouted up at road junctions and on rooftops.[187] The fact that some of these "peace" demonstrations ended in confrontations with confused and nervous Israeli soldiers, and in additional Palestinian casualties, does not detract from the fact that something entirely new was taking hold.

Until September 1993 there would be more clashes, deportations, house demolitions, curfews, and mass arrests, but these were a counterpoint to the peace talks, both the open but futile Madrid process and the successful clandestine talks in Oslo from December 1992 on. The crucial psychological dividing line between mind-sets of confrontation and peacemaking was to be the period between October 1991 and July 1992, when elections in Israel brought Labor back to power with a mandate for peace and territorial compromise.

The prospect of peace held out by the Labor victory propelled the Hamas and Islamic Jihad to redouble their efforts to provoke the Israelis into a cycle of repression that might subvert the process. The Hamas had discovered Israel's psychological weak spot: attacks, especially on young soldiers, *inside* the country. On February 16, 1989, a Hamas team, disguised as Jews in a stolen Israeli car, abducted a hitchhiking soldier. His hastily buried body was not discovered until May. The same Hamas squad carried out a second such murder in May; this soldier's body has never been found.

These abductions effected a sea change in Israel's handling of the fundamentalist threat: At last it was recognized as a mortal danger. On May 18 the GSS jailed Sheikh Yassin and in September, Hamas was declared an "illegal organization." Thereafter the security services mounted periodic sweeps to round up its cadres and to curtail its social, educational, and religious activities.[188] Among those jailed were most of the network responsible for the two murders.

After Yassin's arrest operational command of the Hamas passed to a collective leadership of stalwarts living in the United States, England, and Jordan, headed by Musa Abu Marzuk, an engineer and businessman living in Virginia. (He was detained by the American authorities in July 1996 and was deported to Jordan in May 1997 after Israel withdrew its application for his extradition.) Recruits were trained by Jordanian Hamas–Muslim Brotherhood activists in Amman.[189] Funds sent regularly to the territories and Jordan by fundamentalists in the West and by supportive regimes such as Iran's and Libya's facilitated the reconstruction of the West Bank and Gaza networks after each Israeli sweep.

Between June and December 1991, Hamas's Gaza-based military wing, the so-called 'Izz a Din al-Qassam Battalions, murdered nineteen Gazans suspected of collaboration, and on January 1, 1992, it resumed its attacks on Israelis, ambushing and killing a driver near Kfar Darom, a settlement in the Strip.[190] Often, Hamas and Islamic Jihad operations were planned to foil a specific negotiation between Israel and the PLO or subvert its outcome. But they did not always take place on the intended dates because of successful Israeli (and, later, PLO) countermeasures, such as closure of the territories and arrests.

THE EFFECTS OF THE INTIFADA

The Intifada resulted in a great many casualties, mainly Arab but also Israeli, entailing much bereavement, suffering, and hatred. Many hundreds of Palestinians and dozens of Israelis were permanently crippled. According to

Be'tselem, Israel's security forces killed 1,095 Palestinians in the territories during the period December 1987–December 1993. Another 48 were killed by Israeli civilians—mostly settlers—between December 1987 and December 1991. Of those killed by security forces during the period December 1987–December 1992, 51 were twelve years old and younger and 146 were from thirteen to sixteen.[191]

Palestinian figures are higher than Be'tselem's. IDF figures tend to be much lower; they do not include Arabs killed by nonsecurity personnel or by means other than live fire (such as clubbing), and they appear not to include those who died in hospital of injuries. Moreover, some Arabs killed and wounded by soldiers were never recorded by the IDF. Thus, while the IDF says that by June 1989, the security forces had killed 399 Arabs, Be'tselem puts the number at 548, and Palestinian sources at 682.[192]

During the first three years of the rebellion, an additional 359 Palestinians—almost all of them suspected of collaboration with Israel—were killed by fellow Palestinians.[193]

The number of Arabs injured by truncheons and bullets runs into the tens of thousands. One estimate is that between fifteen and twenty thousand were wounded in the first two years alone.[194]

According to Be'tselem, forty-eight Israeli civilians were killed by Arabs inside Israel between December 1987 and December 1992, and thirty-one in the territories. The number of IDF, police, and GSS personnel killed from the start of the Intifada until the end of 1991 was twenty-two, with eighteen more in 1992 and twenty-five in 1993.[195]

By the end of 1991 the Intifada brought major economic, political, and social changes to the West Bank and Gaza Strip, and also to Israel—chief of which were a polarization of Right and Left and a radicalizing of ideological and political positions. It also altered the political situation in the Middle East overall: The *status quo ante bellum* had become irretrievable, and the Palestinian problem had moved to the top of the international agenda. The Intifada ended in a stalemate, with the Palestinians unable to eject the Israelis from the territories and the Israelis unable to stop the violence. That made the occupation increasingly uncomfortable. As a result, both sides soon fundamentally revised their policies: Within months the PLO agreed to recognize and make peace with Israel, and to establish a self-governing entity in a small part of Palestine. And Israel, some months later, agreed to recognize the PLO and to evacuate much if not most of the West Bank and Gaza Strip. In addition, the United States was to recognize the PLO and reopen its dialogue with it, and Jordan finally severed all administrative links with the West Bank. Ultimately, the result of the Intifada was a basic restructuring of geopolitical realities in the region, one of which was the start of the emergence of a Palestinian state.

The uprising brought about a major economic crisis in the territories, with the standard of living dropping by 35 percent. But the dissolution of economic ties with Israel also led to a relative reduction in dependency. Before 1988 around 90 percent of the West Bank's and Gaza Strip's imports, including materials used in agriculture and industry, had come from Israel.[196] During the Intifada the percentage may have remained the same (with Israel controlling the border crossings, the Palestinians could not import from anywhere else), but the quantities shrank. There was a substantial reduction in industrial production but an increase in new building and in agricultural output, as Palestinians tried to wean themselves from Israeli products. At the same time tens of thousands of laborers continued to commute to work inside Israel, and this remained a major source of income. Moreover, thousands of Arabs continued to work, mainly in construction, in the Jewish settlements (throwing into ironic, and somewhat sad, relief both the Palestinians' dependence on Israel for their livelihoods and the tenuousness of their commitment to the nationalist cause). Israel for its part put an almost complete stop to infrastructure investment and development in the territories.

A major social effect of the Intifada was the replacement of the traditional "notability" leadership in the territories by a new class of activists. From the outset power passed to the local instigators, and to the PLO's direct "representatives," some of whom hailed from notable families (like Faisal Husseini and Sari Nusseibeh) but owed their influence to political affiliation and activity rather than lineage. Clan and family heads were defied by teenagers, who intimidated and harassed their elders (and, often, their social "betters") when imposing commercial strikes and work stoppages.[197]

The Intifada also raised the status of women, amplifying a process that had been slowly under way since the start of the occupation and perhaps even before. A number of women—notably Hanan Ashrawi, a professor of English literature at Bir Zeit University—became prominent politically, and many participated as never before in demonstrations and rioting. According to Schiff and Ya'ari, a full fifth of the Intifada wounded during the first three months were female.[198]

These developments also wrought a deep, perhaps enduring psychological change. From a downtrodden, passive people, the Palestinians overnight became, at least for a time, a defiant, successfully rebellious one, enjoying a sense of moral superiority over their better-armed occupiers.[199] What is more, the uprising nurtured a sense of unity and community and, ultimately, "nationhood" among a people that had traditionally been deeply divided by religious, class, regional, and political differences. A corollary was a strong sense of discipline,[200] which was buttressed by the heavy hand of the "shock committees."

And then there was the Israeli prison system. More than fifty thousand Palestinians served time during the Intifada, many of them studying Hebrew and other subjects and being instilled with a sense of national unity and purpose across regional and party political lines. It was in the prisons that much of the networking took place that resulted in the formation of guerrilla/terrorist cells on the outside.

In Israel, drops in production, exports, and tourism during the Intifada cost an estimated $1.5–2 billion during the first year alone, though the losses gradually declined as the economy adjusted.[201] But the uprising's major effect was political. Within weeks of the outbreak it succeeded in awakening many Israelis to the fact that their country was running a brutal military occupation, and that there was a Palestinian "problem" that had to be resolved if Israel was to have any peace. The Intifada reasserted the existence of the "Green Line," the pre-1967 border between Israel and the West Bank and Gaza Strip, as well as the formally erased but very real line between Jewish West and Arab East Jerusalem. Most people grasped that Israel and the occupied territories were distinct entities and that Jerusalem was not really a "united" city.[202]

Until 1967 Israelis had generally felt that the "Palestinian problem" had somehow gone away. The 1967 conquest and the rise of the resistance movement reawakened the problem, but not to such an extent that it penetrated most people's consciousness. The Intifada changed this—eleven-year-olds stoning troops, open sewage in the shantytowns of Gaza, soldiers beating demonstrators and the GSS torturing prisoners, all entered Israeli homes via television and newspapers day after day, and via the stories of fathers, brothers, and sons who served increasingly longer stints in the territories.

In short order the Intifada radicalized both Left and Right, splitting society perhaps even more definitively than the Lebanese conflict had done. However, the existence since 1984 of the Likud-Labor National Unity Government served to blunt the effects of this polarization.

On the Left, people began to say that Israel had to get out of the territories quickly, and that this could be achieved by dialogue with the PLO and agreement to a two-state solution. The settlements were seen as an obstacle to peace and a burden on security; even Rabin, by no means an emotional left-winger, made no secret of his view that the settlers were an albatross around the neck of the IDF.

The radicalization on the Right was even more dramatic. The settlers, feeling besieged by the Palestinians and ostracized by part of the political establishment, began speaking of left-of-center politicians, and even Rabin, as "traitors" and "murderers" whenever a settler was killed by an Arab. Rehav'am Ze'evi's Moledet ("Motherland") Party, which ran on a "transfer" platform, won two seats in the December 1988 general elections. Mass expulsion once again became, as it had during the 1930s and 1940s, a legitimate subject of public advocacy. One opinion poll indicated that almost half the electorate looked to some sort of transfer solution.[203]

As the Intifada unfolded, the mainstream Right, the Likud, gradually dissociated itself from the wilder settlers and Gush Emunim. A growing number of party supporters came to feel that the status quo was untenable and that "something had to be done." But almost all continued to resist the possibility of talking to the PLO and of a Palestinian state. "Transfer" seemed to hold a simple, decisive way out, though most acknowledged that the Arab world and the West would never accede to the idea.

The Intifada without doubt changed the lifestyle of the settlers, only about a quarter of whom were hard-core, ideologically committed expansionists. The majority had simply sought better housing and quality of life—clean air, space, nice views—on the hilltops of the West Bank, and commuted daily to work in Israel. Now they found their quality of life severely impaired by flying stones on the roads. People moved outside their settlements at their peril; cars and buses traveled in convoy, with close IDF protection; vehicles were fitted with "stone-proof" screens and bulletproof windows. Tension and fear marked every journey, and friends and relatives from Israel proper no longer came to visit. There was also a general sense of political vulnerability. As the months ground on, with rising casualty rates, negative television images, and criticism from abroad, most people came around to the view that Israel must get out of the heavily Arab-populated areas and reach an accommodation with the Arab world, and that this could be achieved only along with or following a settlement with the Palestinians.[204]

The Intifada also damaged the morale of the IDF. Arguments between hard- and soft-liners became a way of life in many units serving in the territories. Most soldiers found it distasteful to confront rioting civilians, especially women and children.[205] To be sure, some took pleasure in the freedom to beat, maim, and kill; and the continuous confrontations with the hostile, jeering, cursing masses led to a degree of bestiality.

The officially sanctioned riot-control measures almost inevitably gave rise to abuse, injury, and killing that went beyond the call of duty and permissible behavior. Sadistically inclined soldiers went on sprees of violence. Only a small minority of these malefactors were brought to book by the army's legal machinery—and were almost always let off with ludicrously light sentences. The civilian courts were just as slow to punish violence by the settlers; for example, a settler who shot and killed a pregnant woman in the West Bank village of al-Jib in December 1995 was sentenced by Jerusalem district court judge Eliahu Ben-Zimra to four months of community service.[206]

During the first three years of the Intifada, some 1,250 cases of IDF abuse were investigated by the military police. These inquiries resulted in 148 soldiers (34 of them officers) being tried on charges including manslaughter, causing death through negligence, grave battery, unlawful use of weapons, and theft of Arab property. Some of the more prominent cases received wide publicity and engendered political controversy. The most senior officer to be tried was Col. Ya'akov Sadeh, the deputy commander of the Gaza Strip division. On July 31, 1989, Sadeh encountered a group of stone-throwers and, at a range of one hundred meters (well outside the range of the stones), fired a plastic bullet at a person he identified as an "inciter." By his own confession, he had aimed at the inciter's shoulder (standing orders were to fire below the knee), but he hit him in the jugular vein and killed him. Sadeh was found guilty and given a six-month prison sentence (suspended) and a severe reprimand.[207]

Another colonel, Yehuda Meir, who commanded the Nablus District, ordered paratroops under his command to round up several dozen youngsters (according to prepared GSS lists), take them to a nearby wood, and (in his phrase) "break their arms and legs." His troops carried out the orders, but, unhappy with the chore, apparently delivered the beatings with restraint and caused no severe injuries. The youngsters were released, and a few were treated for broken limbs in local hospitals. The Red Cross complained to the authorities, who investigated, and Colonel Meir was "severely reprimanded" by CGS Shomron following a disciplinary hearing. The procedure sparked massive public criticism in the media and by left-wing politicians and an appeal to the Supreme Court (sitting as the High Court of Justice). The court, unusually, ruled against the state and ordered that Meir be tried in a criminal proceeding. A special military court was convened, and Meir was demoted to private.[208] Meir argued that he had been carrying out the policy laid down by the defense minister.

Perhaps the most notorious of the Intifada trials, known as "Giv'ati [Brigade] A," involved four infantrymen who, on August 22, 1988, chased a suspected stone-thrower into a house in the Jibalya refugee camp and proceeded to beat the owner of the house, one Hani al-Shami, with their fists, boots, a broomstick, and rifle butts. Al-Shami was then taken to an IDF camp, where other soldiers beat him. A doctor looked him over, pronounced him healthy, and did not treat him. Al-Shami died later that night from internal injuries. The four soldiers were tried for manslaughter and related offenses, and the doctor for negligence; the soldiers who beat al-Shami in the IDF camp were never identified or tried.

At the end of a yearlong trial, the soldiers were convicted of "brutal maltreatment" but not of manslaughter. The judges explained that the fatal blows might have been delivered after al-Shami had reached the camp. Three men were given nine months in prison and nine months suspended, and the fourth six months in prison and six months suspended. The doctor was cleared of all charges. The IDF judge advocate general, General Straschnov, appealed the sentences without success.[209]

Routine beatings by IDF troops were complemented by equally routine abuse and torture of Arab suspects by the army, police, and GSS. In 1987 a judicial commission headed by former Supreme Court justice Moshe Landau officially and explicitly sanctioned the use in interrogations (though not in the preinterrogation detention period) of "psychological pressure" and "moderate physical pressure," in effect giving the GSS, and in some cases the police, blanket permission to use certain forms of torture. A secret appendix specified exactly what was permissible, making it a document unique in the annals of modern Western judicial history. (Landau was subsequently honored by the state with the Israel Prize for jurisprudence.)

Abuse and torture of Palestinian prisoners by the GSS and other security bodies had been routine at least since the early 1970s. In 1977 *The Sunday Times* of London published a series of articles alleging systematic beatings and the use of cold showers and electrical shocks. The charges were dismissed by Israeli government spokesmen and prominent individuals as "Arab propaganda." The Likud government, which took office in 1977, severely restricted the GSS, but an increase in abuse and torture by the service's interrogators was registered from 1984 onward (after the Peres-Shamir unity government took power)—the favored measures being beatings and standing prisoners outdoors in the rain or under a hot sun handcuffed to a metal pipe, with a sack over their heads, for long hours. There was frequent use of cold showers and air conditioners, and denial of food, sleep, and medical attention, as well as threats to family members.[210]

These and other methods were almost routine during the years of the Intifada (especially from mid-1988 on). Be'tselem's investigation of charges brought by Palestinians and foreign human rights organizations resulted in a detailed report issued in March 1991. It described—mainly on the basis of Palestinian testimony—a great many cases of abuse and torture, including five prisoners who died under GSS interrogation during 1988–89. In some of the cases, GSS men and/or police interrogators were tried and lightly punished or reprimanded.[211]

Despite their acute moral discomfort, few soldiers refused to carry out orders or to defy reserve call-up notices. They carried out orders—while lamenting their unpleasantness or immorality. (Israeli columnist Nahum Barne'a dubbed it the *"yorim ve'bochim"*—shooting and weeping—syndrome.) No more than two hundred soldiers, almost all of them reservists, refused to serve in the territories and were jailed, for twenty-one to thirty-five days, in the course of the Intifada. Hundreds more managed to avoid both service in the territories and outright disobedience and prison, usually after reaching "deals" with their commanders.

The Intifada damaged the image and morale of the IDF. Many conscript officers, who otherwise might have contemplated military careers, quit the army. The troops came under increasingly intense media scrutiny and criticism—and many began to view the media as allies of the Palestinians. Rightists in Israel called the army "left-leaning" and "soft on Arabs." Settlers frequently charged that the troops were doing less than their utmost to protect them against the stones and firebombs. Indeed, the settlers repeatedly tried to establish their own "civil guard" or militia to patrol the West Bank's and

Gaza's roads and Arab towns. The IDF staunchly resisted the emergence of such a "second army."

Both within the IDF and in Israeli society, however, the notion that additional territory necessarily provided added security was mortally undermined by the Intifada. The IDF presence in the empty sands of Sinai had certainly given Israel a useful measure of strategic depth (at the same time provoking Egypt into war); but the twenty-to-thirty-five miles added by the occupation of the West Bank was seen to be of equivocal military value at best. It did provide a measure of valuable strategic depth, but it also added a major element of insecurity: The hundreds of thousands of hostile Arab inhabitants were a potentially dangerous fifth column in the rear of the IDF front line on the Jordan.

During the first months of the Intifada there was a pervasive fear among Israelis that the country's 800,000 Arab citizens (as distinct from the residents of the occupied territories) would join the uprising. Indeed, as time went on, many of these Arabs came to identify with their brethren in the territories. The Intifada deepened their sense of a common Palestinian identity, as well as their desire to attain political, social, and economic equality with Israel's Jews. They mounted fund-raising campaigns and demonstrations to support the people of the West Bank and Gaza. [212]

During the early months stones and Molotov cocktails were thrown at Israeli vehicles in a number of Arab-inhabited areas, including Jaffa and Lydda. There were also numerous cases of forest arson. But the Israeli Arab leaders generally managed to restrain their communities. Violence was officially abjured and, by and large, the Intifada failed to cross the Green Line into Israel proper.[213]

EXTERNAL — POLITICAL AND DIPLOMATIC EFFECTS

All during this period, Israel fought an uphill propaganda and political battle to explain why its troops were battling civilians and why it should not give the Palestinians their freedom. A portent of the impact of the Intifada was afforded by the UN Security Council resolution of December 22, 1987, which denounced Israel's response to the West Bank and Gaza violence. The United States had refrained from exercising its right of veto.[214] This time Israel was not going to enjoy automatic American support.

Throughout, Israel came in for condemnation by UN bodies for specific actions, such as deportations, the killing of civilians, and house demolitions.

Criticism also came from the European Community (EC) and the Soviet Union. Prominent international figures such as South Africa's Nobel Peace Prize laureate, Archbishop Desmond Tutu, compared Israel's treatment of the Palestinians to his own country's treatment of its black population. But the Israelis did not take foreign criticism—except that originating in Washington—too seriously. Indeed, President Chaim Herzog, giving voice to the majority view, attributed such sentiments to "a certain strain of latent anti-Semitism."[215] Nonetheless, there was a sense in Israel during the first two years of the rebellion of being internationally embattled and isolated.

The Intifada also placed the Palestinian leadership under intense pressure. Surprised at first, PLO-Tunis had to take control and impose its authority over the rebellious populations of the West Bank and Gaza. The "exterior" struggled under the handicap of being far away, not always fully aware of conditions on the ground or able to impose its will. Moreover, in addition to rivalry with the leadership in the field, PLO-Tunis—and its representatives in the territories—had to vie with the Islamic fundamentalists for the hearts and minds of the population.

The PLO's major challenge was how to translate an indecisive revolt into political and diplomatic gain. The momentum of rebellion had to be maintained, but it could not be allowed to slide into terrorism, which would offend international sensibilities and which Israel could crush far more easily than unarmed protest. Moreover, to make capital out of the Intifada would require the PLO substantially to modify its basic positions, a wrenching political process.

Most of the inhabitants of the territories almost from the start pressed the PLO to seek a political formula that would bring an end to their suffering. Ultimately they demanded that the PLO agree to compromise over the mechanisms of negotiation with Israel and over its possible outcome. But policies often suffer from an inertia that keeps them alive long after they have grown moribund. So it was with the PLO during the first months of the rebellion. And its leadership had also to take account of the large minority, Islamic and secular, inside the territories and outside, that demanded an uncompromising stance until Israel's destruction was achieved.

The Intifada had wrought a "re-Palestinization" of the Israeli-Arab conflict, which during the four preceding decades had effectively been a conflict between Israel and the Arab states. The first diplomatic initiative in the Arab world to try to resolve the problems raised by the rebellion and those that had given rise to it came from Egypt. Cairo had maintained a very cold peace with Israel and had poor relations with the Likud-led government, but President Hosni Mubarak thought it worth a try, particularly as, since Camp David, Egypt had been invested with, or had arrogated to itself, the role of "protector" of the Palestinians.

In January 1988 Egypt proposed the reconvening of a peace conference, to be ushered in by Israel agreeing to stop all settlement activities and both Israel and the Palestinians agreeing to halt the violence for six months. Mubarak's goal was the withdrawal of the IDF from the West Bank and the creation of a Palestinian state. Jerusalem rejected the plan,[216] and Egypt and the other Arab states went into a waiting mode. There was even a waning of interest in the Intifada: The stones were still flying, but the novelty had worn off and the Israeli responses had grown more temperate. It seemed that fewer Palestinians were dying. In June attendees at an Arab summit in Algiers voiced support for the rebellion; but, fragmented by the Iraq-Iran War and along other fault lines, the Arab world could or would do nothing directly for the Palestinians. The Egyptians repeatedly protested against the "brutal" Israeli repression but pointedly refrained from severing diplomatic ties or even recalling their ambassador from Tel Aviv. Mubarak and the others understood that the way to influence Israel was through Washington.

The problem was that the American-Israeli special relationship appeared largely unaffected. The nightly battering of Israel's image on television screens, while temporarily undermining support for it in American public opinion—in January 1989 a *New York Times*–CBS poll found that 64 percent of Americans favored US-PLO contacts and 52 percent were skeptical about Israel's readiness to compromise to achieve peace[217]—failed to dent the relations between the two governments or substantially transform public attitudes. Washington might criticize some measure of repression and look askance at Shamir's expansionist ideology and diplomatic foot-dragging, but it never even came close to considering halting or suspending the annual $3 billion aid package to Israel or the supply of sophisticated weapons to the IDF.

But achieving peace in the Middle East remained a major pillar of American foreign policy. In February 1988 Secretary of State George Shultz launched an initiative of his own. He, too, proposed an "international conference" (as the Arabs demanded), but one that might serve as an umbrella for "direct talks" (as Israel demanded) between a Jordanian-Palestinian delegation and Israel. Both sides rejected the initiative, though in private the Americans were to put most of the blame on Shamir, who automatically opposed any initiative that might lead to an Israeli withdrawal.[218]

Formally the main sticking point was Palestinian representation. The Arabs insisted that the PLO participate in any negotiation, while the Israelis rejected both the idea of separate Palestinian representation and the notion of talking to the PLO. Moreover, the Shamir government opposed the international framework, insisting on direct Israeli-Arab talks to prevent any of the participants from "ganging up" on Israel. The United States proposed an international conference as a means of getting the Arabs to the negotiating table, but supported Israel's rejection of the PLO as a negotiating partner so long as it refused to recognize Israel and renounce terrorism.

The Shultz initiative went the way of Mubarak's. But there was soon to be a major shift in the internal Arab balance of power. As the Israeli troops indecisively battled the stone-throwers, the Jordanian government took fright. Already the Palestinians in Jordan (more than 60 percent of the population), and especially the inhabitants of Amman's refugee camps, were in ferment. The "state of rage," as some called the Intifada, could well spill over into the East Bank and threaten King Hussein's own rule.[219] Amman's efficient security services so far had them well in hand. But who knew what might develop?

On July 31, 1988, King Hussein decided to cut the Gordian knot. In a somber broadcast, he announced that Jordan was severing its "administrative and judicial" links with the West Bank, "in deference to the will of the PLO"—Jordan was washing its hands of the future of the territory and its inhabitants.[220] The move stunned Israel, none more than the leaders of the Labor Party. At a stroke Hussein had virtually abrogated Abdullah's 1950 annexation of the West Bank and shattered Labor's long-held belief in the "Jordanian Option"—that is, that one day Israel would withdraw and hand parts of the West Bank over to Hashemite rather than PLO rule. That way the creation of a dangerous third state between Israel and Jordan would be avoided, and the turbulent population would become the Hashemites' headache.

Now Hussein had indicated that if the West Bank could eventually be wrested from Israeli control, it would become a PLO fief rather than revert to Jordan. In practice, his move meant that the area's municipalities and civil servants would no longer receive Jordanian funds (the sixteen thousand Arab civil administration employees previously collected one-fifth of their salaries from Amman). Jordan's parliament, of which half the representatives came from the West Bank, was dissolved, to be reconstituted exclusively of East Bankers. In time the West Bankers would lose Jordanian citizenship and passports.[221] Hussein's move was the PLO's "first political gain" in the Intifada.[222]

But the most important political consequence of the Intifada lay elsewhere. The year of rebellion and the varied pressures it produced led to the revolutionary November 1988 resolution of the Palestine National Council—the PLO's "parliament." It was augured by the publication, in June of that year, of an equivocal "trial balloon" by Bassam Abu Sharif, Arafat's political advisor, rejecting UN Resolutions 242 and 338 as a basis for negotiation, but speaking of the need for "lasting peace" for both Israel and the Palestinians, and recognizing Israel's legitimate "security" needs. It called for a "two-state" solution and mutual recognition, and expressed sympathy for "the Jewish people's centuries of suffering."[223]

Later that month Palestinian leaders inside the territories, including Faisal Husseini, circulated a document titled "Plan for a Declaration of Independence," which spoke of the need to move from stones and violence to a "political initiative." It suggested setting up a Palestinian state in the borders proposed in the 1947 UN Partition Resolution. Hussein's announcement of dissociation from the West Bank helped this mode of thinking crystallize among the Palestinians. The "Husseini document" reached Israeli hands apparently during a search of his offices as he was being arrested on the night of July 31,[224] and was then leaked to the press.

The PLO had been inching toward moderation for years. The idea of a Palestinian state emerging alongside Israel—instead of a "secular democratic state" in all of Palestine—was first implicitly posited at the PNC meeting in 1974.[225] The seventies and eighties had seen a series of senior PLO—mainly Fatah—figures preaching a "two-state" solution but had also witnessed their assassination by fellow Palestinians of the Abu Nidal faction.[226]

This internal terrorism forced would-be moderates to maintain a low profile. So did repeated declarations by Arafat to the effect that the mooted two-state solution was to be seen merely as a stage in a grand strategy that looked to the eventual takeover of all of Palestine. He told a meeting in Beirut in December 1980: "When we speak of the Palestinians' return, we want to say: Acre before Gaza, Beersheba before Hebron. We recognize one thing, namely that the Palestinian flag will fly over Jaffa." (Acre, Beersheba, and Jaffa are all deep inside the territory of pre-1967 Israel—though all were earmarked by the UN in 1947 for Palestinian Arab Sovereignty.)[227] And why invite a major rift and possible bloody conflict within the Palestinian camp between hard-liners and soft-liners so long as Israel was offering nothing at all? But the debacle in Lebanon initiated the start of a sea-change in mainstream PLO thinking. Clearly, intransigence and war were not working, and the Palestinians might have to agree to a state in less than the whole of Palestine. But only hints of this emerged as Arafat juggled the various factions.

The Intifada at last forced the PLO to take the bull by the horns. The West Bank and Gaza leadership and population, hard-pressed by Israeli repression and eager to win some political gain from the prolonged struggle, forced the leaders of the "exterior" to a decision. They all understood that in order for the Palestinians to cash in on the sympathy generated within Israel and in the international community, and to force the Israelis to offer compromises of their own, they must project political flexibility and suggest an outline for a compromise. The next step was the Abu Sharif article and the Husseini "Independence document."

A token contingent of Intifada activists exiled by Israel put in an appearance at the PNC meeting in Algiers in November 1988, but played no real part in the deliberations. "We're treated like dogs or thieves" by the "exterior," one of them later complained. Arafat was set on denying the local leaders any prominence and assuring the "exterior's" supremacy.[228] But the Intifada itself dominated the proceedings. In his speech (on November 15) Arafat proclaimed Palestinian independence and the establishment of "the State of Palestine," whose capital was "in . . . Jerusalem." Throughout, there was a hard-line/soft-line debate, but the Fatah moderates prevailed in the resolutions. The PLO would demand independence and establish a state in part of Palestine (that is, the West Bank and Gaza Strip). But in his keynote closed-session speech on November 14, Salah Khalaf, Arafat's deputy, reverted to the old plan of taking over Palestine in "stages" (in words reminiscent of Ben-Gurion's 1937 plan for a staggered takeover of Palestine): "This is a state for the coming generations. At first, [the Palestinian state] would be small. . . . God willing, it would expand eastward, westward, northward and southward. . . . I am interested in the liberation of Palestine . . . but . . . step by step."[229]

Khalaf may have been expressing the secret or not-so-secret thinking of many of the delegates. But the concluding "Political Statement" was moderate in tone and innovative, and therefore historically significant, in content. It hailed the glorious Intifada and its martyrs, and declared—following Arafat—the establishment of a Palestinian state on the basis of the 1947 Partition Resolution (UN General Assembly Resolution 181). It accepted the need for a "comprehensive political settlement" and direct negotiations with Israel, and posited the convocation of an international conference on the basis of Resolutions 242 and 338. It explicitly abjured "terrorism in all its forms" but upheld the right to struggle for independence against foreign occupation, implicitly endorsing Intifada violence. The statement passed by a vote of 253 to 46, with 10 abstentions.[230] A few weeks later, Arafat told the German weekly *Der Spiegel* that in Palestine there would be a Jewish state and an Arab state. Within two weeks fifty-five countries—including the Soviet Union, China, and India—had recognized the Palestinian "state."[231]

The Israeli leadership was not exactly won over. The PNC resolution had deliberately left large areas of ambiguity—for example, the references both to UN Resolutions 181 and 242/338 and to the legitimacy/illegitimacy of terrorism and armed struggle. Shamir would have nothing to do with the PLO whatever it declared, and Foreign Minister Peres (rather bizarrely) denounced the Algiers statements as an "even more extreme position" than the PNC had enunciated previously.[232] Nor were the Americans appeased. The State Department continued to regard Arafat as a "terrorist" and denied him a visa to attend the forthcoming General Assembly meeting in New York. But the department had noted the shift in language—and without fanfare, using intermediaries, urged the PLO to further "clarify" its stand in a way that would enable the United States to change its position.[233]

Arafat edged a mite closer to what was being asked of him in his speech at the General Assembly meeting in Geneva (it had been moved there especially to accommodate the Arabs) on December 13. Addressing himself to Israel, he declared: "I come to you in the name of my people, offering my hand so that we can make true peace, peace based on justice . . . together, we can forge peace." Washington responded by saying that Arafat had still failed to dispel the crucial ambiguities relating to 242 and 338, Israel's right to exist, and terrorism.

Arafat ran the necessary extra lap two days later. On December 15 at a press conference in Geneva—after prior Swedish mediation and in coordination with the Americans—he declared: "We completely renounce all types of terrorism, including individual, collective, and state [terrorism]." He added that the PNC had accepted 242 and 338 as "a basis for negotiations with Israel within the context of an international conference."[234]

The Americans, much to Shamir's chagrin, now had what they wanted. At a press conference later that day, Shultz declared himself satisfied. The PLO had accepted 242 and 338, recognized Israel, and renounced terrorism, he said, and went on to announce that Washington had decided to embark on "a substantive dialogue with PLO representatives."[235] American and PLO representatives held several rounds of talks in Tunis during the following weeks.

The start of this dialogue marked a major achievement for the PLO. But it had had to pay for American recognition with substantial concessions. It had accepted the fact that it must do so before it could make political capital out of the Intifada, and the United States had acknowledged that no peace was possible without the PLO. (It would take Israel five more years to reach the same conclusion.)

The Israeli government was stunned: Washington had not kept it informed, and the U.S.-PLO rapprochement filled Shamir with gloom. It failed even to begin to trigger a similar Israel-PLO thaw. Shamir preferred that the PLO remain hard-line and rejectionist, and, therefore, objectionable to the United States. He argued that the shift was merely a tactic, and that the PLO's strategic aim remained the destruction of Israel. But whatever the PLO said or did, Shamir believed that the West Bank and Gaza were an inalienable part of the Jewish people's heritage and must not revert to Arab sovereignty.

Shamir denounced Washington's decision to talk with the PLO as a "blunder" that would "not help the peace process." Only one cabinet minister, Ezer Weizman (who in the early 1980s had joined Labor), welcomed the change as the "start of a new era."[236] But otherwise the leadership remained immovable—and somewhat in the rear of public opinion, which, by late 1988, under the hammer blows of the Intifada, was coming around to the view that Israel-PLO talks were desirable and/or inevitable.[237]

Even Arafat's willingness a few months later to go yet further and in effect renounce the Palestinian National Charter—in May 1989 he told French interviewers "Ç'est caduc" (meaning, "It is null and void")—failed to get a bite out of Peres and Rabin, let alone Shamir.[238] The government refused to talk to the PLO; but American and Arab pressure required that Israel appear to be doing something. The first to break the ice was Rabin, who in January 1989, apparently with Shamir's permission if not his blessing, floated a semiofficial "peace" proposal. Rabin's premise, after more than a year of violence in the streets, was that to end the rebellion, military measures had to be accompanied by a political overture. He proposed that Israel negotiate with a joint delega-tion of Jordanians and Palestinians from the territories (rather than "external" PLO officials); that three to six months of quiet and "political" elections in the West Bank and Gaza, in which Palestinian representatives could be chosen, precede the talks; and that, in line with the Camp David accords, the talks allow for both an interim "expanded autonomy" stage and a final-settlement negotiation.[239] The final-stage negotiations, as envisaged by Rabin (though not Shamir), would result in Israeli withdrawal from parts of the West Bank and the establishment of a Jordanian–West Bank confederation (or of a con-federation of the two with Israel) rather than an independent Palestinian state (again, Labor's traditional Jordanian option).

The PLO rejected the proposals. But they paved the way for the first official Israeli political response to the Intifada, the Shamir "plan," approved by the cabinet on May 14. It reiterated Israel's commitment to the Camp David framework, though it stepped around a solid commitment to 242 or the "land for peace" formula that it embodied. PLO participation and a Palestinian state were ruled out. Israel proposed the "rehabilitation" of the Palestinian refugees in their camps. The core of the proposal was a call for "democratic" elections in the territories, "free from an atmosphere of PLO violence, terror and intim-idation," to elect a delegation that could negotiate a five-year interim arrange-ment in which the Palestinians would enjoy "self-rule" though Israel would continue to retain responsibility for security and defense matters, borders, and foreign relations. The inhabitants of East Jerusalem would be excluded from voting in the prospective elections. The interim arrangement would serve as a test of the two sides' readiness for "coexistence and cooperation" and would be followed by the negotiation of a "permanent agreement."[240]

Whether Shamir was sincerely trying to move toward peace or whether his "plan" was merely a stratagem to buy time (or, as he incautiously let slip at the time, merely "an idle fancy"[241]), the Americans responded as if it was an ade-quate basis for negotiation. The PLO, excluded from the process and denied the prospect of a state, flatly rejected it, and set forth its alternative demands: at least partial Israeli military withdrawal from the territories *before* elections were held; a commitment to full withdrawal within twenty-seven months; acceptance of the refugees' "right of return" to their former homes in Israel and the territories; and agreement to an independent Palestinian state. The PLO was not alone in rejecting the Shamir plan. Mubarak and King Hussein closed ranks behind Arafat during visits to Washington that April.[242]

In any event, within weeks Shamir himself was forced to recant by his own party leadership. Many Likud stalwarts found the proposals too daring and too conciliatory. Meeting in emergency session in July, the Likud Central Com-mittee—guided by Ariel Sharon, David Levy, and Yitzhak Moda'i—tacked on new conditions: East Jerusalemites were to be barred from both running and voting in the elections; the Intifada must end before elections could take place; Israel, whatever the contours of the settlement, would not give up any land; and Jewish settlement activity would be continued.[243]

The plan, with its new preconditions, was dismissed by Faisal Husseini as a "death certificate to a scheme that was born dead."[244] And, indeed, the Shamir plan led nowhere. New Egyptian and American procedural proposals were rejected by the Israeli government, and in March 1990 the Labor Party withdrew from the National Unity Government. By June, Shamir had reconstituted a hardline right-wing government, with Labor relegated to the opposition benches. Shultz's successor, Secretary of State James Baker, reacted by publicly telling the Israelis: "The White House number is 202-456-1414, and when you are serious about peace, call us."[245]

But neither were the Americans overly pleased with the Palestinians. Indeed, on June 20, 1989, they broke off their dialogue with the PLO following a raid on a beach south of Tel Aviv (in which no Israelis were killed) by a team of terrorists belonging to the Palestine Liberation Front, led by Abu al-Abbas. The PLF was a constituent part of the PLO, and Arafat had refused to condemn the raid, as Washington had demanded. The Intifada continued and in effect the peace process went into hibernation for more than a year, to re-emerge only in 1991, against the backdrop of the Gulf War.

THIRTEEN

Peace at Last?

President George Bush, who took office in January 1989, and James Baker, his secretary of state, had set their minds on achieving a breakthrough toward peace in the Middle East. The Intifada, still raging in the occupied territories, provided the impetus. The sudden arrival in Israel of masses of immigrants from the collapsing Soviet empire seemed to add urgency, for they could inundate the West Bank and permanently change its demographic makeup. Moreover, the disintegration of the Soviet Union meant that the Arabs could no longer rely on their former patrons for political and military support and no longer had a realistic war option vis-à-vis Israel.

The United States was now the only superpower. And despite its deep commitment to Israel's security and future, it was generally held (albeit grudgingly by many Arabs and Israelis) to be a relatively objective broker. Washington broke off contact with the PLO when it refused to condemn the abortive PLF raid south of Tel Aviv; but, at the same time, Baker could also bluntly state, on May 22, 1989: "For Israel, now is the time to lay aside, once and for all, the unrealistic vision of a greater Israel. Israeli interests in the West Bank and Gaza—security and otherwise—can be accommodated in a settlement based on Resolution 242. Forswear annexation. Stop settlement activity. . . . Reach out to the Palestinians as neighbors who deserve political rights."[1]

Ironically, American pressure for moderation resulted in the emergence of the most right-wing government in Israel's history. In mid-March 1990 Labor-Likud differences over peace moves resulted in the collapse of the National Unity Government; by June a narrow Likud-led coalition was in office.

By then the Intifada seemed to have lost direction. PLO moves toward moderation had failed to elicit a matching echo from the Israeli government. The Palestinians' perseverance had been eroded by more than two years of repression and economic privation. They had failed to break Israel's hold on the territories. A symptom of the PLO's frustration was the great increase in the killing of suspected collaborators; in 1991 the Israelis killed fewer Palestinians—about 100—than the Palestinians did themselves—about 150. Tension and conflict between various groups of Palestinians—secularists and fundamentalists, Left and Right—also increased considerably.[2]

West Bank sociologist Salim Tamari wrote of "a general malaise in the Palestinian street affecting people's attitudes to the daily routine of the Intifada. . . . What is being questioned here is those tactics whose efficacy has been depleted. What people need today is a reprieve, a breathing space that allows them to rebuild their economy."[3]

This was the situation when the dictator of Iraq, Col. Saddam Hussein, launched an invasion of Kuwait on August 2, 1990, setting in motion the events that led to Operation Desert Storm, in which the United States led a coalition of Arab and Western states (including France, Britain, Egypt, Saudi Arabia, and Syria) under a UN umbrella, to liberate Kuwait and crush Saddam's armies. Going into action on the night of January 16–17, 1991, the Allied air forces pounded Saddam's troops and military and industrial infrastructure for five weeks, and by the time the Allied armored columns began to move, on February 24, it was in effect all over.[4] Within days Kuwait was taken, and most of Iraq's army was scrap metal. Inside Iraq, bridges, roads, and power plants lay in ruins.

Before and during Desert Storm, Iraq tried to link the issues of Kuwait and Palestine in order to drive a wedge through the heart of the coalition. During the fighting Saddam launched Scud ground-to-ground missiles against Israel, calculating that if there were any retaliation, Washington's Arab partners might find it intolerable to be allied with Israel in an attack against an Arab state, and so defect. Altogether thirty-nine Scuds fell, most of them on the Tel Aviv area, causing panic—hundreds of thousands of people fled the stricken coastal cities—much property damage, dozens of injuries, and one or two dead. But thanks to common sense and strong, continuous American pressure, Jerusalem refrained from responding[5] after Washington demonstrated its commitment to Israel by deploying several American-manned Patriot anti-aircraft missile batteries there. (In fact the Patriots proved all but useless in stopping the Scuds.) Some months later it emerged that IDF commandos and the IAF had been set to go into Iraq to hunt for the missile-launchers but had been held back by the cabinet at the last minute. In 1992 the IDF reportedly began planning a commando raid aiming to assassinate Saddam, but it was aborted when, during a dress rehearsal, a missile accidentally killed six men.

From the start, the PLO backed Saddam's conquest of Kuwait and, along with Jordan, openly sided with Iraq. Arafat, in a show of solidarity, visited Baghdad just days before the start of the Allied offensive. Palestinians stood on the rooftops and cheered as the Scuds flew over the West Bank on their way to Tel Aviv;[6] in Jordan, Palestinian crowds mounted anti-American demonstrations. They backed Saddam because he had not only taken on the United

States, but also delivered a mortal blow against Kuwait and implicitly threatened to do the same to Saudi Arabia—and both, despite years of financial
largesse to the Palestinians, were seen as symbols of the prosperous, exploita-
tive, reactionary, pro-Western part of the Arab world. Moreover, Iraq, with its
large army and anti-Zionist, anti-Western rhetoric, was viewed as a possible
agent of Palestinian liberation, while Egypt and Syria, the traditional supporters, appeared to have abandoned the struggle. Palestinians were also annoyed
by what they regarded as the West's double standard—deep concern over the
occupation of Kuwait but relative indifference to Israel's twenty-four-year
occupation of the territories.

Bush and Baker realized that the Gulf War had provided a new opening,
and a new need, for Israeli-Arab peace. Lack of progress could jeopardize the
continued life of the anti-Iraq coalition, whose perpetuation had become a
major American interest. Moreover, the war had demonstrated the potential
destructiveness of a future conflict, with the prospect of barrages of missiles
and the use of nonconventional weaponry.

The PLO had been vastly weakened, having gambled on the wrong horse
and lost the crucial financial and political backing of Saudi Arabia and the
other Gulf States. Moreover, Kuwait expelled some three hundred thousand
Palestinians to Jordan,[7] and remittances to families in the territories, hitherto
at least $400 million annually, dwindled, increasing pressure on the PLO to
reach an accommodation with Israel.[8] This came on top of the severe decline in Palestinian income from work in Israel, as a result of closures of the
territories.

Israel's immigrant influx and the Likud government's settlement policy
both brought home to many that time was against the Palestinians. In 1991
alone, with Ariel Sharon serving as Housing Minister, thirteen thousand new
residential units were started in the territories—in contrast with twenty thousand housing starts there in the twenty-two preceding years. The Jewish population of the West Bank and the Gaza Strip increased by one-quarter during
1990 and by almost as much again in 1991, reaching 112,000, excluding the
Jerusalem municipal area. Moreover, construction of new bypass roads tended
to insulate settlers from Arab violence and stone-throwers, making their lives
easier.[9]

On March 6, 1991, within days of Iraq's defeat, Bush told Congress: "We
must do all that we can to close the gap between Israel and the Arab states and
between Israelis and Palestinians. . . . The time has come to put an end to
Arab-Israeli conflict."[10] Later that month, Baker renewed his Middle East
peace shuttles.

Other developments were to provide Washington with a major lever vis-à-
vis Israel. In May, Israel sought American guarantees for $10 billion in loans,
necessary for the absorption of Soviet immigrants (about 175,000 reached
Israel during 1991 alone[11]). Bush and Baker decided to link the guarantees to

a formal Israeli commitment to refrain from using the funds, directly or indirectly, to establish new settlements or expand existing ones, which they regarded as an obstacle to peace. The Shamir government refused to sign such a commitment. For the rest of the year, hovering over Shamir's head was the implicit threat that failure to play along would result in the loss of the guarantees (without which Jerusalem would have to pay banks much higher interest).

In June, Bush asked Middle Eastern leaders for their views on a prospective international peace conference. Assad, Mubarak, and Hussein all answered affirmatively. Shamir was left with little room for maneuver.[12] On August 1 he sent Bush his conditional agreement to participate. During the following weeks the sides hammered out a list of acceptable Palestinians—that is, residents of the territories who were non-PLO members—who could sit on a joint Jordanian-Palestinian delegation. The PLO, too weakened to hold out for better terms, accepted the list, and by mid-October the final piece of the puzzle was in place.[13]

On October 30 the conference began in Madrid, with Bush and Russian President Mikhail Gorbachev as cochairmen. In attendance were Israel, Egypt, Syria, Lebanon, and the joint Jordanian-Palestinian delegation, which, in fact, functioned as two separate ones. For "the first time in recent history," the Palestinian people were representing themselves "as an almost independent party."[14] During the meetings the Palestinian delegates continuously consulted with and took their orders from PLO-Tunis.[15] The plenary sessions lasted for three days, ending on November 1, after which the delegations met in bilateral sessions until November 4.[16]

The importance of Madrid lay in the actual get-together, not in anything done or said. Among the Palestinian delegation, reported the *New York Times*, "the sentiment . . . is of ecstasy and triumph." One member said: "[W]e have placed the foundation stone for the Palestinian state."[17] At the conference the atmosphere was extremely formal and unfriendly. Each party presented its case and leveled charges against the other side. But at the end all agreed to continue negotiating. Thereafter the various parties met periodically in both bilateral and multilateral tracks, in December 1991 in Washington, in January 1992 in Moscow, and later in several European capitals. The multilateral meetings dealt with such issues as arms control, water rights, and refugees, but no real progress was achieved.

On the bilateral track there was some movement in the Israel-Jordan negotiations, especially on the level of personal chemistry. But the Israeli-Palestinian talks skirted around the core issues and got nowhere. The Palestinian spokeswoman, Hanan Ashrawi, aptly described the negotiations as characterized by "paralysis and inertia. The Israeli delegation lacked the will and the instructions to actually negotiate . . . keeping up a semblance of participation without addressing the real issues. . . . Digressions into trivia, circumvention of substance—these became the key nonmoves of Israel's evasive tactics."[18] Shamir later let slip to an Israeli journalist that, in fact, he had never intended that there be any progress, and that his idea was to drag out the negotiations without result for at least ten years.[19] Shamir subsequently claimed that he had been misquoted.

Opponents of the peace process were not all on the Israeli side. On September 23 and October 7, 1991, Hamas leaflets denounced the impending "conference of surrender" and the "sell-out of Palestine." The process was also denounced by the PFLP, Naif Hawatmeh, and the Islamic Jihad.[20] Intra-Palestinian tensions flared up. On September 21 Fatah and Hamas squads had clashed near Nablus, with one Hamas member killed and four wounded. On the day Madrid convened, October 30, there were mass fistfights in Gaza's Sheikh Radwan neighborhood and the Shati refugee camp. A meeting in Teheran of heads of the "rejectionist" factions denounced the conference. Low-key clashes between PLO and Hamas supporters continued through the winter of 1991–92, and for months a civil war in the streets of the West Bank and the Gaza Strip was a real possibility. Verbal recriminations and exchanges of condemnatory fliers were often followed by violence resulting in injuries and deaths.[21]

In Israel's next general elections, which took place on June 23, 1992, the major issue was the future of the peace process and the situation in the territories. The results constituted a radical upset. The Likud, after dominating all the coalition governments since 1977, was defeated, with Labor winning 44 out of 120 Knesset seats to the Likud's 32 (down from 40 in the 1988 elections). What's more, Labor, this time led by Yitzhak Rabin, was able to form a coalition with the left-wing Meretz Party (12 seats) and the nonparticipatory support of five Arab members. This razor-thin majority of 61 was bolstered by the co-option of the Sephardi ultra-Orthodox Shas Party (6 seats). Rabin, now prime minister, kept the defense portfolio for himself and (reluctantly) named his perennial rival, Shimon Peres, foreign minister. The two, on extremely bad terms since the 1970s (when then Prime Minister Rabin had charged that Peres, his defense minister, had spent much of his energy subverting him), gingerly set about working together to push matters forward.

The immediate postelection months, July–October 1992, were a dead period, with the Labor ministers finding their feet and the United States preoccupied with President Bush's reelection campaign. The multilateral meetings continued. Syria's President Assad spoke of the need for a "peace of the brave" (De Gaulle's name for the Franco-Algerian peace in the early 1960s) and his foreign minister, Farouk a Shar'a, of "total peace for total withdrawal," implying a readiness to fully normalize relations with Israel (embassies, air links, economic ties, and so on) if Israel would give up all of the Golan Heights. But no real movement took place. All awaited the result of the American elections. Bill Clinton, a former governor of Arkansas with no foreign policy experience, was elected president and took over from Bush in January 1993.

THE ISRAELI-PLO BREAKTHROUGH

Labor's assumption of power radically changed the atmosphere in Israel. True, Labor—like the Likud—continued to oppose Palestinian statehood and PLO participation in the peace process. But the party was open to the notion of territorial compromise, and recognized that the Palestinian problem was at the heart of the conflict. As a result of the Intifada, Rabin himself had grudgingly come to understand that Israel could not hold on to the territories indefinitely and would have to talk to the PLO. He saw that the post–Cold War years were a window of opportunity. The Soviet withdrawal from the international arena and the Gulf War had left the Arabs weak and relatively flexible. Moreover, with Muslim fundamentalist forces on the ascendancy throughout the Middle East, how long could the relatively moderate, secular regimes survive? The newly fashioned Russian Federation might arise from the ashes as a pro-Arab world power; and Iran and Iraq might acquire nuclear weapons and project their strength and rejectionism across the Middle East. The golden moment of relative Israeli strength and American superpower dominance— which might last roughly until 1999, in Rabin's estimate—needed to be seized and translated into Israeli-Arab accords.[22]

Rabin, personally unenthusiastic about Arafat, remained opposed to talking with the PLO. Besides, a six-year-old law forbade such contacts. Three months after taking power, Rabin turned down a proposal by Foreign Minister Peres to establish "semidirect" contact with the PLO. Yet a peace process got under way—without the consent or knowledge of the government and in defiance of Israeli law. It was to be a negotiation "propelled by impulse, contingency, improvisation and coincidence"[23]—and it was to prove successful and of great historical significance.

The spark was a meeting between Hanan Ashrawi and Yair Hirschfeld, a Middle East expert teaching at Haifa University, who had periodically met Palestinians in the hope of establishing trust and bridging differences. Hirschfeld and Yossi Beilin, a Labor Party member of the Knesset and confidant of Peres, had intermittently maintained a back channel to the PLO since 1989, through Faisal Husseini, the senior PLO figure in Jerusalem.[24] Ashrawi suggested that Hirschfeld meet with Abu Alaa (Suleiman Ahmed Qurai), the PLO's "finance minister."[25] Hirschfeld flew to London, where at Beilin's suggestion, he contacted Terje Rod Larsen, director of the Norwegian Institute for Applied Social Sciences (FOFA), who also had discussed with Beilin ways of promoting peace. Larsen and Norwegian Deputy Foreign Minister Jan Egeland had met Abu Alaa in Oslo the previous January. Subsequently, Abu Alaa had conveyed to the Norwegians Arafat's desire that Oslo help set up an Israeli-PLO dialogue.

Larsen and his wife, Mona Juul, a senior Norwegian Foreign Ministry official, arranged the Hirschfeld–Abu Alaa meeting, which took place secretly on December 4, 1992, in London.[26] Abu Alaa, to Hirschfeld's mind, blew hot and cold, alternately making conciliatory and extreme statements. But Hirschfeld concluded that the dialogue was worth pursuing. He contacted Beilin, now deputy foreign minister, who was then coincidentally also in London. Beilin voiced no objection to carrying on the dialogue, and Hirschfeld, at a second meeting that evening, told Abu Alaa that he was authorized to continue.

On January 20, 1993—the day after the Knesset repealed the law banning Israeli-PLO contacts—Hirschfeld, now flanked by his colleague, historian Ron Pundak, met with Abu Alaa outside Oslo. Agreement emerged on three ideas: "Israeli withdrawal from Gaza, gradual devolution of economic power to the Palestinians . . . and . . . international economic assistance to the nascent Palestinian entity in Gaza."[27] Between February and early May four more secret rounds of negotiation took place,[28] during which the rudiments of a joint document were hammered out. Eventually to be called the "Declaration of Principles" (DOP), it provided for elections in the territories, Palestinian autonomy during an interim stage before a final settlement, gradual Israeli withdrawal and devolution of powers to the Palestinians, initial implementation in the Gaza Strip ("Gaza first")—where the Palestinians would rule long before the final status was set—and the need for an economic plan for the territories.[29]

During the first week of February, Beilin informed Peres of the secret channel, and Peres notified Rabin. Neither was particularly enthusiastic—Peres once referred to the two Israeli negotiators as "*meshuga'im*" (crackpots). But they were allowed to continue; Rabin and Peres agreed they could always dismiss the talks as unauthorized. Abu Alaa sensed this and repeatedly raised questions about the Israeli academics' authority. Larsen checked with Beilin and reassured Abu Alaa. The Israelis, for their part, were unsure whether Abu Alaa was actually speaking in Arafat's name.

As if to compensate for the radical flexibility that the talks embodied, Rabin cracked down hard on Palestinian terrorism and the Hizbullah in Lebanon, later coining the phrase that he would "fight terrorism as if there was no peace process and pursue the peace process as if there was no terrorism." By the end of 1992 the focus of fundamentalist activity had shifted from the Gaza Strip to the West Bank, where it appeared easier to hide and mount attacks.[30] Following the killing by terrorists of eight Israeli soldiers and policemen during the first two weeks of December 1992, the GSS mounted its largest roundup ever of fundamentalist activists, bagging altogether around 1,600. Of these, 415 Hamas and Islamic Jihad members were singled out for expulsion to Lebanon, which Rabin ordered on December 17. The Lebanese government refused to let them in, and they were left stranded—and much televised—for a year in tents on a bleak hill between Israel's Security Zone and southern Lebanon. Arafat responded by temporarily suspending PLO participation in the Madrid-track talks in Washington (though he did not touch the Oslo back channel). Secretly he may well have been pleased: Israel had, at a stroke, beheaded his chief rival in the territories, the Hamas.

By January 1993, however, the military wings of the Hamas and Islamic Jihad were back in business. In March 1993 the Rabin government responded to a new wave of terrorism, mostly by individual knife-wielders in Jerusalem and Tel Aviv, by sealing off the territories. The closure disrupted terrorist activities, but it left tens of thousands of Palestinian laborers, who depended for their livelihood on work in Israel, unemployed. It effectively resurrected the 1967 borders and underlined Labor's desire to separate Israelis from Palestinians as the best means of assuring the personal security of the Israelis. The settlers and the annexationist Right understood that the result of such measures would be a physical separation of Israel from the territories, facilitating the withdrawal of the IDF and the uprooting of the settlements.

In July 1993 increased attacks on Israeli troops in the Security Zone prompted "Operation Accountability," a massive air and artillery assault against Hizbullah bases in southern Lebanon. Heavy around-the-clock fire, accompanied by warnings delivered by radio, loudspeakers, and air-dropped leaflets, was first directed at the outskirts of the villages and then, once the inhabitants departed, at the villages themselves, many of which were partially demolished. Between July 25 and 31 nearly 300,000 villagers, most of them Shi'ites, fled northward. The IDF plan was that this human floodtide would force the Lebanese government to ask Damascus to rein in the Hizbullah.

The result was only partially successful. The Hizbullah had prepared well, with a profusion of hidden rocket stockpiles, bunkers, and firing positions. On July 25, they fired off about one hundred Katyushas, killing two civilians and injuring fifteen in the town of Kiryat Shmonah in the Galilee Panhandle.[31] Thereafter, though the IAF interdicted many crews, the Shi'ites continued, albeit at a reduced rate, to pepper northern Israel and the Security Zone with shells and rockets, as if to say: *You may have overwhelmingly superior firepower but we have the will and expertise to continue to harass you. You cannot silence us.* The Hizbullah fire resulted in the flight of most of Israel's northern border population. Kiryat Shmonah and Nahariya turned overnight into something like ghost towns, as did most of the moshavim. The Hizbullah, deploying relatively few and primitive means, had managed to achieve a sort of "balance of terror" with the sophisticated IAF and IDF artillery.

It may have been the implicit threat that the IDF would send in armored columns to root out the guerrillas that finally persuaded Syria (and perhaps Iran as well) to call it quits. Damascus probably feared for its improving ties with America, becoming entangled in another war in Lebanon, and causing irreversible damage to the secret peace talks it was engaged in with Israel. Within days of the start of the IDF offensive, Syria acceded to American mediation. Secretary of State Warren Christopher, shuttling between Damascus and Jerusalem, worked out a cease-fire agreement and the shooting stopped on July 31. The unwritten, unsigned accord between Israel, Lebanon, and Syria, as brokered by Washington, stated that the Hizbullah would not shell or rocket Israel so long as the IDF refrained from shelling Lebanese villages. It did not bar Hizbullah attacks on the IDF and SLA in the Security Zone.

On the face of it, the guerrillas had won a major victory. But Rabin had also demonstrated that Israel had red lines, and the Syrians, in recognizing this, had been forced to agree to a cease-fire. Moreover, Rabin's strategy had also been directed at domestic opinion—and he had demonstrated once again that he would brook no nonsense when it came to security matters, an image that was to enhance his ability to pursue peace.[32]

Over months of negotiation Hirschfeld, Pundak, and Abu Alaa slowly worked out a document, with Jerusalem and PLO-Tunis also exchanging ideas indirectly through the Egyptian government. In April 1993 Peres conveyed Israel's readiness to add Jericho and its environs to the "Gaza first" proposal, to make it more palatable. The PLO would get not merely the slums of Gaza but also a foothold in the West Bank, reassurance that Israel intended to continue the withdrawal from that territory as well.[33]

By early May the main lines of agreement seem to have jelled. Indeed, a draft DOP had been ready as early as March, but Abu Alaa had demanded that Israel match his "ministerial" rank with senior officials of its own.[34]

Rabin and Peres agreed, though Rabin vetoed the proposal that Peres himself lead the Israeli delegation. Instead, Uri Savir, the new director general of the Foreign Ministry (and Peres's longtime aide), was appointed, and Yoel Singer, a former IDF attorney, was sent in to assist him. At last the Oslo talks had become official—and had now substantively replaced the open, official Washington channel, which had gone nowhere. Both the Palestinian and Israeli delegations in Washington, while continuing their sparring, were left uninformed of the existence and content of Oslo.[35] Indeed, the Oslo talks, quite miraculously, were to remain completely secret despite an early leak, in May, in the Lebanese daily *An Nahar*, and another in mid-July in the Israeli daily *HaAretz*, which ran a front-page banner headline: JERUSALEM CONDUCTING

SECRET NEGOTIATIONS WITH PLO.[36] Bare-faced government denials and the outbreak along the Israeli-Lebanese border managed to stifle any real follow-up, and the subject dropped from public view until the announcement in September that the talks had been successfully concluded.

The handful of people in the know kept the talks tightly under wraps; only a few generals and intelligence chiefs were told anything. Peres and Beilin were always optimistic about the eventual outcome; Rabin was ambivalent. Peres described him: "Rabin, by disposition always cautious, moved slowly and warily. He was skeptical about the Oslo talks . . . sometimes he wholly disbelieved in them. . . . Nonetheless, he gave me, and the talks, a chance. And ultimately, when the final goal became attainable, he did not draw back."[37]

Savir and Abu Alaa met for their first round of negotiations during the weekend of May 21–23. Abu Alaa above all sought assurance that following the interim autonomy stage a Palestinian state would eventually emerge; Savir, that Palestinian autonomy and whatever followed would be consistent with Israel's security. Both sides were sufficiently satisfied to continue talking. During two further weekends in June they argued over words, paragraphs, and clauses.[38]

During July and August both sides, but especially the Palestinians, tried to gain advantages by reformulating clauses or adding new ones to those that had already been agreed upon.[39] The Palestinians insisted that the PLO be given authority not just over Jericho and the Gaza Strip but over the bridges across the Jordan and the Rafa crossing point between the Gaza Strip and Egypt— effectively, control over entry and exit from the Strip and West Bank. They also demanded extraterritorial road and air corridors between the Strip and Jericho. The Israelis tried to whittle down their initial commitments regarding troop withdrawals. The Norwegians played an important role in mediating, bridging, and smoothing ruffled feathers.[40]

In mid-July the Israelis pulled out a trump card: agreement, on certain conditions, to a long-standing PLO demand for mutual recognition. An indirect exchange of letters—Rabin to Arafat, July 19, and Arafat to Rabin, August 4—also helped break the impasse and clarify a number of issues. The main subject was the nature of Israeli and Palestinian jurisdiction in and authority over Gaza-Jericho and other West Bank areas. Arafat expressed willingness to exclude Jerusalem from the Palestinian self-rule area in the interim settlement—but linked this concession to Israeli agreement on mutual recognition.

Israel's inflexibility on certain political and security issues (Jerusalem, settlements, border crossings) was in part dictated by Rabin's fear of adverse public opinion and by the narrowness of his Knesset majority. The indictment on corruption charges of Arye Deri, leader of the ultra-Orthodox Sephardi Shas Party, one of Rabin's coalition partners, apparently pushed him to speed up the Oslo process. (In March–April 1999, Deri was convicted and sentenced to four years imprisonment.) The fear was that Shas would withdraw its support for the coalition, perhaps leading to an early collapse of the government. As Peres put it: "We must hurry, or we may end up with a peace treaty but no government to sign it."[41]

The finale was reached and last-minute compromises were engineered from Stockholm by Norwegian Foreign Minister Johan Jorgen Holst, in nine telephone conversations (lasting a total of seven hours) with Arafat, Abbas, and Abu Alaa in Tunis during the night of August 18. Peres and his aides were by Holst's side throughout. Rabin, in Tel Aviv, was apparently also consulted.[42] The following day Peres flew to Oslo—ostensibly for another reason altogether—and on August 20 attended the secret ceremony at which the DOP was initialed, with Holst signing as witness.

The Israeli and Palestinian representatives then began to negotiate the instrument of mutual recognition.[43] Peres and Holst flew to an air base near Santa Barbara, California, to brief Christopher and request that the signing ceremony take place with due fanfare in Washington. Israel wanted American backing for the agreement, as well as help in persuading Arab countries to establish diplomatic ties with Israel.[44] This would make it easier for the government to sell the accord to the Israeli public. Back in Israel the news began to leak to the press. On August 30 the agreement was submitted to the cabinet, which, overriding objections by Gen. Barak, chief of the general staff, voted overwhelmingly in favor, with only two ministers abstaining. Rabin also enjoyed wide public support.

For Arafat matters were more complicated. Many Palestinians regarded the agreement as a sellout: East Jerusalem remained firmly in Israeli hands, to be discussed only in the final status negotiations; no settlements were to be uprooted; and the IDF meanwhile was to retain overall control over most of the West Bank and Gaza Strip, including the borders with Jordan and Egypt. All of Arafat's political skills were needed to overcome the opposition, both from within Fatah's ranks and from Islamic and secular rejectionists; the PLO's "foreign minister," Farouk Kaddumi, was among the opponents.[45] Back in Oslo, Holst played a key bridging role in formulating the wording of the mutual recognition accord. The prolonged wrangling ended in Paris on September 4, when Abu Alaa and Savir reached agreement.

The mutual recognition was effected in letters delivered by Holst himself. In his, dated September 9, 1993, Arafat stated that the PLO "recognize[s] the right of the State of Israel to exist in peace and security," "accepts UN Security Council Resolutions 242 and 338," commits itself to the peace process and "to a peaceful resolution of the conflict," "renounces the use of terrorism and other acts of violence," would try to prevent all "PLO elements" from resorting to violence (an implicit affirmation of an end to the Intifada, which the PLO refused to make explicit), affirms that the articles in the Palestinian Covenant that deny Israel's right to exist "are now inoperative and no longer valid," and "undertakes to submit to the Palestinian National Council . . . the necessary changes in regard to the Palestinian Covenant." In his brief response, dated September 10, Rabin stated that "the Government of Israel has decided to recognize the PLO as the representative of the Palestinian people" and to negotiate peace with it.

On September 13, at President Clinton's invitation, Peres and Abbas formally signed the DOP on the White House lawn, with Rabin and Arafat and hundreds of American, Palestinian, and Israeli dignitaries in attendance.[46] Clinton signed as witness. Hirschfeld and Pundak, whom Rabin and Peres had forgotten to invite, came on their own steam and wangled invitations from White House officials.[47] Rabin's body language clearly displayed his distaste for Arafat; Arafat's, his desire for sympathy from the Americans (and perhaps the Israelis as well). Arafat expressed the hope that the DOP would "usher in an age of peace, coexistence, and equal rights" but stressed that "more courage and determination" would be needed to continue the process and reach a just and comprehensive peace. "Putting an end to [the Palestinians'] feelings of being wronged and of having suffered an historic injustice is the strongest guarantee to achieving coexistence and openness between our two peoples," he said.

Rabin injected a somber note:

> We have come from an anguished and grieving land. . . . We have come to try to put an end to the hostilities so that our children, and our children's children, will no longer experience the painful cost of war, violence and terror. Let me say to you, the Palestinians, we are destined to live together on the same soil in the same land . . . we say to you today . . . enough of blood and tears. Enough! We have no desire for revenge. We harbor no hatred toward you.

Nearly two-thirds of Israelis polled supported the agreement. Among Palestinians in the West Bank and Gaza, the figure was similar. But a large minority of those Palestinians who opposed the accord, led by the Hamas and Islamic Jihad, immediately mounted a vigorous campaign to derail the peace process. Terrorist attacks, it was reasoned, would build up right-wing pressure within Israel against the agreement, curtailing Rabin's room for maneuver and flexibility. With the Israelis balking and uncompromising, Arafat would find it difficult to continue with the process.

On September 12, the day before the DOP was signed, 'Izz a Din al-Qassam gunmen ambushed and killed three Israeli soldiers east of Gaza. The day after the signing, a nineteen-year-old Hamas supporter blew himself up in the Israeli police post inside Gaza's Shati refugee camp, but no one else was hurt. Between October 24 and December 25, twelve Israeli soldiers and settlers were killed in a series of terrorist attacks.

The Hamas forbade its men to clash with the PLO. Arafat—also eager to avoid a civil war—refrained from attempting to restrain the fundamentalists' violence against the peace process. (Indeed, Arafat at this time repeatedly called on Rabin to free imprisoned Hamas leader Sheikh Yassin.) The attacks, as Arafat appreciated, constituted pressure on Israel to hasten its withdrawal—while the PLO could devote itself to diplomacy and claim it had abandoned terrorism.

The DOP outlined the framework for future Israeli-Palestinian negotiations and the main interim self-government arrangements for the West Bank and Gaza Strip: The preamble declared that the government of Israel and the PLO had agreed "that it is time to put an end to decades of confrontation and conflict, recognize their mutual legitimate and political rights, and strive to live in peaceful coexistence and mutual dignity and security and achieve a just, lasting and comprehensive peace settlement and historic reconciliation."

The two sides agreed to negotiate the establishment of "a Palestinian Interim Self-Government Authority" in the West Bank and Gaza Strip for "a transitional period" not exceeding five years. This would then lead to a "permanent settlement" based on Resolutions 242 and 338. The DOP provided for free and democratic general elections in the territories, with the Palestinian inhabitants of Jerusalem participating, to elect a council that would be the "Palestinian Authority" (PA) in the territories during the five-year period.

Negotiations between Israel and the Palestinians regarding the final settlement or "permanent status"—involving, among other things, "Jerusalem, refugees, settlements, security arrangements, borders, relations and cooperation with other neighbors"—would begin no later than three years after the start of the interim period.

During the initial period of the interim years, there would be a gradual transfer of "authority"—over "education and culture, health, social welfare, direct taxation, and tourism"—from the Israeli military and civilian authorities to the Palestinians. Moreover, the PA would begin to build a "strong police force" to "guarantee public order and internal security," while Israel would continue to be responsible for "defending against external threats" and for the security of Israelis in the territories.

The DOP stipulated that the parties would, by December 13, "conclude and sign" an agreement on Israeli military withdrawal from the Gaza Strip and Jericho area. The withdrawal would then begin, to be completed within four months. Thereafter the Palestinians would have full control of these areas, save in the fields of "external security, settlements, Israelis, and foreign relations." Responsibility for internal security and public order would be assumed by "the Palestinian police force," which would consist of PLO forces from abroad as well as local recruits. Safe passage between the two areas would be assured.

Agreement on the details of the implementation of "Gaza-Jericho" took not two months but seven. The negotiators found themselves bogged down in items and issues no one had anticipated. The terrorist strikes that punctuated the talks resulted in repeated delays and halts. The bloodiest, and perhaps most threatening, incident was the February 25, 1994, massacre of twenty-nine Muslim worshippers at morning prayer, and the wounding of dozens more, inside Hebron's Ibrahimiya Mosque (the Tomb of the Patriarchs) by Baruch Goldstein, a Jewish settler doctor, who was beaten to death by the survivors. In the riots that followed, IDF troops shot dead about thirty Arabs and injured hundreds. The West Bank and Gaza were in ferment for weeks, curfews were imposed, and the talks were suspended for a month. Goldstein had set out to avenge the victims of Arab terrorism—but probably also to undermine the peace process, which he, along with most of the settlers, feared would result in Israeli withdrawal from the territories. Goldstein was crowned a posthumous hero and martyr by the extreme Right, his grave outside Hebron becoming a place of pilgrimage for Jewish opponents of the peace process.

The "Agreement on the Gaza Strip and the Jericho Area" (usually referred to as "the Cairo agreement") was finally signed in the Egyptian capital by Rabin and Arafat, with American, Soviet, and Egyptian representatives as witnesses, on May 4, 1994. Arafat at first refused to sign the appended maps (he thought the Jericho area allotted to the PA was too small) but eventually was persuaded by his aides and the Americans and Russians. He remained unhappy with the Palestinian concessions and on May 11 called (in a mosque in Johannesburg, South Africa) for a jihad to recover Jerusalem, comparing the accords he had signed to Muhammad's agreement of A.D. 628 with the Jewish Qurayish tribe, which had been a tactical move and which was unilaterally abrogated by the Muslims ten years later.[48] Israeli opponents of Oslo argued that Arafat was, in effect, saying he would go back on the agreements the moment it suited him. However, Rabin and Peres, also unhappy, argued that what counted were Arafat's deeds, not his words.

The agreement effectively transferred control over the bulk of the Gaza Strip and a sixty-five-square-kilometer area encompassing Jericho and its environs to PA control, with Israel remaining in control of the borders between these now-autonomous areas and the outside world and of the Jewish settlements in the Strip. Israel was to have responsibility for the roads leading from these settlements to Israel, and joint Israeli-Palestinian teams were to patrol them. Israel was to assure safe passage for Palestinians between the Strip and the Jericho area. The Palestinian police force was to be under the control of the twenty-four-member PA, and to consist of nine thousand men, of whom seven thousand could come from abroad. They were to be equipped only with light personal weapons, 120 medium and heavy machine guns, and forty-five wheeled armored vehicles. The force was to be responsible for preventing terrorism against Israelis from within the PA areas. The sea off the Gaza Strip was to remain under Israeli control, but the Palestinians were allowed up to eight coastal police vessels. The PA was allowed to operate two helicopters and four fixed-wing transport aircraft between Gaza and Jericho, all subject to Israeli air traffic control and security provisions.

Israel promised to release, within five weeks, about five thousand Palestinian prisoners not involved in fatal acts of terrorism. Prisoners who belonged to groups that opposed the peace process, such as the Hamas and Islamic Jihad, would not be included. The PA undertook not to "prosecute . . . or harm" Palestinians who had collaborated with Israel. Israel retained jurisdiction over offenses committed in the settlements and IDF installations, and by Israelis in the territories. Additional provisions dealt with economic relations, including import-export regulations, tourism, taxation, and monetary policy.[49]

The IDF withdrew from Jericho on May 13 and from most of the Gaza Strip on May 18–19, 1994,[50] and PA police and officials immediately took control. During the first few days there was a spate of attacks on Israeli troops and civilians in and near the Strip. Arafat himself arrived in Gaza to a tumultuous, chaotic welcome on July 1.[51] An exile for almost all his life, he was treading Palestinian soil for the first time since 1967. Much of the PLO-Tunis bureaucracy and thousands of PLO troops—now designated "police"—came with him, and Gaza city was transformed into the PA's capital. The self-government apparatus, including a number of security forces—Arafat was later to be charged with instituting a highly authoritarian, occasionally brutal, corrupt regime, worse, in some respects, than the Israeli occupation it replaced—was mainly manned by people from the "exterior," though PLO activists from the territories were inducted as well.

The PLO, impoverished by the Gulf War, was hamstrung when it arrived in the area. Immediately after the signing of the DOP, thirty-five countries pledged a total of $3.2 billion to set the self-rule areas on their feet, but only a small fraction of this money materialized during the following years. Many donors feared that lack of adequate oversight meant that the funds might not be used for their designated purposes; the chief anxiety concerned PLO corruption. From the start the PA was thus short of cash to pay wages and running costs, and to develop infrastructure. Within weeks Arabs who had welcomed the liberation became disenchanted; peace with Israel and freedom were not leading to instant prosperity. Security problems, by way of Israeli closures of the territories, triggered by terrorist attacks, added to their economic woes. Arafat found his popularity dwindling as support for his fundamentalist rivals grew.

As to security, both the Palestinians and Israel were caught up in a dilemma. The DOP had effectively made Arafat responsible for stopping anti-Israeli terrorism from his areas. But clamping down on the Hamas and Islamic Jihad meant that he would be arresting and torturing those who carried the torch of liberation. "Protecting" the Israelis would alienate a growing number of his own people, especially as, during 1994–96, Israel acted against the militants with mass arrests, curfews, and closure orders. Laborers were prevented from commuting to work in Israel and, sometimes, between Palestinian-populated areas. Palestinians began to question the peace agreement: They had received small slivers of territory, most of them overcrowded and poor, and had committed themselves to reining in their own "freedom fighters." Where were the promised economic benefits and the Palestinian "state" the PLO and Intifada activists had fought for?

As Arafat lost more and more of his support base, he grew less able to grant concessions to Israel, making it that much more difficult for Rabin, himself harried by fundamentalist terrorism and the Israeli Right, to proceed with the process and give the PA more territory and authority—with which Arafat could appease his critics. Rabin understood that only giving the Palestinians more, and quickly, would reduce the number of terrorists, by reducing the motivation to join them.

Arafat's solution, until March 1996, was to go through the motions of curtailing terrorism while allowing the Hamas and Islamic Jihad to mount occasional, dramatic attacks. His security forces would then arrest the foot soldiers—but would generally release them after the spotlight had been turned off. The fundamentalists' infrastructure and leadership were by and large left untouched. Arafat hoped thus to appease Rabin and Israeli public opinion without alienating the Palestinian masses or risking a civil war with the fundamentalists, who were particularly strong in the Gaza Strip. In any case, the occasional jolt to Israel may have satisfied his deep antipathy to the state and people that had humiliated him for decades, and conformed with his understanding of how one could extract concessions.

The 1994–96 period was the heyday of the suicide bombers. Their masters favored Israeli cities on Fridays and Sundays, when IDF soldiers were on their way home for weekend leave or heading back to their bases. (The Islamic Jihad, at this time, as a matter of policy, targeted soldiers; the Hamas generally did not distinguish between soldiers and civilians.) On April 6, 1994, a Hamas terrorist set off a car bomb next to a bus in downtown Afula, in the Jezreel Valley, killing eight (including himself) and wounding forty-three. A Hamas announcement said the bombing was in revenge for the Hebron massacre forty days before.[52] A smaller bomb, again carried by a Hamas suicide, blew up at the entrance to a bus in Hadera's central station a week later, killing five and wounding thirty-two.[53] Israeli closure orders, curfews, and roundups then stymied a number of operations. But six months later, the Hamas struck again. On October 9, two terrorists opened fire on a string of restaurants in Jerusalem, killing one Israeli and wounding twenty before being shot down.[54] The same day a Hamas squad kidnapped an Israeli soldier and held him hostage, demanding the release of Sheikh Yassin and two hundred other fundamentalist prisoners. Israeli intelligence eventually located the hideout, in Bir Naballah, a small village near Ramallah, and on October 14 commandos burst into the house in a rescue attempt. In the gunfire the hostage, his three captors, and one of the raiding party died and ten soldiers were wounded.[55]

On October 19 another Hamas suicide boarded a bus in downtown Tel Aviv's Dizengoff Street and blew himself up, killing twenty-one and wounding forty-three.[56] The shock to Israel was tremendous. Right-wing crowds gathered on street corners and berated the government as "responsible" and Rabin and Peres as "traitors." But the worst—or, from the terrorists' point of view, the most successful—was the attack by two Islamic Jihad suicide bombers, dressed as IDF soldiers, on January 22, 1995, at a refreshment stand crowded with soldiers at the Beit Lid junction, east of Netanya: Twenty-two soldiers, most of them paratroops from a nearby camp, died, and dozens more were injured.[57] Half a year later there were two more Hamas suicide bus bombings—on July 24, 1995, in downtown Ramat Gan, killing five and injuring thirty,[58] and on August 21, when four died and one hundred or so were injured in Jerusalem's Ramat Eshkol neighborhood.[59] Again there were right-wing demonstrations around the country, directed against "Rabin the traitor."

The Oslo process, and the handover of territory to the Palestinians, had led to a major increase in the dimensions and frequency of terrorism, with the focus shifting from the territories to targets inside Israel. For the Hamas and Islamic Jihad, the Gaza Strip and Jericho now served as relatively secure bases. In the eyes of many Israelis, Rabin and Peres had failed to deliver on their promise that peace would halt, or curtail, terrorism. Their response, that it would be a drawn-out affair, with ups and downs, with terrorism vanishing or being substantially reduced only in the long haul, was not completely persuasive or comforting.

Arafat's unwillingness or inability to control the terrorism, in part emanating from his self-rule enclaves, clearly contravened the letter and spirit of the agreements. But Israel too violated a number of important provisions and certainly acted in a manner contrary to the spirit of the accord. It continued to expand settlements and increased construction in and around East Jerusalem in an effort to establish facts on the ground in advance of the permanent status negotiations, in which Jerusalem was expected to figure large. Israel also failed to activate the "safe" corridors between the Strip and West Bank and failed to free all the prisoners it had agreed to release. Moreover, it repeatedly halted, in response to terrorist attacks, the talks on the further withdrawals from the West Bank cities, to which it was committed.

Nevertheless, the talks progressed, eventuating on September 28, 1995, in the main interim agreement that came to be known as Oslo II (the DOP and the exchange of letters of recognition had been Oslo I), signed in Washington by Rabin, Peres, and Arafat. Entitled the "Israeli-Palestinian Interim Agreement on the West Bank and Gaza Strip," it provided for elections in the territories of an eighty-two-man "Council" and a "Ra'is" (or head) of an "Executive

Authority" to take place twenty-two days after the IDF redeployment out of the populated centers of the West Bank. Special arrangements would obtain in Hebron, including IDF withdrawal from most of the city, to take place by March 28, 1996. Israel would retain control of the Jewish suburb of Kiryat Arba, and of the Tomb of the Patriarchs, the adjacent downtown Jewish Quarter, and the "Old City" area. Up to four hundred Palestinian policemen, with one hundred rifles and two hundred pistols, would move into the city.

The PA would take control of the evacuated West Bank areas, bringing in contingents of "police"—whose total should not exceed twelve thousand in the West Bank and eighteen thousand in the Strip. The force would have a total of fifteen thousand light weapons (rifles and pistols), 240 machine guns, forty-five wheeled armored vehicles, and fifteen light unarmed vehicles. The Israelis and the Palestinian police would conduct joint patrols along specified routes in the West Bank and the Strip.

Further IDF redeployments out of the Arab-populated rural areas of the West Bank were to take place gradually, at six-month intervals, within eighteen months of the inauguration of the council. Eventually, Israeli troops would remain only in Jewish settlements and in designated military installations—whose fate would be determined in the permanent status negotiations. Israel guaranteed safe passage to vehicles and passengers traveling between the Gaza Strip and West Bank along a number of designated routes.

Israel would retain responsibility for security along the West Bank's and Gaza Strip's borders and for Israelis and Israeli settlements in the territories. The West Bank was divided into three types of areas: In "Area A," comprising the evacuated cities, the council (or PA) would be responsible for security and public order. In "Area B," containing most of the Arab towns and villages and some 68 percent of the Palestinian Arab population, the PA would wield full civil authority and would regulate public order, but Israel would have ultimate authority over security. In effect, the area would be jointly controlled by Israeli and Palestinian armed forces. In "Area C," covering the largely unpopulated state lands in the West Bank and the Israeli settlements and military camps, Israel would retain responsibility for security and public order, but the PA would have responsibility for the civil services (health, education, and the like) for the Arabs.

The agreement called for a number of Israeli "confidence-building measures," including the release, in three stages, of all Palestinian detainees and prisoners except those involving security offenses that had resulted in "fatality or serious injury." Arab collaborators were not to be subjected to "acts of harassment, violence, retribution or prosecution" by the PA. The PA reaffirmed its commitments to make "the necessary changes" in the Palestinian Covenant and to act against terrorism and terrorists within its area of governance. Last, the agreement stipulated that Israel and the Palestinians would begin negotiating "the permanent status" of the territories—meaning such

issues as "Jerusalem, settlements, specified military locations, Palestinian refugees, borders, [and] foreign relations"—no later than May 4, 1996, which
would lead to the implementation of Resolutions 242 and 338. The implication was that there would be a further, final exchange of "territory for peace."

As to the crucial issue of "Water and Sewage," the two sides agreed that
"Israel recognizes the Palestinian water rights in the West Bank, [but these
will] be negotiated in the permanent status negotiations." For the time being,
Israel agreed to increase the amount of water allocated to the Palestinians, and
the Palestinians agreed to do nothing to imperil the West Bank's and Gaza's
water resources, from which Israel also drew (and draws) much of its supplies.[60]

During November and December 1995, the IDF withdrew from the West
Bank's main towns (apart from Hebron)—Jenin, Qalqilya, Tulkarm, Nablus,
Ramallah–El Bireh, and Bethlehem—and the PA police moved in. Apart from
jeering and the ritual burning of Israeli flags, the transfers of power were
uneventful. On January 20, 1996, the Palestinians voted, and Arafat was overwhelmingly elected Ra'is; his supporters, most of them mainstream Fatah,
won most of the council seats.

Because of another wave of suicide bombings (in February–March) in Jerusalem and Tel Aviv, the Israeli government announced a postponement of the
redeployment in Hebron, which had been scheduled for the end of March. On
April 24, the PNC, meeting in Gaza, voted 504 to 54 (with 214 abstentions) to
amend the covenant to remove those articles calling for the elimination of
Israel.[61] Subsequently, on May 3, 1996, Prime Minister Peres announced that
his government was committed to the Hebron redeployment, which would
take place after the Israeli general elections newly scheduled for May 29.

THE ISRAELI-JORDANIAN PEACE TREATY

The conclusion of the DOP made possible the signing of an Israeli-Jordanian
peace treaty in October 1994. If the Palestinians—Israel's chief victims and
historic enemies—could make peace, King Hussein felt free to do what he
(and his grandfather Abdullah) had wanted to do for decades. The Yishuv, and
then Israel, had a historic rapport with Jordan and its Hashemite rulers, based
on a common anti-Palestinian outlook, pro-Western orientation, the pragmatism and affability of King Abdullah and his grandson Hussein, and a tradition
of clandestine cooperation on the local, practical level in various economic
enterprises, such as the Dead Sea chemical works and agriculture in the Jordan Rift. Over the decades a degree of mutual trust and respect had developed,

and both Abdullah and Hussein saw Israel as a counterweight to—and, *in extremis*, potential ally against—their rapacious neighbors Syria, Saudi Arabia, and Iraq, and the subversive Palestinians.

Since the late 1960s Israel's leaders had periodically met with Hussein and discussed peace, but to no avail.[62] Throughout, the main stumbling block had been the future of the West Bank. Initially Hussein wanted it back; Israel had refused. From the mid-1970s on, as Jordan gradually ceded its proprietary rights to the PLO, the negotiation became more complex, with the Palestinians again constituting the third side of the triangle. From 1977 until 1992, when the Likud either governed Israel or had the last say on major policy issues in the National Unity governments, the possibility of an Israeli-Jordanian deal remained remote. The Likud was ideologically opposed to cession, to any Arab party, of any part of the West Bank. Indeed, the Revisionist wing of Zionism traditionally also regarded the East Bank as an essential part of the Jewish people's domain. During the 1970s and 1980s, senior Likud politicians—such as Ariel Sharon—barely veiled their view that Israel should help topple the Hashemites and transform the East Bank into a Palestinian state (thus relieving the pressure on Israel to cede the West Bank to the Palestinians). Labor leader and Foreign Minister Shimon Peres made, or seemed to make, progress in his talks with King Hussein, as in 1987, when the two concluded a draft agreement about the initiation of formal Israeli-Jordanian negotiations—only to be stymied at the last moment by Prime Minister Shamir.

In January 1991, days before the start of Desert Storm, Shamir and Hussein met in secret in London and apparently agreed on a set of rules of mutual nonbelligerency in the upcoming conflict, in which Hussein was officially backing Iraq (out of fear of what Saddam might do to Jordan if he didn't) and Israel supported the Allied coalition.

Following the Madrid Conference, Israeli and Jordanian negotiators regularly met in two sets of bilateral talks, mainly in Washington and Amman. The two sets ran parallel, those in Washington being official and formal, and the other, secret track involving for the most part Efraim Halevy, the deputy director of the Mossad, and King Hussein and his aides.[63] Substantial progress was made on the basic issues of borders, and war and peace, and by October 1992 agreement had been reached on an "agenda," in which both "the subjects of disagreement were defined and main parameters for a solution" were determined.[64] The signing of the Israeli-PLO Declaration of Principles had a radical and immediate catalytic effect on the negotiations. What previously had been agreed was formalized on September 14, 1993, the day after the signing of the DOP, in "the Israeli-Jordanian Common Agenda."[65]

At the same time the announcement of the DOP came as a shock to the Jordanians, who had believed, since Madrid began, that the Israeli leaders had a Jordanian orientation. Their sudden rapprochement with the PLO seemed to signal a directional change and a drawing together of Israelis and Palestinians, perhaps at Jordan's expense. The talks briefly went into deep freeze. Jordanian fundamentalist Muslim opposition to the process probably contributed to this. But by winter the ice began to thaw. On November 2 Foreign Minister Peres secretly traveled to Amman and was apparently assured by Hussein that Jordan would soon sign a peace agreement. But then Hussein drew back—perhaps because of Peres's subsequent well-publicized hint of what had taken place—and nothing came of the meeting.[66]

But Hussein gradually ripened for agreement. In his late fifties and in ill health (in 1994 he underwent a cancer operation), he may well have felt that it was time to complete what his grandfather had initiated more than four decades before, and for which he had paid with his life at the gates of al-Aqsa Mosque (with Hussein, then a child, looking on). In addition Jordan was feeling the pinch of political and financial isolation by the oil-rich Arabian Peninsula states and the United States, still angry over Hussein's support for Iraq during the Gulf War. Nothing would curry favor with the Americans better than a return to the peace process. The final precipitant may have been the May 1994 Israeli-PLO economic agreement, which Jordan felt threatened its own economic ties with the West Bank.[67]

On May 19 Hussein secretly met Rabin in London, and in June the talks were back on track. During a visit to Washington, Hussein was promised by Clinton that if he took the plunge, the president would move to waive Jordan's $700 million debt to the United States and approve arms and agricultural equipment sales. Despite a lingering fear of Syria's possible reaction, Hussein met Rabin publicly for the first time on July 25. The result was "the Washington Declaration," announcing the end to the state of "belligerency" between their countries, the opening of the border to third-country passport holders, and the establishment of telephone links. The evidence of real warmth between the two leaders, in smiles, body language, and handshakes, was unmistakable. To the PLO's ire, Israel recognized Jordan's "special role" vis-à-vis the Muslim holy sites in Jerusalem (Hussein's grandfather Abdullah and great-grandfather Hussein, the sharif of Mecca, were both buried in the Haram ash-Sharif).

By the end of September a draft was ready; and on October 26, 1994, the Israeli-Jordanian "Treaty of Peace" was signed in a tent in the Arava by Premier 'Abd al-Salam al-Majali and Prime Minister Rabin, witnessed by King Hussein, President Clinton, and Russian Foreign Minister Andrei Kozyrov. The document was far warmer in tone than the 1979 Israel-Egypt treaty. Each country recognized the other's right "to live in peace within secure and recognized boundaries." Each was prohibited from "joining or in any way assisting . . . or cooperating with any coalition, organization or alliance" with the aim of launching acts of hostility against the other or allowing into its territory the military forces of a third country intent on harming the other. There was agreement on full diplomatic, economic, and cultural relations. Israel ceded about three hundred square kilometers in the Arava, areas taken over from Jordan in the 1960s and 1970s, and agreed to allow Jordan to extract, from the area's northern water resources, fifty million cubic meters of water annually in addition to the amount taken in previous years. Jordan, in return, agreed to Israel receiving an additional sixteen-to-twenty million cubic meters of water in the Arava.[68]

ISRAEL AND SYRIA

Following the Madrid Conference of 1991, Israeli and Syrian representatives periodically met in Washington, but to no effect. The change of government in Jerusalem radically invigorated the process, and serious bilateral negotiations, with Washington mediating, began in August 1992. In August 1993 a major breakthrough was achieved when Rabin gave Secretary of State Christopher his "hypothetical" agreement to Israeli withdrawal from the whole of the Golan Heights, should Syria reciprocate with adequate security arrangements and normalization-of-relations measures.[69] However, the Syrians failed to respond with similar largesse, and the meetings were suspended in February 1994, after the Hebron massacre. They were renewed in the summer, with the Israeli and Syrian ambassadors to Washington—respectively Itamar Rabinovich and Walid al-Moualem—leading the delegations. The issues remained the same: the extent and schedule of Israeli withdrawal from the Golan Heights; security arrangements on either side of the new frontier; measures to normalize relations between the two countries in matters such as embassies, trade ties, and air traffic routes.

Rabin held off from issuing a clear public commitment to withdraw from the whole of the Golan but hinted that the "depth" of Israel's withdrawal would be commensurate with the "depth" of the normalization measures to which Syria acceded. President Assad, for his part, declared that Syria had opted to pursue peace as a "strategic choice." But he refused to commit himself to the nature of the normalization and security arrangements so long as Rabin refused to agree publicly to a full withdrawal.

In December 1994 the army chiefs of staff, Hikmat Shihabi for Syria and Ehud Barak for Israel, met in Washington to discuss security measures. Israel wanted Syria to agree to a substantial reduction of its army, especially in armor, and to the removal eastward, away from the border, of key armored units; and to negotiate early warning arrangements, including manned stations on the Golan or Mount Hermon and a deep demilitarized zone on the Syrian side of the border. An American military presence in a buffer zone may also have been discussed. Israel agreed to a small DMZ or limited-forces zone on its side of the border.

Syria demanded "symmetry": Any cutback in its armed forces would have to be matched by a commensurate Israeli reduction in its air power and nuclear weaponry. Shihabi argued throughout that Israel was far stronger than Syria or any likely combination of Arab armies. He refused a foreign early-warning station on Syrian territory—even though Israel offered Syria a station inside Israel, near Safad.

With American officials mediating, Israel's new chief of staff, Gen. Amnon Lipkin-Shahak, and Shihabi met in March 1995. The Syrians eventually agreed to the principle of "asymmetrical" security arrangements, such as a deeper Syrian army pullback from the future border than the IDF's. Israel continued to hint at withdrawal back to the old international (Mandatory Palestine-Syria) frontier. But Syria demanded that Israel agree to withdraw back to the "June 4, 1967, border"—which meant ceding to Syria several small additional areas, such as the northeastern shore of the Sea of Galilee and al-Hama—which otherwise would have been left inside Israel. It is not completely clear whether, by the time Rabin was assassinated on November 4, 1995, Israel had agreed "hypothetically" or otherwise to the June 4, 1967, line, though it appears that he had conveyed such a readiness to the Clinton administration, and that Christopher—perhaps not in accordance with Rabin's wishes—had conveyed as much to Assad. According to the Syrians full agreement was reached between the two sides on this point in July 1994, and Peres, who succeeded Rabin as prime minister, reiterated this commitment after the assassination.[70]

After a brief suspension following the assassination of Rabin, the talks were resumed in December 1995. Peres initially hoped that they could be successfully concluded by the scheduled October 1996 general elections. He would then come to the electorate with a peace treaty with Syria (and possibly Lebanon) in his pocket and be swept back to power. But Assad declined to be rushed, and an exasperated Peres in late January–February 1996 decided to call early elections. Assad was informed that the talks would be seriously renewed after the elections. Peres had chiefly been affected by Assad's refusal to agree to a meeting with him.[71]

Peres narrowly lost the elections at the end of May. Benjamin Netanyahu's assumption of power augured ill for the peace process with Syria and Lebanon. Before the vote he had declared that Israel must not relinquish the Golan Heights. After being elected he announced that he was interested in negotiating peace with Assad. But the new administration's "Basic Guidelines," published in mid-June, stated that "[T]he Government sees in the Golan Heights an area crucial to the security of the state. . . . The maintenance of Israeli sovereignty over the Golan will constitute a foundation for any settlement with Syria."[72] The Syrians, quite naturally, reacted negatively. They insisted that the talks be resumed where they had left off, with Rabin's and Peres's agreement to withdraw to the old border and acceptance of the American-drafted paper, "Aims and Principles of Security Arrangements," which Rabin and Assad had endorsed in late May 1995. The paper outlined the guidelines for the prospective symmetrical and asymmetrical security arrangements. Netanyahu declined to endorse these positions, and the talks remained in suspension.

Syria refused to allow Lebanon to negotiate a separate deal for Israeli withdrawal from the Security Zone so long as the IDF was still on the Golan. During 1997–98, with the Hizbullah harassing the IDF in the Zone, several prominent Israelis, including Labor's ex-minister Yossi Beilin, proposed that Israel withdraw unilaterally (but threaten that should the Hizbullah subsequently attack northern Israel, the IDF would be free to retaliate "massively"). The proposal was reinforced by the crash in February 1997 of two IDF helicopters over the Galilee Panhandle on their way to Lebanon, killing seventy-three soldiers. During 1998 the idea of a unilateral Israeli withdrawal was repeatedly floated, especially after incidents involving IDF casualties, but was repeatedly rejected by the cabinet. The consensus remained that Israel could not risk withdrawing from southern Lebanon without prior agreement with Syria—and Syria would not agree unless Israel first agreed to evacuate the Golan.

THE RABIN ASSASSINATION

Following the signing of the DOP and the implementation of "Gaza-Jericho," the Israeli Right demonstrated frequently and raucously against the peace process. Each Islamic terror bomb brought demonstrations against Rabin's concessions. The Muslim enemies of peace nurtured and activated their Israeli twins. Leaflets handed out to the crowds depicted Rabin in Nazi uniform or Arab headgear, or hugging Arafat; his public appearances were greeted with cries of "Traitor, traitor." The rabbinical establishment, almost to a man, either egged on the opponents of the peace process or kept silent. Some rabbis issued rulings supporting the death penalty for those "who persecute Jews" or "hand over" Jewish property or lives to the enemy. The implication vis-à-vis Rabin and Peres was clear.

But it was not only the rabbis. The political leaders of the mainstream Right—Netanyahu and Sharon, Rafael Eitan of Tzomet, Zevulun Hammer of the NRP—often joined in. Netanyahu said on May 4, 1995, the day before "Oslo II" was signed, "In another hour Rabin will be able to announce that in

Cairo [he] established the Palestinian terrorist state." On May 5, Hammer declared: "The terrorist organizations are being given a state on a silver platter, and they are rejoicing over the blood of our sons and daughters." Sharon implicitly compared Rabin to the Nazis: "I never believed a day would come when a Jewish government (Jewish?) in Jerusalem would deal with selecting which Jews would be protected and which, thrown to the dogs." Eitan, months before, had dubbed Rabin's government "the Judenrat." On November 18, 1994, Sharon had spoken in one breath of Rabin and Adolf Eichmann and "the Jews-for-trucks" deal of 1944. And on January 23, 1995, Eitan had said of the government: "Quislings. That's the term that suits them."[73]

It was partly to offset this agitation that Peace Now, the Labor Party, and Meretz organized a pro-peace demonstration on November 4, 1995, in Kings of Israel Square in Tel Aviv. Nearly 100,000 people participated. There was a strong police presence, as there had been warnings of a possible Arab terrorist attack. The rally was a massive show of support for Rabin and Peres—both were on the dais—and for peace.

At the end of the rally, as the demonstrators began to disperse, the VIPs descended to a police-protected parking area. Just as Rabin was entering his car, Yigal Amir, a twenty-seven-year-old law student at Bar-Ilan, Israel's religious university, darted between two GSS bodyguards and fired three shots. Rabin, hit twice in the back, was shoved into the car and driven off at high speed to Ichilov Hospital, where he died a few minutes later.

Amir, apprehended on the spot, told his interrogators that his aim had been to stop the peace process and the cession of parts of the Land of Israel.[74] Born to Yemenite Jewish Orthodox parents and brought up in Orthodox and ultra-Orthodox schools and yeshivas, he had served in the Golani Infantry Brigade, and was a pro-settlement activist. He had repeatedly told friends that he intended to kill the prime minister. Later, under GSS and police interrogation, he compared the Rabin-Peres government to the Nazi regime and to the collaborationist Judenrats. He said he had "acted to save the Jewish people."

Amir was tried for murder and sentenced to life imprisonment. His brother, Haggai, and a close friend, Dror Adani, were subsequently convicted of conspiracy and received lesser terms. A handful of other people connected to Amir—fellow students, settlement activists, and rabbis, including some who had publicly sanctioned the murder of the prime minister—were questioned but never put on trial. The moment Amir's circle was placed under investigation, the Right began to scream "Witch hunt," denying that there had been incitement. Peres and his colleagues, with an election and future coalition-building to think of, and worried about alienating part of the public, allowed the investigation to peter out. Only one of Amir's friends, Margalit Har-Shefi, was eventually tried and convicted for failing to report his plans.

Amir had eliminated Labor's chief electoral asset. Somehow, owing to a gritty, no-nonsense personality and a glorious military record, Yitzhak Rabin had been able, through the thick and thin of the peace process and the attendant terrorism, to retain the trust of most of the public. As would soon become apparent, the floating vote that had gone Rabin's way in 1992 was to be lost by Peres.

Peres's seven months as prime minister, from November 1995 until the end of May 1996, were overshadowed by the looming general elections, the Oslo-sanctioned IDF pullback from the West Bank's main towns, and the Muslim terrorists' campaign to derail the peace process.

Polls taken in early 1996 indicated that Labor would win handily. The withdrawal from the West Bank towns had passed without a hitch, as had the PA elections on January 20, in which Arafat had won 85 percent of the vote and, thus, a firm mandate to continue the peace process.[75] But the surveys failed to take into account two interlocking developments: Labor's poorly run campaign, and an unprecedentedly savage, concentrated Muslim fundamentalist terrorist offensive. Labor failed altogether to utilize the assassination, or the right-wing incitement that had sired it, and failed equally to exploit Netanyahu's lack of experience or his closetful of personal skeletons (a history of philandering and three troubled marriages, and a chronic failure to pay his bills). Peres's aides had decided to run him as an elder statesman above the daily grind and mud-slinging of political rivalry. They would not stoop to blackening the Right and Netanyahu; they would win regardless.

But this strategy did not allow for the fundamentalist offensive of late February–early March, which the Right devastatingly used during the following weeks to smear Peres personally and to undermine the public's confidence in the peace process. The bombings blocked out the image of Rabin's bloodied shirt and the anger that it had engendered. By election day, May 29, most Jewish Israelis remembered only the dozens of bloodied shirts of the bomb victims and linked them to the Oslo agreements that had facilitated the terrorists' campaign and to Peres's smiles and handshakes with Arafat, the ex-terrorist who had failed to rein in (and had perhaps encouraged) the bombers.

There are indications that Iran, which supplied the Hamas and Islamic Jihad with political backing and funds, hoped to see Peres defeated and the Likud return to power as part of its grand design to halt the peace process. When the election results came, there were, reportedly, celebrations in the headquarters of Iran's Revolutionary Guards and foreign intelligence service. It appears that, starting in November 1995, Iranian officials had egged on the Hamas and Islamic Jihad activists to mount a terrorist campaign to unseat Labor.[76] However, it is unclear whether either group was party to this thinking or was persuaded that a Likud victory was what they wanted. The Likud might well decide to cut its own deal with the Arab world (as Begin had done with Egypt). Moreover, a Likud victory would mean a perpetuation of harsh Israeli rule over the still-occupied parts of the West Bank and Gaza Strip. Perhaps it was better to let Arafat negotiate with Labor and get more territory, even a full-fledged Palestinian state, and then launch the crusade to conquer the rest of "Palestine."

Most likely, different fundamentalist leaders had different views, with those inside the territories tending to prefer that Labor win and those outside wanting a Likud victory and an immediate disruption of the peace process. Many probably failed to distinguish between Labor and Likud, viewing both as equally hateful Zionists. But whatever the long-term political calculation, the bombing campaign had a more immediate cause. Both the Islamic Jihad and the Hamas had been badly, some might say provocatively, hit by Israel's security forces, and had vowed revenge. In October 1995 Mossad agents in Malta assassinated Fathi Shkaki, the leader of the Islamic Jihad,[77] and in January 1996, GSS operatives in the Gaza Strip killed Yahya Ayash, Hamas's chief bomb-maker and terrorist mastermind.[78] The Islamic Jihad had been responsible for a series of major bomb attacks in Israel and the occupied territories during the previous two years, all apparently planned and/or authorized by Shkaki from his hideaway in Damascus. And Ayash—who was known as "the Engineer" because of his bomb-making skills and because he had been a Bir Zeit University engineering student—had been responsible for most of the major terrorist attacks inside Israel during 1994–95. By the GSS's calculation, he and his Hamas operatives had taken the lives of sixty-seven Israelis and injured another four hundred. Hamas's leaders vowed revenge for his death, and Arafat, attending a rally in his honor in the West Bank village of Dura, saluted "all the martyrs, with Ayash at their head."[79]

During the following weeks the Hamas—its military wing now led by Muhammad Dif—prepared its response. Arafat's forces did little or nothing to hinder them. Israel's closing of the territories and roundups of activists delayed the operation several times. To maximize the effect the Hamas and Islamic Jihad jointly decided to carry out a concentrated series of large suicide bombings in Israel's cities.

In early February one of Dif's aides, Hassan Salame ("Abu Ahmad"), traveled from the Gaza Strip to the West Bank and began assembling a network of seminary students. On the morning of February 25, two of his recruits were given bombs—apparently prepared in the Gaza Strip and smuggled into the West Bank by Salame. One student, probably dressed in an IDF uniform, crossed into West Jerusalem and boarded a crowded No. 18 bus. As it approached the central station, he detonated the bomb, which contained from ten to twenty kilograms of TNT.[80] Twenty-five persons were killed and another fifty or so injured, many of them badly. More than half the casualties were soldiers. A few minutes later, at a busy crossroads outside the coastal town of Ashkelon, another recruit, also dressed as a soldier, set off his bomb at a crowded hitchhiking stop. One female soldier died and thirty soldiers were injured.

The scenes televised throughout the day, especially of the inside of the blackened, devastated bus, shocked Israel (and caused jubilation in the Gaza Strip and parts of the West Bank). Two days earlier, on February 23, Peres had lifted the closure of the territories that had been imposed eleven days before, on the basis of intelligence warnings that the fundamentalists were about to launch a terror campaign. The step had probably facilitated the movement of the bombers into Israel. After the explosions irate right-wing crowds gathered in central Jerusalem, Tel Aviv, and elsewhere, chanting both "Death to Arabs" and "Death to Peres."[81]

The following day, February 26, a fundamentalist from the West Bank drove a car into a crowded bus stop in northern Jerusalem, killing a woman and injuring twenty-three people.[82] It is unclear whether this was part of the Dif-directed campaign or just an incidental "bonus."

On March 3, a third suicide recruit detonated a bomb on another No. 18 bus in Jerusalem's Jaffa Street, next to the central post office building. There were eighteen dead and seven wounded. The following day a member of Islamic Jihad who had been smuggled across the Gaza Strip–Israel border by an Israeli Arab truck driver blew himself up at a crowded crossing outside Tel Aviv's Dizengoff shopping center, killing thirteen and wounding about one hundred. (The same day a Hizbullah ambush in the Security Zone killed four Israeli soldiers and wounded seven.)

The effect on the public of this cluster of attacks was traumatic. Middle-of-the-roaders joined the Right in upbraiding the government for its loss of control and their own loss of personal security. There were demonstrations around the country—the tone usually set by the extreme Right— demanding Peres's head and the permanent closure of the territories. In several places Arab pedestrians were beaten.[83] During the following weeks, the Likud and its right-wing partners continuously ran pictures of scenes of the carnage in their election campaign posters and TV clips—and then pictures of Peres shaking this or that Arab's hand. The message was simple and clear.

Belatedly Arafat and his aides grasped the seriousness of the situation and, in wide-ranging sweeps, the Palestinian police arrested most of the fundamentalist leaders and some of their military cadres as well (though not Muhammad Dif). A number of Hamas fighters were killed in firefights with the police; many were beaten and tortured. The PA had demonstrated that it would no longer countenance terrorist attacks on Israel launched from its territory—and that it was willing to risk confrontation with the Hamas and Islamic Jihad.

Moreover, at last delivering partially on long-promised goods, Arafat in late April assembled the Palestine National Council in Gaza—its first meeting ever on Palestinian soil. The assembly annulled the clauses in the Covenant that called for the destruction of Israel but failed to promulgate a new covenant from which these statements were absent—thus enabling the Israeli Right to argue, with a certain cogency, that the old one was still in force.[84]

The Hizbullah also contributed to the chaos of those preelection weeks. On

March 30 and again on April 9, its men let off salvos of Katyusha rockets against Kiryat Shmonah, both times in response to the deaths—the first from Israeli shelling, and the second from an explosive device (of indeterminable origins)—of Lebanese villagers. Seven Israelis were wounded by the rockets. In Kiryat Shmonah, which was largely Likud, there were antigovernment demonstrations.[85]

With the Hizbullah thus challenging him only weeks after the terrorist bombings, Peres had no choice but to demonstrate that he was no softie. He and the IDF brass decided on a sophisticated version of Operation Accountability, again hoping to force the Lebanese to persuade the Syrians to rein in the Hizbullah. The offensive, Operation Grapes of Wrath—involving massive bombardment of Hizbullah centers and Shi'ite villages; a blockade of the Lebanese coastline; and the destruction of major elements of Lebanon's civilian infrastructure, including main roads and two power stations—began on April 11 and ended on the 27th. By the end of the first week some 400,000 Lebanese civilians had fled to Sidon and Beirut. The Hizbullah responded with about five hundred Katyusha rockets on northern Israel. Israeli gunners, airmen, and commandos proved unable to deal with the two- and three-man rocket-launching teams, which moved about the countryside, usually at night, from one prepositioned stockpile and launching position to another.

The Lebanese duly appealed to Syria to rein in the Hizbullah. But then tragedy struck. On April 18, a team of IDF scouts came under rocket fire inside Lebanon and called for fire support. The 155 mm battery that responded sent a salvo of shells crashing accidentally into a UN camp at Kafr Kana. (The Katyushas had been launched from a spot two to three hundred yards away.) The UN personnel were ensconced in their underground shelters, but above ground, unbeknownst to the Israelis, were hundreds of villagers who had taken refuge in the camp. Scores of them, possibly one hundred, were killed and dozens more were seriously injured.[86] The same day Israeli fire also destroyed a house in Nabatiya al Fawqa, killing eleven civilians.

From that point on there was a sharp decrease in the volume of Israeli fire—another such mishap would have been diplomatically disastrous—and an increase in international pressures and efforts to end the shooting. The slaughter at Kafr Kana triggered demonstrations around the Muslim world. In Cairo, fundamentalist gunmen killed seventeen Greek tourists (and an Egyptian) and wounded fourteen more, believing that they were Israelis.[87]

Peres announced that Israel would agree to a cease-fire as soon as the Hizbullah did, but the shelling and counterfire continued for ten more days. Clinton sent Christopher shuttling among Middle East capitals in an effort to achieve an agreement among Israel, Syria, and Lebanon. It was finally concluded on April 26 and a cease-fire went into effect the following day. A refinement of the understanding reached at the end of Operation Accountability, the new agreement barred Israel and the Hizbullah from attacking civilians or civilian settlements and infrastructure. But it left the Hizbullah free to hit the IDF and SLA in the Security Zone and all Israeli targets abroad, and it left open that perennial dilemma: How could Israel respond if the Hizbullah launched attacks from inside villages or their peripheries?[88]

For Peres, Grapes of Wrath was a two-edged sword. The public remembered not only the massive punishment of the Hizbullah but also the hail of Katyushas on Israeli settlements and the inability of the IDF to stop them. Moreover, the operation had ended on a sour note of international reproof and with very little, if any, strategic gain. Once again Peres had emerged as unlucky.

But Grapes of Wrath had another side effect: damage to Labor's electoral prospects. The killing of so many Arab civilians, albeit unintentional (and many Arabs believed it was intentional), soured Israel's Arab minority toward Peres. Many of their leaders argued that there was little to choose between him and Netanyahu, and on election day tens of thousands abstained from voting.

In short, nothing helped Peres—not Arafat's crackdown on the fundamentalists, not the ambiguous annulment of the offensive passages of the Palestinian Covenant, not Grapes of Wrath. He was identified with a peace process that had engendered massive terrorism and loss of security—and with a partner who could not be trusted. Meanwhile, Netanyahu broadcast a simple message: "Peace with security." No, he said, he wasn't against peace. But he would not rush headlong into agreements with "terrorists" like Arafat and, unlike Peres, would make sure that each step was compatible with Israeli security. When pressed about Oslo, Netanyahu neither committed himself to continued implementation nor renounced the agreement (though some of the Likud's leaders, such as Sharon, flatly rejected it).

THE NETANYAHU YEARS

On May 29, Netanyahu won 50.4 percent of the vote for prime minister, with a narrow 29,500 majority out of some 3 million votes cast. Among Jews, his edge was more impressive: 56 percent to Peres's 44. In the Knesset the Likud won 32 of the 120 seats, and its allies of the religious and secular right another 29. Labor won 34 seats and its left-wing and Arab allies 18. Most Soviet immigrants voted for Natan Sharansky's Yisrael Ba'Aliya, giving it seven seats. Netanyahu easily put together a coalition of 66 Knesset members.

In mid-June, as Netanyahu was assembling his coalition, the Likud formulated the new government's "Basic Guidelines." While vaguely promising "to widen the circle of peace with all our neighbors," and to negotiate with Syria and the PA, the document laid out a set of preconditions that offered only bleak hope of progress. It defined the Golan as crucial to Israeli security and promised continued sovereignty over the area. It made no mention of the implementation of the outstanding provisions of Oslo II, speaking rather of "autonomy," and adding: "The government will oppose the establishment of an independent Palestinian state and will oppose the 'right of return' of Arab population to parts of the Land of Israel west of the Jordan." Moreover, the new government would "act to consolidate and develop the settlement enterprise." And, "united Jerusalem, the capital of Israel, . . . will forever remain under [sole] Israeli sovereignty."[89] While visiting Washington a few days later, Netanyahu added that the status of Jerusalem was "nonnegotiable."

There followed three months of inaction, punctuated only by a single, brief, and perfunctory Netanyahu-Arafat meeting on September 4, initiated at American insistence. Both men looked dour and unfriendly, and promised nothing. The Palestinians could be forgiven for concluding that the new government's sole aim was to halt Oslo while appearing to negotiate in order to appease Washington. Meanwhile the closure order imposed on the territories after the February–March bombings remained in force. As the weeks passed without further Israeli troop withdrawals, a prisoner release, or substantive negotiations, but with continuous announcements of intent to expand the settlements, Palestinian tempers frayed. Politicians on both sides warned that an explosion was imminent, but the prime minister remained unruffled.

It was Netanyahu himself who triggered the explosion. On September 24 the authorities, acting under his orders, opened an exit in the Muslim Quarter of Jerusalem's Old City from an archaeological tunnel that ran parallel to much of the length of the Western Wall of the Temple Mount. The aim was both to make access to the tunnel easier for tourists and to highlight the government's determination to "Judaize" all of Jerusalem. The Rabin government had repeatedly put off opening the exit, fearing that—like most things connected to the Haram ash-Sharif—such action would be construed and exploited as a provocation. The Muslims had long charged that Israel was trying to undermine the foundations of the compound in order to topple the al-Aqsa Mosque and the Dome of the Rock, paving the way for the reestablishment of the Temple. Opening the tunnel exit would be seen as a change in the status quo detrimental to the Muslims (although the tunnel actually skirted the Temple Mount), and would ignite religious and political passions.

Netanyahu ignored the warnings, and Jerusalem's Mayor Ehud Olmert, a Likud stalwart who had pressed for the opening, described the new entrance as "a great present for humanity." The Palestinians disagreed. On September 25, with Arafat's encouragement, crowds gathered in protest in PA-controlled towns. In Ramallah and East Jerusalem, the demonstrators marched toward Israeli military and police outposts and pelted them with stones. The jittery, heavily outnumbered troops began firing tear gas and shots into the air, and then rubber bullets into the crowds. The rioting continued for some hours until suddenly, outside Ramallah, a Palestinian fired an automatic weapon at the Israelis. The Israelis fired back, and Arafat's armed police joined in. The gunfire spread quickly, and the exchanges were renewed the following day and the next. The main firefights raged on the outskirts of Ramallah, Nablus, and Bethlehem, and around the Israeli settlements of Netzarim and Kfar Darom in the Strip.

The fighting died down only when the IDF deployed tanks near the PA-held cities and, at several sites, helicopter gunships were unleashed on the Palestinians. Netanyahu and Defense Minister Yitzhak Mordechai warned that if Arafat's troops continued firing, the IDF would have no choice but to push into the cities with armor. American mediation was also crucial to the pacification efforts. A cease-fire was agreed on. During the three days of fighting, about seventy Palestinians were killed and several hundred were injured; fifteen IDF soldiers died and several dozen were wounded.[90]

To defuse the situation, President Clinton summoned Arafat and Netanyahu to Washington, where the two—displaying distrust and animosity—met on October 1–2 and agreed to renew the Hebron negotiations. Clinton obtained an in-principle commitment from Netanyahu to Israeli withdrawal from most of Hebron. But the prime minister refused to commit himself to a target date, or to close the disputed tunnel exit.[91]

For the next three months Israeli and Palestinian negotiators, assisted by Warren Christopher and his aide for Middle East affairs, the indefatigable Dennis Ross, worked out the details of the IDF redeployment. Arafat balked from the first, arguing that the Palestinians had already negotiated and concluded a Hebron deal with the previous government, which Peres had failed to honor. But Netanyahu, having promised his voters "more security," had no choice but to obtain "more," or at least the semblance of something more. Possibly, too, Netanyahu was still playing for time—hoping that Hamas bombers might let him off the hook and abort the negotiation.

Arafat could do nothing but play along. But he too upped the ante, by demanding an airtight commitment to the continuation of the peace process after Hebron, meaning an endorsement of the Oslo process as a whole.

As the talks were nearing completion, yet another Jewish fanatic tried to thwart the process. On January 1, 1997, nineteen-year-old Noam Friedman, a religious soldier from the West Bank settlement of Ma'aleh Adumim with a record of psychological problems, traveled to Hebron and opened fire on the main thoroughfare bordering on the Jewish quarter, wounding seven Arabs before being overpowered by Israeli soldiers. As he was hauled away, he told reporters that he had aimed to halt the talks and the expected IDF withdrawal by killing as many Arabs as possible.[92]

But, apart from prompting Arafat to demand more measures to assure the security of the townspeople, the attack merely strengthened Ross's resolve to conclude the deal. The final details of the redeployment were worked out during the first week of January. There followed additional haggling sessions regarding the next stages. The Palestinians demanded that Israel agree to complete the three stages of withdrawal from the Arab-populated rural areas of the West Bank by September 1997. Oslo II had spoken of such a staggered "redeployment" during the eighteen months following the completion of the IDF departure from the cities.

Netanyahu initially insisted that no date be fixed for the completion of the third stage. Later he suggested that the rural redeployment be completed in 1999, simultaneously with the targeted Oslo II completion date for the permanent-status negotiations. He sought to avoid either any further withdrawal at all or a situation in which Israel had withdrawn from too much of the West Bank before the end of the permanent-status talks.

At the last minute, on January 12, 1997, with Ross about to give up and depart for Washington, King Hussein flew to Gaza and Israel and persuaded Arafat and Netanyahu to agree to the compromise date that Ross had pushed all along—mid-1998. They met on the Gaza-Israel border around midnight on January 14 and initialed the agreement. Essentially it resembled the one reached between the Peres government and the PA in early 1996 and never implemented—though Netanyahu and his aides claimed it was substantively better from the Israeli perspective.

The core of the accord provided for Israel to withdraw from 80 percent of Hebron, leaving under sole IDF control the 20 percent around the settlement zones of Beit Hadassah and Tel Rumeida (into which the Jews had begun to move, in defiance of the military government, in 1979) and the Tomb of the Patriarchs (al-Ibrahimiya Mosque); joint Palestinian-Israeli mechanized patrols at the entrances to Hebron and around the Jewish settlement perimeter; the entry into the Arab-populated parts of Hebron of four hundred lightly armed Palestinian policemen; and a "buffer zone" around the Jewish enclave, in which Palestinians must be unarmed. In a "note for the record" Netanyahu agreed to the release of an unspecified number of prisoners, to the opening of air- and seaports in the Gaza Strip (with details still to be negotiated), and to the activation, as called for in Oslo II, of a safe-passage route between the Strip and the West Bank. Netanyahu also assented to a three-stage additional troop redeployment out of unspecified rural areas of the West Bank by mid-1998. Arafat agreed to dismantle the remaining terrorist infrastructure in PA-controlled territories and to complete the revision of the Covenant so that the clauses calling for the disappearance of Israel would finally be laid to rest.

Separate letters from Christopher to Netanyahu and to Arafat outlined what the United States expected of each side (in a sense, constituting an American commitment to implementation). The Israelis published the letter addressed to them, which included a reiteration of the historic U.S. commitment to Israel's security and to "secure and defensible" borders. Arafat declined to publish his letter.[93]

From the Palestinian perspective, the weak point in both Oslo II and the Hebron agreement was that the Israelis were left with the prerogative of determining how much of the West Bank they would evacuate during the three stages of the rural withdrawal. Against this Arafat now had Netanyahu's promises to Washington and Washington's reassurances to him that Israel would meet its withdrawal commitments and would not try to fob everyone off with merely token redeployments.[94] It was not clear whether Netanyahu had agreed to consult with the PA about the specifics—the extent of the areas to be evacuated and timetables of withdrawal, among other aspects.

On January 16, in the course of twelve hours of bitter debate, Netanyahu managed to ram the agreement down a reluctant cabinet's throat, by a vote of 11 to 7. The majority was secured by the implicit threat that if the accord failed to pass, Netanyahu would dissolve the coalition and form a new National Unity Government with the Labor Party. The small right-wing and religious parties would then become superfluous and end up in opposition. (It was afterward charged that Netanyahu had obtained the support of the two Shas ministers by promising to appoint a new attorney general who would cut a plea-bargain deal with their indicted leader, Arye Deri.) One of the seven dissenters, Science Minister Benny Begin, son of Menachem Begin, resigned ("the air carries the bitter taste of capitulation," he was to tell the Knesset). Infrastructure Minister Sharon, who the previous May had called the Oslo accords "terrible and dangerous," voted against but stayed on.[95] The next day the Knesset approved the accord by a vote of 87 to 17, with sixteen members absent or abstaining; the slim majority of Likud members voting aye was bolstered by the near-unanimous vote of the Labor bloc in support.

In the PA cabinet ten ministers voted for, two against, and three abstained. As expected, the national-religious extremists in both camps—the NRP–Gush Emunim–Moledet and the Hamas–Islamic Jihad—condemned the agreement as a sellout of their respective peoples.[96]

On January 17, the IDF left most of Hebron, and four hundred Palestinian policemen fanned out in the Arab parts of the town, raising the Palestinian flag over the old British police fort that had for three decades served as the local headquarters of the military governor (and as a prison). The changeover passed festively and without incident, though Israeli observers noted that the Palestinians were brandishing more weapons, including prohibited Kalashnikov assault rifles, than allowed for in the agreement. The Israeli settlers mostly stayed indoors, behind the carapace of IDF protection, issuing gloomy predictions.[97]

For the first time, a Likud-led government had withdrawn from a patch of the Land of Israel—small but of great emotive pull and symbolic importance—and handed it over to PLO control. Netanyahu—urged on by international pressure, implicit Palestinian threats, and the weight of Israeli public opinion—had also pushed one vital step forward in the Oslo process, whose guiding principle was trading land for peace, and had committed his government to its continuation.

The year 1997 passed without any further progress. Washington managed a number of times to bring together Israeli and Palestinian negotiators, but nothing was achieved. Essentially, the Netanyahu government was unable or unwilling to continue the Oslo process, which boiled down to trading further chunks of the West Bank for further steps toward peace. Netanyahu's ideology, and that of the bulk of his coalition partners, militated against further withdrawals—and a number of devastating Hamas suicide attacks (a double suicide bombing on July 30 in Jerusalem's Mahane Yehuda market, killing twelve bystanders and injuring dozens; and a triple suicide bombing on September 4 in Jerusalem's Ben-Yehudah Street, killing three and injuring more than one hundred)—provided the government with cause, or excuse, for further delay and for renegotiation of the provisions already agreed on.

Despite a visit by Secretary of State Madeleine Albright in September designed to pressure Netanyahu, the Israeli government failed to carry out the first of the three scheduled redeployments, or withdrawals, from further West Bank rural areas, as called for in Oslo II and the Hebron agreement. And despite direct intercession by President Clinton in early 1998, Israel failed to execute the second withdrawal. Netanyahu also did not release more prisoners, did not allow the Palestinians to open air- and seaports in Gaza, and did not inaugurate the safe-passage West Bank–Gaza routes stipulated in Oslo I and II and reiterated in the Hebron agreement. Nonetheless, he continued to demand Palestinian "reciprocity" as a condition for Israel's fulfillment of its obligations.

For its part, the PA failed to issue a new "National Covenant" or to crush the Hamas and completely end terrorism originating in its cities.

Netanyahu's hard-line stance was probably reinforced by one of the bigger blunders of his premiership (by this time he had clearly staked out his claim as Israel's most incompetent—and mendacious—prime minister, earning from *The Economist* the sobriquet "serial bungler"): the assassination attempt on Khaled Mashal, a senior Hamas official, in Amman on September 25, 1997. The botched operation, in which three Israeli Mossad agents were arrested by Jordanian police, thoroughly embarrassed King Hussein. He immediately demanded that Israel release Hamas leader Sheikh Yassin and two dozen other jailed terrorists in exchange for the Mossad operatives. Yassin was duly released and flown to Gaza, where he received a hero's welcome. The reunion of Yassin with his supporters weakened Arafat's position in the territories.

In December 1997 and February 1998, Albright met Netanyahu and pressed for acceptance of a thirteen percent withdrawal from the West Bank to meet the IDF redeployment commitments entered into in Oslo II and the Hebron agreements. Netanyahu balked, precipitating the resignation from the cabinet, in January, of Foreign Minister David Levy, who with his "Gesher" faction then left the Likud and the coalition. In March the Palestinians, who had demanded that Israel withdraw from fifty percent or more of the West Bank, reluctantly agreed to the thirteen percent.

Levy's resignation, and Clinton's domestic problems (the Monica Lewinsky affair) and troubles with Iraq, strengthened Netanyahu's hand and impaired the American administration's ability to twist Israel's arm. Nonetheless, by April–May 1998, Netanyahu had secretly agreed in principle to thirteen percent (albeit with three percent designated as a "nature reserve")— but on condition that the withdrawal was carried out in three stages, with each stage being matched by the implementation of specific Palestinian concessions. By summer, pressure from Clinton was complemented by increasing pressure from inside the Israeli cabinet (Levy having been replaced as the primary advocate of moderation by Defense Minister Yitzhak Mordechai) and from various Arab quarters. Jordan and Egypt, for example, hinted that in the absence of progress toward Palestinian-Israeli peace, they would shortly be lowering their diplomatic representation in Tel Aviv; and Arafat declared that on May 4, 1999, in line with Oslo, he would unilaterally declare Palestinian independence and statehood, a step which could well throw the region into political and perhaps military chaos.

By September, Clinton and his aides sensed that the Israelis and the Palestinians were close enough to agreement to go the last lap, and invitations went out to Arafat and Netanyahu to attend an open-ended negotiating summit in the United States à la Camp David 1978.

Netanyahu arrived in the United States under intense Israeli right-wing pressure not to concede any territory—most Israeli pundits expected the prime minister to torpedo any possibility of agreement—and accompanied by his new foreign minister, Ariel Sharon, who had defined any concession of more than nine percent as "jeopardizing" Israel's existence.

The summit at the secluded Wye River Plantation in Maryland began on October 15 and concluded with the signing of the "Wye River Memorandum"[98] on October 23. As at Camp David, journalists were completely excluded. Netanyahu was flanked by Sharon, Trade and Industry Minister Natan Sharansky (for a time), and Defense Minister Mordechai; Arafat, by Abu Mazen and Nabil Sha'at. An impassioned surprise appearance by King Hussein, then undergoing cancer treatment at the Mayo Clinic in Minnesota, failed to resolve the differences, and on October 21 the Israelis packed their bags and threatened to leave. But the Americans proceeded to narrow the gap and a deal was painfully hammered out. On the 23rd, at the last minute, Netanyahu informed Clinton that his signature was contingent on the release from prison of Jonathan Pollard, an American spy for Israel; Clinton dismissed the idea as "ridiculous" and agreed only to "reconsider" the Pollard case. Netanyahu gave in.

The agreement was signed in the East Room of the White House by

Netanyahu and Arafat, with Clinton as witness and King Hussein looking on (the king died a few months later, on February 7, 1999, and was succeeded by his son Abdullah). It provided that Israel would cede thirteen percent of "Area C" (territory under full Israeli control) (three percent being a Green Area/Nature Reserve in which the Palestinians could not build or otherwise change the landscape), with one percent reverting directly to "Area A" (full Palestinian control) and twelve percent to "Area B" (mixed Israeli-Palestinian control); another 14.2 percent would be shifted from Area B to Area A. These redeployments were to take place within twelve weeks of the signing. Subsequently, the three parties would discuss one further, last stage of indeterminate size of rural redeployment—which Netanyahu assured the Israeli public would consist of no more than one percent of the West Bank.

The two sides committed themselves to preventing acts of terrorism against each other, and to preventing and punishing incitement to violence and terrorism. The Palestinians agreed to hammer out a "work plan" to combat the "terrorist organizations and their infrastructure," and to "review" its implementation with American representatives on a biweekly basis. The Palestinians would confiscate illegal weapons and prevent the smuggling of further weapons into PA territory. There would be "continuous, intensive and comprehensive" Israeli-Palestinian cooperation in combating terrorism. The Palestinians agreed to round up an indeterminate number of "terrorism suspects" (those appearing on Israel's "wanted" lists, most of them suspected of killing Israelis).

Arafat agreed to a convocation of a joint meeting of the Palestine National Council, the Palestinian Central Council, and Palestinian heads of ministries, to be addressed by President Clinton in Gaza, where they would reaffirm their support for the peace process, and as well for the decisions of the PLO Executive Committee and the Palestinian Central Council concerning the "nullification of the Palestinian National Charter provisions" that were inconsistent with the PLO's commitments to renouncing terror and to recognizing Israel.

In the economic sphere, the two sides agreed on the opening both of an industrial park on the Gaza border and of Gaza's (Dahaniya) airport. Further provisions called for the conclusion of talks on the opening of the safe-passage routes between the Gaza Strip and West Bank and on the opening of a seaport for Gaza.

Lastly, the two sides agreed to reopen "immediately" the "permanent status" (final settlement) negotiations, which were to proceed "continuous[ly] and without interruption," with the aim of achieving a final settlement by May 4, 1999.

All these provisions were to be implemented in five stages, with each Israeli withdrawal on the ground contingent on PA implementation of one of the security provisions (weapons collection, arrest of suspects, etc.). The memorandum was accompanied by a series of clarifying letters from senior

American officials to Israel, including one from U.S. Ambassador to Tel Aviv Edward Walker, Jr., to Israeli Cabinet Secretary Dani Naveh, of October 29, 1998, affirming Washington's opposition to any unilateral declaration of statehood by Arafat, and another, of October 30, 1998, assuring the Israelis that the Palestinians had agreed that there would be no "revolving door" with respect to Palestinian terrorist suspects (that is, that the PA would not briefly arrest and then quickly release such suspects).

If Netanyahu had been propelled into Wye, much against his will, by a combination of domestic, American, and Arab pressures, his return home with the agreement in his pocket was greeted by the right with shocked disbelief: He had signed on the dotted line and committed himself to withdrawal from another thirteen percent (and more) of the West Bank. Netanyahu privately argued that it was all contingent on the Arabs carrying out their part of the bargain, and that this would not happen, and so Israel in the end would not have to deliver. To his moderate coalition partners, and especially Mordechai, Netanyahu explained that he had promised at the time of his election "peace with security," and now he was carrying this out.

Both the right and the left were unconvinced—by now, no one trusted Netanyahu's word. The right feared that Netanyahu would implement Wye, handing over the full thirteen percent (and more); the left, that Netanyahu would halt implementation of the agreement as soon as possible on one pretext or another.

During the months of back-room negotiations before Wye and during the Wye talks themselves the Palestine Authority, using a mixture of carrot and stick, but mostly stick, had kept a tight grip on the Islamic fundamentalists, and in large measure prevented them from carrying out terrorist attacks on Israel. Arafat understood that such attacks would obviate an agreement and further delay Israeli withdrawals. On October 29 the fundamentalists at last managed to launch a suicide car-bomber against a bus packed with settlers' children near Kfar Darom in the Gaza Strip. A courageous last-second interdiction by the IDF jeep escorting the bus prevented the bomber reaching the bus and a major disaster; one soldier was killed and a second badly injured.

On November 17, after some delays, with Netanyahu complaining that the Palestinians had not fulfilled some of Wye's technical clauses, the Knesset approved the agreement by a 79 to 19 vote, and two days later it was—narrowly—approved by the cabinet: 7 to 5, with several ministers abstaining.

On November 20, Israel withdrew from two percent of the West Bank included in Area C, which then became part of Area B, while 7.1 percent in Area B now joined Area A. Most of the areas evacuated were around Jenin, in northern Samaria. Four days later, Gaza international airport officially opened and Israel released 250 Palestinian prisoners, 150 of them common criminals. The Palestinians complained that the understanding was that Israel would release 250 security and political prisoners—but this had not been explicitly written into Wye. On December 14, the PNC meeting jointly with other Palestinian bodies—in President Clinton's presence (the first visit by a U.S. president to PA territory)—reiterated the nullification of those clauses in the Palestinian Charter (Covenant) calling for Israel's destruction.

But by then Netanyahu's right-wing coalition partners (and perhaps the dictates of his own conscience) had persuaded the prime minister to suspend implementation of Wye and call off the further IDF withdrawals from the West Bank scheduled according to the agreement for early January and mid-February 1999. In public, and to Washington, Netanyahu argued that the Palestinians had not fulfilled several of their commitments (the collection of illegal arms, the arrest of wanted terrorists, an end to anti-Israeli incitement). The true difficulty was that the right had threatened to bring down the government should Netanyahu continue the withdrawals.

The hard-liners, however, continued to fear that Netanyahu might yet go through with the agreement—whereas centrist moderates within the coalition (the Third Way Party and Mordechai) threatened to vote no-confidence and topple the government if Wye was *not* implemented. Netanyahu was placed in an impossible position; the coalition lacked a majority for either implementation or non-implementation.

Finally succumbing to these contrary pulls and pressures, on December 21 Netanyahu voted with the Knesset majority (the vote on the key resolution was 81 to 30) to dissolve the government and set early elections. The Likud and Labor eventually agreed on May 17, 1999, as the date for the first round of voting, for the Knesset and the premiership, with a second round for the premiership on June 1, should none of the candidates receive more than 50 percent in the first round.

One reason for the much-criticized half-year gap between the vote for the government's dissolution and the election dates—during which Netanyahu's coalition and cabinet continued to function in a caretaker role—was the two main parties' fears of the electoral potential of the embryonic "Center Party" and its possible candidates for the premiership, Gen. (Res.) Amnon Lipkin-Shahak and former Likud finance minister Dan Meridor. In January 1999, Netanyahu fired the Iraqi-born Mordechai, who was busy clandestinely negotiating with the Center Party, and, with Lipkin-Shahak and Meridor bowing out, Mordechai was selected as the party's candidate for premier. The Likud, inevitably, nominated Netanyahu and the Labor Party, Ehud Barak. Benny Begin, Menachem's son and formerly Netanyahu's energy minister, left the Likud and ran for the premiership as the candidate of the extreme right.

In effect, Wye had become a dead letter, and its implementation was completely suspended for the duration. Arafat, while complaining to Washington about Israel's nonimplementation of the agreement and periodically threatening to declare Palestinian statehood on May 4, maintained his clampdown on the fundamentalists, understanding that anti-Israeli terrorist outrages would only serve to bolster Netanyahu's electoral prospects. London, Paris, Washington, and Cairo persuaded Arafat that a pre-election declaration of statehood would also play into Netanyahu's hands. Beginning in February, Clinton, having survived the impeachment vote in the Senate, sent out subtle and not-so-subtle signals (such as refusing to meet Netanyahu) to the Israeli electorate against returning Netanyahu to office.

The February–May period was dominated by the election campaign. Netanyahu continued publicly to espouse "peace with security" and a vague adherence to the Oslo process and to the Wye agreement while berating Barak as a "softie" who would divide Jerusalem and hand the West Bank to the Palestinians and all of the Golan to Syria, and whose election would result in a resumption of terrorism. Barak, for his part, plugged away at Netanyahu's character defects, principally his mendacity and untrustworthiness, and at the government's failures on the domestic front (rising unemployment, declining services, reduced investment in the economy), the suspension of the peace process, and Israel's isolation in the international arena. Barak promised to extricate the IDF from the quagmire of southern Lebanon "within a year." Mordechai pitched in with a direct assault on Netanyahu's credibility and competence, while Shahak bluntly declared that he was "a danger to Israel." Both men had worked closely with the prime minister.

As it turned out, one round proved sufficient. On May 15–16, the three junior candidates for the prime-ministership—including Mordechai, whose campaign had failed to take off—pulled out, leaving Netanyahu and Barak alone in the ring. Barak's solid military credentials rendered him immune to Netanyahu's charges that he would be "soft on the Arabs," while the Barak-Mordechai assault on the prime minister's character proved effective in the extreme. Netanyahu's last-minute "dirty tricks," including his continued campaigning on election day in defiance of Israel's election laws and his effort to incite Sephardi and ultra-Orthodox passions against "the secular Ashkenazi elites," were unavailing, and on May 17 Barak won 56 percent of the vote to Netanyahu's 44. Barak's campaign had been efficiently run by a group of retired army officers, successfully mobilizing the Left and Center on polling day, while over the years, pummeled by Netanyahu's shenanigans, the heart had gone out of many veteran Likud supporters. The 74 percent election turnout, compared to 80 percent in 1996, indicated that many right-wingers had preferred simply to stay home and abandon Netanyahu to his fate.

In a massive, symbolic celebration of support and relief, hundreds of thousands of Israelis gathered spontaneously in the early hours of the following day in Tel Aviv's central Yitzhak Rabin Square (formerly Kings of Israel Square), where Rabin, Barak's mentor, had been murdered four years before. It was as if the election result were a belated political revenge for the assassination, for which the inflammatory rhetoric of Netanyahu and his fellow Likud leaders had served as background. Indeed, addressing the crowd at 3:00

A.M., Barak suggested that Rabin was looking down on the scene from heaven, and promised to "carry out his legacy."

Barak had been given a clear mandate by the electorate. But the results of the simultaneous parliamentary vote were less clear-cut and left the prime minister–elect with a variety of problematic coalition-building options. Though the Likud's Knesset representation dropped from 32 seats (in 1996) to 19 (most of the lost seats going, ironically, to the party's ultra-Orthodox Sephardi ally, Shas, which emerged with 17), Labor, too, lost seats (declining from 34 to 26), and failed to clinch an obvious, straightforward left-center coalition. Labor's leftist and centrist allies won 30 seats altogether, leaving the emergent "natural" coalition a few seats short of a majority in the 120-seat parliament and so dependent on the votes of the 10 Arab lists' Knesset members. But pushing through, on the basis of such Arab support, a settlement with the Palestinians and/or Syria involving major territorial concessions would necessarily antagonize large sections of the Jewish public. On the other hand, building a wider coalition, with the cooption of right-wing and/or religious parties in addition to Labor and its left-wing and centrist allies, might result in severe constraints on the negotiations with the Arabs.

By mid-June it appeared that Barak intended to opt for this second, wider alternative and to take on board the National Religious Party (with five seats) and Shas, thus substantially neutralizing the type of right-wing and settler antagonism and dissidence encountered by Rabin (with his narrow left-wing coalition) as he had pushed forward with the Oslo process. The Likud, immersed in a succession battle following Netanyahu's election-night resignation as party leader, was expected to stay out of the coalition.

Such was the internal Israeli political situation as this book went to press. Clearly, an upheaval of major historical significance—on a par with Menachem Begin's assumption of power in 1977 after three decades of Labor rule—had taken place, and Barak is expected to renew the peace process suspended during the Netanyahu years and try to clinch peace treaties with Syria, Lebanon, and the Palestinians. The negotiations will be difficult and protracted and—as the country's new leader reiterated in his election victory speech—will require "difficult decisions" (i.e., painful territorial concessions). But the Middle East clearly set out on a new course on May 17.

FOURTEEN

EHUD BARAK'S 19 MONTHS

The May 17, 1999, Israeli general elections ushered in a hope-inspiring but ultimately bloody period in the relations between Israel and the Arab world. Ehud Barak handily beat the incumbent Netanyahu, of the Likud, by a 56 to 44 percent margin, and went on to launch intensive peace negotiations with the Syrians and the Palestinians. But 19 months later, the overture towards Syria was dead in the water and Israel and the Palestinians were locked in bloody struggle around the Jewish settlements and Arab towns in the West Bank and Gaza Strip, and the Israeli electorate had voted Barak out of office and replaced him with a hard-line general whose reputation, at least, offered little hope for Israeli-Arab reconciliation.

One reason for the dismal end of Barak's premiership lay in those 1999 elections. The electorate had given him a clear personal mandate—but at the same time, in the parliamentary vote, had presented him with a political dead end. His own Labor Party (just renamed "One Israel" to give it a less socialist ring) declined from 34 to 26 seats in the 120-seat Knesset and together with four other centrist and left-wing factions mustered only 50 votes. Another 10 votes, held by three Arab parties, could be expected to go along with Barak on the peace process, but the new prime minister was loath to induct them into his coalition and make it dependent on Arab consent. So, in order to form a reasonably stable coalition, Barak was forced to choose between a coalition comprising Labor, its satellites and the Likud (which emerged from the election badly battered with 19 seats) or one comprising Labor, its satellites and the three religious factions, the ultra-orthodox Sephardi Shas Party (17 seats), the ultra-orthodox Ashkenazi United Torah Judaism (5 seats), and the orthodox National Religious Party (5 seats).

Barak chose the second course, assuming that the Likud in government would inevitably frustrate any effort, necessarily involving concessions, at peacemaking. Such a coalition could be expected to swiftly collapse, without achieving peace with either the Syrians or the Palestinians. On the other hand, the religious factions, or at least the main one, Shas, could, Barak reasoned, be "bought off" with economic benefits for their school system and religious legislation in exchange for grudging support for peace making and concessions. At the very least, as had happened with Rabin and Shas back in 1993, the ultra-orthodox could be expected to go some of the way with Barak in the peace process, perhaps providing enough momentum to carry the country through to a popular referendum on whatever agreement emerged.

After lengthy and complex negotiations, Barak on July 6 presented the Knesset with his new government, based on a coalition of 75 MKs, with Labor, Meretz, and Shas as its chief components. The following day the changing of the guard took place in the Prime Minister's Office, with Netanyahu handing over what the Israeli press called "control of the state's strategic weapons systems" to Barak.[1] Barak immediately promised Arafat to abide by and implement the commitments made by Netanyahu at Wye—but also signaled that he preferred to integrate the third-stage Wye pullback from further parts of the West Bank in a "final status," comprehensive peace agreement rather than to continue the piecemeal process (of giving additional slices of territory for additional slices of peace) pursued, and repeatedly stalled, since Oslo in 1993. Barak feared that the end result of the salami process would be that Israel would give up most of its "cards" (i.e., the territory it still retained in the West Bank and Gaza Strip) without getting a comprehensive, final peace settlement.

This integration of Wye with final status negotiations was embodied in the Sharm ash Sheikh Agreement signed by Barak and Arafat, with U.S. Secretary of State Albright, Egyptian President Mubarak and King Abdullah II of Jordan as witnesses, on September 4, 1999. The agreement was in effect an "improved Wye," as one Israeli commentator put it, but the West acknowledged that Israel was now governed by a regime that wanted peace and appeared willing to make concessions to achieve it. The accord provided for three further small Israeli withdrawals from chunks of the West Bank in September and November 1999 and January 2000; the release, in two batches, of 350 Palestinian security prisoners from Israeli jails in September and October 1999; and the start, on September 13, of intensive negotiations on a final status peace settlement (covering borders, Jerusalem, Israeli settlements, and Palestinian refugees), based on UN resolutions 242 and 338. Israel agreed to the start of the construction in Gaza of a Palestinian seaport and to the activation of the Southern Safe Passage route from Gaza to the West Bank from October 1, 1999, and the Palestinians agreed to resume full cooperation with Israeli agencies to stymie terrorism.[2]

But after the promised prisoner releases and after the Israeli implementation of the first stage of the Sharm ash Sheikh–provisioned withdrawal, arguments erupted over how much and which territory was to be handed over to the Palestinians in the second stage (scheduled for November). Moreover, time was wasted in several unfruitful rounds of preliminary final status talks, and Palestinian terrorist attacks inside Israel caused further delays and bad blood. In December, the Palestinians suspended the negotiations citing Israel's continued expansion of West Bank settlements. The Israeli and Palestinian negotiators failed to reach a draft or "framework" final peace accord by February 13, 2000, as Barak had wanted.

By comparison with the Israeli-Palestinian track, the problems dividing Israel and Syria appeared simple. Following Barak's election, a flurry of diplomatic activity presaged the resumption of Israeli-Syrian peace negotiations. For all practical purposes, bilateral negotiations had been suspended in 1996, with the demise of the Rabin-Peres government. During the summer of 1998 Netanyahu had briefly conducted secret talks with the Syrians, with American Jewish millionaire Ron Lauder, a friend of Netanyahu's, acting as go-between. Assad had agreed to the presence on Syrian soil, for 15 years, of early warning stations manned by Americans or Frenchmen as well as by Israelis and to withdraw the bulk of his army eastwards, out of offensive range of Israel. Netanyahu had apparently agreed to an Israeli withdrawal to the 1923 international border or to a line "based on the 4 June 1967 lines," but had refused to present the Syrians with a detailed map indicating what he thought acceptable, as demanded by Assad. In any event, internal pressures by Likud stalwarts, led by Ariel Sharon, had led to the abrupt cessation of the secret contacts in September 1998.[3]

Nonetheless, after Sharm ash Sheikh, Barak decided to try the Syrian track; the issues appeared clear and simple, Syria—unlike the Palestinians—was ruled by a powerful, decisive leader, and giving up the Golan Heights was far less contentious, in terms of internal Israeli politics, than compromise over Jerusalem, the refugees and the fate of the West Bank. The initial indications seemed propitious. In an interview in mid-June 1999, Assad described Barak as "a strong and honest man" who would seek to make peace with Syria. Barak reciprocated with compliments for Assad, saying that he had built "a strong, independent, self-confident Syria—a Syria which, I believe, is very important for stability in the Middle East."

In September, Albright and U.S. Middle East envoy Dennis Ross held talks with Assad in Damascus, and on December 8 President Clinton announced the resumption of the Israeli-Syrian talks "from the point where they left off." The Syrians said that this meant the inclusion of Rabin's (they alleged) agreement to give up all of the Golan in exchange for peace. Barak and Syrian Foreign Minister Farouk al-Shara met on December 15–16 in Washington for an initial round, with a second, fuller meeting taking place at Shepherdstown, West Virginia, during January 3–10, 2000. Al-Shara exhibited a cold and unconciliatory front. Clinton intermittently came down to mediate and the Americans hammered out a draft "Treaty of Peace Between the State of Israel and the Syrian Arab Republic" (dated January 7, 2000) that defined the areas of agreement and disagreement between the two sides.⁴ Barak had apparently agreed to a withdrawal "on the basis of" the June 4, 1967 borders though not necessarily at every point to the June 4 lines. But the Syrians demanded that Israel give Washington an ironclad commitment regarding the June lines, and stressed that they sought a return also to the waterline along the northeastern flank of the Sea of Galilee. The meeting broke up without agreement. Escalating Hizbullah attacks in the South Lebanon Security Zone, which claimed half a dozen Israeli lives in late January and February 2000, were interpreted by Israel as subtle or not so subtle pressure by Assad for Israeli concessions regarding the Golan.

On March 26, 2000, Clinton put his prestige on the line in a face-to-face meeting with Assad in Geneva. Israel (and Washington) assumed that Assad's willingness to meet Clinton—involving, for Assad, a rare sortie abroad—meant that he had softened his stance and was ready to compromise. Clinton was duly disabused when Assad let loose with a lengthy lecture on Israel's abuse of the Arabs and demanded that Israel give up the northeastern shore of the Sea of Galilee so that Syrians could "wash their feet" in the lake. The meeting broke up without result, except embarrassment for Clinton and praise in Arab newspapers for Assad's firm stand.

Barak was willing to give up the Golan Heights but insisted on continued Israeli retention of the complete Sea of Galilee waterline to a depth of several hundred meters. Barak had promised the Israeli public a referendum on whatever draft agreement was reached. He assessed that Israelis would reject a deal that included a handover of the northeastern shoreline to the Syrians. Israeli-Syrian negotiations were effectively suspended.

But soon there were to be significant developments on the Lebanese front. In spring 1999, during his campaign for the premiership, Barak had promised that Israel would withdraw its troops from the Security Zone back to the international frontier "within a year." After taking office, he began to speak of "July 2000" as the deadline. He hoped that the withdrawal would be a part of a general peace agreement with Syria and Lebanon, which would include a Syrian guarantee of the security of northern Israel and, perhaps, a deployment of Syrian troops in South Lebanon. But the deadlock in the Israeli-Syrian peace talks had gradually persuaded Barak that the withdrawal from the Zone would most probably be unilateral and without agreement either with Syria or Lebanon. The IDF General Staff opposed a withdrawal without an agreement; but on March 5, 2000, the Israeli cabinet unanimously endorsed a withdrawal by July, "with or without an agreement," back to the international frontier.⁵ The IDF was instructed to plan for a withdrawal without agreement. In order not to precipitate a collapse of SLA morale, the SLA was not informed. Indeed, SLA wages and armaments were beefed up. In mid-April, Israel informed the UN that it would withdraw from Lebanon by July 7. But last-minute efforts to negotiate with the UN and various western countries an expansion of UNIFIL and its deployment in the Zone hard on the heels of an Israeli departure came to naught: Nobody was willing to tangle with the Hizbullah. In April and May, the Israeli army stepped up its preparations for a unilateral pullout. But events on the ground soon precipitated a premature, dramatic, but ultimately successful IDF pullback.

In mid-May, the IDF handed over several Security Zone positions to the SLA. Israel vaguely promised SLA officers and men at least temporary sanctuary when the final pullback occurred. The Israelis envisaged an orderly process in which several hundred men, with their families, would cross over into Israel while hundreds of others would immigrate to a host of countries, including Germany, with whom sanctuary had been negotiated by Israel. But on May 21, hundreds of Lebanese civilians, apparently spontaneously and unorganized by the Hizbullah, crossed into the Zone from the north, entered the village of Kantara, and pushed toward the SLA position at Taibeh. The soldiers, rather than fire on the crowd, abandoned the position. The Hizbullah took note and immediately began organizing further civilian processions. IDF Northern Command decided not to retake Taibeh, an action that would have involved, it was estimated, massive civilian casualties. During May 22–23 columns of civilians, accompanied by Hizbullah gunmen, marched into the Zone. The IDF refrained from unleashing artillery and helicopter gunships and the SLA began to crumble, position after position. At the northern edge of the Zone, around the town of Hasbaya, the Druze battalion of the SLA quietly shed its uniforms and arms and faded away, apparently after a Hizbullah-Druze deal that assured the soldiers immunity. SLA men and Lebanese officials, who had for years cooperated or collaborated with the Israelis, and their families, spontaneously rushed to the Israeli crossing points at the international frontier. On May 23, the eastern sector of the Security Zone, including the town of Marj Ayoun, was overrun by Lebanese civilians backed by Hizbullah guerrillas. But there were still a handful of isolated IDF positions along the northern edge of the Zone. On the night of May 23–24, in a well-orchestrated operation, backed by columns of heavy Merkava tanks and helicopter gunships, the last Israeli troops pulled out under sporadic Hizbullah fire. The swiftness of the SLA collapse had taken the Hizbullah by surprise; they had failed to mount any effective operation against the retreating Israelis. Israel suffered no casualties, while the Hizbullah lost at least six dead.[6] But they had won the war against the invader who, after 19 years, had left Southern Lebanon palpably as a result of the guerrilla campaign and without any political or military agreement or gain.

All told, about 6,500 SLA men and South Lebanese officials and their families crossed over into Israel. Hizbullah, Druze, and Syrian Social Nationalist Party and Communist militiamen fanned out in the newly evacuated South Lebanese villages and along the border fence, with the Hizbullah in overall control. The guerrillas set up observation posts and Katyusha rocket and mortar emplacements within earshot of the international line. In one or two sites shots were traded with Israeli troops across the fence. Inside the Zone, only a handful of killings and beatings by Hizbullah or other militiamen were reported, though some 1,500 SLA men who had remained behind or had recrossed the border back to Lebanon were taken into custody by Lebanese security agencies and subsequently tried in large mass trials, usually ending up with relatively light sentences.

Barak was able to announce that he had fulfilled a major campaign promise: He had "freed" Israel from Lebanon, and removed the major obstacle to a possible Israeli-Lebanese peace agreement (which had since the early 1980s been viewed, in Jerusalem and Damascus, as an almost inevitable adjunct to an Israeli-Syrian settlement). But the slapdash IDF withdrawal to the frontier and the mad scramble of SLA men and families at the crossing points looked embarrassingly like a hasty retreat, and right-wing Israeli politicians immediately predicted that the Hizbullah would soon renew its military campaign—but this time against the Galilee settlements and from the border itself. In some areas, residential housing is a mere stone's throw away from the border fence.

Weeks later, after some diplomatic squabbling, UN officials and the Security Council (on June 18) confirmed that Israel had withdrawn back to the exact contours of the international demarcation line agreed upon by British and French officials in 1923, in compliance with Security Council Resolution 425. During the following months, the IDF erected a mined fence with electronic sensors the length of the border. But the Hizbullah, backed by Syria, raised objections to Israel's continued retention of some 20 square kilometers of territory in the Shab'a Farms or Har Dov area, at the northeastern edge of the frontier, where Israel, Lebanon and Syria meet. Israel had seized the area in 1967–1969 in the aftermath of the Six Day War and as part of its campaign against the PLO in the Arqoub, which Har Dov dominates. (However, one of the 18 farms was occupied by Israel only in 1982.) Israel claims that the land is Syrian, and therefore its to retain until—and if—it gives back the Golan Heights to Syria; Syria and Lebanon argue that the Shab'a Farms are Lebanese territory, "loaned" before 1967, to Syria.[7] The Hizbullah maintains that Israel has not completed its withdrawal from Lebanon so long as it remains in the Shab'a Farms—and therefore it still has the right and duty to fight on. But in practice, the Hizbullah, bowing to pressure from Syria and from the Lebanese government and population, who fear a renewal of warfare on Lebanese soil, has maintained a relatively stable cease-fire, bar a number of bomb and rocket attacks in the Har Dov sector and the abduction on the border of three Israeli soldiers (and the kidnapping of an IDF reserve colonel in an unnamed Arab state).

Without doubt the abrupt Israeli withdrawal from Southern Lebanon surprised and angered Damascus. The Syrians regarded Israel's entanglement in the

Security Zone as a Syrian "card," with anti-Israeli violence, mostly by proxy Hizbullah forces, to be modulated in accordance with Damascus's needs. Syria would "free" Israel from Southern Lebanon only in return for the Golan Heights. Suddenly Barak had extricated Israel from Lebanon without any Syrian gain. But on June 10, 2000, before Syria could decide how to react, President Hafez Assad, who for three decades and without success had alternatively fought and negotiated with Israel for the return of the Golan, collapsed and died of a heart attack.[8] With him died any hope of an early resumption of Israeli-Syrian peace negotiations. Assad's successor, his 34-year-old son, Bashar Assad, a physician and jumped-up Syrian army colonel, was quickly installed in power by the ruling Ba'ath Party and the Syrian state institutions. A popular referendum confirmed the selection with 97 percent of the votes (he was the only candidate for president). Bashar Assad quickly announced that he would follow in his father's footsteps in demanding that Israel relinquish every last inch of the Golan Heights in return for peace. The prospect of a renewal of Israeli-Syrian negotiations was effectively put on hold as Bashar devoted his energies to consolidating his rule.

Meanwhile, Israeli-Palestinian negotiations on a final status agreement had resumed in March 2000, and Israel agreed, in fulfillment of the terms of the Sharm ash Sheikh accord, to carry out a further hand-over of territory—6.1 percent of the West Bank. Some 341 square kilometeers around Jericho, Ramallah and Jenin were handed over to the Palestinians. But pressure from right-wingers within his coalition, persuaded Barak not to hand over the villages of Anabta and Abu Dis (in effect, an East Jerusalem neighborhood). Nonetheless, the hand-over of chunks of territory and hints that he intended to make further, perhaps large, concessions, as well as problems relating to religious and educational issues—the left-wing Meretz Party was engaged in a running battle with the ultra-orthodox Shas Party over the supervision and financing of Shas's private school system—gradually ate away at the bonds holding together his coalition. On July 9, his government effectively collapsed as the Shas, NRP and Yisrael Ba'aliya (a Russian immigrants' party) ministers resigned. The immediate trigger for the walkout was Barak's refusal to discuss an agreed political line in the impending Israeli-Palestinian summit, which he had pressed Washington to convene.

As if to underline his increasing internal political vulnerability, the Knesset that week voted 54 to 52 in favor of a no-confidence motion—but this fell short of the 61 votes needed by law to topple the government. Barak responded by saying, probably with accuracy, that the Knesset no longer reflected the popular will, which was in favor of peace and supported major concessions to achieve it.

Four days earlier, on July 5, President Clinton had announced that Barak and Arafat would meet at Camp David, starting on July 11, for the "make or break" summit. During July 11–26, Barak and Arafat, with Clinton (assisted by Albright) playing a crucial mediating role, tackled the major issues dividing Israel and the Palestinians: The refugees, Jerusalem, the borders between a future Palestinian state and Israel, the Israeli settlements, and the problem of water supplies and pollution. Over the summit hung the threat by Arafat that, in the absence of a final status agreement, the Palestinians would unilaterally declare statehood (and, presumably, the state's borders) on September 13. A crucial sticking point was Jerusalem. Barak, breaking a long-held, consensual Israeli taboo, agreed to a division of Jerusalem, with the Palestinians to receive sovereignty over most of the Arab-populated neighborhoods in the eastern part of the city. But no agreement was reached on the future of the walled Old City and, more particularly, the Temple Mount (Haram ash Sharif) area within it, containing the Dome of the Rock and the al-Aqsa Mosque as well as the (presumed) underground remains of King Solomon's and Zerubabel's (and Herod's) temples. Arafat stuck firm to his demand that the Temple Mount and the whole of the Old City come under Palestinian sovereignty; he rejected President Clinton's last-minute proposal that the Old City be divided between Israel and the Palestinians, with the Temple Mount to be governed conjointly by the Security Council, Morocco (the permanent president of the Islamic states' "Jerusalem Committee") and the Palestinians. Major disagreement also surfaced over the Palestinian demand for recognition and implementation of "the right of return" of the refugees (based on UN General Assembly Resolution 194, from December 1948) to their homes, villages and towns in Israel (Israel rejected this "right" and the return of millions of refugees, though it agreed to absorb "several thousand" refugees over ten years as part of a "family reunion scheme" and to participate in paying compensation for the refugees' lost property). There was also contention over the Palestinian demand that Israel hand over all of the West Bank and Gaza Strip to Palestinian rule (Barak was willing to concede 84–90 percent of the West Bank and almost all of the Gaza Strip). The summit collapsed, with both the Israelis and Palestinians letting fly with recriminations. In private, Barak (and, to a degree, Clinton) expressed astonishment and anger at the Palestinian rejection of the most far-reaching Israeli concessions ever offered. Arafat, for his part, lambasted the Israeli proposals as inadequate—in his view, they awarded the Palestinians the trappings rather than the reality of sovereignty and, besides, Israel would continue to rule large chunks (the Jordan Valley, the area around East Jerusalem) of the West Bank. The Americans blamed Arafat for the collapse of the talks, charging that, unlike Barak, he had failed to offer any concessions on the important issues.[9]

In Israel, word of Barak's concessions precipitated a series of political tremors. His foreign minister, David Levy, who had refused to attend Camp David, resigned on August 2, further weakening Barak internally. But the Prime Minister, locked on target—a final peace settlement—soldiered on.

Arafat was subjected to mounting Israeli and American pressure to match Israel's flexibility and to delay the announcement of statehood, which all understood would thrown the Middle East into a major crisis. Arafat agreed to the delay (he understood that his "state," if declared, would not receive world recognition), but refused to budge on the substantive issues, even after the new Israeli foreign minister, Shlomo Ben-Ami, proposed that the Temple Mount be placed under UN Security Council control in a final settlement and that 90–95 percent of the West Bank would be handed over to Palestinian sovereignty.

THE AL-AQSA INTIFADA

But the real, historic response of the Palestinians to the Barak peace proposals at Camp David was not diplomatic footwork but the launching of the second Intifada, almost immediately dubbed by the Palestinian leadership "the al-Aqsa Intifada," after the al-Aqsa Mosque, where the rebellion was triggered. The name, with its religious overtones, was useful in mobilizing pro-Palestinian sentiment in the Arab and Islamic worlds.

The spark to what began as a spontaneous, ground-up rebellion was provided by a visit on September 28 to the Temple Mount compound by Knesset member Ariel Sharon, who had succeeded Netanyahu as Likud Party chairman in May 1999. Though a few days before Arafat had cautioned Barak against allowing the visit, his head of the security service in the West Bank, Jibril Rajoub, had promised-predicted that the visit would pass quietly; so had Israel's internal security service, the GSS. Besides, there was no legal bar to an MK visiting the Temple Mount, so long as he did not act or speak provocatively. So Barak had given the visit the green light. Sharon, accompanied by many dozens of policemen, smiling broadly, spent 24 minutes strolling about the compound, then left; he did not approach or enter either of the mosques.

Apparently spontaneously, Muslim crowds gathered in Jerusalem and began rioting, pelting police with stones near the Temple Mount compound. The following day, a Friday, as tens of thousands left the compound after prayer, rioting erupted anew, this time on a grand scale. Israeli police entering the compound were pelted with stones and responded with rubber-coated (and possibly also live) ammunition, killing at least four Palestinians and wounding more than one hundred. The rioting spread throughout Jerusalem. The following day, throughout the West Bank and Gaza, demonstrators (most of them youngsters) clashed with Israeli troops at roadblocks and positions on the edges of the Palestinian-ruled towns and along Israeli-patrolled roads. Within hours, Palestinian Authority (PA) radio and television stations joined in with flagrant anti-Israeli (and occasionally anti-Semitic) incitement. PA leaders fanned the flames with talk of "marching on Jerusalem" and calls for a Jihad. The new Intifada had begun.

But it differed from the Intifada of the late 1980s in at least two important respects. Firstly, during the first days of the clashes the stone-throwing rioters were augmented by Palestinian security men and militiamen firing light weapons at Israeli positions. During the following weeks, the shooting attacks and bomb-planting were to become the essence of the rebellion, with street demonstrations and rock-throwing gradually declining in incidence and prominence. Secondly, this time Israel's million-strong Arab minority joined in. One of those killed on the Temple Mount on September 29 was an Israeli Arab, and this helped trigger a wave of violent mass protests in Arab villages around Israel. During September 30 and the first week of October Israeli Arab rioters, using stones and Molotov cocktails—and occasionally live fire—attacked civilian and police vehicles, blocked main thoroughfares and crossroads around the country, and set fire to gas stations, bank branches and other "Israeli" institutions inside their towns. There was rioting by the Arab minority populations in Jaffa, Acre and Nazareth, as well as in the Galilee, Little Triangle, and Negev beduin villages. The police, using rubber bullets and tear gas, and some live fire, tried to drive the rioters off the main roads back into the villages, often without success. Altogether 13 Israeli Arabs were killed and hundreds injured as well as dozens of policemen. One Israeli driver was killed by a stone thrown along a main road. The Arab minority leaders protested against the killing of "unarmed citizens" and demanded the establishment of a judicial commission of inquiry; Barak reluctantly agreed. (It was investigating these events as this book went to press.)

The cause of the eruption, which without doubt has scarred Jewish-Arab relations in Israel for many years to come, lay in the 52-year history of marginalization of and discrimination against the Arabs in Israeli society[10] and their gradual radicalization, which has included a fast-growing Islamic fundamentalist movement and incendiary anti-Israeli rhetoric by their elected leaders. (Several Arab MKs, for example, issued statements in support of the Hizbullah during 2000.) More immediately, Barak's studied indifference towards this minority and its leaders badly exacerbated existing tensions; after receiving 95 percent of the Arab vote in the 1999 elections, Barak failed to invite the Arab leaders into his coalition or even to consult with them, let alone offer redress for their various grievances, which included high levels of poverty and unemployment, a poor education system and weak infrastructures. When the Intifada erupted in East Jerusalem, and around the uniting religious symbol of the Temple Mount sites (where many Israeli Arabs pray), and was accompanied by the televised spectacle of massive Arab casualties, Israel's Arabs could apparently hold back no longer: Their Palestinian and Muslim identities were being challenged. The villages erupted in spontaneous violence, which their leaders neither wanted nor tried to control. This spontaneity was reinforced, during the following days, by deliberate incitement by PA spokesmen and media.[11]

The country's majority Jewish population was stunned by the outbreak. Many feared that the eruption marked the start of an Israeli Arab irridenta reflecting both a desire to subvert the Jewish state and to tear off Arab-populated chunks of territory and join them to a future Palestinian state. At the very least, the rioting was seen as an effort to help the PA and the West Bank and Gaza populations in theirs struggle against Israel, and as a first stage in a struggle for "territorial autonomy" within Israel.[12]

The causes of the outbreak in the West Bank and Gaza were somewhat different. Here, too, the alleged threat to Islamic control of the Temple Mount mosques—as represented by Sharon's visit—played a part. This was to become the standard PA explanation of the cause of the outbreak. But Israeli officials, with good cause, later described the Sharon visit as an "excuse" for, not as the cause of, the Intifada. Once the initial, spontaneous eruption had occurred, the Palestinian leadership quickly assumed a measure of control and indulged in massive incitement to further action. The leaders appear to have been motivated by a desire to improve the PA's position in the peace negotiations with Israel. This, at least, was the reading of the situation—which probably exaggerated the degree of control exercised throughout by Arafat—presented in the official Israeli report to the international committee of inquiry headed by Senator George Mitchell. For example, the report quoted a statement by senior PA official Abu Ali Mustafa from July 23, 2000, just after the breakdown of the Camp David summit and two months before the Intifada's outbreak: "The issues of Jerusalem, the refugees and sovereignty will be decided on the ground and not in negotiations. On this point it is important to prepare the Palestinian public for the next step, because without doubt we shall find ourselves in conflict with Israel in order to create new facts on the ground ... I believe the situation in the future will be more violent than the [1987–93] Intifada." And months after the outbreak, the PA's Communications Minister, Imad Al-Faluji, told an audience of Palestinian refugees at Ein al-Hilwe that the Intifada was planned by the PA leadership after the breakdown of the Camp David talks.[13]

But these explanations are insufficient—the outbreak owed much more to history and the state of the Palestinians and the peace process. At base, the frustrations and slights endured since the signing in 1993 of the Oslo agreement and, more generally, since the start of the occupation in 1967, had now come home to roost. Indeed, the new Intifada seemed to give release to the pent-up anger of the Palestinians since their initial confrontations with Zionism and the catastrophic loss of Palestine in 1948. The Palestinian population in the West Bank and Gaza Strip had tired of the domination and control over their lives exercised by the Hashemites and the Egyptians between 1948 and 1967, and by Israel (in direct fashion until 1993 and indirectly, but still very palpably, ever since). All Israeli Arabs remained dependent on the Israeli economy for livelihood and basic services; all had to endure the insult and humiliation of searches at IDF roadblocks as they traveled from one island of Palestinian control to another or into Israel or out of the country; and all suffered politically from the absence of real sovereignty and control over their lives and fortunes.

Meanwhile, the Palestinians, many of them, especially in the Gaza Strip, endured harsh living conditions in refugee camps or slums. Oslo heightened expectations of an immediate improvement and release from political bondage. But as one government succeeded another in Jerusalem and as partial agreement succeeded partial agreement, nothing seemed to improve; the longed-for sovereignty and economic boom failed to materialize. True, about 40 percent of the West Bank, with most of the territory's population, and most of the Gaza Strip had come under Palestinian rule. But real control remained in Israeli hands and the poor remained poor. The PA was seen by many as despotic and corrupt, and in many ways collaborationist (hadn't Arafat and his security services for years protected Israel from Hamas and Islamic Jihad militants?). Indeed, for many Palestinians life had been better under direct Israeli rule. By September 2000, the masses apparently had reached a point where they could no longer wait.

And the Hizbullah had just pointed out the route to successful liberation. Without doubt the hasty IDF withdrawal/retreat from Southern Lebanon four months before had a revelatory, almost hypnotic effect on the West Bank and Gaza populations: The message from South Lebanon was that Israel, its sophisticated air force and giant armored divisions notwithstanding, was weak; that the determined guerrilla, with Kalashnikov and grenade in hand, could win; and that Palestine could be "liberated" without "favors" from the Israelis at the negotiating table and without giving anything in return.[14]

Barak's actions during his first year in office had certainly contributed to the explosion. Like Netanyahu before him, he too repeatedly postponed the implementation of Oslo-related IDF pullbacks from parts of the West Bank. And, while not setting up new settlements, the Barak administration had repeatedly approved a significant enlargement of existing settlements. Every Palestinian understood that each settlement expansion meant that much less territory for his people. At the same time, many hundreds of Palestinian security prisoners continued to languish in Israeli jails, despite repeated appeals by Arafat and continuous demonstrations by the prisoners' families in the territories.[15]

Barak's peace proposals of July 2000 at Camp David, paradoxically, also contributed to the eruption. Barak had come to power announcing a complete break with the Netanyahu past and an intention to reach a final settlement with the Palestinians. During the 1980s and 1990s, the PLO leadership had gradually accepted, or seemed to accept, history's verdict: That Israel, in its post-1948 borders, was there to stay—keeping 78 percent of historic "Palestine." But the PLO wanted the remaining 22 percent, the West Bank and Gaza Strip, regarding this as a modicum of justice. At Camp David Barak had endorsed the establishment of a Palestinian state; but he had proposed that it make do with 84–90 percent of that 22 percent—and to underline his point had insisted

that the bulk of the settlers and large concentrations of Jewish West Bank settlements be incorporated into Israel. Also Israel was to control the territory
between a greatly enlarged "Jerusalem" and Jericho, effectively cutting the
core of the future Palestinian state in two, and giving Israel control of the border crossings between the Palestinian state and Egypt and Jordan. To Palestinian eyes, this was not fair or just.

Moreover, one of the basic assumptions of the Barak proposals was the
non-return of the Palestinian refugees to their homes. They could return to
Palestine, i.e., the West Bank and Gaza, but not to the sites of their pre-1948
homes in Israel. For the refugee communities, especially in the camps of the
Gaza Strip and Lebanon, this spelled ideological death. The vision of a return
is what had kept them going, the be-all and end-all of their political existence,
a major part of their identity, during the previous half century. Without doubt,
the refugees who are so prominent in the ranks of the Hamas, Islamic Jihad
and the Fatah's Tanzim and in the front lines of the al Aqsa Intifada, are, at
least to a degree, motivated by this dream of a return and by a desire to prevent
its removal from the agenda.

During its first few weeks, the Intifada violence focused on Israeli positions
and outposts outside the main Palestinian towns—Ramallah, Bethlehem,
Nablus, Rafah, Khan Yunis, Hebron. Daily, hundreds of stone- and Molotov
cocktail–throwing youngsters confronted Israeli soldiers and border policemen
using rubber bullets and tear gas, and some live fire. Armed Palestinians, hiding
behind or among the rioters, joined in with occasional shots. Much of the violence focused on isolated Israeli settlements, such as Netzarim and Kfar Darom
in the Gaza Strip and Psagot near Ramallah. The Palestinian gunmen have been
waging a more or less systematic campaign aimed at unnerving the settlers—
perhaps with an eye to ultimately engineering their evacuation of the territories.
In addition, during the Intifada's first weeks the gunmen directed much of their
anger at Jewish "religious outposts" (which they regarded as both militarily
and religiously provocative), such as Joseph's Tomb in Nablus and Rachel's
Tomb on the northern outskirts of Bethlehem. When Joseph's tomb fell at the
start of October after a two-day siege, the attackers proceeded to demolish the
building with pick-axes and hammers; destruction was also meted out by
Palestinians a few days later to Jericho's ancient synagogue. The PA, which
was seeking sovereignty over major Christian and Jewish religious sites, was
embarrassed and later apologized and restored both buildings.

It could be argued—as Palestinians often did—that Israel's continued
occupation of large parts of the West Bank and Gaza Strip and the continued
control of Palestinian lives was a form of "aggression." But during the al-Aqsa
Intifada—which Arab spokesmen dubbed, in Orwellian style, "The Peace
Intifada" during its first months —Arafat and his colleagues went further, giving voice to a veritable culture of mendacity. They consistently described

what was happening as an Israeli-initiated "war" on the Palestinians. And they repeatedly broadcast barefaced lies about the specifics of Israeli behavior, such as alleging the IDF's use of poison gas (they called it "black gas") and depleted uranium projectiles against Palestinian civilians or attributing the firing on Gilo to Israeli collaborators. They flatly denied, almost as a matter of form, their involvement in the violence.[16] In reality, however, the specific acts of violence of which the Intifada consisted—the stone-throwing, shooting, bomb attacks—were invariably initiated by the Palestinians, often with the involvement or under direct order of PA officials. By and large, Israeli troops—on order to use live fire only in life-endangering situations—acted with extreme restraint in face of acute provocation. The shells and rockets fired by IDF tanks and helicopters—apart from individual assassination operations (during October 2000–January 2001 in Ramallah, Beit Jala, Jericho and the Gaza Strip)—killed no more than three or four Palestinians altogether.

Nonetheless, on October 7 the UN Security Council voted "to condemn the excessive use of force against Palestinians." In part, television coverage was responsible. Israel allowed almost complete freedom to Western, Arab and Israeli television crews covering the events—and what was broadcast, given the IDF's superior armaments and firepower, almost always placed Israel in the dock. The crews almost never arrived on the scene in time to catch who had started a given firefight—but always showed the strong Israeli response. (Which, of course, televised well. Helicopters firing rockets at houses showed up far better and more powerfully than a lone Palestinian gunmen firing from behind a bush.) Symbolic of television's powerful effect on public reaction around the world was the death of Muhammad al-Dura, a 12-year-old boy caught in a Gaza crossfire whose death in his father's arms was captured by TV cameras. What exactly the two were doing at the Netzarim junction that day is unclear; nor was it clear whether the two had been hit by Israeli or Palestinian bullets, though most viewers, at Arab prodding, were persuaded that the IDF was responsible.

By October 10, some 90 Palestinians lay dead and some 2,000 injured. There were only a handful of Israeli casualties as the IDF had prepared well, in terms of reinforced fortifications and cleared lines of fire, since the "Tunnel Incident" in 1996, when Palestinian gunmen had killed some 18 Israeli soldiers during three days of rioting and shooting following Israel's opening of an exit from a Second Temple tunnel that ran parallel to and outside the Temple Mount's Western Wall. Additionally, the Palestinians possessed and used only light weapons, which were barely able to penetrate the Israeli positions (though in the course of the Intifada, Palestinian armaments were bolstered by smuggled shipments of anti-tank, rocket-propelled grenades and, perhaps, a handful of missiles).

On October 12, Palestinian civilians and policemen lynched two Israeli reserve soldiers who had accidentally wandered into Ramallah and been detained by policemen. The bodies were subsequently mutilated. The PA tried but failed to prevent TV footage of the incident from getting out. The televised savagery, which appalled the Israeli public, accurately reflected Palestinian anger and hatred toward Israel. Israel retaliated the same day with a series of helicopter-launched rockets against PA police posts (including the one in which the murders had occurred) and offices in Ramallah and Gaza—but only after warning the Palestinians to clear out of the targeted buildings. No one was killed.[17]

The measure of involvement of the PA and its president, Yasser Arafat, in the initial outbreak and in the subsequent violence is not clear. Israeli intelligence reported that after the breakdown of the Camp David talks in July 2000, various PA agencies began preparing for an eventual outbreak of hostilities by stocking up on certain basic goods; there may also have been an increase in Palestinian efforts to smuggle in arms and ammunition. However, the initial rioting of September 28–29 seems to have been completely spontaneous, though local Fatah cadres certainly were active as inciters and leaders. During the initial bouts of shooting, PA policemen and security men occasionally took part, but not as members of organized units and probably on personal or, at most, local initiative. But as the days wore on, and street riots were either accompanied or replaced by shooting attacks, the Fatah's militia arm, the Tanzim (the Organization, in Arabic), emerged in a dominant role. In each region, the local Tanzim apparatus organized and carried out the attacks; occasionally, squads of PA policemen and security men (especially from among Force 17, Arafat's bodyguard unit, and Muhammad Dahlan's Preventive Security Agency, the main PA security arm in the Gaza Strip) took part, planting bombs or ambushing convoys. Marwan Bargouti, the Fatah and Tanzim secretary general in the West Bank, declared that his party was leading the struggle, and would not stop firing until independence was won and the occupier pushed out. Arafat appears almost from the first to have given "the street" and its activities his benediction without actually authorizing specific attacks—but at the same time keeping his own police and security agencies as such out of the fighting. While he released Hamas and Islamic Jihad activists from his jails in a show of "national" unity, he kept them on a tight leash with respect to terrorist operations in Israel proper. (During the Intifada's first four months, there were surprisingly few terrorist operations inside Israel. This was partly due to GSS and Israeli police interdiction; but it also seems to have been due to a general PA guideline not to overly antagonize the Israelis. Such attacks might prompt the Israelis to hold back on concessions at the negotiating table or energize them into major, painful anti-PA reprisals.) The Israeli (and western) intelligence services spent October–December 2000 debating whether Arafat was controlling and directing the rebellion or was simply "riding the tiger," whether by choice or because he was incapable of controlling his population and gunmen. In public, Arafat generally presented himself as in control, the rebellion's instigator and leader. And, occasionally, when diplomatic foot-work required, Arafat issued behind-the-scenes orders to "the street" to cease fire or lower the intensity of the violence. And by and large, the intensity was reduced, for a day or two, indicating that Arafat had a measure of strategic control over the level of violence but was probably incapable, had he chosen to, of stopping it altogether.

The development of the Intifada created a situation of near-anarchy in the West Bank and Gaza Strip. Power to a degree shifted from the formal, "national" PA institutions, including the security agencies, to the rebel frame-works and squads—Tanzim, Hamas, Islamic Jihad, and plain criminals—in the streets (to a degree duplicating the power-shifts that characterized the first Intifada). In a sense, the PA faded only to be supplanted by a reborn PLO. The PA's major losses of revenue resulted in an inability to pay its employees, con-tributing to its growing weakness. In some measure, actions against Israeli tar-gets became a function of turf struggles between competing Palestinian groups and organizations; killing Israelis garnered popularity. Occasionally, the turf connections were convoluted. For example, the almost daily shooting by a group of Ta'amra beduin tribe gunmen installed in Beit Sahur, a Bethle-hem suburb-village, at the nearby IDF Shdema base—bringing down IDF counterfire against Beit Sahur—ceased for a month in January 2001 after a squad from Beit Sahur travelled to the Teko'a area to the south, the Ta'amra tribe's "homeland," and fired at a nearby IDF post, which brought down IDF counterfire against nearby Ta'amra houses. The frequent firing from the Beth-lehem Christian suburb of Beit Jala by Fatah gunmen at the Jerusalem neigh-borhood of Gilo appears to have been partly motivated by a desire to bring down upon the Christian population IDF counterfire, perhaps to induce it to participate more actively in the rebellion (many Muslims viewed their Chris-tian Arab fellows as insufficiently active). The firing on Gilo ceased (for a month) early in January only after Israeli counterfire produced pressure by Beit Jala's residents (and sympathetic Western churches) on Arafat to halt the attacks.[18]

The IDF initially responded in kind to attacks on settlements and Jeru-salem's Jewish neighborhoods with (usually heavier) machine-gun fire and, occasionally, with tank rounds or helicopter–rocket fire against the offending buildings. But in November 2000, the Israelis compounded this form of response by targeting specific local Fatah, Hamas and Islamic Jihad comman-ders and operatives who were suspected of mounting the attacks. IDF intelli-gence, the GSS, the IAF and select ground units were used in pinpoint strikes: Samih Mal'aba, 28, a Kalandiya refugee camp resident and Fatah activist was killed on December 17 by an exploding cellular telephone, probably a "gift" from the GSS; Hussein Abayat, a local Tanzim commander who led the gun-men shooting almost nightly at Gilo, was killed near Bethlehem in his jeep (along with two innocent bystanders) on November 9 by a rocket fired from a helicopter gunship; Ibrahim Bani Uda, a senior Hamas officer, was killed as the headrest in his car exploded on November 24.[19] On February 13, 2001, Israeli helicopters killed Massoud Ayad, a senior officer in Arafat's presidential guard, Force 17, and a (part-time) Hizbullah agent, responsible for two mortar attacks on Netzarim in January and February. Altogether, some 15 Palestinian operatives were taken out by Israel between November and the end of February. Israel's "liquidation policy" was challenged by Barak's left-wing critics, Arab human rights organizations and criticized by the United States.

Much of the accuracy of the Israeli assassinations was attributed by Palestinians to good intelligence garnered from a network of collaborators and informers. As in the 1970s and 1980s, the PLO had been riddled with Israeli agents, so, too, was the PA and its police and security agencies. These agencies, as well as ad hoc Palestinian activists, sought out, arrested and often killed suspected collaborators. Sometimes, a "kangaroo" trial took place; sometimes not even that. But quite often those killed had had no connection to any Israeli security agency—clans were simply taking revenge on enemy clans, husbands on suspected lovers of their wives, etc. One Israeli source said that of the nine Palestinians officially executed as collaborators during November–December 2000, "less than four" worked for the GSS. Many more were jailed.[20]

Israel responded to the rioting with rubber bullets and tear gas, and to the sniping and machine-gun fire with snipers and machine-guns of its own, occasionally letting loose with a tank shell or a helicopter missile against a building housing gunmen. Care was taken not to hit collateral targets and non-rioting and non-shooting bystanders (though a few died). Ambushes were set along problematic roads and outside PA centers to interdict foraying gunmen. Israel's main anti-Intifada measures were to seal off the territories so that Palestinian laborers (and terrorists) could not reach Israel and Palestinian produce could not be exported; to deny the PA areas various raw materials and goods; and to seal off the various PA-controlled villages and towns from each other with rings of roadblocks and armor. Alongside trouble-prone roads, especially in the Gaza Strip, armored bulldozers destroyed groves and orchards and, occasionally, houses and workshops, to deny Palestinian gunmen cover. Jericho's casino, long the play venue of rich Israelis, was eventually shelled after repeated use of its roof by Palestinian gunmen. But the Israelis generally took care not to escalate the conflict by cutting off electricity or water supplies or telephone services, or by crossing into PA-ruled ("A") areas—partly in order not to antagonize the Americans or provoke the Arab states.

The Israeli measures restricted the violence but didn't end it. Squads of gunmen still managed to evade the IDF, launch an attack, and then escape back into the cities. Particularly attractive targets for these squads were settlers commuting between home and work. At the end of December 2000,

Palestinian gunmen murdered Binyamin Kahane (the son and political heir of Meir Kahane, the head of the extremist Kach party who had also died at Arab hands) and his wife on a road near Ramallah. Palestinian gunmen traded shots almost daily with Israeli guards in the isolated West Bank and Gaza settlements and outposts. Even so, the level of Israeli response was always cautious and restrained. The Israeli right charged that the government was preventing the army from "crushing the Intifada." But Barak and his generals denied this, saying that the army was doing what it deemed appropriate in the circumstances. Clearly, Barak and his generals were trying to avoid a slide into a general Middle Eastern war. During the Intifada's early days, Palestinian rioted in Jordan and Lebanon, and sympathetic students rioted on the streets of Cairo; the Intifada's potential for escalation, by destabilizing and sucking in neighboring states, was palpable.

In a major effort to halt the fighting, Clinton and Mubarak convened a summit in Sharm ash Sheikh on October 16–17, with Arafat, Barak and Jordan's King Abdullah attending. Both sides made a commitment to end the violence but Arafat and Barak failed to sign an agreement or to shake hands. Clinton simply announced that Barak and Arafat had agreed to take steps to end the violence.[21] The parties agreed to the dispatch of a U.S.-led fact-finding mission (the Mitchell Committee) to investigate the events during the first weeks of the Intifada and how to prevent their recurrence, and the U.S. was empowered to seek ways to renew the peace talks.

Immediately afterward, on October 21–22, the Arab leaders convened a summit in Cairo—the first Arab summit since 1996. Most of the leaders, including Mubarak of Egypt, Abdullah of Jordan, and Bashar Assad of Syria, reaffirmed their support for the peace process—alongside condemnations of Israel and support for the Intifada. The summit, at the insistence of Arafat (who all along had been pressing for international intervention in the crisis, including the dispatch of a UN peacekeeping force to the territories), called for an international war crimes tribunal to try Israeli perpetrators of "massacres," supported the Palestinian demand of "the right of return" as sacred, and called for Palestinian sovereignty over all of East Jerusalem, including the Old City and its Temple Mount. The moderate Arab states, Egypt and Jordan, managed to ward off pressures to break their diplomatic ties with Israel—though Egypt withdrew its ambassador and Jordan failed to send a new one to Tel Aviv. Most of the other Arab states with partial diplomatic relations with Israel—Oman, Tunisia, Morocco, etc.—broke off their ties.

EFFECTS OF THE INTIFADA

The first four months of the Intifada left about 350 Palestinians dead and thousands injured, and over 50 Israelis dead and several hundred injured. There was relatively little property damage; both sides deployed, almost consistently, only light weapons.

The most important immediate effect of the outbreak of the Intifada was to precipitate a new American diplomatic initiative, involving concessions to the Palestinians that went beyond what had been offered at Camp David, and tentative Israeli acceptance of these new proposals. Initially, in October 2000, Barak insisted that Israel would not continue to negotiate peace under fire and so the American (and UN, European and moderate Arab) efforts were directed at obtaining a cease-fire. But all international efforts—for example, by Madeleine Albright in Paris on October 4 and Mubarak the following day in Egypt—to broker a cease-fire failed, and by November Barak caved in, agreeing to renew the peace talks against the background of continued Palestinian violence (for which concession he came under scathing criticism inside Israel). Barak was under two ineluctable pressures—the pressure of the rebellion itself, which he understood would end only with a political agreement, and the pressure exerted by two imminent political deadlines—the end of Clinton's presidency on January 20, 2001 (after which he could expect no American mediatory support) and Israel's elections on February 6. He understood that he must use the remaining weeks to clinch a deal with the Palestinians, otherwise there would be, in all probability, no deal for many years—and that in the absence of a deal, he would almost certainly be replaced by a right-wing prime minister.

Following weeks of behind-the-scenes diplomatic footwork, President Clinton dispatched a set of proposals for a comprehensive, final status Israeli-Palestinian peace agreement to Barak and Arafat. Dated December 23, the Clinton proposals called for a hand-over of "94–96 percent" of the West Bank to Palestinian sovereignty and Israeli territorial compensation to the Palestinians elsewhere (presumably in the northwestern Negev, adjoining the Gaza Strip) for the 4–6 percent it would retain; the evacuation of most Israeli settlements; an international force to secure the new borders, particularly between the West Bank and Jordan; early warning stations in the West Bank; the demilitarization of the Palestinian state; the division of Jerusalem according to demographic concentrations, with the Arab districts under Palestinian sovereignty and the Jewish districts under Israeli sovereignty; and some form of Palestinian sovereignty over the Temple Mount and Israeli sovereignty over the Wailing Wall "and the area sacred to the Jews" or "the holy of holies" (meaning the area under the two mosques). As to the refugees, Clinton somewhat confusingly proposed that Israel agree to recognize the physical and moral suffering caused the Palestinian people as a result of 1948; a return of Palestinian refugees to the Palestinian state while Israel might absorb some of them; at the same time, both states should recognize the refugees' "right of return," either to "their homeland" or "historic Palestine"; and he called for international aid for rehabilitating the refugees.[22] Israeli critics charged that Clinton—and, by extension, Barak—had in effect accepted "the right of return"; Barak countered that Israel had agreed only to a refugee "return" to the prospective West Bank–Gaza Strip Palestinian state, alongside a token return of refugees to Israel proper.

At the end of December the Israeli government formally accepted Clinton's proposals as a basis for a settlement; Arafat responded with a long list of questions and objections, amounting to a rejection.[23] As Yasser Abd Rabo, one of Arafat's ministers and peace negotiators, put it: "Clinton's proposals are one of the biggest frauds in history, like the Sykes-Picot Agreement."[24]

During the following weeks, with Washington mediating, the Israelis strove to reach a peace agreement while at the same time to obtain at least a reduction in Palestinian violence so as to make the continued negotiations with the Palestinians palatable to the Israeli public. Israeli officials tried to project optimism ("the two sides have never been closer to agreement") but either there was too little time to make the necessary compromises or the Palestinians were simply uninterested in reaching an agreement that would include their effective abandonment of "the right of return"—which Jewish Israelis almost unanimously agreed would spell suicide for the Jewish state—and of full sovereignty over the Old City of Jerusalem.

Palestinian and Israeli delegations met for a last effort at Taba, in Sinai, during January 21–27 but the talks were continuously undermined by Palestinian acts of terrorism (such as the execution-style murder of two unarmed Israeli civilians by Tanzim operatives in Tulkarm on January 23) and by Palestinian unwillingness to budge from their fixed positions on Jerusalem, the borders, and the refugees. The talks broke up on January 27 with a joint statement that in effect conceded that nothing had been concluded or agreed, though Abu Alaa and Ben-Ami affirmed that "significant progress had been made" and that they had "never been closer to agreement."[25] Again, Arafat had either played Israel along, unwilling simply to make peace with the Jewish state, or, though willing, had simply failed to rise to the occasion and make the best deal he would ever be offered. In either case, the Palestinians, it would seem, had once again missed an historic opportunity in their century-long struggle for independence and statehood. The following day, January 28, Barak called a halt to all talks with the Palestinians (after Arafat's hate-filled speech against Israel at Davos—see following) and devoted the remaining week to his election campaign. The Israeli-Palestinian peace process had ground to an indefinite halt.

The Intifada badly shook the PA-controlled areas of the West Bank and Gaza Strip. The PA appears to have lost much of its authority, and real power passed, at least on the local, day-to-day level, to the armed militia and terrorist groups only informally linked (Tanzim), or not at all (Hamas, Islamic Jihad), to the PA. The old guard running the PA had been somewhat discredited—the years of negotiation with Israel had failed to deliver a full, sovereign Palestinian state or economic betterment—and power began to shift to younger activists, who were running the current Intifada at street level.[26] The extent of this changing of the guard is still unclear; much will depend on the length and military and political outcome of the Intifada and on Israel's behavior.

More easily assessible are the very substantial Palestinians' economic losses due to the outbreak. Israel has held up various payments (mostly of taxes paid to Israel by Palestinian laborers in the past) to the PA, as have Western states and the Arab states (due to the chaos and corruption in the PA and the uncertainty about what would happen to these funds were they to reach the West Bank and Gaza).[27] These losses amounted to several hundred million dollars by February 2001. Israel's partial stoppage of the flow of raw materials and goods into the territories has crippled their industries and hurt their retailers. The almost complete stoppage of exports from the territories has badly hurt agriculture and industry. There was a major drop in PA tax revenues. The closure of the territories has meant that more than 120,000 Palestinian laborers have stopped commuting to and earning wages in Israel. Moreover, the Intifada put an almost complete halt to tourism, one of the mainstay's of West Bank's economy. One estimate put Palestinian losses from these developments at $400–500 million for October–November 2000 alone;[28] another, at $774 million.[29] To this must be added a drop in foreign investments in the territories. According to Terje Larsen, the UN secretary-general's special envoy to the Middle East, the Al-Aqsa Intifada had erased—in its first eight weeks—the gains from the three previous years of economic development in the territories. Unemployment in the West Bank and Gaza, which had stood at 12 percent in 1999, by December 2000 was around 40 percent. Poverty, he reported, affected 32 percent of the population; half the Palestinians lived on some $2 a day.[30]

Without doubt the first four months of the Intifada also had a detrimental—if less serious—effect on the Israeli economy, which had enjoyed a significant improvement since the start of Barak's premiership. There was an instant decline in foreign investments and an almost complete halt to tourism, with most hotels empty, restaurants partly empty, and tourism companies and guides badly hurt. Agriculture and construction, and to a far lesser degree, industry, were marginally hit by the unavailability of Palestinian laborers. It is still too early to accurately gauge the full economic effects of the Intifada.

But the major effect on Israel, of course, was political. New elections had been in the air since mid-2000, as Barak's coalition fell apart, mainly because of his drawn-out peace initiative and proposed concessions to the Palestinians. The outbreak of the Intifada telescoped the process and brought about elections for the prime minister—resulting in Barak's (humiliating) dismissal by the vast majority of the Israeli public and his replacement by the Likud's hard-line leader, Ariel Sharon. Perhaps with more lasting import, the Intifada—as a response to Israel's peace efforts—cast the Israeli left (Labor and Meretz) into major ideological disarray. There was widespread confusion and a sense of betrayal by Arafat. Traditionally, since 1967, what had divided left from right was the left's willingness to compromise and make territorial concessions for peace and, ultimately, to agree to a Palestinian state in the West Bank and Gaza. But now Syria—despite being offered 99 percent of the Golan Heights—had very impolitely turned down the Israeli overture (for a second time), and the Palestinians had belligerently turned down Israel's far-reaching concessions. What's more, the Palestinians had launched a mini-war against the Jewish state, possibly with the intention of sucking in the whole Middle East. Symbolic of what had happened were the speeches by Shimon Peres and Yasser Arafat at the World Economic Forum at Davos, Switzerland, on January 28, 2001: Peres spoke of the need and inevitability of partnership, peace and cooperation between Israel and the Palestinians; Arafat branded the Jewish state "fascistic," "colonialist" and murderous, charged mendaciously that Israel was using uranium-tipped shells against his people, was trying to starve them, and was intent on "destroying the Palestinians." It was as if Oslo and eight years of dialogue, peace-making and Israeli concessions had never happened. In the absence of a partner for peace, what exactly could the left now offer the Israeli voter?

On November 28, 2000, Barak agreed to general elections—and then, on December 9, took everyone by surprise by announcing his resignation, forcing elections for the premiership within 60 days. For a moment it appeared that there would be a repeat of 1999 and that Netanyahu would run against him. But Netanyahu withdrew after the parties rejected his call for Knesset elections as well. Barak was left in the ring with Ariel Sharon. Initially, the opinion polls gave Sharon only a slight lead—but it expanded by leaps and bounds with each new Palestinian attack, especially in the Israeli heartland, and with each new expression of rejectionism by Arafat.

Much as Arafat had won the 1996 elections for Netanyahu against Peres, by allowing the dispatch into Tel Aviv and Jerusalem of Hamas and Islamic Jihad suicide bombers, so he won the election for Sharon on February 6, 2001. Again, it was Arab violence that persuaded the Israeli middle-of-the-road swing vote to move to the right because of the enhanced personal security that it promised. It was a one-issue election, dominated by Arafat's rejection of the Clinton-Barak proposals and by the Intifada, which was seen as the Palestinian response to these proposals. Moreover, the violence in the territories had spread into Israel by inciting the until-then dormant Arab minority to massive demonstrations and violence of its own. The Israeli public responded by throwing out Barak, a leader of vision and tremendous courage, and installing in his place an old and tried warhorse, who could be expected to send a shudder down Palestinian spines, with an overwhelming mandate: Sharon won 62.4 percent of the vote to Barak's 37.6 percent; it was the most decisive win in Israeli history. It was also the most poorly attended, with a 62 percent turnout that helped Sharon. One reason for the almost 25-point margin was that many of Israel's Arabs, obeying their leaders,[31] boycotted the election in protest against what was seen as Barak's brutal response to their rioting in early October and his indifference to their needs and grievances during the previous twelve months. Only 18 percent voted, down from over 70 percent in 1999. Some Arab and Jewish commentators interpreted the vote as representing the start of a sea of change in the Arab minority's attitude toward Israel, a "declaration of independence" and possibly the start of a pro-autonomy or irridentist movement. Another reason for the low turnout was the disappointment and confusion on the left: Some stayed home in protest against Barak's "insufficient" flexibility in the negotiations; others, because he had made too many concessions toward the religious parties (in his effort to keep the pro-peace coalition together); still others, out of despair resulting from Arafat's response to Barak's overtures.

Following his victory, Sharon had two choices: To form a right-wing religious government based on a narrow 62-seat Knesset majority and a hard-line foreign policy platform; or to form a so-called "national unity government," based on a Likud-Labor partnership which would be joined by several religious and centrist factions. A "unity" government would help Sharon fend off Western and Arab political pressures and avoid crippling internal dissidence (of the sort that had undermined his war in Lebanon in 1982).

By press time, Sharon had put together a Likud-Labor "unity" government, to which Shas and Agudat Yisrael and several ultra–right wing parties had been added. Labor held the defense and foreign affairs portfolios (Shimon Peres is Foreign Minister) and the Likud holds the premiership (Sharon) and finance ministry. But it is extremely unlikely, given Arafat's uncompromising positions and the Likud's hard-line stance on settlements, the refugees and an undivided, Jewish-ruled Jerusalem that this government would make any headway in negotiating peace with the Palestinians.

Sharon's election, which under other circumstances might have stunned the world, was greeted with an almost unnatural calm both in Washington and the Arab states. The newly installed Bush Administration, in any case not particularly happy with Clinton's performance on the Middle East, gave Sharon the benefit of the doubt and refused to regard him through the prism of the Lebanon War of 1982. Going even further, it announced formally that the ideas proposed by Clinton for a Palestinian-Israeli peace were Clinton's personally and were no longer official American positions. Indeed, Clinton himself added that now that he was out of office, his proposals no longer obligated anyone.

Barak chimed in by declaring that so long as not everything was agreed upon, nothing was agreed—in effect releasing Sharon from the Clinton proposals and whatever was agreed between the negotiating teams at Taba.

Arafat, with the Arab states in his wake, displayed some trepidation at the advent of Sharon, but announced that they would do business with whatever government was in power in Israel. They all declared that they expected the negotiations to proceed from the point at which they had left off (meaning that they considered the concessions embodied in the Clinton proposals and the Taba talks the basis for future negotiations). But clearly there was deep anxiety in the Arab world. On the ground, the Palestinians stepped up their shooting attacks on Israeli positions, as if to say "we are not afraid of you." The Arab news media, in Palestine and outside, uniformly portrayed Sharon as "the butcher of Lebanon." Arafat and the Palestinians understood that Sharon, while willing to negotiate, was unlikely to offer as much as Barak. The outside Arab leaders feared that an impasse in Israeli-Palestinian negotiations would lead to an escalation of Israeli-Palestinian clashes, which could suck the rest of the Middle East into the conflict. Particularly alarmed were the Jordanians, who feared a spillover of the Intifada into their kingdom and moves by Sharon to translate his long-espoused vision, "Jordan is Palestine," into reality—meaning that he might try to promote a Palestinian overthrow of the Hashemite regime and turn Jordan into the Palestinian state.

Where the Middle East is headed in the short term is unclear. While some commentators suspected that Sharon might try to pull off a "Charles de Gaulle"—the hard-line general who surprised everyone by making grand concessions for peace and extricated France from Algeria—most felt that Sharon, with Labor at his side, would probably aim for a further partial agreement, or a series of further partial agreements, to bring down the level of Palestinian-Israeli violence or end it altogether. With Syria, he would probably try to renew the negotiations though it is doubtful whether he would be as conciliatory as Rabin and Barak. How the Arabs would respond to all this is unclear. Arafat and the Palestinians are likely to continue fighting and to declare statehood in the coming months. Bashar Assad is unlikely to agree to anything less than a 100 percent Israeli withdrawal from the territory lost in 1967. Like Arafat, he probably believes that time is on his side, and has been trained by his father to think in terms of decades and centuries, not months and years.

CONCLUSIONS

ORIGINS

I n 1938, against the backdrop of the Arab rebellion against the Mandate, David Ben-Gurion told the Political Committee of Mapai: "When we say that the Arabs are the aggressors and we defend ourselves—that is only half the truth. As regards our security and life we defend ourselves. . . . But the fighting is only one aspect of the conflict, which is in its essence a political one. And politically we are the aggressors and they defend themselves."[1]

Ben-Gurion, of course, was right. Zionism was a colonizing and expansionist ideology and movement. Classic European colonialism had seen imperialist countries projecting their power and extending their territory by force of arms and by the settlement of their sons in far-flung territories, where they lorded it over disenfranchised native populations and exploited the natural resources. Zionism, as its leaders saw it, served no imperial power but rather a dispersed people that was in need of a piece of territory in which to find a safe haven and reconstruct itself socially, economically, and politically. The movement, focusing on Palestine, where the Jews had lived and ruled during the first millennium B.C., carried this out, starting in the early 1880s, by purchasing—not conquering—land and establishing colonies or settlements. The first colonists did exploit the cheap native labor, but subsequent generations of immigrants tried to avoid this, for reasons both of morality and expediency, aiming at an exclusive, separate Jewish economy as a basis for an autarchic society and state. Paradoxically, but also naturally, this separatist ethos became another source of friction with the Palestinian Arabs.

Zionist ideology and practice were necessarily and elementally expansionist. Realizing Zionism meant organizing and dispatching settlement groups to Palestine. As each settlement took root, it became acutely aware of its isolation and vulnerability, and quite naturally sought the establishment of new Jewish settlements around it. This would make the original settlement more "secure"—but the new settlements now became the "front line" and themselves needed "new" settlements to safeguard them. After the Six-Day War, a similar logic would underlie the extension of Israeli settlement into the Golan Heights (to safeguard the Jordan Valley settlements against Syrian depredations from above) and around Jerusalem (to serve as a defensive bulwark for the districts on the exposed northern, eastern, and southern flanks of the city).

Beyond this inner logic Zionist expansionism also had an "external" one. In the late-nineteenth and early-twentieth centuries, the movement was driven by what seemed to be an ever-growing number of desperate Jews seeking escape from persecution. More and more of Palestine had to be made "Jewish" to accommodate their need for land and housing.

Last, Zionism was politically expansionist in the sense that from the start, its aim was to turn all of Palestine (and in the movement's pre-1921 maps, the East Bank of the Jordan and the area south of the Litani River as well) into a Jewish state. Palestine was seen as too small to absorb the whole people, and it was understood that the ultimate contours of the prospective state would be determined by the extent of settlement: The outer chains of settlement would mark the frontiers.

During the formative decades, between 1881 and 1947, the enterprise expanded outward gradually and by purchase, most of the time finding a useful protector in the British Mandatory government and Arabs ready to collaborate by selling or arranging for others to sell land to Jews. For most of the period, land purchase was restricted more by lack of funds than by Ottoman or British limitations or Arab nationalist pressure.

Subsequently expansion occurred in two brief but massive thrusts—the military offensives of the 1948 and 1967 wars. (A third such effort, the 1956 war, failed to result in lasting territorial gains.) In the first Arab-Israeli war, the Jewish state expanded by two thousand square miles at the expense of the UN-sponsored prospective Palestine Arab state; in 1967, Israel conquered the Sinai Peninsula, Gaza Strip, East Jerusalem, West Bank, and Golan Heights. During the following years Israel launched vast settlement drives which in effect meant the projection or extension of the polity into these territories. Sinai, with its settlements, was given up in 1982 to make peace with Egypt possible, but to date, the other chains of settlements, in the Golan, Gaza, and the West Bank, have substantially hampered the possibility of achieving peace with Syria and the Palestinians.

Almost from the start the Arabs equated Zionism with expansionism. Indeed, their leaders both inside and outside Palestine often charged, citing Scripture, that the Zionists were bent on forging a kingdom stretching from the Nile to the Euphrates. And while one need not always take Arab asseverations at face value, they were solidly anchored in a perception that expansion, whatever its real extent, would be at the expense of their people, principally and initially those living in Palestine itself.

From the start these Arabs—while certainly not a distinct "people" before

1920—resented the influx (they termed it an "invasion") of infidel settlers who might bring some material benefit to the region as a whole but simultaneously were dispossessing tenant-farmers and posing a vague threat to its Arab and Muslim mores and character. Within years the Arabs came to fear for their lands and livelihoods; and, with the onset of national consciousness, began to fear also for the fate of their "country." Paradoxically it was in large part the thrust and threat of Zionism that generated this consciousness of collective self, that is, a distinct Palestinian Arab identity and nationalism.

The Zionist leaders and settlers were only vaguely aware that the movement was having this effect. Indeed, to a very large degree they managed to avoid "seeing" the Arabs, of whom there were about half a million in the country around 1880, about seven hundred thousand in 1914, and 1.25 million in 1947. Herzl's *The Jewish State* makes no mention of the Arabs; memoirs by settlers from the last years of the nineteenth century and the early years of the twentieth rarely refer to their existence. It is as if each Jewish colony was a separate, self-contained universe, with nothing around it.

At work were a number of factors. One undoubtedly was the routine European colonist's mental obliteration of the "natives"; colonists tended to relate to natives as part of the scenery, objects to be utilized when necessary, and not as human beings with rights or legitimate aspirations. Another factor was a self-defense mechanism: Constant consciousness of the surrounding sea of Arabs could have eroded faith in the tenability and future of the Zionist enterprise and the sparse, scattered settlements. How could Zionism succeed against such odds? the settler might well ask. Better not to look at the odds but simply to go about one's daily business while ignoring the existence of "the Arab problem" (as the Zionists eventually came to call it).

A third factor may have been a desire to suppress feelings of guilt. The Zionists were intent on politically, or even physically, dispossessing and supplanting the Arabs; their enterprise, however justified in terms of Jewish suffering and desperation, was tainted by a measure of moral dubiousness. It was better not to dwell on the problem lest it generate an infirmity of purpose which could be politically and psychologically debilitating. Yet, despite the indisputable presence of Arab communities in most areas of the country, the Jews, down to the 1920s, were right on one level: They themselves were the only "nation" or "people" in the country: The Arabs simply did not exist as a Palestinian people—as another, competing nationalism. The small minority of politically conscious Arabs saw themselves as part of the wider "Arab nation" or of the "Greater Syria" polity.

While taking note of the Jewish settlers, the Arabs proved unwilling or unable to understand them. This mutual lack of empathy, to be sure, has characterized the conflict ever since. The Palestinians, from the start, never really understood the Zionist claim to the land. They were not aware of or didn't care about the Jews' roots in the country, and took no interest in their current suffering, the main propellant of Zionism. Had they done so, perhaps they would have fathomed the source of the movement's strength, to their own benefit. The Palestinians' insensitivity to the plight of the Jews heightened Jewish antagonism toward them. This was especially true during the late 1930s and early 1940s, when they resisted the immigration of European Jews to Palestine and when some of their leaders made common cause with Hitler. Nor did the Palestinians ever fathom the centrality of the Land of Israel to Judaism, partly, no doubt, because it was not central to their own identity, as a "national" collective, until well into the twentieth century, and partly because to have acknowledged this would have been tantamount to a partial endorsement of Zionist claims.

The Zionists, for their part, were uninterested in the Palestinian Arabs' nexus with the soil or in Jerusalem's sanctity to Islam. Nor were they able or willing to recognize the Palestinians as a "people" until decades after they had become one, in terms of collective consciousness and political institutions, leadership and aspirations. Thus, the Zionist-Palestinian conflict, which was the origin and remains the core of the Israeli-Arab conflict, has been characterized by a crude and brutalizing perceptional symmetry. This symmetry was to some degree eroded during the late 1980s by the Intifada, during which much of the Israeli public came (mainly through the agency of television) to understand the plight of the Palestinians; it is possible that the suicide bombings of the mid-1990s have had a somewhat similar, obverse impact on some Palestinians (though I have yet to encounter a full, empathetic Palestinian study of the Holocaust and the two thousand years of Christian—and, to a lesser degree, Islamic—persecution of the Jews that preceded it, and of their effect on Zionism and Israeli behavior).

EARLY CONFLICT

As early as the 1880s, Palestine's Arabs displayed scattered, inconsistent hostility toward the settlers (while, at the same time, helping them take root by working in their fields and selling them land). The years immediately preceding World War I were characterized by a series of murderous Arab attacks with clear "nationalist" undertones. Antagonism towards the new enterprise grew apace, as the Zionist presence burgeoned and its aims became clearer.

There were many more Palestinian Arabs than Zionist settlers. But from the first the latter held the advantage. Though the Arabs enjoyed the sympathy of the Ottoman rulers, they were an inchoate, disorganized, and politically primitive mass, in which family, village, and clan were the decisive features of organization and loyalty. The Zionists were few but organized and highly motivated as a national collective, with clarity of purpose and relative efficiency in going about their business. It was Europeans versus Third World people. The Zionists, at least down to the 1990s, enjoyed a competent, efficient leadership with a public-service orientation; not the amassing of wealth or personal influence but the empowerment of the collective was their main concern. Between the two communities in Palestine, there was a crucial forty-to-fifty-year gap in levels of political development and consciousness. This rendered the Arabs' numerical superiority insignificant, supplemented as it was by the divisive deformities and general cultural backwardness of Palestinian society, which was characterized by regionalism, a Muslim-Christian split, clan feuding, a venal aristocracy, general illiteracy, and technological retardation.

Through the first four decades of Zionist settlement, violence against it was disorganized and relatively rare. There was no general mobilization of resources and will. The Palestinians failed in any significant way to prevent Zionism taking root. Moreover, the fact that the Jewish penetration was very gradual and piecemeal probably dulled Arab sensibilities to the unfolding threat. To a degree, the immigrants and their enterprise benefited from both the protection of the European powers and the incompetence and corruption of the Ottoman authorities.

It was only after the defeat of the Ottoman Empire and the arrival of the British, in the last years of World War I, that the Palestinians began their slow maturation toward peoplehood and began to organize against the "invaders." But by then—though it was by no means clear at the time—it was too late, in the sense that the Zionists had already taken root with more than four dozen settlements and enjoyed the political support and military protection of the powerful British Empire. The Zionists might—and did—complain that Britain was not facilitating Jewish immigration and settlement as vigorously as might have been expected from the country that had issued the Balfour Declaration; on occasion, indeed, the British actually hampered Zionist development. But, on the whole, during the period between the two world wars, the enterprise unfolded under the protective carapace of British rifles and under a beneficent and efficient administration that made the tasks of the settlers and their Jewish Agency infinitely easier.

The Arabs periodically tried violence, in order both to kill settlers and to persuade the British to kill Zionism. But even though the British troops were not always efficient, Jewish casualties and material losses were relatively minor and, in effect, Zionism made rapid progress. The bouts of violence, it should be noted, were relatively brief, and the months and years between them saw continued Jewish immigration and growth. And, ironically, the Arab attacks themselves, and Britain's occasional ineffectiveness in repelling them, proved a boon for the Yishuv. Besides endowing the settlers' society with sympathy as the bloodied underdog, it spurred them to improve their militia—the Haganah—and to construct solid communal institutions that might tide them over in times of emergency. These were to serve the Yishuv well as it fought the crucial battles of 1947–49 and turned itself, almost overnight and in extremely trying circumstances, into a state.

By comparison, the Palestinian Arabs, with their fragmented, venal political elite, failed to put together effective national institutions that could have guided them towards self-sufficiency and statehood. Most significantly, they failed to organize self-taxation or a national militia that could counter the Haganah. Faced by the British army and the Jewish militia, the Arab mobs and guerrilla fighters of 1920–21, 1929, and 1936–39 proved able only to dent the surface of the Zionist enterprise. During these episodes of violence, the Arabs introduced to Palestine the "pogrom" and its paraphernalia—the knife, the bludgeon, and the fuel-doused rag—as well as, in the last outbreak, the tactics of guerrilla warfare and terrorism. The Zionists remained strategically on the defensive—and not necessarily because they philosophically preferred the defensive ethos but because, under the Ottomans and the British, they lacked the power to go over to the offensive. Moreover, they were constrained by external, imperial interests and dictates, and they enjoyed the protection of the authorities, which meant that they need do no more than defend themselves.

But the Zionists also proved brutally innovative. While the Haganah generally cleaved to the defensive, the dissident right-wing organizations, the IZL and LHI, introduced into the arena (in 1937–38 and 1947–48) what is now the standard equipment of modern terrorism, the camouflaged bomb in the market place and bus station, the car- and truck-bomb, and the drive-by shooting with automatic weapons (though not the suicide bomber, which was an Arab innovation of the 1980s and 1990s).

During the Arab rebellion of 1936–39, the Zionist movement had to confront its first real political-ideological test since the beginning of the Mandate: the Peel Commission recommendations of July 1937. The movement, which (like the Arabs) had always regarded all of Palestine as its patrimony, was asked to agree to a solution of the conflict based on a judgment-of-Solomon partition. The recommendations offered the Jews 20 percent of the country, with most of the rest going to the Arabs. After painful soul-searching and wrangling, a majority of the Zionist leadership reluctantly and with reservations agreed in principle—better something in the hand than nothing in the bush. But leaders like Ben-Gurion, while saying yes, continued to entertain in their hearts the vision of "the Whole Land of Israel" ("Greater Israel," as it was later to be called). Ben-Gurion repeatedly declared (though not in front of the British) that the ministate London was offering would serve merely as the springboard for future Jewish conquest of the whole land: Palestine was to be taken over in stages. (Half a century later, many Zionists would accuse Yasser Arafat of secretly harboring much the same thoughts and plans as he grudgingly accepted the concept of a Palestinian ministate in the West Bank and Gaza Strip.)

One of the inducements offered to the Zionists by Peel was that the bitter pill of partition and "ministatehood" would be sugared by a transfer of the Arabs out of the intended Jewish areas. Ben-Gurion and his protégés accepted this with alacrity, enthusiastically—the only time in Zionism's history that the mainstream leadership of the movement more or less publicly endorsed the idea of transfer. "I support compulsory transfer. I don't see anything immoral in it," Ben-Gurion declared at a meeting of the Jewish Agency Executive in 1938.[2] But subsequently, after London shelved the Peel proposals, the idea of transfer ceased to be discussed publicly or with frequency.

As we have seen, most of the Zionist leaders, including Herzl, Ruppin, and Ussishkin, had at one time or another supported the idea. Zionism had always looked to the day when a Jewish majority would enable the movement to gain control over the country: The Zionist leadership had never posited Jewish statehood with a minority of Jews ruling over a majority of Arabs, apartheid-style. But how could such a Jewish majority come about? And even if it did, how could a secure, stable state be established with a large, hostile minority in its midst? Throughout, the Zionist leaders hoped that incremental immigration would one day lead to the desired majority, but as the first decades of the twentieth century passed, it became clear that the rate of immigration, while increasing the percentage of Jews in the overall population, was insufficient to radically transform the ratio. Even the massive immigration of the mid-1930s did not effect the necessary change. Moreover, the influx was precipitating intense Arab opposition, which, in turn, led to British curtailment of immigration.

How, then, could the Zionists achieve a Jewish majority? The alternative to immigration was transfer. For decades Arab leaders had loudly proclaimed that Zionism inevitably meant the physical displacement of their people. The Zionist leaders always publicly denied this: Palestine was big enough for the two peoples; there was no need for a transfer of Arabs to make room for the Jews, they argued. But the stark realities of the 1930s, with wholesale persecution in Central and Eastern Europe and with Britain closing the gates to Jewish immigration, seemed to prove the Arabs right. Palestine would not be transformed into a Jewish state unless all or much of the Arab population was expelled. Needless to say, the steady growth of Arab belligerency toward Zionism during the 1920s and 1930s reinforced the imperative of transfer in Zionist minds.

The Zionist leaders preferred a "voluntary" transfer: Perhaps the Arabs could be induced to move to the neighboring states, with the Jews paying appropriate compensation that would enable the transferees to resettle comfortably? But this proved unrealistic. While a few Arabs sold off their land and moved, the mass of the population declined to be bought out.

The Peel Commission recommended "voluntary" transfer. But, it added, if the Arabs refused, then there would have to be a compulsory transfer. The innovation of the Peel recommendations was twofold: The transfer would dovetail with a partition of the country and would encompass only those Arabs living in the area of the Jewish-state-to-be or most of them (some 225,000–300,000); and it would be carried out by the British authorities.

Thereafter, and despite the eventual rejection of the Peel scheme by Whitehall, the floodgates had opened for the Yishuv to think about transfer: If His Majesty's Government could recommend the idea, surely the Jews could discuss and adopt it as well? From then on, the idea won almost consensual approval in the deliberations of the supreme Zionist bodies, including the Zionist Congress and the Jewish Agency Executive. As Ben-Gurion put it yet again in 1944: "I do not reject [the idea of] transfer morally or . . . politically."[3] But he was frequently to caution against discussing the matter in public, lest it antagonize the Arabs and alienate British and world opinion. No important Zionist body ever openly advocated transfer as an element of its platform (though in summer 1937 the Twentieth Zionist Congress, the movement's supreme decision-making forum, accepted the Peel proposals in principle, including transfer). But the idea was in the air from 1937 onward and without doubt contributed in various ways to the transfer that eventually took place, in 1948.

Peel's main recommendation had been partition. And, formally, Ben-Gurion had barreled acceptance through Mapai's executive and the Zionist Congress. The irony was that though this acceptance was at best halfhearted and insincere (certainly on Ben-Gurion's part), the decision of the congress was effectively internalized and amalgamated into mainstream Zionist ideology and, come 1947, when partition—this time more favorable to the Jews—was again proposed by the international community, it was once more accepted and endorsed by the majority, and this time with a greater degree of sincerity. Some, such as Ben-Gurion, Herut, and the (socialist) Ahdut Ha'Avodah faction, continued to harbor expansionist ambitions, and occasionally—in 1948 and 1956—to act upon them. But the heart had gone out of "Greater Israel" expansionism, at least until 1967. Reluctantly, mainstream Zionism, as represented by Mapai and the Labor movement, from 1937 onward progressively reconciled itself to the necessity of partition, of "territorial compromise" between the two "rightful owners" of Palestine (though there always remained within socialist Zionism a hard core of "Greater Israel" supporters).

In 1967, with the conquest of the West Bank and Gaza Strip (and Sinai and the Golan Heights), the original, full dream of Zionism—of Jewish statehood in the whole of Palestine—once again burst forth, to inflame and complicate the conflict. Again the concept of transfer came to the fore, with two to three hundred thousand Palestinians fleeing the newly conquered territories, some of them under duress, and with Israeli policy in the following years geared, at least in part, to squeezing out of East Jerusalem, the West Bank, and Gaza Strip as many additional Arabs as possible. It was appropriate and natural that, in June 1967, representatives of Revisionist Zionism, for whom the dream of Greater Israel was a raison d'être, for the first time were coopted into an Israeli cabinet and, indeed, within years, were to succeed Labor as the leaders of the Zionist movement and state. Since 1977 the Revisionist Herut Party and its successor, the Likud Bloc, have dominated Israeli politics. Fittingly and paradoxically linking the Labor and Likud eras was the towering figure of Moshe Dayan, the first child born on the first kibbutz (Deganya), who served as Ben-Gurion's expansionist IDF chief of staff in 1956, Eshkol's "creeping annexationist" defense minister in 1967, and Begin's peacemaking foreign minister in 1977–80.

As 1937 was the defining moment of Zionism under the Mandate, so the period 1936–39 was to be fateful for the Palestinian Arab national struggle. The Palestinians failed to mobilize properly for the revolt and, under an incompetent crew, shot their bolt, unsuccessfully and prematurely expending what little resources, energy, and unity they had against the British. Came the test against the real enemy, Zionism, in 1948, and the result was a foregone conclusion. The revolt both decimated the Palestinian Arab political and "military" elites and neutered and impoverished the community as a whole. The rebellion and its demise left Palestinian society mortally weakened in the years leading up to 1948.

Moreover, the rebellion was to prove fatal to Palestinian interests in another way. Offered two reasonable solutions to the conflict—by Peel in 1937 and by the White Paper of 1939—the Palestinian leadership, against the advice of much of the outside Arab world, rejected both. It consistently rejected all thought of partition. Amin al-Husseini forever underestimated Zionist strength and overrated the Arabs'. This underlay his unwillingness (or inability) to compromise, and proved to be his people's undoing. By the time a new leadership had learned the art of compromise and grudgingly agreed to the principle of partition, in the 1980s and 1990s, and had begun to reap the rewards of moderation (de facto sovereignty over most of the Gaza Strip and the cities of the West Bank), it was almost too late.

Hard upon the heels of the Arab Rebellion came World War II. The Holocaust had an ambivalent effect on the situation in Palestine: The Zionist movement lost the bulk of its potential manpower, but on the other hand, it received a tremendous boost of motivational energy. The Zionists' message, all along, had been that only Zionism could save the Jewish people from the jaws of European anti-Semitism, and Hitler proved them right. The Holocaust led to an urgent reinvigoration of the demand for a Jewish state. The Zionists thought and acted as if their backs were to the wall—and as if a similar slaughter might occur in Palestine.

At the same time, the Holocaust also mobilized, as could have nothing else, the support of world Jewry, most of which had previously been non- or anti-Zionist, and the Western democracies for the creation of a Jewish state. It may also have influenced Soviet policy in the same direction. The guilty conscience of Christendom translated into support of Zionism, most importantly in the United States. Conversely, the Arabs' association with the Axis cause, by way of the German-backed revolt in Iraq in 1941, the anti-British intrigues in Egypt (for which the young Sadat spent months in jail), and Husseini's activities in Berlin from 1941 to 1945, did nothing to endear the Palestinian cause to the West. Public opinion was particularly swayed by the spectacle of British soldiers preventing Holocaust survivors from reaching the shores of the "Promised Land" and even, on occasion, forcing them to return to Germany.

WARS

Ideologically and politically, the Palestinians acted as though their conflict with the Zionists were a zero-sum game. They refused all compromise. But though they often talked in this manner ("We'll throw the Jews into the sea"), they systematically failed to translate their words into deeds, failed at every stage to organize for total war. They haphazardly "launched" their war late in 1947—but proved unable to see it through. The Yishuv, on the other hand, forewarned by decades of Arab belligerence, had prepared adequately if not optimally—and when it came to the confrontation of December 1947–May 1948, beat them handily and swiftly, in the process shattering Palestinian society.

The Palestinians were thus "knocked out" of the conflict (and, substantially, out of history), only to return to it as major players in the wake of the 1967 war (though without doubt, the catastrophe of 1948 helped to crystallize their sense of national identity). But the exile and refugee status of about 700,000 of them, mainly caused by Israeli arms, was to be a major source of tension and a catalyst to violence almost continuously between the 1950s and the 1980s.

The Yishuv-Palestinian war, the "first half" of the 1948 war, was immediately followed by the war between the Arab states and Israel, which began on May 15–16, 1948, with the invasion of Palestine by the armies of Egypt, Jordan, Syria, and Iraq. The limited communal civil war thus turned into the Israeli-Arab conflict, which was to shake the region, and occasionally the world, in the following decades. It was punctuated by a series of full-scale conventional wars (1956, 1967, 1973, and 1982—a war per decade), with periods of major turmoil, often accompanied by low-level guerrilla warfare and terrorist insurgency and counterinsurgency, in between.

The Arab states, like the Palestinians before them, lost the 1948 war as well as all the subsequent wars (though in 1973 and 1982 they ultimately managed to turn limited military defeat into limited political victory). The main reason for their defeat on the battlefield lay in the cultural and technological gap between the contending societies, which translated into a major discrepancy in levels of organization and national mobilization. Other factors, such as a gap in quality of armaments (the IDF's heavy weapons were more advanced than the Arabs' from the 1960s to the 1990s), military experience and expertise, varying lengths of lines of supply and communications, and political and military unity, also told during the succession of wars. In three of the wars—1956, 1967, and 1982—Israel took the initiative and enjoyed the major advantages of surprise and delivery of the first blow. The results—the destruction of the Egyptian army in Sinai in 1956; the devastation of the Egyptian, Jordanian, and Syrian armies in 1967; and the rout of the PLO and the partial destruction of the Syrian army in Lebanon in 1982—were in accordance. The Arabs enjoyed the advantages of initiative and/or surprise only in 1948 and 1973, and indeed these proved to be Israel's costliest and most difficult wars.

From 1948 on, Israel organized itself as a garrison state perennially at the ready to fend off belligerent neighbors. Internal divisions, such as those between the religious and secular communities and those between ethnic groups, were placed on the back burner, and manpower and other resources were subordinated to national needs, chief of which was security. The economy was directed toward self-sufficiency and industrialization, with rapid growth of arms production capabilities. Democratic norms were frequently subordinated to perceived conflict-related needs; Israel's own 15 to 20 percent Arab minority was regarded, and for long periods treated, as a potential Fifth Column. All eighteen-to-twenty-year-old Jewish males and most females did compulsory twenty to thirty-six months of military service; and males subsequently served for a further twenty to thirty years in reserve formations. Some 20 to 40 percent of the national budget was devoted to security and military expenditure. Many of the best and the brightest made their way into the army or the intelligence services, and such careers often paved the way for later political prominence.

Motivation was another key factor in the Israeli successes in 1948, 1956, 1967, and 1973. There could be no collective return to Europe or North Africa: It was either victory or death. That this may not have been objectively true—that Israel rather than the Arabs initiated the war of 1956 and that Israel was not faced with destruction in 1967 or 1973—is of marginal significance. What is important is that the society as a whole and its soldiers at the front in each of these wars felt that, for the nation, as for individuals, it was a win-or-die situation. The proximity of the front lines to every soldier's home and family only underlined the dire nature of the threat, as did the rhetoric of the Arabs. (The fact that by the late 1960s Israel possessed a nuclear capability, for some reason—perhaps because of the secrecy surrounding the subject—never seemed to blunt the existential fears of the people. The leaders, for their part, seemed to feel that it was an instrument that could never be used; or, put another way, could only be used "too early"—with terrible international political cost—or "too late," that is, after the IDF had been defeated, by which time it might have become irrelevant.)

Until the rise of the Muslim fundamentalist resistance groups in the early 1980s, the Arabs' motivation was generally inferior to that of the Israelis. Individuals and families had a hinterland—the West Bank, Jordan, Lebanon—to which they could flee if necessary. And, in 1948, this is what most did, perhaps in the expectation of a swift return after the Yishuv was destroyed. Motivation, to the point of willing self-sacrifice, only came to the Palestinians decades later, after they had re-emerged from the void of defeat and expulsion, and organized for guerrilla warfare against the occupying power.

As to the soldiers of the Arab states, their motivation throughout the wars was generally much lower than the Israelis'. True, they were conditioned to believe that the Jews were "infidels" and "usurpers" who had "stolen" Muslim lands. But in 1948 the Arab soldiery invaded and were fighting in a foreign land, not for their own homes and families, which were never under threat. In 1956 and 1967, the Egyptian troops were fighting for a piece of desert in which they had very little interest. Even though it is part of Egypt, Sinai is not the Nile Valley. The same might be said to apply to Jordanian and Syrian troops in 1967. In 1973 the Egyptian and Syrian soldiers had been keyed up and persuaded by years of indoctrination of the sanctity of the occupied regions they were about to retake. But again, Sinai and the Golan were not exactly their native soil (though for the Syrians, the IDF's minatory proximity to Damascus was certainly a powerful incentive to do battle).

The exception in this sphere was Lebanon in 1982, where both the Israelis and the Syrians fought on "foreign" soil. And there, clearly, many of the participating Israeli troops were in doubt about the war's purpose and morality. On the other hand, many Palestinians and Syrians fought with great determination, the former in defense of their homes, the refugee camps, and the latter perhaps because they suspected that the Israelis might "turn right" and drive towards Damascus. This accounts for the determination with which the Syrian high command reacted to the Israeli thrust up the Beka'a Valley.

But though motivation was crucial in certain battles, it is only a small part of the story. In 1948 and after, fighting Israel was not a primary interest or concern of the Arabs (though many Israelis believed it was). Each regime and political elite was preoccupied by its own internal problems and agendas, and in large measure regarded its Arab neighbors as a greater threat than Israel. Until 1967–68 the Arab leaders did not take the task of organizing for war with Israel very seriously. Without doubt they wanted Israel to disappear and would have been happy to have brought this about, had they been able to. But they had other priorities and recognized their limitations. And Palestine was not their own country.

The Yishuv, on the other hand, could take no chances: At stake was survival, and the margins of safety were very narrow. Israel's waist, from Tulkarm to the sea, between 1949 and 1967, was no more than ten miles wide; in the 1950s, its population was only one to two million strong. Israel organized itself for total war, carrying on with that mobilization of resources instituted in 1947–48. It established a (relatively) large army, based on conscription and reserves, and launched a formidable nuclear program. The Palestinian Arabs and the surrounding states never got even close to achieving "total" mobilization (save in the field of rhetoric). But taking the Arabs at their word, the Yishuv girded itself for battle and achieved the necessary degrees of material mobilization, unity, and fixedness of purpose (even while its politicians were forever lamenting the "lack of unity" and "disorganization").

Things changed somewhat after June 1967, when Nasser maneuvered himself and the Middle East into a war that he had not anticipated or prepared for. The destruction of the Arab armies was total and humiliating, and the Arab world at last turned its full gaze on Israel—and on itself—and began to take the notion of war seriously. And this time, it was not to be war over a "foreign" country but to recover chunks of the "homeland," Sinai (Egypt) and the Golan (Syria). It was only natural, perhaps, that military men (such as Hafez Assad) achieved positions of political prominence in their respective countries.

By this time, however, Israel had become a very serious adversary indeed. Its conventional military power had been amply demonstrated and its reputed nuclear prowess gave even the most adventurous Arab leaders reason for pause. Thus, in planning for the 1973 war, the Egyptians and Syrians restricted themselves to delivering a blow that would shake loose these territories from Israel's grasp, rather than anything more far reaching. In the end the Egyptian performance on the battlefield resulted in Israel disgorging all of Sinai in exchange for peace—but Syria's failure to retake the Golan left that territory in Israeli hands. But both Arab armies had acquitted themselves infinitely better than in previous wars and felt that they had rehabilitated "Arab honor." Motivation—among the political leadership and the high command, and in the ranks—was a major factor in this (relative) Arab success.

While demographically puny, Israel had always managed to mobilize its manpower in a way that made it possible to field more troops overall (as happened in 1948) and/or to deploy more of them than the Arabs on each important battlefield. Moreover, its troops were almost invariably better trained and more experienced than their foes. This was to prove crucial in 1948, 1956, 1967, and 1973. It was especially true with regard to the officer corps, which was superior to that of each of the Arab armies in each of the wars (with the sole exception of the Arab Legion in 1948).

There were also important qualitative disparities from the 1956 war onward in the two elements crucial to success in wars of movement: air and armor. Israeli air traffic/battle controllers, ground crews, and pilots proved to be infinitely better than their Arab counterparts, on every front; and the IDF's tankmen proved far superior to their counterparts in 1956, 1967, 1973, and 1982. In both areas, it is important to stress, the IDF, for most of the time, also enjoyed a qualitative edge, and often more than an edge, in weaponry (albeit often along with a numerical disadvantage). Successive generations of Israel's French, British, American, and homemade armor were superior to their Soviet-built counterparts. The qualitative gap in aircraft became even more pronounced from war to war.

Only in mid-1948, briefly, was the Haganah/IDF outgunned in most types of heavy weapons (aircraft, artillery, and armor). Otherwise Arab superiority was restricted to the artillery arm—where the far greater numbers were partly offset by the IDF's fuller mechanization and self-propulsion—and infantry weapons. But in the type of blitzkrieg campaigns fought in the latter part of 1948, 1956, 1967, and the latter part of 1973, the decisive arms proved to be air and armor. Infantry weapons were often irrelevant and Arab artillery could barely keep up with and find targets, given the speed of the Israeli advances. During the initial stages of 1973, the Egyptians and Syrians managed to offset IDF armored and aerial superiority by fielding masses of antitank missiles and antiaircraft missiles and gun batteries. But during the war's later stages Israeli tankmen and aircraft managed to overcome this "spoiling" weaponry and by 1982 Israel had taken the measure of the Soviet-built antiaircraft defenses and wiped out the Syrian air defense system in Lebanon in two hours and without loss.

Another factor which told in Israel's favor was unity of command. During the various wars, and nowhere more tellingly than in 1948, the Arab states' lack of political and military unity and coordination proved self-defeating. In two of the wars, 1956 and 1982, the Israelis managed to fight only one state, the rest watching inactively from the sidelines. In the other wars, principally 1948 and 1967, while fighting several Arab armies simultaneously, the IDF benefited from their lack of military coordination and political unity. For most of 1948 and 1967, the Israelis were able to fight and pick off one army (or air force) at a time. Only in 1973 did the two main foes—Egypt and Syria—coordinate their political and military planning and launch a simultaneous two-front offensive—which, indeed, the IDF found difficult to contain and repel. From the military perspective 1973 was the most successful war for the Arabs, even though Israel ultimately badly battered both armies and captured fresh Syrian territory and more Egyptian territory than it lost. Closely connected with this was the question of lines of supply and communication. In 1948, 1956, 1967 and, in the north, 1973, the IDF enjoyed relatively short, internal lines; Arab lines—most notably for the Iraqi expeditionary forces of 1948 and 1973—were generally longer.

Israel won all its wars, albeit with varying degrees of military decisiveness and with varying political results. But the IDF proved less successful in the in-between years of low-level skirmishing and guerrilla and terrorist warfare. Each such period exacted a major toll in lives and morale and, by and large, resulted in the IDF's outright failure or lack of clear success. Indeed, some of these struggles proved more traumatic than the concentrated, conventional wars. The IDF proved relatively unsuccessful in the struggle against the Palestinian (and Egyptian) marauders between 1948 and 1956, in the war of attrition along the Suez Canal during 1968–70, and in the battles against the Shi'ite militants in southern Lebanon since 1983 and the Palestinians in the territories since December 1987. Moreover, while successes were registered against the PLO in the late 1960s and 1970s inside the territories, across the Jordan River, and in Europe, they proved insufficient to knock that organization out of the ring.

There appear to be several reasons for the IDF's different levels of achievement in the two types of warfare. One is that guerrilla/terrorist warfare is mostly fought with light weapons and by relatively small units. The IDF's traditional areas of expertise and superiority, in air and armor, and in the activation of large formations, were rendered irrelevant (though Israel's very able commandos were often used with telling effect). This emerged most starkly during the two large operations in southern Lebanon in 1993 and 1996, when enormous firepower failed to quell a handful of Hizbullah rocket squads.

A second reason was that the groups engaged in this type of warfare were highly motivated, or at least as much so as their Israeli foes.

PEACEMAKING

The conflict, and the wars that punctuated it, paradoxically served as a catalyst to both peacemaking and further wars. The grief, suffering, and great material loss caused by war inclines people to seek peace; this was as true for Israelis as for Arabs after each war between them. But war also breeds hatred, vengefulness, and territorial changes that provoke new bouts, and the Israeli-Arab confrontations have been no exception.

In the early 1950s Ben-Gurion believed that peace with the Arab world would eventually dawn, but only after Israel hit it over the head again and again, until it was persuaded that Israel was too resolute and too strong to beat.

It would then resign itself to Israel's existence and make peace. But he failed to foresee just how many years would have to pass.

From the perspective of the late 1990s it appears that, in essence, Ben-Gurion's prognosis was correct. One at a time, the Arab states have come round to recognizing that Israel is there to stay and have grudgingly moved toward peace. No doubt, most Arabs in some corner of their mind hope and pray for Israel's disappearance or destruction. Many, perhaps, believe that demographic realities and developments may ultimately lead to Israel being overwhelmed by Arab numbers and power or to its gradual transformation into a more acceptable, non-European, Levantine country, akin to their own. But this is for the long term.

In the short and medium term, it would appear that the succession of Israeli-Arab wars have persuaded most of the Arab world of Israel's strength and durability, and have forced it to resign itself to the continued existence of a Jewish state in the heart of the Middle East. Arab leaders such as Anwar Sadat and King Hussein apparently understood that the price of continued warfare would simply be too high. Most of the leadership of the PLO, too, it would seem, reached the same conclusion, and Syria's leaders were possibly similarly minded by the late 1990s.

But the wars did not lead in a direct trajectory to the peace process that started unfolding in the 1970s. Before 1947, by and large, the Yishuv sought an accommodation with the Arabs of Palestine and the world around—to be based on their acceptance of Jewish statehood in all or part of Palestine. However, the Arabs in Palestine and elsewhere—with the exception, at times, of Jordan—rejected this notion and generally declined offers of peace.

Following the war of 1948, there may have been a chance for peace between the new state and one or more of the Arab countries. But both Israel and the Arab world (as a collective) were in no frame of mind for compromise. Though one or two states and regimes were apparently willing to reach an accommodation, they were too weak to take the plunge so long as Israel was not conciliatory.

Without doubt the humiliation suffered by the Arabs in 1948 and the embarrassing refugee problem that emerged in its wake made acquiescence in Israel's existence very difficult. And the problems engendered by the war—infiltration by refugees and border farmers into Israel, terrorism, and border and water disputes in and around the demilitarized zones—as well as the prevalent rejectionist Arab mindset and mutual fears of aggression rendered a second round inevitable.

But that second round, initiated by Israel in 1956, brought the two sides no closer to peace: Indeed, the spectacle of Israel joining the Western powers against Egypt probably deepened the Arabs' suspicions, fear, and antagonism. So, too, did the humiliating experience, from their perspective, of 1967—though this war also gave Israel the territorial assets (the Sinai Peninsula,

Golan, and West Bank) that it could eventually trade for peace. On the other hand, the Six-Day War also gave rise in Israel to a reborn expansionist spirit and territorial greed—quickly expressed in a settlement enterprise—that made the prospect of peace that much more remote.

October 1973 in some ways radically changed the geopolitical situation. Without doubt, the war created conditions that set in train the bilateral peace process that ended in 1979 with the signing of the Israeli-Egyptian peace treaty. The initial Egyptian successes had wiped out the "shame" of 1948 and 1967, enabling Sadat to make peace "with honor" (though, to be sure, he had made an effort to reach some form of settlement with Golda Meir's government even before, in 1970–71, an effort that had been rebuffed). At the same time, the drubbing Israel had received in that war's initial stages made it more amenable to compromise and concessions.

The war of 1982, too, contributed to the advancement of peace. The destruction of the PLO infrastructure and military option in Lebanon, which Menachem Begin and Ariel Sharon had hoped would facilitate Israeli annexation of the West Bank and Gaza Strip, in reality pushed the PLO toward that moderation of its basic policies that enabled the peace process to take off. The invasion of Lebanon, whatever its original goals, served to deliver up the PLO as a (reluctant) peace partner. By 1988 the moderating process had ripened sufficiently for the organization to publicly and formally declare its readiness for a "two-state solution," implying acceptance and recognition of Israel.

But Israel still remained unwilling to contemplate substantive concessions for peace with the Palestinians. Like most nationalist movements, Zionism, once ascendant, was unmarked by feelings of generosity toward its enemies (even though it is clear that a durable peace, and hence real security for Israel, could only be achieved on the basis of generous concessions). The 1970s and 1980s had witnessed a reversal of roles. Before, the Yishuv and then Israel were willing, in principle, to talk and compromise for peace, albeit on somewhat rigid terms, and the Palestinians were, in principle, rejectionist; during the 1970s and 1980s the PLO evolved towards a conciliatory stance while Israel, under the Likud, moved away from it.

Only the Intifada, which started in December 1987, at last propelled the Israeli leadership toward moderation and concessions. At the same time, the realities of the uprising, and pressure from the grass roots in the occupied territories, compelled the PLO-Tunis leadership to move toward further moderation of its positions. It was the conjunction of these two processes and the break-up of the Soviet Union (which denied the Arabs a war option) that in 1991 made possible the Madrid Peace Conference and, ultimately, after a new, moderate government came to power in Jerusalem, the Israeli-PLO Oslo accords, including mutual recognition and the start of Israel's gradual withdrawal from the Gaza Strip and the West Bank.

What emerges from all this is that, over the long haul, the Israeli-Arab wars have had a definite moderating role on the various parties. Or, put another way, in the long run, the only language that either side has understood in this conflict is force: Only the successive displays of persuasive force have made both peoples sit up and contemplate a future of coexistence without violence.

BUT IS IT PEACE?

So far the Zionists have been the winners in this conflict. Each victory can be explained in the light of specific concrete factors, but, viewed as a whole, the success of the Zionist enterprise has been nothing short of miraculous. For how else can one describe the taking root, in a desolate land, in the face of imperial ill will and native hostility, of a small, ill-equipped community of tens of thousands of transplanted Russian Jews; how else describe the growth of that community, albeit under the protective umbrella of British bayonets, in defiance of increasing Arab opposition and violence? How else describe the victory of the minuscule community against the surrounding sea of Arabs and Arab states in 1948; the establishment of a solid, viable state; its successive military victories; and the gradual Arab acquiescence in its existence, as embodied in the peace accords with Egypt, the PLO, and Jordan?

But, from the perspective of early 2001, this victory seems far from final. Fundamentalist Islamic or pan-Arab currents may yet undermine those moderate Arab regimes that have already made peace. Moreover, two of the original "confrontation states," Syria and Lebanon, currently remain outside the process of peace making. And beyond the immediate circle of Israel's neighbors lies a cluster of countries—Iraq, Iran, Libya, Sudan—driven by radical philosophies that include among their foreign policy priorities the destruction of the Jewish state. Some of these states are hard at work trying to acquire non-conventional, including atomic, weaponry that might counter-balance Israel's and that might be used to bring Israel to its knees, or, indeed, destroy it. Some of these states have recently enjoyed the political support of Russia and China, who have been assisting them with missile and other weapons technologies.

Lastly, the Palestinian rejection of the far-reaching Israeli-American peace proposals of December 2000–January 2001 and their unleashing of the second, "al-Aqsa" Intifada—taken together, a major historical development—bode ill for the prospect of an Israeli-Palestinian peace settlement anytime soon. It remains unclear whether the PA leadership is willing or able to make peace with Israel. And in the absence of such a settlement and against the backdrop of continuing hostilities in the West Bank and Gaza Strip, there is a real danger of escalation and a descent into a more general Middle Eastern conflagration. If there is one thing that the past teaches, it is this: That Palestinian violence has repeatedly helped trigger full-scale Israeli-Arab wars; and that the region is prone to slide into these wars despite the wishes of its states' leaders.

NOTES

ONE
PALESTINE ON THE EVE

1. Twain, 464–66.
2. McCarthy, 1.
3. Ibid., chap. 1; Scholch, 19–43.
4. Scholch, 77–240.
5. Vital, 1975, 289.
6. Stillman, 8–19.
7. Stillman, 149–51; Lewis, 11,13, 14.
8. Stillman, 157–58.
9. Gorny, 1985, 21.
10. Stillman, 81.
11. Ibid., 59; Ye'or, 61.
12. Stillman, 281–86.
13. Ibid., 66–67, 76, 81; Ye'or, 61.
14. Lewis, 102.
15. Stillman, 80–81.
16. Lewis, 164.
17. Stillman, 88–91.
18. Lewis, 164–65.
19. Ye'or, 96, n. 11; Lewis, 156–57; and Frankel, *passim.*
20. Vital, 17.
21. Stillman, 357–60.
22. Ye'or, 105.
23. Vital, 1975, 30, 37–42.
24. Hertzberg, 169.
25. Vital, 1975, 179, 310.
26. Ibid., 127.
27. Ibid., 214.
28. Sokolow, Vol. 2, 332–33, "Manifesto of the Bilu (1882)"; Vital, 1975, 85–86.
29. Ibid., 80–2; *Encyclopaedia Judaica,* 16, 1038–39.
30. Vital, 1975, 100.
31. A dunam is a quarter of an acre.
32. Vital, 1975, 178.
33. Ibid., 183.
34. Ibid., 233.
35. Ibid., 244.
36. Hertzberg, 225.
37. Shapira, 1992, 31–32.
38. Be'eri, 89.
39. Ibid., 102.
40. Herzl, *Diaries,* vol. 1, 88, entry for June 12, 1895.
41. Be'eri, 100.
42. Vital, 1975, 287.
43. Herzl, *Diaries,* vol. 2, 581, entry for Sept. 3, 1897.
44. Vital, 1982, 84–85.
45. Hertzberg, 217, 222.
46. Vital, 1982, 84.
47. Ibid., 130.
48. Vital, 1982, 271.
49. Vital, 1982, 239–40.
50. Quoted in Eliezer Tauber, 1993a, 7–8.
51. Zeine, 67, n. 1.
52. Be'eri, 17–18.
53. Tauber, 1993a, 10–14.
54. Ibid., 12, 16–19.
55. Antonius, 90.
56. Porath, 1976, 15–16.
57. Tauber, 1993a, 29.

58. Ibid., 25–32.
59. Ibid., 51.
60. Ibid., 113–17.
61. Ibid., 33–36.
62. Zeine, 75.
63. Ibid., 40–42.
64. Zeine, 79–80.
65. Muslih, 1988, 56–58.
66. Tauber, 1993a, 55.
67. Ibid., 56, 44, n. 8.
68. Ibid., 56–58.
69. Muslih, 1988, 60.
70. Porath, 1976, 16.
71. Zeine, 93–98; Antonius, 109–12.
72. Tauber, 1993a, 121–34.
73. Ibid., 90.
74. Ibid., 90–97.
75. Ibid., 183.
76. Ibid., 198–212.
77. Antonius, 118.
78. Ibid., 153.
79. Tauber, 1993a, 78–79, 87–89.
80. Ibid., 246.
81. Ibid., 245–67, 331–33.
82. Porath, 1976, 5–6.
83. Ibid., 7.
84. Muslih, 158.
85. Tessler, 124.
86. Muslih, 1988, 169.
87. Ibid., 170.
88. Porath, 1976, 88–99.
89. Muslih, 1988, 204–10; Porath, 1976, 89–90.
90. Porath, 1976, 90.
91. For a discussion of the shift to a Palestinian orientation, see Porath, 1976, 56–99.
92. Muslih, 1988, 210.
93. Bar-On, 1996, 12.

TWO
THE BEGINNING OF THE CONFLICT:
JEWS AND ARABS IN PALESTINE,
1882–1914

1. Be'eri, 89–90; Mandel, 47–48.
2. McCarthy, 23–24.
3. Mandel, 20.
4. Ro'i, 1980, 245, n. 2; Mandel, 20.
5. Mandel, 29.
6. Shafir, 41–42.
7. Mandel, 29.
8. Vital, 1975, 290, 292.
9. Mandel, 3, 5.
10. Vital, 1975, 30, 106.
11. Be'eri, 27.
12. Ibid., 78; Mandel, 5.
13. Mandel, 215.
14. Ibid., 216.
15. Ibid., 11.
16. Be'eri, 27.
17. Vital, 1982, 55.
18. Be'eri, 27.
19. Ibid., 137.
20. Shapira, 84–85.
21. Garfinkle, 539–50; and Be'eri, 35–37.
22. Khalidi, R., 1988, 216.
23. Shapira, 91.
24. Be'eri, 38–40.
25. Ro'i, 1980, 247.
26. Be'eri, 41.
27. Shafir, 56.
28. Be'eri, 70.
29. Gorny, 1976, 89.
30. Ibid., 96.
31. Be'eri, 152–53.
32. Shapira, 85.
33. Tessler, 137.
34. Mandel, 31; Teveth, 1985, 5.
35. Teveth, 1985, 7.
36. Mandel, 34.
37. Be'eri, 112–13.
38. Ro'i, 1968, 227.
39. Mandel, 181.
40. Ibid., 39.
41. Ro'i, 1980, 249, n. 22.
42. Be'eri, 43–45.
43. Ro'i, 1980, 155, 188–89.
44. Mandel, 27.
45. Ro'i, 1980, 165.
46. Shapira, 90–91.
47. Ro'i, 1980, 165. See also Be'eri, quoting Hissin, 74.
48. Ro'i, 1980, 174–76, 199.
49. Ibid., 165.
50. Gorny, 1976, 94.
51. Ro'i, 1980, 166.
52. Gorny, 1985, 34.
53. Shapira, 1992, 86–87.
54. Be'eri, 38.
55. Ibid., 38–39.

56. Ro'i, 1981, 256.
57. Ibid., 257–58.
58. Teveth, 1985, 9–10.
59. Shafir, 45.
60. Ibid., 79.
61. Ibid., 143.
62. Ibid., 87.
63. Ro'i, 1981, 261–63.
64. Ro'i, 1968, 223.
65. Be'eri, 182.
66. Gorny, 1976, 93.
67. Ro'i, 1968, 218.
68. Shafir, 139.
69. Ro'i, 1980, 165.
70. Ibid., 162.
71. Be'eri, 59–64; Mandel, 35–36; Shafir, 200–201.
72. Be'eri, 63.
73. Mandel, 37.
74. Laskov, 279–80.
75. Ro'i, 1981, 152.
76. Mandel, 38.
77. Be'eri, 83.
78. Be'eri, 115; Mandel, 26–28.
79. Teveth, 1985, 13.
80. Ro'i, 1968, 206.
81. Gorny, 1985, 27.
82. Mandel, 41; Be'eri, 82.
83. Mandel, 49–54.
84. Eliav, 1977, 303, n. 26.
85. Ro'i, 1968, 199.
86. Be'eri, 121.
87. Shapira, 1992, 74.
88. Gorny, 1976, 77.
89. Shapira, 1992, 74–75.
90. Be'eri, 124–25.
91. Gorny, 1976, 81–82.
92. Shapira, 1992, 78.
93. Gorny, 1976, 83.
94. Ibid., 83, 85.
95. Ibid., 97–98.
96. Be'eri, 65.
97. Eliav, 1977, 305, n. 30.
98. Shapira, 1992, 72.
99. Mandel, 67–69; Teveth, 1985, 14–15.
100. Teveth, 1985, 15–19.
101. Be'eri, 169.
102. Ro'i, 1968, 203–4.
103. Ibid., 228.
104. Ibid., 205.
105. Ibid., 212.
106. Ibid., 214–15.
107. Khalidi, R., 1988, 216.
108. Mandel, 103–4; Khalidi, R., 1988, 220–21.
109. Be'eri, 159; Mandel, 107.
110. Mandel 104–6.
111. Ibid., 217.
112. Ibid., 72.
113. Be'eri, 146.
114. Mandel, 76–78.
115. Ibid., 113.
116. Gorny, 1985, 39.
117. Be'eri, 140.
118. Muslih, 1988, 81.
119. Be'eri, 141–42; Mandel 107–12.
120. Mandel, 122, 128, 139–40.
121. Muslih, 1988, 85.
122. Eliav, 1977, 308–9.
123. Ro'i, 1968, 218.
124. Mandel, 150.
125. Ibid., 159–61.
126. Ibid., 181.
127. Ibid., 174–77.
128. Ibid., 189.

THREE
WORLD WAR I, THE BALFOUR
DECLARATION, AND THE BRITISH
MANDATE

1. Tauber, 1993b, 15.
2. Fromkin, 269.
3. Friedman, 165.
4. Fromkin, 95–105.
5. Ibid., 142.
6. Friedman, 207.
7. Fromkin, 181.
8. Friedman, 123.
9. Antonius, 419–20, Appendix 4, reproducing McMahon to Hussein, October 24, 1915.
10. Kedourie, 65–137; Sanders, 249.
11. Friedman, 88.
12. Sanders, 252.
13. Ibid., 229–55.
14. Fromkin, 164.
15. Ibid., 185.
16. Sanders, 256–62, 275–83, 303–10; Fromkin, 192.
17. Sanders, 308.

18. Fromkin, 235.
19. Friedman, 125.
20. Ibid., 187.
21. Ibid., 8–11.
22. Wasserstein, 1991, 78.
23. Fromkin, 269–70.
24. Friedman, 290.
25. Ibid., 7.
26. Ibid., 128.
27. Fromkin, 283.
28. Ibid., 257.
29. Ibid., 41–42.
30. Ibid., 92.
31. Friedman, 57.
32. Ibid., 278.
33. Fromkin, 292–93.
34. Ibid., 295.
35. Friedman, 268.
36. Ibid., 269.
37. Caplan, 1978, 16.
38. Asiya, 9 and 221, n. 2.
39. Sanders, 652.
40. Friedman, 325–26.
41. Antonius, 267.
42. Ibid., 267–69.
43. Tessler, 155.
44. Friedman, 273.
45. Sanders, 632.
46. Fromkin, 336.
47. Ibid., 364–65.
48. Ibid., 374.
49. Ibid., 321.
50. Ibid., 345.
51. Caplan, 1978, 26–27.
52. Tessler, 153.
53. Wasserstein, 1991, 36.
54. Caplan, 1978, 82.
55. Weizmann, 1977, 292–94; Sanders, 636–37; Fromkin, 324.
56. Sanders, 637–39.
57. Ibid., 639–40.
58. Caplan, 1978, 142.
59. Sanders, 639–40.
60. Fromkin, 375; Sanders, 640.
61. Fromkin, 395.
62. Sanders, 641–42.
63. Ibid., 642–43.
64. Weizmann, 1949, 306–9; Sanders, 643–44.
65. Friedman, 93.
66. Sanders, 644–46.
67. Fromkin, 400.
68. Ibid., 401.
69. Seikaly, S. 400; Kimmerling and Migdal, 26.
70. Efrati, 25; Friedman, 121; Eliav, 1978, 448–49.
71. McCarthy, 26. Shmelz, 39, says the population of Palestine declined overall from 1914 to 1918 from eight hundred thousand to seven hundred thousand.
72. Seikaly, S., 399–406.
73. Storrs, 301.
74. McCarthy, 27.
75. Kimmerling and Migdal, 26.
76. Seikaly, S., 399.
77. Eliav, 1978, 437–38.
78. Tauber, 1993b, 37–38.
79. Ibid., 36.
80. Muslih, 95.
81. Storrs, 371.
82. Antonius, 203.
83. Dinur, vol. 1, part 1, 331.
84. Tauber, 1993b, 38.
85. Muslih, 1988, 90–91.
86. Seikaly, S., 3–4.
87. Dinur, vol. 1, part 1, 322; Eliav, 1978, 440; Seikaly, S., 404–45.
88. Efrati, 19, 52–87; Eliav, 1978, 439–40; Seikaly, S., 405–6.
89. Dinur, vol. 1, part 1, 322; Storrs, 295; Eliav, 1978, 441.
90. Seikaly, S., 404; Eliav, 1978, 442–43, 450.
91. Efrati, 21.
92. Menahem Sheinkin, in Ibid., 20.
93. Efrati, 21.
94. Eliav, 1978, 443.
95. Efrati, 274; Dinur, vol. 1, part 1, 327; Eliav, 1978, 444–45.
96. Shmelz, 31–32; Dinur, vol. 1, part 1, 315; Eliav, 1978, 457.
97. Shmelz, 38. McCarthy, 16–24, convincingly argues that the figure of 85,000 is an exaggeration, though his proposal of 60,000 for the prewar population seems on the low side.
98. McCarthy, 21–23.
99. Efrati, 23.
100. Ibid., 29–30, 40–41, 284–85, 288–95.

101. Ibid., 30.
102. Ibid., 42–43.
103. Friedman, 121.
104. Efrati, 31–32; Dinur, vol. 1, part 1, 353–86; Eliav, 1978, 453.
105. Dinur, vol. 1, part 1, 369–70; Friedman, 184.
106. Antonius, 440–42, Appendix 6, for text of the "Resolution of the General Syrian Congress (Damascus, 2 July 1919)."
107. Wasserstein, 1991, 38, quoting Curzon to Balfour, Jan. 16, 1919.
108. Wasserstein, 1991, 67.
109. Ibid., 22.
110. Ibid., 14, n. 52.
111. Ibid., 14.
112. Ibid., 40.
113. Dinur, vol. 1, 603.
114. Storrs, 367.
115. Wasserstein, 1991, 43.
116. Porath, 1976, 31.
117. Wasserstein, 1991, 31–32.
118. Ibid., 36; Porath, 1976, 104.
119. Porath, 1976, 23–25, 64–69; O'Brien, 143.
120. Shapira, 1992, 164.
121. Weizman, 1977, xxviii, Wasserstein, 1991, 26.
122. Wasserstein, 1991, 29.
123. Ibid., 41.
124. Caplan, 1978, 42.
125. The text of the letter, from Shertok (Istanbul) to friends in Tel Aviv, February 12, 1914, was reproduced in HaAretz, Friday supplement, December 1, 1995.
126. Caplan, 1978, 49–51; Rogel, 159, 165.
127. Dinur, vol. 1, 565–85; Shapira, 141–43.
128. Caplan, 1978, 53.
129. Dinur, vol. 1, 589–91.
130. Porath, 1976, 78–79.
131. Wasserstein, 1991, 61.
132. Porath, 1976, 80–81.
133. Dinur, vol. 1, 607.
134. Ibid., 609.
135. Sakakini, 137.
136. Porath, 1976, 79–80.
137. Sanders, 653; Caplan, 1978, 59.
138. Dinur, vol. 1, 615.
139. Caplan, 1978, 58.
140. Dinur, vol. 1, 615–6.
141. Ibid., 627–28.
142. Fromkin, 447–48.
143. Wasserstein, 1991, 71; Dinur, vol. 1, 623.
144. Wasserstein, 1991, 79–86.
145. Ibid., 149.
146. Ibid., 87.
147. Ibid.
148. Ibid., 91.
149. Ibid., 88.
150. Ibid., 95.
151. Ibid., 96.
152. Muslih, 1988, 153.
153. Porath, 1976, 81–84.
154. Ibid., 87.
155. Ibid., 89.
156. Fromkin, 519.
157. Sykes, 68.
158. Fromkin, 520.
159. Wasserstein, 1991, 97–98.
160. Fromkin, 504.
161. Arnon-Ohana, 1989, 37.
162. Wasserstein, 1991, 98–100.
163. Sykes, 69.
164. Shapira, 1992, 158–59.
165. Wasserstein, 1991, 107.
166. Dinur, vol. 2, part 1, 77.
167. Wasserstein, 1991, 103.
168. Dinur, vol. 2, part 1, 77–109; Porath, 1976, 104–11.
169. Porath, 1976, 111.
170. Wasserstein, 1991, 103.
171. O'Brien, 161.
172. Caplan, 1978, 171.
173. Wasserstein, 1991, 103–5, 110.
174. Ibid., 133.
175. Ibid., 132–3.
176. Ibid., 106.
177. Ibid., 119; Sykes, 88; Weizmann, 1949, 360–61.
178. Fromkin, 516, unnumbered footnote.
179. A Survey, HMSO, I, 19.
180. Caplan, 1978, 95.
181. Ibid., 100–101.
182. Wasserstein, 1991, 241.
183. Caplan, 1978, 40–43.
184. Caplan, 1983, 49.

185. Ibid., 69–70.
186. Ibid., 73.
187. Caplan, 1978, 98–101, 128–29.
188. Ibid., 198.
189. Gelber, 1992, vol. 1, 41–43, 53, 68–70.
190. Weizmann,1949, 406.
191. McCarthy, 26.
192. Ibid.
193. Wasserstein, 1991, 161.
194. McCarthy, 33–34.
195. McCarthy, 31. See also Janet L. Abu-Lughod, "The Demographic Transformation of Palestine," in *The Transformation of Palestine*, edited by Ibrahim Abu-Lughod (Evanston, Ill.: Northwestern University Press, 1971), 139–63.
196. Wasserstein, 1991, 160.
197. Ibid., 140.
198. Ibid., 160–61.
199. Ibid., 140, n. 3.
200. Ibid., 162–3.
201. Ibid., 160.
202. Ibid., 141.
203. Shapira, 1992, 225; Shavit, 1988.
204. Shapira, 1992, 217.
205. Ibid., 218.
206. Lesch, 53.
207. Shapira, 1992, 221–22.
208. Ibid., 234.
209. Ibid., 237.
210. Wasserstein, 1991, 94–95.
211. Ibid., 128–29.
212. Ibid., 109.
213. Ibid., 152.
214. Sykes, 108.
215. Ibid.
216. Ibid., 116.
217. Stein, 1991, 80, n. 43.
218. From articles that appeared in 1934 in an Arab newspaper, quoted in Stein, 1984, 183.
219. Stein, 1984, 67–70.
220. Ibid., 70.
221. Smith, passim.
222. Smith, 3.
223. Wasserstein, 1991, 221, 223.
224. Porath, 1976, 220; Wasserstein, 1991, 225; Kimmerling and Migdal, 89; Sela, 1994, 64–71.
225. Lesch, 138.
226. Porath, 1976, 211–17; Wasserstein, 1991, 225–28; Mattar, 33–49.
227. Wasserstein, 1991, 229.
228. Ibid., 230–31.
229. Dinur, vol. 2, part 1, 312.
230. Arnon-Ohana, 1989, 74.
231. Lesch, 209–10.
232. Wasserstein, 1991, 233.
233. Dinur, vol. 2, part 1, 313.
234. Ibid. Dinur claims that there were only 142.
235. Wasserstein, 1991, 159, 235. See also Dinur, vol. 2, part 1, 313.
236. Dinur, vol. 2, part 1, 319.
237. Wasserstein, 1991, 236.
238. Dinur, vol. 2, part 1, 315.
239. Ibid., 313–20.
240. Ibid., 320.
241. Wasserstein, 1991, 237.
242. Dinur, vol. 2, part 1, 320–23.
243. Ibid., 336–39.
244. Ibid., 325–28.
245. Ibid., 328–32.
246. Ibid., 324–25.
247. Ibid., 325.
248. Ibid., 333.
249. Wasserstein, 1991, 237; and Sela, 1994, 64–71.
250. Shapira, 1992, 250–51.
251. Ibid., 240–42.
252. Porath, 1978, 15.
253. Wasserstein, 1991, 157.
254. Shaw Commission Report, Cmd. 3530, 163.
255. Wasserstein, 1991, 237–38.
256. Stein, 1984, 68, 89.
257. Ibid., 88.
258. Porath, 1978, 20.
259. Kolinsky, 18–34.
260. Stein, 1984, 125.
261. Smith, 86.
262. *A Survey*, HMSO, 1, 28.
263. Weizmann, 1949, 415.
264. Ibid.
265. Caplan, 1978, 110.
266. Ibid., 113.
267. Eilam, 42.
268. Ibid., 50–51.

269. For the development of the Haganah, see Dinur, vols. 1, 2; Eilam, 1979.

FOUR
THE ARABS REBEL

1. Elpeleg, 1995, 52.
2. Seikaly, M., 217–55.
3. Porath, 1978, 38–44.
4. Ibid., 52.
5. Ibid., 55–56.
6. McCarthy, 34. Porath, 1978, 58, gives numbers 5–10 percent higher, because he includes estimated illegal immigrants.
7. Elpeleg, 1989, 41.
8. Lesch, 45–46.
9. Seikaly, M., 217–34.
10. Porath, 1978, 59.
11. McCarthy, 35–36.
12. Teveth, 1985, 166–68.
13. Smith, 98.
14. Porath, 1978, 108–11, 117–20.
15. Kano, 41.
16. Tessler, 176.
17. Porath, 1978, 114.
18. Smith, 109.
19. Porath, 1978, 113–14.
20. Tyler, 1989, 123–62; 1991, 343–73; 1994, 826–59.
21. Adler (Cohen), 197–220.
22. Porath, 1978, 117; Stein, 1984, passim.
23. Porath, 1978, 24–29; Arnon-Ohana, 1989, 80–90.
24. Arnon-Ohana, 1989, 129–32.
25. Ibid., 135.
26. Porath, 1978, 100.
27. Ibid., 101; Arnon-Ohana, 1989, 134.
28. Arnon-Ohana, 1989, 251.
29. Porath, 1978, 101.
30. Ibid., 147–56.
31. Arnon-Ohana, 1989, 161–79; Porath, 1978, 152–56.
32. Porath, 1978, 151–52.
33. Ibid., 29–35.
34. Ibid., 59–67; Arnon-Ohana, 1989, 245–250.
35. Porath, 1978, 161–71.
36. Schleifer, 61–81.
37. Seikaly, M., 244.
38. Porath, 1978, 166.
39. Abu Lughod, 238–39.
40. Shapira, 302.
41. Porath, 1978, 168–71; Arnon-Ohana, 1989, 266–71; Elpeleg, 1989, 42–44.
42. Shapira, 1992, 256–66.
43. Ibid., 285–87.
44. Ibid., 287–88.
45. Marlowe, 140–43.
46. Arnon-Ohana, 1989, 121.
47. Ibid., 149–51.
48. Porath, 1978, 172–73, 193–94.
49. Abu Lughod, 239; Arnon-Ohana, 1982, 21.
50. Dinur, vol. 2, 632.
51. Arnon-Ohana, 1982, 22.
52. Sakakini, 186.
53. Teveth, 1985, 165.
54. Porath, 1978, 313–24.
55. Elpeleg, 1989, 46–48.
56. Arnon-Ohana, 1982, 22–23.
57. Marlowe, 153.
58. Shimoni, 297.
59. Arnon-Ohana, 1982, 25.
60. Dinur, vol. 2, 637–8; Porath, 1978, 195–200; Arnon-Ohana, 1982, 24–26.
61. Porath, 1978, 200–203.
62. Teveth, 1985, 166; Porath, 1978, 209.
63. Abu Lughod, 252–54; Eyal, 90–91, 109–13.
64. Arnon-Ohana, 1982, 33.
65. Porath, 1978, 212–14.
66. Arnon-Ohana, 1982, 33.
67. Ibid., 35.
68. Ibid., 37–38.
69. Porath, 1978, 214.
70. Marlowe, 135.
71. Sykes, 219.
72. Porath, 1978, 213.
73. Ibid., 219–22.
74. Eyal, 247; Teveth, 1985, 373.
75. Porath, 1978, 234–36.
76. Ibid., 213–17.
77. Ibid., 216–17.
78. Ibid., 219.
79. Ibid., 218.
80. Arnon-Ohana, 1982, 11–12.
81. Ibid., 36.
82. Ibid., 26–28.

83. Ibid., 37–38.
84. Porath, 1978, 230–33.
85. Marlowe, 157.
86. Porath, 1978, 231–33.
87. Ibid., 230–32.
88. Ibid., 224–25.
89. Gelber, vol. 1, 1992, 271–81.
90. Hurewitz, 86–88.
91. Arnon-Ohana, 1982, 50–54; Porath, 1978, 225–28.
92. Arnon-Ohana, 1982, 53–54; Porath, 1978, 228–30.
93. Porath, 1978, 241–50.
94. Ibid., 267–68.
95. Ibid., 212.
96. Hurewitz, 71.
97. "Text of a Secret Proclamation sent by the Arab Higher Committee to the Terrorist Gangs," n.d., unsigned, CZA S25-3441.
98. Arnon-Ohana, 1982, 73–75; Porath, 1978, 257.
99. Porath, 1978, 256–58.
100. Mattar, 73.
101. Shapira, 1992, 303–4.
102. Ibid., 305.
103. Ibid., 306–8, 14–15.
104. Ibid., 317.
105. Teveth, 1985, 165.
106. Ibid.
107. Ibid., 166.
108. Shapira, 1992, 310–11.
109. Ibid., 319–51.
110. Teveth, 1985, 173–74.
111. Shapira, 1992, 341–45.
112. Dinur, vol. 2, 671–73.
113. Ibid., 676–97.
114. Porath, 1978, 259–62; Peel Commission Report, Cmd. 5479.
115. Cohen, 1978, 30.
116. Masalha, 54–58; Shlaim, 1988, 58.
117. Shlaim, 1988, 58.
118. Sykes, 212–13.
119. D. Ben-Gurion to A. Ben-Gurion, Oct. 5, 1937, IDFA, Ben-Gurion Correspondence.
120. Shlaim, 1988, 59.
121. Peel Commission Report, Cmd. 5479.
122. Ibid., 391.
123. D. Ben-Gurion to A. Ben-Gurion,
July 27–28, 1937, IDFA, Ben-Gurion Correspondence.
124. Masalha, 14.
125. Ibid., 11–12.
126. Caplan, 1978, 29.
127. Ibid., 31.
128. Masalha, 32.
129. Ibid., 37.
130. Ibid., 50.
131. Protocol of the Meeting of the Jewish Agency Executive, Nov. 1, 1936, S100/20B.
132. David Ben-Gurion Diary, BG Archive.
133. D. Ben-Gurion to A. Ben-Gurion, Oct. 5, 1937, IDFA, Ben-Gurion Correspondence.
134. CZA S5-1543, Aug. 7, 1937. The file contains the original texts of the speeches delivered at the Twentieth Zionist Congress.
135. While the original transcript of Weizmann's speech is missing from file CZA S5-1543, and the section on transfer was omitted from the published versions, a number of other speakers at the congress referred to it in their speeches, the original versions of which are in S5-1543.
136. Protocol of the meeting of the Jewish Agency Executive, June 7, 1938, CZA, S100/24B.
137. Protocol of the joint meeting of the Jewish Agency Executive and the Political Committee of the Zionist Action Committee, June 12, 1938, CZA, S100/24B.
138. The documents are in CZA S25-247; Katz, 167–89; Masalha, 93–106.
139. Hurewitz, 79.
140. Lesch, 121–22.
141. Hurewitz, 79.
142. Lesch, 230.
143. Danin, 35, n. 69; Arnon-Ohana, 1982, 81.
144. Porath, 1978, 278.
145. Mattar, 82.
146. Gelber, 1992, 214; Porath, 1978, 279–81; Mattar, 83.
147. Arnon-Ohana, 1982, 82.
148. Porath, 1978, 309–11; Danin, xxix.

149. Arnon-Ohana, 1982, 89.
150. Ibid., 90–92.
151. Aharon Haim Cohen to Shertok, Nov. 30, 1937, CZA S25-3539.
152. Yishak Darwish's statement in Sasson (Beirut) to Shertok, Sept. 4, 1938, CZA S25-5568.
153. A Survey, I, HMSO, 43.
154. Porath, 1978, 296.
155. Arnon-Ohana, 1982, 84.
156. Porath, 1978, 306.
157. Ibid., 297–98.
158. Danin, 54, 58, 137, etc.
159. Ibid., passim; Porath, 1978, 288–96.
160. Arnon-Ohana, 1982, 95–100, 104–8.
161. Porath, 1978, 282.
162. Naor, 98.
163. Naor, 103–6; Niv, 35–42.
164. Niv, vol. 2, 78; Naor, 120.
165. Niv, vol. 2, 79–80; Naor, 121; Marlowe, 200; A Survey, I, HMSO, 45.
166. Marlowe, 201; Niv, vol. 2, 93–94.
167. Niv, vol. 2, 80–94; Naor, 121–22.
168. Dinur, vol. 2, 939–67.
169. Wallach, 1991, 54.
170. Dinur, vol. 2, 924.
171. Dinur, vol. 2, 921.
172. Wallach, 1991, 54; Niv, vol. 2, 246.
173. Gelber, 1992, vol. 1, 318–36, and vol. 2, 548–61; Black and Morris, 1–34.
174. Porath, 1978, 310–13.
175. Ibid., 280–83.
176. Nahmani, Oct. 3, 1938; Dinur, vol. 2, 818–24.
177. Nahmani, Oct. 27, 1938.
178. E. Danin to R. Zaslani, Nov. 15, 1938, CZA S25-10615.
179. Arnon-Ohana, 1982, 121.
180. Porath, 283.
181. Marlowe, 198–99.
182. Arnon-Ohana, 1982, 119.
183. Ibid., 123.
184. Ibid., 62–63.
185. Ibid., 84–85; CZA S25-4144, unsigned intelligence report, Jan. 3, 1939.
186. Arnon-Ohana, 1982, 117.
187. Danin, 129–31.
188. Arnon-Ohana, 1982, 118.
189. Danin, 9–14.
190. Porath, 1978, 316–17.

191. Danin, 19.
192. Ibid., 68.
193. Porath, 1978, 302.
194. Ibid., 306.
195. Jewish intelligence report, "Acts of Destruction and Robbery . . . ," unsigned, Nov. 6, 1938, CZA S25-10615.
196. Marlowe, 230.
197. Porath, 1978, 321–22.
198. Porath, 1978, 299.
199. Gelber, 1992, vol. 1, 233.
200. Porath, 1978, 306.
201. Ibid., 298.
202. Arnon-Ohana, 1989, 131.
203. Porath, 1978, 301–3; Danin, 114, n. 236; Arnon-Ohana, 1982, 151.
204. Porath, 1978, 304.
205. Ibid., 303.
206. Ibid., 319.
207. Ibid.
208. Cohen, 1978, 4.
209. Porath, 1978, 330.
210. Cohen, 1978, 49.
211. Ibid., 48.
212. Cohen, 1978, 68, citing Bateman, the chargé d'affaires in Baghdad, to the Foreign Office, Aug. 30, 1938.
213. Cohen, 1978, 72.
214. "Palestine Partition Commission Report Presented by the Secretary of State for the Colonies to Parliament by Command of His Majesty, October, 1938," Cmd. 5854, 235.
215. Hurewitz, 96.
216. A Survey, I, HMSO, 47.
217. Hurewitz, 96.
218. Cohen, 1978, 80.
219. Hurewitz, 100.
220. Cohen, 1978, 84.
221. A Survey, I, HMSO, 90–99, for the text.
222. For text of note of rejection, signed by Amin al-Husayni, see Elpeleg, 1989, 177–78.
223. Porath, 1978, 344–45; Hurewitz, 102–3.
224. Porath, 1978, 348.
225. Mattar, 84.
226. Hurewitz 104–6.
227. Ibid., 104–5; Zweig, 4–5.
228. Seikaly, M., 255.

229. Khalaf, 78.
230. Danin, xxxii.
231. Arnon-Ohana, 1982, 140.
232. Mattar, 85.
233. Levenberg, 50.
234. Hurewitz, 113.
235. Ibid., 84.
236. Ibid., 84–85.

FIVE
WORLD WAR II AND THE FIRST ARAB-
ISRAELI WAR, 1939–49
1. Hurewitz, 124–25.
2. Sakakini, 212–13.
3. Segev, 22; Weitz, 353.
4. Segev, 86.
5. Ibid., 89.
6. Zweig, 110.
7. Ibid., 47; Wallach, 1991, 72; McCarthy, 178.
8. Zweig, 67, n. 122.
9. Ibid., 118–30; Wasserstein, 1979, 143ff.
10. Zweig, 88, 146.
11. Hurewitz, 111.
12. Ibid., 117.
13. Ibid., 121.
14. Ibid., 150–52.
15. Ibid., 153.
16. Mattar, 100.
17. Ibid., 104; Hurewitz, 146–55.
18. Elpeleg, 1995, 106.
19. Mattar, 100.
20. Ibid., 105.
21. Ibid., 99.
22. Cohen, M., 1978, 162–63.
23. Zweig, 89–92.
24. Cohen, M., 1978, 93.
25. Ibid., 94.
26. Zweig, 20.
27. Cohen, M., 1978, 100.
28. Ibid., 110–16.
29. Ibid., 123; Dinur, vol. 3, 649–798.
30. Zweig, 112.
31. Ibid., 174, n. 107.
32. Ibid., 135.
33. Bar-Zohar, vol. 1, 417.
34. Cohen, M., 1978, 130.
35. Hurewitz, 158.
36. Bauer, 231, 239–41.

37. "Short Minutes of Meeting Held on Thursday, January 30th, 1941, at 77 Great Russell Street, London, W.C.1," Chaim Weizmann Archive 2271. See also *Yediot Aharonot,* May 25, 1993, and *HaAretz,* March 16, 1993.
38. "Outlines of Zionist Policy," by D. Ben-Gurion, Oct. 15, 1941, CZA Z4-14632. I am indebted to Prof. Yoav Gelber, of Haifa University, for directing my attention to this important document.
39. Bauer, 245.
40. Hurewitz, 201.
41. Ibid., 202–3.
42. Cohen, M., 1978, 129.
43. Ibid., 139.
44. Ibid., 153.
45. Zweig, 175.
46. Cohen, M., 1978, 167.
47. Ibid., 170.
48. Niv, vol. 4, 81–84.
49. Cohen, M., 1978, 179.
50. Ibid., 1988, 162.
51. Hurewitz, 213.
52. Schoenbaum, 32.
53. Ibid.
54. Cohen, M., 1988, 181.
55. Hurewitz, 229.
56. Ibid., 189.
57. Khalaf, 93–95; Hurewitz, 183–84.
58. Hurewitz, 186; Khalaf, 87–89.
59. Porath, 1986, 257–311.
60. Hurewitz, 192.
61. Ibid., 194.
62. Khalaf, 96–98.
63. Ibid., 115–25.
64. Ibid., 129–30.
65. Hurewitz, 232.
66. Zweig, 173, n. 106.
67. Ibid., 165, n. 68.
68. Bauer, 306; Zweig, 165, n. 69.
69. Heller, vol. 1, 125–35.
70. Niv, vol. 4, 20–32, 46–48, 50–57, 60–63; Dinur, vol. 3, 523–27.
71. Niv, vol. 4, 32–36.
72. Hurewitz, 200.
73. Niv, vol. 4, 88–117; Dinur, vol. 3, 531–43.
74. Hurewitz, 225.

75. Ibid., 228.

76. Cohen, M., 1988, 182, 188; Hurewitz, 229–30.

77. Niv, vol. 4, 162–64.

78. Ibid., 167.

79. Ibid., 172–74.

80. Ibid., 179–83.

81. Gil'ad, vol. 1, 629–40.

82. Niv, vol. 4, 183–86.

83. Ibid., 190.

84. Ibid., 191; Wallach, 1991, 82.

85. Gil'ad, vol. 1, 650–8; Niv, vol. 4, 267–69.

86. Wallach, 1991, 83.

87. Zertal, 37–270.

88. Hurewitz, 231.

89. Nachmani, 66–81.

90. Hurewitz, 237–39.

91. Nachmani, 111–13.

92. Ibid., 143.

93. Ibid., 146.

94. Ibid., 161.

95. Ibid., 167.

96. Ibid., 178.

97. Ibid., 187.

98. Crossman, 148.

99. Hurewitz, 249.

100. Nachmani, 205, 208–9.

101. Hurewitz, 254.

102. Cohen, M., 1982, 141–47; Freundlich, 42–49.

103. Hurewitz, 256.

104. Cohen, M., 1982, 162–70.

105. Ibid., 223.

106. Hurewitz, 281–82.

107. Niv, vol. 5, 161–63, 274–80.

108. Cohen, M., 1982, 245.

109. Ibid., 245–46, 249.

110. Black and Morris, 48.

111. Freundlich, 109.

112. Khalaf, 157.

113. Cohen, M., 1982, 264–67.

114. Freundlich, 110–11.

115. Levenberg, 90.

116. Zertal, 182–96; Levenberg, 89–90.

117. Cohen, M., 1982, 250–57; Pappe, 1992, 24–25.

118. Freundlich, 111–12; Pappe, 1992, 27.

119. Cohen, M., 1982, 268–76.

120. Pappe, 1992, 19–20; Freundlich, 87.

121. Cohen, M., 1982, 276–67.

122. Asiya, 37–38.

123. Cohen, M., 1982, 290.

124. Ibid., 295.

125. Khalidi, W., 305–6.

126. Freundlich, 199.

127. Cohen, M., 1982, 292.

128. Kimche and Kimche 48–53; Mayer, 21.

129. Levenberg, 191.

130. Pappe, 1992, 71; Sela, 1996, 139–60.

131. Cohen, M., 1982, 319–20.

132. Sabag, Shmuel (ed.), *Behind the Screen, An Iraqi Parliamentary Committee on the War Against Israel* (Heb.), IDF Press, Tel Aviv, 1954, 66–68; Mattar, 125.

133. Kimche and Kimche, 60.

134. Thomas, 22–23.

135. Cohen, M., 1982, 321; Levenberg, 189.

136. Pappe, 1992, 73–74.

137. Mattar, 125–26.

138. Sela, 1996.

139. Dinur, vol. 3, 1253–55.

140. Ibid., 1322.

141. Milstein, 1981–91, vol. 1, 185–211.

142. Ibid., 1989–91, vol. 2, 25.

143. Ibid., 1989–91, vol. 2, 53.

144. Collins and Lapierre, 40–41.

145. Nahmani Diary, Nov. 30, 1947.

146. Collins and Lapierre, 43.

147. Milstein, 1989–91, vol. 2, 25.

148. "Tuviel, 6.12.47," by "E. L.," Dec. 7, 1947, CZA S25-4015A.

149. Milstein, 1989–91, vol. 2, 32–45.

150. Cohen, M., 1982, 311.

151. Ibid., 1982, 307.

152. Meir, 220–23.

153. Levenberg, 126–54.

154. Ibid., 210.

155. Ilan, 1995, 66–67.

156. Nazzal, 45, 50, 56, 65–66, etc.

157. Gelber, 1995, 229–52.

158. Nazzal, 11.

159. Levenberg, 198.

160. Milstein, 1989–91, vol. 2, 55–68.

161. Ibid., vol. 3, 152.

162. Ibid., 152–3.

163. Ibid., vol. 2, 205–12.
164. Ibid., 46.
165. Ibid., 77–78; Niv, vol. 6, 19–20.
166. Milstein, 1989–91, vol. 2, 78–81.
167. Ibid., vol. 3, 71–73; Niv, vol. 6, 40–41.
168. Milstein, 1989–91, vol. 3, 73–75; Niv, vol. 6, 41. Jewish sources later claimed that one or two of the dead were Arab irregulars.
169. Milstein, 1989–91, vol. 3, 81–84; Black and Morris, 42.
170. Milstein, 1989–91, vol. 2, 107–12.
171. Ibid., 115–18.
172. Ibid., 88–92; Tal, 18.
173. Ibid., vol. 2, 93–4, 119.
174. Ibid., vol. 3, 35–36.
175. Ibid., 51–54; Levenberg, 193–94.
176. Ibid., vol. 3, 39–50.
177. Ibid., 58–9.
178. Ibid., 62.
179. Ibid., 62–68; al-Qawuqji, "Memoirs, 1948," part 1, 27–58.
180. Milstein, 1989–91, vol. 3, 231.
181. Tal, 18.
182. Collins and Lapierre, 173–75.
183. Milstein, 1989–91, vol. 3, 86–88.
184. Levenberg, 202.
185. Milstein, 1989–91, vol. 3, 92–96.
186. al-Qawuqji, "Memoirs, 1948," part 1, 31–34.
187. Levenberg, 203.
188. Milstein, 1989–91, vol. 4, 86–94.
189. Ibid., 118–19.
190. Ibid., 97–124.
191. Ibid., 64–84.
192. Ibid., 125–27.
193. Ibid., 125–39.
194. Cohen, M., 1982, 354–66.
195. Ilan, 1995, 184.
196. Ibid., 185.
197. Milstein, 1989–91, vol. 4, 165–81.
198. Ibid., 182–85.
199. Ibid., 198–200.
200. Ibid., 201–12, 221–50.
201. Milstein (ibid., 257–58) believes that irregulars did participate.
202. Ibid., 258.
203. Lapidot, 160; Milstein, 1989–91, vol. 4, 258.

204. Niv, vol. 6, 78–94.
205. Milstein, 1989–91, vol. 4, 268.
206. See, for example, ibid., 276, qouting Mordechai Ra'anan, the IZL head of the operation.
207. Ibid.
208. "Yavne" (Yitzhak Levy) to "Tene (Dalet)" (Shai southern area), "The IZL and LHI Action in Deir Yassin," Apr. 12, 1948, IDFA 5254\49\\372; "Yavne" to "Tene (Dalet)," "The Dissidents' Action in Deir Yassin," Apr. 13, 1948, IDFA 5254\49\\372; and "Report on Conquest of Deir Yassin," Apr. 10, 1948, by "Eliezer," IDFA 500\48\\29. Milstein (ibid., 273–76) quotes at length from most of the massacre and rape reports but casts doubt on their veracity. In general, he denies that there were any "massacres." Families were indeed slaughtered, he says, but mostly during attacks by Jewish forces on Arab villages in the first half of 1948; similar brutal conquests of villages were carried out by the Haganah and Palmah. But Deir Yassin was subsequently "elevated" by the Yishuv's leadership and the Haganah to the status of a unique massacre and publicized because of their antipathy toward the IZL and in order to focus blame for the various atrocities committed during the war on the IZL and LHI, and to divert blame away from the Haganah, he argues. And, Milstein argues (ibid. 277–80), Ben-Gurion and the left-wing Mapai party deliberately exploited Deir Yassin to prevent the conclusion of a political power-sharing agreement with the Revisionists, which was then being debated in Tel Aviv.
209. *Kol Ha'Ir,* Nov. 25, 1988; Milstein, 1989–91, vol. 4, 274; Levy, 340–45.
210. ISA "Documents," 376, Jewish Agency to Abdullah, Apr. 12, 1948.
211. Morris, 1994, 90.
212. Collins and Lapierre, 283–91.
213. Orren, 84–90; al-Qawuqji, "Memoirs, 1948," part 1; Morris, 1988, 115–19; *Mishmar Ha'Emek at War;* Khalidi, W., 1992, 185.

214. Dinur, vol. 3, 1567.

215. Ibid.; and Gelber, 1995, 234–35.

216. Morris, 1994, 171–76.

217. Ibid., 177–78.

218. Av, 172–217; Morris, 1988, 70–73; Morris, 1994, 179–83.

219. Morris, 1988, 73–95; Carmel, 85–115; Eshel, 347–78.

220. Lazar, 114–239; al-Qawuqji, "Memoirs, 1948," part 1, 50–58; Morris, 1988, 95–101.

221. Morris, 1988, 121–22.

222. Ibid., 102–5.

223. Ibid., 122–24.

224. Ibid., 107–9.

225. Ibid., 125; Coren, 116–26.

226. Giv'ati, 129–31; Dinur, vol. 3, 1427–28; Levenberg, 177–78.

227. Shlaim, 1988, 215; Tal, 36–37; Wallach, 1991, 111.

228. Interview with Ya'akov Edelstein, Oct. 5, 1994.

229. Collins and Lapierre, 361–4; Dinur, vol. 3, 1436–40; Tal, 39–42.

230. Ben-Gurion, 1982, vol. 2, 416.

231. Israel State Archives, 1978, People's Administration, meeting of May 12, 1948.

232. Kimche and Kimche, 160. Arab estimates of Jewish strength at this time, such as Glubb's, of "65,000" or even 100,000, were fanciful.

233. Ilan, 1995, 77.

234. Ibid., 72, 77.

235. Ibid., 76.

236. Ibid., 145.

237. Ibid., 80, 175; Wallach, 1991, 114; Kimche and Kimche, 161.

238. Itzhaki, 127.

239. Glubb, 95; Pappe, 1992, 109–10, 122.

240. Ilan, 1995, 80; Glubb, 94. Pappe (111) estimates that 23,500 Arab soldiers participated in the invasion, and that there were, in addition, 12,000 Palestinian irregulars and foreign volunteers; Wallach (1991, 114) gives a figure of 30,000 Arab troops plus "10,000 local [irregulars]"; Kimche and Kimche (162) speak of 23,000–24,000 invading Arabs, but include "3,000" Lebanese— of whom more later—and "2,000" troops of the ALA already in the country.

241. Glubb, 195.

242. Kimche and Kimche, 152, n.1; Ben-Gurion, 1982, Jan. 5, 1949.

243. Ilan, 1995, 11.

244. Ibid., 14–15.

245. Ibid., 72.

246. Ibid., 107.

247. Collins and Lapierre, 408.

248. Ibid., 157.

249. Ibid., 302; Kimche and Kimche, 153–54; Ilan, 1996, 36–39.

250. Shlaim, 1988, 227–28; and Mayer, 1986.

251. ISA, Protocols of May 12, 1948, meeting of People's Administration.

252. Pappe, 1992, 112.

253. Glubb, 93.

254. Glubb (ibid.) claims that there was not: "There had been no joint planning of any kind. The Israelis subsequently claimed knowledge of an Arab master plan, combining the strategy of all the Arab armies. No such plan existed, nor had any attempt been made to prepare one."

255. Collins and Lapierre, 294–95; Shlaim, 1988, 199. A similar plan is described by Kimche and Kimche, 150. A version of the plan, as understood by Haganah intelligence, is to be found in "The Arab Attack Plan after May 15," unsigned, May 5, 1948, IDFA 5942/49//72.

256. Shlaim, 1988, 226.

257. Ibid., 199–201.

258. PRO FO 816/120, Kirkbride to Secretary of State, May 14, 1948.

259. Kimche and Kimche, 151–52.

260. Shlaim, 1988, 202–3; al-Qawuqji, "Memoirs, 1948," part 2, 3–33.

261. "A Talk with Abdullah 17.11.47," by E. Danin, CZA S25-4004; Shlaim, 1988, 110–17.

262. State of Israel, 1978, Protocol of May 12, 1948, meeting of the People's Administration; State of Israel, 1979, "Meeting of the Arab Section of the Political Department of the Jewish Agency (May 13, 1948)," and Shertok to

Goldmann, May 13, 1948, 789–91; Tal, 48–50; Shlaim, 1988, 205–14.

263. Glubb, 152.

264. Collins and Lapierre, 365.

265. Shlaim, 1990; Elpeleg, 1995, 80–81.

266. Glubb (90) writes of 6,000, though also (92), of "4,500"; Tal, 66, writes of "9,050," plus some auxiliaries. Pappe, 1988 (109), writes of "7,400."

267. Ilan, 1995, 54–55.

268. Ibid., 58.

269. Glubb, 89–92.

270. Ilan, 1995, 60.

271. Ibid., 61.

272. Glubb, 99.

273. Sabag, 144–45, reproducing Mahmud al-Ghussan (Arab.), *The Battle for Sha'ar HaGai*, Amman, n.d. [1950?].

274. Sela, 1992, 623–88.

275. Glubb, 100–107.

276. Ibid., 111.

277. Sabag, 87–89, reproducing Kamal Ismail al-Sharif, *The Muslim Brotherhood in the Palestine War*, Cairo, 1951.

278. Glubb, 114–25; Collins and Lapierre, 473–76.

279. Glubb, 127–31; Tal, 78–112; Lorch, 182–88.

280. Itzhaki, 214, 180–231, 177–78, 253, 238–68; Sabag, 173–77, 183–89; Shapira, 1994, 9–41; Shamir, 1986, 2–60. Itzhaki, 592, speaks of "389" killed.

281. Shapira, 1994, passim.

282. Itzhaki, 292–320, 327–32; Sabag, 194–99 (reproducing al-Ghussan, *The Battle of Sha'ar HaGai*).

283. Itzhaki, 269–82.

284. Ilan, 1995, 260–61.

285. Nasser, 1973, 1–32.

286. Ilan, 1995, 54.

287. Ibid., 51.

288. Ibid., 50.

289. Ben-Gurion, 1982, May 16, 1948.

290. Giv'ati, 53–54; Nasser, 1973, 10.

291. Nasser, 1973, 12.

292. Giv'ati, 57–65; Ayalon, 1963, 41–42.

293. Ayalon, 1963, 111–112.

294. Nasser, 1973, 13.

295. Giv'ati, 103–14; Ayalon, 1963, 109–42.

296. Ayalon, 1963, 142.

297. Ilan, 1995, 42–45, 130.

298. Ibid., 252.

299. Ibid., 45–46, 80.

300. Lorch, 167–68.

301. Glubb, 130.

302. Ilan, 1995, 175.

303. Eshel, 1973, 187–203; Etzioni, 198–219.

304. Ilan, 1995, 262.

305. Ibid., 62–63.

306. Ibid., 64.

307. "Tzuri" to "Tene (Ayin)," May 24, 1948, Haganah Archive, RG 105-126. The report also says that the British "consul" (minister?) simultaneously pressed the Lebanese leaders to join in the invasion, but this seems unlikely. I would like to thank Prof. Yoav Gelber, of Haifa University, for directing me to the archival sources that suggest that the Lebanese kept out of the invasion.

308. "Tzuri" to "Tene (Ayin)," May 21, 1948, Haganah Archive, RG 105-128.

309. "Yediot Tene (Ayin)," June 16, 1948, Haganah Archive, RG 105-126. See also, in the same file, an unsigned "Tene (Ayin)" report of June 17, 1948.

310. See, for example, undated report, "Tzuri" to "Tene (Ayin)," possibly from June 30, 1948, Haganah Archive, RG 105-126. See also "BaTziburiyut Ha'Aravit" ("In the Arab Public"), June 11, 1948, Haganah Archive, RG 105-147, "Tzuri" to "Tene (Ayin)," May 29, 1948 (there is "information that all the Lebanese army personnel who took part in the [battle on] the Malikiya front returned to the Lebanese border").

311. Gil'ad, vol. 2, 293–96; *Stormy Yiftah*, 150–51.

312. Wallach and Lissak, 1978, 35.

313. Lachish, 44–57.

314. "BaTziburiyut Ha'Aravit," Foreign Ministry Political Division/Research Department, June 27, 1948, Haganah Archive, RG 105-147.

315. Lorch, 251.

316. Ilan, 1995, 160, 163, 202–203, 211–12, etc.

317. Israel, State of, 1981, Bernadotte to Shertok, June 27, 1948, 230–34; Ilan, 1989, 125–44.

318. State of Israel, I, 1981, 262–64, Shertok to Bernadotte, July 5, 1948; Pappe, 1988, 143–53.

319. State of Israel, 1, 1981, 298, Shertok to Trygve Lie, July 8, 1948; ibid., 300, Shertok to Eban, July 8, 1948.

320. Nasser, 1973, 19.

321. Giv'ati, 163–70.

322. Ayalon, 1963, 278–92.

323. Ibid., 293–340; Giv'ati, 178–84.

324. Gelber, 1995.

325. Eshel, 1973, 205–24.

326. Ibid., 214–21.

327. Etzioni, 254–77.

328. Eshel, 1973, 227–48.

329. Orren, 1976, 41–42.

330. Itzhaki, vol. 2, 369–86.

331. Glubb, 157–59; Orren, 1976, 42.

332. Itzhaki, vol. 2, 389–475.

333. *HaAretz*, July 16, 1948.

334. Lachish, 44–57.

335. Ilan, 1995, 266 and 305, n. 42.

336. Ibid., 267.

337. There is good reason to believe that Ben-Gurion opposed an offensive on the Central Front and proposed it only after making certain that the cabinet would turn it down. See Itzhaki, vol. 2, 507–8.

338. Ibid., 476–514.

339. Ayalon, 1963, 416–17.

340. Ilan, 1995, 257–58. In corruption charges drawn up by the Egyptian government after the war against some of its senior military officers, it was stated that, in one significant purchase, 42 percent of the ammunition bought was spoiled and "more dangerous to the user than the enemy."

341. Giv'ati, 209–30.

342. Ayalon, 1963, 421–618.

343. Ayalon, 1963, 575–88.

344. Glubb, 198–210.

345. Ilan, 1995, 257.

346. Giv'ati, 231–42.

347. Eshel, 1973, 277–86; Etzioni, 307–12. For some of the massacres, see Morris, 1988, 222–23, 229–34.

348. Ben-Gurion, 1982, 886–87, Dec. 19, 1948.

349. Etzioni, 337–49.

350. Giv'ati, 243–81; *The Negev Brigade,* 197–217; Sabag, 108–14, quoting from Kamal Ismail al-Sharif, *The Muslim Brotherhood.*

351. State of Israel, II, 1984, 319, U. Heyd (Washington) to M. Sharett, Dec. 30, 1948.

352. State of Israel, II, 1984, 331, J. G. McDonald to M. Sharett, Dec. 31, 1948; Ben-Gurion, 1982, vol. 3, 914–18, Dec. 31, 1948.

353. State of Israel, II, 1984, 337, Weizmann to Truman, Jan. 3, 1949.

354. Ben-Gurion, 1982, vol. 3, 912–3, Dec. 30, 1948; Giv'ati, 271–13.

355. Giv'ati, 275–81; Bartov, 63–65.

356. State of Israel, II, 1984, 347, E. Elath to M. Sharett, Jan. 6, 1949.

357. Giv'ati, 280–81.

358. See, for example, Sharett's letter to McDonald of Jan. 3, 1949, stating that "no Israeli troops now remain on Egyptian soil," State of Israel, II, 1984, 335.

359. State of Israel, II, 1984, 349, C. Marriott to H. Beilin, Jan. 8, 1949; DBG-YH, vol. 3, 934–38, Jan. 7–8, 1949.

360. Giv'ati, 283–95; Glubb, 229–32; State of Israel, II, 1984, 482–83, "Meeting: I. J. Linton–M. Wright (London, 9 March, 1949)," Mar. 10, 1949; Shlaim, 1988, 401–6; Ben-Gurion, 1982, vol. 3, 974, Mar. 11, 1949.

361. State of Israel, III, 1983, 382–83, "Israel-Jordan General Ceasefire Agreement," Mar. 11, 1949.

362. Elpeleg, 1995, 29.

363. *Jerusalem Post,* June 15, 1950.

364. Shlaim, 1988, 386–433.

365. State of Israel, III, 1983, "Introduction" and 688–734 for texts of the four general armistice agreements.

366. CZA S-100/24B, protocol of the joint meeting of the Jewish Agency Executive

and the Political Committee of the Zionist Executive, June 12, 1938.

367. CZA S100/42b, protocol of meeting of Jewish Agency Executive, May 7, 1944.

368. Ben-Gurion, 1952, 68–69.

369. Sela, 1996, 134, 140, 167.

370. IDFA 715/49//3, Carmel to brigades, districts, October 31, 1948.

371. Shalom, 266 n. 101, 127–29.

372. For a fuller discussion of the origins of the refugee problem, see Morris, 1988, and Morris, 1994. For critiques of these books, from the traditional Arab and Zionist perspectives, see Finkelstein, 1991, 66–89; Masalha, 1991, 90–97; and Teveth, 1990, 214–49.

SIX
1949–1956

1. Seale, 1987.

2. Ben-Gurion, 1982, vol. 3, 894.

3. Israel cabinet meeting protocol, Dec. 19, 1948, ISA.

4. Caplan, 1993.

5. For payments in 1934 by the agency to Aharon Haim Cohen for transmission to Abdullah, CZA S25-3029.

6. State of Israel, IV, 1986, 68.

7. Ben-Gurion Diary, Feb. 7 and 13, 1951, BGA.

8. For varying views of the Israeli-Jordanian negotiations of 1949–51, see Shlaim, 1988, chaps. 12–19; Rabinovich, 1991, chap. 4.

9. Shlaim, 1988, 465.

10. Pappe, 1988, 188.

11. "Protocol of consultation on peace negotiations with the Arab States," 4.12.1949, ISA FM 4373/13.

12. Morris, 1988, 277

13. Shlaim, 1988, 604.

14. "Protocol of consultation on peace negotiations with the Arab states," 4.19.1949," ISA FM 4373/13.

15. Keeley to State Dept., May 19, 1949, NA RG 84, Tel Aviv Embassy Classified Records 1949, 321.9–Israel-Transjordan.

16. Morris, 1993, 18.

17. Seale, 1987, 61.

18. James McDonald (Tel Aviv) to Secretary of State, May 16, 1949, NA RG 84, Tel Aviv Embassy, Classified Records, 1949, 321.9-Israel-Syria, Secret and Confidential.

19. Rabinovich, 1991, 78–79.

20. I am not arguing that Ben-Gurion was wrong; perhaps land and water resources were more important for a tiny, immigrant-absorbing country than peace. I am, however, arguing that Syria offered peace terms and that Ben-Gurion, apparently with Sharett's full support, failed to give negotiation a chance; decided this without bringing the matter before the cabinet; and then, for decades lied about the Syrians' (and, more generally, the Arab leaders') willingness to talk peace.

21. Ben-Gurion to Sharett (New York), Dec. 4, 1955, ISA FM 2455/4.

22. State of Israel, I, 1981, 632–36; vol. 2, 21–29, 44; Shlaim, 1988, 315–20; Rabinovich, 1991, 172–73.

23. Rabinovich, 1991, 174–76; Shlaim, 1988, 346–48.

24. Rabinovich, 1991, 185–86.

25. State of Israel, VI, 1991, 767–68 and 861–62; and State of Israel, VII, 1992, 292–94.

26. Bar-On, 1992, 421, n. 31.

27. Nasser, 1961, 47, 44, 40.

28. Morris, 1993, 272.

29. Shimon Shamir, in Louis and Owen, 1989, 73–81.

30. Morris, 1993, 286–88; Shamir, in Louis and Owen, 1989,.

31. Divrei Ha-Knesset, 12/2, 3020 (Aug. 19, 1952).

32. Eytan, 1958, 87–104.

33. Morris, 1993, 98–99, n. 4.

34. Dayan, Lecture to IDF officers, 1955, cited in Morris, 1993, 69.

35. Morris, 1993, 78.

36. Ibid., 87.

37. Ya'ari, 1975, 13.

38. Morris, 1993, 97.

39. Ibid., 100–101.

40. "The Security Situation in Tal Shahar, Kfar Daniel, Gimzo and Mishmar

Ayalon," unsigned, Dec. 31, 1951, CZA S-92/17; Y. Berginski at meeting of Jewish Agency Executive, July 1, 1953, CZA S100-87.

41. Morris, 1993, 109.

42. "Orders for Fighting Infiltration," Fifth Brigade/Operations, to Fifty-first Battalion, May 1953 (full date unclear), IDFA 278/54//4.

43. Morris, 1993, 124–31.

44. Ibid., 133.

45. Ibid., 134.

46. Ibid., 135–38.

47. Ibid., 146.

48. "M.M." to *Al HaMishmar* ("on guard," the Mapam Party's daily newspaper), undated, and covering letter, *Al HaMishmar* to the Mapam Knesset faction, June 20, 1950, both in HHA kaf-9/1/6.

49. Morris, 1993, 157–66.

50. Ibid., 165.

51. Ibid., 166–72.

52. Ibid., 173.

53. Ibid., 177.

54. Ibid., 173–83.

55. Ibid., 193–94.

56. Ibid., 203–10.

57. Sharon, 1989, 80.

58. Sharett, 1978, vol. 1, 39.

59. Ibid., 44.

60. "Orders, Operation Shoshana," Maj. Shmuel Meller in the name of Col. Meir Amit, General Staff Branch/Operations, to OC Central Command, OC Unit 101, etc., Oct. 13, 1953; and "Orders, Operation Shoshana," Maj. Alex Sharon, in the name of Central Command's operations officer, Lt. Col. David Elazar, to OC Unit 101, etc., Oct. 13, 1953, both in IDFA 644/56//207.

61. "Statement by Prime Minister David Ben-Gurion," ISA FM 2453/5.

62. Sharett, 1966, excerpt from speech delivered by Sharett, Nov. 1957.

63. BG Diary, Aug. 11 and 18, 1953, BGA.

64. Morris, 1993, 294–300.

65. David Tal, in Golani, 1994, 68, 72–73.

66. "Special Report: The Gaza Incident— Summary and Situation Assessment,"

IDF Intelligence Branch, Mar. 22, 1955, ISA FM 2454/5.

67. Untitled memorandum by Nutting, Mar. 2, 1955, PRO FO 371-115897. VR1092/49.

68. Morris, 1993, 351. More than seventy Egyptian soldiers and one Israeli died.

69. Bar-On, 1992, 173.

70. An IDF corps that combined military training and agricultural settlement.

71. Bar-On, 1992, 68–69.

72. Sharett, 1978, v, 1517, June 28, 1956.

73. Byroade to Secretary of State, Apr. 9, 1956, NA RG 59, 684a.86/4-956, Box 2694.

74. Dayan, 1976, 187.

75. Morris, 1993, 375.

76. Ibid., 379–80.

77. Bar-On, 1992, 124–40.

78. Black and Morris, 1991, 171–74.

79. On Sept. 11 and 13 IDF troops blew up two Jordanian police forts, at Khirbet a Rahwa and Gharandal, killing about thirty soldiers and policemen. On Sept. 25 the IDF blew up the fort at Husan near Bethlehem, killing thirty-seven soldiers, and on Oct. 11 the fort at Qalqilya, killing about eighty soldiers.

80. Dayan, 1976, 255; Bar-On, 1991, 249, 253; Bar-On, 1992, 276–77.

81. Dayan, 1976, 259–60.

82. Kyle, 314–31, 565–67 (text of the Sèvres protocol).

83. Kafkafi, 98.

84. Bandman, 1987, 70–71.

85. Ibid., 71–74.

86. Ibid., 74–75.

87. Black and Morris, 132–33.

88. Bandman, 1987, 80.

89. Ibid., 82.

90. Shemesh and Troen, 310.

91. Bandman, 1987, 81.

92. Ibid., 76.

93. Shemesh and Troen, 310.

94. Ibid., 310–11.

95. Kyle, 385.

96. Bandman, 1987, 85.

97. Tehan, 40.

98. Morris, 1993, 408–9.

99. The best concise description of the IDF's Sinai Campaign is in Tehan, 1–47.
100. Bandman, 1987, 92.
101. Kyle, 432.
102. Ibid., 457.
103. Ibid., 444–76.
104. Ibid., 497.
105. Ibid., 479; Bar-On, 1992, 323.
106. Kyle, 479; Bar-On, 1992, 324.
107. Bar-On, 1992, 331–32.
108. Ibid., 342–74.
109. Dann, 39–107.
110. Nasser, 1961, 58.

SEVEN
THE SIX-DAY WAR, 1967
1. Black and Morris, 211–12.
2. Wallach, Lissak, Shamir, 1980, 26.
3. Ayalon, "Mivtza Magressa," 27–38. Jordanian casualties were fourteen soldiers and six civilians killed, and three dozen wounded. Israel lost one killed and ten wounded.
4. Yonay, 218–19.
5. Ibid., 221–24; Wallach, Lissak, Shamir, 1980, 30; Bartov, vol. 1, 117–20.
6. Haber, 147.
7. Ibid., 146.
8. Ibid., 147.
9. Middle East Journal 46/2 (Spring 1992), 174; Quandt, 1993, 508, n. 4. Gamasy (20) misidentifies the source of the statement and crucially distorts its content, writing: "Rabin actually announced on Radio Israel . . . that 'we will make a lightning attack against Syria and occupy Damascus to overthrow the government there.'"
10. Parker, 1992, 179; Black and Morris, 213.
11. Gamasy, 23.
12. Parker, 1992; 180–81; Gamasy, 23.
13. Gamasy, 23.
14. Gamasy (23–29) criticizes the move into Sinai as "rash and precipitate."
15. Black and Morris, 216.
16. Ibid., 217.
17. Gamasy, 27.
18. Ibid., 26; Parker, 1992, 191–92.
19. Laqueur, 1969, 98–99, 124.
20. Black and Morris, 217; Quandt, 1993, 31.
21. Rabin, 1979, 63; Hadashot, May 22, 1992.
22. Weizmann, 1976, 211–13.
23. Rabin, 1979, 57–59; Hadashot, May 22, 1992.
24. Quandt, 1993, 512, n. 38.
25. Ibid., 1992, 209.
26. Gamasy, 42–43.
27. Ben, "The First Nuclear War."
28. Haber, 161–63.
29. Mardor, 498–99.
30. Cohen, A., 190–210; Peres, 1995, 166–67.
31. Yediot Aharonot, May 25, 1993; Yonay, 243.
32. Haber, 186.
33. Quandt, 1993, chap. 2.
34. Korn, 17.
35. Black and Morris, 217–18.
36. Segev, 365–67.
37. Ibid., 366.
38. Ibid.
39. Narkiss, 327; Mutawi, 108–11.
40. Laqueur, 1969, 59, 105.
41. Bar-On, 1996, 339, n. 5.
42. Dayan, 1976, 427.
43. Quandt, 1992, 219, n. 60.
44. Ibid., 199; Ibid., 1993, 43–48, 53.
45. Segev, 368.
46. Gawrych, 535–59.
47. Ibid., 536–37.
48. Gawrych, "The Egyptian High Command . . ."
49. Gamasy, 40.
50. Ibid., 46–47.
51. Rabin, 1979, 56.
52. Dayan, 1976, 436.
53. Ibid., 445.
54. Narkiss, 328, 338–40.
55. Haber, 222; Narkiss, 329.
56. Bartov, vol. 1, 126.
57. Ibid., 121–22.
58. Yonay, 202–13; Yediot Aharonot, June 6, 1992.
59. Black and Morris, 223–24; Sadat, 1978, 174; Gamasy, 34, 44.
60. Dayan, 1976, 433.
61. Yonay, 233.

62. Ibid., 234.
63. Haber, 207.
64. Black and Morris, 223.
65. Ali, 35; Gamasy, 50; Hussein, 102–4.
66. *Yediot Aharonot,* May 25, 1993.
67. Yonay, 239.
68. Ibid., 241.
69. Rabin, 1979, 81.
70. Dayan, 1976, 433.
71. Weizman, 1976, 226.
72. Yonay, 243.
73. Ibid., 254, 265.
74. Haber, 213.
75. Rabin, 1979, 56.
76. Dayan, 1976, 423.
77. Haber, 246.
78. Ali, 35.
79. Gamasy, 62; Ali, 37.
80. Gamasy, 67–68.
81. Ibid., 62, 64–71; Ali, 38–39.
82. Ali, 37.
83. Ibid., 38.
84. Ibid., 40.
85. Haber, 231.
86. Brecher, Geist, 1990, 100.
87. Haber, 222.
88. Haber, 23; Bartov, vol. 1, 126.
89. Rabinovich, Abraham, 93–98.
90. Dayan, 1976, 437.
91. Mutawi, 123.
92. Narkiss, 329.
93. Haber, 228.
94. Ibid., 229–30.
95. Ibid., 231.
96. Ibid., 232–33; Dayan, 1976, 441.
97. Haber, 231.
98. Bartov, vol. 1, 130.
99. Ibid., 124–25.
100. Haber, 250–53.
101. Bartov, vol. 1, 131.
102. Dayan, 1976, 479–80.
103. Eldar, 1993, 291–310.
104. Interview with Gen. Yoel Ben-Porat, 1990; Erel, 275–77.
105. Haber, 155.
106. Gamasy (79) writes of 9,800 Egyptian dead or missing in action.
107. Wallach, Lissak, Shamir, 1980, 57, 68–69, 82. Altogether, the Arab states lost 452 aircraft (Egypt 318, Syria 61, Jordan 29, Iraq 23, and Lebanon 1). Israel lost 46 aircraft, with 28 pilots killed and 13 captured. Egypt lost 629 tanks and 750 guns. The Syrians lost 85 tanks and Jordan more than 100. Arab civilian dead on all fronts probably numbered no more than 500. A handful of Israeli civilians were killed by Jordanian fire in Jerusalem.
108. Dayan, 1976, 495–96; Gazit, 56–57.
109. *HaAretz,* Oct. 7, 1994. See also Gideon Levy (Heb.), "I Refused an Order," *HaAretz,* June 5, 1998, about a temporary expulsion from the village of Anabta, near Tulkarm.
110. Narkiss, 333–35; Gazit, 53.
111. Dayan, 495–97.
112. Braun, 1997, 153–54; Shashar, 134, 194, 212–13.
113. Laqueur, 1969, 290.
114. See, for example, Hirst, 227–28.
115. *Kol Ha'Ir,* Nov. 8 and 15, 1991.
116. Laqueur, 1969, 290; Gazit, 57–60.
117. Braun, 1997, 173.
118. Ajami, 1981.
119. Eban, 435–36.
120. Korn, 14–15.
121. Segev, 369.
122. Dayan, 1976, 490–92; Haber, 271.
123. Bar-On, 1996, 42–43.
124. Korn, 72; Pedatzur, 1995.
125. Laqueur, 1969, 294.
126. Haber, 275–76.
127. Ibid., 278; Narkiss, 335–36.
128. Narkiss, 343.
129. Ibid., 346.
130. Sprinzak, 44.
131. Ibid., 35–69, 107–66; Newman, 1985; Segal, 26–35.
132. Pedatzur, 1995.
133. Admoni, 22.
134. Ibid., 27.
135. Ibid., 51–54; Sprinzak, 47.
136. Admoni, 49.
137. Narkiss, 333.
138. Admoni, 58.
139. Ibid., 58–59; Narkiss, 356–57; Segal, 17–23.
140. Sprinzak, 47.
141. Kimmerling and Migdal, 240.

142. Braun, 1997, 68. Brigadier General Braun served as Dayan's aide-de-camp.
143. Braun, 1997, 170.
144. Ibid., 163–64.
145. Ibid., 170.
146. Shashar, 1997, 240. Shashar served as a staff officer and then spokesman of the West Bank military government in 1967.
147. Ibid., 240.
148. Kimmerling and Migdal, 260.
149. Gazit, 178–79, 181, 266–302, 324–33.
150. Ibid., 142–43.
151. Ibid., 143–44.
152. Ibid., 313.
153. Ibid., 279.
154. Ibid., 277.
155. Ibid., 306–7.
156. Ibid., 145.
157. Korn, 54–55. Gamasy (95) says that already in late June 1967, during Podgorny's visit to Cairo, Nasser had agreed to give the Soviets naval facilities in Egypt's Mediterranean harbors.
158. Laqueur, 1969, 275–76, 278.
159. Korn, 78.
160. Ibid., 75–76.
161. Ibid., 75.
162. Laqueur, 1969, 276; Sadat, 1978, 179.
163. Ajami, 1981.
164. The United States, Britain, and Israel later agreed that the English-language version of 242 was the authoritative one, as the resolution had been originally submitted in English, by Britain (Korn, 33).

EIGHT
THE WAR OF ATTRITION 1967–73

1. Korn, 56; Gamasy, 93–96.
2. Korn, 96–97; Gamasy, 100–102.
3. Korn, 56–57.
4. Ibid., 89.
5. Ibid., 98.
6. *Al-Ahram,* Mar. 6, 1969, quoted in Korn, 109.
7. Korn, 93, 95. One Israeli source (Peled, 126) maintains that the Egyptian fire had been triggered by earlier Israeli salvos across the Canal.

8. Schueftan, 134; Dayan, 1976, 513.
9. Schueftan, 135.
10. Korn, 106; Schueftan, 152.
11. Korn, 108.
12. Dayan, 1976, 516.
13. Korn, 117; Dayan, 1976, 516.
14. Peled, 129.
15. Eldar, 1993, 373–84.
16. Schueftan, 189–90; Korn, 167.
17. Korn, 118–19.
18. Ibid., 165.
19. Rabin, 1979, 119.
20. Eldar, 1993, 386–414.
21. Yonay, 273–74.
22. Korn, 168.
23. Ibid., 171.
24. Eldar, 1993, 414–21.
25. Zohar, 15–23; Adan, 49–50.
26. Schueftan, 212; Korn, 169–70. Gamasy (111–12) downplays the raid, speaking of only five Egyptian dead.
27. Korn, 170.
28. Yonay, 277–78.
29. Ibid., 276.
30. Bar-Siman-Tov, 1980, 99.
31. Korn, 175–76.
32. Gamasy, 112.
33. Eldar, 1993, 430–44, 438–42; Gamasy, 112.
34. Korn, 160–61.
35. Ibid., 163.
36. Ibid., 163–64; Quandt, 1993, 82.
37. Korn, 185.
38. Ibid., 171–72, 178–79.
39. Ibid., 173.
40. Ibid., 180.
41. Ibid., 181–82.
42. Ibid., 184.
43. Rabin, 1979, 119.
44. Korn, 189.
45. Ibid., 191–92.
46. Ibid., 194.
47. Yonay, 279.
48. Bar-Siman-Tov, 1980, 160.
49. Khrumchenko, 1996; Korn, 183.
50. Korn, 183.
51. Ibid., 198–201.
52. Bar-Siman-Tov, 1980, 132.
53. Khrumchenko, 1996; Korn, 196–97.
54. Bar-Siman-Tov, 1980, 142.

55. Ibid., 1980, 171.
56. Korn, 198.
57. Bar-Siman-Tov, 1980, 156.
58. Wallach and Lissak, 1983, 107.
59. Korn, 203; Wallach and Lissak, 1983, 107; Eldar, 1993, 443–46.
60. Korn, 225.
61. Yonay, 282–83.
62. Korn, 229–30.
63. Korn, 230; Bar-Siman-Tov, 1980, 161–63; Yonay, 283.
64. Yonay, 291.
65. Ibid., 294–97; Korn, 230–31; Bar-Siman-Tov, 1980, 163.
66. Bar-Kochba, 1989, 263–77. The Syrians lost some 40 tanks and 350 killed, the IDF 12 dead and one jet downed.
67. Yonay, 298–302.
68. Ibid., 302–4; Korn, 233.
69. Yonay, 304.
70. Korn, 227.
71. Ibid., 250.
72. Ibid., 254.
73. Years later, Gamasy still maintained that Egypt had moved the missile wall prior to "1:00 A.M. of August 8" (Gamasy, 121).
74. Korn, 266.
75. Ibid., 267, 269.
76. Schueftan, 439; Yonai, 265. From June 11, 1967, until mid-August 1970, the IAF lost 24 aircraft and the Egyptians 137.
77. Korn, 208, speaks of "10,000" Egyptian "casualties."
78. Bartov, 180; Korn, 275.
79. Schueftan, 440.
80. Gamasy, 123.
81. Kimmerling and Migdal, 220; Sayigh, 107–108, 141.
82. Abu Iyad, 88; Wallach, Lissak and Shamir, 1980, 118.
83. Black and Morris, 240.
84. Ibid., 246.
85. O'Ballance, 45–46.
86. Mem, 1984, 22.
87. Abu Iyad, 95–96.
88. Mem, 1984, 29.
89. Ibid., 1984, 18–32; Sayigh, 178–80.
90. Mem, 1984, 29.
91. Ibid., 32.
92. Ibid., 31.
93. O'Ballance, 47.
94. Wallach, Lissak, and Shamir, 1980, 124.
95. O'Ballance, 197.
96. Maimon, 1993; Sharon, 249–62.
97. O'Ballance, 195.
98. Mosko, 1995.
99. O'Ballance, 91.
100. Ibid., 137–90.
101. Quandt, 1993, 99–100.
102. Ibid., 101–15.
103. O'Ballance, 158. Sayigh, 267, speaks of 600 Legionnaires and more than 900 Palestinian fighters killed, with 1,500–3,500 civilians killed.
104. Sayigh, 274–??, O'Ballance, 205.
105. Merari and Elad, 16–17.
106. Ibid., 35–36.
107. Ibid., 37–38.
108. Ibid., 86–87.
109. Ibid., 57.
110. Ibid., 168–69.
111. Halasa, "A Deadly Inheritance."
112. Abu Iyad, 158–66.
113. Ibid., 155.
114. Ibid., 168–74; Bartov, vol. 1, 227–31.
115. Jonas, 262–66 and 299–303. Several Israeli agents were killed by Black September in Europe in 1972 and 1973.
116. Merari, 46.
117. Ibid., 39–49.
118. Peres, 1995, 161–62.
119. Shachan, 167–68.
120. Ibid., 95–97, 192–202.
121. *New York Times,* Aug. 31, 1981; ibid., Aug. 10, 1982.
122. Seale, 1992, 129–30.

NINE

1973: THE OCTOBER WAR

1. Schiff, "A Foreign Ruler Warned,".
2. Bar, 33.
3. Gamasy (130) maintains that Egypt's aim in going to war was "to upset the regional political and military balance." He also maintains (131, 139) that the Egyptian war plan called for crossing the Canal, defeating "the main concen-

trations of enemy forces in Sinai, reaching the mountain passes, and holding this position in preparation for other combat missions." But he concedes that, in the course of the war, disagreements surfaced in the military over whether the army should proceed, after the consolidation of a line some six miles east of the Canal, toward the line of the passes, about thirteen miles farther east. It remains unclear whether the actual, written operational order (which has never been published) spoke of reaching the passes (264–65, 267, 270).

4. Ibid., 138.
5. Bar, 67.
6. Ya'acobi, 65.
7. Rafael, 258–59; Rabin, 1979, 149–50.
8. Sadat, 1978, 219, 279–87.
9. Ya'acobi, 86.
10. Ibid., 76.
11. Ibid., 79–81.
12. Ibid., 91.
13. Bar-On, 1996, 44.
14. Quandt, 1993, 124.
15. Finkelstein, 159.
16. Ya'acobi, 91–92.
17. Ibid., 98; Rabin, 1979, 152–53; Quandt, 1993, 122. Ya'acobi (177–80) gives the texts of the Egyptian (Feb. 15, 1971) and Israeli (Feb. 26, 1971) replies to Jarring.
18. Ya'acobi, 110–11; Dayan, 1976, 526; Braun, 1993, 13.
19. Rabin, 1979, 165.
20. Ya'acobi, 130; Braun, 1993, 16.
21. Braun, 1993, 16.
22. Ibid.
23. Ya'acobi, 173–75.
24. Meir, 334.
25. Ya'acobi, 135, 139–40.
26. Shazly, 105.
27. Sadat, 1978, 225–27.
28. Sadat, 1978, 221, 229–31; Shazly, 195–97; Bar, 25.
29. Shazly, 172–84; Sadat, 1978, 234–36.
30. Gawrych, 1987.
31. Sadat, 1978, 241; Black and Morris, 300.

32. Gamasy, 183; Sadat, 1978, 242.
33. Shazly, 201–3, 205.
34. Gamasy, 181.
35. Ibid., 180.
36. Sunday Times, 85; Sadat, 1978, 239.
37. Shazly, 203–5, 278–79.
38. al-Gridly, 58.
39. Shazly, 18.
40. Ibid., 20.
41. Ibid., 83–84.
42. Ibid., 277.
43. Ibid., 25.
44. Ibid., 53.
45. Ibid., 54–56.
46. Ibid., 41.
47. Bartov, vol. 1, 237.
48. Zeira, 169.
49. Braun, 1993, 21.
50. Ibid., 25.
51. Milstein, 1993, 97, for documentation on which the konseptziya was based.
52. Rafael, 282.
53. Golan, 145.
54. Black and Morris, 292.
55. Heikal, 1975, 15.
56. Bar, 40.
57. Black and Morris, 292; Shazly, 209.
58. Meir, 347–52; Haber, 20.
59. Zeira, 116.
60. Shazly, 206–7.
61. Sari, 63.
62. Black and Morris, 297. Some of Egypt's deceptive military measures are described in Gamasy, 192–202.
63. Braun, 48, 56.
64. Black and Morris, 296.
65. Sadat, 1978, 241–42.
66. Shazly, 208.
67. Gamasy, 187–91.
68. Braun, 18.
69. Ibid., 26.
70. Black and Morris, 301–2.
71. Ibid., 298–312; Wallach and Lissak, 1983, 47.
72. Zeira, 96.
73. Nakdimon, 1993; Schiff, "A Foreign Ruler," 1993.
74. Black and Morris, 308.
75. Edelist, Hadashot.

76. See Black and Morris, 285–88.

77. Zeira, 163, 86–88, 123, 92; Braun, 1993, 68.

78. Braun, 1993, 68–83.

79. Zvi, 21–29; Milstein, 1993, 125.

80. Milstein, 1993, 125–28.

81. Braun, 1993, 44.

82. Milstein, 1993, 203–38.

83. Dromi, 72–76.

84. Yonay, 344.

85. Braun, 1993, 92–93; Yonay, 331–32.

86. Yonay, 310–12.

87. Yonay, 332; Cohen and Lavi (474–76) say 15 Phantoms took part—though perhaps they are referring only to the attacking aircraft, and not to decoys, electronic warfare aircraft, and so on.

88. Yonay, 332–34; Cohen and Lavi 474–76.

89. Braun, 1993, 130.

90. Hersh, 223–40; Aaronson and Brosh, 143–48; Milstein, 1993, 231. One Israeli historian, Martin van Krefeld (*HaAretz,* Aug. 27, 1993), has suggested that the Syrian retreat order issued at noon on Oct. 9, during the finale in "the Vale of Tears" was prompted by the Israeli nuclear warning; there is no proof of this, and it makes little sense. The Syrians had not reached Israel proper and were not threatening Israel's existence. If they were deterred by Israel's nuclear capability on Oct. 9, surely they should have been as deterred if not more so, on Oct. 6, and would have refrained from attacking altogether.

91. Shalit, 1993.

92. Milstein, 1993, 228; *Sunday Times,* 158.

93. Avigdor Kahalani, one of Ben-Gal's battalion commanders, later wrote a vivid memoir of the battle, *Oz 77* (Jerusalem and Tel Aviv: Schocken, 1988).

94. Lieutenant Colonel "Zvi," 27.

95. *HaAretz,* Jan. 1, 1995.

96. Eitan, with Goldstein, 135.

97. Milstein, 1993, 220.

98. Peled, 171–75.

99. "Zvi," 29.

100. Bar-Kochba, 279–99.

101. Braun, 1993, 130–31.

102. Ibid., 130–32.

103. Yonay, 347–48.

104. Interview with Yossi Peled, Jan. 9, 1996.

105. Peled, 175–76.

106. Braun, 158–59, 163.

107. Eitan, 137.

108. Bar-Kochba, 301–13.

109. Eitan, 139.

110. Interview with Yossi Peled, Jan. 9, 1996.

111. Shai, 1977, 8–15; Bar-Kochba, 315–31; Peled, 177–80.

112. Eitan, 140.

113. Yonay, 350–51.

114. Lieutenant Colonel "David," 28–36; Interview with Yossi Peled, Jan. 9, 1996.

115. Peled, 185–97; Shai, 8–15. Altogether, according to official Iraqi figures (which seem very low), the Iraqi forces in Syria suffered 135 dead, 271 wounded, and 73 missing in action. Iraq lost 22 aircraft, 11 tanks and APCs, and 249 other vehicles.

116. Zalman and Dan, 289–90; Wallach and Lissak, 1983, 64–65.

117. Golani lost 55 dead and 79 wounded; the Syrians several dozen dead and a handful of prisoners. The Syrians also lost 13 MiG-17s; the IDF, one Skyhawk fighter-bomber.

118. Milstein, 1993, 105–11.

119. Shazly, 222, speaks of "2,000" guns (probably including medium-caliber mortars and antitank guns).

120. Milstein, 1993, 189.

121. Yonay, 320. Gamasy, 206, describes the air assault as "highly successful" and claims that only 5 Egyptian aircraft were downed.

122. Gamasy, 207.

123. Milstein, 1993, 114, 189.

124. Gamasy, 206–9.

125. Shazly, 223.

126. Milstein, 1993, 70.

127. Shazly, 227–28.

128. Gamasy, 211–12.

129. Bandman, 1984B, 29, speaks of eight completed bridges.

130. Shazly, 213, 225.

131. Milstein, 1993, 98–99; Fishman, 1993.

132. Shai, 1976; Mem, 1992, 12–19.

133. Milstein, 1993, 191.

134. Ibid., 240–2, 192.

135. Shazly, 234. The Israelis put the number of Egyptian tanks on the east bank at the end of Oct. 7 at 400 (see Bartov, vol. 1, 77).

136. Bandman, 1984B, 29.

137. Ibid., 27. On Oct. 7 the IAF managed to knock out two of the Third Army's bridges for twenty-four hours.

138. Gamasy (217) writes that the Egyptian army had suffered only 280 dead during the first day of the war.

139. Sharon, 295.

140. Yonay, 329–30.

141. Braun, 1993, 98.

142. Mem, 1992, 17.

143. Eldad, Nahum, and Zvi, 20–25.

144. Milstein, 1993, 190. Gamasy (210–11) exaggerates the effects of the commando operations. Altogether the Egyptians lost 740 commandos killed (most of them in flight) and 331 captured, and 28 helicopters, in these operations.

145. Mem, 1992, 17–18.

146. Milstein, 1993, 259.

147. Adan, 121.

148. Bartov, vol. 1, 72–88; Braun, 1993, 108–9; Adan, chap. 3; Wallach, Lissak, 1983, 74–75.

149. Dromi, 75.

150. Milstein, 1993, 193.

151. Ibid., 261.

152. Ibid., 193–94.

153. Ibid., 261–63.

154. Ibid., 266.

155. Kedar, 31. One battalion commander later explained: "We were beaten on Hammutal because when . . . [the Egyptian infantryman] is attacked by tanks he doesn't run away but responds with fierce antitank fire; and even when we run them over, they come back and return fire" (Kedar, 44; Adan, 78).

156. Milstein, 1993, 271.

157. Eldad, Nahum, and Zvi, 1992; Wallach and Lissak, 1983, 72–73.

158. Roszanski, 16–24.

159. Bandman, 1984B, 29.

160. Sharon, 306.

161. Bartov, vol. 2, 116; Braun, 1993, 130, 136–37.

162. Yonay, 352.

163. Golan, 2–11.

164. Gamasy (276–77) implies that it was the United States—whose SR-71 spy aircraft overflew the Canal area on Oct. 13–14—which informed Israel that the Twenty-first Division had crossed the Canal.

165. Shazly, 243–48.

166. Sharon, 310.

167. Shazly, 248.

168. The battles of Oct. 14 are described in Ayalon, 9–19; Doron, 20–27; Wallach and Lissak, 1983, 79–80. Gamasy (277) speaks of 250 Egyptian tanks lost on Oct. 14.

169. Braun, 1993, 177.

170. Sharon, 316.

171. Shazly, 253.

172. Gamasy (285) admits that the communiqué was mistaken and writes that, in reality, there were "closer to thirty tanks."

173. Adan, 205.

174. Braun, 1993, 191; Shazly, 254–55.

175. Israelyan, 249.

176. Shazly, 253–54.

177. Adan, 202–3.

178. Ibid., 213.

179. Shazly, 254–55; Yosef, Ilan, and Yosef, 79–83.

180. Yosef, Ilan, and Yosef, 83; Shazly, 260; Adan, 215–21.

181. Sharon, 322.

182. Shazly, 261.

183. Adan, 228; Shazly, 260.

184. Yonay, 353–54.

185. Shazly, 266, 261; Sadat, 262–63; Bar, 65; Shazly and Sadat also date this important meeting differently—Shazly on Oct. 19, Sadat on the 18th.

186. Adan, 248.

187. Ibid., 248–49.

188. David, 22–28.
189. Adan, 254.
190. Israelyan, 255–57.
191. Adan, 270.
192. Ibid., 275.
193. Ibid., 284.
194. Israelyan, 264–65.
195. Adan, 281–82.
196. Ibid., 282–83.
197. Dayan, 1976, 665.
198. Shazly, 181; Adan, 290.
199. Eldar, 1993, 493–99.
200. Braun, 1993, 141.
201. Shazly, 274–75; Wallach and Lissak, 1983, 96.
202. Kissinger, 493.
203. Ibid., 500–502, 512–15.
204. Quandt, 1977, 175; Quandt, 1993, 163.
205. Quandt, 1993, 547, n. 49; Shazly, 275–77; Dayan, 1976, 627. Gamasy seems to blame the American airlift for the "turning of the tables" in the war—but refers to the Soviet airlift to the Arabs only in passing, as if it was of no consequence.
206. Braun, 1993, 145.
207. Ibid., 173.
208. Quandt, 1993, 169.
209. Braun, 1993, 169.
210. Ibid., 166–70.
211. Quandt, 1993, 160–61, 166.
212. Braun, 1993, 213.
213. Gamasy, 261.
214. Quandt, 1993, 197.
215. Ibid., 169–71.
216. Braun, 1993, 232.
217. Kissinger, 569.
218. Quandt, 1993, 172–73.
219. Ibid., 172–77.
220. Ibid., 183–200.
221. Gamasy, 336.
222. Quandt, 1993, 209–15.
223. Ibid., 234–38.
224. Ibid., 239–43.
225. Moore, 1208–23.
226. Braun, 1993, 313–19, 321–23, 325–26, 337–38.

TEN

THE ISRAELI-EGYPTIAN PEACE, 1977–79

1. Brzezinski, 97.
2. Carter, 173–4.
3. Quandt, 1986, 36.
4. Vance, 181.
5. Quandt, 1986, 80.
6. Carter, 291.
7. Quandt, 1986, 82–83.
8. Ibid., 108.
9. Ibid., 91.
10. Ibid., 106.
11. Dayan, 1981, 38.
12. Bar-Siman-Tov, 1994, 29–30.
13. Kimche, 76–77.
14. Haber, Ya'ari and Schiff, 27–28, 128–29.
15. Quandt, 1986, 110.
16. Ibid., 112.
17. Ibid., 115.
18. Ibid., 122–23.
19. Carter, 1982, 294—"I felt particularly embattled at this time . . ."
20. Quandt, 1986, 125–31.
21. Sadat, 1978, 302–4.
22. Tessler, 507–8.
23. Ali, 69.
24. Haber, Ya'ari, and Schiff, 50.
25. Quandt, 1986, 140–41.
26. Fahmy, 257.
27. Ibid., 254–61.
28. Brzezinski, 111, 93.
29. Quandt, 1986, 144–45; Sadat, 1978, 306–7.
30. Fahmy, 266.
31. Haber, Ya'ari, and Schiff, 11.
32. Fahmy, 265–67.
33. Vance, 194.
34. Ibid., 191, 194.
35. Haber, Ya'ari, and Schiff, 51.
36. Weizman, 1981, 19; Bar-Siman-Tov, 1994, 37; Haber, Ya'ari, and Schiff, 54, 71.
37. Bar-Siman-Tov, 1994, 44–45.
38. Haber, Ya'ari, and Schiff, 54. The Egyptians were hardly likely to agree in public that the Jews had built their most prominent, prestigious monuments.
39. Haber, Ya'ari, and Schiff, 60.

40. Weizman, 1981, 25–28.
41. Haber, Ya'ari, and Schiff, 67.
42. Fahmy, 277–79.
43. Bar-Siman-Tov, 1994, 46–47.
44. Haber, Ya'ari, and Schiff, 121–22.
45. Sadat, 1978, 309.
46. Haber, Ya'ari, and Schiff, 124–25.
47. Sadat, 1978, 309.
48. Haber, Ya'ari, and Schiff, 128–29.
49. For text of Sadat speech, see Quandt, 1986, 345–55.
50. Weizman, 1981, 32–3.
51. Ibid., 136–7.
52. Vance, 195.
53. Weizman, 1981, 56.
54. Ibid., 60–61; Haber, Ya'ari, and Schiff, 138–40.
55. Bar-Siman-Tov, 1994, 61.
56. Weizman said at the end of the visit, "If I worked at Lloyd's, I would not issue [Sadat] a life insurance policy." Haber, Ya'ari, and Schiff, 145.
57. Ibid., 146.
58. Cobban, 92–3.
59. Dayan, 1981, 93.
60. Ibid., 97.
61. Ibid., 99–101; Haber, Ya'ari, and Schiff, 146–66; Cobban, 93–4.
62. Bar-Siman-Tov, 1994, 66–9.
63. Quandt, 1986, 155–6.
64. Quoted in Gamasy, 343.
65. Ibid., 343.
66. Ibid., 348–51.
67. Ibid., 340–54; Haber, Ya'ari, and Schiff, 167–71.
68. Quandt, 1986, 159.
69. Gamasy, 358.
70. Kamel, 22.
71. Gamasy, 359–60; Haber, Ya'ari, and Schiff, 182–201.
72. Haber, Ya'ari, and Schiff, 241–2.
73. Quandt, 1986, 159–60.
74. Carter, 303.
75. Haber, Ya'ari, and Schiff, 210–12.
76. Quandt, 1986, 161.
77. Ibid., 164–5.
78. Carter, 310.
79. Gamasy, 367–80.
80. Haber, Ya'ari, and Schiff, 241.
81. Carter, 305.
82. Quandt, 1986, 166 n. 34.
83. Haber, Ya'ari, and Schiff, 243–4.
84. Dayan, 1981, 115.
85. Quandt, 1986, 173–8.
86. Weizman, 1981, 296, 299.
87. Bar-Siman-Tov, 1994, 96.
88. Bar-On, 1985 15–16; Bar-On, 1996, 98.
89. Ibid., 1985, 25–6.
90. Haber, Ya'ari, and Schiff, 286.
91. Gamasy, 389.
92. Haber, Ya'ari, and Schiff, 292.
93. Bar-Siman-Tov, 1994, 105.
94. Kamel, 208–19.
95. Haber, Ya'ari, and Schiff, 296.
96. Carter, 316.
97. Quandt, 1986, 201–2.
98. Carter, 315; Vance, 1983, 217.
99. Quandt, 1986, 204–5; Carter, 318.
100. Bar-On, 1985, 31–2.
101. Carter, 330.
102. Quandt, 1986, 215.
103. Ibid., 207–10; Carter, 321.
104. Carter, 322.
105. Dayan, 1981, 155.
106. Carter, 317–18, 331.
107. Brzezinski, 254.
108. Carter, 342.
109. Haber, Schiff, and Ya'ari, 325.
110. Brzezinski, 237–8.
111. Ibid., 243.
112. Vance, 220.
113. Ibid., 257.
114. Carter, 329.
115. Ibid., 332.
116. Haber, Ya'ari, and Schiff, 305–7.
117. Carter, 340.
118. Quandt, 1986, 221–23; Carter, 340–1.
119. Carter, 342.
120. Haber, Ya'ari, and Schiff, 310–15; Quandt, 1986, 223.
121. Carter, 345–6.
122. Ibid., 346.
123. Haber, Ya'ari, and Schiff, 313.
124. Dayan, 1981, 162.
125. Carter, 349–50.
126. Carter, 351–3; Haber, Ya'ari, and Schiff, 317–20.
127. Carter, 359–60; Haber, Ya'ari, and Schiff, 320–1.

128. Carter, 364.
129. Weizman, 1981, 362.
130. Carter, 367.
131. Quandt, 1986, 227–8.
132. Ibid., 361–8.
133. Carter, 372–79.
134. Brzezinski, 261. See also Brzezinski, 264, for Carter on Begin: "Not quite sure whether the fellow is altogether rational."
135. Dayan, 1981, 156.
136. Carter, 378–9.
137. Vance, 197, 222.
138. Brzezinski, 269.
139. Carter, 379–82.
140. Ibid., 383.
141. Ibid., 383–5.
142. Quandt, 1986, 232.
143. Brzezinski, 263.
144. Carter, 386–7.
145. Quandt, 1986, 235.
146. Haber, Schiff, and Ya'ari, 340.
147. Vance, 224.
148. Dayan, 1981, 171–72; Carter, 392; Quandt, 1986, 238 and n. 1.
149. Vance, 223.
150. Kamel, 352–3.
151. Ibid., 358.
152. Haber, Schiff, and Ya'ari, 342–3.
153. Kamel, 361.
154. Vance, 224.
155. Quandt, 1986, 239.
156. Carter, 391–3; Quandt, 1986, 235–6.
157. Quandt, 1986, 241; Weizman, 1981, 370.
158. Carter, 398.
159. Quandt, 1986, 245–47; Carter, 396.
160. Quandt, 1986, 247–51; Carter, 397. Dayan (1981, 186–88) argues that Begin committed himself to a three-month freeze—and that Carter subsequently understood this but, in order to curb Begin's settlement policy, persisted in claiming that Begin had agreed to something more.
161. Quandt, 1986, 250.
162. Ibid., 251–2 and 251, n. 14.
163. Carter, 398–9.
164. Quandt, 1986, 252–53.
165. Ibid., 253.
166. Ibid., 255.
167. Haber, Schiff, and Ya'ari, 349–50.
168. Dayan, 1981, 188.
169. Carter, 403.
170. "Framework for the Conclusion of a Peace Treaty Between Egypt and Israel" and "A Framework for Peace in the Middle East Agreed at Camp David," Quandt, 1986, 376–83.
171. Ibid., 383–7, contains the texts of the more important letters.
172. Carter, 406–7.
173. Haber, Schiff, and Ya'ari, 354–5.
174. Ibid.
175. Ibid., 359.
176. Ibid.
177. Gamasy, 396, 398–403.
178. Cobban, 100.
179. Ibid., 101–2.
180. Dayan, 1981, 191.
181. Bar-Siman-Tov, 1994, 150.
182. Quandt, 1986, 259.
183. Carter, 409, extract from his diary entry for Nov. 8, 1978.
184. Quandt, 1986, 260–1.
185. Carter, 418.
186. Ali, 112; Quandt, 1986, 269–70.
187. Vance, 235.
188. Quandt, 1986, 275–7; Bar-Siman-Tov, 1994, 158–9.
189. Quandt, 1993, 299.
190. Ibid., 1986, 277.
191. Bar-Siman-Tov, 1994, 161.
192. Quandt, 1986, 278.
193. Ibid., 280.
194. Bar-Siman-Tov, 1994, 162.
195. Ali, 104–8.
196. Carter, 410.
197. Bar-Siman-Tov, 1994, 165.
198. Quandt, 1986, 284.
199. Bar-Siman-Tov, 1994, 166.
200. Quandt, 1986, 289–90.
201. Ibid., 1993, 306.
202. Ibid., 1986, 290–2.
203. Ibid., 296.
204. Ibid., 298–99.
205. Carter, 415, extract of diary entry for Mar. 2, 1979.
206. Vance, 243–4.
207. Quandt, 1986, 301–2; Carter, 413–17.
208. Haber, Schiff, and Ya'ari, 375.

209. Carter, 420–21, diary entry for Mar. 10, 1979; Haber, Schiff, and Ya'ari, 376–7; Quandt, 1986, 303–4.

210. Carter, 421.

211. Bar-Siman-Tov, 1994, 176.

212. Haber, Schiff, and Ya'ari, 379–80.

213. Quandt, 1993, 317.

214. Carter, 422.

215. Quandt, 1986, 309.

216. Bar-Siman-Tov, 1994, 181, 185.

217. Brzezinski, 287.

218. The text of the Israel-Egypt treaty, the annexes, and some of the accompanying letters, are in Dayan, 1981, 332–55; an abridged version of the treaty and the texts of a number of other letters are to be found in Quandt, 1986, 397–406.

219. Quandt, 1986, 313–14.

220. For the texts of these memoranda, see Dayan, 1981, 356–8.

221. 'Ali, 198.

222. Bar-Siman-Tov, 1994, 189–91.

223. Ali, 213–14.

224. Weizman, 1981, 383.

225. Bar-Siman-Tov, 1994, 195–99.

226. Tessler, 520–4; Bar-Siman-Tov, 1994, 209.

227. Bar-On, 1985, 36–40, 148–50.

228. Sagiv, 54–61; Heikal, 1983, 242–63.

229. Bar-Siman-Tov, 1994, 219.

230. Ali, 272.

231. Bar-Siman-Tov, 1994, 220.

232. Ali, 266.

233. Ibid., 267.

234. Tamir, 116–24.

235. Kimche, 119–22; 'Ali, 276–9.

236. Ali, 272–3.

237. Bar-Siman-Tov, 1994, 222–30.

238. Segal, 135.

239. 'Ali, 66.

240. Bar-Siman-Tov, 1994, 233–4.

241. Ibid., 234–6.

242. Shamir, 210; Peres, 1995, 203–4.

243. "The Egypt Israel Arbitration Tribunal, Summary of Award of 29 September 1988," *Israel Law Review* 22:4 (1988), 467–86.

244. Yehuda, 27–30.

ELEVEN

THE LEBANON WAR, 1982–85

1. Eisenberg, 1994, 41; Teveth, 1985, 34.

2. "A Talk with A. Arida, the Maronite Patriarch," unsigned [probably by E. Epstein (Elath)], May 2, 1937, Haganah Archive, Y. Ben-Zvi files, 4; and E. E[pstein] to M. Shertok (Sharett), June 8, 1938, National Library (Jerusalem), Eliahu Elath Papers, ARC.40 1661.

3. Eisenberg, 1994, 99.

4. Ibid.

5. Asher Goren, "Problems of Lebanon as a Christian Country," Apr. 8, 1954, National Library, Eliahu Elath Papers, ARC.40 1661.

6. Fawaz, 47–100.

7. "A Talk with the President of Lebanon, Emile Edde," Beirut 9.22.36, E. Epstein, CZA S25-5581.

8. Eisenberg, 1994, 25.

9. Ibid., 39.

10. Ibid., 93.

11. E. E[pstein] (Jerusalem) to E. Burk, Jan. 17, 1937, CZA S25-10121.

12. Eisenberg, 1994, 30.

13. Ibid., chaps. 1 and 2.

14. Ibid., 31–2.

15. Ibid., 62.

16. "A Reminder," by Dr. H. Yaski, undated (possibly from April 1938), CZA S25-3500.

17. E. Sasson to D. Ben-Gurion, Apr. 16, 1937, CZA S25-5568; Aharon Haim Cohen to Dov Yosef, Sept. 13, 1937, CZA 10097; E. Sasson to M. Shertok, Mar. 15, 1938, CZA S25-5580.

18. See letters from E. Sasson to M. Shertok, Mar. 17, 19, 20, 25, and 26, 1938, all in CZA S25-4550; Caplan and Black, 48–58.

19. Randal, 110.

20. Eisenberg, 1994, 135.

21. Ibid., 134–42.

22. Ibid., 199, n. 96. See also Mubarak to Sandstroem Aug. 5, 1947, CZA S25-5436, and Mubarak to Sandstroem Oct. 13, 1947, CZA S25-9026.

23. Eisenberg, 1992, 147–63; Text of treaty, CZA S25-3269.

24. Salibi, 186–93.
25. Rabinovich, 1984, 17.
26. Z. Zeligson to Y. Shim'oni, July 13, 1948, ISA FM 2565/12; Morris, 1984, 125–44.
27. BGA, Ben-Gurion Diary, entry for May 24: See also entries for June 18 and Dec. 19, 1948.
28. Sharett, 1978, vol. 2, 377; vol. 8, 2397–8.
29. Ibid., vol. 2, 377.
30. Ibid., vol. 4, 996; vol. 2, 377; vol. 8, 2398–2400.
31. Shim'oni to Katz (Jerusalem), June 23, 1953, ISA FM 3745/2; Rafael to Col. B. Givli, Apr. 5, 1955, ISA FM 2396/6 (bet). See also Goren, "Problems of Lebanon as a Christian Country"; and Palmon (Paris) to Rafael, Oct. 15, 1954, ISA FM 3745/2.
32. Sharett, 1978, vol. 4, 996.
33. Ibid.
34. Eban, Israel Embassy, Washington, to Foreign Ministry, May 15, 1958, and Herzog, Israel Embassy, Washington, to Foreign Ministry, May 15, 1958, both in ISA FM 3752/8.
35. P. Eliav, United States Department, Israel Foreign Ministry, to Y. Meroz (Washington), June 20, 1958, and E. Danin to the director general, July 9, 1958, both in ISA FM 3746/1; and Z. Neeman (New York) to M. Sasson, July 30, 1958, ISA FM 3110/5.
36. Sharon, 426, 434.
37. *Kahan Commission Report,* 6.
38. Randal, 25.
39. Avi-Ran, 1986B, 67.
40. Pakradouni, 48–50.
41. Avi-Ran, 1986B, 31–34; Pakradouni, 50–52.
42. Pakradouni, 55–67.
43. Randal, 23, 90.
44. Khalidi, 1986, 29–31; Tessler, 495–8.
45. Wallach and Lissak, 1983, 116–17. While the IDF committed only a small number of atrocities during Operation Litani, involving only a handful of civilians, Israeli-aligned Christian militiamen, commanded by Maj. Sa'ad

Haddad, slaughtered dozens in the village of al-Hiam, north of Metulla (see Klein, 1993).
46. Sela, Alex, 38.
47. Sneh, 3.
48. Naor, 18–19; Pakradouni, 114.
49. Sneh, 2–8.
50. Sela, Alex, 36–9.
51. Schiff and Ya'ari, 1986, 11–12.
52. Randal, 117.
53. Salem, 2–3, 7.
54. Kimche, 132, dates this at "the beginning of 1976"; Randal, 201, says it took place in "early April."
55. Undated thirty-seven–page memorandum by Sharon, Kahan Commission Papers.
56. Avi-Ran, *Syrian Involvement,* 96–97.
57. Ibid., 103; Randal, 118–25.
58. Bergman, 1997.
59. Schiff and Ya'ari, 1986, 24–25.
60. Ibid., 1986, 32; Randal, 214–15.
61. Sharon memorandum, undated, Kahan Commission Papers.
62. Schiff and Ya'ari, 1986, 28–29.
63. Sharon memorandum, Kahan Commission Papers.
64. Naor, 93–94; *Divrei HaKnesset* (Knesset Records), June 3, 1981.
65. *New York Times,* various days in April 1981; Pakradouni, 195–202; Tlass, 67–76.
66. Schiff and Ya'ari, 1986, 28–33; Randal, 224–31.
67. *New York Times,* Apr. 29, 1981.
68. Schiff and Ya'ari, 1986, 1986, 33–4.
69. *New York Times,* July 1, 1981.
70. Avi-Ran, 1987, 78–88.
71. *New York Times,* July 11, 1981.
72. Ibid., July 18 and 19, 1981; Randal, 237–38; Khalidi, 1986, 38; Avi-Ran, 1987, 95–6.
73. *New York Times,* July 20, 1981.
74. Avi-Ran, 1987, 96–105, 113–16.
75. Schiff and Ya'ari, 1986, 36.
76. Avi-Ran, 1987, 120–28.
77. Sharon, 432.
78. Schiff and Ya'ari, 1986, 37–8.
79. A good example of such propaganda is Prof. (Lt. Col., Res.) Mordechai

Gichon's article, "Peace for Galilee: The Campaign," *IDF Journal,* Dec. 1982, in which he states: "The PLO . . . eventually [renewed] their assaults on Israel, the territory held by Major Haddad, and Israeli and Jewish targets abroad. In the period extending from July 24, 1981, till June 6, 1982, the PLO violated the cease-fire on 289 occasions. Matters came to a head when the PLO conducted a twenty-four-hour bombardment of the Galilee and Major Haddad's enclave on June 4–5, 1982. More than thirty barrages were directed at twenty-three towns, villages, and kibbutzim." Only in a footnote a dozen pages later does Gichon explain that the June 4–5 barrages were a response to an IAF "raid"—which was, in fact, a massive bombing campaign—on PLO targets in Beirut and southern Lebanon. Sharon, 455, mentions "290 terrorist attacks" that were "the real casus belli."

80. Naor, 119–20.
81. Khalidi, 1986, 46.
82. Ibid., 17–19.
83. Naor, 120–1.
84. Naor, 16, 73–85, argues that Begin was hoodwinked by Sharon. Schiff and Ya'ari, 42–3, 104, assume Begin understood that ejecting the Syrians would be part of the campaign.
85. Sharon, 436.
86. Schiff and Ya'ari, 1986, 42.
87. Ibid. Sharon, 437, 447. Begin's son, Benny, has always maintained that Sharon tricked his father, who did not know that the IDF was going all the way to Beirut (*HaAretz,* Apr. 3, 1996). In 1993 Sharon sued *HaAretz* for libel. *HaAretz* had printed an article charging that he had deceived Begin and the cabinet about the war's real aims. On Nov. 4, 1997, the Tel Aviv district court found in favor of the newspaper, upholding its charge that Sharon had lied to Begin and his fellow ministers. Sharon has since appealed the judgment to Israel's Supreme Court, and its ruling is pending. Meanwhile, in early 1998, *HaAretz* complained to the police that there were grounds for investigating whether Sharon had bribed and suborned a witness—Gen. (Res.) Avigdor Ben-Gal— in the libel trial. In 1987, Ben-Gal in a public lecture stated that Sharon had during the war implemented "a clandestine plan," unknown to and unapproved by the cabinet. But at the trial, in July 1997, Ben-Gal testified that all talk of such a "clandestine plan" was "malicious nonsense" and "lies." Several weeks before Ben-Gal's appearance in court, he had flown with Sharon—then minister of national infrastructure—to Russia, where the two countries discussed a possible giant natural-gas deal. Ben-Gal, by then a businessman, was interested in getting in on the deal. The *HaAretz* complaint focused on the possibility that Sharon had elicited Ben-Gal's change of mind and testimony with a promise to award him a profitable role in the deal. In 1998, Attorney General Elyakim Rubinstein instructed the police to open a secret investigation into the *HaAretz* complaint. By press time the state attorney's office had concluded that there was insufficient evidence to charge the two men with bribery and witness-tampering (see *HaAretz,* Feb. 14, Apr. 30, and June 25,1999.

88. Naor, 37.
89. Schiff and Ya'ari, 1986, 47–8; Naor, 33.
90. Rabinovich, 124.
91. Sharon, 438.
92. Ibid., 441.
93. Schiff and Ya'ari, 1986, 50; Sharon, 441–2.
94. Sharon memorandum, Kahan Commission Papers.
95. Naor, 33.
96. *New York Times,* Mar. 26, 1982.
97. Naor, 35.
98. *New York Times,* Apr. 4, 1982.
99. Ibid., Apr. 22, 1982.
100. Ibid., May 10, 1982.
101. Schiff and Ya'ari, 1986, 58–60.
102. Naor, 38–9.

103. "The Main Points in the Defense Minister's Version of Events in the Commission of Inquiry," Kahan Commission Papers.

104. Schiff and Ya'ari, 1986, 60.

105. Ibid., 66.

106. Ibid., 56–7.

107. Haig, 332–33.

108. Thomas M. Davis, quoted in Tessler, 572.

109. Haig, 335.

110. Schiff and Ya'ari, 1986, 69–70; Quandt, 1993, 340; Sharon, 450–1.

111. Naor, 42.

112. Schiff and Ya'ari, 1986, 75; Sharon, 451.

113. Naor, 44.

114. Schiff and Ya'ari, 1986, 97–9.

115. Naor, 47–48; Segev, 374–5.

116. *Yediot Aharonot,* June 21, 1982, for Oz, and July 2 1982, for Rosenblum.

117. Segev, 375–76.

118. Naor, 44–5.

119. Schiff and Ya'ari, 1986, 102.

120. *New York Times,* June 5, 1982.

121. Ibid., June 5, 6, 1982.

122. Naor, 47.

123. Ibid., 49.

124. Sharon, 456–7; Naor (49) says Sharon spoke of "24–28 hours."

125. Eitan, 210, 203–4.

126. Naor, 50.

127. Schiff and Ya'ari, 1986, 46.

128. Naor, 47–52; Schiff and Ya'ari, 1986, 103–5. Sharon (457) says that only two ministers abstained.

129. Schiff and Ya'ari, 1986, 106–7.

130. Mem, 1982, 27–28; Dupuy and Martell, 91–94. Herzog (280) speaks of "eight reinforced divisions."

131. Schiff and Ya'ari, 1986, 84. Mem (1982) writes of "250 artillery pieces and some 100 multibarreled [Katyusha] rocket-launchers," but this is probably an exaggeration.

132. Mem, 1982, 27. Dupuy and Martell (86) speak of 300 PLO tanks and more than 350 artillery pieces.

133. In a ludicrous exaggeration, Sharon (433) says that the PLO had "the equiva-lent of normal equipment for four to five full divisions."

134. Schiff and Ya'ari, 1986, 92–3; Avi-Ran, 1987, 198–218.

135. Mem, 1982, 27.

136. Khalidi, 1986, 74.

137. Schiff and Ya'ari, 1986, 134–6.

138. Naor, 46.

139. Avi-Ran, 1987, 163–82.

140. Ibid., 168–9. For Syrian intelligence assessments of Israel's military preparations, see Avi-Ran, 1987, 178–82.

141. Schiff and Ya'ari, 1986, 94.

142. Ibid., 95–6.

143. Ibid., 133.

144. Khalidi, 1986, 75.

145. Ibid., 79, 150.

146. Rabinovich, 1984, 131–2.

147. Mem, 1982, 26–27.

148. See revealing comments by Gen. (Res.) Avigdor Ben-Gal, who commanded the Beka'a offensive, in *HaAretz,* Oct. 3, 1995.

149. Dupuy and Martell, 92–4.

150. Schiff and Ya'ari, 1986, 117–18.

151. Naor, 15.

152. Schiff and Ya'ari, 1986, 60.

153. Ibid., 114–15.

154. Rabin, 1983, 19–20.

155. Sharon, 460.

156. Yair, 22.

157. Avi-Ran, 1986A, 25–29; Yair, 16; Eldar, 1985, 26–34.

158. Avi-Ran, "The Landing," and 28; Schiff and Ya'ari, 1986, 124–5; Khalidi, 1986, 61.

159. Schiff and Ya'ari, 1986, 126–9.

160. Ibid., 129–31.

161. Ibid., 138.

162. Ibid., 139–41.

163. Ibid., 141–42.

164. Ibid., 141–50.

165. Ibid., 145–50.

166. Ibid., 182.

167. Yair, 57.

168. Schiff and Ya'ari, 1986, 154.

169. Eitan, 203–4.

170. Ibid., 212.

171. Avi-Ran, 1986B, 156.

172. Sharon, 464–5; Naor, 59. Schiff and

Ya'ari, 152–4, say that Begin also demanded that Assad withdraw the SAM batteries from the Beka'a.

173. Naor (16–17) tends to the view that Begin genuinely believed that the Syrians would keep out, and that he was duped by Sharon; Schiff and Ya'ari, (104, 155) tend to the view that Begin was as duplicitous as Sharon.

174. Schiff and Ya'ari, 1986, 155.

175. Tlass, 145, 148.

176. "An Armored Force," 41–4; Mem, 1982, 33–4.

177. Schiff and Ya'ari, 1986, 1986 (157) claim that the Israelis fired first; Naor (66), that the Syrians did. Tlass (145) seems to agree with Naor.

178. "An Armored Force," 44.

179. Naor, 66–7; Schiff and Ya'ari, 1986, 156–60.

180. Mem, 1984, 32.

181. Tlass, 153–5, 158–9.

182. Naor, 53.

183. Ibid., 67.

184. Schiff and Ya'ari, 1986, 166.

185. Ibid.

186. Yonay, 368–9; Cohen and Lavi, 615, 617–18. Schiff and Ya'ari, 1986, 167; Tlass, 191–2, and Sharon, 466–7, are all uninformative about the battle.

187. New York Times, 11 June 1982; Yonay, 358. Cohen and Lavi, 616, maintain that three well-hidden SAM-6 batteries were intact in the Beka'a after the attack.

188. Naor, 72; Schiff and Ya'ari, 1986, 166; New York Times, June 10, 1982.

189. Mem, 35; Schiff and Ya'ari, 1986, 168.

190. Yonay, 358.

191. Schiff and Ya'ari, 1986, 168.

192. Ibid.

193. Naor, 76.

194. Quandt, 1993, 342–43.

195. Ibid., 343.

196. Naor, 77–80; Schiff and Ya'ari, 1986, 169–70.

197. Peled, 262, largely blames Maj. Gen. Ehud Barak, the deputy commander of Ben-Gal's army group, for the failure, laying emphasis on his role in the defeat at Sultan Ya'akub, where an IDF tank battalion was briefly trapped by the First Division. Interview with Peled, Jan. 9, 1996; Peled, 264; Michaelson, 1982, 36; Schiff and Ya'ari, 1986, 172–73.

198. Tlass, 195–224, describes the battles of the Beka'a approaches—June 6–9—and the Beka'a—June 9–11—but is unreliable, and mars the narrative with passages of great inventiveness.

199. Tlass, 216.

200. Schiff and Ya'ari, 1986, 190–1; Tlass, 229–44; Khalidi, 1986, 62–3.

201. Naor, 117; Yair, 133–4, 136, 139.

202. Yair, 168.

203. Ibid., 169–70; Schiff and Ya'ari, 1986, 192.

204. Schiff and Ya'ari, 1986, 187.

205. Naor, 90.

206. Ibid., 118; Schiff and Ya'ari, 187–89.

207. Sharon memorandum, Kahan Commission Papers.

208. Schiff and Ya'ari, 1986, 193–4.

209. Naor, 88.

210. Schiff and Ya'ari, 1986, 199–200.

211. Kimche, 155–6.

212. Schiff and Ya'ari, 1986, 203–5; Mem, 1982, 47–8; Naor, 113–16; Tlass, 163–8.

213. "Meeting of Bashir Gemayel and Johnny Abdu with the Defense Minister," July 31–August 1, 1982, Kahan Commission Papers. Sharon commented: "But we must keep the water open on Monday, when [U.S. Secretary of State] Shultz will be meeting with [Israel Foreign Minister] Shamir."

214. "Following from the meeting of Johnny 'Abdu and Bashir Gemayel with the CGS in Beirut on 16.6.82, afternoon," Kahan Commission Papers.

215. Sharon, 484.

216. Ibid., 485.

217. Khalidi, 1986, 88.

218. Tlass, 267–8.

219. Naor, 124.

220. Ibid., 128.

221. Ibid., 126–27.

222. Untitled memo on meeting between Begin and Senior IDF Officers, July 12, 1982, Kahan Commission Papers.

223. Yitzhak Rabin, "Against the Conquest of West Beirut," *Yediot Aharonot,* June 25, 1982.

224. Schiff and Ya'ari, 1986, 211–3; Naor, 129.

225. Khalidi, 1986, 88.

226. Randal, 257.

227. Extract from Protocols of Cabinet Meeting of July 18, 1982, Kahan Commission Papers.

228. Khalidi, 1986, 65.

229. Schiff and Ya'ari, 1986, 220.

230. Khalidi (1986) 95, says "more than 200 sorties."

231. Naor, 132, 137.

232. Tlass, 270–3.

233. Naor, 132.

234. Khalidi, 1986, 115, 127.

235. Ibid., 94–5.

236. Ibid., 163–4.

237. *HaAretz,* Aug. 5 and 6, 1982; Tlass, 273–7; Naor, 132.

238. Schiff and Ya'ari, 1986, 221–2.

239. Khalidi, 1986, 65.

240. Schiff and Ya'ari, 1986, 225. Khalidi (1986), 95, claims that there were "over 220 sorties."

241. Sharon, 492–93.

242. Naor, 138–9; Schiff and Ya'ari, 1986, 225–6.

243. Naor, 116.

244. Schiff and Ya'ari, 1986, 227.

245. Tlass, 304–5.

246. Naor, 140.

247. Schiff and Ya'ari, 1986, 228–29; Tlass, 305; Avi-Ran, *Syrian Involvement,* 162. By the end of the siege of Beirut, the IDF had lost about three hundred dead and fifteen hundred wounded in the battles on the various fronts against the Syrians and the PLO. Syrian losses up to early July 1982 were some four hundred dead and fourteen hundred wounded and captured; and 345 tanks and 70 APCs and 75 artillery pieces destroyed or captured. The IAF lost nine air crew killed and two captured; six aircraft were lost—two fighter-bombers, two attack helicopters, and two medivac helicopters. The Syrians lost ninety-eight aircraft. Palestinian and Lebanese losses were far, far higher, especially in civilian life, but no accurate figures or even reliable estimates exist. One Lebanese police report, from November–December 1982, speaks of 19,085 people killed altogether and 30,000 wounded ('Abudi, 45–8); another report (Khalidi, 1986, 200, n. 5) speaks of 1,100 Arab combatants killed in the battle and siege of Beirut, 45 percent of them Palestinian, 37 percent Lebanese, and 10 percent Syrian. See also Sayigh, 528–43.

248. Tlass, 305.

249. Schiff and Ya'ari, 1986, 231.

250. Ibid., 233.

251. "An Impression of the First Days After the Election of Bashir—Three Days with Bashir and His People 28.8.1982," unsigned but probably by a Mossad official, Kahan Commission Papers.

252. Quandt, 1993, 344–6.

253. Naor, 143; Schiff and Ya'ari, 1986, 233–6.

254. Avi-Ran, *Syrian Involvement,* 163.

255. Ibid.

256. Extracts from Protocols of Israel Cabinet meetings of July 22 and 25, 1982, Kahan Commission Papers; Bar-Kochba, 1986, passim.

257. "The Activities of the LF in the Near Future," Aug. 27, 1982, Beirut, and "Coordination Measures Between Bashir and the IDF in the Near Future," Aug. 27, 1982, both Mossad memorandums, Kahan Commission Papers. At the latter meeting Bashir promised not to harm Major Haddad, and he and Eitan agreed to the ejection of UN observers from southern Lebanon soon after his assumption of the presidency.

258. Sharon, 497–9.

259. Schiff and Ya'ari, 1986, 240–1.

260. Ibid., 238.

261. "Following Bashir Gemayel's Election as President of Lebanon," undated

Mossad memorandum, Kahan Commission Papers. It states: "In general, Bashir is bent on expelling most of the Palestinians from Lebanon."

262. "Meeting Between the Director General and Bashir Gemayel," date illegible, Kahan Commission Papers.

263. Schiff and Ya'ari, 1986, 246; Naor, 146.

264. "Following Bashir Gemayel's Election," Kahan Commission Papers.

265. Schiff and Ya'ari, 1986, 247–49; Randal, 150–51.

266. Undated Sharon memorandum, Kahan Commission Papers.

267. Schiff and Ya'ari, 1986, 253; Sharon, 500–3.

268. Randal, 13.

269. Undated Sharon memorandum, Kahan Commission Report; Naor, 151; Sharon, 495.

270. Naor, 151–2; Schiff and Ya'ari, 1986, 253.

271. Untitled, undated Sharon memorandum, Kahan Commission Papers. Clearly, in trying to defend himself after the massacres, Sharon had a problem: If he argued that the Phalange had appeared bent on revenge, the commissioners might ask why he sent them into West Beirut to clean out the refugee camps; but if he argued—as he did—that they were calm and self-possessed, then the commissioners might well ask: Why did the IDF occupy West Beirut, and why did Begin say the move was motivated by fears that the Phalange might slaughter Muslims and Palestinians to avenge Bashir's assassination?

272. "Characteristics of the Phalange," undated, unsigned intelligence memorandum, Kahan Commission Papers.

273. Sharon memorandum, Kahan Commission Papers.

274. Naor, 152, 154.

275. Schiff and Ya'ari, 1986, 250.

276. Schiff and Ya'ari, 1986, 253–5; Sharon, 503–4.

277. Schiff and Ya'ari, 1986, 258; Sharon memorandum, Kahan Commission Papers.

278. Schiff and Ya'ari, 1986, 258–60.

279. Kahan Commission Report, 22–3.

280. Ibid., 27; Schiff and Ya'ari, 261–3; Naor, 161–3.

281. Kahan Commission Report, 22.

282. Schiff and Ya'ari, 1986, 264.

283. Kahan Commission Report, 35.

284. Ibid., 33–4.

285. Ibid., 36–39; Schiff and Ya'ari, 1986, 268–72.

286. Kahan Commission Report, 40–1; Sharon, 506.

287. Schiff and Ya'ari, 1986, 275–76.

288. Ibid., 279.

289. "Following is from the Meeting between the Chief of Staff and OC Northern Command with the deputy chief of staff of the LF . . . 19 September 1982," by Drori's aide-de-camp, Kahan Commission Papers.

290. Sharon at meeting of Knesset Foreign Affairs and Defense committee, Sept. 24, 1992, Kahan Commission Papers.

291. Tlass, 332–3.

292. Schiff and Ya'ari, 1986, 277–79; Tlass, 312.

293. Schiff and Ya'ari, 1986, 280.

294. Kahan Commission Report, 45.

295. Ibid., 44–5. Kimche, 159, speaks of six hundred killed.

296. Schiff and Ya'ari, 1986, 280.

297. Kahan Commission Report, 49.

298. Schiff and Ya'ari, 1986, 285.

299. Bar-On, 1985, 60.

300. Kahan Commission Report, 57–58.

301. Ibid., 50.

302. Schiff and Ya'ari, 1986, 282; Kahan Commission Report, 29.

303. Kahan Commission Report, 51–3, 56.

304. Ibid., 104–6. The report was published in English under the title *The Beirut Massacre: The Complete Kahan Commission Report* (New York: Karz-Cohl, 1983).

305. Undated report by Menahem Nevot, Mossad, Sept. 20–21, 1982, Kahan Commission Papers.

306. Salem, 41–4; Kimche, 165; Schiff and Ya'ari, 1986, 290–1.
307. Schiff and Ya'ari, 1986, 293.
308. Salem, 84.
309. Kimche, 166–7.
310. Ibid., 169, 183.
311. Text in Salem, 280–9.
312. Rabinovich, 1984, 167.
313. Avi-Ran, 1986B, 179–86.
314. Fisk, 478–80.
315. Ibid., 511–20.
316. Ibid., 580.
317. Salem, 152: "Assad appreciated our decision to abrogate the agreement."
318. Avi-Ran, 1986B, 204.
319. Tlass (335–8) says Israel's territorial designs on Lebanon were only part of a grander design, of an Israel stretching from the Nile to the Euphrates. He claims that the two blue stripes in the Israeli flag represent the farthest reaches of Zionist ambition, the two rivers.
320. Fisk, 547.
321. Avi-Ran, 1986B, 213.
322. Fisk, 567.
323. Ibid., 557–8.
324. Ibid., 552.
325. Avi-Ran, 1986B, 212.
326. IDF intelligence officer quoted in Black and Morris, 393–4.
327. HaAretz, Mar. 30 and Sept. 21 and 23, 1984; Fisk, 562–3, 571.
328. Fisk, 552.
329. New York Times, April 14 1984; Fisk, 561.
330. Fisk, 559, 564.
331. Times (London), July 6, 1984; Fisk, 564.
332. Times (London), Mar. 5, 6, and 7, 1985; Fisk, 578–80.
333. Quoted in Black and Morris, 399.
334. Times (London), Jan. 14, 1985; Fisk, 553.
335. HaAretz, Apr. 10, 1985.
336. Quoted in Avi-Ran, 1986, 214–15.
337. Fisk, 610–11; New York Times, July 10, 1985, and HaAretz, July 10, 1985.
338. Avi-Ran, 1986B, 162.
339. Khalidi, 1986, 200, n. 5.
340. Schiff and Ya'ari, 1986, 301.

TWELVE
THE INTIFADA

1. HaAretz, Nov. 27, 1987.
2. Peretz, 36–37.
3. Shalev, 41; Schiff and Ya'ari, 1986, 1990, 76.
4. Schiff and Ya'ari, 1990, 45.
5. Shalev, 16.
6. Schiff and Ya'ari, 1990, 79–80.
7. Shalev, 19–20.
8. Shalev, 41–42; Tessler 682–83.
9. Shalev, 28–33.
10. Shabi and Shaked, 47.
11. Schiff and Ya'ari, 1990, 225.
12. Ibid., 227.
13. Shabi and Shaked, 85–6.
14. Shabi and Shaked, 47–59.
15. Schiff and Ya'ari, 1990, 226–7.
16. Nakhle, 209–26.
17. Kimmerling and Migdal, 258.
18. Schiff and Ya'ari, 1990, 84.
19. Tessler, 525.
20. Ibid., 524.
21. Gilbar, 20–39.
22. Shalev, 22.
23. Schiff and Ya'ari, 1990, 85–6; Peretz, 24–6.
24. Schiff and Ya'ari, 1990, 90.
25. Ibid., 97.
26. Tessler, 679.
27. Schiff and Ya'ari, 1990 , 92.
28. Tessler, 527.
29. Kimmerling and Migdal, 250.
30. Mishal with Aharoni, 12.
31. Kimmerling and Migdal, 260.
32. Kimmerling and Migdal, 259; Gilbar, 20–39.
33. Tessler, 671–4.
34. Ibid., 548.
35. Peretz, 31.
36. Schiff and Ya'ari, 1990, 76–7; Tessler, 680–1.
37. Peretz, 43.
38. Schiff and Ya'ari, 1990, 94–6; Kimmerling and Migdal, 253.
39. Shalev, 23–4.
40. Ibid., 24.
41. Ibid., 23–5.
42. Frisch, 254–74.
43. Shalev, 36.

44. Ibid.
45. Shabi and Shaked, 62–3.
46. Ibid., 76–83, 128–33.
47. Abu'Amr, 101–2.
48. Ibid., 80.
49. *HaAretz,* Oct. 4, 1987.
50. *HaAretz,* Oct. 9, 1987.
51. Shabi and Shaked, 181–4; Schiff and Ya'ari, 1990, 51–2, 69, 72–3; Abu'Amr, 57–8; Shalev, 36–7.
52. Schiff and Ya'ari, 1990, 75.
53. Shalev, 37.
54. Schiff and Ya'ari, 1990, 75–7.
55. Shalev, 37–8.
56. Peretz, 30; Sprinzak, 236–7.
57. Sprinzak, 279–81.
58. Tessler, 679.
59. *HaAretz,* June 1, 1987, p. 2.
60. *JP,* May 30, 1988; Shalev, 39–41; Schiff and Ya'ari, 1990, 59–62.
61. *HaAretz,* Dec. 9, 1987.
62. Schiff and Ya'ari, 1990, 18.
63. *HaAretz,* Dec. 10, 1987.
64. Schiff and Ya'ari, 1990, 21.
65. Shalev, 74.
66. Abu'Amr, 59.
67. Kuttab, D., 14–23.
68. Schiff and Ya'ari, 1990, 114–15.
69. Ibid., 103.
70. Shabi and Shaked, 102–3.
71. Schiff and Ya'ari, 1990, 215.
72. Ibid., 47, 49.
73. Ibid., 195.
74. Ibid., 106–13.
75. Ibid., 112.
76. Ibid., 192–5.
77. Ibid., 208–9.
78. Mish'al with Aharoni, 9.
79. Shalev, 91–2, 253.
80. Schiff and Ya'ari, 1990, 217.
81. Shalev, 110.
82. Schiff and Ya'ari, 1990, 249–50. The dinar, Jordan's currency (at the time worth about US$3), was in common use in the West Bank. The Israel shekel, which replaced the Israel pound, was then worth about US$0.40.
83. Abu'Amr, 63–4. Schiff and Ya'ari, 1990, 220–2, say it was founded only in February 1988.
84. Schiff and Ya'ari, 1990, 220–2.
85. Shabi and Shaked, 104.
86. Ibid., 135.
87. Abu'Amr, 77.
88. Shabi and Shaked, 34.
89. Ibid., 97.
90. Schiff and Ya'ari, 1990, 234.
91. Ibid., 238.
92. Abu'Amr, 80–3; Shabi and Shaked, 107–17; Schiff and Ya'ari, 1990, 237.
93. Abu'Amr, 26.
94. Schiff and Ya'ari, 1990, 228–9.
95. Ibid., 238–9.
96. Ibid., 196–8.
97. Ibid., 188–219.
98. Shalev, 93.
99. Mish'al with Aharoni, 1989, gives the text (in Hebrew) of most of the leaflets issued in 1988.
100. Schiff and Ya'ari, 1990, 104.
101. Ibid., 104–105.
102. Ibid., 210.
103. Black and Morris, 1991, 466–7; Schiff and Ya'ari, 1990, 216.
104. Schiff and Ya'ari, 1990, 113.
105. Ibid., 124.
106. Shalev, 89.
107. Ibid., 88.
108. Ibid., 79.
109. Ibid., 79, 94–5.
110. Ibid., 81. During the first nine months of the rebellion, 1,650 Israeli buses were hit by stones and 39 were set alight, with 188 passengers and 24 drivers being injured. By early June 1989, 3,136 buses and 337 persons had been hit.
111. Ibid., 96–8. It should be noted that in combating the Intifada, the IDF during 1987–93 destroyed tens of thousands of trees, the Palestinians claiming as many as 160,000 (see Swedenborg, 220–21 n. 46.)
112. Shalev, 82.
113. Schiff and Ya'ari, 1990, 247–8.
114. Ibid., 241–5.
115. Siniora, 3–13.
116. Gabriel, 198–213.
117. Schiff and Ya'ari, 1990, 206–7.
118. Shalev, 102–3.
119. Ibid., 104.

120. Ibid., 104.

121. Kuttab, J. 26–35.

122. Shalev, 100–1.

123. Ibid., 88–9.

124. Straschnov, 111–21; Sprinzak, 149–51.

125. *HaAretz,* Feb. 25 and 26, 1988; Black and Morris, 475–6.

126. Shragai, 343.

127. *HaAretz,* Aug. 7 and 8, 1990.

128. *HaAretz,* Sept. 30, 1990.

129. The events are accurately described in Shragai, 340–63; *HaAretz,* Oct. 9, 1990; Sprinzak, 287.

130. Shragai, 356.

131. Straschnov, 90; Shabi and Shaked, 287–90.

132. Shragai, 363.

133. Ibid., 357–61.

134. Peretz, 42, 44.

135. Schiff and Ya'ari, 1990, 123.

136. Ibid., 25.

137. Shalev, 46–7.

138. Peretz, 43.

139. Shalev, 90–1; Ashrawi, 45–6, 54, 59–60, etc.

140. Shalev, 109.

141. Interview in *HaAretz,* Mar. 17, 1989.

142. Shalev, 114.

143. Ibid., 114.

144. Schiff and Ya'ari, 1990, 117.

145. Shalev, 47.

146. Straschnov, 141–2.

147. Ibid., 144–7.

148. Shalev, 115.

149. Schiff and Ya'ari, 1990, 139.

150. Ibid., 132–39.

151. Ibid., 135–6.

152. Straschnov, 177.

153. Schiff and Ya'ari, 1990, 150.

154. Shalev, 122.

155. Straschnov, 178; Schiff and Ya'ari, 1990, 150, 152.

156. Schiff and Ya'ari, 1990, 150.

157. Ibid., 153.

158. Straschnov, 178, 192.

159. Ibid., 180–98.

160. Ibid., 188–9.

161. Shalev, 122–3; Straschnov, 192–3.

162. Straschnov, 290–1. Straschnov appealed the court's ruling, and one of the three received six weeks in prison and three and a half months suspended. Straschnov (197) summarizes the beatings policy thus: "The political echelon let the brutal demon out of the bottle; the senior military echelon failed to curb and control it . . . and a small number of soldiers and officers allowed their instincts to prevail and threw off all restraint, going so far as to beat people to death."

163. Ibid., 148.

164. Shalev, 124–5; Straschnov, 150.

165. Shalev, 125.

166. Ibid., 125.

167. Be'tselem, 1992, 48–51, 105. Undercover units accounted for 112 Palestinian dead between December 1987 and December 1992, and another 45 between December 1992 and December 1995 (Be'tselem to author, July 8, 1996).

168. Straschnov, 50.

169. Shalev, 86.

170. Straschnov, 72–3.

171. Be'tselem to author, July 8, 1996, based on IDF-supplied figures.

172. Straschnov, 30; Shalev, 120.

173. Schiff and Ya'ari, 1990, 147–8.

174. Straschnov, 87.

175. Shalev, 129; Schiff and Ya'ari 1990, 145–6.

176. According to Be'tselem, altogether 434 houses were demolished between December 1987 and June 1992, with the largest number being destroyed in the first and second years (128 and 163 respectively), the number declining to 88 in the third year, 47 in the fourth year and 8 in the fifth year of the rebellion. During the same five-year period, the IDF sealed off 314 houses—232 of them in the West Bank and 82 in the Gaza Strip. Another 40 houses were partially destroyed, and about 100 partially sealed off (Be'tselem to author, July 8, 1996).

177. Shalev, 127, 229.

178. Straschnov, 104.

179. Ibid., 108.

180. Be'tselem to author, July 8, 1996; Straschnov, 104.

181. Black and Morris, 468–9; Schiff and Ya'ari, 1990, 228.

182. Black and Morris, 469.

183. *New York Times,* April 17, 1988. Previously, Israel had struck in Tunis on Oct. 1, 1985, when IAF F-15s bombed PLO headquarters in retaliation for the murder by Fatah terrorists of three middle-aged Israelis on their yacht in Larnaca harbor, Cyprus, on Sept. 25. The Israeli jets, in a feat of accurate long-range navigation and precision-bombing, took out Arafat's headquarters building and a Force 17 installation. Altogether, 75 persons were killed, 60 of them PLO men, according to Israel (Black and Morris, 453–5).

184. Tessler, 698.

185. Schiff and Ya'ari, 1990, 163–4.

186. Black and Morris, 469–72; *New York Times,* Apr. 17, 1988.

187. Ashrawi, 156–8.

188. Shabi and Shaked, 136–9, 142, 292–4.

189. Ibid., 308–9.

190. Ibid., 298–301.

191. All the figures are from Be'tselem to author, July 8, 1996.

192. Shalev, 80–5; Stockton, 86–95.

193. Straschnov, 140.

194. Tessler, 701.

195. Be'tselem to author, July 8, 1996; and IDF Spokesman's Office to author, undated, summer 1996; partial figures, for 1987–89 in Shalev, 80–5.

196. Shalev, 164.

197. Schiff and Ya'ari, 1990, 126.

198. Ibid., 126.

199. Ibid., 127.

200. Kuttab, J., 26–35.

201. Shalev, 168–71.

202. Tessler, 708.

203. Tessler, 709; Schiff and Ya'ari, 1990, 289–93.

204. Shalev, 137–8.

205. Ibid., 187.

206. *Kol Ha'Ir,* Dec. 29, 1995.

207. Straschnov, 159. Another colonel, Moshe Giv'ati, commanding the brigade responsible for the Hebron area, on April 4, 1988 fired regular rounds from an automatic rifle at a number of sus-

pected stone-throwers who were escaping through the hills near the village of Bani Na'im, killing one. Giv'ati was removed from his post and severely reprimanded by the deputy CGS, Ehud Barak, and resigned from the army (Straschnov, 160–1).

208. Ibid., 261–82.

209. Ibid., 201–27. In another case involving the Giv'ati brigade ("Giv'ati B"), soldiers beat two Gaza Strip residents suspected of stone-throwing. One of them, a 16-year-old boy, later died. The soldiers said they had been ordered to punish stone-throwers by beating them and "to break arms and legs." The investigation failed to reveal where the order originated—with Defense Minister Rabin, OC Southern Command Gen. Yitzhak Mordechai, or a more junior officer. The army subsequently charged a major, a first lieutenant, and two sergeants with causing grievous bodily harm. All four were convicted; the lieutenant received a two-month prison term, and all got suspended terms as well as demotion (ibid., 235–60).

210. Be'tselem, 1991, 26–7.

211. Ibid., 32–5.

212. Schiff and Ya'ari, 1990, 171, 179.

213. Ibid., 131, 170–87.

214. Ibid., 131.

215. Peretz, 163–7.

216. Shalev, 143–4.

217. Tessler, 714.

218. Schiff and Ya'ari, 1990, 296–300; Shalev, 144–5.

219. Tessler, 716.

220. Peretz, 109.

221. Shalev, 147–8; Schiff and Ya'ari, 1990, 270–2.

222. Schiff and Ya'ari, 1990, 273.

223. *Middle East Mirror* (London), June 2, 1988; Peretz, 112, 185.

224. Schiff and Ya'ari, 1990, 273–4; Shalev, 151.

225. Muslih, 1990, 3–29.

226. First to go was PLO representative in London Said Hamami, the first senior PLO official to meet secretly with Israeli peace activists, murdered on Jan.

4, 1978. On Aug. 3, 1978, another moderate PLO diplomat, 'Izz a Din Kalak, was killed in Paris, and on Apr. 10, 1983, Dr. Issam Sartawi, Hamami's heir as the main PLO proponent of dialogue with left-wing Israelis, was murdered in Portugal.

227. Tessler, 536.
228. Schiff and Ya'ari, 1990, 282.
229. Shalev, 153–4; Schiff and Ya'ari, 1990, 283–4.
230. The text of the "Political Statement," as broadcast on the Voice of Palestine radio station on Nov. 15, 1988, is in Shalev, 239–51; Abbas 22–4; Muslih, 1990, 3–29.
231. Tessler, 722.
232. Peretz, 187.
233. Abbas, 23–32.
234. Shalev, 154–5; Abbas, 32–3.
235. Quandt, 1993, 364–75; Peretz, 189; Shalev, 155.
236. Peretz, 189–90.
237. Tessler, 724–5.
238. Tessler, 724.
239. HaAretz, Jan. 20, 1989.
240. Shalev, 158–61, 274–5.
241. Schiff and Ya'ari, 1990, 319.
242. Shalev, 161–3; Tessler, 728–9.
243. Tessler, 729–30; Schiff and Ya'ari, 1990, 320–1.
244. Tessler, 730.
245. Tessler, 734.

THIRTEEN
PEACE AT LAST?

1. Quandt, 1993, 389.
2. Tessler, 747.
3. Tessler, 748.
4. New York Times, Feb. 24, 25, 1991.
5. Shamir, 263–4, 270–2.
6. Tessler, 741.
7. Makovsky, 108; Tessler, 746.
8. Quandt, 1993, 394–9.
9. Tessler, 745.
10. Quandt, 1993, 399.
11. Tessler, 741.
12. Shamir, 272–91.
13. Abbas, 87.
14. Quandt, 1993, 404; Shamir, 285–91.

15. Ashrawi, 141–55.
16. New York Times, Oct. 31 and Nov. 1 and 2, 1991.
17. New York Times, Nov. 1, 1991.
18. Ashrawi, 200.
19. Quandt, 1993, 407; Ma'ariv, June 26, 1992; Jerusalem Post, June 28, 1992.
20. Shabi and Shaked, 258–9.
21. Shabi and Shaked, 256–78.
22. Makovsky, 111–12.
23. Elon, 77–85.
24. Makovsky, 13–14.
25. Ashrawi, 220–1; Abbas, 112–13.
26. Makovsky, 16.
27. Makovsky, 23; Abbas, 119–27.
28. Makovsky, 21. Abbas, 127–41.
29. Abbas, 132–6.
30. Shabi and Shaked, 318.
31. HaAretz, July 26, 1993.
32. HaAretz, Aug. 1, 1993.
33. Makovsky, 36–7; Abbas, 201–3.
34. Makovsky, 43, 45.
35. Ashrawi, 250–4.
36. HaAretz, July 12, 1993.
37. Makovsky, 51.
38. Abbas, 143–59; Savir, Chaps. 1, 2.
39. Abbas, 166.
40. Makovsky, 60–2.
41. Makovsky, 68–9.
42. Abbas, 175–9; Peres, 299.
43. Abbas, 179–83; Savir, Chap. 3.
44. Peres, 303–6; Makovsky, 75.
45. Abbas, 205–7, 209–10.
46. Abbas, 210–13.
47. Elon, 1993.
48. HaAretz, May 23, 1994.
49. Israel, State of, 1994a.
50. HaAretz, May 15, 18, and 19, 1994.
51. HaAretz, July 3, 1994.
52. HaAretz, Apr. 7, 1994.
53. HaAretz, Apr. 15, 1994.
54. HaAretz, Oct. 10, 1994.
55. HaAretz, Oct. 12 and 16, 1994.
56. HaAretz, Oct. 10, 1994.
57. HaAretz, Jan. 24, 1995.
58. HaAretz, July 25, 1995.
59. HaAretz, Aug. 22, 1995.
60. Israel, State of, 1995.
61. Savir, 333–4.
62. Melman-Raviv, 1989.

63. Rubinstein, 1996a.
64. Rubinstein, 1996b, 347–66.
65. *New York Times,* Sept. 15, 1993.
66. Makovsky, 154–5.
67. Makovsky, 155.
68. Rubinstein, 1996a; Israel, State of, 1994b.
69. Rabinovich, 1998, 138–9.
70. "Fresh Light on the Syrian-Israeli Peace Negotiations: An Interview with Ambassador Walid al-Moualem," *JPS,* XXVI/2, Winter 1997.
71. Rabinovich 1998, 24, 256, 259, 271–3, 279–80; Savir, 316.
72. *HaAretz,* June 17, 1996.
73. Barzilai, 1995.
74. *HaAretz,* Nov. 5, 1995.
75. *HaAretz,* Jan. 21 and 22, 1996.
76. Savir, 318.
77. *HaAretz,* Oct. 29, 1995.
78. *HaAretz,* Jan. 7, 1996.
79. *HaAretz,* Jan. 8, 1996.
80. *HaAretz,* Mar. 10, 1996.
81. *HaAretz,* Feb. 26 and Mar. 1, 1996.
82. *HaAretz,* Feb. 27, 1996.
83. *HaAretz,* Mar. 4 and 5, 1996; NYTech, May 19, 1996.
84. *HaAretz,* Apr. 25, 1996.
85. *NYT,* Apr. 10, 1996.
86. *HaAretz* and NYT, Apr. 19, 1996.
87. *NYT* and *HaAretz,* Apr. 19, 1996.
88. *HaAretz,* Apr. 28, 1996.
89. *HaAretz,* June 17, 1996.
90. *New York Times,* Sept. 26–28, 1996.
91. *NYT,* Oct. 2 and 3, 1996.
92. *HaAretz,* Jan. 2, 1997.
93. *NYT,* Jan. 17, 1997, carried the texts of the "Note" and the Christopher-Netanyahu letter.
94. *NYT,* Jan. 15, 1997.
95. *NYT,* May 25, 1996 and Jan. 16, 1997.
96. *NYT,* Jan. 17, 1997.
97. *NYT,* Jan. 18, 1997.
98. State of Israel, "The Wye River Memorandum, The White House, Washington, D.C., Oct. 23, 1998."

FOURTEEN
BARAK'S 19 MONTHS

1. *HaAretz,* July 7, 1999.
2. Israel Ministry of Foreign Affairs, Information Division, "The Sharm el-Sheikh Memorandum on Implementation Timeline of Outstanding Commitments of Agreements Signed and the Resumption of Permanent Status Negotiations," Sept. 4, 1999; and *HaAretz,* Sept. 5, 1999.
3. See Akiva Eldar's columns in *HaAretz* of Jan. 17 and 20, 2000, and Eli Kamir's "The Secret Talks Between Netanyahu and Assad," *Maariv,* Dec. 31, 1999. Netanyahu claimed that he had proposed an Israeli withdrawal only to a line "a few miles" to the east of the 1923 frontier.
4. The text was reproduced in *HaAretz* (English ed.), Jan. 13, 2000.
5. *HaAretz,* Mar. 6, 2000.
6. *HaAretz,* May 24, 2000; and Ron Ben-Yishai, "The Retreat from Lebanon; the True Story," *Yediot Aharonot,* Sep. 29, 2000.
7. Zvi Barel, "The Hizbullah's Play-Corner," *HaAretz,* Dec. 1, 2000.
8. *Haaretz,* Jun. 11, 2000.
9. For Camp David, see Aharon Barne'a, "15 Days in July," *Yediot Aharonot,* July 28, 2000; Danny Rubinstein, "You Want to Attend My Funeral? Asked Arafat," *HaAretz,* Aug. 14, 2000; and *HaAretz,* July 26, 2000.
10. Asa'ad Ghanem and Sarah Ozacky-Lazar, "'Al-Aqsa Intifada' among the Palestinian Citizens of Israel: Motives and Results," Jan. 2001 (Institute for the Study of Peace, Givat Haviva, Israel), pp. 12–25.
11. Ibid. p. 27.
12. See, for example, *Jerusalem Post,* Nov. 16, 2000.
13. *HaAretz,* Feb. 1, 2001.
14. See, for example, IDF Brig.-Gen. (Res.) Efi Eitam's remarks in an interview with Nahum Barne'a, *Yediot Aharonot,* Jan. 12, 2001: "It is clear to me that what is happening in the territories is a direct reflection of what happened in Lebanon. The Palestinians say this openly. The Middle East wit-

nessed something unprecedented: the IDF evacuated an area without leaving behind security arrangements. This is what the Palestinians are trying to do now in Judea and Samaria."

15. See, for example, Gideon Levy, "I Don't Work for You," *HaAretz*, Oct. 27, 2000.

16. See, for example, Danny Rubinstein, "True Lies," *HaAretz*, Dec. 19, 2000.

17. *HaAretz*, Oct. 13, 2000.

18. Amos Harel, "Internal Palestinian Struggles Cause Shooting Incidents," *HaAretz*, Feb. 11, 2001.

19. Ronni Shaked, "Seven Assassinations in a Week," *Yediot Aharonot*, Dec. 19, 2000.

20. Ron Ben-Yishai, "The Cuckolded Husband was Executed as a Collaborator," *Yediot Aharonot*, Jan. 26, 2001.

21. *HaAretz*, Oct. 17 and 18, 2000.

22. *HaAretz*, Dec. 31, 2000.

23. *HaAretz*, Dec. 28, 2000.

24. Danny Rubinstein, "Arafat's Coalition is Also Falling Apart," *HaAretz*, Jan. 1, 2001.

25. *HaAretz*, Jan. 28, 2001.

26. Amos Harel, "Al-Aqsa Intifada Augurs a Change of Generations," *HaAretz*, Jan. 16, 2001.

27. *HaAretz*, Feb. 11, 2001.

28. *HaAretz*, Jan. 4, 2001.

29. *HaAretz*, Nov. 29, 2000.

30. *Yediot Aharonot*, Dec. 7, 2000.

31. An extreme example of this call to boycott was issued on Feb. 4 by Jerusalem's mufti, Sheikh Akrama Sabri, who said that it was forbidden for Muslims to vote for "Zionist candidates" (*HaAretz*, Feb. 5, 2001). The Hamas and Hizbullah both issued statements expressing a preference for a Sharon victory, which they said would serve Arab interests (*HaAretz*, Feb. 6, 2001).

CONCLUSIONS

1. Flapan, 141.

2. Protocols of the joint meeting of the JAE and the Political Committee of the Zionist Actions Committee, June 12, 1938, CZA S100/24B.

3. Protocol of meeting of the JAE, June 20, 1944, CZA S100/42B.

ARCHIVES
Central Zionist Archives (CZA), Jerusalem
Chaim Weizmann Archive, Rehovot, Israel
David Ben-Gurion Archive (BGA), Sde Boker, Israel
Eliahu Elath Papers, National Library, Jerusalem
Haganah Archive, Tel Aviv
Hashomer Archive (Yosef Nahmani diary), Kfar Giladi, Israel
Israel Defense Forces Archive (IDFA), Giv'atayim, Israel
Israel State Archives (ISA), Jerusalem
National Archive (NA), Washington, D.C.
Public Record Office (PRO), London

NEWSPAPERS AND JOURNALS
The Guardian, London
HaAretz, Tel Aviv
Hadashot, Tel Aviv
Jerusalem Post, Jerusalem
Kol Ha'ir, Jerusalem
Ma'arachot, Tel Aviv
Ma'ariv, Tel Aviv
New York Times, New York
The Times, London
Yediot Aharonot, Tel Aviv

BOOKS AND ARTICLES
Aaronson, Shlomo, with Brosh, Oded. *The Politics and Strategy of Nuclear Weapons in the Middle East: Opacity, Theory, and Reality, 1966–1991, An Israeli Perspective.* N.Y.: SUNY Press, Albany, 1992.

Abbas, Mahmoud (Abu Mazen). *Through Secret Channels.* England: Garnet, 1995.

Abu-'Amr, Ziad. *Islamic Fundamentalism in the West Bank and Gaza: Muslim Brotherhood and Islamic Jihad.* Bloomington: Indiana University Press, 1994.

Abudi, Yosef. (Heb.) "The [Israel] Air Force in 'Peace for Galilee.'" *Ma'arachot* 296 (1984).

Abu Iyad (Khalaf, Salah). (Heb.) *Without a Homeland, Conversations with Eric Rouleau.* Tel Aviv: Mifras, 1983.

Abu-Lughod, Ibrahim, ed. *The Transformation of Palestine.* Evanston, Ill.: Northwestern University Press, 1971.

Adan, Avraham. (Heb.) *On Both Banks of the Suez.* Jerusalem: Idanim, 1979.

Adler (Cohen), Raya. "The Tenants of Wadi Hawarith: Another View of the Land Question in Palestine." *International Journal of Middle Eastern Studies* 20:2 (1988).

Admoni, Yehiel. (Heb.) *Decade of Discretion: Settlement Policy in the Territories, 1967–1977.* Tel Aviv: Yisrael Galili Institute/Kibbutz Meuhad, 1992.

Ajami, Fouad. *The Arab Predicament: Arab Political Thought and Practice Since 1967.* Cambridge, England: Cambridge University Press, 1981.

———. *The Vanished Imam: Musa al-Sadr*

and the Shia of Lebanon. Ithaca, N.Y.: Cornell University Press, 1986.

Ali, Kamal Hassan. (Heb.) *Warriors and Peacemakers.* Tel Aviv: Israel Defense Ministry Press, 1993.

"An Armored Force in a Built-up, Mountainous Area: the 'Bnei Or' Task Force in Jezzine, June 8, 1982" (Heb.). *Ma'arachot* 296 (1984).

Antonius, George. *The Arab Awakening.* New York: Capricorn Books, 1965.

Arens, Moshe. *Broken Covenant: American Foreign Policy and the Crisis between the U.S. and Israel.* New York: Simon & Schuster, 1995.

Arnon-Ohana, Yuval. (Heb.) *Peasants in the Arab Revolt in the Land of Israel 1936–1939.* Tel Aviv: Papyrus, 1982.

———. (Heb.) *The Internal Struggle within the Palestinian Movement 1929–1939.* Tel Aviv: Hadar/Dayan Center, 1989.

Ashrawi, Hanan. *This Side of Peace.* New York: Simon & Schuster, 1995.

Asiya, Ilan. (Heb.) *The Focus of the Conflict: The Struggle for the Negev, 1947–1956.* Israel: Ben-Gurion University Press/Yad Ben-Zvi, 1994.

Av, Nahum. (Heb.) *The Struggle for Tiberias, the First City to be Liberated in the War of Independence.* Tel Aviv: Israel Defense Ministry Press, 1991.

Avineri, Shlomo. (Heb.) *Varieties of Zionist Thought.* Tel Aviv: Am Oved/Ofakim, 1991.

Avneri, Uri. (Heb.) *In the Fields of Philistia: A Combat Diary.* Tel Aviv: Twersky, 1949.

Avi-Ran, Reuven. (Heb.) "The Landing on the Awali Coast during the 'Peace for Galilee' War from the Terrorists' Perspective," *Ma'arachot* 302–303 (1986a).

———. (Heb.) *Syrian Involvement in Lebanon (1975–1985)* Tel Aviv: Israel Defense Ministry Press, (1986b).

———. (Heb.) *The Lebanon War—Arab Documents and Sources,* I. Tel Aviv: Ma'arachot, 1987.

———. *The Lebanon War: Documents and Arab Sources, II, The War.* Tel Aviv: Ma'arachot/Israel Defense Ministry Press, 1997.

Ayalon, Avraham. (Heb.) *The Giv'ati Brigade in the War of Independence.* Tel Aviv: Ma'arachot, 1959.

———. (Heb.) *The Giv'ati Brigade Opposite the Egyptian Invader.* Tel Aviv: Ma'arachot, 1963.

———. (Heb.) "Mivtza Magressa." *Ma'archot* 261–262 (1978a).

———. (Heb.) "The 14th of October: Why Was It Erased from Sadat's Memoirs?" *Ma'arachot* 266 (1978b).

Bandman, Yona. (Heb.) "The Arab Legion in the Run-up to the War of Independence," *Ma'arachot* 294–295 (1984a).

———. (Heb.) "The Third Army Crosses the Suez Canal, October 6–8, 1973." *Ma'arachot* 296 (1984b).

———. (Heb.) "The Sinai Peninsula in Egypt's Strategic Thinking, 1949–1967." In G. Gwirtzman, A. Shmueli, et al., eds., *Sinai.* Tel Aviv: Israel Defense Ministry Press, 1987.

Bar, Shmuel. (Heb.) *The Yom Kippur War in Arab Eyes.* Tel Aviv: Ma'arachot, 1986.

Bar-Joseph, Uri. *The Best of Enemies: Israel and Transjordan in the War of 1948.* London: Frank Cass, 1987.

Bar-Kochba, Moshe. (Heb.) "Operation 'Teref,' a Multiforce Day of Battle, July 22, 1982." *Ma'arachot* 305 (1986).

———. (Heb.) *Chariots of Steel.* Tel Aviv: Ma'arachot, 1989.

Bar-On, Mordechai. (Heb.) *Peace Now: A Portrait of a Movement.* Tel Aviv: Kibbutz Meuhad Press, 1985.

———. (Heb.) *Challenge and Quarrel: The Road to the Sinai Campaign, 1956.* Beersheba: Ben-Gurion University Press, 1991.

———. (Heb.) *The Gates of Gaza: The State of Israel's Security and Foreign Policy, 1955–1957.* Tel Aviv: Am Oved, 1992.

———. *In Pursuit of Peace: A History of the Israeli Peace Movement.* Washington, D.C.: United States Institute of Peace, 1996.

Bar-Siman-Tov, Yavakov. *The Israeli-Egyptian War of Attrition: 1969–1970.* New York: Columbia University Press, 1980.

———. *Israel and the Peace Process, 1972–1982: In Search of Legitimacy and Peace.* New York: SUNY Press, 1994.

Bartov, Hanoch. (Heb.) *Dado.* 2 vols. Tel Aviv: Sifriyat Ma'ariv, 1978.

Barzilai, Amnon. (Heb.) "The Sources of Yigal Amir's Hatred." *HaAretz,* November 9, 1995.

Bar-Zohar, Michael. (Heb.) *Ben-Gurion.* 3 vols. Tel Aviv: Am Oved, 1975–77.

Bauer, Yehuda. *From Diplomacy to Resistance: A History of Jewish Palestine 1939–45.* New York: Atheneum, 1973.

Be'eri, Eliezer. (Heb.) *The Beginning of the Israeli-Arab Conflict, 1882–1911.* Haifa: Sifriyat Po'alim/Haifa University Press, 1985.

Beilin, Yossi. (Heb.) *Touching Peace.* Tel Aviv: Yediot Aharonot, 1997.

Ben, Aluf. (Heb.) "The First Nuclear War." *HaAretz,* June 11, 1993.

Ben-Gal, Avigdor. (Heb.) "Blessed Be Those Who Believe in the Indirect Approach." HaAretz Sefarim, Oct. 3, 1995.

Ben-Gurion, David. (Heb.) *As Israel Fights.* Tel Aviv: Mapai Press, 1952.

———. *The War of Independence: Ben-Gurion's Diary.* Edited by Gershon Rivlin and Elhannan Orren. Tel Aviv: Israel Defense Ministry Press, 1982.

Bergman, Ronen. (Heb.) "Dismissal in the Mossad Leadership," *HaAretz,* Jan. 3, 1997.

Be'tselem. (Heb.) *The Interrogation of Palestinians during the Intifada: Abuse, "Moderate Physical Pressure," or Torture?* Jerusalem: Be'tselem, 1991.

———. (Heb.) *The Activity of the Special Forces in the Territories.* Jerusalem: Betselem, 1992.

Bialer, Uri. *Between East and West: Israel's Foreign Policy Orientation 1948–1956.* Cambridge, England: Cambridge University Press, 1990.

Black, Ian, and Benny Morris. *Israel's Secret Wars: A History of Israel's Intelligence Services.* New York: Grove Weidenfeld, 1991.

Braun, Arie. (Heb.) *Moshe Dayan in the Yom Kippur War.* Tel Aviv: Idanim, 1993.

———. (Heb.) *Moshe Dayan and the Six-Day War.* Tel Aviv: Yediot Aharonot, 1997.

Brecher, Michael. *Decisions in Israel's Foreign Policy.* London: Oxford University Press, 1974.

Brecher, Michael, with Benjamin Geist. *Decisions in Crisis: Israel, 1967 and 1973.* Berkeley: University of California Press, 1990.

Brzezinski, Zbigniew. *Power and Principle: Memoirs of the National Security Adviser 1977–1981.* London: Weidenfeld & Nicolson, 1983.

Burns, E. L. M. *Between Arab and Israeli.* London: Harrap, 1962.

Caplan, Neil. *Palestine Jewry and the Palestine Question 1917–1925.* London: Frank Cass, 1978.

———. *Futile Diplomacy I: Arab–Zionist Negotiations and the End of the Mandate.* London: Frank Cass, 1983.

———. *The Lausanne Conference: A Case Study in Middle East Peacemaking.* Tel Aviv: Dayan Center, 1993.

Caplan, Neil, and Ian Black. "Israel and Lebanon: Origins of a Relationship." *Jerusalem Quarterly* 27 (1983).

Carmel, Moshe. (Heb.) *Battles of the North.* Ein Harod: Ma'arachot\Kibbutz Meuhad Press, 1949.

Carter, Jimmy. *Keeping Faith: Memoirs of a President.* Fayetteville: U. of Arkansas Press, 1995.

Cobban, Helena. *The Palestinian Liberation Organisation: People, Power, and Politics.* Cambridge, England: Cambridge University Press, 1984.

Cohen, Avner. "Cairo, Dimona and the June 1967 War." *Middle East Journal* 50:2 (1996).

Cohen, Eliezer, and Zvi Lavi. (Heb.) *The Sky Is Not the Limit: The Story of the Israel Air Force.* Tel Aviv: Ma'ariv, 1990.

Cohen, Michael. *Palestine: Retreat from the Mandate, the Making of British*

Policy, 1936–45. London: Paul Elek, 1978.

———. *Palestine and the Great Powers, 1945–1948.* Princeton, N.J.: Princeton University Press, 1982.

———. *Churchill and the Jews.* London: Frank Cass, 1985.

———. *Palestine to Israel, from Mandate to Independence.* London: Frank Cass, 1988.

Collins, Larry, and Dominique Lapierre. *O Jerusalem!* Great Britain: History Book Club, 1972.

Coren, David. (Heb.) *The Western Galilee in the War of Independence.* Tel Aviv: Yad Takenkin/Israel Defense Ministry Press, 1988.

Crossman, R. H. S. *Palestine Mission: A Personal Record.* New York: Harper, 1947.

Danin, Ezra, (with Ya'akov Shimoni). (Heb.) *Documents and Characters from the Archives of the Arab Gangs in the Disturbances of 1936–1939.* Jerusalem: Magnes Press, 1981.

Dann, Uriel. *King Hussein and the Challenge of Arab Radicalism, Jordan, 1955–1967.* New York: Oxford University Press, 1989.

"David," Lieutenant Colonel. "The Battle for 'Orha.'" (Heb.) *Ma'arachot* 253 (1976).

———. "The Jordanian Army in the Yom Kippur War." (Heb.) *Ma'arachot* 266 (1978).

Dayan, Moshe. "Military Operations in Peacetime." (Heb.) 1955.

———. (Heb.) *Avnei Derekh.* Tel Aviv: Idanim/Dvir, 1976.

———. *Breakthrough: A Personal Account of the Egypt-Israel Peace Negotiations.* London: Weidenfeld & Nicolson, 1981.

Dinur, Ben-Zion, ed. (Heb.) *The History of the Haganah.* (3 vols.) Tel Aviv: Ma'arachot, (1956–73).

Divrei HaKnesset (Knesset Records)

"Doron," Major. "The Battle of October 14 in the Wadi Ma'abuk Sector." (Heb.) *Ma'arachot* 266 (1978).

Dromi, Uri. "Where Is the Air Force?" (Heb.) *Ma'arachot* 289–90 (1983).

Dupuy, Trevor, and Paul Martell. *Flawed Victory: The Arab-Israeli Conflict and the 1982 War in Lebanon.* Fairfax, Va.: Hero Books, 1986.

Eban, Abba. *An Autobiography.* New York: Random House, 1977.

Edelist, Ran. "That Was the Head of the Mossad?" (Heb.) *Hadashot,* Sept. 24, 1993.

Efrati, Natan. (Heb.) *From Crisis to Hope.* Jerusalem: Yad Ben-Zvi, 1991.

Eilam, Yigal. (Heb.) *The Haganah, the Zionist Way to Power.* Tel Aviv: Zmora-Bitan-Modan, 1979.

"The Egypt-Israel Arbitration Tribunal, Summary of Award of 29 September 1988." *Israel Law Review* 22:4.

Eisenberg, Laura. "Desperate Diplomacy, The Zionist-Maronite Treaty of 1946." *Studies in Zionism* 13:2 (1992).

———. *My Enemy's Enemy.* Detroit: Mich.: Wayne State University Press, 1994.

Eitan, Rafael, (with Dov Goldstein). (Heb.) *Story of a Soldier.* Tel Aviv: Ma'ariv, 1991.

"Eldad," Colonel, Lieutenant Colonel "Nahum," and Lieutenant Colonel "Zvi." "Battle with the Egyptian Commandos in the Yom Kippur War" (Heb.). *Ma'arachot* 327 (1992).

Eldar, Mike. "An Outflanking Move in Operation 'Peace for Galilee,' the Landing on the Awali Coast" (Heb.). *Ma'arachot* 299 (1985).

———. (Heb.) *Squadron 13, the Story of the Naval Commando.* Tel Aviv: Sifriyat Ma'ariv, 1993.

Eliav, Mordechai. (Heb.) "First Encounters with the Arab National Question," *Bar-Ilan Yearbook* 14–15. 1977.

———. (Heb.) *The Land of Israel and its Settlement in the Nineteenth Century, 1777–1917.* Jerusalem: Keter, 1978.

Elon, Amos. "The Peacemakers." *The New Yorker,* Dec. 20, 1993.

Elpeleg, Zvi. (Heb.) *Grand Mufti.* Tel Aviv: Israel Defense Ministry Press, 1989.

———. (Heb.) *In the Eyes of the Mufti: The Essays of Haj Amin.* Tel Aviv: Tel Aviv University/Kibbutz Meuhad, 1995.

Encyclopaedia Judaica.

Erel, Shlomo. (Heb.) *Facing the Sea.* Tel Aviv: Israel Defense Ministry Press, 1998.

Eshel, Zadok. *The Haganah's Battles in Haifa.* Tel Aviv: Israel Defense Ministry Press, 1978.

Etzioni, Binyamin. (Heb.) *Tree and Javelin: The Golani Brigade's Route of Battle.* Tel Aviv: Ma'arachot, n.d.

Eyal, Yigal. (Heb.) *The First Intifada.* Tel Aviv: Israel Defense Ministry Press, 1998.

Eytan, Walter. *The First Ten Years.* New York: Simon & Schuster, 1958.

Fahmy, Ismail. *Negotiating for Peace in the Middle East.* Baltimore, Md.: Johns Hopkins University Press, 1983.

Fawaz, Leila Tarazi. *An Occasion for War: Civil Conflict in Lebanon and Damascus in 1860.* London: Center for Lebanese Studies/I. B. Tauris, 1995.

Finkelstein, Norman. "Myths, Old and New." *Journal of Palestine Studies* 21:1 (1991).

———. *Image and Reality of the Israel-Palestine Conflict.* London: Verso, 1995.

Fishman, Alex. "He Still Doesn't Believe War Broke Out." *Hadashot,* Sept. 24, 1993.

Fisk, Robert. *Pity the Nation: The Abduction of Lebanon.* New York: Atheneum, 1990.

Flapan, Simha. *Zionism and the Palestinians.* London: Croom Helm, 1979.

Frankel, Jonathan. *The Damascus Affair.* Cambridge: Cambridge University Press, 1997.

"Fresh Light on the Syrian-Israeli Peace Negotiations: An Interview with Ambassador Walid al-Moualem." *Journal of Palestine Studies* 26:2 (1997).

Freud, Ernst, ed. *The Letters of Sigmund Freud and Arnold Zweig.* London: Hogarth Press, 1970.

Freundlich, Yehoshu'a. (Heb.) *From Destruction to Resurrection: Zionist Policy from the End of the Second World War to the Establishment of the State of Israel.* Israel: Mif'alim Universitaim, 1994.

Friedman, Isaiah. *The Question of Palestine: British-Jewish-Arab Relations.* London: Routledge & Kegan Paul, 1973.

Frisch, Hillel. "The Palestinian Movement in the Territories: The Middle Command." *Middle Eastern Studies* 29:2 (1993).

Fromkin, David. *A Peace to End All Peace: Creating the Modern Middle East 1914–1922.* Penguin Books, 1991.

Gabriel, Judith. "The Economic Side of the Intifada." *Journal of Palestine Studies* 18:1 (1988).

el-Gamasy, Mohamed Abdel Ghani. *The October War: Memoirs of Field Marshal el-Gamasy of Egypt.* Cairo: American University, 1993.

Garcia-Granados, Jorge. *The Birth of Israel: The Drama as I Saw It.* New York: Alfred A. Knopf, 1948.

Garfinkle, Adam. "On the Origin, Meaning, Use, and Abuse of a Phrase." *Middle Eastern Studies* 27:4 (1991).

Gawrych, George. "The Egyptian High Command in the 1973 War." *Armed Forces and Society* 13:4 (1987).

Gazit, Shlomo. (Heb.) *The Stick and the Carrot.* Tel Aviv: Zmora Bitan, 1985.

Geist, Benjamin. (Heb.) "The Six-Day War: A Study in the Setting and the Process of Foreign Policy Decision Making Under Crisis Conditions." Ph.D. diss., Hebrew University, Jerusalem, 1974.

Gelber, Yoav. (Heb.) *Growing a Fleur-de-Lis: The Intelligence Services of the Jewish Yishuv in Palestine 1918–47.* 2 vols. Tel Aviv: Israel Defense Ministry Press, 1992.

———. "Druze and Jews in the War of 1948." *Middle Eastern Studies* 31:2 (1995).

Gichon, Mordechai. "Peace for Galilee: The Campaign." *IDF Journal* 1:2 (1982).

Gil'ad, Zerubavel. (Heb.) *The Book of the Palmach.* Tel Aviv: Kibbutz Meuhad Press, 1954.

Gilbar, Gad, and Asher Susser, eds. (Heb.) *In the Eye of the Conflict: The Intifada.* Tel Aviv: Kibbutz Meuhad, 1992.

Giv'ati, Moshe. (Heb.) *On the Path of Desert and Fire: The History of the Ninth Battalion.* Tel Aviv: Israel Defense Ministry Press, 1994.

Glubb, John. *A Soldier with the Arabs*. London: Hodder & Stoughton, 1957.

Golan, Matti. *The Secret Conversations of Henry Kissinger: Step-by-Step Diplomacy in the Middle East*. New York: Quadrangle/New York Times Books, 1976.

Golan, Shimon. "12/10/1973—The Positions of the Chief of General Staff and the Political Leadership: Crossing the Canal, the Need for a Cease-fire, and the Means of Achieving It." (Heb.) *Ma'arachot* 327 (1992).

Golani, Motti, ed. (Heb.) *Black Arrow: Gaza Raid and the Israeli Policy of Retaliation during the Fifties*. Holon: Ma'arachot/Israel Defense Ministry Press/Haifa University, 1994.

———. (Heb.) *There Will be War Next Summer. . . . The Road to the Sinai War, 1955–1956*. Tel Aviv: Ma'arachot, 1997.

Gorny, Yosef. (Heb.) "The Roots of the Consciousness of the Jewish-Arab National Conflict and Its Reflection in the Hebrew Press in the Years 1900–18" Vol. 4. *HaTziyonut*, 1976.

———. (Heb.) *Zionism and the Arabs, 1882–1948: A Study of Ideology*. Tel Aviv: Am Oved, 1985.

al-Gridly, Hassan. (Heb.) "The Outbreak of the 1973 War Was Unavoidable." *Ma'arachot* 332 (1993).

Haber, Eitan. (Heb.) *Today the War Will Break Out*. Tel Aviv: Idanim/Yediot Aharonot Press, 1987.

Haber, Eitan, Ehud Ya'ari, and Ze'ev Schiff. (Heb.) *The Year of the Dove*. Tel Aviv: Zmora, Bitan, Modan, 1980.

Haig, Alexander. *Caveat: Realism, Reagan, and Foreign Policy*. New York: Macmillan, 1984.

Halasa, Malu. "A Deadly Inheritance." *The Guardian*, Jan. 11, 1997.

Heikal, Muhammad Hassnein. *The Road to Ramadan*. London: Collins, 1975.

———. *Autumn of Fury: The Assassination of Sadat*. New York: Random House, 1983.

Heller, Joseph. (Heb.) *LEHI: Ideology and Politics, 1940–49*. 2 vols. Jerusalem: Zalman Shazar Center/Keter, 1989.

Hersh, Seymour. *The Samson Option: Israel, America and the Bomb*. London: Faber & Faber, 1993.

Hertzberg, Arthur, ed. *The Zionist Idea: A Historical Analysis and Reader*. New York: Meridian Books/Jewish Publication Society of America, 1960.

Herzl, Theodor. Edited by Rafael Patai. *The Complete Diaries of Theodor Herzl*. New York: Herzl Press and T. Yoseloff, 1960.

Hirst, David. *The Gun and the Olive Branch: The Roots of Violence in the Middle East*. London: Faber & Faber, 1977.

Hurewitz, J. C. *The Struggle for Palestine*. New York: Schocken Books, 1976.

Hussein of Jordan, King. *My "War" with Israel*. London: Peter Owen, 1969.

Ilan, Amitzur. *Bernadotte in Palestine 1948: A Study in Contemporary Humanitarian Knight-Errantry*. London: Macmillan, 1989.

———. *The Origin of the Arab-Israeli Arms Race: Arms, Embargo, Military Power and Decision in the 1948 Palestine War*. London: Macmillan/St. Antony's, 1996.

Israel Defense Forces Education Branch. (Heb.) *The Six-Day War*. Tel Aviv: Israel Defense Ministry Press, 1968.

Israel, State of. "Declaration of Principles on Interim Self-Government Arrangements." Sept. 13, 1993, Washington, D.C.

———. "Agreement on the Gaza Strip and the Jericho Area." May 4, 1994, Cairo.

———. "Treaty of Peace Between the State of Israel and the Hashemite Kingdom of Jordan." Oct. 26, 1994, Arava.

———. "Israeli-Palestinian Interim Agreement on the West Bank and the Gaza Strip." Sept. 28, 1995, Washington, D.C.

Israel, State of, and Israel State Archives. (Heb.) *The People's Administration, Protocols, April 18–May 13, 1948*. Jerusalem, 1978.

———. *Documents on the Foreign Policy of Israel*, vol. 1, May 14–September 30, 1948. Jerusalem, 1981.

———. Vol. 2, *October 1948–April 1949*. 1984.

———. Vol. 3, *Armistice Negotiations with the Arab States, December 1948–July 1949*. 1983.

———. Vol. 4, *May–December 1949*. 1986.

———. Vol. 5, *1950*. 1988.

———. Vol. 6, *1951*. 1991.

———. Vol. 7, *1952*. 1992.

———. Vol. 8, *1953*. 1995.

Israel, State of, and Archives, Israel State, and World Zionist Organization. *Political and Diplomatic Documents December 1947–May 1948*. Jerusalem, 1979.

Israelyan, Victor. "The October War: Kissinger in Moscow," *Middle East Journal* 49:2 (1995).

Itzhaki, Arieh. (Heb.) *Latrun, the Battle on the Road to Jerusalem*. Jerusalem: Cana, 1982.

Kafkafi, Eyal. (Heb.) *A War of Choice—The Road to Sinai and Back, 1956–1957*. Tel Aviv: Yad Tabenkin/Society for the Preservation of Moshe Sharett's Heritage, 1994.

Kahalani, Avigdor. (Heb.) *Oz 77*. Tel Aviv: Schocken, 1988.

Kahan Commission of Inquiry. *The Beirut Massacre: The Complete Kahan Commission Report*. Princeton, N.J.: Kars-Cohl, 1983.

Kamel, Mohamed Ibrahim. *The Camp David Accords: A Testimony*. London: KPI, 1986.

Kano, Jacques. (Heb.) *The Land Problem in the National Conflict between Jews and Arabs, 1917–1990*. Tel Aviv: Sifriyat Poalim, 1992.

Katz, Yossi. "The Deliberations of the Jewish Agency Committee for Transfer of Population 1937–1938." *Zion*, 52–53, 1988.

Kedar, Benjamin. (Heb.) *October 1973: The Story of the "Mahatz" Battalion*. Tel Aviv: Tamuz, 1975.

Kedar, Benjamin, and Denys Pringle. "La Feve: A Crusader Castle in the Jezreel Valley." *Israel Exploration Journal* 35 (1985).

Kedourie, Elie. *In the Anglo-Arab Labyrinth: The MacMahon-Husayn Correspondence and Its Interpretations, 1914–1939*. Cambridge, England: Cambridge University Press, 1976.

Khalaf, Issa. *Politics in Palestine: Arab Factionalism and Social Disintegration 1939–1948*. New York: SUNY, 1991.

Khalidi, Rashid. "Palestinian Peasant Resistance to Zionism Before World War I," Edward Said and Christopher Hitchens, eds., *Blaming the Victims*. London: Verso, 1988.

———. *Under Siege: PLO Decision-Making during the 1982 War*. New York: Columbia University Press, 1986.

———. *Palestinian Identity, the Construction of Modern National Consciousness*. New York: Columbia University Press, 1997.

Khalidi, Walid. *Before Their Diaspora: A Photographic History of the Palestinians, 1876–1948*. Washington, D.C.: Institute for Palestine Studies, 1991.

———, ed. *All That Remains, the Palestinian Villages Occupied and Depopulated by Israel in 1948*. Washington, D.C.: Institute for Palestine Studies, 1992.

Kimche, David. *The Last Option: Nasser, Arafat and Saddam Hussein, the Quest for Peace in the Middle East*. New York: Charles Scribner's Sons, 1991.

Kimche, David, & Jon Kimche. *Both Sides of the Hill: Britain and the Palestine War*. London: Secker & Warburg, 1960.

Kimmerling, Baruch, and Joel Migdal. *Palestinians, the Making of a People*. Cambridge, Mass.: Harvard University Press, 1994.

Kirkbride, Alec. *From the Wings: Amman Memoirs 194–1951*. London: Frank Cass, 1976.

Kissinger, Henry. *Years of Upheaval*. London: Weidenfeld & Nicolson/Michael Joseph, 1982.

Klein, Aharon. (Heb.) "A Massacre Known in Advance." *Hadashot*, March 19, 1993.

Kolinsky, Martin. "Premeditation in the Palestine Disturbances of August 1929." *Middle Eastern Studies* 26:1 (1990).

Kollat, Yisrael, ed. (Heb.) *The History of the Jewish Community in the Land of Israel since the First Aliya: The Ottoman Period,* vol. 1. Jerusalem: Israel National Academy of Sciences/Mossad Bialik, 1990.

Korn, David. *Stalemate: The War of Attrition and Great Power Diplomacy in the Middle East, 1967–1970.* Boulder, Colo.: Westview Press, 1992.

Krumchenko, Yuli. (Heb.) "The Surgeon Has Already Made Mistakes Twice." *Kol Ha'Ir,* May 3, 1996.

Kuttab, Daoud. "A Profile of the Stone-Throwers." *Journal of Palestine Studies* 17:3 (1988).

Kuttab, Jonathan. "The Children's Revolt." *Journal of Palestine Studies* 17:4 (1988).

Kyle, Keith. *Suez.* London: Weidenfeld & Nicolson, 1991.

Lachish, Ze'ev. "The Bombing of the Arab Capitals in the War of Independence." *Ma'arachot* 324 (1992).

Lapidot, Yehuda. (Heb.) *Upon Thy Walls.* Tel Aviv: Israel Defense Ministry Press, 1992.

Laqueur, Walter. *The Road to War: The Origin and Aftermath of the Arab-Israeli Conflict 1967–8.* London: Penguin Books, 1969.

——. *A History of Zionism.* New York: Schocken Books, 1976.

Laskov, Shulamit. (Heb.) *The Biluim.* Jerusalem: Hasifriya Hatziyonit, World Zionist Organization, 1980.

Lazar (Litai), Haim. (Heb.) *The Conquest of Jaffa.* Shelah, n.p., n.d.

Lesch, Ann Mosley. *Arab Politics in Palestine, 1917–1939: The Frustration of a Nationalist Movement.* Ithaca, N.Y.: Cornell University Press, 1979.

Levenberg, Haim. *The Military Preparations of the Arab Community in Palestine, 1945–1948.* London: Frank Cass, 1993.

Levy, Yitzhak. (Heb.) *Jerusalem in the War of Independence.* Tel Aviv: Ma'arachot, 1986.

Lewis, Bernard. *The Jews of Islam.* Princeton, N.J.: Princeton University Press, 1984.

Lorch, Netanel. *The Edge of the Sword: Israel's War of Independence, 1947–1949.* New York: Putnam's, 1961.

Louis, W. Roger. *The British Empire in the Middle East 1945–1951: Arab Nationalism, the United States, and Postwar Imperialism.* Oxford, England: Clarendon Press, 1984.

——. *"In the Name of God, Go!" Leo Amery and the British Empire in the Age of Churchill.* London: W.W. Norton, 1992.

Louis, W. Roger, and Owen Roger. *Suez 1956, the Crisis and Its Consequences.* Oxford, England: Clarendon Press, 1989.

Maimon, David. (Heb.) *The Terrorism That Was Beaten: The Suppression of the Terrorism in the Gaza Strip, 1971–1972.* Jerusalem: Steimatzky, 1993.

McCarthy, Justin. *The Population of Palestine: Population History and Statistics of the Late Ottoman Period and the Mandate.* New York: Columbia University Press, 1990.

Makovsky, Davis. *Making Peace with the PLO: The Rabin Government's Road to the Oslo Accord.* Boulder, Colo.: Westview Press, 1996.

Mandel, Neville. *The Arabs and Zionism before World War I.* Berkeley: University of California Press, 1976.

Ma'oz, Moshe. *Ottoman Reform in Syria and Palestine 1840–1861: The Impact of the Tanzimat on Politics and Society.* Oxford, England: Clarendon Press, 1968.

Mardor, Munya. (Heb.) *Rafael: On the Paths of Research and Development for Israel's Security.* Tel Aviv: Israel Defense Ministry Press, 1981.

Marlowe, John. *Rebellion in Palestine.* London: Cresset Press, 1946.

Masalha, Nur. *Expulsion of the Palestinians: The Concept of "Transfer" in Zionist Political Thought, 1882–1948.* Washington, D.C.: Institute for Palestine Studies, 1992.

Mattar, Philip. *The Mufti of Jerusalem: Al-Hajj Amin al-Husayni and the Palestinian National Movement.* New York: Columbia University Press, 1988.

Mayer, Thomas. "Egypt's 1948 Invasion of Palestine." *Middle Eastern Studies* 22:1 (1986).

Meir, Golda. *My Life*. London: Futura, 1976.

Melman, Yossi, and Dan Raviv. *Behind the Uprising: Israelis, Jordanians, and the Palestinians.* New York: Greenwood Press, 1989.

"Mem" (Michaelson), Benny. (Heb.) "The 'Peace for Galilee' War: The Main Military Moves." *Ma'arachot* 284 (1982).

———. (Heb.) " 'Operation Tophet,' A Battle on the East Bank of the Jordan—March 1968." *Ma'arachot* 292–93 (1984).

———. (Heb.) " 'The Operational Pause' of the Egyptian Army in the Yom Kippur War." *Ma'arachot* 327 (1992).

Merari, Ariel, and Shlomi Elad. (Heb.) *Sabotage Abroad: Palestinian Terrorism Abroad, 1968–1986.* Tel Aviv: Kibbutz Meuhad, 1986.

Milstein, Uri. (Heb.) *The History of the Paratroops.* 3 vols. Tel Aviv: Shalgi, 1985.

———. (Heb.) *The War of Independence.* 4 vols. Tel Aviv: Zmora/Bitan, 1989–91.

———. (Heb.) *The Lesson of a Collapse: From Sadat to Arafat.* Seridut/Yediot Aharonot, 1993.

Mishal, Shaul, with Reuven Aharoni. (Heb.) *Speaking Stones: The Words behind the Palestinian Intifada.* Tel Aviv: Kibbutz Meuhad/Avivim, 1989.

Mishmar Ha'Emeq Bama'aracha. Ed. Anon. Tel Aviv: Sifriyat Poalim, 1950.

Moore, John Norton, ed. *The Arab-Israeli Conflict, Readings and Documents.* Princeton, N.J.: Princeton University Press, 1977.

Morris, Benny. "Israel and the Lebanese Phalange: The Birth of a Relationship, 1948–1951." *Studies in Zionism* 5:1 (1984).

———. *The Birth of the Palestinian Refugee Problem, 1947–1949.* Cambridge, England: Cambridge University Press, 1988.

———. *Israel's Border Wars, 1949–1956.*

Oxford, England: Clarendon Press, 1993.

———. *1948 and After: Israel and the Palestinians.* Oxford, England: Clarendon Press, rev. ed., 1994.

Mosko, Yigal. (Heb.) "Thus Operated Ariel Sharon's Death Squad." *Kol Ha'Ir,* June 30, 1995.

Muslih, Muhammad. *The Origins of Palestinian Nationalism.* New York: Columbia University Press, 1988.

———. "Towards Coexistence: An Analysis of the Resolutions of the Palestine National Council." *Journal of Palestine Studies* 19:4 (1990).

Mutawi, Samir. *Jordan in the 1967 War.* Cambridge, England: Cambridge University Press, 1987.

Nachmani, Amikam. *Great Power Discord in Palestine: The Anglo-American Committee of Inquiry into the Problems of European Jewry and Palestine, 1945–1946.* London: Frank Cass, 1987.

Nakdimon, Shlomo. *First Strike: The Exclusive Story of How Israel Foiled Iraq's Attempt to Get the Bomb.* New York: Summit Books, 1987.

———. (Heb.) "Hussein Told Golda: The Syrian Army has Moved into Jump-off Positions." *Yediot Aharonot,* Sept. 29, 1993.

Nakhle, Emile. "The West Bank and Gaza: Twenty Years Later." *Middle East Journal* 42:2 (1988).

Naor, Arye. (Heb.) *Cabinet at War, The Functioning of the Israeli Cabinet During the Lebanon War (1982).* Israel: Lahav, 1986.

———. (Heb.) *David Raziel, The Life and Times of the Commander-in-Chief of the "Irgun" Underground in Palestine.* Tel Aviv: Israel Defense Ministry Press, 1990.

Narkiss, Uzi. (Heb.) *Soldier of Jerusalem.* Tel Aviv: Israel Defense Ministry Press, 1991.

Nasser, Gamal Abdel. (Heb.) *The Philosophy of the Revolution.* Tel Aviv: Ma'arachot, 1961.

———. "Nasser's Memoirs of the First

Palestine War," *Journal of Palestine Studies,* 2:2 (1973).

Nazzal, Nafez. *The Palestinian Exodus from Galilee, 1948.* Beirut: Institute for Palestine Studies, 1978.

The Negev Brigade during the War (Heb.) Tel Aviv: Ma'arachot, n.d.

Newman, David. *The Impact of Gush Emunim: Politics and Settlement in the West Bank.* London: Croom Helm, 1985.

Niv, David. (Heb.) *The Battles of the IZL.* 6 vols. Jerusalem: Klauzner Institute, 1965–80.

O'Ballance, Edgar. *Arab Guerrilla Power, 1967–1972.* London: Archon Books, 1973.

O'Brien, Connor Cruise. *The Siege: The Saga of Israel and Zionism.* London: Weidenfeld & Nicolson, 1986.

Orren, Elhannan. (Heb.) *On the Road to the City: Operation "Danni."* Tel Aviv: Ma'arachot, 1976.

———. (Heb.) "The Repulse of the Arab Liberation Army at Mishmar Ha'Emeq." *Ma'arachot* 294–95 (1984).

Pakradouni, Karim. (Heb.) *The Lost Peace: Elias Sarkis's Presidency (1976–1982).* Tel Aviv: Israel Defense Ministry Press, 1986.

Pappe, Ilan. *Britain and the Arab-Israeli Conflict, 1948–51.* London: St. Antony's/MacMillan, 1988.

———. *The Making of the Arab-Israeli Conflict, 1947–1951.* London: I. B. Tauris, 1992.

Parker, Richard. "The June 1967 War: Some Mysteries Explored." *Middle East Journal* 46:2 (1992).

———. *The Politics of Miscalculation in the Middle East.* Bloomington: Indiana University Press, 1993.

Pedatzur, Reuven. (Heb.) "The June Decision was Cancelled in October," *HaAretz,* May 12, 1995.

Peel Commission. "Palestine Royal Commission Report Presented by the Secretary of State for the Colonies to Parliament by Command of His Majesty, July 1937." Cmd. 5479.

Peled, Yossi. (Heb.) *Soldier.* Tel Aviv: Ma'ariv, 1993.

Peres, Shimon. (Heb.) *Entebbe Diary.* Tel Aviv: Idanim, 1991.

———. *Battling for Peace.* New York: Random House, 1995.

Peretz, Don. *Intifada: The Palestinian Uprising.* Boulder, Colo.: Westview Press, 1990.

Plascov, Avi. *The Palestinian Refugees in Jordan, 1948–1957.* London: Frank Cass, 1981.

Porath, Yehoshu'a. *The Emergence of the Palestine-Arab National Movement, 1918–1929.* London: Frank Cass, 1974.

———. *The Palestine-Arab National Movement, 1929–1939: From Riots to Rebellion.* London: Frank Cass, 1977.

———. *In Search of Arab Unity, 1930–1945.* London: Frank Cass, 1986.

al-Qawuqji, Fauzi. "Memoirs. 1948." Part 1. *Journal of Palestine Studies* 1:4 (1972).

———. "Memoirs. 1948." Part 2. *Journal of Palestine Studies,* 2:1 (1972).

Quandt, William. *Decade of Decisions; American Policy toward the Arab-Israeli Conflict, 1967–1976.* Berkeley: University of California, 1977.

———. *Camp David, Peacemaking and Politics.* Washington, D.C.: Brookings Institution, 1986.

———. "Lyndon Johnson and the June 1967 War: What Color Was the Light?," *Middle East Journal* 46:2 (1992).

———. *Peace Process, American Diplomacy and the Arab-Israeli Conflict since 1967.* Washington, D.C.: University of California Press/Brookings Institution, 1993.

Rabin, Yitzhak. *The Rabin Memoirs.* Tel Aviv: Steimatzky, 1979.

———. (Heb.) *The War in Lebanon.* Tel Aviv: Am Oved, 1983.

Rabinovich, Abraham. *The Battle for Jerusalem, June 5–7, 1967.* Philadelphia: Jewish Publication Society, 1972.

Rabinovich, Itamar. *The War for Lebanon, 1976–1983.* Ithaca, N.Y.: Cornell University Press, 1984.

———. *The Road Not Taken: Early Arab-Israeli Negotiations.* New York: Oxford University Press, 1991.

———. (Heb.) *The Brink of Peace: Israel and Syria 1992–1996.* Tel Aviv: Yediot Aharonot, 1998.

Rafael, Gideon. *Destination Peace: Three Decades of Israeli Foreign Policy.* New York: Stein & Day, 1981.

Randal, Jonathan. *Going All the Way: Christian Warlords, Israeli Adventurers, and the War in Lebanon.* New York: Vintage, 1984.

Rogel, Nakdimon. (Heb.) *Tel Hai: Battlefront without Support.* Tel Aviv: Yariv-Hadar, 1979.

Ro'i, Ya'akov. "The Zionist Attitude to the Arabs 1908–1914." *Middle Eastern Studies* 4:3 (1968).

———. (Heb.) "The Relations Between Rehovot and Its Arab Neighbors (1890–1914)." In *HaTziyonut,* edited by Daniel Karpi. Tel Aviv University Press/Kibbutz Meuhad Press, 1980.

———. (Heb.) "Jewish-Arab Relations in the First 'Aliyah's Colonies.' In *The First Aliya Book,* edited by Mordechai Eliav. Jerusalem: Yad Ben-Zvi, with Israel Defense Ministry Press, 1981.

Roszanski, Rachel. (Heb.) "The 'Mezah' Position in the Yom Kippur War." *Ma'arachot* 258–59 (1977).

Rubinstein, Elyakim. (Heb.) *The Peace Between Israel and Jordan: An Anatomy of a Negotiation.* Tel Aviv: Jaffe Center for Strategic Studies, 1996.

———. (Heb.) "The Peace Treaty with Jordan." *Hamishpat* 3 (1996).

Sabag, Shmuel, ed. (Heb.) *In Enemy Eyes* (excerpts, translated into Hebrew, from three books in Arabic on the 1948 war: Haj Muhammad Nimr al-Khatib, *Following the Disaster*; Kamal Ismail al-Sharif, *The Muslim Brotherhood in the Palestine War*; and Mahmud al-Ghussan, *The Battle for Bab al-Oued*). Tel Aviv: Ma'arachot, 1954.

Sadat, Anwar. *Revolt on the Nile.* New York: John Day, 1957.

———. *In Search of Identity: An Autobiography.* New York: Harper & Row, 1978.

Sagiv, David. *Fundamentalism and Intellectuals in Egypt, 1973–1993.* London: Frank Cass, 1995.

Salem, Elie. *Violence and Diplomacy in Lebanon: The Troubled Years, 1982–1988.* London: I. B. Tauris, 1995.

Sakakini, Khalil. (Heb.) *Such Am I, Oh World!* Jerusalem: Keter, 1990.

Salibi, K. S. *The Modern History of Lebanon.* Westport, Conn.: Greenwood Press, 1965.

Sanders, Ronald. *The High Walls of Jerusalem: A History of the Balfour Declaration and the Birth of the British Mandate for Palestine.* New York: Holt, Rinehart & Winston, 1983.

Sari, 'Abd al-Rahman Salim. (Heb.) "How Hosni Mubarak Saved the Deception Plan." *Ma'arachot* 332 (1993).

Savir, Uri. (Heb.) *The Process.* Tel Aviv: Yediot Aharonot, 1998.

Sayigh, Yezid. *Armed Struggle and the Search for State, the Palestinian National Movement, 1949–1993.* Oxford: Oxford University Press, 1997.

Schiff, Ze'ev. (Heb.) "A Foreign Ruler Warned—Intelligence [Branch] and Golda Ignored It." *HaAretz,* Sept. 15, 1993.

———. (Heb.) "The October Panorama." *HaAretz,* Dec. 12, 1993.

Schiff, Ze'ev, and Ehud Ya'ari. *Israel's Lebanon War.* London: Unwin, 1986.

———. *Intifada, the Palestinian Uprising—Israel's Third Front.* New York: Simon & Schuster, 1990.

Schleifer, S. Abdullah. "The Life and Thought of Izzid-Din al-Qassam." *Islamic Quarterly* 23:2 (1979).

Schoenbaum, David. *The United States and the State of Israel.* New York: Oxford University Press, 1993.

Scholch, Alexander. *Palestine in Transformation 1856–1882: Studies in Social, Economic and Political Development.* Washington, D.C.: Institute for Palestine Studies, 1993.

Schueftan, Dan. (Heb.) *Attrition: Egypt's Postwar Political Strategy, 1967–70.* Tel Aviv: Ma'arachot, 1989.

Seale, Patrick. *The Struggle for Syria: A Study of Post-War Arab Politics 1945–1948.* New Haven, Conn.:Yale University Press, 1987.

————. *Asad of Syria: The Struggle for the Middle East.* London: I.B. Tauris, 1988.

————. *Abu Nidal: A Gun for Hire.* New York: Random House, 1992.

Segal, Haggai. (Heb.) *Dear Brothers: The History of the Jewish Underground.* Jerusalem: Keter, 1987.

Segev, Tom. (Heb.) *The Seventh Million.* Tel Aviv: Keter/Domino, n.d.

Seikaly, Samir. "Unequal Fortunes: The Arabs of Palestine and the Jews during World War I." In *Studia Arabica et Islamica.* Beirut: 1981.

Seikaly, May. *Haifa: Transformation of an Arab Society, 1918–1939.* London: I.B. Tauris, 1995.

Sela, Alex. (Heb.) "The Security Zone: A Look from Within," *Ma'arachot* 311 (1988).

Sela, Avraham. "Transjordan, Israel and the 1948 War: Myth, Historiography and Reality." *Middle Eastern Studies* 28:4 (1992).

————. (Heb.) "The Palestinian Arabs in the 1948 War." In Moshe Ma'oz, and Benjamin Kedar, eds., *The Palestinian National Movement: From Conflict to Acceptance?* Tel Aviv: Israel Defense Ministry Press, 1996.

————. "The 'Wailing Wall' Riots (1929) as a Watershed in the Palestine Conflict." *The Muslim World* 84:1–2, 1994.

Shachan, Avigdor. (Heb.) *Operation Thunderball.* Tel Aviv: Massada, 1993.

Shafir, Gershon. *Land, Labour and the Origins of the Israeli-Palestinian Conflict 1882–1914.* Cambridge, England: Cambridge University Press, 1989.

Shai, Avi. (Heb.) "Egypt on the Road to the Yom Kippur War—War Aims and the Offensive Plan." *Ma'arachot* 250 (1976).

————. (Heb.) "The Iraqi Expeditionary Force in the Yom Kippur War." *Ma'arachot* 258–59 (1977).

Shaked, Ronni, and Aviva Shabi, (Heb.) *Hamas: Palestinian Islamic Fundamentalist Movement.* Jerusalem: Keter, 1994.

Shalev, Aryeh. (Heb.) *The Intifada, Causes and Effects.* Tel Aviv: Yoffe Center for Strategic Studies/Papyrus, 1990.

Shalit, David. (Heb.) "Heroism or Death." *HaAretz,* Aug. 27, 1993.

Shalom, Zaki. (Heb.) *Ben-Gurion, the State of Israel, and the Arab World.* Beersheba: Ben-Gurion University Press, 1995.

Shamir, Shlomo. (Heb.) "The Battles of Latrun: Three Comments and an Assessment." *Ma'arachot* 304 (1986).

Shamir, Yitzhak. (Heb.) *Conclusion.* Tel Aviv: Idanim, 1994.

Shapira, Anita. (Heb.) *Land and Power.* Tel Aviv: Am Oved, 1992.

————. (Heb.) "Historiography and Memory: The Case of Latrun, 1948." *Alpayim* 10 (1994).

Sharett, Moshe. (Heb.) "Israel and the Arabs—War and Peace." *Ot,* Sept. 1966.

————. (Heb) *Political Diary.* Tel Aviv: Am Oved, 1976.

————. (Heb.) *Personal Diary.* Tel Aviv: Sifriyat Ma'ariv, 1978.

Sharf, Ze'ev. (Heb.) *Three Days.* Tel Aviv: Am Oved, 1959.

Sharon, Ariel, (with David Chanoff). *Warrior.* New York: Simon & Schuster, 1989.

Shashar, Michael. (Heb.) *The Seventh Day War.* Tel Aviv: Sifriyat Poalim, 1997.

Shavit, Ya'akov. *Jabotinsky and the Revisionist Movement, 1925–1948.* London: Frank Cass, 1988.

Shazly, Sa'ad el. *The Crossing of the Suez.* San Francisco: American Mideast Research, 1980.

Sheffer, Gabriel. *Moshe Sharett, Biography of a Political Moderate.* Oxford, England: Clarendon Press, 1996.

Shemesh, Moshe, and Ilan Troen, eds. (Heb.) *The Sinai Campaign and the*

Suez War 1956: A New Look. Jerusalem: Ben-Gurion Center/Ben-Gurion University Press, 1994.

Shim'oni, Ya'akov. (Heb.) *The Arabs of Palestine.* Tel Aviv: Am Oved, 1947.

Shlaim, Avi. *Collusion Across the Jordan: King Abdullah, the Zionist Movement, and the Partition of Palestine.* New York: Columbia University Press, 1988.

——. "The Rise and Fall of the All-Palestine Government in Gaza." *Journal of Palestine Studies* 20:1 (1990).

Shmelz, Uziel. (Heb.) "The Decrease in the Population of the Land of Israel during World War I." In Mordechai Eliav, ed. (Heb.) *Under Siege and Trial.* Jerusalem: Yad Ben-Zvi, 1986.

Shragai, Nadav. (Heb.) *The Mount of Dispute: The Struggle for the Temple Mount, Jews and Muslims, Religion and Politics Since 1967.* Jerusalem: Keter, 1995.

Siniora, Hanna. "An Analysis of the Current Revolt." *Journal of Palestine Studies* 17:3 (1988).

Sion, Arye. "The Conquest of the 'Bren Outposts'—1948." *Ma'arachot* 207 (1970).

Sivan, Emmanuel. "Modern Arab Historiography of the Crusades." Tel Aviv University/Shiloah Center, 1973.

Smith, Barbra. *The Roots of Separatism in Palestine.* Syracuse, N.Y.: Syracuse University Press, 1992.

Sneh, Efraim. (Heb.) "Southern Lebanon: A Model for an Israeli Security Zone." *Ma'arachot* 288 (1983).

Sokolow, Nahum, *History of Zionism, 1600–1918,* 2 vols. London: Longmans, Green and Co., 1919.

Sprinzak, Ehud. *The Ascendance of Israel's Radical Right.* New York: Oxford University Press, 1991.

Stein, Kenneth. *The Land Question in Palestine, 1917–1939.* Chapel Hill: University of North Carolina Press, 1984.

——. "One Hundred Years of Social Change," in Laurence Silberstein, ed. *New Perspectives on Israeli History, the Early Years of the State.* New York: NYU Press, 1991.

Stillman, Norman. *The Jews of Arab Lands: A History and Source Book.* Philadelphia: Jewish Publication Society of America, 1979.

Stockton, Ronald. "Intifada Deaths." *Journal of Palestine Studies* 19:4 (1990).

Stormy Yiftah: The Story of the Yiftah–Palmach Brigade (Heb.) Bat-Yam: Yiftah Veterans Press, n.d.

Storrs, Ronald. *The Memoirs of Sir Ronald Storrs.* New York: G. P. Putnam's, 1937.

Straschnov, Amnon. (Heb.) *Justice under Fire: The Legal System during the Intifada.* Tel Aviv: Yediot Aharonot, 1994.

Sunday Times Insight Team. *The Yom Kippur War.* London: Andre Deutsch, 1975.

A Survey of Palestine. London: Her Majesty's Stationery Office (HMSO), 1946–1947.

Swedenborg, Ted. *Memories of Revolt.* Minneapolis: University of Minnesota Press, 1995.

Sykes, Christopher. *Cross Roads to Israel.* London: Collins, 1965.

Tal (Tell), Abdullah. (Heb.) *Memoirs of Abdullah Tal.* Tel Aviv: Ma'arachot, 1960.

Tamir, Avraham. (Heb.) *Peace-Mongering Soldier.* Tel Aviv: Idanim/Yediot, 1988.

Tauber, Eliezer. *The Emergence of the Arab Movements.* London: Frank Cass, 1993A.

——. *The Arab Movements in World War I.* London: Frank Cass, 1993B.

Tehan, Ben-Zion. (Heb.) "The Sinai Campaign." *Ma'arachot,* May 1958.

Tessler, Mark. *A History of the Israeli-Palestinian Conflict.* Bloomington: Indiana University Press, 1994.

Teveth, Shabtai. *Ben-Gurion and the Palestinian Arabs, from Peace to War.* New York: Oxford University Press, 1985.

——. *Ben-Gurion: The Burning Ground, 1886–1948.* New York: Houghton Mifflin, 1987.

——. "The Palestinian Refugee Problem and Its Origins." *Middle Eastern Studies* 26:2 (1990).

Tibi, Bassam. *Arab Nationalism: A Critical Enquiry.* New York: St. Martin's Press, 1981.

Tlass, Mustafa, ed. (Heb.) *The Israeli Invasion of Lebanon.* Tel Aviv: Israel Defense Ministry Press, 1988.

Twain, Mark. *The Innocents Abroad: Or the New Pilgrims' Progress.* New York: New American Library, 1980.

Tyler, W. P. N. "The Beisan Lands Issue in Mandatory Palestine." *Middle Eastern Studies* 25:2 (1989).

———. "The Huleh Lands Issue in Mandatory Palestine, 1920–1934." *Middle Eastern Studies* 27:3 (1991).

———. "The Huleh Concession and Jewish Settlement of the Huleh Valley, 1934–1948." *Middle Eastern Studies* 30:4 (1994).

Vance, Cyrus. *Hard Choices: Critical Years in America's Foreign Policy.* New York: Simon & Schuster, 1983.

Vital, David. *The Origins of Zionism.* Oxford, England: Clarendon Press, 1975.

———. *Zionism: The Formative Years.* Oxford, England: Clarendon Press, 1982.

———. *Zionism: The Crucial Phase.* Oxford, England: Clarendon Press, 1987.

Wallach, Jehuda, ed. (Heb.) *Carta's Atlas of Palestine from Zionism to Statehood.* Jerusalem: Carta, 1972, 1974.

Wallach, Jehuda, and Moshe Lissak, eds. (Heb.) *Carta's Atlas of Israel, the First Years 1948–1961.* Jerusalem: Carta/Israel Defense Ministry Press, 1978.

Wallach, Jehuda, Moshe Lissak, and Shimon Shamir, eds. (Heb.) *Carta's Atlas of Israel, the Second Decade 1961–1971.* Jerusalem: Carta/Israel Defense Ministry Press, 1980.

Wallach, Jehuda, and Moshe Lissak, eds. (Heb.) *Carta's Atlas of Israel, the Third Decade 1971–1981.* Jerusalem: Carta/Israel Defense Ministry Press, 1983.

Wallach, Jehuda. (Heb.) *Carta's Historical Atlas of the Haganah.* Jerusalem: Carta, 1991.

Wasserstein, Bernard. *Britain and the Jews of Europe, 1939–1949.* Oxford, England: Institute of Jewish Affairs/Clarendon Press, 1979.

———. *The British in Palestine: The Mandatory Government and the Arab-Jewish Conflict 1917–1929.* Oxford, England: Basil Blackwell, 1991.

Weitz, Yehiam. "Jewish Refugees and Zionist Policy during the Holocaust." *Middle Eastern Studies* 30/2 (1994).

Weizman, Ezer. *On Eagles' Wings: The Personal Story of the Leading Commander of the Israeli Air Force.* New York: Macmillan, 1976.

———. *The Battle for Peace.* New York: Bantam Books, 1981.

Weizmann, Chaim. *Trial and Error.* London: Hamish Hamilton, 1949.

———. *Letters,* edited by Jehuda Reinharz. Series A, vol 9, Oct. 1918–July 1920. Tel Aviv: Transaction Books/Rutgers University/Israel Universities Press, 1977.

Wilson, Mary. *King Abdullah, Britain and the Making of Jordan.* Cambridge, England: Cambridge University Press, 1987.

Woodhead Commission. "Palestine Partition Commission Report Presented by the Secretary of State for the Colonies to Parliament by Command of His Majesty, October 1938." Cmd. 5854.

Ya'acobi, Gad. (Heb.) *On the Razor's Edge.* Tel Aviv: Idanim, 1989.

Ya'ari, Ehud. (Heb.) *Egypt and the Fedayeen 1953–1956.* Giv'at Haviva: Center for Arab and Afro-Asian Studies, 1975.

Yair, Yoram. (Heb.) *With Me from Lebanon, the Paratroops Brigade in the Peace for Galilee Campaign.* Tel Aviv: Israel Defense Ministry Press, 1990.

"Yehuda," Colonel. (Heb.) "The Multinational Force." *Ma'arachot* 283 (1982).

Ye'or, Bat. *The Dhimmi, Jews and Christians under Islam.* Fairleigh Dickinson University Press/Associated University Presses, 1985.

Yonay, Ehud. *No Margin for Error: The Making of the Israeli Air Force.* New York: Pantheon Books, 1993.

"Yosef," Lieutenant Colonel, Lieutenant Colonel "Ilan," and Lieutenant Colonel "Yosef." "The Battle Next to the Wedge." *Ma'arachot* 289–90 (1983).

"Zalman," Major, and Major "Dan." (Heb.) "Paratroops in the Rear of the Hermon." *Ma'arachot* 289–90 (1983).

Zeine, Zeine. *The Emergence of Arab Nationalism.* Beirut: Khayats, 1966.

Ze'ira, Eli. (Heb.) *The Yom Kippur War.* Tel Aviv: Idanim, 1993.

Zertal, Idith. (Heb.) *From Catastrophe to Power: Jewish Illegal Immigration to Palestine, 1945–1948.* Tel Aviv: Am Oved, 1996.

Zohar, Avraham. (Heb.) "'Escort,' 'Raviv,' Raids on the Gulf of Suez Coast, September 1969." *Ma'arachot* 297 (1985).

"Zvi," Lieutenant Colonel. (Heb.) "The Syrian Offensive in the Golan Heights in the Yom Kippur War." *Ma'arachot* 314 (1989).

Zweig, Ronald. *Britain and Palestine during the Second World War.* Suffolk, England: Boydell Press for the Royal Historical Society, 1986.